Irreducible Mind

TOWARD A PSYCHOLOGY FOR THE 21st CENTURY

EDWARD F. KELLY,
EMILY WILLIAMS KELLY,
ADAM CRABTREE, ALAN GAULD,
MICHAEL GROSSO & BRUCE GREYSON

ROWMAN & LITTLEFIELD PUBLISHERS, INC.
LANHAM • BOULDER • NEW YORK • TORONTO • PLYMOUTH, UK

Published by Rowman & Littlefield Publishers, Inc.
A wholly owned subsidiary of The Rowman & Littlefield Publishing Group, Inc.
4501 Forbes Boulevard, Suite 200, Lanham, Maryland 20706
http://www.rowmanlittlefield.com

Estover Road, Plymouth PL6 7PY, United Kingdom

First paperback edition 2010

British Library Cataloguing in Publication Information Available

Library of Congress Cataloging-in-Publication Data
Kelly, Edward F.
Irreducible mind : toward a psychology for the 21st century / Edward F. Kelly, Emily Williams Kelly, and Adam Crabtree.
p. cm.
Includes bibliographical references and index.
1. Psychology. I. Kelly, Emily Williams, 1949– II. Crabtree, Adam. III. Title.
BF121.K38 2006
150—dc22 2006023474

ISBN: 978-0-7425-4792-6 (cloth : alk. paper)
ISBN: 978-1-4422-0206-1 (pbk. : alk. paper)
ISBN: 978-1-4422-0207-8 (electronic)

™ The paper used in this publication meets the minimum requirements of American National Standard for Information Sciences—Permanence of Paper for Printed Library Materials, ANSI/NISO Z39.48-1992.

Printed in the United States of America

Dedicated to

F. W. H. Myers
a neglected genius of scientific psychology

and to

Ian Stevenson
and
Michael Murphy
two modern bearers of his intellectual legacy

"I had…often a sense of great solitude,
and of an effort beyond my strength"
(Myers, 1893/1961, p. 40)

Contents

Preface and Acknowledgments

This book originated from a seminar directed to theoretical foundations of scientific psychology, initiated in 1998 by Michael Murphy under the auspices of the Center for Theory and Research of Esalen Institute. By the year 2000 our discussions had advanced to the point where we believed we could demonstrate, empirically, that the materialistic consensus which undergirds practically all of current mainstream psychology, neuroscience, and philosophy of mind is fundamentally flawed. We therefore committed ourselves to developing a book-length presentation which would systematically articulate and defend this point of view.

Our general strategy was to assess the overall state of psychology, as it exists here at the beginning of the 21st century, from a perspective that deliberately but selectively takes into account its first hundred-plus years of organized scientific effort. The essential driving idea was to step backward, the better to jump forward—"*reculer pour mieux sauter*." The tactical opportunity for this exercise was to be provided by the centennial of the publication in 1903 of an extraordinary book by a largely forgotten genius, F. W. H. Myers, titled *Human Personality*. Deeply admired by William James and other leading scholars of that period, this two-volume work is unquestionably a great but neglected classic of our science. It advances an elaborate but empirically supported theory of the constitution and functioning of human beings, one that in many ways is sharply at odds with current mainstream thinking, but one that we believe penetrates far closer to the empirical truths of the matter. By framing the relevant issues in the context of Myers's work, we thought, we would be able to justify and to some extent foreshadow what we anticipate will become a major and vitally necessary reworking of central parts of scientific psychology.

The basic plan of the book was to be threefold. First, we would provide an exposition of Myers's theoretical and empirical contributions. Second, we would systematically and critically examine subsequent research on a variety of empirical topics that were central to the theoretical position he developed. Finally, we would attempt to assess, in light of this review, where things now stand in psychology and where we need to go. The goal throughout would be not simply to celebrate Myers's project as he himself left it, but to carry it forward in the context of relevant substantive and methodological achievements of the intervening century.

The large book you hold in your hands realizes these intentions, to the extent permitted by our collective capacities and knowledge. We missed our original deadline, which seemed at first to lie in a far-distant future, by a full three years. This was due not to lack of effort on our part but to the dimensions of the task, which we seriously underestimated. The book could easily have become larger still. The subjects we discuss are individually complex and deeply intertwined, with ramifications that proliferate endlessly in interesting directions. Most chapters and even parts of some chapters could easily become books in themselves, and some probably will. Many chapters also deal with issues that lie at or beyond the currently recognized boundaries of "accepted" science, and therefore pose special challenges for responsible presentation. Despite their intrinsic difficulties, however, these diverse materials combine to produce what we think is a compelling demonstration that current mainstream opinion in psychology *must* change, and in directions that are both theoretically fundamental and humanly momentous. In a nutshell, we are arguing for abandonment of the current materialistic synthesis, and for the restoration of causally efficacious conscious mental life to its proper place at the center of our science. We hope to catalyze the emergence of an enlarged and reunified mainstream psychology, one that does not systematically ignore—as the present-day mainstream does—many large bodies of evidence deeply relevant to our most central and abiding human concerns.

In the interest of effectively promoting this sea-change we have deliberately crafted our book for a primary audience consisting of advanced undergraduate and early-stage graduate students, particularly students in disciplines such as psychology, neuroscience, and philosophy. These are the future leaders of our field, and we want to reach them before they suffer the "hardening of the categories" that all too often accompanies entry into these highly specialized professions. To do so required that our material be presented with a level of currency, detail, and rigor commensurate with that of the other professional materials such persons are exposed to on a daily basis, and we have attempted to meet that standard.

This has necessarily involved some difficult tradeoffs, however, for we also wanted our book to be accessible to anyone of good general education and intelligence who is seriously interested in its subject matter and willing to make the necessary effort. We have tried to ease the burden for such persons in various ways—for example by defining obscure or "jargon" terms, providing interim summaries and abstracts, and relegating many points of more technical or scholarly interest to parentheses and footnotes. However, there is no escaping the fact that some parts of the argument, especially parts of Chapters 1, 4, 7, and 9, are likely to present difficulties, particularly on first encounter. We implore such readers to be understanding and patient with us and persistent in their own efforts, skipping over any particularly challenging sections at first and returning to them later with a better sense of how everything fits into the overall scheme.

Our book has the outward form of an edited volume but is atypical of that genre. It is united throughout by a single theme, our collective drive toward a broadly correct, though necessarily incomplete, scientific picture of the mind as it relates to brain activity. This generalist impulse contrasts sharply with the extreme specialization that characterizes the sciences and other modern professions, and that is often especially pronounced in edited books. Edited volumes in science often address narrow topics and consist of pieces authored in hermetic isolation for small groups of specialists interested mainly in talking to each other. That is emphatically not the case with the present work. The book as a whole and its chapters individually take on big issues and seek to engage large numbers of readers. Several chapters include two or more of us as authors, and all were generated not in isolation but in conformity with an overall plan that emerged through group discussions spanning a period of years.

Our collective professional experience covers a wide range in terms of education, research, and teaching in psychology, psychiatry, neuroscience, and philosophy, and all of us have had the opportunity to read and critique every part of the book, usually in multiple versions. In addition to pooling our own professional expertise in this way, we have sought critical feedback on chapter drafts from outside volunteer readers including both professional colleagues from various disciplines and more general readers representing a diversity of backgrounds. Their efforts and suggestions have led to numerous improvements throughout the book, for which we are grateful. We are acutely aware that many gaps and imperfections remain, and we take full responsibility for these. One of our main points is that what is most urgently needed for further theoretical progress is more and better data of certain critical and specified kinds; this, the greater good, seemed better served by getting the book out now in reasonably finished form than by obsessing further over potentially endless refinements.

Finally, we wish to acknowledge contributions from individuals who have supported this project in various special ways. Among our "test-drivers" we give particular thanks to Carlos S. Alvarado, William Barnard, Frank Benford, Lori Derr, Ross Dunseath, Lorin Hollander, Fritz Klein, Jeff Kripal, James Lenz, Cory Maxwell, Francis McGlone, Michael Murphy, Margaret Pertzoff, Michael Schaffer, Ben Snyder, Ian Stevenson, Pim van Lommel, and Ray Westphal. Seminar participants who have contributed vigorously to the interdisciplinary conversations that helped shape the book include Richard Baker, John and Alyce Faye Cleese, David Fontana, Owen Flanagan, Arthur Hastings, Sean Kelly, Antonia Mills, Michael Murphy, Gary Owens, Frank Poletti, Dean Radin, William Roll, Bob Rosenberg, Marilyn Schlitz, Charles Tart, Jim Tucker, and Eric Weiss. Frank Poletti efficiently managed the logistics of our meetings, and Bob Rosenberg skillfully oversaw production of our digital version of *Human Personality* (see p. xxx of our Introduction). Robert F. Cook provided translations of the many French and Italian passages in *Human Personality* as well as the translation of Théodore Flournoy's review, for the digital version of *Human Personality*. John Cleese rescued us from periodic despondency and financially supported the mechanics of book production. Faye Joseph and Gary Owens provided additional financial support for book production, and the Institute for Noetic Sciences provided support for our meetings. Nancy L. Zingrone generated our camera-ready copy, including the index. Lori Derr, Dawn Hunt, and Martha Stockhausen provided invaluable help in tracking down references. We thank our associates from Rowman & Littlefield, especially Stanley Plotnick, Jon Sisk, and our editor Art Pomponio, for taking strong interest in this project and then sticking with it despite the many subsequent changes in book content and organization that delayed its completion. Above all we thank Michael Murphy for initially conceiving this project, for bringing us together in the spectacularly stimulating environment of Esalen, and for his apparently limitless reserves of comradeship, wit, and wisdom.

Introduction

Edward F. Kelly

The central subject of this book is the problem of relations between the inherently private, subjective, "first-person" world of human mental life and the publicly observable, objective, "third-person" world of physiological events and processes in the body and brain.

Scientific psychology has been struggling to reconcile these most-basic dimensions of its subject matter ever since it emerged from philosophy near the end of the 19th century. Both were fully present in William James's monumental *Principles of Psychology* (1890b), the earliest English-language survey of the new academic discipline that is still widely cited today. James explicitly acknowledged the normally intimate association between the mental and the physical, and he systematically and sympathetically rehearsed what little was then known or surmised about the brain. Unlike many of his scientific contemporaries, however, James resisted premature and facile attempts at neural reductionism. When he recognized limitations on the physiological side, he was content to record his psychological observations and await further progress in neurophysiology. The bulk of the *Principles* therefore consists of masterful expositions, relying heavily on sophisticated observation of his own inner workings, of central properties of mental life such as attention, imagination, the stream of consciousness, volition, and—at the heart of everything—the self (Leary, 1990).

James's person-centered and synoptic approach was soon largely abandoned, however, in favor of a much narrower conception of scientific psychology. Deeply rooted in earlier 19th-century thought, this approach advocated deliberate emulation of the presuppositions and methods—and thus, it was hoped, the stunning success—of the "hard" sciences, especially physics. James was barely in his grave when J. B. Watson (1913) published the founding manifesto of radical behaviorism, the logical culmination of this tradition. Psychology was no longer to be the science of mental life, as James had defined it. Rather it was to be the science of behavior, "a purely objective experimental branch of natural science" (p. 158). It should "never use the terms consciousness, mental states, mind, content, introspectively verifiable, imagery, and the like" (p. 166). Its task was instead to identify lawful relationships between stimuli and responses: "In a system of psychology completely worked out, given the response the stimuli can be predicted; given the stimuli the response can be predicted" (p. 167).

Watson's doctrine quickly took hold, and for the next half-century mainstream American psychology deliberately avoided contact with issues of the sort most important to James. It largely abandoned the first-person perspective of the investigator trying to understand things from within, and adopted almost exclusively that of an external observer whose task it is to predict and control the behavior of a material object, an opaque "black box," the experiential interior of which psychological science can and should ignore. Indeed, the success of physical science could be viewed as resulting in part precisely from its having in a similar way stripped from *its* subject matter all traces of purpose and teleology. In hopes of carrying through Watson's program of discovering units and laws in terms of which all behavior might ultimately be explained, most psychologists thus turned to narrowly behaviorist experimental studies—sometimes of humans but more commonly of simpler organisms, and typically in artificially simplified environments.

The inward dimension of psychology did not altogether disappear, however. The old introspectionist schools lingered on for a while, and introspection continued to play a significant role in areas such as psychophysics and the mainly European movements known as Gestalt psychology and phenomenology. During the same years in which behaviorism was seizing control of the American scientific mainstream, people such as Janet, Freud, Jung, and their followers were elaborating the various schools of depth psychology or "dynamic psychiatry" (Ellenberger, 1970). Even in the darkest days of the early behaviorist period—the rabid and monolithic "Age of Theory" (Koch & Leary, 1985)—major figures such as Morton Prince, Henry Murray, Gordon Allport, and Gardner Murphy steadfastly defended the complexities of human mind and personality against simplistic reductionist onslaughts. More recently, schools of "humanistic" and "transpersonal" psychology have also emerged which openly aspire to bring the deeper parts of human personality back within the framework of scientific psychology. It cannot be denied, however, that for most of psychology's first century these dissident movements have had to wage an uphill battle at or sometimes beyond the margins of the discipline.

The ascendancy of the behaviorist juggernaut thus essentially fragmented the traditional subject-matter of scientific psychology as envisioned by pioneers such as James, and left the fragments in the care of distinct, poorly integrated, and sometimes even mutually antagonistic professional sub-specialties. That the deep divisions it created remain with us even today is conspicuously exemplified by the 1989 schism within the American Psychological Association, which reaffirmed a fundamental split between the experimental and clinical dimensions of the field. These divisions represent, we contend, something much deeper than the ordinary process of specialization within an otherwise unified scientific discipline. Rather, they reflect the continuing failure of scientific psychology to come fully to grips with the inescapably dual nature of its subject matter—in short, with the mind-brain problem that lies at the heart of our discipline.

This has begun to change, however, in part because of the maturation of mainstream psychology itself. The 20th-century co-evolution of mainstream psychology with developments in allied fields such as neuroscience and philosophy of mind began with progressive refinement, but ultimately rejection, of its original behaviorist formulations, which fell by the wayside as their defects and limitations were progressively identified and articulated. Starting in the 1950s, however, a more sophisticated form of behaviorism arose, uniting the philosophical doctrine of functionalism with the logical theory of Turing machines and the applications technology provided by the digital computer. As described in more detail in the following chapter, this "Computational Theory of the Mind" (CTM) liberated cognitive science from the most oppressive strictures of radical behaviorism and has dominated the mainstream ever since. It also is currently driving what appears to many observers and participants to be an ever-deepening and unquestionably successful marriage between psychology and neuroscience.

Any contemporary discussion of mind-brain issues must certainly take into account the enormous advances made during the past century in our understanding of the brain. New manifestations of mind appear everywhere to be closely associated with modifications of structure or process in brains. In evolution, for example, we see an overall correlation across animal species between behavioral complexity and the level of organization of the nervous system. The rapid post-natal mental development of the human infant likewise is associated with massive structural and functional changes in its maturing brain. And as human adults we are all familiar with numerous facts—the normal daily fluctuations of consciousness and the effects of mild cerebral trauma induced by alcohol and other psychoactive substances, fatigue, thumps on the head, and so on—that also reflect in a general way this dependence of mind upon brain. But what about the details?

In recent decades brain researchers have begun "opening up the black box," deploying a formidable array of increasingly sophisticated clinical, pharmacological, biochemical, genetic, neurosurgical, electrophysiological, and behavioral methodologies in efforts to understand what brains can do and how they do it. The last 20 years in particular have witnessed the emergence of an entire family of new "functional neuroimaging" techniques such as high-resolution electroencephalography (EEG), functional magnetic resonance imaging (fMRI), and positron emission tomography (PET), which allow researchers to observe with ever-increasing temporal and spatial precision subtle physiological processes taking place in the interior of intact and functioning human brains.

These techniques have yielded a torrent of new information about the brain. Scientists and philosophers confronting the mind-body problem even as recently as a century ago knew only in a relatively global and undifferentiated fashion that the brain is the organ of mind. Today we know a great deal more, although our knowledge undoubtedly remains in many respects extremely primitive relative to the brain's unimaginable complexity. We know a lot about the structure and operation of neurons and even lower-level constituents. We also know a lot about the *structural* organization of the brain, its wiring diagram, and thanks mainly to the new imaging technologies we have begun to learn a fair amount about its *functional* organization, the manner in which complex patterns of neural activity are mobilized and coordinated across spatially separated regions of the brain in conjunction with ongoing experience and behavior.

The empirical connection between mind and brain seems to most observers to be growing ever tighter and more detailed as our scientific understanding of the brain advances. In light of the successes already in hand, it may not seem unreasonable to assume as a working hypothesis that this process can continue indefinitely without encountering any insuperable obstacles, and that properties of minds will ultimately be fully explained by those of brains. For most contemporary scientists, however, this useful working hypothesis has become something more like an established fact, or even an unquestionable axiom. At the concluding ceremonies of the 1990s "Decade of the Brain," for example, Antonio Damasio (1999) encapsulated the prevailing view:

> In an effort that continues to gain momentum, virtually all the functions studied in traditional psychology—perception, learning and memory, language, emotion, decision-making, creativity—are being understood in terms of their brain underpinnings. The mysteries behind many of these functions are being solved, one by one, and it is now apparent that even consciousness, the towering problem in the field, is likely to be elucidated before too long.[1]

That an enormous amount of methodological and substantive progress has been made by scientific psychology in its first century can hardly be denied, and I do not mean to deny it. But what sort of root conception of human mind and personality has so far emerged from all this effort? There are many rapidly shifting cross-currents and variations of detail amid the welter of current views, but to the extent that any provisional consensus has been achieved by contemporary mainstream scientists, psychologists and neuroscientists in particular, it is decidedly hostile to traditional and commonsense notions and runs instead along roughly the following lines: We human beings are nothing but extremely complicated biological machines. Everything we are and do is in principle causally explainable from the bot-

1. This quotation and others in this book that do not list a page number were taken from sources published on the internet without specific pagination.

tom up in terms of our biology, chemistry, and physics—ultimately, that is, in terms of local contact interactions among bits of matter moving in strict accordance with mechanical laws under the influence of fields of force.[2] Some of what we know, and the substrate of our general capacities to learn additional things, are built-in genetically as complex resultants of biological evolution. Everything else comes to us directly or indirectly by way of our sensory systems, through energetic exchanges with the environment of types already largely understood. Mind and consciousness are entirely generated by—or perhaps in some mysterious way identical with—neurophysiological events and processes in the brain. Mental causation, volition, and the "self" do not really exist; they are mere illusions, by-products of the grinding of our neural machinery. And of course because one's mind and personality are entirely products of the bodily machinery, they will necessarily be extinguished, totally and finally, by the demise and dissolution of that body.

Views of this sort unquestionably hold sway over the vast majority of contemporary scientists, and by now they have also percolated widely through the public at large.[3] They appear to be supported by mountains of evidence. But are they correct?

The authors of this book are united in the conviction that they are *not* correct—that in fundamental respects they are at best incomplete, and at certain critical points demonstrably false, empirically. These are strong statements, but our book will systematically elaborate and defend them. Our doubts regarding current psychological orthodoxy, I hasten to add, are at least in part shared by others. There seems to be a growing unease in many quarters, a sense that the narrowly physicalist contemporary approach to the analysis of mind has deflected psychology as a whole from

---

2. Newton's law of universal gravitation, insofar as it implies instantaneous action at a distance, appears to conflict with this characterization of physical causation, and indeed this feature greatly troubled Newton himself. The idea that matter could influence other matter without mutual contact was to him "so great an Absurdity that I believe no Man who has in philosophical matters a competent Faculty of thinking, can ever fall into it" (Newton, 1687/1964, p. 634). Newton himself presumed that this difficulty could eventually be removed—as indeed it was, more than two centuries later, with the appearance of Einstein's theory of relativity.

3. Just as this introduction was being drafted, a lengthy cover story on "mind/body medicine" appeared in the September 27, 2004, edition of *Newsweek*. This article exemplifies throughout the attitudes I have just described, and it culminates in a full-page editorial by psychologist Steven Pinker, author of *How the Mind Works* (1997), decrying what he terms "the disconnect between our common sense and our best science." Pinker further advises *Newsweek*'s massive readership that contrary to their everyday beliefs "modern neuroscience has shown that there is no user [of the brain]. 'The soul' is, in fact, the information-processing activity of the brain. New imaging techniques have tied every thought and emotion to neural activity." These statements grossly exaggerate what neuroscience has actually accomplished, as this book will demonstrate.

what should be its most central concerns, and furthermore that mainstream computationalist/physicalist theories themselves are encountering fundamental limitations and have nearly exhausted their explanatory resources. The recent resurgence of scientific and philosophic interest in consciousness and altered states of consciousness, and in the deep problems which these topics inherently involve, is just one prominent symptom, among many others, of these trends.

Even former leaders of the "cognitive revolution" such as Jerome Bruner, Noam Chomsky, George Miller, and Ulric Neisser have publicly voiced disappointment in its results. Chomsky in particular has railed repeatedly and at length against premature and misguided attempts to "reduce" the mind to currently understood neurophysiology. Chomsky (1993), for example, pointed out that empirical regularities known to 19th-century chemistry could not be explained by the physics of the day, but did not simply disappear on that account; rather, physics eventually had to expand in order to accommodate the facts of chemistry. Similarly, he argued, we should not settle for specious "reduction" of an inadequate psychology to present-day neurophysiology, but should instead seek "unification" of an independently justified level of psychological description and theory with an adequately complete and clear conception of the relevant physical properties of the body and brain—but only if and when we get such a conception. For in Chomsky's view, shared by many modern physicists, advances in physics from Newton's discovery of universal gravitation to 20th-century developments in quantum mechanics and relativity theory have undermined the classical and commonsense conceptions of *matter* to such an extent that reducibility of mind to matter is anything but straightforward, and hardly a foregone conclusion.

Several contemporary state-of-the-art surveys in psychology—for example, Koch and Leary (1985), Solso (1997), and Solso and Massaro (1995)—provide considerable further evidence of dissatisfaction with the theoretical state of things in psychology and of a widely felt need to regain the breadth of vision of its founders, such as William James. Solso and Massaro (1995) remark in their summing-up that "central to the science of the mind in the twenty-first century will be the question of how the mind is related to the body" (p. 306) and that "the self remains a riddle" (p. 311). David Leary's (1990) essay on the evolution of James's thinking about the self begins by documenting the remarkable degree to which the *Principles* had already anticipated most of the substance of subsequent psychological investigations of the self. He then goes on, however, to emphasize that later developments in James's own thought—developments completely unknown to the vast majority of contemporary psychologists—contain the seeds of an enlarged and deepened conception of the self that can potentially secure its location where James himself firmly believed it belongs, at the very center of an empirically adequate scientific psychology. From still another direction, Henri Ellenberger (1970) ends his landmark work on the discovery of the unconscious with a plea for reunification of the experimental and clinical wings of psychology: "We might then hope to reach a higher synthesis and devise a conceptual framework that would do justice to the rigorous demands of experimental psychology and to the psychic realities experienced by the explorers of the unconscious" (p. 897).

As will become apparent, our book wholeheartedly endorses this historically conscious, ecumenical, and reintegrative spirit. Before proceeding with its very unusual substance, however, we must set forth certain methodological principles that have guided us throughout, and that we strongly encourage our readers to adopt as well.

First and perhaps foremost is an attitude of humility in relation to the present state of scientific knowledge. Although we humans indisputably have learned a great deal through systematic application of our scientific methods, and are learning more at an accelerating rate, we undoubtedly still have a long way to go. There is surely a great deal about the physical world in general, let alone brains, minds, and consciousness, that we do not yet understand. Furthermore, our intimate *familiarity* with the basic facts of mental life—including, for example, our ability to direct our thoughts to states of affairs in the external world, and indeed the fundamental fact of consciousness itself—should not be confused with *understanding,* or blind us to the deeply puzzling and mysterious character of these phenomena. The self-assurance, even arrogance, of much contemporary writing on these subjects seems to us wholly unjustified and inappropriate. From this point of view many old scientific books and papers that purport to explain features of mental life in terms of hypothetical brain processes make fascinating reading, because of the many ultra-confident pronouncements they contain which in hindsight we know to be false. Future readers of many present-day books and papers about brain, mind, and consciousness, we believe, are likely to experience similar reactions.

Second, we emphasize that science consists at bottom of certain attitudes and procedures, rather than any fixed set of beliefs. The most basic attitude is that facts have primacy over theories and that beliefs should therefore always remain modifiable in response to new empirical data. In the forceful words of Francis Bacon (1620/1960), from the beginning of the scientific era: "The world is not to be narrowed till it will go into the understanding...but the understanding to be expanded and opened till it can take in the image of the world as it is in fact" (p. 276).

Although all scientists presumably endorse this idea in principle, there are complications and subtleties in practice, because "facts" and theories are strongly interdependent. As remarked long ago by philosopher F. C. S. Schiller (1905), "for the facts to be 'discovered' there is needed *the eye to see them*" (p. 60). Many of the issues discussed in this book revolve around well-documented empirical phenomena—facts, we will insist—that have been systematically ignored or rejected by mainstream scientists who find them too discordant with prevailing views to take seriously.

This is a tricky and delicate business, however; for when current scientific opinion hardens into dogma it becomes scientism, which is essentially a type of fundamentalism, a secular theology, and no longer science. As William James (1896) remarked, "science means, first of all, a certain dispassionate method. To suppose that it means a certain set of results that one should pin one's faith upon and hug forever is sadly to mistake its genius, and degrades the scientific body to the status of a sect" (p. 6).[4] Although this may seem uncontroversial, even trite, it is easily and often forgotten. The history of science is therefore replete with the sad spectacle of scientists—sometimes even very prominent scientists talking about their own scientific specialties—issuing what later prove to be profoundly erroneous judgments. For example, Badash (1972) studied the last third of the 19th century, when a "malaise of completeness" pervaded the physical sciences. James Clerk Maxwell commented in 1871 that "the opinion seems to have got abroad, that in a few years all the great physical constants will have been approximately estimated, and that the only occupation which will then be left to men of science will be to carry on these measurements to another place of decimals" (p. 50). In 1894 his American counterpart A. A. Michelson declared that "it seems probable that most of the grand underlying principles have been firmly established and that further advances are to be sought chiefly in the rigorous application of these principles to all the phenomena which come under our notice" (p. 52). But the next year brought the discovery of X-rays, and within the decade radioactivity, the electron, quantum theory, and relativity would shake the foundations of physical knowledge. Misjudgments of this magnitude—and many further examples could easily be adduced—should certainly give pause to anyone tempted to presume that today's science defines the limits of the possible.

Although facts have primacy, not all facts are of equal importance. The ones that should count the most, relative to a given problem, are obviously those that can contribute most to its solution. A useful principle that provides orientation and helps guide the search for such facts was stated as follows by Wind (1967): "It seems to be a lesson of history that the commonplace may be understood as a reduction of the exceptional, but the exceptional cannot be understood as an amplification of the commonplace" (p. 238). This lesson has not penetrated contemporary cognitive science, which deals almost exclusively with the commonplace and yet presumes—extrapolating vastly beyond what in reality are very limited successes—that we are progressing inexorably toward a comprehensive understanding of mind and brain based on classical physicalist principles. This serene confidence seems to us unwarranted. It is now evident, for example, that chess-playing computer programs represent progress toward real intelligence in roughly the same

4. The degradation feared by James is exemplified by media figure Michael Shermer, editor of *Skeptic* magazine, in an opinion piece appearing in *Scientific American* (June, 2002). There Shermer not only overtly embraces scientism, apparently unaware of the generally derogatory connotations of this term, but goes on to characterize leading contemporary scientists in quasi-religious terms: "This being the Age of Science, it is scientism's shamans who command our veneration."

sense that climbing a tree represents progress toward the moon. This book will apply Wind's principle by focusing upon a variety of psychological phenomena that any adequate theory of mind and consciousness will have to accommodate, but that we believe cannot be satisfactorily accommodated within the current explanatory framework of cognitive science. This in turn will motivate an effort to identify an expanded framework capable of overcoming these limitations.

Our own empiricism is thus thorough-going and radical, in the sense that we are willing to look at *all* relevant facts and not just those that seem compatible, actually or potentially, with current mainstream theory. Indeed, if anything it is precisely those observations that seem to conflict with current theory that should command the most urgent attention. As James (1909/1986) put it: "When was not the science of the future stirred to its conquering activities by the rebellious little exceptions to the science of the present?" (p. 375). Or again (James, 1890–1896/1910):

> Round about the accredited and orderly facts of every science there ever floats a sort of dust-cloud of exceptional observations, of occurrences minute and irregular and seldom met with, which it always proves more easy to ignore than to attend to....Any one will renovate his science who will steadily look after the irregular phenomena. And when the science is renewed, its new formulas often have more of the voice of the exceptions in them than of what were supposed to be the rules. (pp. 299–300)

The contribution of anomalies such as radioactivity and the photoelectric effect to the rise of quantum theory amply confirms the wisdom of this remark.

To qualify for this navigational role, of course, the relevant facts should also be suitably well-attested, and this caveat provides considerable scope for exercise of personal judgment. Science must always seek an appropriate balance between liberalism and conservatism in the admission of new observations, and it tends naturally and appropriately toward conservatism, amplified in proportion to the depth to which the new observations appear to conflict with expectations based on current understanding. Contrary to the popular mythology of science, however, such judgments often fall short of its professed ideals of dispassionate and open-minded evaluation of evidence.

Real science is saturated, like all other human endeavors, with human failings. It is often portrayed, and likes to portray itself, as reliably marshaling the intellectual virtues of reason and objectivity against retreating forces of religion, authority, and superstition—Galileo's treatment at the hands of the Catholic Church providing a hackneyed example. But especially in more recent times, opposition to new scientific ideas comes principally from other scientists, and often on less than satisfactory grounds (B. Barber, 1961; Kuhn, 1962). Harvey's theory of the circulation of the blood and discoveries by Lister, Semmelweiss, and Pasteur related to the germ theory of disease and the importance of sterilization in hospital environments were at first bitterly resisted by their medical colleagues. Lord Kelvin strongly resisted Maxwell's formulation of the laws of electromagnetism, and he never gave up his belief that atoms are indivisible (B. Barber, 1961). Scalp-level recording of brainstem evoked potentials is now used routinely to verify the integrity of sensory pathways in neonates and major-surgery patients, but its developer Don Jewett has described vividly the difficulties he experienced early on in funding and publishing this work, which conflicted with what his reviewers thought they knew about the behavior of electrical potentials in biological tissue. Wegener's geophysical theory of plate tectonics was similarly ridiculed for decades before being empirically confirmed. Many other examples of this sort could easily be cited. Pioneer of quantum mechanics Max Planck (1950) was perhaps only slightly exaggerating when he said: "A new scientific truth does not triumph by convincing its opponents and making them see the light, but rather because its opponents eventually die, and a new generation grows up that is familiar with it" (pp. 33–34).

This issue of scientific resistance has proved especially troublesome for one particular family of observations among the many kinds we draw upon in developing the central argument of this book—namely, observations adduced in the course of over a century of effort by workers in "psychical research" and its somewhat desiccated modern descendant, "parapsychology." My co-authors and I wish therefore to state immediately and unequivocally our own attitude toward this still-controversial subject. The irrational incredulity that remains characteristic of mainstream scientific opinion in this area seems to us a remarkable anomaly that will provide abundant and challenging grist for the mills of future historians and sociologists of science. Sufficient high-quality evidence has long since been available, we believe, to demonstrate beyond reasonable doubt the existence of the basic "paranormal" phenomena, at least for those willing to study that evidence with an open mind.[5]

Our Appendix contains an annotated bibliography providing useful points of entry into this large and complex literature. I hasten to add that this literature is uneven and imperfect, like any other scientific literature, and that our endorsement does not extend to all parts of it equally. What we do insist upon, however, is that this scientific literature is something entirely different from what one routinely encounters in checkout lines at the super-

5. The popular terms for the main classes of relevant phenomena are "extrasensory perception" (ESP) and "mind-over-matter" or "psychokinesis" (PK). ESP is sometimes broken into subtypes such as "telepathy" (direct or unmediated awareness of the mental state or activity of another person), "clairvoyance" (of distant events or objects), and "precognition/retrocognition" (of future/past events). It is widely recognized by researchers, however, that these familiar terms are unduly theory-laden and may not correspond to real differences in underlying process. Many researchers therefore prefer the more neutral terminology introduced by Thouless and Wiesner (1947)—"psi" for paranormal phenomena in general, occasionally subdivided into "psi gamma" for the input side and "psi kappa" for the output side.

market or in the flood of sensationalized drivel invading our TV and movie screens. The public credulity that enables this industry to thrive is deplorable, and we ourselves deplore it, but this has no bearing on the underlying scientific issue as to whether psi phenomena really exist as facts of nature.

It seems to us axiomatic that no intellectually responsible person, and especially no responsible scientist, should feel entitled to render opinions on this subject without first taking the time and trouble to study the relevant literature. This axiom is regularly violated, however, and in this connection we wish to comment briefly but more generally on the behavior of outside critics of this field, without being drawn into a discussion that could very easily become a book in itself.

The fundamental issue was incisively framed by American philosopher C. J. Ducasse (1969) as follows:

> Although the evidence offered by addicts of the marvelous for the reality of the phenomena they accept must be critically examined, it is equally necessary on the other side to scrutinize just as closely and critically the skeptics' allegations of fraud, or of malobservation, or of misinterpretation of what was observed, or of hypnotically induced hallucinations. For there is likely to be just as much wishful thinking, prejudice, emotion, snap judgment, naïveté, and intellectual dishonesty on the side of orthodoxy, of skepticism, and of conservatism, as on the side of hunger for and belief in the marvelous. The emotional motivation for irresponsible disbelief is, in fact, probably even stronger—especially in scientifically educated persons, whose pride of knowledge is at stake—than is in other persons the motivation for irresponsible belief. In these matters, nothing is so rare as genuine objectivity and impartiality of judgment—judgment determined neither by the will to believe nor the will to disbelieve, but only by the will to get at the truth irrespective of whether it turns out to be comfortably familiar or uncomfortably novel, consoling or distressing, orthodox, or unorthodox. (p. 35)

In our informed and considered opinion, the critiques of psychical research that have so far been offered by outside observers mainly demonstrate the validity of Ducasse's concerns, and routinely though not invariably fail to meet normal standards of scholarly practice. These tendencies were already fully apparent to William James, who took psychical research far more seriously than most present-day psychologists realize (James, 1986; G. Murphy & Ballou, 1960; E. Taylor, 1996), and they have scarcely abated in the subsequent century. We will not dwell on these controversies here, but have included in the Appendix some pointers to recent literature that illustrates their strange character.

We do, however, want to highlight here one particular critical strategy that has been very commonly and inappropriately employed. Most critics implicitly—and some, like Hansel (1966, p. 19), explicitly—take the view that psi phenomena are somehow known *a priori* to be impossible. In that case one is free to invent any scenario, no matter how far-fetched, to explain away ostensible evidence of psi. Because there are no perfect laboratory experiments—nor, for that matter, perfect "spontaneous" cases involving psi experiences occurring outside of a laboratory—any positive result whatever can be discredited in this way, and thus any potential accumulation of evidence aborted.[6] The extent to which many critics have been willing to pursue this strategy reveals the depth of their emotional commitment to current scientific orthodoxy, and is to us nothing short of amazing. Contrast this with the attitude expressed by James (1920): "I believe there is no source of deception in the investigation of nature which can compare with a fixed belief that certain kinds of phenomenon are *impossible*" (p. 248). Can there be any doubt which is the scientifically more responsible attitude?

One further point needs to be drawn out in this connection. Many critics also seem to presume that words like "paranormal" or "supernormal" are synonymous with "supernatural." That is not the case, however. Psi phenomena (and certain other unusual phenomena that we will discuss in this book) are in our view inconsistent only with the current materialistic synthesis, summarized by Broad (1962) in the form of widely accepted "basic limiting principles." They do not obviously or necessarily conflict with more fundamental laws of nature, and indeed to claim such a conflict is to presume that we already know all the relevant laws, which hardly seems likely. The authors of this book emphatically do *not* believe in "miracles," conceived as breaches of natural law. Our attitude is that these seemingly anomalous phenomena occur not in contradiction to nature itself, but only in contradiction to what is presently known to us of nature. The phenomena we catalog here are important precisely because they challenge so strongly the current scientific consensus; in accordance with Wind's principle, they not only *invite* but should *command* the attention of anyone seriously interested in the mind.

Finally, we also wish to make clear immediately that in our view "empirical" research includes but is by no means limited to *experimental* research. Laboratory research using random samples of subjects, control groups, and statistical modes of data analysis can be wonderfully useful, but obsession with this as the only valid means of acquiring new knowledge readily degenerates into "methodolatry" (Bakan, 1967), the methodological face of scientism. Laboratory experimentation certainly does not exhaust the means of obtaining valid and important information. Detailed case studies of special individuals, such as persons displaying rare cognitive skills or having unusual neurological deficits, have often provided unique insights and indisputably can play a valuable role in the evolution of scientific understanding. Pertinent modern examples here are the investigations by Luria (1968) and Sacks (1987) of persons displaying prodigious abilities of memory and calculation. Conversely, the experimental literature itself is replete with examples of supposedly "rigorous" laboratory studies which

6. Statistically knowledgeable readers will recognize that critics of this type are acting in effect like Bayesians who have assigned a prior probability of zero to the existence of psi phenomena (see also Radin, 2006).

were in fact performed under conditions that guaranteed their failure from the outset. A good example here is provided by the many superficial studies of "meditation" carried out by unsympathetic investigators, using as their subjects random samples of undergraduates having little if any experience or interest in meditation (M. Murphy & Donovan, 1997; M. A. West, 1987; see also our Chapter 8).

With these methodological principles in mind, we turn now to the substance of our book. In our opinion, the most systematic, comprehensive, and determined empirical assault on the mind-body problem ever carried out in the suggested spirit, during the entire long history of psychology, is summarized in F. W. H. Myers's (1903) undeservedly neglected two-volume work *Human Personality* (henceforth, *HP*). Myers's friend and colleague William James (1901) declared that "through him for the first time, psychologists are in possession of their full material, and mental phenomena are set down in an adequate inventory" (p. 16). Gardner Murphy (1954) praised "the heroic accumulation of data and amazing integration which the work represents" (p. iv). Ellenberger (1970) described Myers as "one of the great systematizers of the notion of the unconscious mind" (p. 314) and his book as "an unparalleled collection of source material on the topics of somnambulism, hypnosis, hysteria, dual personality, and parapsychological phenomena,...contain[ing] a complete theory of the unconscious mind, with its regressive, creative, and mythopoetic functions" (p. 788). James and various other writers have suggested that to the extent Myers's views are upheld by subsequent research he could rank with Charles Darwin in terms of the character, scope, and originality of his contributions. Myers also powerfully influenced many leading thinkers of the day, including both William James and Pierre Janet, but like James and Janet themselves he was soon pushed aside by the virulent behaviorism nascent at that period. However, just as James and Janet have undergone a major renaissance in recent years, as their central concerns and ideas have begun to reanimate the psychological mainstream, we believe that Myers's work deserves both wider recognition and careful re-examination for the light it can shed on the current situation in psychology.

The balance of our book attempts to further these aims. Chapters 1 and 2 provide essential background. We begin by reviewing modern developments in cognitive science, calling into question the ability of physicalist/computationalist models of the mind in any of their current forms to deal adequately with the most basic, central, and pervasive phenomena of mind and consciousness. We also identify a variety of specific empirical phenomena, and a variety of critical aspects of human mental life, that appear to resist or defy understanding in terms of the currently prevailing physicalist conceptual framework. The central objective of this exercise is to reduce whatever confidence in that framework readers may initially have, and thus to provide justification for revisiting the broader and deeper framework elaborated over a century ago by Myers, James, and their colleagues.

The following chapter summarizes the contributions of F. W. H. Myers to empirical investigation of the mind-body relation. It begins with a brief summary of the relevant 19th-century intellectual background that suggests why Myers and his type of synoptic approach were ultimately ignored by the nascent materialist psychology. After outlining the purposes and principles in which Myers's work was rooted, the chapter goes on to describe Myers's theoretical model of human personality and consciousness, a model that is the most fully worked out example (so far) of "filter" or "transmission" theories of mind (James, 1898/1900; Schiller, 1891/1894), according to which mind is not generated by the brain but instead focused, limited, and constrained by it. The chapter also includes a description of the methodological principles and empirical phenomena which Myers considered essential for a fully comprehensive and adequate science of psychology.[7]

The next six chapters constitute the empirical heart of the book. We focus in detail on selected large classes of psychological phenomena, several of which were investigated in considerable depth by Myers himself, that appear especially challenging to contemporary mainstream views and capable of yielding new insight into the nature of the mind-brain connection. We do not attempt to review these topics exhaustively, but discuss them selectively in relation to their bearing on this central issue. In so doing, we also begin to assess the degree to which Myers's views have been sustained and confirmed, or must be modified or discarded, in light of subsequent work. Following Myers's own practice, we attempt to lead readers by degrees and without obvious discontinuity from phenomena which, though challenging, are well established and seem at least potentially compatible with current orthodoxy, to phenomena which in our view are just as well or nearly as well established, but clearly cannot be accommodated or understood without radical revision of our most fundamental theoretical ideas. The principal topics we discuss include extreme forms of psychophysiological influence, empirical and conceptual difficulties with current "trace" theories of memory, psychological automatisms and secondary streams of consciousness, the family of "near-death" and "out-of-body" experiences and related phenomena, genius-level creativity, and the world-wide psychological phenomenon of "mystical" experience.

In the final chapter we attempt to re-assess Myers's theory of human personality and to draw out additional implications of this book for future psychological theory and research. We underscore that Myers and James made the most comprehensive effort to date to analyze the mind-body rela-

7. This chapter provides a useful introduction to Myers, but it is no substitute for the real thing. With the hard cover version of *Irreducible Mind*, we included a CD containing the entire text of *Human Personality* in Microsoft Reader ebook format, as well as its most significant contemporary reviews and translations of all foreign text. This digital version and the reader are freely available at the Esalen website (http://www.esalenctr.org/display/hp_ctr.cfm) or through the University of Virginia Electronic Text Center (http://etext.lib.virginia.edu).

tion *empirically*, and we urge scientific psychology to return to its great central problems with a comparably synoptic empirical approach, but supported now by the tremendous methodological and technical advances achieved in the intervening century. We further argue that Myers's theoretical scheme and the empirical phenomena he deployed to support it have held up remarkably well, and at many points have been substantially reinforced by subsequent research. Remaining difficulties and weaknesses, however, are also pointed out, together with critical opportunities and problems for further investigation. Finally, we attempt to show how the theoretical framework elaborated by Myers and James, although certainly incomplete and imperfect, can be reconciled with leading-edge contemporary physics and neuroscience, and prefigures an enlarged scientific psychology that can potentially overcome the historical fragmentation sketched above.

Chapter 1

A View from the Mainstream: Contemporary Cognitive Neuroscience and the Consciousness Debates[1]

Edward F. Kelly

The central contention of this book is that the science of the mind has reached a point where multiple lines of empirical evidence, drawn from a wide variety of sources, converge to produce a resolution of the mind-body problem along lines sharply divergent from the current mainstream view.

The goal of the present chapter is to set the stage by sketching the evolution of mainstream psychology itself over the past hundred years, emphasizing modern developments and assessing critically where things presently stand.

The territory to be covered is vast and complex, so my account will necessarily be telegraphic and selective, and strongly colored by personal interests and experience—hence, "A View...." The center of perspective throughout is that of a working experimental psychologist, one whose professional experience includes psychology of language, human functional neuroimaging studies using both high-resolution EEG and fMRI methods, single-unit neurophysiological work in animals, and experimental parapsychology. I regret that I can claim only amateur-level acquaintance with relevant contemporary literature in philosophy of mind and language, although I recognize its value and unlike most of my fellow psychologists have made significant efforts to acquaint myself with it. The recent upsurge in efforts

1. This chapter updates and greatly expands on views more tentatively expressed in E. F. Kelly (1979). I wish to express thanks to Lisette Coly and the Parapsychology Foundation for permission to use parts of that earlier essay. Thanks also to Alan Gauld for especially helpful comments on earlier drafts of this one.

to bring these complementary perspectives simultaneously to bear on our central subject matter in a systematic and mutually informed way seems to me altogether welcome, and long overdue.[2]

The History of Cognitive Psychology: A Thumbnail Sketch

The following three sections summarize the history of mainstream psychology in the English-speaking world from the advent of behaviorism to the present. So brief a sketch must necessarily be impressionistic, but I believe it is faithful to the main outlines of the subject as it has developed so far, and would be so regarded by most workers in the field. Useful general sources for readers wanting additional historical detail include Flanagan (1991), H. Gardner (1985), and Harnish (2002).

From James B. Watson to the Cognitive Revolution

The history of scientific psychology in the 20th century can be characterized, somewhat cynically perhaps, as a movement toward progressively less unsatisfactory analyses of the mind. I will pass quickly over the first half of this history. Noam Chomsky remarked parenthetically during a lecture on linguistics in 1964 that in his opinion the first half century of American experimental psychology would end up as a footnote in the history of science. That was a characteristically provocative Chomsky remark, but even then it seemed more right than wrong. The historian of psychology Sigmund Koch, an early advocate of behaviorism who evolved into perhaps its most ferocious critic, has repeatedly derided the simplistic scientism of the period, and marveled at the degree to which behaviorism, having sprung into existence under the banner of a "consoling myth of natural science rigor and systematicity," had so often "proceeded to liquidate its subject matter" (Koch & Leary, 1985, p. 942). During its heyday, from perhaps the 1920s to the late 1950s, behaviorism enjoyed extraordinary, almost monolithic, institutional and professional power. Even as late as 1990, the chairman of psychology at a major American university, in a symposium celebrating the centennial of the *Principles of Psychology,* characterized James's great book as mainly illustrating what psychology should *not* be; its positive attributes consisted mostly of those few scattered passages where James's observations corresponded to truths revealed by *real* psychology—the natural science devoted to analysis and control of behavior (Kimble, 1990).

Certainly one of the chief lessons to be derived here is that entire generations of industrious and able scientists can be captured by an ideology

2. The symposium recorded in Bock and Marsh (1993) provides an outstanding example, and one we have tried collectively to emulate.

that is fundamentally unsound. I do not mean to say that behaviorism was all bad. Its central methodological impulse, emphasizing the importance of systematic empirical observation and measurement, was certainly healthy and remains so today. Even on that front, however, the early behaviorist program was unnecessarily narrow. Encouraged by the verificationist doctrine associated with the Vienna school of logical positivism (Ayer, 1952), behaviorists simply outlawed in principle all reference to anything not directly observable from the third-person standpoint. Stimuli, responses, and their supposedly lawful connections exhausted the scientifically legitimate subject matter. Even ignoring the often considerable difficulties in defining exactly what constitutes "a stimulus" or "a response," however, this methodological asceticism was not warranted by any independently established conception of the nature of science. Indeed, philosophers of science soon abandoned verificationism in its narrowest construction, recognizing that even classical physics, the archetypal science, did not hesitate to postulate entities and processes that could not be observed directly, but only through their lawful connections to other things that could.

The experimental psychology that began to evolve after Watson's 1913 manifesto can be viewed as a kind of operationalization of 19th-century associationist theories of the mind, in which "ideas" were replaced by behaviors, and complex behaviors were imagined as arising from simple ones through processes of conditioning and reinforcement. The bulk of this work was carried out with simpler organisms such as rats and pigeons, on the view that everything necessary for scientific psychology was present there, and in more accessible form. From the principles that emerged from such studies, it was hoped, we would eventually be able to build a psychology capable of accounting for all the complexities characteristic of human behavior. This specifically included what Descartes had insisted is uniquely ours, and a defining attribute of the mind—our use of language. A few mainstream behaviorists such as Edward Tolman and Egon Brunswick suggested that even the behavior of rats running their mazes might be guided by some sort of inner representation or map, but these suggestions were largely ignored.

Methodological behaviorism was subsequently reinforced for a time by a companion philosophical doctrine called logical or analytical behaviorism, which received perhaps its fullest expression in the influential book by Ryle (1949). It shared Watson's objective of exorcising the mind, "the ghost in the machine," but sought to achieve this objective by redefining mentalistic terms in terms of overt behavior, or dispositions to such behavior. Having a pain, for example, was to be construed as literally consisting in crying out, reaching for the aspirin, and so on. This relentlessly third-person approach to the mind seemed consistent with, and supportive of, the actual practices of behaviorist psychologists, but its problems as a philosophic doctrine soon became apparent.[3] It proved extremely difficult in practice

3. For lucid and accessible discussions of the various philosophic positions briefly canvassed in this section see for example the books of Churchland (1988), Heil (1998), Kim (1998), and Searle (1992).

to specify, in finite detail and without covert reference to other mentalistic terms, the behavioral conditions in terms of which the original mentalistic terms were to be redefined. From a more commonsense point of view it also seemed to leave out precisely the things that are most important to us as human beings—in particular mental causation and our subjective conscious experience. We all know, for example, that *pain* and *pain behavior* simply are not the same thing. One can have a pain but not show it, or act as if in pain without actually being in pain. For these and other reasons analytical behaviorism fell generally out of favor, although echoes are still heard today—a primary source being Ryle's student Daniel Dennett (1991).

Logical behaviorism gave way in the 1950s and 1960s to a family of positions known collectively as identity theory. Its basic doctrine is that the apparent correlation between mental states and brain states is to be interpreted in one particular way. Specifically, it holds that the relevant mental and physical states are in some sense identical, the same things viewed as it were from inside versus outside. This is regarded not as a logical necessity, but as a fact that we have discovered empirically, through advances in psychology and neuroscience, just as we have discovered that the morning star and the evening star are one and the same.

The identity doctrine came in two forms: The first and stronger form, formulated by writers such Herbert Feigl (1958), U. T. Place (1956), and J. J. C. Smart (1959), holds that mental states can be subdivided into discrete natural kinds or *types*, and that each of these types can be identified with a corresponding type of neural process. A stock example is the supposedly general relationship between "pain" and "excitation of c-fibers." The weaker form of identity theory claims only that each individually occurring or *token* mental state is identical with some corresponding brain state. Note that type identity entails token identity, but not vice-versa.

Type-identity is a strong and interesting philosophic thesis which implies the possibility of reduction, and for these reasons many physicalists welcomed it; but it is certainly false. Quite apart from the difficulties of isolating appropriate "natural kinds" or types in either mental life or brain processes, it is certain that many such mental types, if they existed, would arise under wildly varying neurophysiological conditions. For example, linguistic behaviors involve mainly the left hemisphere in right-handed adults, but a mixture of both hemispheres or even mainly the right hemisphere in left-handers. The mind-brain system is in general enormously adaptable or "plastic." For example, superior general intelligence and linguistic functioning have been observed in a man whose entire left hemisphere had been removed at age 5½ for control of seizures (A. Smith & Sugar, 1975). Fully functioning adults are also occasionally discovered who altogether lack major neural structures such as the corpus callosum or cerebellum, structures that are usually thought to be required for such functioning. In some well-studied cases of hydrocephalus, normal or even exceptional mental functioning has been found in persons who have only 3–5% of the normal volume of brain tissue (R. Lewin, 1980). And to take a still more extreme case, high-level forms of learning and memory are certainly present in the octopus, an invertebrate whose nervous organization is radically different from ours. It even lacks a hippocampus, the one structure that everyone agrees plays an essential role in mammalian memory systems (Chapter 4).

Type identity, therefore, has had little appeal for psychologists and neuroscientists, who undoubtedly gravitate in the vast majority—to the extent they think about such things at all—to some sort of token-identity view. This was essentially the position advocated by James in *The Principles*, although he disavowed atomism in all forms and took pains to insist that the level at which the intersection is appropriately sought is that of whole momentary states of consciousness and whole momentary states of the brain. *Token* identity, on the other hand, has had relatively little appeal for philosophers. Among other things it creates a new and serious problem: If the same mental state, say a certain belief, can exist in combination with different sorts of physical states in brains, what is it about all those physical states that makes them "the same" as their common mental counterpart?

A philosophic response to this problem is the doctrine known as *functionalism*, first formulated by Hilary Putnam (1967).[4] Having rejected type identity, on grounds that a given mental state might conceivably occur in extraterrestrial beings, or more relevantly in computers, Putnam went on to propose a novel solution to the problem just noted. His basic idea was to reconceptualize mental states once again, this time not in terms of what they are *made of*, but in terms of what they *do*, their causal role in the functional economy of whatever sort of creature or entity is in question. Just as "cutting tools" can be implemented using rocks, metals, or laser beams, mental states are to be conceived as "multiply realizable"—that is, potentially instantiated in a variety of physical forms including not only token biological states of one or many brains, but also in computers and other suitable kinds of complex physical systems. On this view mental states become simply Xs, defined by their causal relations to stimuli, to other mental states, and to responses, and they can be identified as similar states to the extent they perform similar roles in their respective causal networks.

I will make only a few brief comments on this doctrine, which in various forms has dominated the philosophy of mind for almost 40 years. First, as originally formulated it was inherently and fundamentally third-person and behavioristic, albeit a refined behaviorism that admits the possibility of complex causal processes—mental causes, in effect—mediating between stimuli and responses. Like the earlier forms of behaviorism, it initially avoided all reference to consciousness and subjective features of mental life. This was widely felt to be unsatisfactory, however, and a large part of the subsequent history of functionalism consists of strained attempts to "naturalize" first-person phenomena of these sorts. Second, although functionalism readily affiliates itself with both physicalism in general and token identity theories in particular (and in most of its adherents probably still does), such affilia-

4. But note that Putnam himself subsequently abandoned functionalism, becoming one of its severest critics; see Putnam (1988/1998).

tions are not an essential or inherent aspect of the doctrine. J. Fodor (1981a), for example, pointed out that functionalist principles might perfectly well apply to the operations of immaterial minds and the like, should any such things exist. Finally, it is fair to say, I think, that functionalism arose not so much *sui generis* in philosophy, but rather as a response to some exciting new developments which had already occurred within scientific psychology itself, and with which Putnam was certainly well acquainted. In any event, it was the confluence of these streams that defined the emergence of the 20th century's most distinctive contribution to mind-brain theory, the "Computational Theory of the Mind" (henceforth, CTM). I turn now to the psychological dimensions of this story.

By the late 1950s discontent with behaviorism was rapidly spreading, as its inherent limitations became increasingly apparent. An influential paper by Lashley (1951) had exposed fundamental difficulties in the attempt to explain complex behavior, notably human linguistic behavior, in terms of linear chains of stimuli and responses. B. F. Skinner, the leading behaviorist, responded to this challenge, but his book on verbal behavior was subjected to a destructive and widely circulated review by Chomsky (1959). Most significantly of all, perhaps, a comprehensive state-of-the-science review organized by Sigmund Koch under the auspices of the American Psychological Association and the National Science Foundation resulted in a sweeping, 6000-page, six-volume indictment of the entire behaviorist platform (Koch, 1959–1963).

At the root of these discontents was a recognition that the old associationist explanatory principles, and their behavioral translations, were in principle unable to cope with the hierarchically organized and orderly character of human language and cognition. We needed a richer concept of mechanism. And as it happened, possible means of overcoming these limitations were just then becoming available, due to fundamental developments in the theory and practice of computation.

The old concept of a "machine"—and perhaps for most of us still the everyday concept—is that of a physical contraption which transforms energy by means of pushes and pulls involving gears, pulleys, shafts, levers, and so on. The fundamental insight underlying the modern developments is the recognition that these physical arrangements are really of secondary importance. The essential attribute of the machine is rather that its normal behavior is *bound by rule*. This insight opened the way to an enormous enrichment of our concept of mechanism, beginning with the contribution of logicians and mathematicians in the 1930s and 1940s and continuing into the present day. These developments, moreover, immediately began to have a profound impact on scientific psychology.

For example, it was quickly recognized that machines can transform data or "information" as well as energy, and that a machine can in principle utilize information about its performance to regulate its own behavior. These ideas had immediate and urgent practical application in the construction of servo-controlled antiaircraft systems during World War II, but possible theoretical implications for the understanding of behavior were also apparent. Rosenblueth, Wiener, and Bigelow (1943), for example, argued that from the point of view of an external observer a device constructed on this principle of "negative feedback" behaved purposively—that is, as a teleological mechanism. Thus, mechanism appeared to penetrate one of the last strongholds of old-fashioned vitalist thinking.[5]

These analogies were developed much more systematically by Wiener in his influential book *Cybernetics,* significantly subtitled *Control and Communication in the Animal and the Machine.* In addition to providing a general analytic theory of feedback control processes, Wiener (1961) provided numerous examples of physiological phenomena that seemed to fall within the province of the theory. Nevertheless, the direct applications of cybernetic theory at this level remained relatively limited. The real power of the ideas emerged later on, in conjunction with the extremely flexible applications technology provided by the digital computer.

To appreciate the full significance of these developments, it is necessary to follow the generalization of the concept of "machine" to its ultimate development in the hands of the British mathematician Alan Turing and several others. Turing devised an abstract representation that formalized his intuition of the core meaning of "mechanism," as applied to the theory of computable functions. Any computation can be regarded as the transformation of a string of input symbols into a string of output symbols by a sequence of rule-governed steps. A procedure that is guaranteed to lead to the desired output in a finite sequence of steps is called an "algorithm" or "effective procedure." Turing envisioned a machine consisting of a read/write head operating on an indefinitely extendable tape ruled off into squares. The behavior of the machine is completely specified by a set of five-part rules. Given the machine's current state, and the input symbol written in the current square, these rules instruct the machine to change state, write a new symbol on the tape, and either remain where it is or move one square left or right. By altering the number of states, the size of the vocabulary, and the behavioral rules, an immense variety of behaviors can be realized by such devices. In fact, Turing argued persuasively that *anything* that would naturally qualify as an algorithm can be represented by a suitably constructed machine of this sort. He also proved rigorously that he could construct a "universal" Turing machine that would simulate the behavior of any other Turing machine. The intuitive notion of "effective procedure" was thus explicated in terms of the formal notion "realizable by a Turing machine." That this is not an arbitrary result but in a fundamental sense exhausts the meaning of the concept of mechanism is strongly suggested by the fact that other workers such as Alonso Church and Emil Post arrived at provably equivalent results from widely different starting points.

5. Some observers, however, already resisted this interpretation of the behavioral appearances as truly equivalent to intrinsic purposefulness in the everyday psychological sense; see, for example, Buckley (1968, Part V).

Because of their utter simplicity, Turing machines do even very simple things such as adding two numbers in extremely cumbersome ways. Their significance is theoretical, not practical. But links to brain-mind theory were quickly forged. An influential paper by McCulloch and Pitts (1943) showed that networks constructed from idealized neurons could in principle implement logical behaviors of arbitrary complexity. Both they themselves and other workers further showed that equivalent capacities could be realized using richer elements that more nearly approximated the characteristics of real neurons. Thus it seemed likely that brains in principle have capacities equivalent to those of Turing machines. They might conceivably have additional capacities as well, but if so—and this is the essential point—these capacities may lie beyond the reach of understanding based on computational principles alone.

The final ingredient was provided by mathematician John von Neumann, who in 1947 invented the basic architecture of the modern stored-program digital computer. Von Neumann was entirely familiar with the theory of computability, and he was undoubtedly directly inspired as well by McCulloch, Pitts, and Wiener, all of whom participated with him in an important series of conferences on cybernetics sponsored by the Macy Foundation (Dupuy, 2000). It was evident to all that von Neumann's new architecture provided in effect the logical capabilities of a universal Turing machine, but now at last in a practically useful form. To the extent that mind and brain are governed by formalizable rules, their activities could now in principle be modeled on suitably programmed general-purpose digital computers. To those sufficiently committed *a priori* to mechanistic principles, the very existence of any given class of behavior essentially *entailed* the possibility of such formalization. The relation of mind to brain could be conceptualized as analogous to the relation of computer software to computer hardware, and the mind-brain problem would simply disappear.

There were other more specific theoretical results that further strengthened this emerging point of view. Consider, for example, some of the early results in theoretical linguistics. Chomsky (1963) and others showed that the possible classes of formal models of language (generative grammars) formed a hierarchy, in which the weakest or most highly constrained class (finite-state grammars) was obtained from the strongest or least constrained class (unrestricted rewriting systems) by the application of progressively more severe constraints on the form of the permissible rules of the grammar. The resulting hierarchy of grammars, it turns out, also corresponds to a hierarchy of classes of automata derived from Turing machines in parallel fashion. Formal results from automata studies thus transferred to the analysis of candidate grammatical theories. Chomsky (1957) was able to show that then-existing psychological and linguistic proposals for theories of language, when formalized, corresponded to the weakest or most constrained members of the hierarchy of grammars, and that these grammars were in principle too weak to account for systematic structural properties of many kinds of sentences found in natural languages such as English. He was thus led to his famous theory of transformational grammar as the weakest class of theory which is still strong enough to account for the known grammatical facts of language. The result that the corresponding automata are weaker than Turing machines greatly strengthened the presumption that linguistic behavior might be formalizable for computer modeling.

The central idea that minds, brains, and computers could fruitfully be regarded as variants of a more general class of information-processing mechanisms quickly took root, even among neuroscientists (W. J. Freeman, 1998; von Neumann, 1958). The ground was very well prepared. Indeed, these developments seem to me an inevitable outcome of our Western scientific tradition. This is not meant disparagingly, however. I have stressed these results about Turing machines and so on precisely to underscore the impressive depth of the theoretical foundation on which all the ensuing developments rest, a foundation which I feel has not been adequately appreciated by many critics of this kind of work, such as Edelman and Tononi (2000), nor even by some of its enthusiastic supporters, such as H. Gardner (1985).

In practice, the applications came a bit slowly at first. In part this was due to purely technical factors. The early computers were small, slow, and highly prone to malfunction. More importantly, in the early days programming a computer was an exasperating business requiring detailed familiarity with low-level details of the hardware organization. Indeed, the basic elements of the available programming languages referred to data structures and operations virtually at the hardware level. As the technology advanced, however, machines grew larger, faster, and more reliable, and so-called "higher-order" languages were created, such as FORTRAN, whose primitives referred to data structures and operations at a level relatively natural for human problem-solvers. Special-purpose applications programs written in a higher-order language congenial to the user could then be translated by general-purpose "compiler" or "interpreter" programs into the internal language of the computer for execution by the hardware.

I mention these details because they relate to the other main reason for the delay, which is more theoretical in nature and involves a basic question of strategy. The fantastic complexities of the brain can obviously be studied at many different levels from the cellular or even sub-cellular on up. At what level shall we seek scientific explanations of human mental activity? Many scientists, particularly those working at lower levels of the hierarchy of approaches, assume that events at the higher levels are in principle reducible to events at lower levels, and that reductive explanations employing the concepts of the lower levels are necessarily superior or more fundamental. Like many other psychologists, I strongly disagree with this view.

Consider, for example, the problem of understanding the behavior of a computer playing chess under the control of a stored program. It seems obvious that we might observe the behavior of the computer's flip-flops forever without gaining the slightest real understanding of the principles that are embodied in the program and explain its behavior. One of the essential characteristics of both human and animal behavior is that functional invariance at a higher level may be coupled with extreme diversity at lower levels.

For example, the rats whose cortex Lashley (1950) progressively destroyed in efforts to locate the memory trace could wobble, roll, or swim to their food box, and I can write a given message with either hand, or probably even with my feet if necessary. Attempted explanations based on activities of the participating muscle-groups, neurons, and so on would never get to the essential common feature, which is the approximate invariance of the final behavioral outcome.

Thus it seems appropriate in general to seek a higher and perhaps distinctively "psychological" level of explanation for human cognitive processes. For the computer simulation approach this involves identifying an appropriate set of elementary information structures and processes that seem powerful enough in principle to account for the relevant behaviors. The hypothesized structures and processes should perhaps also be potentially realizable in the brain, given its known properties—or at least not demonstrably inconsistent with these properties—but successful use of the computer as a tool of psychological understanding does not require the obviously false presumption of literal identity between digital computers and brains.

By the late 1950s and early 1960s, a number of higher-order programming languages had been created which emphasized the capacities of computers as general-purpose symbol-manipulating or information-transforming devices, rather than their more familiar "number-crunching" capacities. These languages (such as IPL-V, LISP, and SNOBOL) provided facilities, for example, for creating and manipulating complex tree-like data structures consisting of hierarchically ordered and cross-referenced lists of symbols. Structures of this sort played a central role in theoretical linguistics, and in this and other ways the new languages seemed to many workers to fall at about the right level of abstraction to support realistic efforts to model important aspects of human cognition.

Previous generations of workers had been obliged either to try to force human mental processes to conform to artificially simple but relatively rigorous behavioristic models, or to lapse into the uncontrolled introspection and mentalistic speculations of an earlier era. Now suddenly we were provided with a conceptual and technical apparatus sufficiently rich to express much of the necessary complexity without loss of rigor. The "black box" could be stuffed at will with whatever mechanisms seemed necessary to account for a given behavior. A complicated theory could be empirically tested by implementing it in the form of a computer program and verifying its ability to generate the behavior, or to simulate a record of the behavior. Progress toward machine intelligence could be assessed by means of "Turing's test"—the capacity of a computer program to mimic human behavior sufficiently well that a physically remote human interlocutor is unable to distinguish the program from another human in an "imitation game" (Turing, 1950). The seminal modeling ideas of Craik (1943) could at last be put into practice.

Enthusiasm for the computational approach to human cognition fairly crackles through the pages of influential early books such as G. A. Miller,

Galanter, and Pribram (1960), Lindsay and Norman (1972), and Newell and Simon (1972). Their enthusiasm seemed justified by the ensuing flood of theoretical and experimental work based on these ideas. In addition to the specific efforts at computer modeling of cognitive functions that is my main concern here, the rise of the computer-based information-processing paradigm also stimulated a healthy reawakening of broader interests in many of the old central concerns of psychology, such as mental imagery, thinking, and even consciousness. I must also acknowledge here that I myself initially embraced the computational theory practically without reservation. It certainly seemed an enormous step forward at the time. Fellow graduate students likely remember my oft-repeated attempts to assure them that the CTM would soon solve this or that fundamental problem in psychology. But all was not well.

Problems in Classic Cognitivism

With the appearance of suitable higher-order languages, numerous research groups set to work to endow computers with capacities for various kinds of skilled performance, including game-playing (especially complex games such as chess), problem-solving (for example, proving theorems in the propositional calculus), pattern recognition (such as recognizing sloppy hand-written characters), question-answering (in restricted domains such as baseball), and natural language translation. An important strategic difference quickly appeared, dividing these efforts roughly into two streams often called computer simulation (CS) and artificial intelligence (AI), respectively. Workers in CS remained faithful to the aim of increasing psychological understanding, in that they sought not only to reproduce particular kinds of human performance, but also to identify testable models of the means by which humans achieve that performance. AI workers, by contrast, disavowed any direct interest in psychology and sought rather to achieve high-level performance by whatever means possible.

I will not attempt to review the substantive accomplishments here.[6] Suffice it to say that many of the individual contributions represented considerable intellectual and technical achievements. Especially dazzling for me was "SHRDLU," a virtual robot that could interact with its handler in more or less ordinary-appearing language while carrying out complex sequences of requested operations on toy blocks of varied color, size, and shape (Winograd, 1972).

However, without intending to disparage these attainments I must add that they still fell very far short of what anyone could plausibly describe as general intelligence. I mention this only because of the extremely inflat-

6. Readers interested in following the history of such work can refer to landmark publications such as Feigenbaum and Feldman (1963), Minsky (1968), Schank and Colby (1973), Winograd (1972), and Winston (1975), or for an overview H. Gardner (1985).

ed image which many outside observers had at the time of the progress of this work, an image aggressively promoted by some of the research workers themselves. Many extraordinarily grandiose statements and predictions were being bandied about on the basis of very modest concrete accomplishments. Of course the predictions could conceivably have been correct; after all, the theoretical foundation is deep, and the work was still in its infancy. Perhaps we were simply in the early stages of an evolutionary process in which machines would inevitably attain at least the equivalent of human cognitive abilities.

My own confidence in the new paradigm was severely shaken, however, by extensive and sobering experience associated with my dissertation research in the area of natural language processing. The group with which I was working was principally concerned with the applied technical problem of reducing lexical ambiguity in English text, the practical aim being increased precision and power of automated computer-based content analysis procedures. In approaching this problem, we constructed an alphabetized concordance of some half-million words of "typical" behavioral science texts sampled from a variety of sources. This keyword-in-context listing (KWIC) identified the most frequently occurring words and supplied information about their typical patterns of usage. It turned out that about 2,000 *types* (in this context, dictionary entries) covered around 90% of the *tokens* (occurrent words) in an average running text. The striking regularities of word usage evident in the KWIC enabled us to build for each such dictionary entry a small computer routine that could scan the context in which each new token instance of that entry appeared and attempt to determine which member of a pre-established set of meanings was actually present. Crude as it was, the resulting system worked surprisingly well, achieving about 90% accuracy in a large new sample of text (E. F. Kelly & Stone, 1975). So at a practical level the project was rather successful.

My own primary interest, however, lay in determining whether the brute facts of everyday language as we were seeing them could successfully be captured by existing computationalist theories of semantic representation. The main such theory at the time was that of J. J. Katz and Fodor (1964). Their theory built upon the central notions of Chomsky's transformational linguistics and embodied the essential doctrines of the classical computationalist program as subsequently formalized by J. Fodor (1975), Pylyshyn (1984), and others. Specifically, it depicted determination of the meaning of a sentence as resulting from a rule-bound calculation, governed by the syntactic analysis of that sentence, which operates upon pre-established representations of the meanings of its constituent words. The possible meanings of the words themselves were treated as exhaustively specifiable in advance, with their essential semantic contents represented in terms of an underlying universal set of discrete "semantic markers"—in effect, atoms of meaning—or logical structures built out of such markers. In a nutshell, syntax was to provide for the generativity of language, our ability to make "infinite use of finite means," and semantics would go along for the ride.

Although Katz and Fodor had made their account appear at least semi-plausible for a few carefully contrived examples, it failed totally to account for obvious and pervasive features of the language in our database, language as actually used by ordinary speakers for ordinary purposes. For one thing, it was clear that resolution of lexical ambiguity routinely relied upon all sorts of linguistic and non-linguistic knowledge, and not just on some supposedly "essential" knowledge of pre-established word meanings. More importantly, sentence interpretation could not plausibly be viewed as a matter of context-driven *selection* from large numbers of pre-established and highly specific word meanings. Rather, it clearly involved *generation* of appropriate interpretations based on much smaller numbers of more general meanings (see, e.g., the entries provided by different dictionaries for common workhorse words such as *among*, *find*, *fine*, and *line*, and note that all major parts of speech display these properties). Any scheme based on atomization of meaning would necessarily fail to capture what to me had become the most characteristic property of word-meaning, a felt Gestalt quality or wholeness, at a level of generality that naturally supports extensions of usage into an indefinite variety—indeed whole families—of novel but appropriate contexts. The existing proposals could only represent the content of a general term such as "line" by some sample of its possible particularizations, and in so doing rendered themselves systematically unable to distinguish between metaphorical truth and literal falsehood. It seemed especially ironic that Katz and Fodor, for all their transformationalist invective about the need to respect the productivity of language, had erected a semantic theory which in effect elevated the commonplace to a standard of propriety and denied creativity at the level of words or concepts. Their theory failed to account even for *identification*, let alone *representation*, of linguistic meaning (E. F. Kelly, 1975).

I also noted with a certain degree of alarm that this crucial property of generality underlying the normal use of words seemed continuous with developmentally earlier achievements. Skilled motor acts and perceptual recognition, for example, require similar on-the-fly adaptations of past learning to present circumstance. It seemed at least vaguely conceivable that these difficult but undeniably fundamental qualities of embodied action and cognition might somehow be rooted in lower-level properties of the nervous system as a particular kind of computing machine. Early discussions had emphasized similarities between brains and digital computers, for example treating the all-or-nothing neural spike discharge or action potential as the equivalent of a digital relay. In more recent times, however, we had become increasingly sensitized to the ubiquitous presence in real nervous systems of inherently more continuous or "analog" processes, such as the spatial and temporal summation of neural input that leads to spike formation, and the rate and pattern of the resulting spike discharges. Workers in CS and AI had been relying heavily on their doctrine of "multiple realizability," assuming perhaps too cavalierly that they could safely disregard such low-level "hardware" details and pitch their efforts at a level of abstraction that happened to be congenial both to them and to the available computers. What seemed now to be emerging, however, was that these low-level neurophysiological properties might enter into the overall computational possibilities of the brain in a much more fundamental way than previously suspected. Perhaps the "missing" cognitive attributes were dependent upon such low-level characteristics. Most neuroscientists, of course—even while adopting more or less wholesale the new computationalist or "information-processing" paradigm—had always presumed this would be so.

The net result of all this was to make me much more skeptical and pessimistic regarding the prospects for computational cognitivism as it was then being practiced. To be sure, others had noted similar problems and were trying to do something about them. The importance of incorporating more general knowledge of the world into language-processing models, for example, had already begun to be recognized, and new formal devices were being introduced to represent what the computer needed to know (what we ourselves know) about various sorts of "typical" situations it might encounter. But it seemed clear to me that all of these knowledge-representation devices, such as "frames" (Minsky, 1975), "scripts" (Schank & Colby, 1973), and "schemata" (Neisser, 1976), suffered essentially the same problems I had identified in the Katz and Fodor account of word meaning. Specifically, they required the possible scenarios of application to be spelled out in advance, in great but necessarily incomplete detail, and as a result ended up being "brittle," intolerant of even minor departures from the pre-programmed expectations. I also pointed out that Winograd's undeniable success with SHRDLU had derived in considerable part precisely from his careful *a priori* restriction of the problem domain in a manner that allowed him essentially to circumvent this whole complex of very difficult issues.[7]

Many of the themes just sounded have been confirmed and amplified in more recent work. On the positive side, our knowledge of the content, organization, and development of the human conceptual system has increased enormously. The old Socratic idea that concepts must be defined in terms of necessary and sufficient features has given way to a recognition of the role of perceptual-level examples, prototypes, and family resemblances in the content of real human concepts (Medin & Heit, 1999; Rosch & Lloyd, 1978; E. E. Smith & Medin, 1981). The contributions of a fundamental human capacity for *metaphorizing* at levels ranging from everyday language to the highest flights of creativity, are also now more widely appreciated (Gentner, Holyoak, & Kokinov, 2001; Hofstadter & FARG, 1995; Holyoak & Thagard, 1995; Lakoff, 1987, 1995; see also our Chapter 7). Computer language-processing systems have tended to move, as I predicted, toward a relatively simplified and "surfacy" syntax coupled with richer representations of the lexicon, and they sometimes attempt to resolve residual ambiguities with the aid of statistical data derived from large databases.

More crucial to the concerns of this chapter, however, are major subsequent events on the negative side. Shortly after I completed my disser-

7. For further details see E. F. Kelly (1975).

tation, Hubert Dreyfus (1972) systematically questioned both the progress and the prospects of CS and AI. He began by reviewing the early work in game-playing, problem-solving, language translation, and pattern recognition. Work in each domain was characterized by a common pattern consisting of encouraging early success followed by steadily diminishing returns. Subsequent work in artificial intelligence, according to Dreyfus, had fared little better, achieving its limited successes only by operating in artificially constrained environments that do not exemplify fundamental difficulties handled with conspicuous ease by everyday human intelligence. Dreyfus argued that the extreme efficiency of human intelligence—which becomes progressively more apparent as we move toward problem domains more typical of its ordinary application—rests on a complex of interrelated abilities which he termed fringe consciousness, ambiguity tolerance based on efficient use of context, essential-inessential distinctions, and perspicuous grouping. Most critically of all, human cognitive performance is characteristically guided by *insight,* an overall grasp of the problem situation, with essential aspects at the foreground of attention set against an organizing but largely implicit background. Phenomenologically, the *situation* is primary; specific facts or features of the situation may only become evident through a deliberate attentive effort of a quite secondary sort. By contrast, Dreyfus argued, for the computer all facts must be specified in advance as explicit bits of atomic data; whatever crude representation of the situation the computer can achieve is necessarily constructed by explicit calculation upon these situation-independent facts. Ironically, AI seemed to have adopted the conceptual framework of Wittgenstein's *Tractatus* shortly after the realities of language use had driven Wittgenstein himself to abandon it. Building upon these and related observations, Dreyfus attempted to establish his main thesis, that central human mental skills are *in principle* not reproducible on digital computers.

Dreyfus's concerns clearly overlapped with mine, and I therefore had no doubt that he had identified a cluster of problems which at the very least constitute extremely difficult problems of practice, although I was not yet convinced that these problems were insoluble in principle. Hardcore AI partisans experienced no such unease, attacking Dreyfus immediately and viciously as merely an ignorant outsider. Shortly afterward, however, Joseph Weizenbaum, a prominent AI insider,[8] expressed broadly similar kinds of misgivings, although he was less confident than Dreyfus in theoretical arguments against the possibility of machine intelligence, and relied primarily on a moral argument to the effect that there are many kinds of things, including psychotherapy, which computers should never be permitted to perform (Weizenbaum, 1976).

8. Among other things, Weizenbaum was author of the widely known ELIZA program, which simulates a non-directive psychotherapist by means of various simple technical devices that involve no "understanding" whatever. Weizenbaum had been horrified to discover many persons interacting with this program as though it were an actual human being.

The most significant by far of these rumblings from within, however, occurred a decade later when a consummate insider, Terry Winograd himself, publicly defected from the program of classical AI. Winograd and Flores (1986) explicitly embraced most of the points already raised above, emphasizing in particular that large parts of human mental life cannot be reduced to explicit rules and therefore cannot be formalized for production by a computer program. Their detailed and fully-informed argument should be required reading for anyone interested in these issues.[9] The best we can hope for along classical lines, they concluded, is special-purpose expert systems, adapted to carefully circumscribed domains that lend themselves to such formalization. Current examples, of course, include things like chess-playing, integration and differentiation of mathematical formulae, and perhaps certain areas of medical diagnosis.

The Second Cognitive Revolution: Connectionism and Dynamic Systems

Since the late 1970s psychology has taken a strongly biological turn, and cognitive science has evolved into cognitive neuroscience. This came as somewhat of a surprise to persons like myself who had been reared in the intellectual tradition of classical or "symbolic" cognitivism and had expected to do all their proper business with little or no reference to biology. When I was a graduate student, for example, the required course in physiological psychology consisted essentially of a smattering of neuroanatomy followed by a lot of boring stuff about appetitive behavior in lower organisms, and that was pretty much that.

I will single out four main threads of this evolution. The first arose within classical cognitivism itself. As indicated above, there was a lot of ferment in the early days as researchers sought to identify appropriate forms of representation for the sorts of knowledge we humans can bring to bear in our thinking, speaking, and so on. Largely reflecting its own historical origins and the available *means* of representation, cognitive theory initially focused almost exclusively on linguistic or propositional forms of knowledge representation. Mental imagery, however, had recently been readmitted onto the roster of acceptable research topics (R. R. Holt, 1964), and a number of important new experimental studies were being carried out, especially by Roger Shepard, Stephen Kosslyn, and various others. On the strength of these investigations Kosslyn (1973) ventured to advance an information-processing theory of visual imagery in which the underlying knowledge structures hypothesized to support the generation of imagery were themselves essentially pictorial and spatial in nature. This provoked an intense reaction from

9. Fundamentally similar views have also been advanced by writers such as Polanyi (1966) and Searle (1992, chap. 8). It is ironic, and perhaps symptomatic, that CTM advocate Robert Harnish (2002, pp. 107–123) reports enthusiastically on SHRDLU without even mentioning Winograd's defection.

Zenon Pylyshyn (1973), who reaffirmed the classical cognitivist view that *all* knowledge is linguistic or propositional in character (J. Fodor, 1975). The ensuing imagery debate has raged on more or less ever since, its intricate experimental details of interest primarily to the participants.[10] For present purposes the critical event was an important theoretical paper by John R. Anderson (1978). Anderson argued that since *both* kinds of representations (and potentially many others as well) could be made internally coherent, and would lead to identical behavioral predictions, a fundamental theoretical indeterminacy had emerged. Considerations of parsimony and efficiency might lead us to *prefer* one such theory to its competitors, but only physiological observations could potentially determine which was in fact *correct*. Thus it became evident, more generally, that neurophysiological data can sometimes provide important constraints on psychological theory.

The second thread was the emergence and consolidation following World War II of neuropsychology as a scientific discipline. An outgrowth and companion of the medical discipline of neurology, neuropsychology seeks to gain insight into the nature and operations of the mind through careful observation and analysis of the mental disturbances, sometimes highly specific and bizarre, that are produced by gunshot or shrapnel wounds, strokes, degenerative diseases, and other forms of injury to the brain.[11] The general thrust of this work was to suggest that skilled cognitive performances of all kinds characteristically involve cooperation of a number of localized cortical and subcortical regions of the brain, each presumptively specialized for some particular role in the overall performance. Classical cognitivism quickly adapted to this emerging picture of things, assimilating its fundamental theme of the mind as a computational or information-processing mechanism to a "modular" view of its components and internal organization (J. Fodor, 1983; Pinker, 1997).

The third development was the advent and maturation of the functional neuroimaging technologies mentioned in the Introduction, which enable us to observe directly, without opening up the skull, the activity of the working human brain. Two principal classes of such methods are currently available, although others are under development.[12] The first provides measures of the electric and magnetic fields directly generated by neuroelectric activity in populations of suitably located and oriented cortical neurons (elec-

10. But see Brann (1991) and N. J. T. Thomas (1999) for excellent third-party reviews.

11. Some important early landmarks here are books by H. Gardner (1976), Luria (1966), Sacks (1987), and Shallice (1988).

12. In addition to the "macro" technologies described in the text, which operate on scales from the whole brain down to roughly naked-eye-sized parts of it, contemporary neuroscience has developed an impressive arsenal of "micro" technologies, suitable mainly for use in animal studies, that operate down to the cellular or even subcellular level. Other emerging developments at the macro level that look especially promising for future work in humans include transcranial optical imaging and transcranial magnetic stimulation.

troencephalography [EEG]; magnetoencephalography [MEG]). The second provides measures of hemodynamic or metabolic consequences of neural activity such as local changes of blood flow, glucose consumption, or blood oxygenation (especially positron emission tomography [PET]; and functional magnetic resonance imaging [fMRI]). All these technologies are complex and expensive, and they tend within and between classes to have complementary strengths and weaknesses (see, e.g., Nunez & Silberstein, 2000; Toga & Mazziotta, 1996; Wikswo, Gevins, & Williamson, 1993). Together, they undoubtedly constitute a major methodological advance for cognitive neuroscience. Indeed, scarcely an issue now goes by of any cognitive neuroscience journal that does not contain one or more papers featuring images outfitted with colored spots identifying regions of "significant" brain "activation" produced by some stimulus or task.[13]

The final thread is the one most directly germane to our primary subject, the computational theory of the mind (CTM). Specifically, discouragement with the progress of classical or symbolic cognitivism led in the 1980s to an enormous resurgence of interest in a fundamentally different style of computation that also seems more directly comparable to what actually goes on in brains—namely, propagation of activity through large networks of basically similar elementary units.

I say "resurgence" because this approach actually harks all the way back to the seminal work of McCulloch and Pitts (1943), Hebb (1949), and others. There had been some promising early steps in this direction, notably the work of Rosenblatt (1962) on "perceptrons," but mainstream interest had largely faded under the impact of a devastating critique by AI partisans Marvin Minsky and Seymour Papert (1968). These authors, mathematicians by training, proved rigorously that simple one-layer perceptrons cannot compute even simple things such as the elementary logic function "exclusive OR" (that is, either A or B but not both). In their conclusion, summing up the implications of these results, they conjectured that more complicated networks would fare little better. In effect they urged the field to stay focused on the CTM in its classic symbol-processing form. One of the great ironies here, as pointed out by Dupuy (2000), is that whereas John von Neumann, the great mathematician, had been interested in expanding the possibilities of computation by reference to the actual behavior of the brain, Warren McCulloch, a neuroscientist, had in effect abstracted from the brain a logic machine; and now here was Minsky, who had been von Neumann's doctoral student at Princeton, promoting McCulloch-style symbolic computation in preference to the neurophysiologically grounded approach advocated by his own illustrious mentor.

13. Most cognitive neuroscientists clearly regard such work as repeatedly and unambiguously confirming the basic mind-brain doctrine of contemporary physicalism, but many significant technical uncertainties remain regarding procedures for acquisition, processing, and interpretation of imaging data, and some of the available results actually conflict with that doctrine. We will touch upon these issues later in this chapter, as well as in our Chapters 4 and 9.

At any rate the net effect was to drive neural-network models temporarily to the margins of the field, although a few dedicated souls such as James Anderson and Stephen Grossberg soldiered on. The subject burst back into the mainstream, however, with the publication of a two-volume handbook on parallel distributed processing (PDP) or "connectionism" as it came to be called (Rumelhart & McClelland, 1986).[14] Connectionism has subsequently emerged as a serious rival to classical cognitivism, but I will give here only the briefest account of these developments.

The fundamental faith of connectionists is that intelligence emerges from the interactions of large numbers of simple processing units organized in a network of appropriate structure. By modifying features of network architecture such as the number of elementary units, the number of layers, their connectivity patterns (feed forward only vs. recurrent), the rules for activating units (simple thresholds, sigmoid functions), and the rules for modifying the connection strengths among units in light of network performance or experience (Hebb, delta, generalized delta), an enormous variety of interesting behaviors can be produced. Networks have proved especially good at some things at which classical models were conspicuously bad, such as pattern recognition, perceptual learning and generalization, and filling in of incomplete input. They also display psychologically interesting and desirable properties such as content-addressable memory and "graceful degradation"—the tendency, as in Lashley's rats, for performance to decline smoothly and continuously as units are progressively removed. It is perhaps not surprising, given these properties, that unbridled optimism soon reappeared within the field. One leading connectionist, Smolensky (1988), has proclaimed that "it is likely that connectionist models will offer the most significant progress of the past several millennia on the mind/body problem" (p. 3). Many contemporary psychologists agree, and even some philosophers of mind, including in particular Daniel Dennett and the Churchlands, are no less enthusiastic.

Significant problems have also come to light, however. Although network models are often said to be "neurally inspired," the current level of neurophysiological realism is typically very low. Both the "neurons" themselves and their connectivity patterns are routinely idealized and distorted, and the most successful learning rule ("back propagation" or generalized delta) still has no generally recognized counterpart in the nervous system (Crick, 1994). Models often have large numbers of free parameters which must be adjusted to fit specific situations, raising doubts about their generality. Similarly, generation of a targeted behavior is sometimes strongly and unrealistically dependent on the exact content and order of previous network experience or training. Many observers, including Papert (1988), also worry that problems of catastrophic interference between previously learned behaviors will emerge as networks are scaled up to more realis-

14. Excellent general introductions are provided by Bechtel and Abrahamsen (2002) and Harnish (2002), and many of the most important early papers are reprinted, with illuminating commentaries, by J. A. Anderson and Rosenfeld (1988).

tic dimensions. Most important of all, networks have particular difficulty capturing precisely those characteristics of human cognition to which the classical cognitivist approach seems best suited—features such as its hierarchical organization, temporal orderliness, and productivity. Indeed, despite some new technical wrinkles, connectionism can be viewed as amounting in large part to a modern revival of 19th-century associationism. To the extent that this characterization is correct, connectionism therefore inherits the very same problems that led to the rise of classic cognitivism in the first place (J. Fodor, 2001; Pinker & Mehler, 1988).

The last 20 years or so of computational modeling of the mind have been dominated by the attempts of these two warring paradigms to refine themselves and work out their relationship. Classical symbol-manipulation modelers, for example, are trying to find ways to make their models more adaptable and less brittle, while connectionists are looking for better ways of generating orderly behavior in the absence of explicit rules. Each paradigm clearly aspires to absorbing the other, but some workers are also exploring "hybrid" computational systems in which the connectionist part takes care of things like perceptual learning and category formation—the subsymbolic level or "microstructure" of cognition—while a more classical symbol-manipulation part deals with things like problem-solving and language. It is not at all clear how things will sort out, although the connectionist faction seems presently ascendant.

I must also mention, however, one further recent development emerging from within connectionism itself, one that threatens in effect to devour it from the other side. This movement, dynamic systems theory, has close ties to modern technical developments in the physics and mathematics of complex systems. There can be no doubt that the brain, with its vast network of reciprocally interconnected and non-linear elements, is an example of the kind of systems to which these new developments apply. Dynamic systems theorists often use typical connectionist technical apparatus to synthesize network models, but they bring to bear additional mathematical and graphical tools to characterize and analyze the temporal dynamics of network behavior. The most distinctive property of this school, however, is its more radical theoretical position. In contrast with mainstream connectionism, which it regards as a kind of halfway-house or unholy compromise with classical cognitivism, it advocates abandoning altogether cognitivism's next deepest commitment after computation itself—namely, the concept of a *representational level.* From the dynamicist point of view what goes on inside our heads is nothing like what the classical formulation presumes, with computational processes operating on stored symbolic knowledge-representations of one or more sorts. There is instead only the mechanical operation of a vast neural network in accordance with deterministic rules. As Dupuy (2000) observed, this is clearly the direction in which the early cyberneticians such as von Neumann were headed. It is also the view of leading contemporary neuroscientists and modelers such as Edelman and Tononi (2000) and Walter Freeman (1999, 2000).[15]

I shall not attempt here to adjudicate among these various schools of computationalism on their own terms. Readers interested in getting a more complete picture of this enormous and thriving industry in all its facets can probably do no better than to sample the contents of the *MIT Encyclopedia of the Cognitive Sciences* (MITECS) (R. A. Wilson & Keil, 1999). For the record, my own overall sense is that the accomplishments, although certainly substantial, continue to lag the "hype" by a wide margin. This seems especially true in the area of language processing, which, as Descartes and Chomsky in particular have insisted, should be viewed as a crucial test case. Despite my skepticism, however, I believe that persons of all philosophic or methodological persuasions should strongly support further efforts along all of these lines. As the computational theories evolve, they are constantly sharpening our understanding not only of what the various kinds of computational models can do, but also of what we ourselves do in a broad range of situations. Even apart from its ultimate success or failure, each new attempt to extend computer modeling into a novel domain of human cognitive performance forces us in the first instance to try to understand in detail what capacities are presupposed by that performance. As our understanding of the capacities of minds deepens and becomes more detailed, it should become increasingly possible to judge precisely which of those capacities may be explainable, and to what extent, in terms of such models.

There are good reasons, however, to believe that computationalism alone, in *any* of its forms, cannot provide a complete account of the mind. I turn next to these. All readers, but especially newcomers to these issues, are advised that from this point forward my discussion becomes more tendentious and increasingly at odds with current mainstream opinion.

John Searle's Critique of Computational Theories of the Mind

Many persons both inside and outside of psychology have expressed reservations of one sort or another about computationalism, but without doubt the most sweeping, searching, and sustained attack on the CTM has come from Berkeley philosopher John Searle.

Briefly, Searle has two principal arguments.[16] The first, the famous "Chinese Room" argument, was directed at the central claim of strong artificial intelligence—specifically, the idea that running a computer program can of itself be sufficient for, or constitutive of, understanding (Searle, 1980, 1984, 1990). The essence of this thought experiment is that a person who

15. For useful general introductions to dynamic systems see Bechtel and Abrahamsen (2002, chap. 8), A. Clark (2001), Dupuy (2000), Kelso (1995), Port and van Gelder (1998), and papers by Beer (2000) and van Gelder (1998).

16. Parenthetically, a neglected paper by Heil (1981) argued on very similar grounds that the computationalism of J. Fodor (1975) is fundamentally mistaken.

knows no Chinese, but who appropriately answers questions in Chinese by virtue of manipulating symbols according to the rules of a (hypothetical) computer program, would not thereby understand any part of the resulting "conversation." Computing is by definition purely syntactical, and consists only of manipulation of uninterpeted formal symbols according to the explicit rules of a program. The occupant of the Chinese room does all that but understands nothing. Hence, semantics is something over and above syntax, and strong AI is false.[17] Moreover, the Turing test is clearly inadequate; *simulation* is not *duplication,* and to act *as if* one understands Chinese does not guarantee that one does.

Classical cognitivism in its more general forms, however, might seem to escape the force of this simple argument, insofar as the computational component is no longer regarded as constituting or providing the semantics, but only as manipulating, in a manner that mirrors and "respects" their content, semantic representations that are provided elsewhere in the theory (as, e.g., in the theory of J. J. Katz & Fodor, 1964). Against this move Searle mounts a further and deeper argument. The most basic underlying assumption of classical cognitivism is that the brain, although certainly different from von Neumann machines, literally *is* a computer. However, Searle argues, "computation" and "information-processing" are not observer-independent features of the world that we empirically discover, like mass, gravity, photosynthesis, and digestion. Rather, these are observer-relative properties that we assign to certain systems for our own purposes. In short, the claim that the brain is a computer is not false, but incoherent. Not only is semantics not intrinsic to syntax, as shown by the Chinese Room, but syntax is not intrinsic to physics, or to the neurophysiology of the brain (Searle, 1992, 1997).

The details of Searle's arguments, and the firestorms of controversy they have provoked over the years, are far too numerous and complex to sort out here, but I wish to make a few summary remarks.

First, like other critics of the CTM such as Dreyfus (1972) and Penrose (1989, 1994), Searle has been startled by the intensity of the reactions he provokes:

> Oddly enough I have encountered more passion from adherents of the computational theory of the mind than from adherents of traditional religious doctrines of the soul. Some computationalists invest an almost religious intensity into their faith that our deepest problems about the mind will have a computational solution. Many people apparently believe that somehow or other, unless we are proven to be computers, something terribly important will be lost.[18] (Searle, 1997, p. 189)

17. According to Dupuy (2000, pp. 141–142), Kurt Gödel himself specifically stated that irreducibility of semantics to syntax was the "real point" of his incompleteness theorem. See also Penrose (1989, 1994).

18. See Searle (1980) for some choice examples of these reactions. Additional examples of the quasi-religious fervor of hard-core compuphiliacs can be found in Brockman (2003). Michael Grosso informs me that this kind of investment of re-

Second, this "passion" undoubtedly accounts for the apparent inability of many psychological and philosophical defenders of the CTM even to report Searle's message accurately, let alone to appreciate its force. Without dwelling upon the details, see for example Bechtel and Abrahamsen (2002, pp. 303–304), Boden (1990), Chalmers (1996, chap. 9), H. Gardner (1985, pp. 171–177), Harnish (2002, chap. 9 & chap. 13), and Pinker (1997, pp. 93–96). Many others, such as Minsky (1985), Newell (1990), and Thagard (1998), essentially ignore him altogether. Searle defends himself much better against his critics than I could do on his behalf, and fortunately he has taken a number of opportunities to do so. In addition to the original debate over the Chinese room (Searle, 1980), see in particular his encounters with the Churchlands (Searle, 1990) and with Dennett (Searle, 1997).

Third, although the initial targets of Searle's arguments were strong AI and cognitivism in its now classic "symbol-processing" formulation, there is no doubt that his arguments apply to computationalism in all of its forms. Searle made this explicit for standard forms of connectionism in his exchange with Dennett (Searle, 1997), and I think he would certainly do so for dynamic systems theory as well, and for the same reasons. The fundamental commonality of the different sorts of models is underscored by the fact that they all are typically implemented in the same sort of physical architecture, the standard von Neumann architecture used in garden-variety personal computers. Specifics of the computing architecture can profoundly influence the speed and efficiency of computation, but this does not alter its fundamental character and has no bearing on the core theoretical issues.[19]

In sum, I feel sure that Searle's negative judgment regarding the computational theory of the mind will be sustained. Like Nagel (1993a), I have come to regard the CTM as one of the dominant illusions of our age. I hasten to add that this judgment has little *practical* import for cognitive science; for as Searle himself points out, and as I remarked above, use of computers to model particular cognitive functions is a perfectly legitimate and undoubtedly useful scientific activity. But for a fundamental theory of the mind we must look elsewhere.

To the extent that physicalist accounts of the mind are identifiable with the CTM, Searle and his allies have already discredited them. However, physicalism has not yet exhausted its resources. Searle's further and positive contribution is to advocate a novel philosophic position which he calls "biological naturalism," a position which in fact closely approximates the views of many leading neuroscientists. I turn next to this.

---

ligiosity in materialism as a philosophic doctrine goes back at least as far as Empedocles, who was called "soter" (savior) by his followers.

19. Parenthetically, shifting the effective *locus* of the computations to a level above (E. L. Schwartz, 1999) or below (Penrose, 1989, 1994) that of single network elements also has no bearing on these issues.

Biological Naturalism: The Final Frontier

To set the stage I will quote the most trenchant statement known to me regarding the current status of the mind-body problem. It is from philosopher Thomas Nagel (1993b):

> The mind-body problem exists because we naturally want to include the mental life of conscious organisms in a comprehensive scientific understanding of the world. On the one hand it seems obvious that everything that happens in the mind depends on, or is, something that happens in the brain. On the other hand the defining features of mental states and events, features like their intentionality, their subjectivity and their conscious experiential quality, seem not to be comprehensible simply in terms of the physical operation of the organism. This is not just because we have not yet accumulated enough empirical information: the problem is theoretical. We cannot at present imagine an explanation of colour perception, for example, which would do for that phenomenon what chemistry has done for combustion—an explanation which would tell us in physical terms, and without residue, what the experience of colour perception *is*. Philosophical analyses of the distinguishing features of the mental that are designed to get us over this hurdle generally involve implausible forms of reductionism, behaviouristic in inspiration. The question is whether there is another way of bringing mental phenomena into a unified conception of objective reality without relying on a narrow standard of objectivity which excludes everything that makes them interesting. (p. 1)

Searle believes he has a good physicalist answer—indeed, in its general form the only *possible* answer—to Nagel's question. It goes like this: One can accept the reality of conscious mental life without lapsing into dualism, which (he thinks) would be tantamount to abandoning 400 years of cumulative scientific achievement. Consciousness is a biological process as physical as digestion, caused by low-level neurophysiological events in the brain such as neuron firings and the like. But consciousness is not a separate something, over and above the brain action; the causality is not of the boy-hits-ball-then-ball-breaks-window sort. Rather, consciousness *emerges*, in roughly the same way that solidity emerges when water freezes upon reaching a certain critical temperature. It is a system-level property of the brain. And this is not epiphenomenalism, the idea that consciousness is real but ineffectual; like the solidity of ice or other emergent physical properties, consciousness has causal consequences, causal powers.

Although consciousness is thus at least in principle *causally* reducible, it is not *ontologically* reducible; for this would involve showing that what appears to us as consciousness is in reality something else, but in the case of consciousness itself, unlike the apparent rising and setting of the sun, the appearance *is* the reality. For Searle the CTM was on the right track, insofar as it was a materialist theory of the mind, but it was not nearly materialistic enough. To imagine that the mind can be instantiated in computer programs of any kind is to entertain a kind of residual dualism. The brain generates mind and consciousness by physical, causal mechanisms inherent in our biology, and we need to respect that unique biological reality. This does not entail that mind and consciousness could not appear in other places, for example in some sort of suitably constructed artifact; but in order for this to occur, the physical substrate of the artifact would need to embody causal powers at least equivalent to those inherent in the brain itself.

That summarizes the central theoretical part of Searle's position. He also goes on to characterize the phenomenology of consciousness in ways that are strikingly reminiscent of James (1890b), and considers in general terms how best to pursue its scientific study. Clearly, given his theoretical commitments, the main order of business is to study the associated neurophysiology. Searle (1997) singled out for special praise neuroscientists such as Gerald Edelman and Francis Crick who were in effect carrying out this program. His admiration for real neuroscience is certainly justified, and it is apparently reciprocated; in a recent paper in the *Annual Review of Neuroscience* he again summarizes his theoretical views regarding consciousness and offers a variety of additional suggestions, both shrewd and detailed, for further neuroscientific investigation (Searle, 2000).

To summarize: In my view John Searle deserves enormous credit for having almost single-handedly altered the terms of the mind-brain controversy. On the negative side, his destructive critique of the CTM should eliminate from contention a family of views that have dominated the past half-century, especially in psychology. On the positive side, his effective advocacy of "biological naturalism" has focused attention clearly and sharply on the position that I believe represents the ultimate development, the necessary culmination, of a conventional physicalist approach to the mind. The fundamental question before us now reduces starkly to this: Can everything we know about the mind be explained in terms of brain processes?

Problems with Biological Naturalism

First, briefly, some conceptual issues. I am not at all persuaded that Searle has succeeded in making meaningful distinctions between his philosophical views and those of a host of others who would describe themselves as advocates of token identity or even property dualism. In particular, his abstract account of the "emergence" of consciousness strikes me as verging upon intellectual sleight of hand. Can mental properties simply be stipulated into physicality in this way? The analogies seem faulty. In the water/ice situation, for example, both ends of the causal relation are indisputably physical things that we know how to observe and measure in conventional physical ways. But that is exactly what is at issue in the relation of brain to mind, as Nagel pointed out.

Related to this, and also captured by Nagel's remarks, we do not in fact have anything even remotely resembling a full causal account of consciousness, let alone an account that we can understand in the way we understand the freezing of water. Intelligibility of causal accounts is surely something we would like to have, but in this case it seems singularly difficult to imagine how we could possibly get one. I will leave aside here, however, the more philosophic issue whether we should require that a satisfactory causal account be *intelligible*, and focus instead on the prior empirical question whether we can get one *at all*.

For Searle it is virtually axiomatic, a given, that brain processes causally generate every detail of our conscious mental life. Throughout his writings he characterizes this as a demonstrated fact, something we know with complete certainty and beyond any possibility of doubt. In the discussion of his paper in Bock and Marsh (1993), for example, he candidly exclaims "frankly, I just can't take it seriously that my point of view, that brain processes cause consciousness, is denied!" (p. 77).

The vast majority of contemporary neuroscientists and psychologists undoubtedly would agree with Searle in accepting without hesitation this basic premise, although many would perhaps question, as I do, details of his account of the emergence, and his confidence that we will be able to achieve a biological theory that is both adequately complete and theoretically satisfying.[20] As noted in the Introduction, the assumption that brain generates mind—that the mind is what the brain does, full stop—seems plausible in light of much prior scientific experience, and has generally served us well as a working hypothesis. It will undoubtedly continue for most scientists to do so. And this is not a bad thing; for as Dupuy (2000) remarked: "The only way to prove the falsity of materialism is to give it every benefit of doubt, to allow it to push forward as far as it can, while remaining alert to its missteps, to the obstacles that it encounters, and, ultimately, to the limits it runs up against. Any other method—fixing its boundaries in advance, for example—is bound to fail" (p. 25).

I agree strongly with this view. I also appreciate that the human brain is a fantastically complex biological system which undoubtedly harbors layer upon layer of neurophysiological mechanism still to be unraveled by our steadily deepening scientific inquiry. New discoveries are constantly being made, some of which profoundly enrich our appreciation of the brain's resources. For example, the old idea that neurons communicate exclusively

20. I think this characterization applies to contemporary philosophers as well, although I am not sufficiently well informed to be sure of this. Nagel appears to accept that there must be such a causal linkage, while doubting that we can make it intelligible. Colin McGinn (1999) has staked out a similar position which accepts the existence of causal connections but attempts to deny on principled grounds (unsuccessfully, I think) that we can ever understand them. Searle's most radical philosophical opponent, however, is undoubtedly David Chalmers (1996). Chalmers argues that "zombies," beings exactly like us behaviorally but completely unconscious, are logically conceivable, and that consciousness must therefore be something above and beyond the recognized physical order. Searle will have none of this, but his rebuttal again presumes what is in question, that low-level physical processes in the brain cause consciousness. See their exchange in Searle (1997).

by means of direct and specific synaptic connections has been enriched by discovery of complementary "volume-conduction" effects caused by diffusion of neurotransmitters through the local extracellular space (Agnati, Bjelke, & Fuxe, 1992). Again, neuroscientists had long believed that the dendrites which make up the input arbor of a typical cortical neuron are essentially passive cables; but in recent years we have discovered that they are enormously more complex and contribute actively to the overall electrical behavior of the cell (see, e.g., the special issue of *Science*, October 27, 2000). Similarly, it had long been believed that glial cells provide only structural and metabolic support for the really important elements, the neurons (which they greatly outnumber), but it has recently been demonstrated that by scavenging potassium ions from the extracellular space, glia can also directly modify the electrical behavior of local neural populations (Kohn, Metz, Quibrera, Tommerdahl, & Whitsel, 2000; Kohn, Metz, Tommerdahl, & Whitsel, 2002).[21]

Other examples could readily be provided, but the point should already be clear: No one can prophesy with certainty how far or even in precisely what directions our evolving understanding of brain mechanisms may lead. Nevertheless, and unlike Dupuy (2000), I believe that sufficient information is already in hand to demonstrate that biological naturalism as currently conceived is not only incomplete but *false* as a theory of the mind.

At this point we make the empirical turn that is the central and distinctive contribution of this book. I will begin by outlining the conceptual framework that underlies our presentation. Imagine if you will two complex streams of activity flowing through time in parallel, one consisting of your conscious mental experience, the other of the myriad physiological processes going on in your brain. Imagine further, even though it is scarcely feasible in practice, that we could divide both streams individually into a sequence of states, and in such a way that the mental states correspond to the brain states. Suppose still further, and again counterfactually, that perfect 1:1 correspondence between the two sequences has been established empirically. We have discovered the Holy Grail of neuroscience and psychology, the neural correlates of consciousness.

All the traditional philosophical positions on the mind-body problem arise from different ways of interpreting this correlation. The current mainstream consensus is that brain processes generate or constitute mental processes, but this is not the only possible interpretation.

Note first that even perfect correlation would not necessarily entail *identity*. For example, like all other mammals we have both hearts and lungs, but hearts and lungs are not identical. It remains at least conceptually possible that minds and brains are distinct, though functionally closely linked.

---

21. Perhaps not coincidentally, detailed postmortem anatomical investigation of Einstein's brain revealed that the most striking respect in which it differed from ordinary brains was in having significantly larger numbers of glia (Diamond, Scheibel, & Harvey, 1985).

The fundamental scientific strategy for sorting out the causal structure underlying observed correlations is of course to attempt to determine what influences what by manipulating the two sides of the correlation. It is evident, and everyone agrees, that physical events such as sitting on a tack can influence mental events. But what about the other way around? It seems equally obvious, naively, that mental events cause physical events, too. For example, as Searle likes to say, I decide to raise my arm and it goes up. But there is a hitch here, an asymmetry in the causal structure. Physicalists can normally reply, and do in their preferred fashion, that the causality in such cases resides not in the mental *per se* but in its physical equivalents or accompaniments. In sum, we can cleanly, simply, and directly manipulate the *physical* side of the correlation, but not so the *mental*, at least under ordinary conditions.

Nevertheless, we will argue, the correlations we actually observe are not simply incomplete but demonstrably imperfect. There exist certain kinds of empirically verifiable mental properties, states, and effects that appear to outstrip in principle the explanatory potential of physical processes occurring in brains.[22] Facts of this sort, moreover, can often be accommodated more naturally within an alternative interpretation of the mind-brain correlation, one already developed in abstract form by William James (1898/1900).

James pointed out that to describe the mind as a function of the brain does not fully specify the character of the functional dependence. Physiologists routinely presume that the role of the brain is *productive*, the brain generating the mind in something like the way the tea kettle generates steam, or the electric current flowing in a lamp generates light. But other forms of functional dependence exist which merit closer consideration. The true function of the brain might for example be *permissive*, like the trigger of a crossbow, or more importantly, *transmissive*, like an optical lens or a prism, or like the keys of a pipe organ (or perhaps, in more contemporary terms, like the receivers in our radios and televisions).

More generally, one can at least dimly imagine some sort of mental reality, which in James's view might be anything from a finite mind or personality to a World Soul, that is closely coupled to the brain functionally but somehow distinct from it. Within this basic framework James himself spoke variously of the brain as straining, sifting, canalizing, limiting, and individualizing that larger mental reality existing behind the scenes. He also quoted approvingly Schiller's (1891/1894, pp. 293, 295) characterization of matter as "an admirably calculated machinery for regulating, limiting, and restraining the consciousness which it encases.…Matter is not that which *produces* Consciousness, but that which *limits* it, and confines its intensity within certain limits" (James, 1898/1900, pp. 66–67). James also explicitly portrayed the brain as exerting these various effects in a manner dependent

22. In Chapter 3 we begin to redress the asymmetry by describing numerous empirical phenomena of just this kind.

on its own functional status, and linked this idea to Fechner's conception of a fluctuating psychophysical threshold (pp. 24, 59–66).

Much can immediately be said in favor of such a picture, James then argued. It is in principle compatible with all of the facts conventionally interpreted under the production model, and however metaphorical and incomprehensible it might at first seem, it is in reality no more so than its materialist rival. It also has certain positive superiorities. In particular, it appears potentially capable of explaining various additional facts such as those being unearthed by F. W. H. Myers and his colleagues in psychical research (pp. 24–27).

In sum, "transmission" or "filter" models are logically viable, and they should rise or fall in the usual scientific way in terms of their capacity to accommodate the available empirical evidence.[23]

The remainder of this book consists primarily of a systematic though necessarily incomplete marshaling of evidence and argument supporting filter models in general as an abstract class. Only in Chapter 9, after all this material has been put on the table, will we attempt to identify in greater detail the specific forms we think such theories might take. To complete the present chapter, I will next set forth in brief compass a catalog of types of mental phenomena that appear especially resistant to explanation in conventional mechanistic, biological terms. Most though not all of these phenomena will be discussed in detail in the chapters that follow.

Psi Phenomena

Like James (1898/1900) and McDougall (1911/1961), among many others, I will immediately appropriate the entire body of evidence for psi phenomena in service of our central thesis. Such phenomena by definition involve correlations occurring across physical barriers that should be sufficient, on presently accepted principles, to prevent their formation (Broad, 1962). This occurs for example when a subject successfully identifies randomly selected targets concealed in opaque envelopes, or displayed in a remote location. It is not difficult to set up controlled experiments of this sort and to evaluate their outcomes using rigorous statistical procedures. As stated in the Introduction, and documented in our Appendix, a considerable amount of work

23. As indicated by an 1897 letter to Schiller (Perry, 1935, vol. 2, pp. 133–134), James thought initially that the transmission theory was his own invention, but it certainly has a much longer history. By the time of the Ingersoll lecture James himself had identified the following passage from Kant's *Critique of Pure Reason*: "The body would thus be, not the cause of our thinking, but merely a condition restrictive thereof, and, although essential to our sensuous and animal consciousness, it may be regarded as an impeder of our pure spiritual life" (1898/1900, pp. 28–29). Michael Grosso informs me that the filter concept can also be detected in a number of the Platonic dialogues, including *Phaedo*, *Phaedrus*, and *Ion*. Clearly, a definitive history of the filter model is yet to be written.

has been carried out along these lines, with results more than sufficient to convince me and the other authors of this book that the sheer existence of the basic input/output phenomena—ESP and PK, or in the more theory-neutral terminology of Thouless and Wiesner (1947), "psi"—is an inescapable scientific reality with which we must somehow come to terms.

In this light the anti-psi polemic recently advanced by psychologist/philosopher and long-time skeptic Nick Humphrey (1996) is particularly startling. Throughout his book Humphrey alludes to a supposed killer argument that he will later deploy to demonstrate the impossibility of psi. When we finally get there (Chapter 26), the argument turns out to be that he cannot imagine any possible scenario under which ostensible psi effects could be achieved by some combination of known physical mechanisms. Therefore the reported effects cannot and do not happen, Q. E. D. But whether we like it or not, such effects *do* happen, as a matter of empirical fact (see the Introduction and the Appendix). That is the whole point, and what makes the phenomena theoretically interesting in the first place! Humphrey's "argument" amounts in my opinion to little more than an expression of his deeply felt wish that the phenomena should simply go away. In this he is of course adopting a strategy that has been widely practiced by contemporary scientists and philosophers.[24]

Psi phenomena in general are important because they provide examples of human behavioral capacities that seem extremely difficult or impossible to account for in terms of presently recognized computational, biological, or physical principles. Even more important for our purposes, however, is a further body of evidence suggestive of post-mortem survival, the persistence of elements of mind and personality following bodily death. It is simply false to declare, as does Paul Churchland (1988), that "we possess no such evidence" (p. 10). We in fact possess a lot of such evidence, much of it of high quality (see the Appendix). Ironically, the primary threat to the survivalist interpretation of this evidence arises not from considerations of evidential quality, but from the difficulty of excluding alternative explanations based upon paranormal interactions involving only living persons.

Quite apart from any personal or theological interests readers may bring to this subject, it should be evident that post-mortem survival in any form, if it occurs, demonstrates the presence of a fundamental bifurcation in nature, and hence the falsehood of biological naturalism. We will touch upon various facets of the survival evidence later in the book and summarize our collective sense of the empirical status of the problem in Chapter 9.

Evidence for the occurrence of psi phenomena in general and post-mortem survival in particular thus plays an important though largely implicit

24. A curious and relevant historical precedent is provided by Turing (1950), who explicitly considered the possibility that telepathy could undermine his proposed Turing-test procedures in favor of the human. Indeed, he evidently took this rather seriously, since it appears last in a list of objections ordered at least roughly in terms of increasing difficulty. His "solution" to the problem, however—putting the human into a "telepathy-proof room"—is patently defective, as he himself probably knew.

role in our overall argument. Our efforts in this book will be amply rewarded if they lead scientifically-minded readers to take these subjects more seriously than they otherwise might. There are many other kinds of evidence, however, that point in the same general direction.

Extreme Psychophysical Influence

Under this heading comes a variety of phenomena especially suggestive of direct mental agency in the production of physiological or even physical effects. Chapter 3 discusses many such phenomena in detail, but I will give a few examples here to capture their flavor.

Placebo effects and related kinds of psychosomatic phenomena have long been informally recognized and are now widely accepted, but they were accepted by modern medical science only grudgingly, as new mechanisms of brain-body interaction came to light that seemed potentially capable of accounting for them. There remain many types of kindred phenomena, however, that pose progressively more severe challenges to explanation in such terms.

Myers, for example, was interested in hysterical "glove anesthesias," in which a patient loses sensation from the skin of a hand in the absence of organic lesion. In such cases the anesthetic skin region typically corresponds only to a psychological entity, the patient's idea, in complete disregard of the underlying anatomical organization. At the same time, curiously, something in the patient remains aware of the afflicted region and protects it from injury.

Related phenomena have been reported in the context of hypnosis. For example, highly suggestible persons who can vividly imagine undergoing an injurious circumstance such as receiving a burn to the skin sometimes suffer effects closely analogous to those that the physical injury itself would produce, such as a blister. More rarely, the correspondence between the hypnotic blister and its imagined source extends even to details of geometric shape, details which appear especially hard to account for in terms of known mechanisms of brain-body interaction. A closely related and well-documented phenomenon is that of "stigmata," in which fervently devout or pious believers in Christ develop wounds analogous to those inflicted during his crucifixion. The injuries to the skin are again localized and specific in form, and they differ in locus and character in accordance with their subjects' varying conceptions of Christ's own injuries. Similarly dramatic phenomena have occasionally been documented in psychiatric patients in connection with their recall of prior physical trauma.

The conventional expectation, of course, is that even the most extreme of the phenomena just mentioned can ultimately be explained in terms of brain processes. Continuing allegiance to this expectation, despite the explanatory difficulties, is undoubtedly encouraged by the fact that the phenomena described so far all involve effects of a person's mental states on that person's own body. Even more drastic explanatory challenges are posed, however, by additional and related phenomena in which one person's mental state seems to have directly influenced *another* person's body. Such phenomena include "maternal impressions" (birthmarks or birth defects on a newborn that correspond to an unusual and intense experience of the mother during the pregnancy), distant healing, experimental studies of distant mental influence on living systems, and cases in which a child who claims to have memories of the life of a deceased person also displays unusual birthmarks or birth defects corresponding closely with marks (usually fatal wounds) on the body of that person. In addition, there has been a considerable influx since Myers's time of other experimental evidence demonstrating the reality of psychokinesis (PK), which by definition involves direct mental influence on the physical environment.

Chapter 3 presents selective and focused discussions of phenomena of these various types, emphasizing their strong association with factors such as emotion, strong beliefs, and unusually vivid mental imagery, and drawing out their implications for an adequate theoretical picture of consciousness, volition, and the mind-body problem. Within-subject phenomena such as placebo effects, hypnotically induced blisters, and stigmata are also more carefully situated in relation to modern developments in "psychoneuroimmunology" and mind-body medicine. The common threads of the chapter are, first, to point out the many, varied, and well-documented phenomena of extreme psychophysical influence for which no conventional physicalist explanation is presently available, or in some cases even seems possible; and, second, to point out the theoretical continuity between normal, conscious volitional acts and these less common phenomena that suggest unconscious (or subliminal) volitional activity, sometimes of wider scope than conscious volition itself. The chapter also provides striking examples of the sometimes pathological interplay between scientific theories and scientific "fact."

Informational Capacity, Precision, and Depth

A number of well-documented psychological phenomena involve levels of detail, precision, or logical depth that seem hard to reconcile with what can be achieved by a fundamentally analog mechanism operating in a statistical way with neural components of low intrinsic precision and reliability. I will give three examples of the sort of thing I have in mind.

The first comes from a case of "automatic writing" observed by James (1889). The subject wrote with his extended right arm on large sheets of paper, his face meanwhile buried in the crook of his left elbow. For him to see what he was doing was "a physical impossibility." Nevertheless, James continues: "Two or three times in my presence on one evening, after covering a sheet with writing (the pencil never being raised, so that the words ran into each other), he returned to the top of the sheet and proceeded downwards, dotting each *i* and crossing each *t* with absolute precision and great rapidity" (p. 44).

This extraordinary performance illustrates two features that have often appeared together in the substantial but neglected scientific literature dealing with automatic writing (Koutstaal, 1992; Stevenson, 1978): The subject is in an altered state of consciousness, and the motor performance, itself extraordinary, is apparently guided by an extremely detailed memory record, an essentially photographic representation of the uncompleted page.

The latter property relates to the phenomenon of eidetic imagery, my second example, study of which was revived in modern times by the Habers (see Obler & Fein, 1988, for an overview). Probably the most dramatic demonstration of its psychological reality has been provided using Julesz random-dot stereograms (Stromeyer, 1970; Stromeyer & Psotka, 1970; see also Julesz, 1971, pp. 239–246). These are essentially pairs of computer-generated pictures, each of which by itself looks like a matrix of randomly placed dots, but constructed in such a way that when viewed simultaneously (by presentation to the two eyes separately) a visual form emerges in depth. Stromeyer and Psotka adapted this technology to their aims by presenting pictures of this type to the eyes of their single subject, a gifted female eidetiker, at different *times,* ultimately as much as three days apart. Under these conditions, the subject could only extract the hidden form if she could fuse current input to one eye with an extremely detailed memory-image of previous input to the other eye. Remarkably, she was able to succeed under a wide variety of increasingly severe demands. The original stereograms, for example, were 100 x 100 arrays, but she ultimately succeeded under double-blind conditions with arrays as large as 1000 x 1000, or a million "bits," viewed up to four hours apart.

These results were understandably shocking to many psychologists, who sought to escape their force by pointing to the dependence on a single gifted subject and the absence of replications (R. Herrnstein, personal communication, October, 1972). At least one successful replication has subsequently occurred, however. Specifically, Crawford, Wallace, Nemura, and Slater (1986) demonstrated that their highly hypnotizable subjects were able to succeed with the small (100 x 100) stereograms, but only when they were hypnotized. Moreover, the literature already contains many additional examples of prodigious memory. Stromeyer and Psotka themselves mention the mnemonist intensively studied by Luria (1968) and the case of the "Shass Pollaks," who memorized all 12 volumes of the Babylonian Talmud (Stratton, 1917). Sacks (1987, chap. 22) has reported a similar case of a person who among other things knew by heart all nine volumes and 6,000 pages of Grove's *Dictionary of Music and Musicians.* Other examples could easily be cited. Prodigious memory of this sort appears to be a real psychological phenomenon.

Third in this group is the whole family of "calculating prodigies." Of special interest is the "savant syndrome," often associated with infantile autism, in which islands of spectacular ability appear in the midst of generalized mental disability (Obler & Fein, 1988; Treffert, 1989). The abilities are of many types, but almost invariably involve prodigious memory. The depth of the problems they pose for brain theory is exemplified by the case of "The Twins," also described by Sacks (1987). These individuals, unable to perform even simple additions and subtractions with any accuracy, nonetheless proved able to generate and test prime numbers "in their heads." Sacks was able to verify the primacy up to 10 digits, but only by means of published tables, while the twins themselves went on happily exchanging ostensibly prime numbers of even greater length, eventually reaching 20 digits. Sacks makes the intriguing suggestion that they seem not to be literally *calculating* these enormous numbers, but *discovering* them by navigating through some vast inner iconic "landscape" in which the relevant numerical relations are somehow represented pictorially. The twins themselves of course cannot say how they do it.

Phenomena of the sorts described in this section look hard to explain in terms of brain processes. The most serious attempt to do so known to me (Snyder & Mitchell, 1999) is in fact devoid of specific neural mechanisms. Its central argument is rather that early-stage brain processes like those subserving visual perception, for example, must also be rather savant-like in terms of their speed, precision, and informational capacity; what is unusual about savants, therefore, may consist merely in their access to these mechanisms. This "explanation" of course presupposes a positive answer to the fundamental question at issue, whether the brain alone can accomplish *any* of these things, including perceptual synthesis itself (see below).

I will make just one further observation before leaving this fascinating and challenging subject. The biocomputational approach leads to one further expectation that could readily be tested using brain imaging methods but to my knowledge has not. As proved by von Neumann (1956), the only practical way to get increased arithmetical depth and precision out of individually unreliable computing elements is to use more of them. Although I do not know how to quantify this in a rigorous way, the biocomputational perspective clearly implies that calculating prodigies must use very large portions of their brains in very abnormal ways to achieve the observed effects. The cognitive losses that often accompany savant skills could perhaps be a reflection of such substitution, but we must remember that savant-type skills sometimes also occur in geniuses such as the mathematicians Gauss and Ampére (see also Obler & Fein, 1988, chap. 23).

Memory

The previous section focused on phenomena such as prodigious memory that appear potentially incompatible with the physical properties of the brain considered as a kind of computing device. Problems also arise, however, in regard to memory in its more familiar and everyday forms. Here I provide a brief sketch of the relevant issues, which are discussed in depth in Chapter 4.

Memory is increasingly recognized as central to all human cognitive and perceptual functions, yet we remain largely ignorant of where and in what forms our past experience is stored and by what means it is brought to bear upon the present. Generations of psychologists and neurobiologists have taken it as axiomatic that all memories must exist in the form of "traces," physical changes produced in the brain by experience, but there has been little progress toward scientific consensus on the details of these mechanisms despite many decades of intensive research.

Significant progress *has* recently been made, to be sure, in regard to "learning" and "memory" in simple creatures such as the sea-slug (*Aplysia*), and more generally in regard to what might be called "habit memory" (Bergson, 1908/1991), the automatic adjustments of organisms to their environments. But these discoveries fall far short of providing satisfactory explanations of the most central and important characteristics of the human memory system, including in particular our supplies of general knowledge (semantic memory) and our ability to recall voluntarily and explicitly our own past experience (autobiographical or episodic memory). Furthermore, recent functional neuroimaging studies, although generating vast amounts of "data," have yielded little if any progress toward a comprehensive and coherent account of memory based on trace theory.

Meanwhile, deep logical and conceptual problems have been identified in the root notion of the memory "trace" itself, as well as in allied components of current mainstream doctrine such as "information" and "representation." Most challenging of all to mainstream views is the substantial body of evidence that has accumulated—much of it since Myers's original efforts along these lines—suggesting that autobiographical, semantic, and procedural (skill) memories sometimes survive bodily death. If this is the case, memory in living persons presumably exists at least in part *outside* the brain and body as conventionally understood. At the very least this evidence raises profound and interesting issues of both philosophical and practical importance in regard to our criteria and procedures for determining personal identity.

I believe that the evidence and issues discussed in Chapter 4 collectively suggest the need for a radical reconceptualization of human memory along lines suggested a century ago by Myers, James, and Bergson. We will return to this theme in Chapter 9.

Psychological Automatisms and Secondary Centers of Consciousness

Phenomena catalogued under this heading involve what looks like multiple concurrent engagement, in potentially incompatible ways, of major cognitive skills (linguistic skills, for example) and the corresponding brain systems. Let me explain.

The current mainstream view pictures the mind or "cognitive system" as a hierarchically ordered network of subprocessors or "modules," each specialized for some particular task and corresponding (it is hoped) to some particular brain region or regions. Leaving aside major issues regarding the details of its specification, this picture seems broadly consistent with the overall manner in which our minds seem normally to operate. Our basic way of doing things, that is, is essentially one at a time in serial fashion. Although psychologists recognize that with suitable training people can do more things simultaneously than they customarily suppose, this generalization applies mainly to relatively divergent things, and conspicuously fails as the simultaneous tasks become more complex and similar (Baars, 1997; Neisser, 1976; Pashler, 1998).

Nevertheless, a large body of credible evidence, some dating back to the late 19th century, demonstrates that additional "cognitive systems," psychological entities indistinguishable from full-fledged conscious minds or personalities as we normally understand these terms, can sometimes occupy the same organism simultaneously, carrying on their varied existences as it were in parallel, and largely outside the awareness of the primary, everyday consciousness. In essence, the structure that cognitive psychology conventionally pictures as unitary, as instantiated within and identified with a particular organization of brain systems, can be functionally divided—divided, moreover, not *horizontally*, leading to isolation of the normal cognitive capacities from each other, but *vertically*, leading to the appearance of what seem to be two or more complete cognitive systems each of which includes all of the relevant capacities. Even worse, it sometimes happens that one of these "multiple" or "alter" personalities appears to have direct access to the conscious mental activity of one or more others, but not vice versa.

Investigation of such phenomena, and more generally of "consciousness beyond the margin" (E. Taylor, 1996) was central to the early work of Myers and James among many others. Two brief examples may serve to convey a more concrete initial sense of the character of these phenomena.

The first comes from Myers (*HP*, vol. 2, pp. 418–422), who quoted from a report by Oxford philosopher F. C. S. Schiller on automatic writing produced by his brother. As is characteristic of this genre of automatisms, the writer typically had no consciousness of the content of his writing, which went on continuously while he was fully and consciously engaged in some other activity such as reading a book or telling a story. Of particular relevance here, however, were occasions on which he wrote simultaneously with both hands and on completely different subjects, one or the other of these streams of writing also sometimes being in mirror-image form.

The second example is the case of Anna Winsor, described both by James (1889) in his report on automatic writing and by Myers (*HP*, vol. 1, pp. 354–360). The case was protracted and bizarre, but only superficially resembles the neurological "alien hand" (Dr. Strangelove) syndrome. Its central feature is that the patient, Anna, at a certain point lost voluntary control of her right arm, which was taken over by a distinctive secondary personality. This personality, whom Anna herself named "Old Stump," was benign, often protecting Anna from her pronounced tendencies toward self-injury. As in the case of Schiller's brother, Stump also typically wrote or drew while Anna herself was occupied with other matters. But Stump also continued writing and drawing even when Anna was asleep, and sometimes in total darkness. This secondary personality also remained calm and rational during periods when Anna herself was feverish and delusional, and it manifested knowledge and skills which Anna did not possess.

The enormous literature on these subjects is reviewed systematically, and its implications discussed, in Chapter 5. The chapter specifically argues for the psychological reality of the phenomenon of co-consciousness (as distinguished from unconscious cerebration and alternating consciousness), which is fundamental both to Myers's own theoretical framework and (as discussed in Chapter 8) to James's later application of that framework to problems in religion and philosophy.

The Unity of Conscious Experience

Under this heading I will briefly address two interrelated problems. The first and narrower is the so-called "binding" problem. This problem emerged as a consequence of the success of contemporary neuroscientists in analyzing sensory mechanisms, particularly in the visual system. It turns out that different properties of a visual object such as its form, color, and motion in depth are handled individually by largely separate regions or mechanisms within the visual system. But once the stimulus has been thus dismembered, so to speak, how does it get back together again as a unit of visual experience?

Only one thing is certain: The unification of experience is not achieved anatomically. There are no privileged places or structures in the brain where everything comes together, either for the visual system by itself or for the sensory systems altogether. McDougall (1911/1961) was already fully aware of this, and used it as a cornerstone of his argument against materialist accounts of the mind. In his view, the evident disparity between the multiplicity of physiological processes in the brain and the felt unity of conscious experience could only be resolved in physicalist terms by anatomical convergence, and since there is no such convergence, physicalism must be false.[25]

---

25. There is an important historical irony here. Dennett and Kinsbourne (1992) also focus on the absence of anatomical convergence, apparently thinking this is something new, but use it in a completely different way. Whereas McDougall (1911/1961) took the unity of conscious experience as a fundamental and undeniable empirical reality, one which physicalism could not explain, Kinsbourne and especially Dennett (1991) want to use the physiological diversity to undermine that appearance of unity itself, along with other supposedly pre-scientific "folk-psychol-

McDougall's original argument, although ingenious, relied upon the faulty premise that the only possible physical means of unification must be *anatomical*. All current neurophysiological proposals for solving the binding problem are instead *functional* in nature. The essential concept common to all of them is that oscillatory electrical activity in widely distributed neural populations can be rapidly and reversibly synchronized in the "gamma" band of frequencies (roughly 30–70 Hz), thereby providing a possible mechanistic solution to the binding problem (von der Malsburg, 1995).[26]

A great deal of sophisticated experimental and theoretical work over the past 20 years has demonstrated that such mechanisms do in fact exist in the nervous system, and that they are active in conjunction with normal perceptual synthesis.[27] Indeed, Searle's doctrine of biological naturalism has now crystallized neurophysiologically in the form of a family of "global workspace" theories, all of which make the central claim that conscious experience occurs specifically and only in conjunction with large-scale patterns of gamma-band oscillatory activity linking widely separated areas of the brain (Crick, 1994; Dehaene & Naccache, 2001; Edelman & Tononi, 2000; A. K. Engel, Fries, & Singer, 2001; W. J. Freeman, 2000; Llinás, Ribary, Contreras, & Pedroarena, 1998; Newman & Baars, 1993; Singer, 1998; Varela, Lachaux, Rodriguez, & Martinerie, 2001).[28]

---

ogy" intuitions about the nature of consciousness. See also Searle (1997, chap. 5), later sections of this chapter, and our Chapter 9.

26. This paragraph summarizes decades of cumulative progress in the neurobiology of sensory coding. The early work, inspired by Hubel and Wiesel (1962), emphasized "feature detection" by single sensory neurons, and provided for detection and representation of higher-order features or conjunctions of features by means of suitable anatomical connectivity. It was subsequently recognized, however, that combinations of elementary features could potentially occur in numbers far too large to manage exclusively in this anatomically-based way. The new functional proposals overcome the combinatorial explosion by providing for rapid and reversible linkages among groups of cells responding to more elementary properties.

27. Note that this characterization does not imply or require that the oscillatory activity itself satisfactorily *explains* binding. That it does not has already been argued by neurophysiologists such as Crick and Koch (2003) and Shadlen and Movshon (1999). See also the following paragraphs.

28. Although the "global workspace" terminology originated with Baars (1988, 1997), we will use it throughout this book in the more generic sense supplied in the text. Baars certainly deserves much credit for emphasizing that we need somehow to reconcile the unity of conscious experience with the multiplicity of associated neurophysiological processes in the brain, and for stimulating new imaging studies that seek to identify more precisely the critical neurophysiological conditions themselves (see, e.g., Dehaene & Naccache, 2001). His own specific version of a theory of this type, however, is less than satisfactory. In particular, his extended allegory of the "theater of consciousness" (Baars, 1997, pp. 41–47), although providing a colorful vocabulary with which to describe or interpret a variety of psychological phenomena, is conceptually incoherent in a multitude of ways.

The neurophysiological global workspace, however, cannot be the whole story. A sizeable body of recent evidence demonstrates that organized, elaborate, and vivid conscious experience sometimes occurs under physiological conditions, such as deep general anesthesia and cardiac arrest, which preclude workspace operation. Experiences of this sort fall under the more general heading of "near-death experiences" or NDEs, which are discussed in detail in Chapter 6 together with related phenomena such as "out-of-body experiences" (OBEs) and lucid dreams. In short, it appears to us that McDougall was right after all, albeit for the wrong reason. In effect, we will argue, recent progress in mainstream physicalist brain theory has provided new means for its own falsification as a complete account of mind-brain relations.

Availability of this emerging evidence emboldens me to make some further and even more contentious remarks regarding the larger problem of perceptual synthesis, and the direction in which things seem to me to be moving.

It is an historical fact that mainstream cognitive psychology has always tended on the whole to try to solve its problems "on the cheap," with as little reference as possible to what all of us experience every day as central features of our conscious mental life. The early workers in "mechanical translation," for example, imagined that they could do a decent job simply by constructing a large dictionary that would enable substitution of words in one language for words in the other. This approach failed miserably, and we were slowly driven, failed step by failed step, to the recognition that truly adequate translation presupposes *understanding*, or in short a full appreciation of the capacities underlying the human use of language.

A similar evolution is underway in regard to perceptual theory. Most of the work to date has taken a strongly "bottom-up" approach, along lines formulated in the seminal book of Marr (1982). This school views perceptual synthesis as a kind of exhaustive calculation from the totality of input currently present at our sensory surfaces. Machine vision and robotics, for example, necessarily took this approach, and even in neuroscience it seemed to make sense to start with the most accessible parts of the perceptual systems—the end organs and their peripheral connections—and work our way inward. The great sensory systems themselves—vision, audition, somatosensation, and so on—were also presumed to operate more or less independently, and were in fact typically studied in isolation.

A separate tradition dating back at least to Kant and the early Gestalt theorists, and carried forward into the modern era by psychologists such as Neisser (1967, 1976), has been sensitive to the presence of "top-down" influences, both within and between sensory modalities. Although a few perceptual subsystems (such as those that engender the Müller-Lyer and other incorrigible visual illusions) may be truly autonomous or "cognitively impenetrable" in the sense of J. Fodor (1983), these seem to be isolated and special cases. A very different overall picture of perceptual synthesis is currently emerging in which top-down influences predominate. On this view perceptual synthesis is achieved not *from* the input, but *with its aid*. This is necessarily the case for example in regard to ambiguous figures, where the stimulus information itself is not sufficient to determine a uniquely "correct" interpretation. More generally, we routinely ignore information that is present in the input and supply information that is not, speed-reading providing a characteristic example.[29] Something within us, a sort of cosmogenic, world-generating, or virtual-reality system, is continuously updating and projecting an overall model of the perceptual environment and our position within it, guided by very limited samplings of the available sensory information (Simons & Chabris, 1999; Tart, 1993).

As in the case of understanding spoken or written language, an enormous amount of general knowledge is constantly mobilized in service of this projective activity, which freely utilizes any and all relevant sensory data available to it. Top-down and cross-modal sensory interactions have recently been recognized as the rule rather than the exception in perception (A. K. Engel et al., 2001; Shimojo & Shams, 2001). Neuroscientist Rodolfo Llinás and his co-workers have even advanced the view, which I believe is profoundly correct, that *dreaming*, far from being an odd and incidental part of our mental life, represents the fundamental form of this projective activity. Ordinary perceptual synthesis, on this inverted view of things, amounts to oneiric (dreamlike) activity constrained by sensory input (Llinás & Paré, 1996; Llinás & Ribary, 1994). Hartmann (1975) had proposed similar ideas in regard to hallucinatory activity more generally, with dreaming included. On his view such activity is again a ubiquitous and fundamental feature of our mental life, and the critical question is not "why do we sometimes hallucinate?" but rather "what keeps us from hallucinating most of the time?" The answer, he thought, lies in inhibitory influences somehow exerted by the brain activity that accompanies ongoing perceptual and cognitive functions of the ordinary waking sorts. Similar arguments for the primacy and importance of this cosmogenic capacity have more recently been advanced by Brann (1991) and Globus (1987).[30]

---

29. Yuo mgiht aslo be srupsired to fnid taht yuo can raed tihs ntoe wtihuot mcuh truoble.

30. Another relevant phenomenon, and one that deserves more attention, is spontaneous hallucinatory experience in normal and awake persons. That such experiences commonly occur was initially demonstrated by the founders of the Society for Psychical Research (Gurney, Myers, & Podmore, 1886; H. Sidgwick et al., 1894) and has subsequently been confirmed repeatedly by others (Bentall, 2000). The mere fact of their occurrence demonstrates that the projective activity can sometimes partially or even wholly *override* current sensory input. Waking apparitions also share with dreams a tendency to incorporate massive amounts of information about physically remote events (Gurney et al., 1886). Critical readers should not indulge any temptation they may experience to dismiss these case reports wholesale as mere "anecdotes," for they are massively and carefully documented. Penetrating analysis of the pitfalls of eyewitness testimony did not begin with Loftus (1979), as commonly supposed: See Gurney et al. (1886), its review by James (1887), and Chapters 2 and 6.

So far so good, but where exactly is the "top," the ultimate source of this projective activity? The mainstream neuroscientists who have already recognized its existence invariably presume that it arises entirely within the brain itself. Evidence such as that assembled in Chapter 6, however, like the more direct evidence of post-mortem survival, strongly suggests that it originates outside the brain as conventionally understood. We will return to this in Chapter 9.

Genius-Level Creativity

In the Introduction we quoted Edgar Wind's guiding principle, that "the commonplace may be understood as a reduction of the exceptional, but the exceptional cannot be understood as an amplification of the commonplace." That principle applies with particular force and poignancy, I think, to the topic of this section. Any scientific theory of personality and cognition truly worthy of the name surely must help us to understand this humanly vital topic, but by this standard we have so far made distressingly little progress. The reason, in my opinion, is that for the most part we have violated Wind's principle by trying to understand the exceptional—real genius, in its fullest expressions—as an amplification of the commonplace—"creativity," as we find it in random samples of undergraduates and the like.

Myers and James consciously and deliberately approached the subject from the other end, and in connection with the enlarged conception of human personality which they were struggling to articulate. In Chapter 7 we discuss genius from this point of view, describing Myers's account in some detail and situating it in relation to the main trends in contemporary creativity research. Focusing primarily on the creative process and creative personality structure, we argue that Myers anticipated most of what has been good in more recent work, while also accommodating in a natural way a variety of additional phenomena—including psychological automatisms and secondary centers of consciousness, altered states of consciousness, unusual forms of symbolic thinking, and psi—that are inescapably bound up with this topic but scarcely touched upon in contemporary mainstream accounts. We also show that various expectations flowing from Myers's account of genius have been strongly confirmed by more recent empirical observations.

Mystical Experience

Experiences of this type lie at the core of the world's major religious traditions and have continued to occur throughout history and across cultures. Their existence as a distinctive and important class of psychological phenomena can scarcely be denied. Yet they have largely been ignored by mainstream psychology and neuroscience, and generations of reductionist clinical psychologists and psychiatrists have consistently sought to devalue and pathologize them. Even when acknowledging that such experiences are often life-transforming and self-validating for those who have them, the historically standard epistemological approaches in psychology and philosophy—beginning with William James in his *Varieties of Religious Experience*—treat them as purely subjective events having authority only for those who experience them, and thus deny their objective significance and the testability of the associated truth-claims. However, a large though scattered literature testifies to the occurrence in such experiences, or in individuals who have them, of genius-level creativity and many other unusual empirical phenomena of the sorts discussed in this book. Mystical-type states of consciousness are also now known to be at least partially reproducible by pharmacological means (psychedelics), and they can also be induced by protracted self-discipline involving transformative practices such as the various forms of meditation. A more objective, informed, and sympathetic appraisal of mystical experience finds within it much additional support for a Myers-type theory of human personality, and many new opportunities for empirical research. Chapter 8 will develop these themes in detail.

The Heart of the Mind

In this final section I wish to comment briefly on a hornet's nest of theoretical issues lying at the very core of our mental life, issues that have been the focus of extensive recent debates, especially in the philosophical literature.[31] These issues are deep, individually complex, and densely interconnected. What I have to say will necessarily amount to little more than a summary of my own opinions, but I believe that this statement derives support both from earlier sections of this chapter and especially from the chapters that follow.

The crucial point I want to make, especially to my fellow psychologists, is this: Our *a priori* commitment to a conventional physicalist account of the mind has rendered us systematically incapable of dealing adequately with the mind's most central properties. We need to rethink that commitment.

Consider first the issue of semantic or intentional content, the "meaning" of words and other forms of representation. Throughout our history, we have tried unsuccessfully to deal with this by "naturalizing" it, reducing it to something else that seems potentially more tractable. An old favorite among psychologists, traceable at least back to Locke and Hume, is that representations work by *resembling* what they represent, by virtue of some sort of built-in similarity or structural isomorphism. Any hope along these lines was long ago exploded in philosophical circles, as shown for example

---

31. See also Chapter 4, which discusses several of these issues in the specific context of memory theory, and Gauld (1989), which develops views similar to those expressed here more systematically and generally in regard to the "entrapment" of cognitive science by its current conceptual framework.

by Goodman (1972) and by Heil (1981) in his destructive review of J. Fodor (1975). The central move subsequently made by classical cognitive psychology is essentially the semantic counterpart of the prevailing functionalist doctrine in philosophy of mind: Meanings are not to be conceived as intrinsic to words or concepts on this view, but rather as deriving from and defined by the functional role those words or concepts play in the overall linguistic system. Currently, there is great interest in "externalist" causal accounts of this functionalist type. In connectionism, dynamic systems theory, and neuroscience, for example, the "meaning" of a given response, such as the settling of a network into one of its "attractors" or the firing off of a volley of spikes by a neuron in visual cortex, is typically identified with whatever it is in the organism's environment that produces that response. But this simply cannot be right. How can such an account deal with abstract things, for example, or non-existent things? Responses do not qualify *ipso facto* as representations, nor signs as symbols. Something essential is being left out. That something, as Searle (1992) so effectively argues, is precisely what matters, the semantic or mental content (see also the detailed discussion of "representations" in Chapter 4).

Closely related to this is the more general and abstract problem of *intentionality,* the ability of any and all representational forms to be *about* things, events, and states of affairs in the world. Mainstream psychologists and philosophers have struggled to find ways of making intentionality intrinsic to the representations themselves, but again it just does not and cannot work, because something essential is left out. That something is the *user* of the representations. Intentionality is inherently a three-way relation involving users, symbols, and things symbolized, and the user cannot be eliminated. As Searle puts it in various places, the intentionality of language is secondary and derives from the intrinsic intentionality of the mind. Searle thus agrees in part with Brentano (1874/1995), for whom intentionality was the primary distinguishing mark of the mental. At the same time, however, Searle ignores the other and more fundamental part of Brentano's thesis, which is that intentionality cannot be obtained from *any* kind of physical system, presumably including brains (see Puccetti, 1989, and Dupuy, 2000, for useful discussions of this issue from opposing points of view).

Talk of "users" and the like raises for many contemporary psychologists and philosophers the terrifying specter of the homunculus, a little being within who embodies all the capacities we sought to explain in the first place. Such a result would clearly be disastrous, because that being would evidently need a similar though smaller being within itself, and so on without end. Cognitive modelers seeking to provide a strictly physicalist account of the mind must therefore do so without invoking a homunculus, but they have not succeeded. Often the homuncular aspect is hidden, slipped into a model by its designers or builders and covertly enlisting the semantic and intentional capacities of its users or observers. The semantic theory of J. J. Katz and Fodor (1964), mentioned earlier, provides one example of this, in that the notation they used to designate their "semantic markers" progressively took on characteristics of telegraphic speech as the theory evolved (E. F. Kelly, 1975). Much of the contemporary work on computational modeling of metaphor has similar problems (Chapter 7).

Sometimes, however, the homunculus is more brazenly evident. One example is Marr's account of vision, which applies computations to the two-dimensional array of retinal input in order to generate a "description" of the three-dimensional world that provided that visual input, but then needs someone to interpret that description (Searle, 1992). Another is Kosslyn's model of visual imagery, which essentially puts up an image on a sort of internal TV screen, but then needs somebody else to view that image. Draaisma (2000) and our Chapter 4 identify similar homunculus problems in the context of contemporary memory models.

Particularly in its more blatant forms the homunculus problem has attracted the attention of physicalists such as Dennett (1978), who have sought to remove its philosophic sting. Dennett's solution is to "discharge" the homunculus by a process of "recursive decomposition." The basic idea is that the "smart" homunculus appearing at the top of a model can be replaced by progressively larger numbers of less smart homunculi, until we get to a vast bottom layer corresponding to the "hardware" level of computer flip-flops or neuron firings. But as Searle (1992) pointed out, this maneuver fails, because even at the bottom level there has to be something outside the decomposition, a homunculus in effect, that knows what those lowest-level operations mean. Cognitive models cannot function without a homunculus, in short, precisely because they lack what we have—minds, with their capacities for semantics, intentionality, and all the rest built in.

No homunculus problem, however, is posed by the structure of our conscious experience itself. The efforts of Dennett (1991) and others to claim that there *is* such a problem, and to use that to ridicule any residue of dualism, rely upon the deeply flawed metaphor of the "Cartesian theater," a place where mental contents get displayed and I pop in separately to view them. Descartes himself, James, and Searle, among others, all have this right; conscious experience comes to us whole and undivided, with the qualitative feels, phenomenological content, unity, and subjective point of view all built-in, intrinsic features. I and my experience cannot be separated in this way.

Finally, I wish simply to record, without argument, my own deepest intuition as to where these issues lead. All of the great unsolved mysteries of the mind—semantics, intentionality, volition, the self, and consciousness—seem to me inextricably interconnected, with consciousness somehow at the root of all.

The consciousness I have in mind is emphatically *not* that of Chalmers (1996), irreducible but ineffectual, consisting merely of phenomenological properties or "qualia" arbitrarily tacked on to a strong artificial intelligence that does all the cognitive work. Ordinary perception and action are saturated with conceptual understanding, and conceptual understanding is saturated with phenomenological content. Volition too has an intentionality aspect, for as Nietzsche somewhere remarked, one cannot just *will*, one must will *something*. Each individual word is in effect "a microcosm of human consciousness" (Vygotsky, 1986/2000, p. 256), and "all *meaning* is in some way ultimately grounded in *being*" (Cassirer, 1957, p. 94). And as William James so forcibly argued at the dawn of our science, all of this perceptual, cognitive, and volitional activity somehow emanates from a mysterious and elusive "spiritual self," which can often be sensed at or behind the innermost subjective pole of our ongoing conscious experience.

Consciousness, in short, far from being a passive epiphenomenon, seems to me to play an essential role—indeed *the* essential role—in all of our most basic cognitive capacities. I can find no better way of ending this section than simply to stand back and applaud the trenchant conclusion drawn by philosopher E. J. Lowe (1998), which encapsulates my own views and the central contention of this book: "Reductive physicalism, far from being equipped to solve the so-called 'easy' problems of consciousness, has in fact nothing very useful to say about *any* aspect of consciousness" (pp. 121–122).

Conclusion

In regard to the deep theoretical issues broached in the previous section, my views as a psychologist closely parallel those of a small minority of modern philosophical writers including E. J. Lowe, Thomas Nagel, and John Searle. I feel an enormous debt of gratitude to them for so vigorously defending, like James (1890b), the reality and importance of our conscious mental life. I find it altogether astonishing, and predict that it will be found so as well by our intellectual descendants, that so much of our science and philosophy from James to the present has sought—consciously!—to slight or ignore these first-person realities of the mind, and sometimes even to deny that they exist. There is perhaps no better example of the power of theory to blind us to facts.

But that has now all changed. We have come full circle and surely will not turn backward again. The question that now confronts us, as it confronted James, is whether all this richness of our conscious mental life really can be accounted for in terms of physical operations in the brain. Searle himself, of course, is sure that it can, at least in principle. But this is just a pious hope, the latest form of "promissory materialism" (Popper & Eccles, 1977, p. 96). Even philosophers fundamentally sympathetic to Searle's point of view are not nearly so confident. Consider for example the gloomy conclusions of physicalist Jaegwon Kim (1998):

> We find ourselves in a profound dilemma: If we are prepared to embrace reductionism, we can explain mental causation. However, in the process of reducing mentality to physical/biological properties, we may well lose the intrinsic, subjective character of our mentality—arguably, the very thing that makes the mental mental. In what sense, then, have we saved "mental"

> causation? But if we reject reductionism, we are not able to see how mental causation should be possible. But saving mentality while losing causality doesn't seem to amount to saving anything worth saving. For what good is the mind if it has no causal power? Either way, we are in danger of losing mentality. That is the dilemma. (p. 237)

In this passage Kim, a determined but scrupulously honest physicalist, has clearly moved within a hair's breadth of the more skeptical and agnostic Nagel. This surely is a development that ought to worry other physicalists. But whereas *their* troubles with physicalism arose primarily via conceptual analysis, and have led them to no definite conclusion, *ours* are primarily empirical in character, and actually falsify biological naturalism. That is the central contention of this book. We believe strongly that in order to get an adequate scientific account of the mind we *must* be prepared to take seriously all relevant data and to modify as necessary even our most fundamental theoretical ideas. Some of the most relevant kinds of data, however, have been systematically excluded from contemporary scientific and philosophic discussions.

Following chapters, as indicated, will discuss a number of these neglected topics in depth. Let me conclude by briefly recapitulating the argument as it has developed so far: Despite its many significant accomplishments, a century of mainstream scientific psychology has not provided a satisfactory theory of mind, or solved the mind-body problem. Physicalist accounts of the mind appear to be approaching their limits without fully accounting for its properties. The computational theory of the mind has been overthrown, forcing physicalism to retreat into what necessarily constitutes its final frontier, the unique biology of the brain. But this biological naturalism appears destined to fare little better. Some critical properties of mental life can already be recognized as irreconcilable in principle with physical operations of the brain, and others seem likely to prove so as well.

These failures warrant a serious attempt to rethink the entire subject of mind-brain relations from a different perspective—specifically, from the perspective provided by James's generic "transmission" theory. There is no better way to begin such an effort than by reviewing the extraordinary contributions of F. W. H. Myers, James's colleague and friend, who provided the most fully developed version so far of a theory of this type.

Chapter 2

F. W. H. Myers and the Empirical Study of the Mind-Body Problem

Emily Williams Kelly

> Psychology sometimes seems to suffer from a memory loss that borders on the pathological. Not only is the number of rediscoveries shamefully high, but valuable empirical and conceptual work carried out in older traditions has disturbingly little impact on present-day research. The result is that certain defects in theory formulation diagnosed as long ago as the nineteenth century, are repeatedly reintroduced in psychology. (Draaisma, 2000, p. 5)

The Historical Context

As the above quotation suggests, psychology as a research discipline has not been a steadily progressing advance of knowledge, each generation building on the discoveries and achievements of its predecessors in a systematic march toward new knowledge. Even in the physical sciences, in which there has been a somewhat more linear progression of achievement, many scientists take the all too parochial view that the insights and observations of previous generations have been superseded by the technological, methodological, empirical, and even conceptual developments of the present. Few modern working scientists consider it likely that an examination of the history of their field might not only broaden their perspective on contemporary problems, but even suggest new (or renewed) avenues for attacking those problems. Over a century ago, however, that quintessential spokesman for modern science, Thomas Huxley, lamented the historical ignorance of scientists in his own day and urged them to study their history because "there is assuredly no more effectual method of clearing up one's own mind on any subject than by talking it over, so to speak, with men of real power and grasp, who have considered it from a totally different point of view" (T. H. Huxley, 1874, p. 556).

In the second half of the 19th century, psychology was undergoing a major and rapid transformation from moral philosophy to naturalistic science, and central to this transformation were efforts to grapple with questions as fundamental to psychology as the nature of mind, the nature of the relationship between mental and physical processes, and the relationship of psychology to the rest of science. By the early years of the 20th century, however, such fundamental questions had, for all intents and purposes, been written off as "metaphysical" problems unsuitable for a scientific psychology. Psychology was well on its way to the fragmentation and conceptual impasses characteristic of contemporary psychology, as described in the Introduction and Chapter 1. What led to this abandonment of fundamental questions? Can a return to them aid psychologists in moving the science of psychology forward, both by bringing psychology conceptually into the 21st century and, perhaps even more importantly, by advancing knowledge about issues that are of interest and concern to the general public?

It is our contention in this book that such a return to fundamental questions is not only desirable but essential to psychology, and that a few "men of real power and grasp" in the late 19th century—including in particular F. W. H. Myers and William James—had opened up avenues for attacking these questions empirically, avenues that were quickly closed off by assumptions and beliefs that still overwhelmingly permeate modern psychology. In this chapter, I will first describe briefly the intellectual context in which scientific psychology developed in the 19th century, and then provide an overview of the work of F. W. H. Myers.

The Roots of Scientific Psychology: Dualism, Mechanistic Determinism, and the Continuity of Nature

Science, from Copernicus to the present, has undoubtedly been the single most important influence on the modern world, its reach extending far beyond technological advances to the fundamental changes it has brought to the way humans view themselves and the world around them. The scientific revolution had its roots in ideas that, with every subsequent accomplishment and advance in science, have become ever more entrenched in modern thinking. An important impetus to the development of Western science was the clear articulation of a dualism that split the phenomenal universe into two radically different domains. With Descartes' distinction between extended, mechanical matter and unextended, volitional mind, and Galileo's distinction between primary, objective properties (such as mass) and secondary, essentially subjective properties (such as color), the material, mechanical, objective side of nature became the domain of science. The physical universe was conceived as operating according to a uniform and unvarying mechanical system of causes and effects—a view in distinct contrast to the old, pre-scientific view of the world as subject to the varying and unpredictable actions of personal forces, whether human or divine. By observing and measuring events, scientists could identify and describe these unvarying sequences, or natural laws, and thus predict future events. Closely related to this idea of mechanistic determinism was the principle of atomistic reductionism, or the assumption that physical systems could be understood in terms of the actions and reactions of their simplest or lowest-level parts. A major goal of science was therefore to identify and describe with ever greater precision the basic elements and processes from which a physical system is built.

This assumption of mechanistic determinism was what made the physical sciences so immensely successful throughout the 17th, 18th, and 19th centuries, and each new success further entrenched the assumption that the world is primarily a kind of machine. Scientific determinism culminated in the views of the astronomer Laplace, who, in an often quoted passage, insisted that all events without exception "obey the great laws of nature" and that what we perceive as happening by chance or by free will simply reflects our ignorance of the causes. Thus, for "an intelligence that, at a given instant, could comprehend all the forces by which nature is animated and the respective situation of the beings that make it up...nothing would be uncertain, and the future, like the past, would be open to its eyes" (Laplace, 1825/1995, p. 2). Perhaps inevitably, a corollary of this thorough-going determinism emerged as epiphenomenalism, the view that mind and free will—the other half of dualism—are either illusions or, at best, secondary, ineffectual byproducts of the physical, mechanical world.[1]

Further advances in science during the 19th century lent increasing support to another important and spreading assumption about the universe, one that, ironically, began to undermine the dualism from which modern science had developed. One major development was the formulation of the principle of the conservation of energy, introduced to the general scientific world primarily through Helmholtz's famous 1847 lecture to the Physical Society of Berlin. This law stated that the total sum of energy in the universe is constant, energy never being either lost or gained but simply transformed from one kind to another (including, Einstein later determined, from and

1. Laplace's determinism and belief that "conscious will is an illusion" are still very much a part of modern philosophy and science: "If [scientific psychologists] somehow had access to all the information they could ever want, the assumption of psychology is that they could uncover the mechanisms that give rise to all your behavior and so could certainly explain why you picked up this book at this moment" (Wegner, 2002, p. 1).

into mass). The law thus became the specific foundation for belief in the unity of all nature in a closed, causal system. Another important development was Darwin's theory that all biological organisms have evolved through the mechanism of natural selection. With the application of evolutionary ideas to biology, not only were all forms of life presumed to be subject to the same universal mechanisms, but all forms of life could be seen as having developed from the same elementary organisms.

From these and other descriptions of natural laws emerged the principle of continuity, or the assumption that the universe is a unitary, not dualistic, phenomenon. All elements of the universe are not only inextricably related, but they all function according to the same basic, deterministic principles of cause and effect and are all, in the final analysis, of the same basic essence or nature. A corollary of this belief in continuity was the growing conviction that, if the world is ultimately a unity, all phenomena must be subject to the same tools of knowledge—that is, the methods of classical science that had already proved so successful. Because scientific method relied so completely on observation, it followed that only phenomena that are observable, directly or indirectly, could provide the contents of science.

Psychology as Science: A Fundamental Conflict

Among those increasing numbers of people who understood the power of scientific inquiry and felt the impact of its accomplishments, there arose the convictions that the principle of continuity demanded the unity, not duality, of the psychophysical organism; that mental phenomena, like physical ones, are natural phenomena; and thus that psychology could be subjected to the same empirical methods that had so revolutionized other branches of natural philosophy and transformed them into science. The attempt to transform psychology into a science, however, raised some unique problems. The phenomena of psychology are unlike those of any of the physical sciences in that they are, above all else, *mental.* At the theoretical heart of psychology, therefore, are the questions, What are mental phenomena and what is their relation to physical phenomena? Is mind "an elementary force in nature," as primary and fundamental a characteristic of nature as matter, or is it the "resultant of the really elementary forces," an evolved, emergent, or epiphenomenal characteristic of matter (James, 1902/1958, p. 105)? Of particular theoretical importance for psychology is the question of mental causality, or volition: Can mental phenomena initiate changes in the physical world? If so, what are the parameters and laws of such mental causality, and what do they imply about the question of whether mind is a fundamental or a derivative aspect of nature? Is mind, in short, *caused* or *causal*?

Scientists of other fields found no need to ask such questions. The physical sciences had progressed, in fact, specifically by rejecting mental, "spiritual," or personal causality as operative in nature in favor of a view of nature as governed wholly by impersonal, mechanistic laws. The notion of mental causality was increasingly dismissed as a vestige of primitive, "supernatural" ways of thinking.[2] The resulting intellectual turmoil of the 19th century, however, was more than a conflict between an old, dying order and a new, more advanced one, or even, as it is so often portrayed, between Religion and Science. It was, in essence, a conflict between experience and knowledge (Daston, 1978): Individual first-person experience suggests one kind of world—one of personal agency—but the cumulative third-person knowledge produced by science was suggesting quite a different world—one of impersonal agency. Scientific psychology became the point at which those two world views collided, thus presenting science with the most serious challenge to the strength and sufficiency of its assumptions, principles, and methods.

The potential incorporation of psychology into science, in sum, seemed to present a threat to both. If the "anomaly" of mind, with its apparently volitional, teleological, and subjective phenomena, was to be reconciled with the otherwise increasingly uniform picture painted by Western science of mechanistic, atomistic, physical determinism, then either the concept of mind or the assumptions of modern science would have to be altered. Psychologists could redefine, or reconceptualize, psychology in such a way that it excludes whatever does not fit the framework of the physical sciences, such as consciousness or volitional agency; or they could use the phenomena of psychology to modify the model of science that limits causal agency to physical determinism. They could, in short, either narrow psychology to fit science as it was then understood, or expand science to accommodate psychological phenomena. The nearly unanimous choice of 19th-century scientists was the former course, to force psychology into the framework of assumptions derived from the classical physical sciences, rather than entertain the idea that science might have to be enlarged to accommodate mental phenomena and causality on an equal footing with physical phenomena and causality (Cook [Kelly], 1992). As Boring (1933) succinctly stated: "Historically science is physical science. Psychology, if it is to be a science, must be like physics....The ultimate abandonment of dualism leaves us the physical world as the only reality. Consciousness will ultimately be measured in physical dimensions" (pp. 6, 8).

The Naturalization of Mind: Limiting Psychology

The first major task for the mid-19th-century scientists who sought to transform psychology into science was to reconceptualize mind as a natural, not supernatural, phenomenon. Several lines of influence contributed importantly to this process. The 17th- and 18th-century empiricist philosophy of associationism, which held that all mental phenomena derive solely

2. Today concepts such as volition (along with "belief, desire, fear, sensation, pain, joy, and so on") are similarly dismissed by many as vestiges of "folk psychology" (Churchland, 1988, p. 44).

from experience (specifically, elementary sensations that bond together to form complex perceptions and ideas) was of immense importance in providing a model of mind that seemed consistent with the scientific model of the physical world as atomistic and deterministic. Advances in physiology, particularly in the localization of function in the brain and nervous system, together with a reflex model of sensorimotor processes that also dovetailed with atomism, associationism, and mechanistic determinism, strongly supported a view of mind as produced by the brain, and thus of physiology as the basis for a science of psychology. The doctrine of the conservation of energy made it increasingly difficult for many scientists to accept the idea of mental processes that could break into the closed causal chain of energy. It also provided a new notion, derived particularly from the physicist Gustav Fechner (considered by many to be the founder of experimental psychology), of mind as a form of energy, the product of a nervous system whose function is to translate physical energy into psychophysical activity. Last, but certainly not least, the biological sciences, in the form of Darwin's theory of evolution and natural selection, played an immense role in undermining old ideas about the uniqueness of human minds and weakening whatever remained of any belief among scientists in teleological or volitional processes in nature.

The naturalization of mind, however, was as revolutionary an idea as Darwinism, and for similar reasons. In the firsthand, subjective experience of all humans, mind seems an indivisible unity, an "I" that is a free, active, causal agent in an otherwise deterministic nature. This concept was being assaulted on many scientific fronts, however, and was rapidly being replaced by a concept of mind as solely the product of a nervous system shaped over the course of evolution in response to the demands of the environment. I use the term "assaulted" deliberately, because this new concept of mind was so antithetical to longstanding and seemingly commonsense ways in which people view their mind, or self, that it quickly became a battleground in which the emerging forces of modern science were arrayed against the old guard of religion, theology, and metaphysics. This war pitted naturalism and the principle of continuity against supernaturalism and dualism; and it was not simply an intellectual matter, but one with enormous implications for the way humans would view themselves, their society, and the world around them. Because so much was at stake, positions rapidly became rigidly polarized, and many of the most well-known and vocal of the scientists advocating for a new science of mind took strong anti-dualistic, anti-teleological views that left no room for compromise.

One of most important results of this militant dichotomization of scientific naturalism and metaphysical dualism was that there was no room in the former for a concept central to the latter, namely, mental causality or volition. A major phenomenon of psychology was therefore automatically excluded because of the assumption that materialistic determinism constitutes the essence of science. For many scientists, causative volition was a nonsensical concept because (they said) it required the introduction of new energy into what was otherwise a closed system. Moreover, allowing for the concept of volition in psychology was "a back-door attempt to reintroduce an active ego or soul into the new psychology" (Daston, 1978, p. 202). Volition became "a taboo concept" because scientists thought "it would pull psychology back to its prescientific, mystical days" (Decker, 1986, p. 52). Thomas Huxley (1887/1892), "Darwin's bull-dog" and the personification of the so-called science-religion debate of the 19th century, asked: "The ultimate form of the problem is this: Have we any reason to believe that a feeling, or state of consciousness, is capable of directly affecting the motion of even the smallest conceivable molecule of matter?" (p. 292). His answer, and that of many others, was, certainly not: "If anybody says that the will influences matter, the statement is not untrue, but it is nonsense....Such an assertion belongs to the crude materialism of the savage. Now the only thing which influences matter is the position of surrounding matter or the motion of surrounding matter" (Clifford, 1874, p. 728). Mental as well as physical events are part of a deterministic chain in which one event is the direct antecedent of, and gives rise to, the next event; but "volitions do not enter into the chain of causation...at all....[T]he feeling we call volition is not the cause of a voluntary act, but the symbol of that state of the brain which is the immediate cause of that act. We are conscious automata" (T. H. Huxley, 1874, pp. 576–577).[3]

Huxley's statement expresses another central assumption of the 19th-century founders of scientific psychology—the assumption that matter is the primary, independent factor in the universe and that mind is a secondary, dependent byproduct of it. Henry Maudsley, a prominent physician and physiologist whose *Physiology and Pathology of Mind* (1868) became "a turning point in English psychiatry" (Lewis, 1951, p. 269), summed up the views of many of his scientific contemporaries when he defined materialism as the belief that "mind is an outcome and function of matter in a certain state of organization" (Maudsley, 1879, p. 667). Huxley (1892) argued that "so far as observation and experiment go, they teach us that the psychical phenomena are dependent on the physical...called into existence" by physical processes (p. 43). Alexander Bain (1872/1874), one of the most influential psychologists during the formative years of scientific psychology, argued that all feelings, intellectual capacities, and volitional activities are directly correlated with and dependent on brain states. In France also, prominent psychologists left no room for doubt that mind and consciousness are wholly dependent on physiological processes. Théodule Ribot (1898), Professor of Experimental and Comparative Psychology at the College of France, stated unequivocally that "the organism and the brain...constitute the real personality," and the apparently psychological problem of "the unity of the ego is, in its ultimate form, a biological problem" (pp. 154–156). Early in his career, Ribot had argued, like Huxley, for an automaton theory in which "consciousness is only an adjunct of certain nervous processes, as incapable of reacting upon them as is a shadow upon the steps of the traveler whom

3. For a 21st-century advocate of such views, see Wegner (2002).

it accompanies" (Ribot, 1882, p. 11). He later modified this extreme view to say that mind, once called into existence by the brain, could have some efficacy.[4] Nonetheless, "the fundamental and active element is the nervous system, [and] the other [i.e., consciousness] is only a concomitant" (Ribot, 1898, pp. 11–12). Psychologists, he said, may treat mental states as causal phenomena, so long as they do not forget that all mental states "have their roots in the organism and are pre-determined by it…[and] that these [mental] causes are in their turn effects" (p. 51). Even a clinician such as Pierre Janet (1893/1901), who described the disturbances he observed as functional and mental rather than organic, emphasized that psychological phenomena are of "cortical origin"(p. 27): "You will understand, once for all, that the word 'mind' represents the highest functions of the brain and probably the functions of the cortex" (p. 52). In sum, for many in the first generation of scientific psychology, the thorough-going unilateral dependence of mind on brain was "a practical certainty.…There are numbers of questions relating to the connection of the mind with the body which have ceased to be open questions, because Science has had her word to say about them" (Clifford, 1874, pp. 734, 715).

The Unresolved Dilemmas of Psychology

The principles of 19th-century scientific naturalism took firm hold in psychology. Mechanistic determinism and reductionistic atomism had been pitted against the old "commonsense" or "folk-psychology" principles such as teleology, meaning, and volition, and had apparently emerged victorious. Nevertheless, humanistic principles were not easily relinquished. Throughout much of the 19th century, the conflict between scientific determinism and human volition remained a central dilemma of the age (Chadwick, 1975, pp. 204–205; Daston, 1978, 1982).

In particular, the denial of volition, or mental causality, left some major problems unresolved. Not only did such a conclusion contradict the daily experience of all humans; it also presented major social and ethical problems. If human beings are products of deterministic processes, how can they be held accountable for their actions under any social or ethical codes? Even Huxley (1892), who had contemptuously dismissed "the primitive dualism of a natural world 'fixed in fate' and a supernatural, left to the free play of volition" (p. 4), felt this dilemma so keenly that he was ultimately forced to construct his own "primitive dualism" of Nature and Society, the former characterized by law, the latter by volition or free will (e.g., T. H. Huxley, 1888/1898). The undeniably dual nature of human experience, together with the social and moral necessity for a belief in volition, presented psychologists with paradoxes and problems that seemed insoluble without sacrific-

4. More recently, the eminent neuroscientist Roger Sperry (e.g., 1980) has expressed a similar view.

ing either human principles on the one hand or scientific principles on the other.

Another major problem that the new psychology not only left unresolved, but actually exacerbated, was the question of whether to view mind as fundamentally a unity or a multiplicity. Is mind an indivisible whole that is the cohesive, organizing factor of mental life, or is it a structure built up from innumerable elements or experiences? Is mind the sum of the parts, or the factor drawing the parts together in the first place? In brief, is mind best understood from the bottom up or the top down? In the 19th century, this problem was central to the conflict between the old dualistic psychology and the new materialist psychology; it was a battle "which pitted the metaphysical 'unity of self' against the scientific 'multiplicity of selves'" (Robinson, 1978, p. 349). The first was the traditional notion of self, and even an associationist such as J. S. Mill (1843/1874) found this a compelling idea: "There is a something I call Myself, or, by another form of expression, my mind, which I consider as distinct from these sensations, thoughts, etc.; a something which I conceive to be not the thoughts, but the being that has the thoughts" (p. 56).

In direct opposition to this view was the "colonial" view of consciousness as a multiplicity built up from innumerable elements of the nervous system working in coordination: "Physiology shows that this verdict [of unity of mind] is an illusion....The apparently simple is, on analysis, found to be complex" (Ribot, 1882, pp. 42, 45). Mill (1843/1874), after acknowledging the compelling sense we all have of a unified self, went on to say that we can have no knowledge of what this something is ("though it is myself") but only of "the series of its states of consciousness" (p. 57). For an increasing number of 19th-century scientists, that knowable "series" was the only conception of mind that psychology needed, especially since the view of mind as a multiplicity conformed much better to the analytic method of science and the atomistic view of matter in 19th-century physics than did the concept of a unitary, indivisible self.

Nevertheless, most psychologists recognized that the multiplicity view of mind left fundamental problems unresolved. As McDougall (1911/1961) later said, the basic problem for all theories of mind is: "What holds consciousness together?" How do we get psychical unity out of physical multiplicity, "the hanging together of a multiplicity of conscious processes in a numerically distinct or individual stream" (p. 164)?[5]

The problem of whether mind is a unity or a multiplicity also raised the problem of whether the traditional analytic methods of the physical sciences are adequate for a science of psychology. If mind is basically a composite structure built up from numerous psychological elements, then such methods are appropriate for psychology. If, however, mind is most fundamentally a unity, then new methods, going beyond quantitative analysis, may be required. In the late 19th and early 20th centuries, a few psycholo-

---

5. The problem, known today as "the binding problem," remains a fundamental one in psychology and the neurosciences (see Chapter 1).

gists continued to insist, in opposition to most of their colleagues, that the analytic method alone is insufficient for psychology. To these psychologists (who included William James, James Ward, and G. F. Stout), when experience is "decomposed into elements" in the interests of conforming to the analytic scientific method, an important datum—the whole—has been lost (Daston, 1982). G. Murphy (1929), specifically discussing the limitations of the quantitative method when applied to human experience, suggested: "It may well be that psychology, precisely because of its concern with problems refractory to existing methods, will be the means of wresting from nature new methods and realities" (p. 415). Similarly, the historian Brett (1921), in the context of discussing the unity-multiplicity problem, said simply: "The central problem [in psychology] is the question of method" (p. 148).

The unity-multiplicity problem is also important because it raises in yet another form the question of the relationship of mind and body, that is, whether mind is caused or causal. Can mind be understood adequately as the product of simple physiological sensations or processes? Or is it itself a fundamental, elementary, and causal principle in nature? In essence, the unity-multiplicity debate is a variant of the primary problem facing scientific psychology: whether—and how—the concept of volition can be accommodated within a deterministic scientific understanding of nature.

An Attempted Solution: Methodological Parallelism

In short, psychologists had worked themselves into an impasse: They had set up an implacable dichotomy of naturalistic (or physicalistic) versus supernaturalistic (or dualistic) ideas about mind, but most of them were unable to throw themselves wholeheartedly on the side of naturalism as they had defined it, which logically required the denial of such "supernaturalistic" ideas as volition and the unity of human personality. Many psychologists sought to escape these discomforts by adopting a methodological parallelism, based on a doctrine of mind-brain concomitance enunciated by the neurologist Hughlings Jackson. Like Huxley, Clifford, Wundt, Bain, and many other 19th-century scientists, Jackson had expressed the view that, if he could be convinced that mind had interacted with and influenced matter, he would be forced to give up neurology altogether, "the implication being that dualism means the negation of law"—and, hence, of science (Engelhardt, 1975, p. 145). In other words, because of the law of the conservation of energy, there can be "no interference of one with the other" (Jackson, 1931–1932, vol. 2, p. 72).[6] Jackson therefore adopted the position that states

6. This belief that mental efficacy is a violation of the conservation of energy lies behind much of contemporary rejection of any form of dualism in which consciousness is understood as an active force in nature (see, e.g., Dennett, 1991). Similarly, it is also behind much of the rejection of psi phenomena, the assumption being that the mental efficacy implied by such phenomena "den[ies] the universal validity of one of the greatest triumphs of nineteenth-century science, the laws of

of consciousness are different in kind from nervous states; the two occur together, that is, in correlation; but there is no interaction or interference between them. Mental phenomena and physiological phenomena, in other words, constitute two parallel, completely closed, yet somehow correlated causal chains; but the relationship between the two chains, the nature of the concomitance, is a metaphysical, and not scientific, problem.

Few psychologists adopted a specific philosophical doctrine of parallelism such as that of Leibniz. Most insisted instead that this parallelism was not ontological, but methodological or linguistic only. Increasingly, they began to argue that the impasses to which the naturalization of mind had led are the result of mixing conceptual categories or realms of discourse (e.g., Janet, 1893/1901). Adopting a methodological parallelism of psychological and physical processes allowed psychologists the "luxury of ontological agnosticism while they got on with their work" (R. M. Young, 1970, p. 233), because it freed them to study psychological processes in their own right, without needing to relate them back in any specific way to their physiological substratum.

Even more fundamentally, psychologists began to argue that the impasses in psychology reflected limits beyond which scientific method cannot go. John Tyndall (1879), one of the most thoughtful exponents of scientific monism, argued that, although the absolute correlation of mental phenomena with brain phenomena is known, the ultimate nature of that relationship is not only unknown but unknowable. A neutral statement of the "invariable" correlation, or parallelism, is as far as science can go; science can *describe* the mind-matter relationship but it cannot *explain* it, because, with mind or consciousness, "the methods pursued in mechanical science come to an end...[and] logical continuity disappears" (pp. 390–391). Tyndall (1874/1879) therefore insisted that he must remain agnostic on the question of whether mind is a causal factor in physical events, or merely a by-product of them, because

> the production of consciousness by molecular action is to me quite as inconceivable on mechanical principles as the production of molecular motion by consciousness....I, however, reject neither, and thus stand in the presence of two Incomprehensibles, instead of one Incomprehensible.

---

thermodynamics" (Deese, 1972, p. 115). More generally, as the long-time editor of the *Journal of Nervous and Mental Disease* put it, "paranormal phenomena...are intrinsically unacceptable—there is no way to make them compatible with the total accumulated body of scientific knowledge....The problem lies...in the body of knowledge and theory which must be abandoned or radically modified in order to accept it" (E. G. Brody, 1979, pp. 72–73). Phenomena of mental efficacy (such as those described in Chapter 3 and in works listed in the Appendix) may indeed require a "radical modification" of certain assumptions in modern science, particularly about the nature of mind and matter. They in no way, however, require the "abandonment" of accumulated scientific knowledge—provided we distinguish *assumptions* from *knowledge*.

> While accepting fearlessly the facts of materialism dwelt upon in these pages, I bow my head in the dust before that mystery of mind. (p. 224)

Even William James, who could hardly be accused of wishing to put psychology into a theoretical or methodological straitjacket, nevertheless argued in *The Principles of Psychology* for a methodological parallelism: "Empirical parallelism...[is] the wisest course....[N]ature in her unfathomable designs has mixed us...of brain and mind,...the two things hang indubitably together and determine each other's being, but how or why, no mortal may ever know" (James, 1890b, vol. 1, p. 182).[7]

In fact, however, the professed ontological neutrality was usually anything but that. Behind the methodological parallelism, and the associated call to get on with studying and describing psychological processes in and of themselves, was the often thinly disguised assumption that mental phenomena are a secondary byproduct of the fundamental constituent of the universe, matter. T. H. Huxley (1892), summarizing his own position, spoke for many of his scientific contemporaries: "I have frequently expressed my incapacity to understand the nature of the relation between consciousness and a certain anatomical tissue...[but] so far as observation and experiment go, they teach us that the psychical phenomena are dependent on the physical" (p. 43). Thus, in the same breath, he expressed both an inability to understand the nature of the mind-matter relationship and a fundamental conclusion about its nature. Huxley was agnostic, therefore, *not* concerning the nature of the relationship of mind and matter—he was convinced that mind is ultimately dependent on (because derived from) matter—but only concerning the specific nature of that dependence. In short, for Huxley as for many other 19th-century scientists, the exact nature of the dependence of psychical processes on physical ones was an open—though unresolvable—question; but the general dependence of mind on matter was a resolved—and thus closed—question.

The outcome of adopting this methodological parallelism in psychology was not difficult to foresee. Psychologists could get on with the business of simply describing psychological processes, professing a vague working assumption of mind-brain unity without having to deal with fundamental theoretical issues such as the nature of mind-brain concomitance and the associated problem of the efficacy of mind in the physical world. The dismissal of such problems as "metaphysical" only, and not "scientific," effectively foreclosed any challenge to the assumption underlying psychology of a unilateral dependence of mind on brain. Although the nature and extent of mind-brain correlation should have become the major empirical problem for a psychology that sought theoretical understanding of its subject matter, it was instead altogether avoided. Perhaps even more problematically, 19th-century psychology had been built on a rigid and unyielding dichotomy of physicalistic naturalism versus dualistic supernaturalism, and the rigidity

---

7. This view that the mind-body problem is insoluble is essentially the "mysterian" position of McGinn (1999).

of the dichotomy precluded any serious consideration of the possibility that the solution to its paradoxes and problems might lie in a close and critical examination of prevailing assumptions about naturalism itself—that is, about whether the equation of naturalism with physicalism and determinism, and of mental efficacy with supernaturalism and lawlessness, exhausted the possibilities.

Scientists instrumental in the development of 19th-century psychology thus in general had chosen to conceptualize science primarily not as a method with which to confront basic questions posed by contradictory aspects of human experience, but as a doctrine to which psychology, if it is to be a science, must conform. Because so many 19th-century scientists refused to question or even critically examine the assumptions of the physical sciences and the world view derived from them, and thus avoided theoretical problems that psychological phenomena alone raised, those assumptions, that world view, and the pattern of avoiding basic theoretical issues became the foundation upon which modern psychology was built. During its subsequent history, psychology, despite its broad expansion in the 20th century, has for the most part remained within that framework:

> Ever since its stipulation into existence as an independent science, psychology has been far more concerned with being a science than with courageous and self-determining confrontations with its historically constituted subject matter. Its history has been largely a matter of emulating the methods, forms, symbols of the established sciences, especially physics. In so doing, there has been an inevitable tendency to retreat from broad and intensely significant ranges of its subject matter, and to form rationales for so doing which could only invite further retreat. (Koch, 1961, pp. 629–630)

F. W. H. Myers: Purposes and Principles

Not all psychologists acquiesced in this retreat from major problems and theoretical issues in psychology. William James, for one, was acutely aware that parallelism, or the Jacksonian doctrine of concomitance, avoided, and did nothing to help resolve, the basic problems of mental causality inherent in psychology. To the injunction of his colleague Charles Mercier—"Having firmly and tenaciously grasped these two notions, of the absolute separateness of mind and matter, and of the invariable concomitance of a mental change with a bodily change, the student will enter on the study of psychology with half his difficulties surmounted"—James replied: "Half his difficulties ignored, I should prefer to say. For this 'concomitance' in the midst of 'absolute separateness' is an utterly irrational notion" (James, 1890b, vol. 1, p. 136). Although he himself had urged psychologists to adopt an empirical or methodological parallelism, he also cautioned them that this was "certainly only a provisional halting-place, and things must some day be more thoroughly thought out" (p. 182). James's close friend and colleague,

F. W. H. Myers, was one of the few psychologists who attempted to do just this. In numerous papers published between 1880 and his death in 1901, culminating in his (1903) posthumously published *Human Personality and Its Survival of Bodily Death* (*HP*), Myers dissented from the determination of his scientific contemporaries to exclude from psychology its most basic questions.

Myers was born at Keswick, England, in 1843, the son of a liberal clergyman who died when Myers was eight. He went up to Cambridge University in 1860 and lived in Cambridge until his death in 1901. At Cambridge he earned a First Class in both the Classical Tripos and the Moral Sciences Tripos, and he began reading for the Natural Sciences Tripos. In 1865 he was appointed to a fellowship and lectureship in classics at Cambridge, which he held until 1869, when, influenced by J. S. Mill's liberalism, he resigned his fellowship to work for the movement to broaden higher education, and particularly women's education, in Britain. After the passage of the Education Act of 1870, he began work in 1872 as a government school inspector, and in 1875 he was appointed school inspector for the Cambridge District, a position he held for the next 25 years.

Myers's work in education, however, eventually provided simply the background and part of the financial support for the real work of his life. Like many of the intellectual leaders of the mid-19th century, he had rejected the Christianity in which he had been raised because of its insufficient rational basis and "the need of an inward make-believe" (Myers, 1893/1961, p. 36). Although scientists such as those referred to earlier in this chapter were giving widespread currency to the new assumption that mind is a secondary byproduct of elementary material processes, this too seemed to him a gratuitous assumption that required closer scrutiny. To examine this assumption with novel lines of empirical research, Myers helped found the Society for Psychical Research (SPR) in 1882, an organization whose stated aim was "to approach these various problems without prejudice or prepossession of any kind, and in the same spirit of exact and unimpassioned inquiry which has enabled Science to solve so many problems, once not less obscure nor less hotly debated" (Society for Psychical Research, 1882, p. 4).

In the SPR's early years, the phenomena studied included most prominently the study of hypnosis and mesmerism, telepathy, mediumship, and hallucinations. The larger purpose of psychical research, however, as conceived by its most prominent founders, was to examine such phenomena in light of their bearing on questions about the nature and place in the universe of mind or human personality. In addition to Myers, founders and early members of the SPR included prominent scientists and intellectual leaders such as Arthur and Gerald Balfour, W. F. Barrett, W. E. Gladstone, Sir Oliver Lodge, Lord Rayleigh, John Ruskin, F. C. S. Schiller, Henry Sidgwick, Eleanor Sidgwick, Balfour Stewart, Lord Tennyson, and J. J. Thomson, all of whom sought a more satisfactory understanding of human nature than the intellectual climate of the 19th century was providing. For the first two decades of the SPR's existence, Myers was one of its most active investigators and prolific writers; and his model of human personality, which he began to formulate in the early 1880s and then presented in detail in the 1890s in a series of nine papers on the Subliminal Self, became the theoretical framework for psychical research, and remained so for decades.[8]

It is readily apparent from even a brief glance at Myers's writings that his ultimate concern was with the question of whether individual personality survives death: "The question for man most momentous of all is...whether or no his personality involves any element which can survive bodily death. In this direction have always lain the greatest fears, the farthest-reaching hopes, which could either oppress or stimulate mortal minds" (*HP*, vol. 1, p. 1). His interest in psychology therefore was not purely academic. Although initially a poet and classicist, he turned to science and psychology because he understood that the question of post-mortem survival was, in essence, the problem of the relation of mind and body, a problem not to be left to "inward make-believe" (Myers, 1893/1904, p. 42) but to be attacked by empirical methods. As William James (1901) said at the time of Myers's death:

> Myers had as it were to re-create his personality before he became the wary critic of evidence, the skillful handler of hypothesis, the learned neurologist and omnivorous reader of biological and cosmological matter, with whom in later years we were acquainted. The transformation came about because he needed to be all these things in order to work successfully at the problem that lay near his heart. (p. 214)

Armed with a fervent belief in the power of scientific method, Myers fought the prevailing tendency in late 19th-century psychology to exclude its most fundamental problems and argued instead for an expansion of psychology's empirical base, the development of its own methods, and an examination of the theoretical assumptions about mind and scientific naturalism that were contributing to the narrowing of psychology.

Before examining Myers's theory of human personality and the avenues of research that he believed important for approaching the mind-body problem empirically, it is first essential to understand some of the purposes and principles that provided the foundation for his thinking. Myers and the field of psychical research in general, for which he was the primary spokesman and theoretician in its first decades, have too often been misunderstood, erroneously portrayed, and contemptuously dismissed as representing "pseudo-science" characterized by "magico-religious belief" and "irrationality" or even "anti-rationality" (see, e.g., Alcock, 1981; Zusne, 1985), or as threatening to return Western society to the superstitious belief in "the operation of 'hidden,' 'mysterious,' or 'occult' forces in the universe" (Kurtz, 1985, p. 505). Nothing could be further from the truth. The central principles guiding Myers were in fact precisely those of most of his scientific contemporaries, including "our modern ideas of continuity, conservation,

---

8. These nine papers are: Myers, 1892b, 1892c, 1892d, 1892e, 1892f, 1893a, 1893b, 1895d, and 1895e.

evolution" (*HP*, vol. 2, p. 251), and a central purpose was to encourage the expansion of science and scientific method to address the most fundamental questions about the nature of human personality. For Myers and his colleagues, the "very raison d'être [of psychical research] is the extension of scientific method, of intellectual virtues....into regions where many a current of old tradition, of heated emotion, even of pseudo-scientific prejudice, deflects the bark" (Myers, 1900a, p. 459).[9]

Tertium Quid

In the midst of revolutionary new ideas in the 19th century about the nature and study of mind, not everyone agreed that the rigid dichotomy of the old, theological, personal world view and the new, scientific, impersonal world view, or the acquiescent methodological parallelism to which this dichotomization had led, is the final word. In the introduction to a two-volume collection of some of his essays, Myers's close friend and fellow psychical researcher Edmund Gurney (1887d) wrote:

> Most of the papers deal with matters of contemporary controversy, as to which two antagonistic opinions have been strongly entertained and enforced....In most of these questions I am conscious of "a great deal to be said on both sides",...[and] the truer view seems to me...not one that would extenuate differences...[but one whose] immediate tendency, on the contrary, is rather to make each of the duels triangular. In short, it is a *tertium quid*. (pp. v–vii)

John Stuart Mill had been the leader and exemplar of mid-19th-century liberal thinkers who believed that the cause of knowledge is best served, not by partisans, but by "those who take something from both sides of the great controversies, and make out that neither extreme is right, nor wholly wrong" (Mill, 1910, vol. 2, p. 360). The impact of Mill was particularly strong on intellectual circles at Cambridge in the 1860s; and Myers, Gurney, and other early leaders of psychical research educated at Cambridge fully absorbed this "tertium quid" approach. Fundamental both to Myers's thinking and to psychical research in general, therefore, was the belief that conflicts between ideas or points of view are best settled not by contentious

9. In the same paper, he went on to say that "we have more in common with those who may criticise or attack our work with competent diligence than with those who may acclaim and exaggerate it without adding thereto any careful work of their own" (p. 459). Unfortunately, most critics of parapsychology and psychical research, past and present, have *not* "criticise[d] or attack[ed] our work with competent diligence," nor have they added any work, careful or otherwise, of their own. With such "critics" in mind, as well as those who "acclaim and exaggerate," Myers (1894–1895) also pointed out that "between the scornfully sceptical and the eagerly superstitious we have virtually had to create a public of our own" (p. 190). Unfortunately, that public still remains small.

debate but by increased knowledge, and that knowledge advances not by the interminable clashing of old antagonists but by the application of both new methods and new perspectives to old problems. Behind Myers's work was thus a conscious and sustained attempt to move beyond the increasingly polarized, dichotomous positions of 19th-century thought and to seek different, broader perspectives in which aspects of both (or all) sides may have a place. As he put it, "something is gained if, having started with the preconception that 'all which is not A is B,' we have come to the conclusion that our own subject-matter is neither A nor B, but X" (Myers, 1890a, p. 248).

Continuity

For Myers, as for so many 19th-century scientists, the continuity or uniformity of nature had emerged as the one most fundamental principle guiding modern scientific knowledge: "If Nature is to be intelligible to our minds she must be continuous; her action must be uniformitarian and not catastrophic" (Myers, 1895a, p. 22). Myers thus believed that all phenomena—mental and material, normal and abnormal, commonplace and rare—are in some sense continuous, coherent, and amenable to the rational, empirical methods of science. The further implication of this belief in continuity was the belief that scientific knowledge would advance qualitatively only when scientists address *all* phenomena, and particularly those that do not readily fit into current views:

> If any phenomenon...seems arbitrary, or incoherent, or unintelligible, she [science] does not therefore suppose that she has come upon an unravelled end in the texture of things; but rather takes for granted that a rational answer to the new problem must somewhere exist,—an answer which will be all the more instructive because it will involve facts of which that first question must have failed to take due account. (Myers, 1900b, p. 120)

Empiricism

A corollary of this belief in the continuity of the universe was that the only reliable means of obtaining knowledge, not only about the physical world but about mind, is scientific method, "those methods of inquiry which in attacking all other problems [man] has found the most efficacious" (*HP*, vol. 1, p. 1). Myers did not believe that science is the *only* way of knowing. A person whose intensely poetic and emotional nature was vividly apparent in all his writings, he recognized that science and intellect may not provide a person's "only or his deepest insight into the meaning of the Universe," and that "contemplation, revelation, ecstasy, may carry deep into certain hearts an even profounder truth" (Myers, 1900b, p. 114).[10] Science undoubtedly has its limitations,

> just as we admit the inadequacy, the conventionality, of human speech itself. Speech cannot match the meaning which looks in an hour of emotion from the eyes of a friend. But what we learn from that gaze is indefinable and incommunicable. Our race needed the spoken and written word, with all its baldness, if they were to understand each other and to grow to be men. So with Science as opposed to Intuition. Science forms a language common to all mankind; she can explain herself when she is misunderstood and right herself when she goes wrong; nor has humanity yet found...that the methods of Science, intelligently and honestly followed, have led us in the end astray. (Myers, 1900b, p. 114)

Expanding Psychology

Despite his recognition that science has its limits, Myers objected vehemently to the growing segregation in the 19th century of science and metaphysics, science and religion, volition and determinism, or mind and matter. In keeping with his "tertium quid" approach, he believed that the challenge to science does not end but *begins* precisely when one comes up against two contradictory findings, positions, or theories, and that breakthroughs occur when one continues to work with conflicting data and ideas until a new picture emerges that can put conflicts and paradoxes in a new light or a larger perspective.

For Myers, those who banned certain phenomena or topics from scientific inquiry showed "a want rather than an excess of confidence" in "the immutable regularity" of nature (Myers, 1881, p. 99). The reach of science is limited only by our ingenuity in translating large, metaphysical problems into finite, empirical ones (Myers, 1885d, p. 127). In psychical research in particular, "such confrontations with metaphysical problems reduced to concrete form are a specialty of our research" (Myers, 1894, p. 421). Myers's (1891c) superb review of William James's *Principles of Psychology* was a plea, in opposition to the deliberate separation of metaphysics and psychology advocated in that book, to try instead to translate the former into the latter, and thus to attack large questions by an "attempt to give [them] a precise, an experimental character" (p. 132). Whereas James had warned that the data of psychology cannot provide answers to fundamental, metaphysical questions, Myers turned the issue around and argued instead that fundamental questions provide the guidance and direction for producing the data—and ultimately the knowledge—of psychology.[11] Whereas James had empha-

---

10. For more in-depth discussions of this other kind of "knowing," see Chapters 7 and 8.

11. In his 1894 Presidential Address to the American Psychological Association, James (1895/1978) abandoned his earlier attempt to separate metaphysics and psychology.

sized the limitations of psychology, Myers, in contrast, wanted to awaken scientists to a sense of the potential power and scope of psychology. We may, he said, so far have insufficiently appreciated "how very far...the possibility of experiment may extend" (p. 119). Myers thus (like James) warned of the danger to science of "the instinct of system, of a rounded and completed doctrine" that prematurely limits what science can and cannot address: A "determined protest against premature synthesis is as much needed now as ever" (Myers, 1889h, p. 392).

In particular, Myers protested against limiting science to the existing subject matter, methods, and concepts of the physical sciences by conceding prematurely that questions about the nature of the relationship between mental and physical phenomena—going beyond the prevailing but ultimately vague assumption of concomitance—are scientifically unapproachable. Instead, "the only line of demarcation which science can draw,...is between things which can, or which cannot, be cognised by our existing faculties," a line which is by no means "permanent and immovable....On the contrary, it is the continual work of science to render that which is incognisable cognisable, that which is imperceptible perceptible....Aristotle...relegated his unknowable to the fixed stars...but we have no more reason than he had to take our [present] mental horizon for an objective line" (Myers, 1881, p. 103).

In addition to lamenting the premature limitation of psychology's subject matter and methods, Myers would also have lamented the current breach in psychology (and indeed in current parapsychology) between its experimental and humanistic or transpersonal branches, that is, between empirically oriented persons who emphasize the objective scientific method and experientially oriented persons who emphasize a more subjective or intuitive approach. The challenge to psychologists—not an easy one, obviously—is to bring the objective method to bear on psychological phenomena without losing sight of their inherent subjectivity. This challenge of bringing scientific method to bear on highly personal experiential phenomena becomes particularly apparent in the study of mystical experience (see Chapter 8).

Psychophysiological Concomitance

Clearly, the most basic problem in psychology needing to be translated from metaphysical to empirical form is the question of psychophysiological correlation. As I discussed earlier, most scientists (then and now) concluded that the mind-body problem is no longer an open empirical question, because advances in physical science seemed to render it certain that mind is a product of the nervous system and wholly dependent on it. For Myers, however, the mind-matter problem was still very much an open empirical problem—and *the* basic theoretical question at the heart of psychology. He argued that the principle of concomitance, or correlation, which states simply that "for every mental state there is a correlative nervous state" (Jackson, 1931–1932, vol. 2, p. 72), has not closed off the empirical question of the causal relationship between mind and brain, because it is essentially a neutral statement: "Accompanying the mental phenomena—states of consciousness, there are physical phenomena—brain changes; but no knowledge of the one throws any light on the other" (*HP*, vol. 1, p. 13n). Moreover, merely continuing to observe the parallelism will not advance our knowledge in any qualitative sense:

> However exactly the parallelism between psychical and cerebral energies may be established, the exacter correlation can tell us little more than the vaguer told us—little more than we had always known....But as to the origin or essential significance of this close connection...we avowedly know nothing at all. We do not know whether the mental energy precedes or follows on the cerebral change, nor whether the two are, somehow, but different aspects of the same fact. (Myers, 1891d, p. 635)[12]

Psychologists had in fact limited their observations of mind-brain correlation primarily to situations in which brain is essentially the independent variable and mind the dependent. The observer creates or looks for a condition of damage or alteration to the nervous system and then describes the effects on mental functioning or, at best, looks at a mental state and attempts to identify an associated physiological state. Such essentially one-sided observations are, in Myers's view, bound to lead to inadequate conclusions. When, he said, we look at a partially illuminated globe, the result is

> a familiar optical illusion. When we see half of some body strongly illuminated, and half of it feebly illuminated, it is hard to believe that the brilliant moiety is not the larger of the two. And, similarly, it is the increased definiteness of our conception of the physical side of our mental operations which seems to increase its relative importance,—to give it a kind of priority over the psychical aspect of the same processes. Yet...the central problem of the relation of the objective and subjective sides of the psychoneural phenomena can in no way be altered by any increase of definiteness in our knowledge of the objective processes which correspond to the subjective side. (Myers, 1886a, p. xl)

The Study of Subliminal Phenomena[13]

Achieving a more balanced approach to the problem of mind-brain concomitance requires a thoroughgoing empirical study of mental efficacy, that is, the study of phenomena which suggest that a change in mental state

12. Those confident that modern neuroimaging techniques confirm the view that mind is a product of the brain would do well to remember this cautionary statement.

13. As I will explain later in this chapter, Myers proposed that the word

has produced some change in a physiological or physical state (I will discuss such phenomena in depth in Chapter 3). To advance our understanding of the relationship between mind and brain beyond the long-recognized but little-understood parallelism, Myers believed that psychologists needed to begin to single out for special attention situations in which the ordinary relationship between mental and physical functioning seems to be altered or thrown out of gear. In particular, he believed that a newly emerging field—namely, the study of subliminal phenomena in all their myriad forms—had enormous potential for increasing scientific knowledge about the relationship of mental and physical processes. These phenomena are especially important because in them the normal equilibrium, as Myers put it, between mental and physical functioning often seems to be upset, and mental and physical processes operate in unaccustomed and unusual ways. Such phenomena thus suggest that the correlation of mind and brain might not be as straightforward as it appears under normal circumstances.

Myers also believed that such phenomena are important because they sometimes reveal latent mental processes or abilities not apparent in the context of ordinary psychophysiological functioning. The study of subliminal phenomena, which was expanding rapidly during the 19th century (see, e.g., Ellenberger, 1970; Gauld, 1992), increasingly turned up phenomena difficult to reconcile with the prevailing physiological, mechanistic theory of mind. For example, psychosomatic phenomena such as those associated with hypnosis and hysteria suggest that alterations in mental states or processes can have dramatic effects on physiological processes. Such phenomena thus reveal the possibility of experimentally manipulating mental states as the independent or causal variable and observing the effects on physical processes. Moreover, many subliminal phenomena such as hysterical anesthesia or hypnotic hallucinations, occurring in conditions where physical pathology is unlikely, nonetheless sometimes resemble phenomena that are clearly associated with neuropathology. These phenomena suggest that similar effects might not always have similar causes; a blister, for example, might have either a physical cause (a burn) or a mental cause (an hypnotic suggestion). Myers urged the importance of studying such phenomena to determine whether, and under what conditions, mind might be an active initiating factor. Finally, more extreme phenomena such as telepathy[14] even

"subliminal" be used, rather than "subconscious" or "unconscious," to denote psychological phenomena occurring outside one's normal waking consciousness.

14. The word "telepathy" was introduced by Myers in 1882 (W. F. Barrett, Massey, et al., 1883, p. 147; Myers, 1896a, p. 174) to refer to the phenomenon of one person apparently deriving information directly from another person's mind. Although telepathy and clairvoyance were, and still are, much more controversial than, for example, hypnosis or hallucinations, Myers and his colleagues believed that they had sufficient evidence, both from experiments and from spontaneous experiences, to try to incorporate such phenomena into a broader understanding of the nature of mind; and we agree. We again urge readers to consult the Appendix for references to the serious literature on psychical research.

more clearly suggest that mental and physical processes do not always operate in the accustomed manner (e.g., Gurney et al., 1886).

To Myers, therefore, subliminal phenomena are particularly important because they suggest that mind is something greater, not only in extent but in capacity, than ordinary psychological phenomena reveal. He argued, however, that the investigation of subliminal phenomena must be approached from a larger perspective than that of most previous studies, which were primarily undertaken for medical or clinical purposes. Although subliminal phenomena were beginning to be widely studied by clinicians (especially in France by Janet, Charcot, Binet, and many others), Myers believed that they should also be examined for their bearing upon central theoretical problems in psychology. The study of hallucinations, for example, "has usually been undertaken with a therapeutic and not with a purely scientific purpose," with the result that pathological aspects of hallucinations have been noted and emphasized, rather than their "absolute psychological significance" (Myers, 1892d, p. 342). Similarly, as I will discuss in more detail later, Myers believed that hypnotism is potentially one of the most effective methodological tools for theoretical psychologists. Yet, here too, in the burgeoning study of hypnosis

> we have to regret the lamentable scarcity of purely psychological experiments over the whole hypnotic field. We are habitually forced to base our psychological inferences on therapeutic practice; and in directions where there has been no therapeutic effort there are gaps in our knowledge, which those hypnotists who have good subjects at their disposal should be invited to fill up as soon as may be. (*HP*, vol. 1, p. 191)

Even hysteria, clearly a severe clinical problem and understandably emphasized as such, is also an important potential source of knowledge about psychophysiological functioning (Myers, 1893a; *HP*, chap. 2). Hysterics often show subliminal control over physiological functioning, producing effects, such as hysterical anesthesias or stigmata, that are practically unknown under normal conditions. A comparison of hysterical and neurological disorders might therefore reveal much about the nature and extent of psychological processes as causal processes, especially the degree to which they are dependent on neurological conditions or, conversely, may themselves alter these conditions.

The New Physics

Just as subliminal phenomena were showing mind to be more extensive and of a different nature than previously assumed, so late 19th-century physics was showing the physical universe to be more extensive—and even of a different nature—than previously assumed. Perhaps its greatest accomplishment was in beginning to reveal just how limited our normal, unaided sensory perception is, in comparison with the character and extent of the surrounding universe. Myers recognized the potential importance to the mind-matter problem of this dawning realization. To those whose thinking about the nature of psychophysical processes has been circumscribed by the assumption that our everyday perception of the physical world is somehow a benchmark, Myers (1881) cautioned that "Science, while perpetually denying an unseen world, is perpetually revealing it" (p. 103).

The discovery and study of electromagnetic radiation in particular had begun to reveal just how narrow and limited our sensory perceptions are. The expansion of our knowledge "into regions of rays which no senses born within us have enabled us directly to discern" (Myers, 1894–1895, p. 196) implies that we have not yet exhausted our potential knowledge of aspects of the universe co-existing, undetected, with the perceivable world. Science cannot "conjecture beforehand how many distinct but coexisting environments may now surround us....Her own history has been one of constantly widening conceptions" (Myers, 1894–1895, p. 195). In a prescient remark anticipating the upheavals in scientists' conception of space, matter, and time brought on by 20th-century physics, Myers cautioned that we "must be ready to conceive other invisible environments or co-existences, and in a sense to sit loose to the conception of Space, regarded as an obstacle to communication or cognition" (*HP*, vol. 2, p. 262).

Yet he also emphasized repeatedly that such "unseen" environments must somehow be "fundamentally continuous" and interrelated with the one we know directly; "if an unseen world exists...we must in some sense be in it" (Myers, 1891d, p. 634): Like "a tadpole...who had learned theoretically that what he was breathing in his pond was not the water but the oxygen dissolved therein,—and who then should...raise his head above water...[and] perceive frogs and other animals respiring the translucid air" (*HP*, vol. 2, p. 526), scientists too would probably continue to discover unsuspected environments, co-existing and continuous with the familiar world we perceive directly, even if also differing from it in certain respects.[15]

Mind and Matter

Myers therefore was in a real sense motivated by the expectation that a combined study of the unsuspected range of mind and the previously unsuspected properties and extent of matter would begin to suggest new

---

15. An important concept in late 19th-century physics was that of the ether. The discovery of radiation had led many scientists to postulate a homogeneous, frictionless, non-material substance filling what we perceive as "empty" space and serving as the transmitting medium for light and electromagnetic forces. Although 20th-century physics abandoned this *particular* concept of ether, it nonetheless added significant support for the larger idea behind the concept of ether—and the one that was of especial significance to Myers—that the imperceptible range of the material universe far exceeds the few aspects of it that are perceptible by our normal, unaided senses.

and unprecedented ways of understanding the relation between the two. Because 19th-century physics and the study of subliminal phenomena were showing that our conceptions of both matter and mind are inadequate and incomplete, so too, Myers concluded, must be the old dichotomy of dualism and materialism which had derived from them. Myers (1890a) therefore cautioned that "the categories 'material' and 'immaterial'...may be quite inadequate" (p. 247): "The line between the 'material' and the 'immaterial,' as these words are commonly used, means little more than the line between the phenomena which our senses or our instruments can detect or register and the phenomena which they can *not*" (Myers, 1886b, p. 290). Anticipating a question that became of central importance after his death, in the wake of theoretical advances in 20th-century physics, Myers asked how one can define the distinction between subjective and objective when matter, which appears to have certain characteristics from one perspective, has different characteristics from another: "The impenetrability of matter, which seems our ultimate sensory fact, may be as relative and contingent a property as colour itself" (Myers, 1890a, p. 247; *HP*, vol. 1, p. 277). In short, both the new psychology of the subliminal and the new physics led him to the conviction that "it is no longer safe to assume any sharply-defined distinction of mind and matter....[O]ur notions of mind and matter must pass through many a phase as yet unimagined" (Myers, 1886c, pp. 178–179).

An Expanded Naturalism

In keeping with his commitment to the "tertium quid" approach as the most productive route to advancing science, Myers also rejected the idea that physicalistic naturalism and supernaturalism exhaust the possible views on the nature of the world. The choices are not, he thought, limited either to the assumption that nature consists entirely of what we can now perceive or otherwise infer from our present understanding of matter, or to the assumption that the universe is essentially lawless and capricious, liable to disruption by whim or vagary. Naturalists believe there is only one world, the "orderly world of Nature" (T. H. Huxley, 1892, p. 3); supernaturalists believe there are two worlds, nature and a world above or beyond nature, the latter not subject to the orderly determinism of nature. In one sense, Myers was a strict naturalist, believing in the continuity of all phenomena in one world and the invariability and universal application of natural laws. Thus he rejected the concept of miracles, conceived as "violations of natural law" or "exceptions" to natural law "permitted by Providence," because, he said, "we know now that natural laws are never violated" and "that all phenomena alike take place in accordance with the laws of the universe" (Myers, 1881, p. 99; 1889d, p. 14).

Where Myers differed with most scientific naturalists was on the question of whether "Nature" should be assumed to be synonymous with "Matter" as then understood. For him, belief in one continuous, orderly world did not automatically imply that the known laws of matter provide the sole and fundamental foundation of that world: "Accepting as perfectly valid every law which recognised science can establish" does not preclude the supposition that there may also be "further laws, of a different kind it may be," but still "susceptible of rigorous investigation" (Gurney & Myers, 1884a, p. 792). The modern belief that the universe is "inevitably naturalistic, cosmical, evolutionary" and never the result of "specially-authorised interference" does not exclude the belief that there may be "a scheme of laws...of which our sciences of matter are...powerless to take account," but which new sciences—particularly psychology—might discover (Myers, 1890b, p. 329).

Myers thus rejected *both* supernaturalism and the prevalent form of naturalism in favor of a different, expanded concept of scientific naturalism: "This distinction [between natural and supernatural] we altogether repudiate" (W. F. Barrett, Massey, et al., 1883, p. 150). In an early essay, Myers (1881) expressed his belief that it is possible to reconcile "the conflict between science and orthodoxy [religion]...which...too often assumes [the form] of a sheer and barren contradiction"; but to do so, it is first necessary to "reject all *question-begging* terms—all phrases such as 'violations of the order of Nature'" (p. 96). He endorsed the general belief behind St. Augustine's statement that "God does nothing against nature." *No* phenomena violate the laws of nature; nevertheless, some phenomena may indeed go "against Nature *as we know it*—in its familiar and ordinary way." Therefore Myers urged antagonists in the controversy between naturalism and supernaturalism to move beyond the divergent and polarized positions in which their assumptions have fixed them: "Let us not oppose *law* and *miracle*....Let us not oppose the *natural* and the *supernatural*." Such "polemical antitheses" derive from the fact that "on each side of the controversy we find a reasonable prepossession pushed too often to an unreasonable extreme" (pp. 96–97). As a first step toward resolving or reconciling the apparent contradiction between naturalism and supernaturalism, Myers rejected the word "supernatural" altogether as a meaningless word. Instead, he

> ventured to coin the word "supernormal" to be applied to phenomena which are *beyond what usually happens—beyond*, that is, in the sense of suggesting unknown psychical laws. It is thus formed on the analogy of *abnormal*. When we speak of an abnormal phenomenon we do not mean one which *contravenes* natural laws, but one which exhibits them in an unusual or inexplicable form. Similarly by a supernormal phenomenon, I mean, not one which *overrides* natural laws, for I believe no such phenomenon to exist, but one which exhibits the action of laws higher, in a psychical aspect, than are discerned in action in everyday life. By *higher* (either in a psychical or in a physiological sense) I mean "apparently belonging to a more advanced stage of evolution." (Myers, 1885b, p. 30n)

These, then, were the general purposes and principles on which Myers based his approach to psychology: first, to maintain a belief in the ultimate rationality and continuity or interrelatedness of all phenomena, mental as well as physical; and second, to attempt to forge a new perspective on old problems concerning the nature of mind by extending psychology's range of observation and data beyond ordinary, familiar phenomena and by broadening its concepts through continually examining assumptions, hypotheses, and views contrary to those currently prevailing. On the basis of this "tertium quid" approach, Myers went on to make two major contributions to psychology. First, he developed a theoretical model of mind that was an important attempt to move beyond the two predominant, but diametrically opposed, views of mind and to develop a more comprehensive view. Second, he identified numerous lines of research by which he thought that the mind-matter problem could be approached, and potentially resolved, empirically. In the rest of this chapter, I will first describe Myers's model of mind and then, by giving a brief overview of his book *Human Personality*, introduce some of the kinds of research that he believed essential for developing an adequate theory of mind.

Myers's Theory of Human Personality

The engine that drove all of Myers's thinking and work was his passionate desire to learn whether or not individual consciousness survives death. As a scientific naturalist in the broad sense, however, he fully recognized that such an enormous question cannot be answered until that problem, and any empirical phenomena relevant to it, can be situated in a framework that makes them theoretically continuous and congruent with other psychological and biological phenomena. This does not mean *reducing* the unknown to the already known, the approach taken in so much of scientific psychology, but instead *linking* the unknown to the already known in a continuous series. Developing such a series, from normal to abnormal to supernormal psychological phenomena, formed the methodological and organizational basis for all of Myers's work.

The immediate challenge for a psychology that might ultimately deal with the question of post-mortem survival is to determine whether human personality is of such a nature that it could even conceivably survive the destruction of the biological organism. In other words, survival research can be conducted productively only within the broader context of psychological research on the nature of mind or consciousness in general: "It became gradually plain to me that before we could safely mark off any group of manifestations as definitely implying an influence from beyond the grave, there was need of a more searching review of the capacities of man's incarnate personality than psychologists...had thought it worth their while to undertake" (*HP*, vol. 1, pp. 8–9). Translating the mind-body problem into an empirical research problem thus became for Myers the primary challenge and task for psychology. It is important to emphasize again that the principle of psychophysiological correlation itself is not what was at issue;

that there is some fundamental relationship between normal, waking consciousness and the state of the brain was and is evident to scientists and non-scientists alike. Nevertheless, recognizing this correlation still leaves open the question of what it signifies.

The first step toward translating the mind-body problem into an empirical problem, therefore, is to recognize that there is more than one way to interpret mind-brain correlation. A few individuals have suggested that the brain may not *produce* consciousness, as the vast majority of 19th- and 20th-century scientists assumed; the brain may instead *filter*, or shape, consciousness. In that case consciousness may be only partly dependent on the brain, and it might therefore conceivably survive the death of the body.[16]

Myers presented what is so far the most thoroughly worked out and empirically grounded version of this filter interpretation of mind-body correlation. Myers himself did not refer to the brain specifically as the filter, nor does he refer to the transmission model of consciousness as described by James (1898/1900) or Schiller (1891/1894). Nevertheless, his huge body of published writings is largely an elaboration of the view that certain phenomena of psychology, particularly of abnormal psychology and psychical research, demonstrate that human personality is far more extensive than we ordinarily realize; that our normal waking consciousness (called by Myers the supraliminal consciousness) reflects simply those relatively few psychological elements and processes that have been selected from that more extensive consciousness (called by Myers the Subliminal Self) in adaptation to the demands of our present environment; and that the biological organism, instead of producing consciousness, is the adaptive mechanism that limits and shapes ordinary waking consciousness out of this larger, mostly latent, Self. In sum:

> There exists a more comprehensive consciousness, a profounder faculty, which for the most part remains potential only...but from which the consciousness and faculty of earth-life are mere selections....[N]o Self of which we can here have cognisance is in reality more than a fragment of a larger Self,— revealed in a fashion at once shifting and limited through an organism not so framed as to afford it full manifestation. (*HP*, vol. 2, pp. 12, 15)

16. For some persons who have seriously considered this "filter" or (as James called it) "transmission" interpretation of mind-brain relations, see Bergson (1913), Broad (1953), Burt (1968, pp. 58–59), A. Huxley (1954/1990, p. 23), James (1898/1900), and Schiller (1891/1894, pp. 293–295). See also our Chapters 1, 8, and 9.

The Unity-Multiplicity Problem: "Unitary" versus "Colonial" Views of Mind

Myers's view of human personality had grown out of his attempts, begun in the early 1880s, to bridge the major theoretical gulf between the old, philosophical, mentalistic psychology and the new, scientific, physiological psychology. As in physics—which throughout its history had seen the recurrent waxing and waning of wave versus particle theories of light—psychological theorizing vacillated between, in essence, a wave theory of mind, in which mind is seen as an indivisible unity, and a particle theory, in which mind is seen as the composite product of individual sensations or other "atomistic" psychological elements. Myers quoted from the 18th-century philosopher Thomas Reid to describe the view of mind as an indivisible whole:

> The conviction which every man has of his identity...needs no aid of philosophy to strengthen it; and no philosophy can weaken it....I am not thought, I am not action, I am not feelings; I am something that thinks, and acts, and suffers. My thoughts and actions and feelings change every moment...; but that *self* or *I*, to which they belong, is permanent....[A] person is a *monad*, and is not divisible into parts. (Myers, 1885c, p. 639; *HP*, vol. 1, p. 10)

In the new physiological psychology, in contrast, mind was seen as an aggregate of elements. Its perceived unity derives entirely from the evolved coordination of the parts and processes of the bodily organism, and it is subject to disintegration under pathological conditions. Ribot provided Myers with his description of this "colonial" view of mind:

> It is the organism...which constitutes the real personality....The conscious personality is never more than a small fraction of the psychical personality. The unity of the Ego is not therefore the unity of a single entity diffusing itself among multiple phenomena; it is the co-ordination of a certain number of states perpetually renascent, and having for their sole common basis the vague feeling of our body. This unity does not diffuse itself downwards, but is aggregated by ascent from below...; *the Self is a co-ordination.* (*HP*, vol. 1, p. 10; see Ribot, 1898, pp. 154–155)

These two views seemed completely opposite in nature and apparently "hopelessly incompatible" (*HP*, vol. 1, p. 11); and yet each was supported by empirical observation—"the one by our inmost consciousness," or personal experience, and "the other by [the] unanswerable observation and inference" of advancing scientific analysis (*HP*, vol. 1, p. 11). In keeping with his "tertium quid" approach, however, Myers believed that "the reconcilement of the two opposing systems in a profounder synthesis" is possible (*HP*, vol. 1, p. 11). Neither view, he argued, is wrong; both are simply incomplete. Myers agreed with the colonialists that mind is not the simple unity we generally take it to be (Myers, 1885c, p. 638; *HP*, vol. 1, p. 11): "The old-fashioned conception of human personality as a unitary consciousness known with practical completeness to the waking self need[s] complete revision" (*HP*, vol. 2, p. 81). The rapidly multiplying observations of experimental psychology, neurology, psychopathology, and hypnotism clearly showed that the human mind is far more extensive than ordinarily thought, since much psychological functioning remains outside the range of our conscious mental life; that higher mental processes had evolved from lower ones; and that under certain conditions, the ordinary unity of consciousness can break down.

Nevertheless, Myers also believed that even though these observations were correct, the theoretical conclusion drawn from them—that human personality is a mere aggregate of separate elements—is a premature and superficial conclusion. He believed that, when psychologists probe more deeply into the problem, the analysis, paradoxically, reveals an underlying continuity, and a fundamental unity, of human personality.

An Expanded View of Consciousness

An important first step that Myers took in this direction was to try to clear up the confusion that many people—then and now—have felt about the notion of an "unconscious mind." Most people naively equate their mind, and especially the term "consciousness," with their ordinary awareness. To propose that there are unconscious mental states, therefore, seems an oxymoron. This belief gave rise in the 19th century to interpretations of unconscious phenomena such as the physiologist William Carpenter's hypothesis of unconscious cerebration, according to which all unconscious processes, being by definition devoid of conscious awareness, are reflexes of the brain (Carpenter, 1874/1882).[17]

This hypothesis was severely challenged, however, by multiple kinds of evidence then emerging for complex mental functioning that occurred outside an individual's ordinary waking awareness. Such evidence included in particular the alterations in consciousness seen in connection with mesmerism and hypnosis, as well as numerous clinical reports of cases involving alternate, or secondary, personalities, with what appeared to be separate memory chains, streams of consciousness, and thus self-identity comparable in kind (if not always in degree) to the original personality.[18] In these situations, processes occurring beyond the margins of ordinary consciousness displayed all the characteristics that we attribute to conscious beings, such as memory, intention, volition, and creativity. Myers unequivocally denied that any variant of the "unconscious cerebration" hypothesis can accommodate such observations: "I wish to protest against the undue extension of such phrases as 'unconscious cerebration,' and to insist that we have as good ground for attributing consciousness to some at least of these subliminal

17. The same idea lives on today in the form of "the cognitive unconscious" (see Chapter 5).

18. See, for example, Binet (1890, 1891/1896), M. Prince (1905/1908), Sidis (1898/1906, 1912), and Sidis and Goodhart (1905). See also Chapter 5.

operations in ourselves as we have for attributing consciousness to the intellectual performances of our neighbors" (Myers, 1892c, p. 327).

Myers was thus led to a definition of "conscious" radically different from our usual equation of it with what goes on in our ordinary, waking, aware self. For him "*conscious* means *memorable*," that is, something that is "capable of being comprehended within some chain of memory," either of the primary consciousness or of a secondary one, given the appropriate conditions (Myers, 1885d, p. 129; 1891c, p. 117):

> When we conceive any act other than our own as a conscious act, we do so either because we regard it as *complex*, and therefore *purposive*, or because we perceive that it has been *remembered*....The *memorability* of an act is, in fact, a better proof of consciousness than its complexity....I cannot see how we can phrase our definition more simply than by saying that any act or condition must be regarded as conscious if it is *potentially memorable*. (*HP*, vol. 1, pp. 36–37)

In other words, something is "conscious" if it is capable of entering waking awareness, given the appropriate condition or the discovery of an "appropriate artifice" or experimental method to elicit it (Myers, 1891c, p. 115). Given this new, expanded conception of what is "conscious," Myers (1892b) therefore considered such terms as "'Unconscious,' or even 'subconscious,'...[to be] directly misleading," and he proposed instead the words "supraliminal" and "subliminal" to distinguish between streams of consciousness that are and are not, respectively, identifiable with ordinary awareness (p. 305).

This notion of something within us being conscious, even though it is not accessible to our ordinary awareness, is an exceedingly difficult one for most of us to accept, since it is so at variance with our usual assumption that the self of which we are aware comprises the totality of what we are as conscious mental beings. Nevertheless, it is essential to keep in mind Myers's new and enlarged conception of consciousness if one is to understand his theory of human personality as something far more extensive than our waking self.

A Jacksonian Model of Mind

Myers's model of mind was deliberately patterned on Hughlings Jackson's hierarchical model of nervous system functioning, which in turn had derived from the 19th-century philosopher Herbert Spencer's ideas about the evolution and dissolution of complex systems (Jackson, 1884). Jackson described the nervous system as a hierarchy of three general levels, ranging from the oldest and most basic biochemical processes, shared with primitive organisms, to mid-level sensorimotor processes, to the most recently evolved cerebral centers with which the higher mental processes are associated. Development occurs as older processes, through repeated functioning, become more organized, automatic, unconscious, and stable. Receding, as it were, from center stage and into the background of consciousness, these processes continue to function automatically, providing the basis upon which higher and more complex processes develop. The higher processes, being newer, are less organized, less automatic, and less stable, and require, because of their relative unfamiliarity, more conscious attention. When injury or disease strikes the nervous system, the higher processes—being less stable—are the first to be affected and impaired, and when the higher processes can no longer function, lower functions re-emerge from the background. According to Jackson (1884), therefore, dissolution of the nervous system proceeds in an order inverse to its original development, and pathological functioning, including the symptoms of insanity, reflect simply whatever lower-level nervous system processes remain functional when higher-level ones have become impaired (p. 591). This model of a hierarchical system that is in a constant state of change—or evolution and dissolution—in response to the organism's environment became the model for Myers's conception of mind, or human personality.

Myers's observations of the numerous forms and varieties of mental functioning outside ordinary awareness led him to recognize that the distinction between subliminal and supraliminal aspects of consciousness is not as simple as a dichotomy between "conscious" and "not conscious" (Myers, 1885a, p. 234). It is also "far more complex than a mere fission into two [or more] personalities" (Myers, 1889f, p. 211), which many psychologists and clinicians were proposing as an alternative to the unconscious cerebration hypothesis. Mind is instead a complex, fluctuating, and ever-changing interaction of subliminal and supraliminal elements or processes.

Moreover, our ordinary waking, supraliminal consciousness is not a pinnacle or the tip of an iceberg:

> There seems no reason to assume that our active consciousness is necessarily altogether superior to the consciousnesses [or processes] which are at present secondary, or potential only. We may rather hold that *super-conscious* may be quite as legitimate a term as *sub-conscious*, and instead of regarding our consciousness (as is commonly done) as a *threshold* in our being, above which ideas and sensations must rise if we wish to cognize them, we may prefer to regard it as a *segment* of our being, into which ideas and sensations may enter either from below or from above. (Myers, 1885a, p. 234)[19]

19. "Subliminal" was thus perhaps an unfortunate choice of terminology, since it means "below the threshold." Myers used the word "subliminal" to refer to "*all* that takes place beneath the ordinary threshold [of consciousness], or say, if preferred, outside the ordinary margin of consciousness" (*HP*, vol. 1, p. 14). In Myers's model of mind, waking consciousness is *not* at the top of a hierarchy, with an "unconscious" or "subconscious" beneath. Instead, it is a segment taken, as it were, from the middle of the entire spectrum of consciousness. The words "subliminal" and "supraliminal" are adequate to convey the idea that certain aspects of experience enter into our ordinary conscious awareness whereas others do not; but they are *not* adequate to convey the more complex model of mind that Myers developed to

To illustrate this view of our ordinary self as a "segment" of a larger Self, Myers used an analogy with the electromagnetic spectrum. Specifically, he suggested that the Individuality or larger Self can be thought of as analogous to a ray of light which, when filtered through a prism, appears as a continuum, or spectrum, of colors. Our ordinary waking consciousness corresponds only to that small segment of the electromagnetic spectrum that is visible to the naked eye (and varies from species to species); but just as the electromagnetic spectrum extends in either direction far beyond the small portion normally visible to us, so human consciousness extends in either direction beyond the small portion of which we are ordinarily aware. In the "infrared" region of consciousness are older, more primitive processes—processes that are unconscious, automatic, and primarily physiological. Thus, "at the red end (so to say) consciousness disappears among the organic processes" (Myers, 1894–1895, p. 197). Sleep, for example, and its associated psychophysiological processes are an important manifestation of an older, more primitive state (Myers, 1892e; *HP*, chap. 4). In contrast, in the "ultraviolet" region of the spectrum are all those mental capacities that remain latent because they have not yet emerged at a supraliminal level through adaptive evolutionary processes. In the "ultraviolet" region, therefore, are those new modes of functioning that appear—rarely, fitfully, and briefly. They are the "*super-conscious* operations" that are "not *below the threshold*—but rather *above the upper horizon* of consciousness" (Myers, 1886b, p. 285), supernormal phenomena that "indicate a higher evolutionary level...above the norm of man rather than outside his nature" (Myers, 1896a, p. 174; see also 1885b, p. 30n). Such latent, "ultraviolet" capacities include telepathy, the inspirations of creative genius, mystical perceptions, and other such phenomena that occasionally emerge.

An Evolutionary View of Mind

Consciousness, in sum, is not to be equated with that relatively small fragment of it that we know as our waking awareness, perception, or memory, because that fragment has been selected from a larger whole. Myers went on to suggest that the nature and extent of the waking, or supraliminal, portion of consciousness, whether in a species or an individual, has been determined by the same mechanism that has determined what portion of the electromagnetic spectrum itself is visible: selection in response to the demands of the organism's environment. Out of the innumerable potential sensory or psychological processes, only those most useful for survival have thus far emerged: "My waking consciousness may embrace only such part of my whole range of faculties as it has been useful for my ancestors to keep under immediate control in their struggle for terrene existence....[T]he

differentiate various kinds of subliminal phenomena. It might have been better if he had used the alternate words he suggested, "intra-marginal" and "extra-marginal" or "ultramarginal" (*HP*, vol. 1, p. 14n).

range of perception which rises above the threshold—the spectrum, as I call it, of my supraliminal consciousness—may merely have been determined by natural selection" (Myers, 1894–1895, p. 197). The ordinary waking self is not the *only* possible self that could have developed out of the entire, mostly latent Self; nor, as Myers frequently emphasized, is it necessarily psychologically superior to or more important than the rest of the spectrum of consciousness:

> I hold that we each of us contain the potentialities of many different arrangements of the elements of our personality....The arrangement with which we habitually identify ourselves,—what we call the normal or primary self,—consists, in my view, of elements selected for us in the struggle for existence with special reference to the maintenance of ordinary physical needs, and is not necessarily superior in any other respect to the latent personalities which lie alongside it. (Myers, 1888a, p. 387)

Myers's model of the evolution of mind echoed certain further ideas of Spencer, from whom Jackson had derived his model of the evolution and dissolution of the nervous system. In Spencer's evolutionary theories, the universe—like an embryo—began as a simple homogeneity, or formless unity, which began to divide and differentiate into parts, and then integrated to form new units that become increasingly complex in the ongoing process of adapting to their environment. Jackson had applied these general ideas about the evolutionary differentiation and increasing complexity of systems to physiology and the nervous system in particular (R. M. Young, 1968, 1970).

Implicit in these ideas about the evolution of the universe from a formless homogeneity to complex forms of life was the idea that all of the latter were somehow inherent in the former. An important aspect of Myers's ideas about the evolution of mind or consciousness, therefore, was that, just as the forms of all living organisms were somehow latent in the original homogeneity, or "primal germ," from which all life developed, all forms of consciousness were likewise inherent in the homogeneous primal germ. All life "starts from an *X* of some sort; and for my present argument it matters not whether you call *X* a carbon-atom or an immortal soul. Whatever it was, *X* had certain propensities, which must have dated in any case from some age anterior to its existence upon our recent planet...[and] on which earth's forces began their play" (Myers, 1892b, p. 318).

Thus, Myers suggested, there had been a "primitive simple irritability" (*HP*, vol. 1, p. 95), or "undifferentiated sensory capacity of the supposed primal germ" (Myers, 1896a, p. 167), which he called *panaesthesia*. Out of this homogeneous or undifferentiated sensibility have developed the particular senses we now have. For example, the evolutionary process eventually reached "a point...where vision differentiate[d] itself from various indefinite forms of perception...with the growing sensibility of the pigment-spot to light and shadow" (*HP*, vol. 1, p. 224). Similarly, other senses evolved out of some pre-existing latent potential. Just as importantly, other forms of perception may yet be emerging and evolving:

> Whatever be the part which we assign to external influences in its evolution, the fact remains that the germ possessed the power of responding in an indefinite number of ways to an indefinite number of stimuli. It was only the accident of its exposure to certain stimuli and not to others which has made it what it now is. And having shown itself so far modifiable as to acquire these highly specialised senses which I possess, it is doubtless still modifiable in directions as unthinkable to me as my eyesight would have been unthinkable to the oyster. (Myers, 1889e, p. 190)

Myers also pointed out that, on both the individual and evolutionary levels, the process of evolution has involved not simply the adaptation of an organism to its environment, but also, with increasingly complex sensory processes, the widening perception of that environment, the "gradual *discovery* of an environment, always there, but unknown" (*HP*, vol. 2, p. 95). The implication for Myers was that, as physics was also revealing, there probably are "unseen" environments, imperceptible to our senses as they have so far evolved, but nonetheless "fundamentally continuous" and interrelated with what we do perceive.

Human beings have "evoked in greatest multiplicity the unnumbered faculties latent in the irritability of a speck of slime" (*HP*, vol. 1, p. 76). Nevertheless, it does not thereby follow that our present sensory capacities and our normal waking consciousness mark the final point of the evolutionary process: "To anyone…who takes a broad view of human development, it must seem a very improbable thing that that development should at this particular moment have reached its final term" (*HP*, vol. 1, p. 186). Just as in the individual spectrum of potential consciousness some contents and capacities have become supraliminal and some remain subliminal, so in the evolutionary spectrum of consciousness, some faculties have been evoked and some remain latent (*HP*, vol. 1, p. 119); but there is "no apparent reason why these latent powers should not from time to time receive sufficient stimulus" to appear sporadically, and even ultimately to develop more fully (*HP*, vol., 1, p. 186).

The Subliminal Self: A "Tertium Quid" Theory of Consciousness

With this evolutionary model of a larger Self whose latent capacities gradually emerge and whose emergent manifestation grows increasingly complex in response to the demands of the environment, Myers thought that psychology could resolve the apparent conflict between the old concept of mind as a unity and the new concept of mind as a multiplicity, and affirm that *both* views are in fact correct, although incomplete: Consciousness is, he insisted, "at once profoundly unitary and almost infinitely complex" (*HP*, vol. 1, p. 34). The Subliminal Self or Individuality—the original whole light ray, in the metaphor of the electromagnetic spectrum—registers or otherwise incorporates within itself everything that comes within its range of experience. These are "the elements of our personality," and those few "elements selected for us in the struggle for existence" are bound together in a more or less stable chain of memory, our ordinary waking self (Myers, 1887b, p. 387). In certain circumstances, however, other chains of memory or groupings of elements may form: "The letters of our inward alphabet will shape themselves into many other dialects;—many other personalities, as distinct as those which we assume to be *ourselves*, can be made out of our mental material" (Myers, 1889e, p. 195). Moreover, the number of such groupings or personalities is potentially endless: "The fresh combinations of our personal elements...may be evoked, by accident [e.g., spontaneous somnambulism or multiple personality] or design [e.g., hypnosis or suggestion], in a variety to which we can at present assign no limit" (Myers, 1888a, p. 387). If any of these new chains of memory become sufficiently complex and stable, they thus develop into one or more secondary personalities, or subliminal selves.

Nonetheless, behind the "shifting" elements and groupings of elements of our being, there is a "perdurable Unity" (Myers, 1889g, p. 343; see also 1885a, 1885c). It is erroneous, he thought, to conclude that the analysis of personality into many components means that there is no ultimate unity behind it (1887a, p. 260). Myers found it particularly significant that, in certain hypnotic and psychopathological cases, the various personalities were not totally isolated; some of them were, in varying degrees, aware of others. In Janet's case of Léonie (or Madame B.), for example, the secondary personality, Léontine, was fully aware of Léonie, although Léonie was unaware of her; and the third personality, Léonore, possessed the memories of both the other two, even though they were both unaware (directly) of her existence (see *HP*, vol. 1, pp. 322–326). Similarly, in Morton Prince's case of Christine Beauchamp, there was a hierarchy of selves in which each one knew about the one(s) lower in the hierarchy, but not the one(s) above it (Prince, 1900, 1905/1908). Although this "hierarchy" of memory was not straightforward or even present in every case of multiple personality, it was a common enough feature to be noteworthy, and particularly because the same sort of hierarchy could also be evoked experimentally by hypnosis (Gurney, 1884, 1887c): "We all know that the hypnotised subject as a rule remembers waking life, but that the awakened subject as a rule has wholly forgotten the effects of this hypnotic trance. The full significance of this fact...has hardly yet, I think, been realised in any quarter" (Myers, 1892b, p. 303). The significance is that there may in fact be an underlying unity to human personality.[20]

---

20. Hilgard (1977) has more recently called attention to the importance of the "covert" contents of consciousness that can be uncovered by means such as hypnosis. Observing that people who profess to be unaware of events occurring while they were hypnotized can sometimes recover memories of these events when re-hypnotized, Hilgard proposed his "neo-dissociationist" model of hypnosis,

Many critics of Myers's theory (e.g., Jastrow, 1906; Mallock, 1903; McDougall, 1926, p. 523) have mistakenly attributed to him the view that the subliminal and the supraliminal selves act as two co-existing, discrete selves. This completely misrepresents his actual view. Myers's theory was not simply a hypothesis of the multiplicity of personality, but went further and tried to reconcile the paradoxical multiplicity *and* unity of human personality. Myers in fact explicitly said: "I do not...assume that there are two correlative and parallel selves existing always within us" (*HP*, vol. 1, p. 15):

> My contention is, *not*, as some of my critics seem to suppose, that a man (say Socrates) has within him a conscious and an unconscious self, which lie side by side, but apart, and find expression alternately, but rather that Socrates' mind is capable of concentrating itself round more than one focus, either simultaneously or successively. I do not limit the number of *foci* to *two*. (Myers, 1885d, p. 129)

One contemporary historian has even alleged that "the cornerstone of his [Myers's] conception was the fact that consciousness had no essential unity" (E. Taylor, 1996, p. 81), an assertion that clearly misses the essence of Myers's theory of human personality, his oft-stated conclusion that there *is* a "perdurable Unity."

To understand that in Myers's theory mind is *both* a unity and a multiplicity, it is essential to understand the clear distinction that he drew between "Individuality" and "personality." By *Individuality*, or *Self*, he meant to refer to "the underlying psychical unity which I postulate as existing beneath all our phenomenal manifestations"; by *personality*, or *self*, he meant those "more external and transitory" chains of memory, including the ordinary or supraliminal self of which we are customarily aware, as well as the potentially infinite number of selves that may be formed from "the elements of our being" (Myers, 1892b, p. 305; 1888a, p. 387). Each of us is *one* of the former, even though *many* of the latter may be formed from that larger Self: "The human individuality [is] a practically infinite reservoir of personal states;—as a kaleidoscope which may be shaken into a thousand patterns, yet so that no pattern can employ all pieces contained in the tube" (Myers, 1892e, p. 363).[21]

---

suggesting that hypnosis creates an amnesic barrier preventing mentation in the hypnotic state from entering ordinary waking consciousness. In important respects, therefore, Hilgard's hypothesis of a "Hidden Observer" who has access to these covert memories is similar to Myers's hypothesis of an underlying Subliminal Self who, as hypnosis sometimes shows, is aware of events that the supraliminal consciousness is not. Hilgard, however, distances his theory decisively from any theories of another "self," primarily because, unlike Myers, his theory is built on the assumption that all forms of consciousness, covert as well as overt, are brain processes alone. See Chapter 5 for further discussion of Hilgard's views.

21. Oxford philosopher F. C. S. Schiller (1891/1894, pp. 279–282) drew a similar distinction between the phenomenal "self" and the transcendental "Ego." Like Myers, he emphasized that the Ego is not a second self, but that the ordinary self

Understanding the distinction Myers drew between "Individuality" and "personality"—or between "Self" and "self"—can help clear up the sorts of confusion that Gauld (1968) apparently experienced with regard to Myers's theory. Gauld complained about "the abstruseness and complexity of the concepts central to his theory, such as consciousness, mind, soul, spirit, personality, psychical activity," and he argued that in Myers's theory the "soul," *not* the "subliminal self," is the "unifying principle...'behind' all mental phenomena....The concept of the 'subliminal self' is simply not qualified to act as a unifying theoretical principle" (Gauld, 1968, pp. 278, 295). Further, Gauld complained, "Myers offers little elucidation of these terms" (p. 278).

Some of this confusion undoubtedly derives in part from Myers's own somewhat inconsistent use of the terms "subliminal self" or "subliminal consciousness." On some occasions, he used the term "subliminal" to refer in general to "all which lies below that threshold [of ordinary consciousness]" (Myers, 1892b, p. 305). On other occasions he used it to refer more specifically to secondary personalities or chains of memory such as those that occur spontaneously, in hysteria or multiple personality, and those that are artificially induced, as in hypnosis. On still other occasions, he used the term "subliminal self" (usually, but unfortunately not consistently, spelled with capital letters as "Subliminal Self" or "subliminal Self") to refer to the underlying unity or larger Self. These "concepts central to his theory" are undoubtedly difficult, but despite some inconsistency in his usage or spelling Myers was quite clear in his intent to distinguish between a subliminal "self" (a personality alternate or in addition to the normal waking one) and the Subliminal "Self" or "Individuality" (which is his real "unifying theoretical principle"). In this book we will try to keep the distinction clear in readers' minds by using the term "subliminal consciousness" to refer to any conscious psychological processes occurring outside ordinary awareness; the term "subliminal self" (lower case) to refer to "any chain of memory sufficiently continuous, and embracing sufficient particulars, to acquire what is popularly called a 'character' of its own" (pp. 305–306n); and the term "Individuality" or "Subliminal Self" (upper case) to refer to the underlying larger Self.

The Permeable Boundary: A Psychological Mechanism

In Myers's model, evolution of consciousness involves the shifting of the supraliminal segment up the spectrum into the ultraviolet region, as more and more psychological processes are mastered and then relegated to the

---

is an extract of the Ego (p. 410). In many respects, in fact, Schiller's and Myers's theories of mind are parallel; and in a review of Morton Prince's *The Unconscious* (Schiller, 1915), Schiller specifically advocated Myers's theory of human personality as providing the best account of the facts described by Prince. Ducasse (1951, p. 495) later drew a similar distinction between individuality and personality.

infrared region, while, simultaneously, latent psychological capacities or processes are drawn out of the ultraviolet region and into the supraliminal range. The supraliminal consciousness has been shaped and is maintained by a kind of psychological "membrane" that controls the passage of psychological elements and processes between the supraliminal and subliminal regions of consciousness. Thus, the boundaries between the supraliminal and the various subliminal portions of the Self are neither fixed nor even precise, but fluid and continually shifting. In other words, the boundaries are "permeable," such that there is a constant exchange of material between regions. An evolutionary model, in fact, demands such lability if there is to be adaptation in the face of changing circumstances: "Self-adaptation to wider environments must inevitably be accompanied...by something of nervous instability" (*HP*, vol. 1, p. 92). As a consequence, during the course of evolution there is "a continual displacement of the threshold of consciousness" (*HP*, vol. 1, p. 16). Similarly, on the individual level, "the personality of each of us is in a state of constantly shifting equilibrium" (Myers, 1893a, p. 9), as the range of our supraliminal awareness expands, contracts, and shifts, and as the processes over which we have conscious, or supraliminal, control become increasingly complex. *All* alterations of consciousness are the result, in short, of an instability or "permeability" of the psychological boundaries between supraliminal and subliminal processes.[22]

Evolutive and Dissolutive Phenomena

An important corollary of this concept of a permeable boundary between regions of consciousness is that such lability or "nervous instability" can bring changes in *either* direction—retrogressive *or* progressive. Hughlings Jackson (1884) had described the ongoing process of both evolution and dissolution ("the reverse of the process of evolution") in the nervous system. Myers extended Jackson's hypothesis to insist that an evolutionary hypothesis of mind implies that there will be *both* "phenomena of degeneration [dissolution] and phenomena of evolution" in mental functioning (*HP*, vol. 2, p. 194). Deviations from the usual psychological state are not neces-

22. More recently, Hartmann (1989, 1991) has proposed a similar model in which what he calls "boundaries" between various "regions, parts, or processes" in the mind (Hartmann, 1991, p. 4) can be "thick" or "thin" and thus contribute to individual differences in fantasy-proneness, absorption, hypnotizability, dream recall, lucid dreaming, and related psychological processes. He also argued, as Myers did, that thin boundaries can be either adaptive or maladaptive, as seen especially in the "relationship between boundaries and creativity or madness" (p. 8). In his chapter on "Predecessors of the Boundary Concept," however, he makes no mention of Myers, and therefore believes, erroneously, that "the concept of thin and thick boundaries has not...been previously used as I am using it—that is, as a broad dimension of personality and an aspect of the overall organization of the mind" (p. 49). Thalbourne (1998; Thalbourne & Delin, 1994) has also proposed a similar model, based on a factor that he calls "transliminality."

sarily always pathological or "dissolutive"; they may also be beneficial or "evolutive."

In contrast, most 19th-century scientists took the view that all "abnormal" phenomena are degenerative or pathological. This was the prevailing view among French clinicians such as Janet, and scientists such as Maudsley and Cesare Lombroso had carried it to an extreme, insisting that even such apparently beneficial phenomena as genius are symptoms of disease, "degeneracy," or insanity. Many scientists (and, increasingly, other persons) "know well that man can fall *below* himself; but that he can rise *above* himself they can believe no more" (Myers, 1886a, p. lvi). As I mentioned earlier, Myers introduced the term "supernormal" in 1885 as one cognate to "abnormal" but implying evolutive rather than pathological abnormal phenomena. He summed up the distinction as follows:

> [I] regard all psychical, as well as all physiological activities as necessarily either developmental or degenerative, tending to evolution or dissolution. And further, whilst altogether waiving any teleological speculation, I will ask [the reader] hypothetically to suppose that an evolutionary *nisus*, something which we may represent as an effort towards self-development, self-adaptation, self-renewal, is discernible especially on the psychical side of at any rate the higher forms of life. Our question, Supernormal or abnormal?—may then be phrased, Evolutive or dissolutive? And in studying each psychical phenomenon in turn we shall have to inquire whether it indicates a mere degeneration of powers already acquired, or, on the other hand, "the promise and potency," if not the actual possession, of powers as yet unrecognised or unknown. (Myers, 1885b, p. 31)

An understanding of abnormal phenomena as potentially evolutive as well as dissolutive is particularly important if a purely psychological (or theoretical), as opposed to medical, understanding of them is to be achieved. Clinicians, not surprisingly, see primarily the morbidity and losses associated with abnormal processes, and their purpose is to restore the patient to an ordinary level of functioning (Myers, 1898b, p. 103; 1900c, p. 384). Myers (1892b) thought that the psychologist, in contrast, should be interested also in what capacities may be *gained* in abnormal states (p. 315). In a review (1900c) of Janet's *Névroses et Idées Fixes* and Flournoy's *Des Indes à la planète Mars*, Myers contrasted their approaches to, and perspectives on, abnormal subconscious processes, with Janet's being the "therapeutic" or clinical, and Flournoy's the psychological or theoretical.

Myers was careful to emphasize, however, that in his insistence on acknowledging evolutive aspects of subliminal function, he did "not mean to imply that [subliminal] mentation is *ipso facto superior* to supraliminal... that all our best thought was subliminal, or that all that was subliminal was potentially 'inspiration'" (*HP*, vol. 1, pp. 71–72). Clearly, many abnormal psychological phenomena *are* degenerative and harmful: "Hidden in the deep of our being is a rubbish-heap as well as a treasure-house;—degenerations and insanities as well as beginnings of higher development" (*HP*, vol. 1, p. 72).[23] Nonetheless, there is "real psychological danger in fixing our conception of human character too low. Some essential lessons [concerning the nature and functioning of human personality] are apt to be missed" (*HP*, vol. 1, p. 50).

On the other hand, our waking or supraliminal consciousness is also not inherently superior, or even necessarily "the most important part of the psychical operations which are going on within us" (Myers, 1887a, pp. 258–259). Myers agreed with Jackson (1884), who, when discussing the evolution and dissolution of the nervous system, had insisted that manifesting states are the "'fittest,' not 'best'....[T]he evolutionist has nothing to do with good or bad" (p. 591). The distinction, Myers emphasized repeatedly, between the subliminal and the supraliminal, as well as between the evolutive and dissolutive, is "a purely psychological one" (Myers, 1900d, p. 289; *HP*, vol. 1, p. 72).

To those, therefore, who asked: "Are we then to believe that the subliminal self is both wiser and more foolish, truer and more false, more understanding and more ignorant, more reliable and more untrustworthy than the normal self?" (Dallas, 1900, p. 288), Myers's answer was "Yes." Depending on the conditions under which they emerge, the elements of the Subliminal Self or Individuality can fall into numerous patterns or even "selves," running the gamut from the most primitive, elementary, fragmentary, and pathological to the most advanced, complex, complete, and beneficial.

23. Jastrow was among those who mistakenly thought that Myers's hypothesis of human personality was based on the notion that subliminal processes are "ipso facto" superior to supraliminal ones (see, e.g., Jastrow, 1906, p. 537). Jastrow seems, however, to have completely misunderstood Myers's hypothesis in general. He criticized it as based "upon a fundamental emphasis on the schism of conflicting personalities," and went on to argue that his own hypothesis of the "subconscious as a natural function with the most intimate relations to consciousness,...both parts of a common synthesis,...is diametrically opposed to that of the subliminal self" (1906, pp. 537, 539–540). Elsewhere (1903) he criticized Myers's hypothesis as one of discontinuity and argued that the concept of the subconscious will not be recognized in psychology as important until the hypothesis of the discontinuity of consciousness and the subconscious is replaced by one recognizing their underlying continuity. Jastrow's hypothesis, in fact, was in many ways closely similar to Myers's hypothesis, *particularly* with regard to the ultimate continuity of conscious and subliminal processes. Some of the larger implications that Myers drew from the same premises (such as the potential post-mortem survival of human personality) were undeniably different from Jastrow's conclusions; and this may explain why Jastrow (and others) have been so prone to misread and misrepresent Myers's hypothesis. It may also help explain why Jastrow (1900) and others have also been so prone to misread and misrepresent psychical research generally.

Automatisms and the Expression of Subliminal Functioning

Another important concept in Jackson's model of nervous system functioning that was paralleled in Myers's model of mind was that of automatisms.[24] Jackson (1884) had proposed that the older and more habitual a process became, the more stable, unconscious, and automatic its execution became, leaving the organism free to develop more advanced and complex processes. Similarly, according to Myers, as a species evolves or an individual develops, older psychological processes become more stable and automatic. There is, he pointed out, an evolutionary advantage to "relegating voluntary ends to automatic execution," because learned, stable, automatic processes get "the needed thing done...with a verve and a completeness which conscious effort finds it hard to rival" (Myers, 1900c, p. 415). But Myers's concept of automatisms went beyond that of Jackson to include not only the automatic execution of older, more established modes of functioning (those in the "infrared" region), but also the emergence of new, more complex processes originating in the "ultraviolet" region. Myers therefore defined psychological automatisms generally as any form of communication or exchange of material from the subliminal regions of the psychological spectrum to the supraliminal. They include dreams, secondary personalities, hypnosis, automatic writing, trance speaking, and the "uprushes" of subliminally generated creative inspirations into supraliminal expression. Automatisms, moreover, may take the form of influence upon primarily organic processes over which the supraliminal self ordinarily has no control (as in the phenomena of hysterical or hypnotic anesthesia), as well as of new and sporadically occurring processes (such as telepathy) over which the supraliminal similarly has little or no control.

On Myers's model of mind, subliminal processes emerge when consciousness is deflected from its normal, supraliminal functioning: "To some extent at least the abeyance of the supraliminal life must be the liberation of the subliminal" (*HP*, vol. 1, p. 122). More specifically, "it seems as though this supersensory faculty assumed activity in an inverse ratio to the activities of everyday life" (Myers, 1886b, p. 287). Supernormal processes such as telepathy do seem to occur more frequently while either the percipient or the agent (or both) is asleep, in the states between sleeping and waking, in a state of ill health, or dying; and subliminal functioning in general emerges more readily during altered states of consciousness such as hypnosis, hysteria, or even ordinary distraction. Thus, whereas supraliminal functioning usually reflects "the familiar parallelism between bodily and mental states," subliminal mental processes might vary "inversely, rather than directly, with the observable activity of the nervous system or of the conscious mind" (Myers, 1890b, p. 320; 1891d, p. 638). For Myers, therefore, the importance of studying psychological automatisms and other aspects of

---

24. Because the concept of automatisms is so central to Myers's model of consciousness, and so important to address adequately in any attempt to understand consciousness, we have devoted an entire chapter to this topic (see Chapter 5).

subliminal functioning derives largely from the light it might shed on mind-body relations.

Myers also proposed that the emergence of subliminal material in automatism may be more likely when one's habitual "paths of externalisation"[25] are in abeyance. As a possible example, he suggested that because the left hemisphere, the seat of verbal capacity, has become the predominant expressive vehicle for cognitive and other intellectual functioning, then subliminal functioning, or automatisms, might more readily emerge when the left hemisphere is damaged, inhibited, or otherwise prevented from functioning fully: "In graphic automatism [automatic writing] the action of the right hemisphere is predominant, because the secondary self can appropriate its energies more readily than those of the left hemisphere, which is more immediately at the service of the waking mind" (Myers, 1885b, p. 43).[26]

This suggestion that the subliminal portions of our spectrum of consciousness might find their "readiest path of externalisation" through the right hemisphere has received modest support from modern observations indicating that right-hemisphere functioning (in right-handers, at least) is for the most part nonverbal (see, e.g., Springer & Deutsch, 1985). Myers had noted that "our subliminal mentation is less closely bound to the faculty of speech than is our supraliminal" (*HP*, vol. 1, p. 98). More specifically, the "language" of subliminal consciousness seems to be primarily pictorial and symbolic, rather than verbal and propositional (e.g., Myers, 1892f, p. 460; 1897, p. 70; *HP*, vol. 1, pp. 100, 277), and he suggested that the "study of visual and motor automatism will afford us sufficient proof that symbolism, at any rate pictorial symbolism, becomes increasingly important as we get at the contents of those hidden [subliminal] strata" (*HP*, vol. 1, p. 100). Thus, he said, art, music, and even poetry (whose "material...is the very language which she would fain transcend") are expressions of this subliminal language (Myers, 1897, p. 70; *HP*, vol. 1, p. 101).

---

25. This phrase refers to a common belief in the 19th century (and one that remains with us today; see Chapter 4) that psychological functioning produces physical changes or "traces" in the brain and that the nerve-currents accompanying psychological processes take the "paths" of least resistance, carving out "established" paths that subsequent nervous activity will become more likely to follow (see, e.g., Carpenter, 1874/1882, p. 442; James, 1890b, vol. 1, pp. 108, 563, 659). In contrast, Myers was concerned to emphasize that here, as elsewhere, psychologists and physiologists still have no real understanding of mind-brain correlation. Therefore, to forestall readers who might be tempted to take his terminology of "brain paths" literally, Myers (1889a) explained that he was using the terminology as a metaphor and *not* "a real transcript of the unknown processes which actually occur" (p. 535).

26. In the wake of discoveries of the localization of function in the brain (beginning especially with Broca's localization of a center for spoken language), the concept of hemispheric asymmetry and differences became an important one in the late 19th century (see Harrington, 1987). Myers was one of the earliest to suggest that subliminal phenomena might find their readiest expression through what was considered the non-dominant hemisphere.

Myers also proposed that variations in the complexity of subliminal functioning or automatisms might be correlated with the amount of time a person has spent, say, doing automatic writing or in an hypnotic state or secondary personality. He noted the observations of Elliotson and Janet about variations in "the amount of personality which the hypnotised subject is able to manifest" (Myers, 1888a, p. 390) and suggested that such differences depend on the stock of memories accumulated in the secondary state. Hypnotize a person once or a few times, and the "little scrap of memory" associated with these states is wholly insufficient "to dignify...with the name of a secondary personality. Repeat the process, however, many hundred times, and at last the time spent in the hypnotic trance, the experience gained therein, will become comparable with the time spent in normal existence, and the experience gained in the common routine of life." For example, "Mme. B. has been so often hypnotised, and during so many years,...that Léontine has by this time acquired a very considerable stock of memories which Mme. B. does not share" (p. 391).

Myers also offered a possible explanation for a frequently noted characteristic of automatisms: the puerile, silly, trivial nature of much of the content, "quite independent of the intellectual level of the automatist" (Myers, 1887a, p. 212). This feature had, perhaps understandably, made automatisms a target for much levity and repugnance,[27] but Myers suggested that automatisms, such as the "much-derided phenomenon of 'table-tilting'," might be early, rudimentary attempts at subliminal communication, just as gestures or sounds of animals are early forms of communication (*HP*, vol. 2, p. 92). Thus, "the interest [of most automatisms]...certainly does not lie in the wisdom of the oracle received" (Myers, 1885a, p. 239). The interest lies instead in the possibility of finding means of gaining greater access to subliminal regions of our consciousness: "If once we can get a spy into the citadel of our own being, his rudest signalling will tell us more than our subtlest inferences from outside of what is being planned and done within" (*HP*, vol. 2, p. 91).

A Law of Mental Causality

Myers fully expected that there are laws of mental causality, or psychological laws in addition to those of the physical world and not derived from these. Moreover, he believed that some such concept as telepathy—the hypothesis that individual minds (or Selves) can, at some now-subliminal level, interact directly with other minds—will be an important element in

27. Huxley (1913), for example, spoke contemptuously of the "twaddle" produced by many spiritist mediums (vol. 2, p. 144). Stevenson (1978), commenting on the "vapid writings" that an automatic writer had attributed to the deceased William James, remarked that survival of death with such "a terrible post-mortem reduction of personal capacities...makes it, at least to me, a rather unattractive prospect" (p. 323).

the major law or principle of psychology that remains to be discovered. Myers thought that this "law" of psychology would demonstrate in general "the Interpenetration of Worlds," that is, the interaction between the physical world that our senses have evolved to perceive and what he called the "metetherial" world, the larger universe that is beyond our direct sensory perception but that "co-exist[s] with, and manifest[s] itself through, the material universe that we know" (Myers, 1892f, p. 534). The belief that there is a world beyond the known physical one has of course been fundamental in most religions (although many religions, particularly Western ones, have, in contrast to Myers, traditionally seen the physical and the spiritual worlds as discontinuous); but Myers believed that the demonstration of "telepathy...would be the first indication of a possible scientific basis" for this belief (Myers, 1886a, p. lvii).

Myers found an important hint to what the new law of psychology might look like in a concept from mesmerism. Many mesmerists believed that the effects they were able to elicit from their subjects result from a yet unknown physical radiation or force passing from the mesmerist to the subject, creating a connection that they called *rapport*. Myers and Gurney believed that the mesmerists might have been on the right track, but that instead of being a physical phenomenon, the influence might be a psychological one, some kind of "a specialised relation between two minds," a resonant link, or a "subtle inter-communication" between subliminal minds (Myers, 1886a, p. lvii; 1886b, p. 287; *HP*, vol. 1, p. 209). This notion of a psychological link between minds became the basis for Myers's concept of telepathy and, indeed, his concept of all supernormal interaction. The nature of the relation remained entirely unknown, as it had for the mesmerists. Certain people made good mesmerists or hypnotists, but no one understood why. The "rapport" does not seem clearly related "either to kinship or to affection" (1884–1885, p. 100), and there are even some telepathic or other such cases in which the nature of the presumed rapport is particularly puzzling, since the people involved are strangers (1884–1885, p. 122). Myers suggested, however, that in some sense this telepathic or mental "rapport" might be the psychological equivalent of the concepts of molecular attraction (Gurney & Myers, 1884a, pp. 814–815) or of gravitation (*HP*, vol. 1, p. 38) in the physical world; and it remained for psychologists to identify and describe this link more adequately.

Methods for Psychology

Myers's vision for a new psychology included more than a theoretical model of mind that could carry psychology beyond the dichotomy of the old mentalistic psychology and the new materialistic one. He also repeatedly emphasized the need for psychologists to develop their own unique methods, suitable to the particular problems and phenomena of psychology and not modeled solely after those of the physical sciences. Unfortunately, psychology still "remains in that early stage...when the methods of experiment are such as other sciences have suggested, not such as this special branch of inquiry suggests for itself, or can use with unique effect." The methods successful in the physical sciences, however, are insufficient for psychology: "They help us rather to define accurately facts already roughly known, than to get at underlying facts of which common consciousness does not inform us. To do this we must pass from general mechanical artifices to artifices special to psychology" (Myers, 1892f, p. 443).

In other words, if psychology is to move beyond merely describing in more detail what we already know, more or less clearly, on the basis of our ordinary experience, then the important work of psychology lies in going beyond what we commonly observe. Major theoretical advances in psychology will come primarily from examining, not normal psychological processes and behavior, but the unusual, often rare phenomena associated with subliminal functioning, and appropriate methods must be found for eliciting them. The primary methodological challenge to psychology, therefore, lies in developing methods, or "artifices," for extending observations of the contents and capacities of mind beyond the visible portion of the psychological spectrum, just as the physical sciences have developed artificial means of extending sensory perception beyond its ordinary limits (*HP*, vol. 1, pp. 17–18).

Myers also emphasized that all sciences must go through a developmental process in which their methods, initially crude and imperfect, are gradually improved and strengthened. The apparent reluctance of psychologists to develop their own special methods reflected, Myers thought, their reluctance to put themselves back in the primitive methodological state where all sciences must begin and where they must return every time they attack new and different problems: "I allude to the ever-growing dislike felt by the votaries of advanced and established sciences to the rude approximate work which has been needed in the infancy of every science; and needed in greater degree as each new science involved a wider scope." There is, he warned, "danger...for Experimental Psychology in the temptation to cling too exclusively to the safe methods of sciences exacter than ours can as yet in reality be." If psychologists "will make only such experiments as admit of precise numerical results," the danger is that psychology will become "no more than a curious appendage to Neurology," rather than its own science, making its own real discoveries: "Men who insist on electric lamps along their road will never reach the centre of Africa" (Myers, 1894–1895, p. 191).

The gap between many psychologists and Myers and his colleagues in psychical research increasingly grew to be one between those who preferred the established, precise methods of other sciences and who narrowed the scope of their researches accordingly, and those who preferred to keep their sights set on fundamental problems, however inadequate the methods might so far be. In reviews of two issues of *L'Année psychologique*, published near the end of his life, Myers conveyed his deep disappointment with what he saw as the resulting superficiality and triviality of much of modern psychology. In the first review (1898c), he contrasted the safe "surface-mining" of most psychological researchers with the riskier "deep-level mining" of the psychical researchers (p. 147). The second review (Myers, 1900e) was more blunt:

> The subjects of research seem scarcely of sufficient importance to occupy for long the attention of scientific minds. The elaborate Bibliography...represents a great mass of intellectual effort, from which, perhaps, fewer leading ideas have in fact emerged than might have been hoped in an age where really illuminating generalisations in science are wont to be so promptly pursued. (p. 106)

The reason for this triteness, he thought, lay in the overwhelming tendency of many psychologists "to treat the *easy* parts of the subject...and to ignore altogether those *difficult* parts," with the result that the research does little more than re-affirm "obvious common-sense" and brings no real advance in knowledge (p. 106). Those involved in psychical research, in contrast, attempted to push beyond the commonplace and treat the difficult parts, inevitably with some risk that they "must make many mistakes" (Myers, 1895c, p. 233). Myers summarized these contrasting approaches to psychology as follows:

> First come the many new Professors and Lecturers in Germany, France, America, and elsewhere who are making accurate experiments on everything in man which they can manage to get at;—the nervous system in general, vision, audition, orientation, tactile sensibility, reaction-times, fatigue, attention, memory, mental imagery,—with a host of cognate inquiries. Much of this is delicate quantitative work, and is performed with instruments of precision. The drawback is that such methods and such apparatus are better adapted to give accuracy to facts already roughly known than to carry the inquirer much farther into the depths of our being. It is work preparatory to discovery, rather than discovery itself.
>
> At the other end of the range a group still small...is attacking psychological problems of the highest importance, but which admit as yet of only approximate and tentative methods of inquiry. This is work of discovery indeed; but it is rough pioneer's work—preparatory also in its own way to the ultimate science to which we all aspire. (p. 233)

In keeping with his "tertium quid" approach, Myers believed that that "ultimate science" requires above all else the examination and inclusion, not only of data supporting one's own position, but even more importantly, of data supporting conflicting positions. He therefore repeatedly cautioned about the too-frequent temptation to draw conclusions based on a limited range of observations. He advocated instead amassing a broad range of pertinent data—broad not just in *quantity* but especially in *kind*—in order to prevent the premature assumption of a hypothesis or view that may be, not necessarily wrong, but misleadingly narrow and incomplete. For example, he said, Carpenter's hypothesis of unconscious cerebration to explain subliminal phenomena in general, and Faraday's hypothesis of unconscious muscular action to explain table-tilting in particular, "were, so far as they went, not only legitimate, but the most logical...to explain the scanty evidence with which alone Faraday and Carpenter attempted to deal"; they were not, however, hypotheses applicable to the full range of available and pertinent data (Myers, 1886a, p. lxii). Similarly, Janet's observations of automatic writing had been confined to hysterical patients, and to relatively few even of them, and as a result "a good many passages of M. Janet's...seem to me...lacking in width of purview," although containing "much which I hold to be true and important" (Myers, 1889e, pp. 189, 191).

Myers and his SPR colleagues thought also that the conflict between "mesmerism" and "hypnotism" was probably the result of limited observations on both sides (W. F. Barrett, Gurney, Myers, et al., 1883). Mesmerists believed that the phenomena produced by Mesmer and his successors were the result of an actual physical force or "effluence" passing from the mesmeriser to the subject. The new hypothesis of hypnotism, in contrast, attributed the phenomena to suggestion, or the subject's belief that a certain procedure or cause will lead to a certain result. In Myers's view, both theories were inadequate because advocates on both sides often confined their observations to too narrow a range. In the case of hypnosis in particular, there was often a "confinement of attention to some few of the commoner and more obvious manifestations" (Myers, 1898b, p. 101).

Likewise, he said, the Nancy view of hypnosis as a psychological phenomenon of suggestion had prevailed over the Salpêtrière view of it as primarily a physiological phenomenon, because advocates of the former, such as Bernheim and Liébeault, had experimented with more, and more varied, subjects than had Charcot and his colleagues at the Salpêtrière.[28] Now, however, the Nancy school was itself in danger of becoming trapped in its own brand of dogmatism by "insisting that *all* in hypnotism is suggestion....I must adhere to the view which I have often expressed....Has not the history of hypnotism thus far been a slow but repeated justification of those who, in each successive controversy, took the wider and less exclusive view?" (Myers, 1889e, p. 198). In appealing for a wider gathering of data, he thus urged "a freer communication between opposing schools" in a joint effort to attack the problems involved (Myers, 1892b, p. 326).

Myers similarly cautioned against the too rigid dismissal of hypotheses alternate to one's own. He defended the approach of explicitly maintaining multiple hypotheses as working possibilities, believing that this breadth of view might enable one ultimately to identify some more comprehensive or "tertium quid" principle that encompasses aspects of the competing hypotheses as well as a wider range of data. His attempt to reconcile the unitary and colonial views of mind exemplified how he thought conflicting views could be reconciled within a larger perspective. Maintaining mul-

---

28. For a discussion of the Salpêtrière and Nancy schools and their differences, see Gauld (1992), especially pp. 306–362.

tiple hypotheses or interpretations as working possibilities is also important because this encourages a broader range of observations. With regard to mesmerism/hypnotism, for example, people who favored the mesmeric hypothesis usually emphasized quite different kinds of phenomena than did those who favored the suggestion hypothesis.

Myers believed that the study of phenomena and beliefs found among ancient cultures and so-called primitive peoples should also play an important part in expanding psychology. One of his earliest papers was an attempt to suggest some parallels between ancient Greek oracles and divination practices and more recent phenomena such as table-tilting and automatic writing (Myers, 1880/1888). He contended that primitive beliefs and reports were not necessarily invalid superstitions simply because of their origin. At a time when most Westerners regarded non-Westerners as "childish" savages, Myers (1886a) urged the potential importance of comparative ethnology and anthropology to psychology and "hoped that shamans and medicine-men will not vanish before the missionary until they have yielded some fuller lessons to the psycho-physicist [i.e., psychologist]" (p. xlv).

Thus, instead of judging "the worth of ideas by tracing their *origins*," as scientists following in the footsteps of E. B. Tylor, Sir John Lubbock, and Herbert Spencer tended to do, Myers urged that we adopt "a somewhat more searching criterion. Instead of asking in what age a doctrine originated—with the implied assumption that the more recent it is, the better—we can now ask how far it is in accord or discord with a great mass of actual recent evidence" (*HP*, vol. 2, p. 91). Gurney's comprehensive survey of witchcraft literature, for example, had shown that firsthand (*not* secondary) accounts of phenomena attributed to witchcraft bore a remarkable resemblance to modern phenomena of hypnotism and hysteria (Gurney et al., 1886, vol. 2, pp. 116–120, 172–185). This example suggests that, faced with unusual or abnormal phenomena, one is not limited to accepting traditional explanations and beliefs about them in their original form or to rejecting the observations altogether. Invalid or insufficient interpretations may have derived from perfectly valid observations. The important question to ask is "whether hypotheses, now admitted to be erroneous, had ever been based in past times on evidence in any way comparable to that which we have adduced" (Myers, 1886a, p. lxix).

In addition to considering a breadth of phenomena and of explanatory hypotheses, Myers believed it was equally important to maintain a breadth of method. The ultimate goal of any science, he said, is to arrive at an explanation of a phenomenon sufficient to allow one to predict or produce that phenomenon (Myers, 1880/1888, p. 56). All sciences, however, must pass through two prior methodological stages before reaching that advanced stage: "First, [the phenomena] will occur spontaneously. Next, they will be empirically produced. And lastly they will be produced scientifically; produced, that is to say, with real knowledge of the conditions on which they depend." Psychical researchers and others attempting to push psychology beyond the commonplace and toward "real discovery" were, he thought, "just entering" the second stage, that is, the early experimental stage "at which we can sometimes set the machinery going, but have no notion how it works." Nevertheless, as long as one remains at this second stage, and has not yet progressed to the third stage of understanding fully how to produce the phenomena, then the observational method must continue in conjunction with the experimental work. It remains "important to take stock, so to say, of the whole range of *spontaneous* phenomena corresponding to the phenomena which we are endeavouring to produce. We shall thus learn how far we are likely to be able to go, and we may get hints as to the quickest line of progress" (Myers, 1892c, p. 333).

In short, the methodological approach for psychology that Myers advocated was above all else a comparative one: comparing observations from widely differing conditions, places, or times; comparing spontaneous phenomena and experimentally produced phenomena; comparing different hypotheses or perspectives. Furthermore, because of his fervent belief in the ultimate continuity of all phenomena, he emphasized the necessity of showing continuity and interrelationship among apparently disparate phenomena. It was particularly important to understand the continuity between normal psychological phenomena and the refractory and rare abnormal and supernormal phenomena of psychology and psychical research, not only to bring the latter out of the realm of superstition and into the realm of science, but also to strengthen science itself by expanding its framework to include, not just some, but all phenomena of human experience. As James summarized this, Myers brought "unlike things thus together by forming series of which the intermediate terms connect the extremes":

> Myers's great principle of research was that in order to understand any one species of fact we ought to have all the species of the same general class of fact before us. So he took a lot of scattered phenomena, some of them recognized as reputable, others outlawed from science, or treated as isolated curiosities; he made series of them, filled in the transitions by delicate hypotheses or analogies, and bound them together in a system by his bold inclusive conception of the Subliminal Self, so that no one can now touch one part of the fabric without finding the rest entangled with it....Through him for the first time, psychologists are in possession of their full material. (James, 1901, p. 16)

Empirical Phenomena for the Study of Mind: An Introduction to *Human Personality*

In addition therefore to outlining a new model of mind and urging the development of methods uniquely suited to psychology, Myers sought to call the attention of psychologists to "their full material" by describing an enormous range of phenomena, both spontaneously occurring and experimentally induced, that he thought not only must be accounted for in any adequate theory of human personality but also are essential for stimulating the development of such a theory. The most fully developed and complete form in which the theoretical, methodological, and empirical themes of Myers's work were presented is the massive two-volume *Human Personality and Its Survival of Bodily Death* (1903). Although it was published posthumously, two years after Myers's death, most of it had been finished and was ready for publication at the time of his death, large parts of it having been drawn from or based upon his numerous publications from the 1880s and 1890s.[29] As Myers had requested when he realized that he was seriously ill and might die soon, Richard Hodgson and Alice Johnson served as editors after his death.[30] When the book appeared, it was quickly reviewed in numerous journals and periodicals.[31]

Human Personality consists of 10 chapters and lengthy Appendices that present much of the empirical data and case reports supporting the primary material. In the first chapter Myers introduces his overall purpose and his theory of the Subliminal Self. In Chapters 2 and 3 he provides a more detailed account of the theory by discussing two seemingly different kinds of phenomena that he believed are closely related psychologically, namely, hysteria and genius. In Chapters 4 and 5 he discusses the emergence of sub-

29. The William James scholar Eugene Taylor (1984, p. 179; 1996, p. 147) made an egregious error when he stated that *Human Personality* was published posthumously by Myers's widow and son because Myers himself had largely abandoned the project. He further seriously misrepresented the facts when he opined that Myers had not completed the book because he had "dallied around" during the 1890s (Taylor, 1996, p. 147). In fact, Myers published nearly 50 papers and reviews in the 11 years before his death, including the important series of nine lengthy papers on the Subliminal Self, published between 1892 and 1895 (see footnote 8 for the references), on which much of *Human Personality* was based. Would that we could all "dally" like this.

30. Although the primary task remaining for the editors was to put the unfinished Chapter 9 and the Appendices in order, at least two major changes occurred that probably deviated sharply from Myers's own wishes. First, as I shall discuss further below, a large body of material that Myers had intended to include in Chapter 9, concerning the medium Mrs. Thompson, was omitted. Secondly, Myers himself had apparently intended a different title for his book than the one that appeared. James (1902/1958, p. 386n) stated that it had already been announced by Longmans, Green, and Company as in press under the title *Human Personality in the Light of Recent Research*—a title that far more accurately reflected Myers's approach than did the title that was ultimately used. The change was apparently made at the last minute by the editors or the publishers and, I suspect, would not have been approved by Myers himself. As I have already mentioned, although the question of survival after death was certainly Myers's central concern, he fully understood that it could be approached adequately only within the much larger context of the nature of consciousness. Unfortunately, the title that was used has probably turned away many scientific readers who would have examined the book if Myers's own title had been used.

31. We have placed the most significant of these contemporary reviews (Flournoy, James, McDougall, Stout) on our digital version of *Human Personality* (see our Introduction, p. xxx). See also Gauld (1968, chap. 12).

liminal functioning in two altered states of consciousness: sleep and hypnosis. In Chapters 6 through 9 he presents a wide variety of evidence, both spontaneous and experimental, for psychological "automatisms" of subliminal origin. Chapters 6 and 7 deal with sensory automatisms, or "messages which the subliminal self sends up to the supraliminal in sensory form," especially visual or auditory form, "externalised into quasi-percepts" (*HP*, vol. 1, pp. 23, 222). Chapters 8 and 9 deal with motor automatisms, or subliminal impulses or ideas expressed through motor functioning, whether "by movement of limbs or hand or tongue" (*HP*, vol. 1, p. 222). The final chapter is an Epilogue assembled by the editors from some of Myers's more speculative writings. It consists largely of a "Provisional Sketch of a Religious Synthesis" and several appendices in which Myers outlines his hope and belief that science ("that great wedding between Reason and Experience" [*HP*, vol. 2, p. 295]) and religion ("the sane and normal response of the human spirit...to the known phenomena of the universe, regarded as an intelligible whole" [*HP*, vol. 2, p. 284]) will come together so that the methods of science can be directed toward questions that religion alone has thus far asked (*HP*, vol. 2, p. 305).

In the remainder of this chapter, I will briefly sketch, using as an outline the chapter divisions of *Human Personality*, some of the many types of phenomena and lines of research that Myers believed important for a truly comprehensive and instructive science of psychology. This skeletal presentation, however, can provide only a glimpse of the richness, depth, and orderliness of the evidence that Myers marshaled in support of his theory. As Gardner Murphy (1954) cautioned years later,

> The reader who would grasp what Myers is doing must simply keep his fingers in the appendices, often the appendices of both volumes, and indeed sometimes several fingers at once, to trace out the carefully marshalled evidence which is offered by the author at each point to support the generalization which he offers. This is the only way in which the documentary strength and philosophical significance of Myers can be understood. (p. iv)

Chapters 2 and 3: Hysteria and Genius

Myers noted that Breuer and Freud had been puzzled by their seemingly paradoxical observation "that amongst hysterics we find the clearest-minded, the strongest-willed, the fullest of character, the most acutely critical specimens of humanity" (translated and quoted by Myers, 1893a, p. 14;[32] see Breuer & Freud, 1893/1957, p. 13). More generally, the apparent relationship between genius and insanity had long been noted and debated (and still is; see our Chapter 7). In Myers's model of mind, this relationship is to

32. This paper (Myers, 1893a, pp. 12–15) provided the first published account of Freud's work in English (Fuller & Fuller, 1986; E. Jones, 1961, vol. 1, p. 250).

be expected. He considered both to be manifestations of the same general psychological mechanism—that is, an unusual "perturbation," instability, or permeability in the boundary between subliminal and supraliminal processes. "Normal" individuals, in contrast, have a relatively stable, less permeable barrier, and are correspondingly less variable: "The man who is in but small degree thus permeable, who acts uniformly on supraliminal considerations,...is likely to be safe in prudent mediocrity" (*HP*, vol. 1, p. 116). The difference between hysteria and genius is a qualitative, not psychological, one. Hysteria (which Myers called a "self-suggestive malady" or "disease of the hypnotic stratum") is for the most part (although not entirely) a dissolutive process, whereas creative genius is primarily evolutive. When there is "a lack of liminal stability, an excessive permeability, if I may so say, of the psychical diaphragm which separates the empirical [supraliminal] from the latent [subliminal] faculties of man," then there may be either an expansion of consciousness (an "uprush" of latent material from the subliminal into the supraliminal) or, conversely, a narrowing of consciousness (a "downdraught" from the supraliminal into the subliminal). The former is genius, the latter is hysteria (Myers, 1893a, pp. 8, 16; *HP*, vol. 1, pp. 20, 66).

As I mentioned earlier, Myers had long urged psychologists to study hysteria as a psychological, as opposed to a clinical or medical, phenomenon. The purely descriptive, clinical approach had yielded little true understanding of hysteria. A nosological definition of hysteria had proven "impossible," since symptoms seem almost infinitely variable. A more adequate definition, he urged, will come only when we "seek it from some psychological standpoint" (Myers, 1893a, p. 5).

The study of the dissolution of personality might also reveal much about its evolution, or integration, and how the "normal" personality maintains a relatively stable integration (*HP*, vol. 1, pp. 19, 35). Unlike Janet and most French clinicians, Myers (1893a) believed that the ordinary or "normal" personality is "no true ideal, no stable synthesis, but rather a transitory and shifting compromise....The personality of each of us is in a state of constantly shifting equilibrium" (pp. 6, 9). More fundamentally, all manifestations of personality involve a narrowing of the field of consciousness so "that it can take in the minimum of sensations necessary for the support of life" (p. 17). The narrowing of the hysteric's field of consciousness, therefore, differs more in degree than in kind from that of the normal person. Thus, unlike organic losses of function, hysterical symptoms are "the mere subsidence of these powers to a level where the empirical will can no longer reach them," but from which they can potentially be recalled (p. 16). They are, in short, not "extinguished" but submerged (*HP*, vol. 1, pp. 46–47).

Myers thus predicted that experiments on hysterics would show that, at some level of consciousness, hysterics retain sensations and memories that they seem to have lost—as in fact experiments of Binet, Pierre Janet, and Jules Janet were showing (Myers, 1893b, pp. 201–204; 1889c, pp. 217–219; 1893a, pp. 16–22; *HP*, chap. 2). Pierre Janet, for example, had observed "how rare a thing it was that any accident or injury followed upon hysterical loss of feeling in the limbs" (*HP*, vol. 1, p. 47). Some deeper level of personality, it seems, retains awareness and maintains some subliminal supervision over the individual's functioning. Similarly, Janet showed that, although an hysteric might have lost the ability to carry out a motor task when her attention was directed to it, she actually retained the capacity at a subliminal level (Myers, 1893a, pp. 21–22). Janet also followed Myers's lead in utilizing automatic writing as a means of accessing the subliminal content of consciousness, thus revealing that psychological traumas often contribute to the development of hysterical symptoms, although they remain out of the patient's conscious awareness (Janet, 1889). Myers encouraged such experiments, not only to determine how deep the hysterical losses of sensation and memory really go and to what extent subliminal awareness of "lost" areas of consciousness might still be influencing supraliminal functioning, but also to demonstrate, as he believed they would, an underlying unity and continuity beneath the hysteric's apparently dissociated personality.

Finally, cases of hysteria provide "one of the most fertile sources of new knowledge of body and mind" (*HP*, vol. 1, p. 43). Hysteria is not solely an excessive narrowing of consciousness, and phenomena such as hysterical anesthesia, blindness, or paralysis (e.g., Binet, 1890; Binet & Féré, 1888; Janet, 1893/1901, 1907/1920) are not, according to Myers, simply the *losses* of sensory or motor capacity that they appear to be. Moreover, they are not organically caused: They do not fit any anatomical pattern; they might periodically change location; and they can often be cured or made to disappear by suggestion. Hysterical symptoms are instead "phantom copies of real maladies of the nervous system" (*HP*, vol. 1, p. 43). As such, they are evidence for a level of control over physiological processes, latent in the subliminal consciousness of the individual, that is beyond the capacity of the supraliminal consciousness. This apparent ability of the hysteric's subliminal consciousness to initiate and control, at some level, physiological processes that are normally beyond conscious control seemed to Myers to be a *gain* rather than a *loss* of function and to have important implications for an understanding of the relationship of mind and body. In Chapter 3 I will discuss in more detail these important phenomena, as well as closely related phenomena such as stigmata, "faith" healing, and maternal impressions, to which Myers also called attention.

In short, Myers believed that hysteria, when viewed as a psychological phenomenon, gives "striking" support to "my own principal thesis" (*HP*, vol. 1, p. 19), namely, that *all* personality is a filtering or narrowing of the field of consciousness from a larger Self, the rest of which remains latent and capable of emerging only under the appropriate conditions. The hysterical personality, in essence, bears the same relationship to the normal, healthy, supraliminal personality as the latter bears to the ideal, totally integrated Self or Individuality of which it is an extract.[33]

---

33. Myers (1893a), perhaps a trifle facetiously, compared the hysteric's frequent unawareness of and indifference to her limitations to the indifference of most normal people to learning more about the nature and extent of their own minds: "If

Similarly, Myers argued that the study of genius can teach us about the structure and evolutionary dynamics of mind, since the same psychological mechanism that produces a narrowing of consciousness in hysterics produces an expansion of consciousness in geniuses (Myers, 1892d; *HP*, chap. 3): Both involve an unusual instability or permeability of the barrier or filter between the subliminal and supraliminal, in one case leading primarily to a "down-draught," in the other to an "uprush." Believing that the evolution of mind involves a general process of "gaining a completer control over innate but latent faculty," Myers defined genius as "an emergence of hidden faculty" (Myers, 1895b, p. 6). In particular, it involves "a power of utilising a wider range than other men can utilise of faculties in some degree innate in all," as well as "a *subliminal uprush*, an emergence into the current of ideas which the man is consciously manipulating of other ideas which he has not consciously originated, but which have shaped themselves beyond his will, in profounder regions of his being" (*HP*, vol. 1, p. 71). As an "uprush," an inspiration of genius is a psychological automatism, a subspecies of subliminal phenomena. What distinguishes the phenomena of genius, however, is that they involve not so much the emergence of new faculties as the intensification of familiar ones (*HP*, vol. 1, p. 96). In the analogy of the spectrum, they "make the bright parts of the habitual spectrum more brilliant," rather than drawing on subliminal faculty "beyond the limits of the ordinary conscious spectrum" (*HP*, vol. 1, p. 78).

Myers's conception of genius was thus quite different from that of Maudsley, Lombroso, and others who considered genius to be indicative of pathology (Myers, 1889e, p. 192; *HP*, vol. 1, p. 71). Unlike them, he believed that geniuses, with their "perceptions of new truths and powers of new action," represent instead the "highest product of the race" (*HP*, vol. 1, pp. 96, 71). Because genius and madness both involve similar psychological mechanisms—namely, a permeability of the psychological boundary—it is to be expected that they might frequently occur in the same person (Myers, 1885d, p. 130; 1892d, p. 355); but any nervous disorders that accompany genius signal, not dissolution, but a "*perturbation which masks evolution*" (*HP*, vol. 1, p. 93).

Genius is customarily associated with an unusually high level of intellectual functioning or extraordinary artistic achievements of a scientist, writer, artist, musician, or dancer. Psychologically speaking, however, any uprush of heightened faculty belongs to the same class: "A man may have a sudden and accurate inspiration of what o'clock it is, in just the same way as Virgil might have an inspiration of the second half of a difficult hexameter" (*HP*, vol. 1, p. 78). A psychological conception of genius, Myers insisted, is entirely different from the aesthetic conception. Whereas from the aesthetic view the important consideration is the perceived quality or value of the product, from the psychological perspective the important consideration

---

we had been a populace of hysterics we should have acquiesced in our hysteria. We should have pushed aside as a fantastic enthusiast the fellow sufferer who strove to tell us that this was not all that we were meant to be" (p. 25).

is the psychological mechanism behind the phenomenon, that is, a sudden uprush from the subliminal that is "*incommensurable*" with ordinary conscious effort (Myers, 1898b, p. 104; *HP*, vol. 1, pp. 75, 99). Two works of art or two different kinds of phenomena may thus be "in the same *psychological* class" without being "in the same *artistic* class" (*HP*, vol. 1, p. 75).

In Chapter 7 we will return to a discussion of the phenomena of genius, including one that Myers thought particularly useful for studying the psychological mechanism involved, namely, arithmetical prodigies. According to Myers, the "calculating boy" is of the same psychological genus as a Shakespeare, although clearly not of "the highest order of art" (Myers, 1898b, p. 104; 1892d, p. 349). Nevertheless, the products of the calculating prodigy, unlike those of the artist, can be judged on purely objective grounds; the answer is either right or wrong. Thus, the study of such persons may provide a relatively objective way to study the otherwise subjective processes of inspirational uprush (Myers, 1892d, pp. 356, 360; *HP*, vol. 1, pp. 78–85).

Chapter 4: Sleep

Myers believed that the study of sleep and dreams should occupy a prominent position in psychological research. In keeping with his view that consciousness has evolved out of a primitive "panaesthesia," Myers described the evolution of consciousness as a process in which, in response to environmental demands, we become "more and more awake." Sleep is thus a reversion to an earlier stage of development. Furthermore, just "as sleep precedes vigilance, so do dreams precede thought" (Myers, 1892e, p. 363); dreams, he thought, represent "the kind of mentation from which our clearer and more coherent states may be supposed to develop" (*HP*, vol. 1, p. 58).

Myers's (1898b) psychological definition of sleep, therefore, was that it is "an alternating phase of our personality" (p. 105) in which the organism reverts to a more primitive state of consciousness for reparative purposes: "It is a fully admitted, although an absolutely unexplained fact, that the regenerative quality of healthy sleep is something *sui generis*, which no completeness of waking quiescence can rival or approach" (*HP*, vol. 1, p. 123). Myers attributed this characteristic feature of sleep to its being a primitive, now subliminal, state of consciousness. Just as in Jackson's hierarchical theory of nervous functioning a lower level takes over when a higher level ceases to function, so in Myers's theory, when waking consciousness ceases, the infrared portion of the spectrum of consciousness, with its "increased control over organic functions at the foundation of life" (*HP*, vol. 1, p. 123), takes over and makes sleep the "regenerative phase of our personality" (*HP*, vol. 1, p. 152; 1898b, p. 105).

For Myers (1892e), therefore, sleep was "no mere abeyance of waking activities, but rather a phase of personality with characteristics definitely its own" (p. 365). The most obvious and important of these characteristics are the reparative organic processes; but there are also others indicating a kind of psychological functioning different from that in the supraliminal waking state. Because of the "heightening effect of sleep" in allowing subliminal impressions "to cross the threshold of consciousness," particularly by appearing in dreams (W. F. Barrett, Massey, et al., 1883, p. 140), sleep and dreams can provide an important source of knowledge about subliminal functioning.

First, Myers argued, dreams provide a readily available means of studying the "language" of the subliminal, a language that may underlie other, less common forms of automatism or subliminal processes. Just as sleep is not simply an absence of waking functioning, dreams are not just "echoes or fragments of waking experience, fantastically combined" (Myers, 1892e, p. 365). Dreams are the evolutionary precursor of thought (p. 363), expressed in a form or language that is often symbolic in content rather than literal. So that psychologists might begin to learn this symbolic, primarily nonverbal language, "dreams should be subjected to an analysis far more searching than they have as yet received from any quarter" (pp. 365–366).

The study of sleep and dreams might also provide information about enhanced or even novel psychological processes emerging in subliminal functioning (1892e; *HP*, chap. 4). For example, dreams most commonly, but also hypnagogic and hypnopompic[34] illusions, reveal a latent capacity for internally generated imagery going far beyond the person's ordinary voluntary waking capacity. For many people, in fact, dream imagery is "the highest point" that their visualizing faculty reaches (Myers, 1892e, p. 370). Moreover, in most people dreams display a creative and dramatizing capacity far greater than they normally show (p. 371); and in some dreams cognitive or problem-solving processes seem to have been enhanced, as in cases in which solutions to mathematical or scholarly problems have appeared in dreams (pp. 392–397; *HP*, vol. 1, pp. 134–135, 372–379).

Another cognitive function that can be enhanced in dreams is memory. For example, "we occasionally recover in sleep a memory which has wholly dropped out of waking consciousness," a phenomenon Myers considered common enough so that "no one will raise any doubt about it" (Myers, 1892e, pp. 380–381). More interestingly, however, there are also occasional dreams involving facts of which the person had never supraliminally been aware (pp. 381–392). Such extensions of memory suggested to Myers that, in sleep as well as in other subliminal states of consciousness, memory may be more wide-ranging than is supraliminal, waking memory—even if it is also less focused or controlled than supraliminal memory (*HP*, vol. 1, p. 129). In other words, the study of enhanced memory, or hypermnesia, in dreams—including the memory of events once known but now forgotten, as well as events perceived with the normal senses but never consciously

34. Myers (1892b, pp. 314–315) coined this word to refer to images that may occur as a person is waking up, comparable to the hypnagogic imagery that precedes sleep.

noted—is of interest in showing that both memory and sensory perception extend beyond our ordinarily noted supraliminal range. Furthermore, Myers believed that the study of memory in dreams will reveal an underlying continuity of memory between the dream state and related conditions such as hypnotic and somnambulistic states, and thus provide further support for his theory of a fundamental unity of human personality behind its multiple and often seemingly disparate manifestations (Myers, 1892e, pp. 378–379; *HP*, vol. 1, pp. 128–134, 370–372).

Myers's model of mind predicts that if sleep is a state of consciousness in which subliminal processes take over from supraliminal ones, then sleep should facilitate subliminal functioning, not only in the organic or "infrared" region, but also in the "ultraviolet" range of the psychological spectrum, such as the emergence of telepathic impressions in dreams. This does, in fact, seem to be the case (W. F. Barrett, Massey, et al., 1883, p. 140; *HP*, vol. 1, pp. 135–150, 379–436).[35] Moreover, Myers (1892e) conjectured that dreams which seem particularly vivid or otherwise impressive to the dreamer—and especially dreams that lead the dreamer to take some action once he or she wakes up—might more often be those which later prove to have been supernormal (pp. 366–367). He thus suggested studying the qualitative intensity of dreams as part of an effort to identify supernormal dreams more readily.

Although dreams, by their very nature, are spontaneously occurring phenomena, Myers nevertheless believed that they can occasionally be brought under some experimental control:

> I have long thought that we are too indolent in regard to our dreams; that we neglect precious occasions of experiment for want of a little resolute direction of the will....[W]e ought to accustom ourselves to look on each dream, not only as a psychological *observation*, but as an observation which may be transformed into an *experiment*. We should constantly represent to ourselves what points we should like to notice and test in dreams; and then when going to sleep we should impress upon our minds that we are going to try an experiment;—that we are going to carry into our dreams enough of our waking self to tell us that they *are* dreams, and to prompt us to psychological inquiry. (Myers, 1887a, p. 241)

What he was proposing was the study of what today we call lucid dreams, a phenomenon now generally acknowledged even though, like many of the phenomena Myers thought important for psychologists to study, it first had to go through a prolonged period of resistance on the part of many scientists (Green, 1968a; LaBerge, 1985; see also our Chapter 6).[36]

---

35. Numerous studies of spontaneous supernormal phenomena since Myers's time have shown dreams to be a frequent vehicle for telepathic impressions (e. g., Stevenson, 1970, p. 2) ; and for more recent experimental evidence of the facilitating effects of sleep on psi functioning, see Child (1985) and Ullman and Krippner, with Vaughan (1973).

36. Myers put himself to the task that he proposed, even though he knew that he

Chapter 5: Hypnotism

From the spontaneous subliminal phenomena associated with sleep, Myers moved on to what he called "that great experimental modification of sleep," hypnotism (*HP*, vol. 1, p. 152). Gurney and Myers had long argued that hypnosis is far more important than a curious anomaly or stage entertainment (Gurney & Myers, 1885, p. 422; *HP*, vol. 1, p. 158). The method that had evolved from Mesmer's original discovery had, in fact, been "the first really intimate, really penetrating method of psychological experiment" (Myers, 1892f, p. 444) and could provide a "corner-stone of a valid experimental psychology" (Gurney & Myers, 1885, p. 422; Myers, 1885c, p. 641n). Its psychological importance lay for them in its potential as "an experimental method of reaching the subliminal self" (Myers, 1891b, p. 83).

As a psychological method, however, hypnosis was in its infancy. It had been used in clinical therapy, but its theoretical implications remained largely unexamined (*HP*, vol. 1, pp. 22–23). As I mentioned earlier, Myers repeatedly emphasized that the usefulness of hypnosis as an experimental method depended on an adequately broad conception of the nature, and hence the phenomena, of hypnosis. Although the terms "mesmerism" and "hypnotism" are sometimes used loosely or interchangeably, the former being considered simply an older term for the latter, there is in fact a distinct difference between the two concepts, and the two schools of thought emphasized not only different interpretations of the phenomena, but even radically different phenomena. One major motivation behind the work of Myers and Gurney on hypnosis was to keep alive both sets of interpretations and observations and arrive at a better, more comprehensive view. They believed that both the mesmeric hypothesis and the hypnosis hypothesis had merit, since both had empirical observations supporting them. On the other hand, they also believed that both remained inadequate. The "effluence"—whatever it is that seemingly emanates from the hypnotist to cause an effect in the subject—is probably not a new physical force, as the mesmerists thought, but a psychological one. Likewise the concept of "suggestion," central to the hypnosis view, is inadequate because suggestion itself is wholly unexplained. They thus cautioned against a too-thorough abandonment of the old mesmeric hypothesis and a too-eager readiness to adopt the suggestion hypothesis as the new dogmatism (see, e.g, Gurney & Myers, 1883).

A point to which Myers returned frequently, however, stemmed from his fear—justified, in light of what actually happened after the turn of the century—that the problem of hypnosis as a theoretical issue in psychology would not be adequately pursued because of the mistaken perception that it has been "explained" in terms of suggestion. Suggestion, it is said, produces effects because in a "suggestible" person it leads to the suspension of

---

was both a poor dreamer (Myers, 1887a, p. 241) and a poor visualizer (Myers, 1892e, p. 370). Perhaps predictably, he succeeded on only three nights out of nearly 3,000 on which he tried (Myers, 1887a, p. 241).

volition or will, to the person's complete absorption in some idea, and to the "increased internal responsiveness of the organism" (Gurney & Myers, 1883, p. 699; *HP*, vol. 1, p. xxxv). This "suggestion hypothesis," however, is simply a *description* of the subject's condition and "not in any way an *explanation*" of *how* the condition is brought about (Gurney & Myers, 1883, p. 699). There is obviously a "profound nervous change"; but how is it effected? Many people "use the word *suggestion* as though this were in itself an explanation of the way in which the phenomena are produced,...[but] they...seem hardly to think it needful or possible to inquire how it comes to pass that a sane man's psychical balance is capable of being thus suddenly disturbed"—and particularly by a method that would seem to have "little more efficacy than the mere utterance of a charm" (Myers, 1892b, pp. 300–301). In short, the words "suggestion," "self-suggestion," and "suggestibility" are "mere names which disguise our ignorance" (*HP*, vol. 1, p. 153).[37]

Myers thought that all the phenomena of suggestion or hypnosis are, in the final analysis, phenomena of *self*-suggestion, because suggestion is a process that activates the subliminal consciousness, or at least a portion of it (Myers, 1891a, p. 170; 1892f, p. 446; *HP*, vol. 1, p. 169). As he clearly recognized, this definition of suggestion also fails to provide an explanation; nevertheless, he thought that it could help advance our understanding—and direct our empirical research—by clearly making hypnosis and suggestion part of a larger problem of psychology, namely, that of the activation of subliminal functioning in general (*HP*, vol. 1, p. 169).

Myers believed that psychological research on hypnosis supported his view of the continuity of consciousness underlying the fragmented manifestations of it. In the spontaneous "fugue" case of Ansel Bourne, for example, the secondary personality, of which the primary personality was unaware, re-emerged under hypnosis (R. Hodgson, 1891; James, 1890b, vol. 1, pp. 390–393). Gurney, who "practically opened up in England a whole department of experimental psychology" (Myers, 1888b, p. 368), studied the content and persistence of memories in different hypnotic states, showing not only that hypnotic states have and maintain distinct memory groupings, but also that they in some sense persist and continue to operate even when not overt (Gurney, 1884; Myers, 1888a, p. 377).

A related problem is the process by which separate memory chains are formed. Janet, Elliotson, Gurney, and others had noted "how very different, in different cases, is the *amount of personality* which the hypnotised

37. As Andrew Lang (1911) put it, "to 'explain the explanation' is the task for the future" (p. 546). Contemporary psychologists have not advanced much further. Claims that "we can now understand hypnosis, in part, as a conditioning phenomenon" (Neher, 1980, p. 295) are distressingly common and similarly disguise scientists' ignorance about the essential mechanism underlying hypnosis. Gauld (1992, chap. 25) has provided an excellent overview of contemporary definitions of hypnosis, suggestion, and related concepts; and he concludes that none of them "have any greater explanatory validity than [those of the 19th century]. A truly viable concept of hypnosis remains to be achieved" (p. 610).

subject is able to manifest" (Myers, 1888a, p. 390), ranging from simple states of mono-ideism to seemingly full-blown, fully functioning personalities. As I mentioned earlier, Myers (1888a) suggested that "the time spent in the hypnotic trance, the experience gained therein," was the crucial factor, just as in spontaneous somnambulistic cases: The more the secondary state functioned, the more memories and experience it would accrue, and the more it would come to resemble the primary state in scope and capacity (pp. 391–392).

Like Janet's observations of hysteria, research further suggested that sensations or memories that disappear because of an hypnotic suggestion are not in fact destroyed or lost, but are simply submerged in other strata of consciousness, from which they can potentially be re-evoked (Myers, 1888a, pp. 385, 393): "The problem thus suggested is one of wide-ranging importance...[because it] ultimately involves the question of the relation of our assumed underlying individuality [or 'Self'] to the various personalities through which it finds partial and temporary expression" (Myers, 1892b, p. 324).

Myers thought that hypnosis, like hysteria, has too often been regarded from the perspective of functions *lost* or diminished, rather than of those *gained*. In contrast, he argued that the most fundamental characteristic of hypnosis is not the inhibition, but the enhancement of functions: "No mere inhibition will produce hallucinations....The real kernel of the phenomenon is not the inhibition but the dynamogeny;—not the abstraction of attention or imagination from other topics, but the increased power which imagination gains under suggestion" (*HP*, vol. 1, p. 189). Even when hypnosis produces a clear loss of function, as in suggested anesthesia, analgesia, or negative hallucinations (i.e., an inability to see something that is actually there), the resulting lack of sensation seems more than a withdrawal of attention or even inhibition of sensation. More importantly, it suggests an enhanced ability of subliminal levels of consciousness to control psychophysiological processes that are not ordinarily under conscious control.

Hypnotic alteration of physiological processes is one of the most important of the phenomena that Myers thought could advance our understanding of mental efficacy and the relationship of mind and brain; and we have therefore devoted an entire chapter in this book to a discussion of this and related phenomena (Chapter 3). Another potentially important phenomenon is the effect of hypnotic suggestion on perception, especially the production of hallucinations (W. F. Barrett, Gurney, Hodgson, et al., 1883, pp. 22–23; Myers, 1888a, pp. 383–385; 1892f, pp. 445–449; *HP*, vol. 1, pp. 188–191). Hypnotic production of hallucinations is not only common, but also "one of the most striking of all our indications of latent faculty" (Myers, 1898b, p. 105). Although the phenomenon is routinely attributed to suggestion and to the subject's motivation to obey the hypnotist, it clearly involves more than the subject's compliant use of a familiar voluntary faculty: "Under ordinary circumstances my subject simply *cannot* see a tiger at will; nor can I affect the visual centres which might enable him to do so" (*HP*, vol. 1, p. 233).[38]

Myers also believed that studying experimentally induced hallucinations is "an important prerequisite" for understanding spontaneous hallucinations (Myers, 1892b, pp. 319–320). For example, he conducted some experiments (Myers, 1892f, pp. 460–461) in which two hypnotized subjects were given different suggestions about what they would see on a blank surface or speculum. They were then brought together and asked to describe what they saw. Each subject described what had been suggested to him, and neither was able to influence the other to see or report anything else. Such experiments clearly are pertinent to the question of collective hallucinations and particularly the hypothesis that the comments or reactions of one person having an hallucination influenced others present to have an hallucination they otherwise would not have had.

Additionally, some hypnotic phenomena appeared to involve hyperesthesia, or the enhancement of the normal five senses. The philosopher Henri Bergson, for example, reported a case of a boy who could, while hypnotized, identify objects reflected in the corneas of the experimenter's eyes (Myers, 1887b; *HP*, vol. 1, pp. 477–479). Recognizing and ruling out such sensory hyperesthesia is, of course, necessary before one invokes an explanation involving psi phenomena such as telepathy or clairvoyance.[39]

In addition to enhanced control over perceptual processes, the phenomena of hypnosis sometimes involve enhancements of cognitive processes. Experiments in post-hypnotic suggestion by Gurney (1887b; 1888), Delbœuf (1892), and Bramwell (1896) showed that some level of subliminal consciousness can conduct complicated arithmetical calculations or keep track of a specific, often lengthy lapse of time (see *HP*, vol. 1, pp. 502–510). Such experiments might contribute, for example, to an understanding of arithmetical prodigies or the claims of some people that they can awaken themselves at pre-determined times (Myers, 1898b, p. 104; H. Sidgwick & Myers, 1892, pp. 605–607).

Finally, from Myers's conception of hypnosis as a means of accessing subliminal strata of consciousness, it follows that phenomena suggestive of supernormal modes of perception, such as telepathy or clairvoyance, would

38. Modern social psychological theories of hypnosis, which attribute hypnotic effects primarily to the compliant behavior of subjects wishing to fulfill the role of good subjects, still fail to address this fundamental question about *how* subjects comply with effects not ordinarily under their conscious control. This failure in large part is surely because of what Myers (1898b) had lamented as "confinement of attention to some few of the commoner and more obvious manifestations" (p. 101; see also our Chapter 5). I will discuss this problem more fully in Chapter 3.

39. Nonetheless, Myers also warned against carrying such explanations to unreasonable extremes. For example, he noted, someone had proposed that subjects hypnotized at a distance had fallen into trance because they heard "the changed sound accompanying the hypnotiser's quickened circulation" (Myers, 1887b, p. 535).

also be observed in connection with hypnosis (see, e.g., *HP*, vol. 1, pp. 543–546, 553–559). Indeed, such phenomena had long been reported in the older mesmeric literature (Gauld, 1992); and SPR members conducted experiments with hypnosis in which the hypothesis of some supernormal mode of perception had to be considered (see, e.g., Gurney et al., 1886, chap. 2). In the century since these early experiments, many other studies have supported the prediction from Myers's model that hypnosis can sometimes elicit or enhance supernormal functioning (for reviews, see Honorton & Krippner, 1969; Schechter, 1984; Stanford & Stein, 1994; van de Castle, 1969).

Chapters 6 and 7: Hallucinations—Sensory Automatisms and Phantasms of the Dead

Myers considered research on hallucinations particularly important, because they provide an instructive means of studying the relationship between "subjective," mental, internal perception and "objective," physical, external reality. As Myers noted, even our senses do not provide us with an entirely objective representation of external reality; sensory perception is itself a mental construct that "is in its own way highly symbolic" (*HP*, vol. 1, p. 277). Likewise, hallucinations "further...confound our already doubtful contrast between objective and subjective,...between 'real' and 'unreal' things" (Myers, 1891c, p. 125).

The study of hallucinations, however, had to be carried out in conjunction with attempts to understand the relationship of hallucinations to other modes of perception and imagery (*HP*, vol. 1, pp. 224–231). Myers and Gurney had first attempted to fit hallucinations into a general scheme of perception in 1884 (Gurney & Myers, 1884b, pp. 77–82; see also Gurney, 1885). They argued that visual perceptions and hallucinations are produced by the same neurological sensory apparatus, but in the former the primary stimulus has come from peripheral sensory mechanisms, whereas in the latter the stimulus has come from mental processes directly activating the relevant cortical areas. Hallucinations therefore fall on a continuum with other perceptual processes, including not only normal sight, but after-images, illusions, memory images, and dreams (*HP*, vol. 1, pp. 224–231).

Myers further argued that not all hallucinations are pathological, as most psychologists then (and now) assumed. Many hallucinations are indeed generated by pathological, physiological agents such as drugs, alcohol, or disease, but others represent internal imagery generated spontaneously or by suggestion. One of the most important accomplishments of Myers, Gurney, and their colleagues in psychical research was in demonstrating the previously unsuspected, but as it turns out not infrequent, occurrence of hallucinations in normal, healthy individuals. In contrast to psychologists such as Janet, who believed that hypnotic phenomena such as post-hypnotic hallucinations could be produced only in hysterical subjects (Janet, 1893/1901, p. 277), the psychical researchers were showing that normal individuals could in fact be hypnotized and induced to experience vivid hallucinations (e.g., Myers, 1892f, p. 470). In addition, they demonstrated the frequent occurrence of spontaneous hallucinations among normal persons, conducting extensive investigations of hundreds of such cases (e.g., Gurney et al., 1886; E. M. Sidgwick, 1922), as well as two major surveys (Gurney et al., 1886, chap. 8; H. Sidgwick et al., 1894). In both the first survey (which yielded 5,705 replies) and the second (17,000), the results showed that approximately 10% of the persons questioned reported having experienced an hallucination of sight, sound, or touch when awake and in good health. These early estimates of the prevalence of hallucinations among normal persons have proved remarkably accurate (see Bentall, 2000, pp. 94–95, for a review).

These studies and surveys also demonstrated that such hallucinations are not always purely subjective in origin. Some, in fact, are veridical—that is, they involve seeing, hearing, or otherwise sensing some event happening at a physically remote location. For example, many of the experiences reported to Gurney, Myers and their colleagues involved seeing an apparition of someone who was undergoing some kind of crisis (usually death) at about the same time.[40]

In these studies, the researchers dealt with two major issues. First they addressed the all-important question of the reliability of the evidence, and in the problems that they identified and the standards of evidence that they set for their material, they were pioneers in the psychology of eyewitness testimony (Gurney et al., 1886, chap. 4). Second, they asked whether the observed correspondences between hallucinations and crisis events could have occurred by chance. Using their own figures for the frequency with which people report having hallucinations in a waking, healthy state, together with statistics regarding the incidence of death in the United Kingdom, they concluded that hallucinations coinciding with a death happened too frequently to be attributable to chance (Gurney et al., 1886, chap. 8; H. Sidgwick et al., 1894).

Veridical hallucinations are, however, in some sense *both* subjective and objective. Even when the stimulus for the hallucination is external and objective, as seems to be the case with veridical hallucinations corresponding to some real but distant event, the percipient's mind often contributes by modifying that original stimulus in idiosyncratic ways, such that the hallucination may take symbolic, expected, or familiar forms (Gurney & Myers, 1884b, pp. 81–82; see also Tyrrell, 1943/1953). Hallucinations "are not mere crude externalisations....They are in most cases elaborate products—complex images which must have needed intelligence to fashion them" (*HP*, vol.

40. Although no subsequent study of veridical hallucinations has approached those of the early SPR in scope or thoroughness of investigation, such experiences have continued to be reported (see, e.g., Dale, White, & Murphy, 1962; Green, 1960; Stevenson, 1970, 1995; S. H. Wright, 1999). An ongoing study at our research unit in the University of Virginia over the past several years has identified more than 200 cases of dreams, telepathic impressions, or hallucinations occurring at the time of some crisis (usually death) occurring to a person at a distance.

1, p. 234). To further understand the relative contribution of subjective and objective elements, Myers believed that it is necessary to examine *both* sides of a case—that of the percipient and that of the person undergoing the crisis, including the state of consciousness of each and the emotional relationship between them (W. F. Barrett, Massey, et al., 1883; Myers, 1884–1885). Myers particularly warned against "the error of attributing too much importance to the person who sees the phantom, because his account of the matter is the only one which we can [or do] get" (1886b, p. 301).[41]

Undoubtedly, the cases that raise in particularly acute form the problem of the subjectivity versus objectivity of hallucinations, and the ones that Myers believed to be the most important to study, are collective cases, in which more than one person perceives an apparition simultaneously (see, e.g., Myers, 1886b; 1886d; 1890b; 1898a). Because collective cases suggest some kind of objective stimulus for the hallucinations, they raise "this perplexing problem of the relation of psychical operations to space" (Myers, 1886b, p. 302). Myers proposed the idea that subliminal elements of Person A's mind may be drawn to a particular place, perhaps by some form of psychological "rapport" with one or more people there. These subliminal elements then, in some yet unknown way, modify an actual point in space, not in a material way perceptible to ordinary senses, but nonetheless in some manner sufficient to stimulate perception of Person A at subliminal levels of the percipients' minds. His hypothesis was, in short, a *spatial* one without being a *sensory* one (Myers, 1886b; 1898a, pp. 323–325). It resulted from his attempt to find a more satisfactory view than, on the one hand, the animistic interpretation of apparitions as some kind of objective "ghost" that multiple people present will see and, on the other hand, Gurney's hypothesis that apparitions are subjective hallucinations produced by a telepathic impression, with collective cases involving further telepathic transfer of this impression from a primary percipient to bystanders. There is still no consensus in sight on this complex and theoretically important phenomenon (for a review, see Gauld, 1982, chap. 15).

Like crisis apparitions of persons who may be dying but not yet deceased, apparitions of people that the percipient already knows to be dead have been reported in all times and cultures, and numerous such cases were reported to the SPR. Although most such cases cannot be attributed to anything other than subjectively generated imagery, some cases do suggest a more objective origin, including collective hallucinations of a deceased person; cases in which veridical information unknown to the percipient was conveyed by the apparition; and cases in which the apparition was later recognized by the percipient in a photograph of someone he or she had not known in life (Myers, 1889d; 1890b; *HP*, chap. 7).

Myers also called attention to hallucinations perceived by a seriously ill or dying person, experiences that in recent years have been called near-death experiences and deathbed visions. We have devoted a whole chapter to this topic (Chapter 6) because such experiences seem to us particularly

41. Stevenson (1987, pp. 106–107) has since had to repeat this warning.

important, suggesting as they do "the persistence...of consciousness under pathological conditions which would seem to negative its possibility"(Myers, 1891c, p. 116).

I have already referred to the importance Myers placed on the study of hypnotically induced hallucinations. Another important method for inducing hallucinations—one that leaves the subject more or less in an ordinary state of consciousness, "undisturbed" by suggestion from another person—is "scrying" (Myers, 1892f, p. 449). Throughout history and across cultures, people have deliberately generated visual and auditory hallucinations with various forms of speculum (or crystal) gazing and "shell-hearing." Although such methods have long been associated with occultism and superstition, Myers believed that they could be usefully adapted and developed as an experimental method in psychology (pp. 458–459, 465).[42]

In early attempts at scrying the content will often be nothing more than "confused reminiscences" or other more or less random imagery (Myers, 1892f, p. 483). In keeping with his idea that the complexity and extent of subliminal functioning correlate with the amount of time spent in the altered state, Myers suggested that, as the scrying is pursued further and develops, the material will become more complex. As with dreams, there may be material once known but now forgotten, or material that had been within one's sensory range but never consciously perceived. Most importantly, but most rarely, the hallucinations may contain information not known normally by the automatist (Myers, 1892b, pp. 318–319; 1892d, p. 348; 1892f; 1899; *HP*, vol. 1, pp. 575–598). Because he believed that complex material, and particularly the latter kinds, will emerge only with sustained attempts, Myers (1896b, 1899) chastised those whose efforts at inducing automatisms had been brief and superficial and who had drawn their conclusions from those limited observations.

Chapters 8, 9, and the Epilogue: Motor Automatisms, Trance, Possession, and Ecstasy

When subliminal material is expressed through motor functioning, Myers classified it as an active, or motor, automatism. For example, if attention is sufficiently diverted from the act of writing, certain persons may produce automatic writing, something more than the simple doodling common to many people, and often attaining "a degree of complexity hitherto little suspected" (Myers, 1885a, p. 248). Because of this complexity, together with the conviction of most automatists that the writing seems not to have originated within themselves, many people believe the phenomenon is produced

42. He was right: The Ganzfeld method now widely used in parapsychology can be viewed as a modern variant of the crystal-gazing and shell-hearing techniques that Myers advocated for psychological research, in that a uniform visual and auditory field is used to heighten internal imagery and focus the subject's attention on it (for some references, see the Appendix).

by some external agency (usually, the spirits of deceased persons). Against this popular interpretation, Myers (1893b) argued that "the great majority of such communications represent the subliminal workings of the automatist's mind alone" (p. 41). As such, automatic writing is potentially another important method available to psychologists for "throwing light upon the workings of the subconscious strata of the mind" (Myers, 1890c, p. 671), and several of Myers's earliest papers (1884, 1885a, 1885b, 1887a) were therefore devoted to this topic.[43]

Other motor automatisms include dowsing, automatic drawing or painting, and telekinesis (now called psychokinesis or PK), the movement of objects involving no tactile or other normal physical contact with the object. Myers placed particular emphasis, however, on another means (in addition to automatic writing) of expressing subliminal mentation verbally—namely, automatic or trance speaking.[44] As with automatic writing, much of the material is gibberish (Myers, 1885b, p. 46), but in certain persons it develops into far more than this. In Myers's lifetime, Mrs. Piper, a trance automatist studied extensively by William James and Richard Hodgson, and Mrs. Thompson, an automatist identified and studied extensively by Myers himself (1902),[45] provided the most important examples of supernormal functioning in the trance state—so important that Myers was ultimately convinced by sittings that he had with them that he had obtained evidence of personal survival after death (Myers, 1893/1961, pp. 40–41; 1902, p. 73).[46]

---

43. We will return to the topic of automatic writing in Chapter 5.

44. Although the phenomenon is more widely referred to as "mediumship," Myers preferred the term "automatist" to "medium," because the latter is question-begging, implying that the material spoken has come from a deceased person, whereas the term "automatist" reflects more generally the means by which the material is produced, rather than a purported source.

It is worth noting here also that most of the best mediums studied extensively in the late 19th and early 20th centuries were *trance* automatists. Although mediumship has in recent years become a topic of interest to the general public, and hence the media, few of today's mediums seem to go into an altered state, much less a "trance" or alternate personality state. On Myers's theory, the abeyance of the supraliminal is conducive, if not absolutely necessary, for the emergence of subliminal mentation, whether from one's own mind or from that of a deceased person. This notable difference between mediums of today and the automatists of the past may explain why, in my view, the material produced by today's mediums is generally of far lower evidential quality.

45. The research with Mrs. Thompson occupied much of the last two years of Myers's life. He had originally intended to include a report of his work with her in *Human Personality*, but for reasons that are not clear what he had written was omitted after his death (see Gauld, 1968, p. 325; Piddington, 1903, pp. 74–76). Unfortunately, none of the records of his 150 sittings with her survive.

46. For an introduction to and review of the literature on Mrs. Piper, as well as important mediums studied after Myers's death, see Gauld (1982). We will return to the topic of mediumship in Chapters 4 and 5.

Myers believed that trance can develop in two directions (*HP*, vol. 2, p. 217). On the one hand, trance may involve an apparent "possession," either by the automatist's own (subliminal) mind or by the mind of another person, living or deceased. Most such cases, however, are neither all one type of possession nor all the other, but instead involve a more complex "admixture...of elements which come from the sensitive's own mind with elements inspired from without" (*HP*, vol. 2, p. 249). On the other hand, trance may lead to a phenomenon "common to all religions" (*HP*, vol. 2, p. 260), and that is "ecstasy." In Myers's view, aspects of a person's consciousness can sometimes make "excursions" beyond its normal bounds and thereby make contact with aspects of the universe with which it ordinarily does not. Such excursions can range from clairvoyance, which is an "incipient" type, to the full-blown ecstatic experiences of mystics or other persons.[47] He also pointed out that the two types of trance are "complementary or correlative," one involving some sort of "entry" of an external mind into another person's body ("possession"), the other involving some sort of "excursion" out of one's body into a larger environment ("ecstasy") (*HP*, vol. 2, p. 259). Although he used words such as "enter" and "go out," "inside" and "outside," he emphasized that the unknown processes behind these phenomena, as well as related phenomena such as clairvoyance, "need not be...*spatial*" (*HP*, vol. 2, p. 259).

We will discuss ecstasy and mystical experiences more fully in Chapter 8. It is important to note here, however, the spiritual motivation so central to all of Myers's work and permeating especially Chapter 9 and the Epilogue of *HP*. This attitude, and in particular what Gauld (1968, p. 276) called the "Cosmic chant" of some of Myers's more lyrical writing, has surely contributed to the misunderstanding and dismissal of Myers by other scientists. He himself readily acknowledged this motivation: "For my own part, I certainly cannot claim such impartiality as indifference might bring. From my earliest childhood—from my very first recollection—the desire for eternal life has immeasurably eclipsed for me every other wish or hope." Nevertheless, he went on to say, "*desire* is not necessarily *bias*," and he believed that "my wishes do not strongly warp my judgment...sometimes the very keenness of personal anxiety may make one afraid to believe, as readily as other men, that which one most longs for" (*HP*, vol. 2, p. 294). Believing that all aspects of the universe and human experience are part of some unified whole, he insisted that science and religion are not separate, or even separable, and his goal was, by bringing religion and science to bear on each other, to expand and strengthen both. On the one hand, therefore, he believed that science could "*prove the preamble of all religions*" (*HP*, vol. 2, p. 297)—namely, that the universe extends far beyond the perceptible material world. On the other hand, religion could contribute to "the expansion of Science herself until she can satisfy those questions which the human heart will rightly ask, but to which Religion alone has thus far attempted an answer" (*HP*, vol. 2, p.

47. Shortly after Myers's death, James addressed in detail the phenomenon of ecstasy, or mystical experience, in his 1902 Gifford lectures (1902/1958).

305). Whatever one thinks of the personal religious convictions that Myers drew from his work, his general goal of expanding science and psychology to include *all* aspects of human experience, from the most primitive physiological reflexes to the highest manifestations of creativity and mysticism, was one to which, we contend, scientists must return after more than a century of avoiding those "larger questions which the human heart will rightly ask."

Conclusion

Aldous Huxley (1961), comparing *Human Personality* to better-known writings on the "unconscious" by Freud and Jung, said: "How strange and how unfortunate it is that this amazingly rich, profound, and stimulating book should have been neglected in favor of descriptions of human nature less complete and of explanations less adequate to the given facts!" Evaluations of Myers and his work, however, both by his contemporaries and by later psychologists or historians of psychology, have been extraordinarily varied, both in the accuracy with which they have portrayed his ideas and in the conclusions they have drawn about the value of his work. Myers himself recognized that his ideas and theories were far-reaching and at many points possibly premature; but his conjectures and speculations were part of a deliberate attempt to encourage further empirical research: "My excuse for the bold and comprehensive way in which I have set forth [my] hypotheses ...[is that if] there is to be widespread effort there must be widespread interest; and such interest can only be evoked by an understanding of the vast importance of the discovery to which these small and scattered inquiries do manifestly, although remotely, tend" (Myers, 1892f, p. 534).

One of the most cogent evaluations of Myers was that of his friend and colleague William James,[48] upon whom Myers's ideas had a considerable and lasting impact.[49] Myers, he said, had identified psychology's most important

48. James's discussion of Myers's contributions to psychology (James, 1901) and his review of *Human Personality* (James, 1903) are reproduced in our digital version of *HP*.

49. Some James scholars have mistakenly credited James with developing the idea of the subliminal consciousness, upon which Myers then drew. Barzun, for example, claims that James, "with his usual generosity," gave credit to Myers, even though "two years before Myers, he [James] had written an article on 'The Hidden Self'" (Barzun, 1983, p. 230n); and McDermott (1986, p. xviii) echoes Barzun's claim. These writers are clearly unaware that Myers's ideas about a subliminal consciousness long predated the series of nine papers on the Subliminal Self that he began publishing in 1892 (see, e.g., Myers, 1884, 1885a, 1885b). As we will discuss further in Chapter 5, James himself said that the "discovery" of a consciousness "extra-marginal and outside of the primary consciousness" was made in 1886 (James, 1902/1958, p. 188). Although matters of priority are often difficult to sort out, especially since important ideas usually do not spring suddenly out of a void,

problem: "*The precise constitution of the subliminal*...is the problem which deserves to figure in our science hereafter as the *problem of Myers*" (James, 1901, pp. 17, 18). Moreover, "Myers has not only propounded the problem definitely, he has also invented definite methods for its solution....He is so far the only generalizer of the problem and the only user of all the methods" (p. 17). James similarly appreciated the vast range of psychological phenomena that Myers identified as pertinent to the problem (p. 16).

Additionally, James considered Myers's theory of human personality to be an important one: "It is a vast synthesis, but a coherent one....No one of the dots by which his map is plotted out, no one of the 'corners' required by his triangulation, is purely hypothetical. He offers empirical evidence for the concrete existence of every element which his scheme postulates and works with" (James, 1903, p. 30). To those who found Myers's theory "unsatisfactory," James pointed out that "no regular psychologist has ever tried his hand at the problem....Myers's map is the only scientifically serious investigation that has yet been offered" (p. 33).

James (1903) did express some reservations, to which we will return in Chapter 9, but one particularly worth noting here is:

> Most readers, even those who admire the scheme as a whole, will doubtless shrink from yielding their credence to it unreservedly....The types of case which he uses as stepping-stones are some of them, at present, either in quality or quantity, decidedly weak supports for the weight which the theory would rest upon them, and it remains at least possible that future records may not remedy this frailty. (p. 31)

In the remaining chapters of this book, we will examine many of the "stepping-stones" to which James refers, and we will argue that "future records" *have* to an unappreciated extent remedied their frailty. In the century since Myers's death, many of the observations he made have been powerfully reinforced by subsequent research. Perhaps more importantly, the intervening century of psychological research has reinforced the need for a theory of human personality which—like his—encompasses the full range of human experience.

---

it seems clear that the basic outlines of Myers's theory of subliminal consciousness were well in place in the 1880s.

Chapter 3

Psychophysiological Influence[1]

Emily Williams Kelly

> Phrases about "the influence of the mind on the body" are so often loosely adduced as though they were themselves the explanation needed, that it is as well to keep the real obscurity of the physiological problems in view. (Gurney, 1887a, p. 105)

The naturalization of mind begun in earnest in the 19th century has continued unabated, and the assumption that mind is wholly derivative from brain processes has strengthened and grown more pervasive over the last century. The consensus of nearly all scientists and philosophers today is that all aspects of mind and consciousness are byproducts of an evolving nervous system; and extremists such as the "eliminative materialists" even hold not only that all mental processes and concepts are in principle reducible to brain processes but that any reference to them in language other than that of physiology constitutes mere pre-scientific "folk psychology," to be abolished through further advances in physiology.

This widespread presumption of equivalence between mind and brain is based on the observations, both scientific and everyday, that the evolution of mind is correlated with the evolution of the nervous system and that changes in or injuries to the brain result in changes in or even abolition of consciousness. It is easy to forget, however, that correlation is not causation. As I pointed out in Chapter 2, the assumption that the correlation implies a

1. This chapter has been inspired largely by two great works, both of a remarkable breadth and depth of scholarship: *Reincarnation and Biology*, by Ian Stevenson (1997), and *The Future of the Body*, by Michael Murphy (1992).

unilateral dependence of consciousness on the brain has been exacerbated and entrenched because observations of the mind-brain relationship have been limited primarily to situations in which a change on the side of the brain is the independent variable and changes on the side of behavior or consciousness the dependent. What happens, however, when we expand our observations to phenomena in which a change in mental state clearly seems to be the initiating cause, and a change in a physiological or physical state the result—phenomena, in brief, relevant to a problem long neglected by psychologists, namely, the problem of volition?

In *Human Personality*, Myers laid out a wide variety of phenomena that had to be addressed by scientific research before the books were closed on the question of the nature of mind-brain correlation. Some of these—previously ignored, denied, or derided by scientists because they resisted a ready physiological explanation and seemed instead to harken back to a pre-scientific, magical way of thinking—are now finding their way back to the mainstream of scientific and medical thinking. This has happened not only because the phenomena continue to be observed, but much more importantly because scientists have begun to identify neurobiological processes that seem to bring them safely within the framework of the prevailing physiological model. But how complete and adequate are such models, even in principle if not yet in actuality, to explain the enormous variety of phenomena in which a mental state seems to have triggered a physiological reaction? As we will see, it is less than fully clear that they succeed even for phenomena that are becoming more widely acceptable. Moreover, many additional phenomena discussed by Myers continue to remain outside the mainstream of scientific and medical thinking, still ignored, denied, or derided, even though observations of these too have continued and, in some instances, grown substantially in number and quality.

There is, in short, a continuum of phenomena suggesting effects of mental state on physiological processes, ranging from those now increasingly accepted by the scientific community and seemingly explainable by physiological mechanisms to phenomena still routinely dismissed by most scientists as outside the explanatory framework of science. In this chapter I take the position that many of the latter phenomena rest on just as firm an empirical basis as the former and that, like the former, they must somehow be brought within the framework of science—science, that is, as a method and not as an ideology—before we can arrive at an adequate understanding of consciousness and volition. I will begin with phenomena of mind-body interaction that have gradually become accepted by scientists, and the theories that have begun to make them more acceptable, and then move further along the continuum to address phenomena that become progressively more difficult to account for within present models of mind and brain. For most of these phenomena there is an extensive amount of biomedical literature, which I will certainly not attempt to review exhaustively. The primary purposes of this chapter, rather, are: first, simply to call attention to the extraordinarily wide range of documented phenomena of psychophysical influence which seem to originate in or depend upon a person's beliefs or expectations, however those were generated; and second, to show how the more extreme and unusual of these phenomena challenge physiological models of any conventional sort.

I will begin by briefly describing the revolutionary developments of the last few decades in regard to mind-body medicine and "the faith that heals."[2] It is no exaggeration to say that there has been an explosion of interest in recent years in the question of whether, and when, psychological states or traits affect physical health, promoting both health and disease. Medical journals as well as the popular press have published numerous reports on studies of the relationship between physical health and spirituality, religion, personality, stress, depression, humor, imagery, meditation, and—that quintessential emblem of patient expectation and faith—the placebo. To be sure, many physicians and other scientists still support a statement made 20 years ago by a former editor of the *New England Journal of Medicine*: "The venerable belief that mental state is an important factor in the cause and cure of disease...is largely folklore" (Angell, 1985, pp. 1571–1572). Such resistance may be breaking down, however.

What has led to this increasing breakdown in resistance to, and the explosion of interest in, phenomena suggesting that mental factors contribute importantly to physical health? In this section I will first review developments in psychosomatic medicine and especially the burgeoning field of psychoneuroimmunology (PNI) that have recently made the concept of psychological influence on health more palatable to scientists. I will then briefly review how the findings of PNI have been applied to various phenomena. Finally, I will discuss research on the placebo effect, which illustrates the general shift in scientific opinion about mind and health.

Psychosomatic Medicine

Many physicians and historians of medicine have maintained that Western medicine is deeply tied to Cartesian-style dualism (see, e.g., G. L. Engel, 1977; Lipowski, 1984) and that "from Hippocrates on [it] has tended to be staunchly naturalistic and somatic, or physiologic" (Lipowski, 1984, p. 159). With the growing identification of specific agents of diseases in the 19th century, medicine became increasingly wedded to reductionism and a mechanistic model of disease in which the role of medicine was to repair malfunctioning of the biological machine. It is a mistake, however, to attribute a reductionistic view of disease and "noninteractionist" dualism to Des-

---

2. Two articles with this title have appeared in medical journals (Frank, 1975; Osler, 1910), and, although separated by 65 years (and even by culture, if the distinct difference in linguistic style can be taken as a measure of that), they both conveyed the same message: the importance in medicine of releasing the patient's own powers of healing.

cartes himself. Interaction of the two ontologically distinct "substances," mind and body, was in fact a central feature of Cartesian dualism; Descartes famously proposed that this interaction perhaps took place in the pineal gland. It was, in fact, chiefly this aspect of Cartesian dualism that has caused philosophical problems for many people ever since Descartes' time, because they cannot imagine how two substances so unlike can interact.[3] As a result, although the rigid separation of the workings of mind and body cannot be attributed to Descartes himself, it is nonetheless true that it was the influence of his substance dualism that led to the subsequent separation of physical and psychological processes and to a mechanistic determinism in medicine, and indeed in virtually all of modern Western science.

As Lipowski (1984, 1986) has described, modern psychosomatic medicine emerged in the early decades of the 20th century as a reaction against biological reductionism in medicine. It was initially focused around two concepts, namely, psychogenesis—the notion that psychological factors can cause and influence physical disease—and holism—the notion that mind and body are an indivisible unity. Although the initial purpose of psychosomatic medicine was "to bridge the gap that exists between the universe of psychological functioning and the universe of physiological functioning" (Ruesch, 1947, p. 291), more recently people have begun to argue that modern psychosomatic medicine has instead perpetuated dualism and deviated from holism (e.g., Fava & Sonino, 2000; Karlsson, 2000; Lipowski, 1984, 1986). Lipowski (1986), for example, has argued that the very concept of psychogenesis, with its implication that mental factors ("something 'psychic'") are a causative agent in disease ("something 'somatic'") (p. 4), is rooted in "unresolved issues of causality and dualism, and should best be buried" (Lipowski, 1984, p. 162). More bluntly, "the traditional concept of psychogenesis is obsolete" and "undermine[s] a much-needed holistic approach to the practice of medicine" (Lipowski, 1986, p. 4; 1984, p. 155).

Engel (1977) argued that not only psychiatry but "all medicine is in crisis...[because of its] adherence to a model of disease no longer adequate" (p. 129)—that is, the reductionistic model deriving from classical dualism. He proposed a new model that he christened "biopsychosocial." The hallmark of this model is the "psychobiological unity of man," which requires a "general systems" approach to health and disease in which all levels, from the molecular to the social and environmental, are linked (p. 134). Psychosomatic medicine therefore is no longer to be defined in traditional psychogenic terms as "the role of psychological factors in causing disease," but instead as "an integrative approach...based on a biopsychosocial view of illness" (Sharpe, Gill, Strain, & Mayou, 1996, p. 101).

This holistic or multifactorial view and the related systems approach have rapidly become widespread and influential, not only in medicine but also in psychology. This new perspective has contributed importantly to

3. More specifically, as I pointed out in Chapter 2, such interaction has seemed to many people necessarily to conflict with the law of energy conservation and hence to invite an abandonment of science.

breaking down the resistance to the idea that psychological factors can influence the body, because it essentially erases the problem by insisting on the unity, if not identity, of mind and brain. In essence, however, the change to the classical psychosomatic models consisted of recasting the "psychological" part as itself biological, with ideas, beliefs, expectations, and the like to be understood as patterns of neural activity. In consequence, some scientists have begun to speak of this unified psychophysiological entity as "the brain-mind" (e.g., H. Spiegel, 1997, p. 617).

A few authors have cautioned that there has been a too eager abandonment of the original "psychogenic" idea that psychological factors play "an important etiologic role in the production of disease" (Nemiah, 2000, p. 299). Moreover, although the currently prevailing view is that "the mind-body problem...cannot be viewed as the subject matter of psychosomatic medicine" (Lipowski, 1984, p. 168), a minority still think that "as a discipline, psychiatry should be deeply interested in the mind-body problem" (Kendler, 2001, p. 989). It is important to note also that the theoretical assumption of mind-body unity, or holism, is nevertheless itself frequently accompanied by a methodological dualism: "Mind and body may be regarded as abstractions derived for methodologic purposes," and the "most appropriate" position for medicine is "a *methodologic* and *linguistic* approach to the mind-body problem rather than a metaphysical one" (Lipowski, 1984, pp. 168, 161). The editor of the *American Journal of Psychiatry* spoke for many when she suggested that "the relationship between mind and brain has been extensively discussed...without any decisive resolution....One heuristic solution, therefore, is to adopt the position that the mind is the expression of the activity of the brain and that these two are separable for purposes of analysis and discussion but inseparable in actuality" (Andreasen, 1997, p. 1586).

As I discussed in Chapter 2, however, this methodological parallelism not only permits but encourages the evasion of important questions about the "how" of psychophysical interaction. In rejecting dualism and embracing a holistic systems model, "we have been evading the question of the 'how' of physical symptom formation, and so far extremely limited attention has been given to the matter of transition from a purely mental concept, such as consciousness, to very specific somatic alterations" (Sheikh, Kunzendorf, & Sheikh, 1996, p. 153). Moreover, most contemporary scientists go much further and believe that this assumption of mind-body inseparability is not simply a "heuristic solution" but an established fact: "We *know* that mind and brain are inseparable....Mental phenomena arise from the brain" (Gabbard, 2000, p. 117).

Psychoneuroimmunology

Resistance to the idea that mental factors can influence physical states has primarily been rooted in the lack of any theory to explain the interaction: "Physicians and scientists until recently dismissed such ideas as nonsense, because there did not appear to be a plausible biological mechanism to explain the link" (E. M. Sternberg, 2001, p. 16). The expression of an anti-dualistic, holistic approach to mind and body in the biopsychosocial model laid the groundwork, but the most important impetus to the readmittance of the idea that mental factors influence the body has come from a burgeoning field that seems to many scientists to provide a plausible biological mechanism, namely, psychoneuroimmunology (PNI). This field had its roots in the work of the physiologist Walter Cannon, the physician Hans Selye, and others, who showed that the body maintains its proper state of functioning by a self-regulating internal process (called by Cannon "homeostasis") and that stress is an important factor in upsetting the normal balance because, reflecting the body's reaction to environmental changes, it has widespread biochemical and neurophysiological effects. Solomon and Moos (1964) extended this picture by hypothesizing that stress could be immunosuppressive and in this way could influence health, but there was much resistance to this idea because it was then widely assumed that the immune system is autonomous and beyond the reach of influence by the central nervous system (see, e.g., Solomon, 1993; E. M. Sternberg, 2001).

Although evidence continued to accumulate, especially in psychosomatic medicine, for the influence of psychological factors on disease and health, and although it seems intuitive that "the two great systems that relate the organism to the outside world [that is, the nervous system and the immune system] 'ought' to talk to each other" (Solomon, 1993, p. 357), it took an experiment by Ader and Cohen (1975) to demonstrate such interaction conclusively. Using a classical conditioning paradigm, Ader and Cohen showed that the immune system of rats could be suppressed by exposing them first to an immunosuppressive drug coupled with saccharine, and then to the saccharine alone. Once the immune system had been shown to be responsive to conditioning of the central nervous system, this finding could be extended to account for the interaction between the immune system and central nervous system activity in response to stress.

PNI seeks to delineate physiological and functional connections between the brain and the immune system, and as such has been dubbed "the field of mind-body communication" (E. M. Sternberg, 2001, p. xi). The literature of PNI is now vast, but the key point for purposes of this chapter is that "even the greatest skeptic must now admit that a wealth of evidence exists to prove in the most stringent scientific terms that the functions of the mind do influence the health of the body....This level of proof [provided by PNI] of the myriad connections between the brain and the immune system was needed" (E. M. Sternberg, 2001, p. xvi). In particular, "by understanding these [mind-body] connections in modern terms, in the language of molecules and nerve pathways, electrical impulses and hormonal responses, scientists can finally accept that such effects are real" (E. M. Sternberg, 2001, p. 7). In the next few pages I will describe how scientists have begun to explain in these terms some specific psychophysical phenomena that had previously been viewed with suspicion, disbelief, and even disdain. The fundamental idea is that anything which produces prolonged stress or other strong emotions leads to biochemical changes that, by affecting systems such as the immune or cardiovascular system, can produce disease;[4] and, conversely, anything that relieves the stress can help reverse those effects, restore homeostatic balance, and, perhaps, improve health.

Mind and Disease

We begin with some phenomena of apparently psychogenic disease. There have been occasional reports of "mass hysteria" among co-workers, students, or other closely associated groups (see Hahn, 1997, pp. 63–64). When the symptoms are of a general systemic nature, they can perhaps best be explained by the stress associated with the sudden shared expectation or fear of becoming ill. Much more commonly reported and widely studied, however, has been the relationship between chronic negative emotions such as depression or hopelessness and illness (for a review see Wulsin, 2000; Wulsin, Vaillant, & Wells, 1999). For example, a study of over 2,400 patients in Finland showed that hopelessness, as measured by a simple two-item scale, was significantly correlated with higher rates of death from cardiovascular disease, cancer, and violence or injury, as well as with a higher incidence of nonfatal cancer and myocardial infarction (Everson et al., 1996). A feeling of hopelessness may have also been a major contributing factor in two other studies (D. P. Phillips, Ruth, & Wagner, 1993; D. P. Phillips et al., 2001), in which a complex of beliefs in traditional Asian medicine and astrology seemed to have contributed to mortality among people who held these beliefs, presumably because these beliefs led them "to feel helpless, hopeless, or stoic" (D. P. Phillips et al., 1993, p. 1142). Other studies have homed in more directly on the association between depression or hopelessness and cancer (e.g., M. Watson, Haviland, Greer, Davidson, & Bliss, 1999; see also Holden, 1978) or cardiovascular disease (e.g., Schulz et al., 2000). In addition to epidemiological studies, there is also evidence from prospective studies of healthy subjects for an association between depression and coronary heart disease (Haas et al., 2005).

---

4. In "modern" terms, "stress leads to increased adrenal cortical activity and consequent deficiency of T cells, [and] impairment of host defense system," and "the cost of chronic exposure to fluctuating or heightened neural or neuroendocrine response" and of "increased hypothalamic-pituatary-adrenal axis (HPA) activation" may be disease (Lipowski, 1977, p. 240; Fava & Sonino, 2000, p. 187; see also E. M. Sternberg & Gold, 2002).

Bereavement and Mortality

One of the most poignant examples of the relationship between negative emotions and disease comes from the numerous studies showing increased mortality after bereavement. As Jacobs and Ostfeld (1977) pointed out, the study of conjugal bereavement is particularly useful for examining the relationship between stress and illness, both because of its specificity and because of its severity. Jacobs and Ostfeld reviewed eight studies that had been conducted up to that time, all showing an increased risk of mortality during the first two years after bereavement, and especially among men during the first six months. McAvoy (1986) and J. R. Williams (2005) provide more recent reviews. In addition, Williams provides a brief review of studies showing both an increased incidence of depression among the bereaved and an association between depression and increased mortality from cardiovascular disease. In a large prospective study of nearly 100,000 widows and widowers, Kaprio, Koskenvuo, and Rita (1987) found a significantly higher rate of mortality immediately after bereavement, even as early as the first week.

Although most of the studies of the relationship between bereavement, depression, and mortality are epidemiological studies, some studies have attempted to pinpoint physiological mechanisms underlying the increased mortality. Bartrop, Lazarus, Luckhurst, Kiloh, and Penny (1977) measured lymphocyte function in 26 bereaved spouses, both two weeks and six weeks after their spouse's death. Their findings of depressed T-cell functioning showed "for the first time...a measurable abnormality in immune function" resulting from severe psychological stress (p. 834). Schleifer, Keller, Camerino, Thornton, and Stein (1983) replicated and extended this study by measuring lymphocyte stimulation responses in the spouses of 15 women with advanced breast cancer, measuring the responses several times before the spouse's death, as well as two months and one year after the death. The responses were significantly weaker after bereavement than before, "demonstrat[ing] that suppression of mitogen-induced lymphocyte stimulation in widowers is a direct consequence of the bereavement event" and not "a preexisting suppressed hormone state" (p. 376).

Sudden and "Voodoo" Death

Another example of the association between depression, bereavement, cardiovascular disease, and increased risk of death is the phenomenon of sudden death. Engel (e.g., 1966, 1968) wrote extensively on the relationship between stress, hopelessness, and mortality, which he called the "giving up-given up" complex, a phenomenon that had been demonstrated earlier in experimental studies of rats exposed to conditions of danger accompanied by hopelessness (Richter, 1957; see also G. L. Engel, 1978). In particular, Engel (1971) discussed numerous examples of people who have died suddenly, usually from cardiac arrest, shortly after receiving a sudden shock, such as news of a death or other serious loss, a sudden fright, or, occasionally, at a time of unusual joy. Although Engel's cases were ones he learned about anecdotally, either from media reports or from medical colleagues, a systematic study of 26 men who died suddenly found that both depression and an event causing acute anger or other emotion immediately preceded the death (W. A. Greene, Goldstein, & Moss, 1972); and a study of 100 men under the age of 70 who died suddenly found that the vast majority of them had been under unusual stress, within 30 minutes, 24 hours, or six months before the death (A. Myers & Dewar, 1975, p. 1137).

I mentioned above that some sudden deaths have occurred at a time of fear. Among the most well known of these cases of being "scared to death" are those commonly labeled "voodoo death," but also "hex death," "bone-pointing," or death by sorcery. In such cases, a person who has been cursed or otherwise led by another, usually authoritative, person to believe that he or she is going to die at a particular time does in fact die. The phenomenon has periodically been discussed in the Western medical and anthropological literature ever since physiologist Walter Cannon's 1942 paper describing some cases reported by anthropologists and physicians and proposing a physiological mechanism for them. It is often assumed that such cases are found primarily in preliterate societies. Despite the many difficulties in penetrating preliterate cultures by Western investigators and in obtaining adequate medical documentation in connection with suspected voodoo deaths, medical observers have continued to report similar observations. A. A. Watson (1973), for example, reported witnessing 9 or 10 such cases (in about four years) while he was medical officer at a small mission hospital in Zaire. One of them involved a native nurse who, now a Christian, had been "outspoken on the foolishness of accepting the belief in the death curse," but who nonetheless died within three days of learning that he himself had been cursed (p. 194). Even in the United States, belief in voodoo death, and associated cases, persist among particular sociocultural groups such as African-Americans (Golden, 1977, 1982; Tinling, 1967).

Such cases, however, are by no means limited to preliterate or "folk" societies; they also occur in modern Western cultures. Although superficially different, the general phenomenology of Western cases parallels that found in aboriginal or preliterate cultures. The belief that one is going to die may be generated, not by a witch doctor's curse, but by more culturally congruent phenomena such as a fortune teller's prediction (Barker, 1968), a doctor's pronouncement of a hopeless condition (Milton, 1973), or some other suggestion accepted by the patient. Both Myers (1895e, pp. 528–529) and Tuke (1884, pp. 112–113) described cases in which a prediction of death seemed to have contributed to the person's sudden death. More recently, Boitnott, Friesinger, and Slavin (1967) reported a case in which a midwife who had delivered three babies on the same day had predicted that the first would die before her 16th birthday (she did so, in an automobile accident), the second would die before her 21st birthday (she died on her 21st birthday), and the third (the subject of the report) would die before her 23rd birthday. This woman was admitted to the hospital, anxious, "terrified," and convinced that she was "doomed" because of the prediction; and she died there two weeks later, the day before her 23rd birthday, apparently of pulmonary hypertension.

Walters (1944) described a case of a woman who, because of a complex family situation, believed that she would die at the same age (42) as her mother. As Walters described the events: "Her last two weeks were marked by extreme excitement and fearfulness....She lapsed into a coma on the anniversary of her mother's death and died the day after, in the seventh month of her forty-second year....It is probable that the cause of death was renal failure brought about by acute emotionalism" (p. 84).

Another Western case more closely resembles voodoo death. Mathis (1964) reported the case of a man who first developed asthma at the age of 53 and died nine months later of an asthmatic attack. A closer examination of his history revealed that he suffered his first attack two days after his mother had cursed him for going against her wishes, saying "something dire will happen to you" as a result. His attacks all seemed to be precipitated by similar encounters with his mother. On the day of his death, at a 5:00 p.m. interview with a physician, "he was in excellent physical and mental condition." At 5:30 p.m. he had a telephone conversation with his mother, in which she repeated her warning. At 6:35 p.m. he was found semicomatose, and at 6:55 p.m. he was pronounced dead.

A letter to the editor of the *British Medical Journal* in 1965 (Elkington, Steele, & Yun, 1965) described the case of a 43-year-old woman who died following a minor operation. Years earlier she had been told by a fortune teller that she would die at 43, and before her operation she told both her sister and a nurse that she would not survive the operation. This report precipitated numerous additional letters to the editor, in many of which physicians reported their own observations of similar cases (e.g., Barker, 1965; Ellis, 1965; Hunter, 1965; Nelson, 1965; Nixon, 1965; P. J. W. Young, 1965). Barker (1965, 1966) appealed in two major medical journals for other cases of "auto-suggestion," particularly those generated by remarks of fortune tellers, and he subsequently published a short book on this and related phenomena (Barker, 1968).

A corollary of the belief in voodoo death is the belief that the curse can be overridden by the counter measures of a more powerful figure. Kirkpatrick (1981) described the case of a 28-year-old Philippine-American woman diagnosed with and treated for systemic lupus erythematosus. Although the treatments were at first successful, when her illness recurred she refused further treatment and returned to the Philippines, where her village's witch doctor "removed the curse placed on her by a previous suitor." She returned three weeks later, apparently cured, and continued in good health with no further conventional treatment for at least two years, when she gave birth to a child. Golden (1982) similarly described the case of an American man, admitted to a Veterans Administration hospital, whose wife had put a "spell" on him, but who "began to recover upon administration of a placebo liquid, with considerable emphasis as to its potency by the physician" (p. 40). Even more dramatic is a case described by Meador (1992) of an American man who was considered "doomed" by himself and his family because of a hex put on the patient by a voodoo priest. His physician likewise considered him to be "near death"; but he was successful in overriding the hex and setting in motion an almost instantaneous and rapid recovery by fully entering into the belief system of the patient and his family and conducting an elaborate and convincing counter-hex (pp. 244–245). The physicians in Golden's and Meador's cases, as well as the Filipino witch doctor in Kirkpatrick's case, had apparently gained the patient's confidence that they were more powerful than the original hexer.

Meador's paper is interesting and important in a more general sense, because the two cases he described blur the lines between deaths associated with "primitive" folk beliefs and those occurring in modern medical circumstances. In the case described above, both the illness and subsequent cure were strongly associated with the patient's belief in hexing. The other case involved an elderly man who had been given the diagnosis of widespread, incurable liver cancer. He and everyone around him believed in the finality of this diagnosis, and he died shortly thereafter. An autopsy, however, revealed that the diagnosis had been a false positive; only a small cancerous nodule was found, insufficient to have caused death.

Meador's (1992) second case in fact illustrates several aspects of the relationship between psychological factors and disease. The patient had lost his wife under particularly tragic and sudden circumstances; as he described it, "everything I ever loved or wanted in my whole life vanished. Gone forever....My heart and soul were lost in the flood that night" (p. 246). Within six months of her death, he was diagnosed with cancer. When he was told in October that he had only a short time to live, he said he would like to live through Christmas for his family's sake. He was seen at monthly intervals and "looked quite good on each visit," but in early January he was readmitted to the hospital and died 24 hours later. The case is a vivid example of the relationship between bereavement and depression in the onset of disease, the apparently deliberate postponement of death until after a significant occasion (to be discussed more fully below), and death associated with suggestion. Meador considered both cases to be examples of "hex death," defining a hex death as "a ritualized pronouncement of death by someone perceived by the subject to have immense power and authority" (p. 244); and he asked "are we so different from our ancient and primitive witch doctor colleagues?" The only difference is cultural; and in modern culture "the idea that words or symbolic actions can cause death...challenges our biomolecular model of the world...and we tend to deny that a phenomenon exists until it can be explained in molecular terms" (p. 247).

Possible Mechanisms Behind Psychological Factors in Mortality

Noting that before the 20th century physicians routinely took into account the influence of mental state on the health of patients, Engel (1968) asked: "How is it that such insights could have vanished so completely from medical writings for so long?" (p. 363). In a later paper he further commented that "consideration of the relationship between emotion and sudden death has virtually disappeared from the medical literature, or at best the idea is greeted with scepticism if not incredulity or downright ridicule" (G. L. Engel, 1971, p. 772). Since Engel made those remarks, and perhaps to a great extent because of him, the relationship between stress and illness or death has become a major focus of research, the attitude shifting from incredulity to a search for the underlying physiological mechanisms.[5] As I mentioned earlier, that search has been prompted primarily by the findings of PNI that stress and associated strong emotions produce physiological effects which can precipitate disease. Phenomena such as voodoo death have thus begun to be taken more seriously precisely because of the growing belief that "such deaths may be explained in physicalistic terms" (Lachman, 1982–1983, p. 347).

Particularly important to this change in attitude has been research showing that the activation of the hypothalamic-pituitary-adrenal (HPA) axis by stress leads to the release of corticosteroids, which have profound effects on the immune system. Explanations along these lines have been proposed in particular for the mechanism by which stress and emotion can lead to sudden death. Cannon (1942) himself suggested that voodoo death was the result of "the persistent excessive activity of the sympathico-adrenal system," precipitated by extreme fear and unrelieved by any action on the part of the victim, who believes that he can do nothing to prevent his death.[6] In an editorial on the 60th anniversary of the publication of Cannon's paper, E. M. Sternberg (2002) credited his work with "form[ing] the basis of much of our modern understanding of the physiological response systems

---

5. See, for example, an extensive review of studies showing a relationship between psychological factors and cardiovascular disease, as well as a discussion of some physiological mechanisms that may be behind the relationship (Rozanski, Blumenthal, & Kaplan, 1999).

6. Similarly, Fry (1965) and, more recently, Wittstein et al. (2005) have suggested that increased activity of the sympathetic nervous system produced by stress can lead to sudden death. In contrast, Spieker et al. (2002) thought that "a contribution of the sympathetic nervous system to the derangement of vascular function after mental stress could be excluded" (p. 2819); and Richter (1957) suggested that the deaths of the rats in his study seemed to involve overactivity of the parasympathetic nervous system. Other researchers (G. L. Engel, 1971, 1978; Lex, 1974) have proposed that *both* the sympathetic and the parasympathetic systems—or, in more operational terms, the "flight-or-fight" and "conservation-withdrawal" reactions of the biological defense system—are involved. Such debates, however, concern only the detailed mechanisms involved, and not the basic premise that stress has profound effects on the body.

involved in linking emotions, such as fear, with illness" (p. 1564). Moreover, she concluded that "most of Cannon's proposed explanations" have been upheld by subsequent research on the role of the massive release of stress hormones and other neurochemicals in causing disease. The picture remains complicated, because research on the relationship between depression and specific immune system measures and diseases (such as HIV) has often produced inconsistent results (M. Stein, Miller, & Trustman, 1991). Nonetheless, increased understanding of the mechanisms seems likely to come from advances in basic PNI research. Meanwhile, perhaps the best lesson to take away from all these phenomena is that "unless you have something to live for you die before your time" ("Pertinax," 1965, p. 876).

Mind and Health

The relationship between psychological factors and health is not limited to the role of mental states in the etiology or prognosis of disease. If negative emotions can contribute to disease and even death, positive ones ought conversely to contribute to improvements in health or even healing. Cousins (1976) was instrumental in bringing widespread attention to this idea. Confronted with a serious illness with little hope of full recovery, he recalled Selye's (1956) demonstration that stress and negative emotions can lead to illness, and he wondered whether the opposite might not also be true. As a result, he undertook a regime that consisted, among other things, of improving his psychological state by daily doses of humor and laughter. He recovered, and concluded that "the will to live is not a theoretical abstraction but a physiologic reality" (p. 1462). Since then he has supported research on the relationship between positive emotions and health, including the study of laughter and its impact on stress hormones and other physiological measures (Berk et al., 1989). More generally, numerous studies have shown the efficacy of interventions such as relaxation training, meditation, imagery, biofeedback, and hypnosis in alleviating pain and perhaps also in improving conditions associated with cancer, cardiovascular disease, and surgery (for a review, see Astin, Shapiro, Eisenberg, & Forys, 2003).

Postponement of Death

One example of the "will to live" described by Cousins is that some people seem to have postponed their death until after some meaningful occasion, such as the arrival of a loved one or a significant day (Callanan & Kelley, 1993). I mentioned above Meador's (1992) patient, who announced his desire to live through Christmas, and then died shortly afterward. A more famous example is that of Thomas Jefferson and John Adams, both of whom died on July 4, 1826, exactly 50 years after the Declaration of

Independence was signed. Although there is no direct evidence that either one expressed the wish to live until that date, Jefferson's last words—"Is it the Fourth?"—suggest that this meaningful occasion was prominent in his mind (Peterson, 1970, p. 1008). More generally, some epidemiological studies (D. P. Phillips & King, 1988; D. P. Phillips & Smith, 1990) have shown a significant dip in mortality rate just prior to an event culturally significant to the individual and a subsequent rise in mortality immediately afterward, again suggesting that the "will to live" may keep a person alive, but only until the event has passed.

Religion and Health

A more general manifestation of the relationship between positive mental factors and health is one that has received an enormous amount of attention in recent years in both the medical literature and the popular media—namely, the effect of religious involvement on health. Reviews over the past decade (e.g., Koenig, McCullough, & Larson, 2001; Levin, 1994; Luskin, 2000; Matthews et al., 1998; Mueller, Plevak, & Rummans, 2001; L. H. Powell, Shahabi, & Thoresen, 2003) have shown not only that there has been growing, widespread interest in the relationship, but also that the "quantity as well as methodological quality" of studies conducted since the 1990s have increased "markedly" (W. R. Miller & Thoresen, 2003, p. 26). Matthews et al. (1998), for example, looked at the relationship between religious commitment and prevention of illness, coping with illness, and recovery from illness, and concluded that a "large proportion of published empirical data" suggests a positive correlation (p. 118). Luskin (2000) looked primarily at the association with cardiovascular and pulmonary disease, and he too thought that the evidence, although primarily from correlational studies, is "suggestive." In a much more extensive review, Koenig et al. (2001) examined over 1,300 studies on the relationship between religious factors and various aspects of mental and physical health. In particular, the studies looking at physical health suggested that religious involvement correlates with improved immune system function and a lower risk of cardiovascular disease, hypertension, stroke, pain, and mortality in general. Levin (1994), reviewing "hundreds of studies," concluded that as a body of evidence they show "statistically significant, salutory effects of religious indicators on morbidity and mortality" (p. 1475). Cautioning that correlation does not imply causation, he broke the problem down further by asking: "Is there an association?"; "Is it valid?"; and "Is it causal?" On the basis of the studies reviewed, he answered the first question "yes"; after reviewing a variety of possibly confounding variables, he answered the second "probably"; and after emphasizing the multifactorial nature of causality for such a phenomenon, he answered the third "maybe."

There have also, however, been strong critics of this literature. Sloan, Bagiella, and Powell (1999) in particular have criticized such studies as inconsistent and often methodologically weak. Moreover, they regard the introduction of spirituality and religion into medical practice as ethically suspect. As a result of both problems, they argued that "suggestions that religious activity will promote health, [and] that illness is the result of insufficient faith, are unwarranted" (p. 667). Nearly all reviewers on this subject have acknowledged that most research to date is based on epidemiological data or on prospective cohort studies, and not on randomized clinical trials where contributing factors can be more carefully controlled (e.g.,, Koenig et al., 2001, p. 382). Most researchers, however, have considered this weakness as one to be remedied in future research, and not as a reason for dismissing what has already been done (e.g., McCullough, Larson, Hoyt, Koenig, & Thoresen, 2000, p. 220; L. H. Powell et al., 2003, p. 50).

Moreover, recent statistical and methodological reviews have shown that there have in fact been studies methodologically sufficient to warrant further research. In a series of papers in the *American Psychologist* (W. R. Miller & Thoresen, 2003; L. H. Powell et al., 2003; Seeman, Dubin, & Seeman, 2003), the authors used a levels-of-evidence approach in which they judged and ranked studies in terms of methodological soundness. The strongest finding was of "a strong, consistent, prospective, and often graded reduction in risk of mortality in church/service attendees" (L. H. Powell et al., 2003, p. 36). Consistent with this finding is a study that used a meta-analytic, rather than levels-of-evidence, approach (McCullough et al., 2000). In 42 independent studies based on samples of almost 126,000 people, the meta-analysis also revealed a significant correlation between religious involvement and reduction of mortality from a variety of causes.

Meditation and Healing

Another strong finding from the analyses in the *American Psychologist* series concerns the relationship between meditative practices and better health (Seeman et al., 2003). I will return to the topic of meditation below in regard to the apparent ability of yogis and other contemplatives to control autonomic functions; but here I will mention just briefly a few additional meditation studies not covered by Seeman et al. G. R. Smith, McKenzie, Marmer, and Steele (1985) described the case of "an experienced meditator" with a hypersensitivity to a viral antigen. Apparently by a combination of her usual daily meditation and a process of visualization, she "could voluntarily modulate her immune responses by a psychic mechanism....the subject, acting with intention, was able to affect not only her skin test response but also the response of her lymphocytes studied in the laboratory" (p. 2111).

Meares (e.g., 1977, 1979, 1980) has described his work with advanced or terminal cancer patients who undertook, under his training and supervision, an intensive program of meditation. Of 73 patients thus treated, nearly all received relief from pain and anxiety. In about 10% of the patients the growth of the tumor was slowed, and another 10% also "far outlived" the original prognosis of their oncologists (Meares, 1980, p. 323). More dramatically, five had a complete regression "in the absence of any organic treatment which could possibly account for it," and five more seemed "well on their way" to a similar regression. Meares (1981, 1983) proposed a mechanism for the remissions: On the assumption that cancer is related to a failure of the immune system, he proposed that meditation, by lowering the patient's anxiety and feelings of stress, also lowers cortisone production, adrenaline levels, and the activity of the sympathetic nervous system, thus boosting the functioning of the immune system.[7]

Meares suggested that a similar process might explain some cases of spontaneous regression of cancer (Meares, 1977, p. 133). There have been several reviews of this phenomenon (see in particular Challis & Stam, 1990; O'Regan & Hirshberg, 1993). All defined spontaneous regression as the partial or complete disappearance of a malignancy in the absence of any treatment, or with treatment generally considered inadequate to bring about the observed results (Challis & Stam, 1990, p. 545). Even with this restrictive definition, it is clear that hundreds of such remissions have been reported in the medical literature, and furthermore that the usual "explanation" in terms of mistaken diagnosis is wholly inadequate. Unfortunately, however, practically none of the reports include a description of the psychological conditions surrounding the remission (one exception is Ikemi, Nakagawa, Nakagawa, & Sugita, 1975, but their report was limited to five cases). Any attempt to evaluate either Meares's hypothesis or any other more comprehensive, "biopsychosocial" view of remissions must await more detailed reports.

Faith Healing

The phenomenon known as faith healing, spiritual healing, and a variety of other names has been defined as "any purely mental effort undertaken by one person with the intention to improve physical or emotional well-being in another" (Targ, 1997, p. 74). The medical community has occasionally responded to the continuing reliance among the general public on such healing by examining the history and claims for alternative forms of healing (see, e.g., a section of the 1910 *British Medical Journal* devoted to this topic). In 1893 Myers and his brother A. T. Myers, a physician, published a paper in response to the then widespread interest in apparent cures of diseases

7. Another contributing factor may have been Meares himself. In line with my earlier discussion of the role of authoritative figures in creating or removing a "curse" of death, Meares's own apparent conviction of the efficacy of meditation in healing, together with his insistence on a particular practice—even ritual—that was not to be deviated from, may have profoundly influenced his patients' beliefs and expectations. A similar factor seems to be involved in placebo/nocebo effects, which I discuss later in this chapter.

with mesmerism, at the shrine at Lourdes, and by "mind-healers." Although deploring the too frequent lack of firsthand or medical testimony in such cases, they concluded that the *occurrence* of some such cures was "certain....Cures are and always have been effected by other than demonstrably physiological means" (Myers & Myers, 1893, p. 164). What was still very much unresolved was the *explanation* of the cures. In their view there was at that time no adequate evidence for any mechanism beyond the activation of the person's "own inward forces" by self-suggestion (p. 207). Nevertheless, even if healing is the result of self-suggestion, the mechanism—be it faith in mesmerism, in Lourdes, in the healer, or in something else—is not to be dismissed as insignificant. In the first place, the mechanism behind self-suggestion has shown "the power of evoking the imagination to a degree and in a manner in which nothing else has ever evoked it" (Gurney & Myers, 1885, p. 406). Also, it remains unknown how the "imagination" or faith can activate these self-healing forces—themselves yet another unknown.

Now once again, with the recent burgeoning of alternative and complementary medicine in this country and in Europe, the scientific and medical community has turned its attention to evaluating seriously some of these claims. In the United States, the Office of Alternative Medicine (now the National Center for Alternative and Complementary Medicine), at the National Institutes of Health, was founded in 1992, and its budget grew from $2 million in 1992 to $123.1 million in 2005. Among the many topics of interest, especially among the general public, has been faith or spiritual healing. Such healing includes not only that occurring under the auspices of a particular religion, but also healing by practitioners who profess no faith except in their ability to heal by transferring some power or energy to the patient, usually to correct some imbalance thought to be causing the disease and to activate the patient's self-healing capacities (R. D. Hodges & Scofield, 1995, p. 205). I will discuss the phenomenon of distant healing and prayer under double-blind conditions later in the chapter, but here I limit the discussion primarily to healing in a context in which patients know they are being treated by a healer and hence in which self-suggestion seems likely to be a factor.[8]

One example of healing apparently through some form of faith on the part of the patient is that of John Fagan, which received widespread publicity. A physician knowledgeable about this case published a report concerning its medical aspects (Curran, 1976). Diagnosed with and operated on for invasive cancer of the stomach in the spring of 1965, Fagan slowly deteriorated for the next two years. By 1967 he had deteriorated to the point that during the weekend of March 4th–5th his doctor said that his death was imminent. On March 6th, however, he roused, asked to eat, and from

8. I emphasize here that self-suggestion is likely to be *a* factor, perhaps even the most important one; but it is important to keep in mind that the source of the effect is not always clear. As I will discuss later in the chapter, there is also strong evidence supporting the idea that one person can deliberately influence the physiology of another person.

then on "made an uninterrupted recovery" (p. 333). Clinical and radiological examinations carried out in 1971 showed no sign of the tumor. The only intervention apparent at the time his recovery began consisted of "the family appeal to the intercession of the Blessed John Ogilvie [a 17th-century Scottish Reformation martyr]," accompanied by prayers and novenas on the part of local parishioners (p. 333). The case was offered in support of Ogilvie's canonization, and in accordance with the formal procedures of the Catholic Church the testimony of many medical witnesses was gathered. As Curran noted (p. 335), contrary opinions were expressed by some other medical specialists, "but invariably without a full knowledge of all the relevant details."

In another case, the role of "faith," and hence of self-suggestion, is somewhat less clear. Dunbar (1954) described a 1931 report in a medical journal of a case involving a professor with chronic and longstanding eczema who was cured in one day after going to a woman known for her cures by prayer. He had originally refused to go to her because he was an atheist, but he finally went at his family's urging and out of desperation for relief (p. 617).

R. Gardner (1983) reported seven cases, most of them observed by British physicians (including himself) between 1951 and 1982, in which healing of a variety of serious and even life-threatening conditions began shortly after the patient had been prayed for. In six of these cases the patient was an adult present during the prayers (although unconscious in at least two cases). One involved a young physician in Wales with meningitis that developed into Waterhouse-Friderichsen syndrome, an adrenal gland failure that is often fatal. Although "no such case had ever survived in that hospital," she recovered suddenly and swiftly after several groups prayed for her (p. 1929). Two cases—one involving severe hemorrhaging prior to and after a caesarean delivery, the other involving abdominal hemorrhage from a ruptured spleen—occurred in remote places in which medical facilities and supplies were minimal. The missionary physicians present attested to the rapid and complete healing after the patients were prayed for, despite the almost complete lack of conventional treatment available. A nun in Germany recovered from a broken pelvis unusually rapidly and also without conventional treatment, her recovery clearly beginning almost instantly after prayers and "laying on of hands" by other nuns. In the fifth case, a young girl with a serious and longstanding leg ulcer asked for healing at a prayer meeting: "By next morning almost the whole ulcer had dried up with healthy skin covering; but one spot continued to exude pus." A week later the group conducted more prayers and "laying on of hands," and "healing became immediately complete" (p. 1932). In the sixth case involving an adult, no diagnosis was given, but the patient, a villager in Thailand, was thought to have died by missionaries and villagers present. The missionaries prayed for her, and "twenty minutes later she sat up" (p. 1932). Although, as Gardner pointed out, there is "not the slightest proof that...[she] actually died," her almost instantaneous recovery after the praying, from whatever condition she was in, is at least noteworthy.[9]

In the seventh case reported by Gardner, attributing the recovery to the patient's "faith" or to self-suggestion again becomes more problematic. This case involved an infant in England diagnosed with advanced fibrosing alveolitis, for which the prognosis "is *almost* uniformly fatal" in such a young child (p. 1928). He failed to respond to conventional treatment and after three months in the hospital was discharged home with a "hopeless" prognosis, with "maintenance" medication only. After being taken to a local prayer service—at the suggestion of his physician—he began a rapid and ultimately complete recovery.

Gardner compared these contemporary cases, in most of which there is "no doubt as to the accuracy of the diagnosis or clinical details" (p. 1930), with similar cases reported by the historian Bede in the 7th century; and he concluded from the similarities that older cases lacking in adequate medical documentation are not necessarily to be dismissed on that account alone. Moreover, one might add, cases with clear medical documentation cannot be ignored or dismissed as "anecdotes" or on the grounds that the reporters had, like Bede, a Christian orientation and, presumably, interpretation of the healings. Another physician has published reports of "miraculous" healings in a strongly Christian context (Casdorph, 1976). Casdorph described 10 cases of rapid and complete healing of serious and longstanding illnesses, including rheumatoid arthritis, multiple sclerosis, various kinds of cancer (bone, brain, and kidney), and other debilitating and life-threatening diseases that had not been, or could not be, cured by conventional medical treatment. All occurred during the 1970s either during or shortly after the patient attended a large public service conducted by the well-known healer Kathryn Kuhlman; and all are extensively documented with medical records studied by Dr. Casdorph, as well as by testimony obtained from the patients and the physicians involved.

Although Gardner's report was published in the *British Medical Journal*, most medical journals have refused to publish studies on faith healing (Benor, 1990, p. 9).[10] As a result, almost all of the research studies, as well as reviews of them, have been published in relatively obscure specialty journals, such as parapsychology journals (which are, however, peer-reviewed) or ones devoted to alternative and complementary medicine (e.g., Abbot, 2000; Benor, 1990; Schouten, 1993a, 1993b; Solfvin, 1984).

---

9. Interestingly, although this case occurred in rural Thailand in 1963, the woman also described an experience that seems much like the near-death experiences that have been widely reported in the West in recent decades (see our Chapter 6): She said that "she had met Christ, had seen into heaven, but was told she must go back and report what she had seen" (Gardner, 1983, p. 1932).

10. Casdorph has published research papers on other topics in prestigious medical journals, but his reports of unusual healings were published in a popular book. One wonders whether he tried, without success, to publish these reports in professional journals.

Most reviewers have covered a highly heterogeneous group of studies, including studies conducted on nonhuman targets, on human subjects aware of the intended intervention, and on human subjects kept blind as to whether or not they were being treated. Abbot (2000), for example, reviewed 22 studies involving randomized clinical trials, which were almost evenly split between distant healing studies and studies involving contact between the healer and the patient. The results of the studies were also almost evenly split, with 10 showing a significant positive effect (five of them involving distant-healing and five direct contact). Moreover, there did not seem to be a relationship between the methodological quality of the study and the results. Because of these mixed results, and because of the "significant heterogeneity" in the studies with regard to healing method used, medical condition treated, outcome measure, and control intervention, Abbot decided—as have most other reviewers and researchers—that no firm conclusion can yet be drawn, but that there has been enough positive evidence from studies of good quality to warrant further and better research on faith healing.[11]

---

11. I mentioned earlier that few medical journals would publish results of faith or spiritual healing studies, regardless of their quality, until recent years. When the prestigious *JAMA* (*Journal of the American Medical Association*) finally broke this ban in its pages, it did so in an unusual and revealing way. Specifically, in 1998 the editors of *JAMA* published a science-fair project of a 9-year-old 4th-grader who herself had designed and carried out an experiment to test the practice of Therapeutic Touch (TT), and in particular "whether TT practitioners can actually perceive a 'human energy field'" (Rosa, Rosa, Sarner, & Barrett, 1998, p. 1005). Finding that the "practitioners were unable to detect the investigator's 'energy fields,'" the authors concluded that this study provided "unrefuted [sic] evidence that the claims of TT are groundless and that further professional use is unjustified" (p. 1005).

However, as 12 letters to the editor about this paper unanimously pointed out, such a sweeping conclusion was premature, biased, and irresponsible. One clinician summed up the study as "simpleminded, methodologically flawed, and irrelevant" (Freinkel, 1998, p. 1905). Several others described some of its serious methodological flaws. Others recognized that the authors failed to make the important distinction between the efficacy of the method and the theoretical underpinning proposed by practitioners: "The definitive test of a healing practice is whether healing takes place, not whether the practitioners have a flawless grasp of the natural forces at work" (Lee, 1998, p. 1905). It is remarkable—but unfortunately not uncommon—that the editors of this major journal would publish a paper that sweepingly dismisses a whole complex and controversial phenomenon solely on the basis of one small and highly flawed study—especially since they have not, to my knowledge, published a review or research paper with more moderate and reliable conclusions. One can only conclude that this affair reflects a deep-seated bias on the part of the editors, where "one would expect medical professionals to be more concerned with whether real healing takes place" (Lee, 1998, p. 1906). It is not difficult to guess what would have been the fate of a paper submitted by similar authors, with similarly flawed methodology and conclusions, if the results had been positive and not in accord with editorial bias. For more responsible reviews of TT, see Astin, Harkness, and Ernst (2000), Peters (1999), and Wardell and Weymouth (2004).

I turn now to cases, like that of John Fagan, in which the healing agency seems not to have been another person deliberately attempting to heal someone, and in which the hypothesis of healing by self-suggestion is therefore particularly strong. One of the most well-known—and controversial—of the claims involving "faith healing" is the venerable belief that visits to certain places or shrines, such as the hundreds of healing temples of ancient Greece, can result in healing. The best known of such places is the shrine at Lourdes, in France. Since 1858, when a young girl claimed to see an apparition of the Virgin Mary at a spring, millions of people have visited the place in the hope of being cured, and there has been an ongoing and still very much unresolved debate about the nature of the cures that have occurred: The faithful attribute them to miracles, while the skeptical pronounce them instances of misdiagnosis, chance spontaneous recovery, or psychosomatic recovery from functional rather than organic ailments. Lourdes is unique as a healing shrine, in terms of the level of involvement of physicians in the evaluation of the cases. One prominent physician—a Nobel laureate in medicine—himself witnessed the sudden and to him unprecedented recovery of a woman near death from tubercular peritonitis (Carrel, 1950). More generally, since the late 19th century there have been investigative bodies of physicians charged with evaluating claims of cures. Dowling (1984) gives a good brief description of the history, procedures, and standards of medical evaluation at Lourdes.

Not all observers, however, have found the medical evaluations adequate. D. J. West (1957), a physician, examined 11 cases that occurred between 1937 and 1952, the only cures during that time period ultimately pronounced "miraculous" by an Ecclesiastical Commission after first passing through two levels of medical evaluation (the Lourdes Medical Bureau and then a Medical Commission in Paris). He arrived at a conclusion similar to that of Myers and Myers (1893) 64 years earlier—namely, that the medical documentation in all the cases was too incomplete (and sometimes even biased and distorted) for a reliable assessment of the patient's condition before and after the visit to Lourdes. In his review West had two aims. The first was to determine whether the Lourdes cures were of "a remarkable kind, such as are not ordinarily encountered in medical experience" (p. 11); and his answer was "No." There was no restoration of lost limbs, for example, and "in no case is a sudden structural change confirmed by the evidence of X-rays taken just before and just after the event" (p. 122). Instead, "the great majority of cures concern potentially recoverable conditions and are remarkable only in the speed and manner in which they are said to have taken place" (p. 122). Secondly, West asked whether the cures were "inexplicable," and again he answered "No," insisting that many of even the best cases "are in fact readily explainable in ordinary terms" (p. 122). He favored the view that most of the cases are the result either of the psychosomatic healing of a functional disease that had been misdiagnosed as an organic one, or that they were the result of a spontaneous, naturally occurring recovery in patients "whose recuperative powers seemed suddenly to reassert themselves" (p. 13).[12]

West was quite right to point out that what occurs at Lourdes is not unique, in that similar cases can be found in other contexts. Nonetheless, was he right in saying that there is a "rational physiological basis" (p. 119) for the Lourdes cures and that they are thus "readily explainable"? Even if a disease is "functional" and not "organic"—a distinction that West himself emphasized is not one that can be clearly made—do we understand what these "recuperative powers" are or how and when they work? Do we really understand the physiological basis of rapid healing by hypnosis or any other means of suggestion? Such questions are fundamental, not only in connection with Lourdes cases, but in connection with all the phenomena that I am discussing in this chapter, including the effects of self-suggestion on physiological conditions.

Since 1954, moreover—and therefore after the occurrence of the cases examined by West—the medical evaluation at Lourdes has been extended such that medical dossiers on cases that seem worthy of further follow-up have been passed on to an international body of physicians. This committee examines all available medical documentation to determine whether a correct diagnosis was made; whether the disease was both organic and serious; whether there was a possibility that the disease disappeared spontaneously or in response to medical treatment; whether the symptoms disappeared; how sudden and complete the cure was; and how long the cure persisted. Out of 38 dossiers sent to this committee between 1954 and 1984, 19 have been judged "medically and scientifically inexplicable" (Dowling, 1984, p. 637).[13]

Much of the literature on Lourdes is in French. There are, however, several good sources in English published after West's book, and also after the 1954 establishment of the international body of medical evaluators (e.g., Dowling, 1984; Garner, 1974; M. Murphy, 1992, pp. 267–271). These report several cases not discussed by West, including one older case (the 1923 case of John Traynor) and three more recent ones (those of Vittorio Micheli [1963], Serge Perrin [1970], and Delizia Cirolli [1976]), in all four of which there was extensive medical documentation. In the case of Vittorio Micheli, for example, X-rays showed "an almost complete destruction of the left pelvis" as a result of sarcoma (Garner, 1974, p. 1257). At Lourdes in May 1963, Micheli felt an immediate disappearance of his long-standing pain and a subjective sense that he was cured. Within a month, he was walking, and within three months X-rays "showed that the sarcoma had regressed and the bone of the pelvis was recuperating" (p. 1259). In a similar case, 12-year-

12. As examples of such recuperative powers, he cites (pp. 19–20, 119) some of the kinds of phenomena that I will discuss at greater length later in this chapter, such as accelerated healing of skin diseases by hypnosis.

13. As Dowling and others have emphasized, however, declaring a cure "medically inexplicable" is *not* synonymous with declaring it a "miracle"—the latter being a theological, not scientific, designation.

old Delizia Cirolli went to Lourdes in August 1976 with a diagnosis (made by X-rays and a biopsy) of a bony metastasis of a neuroblastoma. There was no improvement, and she continued to decline, X-rays in September showing further growth of the cancer. Villagers prayed for her, however, and her mother regularly gave her Lourdes water. By Christmas, weighing less than 50 pounds, she began to recover. Subsequent X-rays showed the bone repairing, and ultimately cured. Although "there was no doubt she had been cured," the exact nature of the diagnosis was in some doubt. Doctors ultimately decided that Ewing's tumor was more likely than a neuroblastoma; but whether a neuroblastoma or a Ewing's tumor, spontaneous remissions are either rare or unknown (Dowling, 1984, p. 636).

Again, what are we to make of such cases? Clearly we cannot dismiss them as based on unreliable or distorted "anecdotes." But is it then an adequate explanation simply to say that some self-healing power, perhaps within the neuroimmunological system, has been activated in some unusually potent way? What is this self-healing power, how is it activated, and how does it work, not only in the repair of a bone seriously damaged by cancer, but even in less dramatic illnesses? Do "spontaneous" cures and remissions—whether those that are frequently seen or those that are rare—occur only by "chance"?

Placebo and Nocebo

Closely related to all the phenomena I have discussed so far—some now accepted as genuine, some still viewed with considerable skepticism—is a phenomenon that has occupied an odd place in the history of modern medicine, namely, the placebo effect and its obverse, the nocebo effect. Scientists have struggled even with the problem of *defining* placebo/nocebo[14]—let alone explaining it—primarily because most of them wish to avoid charges of dualism, and thus they reject definitions that involve any "tortuous attempts to define the placebo as a belief state separable from the purely physical effect of a drug or of surgery" (Wall, 1996, p. 163). Many insist, as we saw earlier, that mind and body are a unified entity—"brain-mind"—and on this basis some have suggested, rather vaguely, that placebo/nocebo effects are "meaning responses" (Moerman, 2000, p. 56) or "context effects" (Kleijnen, 2000). As I will argue throughout this chapter, however, such assumptions and terms provide neither definitions nor explanations.

A placebo (or nocebo) is an intervention that has no known direct physiological consequences but nevertheless improves (or worsens) a person's health. For a more precise definition, however, "dualistic" terms seem unavoidable to convey the basic idea that a psychological factor seems to have precipitated a change in a physiological condition. As Kihlstrom

14. Thompson (2005) discusses the problem of defining placebo (pp. 27–28) and provides a table listing 18 different dictionary definitions from 1785 to 2001 (pp. 18–21).

(1993a) cautiously recognized, the placebo response suggests "the reverse of the conventional way of thinking about the mind-body problem. We usually think about mental states as emerging from physiological processes. In placebo, there is a mental state that seems to alter physiological processes" (p. 215).

There has thus been widespread resistance to and skepticism about the notion of a placebo effect—despite the professed belief of many scientists in a unified "brain-mind"—because "it poses a serious challenge to much of the ideology of biomedicine...[that] disease is a mechanical phenomenon" (Moerman, 2000, p. 65). The placebo's odd place in the history of modern medicine derives from the conflict between this relatively new but now prevailing mechanistic assumption in Western medicine and the old, long-standing assumption in medicine that "faith heals." The issue came to a head after the 1940s with the emergence of the double-blind, randomized clinical trial as the standard for medical research, and also with the publication of some influential papers, especially that of Beecher (1955), that seemed to show "the oxymoron-like enigma of an effect produced by something that is inert" (Kaptchuk, 1998, p. 1723). In clinical research, it became essential to show that a new procedure or therapy was better than "non-specific effects" produced by a placebo, and placebo thus became simply the control condition, a "nuisance" to be eliminated in the search for truly effective treatments.[15]

Placebo's "odd" place, therefore, is that, on the one hand, it has been so thoroughly accepted by the medical community that it is now an obligatory factor in the experimental design of studies of the efficacy of medical treatments; and yet on the other hand, there has been virtually no effort until recently to understand the "enigma" of the placebo itself and its apparent conflict with the biomedical model. As Kaptchuk (2002) cautioned, "dismissing a treatment as 'just a placebo' may not be enough" (p. 817).

Benson and Epstein (1975) were among the first to urge scientists to drop their "disdain" for the placebo and study it as a phenomenon in its own right, but 24 years later some researchers were still asking "why the bald facts of the placebo phenomenon...have not yet launched a thousand inquiries into the mind's treatment powers" (Dientsfrey, 1999, p. 233). Efforts to understand the placebo itself, however, have increased in recent years, largely because a physiological hypothesis emerged that "gave it instant respectability in 20th century terms" (Wall, 1993, p. 197). Specifically, J. D. Levine, Gordon, and Fields (1978) reported a double-blind study in which 40 post-dental-surgery patients were given a placebo as a pain-killer. An hour

---

15. This attitude that the placebo is simply a nuisance to be eliminated, rather than an important phenomenon begging to be explained both for theoretical reasons and so that it might perhaps be used deliberately, remains the dominant one. For example, two physicians (both of them, incidentally, supported by grants from drug companies) recently said that "a detailed understanding" will allow scientists "to decrease placebo response in clinical trials" (D. J. Stein & Mayberg, 2005, p. 442).

later 17 were randomly chosen to receive another placebo, and the remaining 23 were given naloxone, a substance that blocks the analgesic effect of endogenous opiate-like substances such as endorphins. Those given the naloxone reported significantly more pain than those given a second placebo, leading the authors to hypothesize that because naloxone undid the analgesic effects of the placebo, the original placebo effect had been the result of opiate release. With this paper, "the neurobiology of placebo was born" (Amanzio & Benedetti, 1999, p. 484), and subsequent studies have supported a relationship between placebo analgesia and release of endogenous opiates (Rowbotham, 2001; ter Riet, de Craen, de Boer, & Kessells, 1998).

Despite the gradual shift from considering the placebo as only a control condition for research to investigating the placebo effect itself, not all scientists are convinced that there is any placebo effect to be studied. For some (Bailar, 2001), the belief that placebos have powerful clinical effects is a "myth." Others (Kienle & Kiene, 1997) have argued that the "placebo topic seems to invite sloppy methodological thinking" (p. 1311). Most of this criticism stems from the fact that there are relatively few studies in which there were three conditions: a treatment condition, a placebo condition, and a true no-treatment condition. This is perhaps understandable in that, up until recently, the placebo itself was considered the control condition. Nevertheless, it is argued, without a true control condition with which to compare them, effects seen in the placebo condition may simply be the result of naturally occurring effects, such as spontaneously occurring fluctuations in, or even recovery from, the illness (Ernst & Resch, 1995; Kienle & Kiene, 1997). In a recent review of studies (Hróbjartsson & Gøtzsche, 2001) in which there was a true control (no-treatment) condition as well as a placebo condition, the authors claimed to find "little evidence that placebos in general have powerful clinical effects" (p. 1599), and they further claimed that the few effects that do occur are subjective only, especially in pain relief (see also S. Fisher, 2000; Spiro, 2000).

The responses to such skepticism about the existence of placebo effects have primarily been two: First, the review of Hróbjartsson and Gøtzsche suffered from methodological problems of its own, in that it "lumped together studies ranging across 40 different maladies," some susceptible to placebo effects, some not (Stewart-Williams & Podd, 2004, p. 326). The review "is the classic apples and oranges problem in meta-analysis....What this study shows is not that placebos do not improve anything, but rather that they do not improve everything" (D. Spiegel, Kraemer, & Carlson, 2001). The second and more robust response has been that placebo *has* in fact been shown to have objective, and not simply subjective, consequences. I will now examine some of these more objective manifestations of the placebo effect that must be considered in the debate about its existence and nature.

There have perhaps been more studies of the relationship between placebo and pain than any other studies involving a placebo treatment, probably because pain seems especially responsive to placebo (Ernst & Resch, 1995, p. 552). This observation has led many to conclude that placebo works primarily on subjective perceptions—although one might then ask, as one researcher did, "If it's all in your head, does that mean you only think you feel better?" (Ader, 2000, p. 7). I have already mentioned studies showing a relationship between placebo and the release of endogenous opioids. More recent studies on pain and placebo have added to the evidence that placebo can produce highly specific and objectively measurable physiological changes. For example, two brain-imaging studies, one with positron emission tomography (PET) (Petrovic, Kalso, Petersson, & Ingvar, 2002), and one with functional magnetic resonance imaging (fMRI) (Wager et al., 2004), have shown decreased activity in brain areas associated with pain (such as the thalamus, insula, and anterior cingulate cortex) in response to placebo administration as an analgesic. In another study (Zubieta et al., 2005) PET imaging specifically showed activation of the endogenous opioid system in response to a placebo analgesic.

Another condition whose responsiveness to placebo might be thought purely subjective is depression. Effects of placebo on depression have been recognized since the introduction of pharmacologic treatments (e.g., Malitz & Kanzler, 1971), and a meta-analysis of studies in which patients had been assigned randomly to an antidepressant medication or to a placebo provocatively suggested that much of the effect of the medications themselves is attributable to placebo effects (Kirsch & Sapirstein, 1999). Most studies have indeed used subjective measures of effectiveness, such as scales in which patients rate the severity of particular symptoms; but at least two recent studies have focused on more objective outcomes. Both studies found alterations in brain activity, one using electroencephalography, or EEG (Leuchter, Cook, Witte, Morgan, & Abrams, 2002), the other using PET (Mayberg et al., 2002); and both also found that the physiological response to placebo was in some way different from that to the antidepressant. Such findings suggest not only that placebo is an active, and not a "no-treatment," condition, but also that "the two treatments [placebo and pharmacological] are not physiologically equivalent" (Leuchter et al., 2002, p. 125).

Other conditions known to be responsive to psychological factors, such as asthma and ulcers, have also been responsive to placebo, and several studies have measured physiological reactions to placebo treatments of these conditions. For example, asthmatic patients given a nocebo (an inhalant of saline solution that they were told was an allergen) showed a significant increase in airway resistance; all the resulting asthmatic attacks then responded to a placebo (the same saline solution that they were now told was a medication) (Luparello, Lyons, Bleecker, & McFadden, 1968; McFadden, Luparello, Lyons, & Bleecker, 1969; see also Butler & Steptoe, 1986). Moerman (1983, 2000) reviewed numerous studies comparing placebo and the drug cimetadine in the treatment of ulcers, in which the effect was determined by an objective measure (an endoscopic examination). The studies showed "broad variation—from 0 to 100 percent—in placebo effectiveness rates" (Moerman, 2000, p. 51). Related to this, in one of the earliest studies to obtain objective measures of placebo (and nocebo) response, Sternbach (1964) reported a small study in which six subjects were given three pills on separate occasions. They were told that one was a stimulant to stomach activity, one was a relaxant, and one was a placebo. In fact, all three pills were placebos, but in four of the six subjects the measured gastric motility rate reflected what the subject thought was the nature of the pill—that is, highest for the "stimulant," lowest for the "relaxant," and intermediate for the "placebo."

Placebo treatment has not been confined to the use of dummy pills or saline solution. There are some indications that the type of placebo used may influence the strength of the response, and specifically that a type of intervention believed by the patient to be more effective might produce a stronger response.[16] Placebo injection, for example, may have more efficacy than a placebo pill (Kaptchuk, Goldman, Stone, & Stason, 2000). If so, it would be surprising if surgery, one of the most radical interventions possible, did not occasionally show a placebo response. There are, of course, ethical issues that often preclude sham surgery (Hornig & Miller, 2002), and because of methodological problems, the results of such studies can be considered only suggestive (for example, there are no studies comparing the surgery and sham surgery with a third, no-treatment condition). Nevertheless, surgeons themselves have recognized that surgery, like medications, should be evaluated when possible for a placebo effect (A. G. Johnson, 1994), and there have been a few studies comparing the effects of certain surgical procedures with those of a sham surgery.

Among the earliest such studies were several in the 1950s involving a procedure for the treatment of angina, in which mammary arteries were tied off in the belief that this would increase blood flow through other channels. Suspicion about the rationale of this procedure led to the testing of it with sham surgery. Neither the patients nor the physicians evaluating them after the surgery knew which group they were in. In one study (Cobb, Thomas, Dillard, Merendino, & Bruce, 1959), both groups improved with regard to the number of nitroglycerine tablets taken, with the sham-surgery group showing a slightly greater reduction than the real-surgery group. The sham-surgery group also reported slightly greater subjective improvement, the most dramatic improvement being that of a sham-surgery patient. Neither group improved significantly with regard to exercise tolerance or electrocardiographic changes, but the only three patients who did show improvement on these measures were all from the sham-surgery group. In another study (Dimond, Kittle, & Crockett, 1958), there was significant improvement in 10 of 13 real-surgery patients, as well as in all five sham-surgery patients. Apparently the success of this procedure had depended more on the enthusiasm of the surgeons performing it than on the procedure itself (Beecher, 1961; Benson & McCallie, 1979). More recently, two physicians suggested that laser treatment for angina may also have "a potentially marked placebo effect" and that, because it has been evaluated primarily with subjective measures and by physicians "presumably enthusiastic" about the pro-

16. For some references to studies suggesting that the size and color of a placebo pill may influence its effectiveness, see Thompson (2005, p. 41).

cedure, more objective studies are needed to determine how much of the reported success with the procedure may have been the result of a patient's (and physician's) belief that laser therapy "is synonymous with state-of-the-art, successful therapy" (R. A. Lange & Hillis, 1999).

Studies have also been carried out recently comparing arthroscopic knee surgery with placebo sham surgery (Moseley et al., 2002). Patients received either the real surgical treatment, or arthroscopic lavage only, or simulated surgery. Neither the patients nor the physicians who evaluated them for 24 months after the surgery knew which group they were in. Outcome was measured both by patient reports of pain and level of function and by more objective tests of walking and stair climbing. Overall, there were no differences between the three groups; patients in all three groups reported less pain and improved function. More significantly, on the measures evaluated by physicians, "objectively measured walking and stair climbing were poorer in the debridement [surgery] group than in the placebo group" (p. 84). The authors thus cautioned that the study showed "the great potential for a placebo effect with surgery" and that "health care researchers should not underestimate the placebo effect, regardless of its mechanism" (p. 87).

Another attempt to evaluate objective responses to placebo surgery involved ultrasound therapy for patients following dental surgery (Hashish, Harvey, & Harris, 1986). There were three groups of patients: those receiving ultrasound therapy, those receiving a mock ultrasound treatment, and those receiving no treatment. All three groups were given both antibiotic and analgesic pills. Results were evaluated not only by subjective reports of postoperative pain, but also by objective measures of inflammation and facial swelling. There was significant reduction in all three measures in both the ultrasound and placebo groups, as compared with the control group. The authors concluded, moreover, that the "majority of the anti-inflammatory activity was attributable to the placebo effect" (p. 77). In a follow-up study (Ho, Hashish, Salmon, Freeman, & Harvey, 1988) designed to rule out possible massage effects of contact with the ultrasound equipment, as well as emotional factors such as anxiety, the researchers again found that "swelling was reduced by a placebo effect of ultrasound" (p. 197).

A more serious and debilitating condition that has also occasionally responded to placebo, on both subjective and objective measures, is Parkinson's Disease (Shetty et al., 1999; Stoessl & de la Fuente-Fernández, 2004). Some investigators have looked at objective measures of placebo effects in conjunction with drug treatments for Parkinson's. For example, Goetz, Leurgans, Raman, and Stebbins (2000) found that some placebo-treated patients showed improvement in a standardized evaluation of motor function. (Patients also, interestingly, reported a variety of noxious side effects of the placebo, including upper respiratory symptoms and nausea.) Other researchers (de la Fuente-Fernández et al., 2001), using PET, have found a "substantial release of endogenous dopamine" in response to a placebo injection, an effect "comparable to that of therapeutic doses of levodopa… or apomorphine" (p. 1164; de la Fuente-Fernández, Phillips et al., 2002).

Another study (Benedetti et al., 2004) showed changes in neuronal activity in association with a placebo saline injection (in contrast to a no-treatment control group), and the authors concluded that "these STN [subthalamic nucleus] neuronal changes are likely to be induced by the placebo-activated dopamine" (p. 588).

Placebo effects have also been found in some studies of a surgical procedure to implant fetal (nigral) tissue in the brains of Parkinson's patients, again prompting some physicians to emphasize the need to include, when possible, a placebo (sham surgery) in studies to evaluate the effectiveness of such surgery (Albin, 2002; T. B. Freeman et al., 1999). In one such study (Freed et al., 2001), among patients reporting improvement there was no difference between the real and placebo treatment. In a later reanalysis of the same data (McRae et al., 2004), expectation seemed to produce a "very strong" placebo effect, because those who *thought* they had received the real treatment had better scores, regardless of which treatment they had in fact received. Similarly, a study (de la Fuente-Fernández, 2004) of patients who had received both real and simulated deep-brain stimulation for Parkinson's showed that the magnitude of effect was equivalent in both conditions, as measured objectively by a standardized scale of motor function.

Despite recent studies of placebo showing objective measures of improvement, many physicians still insist that, regardless of its mechanism, placebo "helps people to feel better..., but it cannot cure diseases"; or more specifically that "evidence that diseases like cancer yield to placebos are [sic] limited to anecdotes, few, if any, of which can be believed....no one has yet convinced me that tuning up the nervous or immune systems repels the overwhelming forces of disease" (Spiro, 2000, p. 26).

One of the "anecdotes" to which Spiro may have been referring is the well-known case reported by Klopfer (1957). In this case, a patient who was clearly near death from lymphosarcoma learned that his hospital was to participate in studies of a promising new drug, Krebiozen. Although he did not qualify for the study because he was so close to death, he was so insistent on receiving the drug that his doctor agreed. Within three days of his first injection, he was up and walking, and his "tumor masses...were half their original size." In 10 days he was discharged, and he continued in "practically perfect" health for two months. At this time, he began to see in the media conflicting reports about the drug; as a result, "he began to lose faith...[and] relapsed to his original state." His doctor decided to tell him not to believe what he had read because there was an improved, stronger version available, and "with much fanfare" he gave him an injection—this time, of water. The patient again recovered, the results "even more dramatic" than before, and the water injections were continued for another two months. When, however, the patient learned that further studies had shown the drug to be worthless, he almost immediately declined again and died within days (pp. 337–339).

Recovery from such serious conditions in response to a placebo treatment is undoubtedly rare, and necessarily such reports must be "anecdotal," if what is meant by this is a case report and not an experimental study.

Nevertheless, there is no good or compelling reason to dismiss such reports in the absence of evidence of fraud or incompetence. Moreover, Klopfer's report is not unique. Earlier I discussed cases of remission of cancer in connection with Lourdes and with meditation, again reported by presumably competent physicians, and I suggested that, without more knowledge of the psychological conditions involved in the numerous reports of spontaneous remissions of cancer, it is premature to dismiss them as attributable solely to chance.

In sum, we have convergent evidence, not only from formal studies of placebo but also from other phenomena such as those I have so far discussed, that health can be significantly influenced by psychological factors such as belief or suggestion. It seems more useful at this point, therefore, to ask not *whether,* but *how,* this occurs. As I mentioned earlier, PNI studies suggest strongly that psychological factors such as stress or anxiety, or converse conditions such as relaxation or hope, can, through the interaction of the nervous and immune systems, significantly impact a person's health. In placebo studies in particular, there have been two primary candidates for a more specific mechanism. Some have argued, in the wake of the Ader and Cohen (1975) study that essentially launched PNI, that placebo is a conditioned response (e.g., Ader, 1997), but others (e.g., Kienle & Kiene, 1997) have pointed out the weaknesses of evidence for relevant conditioning in most clinical situations (pp. 1314–1315). In particular, how can there be "conditioning" of responses that have not occurred before? The other and more common proposal, therefore, is that the response to placebo depends on the patient's expectations (e.g., de la Fuente-Fernández, Schulzer, & Stoessl, 2002). G. H. Montgomery and Kirsch (1997), for example, concluded that "conditioning...is completely mediated by expectancy" (p. 111); the "effect of placebos depends on the strength of the person's expectations, not on how those expectations were formed" (p. 108). In practice, however, disentangling a conditioned response from the influence of expectation in an adult human is not straightforward, and studies comparing the two hypotheses have found that both are in fact involved, perhaps in different ways (Amanzio & Benedetti, 1999; Benedetti et al., 2003; Stewart-Williams & Podd, 2004). For example, Benedetti and his colleagues found that expectation seemed to be the primary factor in the release of endogenous opioids in response to placebo given for pain relief, whereas conditioning seemed more involved in the release of hormones such as dopamine in Parkinson's patients (Amanzio & Benedetti, 1999; Benedetti et al., 2003).

Whether expectation, conditioning, or both are involved, a much more fundamental problem remains. Placebo has received increased attention in recent years because of evidence that it activates physiological mechanisms, such as the release of dopamine or endogenous opioids or a more basic reaction of the immune system in general. Similarly, other phenomena such as "voodoo death" or faith healing can be taken more seriously as the mutual interaction of the nervous and immune systems. But how adequate are these explanations? Even if we assume that expectation is the fundamental factor, "a remaining question is how these expectancies then generate the corresponding responses" (Kirsch, 2004, p. 341). More directly, "how does a social situation, a psychosocial factor, initiate a physiological process in the body?" (Dienstfrey, 1999, p. 230). As the neurophysiologist Wall cautioned (1993), explanations offered so far seem to be no more than "labelling an unknown process" (p. 214).

Behind these vague descriptions of psychophysiological mechanism, however, is the presumption that has grown steadily over the past century or more—discussed throughout this book—that mind and brain are not separable but are in fact coterminous, different words for the same phenomenon. With regard specifically to the placebo, Byerly (1976) proposed an "alternative to either a physicalistic or mentalistic interpretation," in which "physical and psychological factors are not treated as two separate substances"; with this "softening of the distinction," the problem of "how mind and body can causally interact seems less of a problem" (p. 433). Similarly, H. Brody (1980) devoted an entire volume to placebo as seen by the new "philosophy of medicine," an anti-Cartesian, holistic search for "theories which avoid the rigid distinction between mental and bodily phenomena" (p. 23). Numerous others writing about the placebo effect have rejected the "outmoded dualism" (Wall, 1977, p. 365) and "misleading dichotomy" of mind and brain (Cardeña & Kirsch, 2000, p. 16) that "obfuscates and stigmatizes" such phenomena as placebo (Hahn & Kleinman, 1983, p. 16). Instead, the new "conceptualization [is that]...mind and beliefs are literally *embodied* and, conversely, the bodies of persons literally *mindful*" (Hahn & Kleinman, 1983, p. 16), and "without the Cartesian straightjacket, the issue then becomes not whether mental, 'non-material' processes can bring about significant changes, but rather whether one type of physical events can have a substantial effect on others" (Cardeña & Kirsch, 2000, p. 16). Underlying this "holistic" approach to psychophysiology, however, is a very clear-cut assumption: Most scientists today take a "neuralist" view that "obviates the mind-body mechanism problem because it treats subjective phenomena (the conscious mind) as products of nervous system activity....this neuralist approach avoids the problem of how subjective 'mind' could act on the objective and physical body" (Fields & Price, 1997, p. 94).

The noteworthy word in this last quotation is "avoids." In their determination not to be saddled with the stigma of dualism—a word synonymous for most modern scientists with "unscientific"—scientists have opted for a position that in fact explains nothing and is really only an empty restatement of the obvious, that we are psychophysiological beings. One can readily embrace the "biopsychosocial" view of humans as products of inextricably interwoven factors, and one can also reject the view—mistakenly called Cartesian dualism—that mind and body are separate entities that cannot interact. But we cannot—or should not—gloss over the problem that remains. Despite statements and assumptions about "holism" or "unity," we observe that there are mental events and physical events, and few would argue that they are not somehow related. No one, however, can say how. *How*, for example, does "a person's belief in a sham treatment...send a message to his or her pituitary gland to release its own endogenous pharmaceuticals" (Harrington, 1997, p. 5)? It is a difficult enough question when, as with most of the phenomena discussed so far, the initiating factor seems to be a general state such as fear, depression, or belief, and the effect seems to be a general systemic one which then leads to the waxing or waning of one or another disease. The question becomes still more difficult, however, when particular ideas somehow translate into more specific physiological reactions. I will next describe examples of this more problematic kind.

Specific Physiological Changes Appearing Spontaneously

Sudden Whitening of Hair or Skin

Many of the phenomena we have discussed thus far have involved stress that seems to have resulted in a general breakdown in the immune or cardiovascular systems, as in cases of sudden or "voodoo" death. A much more specific physiological response—less catastrophic, but probably related to these sudden-death cases—involves hair turning white suddenly, even within a few hours, usually after a severe fright. Such cases have been reported for centuries, both in the medical literature (for reviews, see Barahal, 1940; Ephraim, 1959; Stevenson, 1997, vol. 2, pp. 1726–1731) and in the non-medical historical literature (see Jelinek, 1973). A frequently cited example is the case observed by Parry, a surgeon, in 1859, of a Bengali prisoner whose hair turned from glossy black to grey within a half hour, apparently because he was "stupefied with fear" (Parry, 1861). This case is by no means unique, as the above-mentioned reviews demonstrate. Similarly, there have been reports of a sudden change of pigmentation in patches of skin (for a review and some photographs of the phenomenon, see Stevenson, 1997, vol. 2, pp. 1731–1735). Despite the numerous reports, often by apparently qualified medical observers, there has been, and remains, much skepticism about the phenomenon. For many scientists, "the structure and physiology of hair seems incompatible with the sudden spontaneous change in the hair color" (Helm & Milgrom, 1970, p. 103), and "despite the reports of otherwise trustworthy observers," the cases thus are dismissed as "legendary tales" or even "fiction" (Ephraim, 1959, p. 233). Some have suggested that many reports are exaggerations, transforming the "weeks or months in reality" to "overnight" (Jelinek, 1973, p. 530)

Others have taken the phenomenon seriously and suggested possible explanations. One of the earliest was that microscopic air bubbles have developed in the hair and that these reflect light and create an illusion that the hair changed color. The explanation seemed supported by "the fact that emotional states such as shock, rage, or fear, produce histamine-like substances in the skin with a subsequent lowering of the surface tension of the fluid in the hair shaft, producing a release of gaseous bubbles" (Barahal

& Freeman, 1946, pp. 35–36; see also Barahal, 1940; and R. Jones, 1902). Some (Ephraim, 1959, p. 233) have thought that this mechanism has been confirmed in some cases, whereas others (Jelinek, 1973, p. 529) have thought not, but in any event air bubbles cannot account for cases, by far the most common type, in which the change was permanent.

Another proposed explanation has been that a sudden loss of hair in which dark pigmented hairs fall out, but white ones do not, would give the illusion that the hair had changed color rapidly (Helm & Milgrom, 1970; Jelinek, 1973; P. R. Montgomery, 1967): "In recent years, most patients with rapid whitening of scalp hair have been found to have either alopecia aleata [loss of hair] or vitiligo [whitening of patches of the skin]" (Guin, Kumar, & Petersen, 1981, p. 577). Although this explanation almost certainly covers some cases, it cannot cover all, especially those in which the patient had originally had no (or very few) white hairs and those in which the reporting physician denied any substantial hair loss (see Stevenson, 1997, vol. 2, p. 1730).

Because sudden stress or other intense emotion affects the immune and nervous systems, resulting biochemical changes might somehow contribute to loss of pigment (Ephraim, 1959, p. 233; Ornsteen, 1930); and Guin et al. (1981) have pointed out that both alopecia aleata and vitiligo have been associated with immune disorders. Clearly, however, sudden whitening of hair or skin pigment involves a more precise mechanism than that behind the general systemic responses in the conditions I have discussed so far, and it remains "physiologically difficult to understand how the hair, which, once formed, is a structure without nerves or blood supply, can throughout its length undergo rapid physicochemical changes directly due to emotional influences" (Ephraim, 1959, p. 228).

False Pregnancy

In contrast to general stress, a quite specific idea seems to have precipitated a specific physiological response in the condition known as pseudocyesis, in which a woman who falsely believes herself to be pregnant shows many of the physiological symptoms of pregnancy (for a succinct review, see Small, 1986). The condition has been known to physicians at least since the time of Hippocrates, who described 12 cases that he had observed. Another well-known case from antiquity was that of Mary Tudor (Aldrich, 1972). Pseudocyesis also is—or was—not an uncommon condition. Bivin and Klinger (1937) reviewed 444 cases, most from the English-language literature of the 19th and 20th centuries, and another review 22 years later by Murray and Abraham (1978) reported an additional 68. T. X. Barber (1984) commented that a "surprisingly large number of...excellent hypnotic subjects (60% of those asked)" in one of his studies had experienced pseudocyesis on one or more occasions (p. 112). There have been reports of other cases since 1978 (e.g., five in Devane, Vera, Buhi, & Kalra, 1985;

six in Whelan & Stewart, 1990; and six in Signer et al., 1992), but it is clear that the reported incidence (if not the real incidence) is declining, probably because of several factors. Improved diagnostic techniques, for example, do not allow a woman to maintain the illusion of pregnancy for long; and increased sociocultural options for women besides motherhood may have lessened the pressure to become pregnant that many women probably felt in earlier times (L. M. Cohen, 1982).

The symptoms are often objective ones, so much so that the condition "may tax the diagnostic abilities of the ablest physician" (Fried, Rakoff, Schopbach, & Kaplan, 1951, p. 1330). In one study of 27 cases occurring between 1937 and 1952, in every case at least one doctor had concurred with the woman's belief that she was pregnant (Schopbach, Fried, & Rakoff, 1952, p. 130). The commonest symptoms are, in order of incidence: abdominal enlargement, often progressing at approximately the rate of a normal pregnancy; menstrual disturbances (usually a complete cessation of menstruation for several months); sensation of fetal movements, felt not only by the woman but by others (including doctors); nausea and other gastrointestinal symptoms; breast changes, including secretions; labor pains; enlargement of the uterus; and changes in the cervix (Bivin & Klinger, 1937). Most authors since 1937 have reported similar symptoms.[17]

Some physicians have hypothesized that pseudocyesis represents a psychosomatic response to conflicting wishes and fears of pregnancy (e.g., Bivin & Klinger, 1937; Bressler, Nyhus, & Magnussen, 1958; Fried et al., 1951). According to this interpretation, it is a kind of conversion disorder, that is, a condition in which "a change in physical functioning mimicks a physical condition as an expression of a psychological conflict or need" (O'Grady & Rosenthal, 1989, pp. 506–507). Many cases of pseudocyesis do seem to have occurred at times of psychological distress, although few patients have been considered hysterical, as are most individuals in whom conversion reactions are commonly observed. More generally, Pawlowski and Pawlowski (1958) suggested that the extent to which the pseudo-pregnancy progresses depends in large part on "the extent to which the idea of pregnancy takes possession of the patient's entire personality" (p. 439). Clearly, however, such psychological interpretations constitute at best descriptions of the precipitating conditions, and not an explanation.

Most observers of pseudocyesis therefore have emphasized a psychophysiological approach according to which disturbances in the hypothalamus, perhaps brought on by depression or anxiety, have led to alterations in

17. There have even been a few cases reported of pseudocyesis in a male, although the symptoms are generally much less pronounced than in women. Also, unlike women, the men almost invariably have severe psychological disorders contributing to the delusional belief that they are pregnant (see Silva, Leong, & Weinstock, 1991, for references to reports of such cases). A related and much more common phenomenon is that of couvade, in which someone (usually the father), witnessing the expectant mother's symptoms and suffering, experiences similar ones in apparent empathy (Klein, 1991).

neuroendocrine function and hormonal levels. Among the first to propose this mechanism were Fried et al. (1951; see also a second paper by the same group [Schopbach et al., 1952]). They proposed that "psychic factors acted on the endocrine system by utilization of pathways from the cortex through the hypothalamus to the anterior pituitary gland causing release of the luteotropin and suppression of the follicle-stimulating hormone" (p. 1334). E. Brown and Barglow (1971) attempted to pinpoint the initiating "psychic factor" more precisely, suggesting that this is depression, which "is associated with alterations in the neuronal networks connecting the higher brain centers [cerebral cortex and limbic system] with the median eminence of the hypothalamus," and more specifically with a decrease in biogenic amines (p. 227). Signer et al. (1992) reported six cases of pseudocyesis associated with depression, but they cautioned that "pseudocyesis does not appear to be a single, coherent entity" (p. 322).

Starkman, Marshall, la Ferla, and Kelch, (1985) tested Brown and Barglow's theory with psychiatric and neuroendocrine profiles of two of their patients, and they also looked at the neuroendocrine profiles of four additional patients previously reported in the medical literature. In these six patients, Brown and Barglow's hypothesis was not supported. One of Starkman et al.'s two patients showed no clinical symptoms of depression, and, more significantly, the neuroendocrine profiles among all six varied both from each other and from the predictions of Brown and Barglow. In particular, the prolactin levels varied and could not therefore explain the cessation of menstruation in the patients (p. 55).

Because endogenous opioid peptides in the hypothalamus had been shown to have an "inhibitory effect in the neuroendocrine regulation of gonadotropin secretion," and because women with organic hypothalamic amenorrhea have responded to injections of naloxone, Devane et al. (1985) predicted that women with pseudocyesis would likewise respond to naloxone. They did not, leading the authors to the "unexpected" conclusion that "opioid peptide modulation is not perturbed in patients with pseudocyesis." More significantly, the authors commented that "the prompt clinical recovery after disclosure of the diagnosis [of pseudocyesis] is evidence that organic hypothalamic dysfunction was not present" (p. 187).

Although it seems likely that pseudocyesis is the result of some psychophysiological process in which an emotional state has triggered changes in neuroendocrine and hormonal levels, there has so far been no consistent pattern observed either in psychological state or in neurophysiological findings. Because of the "lack of consistent endocrinologic findings" some have argued again, as did Engel, that the biomedical "linear model of psychogenic or biological causation" is inadequate and that what is needed instead is a biopsychosocial model (Whelan & Stewart, 1990, p. 104). Pseudocyesis is certainly a striking example of the complex interplay of psychological, biological, and sociocultural factors in disease; but I repeat that this "systems" approach provides a description, not an explanation, of the phenomenon. Statements such as "the usually accepted mechanism is that the symptoms [of pregnancy] generated by the individual...reduce anxiety" (O'Grady & Rosenthal, 1989, p. 507) or a "depressive mechanism induces neuroendocrine changes through cortical or limbic connections at the level of the hypothalamus" (Whelan & Stewart, 1990, p. 105) tell us nothing about how such changes are "generated" or "induced."

In sum, there is much evidence for an association between a woman's belief that she is pregnant and objective physiological changes in her body consistent with that belief, but so far the mechanisms underlying this association remain unknown. Unfortunately, although "the role of psychogenic factors in the control of the neuroendocrine system is becoming one of the most exciting areas of psychosomatic medicine" and pseudocyesis has been called "a paradigm of psychosomatic research" (Murray & Abraham, 1978, pp. 629, 631), opportunities for understanding the condition may be diminishing.[18] Pawlowski and Pawlowski (1958) predicted that, as diagnostic methods improve and especially "as people become more cultured and sophisticated, their emotional conflicts will seek a more profound, sophisticated mode of expression than that of spurious pregnancy" (p. 440).[19] If so, this is unfortunate (from a scientific point of view), because not only do we not have an adequate picture of the psychophysiological mechanisms involved, we are even less knowledgeable about how the specific idea of pregnancy can trigger the specific physiological systems necessary to produce the symptoms.

Stigmata

Among the most well known and hotly debated of the phenomena I discuss in this chapter are cases of stigmata, in which a person develops marks, and even bleeding, corresponding to the sites of wounds Christ is thought to have suffered at his crucifixion. Hundreds of cases have been reported from the 13th century to the present time, although one of the early reviewers of the phenomenon concluded that up to his time only 50 had been reported with adequate testimony (Thurston, 1952, p. 121). Most of the cases have

18. The neuroscientist V. S. Ramachandran (Ramachandran & Blakeslee, 1998) likewise thought that "pseudocyesis provides a valuable opportunity for exploring the mysterious no-man's-land between mind and body" (p. 218). He also noted (p. 216) that the incidence has declined from 1 in 200 pregnancies in the late 18th century to about 1 in 10,000 today, but unfortunately he gives no source for these figures.

19. An alternative (or additional) explanation for the decline of reports of cases of pseudocyesis is one that applies more generally to many types of controversial phenomena: The decline may represent not so much a decline in the *incidence* as a decline in the *reporting* of such cases. Because such cases do not fit with our current understanding of the possible mechanisms, observers may fail to report them or, at another level, journal reviewers and editors may decline to publish reports, believing that such cases cannot really occur.

occurred in young, single females, often Catholic and usually highly religious. The marks are usually on the palms, the backs of the hands, and the soles and top of the feet, corresponding to sites where nails were thought to have pinned Christ to the cross. Another common site is in the side, corresponding to the spear wound. Less common but still repeatedly reported are marks on the head, back, or shoulders (corresponding to the crown of thorns, the lashings Christ received, and the site where he bore the cross), and, more rarely, bloody tears. Although usually called "wounds," the marks vary in nature from relatively simple red marks to blisters to actual bleeding. Rarely are actual lesions seen; the bleeding instead seems to erupt from unbroken skin. The emergence of the marks is almost always periodic and regular, usually occurring on Fridays and repeating weekly for years. They frequently appear when the stigmatic is in some kind of altered state of consciousness, such as an ecstatic state or trance. Finally, however severe the nature of the wounds or bleeding, no sepsis or inflammation occurs, and the wounds disappear rapidly, leaving little or no mark, until the next recurrence.[20]

Among the most well known cases are those of St. Francis of Assisi in the 13th century, usually considered the first stigmatic, and cases from the 19th and 20th centuries, such as Louise Lateau, Gemma Gelgani, Thérèse Neumann, and Padre Pio. Stigmata are, however, still occurring. Early and Lifschutz (1974) reported the case of a 10-year-old girl in California who was "intensely religious" and strongly identified with Christ. She showed no signs of psychopathology. Unlike most cases, in this one the stigmata appeared on only one occasion, a period of 19 days just preceding Easter 1972. A week before the stigmata appeared the girl had read a book about the crucifixion, and three days later she had seen a movie depicting it. Both portrayals of the crucifixion apparently affected her deeply, and on the night she saw the movie she also had a vivid dream about it. Her stigmata consisted of bleeding from the usual sites, including the hands, feet, and forehead. As in many cases, there were no lesions; the blood seemed instead to ooze from the skin. Although the physician (one of the authors) never saw the actual onset of bleeding, on one occasion she "observed the blood [on her palm] to increase in volume four fold" (p. 199). Bleeding from all sites occurred for the last time on Good Friday; up to the time of publication of the report they had not recurred.

Whitlock and Hynes (1978) reported the case of Mrs. H., a Polish Catholic woman who had wanted to enter a convent as a young girl, but became pregnant at age 16. After years of unhappiness, in 1958 at age 49 she developed hysterical anesthesia and began having visions and pains in her limbs. Shortly afterward a weekly cycle began in which every Friday she would pass into a trance state and late that afternoon blood would appear "below her closed eyelids." Because the blood seemed to be oozing from the skin

20. For some reviews and summaries of cases in English, see Klauder (1938), M. Murphy (1992, pp. 484–502), Ratnoff (1969), Stevenson (1997, vol. 1, pp. 34–53), Thurston (1922, 1952), and Whitlock and Hynes (1978).

and there were no lesions or broken blood vessels, the authors conjectured that the bloody secretions came from her tear ducts (p. 191). She remained under the care of one of the authors of the paper until her death in 1963, and the authors were "satisfied that the phenomena of trance, muscular rigidity and the blood on her eyelids were genuine and not fraudulent" (p. 192). Like many stigmatics, Mrs. H. was "generally regarded as hysterical" (p. 192); but, unlike most, her stigmata took only one form—bloody tears. Moreover, that form is one of the most rare, having been reported in only a few other cases, such as those of Thérèse Neumann, Gemma Galgani, Elisabeth K., and Delfina (Stevenson, 1997, vol. 1, p. 39; Whitlock & Hynes, 1978, p. 198).[21]

J. G. Fisher and Kollar (1980) reported the case of a 23-year-old Mexican-American woman, who was initially raised Catholic but later became Pentacostal. Her religiosity intensified when she married a man equally active in the Pentacostal church. In 1971, six months after her marriage, stigmata began to appear, first on her hands, later on her feet, head, back, and left side, "usually (but not always) associated with religious ecstasy" (p. 1461). The authors began psychological and physiological studies (an MMPI that "revealed a normal profile," with no signs of psychopathology), but unfortunately they were unable to complete their studies because she and her husband "disappeared abruptly without notice" (p. 1462).

An even more recent case was phenomenologically quite different from either Mrs. H. or Early and Lifschutz's patient. Margnelli (1999) reported the case of Anna Maria T., an Italian Catholic woman whose stigmata first appeared in 1990, when she was 64. They continued to appear regularly on the first Friday of every month and would last two to three days before suddenly disappearing, leaving no scars. They were still continuing to appear regularly up to the time of the publication of the report. The marks occurred only on her palms and consisted of red rounded blotches, and sometimes blisters, that most closely resembled a burn but never bled. Anna Maria was not unusually religious, but she did pray and go to mass once a week, especially after the death of her husband in 1987, and she was an admirer of St. Francis and Padre Pio (both of them stigmatics themselves). Unlike most stigmatics, she apparently did not go into a trance-like state, although the stigmata had begun when, while praying, she had a vivid vision of Jesus approaching her and taking her by the hands.

She was closely followed by the author for five months, during which time color and infrared photographs were taken, various physiological reactions measured, and psychological tests (MMPI and Rorschach) administered. Measurements and photographs were made on days when the stigmata were present as well as on days when they were not. Physiological measurements showed differences in temperature, blood flow, and electrodermal response

21. Related to this phenomenon may be that of the secretion of bloody sweat under emotional circumstances, of which there have also been a few reports, usually among persons who were not religious stigmatics (Dunbar, 1954, p. 608; Tuke, 1884, p. 295).

between the stigmatic areas and surrounding skin, as well as differences between the days when stigmata were present and "control" days when they were not. The psychological tests showed no signs of psychopathology, including low scores on the hysteria scale. She did have a high score on the schizophrenia scale of the MMPI, but her high scores were primarily attributable to items about experiences that the American Psychiatric Association now considers nonpathological, such as religious and mystical visions (Margnelli, 1999, p. 479).

Myers pointed out that people usually react to reports of stigmata with one of two polarized views: "*ou supercherie ou miracle*"—either fraud or miracle (*HP*, vol. 1, p. 492). Although fraudulent cases have certainly occurred, many others have been studied and reported carefully enough that it is "beyond doubt that the pertinent lesions were not created artifactually" (Stevenson, 1997, vol. 1, p. 35). With reports of the psychological profiles of stigmatics increasingly available, the dichotomy of opinion has been modified to "pathology or miracle" (Simpson, 1984). It has become clear that many stigmatics have shown symptoms of hysteria (Thurston, 1952, p. 124), often having a prolonged period of ill health and strange symptoms, sometimes followed by "a 'miraculous' healing" and then by the onset of the stigmata (Whitlock & Hynes, 1978, p. 187). For years, therefore, hysteria has had "pride of place" as the explanation, usually as a "denigratory label, which in the minds of some writers is barely to be distinguished from conscious malingering"—the old assumption, that is, of fraud (Whitlock & Hynes, 1978, p. 194). As I pointed out earlier, however, in some recent, well-studied cases (Early & Lifschutz, 1974; Margnelli, 1999) there have been no signs of hysteria or other psychopathology.

The problem of stigmata, however, lies much deeper than asking whether they are symptoms of psychopathology or not. Clearly, "calling a phenomenon hysterical is no explanation" (Whitlock & Hynes, 1978, p. 194); "we are just substituting one poorly understood diagnosis (stigmata) with another (hysterical conversion)" (Simpson, 1984, p. 1748). As I discussed in Chapter 2, with regard to all the phenomena about which he wrote, including stigmata, Myers attempted to go beyond the usual polarized positions and find a more comprehensive explanation. A century later Stevenson (1997) echoed this approach when he argued that, instead of reducing stigmata to hysteria or elevating them to miracles, it is "possible to appraise stigmata without using the vocabulary of hagiology or that of psychopathology" (vol. 1, p. 34). Indeed, it is not only possible, but essential.

Some writers have attempted to interpret stigmata in psychoanalytic terms, noting not only the hysterical symptoms but the parallel between stigmata and menstruation (e.g., Lifschutz, 1957). "Interpretations are not explanations," however, as Whitlock and Hynes (1978, p. 199) succinctly stated, and more recently scientists have looked to psychophysiology for explanations, particularly in the wake of our increasing awareness of the relationship between emotions and the immune system. Some have suggested that the general ill health of many stigmatics, perhaps exacerbated by prolonged fasting, may have led to a general depletion of the immune system resulting in diseases such as herpes simplex (Simpson, 1984, p. 1747; Whitlock & Hynes, 1978, pp. 198–199). Others have noted that in hemophiliacs, as in stigmatics, bleeding sometimes occurs in connection with severe emotional stress (Ratnoff, 1969, p. 157; Whitlock & Hynes, 1978, p. 196).

The most specific suggestion, however, has come from Ratnoff (1969), who compared stigmata cases with a phenomenon known as autoerythrocyte sensitization (AES), "the lay equivalent of stigmata" (p. 162). AES is a rare condition in which the patient, usually a woman, has suffered some severe physical trauma and subsequently develops bruising, inflammation, pain, swelling, or other internal bleeding at times of emotional stress. Because the symptoms can be induced by injecting small amounts of their own blood into patients, it has been suggested that the original trauma created an unusual sensitivity to their own blood, a sensitivity apparently somehow activated by subsequent stress. It has further been suggested that AES is an autoimmune disorder, but tests have not yet demonstrated this (Ratnoff, 1969, p. 160).

The psychological similarities between AES patients and stigmatics are notable. Like stigmatics, AES patients are nearly all women, their symptoms "sound like the table of contents of a monograph on hysteria," and most patients were "under severe emotional stress when symptoms first appeared" (Ratnoff, 1969, pp. 161–162). The physiological parallels, however, are not so clear-cut. Stigmatics do not develop bruising or inflammation, the hallmark of AES. J. G. Fisher and Kollar (1980) concluded that AES was an unlikely diagnosis in the case they investigated, and, moreover, "our review of the literature failed to identify any stigmatic in whom this interesting psychosomatic entity would have been a likely mechanism" (p. 1463).

Phenomena Related to Stigmata

Any proposed mechanism of stigmata will also have to take into account that it is not an isolated phenomenon. There have been many reports of similar, but "non-religious" cases in which strong emotion seems to have produced a specific physiological reaction related to the emotion, in particular, "somatic repetitions of previous experiences" (R. L. Moody, 1948). Stevenson (1997, vol. 1, p. 68–78) has reviewed many such cases. In some cases the rush to psychoanalytic interpretations unfortunately overshadowed the re-porting of the phenomenon itself. In one of these, a 31-year-old man bled on the palms of his hands on three occasions, all involving a stressful situation (Needles, 1943). In another case a man was reported to have bled from his armpits, in the absence of any visible wound, for four to five days every month for at least seven months (Hadley, 1929–1930).

Other cases that have also been interpreted psychoanalytically may have been related to AES, since the somatic reactions reflected an earlier injury. In a case reported by Graff and Wallerstein (1954), a male patient in a psychiatric ward developed, on two occasions, some unusual swelling on one of his several tattoos. The reactions occurred two days apart, both times after a psychiatric interview in which he talked about various traumatic memories. Because the wheals remained for 24 hours after the first occasion, photographs and plaster casts of them were made (pp. 510, 512). In another case (Lifschutz, 1957) a patient reported that, when she was 13, her father had "scratched her down her back with his fingernails, leaving three long scars." Four years later she left home, but when her father announced he was coming to visit her, the scars, healed for four years, bled, and they did so again on several subsequent occasions when her father was coming to visit (p. 529). Dunbar (1954) described two similar cases. In one of them a patient, recalling that a physician treating her for typhoid fever would "jokingly...grasp her neck with his hand," developed a red spot on the left side of her neck and three red spots ("of the size of a finger tip") on the right side (p. 614). In the other case, a woman developed a bruise and swelling on an arm in association with recalling her husband beating her (p. 622).

Two of the most remarkable cases were witnessed and documented by R. L. Moody (1946, 1948). In one, a man was hospitalized for several months in 1935 because of frequent somnambulism. On one occasion, to restrain him from his wanderings, his hands were tied behind his back while he slept. Nine years later he was again hospitalized because of somnambulism, as well as aggressive behavior. One night he was seen writhing on his bed with his hands clasped behind his back, after which he got up and walked outside in a somnambulistic state, his hands still behind his back. Because of the patient's aggressive behavior, Moody had ordered that he not be followed in his somnambulistic wanderings "for the safety of the staff." He returned 20 minutes later in an apparently normal state. The nurse then saw "deep weals like rope marks on each arm" (1946, p. 934). They remained and were observed by Moody and others for two days. On the evening after they disappeared, "the incident was abreacted under narcosis."[22] While he was in an apparently "completely dissociated state" and being observed by Moody, "weals appeared on both forearms; gradually these became indented; and finally some fresh petechial hæmorrhages appeared along their course" (p. 934). Although trickery could not be ruled out on the first occasion, since the patient was unobserved just before the marks were noticed by the nurse, on the second occasion the marks appeared under Moody's direct observation. These remained until the next morning, when they were photographed. The photograph published by Moody shows the many indentations on the arm and their close resemblance to rope marks (p. 935; reproduced in Stevenson, 1997, vol. 1, p. 72).

In another case, of a woman whose father had beaten her repeatedly when she was a child, "swelling, bruising, and bleeding were observed by me on at least thirty occasions" while she was reliving various traumas she had suffered (R. L. Moody, 1948, p. 964). Moody described several examples,

22. R. L. Moody (1946) defined "abreaction" as "an uninhibited reliving of the traumatic incident...[that] differs fundamentally from the mere recall of a forgotten event" (p. 934).

including bruises that appeared on her left buttock;[23] a red, bleeding mark on her left shoulder; the flushing, hemorrhaging, and flaking of a scar left from a childhood accident; red streaks appearing on her leg while she was recalling another accident; and a "test case" in which Moody, in the presence of a colleague, produced an abreaction of an event in which her father had struck her across the palms with a whip, and "transverse red streaks" appeared on her palms and later bled. The most interesting occurrence, however, was when she was reliving an incident in which her father had struck her with an "elaborately carved stick," and a bruise developed with "a curious sharply defined pattern" that apparently resembled the stick.

In addition to vivid recall of a past event, vivid dreams may also sometimes lead to a physiological response. Tuke (1884) reported a case in which a man dreamed that he had been hit in the chest with a stone: "The vivid shock awoke him, and then he found that there was on his chest…a round mark, having the appearance of a bruise" (p. 286). Because it was also swollen the next day, he went to a doctor for treatment, and it soon healed. Stevenson (1997, vol. 1, pp. 76–78) reported a case in which an Indian man, while seriously ill with typhoid fever, had a vivid experience in which he thought that he had died and that, as he was struggling to return to life, persons in the "other realm" had subdued him by cutting off his legs at the knees. When he recovered, "he was found to have some unusual horizontal scars in the skin across the front of both knees," and the "scars" persisted so that years later Stevenson was able to photograph them (p. 78).

Stevenson (1997, vol. 1, pp. 54–56) has also reviewed several cases in which a person's emotional reaction to seeing wounds on another person has resulted in similar wounds on the observer. Kerner, for example, reported an 1812 case of a man who observed severe wounds being inflicted on a soldier, and shortly afterward he developed similar wounds which "bled and…[had to be] treated medically." Pabst described the case of a woman who, at the time her soldier-brother was being beaten on the back for some misbehavior, developed bleeding wounds on her own back. Carter reported a case in which a woman witnessed her child's three middle fingers being cut off when a window sash fell on them. The surgeon treating the child noted that the corresponding three fingers on the mother's hand were swollen and inflamed, so that pus had to be drained from them the next day.

Tuke (1884, pp. 285–287) reported similar cases, such as that of a woman "whose lips and mouth became suddenly enormously swollen" when she thought a child was about to cut itself on the lip with a knife (p. 287). In another case, a woman "well known" to Tuke saw the near-crushing of a child's ankle by a heavy iron gate. She immediately felt intense pain in her own corresponding ankle and walked home with difficulty, at which time she "found a circle around the ankle, as if it had been painted with red-

23. Stevenson (1997, vol. 1, p. 75) reported two similar cases, related to him by colleagues, in which a patient developed wheals on the buttocks when recalling a beating.

currant juice." The next day it was inflamed, and it kept her bedridden for several days (p. 285).

Such cases "cause initial incredulity" (Stevenson, 1997, vol. 1, p. 74), especially when they occur in times and places other than our own. More recently, however, Rantasalo and Penttinen (1959) reported the case of a mother who, on six occasions, developed blisters on her arm. The six occasions were, first, during her first pregnancy, then on each of the four occasions when her three children were vaccinated, and finally during a time of stress again involving the welfare of her children.

Later in this chapter I will discuss the numerous instances in which bleeding, blistering, or other marks have been induced deliberately, usually by hypnotic suggestion, but one such case is worth mentioning in this section because it is apparently the only one in which wounds closely resembling religious stigmata have been produced by hypnotic suggestion. This is the case of Elisabeth K., a German girl observed by Lechler beginning in 1929. Lechler's report has never been translated; the best summary of the case in English, including five photographs of the stigmata, is by Stevenson (1997, vol. 1, pp. 43–49). Similar to the cases reported above of people who developed reactions in response to seeing another person's injuries, Elisabeth had an "extraordinary capacity to translate images" of another person's suffering into similar symptoms on her own body (p. 44). After attending a lecture on the crucifixion on Good Friday 1932, she reported to Lechler that she had felt severe pain in her hands and feet while watching depictions of Jesus nailed to the cross. Lechler had been hypnotizing her for several years for treatment of a variety of hysterical symptoms, and he decided to test her apparent ability to produce symptoms in sympathy with other people's suffering. He hypnotized her and suggested that she would dream that night of nails being driven into her hands and feet. The next day she had red, swollen areas, "with the skin somewhat opened up," at the suggested sites. Lechler told her about the hypnotic suggestion and, with her consent, gave her the further suggestion that the wounds would become deeper and that she would produce bloody tears—suggestions that were also effective. On subsequent occasions he was able to induce actual bleeding, as well as swollen red marks on her forehead and shoulder. The marks on the forehead, flecked with blood, were especially interesting because some of them were "distinctly triangular in shape, and therefore corresponding to the wounds that real thorns might sometimes make" (Stevenson, 1997, vol. 1, p. 45; photographs of these triangular marks are on p. 48). After the first inductions, she was kept under constant surveillance, and Lechler witnessed the onset of the bleeding on several occasions.

Specificity of the Wounds

An adequate explanation of stigmata will have to take into account not only the existence of these other kinds of cases, both spontaneous and induced, but also several further noteworthy features. First, as we have seen in the above examples, marks appear at quite specific locations corresponding to the image in the person's mind, whether the image is of Jesus' wounds or of wounds on someone else. For example, stigmata corresponding to the spear wound on Jesus' side may be located on either the left or the right side, apparently reflecting the stigmatic's belief about the location of that wound (Stevenson, 1997, vol. 1, pp. 40–41): "There seems to be little doubt that the representation of this wound in pictures or sculptural crucifixes had a powerful influence on which side of the body the lesion appeared" (Whitlock & Hynes, 1978, p. 187). Some stigmatics have had wounds in the palms of their hands, others wounds in the wrists (Stevenson, 1997, vol. 1, pp. 38, 41). An additional example of the specificity of location is provided by a rare phenomenon known as "espousal rings," in which a red line, often accompanied by thickening of the skin, appears encircling a finger, apparently as a symbolic token of the person's devotion to Jesus (Thurston, 1952, pp. 130–140). One example was the case of Marie-Julie Jahenny, a 19th-century Breton girl whose stigmatic ring appeared in 1874 and was still visible in 1891 (M. Murphy, 1992, pp. 491–492; Thurston, 1922, pp. 206–208).

In addition, wounds often take specific shapes, again corresponding to the image in the person's mind. The triangular marks on Elisabeth K.'s forehead provide one example. In the case of Anna Emmerich, Y-shaped stigmata on her chest resembled a Y-shaped cross at the church of her childhood (M. Murphy, 1992, pp. 486–488; Stevenson, 1997, vol. 1, p. 42). I have already mentioned the detailed shape of rope marks on one of R. L. Moody's patients; Stevenson (1997, vol. 1, pp. 38–39) describes three similar cases among stigmatics (two from the 17th century and, again, Marie-Julie Jahenny in the 19th century), in which rope marks on the wrists appeared, apparently corresponding to images of Jesus being bound to the cross by ropes rather than by nails.

Other features of stigmata cases are difficult to reconcile with the notion that they are the result of some normal disease such as herpes simplex. One is their temporal regularity: Many recur regularly, often for years, at a specific time, usually Friday. Another is "the almost invariable absence of sepsis when they were open or healing" (Whitlock & Hynes, 1978, p. 188). Additionally, the wounds disappear and heal rapidly, usually leaving no scars, inflammation, or other residue. Thurston (1922) summed up the problem presented by features such as these: "For the symmetrical arrangement and narrowly limited area, the periodicity extending over a long term of years, and for such deep wounds...—wounds that never suppurate but heal with extraordinary rapidity—there seems to be no adequate analogy" (pp. 200–201). More recently, Margnelli (1999) asked what "activates the nerve trunks, the contained area of the lesions, the wounds' topographical precision and their long duration" (p. 464).

Predisposing Characteristics

Certain psychological characteristics or conditions seem conducive to psychophysiological phenomena such as stigmata. The "unmistakable symptoms of hysteria" in many stigmatics is a clue (Thurston, 1952, p. 122), but the essential factor does not seem to be psychopathology per se, but rather a trait variously manifesting as suggestibility, absorption or intense concentration, capacity for vivid imagery, hypnotizability, or dissociation. As M. Murphy (1992) put it, "images, it seems, often work upon the flesh most effectively in states of deep mental absorption" (p. 500), and clearly an important feature in most cases has been the person's heightened, intense "monoideism" or concentration on the relevant images (Stevenson, 1997, vol. 1, pp. 50–51, 80–83).

Another characteristic is what has been called "abnormal suggestibility" (Thurston, 1952, p. 122) or unusual "impressionability" (Stevenson, 1997, vol. 1, p. 52). Stigmatics seem to be "model hysterics in whom suggestibility/auto-suggestibility would reach the maximum visibility" (Margnelli, 1999, p. 464). Ratnoff (1969) likewise noted the importance of suggestibility among patients with AES syndrome (p. 162).

Related to both absorption and suggestibility is the observation that stigmata frequently occur when the person is in some kind of altered state of consciousness, such as religious "ecstasy" or a trance (Margnelli, 1999, pp. 466–467; Whitlock & Hynes, 1978, pp. 187, 189). Such an altered state may also be conducive in non-religious cases, as seen in that of R. L. Moody (1946) in which the marks appeared during a somnambulistic state. Such altered states figure so frequently in these cases that Whitlock and Hynes (1978) called them "essential precursors" of stigmata-like lesions: "One fact appears to be fairly well established: the existence of a state of trance or some other altered state of consciousness seems to have a facilitatory effect on the production of changes that culminate in bleeding from open wounds in the skin" (p. 500).

Another important factor, and one surely tied to the absorption in relevant imagery, is the intense emotion accompanying stigmata and related cases. Many people have noted, and many of the phenomena described in this chapter suggest, "that intense emotional experience can activate specific psychophysiological mechanisms" (Whitlock & Hynes, 1978, p. 200). The fundamental question, however, behind stigmata as well as all the other phenomena described in this chapter, is "How?" Although some may presume with R. L. Moody (1946) that "neural pathways undoubtedly exist by which psychic contents may be projected on to the body in a highly specific manner" (p. 935), we must ask what exactly are the neural pathways underlying a physical symptom, such as stigmata, with a highly specific form, location, and temporal occurrence: "It is difficult to see how underlying systemic disorders on their own could cause painful recurrent bleeding, often for periods of many years" (Whitlock & Hynes, 1978, p. 199). More specifically, "we have no understanding of how the brain could instruct local blood vessels and other tissues to represent the various forms in the skin" (Stevenson, 1997, vol. 1, p. 87); and vague suggestions that "an anomalous activation of nerve fibers...induc[es] the liberation of histamine in points where the lesions are formed" are—or should be—clearly inadequate (Margnelli, 1999, pp. 463–464).

Hysteria

As I mentioned above, the association between stigmata and hysteria may provide a clue to some more fundamental underlying characteristic, such as suggestibility or absorption, that can lead to both. It should thus not be surprising that hysteria involves other psychophysiological effects; indeed, hysteria is defined as "symptoms of a neurological nature—paralysis, anaesthesia, aphasia, blindness, amnesia, fits, etc.—for which there is no apparent neurological cause" (Lader, 1973, p. 265). Moreover, the symptoms are not only not caused by organic damage, but they also "cannot be mapped on to conventional neuroanatomical knowledge" (Sierra & Berrios, 1999, p. 267). Discussing hysterical anesthesia, Myers noted that "the anæsthetic belts or patches do not always, or even generally, correspond with true anatomical areas, such as would be affected by the actual lesion of any given nerve. They follow what may be called fancy arrangements;—sometimes corresponding to rough popular notions of divisions of the body,—sometimes seeming to reflect merely childish caprice" (*HP*, vol. 1, p. 45).

Because of the paradox in the biomedical model of a disease with no apparent pathophysiology, there has been much controversy over the years about the validity of hysteria as a diagnosis or even a concept. Some physicians have considered it merely "a cloak for ignorance" (Marsden, 1986, p. 285). Nonetheless, "a tough old word like hysteria dies very hard. It tends to outlive its obituarists" (Lewis, 1975, p. 12), in large part because observation of the symptoms persists. Thus, despite the waxing and waning of hysteria as a diagnostic category, "the concept of 'hysteria' is alive and well in the practice of medicine" (Slavney, 1990, p. 3). Without further understanding of the mechanisms involved, however, some physicians have suggested that it be considered, not a diagnosis, but simply a "descriptive neurologic shorthand" (Marsden, 1986, p. 286).

The theoretical importance for psychology of hysterical symptoms was not lost on Myers. He repeatedly emphasized that such phenomena provide a potential source of important knowledge about psychophysiological functioning in general, precisely because they are "phantom copies of real maladies of the nervous system...due...not to purely physiological but rather to intellectual causes" (*HP*, vol. 1, p. 43). Cases of hysteria provide "one of the most fertile sources of new knowledge of mind and body" because they are "in some ways a better dissecting agent than any other" for isolating, manipulating, and studying the psychological and organic contributions to the symptoms, especially when hysterical symptoms can be compared with organically caused neurological cases that they resemble (*HP*, vol. 1, pp. 43, 65). Noting also (as many others have) the parallels and similarities between hysteria and hypnosis, Myers considered both to be manifestations of an unusual instability or permeability in the boundary normally separating subliminal and supraliminal processes. He thus considered hysteria to be a "self-suggestive malady" or "disease of the hypnotic stratum" (Myers, 1893a, p. 5). By studying the two together therefore—hysteria as the spontaneously occurring phenomenon, hypnosis as the experimental production of the same or similar phenomena—we might begin to unravel the "paradoxical" notion of a physical symptom induced by an idea.

As with all the phenomena I am discussing in this chapter, most attempts to explain hysteria have "wavered between the two terms of Cartesian dualism" (Ey, 1982, p. 11), considering them either "real" (that is, organic) or "imaginary" (that is, psychological or malingering). The term "hysteria" itself derived from the longstanding belief that the disease, far more common in women, resulted from a disorder of the uterus; but the 18th-century physician Robert Whytt proposed that it was instead a derangement of the nervous system, not the uterus, and 19th-century scientists took up this idea enthusiastically (Slavney, 1990, pp. 22–24). Maudsley, for example, vaguely attributed hysteria to an underlying "molecular disorder" in the nervous system. Janet thought it was a deficiency in neural "energy" resulting in an inability to integrate sensory input and thus a "dissociation" of sensorimotor processes. Some thought it primarily a disorder "in the higher cerebral centers" (Yazící & Kostakoglu, 1998, p. 166); and others have suggested that the symptoms are the result of changes in cerebral blood flow (Sierra & Berrios, 1999, p. 272).

In the absence of detailed knowledge of the physiology involved, however, such explanations amounted to "the delineation of a metaphor, not the demonstration of a mechanism" (Slavney, 1990, p. 24). Psychodynamic interpretations thus began to take over. Breuer and Freud, for example, proposed that the primary mechanism is the conversion of a strong idea or emotion into somatic expression—specifically, the observed symptoms of motor or sensory dysfunction or loss—"in much the same way as kinetic energy can be converted into various forms of movement and power" (Whitlock, 1967, p. 146).

The conversion hypothesis, however, is itself metaphoric and does not explain but *embodies* the problem. It "fails to state how it bridges the gap between the mental and the physical. How does the psychic energy or libido actually become transformed into something physical to produce, say, a paraplegia?" (E. Miller, 1987, p. 166). Psychological explanations such as conversion have seemed to many to be "very much tied up with dualist notions of mind/brain relationships" (E. Miller, 1999, p. 188), and, because of the modern determination to avoid at any cost the "pain of Cartesian dualism" (Halligan & David, 1999, p. 161), the pendulum has swung away from psycho-dynamic interpretations of hysteria and back again to seeking neurophysiological mechanisms—but this time rooted more squarely in the notion of the "brain-mind," that mysteriously unified entity in which the terms on either side of the hyphen are, in the final analysis, synonymous.

It has been known since the late 19th century that the sensorimotor functioning of an hysterical patient remains intact at some level, although part of it is prevented somehow from reaching the patient's awareness. For example, a patient suffering from hysterical blindness may, when hypnotized or producing automatic writing, give evidence of having perceived a particular visual stimulus when he or she is unaware of having done so. Similarly, patients with hysterical anesthesias rarely suffer any injury to the affected area, as often happens when sensation is blocked by, say, chemical anesthesia (*HP,* vol. 1, pp. 46–47). Since the 19th century, therefore, neurophysiological theories have described hysteria not so much as a *loss* but as an *inhibition* of normal sensorimotor processes, with a resulting dissociation of sensory input and perceptual awareness. Ludwig (1972), for example, attributed hysteria to "a dysfunction of attention and recent memory due to increased corticofugal inhibition of afferent stimulation" (p. 771).

Building on such proposals, researchers in recent years have attempted to identify more specifically the neural correlates of hysteria. There have not yet been many such studies. Some writers (Athwal, Harrigan, Fink, Harshall, & Frackowiak, 2001) have expressed surprise at the "dearth of relevant neuropsychological or anatomicophysiological reports in the literature" (p. 217); but the development of neuroimaging techniques has encouraged scientists that we now have the "means of elucidating the neural correlates of conversion disorder" (Yazící & Kostakoglu, 1998, p. 163). The earliest neuroimaging studies involved EEG recordings of evoked potentials, using somatosensory, visual, or auditory stimuli corresponding to the clinical deficits. In general these studies have tended to show that there is little or no alteration of "early" components (those closely tied to physical aspects of the stimuli), but significant changes in later components associated with attention and other aspects of psychological response (Lader, 1973; Marsden, 1986; Sierra & Berrios, 1999). Other evoked potential studies have similarly supported a "gate control theory" of pain, in which pain is prevented somehow from reaching consciousness (Sierra & Berrios, 1999, pp. 276–277; Slavney, 1990, p. 28), even though the painful stimulus appears to be processed normally up to the cortical entry level.[24]

Tiihonen, Kuikka, Viinamäki, Lehtonen, and Partanen (1995) used SPECT imaging to measure changes in cerebral blood flow in a patient with both paralysis and loss of sensation in her left arm. They took measurements during the time she was symptomatic and after she had recovered, and found differences suggesting that the hysterical symptoms were "associated with the simultaneous activation of frontal inhibitory areas and inhibition of the somatosensory cortex" (p. 134).

Two years later Marshall and colleagues reported a study with a woman suffering from left-sided hysterical paralysis of her arm and leg (Marshall,

24. It remains unresolved at this point whether hysterical sensory deficits do sometimes reach down to earlier levels of the corresponding pathways, as suggested by Levy and Mushin (1973) and some other early studies. An ideal way of pursuing this question would be to use natural tactile stimuli (not electrical stimuli, which bypass the tactile receptors in the skin) applied to anesthetic versus normal hands in the same subjects. This would circumvent the problems that arise in connection with visual and auditory stimuli stemming from changes of head or gaze orientation and provide each "hysterical" evoked response with a natural within-subject control.

Halligan, Fink, Wade, & Frackowiak, 1997; a more complete report is in Athwal et al., 2001). They used PET to measure regional cerebral blood flow both when she attempted to move her left (paralyzed) leg and when she attempted to move her good leg. Unlike attempts with the good leg, which activated contralateral motor cortex in the expected way, those with the paralyzed left leg "failed to activate right motor cortex"; instead, there was significant activation of the right orbito-frontal and right anterior cingulate cortex, two areas that are "implicated in action, emotion, and motor inhibition" (Marshall et al., 1997, pp. B1, B5). Like Tiihonen et al., they concluded that hysterical paralysis involves the inhibition of the relevant sensorimotor areas by activation of frontal inhibitory mechanisms.

Other studies (Yazící & Kostakoglu, 1998; Vuilleumier et al., 2001) have also shown alterations in cerebral blood flow suggesting "regional cortical inhibition associated with conversion symptoms" (Yazící & Kostakoglu, 1998, p. 167). In two additional studies, researchers used imaging methods (evoked potential methods in Lorenz, Kunze, & Bromm, 1998; PET in Spence, Crimlisk, Cope, Ron, & Grasby, 2000) to try to distinguish between patients with hysterical sensorimotor losses and healthy persons feigning such losses. Researchers in both studies concluded that hysterical sensorimotor loss can be "neurophysiologically distinguished from malingering" (Lorenz et al., 1998, p. 191). In the first of these, an hysterical patient failed to produce an "oddball" evoked response at the cognitive level (P300) to rare stimuli applied to his anesthetic right hand, even though the sensory pathways themselves were apparently intact since the potentials evoked by both electrical and thermal (laser) stimulation of that hand were otherwise normal. This finding supports the early conjecture of Ludwig (1972) that the deficit is not at the sensorimotor level, but at some higher, cognitive level. In the second study, which compared three patients showing hysterical motor weakness of an arm with two feigners and six control subjects, Spence et al. (2000) found evidence suggesting that the patients' hysterical motor symptoms were associated with reduced blood flow in left dorsolateral prefrontal cortex, an area associated with volition.

Neurophysiological studies such as these are all converging on the idea that the physiological symptoms of hysteria are produced by some inhibitory mechanism, operating at a "high level of cognitive processing," that "inhibits processing of information at levels necessary for awareness," and moreover that prefrontal structures are the "likely substrate" because they are part of the "network that integrates attentional responses and generates awareness" (Sierra & Berrios, 1999, pp. 283, 279). Neuropsychiatrists, in short, may be closing in on physiological expressions of the mechanism by which "distressing psychological events...alter the neurophysiology of the human brain in a specific way and trigger [specific] symptoms...through activating or inhibiting critical areas of the brain" (Tiihonen et al., 1995, pp. 135–136). But the critical question—with regard not only to hysteria and all the phenomena discussed in this chapter, but also to "normal" volitional phenomena such as raising one's arm—is not *whether* this or that area of the brain is activated, inhibited, or in some other way altered; obviously, "hysterical paralysis must express itself through the physiological medium of brain anatomy" (Athwal et al., 2001, p. 216). The critical question is *how* the physiological change producing the symptoms is set in motion in the first place: "How is the meaning of events translated into the pathophysiology of neurons?" (Slavney, 1990, p. 29); "how the neurotransmitters were affected by the psychological state...still requires explanation" (E. Miller, 1999, p. 188); "how [do] psychological mechanisms translate (convert) from an emotional reaction into physical symptoms" (Halligan & David, 1999, p. 161)? The problem, again, is particularly acute when the symptoms "do not reflect known anatomical functions, do not correspond to known neurological pathways...,and do not follow known principles of neurophysiologic response patterns" (Ludwig, 1972, p. 771).

The problem becomes still more acute when we recognize what has made hysteria so notoriously difficult both to diagnose and to define nosologically—namely, its protean nature. Symptoms may change location, may respond to suggestion, or may reflect some meaningful response to psychological precipitating conditions. Another important point is one that Myers called attention to more than a century ago, but has rarely been appreciated: Both hysteria and hypnosis involve not just a functional *loss* or *inhibition* but also a *gain,* in that the hysteric or the hypnotized person seems to have attained a level of control—albeit at a subliminal level—over processes not ordinarily under volitional control. Moreover, physiological studies of hysteria seem to be showing that there is no underlying organic damage and that the nervous system is operating normally—"the brain receives normal sensory input...and can issue normal motor commands." What seems to be affected, instead, is the cortical activity ordinarily associated with consciousness, and "it is here that contemporary neurobiology faces a major challenge. The cerebral mechanisms of consciousness are not understood" (Marsden, 1986, p. 287).

In sum, as in the case of stigmata an adequate account of hysterical conversion will have to account for the specificity of the symptoms, as well as for the facts that they often do not fit any anatomical pattern (as in "glove anesthesias"), may change location, and can often be changed, alleviated, or cured by suggestion. General psychophysiological mechanisms, therefore, such as that behind "the tears that follow tragedy and the facial flushing that accompanies shame" (Slavney, 1990, p. 23) or the perspiration, tachycardia, and other symptoms accompanying stress, anxiety, or fear cannot adequately account for the "more dramatic" symptoms of hysteria (E. Miller, 1999, pp. 186–187). Scientists may increasingly be "elucidating the neural correlates of conversion disorder" (Yazící & Kostakoglu, 1998, p. 163), but, as Myers frequently emphasized, "correlates" is a neutral term and implies nothing about causation. Describing what is happening at the physiological level in the modern terminology of the neurosciences brings us no closer to an adequate theoretical understanding of the phenomena than we were a century ago. Modern neurophysiological terminology, like the old psychodynamic terminology, can too easily "distract attention from careful investigation of how beliefs and related mental images about the body come to implement physiological changes in the persons affected" (Stevenson, 1997, vol. 1, p. 53n).

The search for an adequate theoretical model, however, has been hampered by the fear of being chained to an outmoded dualism. Like most modern scientists, those addressing the problem of hysteria have called for a reconceptualization of the phenomenon that avoids the pitfalls of dualism (E. Miller, 1999) and offers instead "a more all-embracing concept" that integrates rather than separates *"the organic and functional, somatic and psychological"* (Ey, 1982, p. 18). Again, however, I emphasize that such "holism" also brings us no closer to a real understanding of psychophysiological phenomena and too often leads instead to such vacuous statements as "an individual's hysterical symptoms correspond to his/her ideas about what his/her symptoms should look like [because] his/her symptoms are his/her ideas" (M. Turner, 1999, p. 200).

Multiple Personality and Dissociative Disorders

Another phenomenon involving profound altered states of consciousness, and closely related to hysteria, is multiple personality disorder (MPD), now more generally called dissociative identity disorder (DID). The main feature of MPD is not, as in hysteria, the so-called conversion or somatic symptoms, but the dissociation. Nonetheless, perhaps not surprisingly, there are frequent reports of MPD patients manifesting strikingly different physiological characteristics or symptoms in association with different "alter" personalities. In Chapter 5 we will discuss MPD in detail. In this section, I will concentrate on neurophysiological findings in MPD patients, especially from the point of view of their relevance for the central message of this chapter, namely, that "experimental investigations of the processes by which persons with MPD accomplish such changes may eventually aid the understanding of normal mind-body processes" (S. D. Miller & Triggiano, 1992, p. 57).

There have been several reviews of psychophysiological changes associated with MPD (Birnbaum & Thomann, 1996; Coons, 1988; S. D. Miller & Triggiano, 1992; F. W. Putnam, 1984, 1991). Systematic observation and research in this area was initially motivated by continuing skepticism and controversy over the clinical validity of MPD and the hope of determining whether it was "real" or simply an extreme form of role-playing. But as Putnam (1991) pointed out, hoping to "prove" the reality of MPD with psychophysiological studies is probably unrealistic, since "there are few physiological measures that can readily distinguish between separate people" (p. 491). Thus, the goal of research on the psychophysiology of MPD has gradually shifted away from trying to "prove" the reality of MPD and instead toward trying to identify the neurophysiological processes underlying MPD and thereby aid in our understanding of the mechanisms of consciousness in general (e.g., S. D. Miller & Triggiano, 1992, p. 57; F. W. Putnam, 1991, p. 493; Reinders et al., 2003)—a goal more in line with Myers's approach of studying abnormal and unusual phenomena to shed light on normal psychophysiological processes. All the reviewers have emphasized that research in this area is in its infancy: There have been few studies yet with adequate experimental controls, and many of them are unpublished, presented only in conference reports. Nonetheless, these preliminary studies, as well as frequent clinical observations, have shown that psychophysiological changes associated with MPD constitute a robust and potentially important phenomenon.

Psychophysiological changes between alter personalities have been observed "in virtually every organ of the body" (Coons, 1988, p. 47). Although such observations are often derisively labeled as mere "anecdotes," the persistence and number of them was what suggested the need for more controlled studies in the first place. Many of the changes, in fact, are sensorimotor changes similar to those seen in hysterical conversion. There have been reports, for example, of anesthesia or analgesia in one personality but not others (e.g., B. G. Braun, 1983a, pp. 87–88; Ludwig, Brandsma, Wilbur, Bendfeldt, & Jameson, 1972, pp. 305–306); estimates of the incidence of these are 25–38% (Coons, 1988, p. 48; F. W. Putnam, Guroff, Silberman, Barban, & Post, 1986, p. 287). Related phenomena such as deafness or auditory hallucinations, or muteness or speaking with different accents, have also been reported (Coons, 1988, p. 48; S. D. Miller & Triggiano, 1992, pp. 54–55).

There have also been reports of changes in handedness or handwriting across personalities (Coons, 1988, p. 49); in one study, 37% of the 100 patients surveyed showed changes in handedness (F. W. Putnam et al., 1986, p. 289). As many as 26% of MPD patients show allergies in some personalities but not in others (F. W. Putnam et al., 1986, p. 289). In their book about their famous patient "Eve," for example, Thigpen and Cleckley (1957, p. 132) reported that the alternate personality Eve Black had an allergic reaction when she wore nylon stockings, whereas the original personality Eve White did not. B. G. Braun (1983b) described a case in which one personality could eat oranges normally, whereas all the other personalities were allergic to citrus. In another case one personality was allergic to cats, whereas another was not. In still another a woman had an allergic response to smoke in one personality but not in another. In a survey of 100 cases, 35% involved alter personalities which responded differently to foods, and in nearly half the cases they responded differently to medications (F. W. Putnam et al., 1986, p. 289). For example, B. G. Braun (1983a) reported a case in which a woman who developed adult-onset diabetes "required variable amounts of insulin depending on which personality had control" (p. 87).

Related to stigmata and the recurrence of traumatic wounds in some psychiatric patients are phenomena that B. G. Braun (1983b, p. 127) observed in two patients. One woman, whose mother had repeatedly burned her with cigarettes, developed several red marks on her skin while recalling the abuse in one personality, and they would reappear whenever that particular personality emerged.[25] In another case Braun observed stripe marks develop across a patient's arms, shoulders, and neck, apparently reflecting the patient's memory of being whipped by his mother with a bull-whip. Similar cases appear in unpublished reports. Ewin (1979; see also B. G. Braun, 1983b, pp. 127–128) had a patient who had suffered severe burns in a motel fire. Ten years later, after he learned about a boy who had similarly been burned in a hotel fire, "the area from which his skin grafts had been taken became quite red, painful, and swollen" (p. 271). Densen-Garber (unpublished data cited in Coons, 1988, p. 50, and in S. D. Miller & Triggiano, 1992, p. 56) reported on stigmata-like phenomena in two cases. In one, a woman addicted to heroin in one personality (but showing no withdrawal symptoms in the others) would develop needle track marks when she switched to that personality. In another, a man beaten as a child would develop welts and marks on his back and legs when he switched to his child personality.

Sensory changes, especially visual ones, have also been described. An early case was that reported by Dufay in 1876 (Alvarado, 1989, p. 162; *HP*, vol. 1, pp. 133–135), in which a woman who had severe myopia requiring glasses could, when in a somnambulistic state, do needlework and even thread the needle easily without her glasses and in poorer light. Condon, Ogston, and Pacoe (1969) studied film recordings made of "Eve" and discovered that the three personalities all showed strabismus (divergent eye movements in which the two eyes move in different directions and/or at different speeds). The "least stable personality" showed by far the largest number of such divergent movements, whereas the personality who later became the dominant personality showed very few. B. G. Braun (1983a, p. 86) reported color-blindness in a patient ("documented by the isochromatic color blindness test") that disappeared following successful integration of the personalities. Birnbaum and Thomann (1996) reported a case remarkably similar to cases of hysterical blindness, in which the patient briefly showed a severe loss of peripheral vision in her right eye during a particularly stressful time in her psychiatric therapy. The same patient required different corrective lens for her primary and an alter personality, and there were also differences between them in corneal curvature and astigmatism.

It is in studies of optical changes across personalities that we begin to find experimental studies assessing these differences. So far there have been three such studies (S. D. Miller, 1989; S. D. Miller, Blackburn, Scholes, White, & Mamalis, 1991; the third, a 1985 study by Shepard & Braun, is unfortunately unpublished, but is described briefly by Miller, whose studies

---

25. Braun reports that he confirmed this particular abuse with outside sources. Whether the memories of abuse by patients reflect real events or are false memories has been a matter of much controversy and debate in psychiatric and legal forums (see, e.g., Braude, 1995; D. Schacter, 1996), but for purposes of the issues I am discussing in this chapter, resolving that debate is unnecessary. The crucial point here is that mental changes, whether rooted in reality or fantasy, can lead to unarguably real physiological changes.

were intended as a replication). In the first study Shepard and Braun, examining seven MPD patients, found "clinically significant optical differences between alter personalities" on six measures: visual acuity, manifest refraction, color vision, pupil size, corneal curvature, and intraocular pressure (S. D. Miller, 1989). On two additional measures, eye muscle balance and visual fields, there were no significant changes except in one patient. In his attempt to replicate this study, Miller added a control group of nine people who attempted to simulate alter personalties, for comparison with nine MPD patients.[26] An ophthalmologist, blind to which persons were the patients and which the simulators, administered and evaluated the ophthalmological tests. He tested these 18 people on five of the eight measures that Shepard and Braun had used: visual acuity (both with and without correction), manifest refraction, pupil size, eye muscle balance, and visual fields. There were 4.5 times more changes among different personalities in MPD patients than in those of the simulating controls. Some of the measures are "subjective," requiring the responses of the person being examined, whereas others are "objective," or measured directly by the ophthalmologist; but Miller questioned whether even the subjective measures were "transparent" enough so that a feigning patient would know the appropriate responses to make, and furthermore whether patients would be knowledgeable enough to produce the consistent results observed over multiple trials (p. 485).

S. D. Miller et al. (1991) replicated this study, extending it to 20 MPD patients and 20 simulating controls, and they again found significantly greater differences, both statistically and clinically, between the alter personalities of the MPD patients than between the "simulated" personalities of the controls. In a table summarizing the results of the three studies, however, they also show that the measures on which significant changes were found were not the same across all three studies, with changes in visual acuity and manifest refraction being the most consistent.

In addition to these controlled comparisons, Miller, like clinicians before him, noted some "highly unusual personality-specific" physiological changes that were "not amenable" to statistical study (p. 483).[27] In one

26. Although experimental studies with "control" subjects are usually considered the ideal to which all psychological research must conform to be acceptable, studies of MPD involving simulating controls raise the question of how useful such a research model is when confronting phenomena produced by highly unusual subjects. This question arises again in connection with experimental studies of hypnosis that fail to acknowledge the importance of using highly hypnotizable subjects (discussed later in this chapter) and in connection with phenomena associated with creativity, genius, and mystical experience (Chapters 7 and 8).

27. S. D. Miller and his colleagues (1991) caution that there has been no systematic research on whether observed differences are consistent over time within personalities, and that "psychophysiological differences between personalities may be more labile than previously thought." Nevertheless, they believe that the study of such differences should move away from demonstrating the phenomena toward seeking the "underlying processes by which these patients develop such differences" (p. 135).

patient, for example, a condition known as accommodative-type esotropia, or a rotation of the eyes that sometimes appears in 4- to 5-year-old children but eventually corrects itself, was observed only in a personality that was four years old, and not in the adult personalities. In another case, an adult personality showed presbyopia, or deterioration of the ability of the eye to adjust thickness and curvature of the lens, whereas two child personalities did not, consistent with normal aging of eyesight. One personality of a third patient had 20/15 visual acuity in both eyes and no muscle balance problems; but in another personality, vision "markedly deteriorated to 20/30 in the right eye, and 20/50 in the left eye," and there was also a muscle balance disorder (a rotation outward of the left eye). Both conditions "*completely* resolved" when the patient switched back to the first personality (p. 484).

As with hysterical conversion, the development of neurological measuring techniques has prompted studies looking at measurable physiological differences between MPD alter personalities. Unfortunately, most of these studies date from the 1970s and 1980s, when techniques were less developed than they are now, but they are worth noting because many of them did demonstrate quantitative differences between personalities that could, and should, be followed up using more sophisticated imaging and statistical techniques.

The first such study, published nearly 100 years ago (M. Prince & Peterson, 1908), looked at galvanic skin response (GSR), or changes in skin resistence, in three personalities of one patient. Presented with emotionally laden words, the personalities reacted differently to them, as measured by the GSR. It took more than 60 years for someone to follow up on these promising results, but in 1972 one study measuring, among many other things, GSR in four personalities was reported (Ludwig et al., 1972). Emotionally laden words were determined for each of the four personalities and presented to the appropriate personality; again there were differential responses consistent with the clinical picture. In a second study, however, with a different patient who also had four personalities, Ludwig and his colleagues (Larmore, Ludwig, & Cain, 1977) found no unusual changes in GSR. Two additional studies involving measurement of skin conductance (Bahnson & Smith, 1975, p. 86, and Brende, 1984) found changes that "var[ied] by emerging personality." More recently, F. W. Putnam, Zahn, and Post (1990) looked at skin conductance in the context of other activity of the autonomic nervous system (ANS), such as heart and respiration rates. They found overall differences among the alter personalities of nine MPD patients, but they also found differences among the alter personalities of five simulating control subjects. Nevertheless, the patterns in the various changes led the authors to suggest the "differences in ANS activity between alter personality states may be arrived at in different ways" by MPD patients and controls (p. 256).

Several studies have used EEG methods to look for possible differences among personalities, not only in patterns of spontaneous electrical activity but also in average evoked responses, usually from visual stimulation. Two studies—one of Eve in the 1950s by Thigpen and Cleckley, and another by Morselli of a patient named Marisa—found EEG differences in background alpha frequency, as well as in muscle tension (F. W. Putnam, 1984, p. 33; Thigpen & Cleckley, 1954, p. 145; 1957, pp. 141–142). Similarly, Ludwig et al. (1972) found "dramatic differences in [EEG] activity," including differences in alpha blocking (Ludwig, 1983, p. 95). The personalities in Larmore et al.'s (1977) patient also showed changes in alpha abundance, but not significant enough for any "definite conclusions" (p. 39).

As S. D. Miller and Triggiano (1992) remarked, "psychophysiological research using evoked potentials has provided some of the most consistent and convincing experimental evidence for the existence of MPD as a clinical entity, as well as for the distinctness of the personality states" (p. 50). In the pioneering study of Ludwig et al. (1972), there were "definite qualitative differences in the VER [visual evoked response] records in the [four] different states" (p. 305), and these findings, together with the other physiological and psychological measures taken, led the authors to suggest that the personalities represent "different altered states of consciousness" (p. 308). Ludwig and his colleagues (Larmore et al., 1977) stated this conclusion even more forcefully in the report of a second patient, in which the physiological findings were in general unremarkable, with the notable exception of the visual evoked response: "The average visual evoked responses (AER) for each personality [four] were quite different from each other," and in fact, "each personality had its own individual AER type, as if four different people had been tested" (p. 40).

In an attempt to replicate Larmore et al., F. W. Putnam and his colleagues (Putnam, 1984, pp. 35–36; Putnam, 1986, p. 112; Putnam, 1991, p. 493) conducted a study in which they compared the visual evoked potentials of MPD patients with simulating controls. The results showed "significant differences in evoked and spontaneous central nervous system (CNS) activity across MPD personality states that were not duplicated by the simulating controls" (Putnam, 1991, p. 493). Specifically, "the MPD alter personalities looked significantly less like each other on the measures of amplitude and latency for the P100, N120, and P200 visually evoked potential components than did the 'alternate personalities' of the simulating control subjects" (Putnam, 1986, p. 112). More generally, because within an individual the visual evoked response seems to be "relatively reliable and time-stable" and "fluctuations...[are] extremely limited" (Larmore et al., 1977, p. 40), it seems unlikely that MPD patients were feigning these differences.

There have been a few other studies of visual evoked responses. In a preliminary study of two patients who had been successfully integrated using hypnotherapy, B. G. Braun (1983a) found differences in the scalp topography of the P100 component of visual evoked responses between personalities and following the integrations. Pitblado and Cohen (1984) reported "significant and longitudinally stable differences among the five personality states in amplitudes, latencies, and right-left asymmetries." Two other (unpublished) studies similarly found "a significant personality effect on the evoked potentials" (S. D. Miller & Triggiano, 1992, p. 50).

More recent studies have involved contemporary neuroimaging techniques, including mapping of EEG frequencies (Hughes, Kuhlman, Fichtner, & Gruenfeld, 1990), SPECT (Saxe, Vasile, Hill, Bloomingdale, & Van der Kolk, 1992), and PET (Reinders et al., 2003). Although the results have again suggested reproducible differences between alter personalities in individual patients, these studies can at best be considered preliminary only, given the large number of problems that have yet to be satisfactorily controlled. Nonetheless, discussion of the possible mechanisms and implications of physiological differences between alter personalities of MPD patients has begun. F. W. Putnam (1991) outlined the five primary models that have been proposed—namely, that alter personalities are the product of: (1) an autohypnotic or trance-like state; (2) a functional disconnection between the cerebral hemispheres; (3) epileptic-type seizures in the temporal lobes; (4) discrete psychophysiological and behavioral states produced by mechanisms such as conditioning or state-dependent learning and memory; and (5) feigning or role-playing. Putnam concluded that there is little if any evidence thus far to support (2) or (3) and considerable evidence to refute (5). The "most congruent" model to Putnam seems to be (4), although he also pointed out, in support of (1), the relationship between hypnotizability and clinical dissociation in adults.

Much of the neurophysiological evidence to date can, in fact, be viewed as supporting a Myers-like view of alter personalities as the products of an hypnotic-like state in which some "slackening of the centralising energy" can start a process leading to "a new mnemonic chain" in which state-dependent learning and memory can accrue and eventually form a new personality. Moreover, he believed, these "fresh combinations of our personal elements...may be evoked, by accident or design, in a variety to which we can at present assign no limit" (Myers, 1888a, pp. 383, 387).[28] Since Myers's time, much more data has accumulated suggesting the high hypnotizability of MPD patients (already well recognized in the late 19th century by Myers, Charcot, Janet, and others), as well as in support of a Myers-like "behavioral state model...that alter personalities represent discrete behavioral states of consciousness with personality state-specific encoding of certain types of memory, behavior, and psychophysiology" (F. W. Putnam, 1991, p. 499)—in short, that partly distinctive personalities can develop within the same organism and influence it in somewhat divergent fashions.

The major remaining question, however, is not so much why, but how these states form and, especially, how the accompanying physiological changes are produced. The one finding on which probably all observers of MPD can agree is the central role of emotion, and especially stress, in

28. Some of these conditions of "accident" and "design" which Myers suggests can produce these new chains of consciousness include dreams, somnambulism, automatic writing, trance, certain intoxications, hysteria, and hypnotism (Myers, 1888a, p. 387; see also our Chapters 2 and 5).

engendering and maintaining dissociative states; and certainly the general importance of emotional states in altering both the autonomic and central nervous systems is well known. It seems likely, therefore, that EEG, blood flow, and GSR or other autonomic changes reflect the different emotional states of the various personalities, because of changes in arousal, anxiety, muscle tension, and the like that must accompany these emotional changes (Coons, Milstein, & Marley, 1982; F. W. Putnam et al., 1990). Ludwig et al. (1972), for example, found that psychophysiological changes are prominent in "emotionally relevant areas" but "tend to disappear for most emotionally neutral or non-affect-laden material" (p. 308). Mathew, Jack, and West (1985) found marked changes in regional cerebral blood flow in the right temporal lobe between alter personalities in two patients, and they suggested that, because the right hemisphere plays an important role in general in emotional states, it follows that it would play a similar role in dissociative states.

Such explanations may well be correct for generalized physiological changes, but the picture becomes more complicated when we encounter more specific and selective changes, such as the vision changes found by S. D. Miller and his colleagues, different allergic responses, anesthesias, or state-specific stigmata-like reactions, all of which have been reported repeatedly and for years. For such effects, researchers have so far suggested only rather vague models involving some kind of inhibition of function. B. G. Braun (1983b), for example, speculated that when patients do not show an allergic reaction in one state that they have in others, this is because "the final common pathway, the allergic response, can be blocked" (p. 133). Reinders et al. (2003) similarly suggested "an inability…to integrate visual and somatosensory information," that is, a "'blocking' of trauma-related information" (p. 2122), and Forrest (2001) concluded that the orbitofrontal cortex produces "a pattern of lateral inhibition between conflicting subsets of self-representations which are normally integrated into a unified self" (p. 259).

But do such proposals really constitute an explanation of the mechanism leading to specific physiological changes? Or are they merely redescriptions of the original phenomena in more "modern," physiological terms? As with studies of hysteria, scientists may be starting to close in on some neural correlates of some dissociative phenomena. But, once again, the larger underlying problem is: How is the differential and often quite specific and time-limited release of particular neurotransmitters, or the "blocking" of somatosensory information, or the "lateral inhibition" between the various states accomplished? This central problem, already serious enough in the context of the spontaneously occurring phenomena I have discussed so far, becomes even more serious when we consider psychophysiological changes that are induced *deliberately*. I turn next to these.

Specific Physiological Effects Induced Deliberately

Deliberately induced changes in autonomic processes that are not ordinarily under voluntary control have long been reported (Tuke, 1884), particularly in connection with yogic, Zen, or other meditative practices intended to alter the ordinary influences of physical, and particularly sensory, processes on consciousness.[29] In this section, I will describe some of the autonomic changes that have been observed and some proposed explanations, concentrating especially on phenomena suggesting unusual kinds or levels of deliberate, volitional control over autonomic processes.

I begin with two cases, reported in a medical journal and later described by Dunbar (1954), that are reminiscent of cases I described earlier, such as those of R. L. Moody (1946, 1948), in which a person remembering a traumatic experience developed marks or wounds on the skin corresponding to injuries suffered during that experience. Dunbar described two people who could apparently deliberately produce urticaria, or wheals on the skin. One was a physician who had been "able from childhood to produce urticaria on his arms and trunk 'by the strength of his will'." The other was "able, under the eyes of the physician, to produce an urticarial wheal at any designated spot on his forehead just 'by thinking about it,' without any previous touching of the spot" (p. 612).

Among the earliest studies describing deliberately induced autonomic changes were several of persons who claimed to be able voluntarily to increase their heart rate. The physician Tuke (1884, pp. 371–372) confirmed the claim of an acquaintance that he could voluntarily increase his heart rate 10 to 20 beats a minute; on the occasion that Tuke observed, his pulse went from 63 to 82 in two minutes. Tuke was inclined to think "the mere direction of the Attention to the heart is sufficient," but because few people can accomplish this feat, it might have been more appropriate to suggest that a focus of attention on the heart might be necessary, but certainly not sufficient. Between 1872 and 1968 at least 18 more such cases were reported in the scientific and medical literature. Favill and White (1917), for example, reported Favill's own ability to increase his heart rate by 30 to 96 beats a minute, the increase usually beginning immediately and reaching its peak after "several beats." Another example is Luria's (1968) remarkable subject S., who demonstrated for Luria his ability to control his heart rate by first raising it to 100 from a resting state of 70 to 72 and then lowering it to 64 to 66 beats a minute. He said that he did the first by imagining himself running to catch a train, and the second by imagining himself in bed trying to fall asleep (p. 139). Most observers of these effects reported no correlation with respiration rate, and most subjects could shed little light on how they were able to produce them. Some reported, rather vaguely, exerting considerable

29. For a comprehensive bibliography of about 1,700 studies of physical and psychological effects of meditation from 1931–1996, see M. Murphy and Donovan (1997).

mental effort. At least one person said specifically that he did *not* conjure up appropriate imagery or emotion, but was able to raise his heart rate in the same way—whatever that is—that one raises an arm: "It is probably no more—*and no less*—mysterious than is, for example, the flexing of a biceps muscle" (Ogden & Shock, 1939, p. 320; italics added).

I have added italics to this important sentence because, despite its familiarity, volitional control of our muscular activity—how the intention to raise an arm translates into the appropriate motor response—remains a mystery, encapsulating the mind-body problem in its essence, and not magically erased by simply asserting that the intention and the response are both brain processes. This point is underscored by the work of Basmajian (1977) on voluntary control of single motor units in skeletal muscles. Specifically, when provided with suitable auditory feedback derived from a fine-wire electrode inserted into skeletal muscles (such as biceps), most subjects can rapidly learn to enhance selectively the activity of any given motor unit within the area sampled by that electrode, while suppressing that of neighboring units. Virtuoso subjects can not only raise or lower the overall rates at which such isolated units generate motor potentials, but control their temporal spacing as well, some even producing complex rhythmic sequences such as "drum rolls" on demand. Two further points are especially significant here: First, successful subjects have no idea whatever *how* they exercise this control; they simply learn to do so, much as an infant learns to control its limbs. Second, the control in this case is certainly direct, as there is in general no naturalistic situation a person might recreate in imagination that would produce a corresponding specificity of motor unit behaviors.[30]

The increased heart rate in the cases described above was usually accompanied by other autonomic changes, such as a rise in blood pressure and dilation of the pupils. Although these were normally involuntary accompaniments, Tuke (1884, pp. 375–377) also reported on two men each of whom could "in the same light contract or dilate his pupil at will" and, at least in one of the cases, "with as much facility as he can open and shut his hand." One of these men produced the changes by imagining himself in a bright or a dark place; but the other said specifically that he did not use any such imagery. Similarly, Luria's subject S. showed a cochlear-pupil reflex when he imagined a piercing sound and a depression of alpha waves when he imagined that a strong light was flashing in his eyes (Luria, 1968, p. 142).

---

30. There is also an enormous literature on the control of autonomic processes through biofeedback training, such as the regulation of blood flow to the hand, and hence hand temperature, in Raynaud's disease. (I will discuss later in the chapter efforts to influence blood flow in Raynaud's disease by hypnotic suggestion.) Biofeedback studies are obviously relevant to understanding the relationship between volition and physiological processes, but so as not to make this chapter even longer than it already is, I will simply refer readers to sources such as Kamiya et al. (1971), Lehrer and Woolfolk (1993), and G. E. Schwartz and Beatty (1977).

Yogis

I turn now to autonomic changes voluntarily induced by yogis or other trained meditators. A frequent claim is that some yogis are able to survive long periods of time in a meditative state without food, water, or even air. Several studies have examined the hypothesis that they do this by lowering their metabolism, one indication of which would be a decrease in heart rate and hence in oxygen consumption. Although a lowered heart rate could be presumed to be the result of the relaxation, at least one case suggested that something more may be involved. Hoenig (1968) observed that, while the yogi was in a meditative state (maintained in the experiments for up to nine hours), there was an unusual pattern in his heart rate: It gradually decreased from 100 to 40, and then gradually increased again to 100, in regular cycles of 20 to 25 minutes. Despite the unusual pattern, Hoenig suggested that it was probably "a by-product of relaxation of an extreme degree" (p. 88).

Some yogis have claimed that they can survive conditions of deprivation not simply by lowering heart rate, but by stopping the heart altogether. Again, Tuke (1884, pp. 372–373) provided examples of Westerners who have made such claims; but when modern devices such as EEG and EKG allowed better examination, in most cases it was found that the heart did not actually stop. The heart sounds and the pulse were reduced enough not to be detectable by ordinary examination, and thus the heart seemed to have stopped without actually having done so. This reduction was apparently accomplished by some variation on the Valsalva maneuver, in which contraction of chest muscles, while holding the breath, puts pressure on the heart. Again, however, the picture is not quite so simple because in at least two cases EKG seemed to show that the heart *had* in fact stopped. McClure (1959) reported the case of a non-yogi in which EKG showed "slowing of the sinus rate progressively to the point of sinus arrest for a period of a few seconds" (p. 440). Moreover, no breath-holding or Valsalva maneuver was observed; "the patient simply abolished all sympathetic tone by complete mental and physical relaxation" (p. 441).

A much more extreme case, observed and reported by Kothari, Bordia, and Gupta (1973a, 1973b), involved a yogi who was confined to a small underground pit for eight days, connected to an EKG with 12 leads "short enough not to allow any movement" (1973b, p. 1646). Almost immediately after the pit was sealed, a significant sinus tachycardia developed and progressed until it reached 250 beats per minute, but without any sign of ischemia. This tachycardia continued for 29 hours when, suddenly and with no prior slowing of the heart rate, "a straight-line had replaced the [EKG] tracing" (p. 1647; a reproduction of the tracings is in the report). The investigators wanted to terminate the experiment, understandably fearing that the yogi was dead, but his attendants insisted that it continue. The flat-line state persisted for five more days until, half an hour before the experiment was scheduled to end, sinus tachycardia again developed. This continued for two hours after the yogi was removed from the pit, when his heart rate finally returned to normal (98 beats per minute). The obvious explanation, that the EKG leads had been disconnected, was ruled out, first because the machine was immediately checked for any malfunctioning, but more importantly because no electrical disturbance ever appeared, such as would accompany the disconnection of the leads; subsequent attempts by the investigators to disconnect the leads always produced "gross and irregular electrical disturbance." Moreover, malfunction of the machine was highly unlikely, since "the [EKG] re-appeared spontaneously on the last day" (p. 1649), an "extraordinary coincidence" if it had been a malfunction of the machine (M. Murphy, 1992, p. 535).[31] Having ruled out such explanations, the authors candidly admitted that they were "not prepared" to accept that the yogi had voluntarily stopped his heart for five days and survived; but they could "offer no satisfactory explanation for the [EKG] record before us" (p. 1649).

Other studies (Anand, Chhina, & Singh, 1961b; Hoenig, 1968; Karambelkar, Vinekar, & Bhole, 1968; Vakil, 1950) have also involved putting yogis in underground pits, for periods ranging from hours to days, and observing metabolic changes including oxygen intake and carbon dioxide output. Most have shown a significant decrease in oxygen consumption, "much more than what could be produced even by sleep" (Anand et al., 1961b, p. 89), a finding replicated in the studies by Wallace and Benson (Wallace, 1970; Wallace & Benson, 1972) of Transcendental Meditation practitioners. Concurrently, there is usually a significant decrease in carbon dioxide output.

Most investigators have concluded that yogis can survive these conditions not only because of their reduced metabolism but also because "airtight" underground pits are not, in fact, airtight, even when sealed; oxygen and other gases seep in from the surrounding earth. In one study (Anand et al., 1961b), however, the pit actually was airtight, not one dug in the earth but a specially constructed metal box. In these conditions the yogi showed that he could voluntarily "reduce his oxygen intake and carbon dioxide output to levels significantly lower than his [ordinary] requirements" (p. 87).

Other physiological changes suggest even more direct control of autonomic functions. Luria (1968, pp. 140–141) reported that S. deliberately raised the temperature of one hand by 2° C and then immediately lowered the temperature on the other hand by 1½° C. He said that he did this by imagining one hand being placed on a hot stove and the other being immersed in cold water. Similarly, a yogi was reportedly able to induce an 11° F difference in the temperature of the left and right sides of the palm of one hand, with the color of the skin changing to pink on the hot side and grey on the cold side (M. Murphy, 1992, p. 532). Wenger and Bagchi (1961) observed a yogi who could produce forehead perspiration within 1½–10 minutes of being asked to do so; moreover, the temperature on his forehead

31. The sudden reappearance of the heart beat half an hour before the scheduled end of the experiment also suggested an unusually precise internal clock, since the yogi had been in complete isolation and darkness for eight days (M. Murphy, 1992, p. 535).

and on his arm was found to have risen. To warm himself while meditating for long periods in cold mountain caves, he had taught himself to do this by imagining himself in a warm place. Similarly, Benson et al. (1982) found that three practitioners of g Tum-mo (or heat) yoga, who also learn to warm themselves while meditating in cold Himalayan mountain conditions, could deliberately and significantly raise the temperature of their fingers and toes, by amounts ranging from 3.15° C up to 8.3° C.

Body temperature can apparently also be lowered. For example, the yogi studied by Kothari et al. (1973b), who had such extreme and deliberately produced fluctuations in heart rate, including a straight-line EKG for five days, had also induced a marked hypothermia. The investigators reported that his body temperature was "abnormally cold" (34.8° C / 94.6° F) when he was removed from the pit, and he shivered severely for two hours afterward, although the temperature in the pit had been normal and comfortable (24–33° C) for the entire eight days (pp. 1648–1649).

Several hypotheses have been suggested for metabolic changes such as these. Wenger and Bagchi (1961) suggested that the ability of the yogi who could voluntarily produce perspiration on his forehead was "a conditioned ANS response pattern to visual imagery based on reaction to the ambient temperature in the caves" in which he meditated, which the authors estimated was about 0° C (pp. 313–314). This argument seems rather circular, however, since it is difficult to understand what produced the original, unconditioned rise in local skin temperature that provided the basis for such conditioning. Benson et al. (1982) said that the "most likely mechanism" was not controlling metabolism but controlling vasodilation, or blood flow (p. 235). Similarly, Frederick and Barber (1972) concluded that "the principles involved," both in yogis and in hypnotized subjects (as I will discuss later), are "localized vasoconstriction and vasodilation...induced by various types of suggestions," whether from oneself or from another person. In other words, "the process of vividly imagining cold water gives rise to vasoconstriction and the process of vividly imagining warmth gives rise to vasodilation" (p. 860). However, as with most pronouncements that a response is the result of "suggestion" or "imagining," such an "explanation" is no more than a restatement of the phenomena in biological terms, and the deeper problem still lurks: *How* are these hypothesized mechanisms activated in the first place, particularly in instances of specific and localized, rather than general or systemic, changes?

Specific Physiological Changes Induced by Hypnosis

I turn now to phenomena apparently induced at the "suggestion" of another person; but it is important to keep in mind here Myers's definition of suggestion as "successful appeal to the subliminal self" (*HP*, vol. 1, p. 169) and its implication that many phenomena ostensibly produced by suggestion from another person may in large part be attributable to auto- or self-suggestion.

Psychophysiological changes have been deliberately induced most frequently through hypnosis. (As we will see in the following pages, however, many of the same phenomena have been produced by suggestions that did *not* involve a formal hypnotic induction.) Like other phenomena discussed in this chapter, hypnosis (and its predecessor, mesmerism) has a long, complicated, and often contentious history, and there is an enormous literature about it. The definitive history may be found in Gauld (1992). In this section I will limit the discussion to an especially important aspect of hypnosis—the localized and often quite specific physiological changes that have been induced by hypnotic suggestion.

It is first important to emphasize, as have Myers and others, that hypnosis is much more than an entertaining oddity. Myers (1885c) considered hypnotism "as above all things *a method of psychological experiment*" (p. 641n), "an experimental method of reaching the subliminal self," and particularly a "means of artificial displacement of the psycho-physiological threshold" (Myers, 1891b, p. 83). Others since Myers have echoed its importance. For example, Bramwell (1903, p. 176) remarked that, although its therapeutic use in surgery and medicine is necessarily limited because only a small proportion of patients are sufficiently responsive to it, it is nonetheless of great theoretical importance for both psychology and physiology. T. X. Barber (1984) said bluntly that because suggestion can produce physiological changes, "the royal road to solving the mind-body problem involve[s] unraveling the mystery of hypnosis" (p. 77).

Much of the research on hypnosis over the past century has revolved around the question of whether hypnosis is a discrete "state" with its own unique phenomena, or whether it is simply an extension or variation of normal states of consciousness and psychological processes associated with suggestion. The variety of positions taken over the years on this question has prompted a corresponding variety of attempted explanations for the physiological changes induced by hypnosis, especially hypotheses about the role of cortical inhibition or alterations in blood flow, and about the central role of emotion, imagery, and belief. I will return to the question of the adequacy of these explanations after I have provided some examples of specific psychophysiological changes induced by hypnotic suggestion.[32] In the meantime, there are two important points to keep in mind. First, those (like Barber) who have repeatedly argued that many phenomena produced by hypnotic suggestion can also often be produced by non-hypnotic suggestion or by voluntary efforts are certainly correct. One of the main points of this chapter is, as Myers emphasized, the continuity and interrelationship of phenomena such as I have been discussing, both with each other and with other psychophysiological processes. We will see, therefore, that many

32. For reviews of such phenomena, see T. X. Barber (1961, 1965, 1978, 1984), Crasilneck and Hall (1959), Gorton (1949), M. Murphy (1992, chap. 15), and Stevenson (1997, vol. 1, pp. 56–68).

unusual phenomena described earlier, including stigmata and other skin changes, changes in allergic reactions, sensory changes such as anesthesia and analgesia, changes in heart rate and other autonomic functions, and the healing effects associated with placebo, occur not only in waking states involving intense emotion, imagery, or belief, but also with hypnosis. Hypnosis may in some way facilitate these phenomena, but there seem to be no phenomena absolutely unique to hypnosis.

The other crucial point to keep in mind is that effects seen in connection with hypnosis often go far beyond general systemic effects of stress or relaxation, in terms of their specificity of location and other characteristics, and that any adequate explanation must address this specificity. Many theorists have contended that hypnosis is a simple extension of "normal" psychological processes, produced by compliance with the experimenter's instructions, "role-playing," or outright feigning.[33] They have been able to do so, however, only by confining their observations primarily to studies involving the most elementary, commonplace phenomena, and conducted with ordinary, even non-hypnotizable, subjects.[34] I therefore dissent sharply from the position taken by McDougall (1908). Contrasting himself with those such as Myers who "fix their attention on the most strange and perplexing of the phenomena of hypnotism," McDougall regarded as "more sober" and "more consistent with scientific principles" an approach that "concentrate[s] attention upon the simplest and least astonishing of them" (p. 242). I instead agree with Myers, who, as I pointed out in Chapter 2, believed that confining one's observations to a narrow range can lead only to a position that, lacking "width of purview," may be completely misleading.[35] In this section, therefore, I will concentrate on the more rare, extreme phenomena that are too often ignored in theorizing about hypnosis.

Most of the research on physiological effects of hypnosis, as well as most of the extreme phenomena reported, have occurred in connection with the effects of hypnosis on pain and on a variety of conditions involving the skin. Before turning to these two primary areas, I will first mention briefly some effects that have been induced by hypnosis on autonomic and sensory processes.

Autonomic Effects

Many studies have examined changes induced by hypnosis in autonomic functions such as glucose level, gastrointestinal effects, skin temper-

33. For a detailed discussion of this "sociocognitive" position, see Chapter 5.

34. This "college sophomore as subject" methodology has been a major factor in the inadequacy of much psychological research and has led, in our view, to the trivialization not only of hypnotic phenomena, but also of important areas of human experience such as creativity, meditation, and mysticism (see also Chapters 7 and 8).

35. I remind readers here of "Wind's principle," quoted in the Introduction.

ature, salivation, and heart rate, but the conclusion of most reviewers of the phenomena has been that these changes are secondary results of changes in emotional arousal (e.g., T. X. Barber, 1961, 1965; Crasilneck & Hall, 1959; Gorton, 1949; Reiter, 1965). In one patient, for example, temporary cardiac arrest was induced by suggesting that the patient recall previous episodes of fainting (Raginsky, 1959), an effect perhaps related to the emotion generated by the memories. In another study, however, reminiscent of the deliberately induced changes in heart rate among yogis and other persons, a dramatic acceleration of heart rate was induced by hypnosis, an effect apparently induced directly and not by any suggested or accompanying emotions (van Pelt, 1965).

I mentioned earlier some cases of multiple personality disorder in which the subject, while exhibiting the personality of a young child, showed physiological effects appropriate to that age: In one case, the child personality had a childhood eye muscle disorder that disappeared in the adult personalities, and in another the older personalities had myopia, whereas two child personalities did not (S. D. Miller, 1989). A similar age-specific alteration in myopia was induced hypnotically by Erickson (1943). An even more important study was reported by Gidro-Frank and Bowersbuch (1948), in which three subjects, regressed to the age of about five to six months and below, consistently exhibited the Babinski reflex, a reflex that is produced by stroking the sole of an infant's foot, and that normally disappears and gradually changes to a different kind of reflex by the age of about one year. The Babinski reflex appeared spontaneously, with no specific suggestion for it by the experimenters and in subjects unaware of its existence and properties. One reviewer (Gorton, 1949) commented shortly after the publication of this study that it was "the best single piece of evidence available at present to support the thesis that hypnotic suggestion *properly administered to suitable subjects* can bring about psychobiological changes in the total organism which are impossible of attainment in the waking state" (p. 478; italics added).

Another interesting case involving autonomic changes is related to the phenomenon of false pregnancy, discussed earlier. Its subject, a male undergoing hypnotherapy in an attempt to quit smoking, was on one occasion given the suggestion to imagine himself as the person he would like to be. Instead of imagining himself as a non-smoker—presumably the hypnotist's intention—he imagined himself as a pregnant woman. A homosexual whose partner had recently died, he had long thought of himself as a woman and had wished he could bear a child. After the initial suggestion by the hypnotherapist, the patient continued on a daily basis to produce vivid imagery of himself as a pregnant woman, and by the time he came to a hospital three months later, he had an enlarged abdomen, morning nausea, nipple secretion, and "noticeable" enlargement of one breast (D. Barrett, 1988).

A related series of studies similarly suggests that strong imagery in connection with suggestion can contribute to structural changes in the body. In these studies 70 women who wished to increase the size of their breasts were given several relevant suggestions while in a hypnotic trance. They were instructed, for example, to feel sensations of warmth and tingling in their breasts and to visualize themselves as they wished to look. Nearly all the women succeeded to some extent in increasing their breast size, with an average increase across the studies of 1½–2 inches.[36] Moreover, one of the researchers (Willard, 1977) found that those women who could "obtain visual imagery, quickly, easily, and a large percent of the time that they attempted it" had the greatest success (p. 197). T. X. Barber (1978) proposed that "this kind of focused, believed-in thinking, imaging, and visualizing can lead to increased blood flow to the breasts which, in turn, could stimulate breast development" (p. 20). As with many explanations this sounds at least vaguely plausible, but it is in fact only a *description* of a possible mediating mechanism. It is in no way an explanation of *how* imagery sets in motion the specific and focused blood flow necessary to produce the imagined result.

Sensory Effects

For more than two centuries there have been frequent reports of sensory changes, in all modalities, that occur as a result of hypnotic (or mesmeric) suggestion. These include, for example, increased acuity of senses (hyperaesthesia) and hallucinations (whether positive ones, to perceive something for which there *was* no physical stimulus, or conversely negative ones, *not* to perceive something). The philosopher Henri Bergson reported in 1876 a case of hyperaesthesia in which the ability of a hypnotized boy to identify "clairvoyantly" a playing card being looked at by the experimenter turned out instead to be an ability to see the card reflected in the experimenter's eye (*HP*, vol. 1, pp. 477–479). More recent if less dramatic studies have demonstrated improvements of visual acuity with hypnosis in highly hypnotizable subjects (e.g., Davison & Singleton, 1967; Kline, 1952–1953; Weitzenhoffer, 1951). Other people, however, have noted that similar improvements can be induced by suggestion only, not accompanied by hypnosis (e.g., Sheehan, Smith, & Forest, 1982). They have thus attributed such feats, not to some special ability associated with the hypnotic "state," but to processes such as increased (or decreased) attention to stimuli or to feigning or "role-playing" (whether deliberate or not) in compliance with the hypnotist's instructions. To address this issue, much emphasis has been placed on examining more objective changes, especially changes not ordinarily under volitional control.

For example, changes in normal dilation or contraction of the pupils during hypnosis have occasionally been reported. One of the earliest to observe this was the surgeon Esdaile (1846), who described several occasions in which the pupils of a hypnotized patient remained dilated even

---

36. For references to these studies see T. X. Barber (1978) and M. Murphy (1992, pp. 336–337).

when exposed to full Indian sunlight: "The muscles of the eye, and iris,... lose their contractibility, and the eye becomes as motionless and insensible to light as that of a dead man" (pp. 46, 82–83). Similarly the French physician Féré reported that the pupils of two hysterical patients contracted and dilated appropriately in response to a suggestion given in the "cataleptic" (or deep hypnotic) state, but not to the same suggestions when they were in a normal state (Tuke, 1884, p. 377). More recently, Schwarz, Bickford, and Rasmussen (1955) found that in two of three subjects who responded to a hypnotic suggestion of total blindness, the pupils became "much more dilated and sluggish in their reaction to light" (p. 567). More dramatically, Erickson (1977) reported "subjects who would dilate the pupil of one eye and contract the pupil of the other in hypnotic trance, when looking at the same light" (p. 9). Unfortunately, he published no detailed report of these observations; but he did describe (1965) the case of one girl who could produce unilateral pupillary responses even when *not* hypnotized, reminiscent of the three subjects reported by Tuke and Luria (discussed earlier) who could voluntarily control pupil contraction or dilation. Significantly, this girl was "an excellent hypnotic subject"; she had extensive experience with producing suggested visual hallucinations, and she was also "remarkably competent in developing autohypnotic trances to obliterate pain."

Whether changes of these sorts have been induced by hypnosis or by nonhypnotic suggestion, our oft-repeated question remains: How? To say that it is simply a matter of voluntarily, or even involuntarily, diverted attention (see, e.g., T. X. Barber, 1961; McPeake, 1968) demonstrates the inadequacy of explanations that deal only with the more commonplace phenomena. The hypothesis of diverted attention becomes somewhat strained when one considers a report in which a hypnotized subject did not react "even when a pistol was discharged close beside him" (Esdaile, 1846, p. 278). Perhaps the important diverted attention here is not that of the subject from the relevant stimulus, but that of the theoretician from the relevant phenomena.

Recent imaging studies seem to be moving us in the direction of seeing hypnosis more comprehensively, neither as a mere extension of normal capacities nor as a discrete and homogeneous altered "state" associated with unique phenomena, but instead as a means of facilitating—in ways still unknown—physiological changes that go far beyond those producible by simple imagining or role-playing. For example, two recent PET studies of hypnotically induced hallucinations (Kosslyn, Thompson, Costantini-Ferrando, Alpert, & Spiegel, 2000; Szechtman, Woody, Bowers, & Nahmias, 1998) both found changes in regional cerebral blood flow consistent with what is seen during "real" sensory perception, but unlike the changes seen with nonhypnotic imagery. As the authors of one of these studies concluded, "hypnosis is a psychological state with distinct neural correlates and is not just the result of adopting a role" (Kosslyn et al., 2000, p. 1279).

Autonomic and sensory changes such as I have been discussing present a significant enough challenge for those seeking to develop an adequate theoretical understanding of hypnosis and suggestion. When we examine the phenomena of hypnotic analgesia and effects involving the skin, we encounter even more serious challenges.

Hypnotic Analgesia

Hypnosis—or, more properly in this context, mesmerism—developed primarily as a therapeutic tool in late 18th- and early 19th-century medicine, but observers quickly realized that perhaps its most powerful medical use, in the days before chemical anesthesia, was as a means of reducing and even eliminating the severe pain that otherwise accompanied every surgical procedure. The heyday of mesmeric analgesia occurred between 1829, when a cancerous breast was removed from a mesmerized patient who showed no signs of pain and no changes in pulse or breathing during the surgery, and 1854, when a similar surgery was performed in the presence of several observing physicians (see Gauld, 1988). By far the most surgeries carried out in conjunction with mesmerism were performed by James Esdaile in Bengal between 1845 and 1851. These surgeries included amputations of breasts, limbs, and penises, as well as less severe operations, but the largest number (161) were for removal of often enormous (up to 80 pounds) scrotal tumors, a condition distressingly common in those days in Bengal. Even after the introduction of chemical anesthesia in the mid-19th century, which quickly superseded the need for any other kind in most cases, mesmeric or hypnotic analgesia continued to be used occasionally, especially in situations when a chemical agent might have been dangerous. Bramwell (1903, chap. 9), for instance, described numerous cases of his own as well as those of other physicians, particularly for the removal of teeth (an excruciatingly painful procedure without anesthesia), but also for eye surgery, removal of tonsils and uterine and breast tumors, and childbirth. Even in more recent years, numerous painless surgeries under hypnosis have been reported (for a list of 32 reports of such surgeries between 1955 and 1974, see Hilgard & Hilgard, 1975/1983, p. 134).

As with hypnosis in general, attempts to explain hypnotic analgesia have fallen primarily into two camps, which can be roughly described as (1) physiological theories that seek an explanation in terms of changes in the brain, especially the inhibition of memory, attention, or perceptual processes; and (2) psychological theories that seek an explanation in terms of normal psychological processes such as expectation, relaxation and anxiety reduction, or "role-playing" enacted in compliance with the social or interpersonal context. These two groups of theories are by no means mutually exclusive. Nevertheless, the acceptance of hypnotic analgesia has been hindered by the frequent contention that hypnosis has not really produced analgesia, but has only prompted subjects to adopt a variety of strategies either for coping with the pain or for hiding it from observers. Thus, as with other phenomena I have been discussing, some investigators have tried to go beyond relying on verbal reports of patients and have sought more objective physiological indicators of pain, or the lack of it.

Even as early an investigator as Esdaile had gone beyond the almost invariable verbal reports of his patients that they had felt no pain, and also beyond the observations by himself and numerous others that patients had endured the surgeries without showing overt behavioral signs of pain. He also reported that, in addition to the behavioral signs, physiological signs of pain—ones not readily amenable to volitional control, such as changes in pulse rate or pupil reaction—were absent. Decades later, other investigators began again to look at objectively measurable changes such as galvanic skin response, facial flinching, respiration and pulse, vasomotor changes, and pupil changes (for a review, see Gorton, 1949, pp. 468–473).

The recent emergence of brain imaging techniques has led to renewed interest in identifying physiological markers for, and explanations of, hypnotic analgesia (for a review, see Crawford, Knebel, & Vendemia, 1998). One early study (Goldstein & Hilgard, 1975), confirmed by later ones, weakened the hypothesis that hypnotic analgesia, like placebo analgesia, might result from the release of endogenous opioids: The analgesia persisted even after the injection of naloxone, which blocks opioid release. More recent studies, however, have begun to suggest other possible neurological mechanisms. D. Spiegel, Bierre, and Rootenberg (1989), for example, found changes in somatosensory cortical event-related potentials following hypnotic suggestions—but only among highly hypnotizable subjects—leading them to suggest (rather vaguely) that hypnotic analgesia involves "alterations in perceptual processing" (p. 753). Since then, other researchers have reported changes in event-related potentials in the anterior frontal cortex (Crawford, Knebel, Kaplan, et al., 1998; Kropotov, Crawford, & Polyakov, 1997).

In what one commentator (Gracely, 1995) called "a pivotal study" in the controversy between social-psychological and physiological schools of thought, Kiernan, Dane, Phillips, and Price (1995) found that a spinal pain reflex (the RIII) was reduced when hypnosis was effective in reducing pain, leading the authors to conclude that "hypnotic sensory analgesia is at least partly mediated by...mechanisms in the spinal cord" (p. 44). The picture was complicated, however, by a study that measured RIII, somatosensory evoked potentials, changes in spontaneous background EEG, and autonomic responses (heart rate and respiration). Although all 18 highly hypnotizable subjects reported significant reduction of pain and showed changes in the RIII spinal reflex, for some of the subjects the spinal reflex *decreased* in connection with the hypnotic analgesia, whereas in the rest it *increased.* The authors could only suggest that there must be individual differences in mechanisms for modulating pain (N. Danziger et al., 1998).

Still other neuroimaging studies support the emerging concept that multiple brain regions contribute differentially to the experience of pain (and thus to hypnotic analgesia), and that these "are highly interactive" (Rainville, Duncan, Price, Carrier, & Bushnell, 1997, p. 970). Using hypnosis as a tool to differentiate these regions, researchers have begun to suggest that the sensory and discriminative aspects of painful stimuli are handled primarily by somatosensory cortex, whereas aspects of emotional response, such as judgments of pain unpleasantness, are handled by anterior cingulate cortex and related frontal structures (Faymonville et al., 2000; Rainville, Carrier, Hofbauer, Bushnell, & Duncan, 1997, 1999). Hypnotic analgesia may therefore in part involve a functional dissociation between these normally cooperating parts of the brain, which in turn enables a blunting of the pain experience.

Although research on the neurophysiology of hypnotic analgesia (and of hypnosis in general) is becoming a robust activity, two major questions remain. The first, asked repeatedly throughout this chapter, is—*how* does it occur? Over a century ago, neurophysiologists were already suggesting that hypnosis involves the inhibition of higher cortical centers, and most neurophysiological theories since then have suggested one or another cortical or subcortical process as being inhibited or otherwise blocked from functioning normally during hypnosis. But how is this inhibition effected? What sets in motion the complex and specific processes involved in, say, complete analgesia of the right forearm or a left lower wisdom tooth? Some neurophysiologists have recently begun to recognize, as Myers (1886a) already had, that hypnosis involves more than "inhibitory cerebral action" (p. xlii). Crawford, Knebel, and Vendemia (1998) have suggested that hypnotic analgesia requires the "activation of a supervisory attentional control system...involving the anterior frontal cortex" (pp. 22, 29). But, again, what activates this "supervisory control system," and how does it know to release the relevant neurochemicals, or block the relevant neural pathways, or do whatever else is required to produce the desired result?

The second primary question lurking behind all the numerous and varied studies of hypnotic analgesia over the past century is prompted by the uneasy feeling that should be felt by anyone who has paid sufficient attention to what has actually been reported in connection with mesmeric and hypnotic analgesia—specifically, a feeling that somewhere along the way we have missed the boat, or, perhaps more precisely, that scientists have become so focused on the minor leaks in the hold that they have failed to go on deck and see the typhoon bearing down on the boat. I am referring here to the question of how adequate all proposed theories—neurological as well as psychological—are to account for the more extreme phenomena that have repeatedly been reported by qualified medical observers. For many people, there is "astonishment" when reading reports of these phenomena, because they challenge the belief "that hypnotic states are really no more than states of heightened awareness or attentiveness [or] states of conscious conformity and obedience" (Robinson, 1977, p. xxvi). The usual response of such people is simply to dismiss the reports as "anecdotes" that can be ignored in light of more "rigorous" experimental and clinical studies (Spanos & Chaves, 1989). This is bad enough, but it is even more intellectually irresponsible to distort and misrepresent what was actually reported, as T. X. Barber (1963) does to Esdaile's reports. Barber suggests that Esdaile's patients "may not have been free of anxiety and pain," because they "moved" or "gave a cry." He fails to mention, however, that such signs were extremely infrequent, as Esdaile himself reported, or that such signs of "moving" or "moaning" also occur occasionally in connection with chemical anesthesias such as ether, chloroform, or nitrous oxide (Gauld, 1988, p. 21). Moreover, Esdaile recognized that some patients were less responsive to suggestion than others, and may have felt some pain, and thus he soon introduced measures to ensure that a patient was adequately analgesic before proceeding with the surgery.

Moreover, as Bramwell (1903) and others have pointed out, there is a vast difference between (in Bramwell's terms) the "pinprick" involved in most experimental studies and the "faradic brush" (an extremely painful DC electrical stimulus) involved in other situations (p. 94). Most contemporary experimental studies use relatively minor and brief pain stimuli (understandably, given ethical considerations). The reports of surgical procedures, however, are quite another matter. There are, as I mentioned earlier, numerous reports of major surgeries, including amputations. Gauld (1988) points out that one response of some contemporary theorists has been to suggest that "the pain caused by surgical procedures is not as great as is commonly supposed"; but he cautions us to recognize that "it is easy, in these comfortable days, to forget what pre-anaesthetic surgery was like for the patient" (pp. 20–21).[37]

A few examples, selected from numerous similar ones, should illustrate the kind of extreme phenomena that need to be accounted for, and not dismissed cavalierly as "anecdotes," fabrications, or exaggerations. Moll (1901) cites "a cynical experiment of the American physician, Dr. Little, who thrust a needle through the cornea of a subject whom he suspected of simulation" (p. 113). A dental surgeon reported operating on several of Bramwell's hypnotized patients, extracting in all about 40 teeth, including a young girl's "two left lower molars, which were decayed down to a level with the alveolus, with pulps exposed; also two right lower molar stumps, and a lower bicuspid: all difficult teeth" (Bramwell, 1903, pp. 162–163). Mason (1955b) reported the case of a woman who had two impacted wisdom teeth extracted under hypnosis, involving an incision in the gum and removal of bone by chisels. Later, also under hypnosis alone, she had a follow-up surgical bilateral mammoplasty in which scars, skin, breast tissue, and fat were cut out and the breasts completely reshaped. This procedure took 70 minutes, during which time she showed no sign of pain or shock. She later said that she felt and remembered nothing.

---

37. Darwin, who ultimately rejected a medical career in part because of his inability to tolerate the suffering he witnessed, reminds us of this: "[I] attended on two occasions the operating theatre in the hospital at Edinburgh, and saw two very bad operations, one on a child, but I rushed away before they were completed. Nor did I ever attend again, for hardly any inducement would have been strong enough to make me do so; this being long before the blessed days of chloroform. The two cases fairly haunted me for many a long year" (Darwin, 1892/1958, p. 12).

One of Esdaile's nearly 300 surgeries illustrates in particularly vivid detail that we are not here talking about the "pinpricks" of most contemporary experimental studies.[38] The case was that of a man who for two years had suffered from "a tumour in the antrum maxillare; the tumour has pushed up the orbit of the eye, filled up the nose, passed into the throat, and caused an enlargement of the neck" (Esdaile, 1846, p. 147). Although the patient proved difficult to mesmerize, Esdaile finally succeeded in doing so. Then, he reports,

> I performed one of the most severe and protracted operations in surgery.... I put a long knife in at the corner of his mouth, and brought the point out over the cheek-bone, dividing the parts between; from this, I pushed it through the skin at the inner corner of the eye, and dissected the cheek back to the nose. The pressure of the tumour had caused the absorption of the anterior wall of the antrum, and on pressing my fingers between it and the bones, it burst, and a shocking gush of blood, and brain-like matter, followed. The tumour extended as far my fingers could reach under the orbit and cheek-bone, and passed into the gullet—having destroyed the bones and partition of the nose....The man never moved, nor showed any signs of life, except an occasional indistinct moan.[39] (pp. 148–149)

With this description firmly in mind, consider now this statement by T. X. Barber (1963), who purports to explain hypnotic analgesia in terms of the patient's "motivation for denial of pain":

> [He] has often formed a close relationship with the physician-hypnotist and would like to please him or at least not to disappoint him....[He] is aware that if he states that he suffered, he is implying that the physician's time and energy were wasted and his efforts futile....this may at times be sufficient for him to try to inhibit overt signs of pain such as moaning, wincing, or restlessness....[The patients] "bravely made no signs of suffering at all." (pp. 306–308)

---

38. T. X. Barber (1963) contemptuously dismisses those who "almost always rel[y] heavily on Esdaile's series" in support of their contention that truly painless surgeries have been performed under hypnotic analgesia alone (p. 316). Similarly, Spanos and Chaves (1989) "view with alarm the retreat to nineteenth century anecdotes" (p. 131). I make no apologies for being another who is profoundly impressed with Esdaile's reports. I can only wonder at the intransigence of those who simply dismiss reports that run counter to their beliefs, and moreover in doing so grossly misrepresent them. Furthermore, the suggestion that such reports are limited to one reporter or to the 19th century or any other "pre-modern" or "pre-scientific" period is simply false (again, see Hilgard & Hilgard, 1975/1983, p. 134).

39. A "moan," no doubt, that was behind Barber's dismissal of this case as not being truly painless—but as Esdaile commented later, "he declares most positively, that he knew nothing that had been done to him ...—and I presume he knows best" (p. 150).

It seems hardly necessary to point out the utter insufficiency of such "explanations" for cases like those of Esdaile.[40] Perhaps those who suggest that the pain is not as severe as we might imagine, or explain hypnotic analgesia in terms such as "role-playing" or "bravely" hiding their pain, would be willing to test their theories by submitting themselves to removal of a tooth, amputation of a leg, or probing of an exposed sciatic nerve without chemical anesthesia. The juxtaposition of Esdaile's report and Barber's explanation should demonstrate unequivocally the danger of relying too heavily, when theorizing about these or any other phenomena, on laboratory experiments divorced from real-life situations.

Skin Conditions: Healing

Many of the most profound analgesic effects of hypnosis have been obtained in situations involving severe trauma to the skin, such as surgery or burns (Dahinterova, 1967; Ewin, 1979; Hammond, Keye, & Grant, 1983, p. 56). Dunbar (1954) commented on the importance of the skin as a means of expressing emotion through physical symptoms. She surmised that, as "the boundary between the self and the outer world, the skin...seems to be peculiarly susceptible to suggestion" (p. 647). Not surprisingly, therefore, the other major area in which hypnosis and mesmerism have produced striking physiological responses has involved various skin conditions. In this context it has been used both to heal or remove such conditions and to *produce* conditions that were not already present. I will begin with the former, noting particularly what Sulzberger and Wolf (1934) pointed out long ago, that "dermatology [was] one of the first branches of medicine to recognize officially the curative powers of suggestion on organic ailments," because the effects were clear-cut: "lichen planus, psoriasis, warts, and dermatoses in general are either present, clearly visible, tangible and palpable—or they are gone" (p. 552). Results, in short, are objective.

Allergies

In a massive review of psychological factors in both the etiology and the treatment of skin diseases, Dunbar (1954, chap. 14) discussed the importance of emotion in connection with allergies, and she cited in particular a 1931 experimental study in which reactions to an allergen were significantly reduced or increased in response to hypnotic suggestion (pp. 628–

40. Such explanations are also not new. In a book full of reports of cases like Esdaile's, Elliotson (1843) described the amputation of a leg, in words as graphic as Esdaile's, and the subsequent reaction of a surgeon that "the man had been trained to it" and "had disciplined himself to bear pain without expressing his feelings" (pp. 7, 8). Like others since then, however, the skeptical surgeon ignored some crucial details, such as the report that during the surgery the "divided end of his sciatic nerve was...poked with the points of a forceps, and he gave no sign of suffering" (p. 11).

629). Decades later T. X. Barber (1984) concluded that "abnormally reactive (allergic) skin responses to pollen, house dust, tuberculin, and many other allergens can be reduced and at times totally blocked by suggestions not to react," particularly among highly hypnotizable persons (p. 75). Mason (1960), for example, reported that the lesions caused by skin allergies were improved in eight of nine patients by hypnotic suggestion. Among the most interesting studies, however, have been those in which allergic reactions to a skin test have been abolished. Mason and Black (1958) reported a case in which not only the patient's symptomatic signs of asthma and hay fever, but also her reactions to a skin test with the allergens that had previously affected her were abolished. Mason (1960) also reported a case in which he injected both of a patient's arms with tuberculin, but told the patient that one arm was being injected with water only. The skin reaction, as indicated by the Mantoux test, was inhibited in that arm, but normal in the other arm. Several weeks later, the test was repeated, with the experimental ("water"-injected) and control (tuberculin-injected) arms being reversed, and again the reaction was inhibited only in the arm that the patient believed had been injected with water (p. 336).

Black, Humphrey, and Niven (1963) extended this study to four more Mantoux-positive patients, this time evaluating not only the observed swelling and redness but also skin biopsies. Again, there was significant reduction in the overt symptoms, but no changes were found in the cellular patterns in biopsy specimens. They concluded that the reactions to hypnotic suggestion took place, not at the cellular level, but at the level at which fluids are exuded, suggesting "a vascular constituent...in the mechanism of inhibition" (p. 1652). Similarly, in a review years earlier of hypnosis and allergies, Gorton (1949, pp. 337–339) had suggested that the effect was on the "cutaneous reaction" and not on the underlying "allergic constitution."

In a more recent study (Laidlaw, Booth, & Large, 1996), 32 of 38 subjects were able to reduce significantly the size of skin wheals produced in reaction to a histamine solution when exposed to a hypnotic-like procedure involving relaxation, imagination, and visualization.[41]

Bleeding

Hypnotic suggestion has also been successful in controlling bleeding, an especially important use for hemophiliacs. Myers (*HP*, vol. 1, p. 490) had called attention to this phenomenon, particularly in connection with a case in which a young boy was cured of "a most desperate case of hæmorrhagy." But possibly the best-known case is that involving the Russian monk Rasputin, who was said to have been able to stop the bleeding of the hemophiliac son of the Czar by hypnotic suggestion (Stevenson, 1997, vol. 1, p. 58). Blood flow has also been slowed or stopped in an effort to

41. The subjects had been chosen randomly, all had comparable reactions to the histamine solution in a pretest, and all were given a hypnotic susceptibility scale, but there was no relationship between hypnotizability and the response of the skin reaction to the hypnotic suggestion (p. 245).

promote healing. McCord (1968) reported that, in a patient whose frequent and severe nosebleeds had responded only "poorly" to conventional treatments, a single hypnotic suggestion ("given...in a definite and purposeful manner") stopped the bleeding entirely, at least up to a three-month followup. Clawson and Swade (1975) reported immediately stopping the bleeding of a severe laceration. Bleeding that does not involve the skin has also been stopped, for example with severe gastrointestinal bleeding from ulcers (Bishay, Stevens, & Lee, 1984; L. E. Fredericks, 1967). Perhaps the most common use, however, has been to control bleeding in dental surgery, particularly with hemophiliacs (for reviews, see T. X. Barber, 1984, pp. 95–96; Crasilneck & Hall, 1959, pp. 15–16).

Hypnosis has also been used to increase blood flow. I noted earlier in the chapter reports that yogis could raise or lower the temperature in a hand, sometimes unilaterally. Similar results have been obtained with hypnosis (see T. X. Barber, 1978; Conn & Mott, 1984; McGuirck, Fitzgerald, Friedmann, Oakley, & Salmon, 1998; *HP,* vol. 1, p. 491). Because altered blood flow produces such temperature changes, a few investigators have asked whether hypnotic suggestion could help patients suffering from Raynaud's Disease, a painful condition caused by low peripheral blood flow, usually to the fingers or toes. Grabowska (1971) and Conn and Mott (1984) reported significant increases in blood flow in four patients, and Crasilneck and Hall (1975, pp. 127–128) reported that among 48 patients whom they had treated between 1950 and 1975, there was remission or marked improvement in about 60%.

Burns

In light of studies such as these showing that hypnotic suggestion can affect blood flow to specific sites (T. X. Barber, 1978, 1984), the hypothesis that healing of wounds might be accelerated by hypnosis seems more than plausible. In one study (Ginandes, Brooks, Sando, Jones, & Aker, 2003), for example, surgical incision wounds healed faster in a hypnotic suggestion group than in two control groups. In addition to—or perhaps because of—its effectiveness as an analgesic, hypnotic suggestion has also been used successfully to promote healing of severe burns. Most of the reports have been of clinical cases, such as that of Ewin (1979), who reported that 13 of 14 severely burned patients "healed rapidly and without scarring," including a man whose right leg had briefly been immersed up to the knee in 950° C (1750° F) molten aluminum. The 14th patient had "scoffed at the idea" of hypnosis, perhaps contributing to a self-fulfilling *lack* of effect.

Few controlled studies have been conducted, but in 1983 some preliminary findings were reported (Hammond et al., 1983; Margolis, Domangue, Ehleben, & Shrier, 1983; Moore & Kaplan, 1983). Two of these provided suggestive results consistent with accelerated healing, but the results in the third (Moore & Kaplan, 1983) were even more impressive. The patients served as their own controls in that each had suffered similar burns on both sides of the body (usually both hands), and the hypnotic suggestion was directed at one side only, randomly chosen. Four of the five patients "demonstrated clearly accelerated healing on the treated side," as judged by a physician unaware of which side had been treated. The fifth patient had temperature increases and rapid healing on both sides, and among the other four patients, after about the third day of treatment, there was no further acceleration in the difference between the two sides. However, there was surely motivation in the patients—understandably—to heal *both* sides and not conform to the experimental protocol to heal just one, and the authors pointed out some evidence suggesting this explanation of the results (p. 17).

Warts

Another situation in which hypnotic healing of a skin condition has been studied involves the treatment of warts. "Old-wives" remedies have been numerous, varied, and persistent for centuries. Such methods have included passing the warts to someone else by means of a knotted ribbon (Gravitz, 1981, p. 282), rubbing the warts with beef stolen from a butcher's shop (Tuke, 1884, pp. 403–404), or making a drawing of the warts and then burning the paper (Sulzberger & Wolf, 1934). "There are as many such methods as there are lands and customs" (Sulzberger & Wolf, 1934, p. 553), and the common element, clearly, is suggestion. As we have seen throughout this chapter, suggestion and accompanying psychological reactions can have profound effects in the absence of specific hypnotic induction techniques; and the removal of warts is no exception.

Dunbar (1954, chap. 14) said that the contribution of psychological factors to the etiology as well as cure of warts is "a subject...which illustrates particularly well certain phases of medical thinking," because folk treatments have "always" been around, but physicians ignored the phenomena until Bloch "had the moral courage and scientific objectivity to take up these matters and investigate them systematically" (pp. 623–624). She was referring here to the German physician Bloch, who in the 1920s developed an elaborate procedure in which patients were blindfolded and their warts exposed to the (non-existent) "X-rays" from a noisy and intimidating-looking machine. The warts were then painted with a topical treatment (actually, only a dye) and the patient warned not to touch the warts or wash off the "medicine" until it had faded. Bloch became famous for his successful cures of warts. In a group of 179 patients who were followed up, 31% were cured after the first treatment, and 78.5% overall were eventually cured. Moreover, the cures occurred usually within weeks, even though many of the patients had had their warts for months or even years, and previous medical treatments had been unsuccessful (T. X. Barber, 1984, p. 80; Sulzberger & Wolf, 1934, pp. 553–554). After Bloch, "the treatment of warts by suggestion [became] more or less respectable" (Dunbar, 1954, p. 624), and references to subsequent instances of successful treatment of warts by non-hypnotic suggestion can be found in several reviews (e.g., Sulzberger & Wolf, 1934; Surman, Gottlieb, Hackett, & Silverberg, 1973; Ullman, 1959).

A few investigators have compared the efficacy of hypnotic and nonhypnotic suggestion. The first such study was by R. F. Q. Johnson and Barber (1978), who gave the same suggestions to a group exposed to an hypnotic induction procedure and to another group instructed in "focused contemplation." Three of 11 patients in the hypnotic group were cured, as opposed to none of the "focused contemplation" group. Because these numbers were so small, Spanos and his colleagues attempted to replicate and extend these findings. In one experiment the hypnosis group did better than either a placebo or a no-treatment group. In a second experiment both a group given an hypnotic suggestion and a group given a suggestion without hypnotic induction did better than a control group (Spanos, Stenstrom, & Johnston, 1988). In a third experiment the hypnosis group did better than a medication-treated group, a placebo group, and no-treatment group (Spanos, Williams, & Gwynn, 1990).

All four studies provide some evidence for the effectiveness of hypnotic treatment, even though the subjects were not chosen on the basis of their hypnotizability, but solely because they had warts and volunteered for the study. Nonetheless, Spanos and his colleagues did find that subjects who lost their warts, whether in the hypnosis, suggestion, or placebo groups, reported more vivid imagery than those who did not. Similarly, two studies (Asher, 1956; Ullman & Dudek, 1960) found that patients capable of deep trance fared significantly better in being cured of their warts by hypnosis than did those who were not.

Others have reported the successful treatment of warts with hypnosis (e.g., Clawson & Swade, 1975; Ewin, 1974), but many such results have been criticized because they could not exclude the possibility of spontaneous remission, which does occur frequently. Recognizing this problem, Clawson and Swade (1975, p. 165) had remarked that a better experiment than curing all warts would be one in which specific warts were targeted. Successful experiments of this kind would weaken the explanation that the warts had disappeared spontaneously, as part of their "natural history," such as some general systemic change in the patient's immune system or vasomotor processes. In fact, there have been some studies in which patients had warts on both sides of the body (usually on their hands), the experimenters suggested that the warts on only one side would disappear, and only the selected warts were cured (Dreaper, 1978; Sinclair-Gieben & Chalmers, 1959).[42] In

42. Several other studies have *not* provided evidence for a side-specific effect, in that in these studies the warts disappeared on *both* sides and not just on the selected side (R. F. Q. Johnson & Barber, 1978; Spanos et al., 1988; Surman, Gottlieb, & Hackett, 1972; Surman et al., 1973); but there may be a fairly straightforward explanation. In a study that produced significant healing but not a side-specific effect, Spanos et al. (1988, p. 257) noted that the effect of suggestion was greater on the hand that had the most warts, whether it was the target or control side; and in their highly successful study, Sinclair-Gieben and Chalmers (1959, p. 481) had always selected the hand with the most or the largest warts as the target hand. As with burn cases, therefore, it seems likely that the patient's primary motivation would be to cure the worst, and preferably all, of the warts, rather than comply with the experi-

Dreaper's case, when treatment was begun the intention was to remove all warts, which were on both sides of both hands. When they began to shrink, however, he suggested to the patient that she allow one wart to remain, as a control; and "after ten months' treatment the only wart remaining was the suggested one" (p. 308). Attention was then directed to the remaining wart, and it too disappeared after two months.

Sinclair-Gieben and Chalmers thought that, to be successful, subjects had to reach a depth of hypnosis such that they could carry out a post-hypnotic suggestion—a logical hypothesis since the gradual disappearance of warts after hypnosis is, in essence, the continuing operation of a post-hypnotic suggestion. In their study, in nine of the 10 patients who could reach this level of hypnosis the warts disappeared on the treated but not on the untreated side.

Nearly all the proposed explanations of curing warts by suggestion have been variations on the idea that the blood supply to the warts has been altered, a change produced by some vaguely characterized neurological mechanism. Sulzberger and Wolf (1934) were among the earliest to propose this kind of explanation, saying that the "permeability of the capillaries may be affected by psychic influences," and more specifically that the hypothalamus receives impulses from the cortex, "which are, in turn, transmitted to the sympathetic and parasympathetic nerve fibres leading to the particular part. In this way, vasomotor and other changes are brought about which, in turn, can cause local trophic and physico-chemical changes. These changes are probably sufficient to make the soil unsuitable for further activity of the wart virus" (p. 555). In reviewing and summing up similar theories, Ullman (1959) emphasized the important role of emotion, and particularly "vasomotor effects emotionally induced": "The mechanism of healing in the case of cures by suggestion is in all likelihood dependent on local vascular changes brought about by vegetative impulses concomitant with the affective changes experienced by the patient" (p. 483).

Sulzberger and Wolf (1934), however, also cautioned that such descriptions "may, at first, seem to be a satisfactory explanation—but, on further analysis, how utterly hypothetical and incomplete!" (p. 556). We would do well to remember this cautionary remark, even—perhaps especially—now. I have asked repeatedly throughout this chapter whether more precise identification of physiological effects accompanying the phenomena discussed, even if correct, really gets us any closer to understanding what has set those effects in motion, particularly when they involve not simply a generalized systemic response to stress, relaxation, fear, or some other emotion, but instead a specific and localized response. As Dreaper (1978) asked, when commenting on his own impressive case in which the "mechanism" allowed one single wart among many to remain, "what can be the mechanism...

mental goal of removing only the randomly chosen ones. More clear-cut results might be obtained, therefore, by assuring patients that after the "target" warts have been removed, the treatment will later be directed toward the "control" warts.

[that] could cause the geographically selective destruction of warts" (pp. 308–309)?

Whatever the mechanism, most observers of the phenomena agree that, because warts are a kind of skin tumor produced by a virus, if warts "can be cured by suggestion, then we are forced to admit that we are concerned with something which deals with the most fundamental processes in medicine" (Sulzberger & Wolf, 1934, p. 553). Understanding this phenomenon might, therefore, lead to an "understanding of the bodily mechanisms involved in immunity, resistance against disease, malignancy, and other vital problems" (Gravitz, 1981, p. 282). More specifically, Clawson and Swade (1975) called warts "a model for metastasizing tumors," and they conjectured that if suggestion can cure warts by stopping the blood flow to the capillaries nourishing them, then "we think likewise tumors can be destroyed" (p. 165).[43]

Other Skin Diseases

Although the remission of tumors by hypnotic suggestion remains a hypothetical suggestion for now, hypnosis has nevertheless already been used successfully to treat skin diseases far more serious than warts. For example, Osgood (see *HP*, vol. 1, pp. 471–472), Bramwell (1903, p. 264), Asher (1956, pp. 311–312), Mason (1960), and others (see Crasilneck & Hall, 1959, p. 15) have reported curing or significantly improving cases of eczema with hypnotic suggestion, and Frankel and Misch (1973) reported significant improvement in a case of psoriasis that had resisted 20 years of conventional treatments. Dunbar (1954, pp. 616–623) reviewed numerous reports of cures, often almost instantaneous, of longstanding eczema, psoriasis, and other skin disorders. She also described a case of a physician who had suffered a severe X-ray burn, the effects of which had persisted for 14 years as painful swelling, eczema, and scars so severe that another physician had recommended amputation. The symptoms were almost completely cured after four weeks of hypnotic treatment, and a year later were completely healed.

Most striking, however, have been reports of the improvement in some cases of congenital ichthyosiform erythrodermia, or "fish-skin disease," a congenital disease appearing at birth or shortly thereafter in which a thick, black, horny layer of skin, inelastic and subject to painful lesions, covers part or even all of the body. There have been 10 cases in which this disfiguring and painful condition has responded favorably, with varying degrees of success, to hypnotic suggestion, improvements that were initially "unbelievable" to T. X. Barber (1984, p. 77), given that spontaneous remissions, or

43. Whereas patients can see warts and the effect that suggestion may be having on them, most tumors are not visible to the patient, and this may hinder the effectiveness of any suggestive techniques. Now, however, tumors can be viewed directly with imaging techniques, and it is worth considering that patients given appropriate suggestions together with the feedback of such images might respond to suggestion as effectively as patients with warts have done.

even significant improvement in response to conventional treatments, are practically unknown.

The first and most dramatic case was reported by Mason (1952). The patient was a teen-age boy in whom the disease affected nearly his entire body. Mason began the treatment by focusing suggestions on the left arm, with results both quick and striking: "Five days later the horny layer softened, became friable, and fell off. The skin underneath became pink and soft within a few days....At the end of 10 days the arm was completely clear from the shoulder to the wrist" (p. 422). Mason then treated the other arm, and 10 days later the legs and the trunk. The improvements ranged from 50–95% for various parts of the body. There was "rapid and dramatic" improvement in the first few weeks, but little further improvement after that. As Mason (1955a) reported later, however, four years after the treatment "not only has there been no relapse, but his skin has continued to improve...without further treatment of any sort, hypnotic or otherwise" (p. 58).

Inspired by Mason's results, other physicians tried hypnotic suggestion in similar patients, usually as a last resort when all other treatments had failed, and they too reported varying degrees of success. Mullins, Murray, and Shapiro (1955) reported a case of pachyonychia congenita, a condition similar to ichthyosis. Like Mason, they focused first on a specific area, in this case the left hand, and "within three days there was noticeable softening of the keratotic material on the left hand." The treatment continued, and the authors published photographs showing the dramatic improvement in the soles of the patient's feet. When the patient was admitted to the hospital, the condition was so painful that he could not walk and was confined to a wheelchair. By the 13th day of treatment, "he stood on his feet without pain for the first time in his life that he could remember," and by the 17th day "he was able to walk the length of the ward without pain." Five months later he was walking "with only slight impairment" (p. 267).

Mason (1955a), commenting on this case, noted that it "shows that the treatment is repeatable in other hands and that the improvement in the case I reported is not a freak occurrence." Other repetitions followed, with varying results that began to indicate the complex nature of such treatment. Kidd (1966), for example, called attention to the potential importance of the depth of trance attained. He had treated two patients suffering from ichthyosis, a father and his 4-year-old son. The father was able to achieve a sufficient depth of trance, and within five weeks there was 90% remission of his symptoms, a near-complete cure. In contrast, the child was "inattentive and easily distracted," able to achieve only a "light" and "superficial" trance, and he showed only 30% improvement. Similarly, Wink (1961) reported treating two sisters, and the sister who reached a deeper trance showed more improvement than the other.

Schneck (1954, 1966) reported two ichthyosis cases in which the response to the hypnotic treatment was more moderate and also took a more up-and-down course, apparently in part because the patients had ambivalent feelings about being cured; and at the end of his second report he commented that "no total cure has been effected" (1966, p. 234). He was apparently unaware, however, of two cases in which a total cure was achieved (Bethune & Kidd, 1961). In the first, after seven weeks of treatment, "the patient had reached a state of complete naked-eye remission," and four years later she remained cured. The second case was somewhat more complicated. The early results were "not so striking" as in the first case, and after about six months the patient had a partial relapse. This relapse prompted "a determined redirection of drive by the patient himself," which almost immediately produced "a complete remission, which has remained" (p. 1421).

The difficulty of explaining such effects is complicated by the undeniable fact that positive results are more the exception than the rule. Mason himself (1961), whose first case stimulated the rest, failed with eight subsequent ichthyosis patients with whom he tried hypnosis, and "why one case responded and the others did not still remains a mystery." One strong candidate for an explanation (not, however, mentioned by Mason) is that the first patient may have been highly hypnotizable, whereas the others may have been less so.

Whatever the reason, the cases that have been successful cannot simply be ignored because other attempts have failed.[44] Mason's first case report prompted numerous letters to the editor of the *British Medical Journal,* many of them skeptical and dismissive. One of the correspondents, however, who had himself actually seen Mason's patient, had this to say: "It is surprising that it [congenital ichthyosis] should respond to any kind of treatment; that it should respond to hypnotic suggestion demands a revision of current concepts of the relation between mind and body. If this case does not surprise Dr. Freeman [one of the skeptics], nothing ever will" (Bettley, 1952).

T. X. Barber (1984) also commented on the importance of such cases for an adequate understanding of the mind-body problem, concluding that these reports of cures of ichthyosis alone are "sufficient to topple the dualistic dichotomy between mind and body." Insofar as "dualism" is understood—incorrectly—to imply the impossibility of interaction between mind and body, Barber is correct. As I discussed earlier, however, a mere assertion of the unity of mind and body gets us no further in understanding *how* (as Barber described it) "abnormally functioning skin cells begin to function normally when the individual is exposed to specific words or communications (suggestions)," and his explanation—that "suggestions are associated with dramatic skin changes when they are experienced and accepted at a deep emotional level"—is clearly no help in that regard (p. 79).

Other attempts to explain the amelioration of ichthyosis by suggestion are similarly inadequate. Most investigators have simply "presumed that the effect of suggestion on the patient activates the nervous system and sets in motion complex physiological adjustments" (Bethune & Kidd, 1961, p.

44. This point might seem too obvious to have to make, but, in fact, in many instances involving controversial phenomena, it has apparently been too tempting, because easier, to ignore positive results rather than to dig deeper into conditions behind, and hence reasons for, the successes versus the failures.

1420). Others have tried to be more specific, noting for example that "the skin is a sensitive indicator of emotional disorder" such as stress (p. 1419). Thus, the presumed changes in blood flow occur when "a state of emotional high drive...initiates activity of the central nervous system [and] the subjective feeling of the physiological response directs efferent nerve impulses to the organ or part which is now the seat of subjective sensations" (p. 1420). In short, "efferent nerve impulses act on the vascular bed of the affected skin areas" (Kidd, 1966, p. 107). But how does an idea, an image, or an emotion activate nerve impulses that target a specific location on the skin? Kidd thought it "easy" to understand that psychological methods may be successful "in treating diseases that are of psychogenic as well as organic origin" (p. 103). Is it, though? As Wink (1961) pointed out, cases in which there is "a generalized beneficial effect, rather than a local and specific effect" may be more easily understood, but cases involving "correspondences between specific suggestions and the changes consequent upon them...indicate the influence of a psychological process acting directly on local tissue metabolism...and it is difficult to see by what pathways such an influence could be mediated" (p. 742). Wink's two cases, like those of Mason (1952) and Mullins et al. (1955),

> both showed some definite conformity to the suggestions, though this conformity was not exact, for the response included improvement extending outside the designated areas, and a relative failure in other areas which were intended to respond. Finally, though there was a mild improvement in undesignated areas, it was quite overshadowed by the changes in those intended to benefit. (Wink, 1961, p. 743)

Moreover, as even Kidd (1966) acknowledged, the severity and undeniable organic etiology of ichthyosis make it "less easy to understand how [it] ... can be so spectacularly affected by a psychological process" (p. 103).[45]

Skin Conditions: Induction of Bleeding, Blisters, and Markings

Hypnosis clearly can have beneficial therapeutic effects, but it is perhaps even more important theoretically, as Myers so strongly argued. In this context numerous experimental attempts have been made, not to remove a pathophysiological condition that already existed, but to induce one that did not. As a transition into this next section, I will mention one particularly important study that combined the elements both of therapeutic healing and of experimental induction of a skin condition. I mentioned earlier

45. Kidd (1966) also pointed out, first, that "there is no evidence that any psychological component influenced either cause or chronicity" of ichthyosis (especially considering that it is usually present from birth), and, second, that hypnotic suggestions "seem to operate without direct reference to the emotional state of the patient" (p. 104).

some studies in which asthmatic patients, given a nocebo that they were told was an allergen and then a placebo that they were told was a medication, responded appropriately to these suggestions. In a similar study, this one involving hypnosis, Ikemi and Nakagawa (1962) reported five experiments involving teenage boys, some of whom were allergic to the leaves of lacquer and wax trees, developing severe dermatitis when exposed to the leaves, and some of whom were not. In one experiment involving 13 subjects who were severely allergic, five were given the suggestion when hypnotized, and eight were given the same suggestions in a waking state. All were touched on one arm with a lacquer or wax tree leaf but told that it was that of a chestnut tree (to which they were not allergic). They were touched on the other arm with a chestnut tree leaf but told that it was a lacquer or wax tree leaf. Four of the five hypnotized subjects and seven of the eight non-hypnotized subjects developed dermatitis in response to the inert substance that they thought was the allergic agent, and conversely showed no reaction to the real allergic agent that they thought was inert. The other two subjects showed an allergic response to both substances, *including* the inert one.

In another experiment, this one involving 15 (non-hypnotized) subjects who were moderately allergic, all subjects were touched on both arms with the actual allergic agent, but they were told that one was the agent whereas the other was only water. The subjects were observed for five days. At the end of that time eight of the 15 subjects had developed a normal allergic reaction on one arm, but *not* on the arm that they thought had been touched with water. In three other subjects, the allergic reaction on the "water" arm took longer to develop than it did on the other arm.

Some subjects had claimed that they did not even have to touch the leaves, but had only to walk under the trees to develop an allergic reaction. The conventional explanation was that they had in fact been exposed to minute particles of the leaf in the air under the tree. To test this, the authors took one of the boys and had him walk under a lacquer tree that he knew to be such; he developed the usual reaction. On a second occasion he was taken under an oak tree in which lacquer tree leaves had been placed without his knowledge. On this occasion, he did *not* develop an allergic reaction. Another boy developed an allergic reaction both when he was taken under a lacquer tree that he knew to be such and when he was taken under a tree that he was told (falsely) was a lacquer tree.

The authors concluded that there is a psychological component in the development of allergic reactions, revealed by their success in both suppressing and inducing the physiological response by means of suggestion. But what known mechanism can selectively turn on the allergic response in one arm while simultaneously turning it off in the other?

I turn now to cases in which a stigmata-like skin reaction, such as an area of redness, a burn or blister, or even bleeding, has been induced by hypnotic suggestion. I discussed earlier the spontaneous cases of redness, bleeding, and blistering occurring at specific sites, most notably in connection with stigmata and with the recall of previous traumatic or emotional experiences. Similar but deliberately induced phenomena have been reported since the earliest days of mesmerism (Gauld, 1990), although the heyday was certainly in the late 19th and early 20th centuries. There have been several useful reviews, of varying comprehensiveness (e.g., Dunbar, 1954, pp. 601–603; Gauld, 1990; Moll, 1901, pp. 130–138; *HP,* vol. 1, pp. 493–498; Pattie, 1941; Paul, 1963; Stevenson, 1997, vol. 1, pp. 60–67; Weitzenhoffer, 1953, pp. 142–144), and M. Murphy (1992, p. 337) estimated that several hundred such cases have been reported. Relatively few of these have been reported in detail, but the above reviews provide summaries of, and references to, important experiments that were conducted and reported by scientific observers.

As with cases of spontaneous stigmata, a common criticism has been that in many cases the subjects were not adequately watched to ensure that they had not deliberately induced the wounds, whether deceitfully or out of a compulsion to obey the hypnotist in whatever way. The suspicion of fraud (conscious or unconscious) was increased by the observation that many subjects who responded to suggestions of blistering were undoubtedly hysterical. Some extremely interesting reports, therefore, are inconclusive because the subjects were left unattended. Biggs (1887), for example, reported three such cases. In the first, he suggested that a cross would appear on the subject's right arm and remain until he told it to go away. It appeared after three days, in the form of "a dusky-red cross, four or five inches long and about three inches wide." Although the subject was not kept under surveillance for those three days, the fact that the mark persisted for several months, and disappeared only when she returned to Dr. Biggs in desperation to have it removed by suggestion, makes deliberate deception seem unlikely. In another case, Biggs suggested that a red cross would appear on the subject's chest every Friday, and that eventually the words "Sancta" and "Crucis" would appear and the cross would bleed. The cross appeared on the first Friday after the suggestion was given, and re-appeared consistently for many weeks thereafter—not being visible on any other day of the week. On one occasion only, bleeding occurred and part of a letter "S" appeared in the suggested spot. In the third case, a cross was also induced, but, unlike the other two cases, it appeared long after the suggestion (six weeks), by which time Biggs thought that the experiment had failed. Moreover, it lasted only two to three days.[46]

In response to the criticism that unwatched subjects may have deliberately injured themselves, some investigators have attempted to prevent self-injury either by suggesting the mark at a location out of the subject's reach or by bandaging the relevant area and, usually, securing it with a seal. For example, in one 1886 experiment, eight postage stamps were applied to a hypnotized woman's back, out of her reach, and she was told that they

46. One might ask why Biggs (and others) repeatedly used the image of a cross with his subjects; but this is understandable if one considers that emotional salience may be an important factor. We do not, however, have information about the religiosity of these three subjects.

were a blistering agent. The area was then bandaged. The next day the still intact bandages and stamps were removed. The area was "thickened, deadened and of a whitish-yellow colour," surrounded by a reddened and swollen area, and later that day a blister appeared (Gauld, 1990, p. 143; Pattie, 1941, pp. 63–64; Stevenson, 1997, vol. 1, p. 61).

Similarly, Hadfield (1917) reported that he had induced a blister in a patient by touching him lightly on the arm with his finger, but telling him that it was a "red-hot iron." A blister formed after half an hour, but because the patient had been unobserved during that time, Hadfield considered this inconclusive. Consequently, he attempted another experiment, but this time covered the area with "a large roller bandage, so that it would be impossible for [the patient] to interfere with the area touched." The bandage was then fastened with a safety pin and the pin sealed with sealing wax. Nonetheless, six hours later, a blister had formed, and it soon increased in size and developed a large quantity of fluid.

Other experimenters used different means of securing the area. In one experiment, a sealed cardboard tube was placed around the area (Paul, 1963, p. 236). In two others a glass covering was applied instead of a soft bandage, a covering "that would seem to preclude any attempt to scratch the indicated area" (Stevenson, 1997, vol. 1, p. 61).

Even with such coverings, however, doubts can remain, particularly since in at least one case the subject was apparently still able to scratch herself through the bandage (Gauld, 1990, p. 144). An alternative or additional measure is to keep the subjects under close surveillance until the mark or blister appears. Hadfield himself was not satisfied with the bandaging method, and in a third experiment with his subject, he instituted "still stricter conditions" in which the patient's arm was bandaged as before, and he was watched continuously for 24 hours. The bandage was then removed, and Hadfield and three other surgeons observed "the beginning of a blister..., which gradually developed during the day to form a large bleb with an area of inflammation around it."

One might argue that 24 hours is a long time to keep someone under observation without lapses of attention, even with multiple observers. However, in most cases in which the subject was closely observed, the time until the mark developed was much shorter, and in numerous cases the mark in fact developed almost instantly. For example, one subject had spontaneously begun crying bloody tears, which we encountered earlier in some of the stigmata cases. The tears could also be evoked by hypnotic suggestion, but not halted, and so on one occasion the physician suggested instead that the bleeding be transferred to her hand. Several minutes after she was awakened, "blood seemed to well up in the lines of the hand much as a profuse sweat would have done." Moreover, the process "took place before our eyes" (see Gauld, 1990, pp. 141–142; *HP,* vol. 1, p. 498). Similarly, Smirnoff described two instances in which a blister appeared shortly after the suggestion, and he could rule out self-injury because "the whole process ran its course before our eyes" (Gauld, 1990, p. 147; Stevenson, 1997, vol. 1, p. 63).

Liébeault suggested to two subjects that when they were awakened, they would go to a stove and touch it, suggesting further that the stove was red-hot. They did so, and although the stove was in fact cold, both subjects developed immediate reactions, one "a lively reddening" and the other "an actual burn from which the skin subsequently came away" (Gauld, 1990, p. 142; Madden, 1903). Bellis (1966) suggested to a patient that she imagine herself on the beach on a sunny day, not intending to induce anything but relaxation. Instead, immediately upon awakening her, he saw that her face had become "beet-red...[and the] redness extended over her shoulders and half-way down her arms." Ullman (1947) gave a soldier the suggestion that a molten shell fragment had hit his hand. An "immediate pallor" developed, and 20 minutes later a "narrow red margin appeared." In an hour a blister began to form, ultimately becoming a second-degree burn. Most importantly, the "patient had remained under the observation of the author and another medical officer...for the entire period" (p. 829).

Some observers were not satisfied even with such immediate reactions. Schrenck-Notzing, whose experiences with a subject who was probably guilty of self-injury had led him to issue a strong plea for adequate control in these experiments, watched a red mark develop "almost immediately" on one of Liébeault's hysterical patients. Not convinced, he and a colleague paid a surprise visit to the patient's house, and while there they commented that she seemed to have been bitten by an insect because they saw a red spot under her left ear (nothing, in fact, was there). They reinforced the suggestion by saying that it seemed to be getting worse and must be painful. Although concerned, she did not touch the spot, and within three minutes they saw that an area of redness had developed in the spot suggested (Gauld, 1990, p. 144).

Perhaps the most striking case of immediate observation, however, involved a patient of Schindler (see Pattie, 1941, p. 70; Paul, 1963, p. 237; Stevenson, 1997, vol. 1, p. 62), who had suffered from spontaneous and apparent psychogenic bruising (the phenomenon later called autoerythrocyte sensitization, discussed earlier). Schindler was able to induce bruising in this patient by hypnotic suggestion, and on one occasion he suggested that a blister would develop, which it did. Ultimately, according to an entry in his log, "it is now *possible to regulate the occurrence of the blister to the minute.* It shoots up before the eyes of the physician at the regulated time, becoming fully developed within five minutes" (Dunbar, 1954, p. 603).

Fraud (or unconscious compliance, if one wishes to be more generous in the interpretation) thus seems to be ruled out as a general explanation. Other more "normal" explanations have been suggested, however, relying especially on the idea that the subject's skin is unusually sensitive and therefore that the phenomena observed involve either dermographia (a condition in which even light touch can produce marked reactions) or contact dermatitis (in which ordinarily harmless materials, usually metal, produce an allergic reaction). Paul (1963), for example, attributed most (but not all) cases to such reactions, and he even extended the hypothesis to suggest that in cases in which a bandage was applied to control the subject's access to the site, the bandage *itself* caused the wound: "In their zeal," he said, the investigators "have in fact induced the 'injury' themselves" (p. 239). In many cases the site of the blister had been lightly touched to reinforce the suggestion. Sometimes the stimulus was simply the physician's finger, and sometimes it was a small object such as a coin, a metal file, or a pencil, especially when the suggestion given was that the hypnotist was burning the patient with a hot object.

However, in one early study examining the possibility that hysterical patients showing unusual skin reactions have abnormally reactive skin, Haxthausen (1936) found that none of the eight hysterical patients examined did. Gauld (1990, pp. 148–149) and Stevenson (1997, vol. 1, pp. 64–65) have also pointed out that, although some subjects have had unusually sensitive skin, not all have. More importantly, in cases in which the stimulus was an everyday object, such as a button, a matchstick, or a cold stove—or the physician's finger—it is "absolutely inconceivable" that a contact dermatitis sufficient to produce blisters would not have been known before to the subjects or their doctors (who were often the hypnotists) (Gauld, 1990, p. 149).

Myers seems to have been the first to recognize the need to provide appropriate controls for unusual skin reactions. In an 1885 experiment in which he and Gurney participated, Liébeault "slightly pricked" the back of the hand of his patient Mlle. A. E., suggesting that a patch of redness would form there. At the same time, Myers scratched her arm, with no suggestion of any reaction, as a control. On the place touched by Liébeault, a red patch appeared almost immediately; on Myers's control scratch, no reaction was observed (Myers, 1886c, pp. 167–168n). Forel later made a similar experiment in which he drew a cross on each forearm with a blunt knife. He suggested that blisters would appear, but on the right side only, and after five minutes a reddish swelling and a wheal, "somewhat in the shape of a cross," appeared on that side only (Moll, 1901, pp. 136–137). In a similar case, performed by a German physician, Oskar Kohnstamm, before a group of neurologists, some of whom kept the hypnotized subject under constant observation, a cross was traced on both arms with a pencil, with the suggestion that a wheal would form on the left side only. A wheal appeared an hour later, *only* on the left arm (Dunbar, 1954, p. 613).

Similar cases are those in which a suggestion of analgesia was given to one arm, but not to the other, to see whether the suggested analgesia would affect the skin response. Delboeuf, for example, suggested to a hypnotized subject that her right arm was analgesic, and he then burned both arms with a red-hot iron rod.[47] The left arm showed a normal reaction, with a large, inflamed, and blistered wound, but the right arm had only a small bump, with no redness or inflammation (Stevenson, 1997, vol. 1, pp. 65–66). In another experiment performed by the physician Kohnstamm before a

47. Delboeuf had obtained her permission to do this before he hypnotized her, but probably few subjects (or university review boards) would agree to such a procedure today.

medical audience, a deeply hypnotized subject was given the suggestion that one finger would be analgesic. When that finger was punctured with a large pin, no bleeding occurred, although the corresponding finger on the other hand bled normally when similarly punctured (Dunbar, 1954, p. 608). Chapman, Goodell, and Wolff (1959) reported a more extensive experiment of this kind, involving 13 hypnotized subjects in 40 experiments. In 39 of these the subjects were given the suggestion that one arm was either normal or anesthetized and that the other arm was especially "vulnerable"; and in the other the suggestion was that one arm was normal and the other was anesthetic. A "standard noxious [thermal] stimulus" was then applied to three spots on each arm. In 30 of the 40 experiments, the arm suggested to be the more "vulnerable" showed greater inflammatory reaction and damage than did the anesthetic or normal arm. The reaction clearly depended on the subjects' beliefs or expectations about being burned, and not on an unusually sensitive skin condition.

An equally important argument against dermographia or contact dermatitis as general explanations is that there are numerous cases in which the site that developed the reaction was not touched. In the Myers/Liébeault case, described above, Liébeault had suggested that a red mark would appear on both hands, although he touched only one of them. A red mark developed also on the hand he had not touched, although "a little less red and distinct" than the other mark (Myers, 1886c, pp. 167–168n). In Bellis's case of induced sunburn, no tactile contact was made with the patient's face, arm, or shoulders; and in Schindler's case, also cited above, many of the instances of bruising and blistering involved suggestion only, with no touch (Paul, 1963, pp. 237, 241). Charcot suggested to a patient, "without touching it," that her arm was covered with burning wax. She was continuously watched, and within a few minutes she developed "a veritable burn" (Gauld, 1990, p. 146). Ullman (1947, pp. 829–830) suggested to his patient (the soldier mentioned above) that he was "rundown and debilitated" and that a fever blister would develop on his lower lip in the right corner. The area was not touched. The patient was kept under observation, and 24 hours later one large blister and multiple smaller satellite blisters had developed at the suggested site.

Other cases that cannot be explained by skin sensitivity are those in which the mark appeared at a site other than the one either suggested or touched. Podiapolsky (1909) described a case, again one in which the subject was closely watched by several people, in which a coin and then the bottom of a thermometer case were lightly pressed against her skin in two locations on her back, with the suggestion that she was being burned, as with a hot coal. Several hours later, blisters had appeared in both spots, but "not quite in the right place." One was a grouping of three or four blisters about 3 cm below and to the left of the site touched, and the other a larger, broken blister about 1 cm above that site. Similarly, Smirnoff placed a button on his subject's hand, suggesting that it was "glowing hot." Immediately after she was awakened, a red patch appeared, and 15 minutes later a blister surrounded by reddening appeared—"not on the spot where the button had been laid, but somewhat lower." Four days later Smirnoff tried the same experiment, placing a copper letter C near the previous burn. At first the site of the previous burn, not the present site, turned red; and then this disappeared and a blister developed between the site of the previous burn and the site where the copper had been placed (Gauld, 1990, p. 147).

A particularly interesting example of marks appearing at a site different from the one touched was that of Ilma Szandor, who was described as "almost dangerously susceptible to hypnotic blistering," sometimes developing reactions "much worse than the experimenters intended" (Gauld, 1990, p. 143). After an initial incident in which a medical student had laid a pair of scissors on her chest, suggesting that they were red-hot and thus producing a serious burn, Drs. von Krafft-Ebing and Jendrássik began to experiment with her, but making more "humane" suggestions such as red marks (*HP,* vol. 1, pp. 495–496). Ilma was an hysteric whose right side was "permanently anesthetic," and, interestingly, when objects were placed on her left side, with the suggestion that they were hot, the mark appeared, not where the object had been placed, but instead on the corresponding spot on her (anesthetic) right side (Gauld, 1990, p. 143; *HP,* vol. 1, p. 496; Pattie, 1941, p. 64).

Another case illustrates again that the reaction depends more strongly on the patient's "idea" (in Myers's term) than on the actual stimulus. The famous hysterical subject Louis V. had developed the idea that gold would burn him. An investigator, Voisin, reported that when he touched Louis with gold, a burn and blistering would indeed occur; but "if the subject was unaware that the object was gold, there would be no effect and, conversely, if he thought he was touched by gold or mercury when he was not, a burn would appear" (Gauld, 1990, p. 146).

The case of Ilma, mentioned above, is important for another reason. I have so far been describing mainly cases in which the reaction was precise in terms of location. Ilma's case is one of many in which the specificity was not just in location, but also in *shape*. On one occasion, for example, a letter K was pressed against her left shoulder, and "in a few hours a K-like blister, 'with quite sharp outlines,' came on the corresponding spot on the right side." Even more interestingly—given the fact that it had appeared on the opposite arm rather than the one that received the stimulus—this and other marks on Ilma appeared reversed, as in a mirror-image (*HP,* vol. 1, p. 496; Stevenson, 1997, vol. 1, p. 64). Moreover, in the case of the letter K it was not "an exact reproduction" of the original K stimulus, but in a different style, as if in "another person's handwriting" (*HP*, vol. 1, p. 496). On another occasion a ring with a notch in it was placed on her left arm, and again the mark appeared on the right arm instead, in the "shape of the ring with an indication of a notch" (Stevenson, 1997, vol. 1, p. 64).

Madden (1903) considered Ilma a fraud, in part because he considered her a "degenerate" and "cunning but evil-minded" hysteric, in part because he believed that she had not been adequately controlled, and in part because of the supposedly "fatal defect" that it took 24 hours or more for her blisters to develop. It is not clear why this lapse of time should necessarily be considered a defect; but in any case, like many such "skeptics" he was less than accurate in his portrayal of the facts. It is not true that "in no case" with Ilma was the interval less than 24 hours; nor is it true that there was no description of the means by which Ilma was controlled. Jendríssik, for example, had reported an instance (the one involving the ring) in which the blister had developed after five hours, during which period of time she had been watched continuously (Gauld, 1990, p. 143; Stevenson, 1997, vol. 1, p. 64). Another "condemning fact" to Madden was that, according to him, a "burn just like a K" appeared on the shoulder touched. In reality, the mark appeared not on the left shoulder, but on the untouched right shoulder, and was both reversed and more like an H than a K in shape.

Myers took quite a different view of the reversal and distortion of the K than Madden's "conviction" that such distortions were "the very strongest evidence for deceit." For him, Ilma's case was a "striking example" of "the *intellectual* character, as I have termed it, of the organic process which responds to suggestion" (*HP,* vol. 1, p. 495). The fact that the mark was not an exact reproduction suggested to Myers that, just as the marks in Dr. Biggs's three cases had corresponded to "the idea of cruciformity," so in this case it "corresponded to an intellectual idea," that is, "the idea of K-shape," an idea that "underwent some idiosyncratic modification in the subject's subliminal intelligence" (*HP,* vol. 1, p. 496)—one of those modifications, common in other automatisms such as automatic writing, being mirror-image writing (Myers, 1885b).

Other marks corresponding to a suggested shape have been reported. Earlier in the chapter I described several cases of this kind. By hypnotic suggestion Lechler was able to induce on the forehead of his patient Elisabeth K. several marks having the triangular shape of thorns. Ilma K. developed on her right arm a blister in the shape of a ring with the additional detail of a notch in the ring, corresponding to the shape and appearance of a ring that had been pressed against her left arm. Similarly, several stigmatics have developed marks, called "espousal rings," encircling a finger (Thurston, 1952, pp. 130–140). Another case, this one not involving hypnosis, was R. L. Moody's patient, on whose arm appeared marks clearly showing indentations resembling rope marks. I have also already mentioned Biggs's three subjects, who developed marks in the shape of a cross. More significantly, one of them also developed a mark, in a place that had not been touched, that was the beginning of a letter S, in response to the suggestion that the word "Sancta" would appear. In Bellis's case of induced sunburn, the redness conformed to the lines of the patient's dress. Louis V., who showed numerous physiological reactions to suggestions, on one occasion developed a bleeding V on his arm after that had been suggested to him (Myers, 1886c, pp. 168–169; Stevenson, 1997, vol. 1, p. 63). One of Liébeault's patients developed a mark resembling a cross in response to a post-hypnotic suggestion (Gauld, 1990, p. 144), as did Forel's subject (Moll, 1901, pp. 136–137).

Janet reported three cases, the first illustrating again what Myers called "the intelligence presiding over these organic suggestions" (*HP,* vol. 1, p. 496). Specifically, Janet suggested to his patient Rose that he was applying a mustard plaster to her abdomen, although he did not in fact do so. After a few hours, a swollen and red rectangular area appeared, but it had the odd characteristic that it looked as though the four corners had been cut on a diagonal. When Janet commented on this, Rose said that it was the custom where she came from to cut the corners at an angle; it was thus her own notion of mustard plasters, and not the suggestion from Janet, that determined the particular form. On another occasion, Janet suggested to Rose that he was applying a mustard plaster in the shape of a six-pointed star, and a red mark appeared with "exactly" (Janet's term) that shape. In the third instance, this one involving his patient Léonie, Janet suggested a mustard plaster in the shape of an S, and a mark in that shape appeared on her chest (*HP*, vol. 1, pp. 496–497; Stevenson, 1997, vol. 1, p. 64).

Another remarkable case involving skin marks corresponding closely to suggested images was that of Olga Kahl. Among her abilities was that of producing thin red lines in the skin of her forearms or chest, closely corresponding to target images chosen sometimes by her, sometimes by the investigators.[48] This ability was studied in detail by the physician Osty and the physiologist Richet (Osty, 1929). Their experiments were conducted with Olga under observation in full daylight. The marks were generally both clear and large, occupying for example a sizeable part of Olga's ventral forearm. They usually took some tens of seconds to form and then faded within a minute. Unfortunately, there are no photographs of these marks (as there are in R. L. Moody's cases, in the case of Lechler's Elisabeth K., or in Hadfield's case), but Osty made drawings of 10 of them, which have been published (Osty, 1929, pp. 129–131; Stevenson, 1997, vol. 1, pp. 97, 98, 101). Three of the targets were complex line drawings, all reproduced fairly closely in Olga's skin writing, although somewhat distorted or missing some lines. When the number 8 was suggested, for example, an X first appeared, and then a rounded line at the bottom appeared, giving the X the appearance of part of an 8. When a water goblet was suggested, lines appeared that closely resembled one side of a drawing of a goblet. In the remaining five instances, names were suggested, and in all cases letters appeared on her arm, one after the other, partially spelling out the name. Thus, the name "Rosa" yielded "Ro," the name François yielded "FrAN," and the name "Sabine" yielded an odd-looking S, followed by an A, a B, a blank space, and then an N and a straight vertical line. The name "Yolande" yielded an odd-looking Y, followed by a blank space, then an L, a distorted a, an n, a distorted d, and an e. Perhaps the most interesting, however, was "René," which came out upside down on her arm in the form "REH." Olga was Russian, and in the Russian alphabet N is written like H. Although there had

48. As I will discuss later in the chapter, an important feature of this case is that, when the target was chosen by the investigators, Olga herself was usually neither told nor allowed to see what the target was.

been no touching or tracing of the images on Olga, she was tested for dermographia, and showed only a "feeble" response (Stevenson, 1997, vol. 1, p. 102).

Attempted Explanations of Hypnotic Skin Marking and Related Phenomena

It seems clear that there have been cases of skin marking and blistering that cannot be explained in terms either of fraud or of unusually sensitive skin. What other "normal" explanations might be available? Several have been proposed. One of the most common focuses on the fact that in many instances of hypnotic or non-hypnotic skin reactions, as well as many of the other phenomena discussed in this chapter, emotion plays an important role. Clearly, emotion can engender physiological reactions, such as the blushing that occurs when one feels embarrassment or the increase in heart rate when one is frightened. Blushing or changes in heart rate, however, are a far cry from a clearly outlined letter K at a specific spot on the skin. As Stevenson (1997, vol. 1, pp. 102–103) put it, "blushing shows neither the voluntariness nor an ability to control the sites of vasodilatation, let alone that of dilating blood vessels to represent particular forms." Madden (1903) was more specific: "No one ever saw a blush in the shape of a K of such intensity that it caused a burn" (p. 289).

Others have suggested that the abnormal reactions are, in essence, a conditioned response produced when the person recalls suffering a similar injury in the past (see, e.g., Paul, 1963, p. 242). Podiapolsky (1909), for example, had found that a certain patient did not respond, as Janet's patients had, to suggestions that a mustard plaster was being applied, but he then learned that this patient had never experienced a real mustard plaster. He concluded that subjects must have previously experienced the sensations of a particular stimulus before the suggestion would "take." Similarly, as we saw earlier, Ewin (1979, p. 271) reported the case of a man who developed redness and swelling when he was vividly reminded of a serious burn he had suffered 10 years earlier; R. L. Moody's patient developed rope marks on his arm when recalling a traumatic experience of being tied down with ropes; and Bellis's patient developed a sunburn in reaction to her memory of a severe sunburn she had previously experienced. Weitzenhoffer (1953) believed, much like Podiapolsky, that "for the suggestion to be effective the subject must have previously experienced traumatic situations leading to blister formation," because the "re-experiencing" elicits a conditioned response that "brings about reflexedly the somatic changes that were once associated with the previous reaction" (pp. 298, 296).[49]

---

49. To Weitzenhoffer's credit, he acknowledged that the hypothesis of conditioning can explain only generalized responses, and not phenomena involving "specific localization." In what was surely a remarkable understatement, he admitted that the latter phenomena require "further refinement" of the hypothesis (p. 196).

It is worth describing here in some detail a modern experiment that supposedly supports this "conditioned-response" theory of skin-markings, in part because this experiment is a particularly egregious example—provided by an important contemporary experimenter—of how *not* to study this psychological phenomenon. To investigate claims of hypnotic skin markings, R. F. Q. Johnson and Barber (1976) decided to develop a protocol that would rule out supposed "weaknesses" of previous studies, including the facts that most such studies involved one subject only and that the subjects had often been hysterical or "somnambulistic." Their subjects were instead 40 student nurses who had never before been hypnotized. All were told explicitly that the purpose of the study was to induce blisters by hypnosis. After a formal hypnotic induction procedure, for 20 minutes the experimenter suggested to the subject that she was frying bacon and burned her hand when she accidentally touched the hot pan. After five minutes and 10 minutes, the suggestion was interrupted to ask the subject whether she felt anything yet. Of the 40 subjects, only one produced a reddening (but not a blister) on her hand. This reaction developed within five minutes after the verbal suggestions were begun, was clearly visible to both the subject and the experimenter, and disappeared within three minutes after the completion of the 20-minute session. That subject, as it turned out, had been burned by hot grease at that spot some years earlier; and she further reported that the experimental mark closely resembled in shape the earlier burn. On this basis the authors concluded that previous trauma and some associated conditioning are necessary in general for a reaction.

It is hard to imagine an experiment *less* likely to produce the desired result (even assuming—doubtful in the case of Barber and his colleagues—that the desired result *was* in fact the hypnotic production of blisters). A mere 20 minutes, in subjects who had never before experienced hypnosis, and with an interruption every few minutes, could hardly be conducive to the deep state of absorption that has clearly been a factor in most successful suggestions. Additionally and perhaps more importantly, the use of unselected subjects for whom there is no empirical or theoretical reason to think they would be *able* to react in such an extreme way to suggestion is almost guaranteed to ensure failure. Johnson and Barber argued that this is an invalid objection because 12 of the 40 subjects scored above the median on a test of hypnotic susceptibility. "Above the median," however, is hardly equivalent to being highly hypnotizable, let alone "somnambulistic."[50] Finally, given Barber's well-known skepticism about "this purported relationship between blister formation and hypnotic suggestion" (Johnson & Barber, 1976, p. 172), it seems more than likely that there was a negative "demand characteristic"—that is, an implicit suggestion not to respond—

50. Barber (1984) later apparently acquiesced somewhat on this point when he described "all of the individuals" who had produced blisters as "superb" or "excellent" hypnotic subjects (p. 92).

operating in this experiment.[51] In short, this experiment is a quintessential example of an all-too-familiar characteristic of experimental studies in psychology, that of allowing "methodolatry" to triumph over a sincere attempt to learn something important about a controversial but theoretically significant phenomenon. The fact that, even under such non-conducive conditions, Johnson and Barber still had one subject respond mildly is perhaps a surprising testament to the robustness of this phenomenon.

Emotion and a kind of "memory" or "conditioning" associated with previous injuries may indeed play some role, in some cases, but this clearly cannot provide an adequate general explanation since neither emotion nor relevant previous trauma are present in all or even most of the reported cases. We encounter even more serious limitations, however, when we examine other attempts to provide purely biological explanations.

As I discussed at the beginning of this chapter, most contemporary scientists take the position that understanding the "how" of psychophysiological interactions presents no problem because the "psychological" parts of these interactions are themselves ultimately biological, involving nothing more than patterns of electrochemical activity in the central nervous system. "Thoughts" and "emotions" simply represent certain aspects of this biologically unitary mind-brain system, while "warts and allergic responses" represent others, and there is thus no particular problem in understanding, at least in principle, how the former might produce or influence the latter (T. X. Barber, 1984, p. 84). Indeed, to suggest anything different is automatically viewed with horror as threatening a return to outmoded forms of dualistic thinking. As a consequence, many scientists will let pass without comment a statement such as that of Grabowska (1971): "The most probable explanation [in this case, for elevation of skin temperature in response to hypnotic suggestion] is that the word 'warmth' becomes...a stimulus equally strong (and perhaps even stronger) than the action of heat in the waking state" (p. 1050). But surely it is legitimate here to ask, how?

The viability of this basic conceptual scheme of mind-brain identity has simply been assumed by most modern students of skin-marking and blistering by suggestion. Most of the resulting accounts, however, proceed at a very general level, without adequate attention to the details. S. I. Cohen, Bondurant, and Silverman (1960), for example, speak vaguely of how emo-

51. The "experimenter effect," in which the experimenter's explicit or implicit expectations can profoundly influence the experimental results, has become increasingly recognized in psychology (Rosenthal & Rubin, 1978), and perhaps even more so in parapsychology (e.g., Kennedy & Taddonio, 1976; R. A. White, 1976). A striking illustration in the specific context of the hypnotic production of blisters was described by H. Spiegel (1997). Spiegel hypnotized an army corporal and touched him on the arm with a pencil, telling him that it was a hot iron. Within a few minutes a blister appeared. During the next month, the experiment was repeated successfully four times; but on a fifth occasion "the experiment was repeated...in the presence of a high-ranking officer who voiced doubts about the genuineness of the experiment. After being belittled and humiliated by this authority figure, this subject never again responded to the hypnotic suggestion" (p. 617).

tionally charged words cause activation of the hypothalamus, which in turn regulates the autonomic nervous system, thus producing the required effects on localized blood vessels. Weitzenhoffer (1953, p. 296n) similarly found it "plausible" that suggested blistering can be produced by the central nervous system by way of its close connections with the autonomic nervous system, which is known to regulate peripheral vascular changes. Chapman et al. (1959), who conducted research on inflammatory responses generally as well as research specifically on the influence of suggestion on inflammatory skin reactions, blandly proposed that a person's "perceptions and attitudes are relevant to neural activities that engender or enhance inflammatory reactions" (p. 104). Paul (1963) epitomized the lot when he declared that there is "little doubt that the anatomical structure of the brain contains the necessary circuits and pathways to allow such cortical influence on subcortical and brain stem structures" (p. 242), and hence to create whatever localized reactions of blood vessels and other physiological components of the skin are necessary to produce the phenomena of interest. Paul notwithstanding, however, there is considerable doubt.

This kind of vapid and generic theorizing reached new depths in an important paper by T. X. Barber (1984), in which after many years of dogged resistance he announced that he had finally come to accept the existence of some psychophysiological phenomena of hypnosis that he had earlier (e.g., 1961) dismissed as mere "compliance." The reason, it turns out, is that he had finally found a satisfactory explanation for them, one that "should, once for all, topple the dualistic dichotomy." Here is his explanation:

> The meanings or ideas imbedded in words which are spoken by one person and deeply accepted by another can be communicated to the cells of the body (and to the chemicals within the cells); the cells then can change their activities in order to conform to the meanings or ideas which have been transmitted to them. (pp. 115–116)

Similarly, Barber asserts, beliefs "alter microphysiological processes" (p. 116), "abnormally functioning skin cells begin to function normally when the individual is exposed to specific words or communication (suggestions)" (p. 78), and "feelings...instruct the cells to behave the way they would if a burn was occurring, warts were regressing, or mammary glands were growing" (p. 118).

Barber undoubtedly believed in all sincerity that with this kind of talk he was "posing an explanation" (as he entitled the section beginning on p. 24 in the version of his 1984 paper published in the journal *Advances*); but it is surely more accurate to characterize it instead as "posing *as* an explanation." What Barber and others of this general persuasion typically do is essentially to focus primarily on the bookends of the process—an idea or image and the corresponding physiological change—while simply presuming that the passage from the former to the latter can be fully accounted for in conventional biological terms.

Those intermediate connections, however, are all-important. In the first place, as I have emphasized throughout this chapter, identification of central nervous system correlates of an "idea," even if far more precise than those currently available, would not obviously or necessarily bring us any closer to understanding *how* the various mechanisms required to produce the desired outcome—and *only* those—are set in motion. As Myers (1891d) put it, "however exactly the parallelism between psychical and cerebral energies may be established, the exacter correlation can tell us little more than the vaguer told us" (p. 635).

Secondly, just how exceedingly complex and specific these subsequent biological steps themselves must often be has not been adequately appreciated by most contemporary workers. T. X. Barber (1984), for example, echoing a suggestion originally made by Gurney (1887a), proposed that a vivid hallucination, such as that of heat at a particular skin location, provides "an important mediating step" in producing a blister at that location; but he made no serious attempt to explain more precisely *how* it does so. Barber merely asserted, in words remarkable only for how they skip over rather than address the underlying problem: "When individuals experience (hallucinate) a suggested burn in virtually the same way as they experience an actual burn, the central nervous system can react in virtually the same way as it reacts to an actual burn" (p. 92).

Others, to their credit, have felt some unease with regard to the prospects for providing an adequate account in such terms. Bowers (1979), for example, evidently accepted Barber's basic picture, suggesting that the production of highly specific or "focused" effects such as blisters is rooted in "the central nervous system's capacity for imagery and symbolism" and involves "the transduction of information from a semantic to a somatic level, possible through the mediation of imagery." Yet Bowers also acknowledged openly, unlike Barber, that "the specifics of this transduction process are...a mystery of the profoundest sort, with all sorts of implications for the so-called mind-body problem" (pp. 269–270).

A very few others have been more explicit in raising questions about this "transduction." McDougall (1911/1961), for example, asked how "the neural impulses initiated in the auditory nerve by the sound of the words, 'Your left eye is blind,'...find their way to the fibres of the left optic nerve...[or] paralyse the conductivity of the nerve" (p. 352).[52] Myers (1892c) remarked, more poetically, that the hypnotist's "command, 'Feel pain no more!', is no more a scientific instruction *how* not to feel pain than the prophet's 'Wash in Jordan and be clean!' was a pharmacopoeal prescription for leprosy" (pp. 331–332).

The biologist, physician, and author Lewis Thomas (1979) regarded phenomena such as hypnotic healing of warts as "one of the great mystifications of science," and he was explicit and eloquent in stating his views as to where an adequate explanation must be sought. As he put it, it is "hardly enough

52. In answer to his own question, McDougall could only say that it was "utterly impossible to conceive."

for the mind to say, simply, get off, eliminate yourselves, without providing something in the way of specifications as to how to go about it." Given that warts are caused by a virus and often gotten rid of by immunological mechanisms rejecting them, the process of eliminating them by suggestion probably involves not only selectively shutting down the local blood supply, but also activating the appropriate lymphocytes while simultaneously "exclud[ing] the wrong ones." Again, he insisted, "it wouldn't do to fob off the whole intricate business on lower centers without sending along a quite detailed set of specifications, away over my head." Thomas concluded that there must be a "Person in charge," a "kind of superintelligence in all of us" that knows how to do this, one that is "infinitely smarter and possessed of technical know-how far beyond our present understanding." Yet

> there ought to be a better word than Unconscious, even capitalized, for what I have, so to speak, in mind. I was brought up to regard this aspect of thinking as a sort of private sanitarium, walled off somewhere in a suburb of my brain, capable only of producing such garbled information as to keep my mind always a little off balance.
>
> But any mental apparatus that can reject a wart is something else again. This is not the sort of confused, disordered process you would expect at the hands of the kind of unconscious you read about in books, at the edge of things making up dreams or getting mixed up on words, or having hysterics. (p. 59)

The type of "Unconscious" that Thomas seems to have in mind is, in fact, precisely what Myers meant by his notion of a Subliminal Self—a kind of hidden, larger intelligence guiding and producing the protean and ever-shifting symptoms of hysteria, knowing how to turn on and off the inflammatory processes behind stigmata or hypnotically produced blisters, or accomplishing in ways unknown to our ordinary consciousness the goal of expressing an idea such as that of a "K" or a cross in somatic form. As I discussed in Chapter 2, one of the central issues Myers was addressing was the problem of volition, and he specifically suggested that, just as it had been a mistake to identify *mind* with that portion of it of which we are aware, so it might be a mistake to limit *volition* to the relatively small supraliminal fragment of the total spectrum of consciousness. Volition should instead be considered the function of an individual's mind as a whole, subliminal as well as supraliminal, and not be limited to those acts an individual is aware of initiating consciously and voluntarily (*HP*, vol. 2, pp. 518–523). An hypnotic or other suggestion is effective because the larger subliminal intelligence "carries out the idea as well as it can, unhindered by the mistakes or clumsiness of the conscious mind" (Myers, 1886e, p. 448). How that "Person in charge" does so is, of course, no more clear to us than how the brain might do so; but it seems likely that the process is a volitional and goal-oriented one, rather than an automatic brain reflex or even, as Thomas described it, one in which some "mental apparatus" understands and carries out each individual step along the way. And this brings us once again face to face with a fundamental problem with which few psychologists have been willing to grapple—namely, the problem of volition and what all volitional phenomena, from deliberately raising one's arm to deliberately raising a blister, imply about the nature of mind.

Even Thomas, however, may not have fully appreciated the magnitude of the problems he was pointing out. I have already stated several times that attempted explanations of phenomena of psychophysiological influence in conventional biological terms become progressively strained and unsatisfactory as we move from the level of commonly occurring global or systemic effects to phenomena of the more localized, dramatic, and uncommon sorts. In fact, I will now argue, in extreme cases like those of blistering and skin marking the conventional approach breaks down altogether, because the brain and body demonstrably lack output mechanisms capable of producing the observed effects. It is imperative to note also that this argument, if sustained, casts retrospective doubt on the conventional interpretations of all seemingly less complex phenomena of psychophysiological influence, including that everyday phenomenon which we so readily take for granted—namely, our ability to raise our arm whenever we intend to do so.

Consider first the case of hypnotically induced blisters. Gurney (1887a) examined these thoughtfully in relation to his own suggestion that vivid mental imagery might be a causative factor in their production. The more primitive manifestations, such as a generalized reddening of an area of skin when attention is focused on it, seemed to him possibly within the reach of a biological explanation. However, he cautioned, "difficulties increase as we go on." In particular, he recognized clearly the difficulties of identifying any mechanism by which a suggested idea—hypnotic or non-hypnotic, emotional or non-emotional, hallucinatory or not—could produce a "minutely localised erethism...[that] corresponds with the idea to the extent of being cruciform" (p. 105). Gurney was even willing to allow—wrongly, as we now know—the possibility "that the cerebral area involved in the idea of a cross should itself be cruciform." That would not help explain the cruciform blister, however:

> No one has ever supposed that a nervous impulse transmitted from ideational tracts to lower centres, and thence to the periphery, was conveyed by fibres which retained precisely similar spatial relations, so that the course of the discharge, wherever cut across, would present a similar section. Passing inwards from the periphery along the track of nervous disturbance, should we find cruciformity of area all the way? And if not, where does it stop? And if it stops anywhere, what is the connection between the cruciform effect at the periphery, and the cause (even if we assume that to be cruciform) in the brain? (Gurney, 1887, p. 105)

Others since Gurney have also clearly recognized the severe explanatory challenge posed by blisters of this type. Madden (1903) outlined arguments that are in fact quite similar to Gurney's, but unlike Gurney he concluded on that basis that "vesication by suggestion is a physiological impossibility" and therefore that all previous investigators had been deceived. Pattie (1941) was more cautious, acknowledging the strength of the evidence, but maintaining "an attitude of suspended judgment, an attitude due mostly to [my] inability to understand by what physiological processes suggestion—or the central nervous system—could produce *localized and circumscribed* erythemas or blisters" (p. 71).

The essence of the problem in more modern terms is that although we have learned a great deal in recent decades about the processes of neurogenic inflammation that give rise to blister formation in the case of, say, a burn, we have no credible idea as to how those processes could be engaged directly by the central nervous system, in the absence of the tissue injury and activation of pain receptors that normally precipitate local release of substance P and related vasoactive agents. Pattie himself thought that this had to occur "independent of the central nervous system," and in this he seems almost certainly correct.

But how then might it happen at all, if the central nervous system cannot itself directly produce the necessary effects in the skin, with the requisite precision? The only remaining hope for a neurological explanation amounts essentially to transferring control of blister shape to the corresponding tactile stimulus, such as Janet's mustard plaster in the shape of a six-pointed star. The basic idea is that an abnormal state of the central nervous system, such as deep hypnotic trance, might somehow sensitize the skin in such a way that light touch with the star activates local mechanisms of blistering in the same way that they would normally have been activated had the star actually been burning hot. Although skin-based mechanisms capable of producing such local sensitization are known to exist (Willis, 1999), it is not known whether they can be mobilized by hypnosis, directly from the central nervous system, in the necessary form and extent. Furthermore, and more decisively, these mechanisms could not in any event provide a general explanation of hypnotic blistering because, as we have seen, blisters sometimes appear, not at the location touched by the hypnotist, but at some other location, or even in the absence of any touch stimulus whatever.

Let us go on to a second and even more challenging case, the skin-writing of Olga Kahl.[53] The marks in this case were in or below the skin, and not on the skin, because they were not altered by attempts to wash them away (Besterman, 1929, p. 428). Osty (1929), a physician, regarded this skin-writing phenomenon as an inspiring example of generally unrecognized potentials of the human organism for physiological self-control, and he made a serious attempt to understand it in terms of the neurophysiology of the day. The red color, apparent depth, and spatial precision of the lines clearly required an extraordinary degree of control of the peripheral circulation. Osty (p. 137) assumed that this control had to be exerted at the level of the capillary bed, through local dilation of capillaries, and by a central nervous

53. I will leave aside here the psi-related aspects of this case, discussed later in the chapter, and consider only the challenge it poses as a purely psychophysiological phenomenon.

mechanism of exquisite precision. There was a problem, however. Physiologists already knew most of what we know today about autonomic control of the peripheral vasculature, and had demonstrated its existence only to the insufficiently precise level of arterioles terminating prior to the capillary level. Osty, confident that his biological assumptions must be correct, therefore postulated that a similar but more delicate control system exists within the capillary bed itself, and he challenged anatomists to find it.

Osty's hypothesis was bold and reasonable at the time, but we now know that it is false, and for several reasons. First and already decisive is the fact that the requisite neuroanatomical structures within the capillary bed simply do not exist. Second, it has become clearer that the autonomic nervous system—more specifically, the sympathetic outflow from the stellate ganglion that supplies forearm skin—is designed primarily for relatively global and spatially imprecise tasks such as thermoregulation, relying on unmyelinated and highly branched neurons to achieve these effects. Finally, it does not appear to be the case, as Osty also assumed, that any of these sympathetic neurons produces active vasodilation in peripheral vasculature. Rather, their primary effect is vasoconstriction, and although a modest and diffuse vasodilatory effect can be achieved by relaxation of this sympathetic vasoconstriction, active vasodilation in the skin now appears to be dominated instead by non-neural mechanisms involving release within the skin of various vasoactive chemical agents from structures such as mast cells, the capillary endothelium, and "varicosities" in the sympathetic fibers themselves (Berne & Levy, 1993; Brading, 1999; Hamill, 1996; Jänig, 1990; Kandel, Schwartz, & Jessell, 1991; Roddie, 1983; Ryan, 1991; Willis, 1999).

In short, Olga's skin-writing, like the formation of cruciform hypnotic blisters, appears to be mediated by some sort of abnormal and yet spatially precise operation of these local chemical mechanisms of inflammation and vascular control. How such control could be exerted remains a mystery, but it is worth pointing out that both situations offer numerous opportunities for further physiological investigation, if suitable subjects can be found. Sympathetic nerve-block, for example, should not abolish the effects. Similarly, more detailed time-course-information could help to identify which vasoactive agents are potentially involved, with follow-up experiments using selective agonists/antagonists of these agents helping to pinpoint their contributions. Substance P and similar peptides activated in dermographia, for example, appear unlikely candidates for a role in Olga's skin-writing, because their time courses are on the order of minutes to hours rather than the tens of seconds in which Olga's skin-writing appeared.

In sum, I have now provided two examples of extreme psychophysiological influence for which no explanation in conventional biological terms seems even possible, let alone anywhere in sight. Like Gurney (1887a), I do not wish to insist too strongly on the impossibility; but I do insist that *at minimum* serious explanatory gaps currently exist, and that these gaps cannot simply be papered over with glib and vague invocations of the principle of psychophysical equivalence, or mind-body unity, that has been relied upon by nearly all contemporary investigators. Similar gaps exist with regard to nearly all the other phenomena I have discussed so far in this chapter.

Changes in Another Person's Body

By this point it should be abundantly clear that there are numerous types, and many well-attested instances, of phenomena demonstrating that an emotion, a belief, vivid imagery, or some other psychological process can sometimes produce striking physiological changes which, in terms of their specificity of location and form, go far beyond the generalized responses of the body and nervous system to stress or other emotions. The belief that all phenomena of psychophysiological influence *must* be explainable in purely biological terms can perhaps be sustained, in those sufficiently committed to it, so long as we confine our attention—as we have so far—to phenomena involving the apparent effects of mental states on a person's own body.

This promissory materialism, however, is further undermined by related types of phenomena in which one person's mental state seems to have influenced *another* person's body. Although most scientists, and many others, are unwilling even to entertain the idea that such phenomena can occur, they do in fact occur, and pose essentially the same problem as phenomena of psychophysiological influence involving only one person. Both types are examples of volition, or the carrying out of some kind of intention or purpose by some kind of intelligence. Even in its simplest and most basic forms, as I have said before, volition remains a mystery: How does the idea to raise one's arm translate into the complex motor processes that carry out that intention? The phenomena that I will discuss in the remainder of this chapter are simply an extension of that basic problem, but they are especially important because they call even more seriously into question glib assertions of mind-body "unity" as the basis of all psychophysical interactions. How on such views can a brain process in one person set in motion its physiological expression in the body of another person? The problem of volition, from the most common everyday acts to the rarest and most extreme of the phenomena examined in this chapter, will remain a mystery without some understanding of the relation of mind and brain that goes deeper than either an absolute separation of non-interactive mind and brain or the currently popular, but ultimately superficial, assertion of mind-brain unity.

Myers suggested that all supernormal phenomena, including those in which the thoughts of one person seem to have affected the body of another person, may reflect an ability to act on other bodies "such…as the living energy, whatever it be, in each of us is wont to exercise upon the brain" (Myers, 1894, p. 417), a process he called *"telergy"* (*HP*, vol. 2, p. 52). The extension of this volitional power from one's own body to another person's body may seem radical, but, as Myers (1894) summarized the situation, we are as ignorant about the nature of the former as about the latter:

> It is the very secret of life which confronts us here; the fundamental antinomy between Mind and Matter....I here say only that since this problem does already exist,...we have no right to take for granted that the problem, when more closely approached, will keep within its ancient limits, or that Mind, whose far-darting energy we are now realising, must needs be always powerless upon aught but the grey matter of the brain. (p. 421)

One important point to emphasize, however, is that the distinction I am making here between effects on one's own body and effects on another person's body is often harder to draw, in practice, than one might expect. In the first place, it seems likely, as Myers pointed out (e.g., *HP,* vol. 1, p. 213), that most if not all psychophysiological effects of direct suggestion—whether produced by suggestions arising from within oneself or by suggestions coming from another person (such as a healer or a hypnotist)—are ultimately the result of self-suggestion. For most of the phenomena discussed in this chapter, moreover, any suggestions received from other persons are perceived in the normal way. In other cases, however, it seems reasonable to extend this picture by proposing, based on the extensive evidence for psi (see the Appendix), that a suggestion has been received in some supernormal way. Whether perceived normally or supernormally, the suggestion takes root in the person's mind and sets off whatever psychophysiological processes in his or her own body are necessary to produce the observed phenomena.

In cases of this latter type, however, we must also keep in mind the possibility that, in addition to a physiological process set in motion by self-suggestion, there may also have been some more direct influence by the other person; and it is often not clear-cut when, or to what extent, the former process may leave off and the latter take over. This will become particularly apparent when we come to cases in which the other person was making a deliberate attempt to alter the physiology of the subject.

Keeping in mind these cautionary remarks about possible sources of the influence, I will next briefly survey phenomena of psychophysiological influence that involve, not just one, but two people—that is, evidence indicating that one person can somehow induce physiological changes in *another* person's body. The section will be relatively brief, because this topic lies so far beyond ideas that most contemporary scientists are willing to entertain that research has been severely limited both by the number of people willing to undertake it and by the serious lack of funding for it. Nonetheless, as I will try to make evident, there has in fact already been a substantial amount of serious scientific research on these topics, the results of which cry out for further research.

Spontaneously Occurring Phenomena

Sympathetic Symptoms

The difficulty of making the distinction between effects on one's own body and effects on another person's body is illustrated by cases that might be considered “transitional.” In the cases that comprise this category, one person takes on the pains or other symptoms of another person’s suffering, apparently in sympathy with that person, a phenomenon that has been called “compathy,” or “the physical equivalent to empathy” (J. M. Morse & Mitcham, 1997). I mentioned earlier the well-known phenomenon of couvade, in which a man suffers some of the symptoms of his pregnant wife, such as nausea during the pregnancy or abdominal or other pains during the childbirth. I also mentioned earlier cases described by Stevenson (1997, vol. 1, pp. 54–56) and Tuke (1884, pp. 285–287), in which a person developed bleeding, blisters, swelling, or other adverse reactions after witnessing a corresponding injury on another person.[54]

I also earlier discussed what is in fact another, more extreme example of this phenomenon, namely, stigmata. Stigmata seem essentially to be symptoms of the stigmatic’s sympathy for the suffering of Jesus; and so it is perhaps not surprising that other sympathetic symptoms have also occasionally been reported in connection with stigmatics. Thérèse Neumann, for example, apparently developed symptoms comparable to those she witnessed in other people (Klauder, 1938, p. 653), as did Anna Emmerich and Elizabeth K., the subject in whom Lechler had induced stigmata with hypnosis (Stevenson, 1997, vol. 1, pp. 43–44). Likewise, Olga K., not a stigmatic in the religious sense but a person capable of producing similar skin symptoms, is reported to have developed pain in her cheek, and later an abscess on the inside of her cheek that penetrated through it, as a reaction to having seen in Turkey some dervishes who thrust skewers through their cheeks (Stevenson, 1997, vol. 1, p. 95). People such as stigmatics who develop symptoms in response to the suffering of others may share certain personality traits that make them susceptible to this and other kinds of psychophysiological responses. A hint might be provided by Barber’s finding (1984) that a large number of highly hypnotizable and fantasy-prone individuals experience not only false pregnancy, as I mentioned earlier, but also “another person’s symptoms when they hear or read about them” (p. 113).

It seems relatively clear-cut in these cases that the effect is the result of self-suggestion. The problem becomes more complicated, however, when we come to the many similar cases in which the person did not actually witness, or even know normally about, the condition of the other person. In one case, for example, a woman suddenly “doubled over, clutching her chest as if in severe pain and said, ‘Something has happened to Nell [her daughter], she has been hurt.’” Two hours later she learned that Nell had died in a car accident, from wounds incurred when the steering wheel pierced her chest (Rhine, 1962, p. 107). In cases such as these, did the subject of the case perceive the distant event in some supernormal manner and develop sym-

54. For two additional cases reported by Stevenson—including that of a man who, shortly after a friend died of lung cancer, developed pains that persisted for more than four years and seemed to correspond to the pains suffered by his friend—see Stevenson, 1965, pp. 1232–1233; 1970, p. 108.

pathetic symptoms by self-suggestion? Or did the distant person exert some sort of influence on the body of the subject? Or both?

Stevenson (1970, pp. 108–114; 1997, vol. 1, pp. 92–93) has provided reviews of numerous similar cases, and Rhine (1967) published a paper in which she analyzed 169 cases reported to her in which someone described having had a "somatic experience" corresponding to the injury or illness of a distant person. Of these 169, 58 had occurred at the time of death of the distant person, 52 involved non-fatal accidents, 33 corresponded to illnesses or operations, and 26 were related to childbirth (p. 115). In one case, for example, the person "suddenly got violent pains in my right eye"; she soon learned that her son had suffered an injury to his eye at about that time from the backfiring of an engine (p. 115). In another, a man "suddenly...felt a severe shock to my temple" and said to his wife that he felt that his brother had just shot himself; four hours later he received a telegram confirming this (p. 120). In another, similar to hysterical cases of limb paralysis, a person suffered a temporary paralysis of a leg at about the time the other person had been fatally wounded in the hip and leg (pp. 121–122). In still another, reminiscent of stigmata cases, the person developed a mark on one arm, which lasted for several days and apparently corresponded to an intravenous injection in the arm of a friend then hospitalized.

Because in these cases the condition of one person was not known about normally by the person who developed a symptom corresponding to it, they may seem to some readers to be of a qualitatively different kind than those in which the subject *did* see or hear about the stimulus. Yet, given the phenomenological similarity of the two, and given also the extensive evidence that people can learn about events in some way other than through ordinary sensory functioning (see the Appendix), it is possible that the essential difference lies only in the manner in which the idea providing the stimulus for the physiological response reached the subject's mind.

Maternal Impressions

There have been numerous cases, reported throughout history, in which an idea in the mind of a pregnant woman, usually triggered by her perception of another person's injury or deformity, seems to have resulted in a similar deformity in a third person—her unborn baby. Such phenomena have been called "maternal impressions," and Myers urged the study of them:

> If [some] shock fall upon the mother during the embryo's life, and if it chance...to reach the mother's subliminal self in effective fashion, it may then transfer itself to the embryo, and imprint upon the child the organic memory of the mother's emotion of admiration, disgust, or fear....I believe that there is evidence enough...to show that isolated and momentary suggestions—as the sight of a crushed ankle or missing finger—may produce a definite localised effect on the embryo in much the same way as a hypnotic suggestion may produce a localised congestion or secretion. (Myers, 1895d, p. 349; also *HP,* vol. 2, p. 267)

Most modern medical scientists deny the reality of maternal impression cases. E. M. Sternberg (2001), for example, referred to them as "the fifteenth century belief in monster births if a pregnant woman was exposed to a fright," a belief "carried through to the nineteenth century and, in transmuted form, on into the twentieth century, in grandmother's warning that if mother spilled coffee on her leg, baby would be born with a birthmark on the thigh." She concluded that such "magical thinking" has now, in the 21st century, fallen "by the wayside," remaining only in "the realm of popular culture" (p. 8).

But can reports of maternal impressions be dismissed so quickly as mere superstition? Contrary to what Sternberg and many others may assume, the phenomenon is not confined to folklore or legend: Numerous cases have in fact been observed by physicians and reported in medical journals. Myers (*HP,* vol. 1, pp. 455–458) called attention to two cases reported by physicians in medical journals in the 1890s. The first involved a "very suggestible" woman who during her pregnancy encountered a woman with a birthmark covering one whole side of her face. Thereafter, throughout her pregnancy, she had the hallucination that the faces of all passers-by in the street were similarly marked. Interestingly, she did *not* expect her unborn child to have the mark; but it did. The second case was slightly different, in that the pregnant woman had the misfortune to be present when her husband was shot in the left side of his chest. He survived, but while trying to help him, she had gotten blood all over her face; and, as she confided to their doctor that same day, she was convinced that her child would be born with a "bloody face." Instead, as the doctor observed nearly eight months later, the baby was born with "bright red marks" that were "elevated nævi...easily to be seen at a distance of a hundred feet." Moreover, "they were on the left side of the chest, and although not in the exact anatomic location of the wound on the father's chest, still so near the spot that they are easily recognised as resulting therefrom. The mother had seen the wounds in her husband's chest, and had told me during his illness that they made her sick every time she looked at them."[55]

Stevenson (1992a, 1997, vol. 1, pp. 104–175) has provided an important review of this phenomenon, with a detailed survey and analysis of 50 cases selected from several hundred that he identified in the literature.[56] The 50 cases were chosen by the following criteria: First, in many of them the physician (usually also the author) had seen not only the baby and its birthmark or birth defect, but also the person whose similar deformity had impressed the

55. An interesting variation on this may have occurred in connection with a stigmata case. I mentioned earlier a case reported by J. G. Fisher and Kollar (1980) of a young Mexican-American woman who developed stigmata shortly after her marriage. About a year and a half later, she gave birth to a child who "also had the stigmata (hands, feet, crown of thorns) five times, the first at age 2½ weeks" (p. 1462). This is a "variation" on maternal impression cases because the marks developed, not in utero, but shortly after the child's birth.

56. For a summary of all 50 cases, see Stevenson (1997, Table 3.2, pp. 111–134).

pregnant woman. Second, Stevenson chose cases in which the most detail had been given (although in many of them still more detail would have been desirable). Third, he chose cases in which the correspondence between the two marks or deformities was close. Finally, and perhaps most importantly, he gave preference to cases in which the marks in question were unusual, thus lessening the likelihood of chance correspondence.

For example, 32 of the 50 cases involved birth defects, usually the congenital absence of all or part of a limb. In one (from the 1890s), a child of the pregnant woman had accidentally been cut severely with a wood chopper across the middle, ring, and little fingers of the left hand; and the child born subsequently was also missing the middle, ring, and little fingers of the left hand. In another (from 1949) the pregnant woman saw a man whose ear had been cut off by a sword in a war, and her child was born without an external left ear. In a third case (from 1863), a pregnant woman who had seen her brother's genitalia after his penis had been amputated for treatment of cancer later gave birth to a male child lacking a penis. The physician in this case confirmed the condition of both the woman's brother and her baby. This case particularly calls into question the hypothesis of chance coincidence: Surgical amputation of a penis is not a common occurrence, and the incidence of congenital absence of the penis is similarly exceedingly rare. Stevenson (1997, vol. 1, p. 140) cites an 1898 study in which the incidence of congenital absence of the penis was estimated at 1 in 30,000,000 births and another study showing that only 15 such cases had been reported in the medical literature up to 1951.

In the remaining 18 cases, involving what would be more accurately described as birthmarks rather than birth defects, the two conditions were also often unusual ones. In one case (from 1877), a pregnant woman's 2-year-old son cut his upper lip severely, requiring surgical repair and leaving a scar. The child born subsequently had a linear scar on the upper lip at the same place. In another case, a woman had seen her husband after he had been slapped on the face and neck by someone whose four bloody fingers had left bloody marks on his face. The child was born with marks on the face and neck resembling the four finger marks.

The cases are not confined to earlier times. Similar cases are still occasionally reported, even in medical journals (e.g., H. C. Williams & Pembroke, 1988). Stevenson himself has investigated and reported six such cases (1997, vol. 1, pp. 142–173).[57] One of these (Stevenson, 1985, 1989, 1997, vol. 1, pp. 160–169) occurred in the 1980s in Sri Lanka. In 1974 the father and uncle of Sampath, the subject of the case, murdered a man in their village by cutting off his arms and legs. The victim's mother repeatedly cursed the family and wished them to have a deformed child. Sampath's mother feared that the curse would be effective, but when her next child was born a few years later,

57. Additionally, some of the more than 200 cases that Stevenson (1992b, 1997) has reported of birthmarks or birth defects attributed to the effects of a previous life (which I will discuss later in the chapter) may possibly be attributable instead to maternal impression.

it was normal and she believed that the curse had somehow been negated. The next child, however, born in 1982, was severely deformed, lacking both of his arms and having seriously deformed legs.

A curse of this kind is an unusual form of maternal impression, but we encountered similar kinds of cases earlier in the chapter in connection with hexing or voodoo deaths. Moreover, Sampath's case is not alone. A pediatrician in Australia reported a remarkably similar case (E. K. Turner, 1960), in which a young girl became pregnant by a man of whom her parents disapproved. From the second month of her pregnancy,[58] her mother repeatedly cursed her and declared that the baby would be born "without arms and legs, and blind." The girl nonetheless persisted in the pregnancy, and when the child was born he was missing both legs and had severe deformities of the arms, although he did not seem to be blind. He died six months later. The author attributed the deformities to severe stress that aborted the development of the child's limbs.

E. M. Sternberg (2001) likewise believes that stress or other strong emotion can explain such cases, because of the findings of psychoneuroimmunology, discussed earlier in this chapter, showing a relationship between emotion and the immune system. Thus, she claims, maternal impression cases have been "removed from the realm of the magical" (p. 8). But can anyone really take seriously the "explanation" that "stress" produced the specific, localized, and often rare marks and deformities encountered in many of these cases?

Unfortunately, opportunities for scientists to find a more adequate explanation by studying cases at first hand may be diminishing. In earlier centuries physicians believed that the fetus was directly connected to the mother's body by nerve or blood vessels and that the cases could be "explained" as an effect of the mother's mental processes on her own body. As long they believed in this as a plausible explanation, maternal impression cases were regularly reported in the medical literature. In the 20th century, however, scientists learned that there are no such neural or circulatory connections. There is transfer of some substances across the placenta, but this clearly cannot explain how an idea in one person's mind (the mother's) could translate into correspondingly specific and localized effects on another person's body (the baby's). Apparently because there was no longer an acceptable explanation, reports of such cases in the medical literature declined precipitously. Perhaps even more importantly, however, as Stevenson (1997, vol. 1, p. 174) has pointed out, the *real* (and not just the *reported*) incidence of such cases may also be falling off, since the belief in such an effect among the general public may be dying away, in the West at least.

---

58. This case illustrates an interesting finding by Stevenson (1997, vol. 1, pp. 138–139), namely, that the stimulus in maternal impression cases was significantly more likely to occur in the first trimester than in the other two. Assuming that a pregnant woman would be equally likely in any trimester to encounter a stimulus, Stevenson suggested that this finding is "medically significant," because the 1st trimester is also the one in which the developing fetus is most vulnerable.

Distant Mental Influence on Living Systems

The cases of "sympathetic symptoms," described earlier, occurred spontaneously, often at a time of crisis for the person whose injury seemed to provide the stimulus. In this section I will discuss some of the evidence for closely related phenomena, in which one person has deliberately attempted to influence physiological processes in another person. Here in particular we encounter again the problem of deciding whether the effect is really some direct influence *on* the subject by the other person or rather the result of self-suggestion *within* the subject, engendered by information obtained in some supernormal fashion. Support for the former possibility derives from the large experimental literature concerning direct mental influence on inanimate or non-human living targets, otherwise known as psychokinesis, or PK.[59]

Community of Sensation

Some of the early mesmerists had reported that a mesmerized subject sometimes seemed to experience a sensation comparable to one that the mesmerist was feeling, usually a taste or a pain—although, as Gauld (1992, pp. 234–235) pointed out, rarely was there any indication that auditory or olfactory cues had been adequately controlled for. Later in the century, Esdaile, Elliotson, and others also reported experiments along these lines (for a brief review, see Gurney et al., 1886, vol. 2, pp. 324–329), and still later Gurney, Myers, and other members of the SPR undertook similar experiments (for a review, see Gurney et al., 1886, vol. 1, pp. 51–58; *HP,* vol. 1, pp. 540–543).

Another series of experiments that might be considered a variation on the "community of sensation" phenomena were those, described earlier, in which Olga Kahl was able to reproduce on her skin target pictures or writing. It was remarkable enough, as described above, that she could somehow translate an image presented to her normally into corresponding marks within her skin. Even more remarkable was that the target information often had not been conveyed to her in any normal sensory way. In a typical experiment of this sort, an investigator would write a name or other target on a piece of paper and then concentrate on it, always taking care of course that Olga did not see it, sometimes by going into a different room. The investigators also sometimes designated at the time of the experiment the skin location where they wanted the marks to appear. Within a short time, corresponding letters or lines would begin to form in Olga's skin (Stevenson, 1997, vol. 1, pp. 94–103). Somehow, it seemed, information in one person's mind was transferred, within seconds or minutes, into a highly specific physiological reaction in another person. Olga's case invites the interpretation that it was the image that arose in her mind, rather than a direct PK effect from the other person, that somehow controlled the reaction: Recall,

59. I will not attempt here even to summarize this literature, let alone discuss it adequately, but for pointers into it see the Appendix.

for example, that when the target was the name "René," the "N" came out looking like an "H," as in the alphabet of Olga's native Russian.

Suggestion at a Distance

The possibility of direct, PK-like influence from experimenters or other persons, however, seems stronger in some other experiments in which a more generalized physiological response was induced in a distant subject. For example, Janet, Richet, and others undertook experiments in "suggestion at a distance," in some of which Myers participated (Janet, 1886/1968a, 1886/1968b; Myers, 1886c, pp. 127–137; Richet, 1888, pp. 32–52).[60] In 18 of 25 trials Janet and his colleague Gibert were able to induce a trance in their hysterical subject Léonie at distances varying from ¼ to 1 mile. In most of these, the experimenter made the suggestion while another person was with Léonie and could observe her. To rule out the possibility that the observer might have inadvertently conveyed normally to her a suggestion that she fall into an hypnotic trance, some trials were made when the observer did not know that an attempt was being made. Moreover, she was rarely found to have fallen into a trance spontaneously, "not provoked by our order" (Janet, 1886b, p. 263). Recognizing the importance of such experiments, Myers suggested that they be extended with experiments on the distant influence of a subject's physiological state (such as vasomotor, circulatory, or respiratory systems) (1886e, p. 450; 1893b, pp. 31–32).[61]

Myers had thought that Janet and his colleagues "are not likely to drop the inquiry; and we may hope that the experiments...are but the first instalment of what they may yet achieve" (1886e, p. 450). Regrettably, they *did* soon drop the inquiry. Even worse, years later Janet downplayed their significance, apparently retrospectively embarrassed by his own results. In reporting his experiments in 1886, he had said that "there is a sort of faculty, I don't know what sort, by which she [Léonie] is able to perceive the thoughts of others" (Janet, 1886/1968a) p. 130); but in 1930 he declared that he had always been "skeptical as to mental suggestion and hypnotism from a distance" (Janet, 1930/1961, p. 125). He even rebuked those who had tried to urge the importance of such research. Apparently, the suggestion that such studies might imply "unknown faculties of the human mind" (p. 125) was unacceptable enough to lead him to repudiate this line of research—even his own—altogether.[62]

---

60. For a description of Richet's experiments in English, see A. T. Myers (1888) and Podmore (1894, pp. 113–116).

61. Researchers in recent years have successfully taken up this suggestion to study distant influence on physiology—but we have here another cautionary example of the consequences of ignoring one's history. No current parapsychologist conducting research on distant mental influence seems aware of Myers's suggestion, and it was decades before research along these lines was begun.

62. Janet's "retrocognitive dissonance"—to use a phrase coined by Brian Inglis (1983)—reflects an all too common reaction to supernormal phenomena, even those produced in careful experiments witnessed or even conducted by oneself.

Fortunately, not everyone agreed with Janet. Other experiments of this kind were carried out later by Russian scientists, especially the physiologist L. L. Vasiliev of the University of Leningrad (for an overview, see Vasiliev, 1976). During the years 1933–1934, Vasiliev and some colleagues conducted 260 trials with three subjects (two of them hysterical patients, one normal). In these, an observer stayed in the room with the subject while another experimenter attempted, at randomly chosen times unknown both to the subject and to the observer, first to put the subject into a hypnotic trance and then to awaken him or her, solely by sending a mental command. There were four conditions, involving varying degrees of screening the subject from sensory cues: In the least restrictive trials (n = 65), the "sender" was in the same room as the subject, a few meters away, but out of sight. In the rest the sender and subject were nearly always in different rooms, separated by two passages whose doors were shut. In 68 trials the sender was in a "perfect screening chamber" (p. 116), and in 32 of these the subject was in a Faraday chamber (to screen out electromagnetic radiation). In only about 10% of the trials did the subject fail to go to sleep or wake up within a few minutes of the command; and there was no overall statistical difference between the four conditions (p. 126). Vasiliev also conducted another series of 12 trials with distances ranging from 25 meters to 1700 kilometers, and in most of these, the subject fell asleep or woke up within one to two minutes of the distant command (p. 153).

Like Janet, Vasiliev also reported that on very few occasions did the subjects fall into, or awaken from, a hypnotic trance spontaneously (p. 129). This, together with the fact that many trials were successful even when the time of induction was randomly chosen by the "sender" and unknown to both the subject and the observer, weakens the hypothesis that trances were induced by the subject's expectations.

In recent years, there have been many other kinds of studies designed even more tightly to rule out expectation as an explanation. Before turning to the laboratory studies, I will first comment briefly on one particular variety of distant-influence studies that has been highly controversial, highly publicized, and (so far) inconclusive—namely, attempts to heal a distant person, either by prayer or by a "psychic healer."

Distant Intentionality Studies: Clinical

Studies of alternative healing methods such as Therapeutic Touch (discussed earlier) are so far "inconclusive because of the required presence of the practitioner" (Targ, 1997, p. 76) and the resulting strong likelihood that any effects seen are placebo effects (themselves requiring explanation, as I have argued). Within the enormous literature on complementary and alternative forms of healing, there have been relatively few studies that have attempted to control for such effects by conducting the healing intervention at a distance and unknown to the patient.[63] Some of these have involved

63. Such studies, however, still do not entirely rule out placebo, or self-suggestion, effects. There remains the possibility that patients detected the attempted influence

self-identified alternative healers; some have involved ordinary people praying for the sick person. Reviews of these studies (Abbot, 2000; Astin et al., 2000; Ernst, 2003; Targ, 1997) have acknowledged the methodological problems and equivocal results, but most also cautiously conclude that there is sufficient evidence to warrant further research. For example, among the 13 distant-healing studies reviewed by Abbot and by Astin et al., six produced significant results.

Of the three most often cited and apparently well-conducted studies yielding positive results, two involved prayer (Byrd, 1988; Harris et al., 1999) and one involved distant healing (Sicher, Targ, Moore, & Smith, 1998). All have methodological problems that the authors themselves were the first to acknowledge.[64] Clearly, the results so far are inconclusive, and the only way to resolve the question is with more thorough and better-designed studies. But some general comments about these studies are in order here. First, perhaps more notable than the studies themselves have been the reactions to them. For a microcosm of these reactions, one has only to look at the 15 letters to the editor of the *Archives of Internal Medicine* prompted by the Harris et al. study. Harris and his colleagues attempted to replicate the findings of Byrd with a large-scale study involving 990 patients admitted to a cardiac care unit (CCU); 466 were randomly assigned to be prayed for by distant persons who did not know them, and the rest were given standard care only. The patients not only did not know which group they were assigned to, they also did not even know that such a study was being conducted. A person unconnected with the CCU assigned patients randomly to the groups, and no one who had any contact with or evaluated the patients knew which group they were in. Because the prayers were simply for a speedy recovery, the investigators expected a global effect, rather than any specific outcomes; and they did find that the patients in the "prayer" group had "lower overall adverse outcomes" in the CCU.

Of the 15 letters to the editor, only one was positive; the rest criticized the study on various methodological, statistical, or ethical grounds, some of which are valid concerns. The predominant motivation for the critiques, however, seems to have been that religion and science cannot and should not be mixed, some protesting that if prayer is effective we will "need to reassess 500 years of scientific achievement" (Sandweiss, 2000), others arguing that "God's omnipotence is beyond our ability to add or detract" (Galishoff, 2000).

The first critique is one that has repeatedly been leveled against studies of all phenomena suggesting a primary role for volitional or mental causation—particularly psi phenomena, but also nearly all the phenomena discussed in this chapter. As I pointed out in Chapter 2, Myers and most others

in some supernormal manner.

64. Unlike Galton, apparently the first person to attempt a scientific study of prayer, most people have recognized that such research is anything but "a simple statistical question" (Galton, 1872, p. 126) and involves numerous logical and methodological problems (see, e.g., Chibnall, Jeral, & Cerullo, 2001, pp. 2529–2530).

who have taken seriously the evidence for such phenomena have insisted that the only consequence of accepting them is not the negation but the expansion of modern science—rightly understood as an epistemological method and not an ideology. One can fully accept the fundamental scientific premise of the underlying continuity and lawfulness of nature without also assuming that we currently know all relevant principles. Accepting evidence that consciousness can have an influence on distant minds or matter clearly implies rejection of the modern equation of the natural order with the physical universe as classically conceived—but not of science itself.

The second critique of prayer studies—the need to keep science and religion separate because questions about God are beyond the scope of science—betrays a limited view of what prayer studies really imply. Much of the visceral reaction against studies of the efficacy of prayer seems to be based on this assumption: "The most fundamental problem is that experiments to test the power of prayer...require God...to work miracles. The whole enterprise is therefore not really about prayer as a practice, but about the existence of God" (Thomson, 1996, p. 534). And again: "God is the purported mechanism in these studies....We maintain that studies of distant prayer have had this feature not to test the effect of prayer on human illness, but to test for God's intervention in response to human intercession" (Chibnall et al., 2001, p. 2532).

Such statements are simply false. I cannot of course comment on the personal motivations of individual researchers, but prayer studies broadly understood are *not* about the existence of either God or miracles. As Harris et al. insisted, "it was intercessory prayer, not the existence of God, that was tested here" (p. 2277). Prayer studies are, in fact, a subset of the much larger body of research intended to examine the question of whether consciousness can directly affect, not just the healing of another person, but more generally material objects (psychokinesis, or PK studies; see the Appendix) and biological systems (the experimental studies to be discussed in the next section). Given this larger context of numerous studies suggesting the existence of such effects, it would be surprising if intercessory prayer—understood as the intentional direction of one's thoughts toward another person—were *not* effective under appropriate circumstances (those circumstances, of course, to be determined by further research).

A more valid criticism of prayer studies has been that the use of blinded intercessors—persons praying for a distant person not known to them—makes little psychological sense (Chibnall et al., 2001).[65] These authors suggest placing the intercessor surreptitiously outside a patient's room where they can "direct their intention right at the patient" (p. 2532). As an alternative, remote healers or persons praying could view the patient on a video monitor. As we will see in the next section, numerous successful experiments in distant influence have been conducted in this way, and I would

65. Three recent large-scale studies of prayer and healing that did not produce significant results suffered from this same methodological weakness, one I consider serious (Aviles et al., 2001; Benson et al., 2006; Krucoff et al., 2005).

expect the results of prayer studies to improve greatly under more personal and directed conditions.[66]

Distant Intentionality Studies: Experimental

I said earlier that prayer studies are, in fact, a subset of a much larger body of research intended to determine whether a person's conscious intention can directly affect distant biological systems, without any normal communication of the intention. A body of studies much more robust than the prayer studies, in terms of both numbers and results, consists of what have previously been called bio-PK, distant intentionality, or healing analog studies, and are now generally called DMILS, or "distant mental influence on living systems."[67] These studies include not only those in which a physiological response of another person is the target, but also numerous studies in which non-human organisms, from bacteria or yeast to small mammals, have been the targets. Over the past few decades there have been more than 150 such studies (for reviews, see Benor, 1990; Braud, 1993, 2003; Solfvin, 1984). In this section, however, I will concentrate on research involving humans, of which there have also been several reviews (Braud & Schlitz, 1989, 1991; Delanoy, 2001; Schlitz & Braud, 1997; S. Schmidt, Schneider, Utts, & Walach, 2004).

The basic method for these studies has been for one person (the "agent") to direct some specified intention at another person (the subject or target person), such as the intention to calm or conversely to arouse that person. In nearly all of the studies, the response of the target person to the intentions of the agent has been measured by reactions of the autonomic nervous system (usually skin conductance or other measures of electrodermal activity). Because this response reflects a level of arousal in the target person that is not under conscious control, the assumption has been that such a measure is a better indicator of an effect than are conscious attempts to respond to the agent's intentions, such as by guessing when he or she is directing the intention. Experimental methods have been designed specifically to rule out conventional explanations for any response seen in the target persons, such as suggestion or expectation, sensory cues, naturally occurring internal rhythms in the autonomic nervous system, recording errors, arbitrary selection of data, and chance. For example, the two persons are isolated in separate rooms with no sensory contact possible, experimental and control periods are randomly interspersed in an order that is automatically generated, and responses are recorded automatically.

---

66. I remind readers of Myers's concept of "rapport" (discussed in Chapter 2)—that is, some kind of link or interconnectedness between persons at a subliminal level that may contribute to spontaneous occurrences of supernormal phenomena, to effective induction of hypnotic trance and associated phenomena of suggestion, and to successful psi experiments, including distant healing studies.

67. Another translation of DMILS is "direct mental interaction with living systems."

Under these general conditions, the results over numerous studies have been reasonably consistent and robust. In an overview of 19 studies conducted at three labs, Schlitz and Braud (1997) found an overall success rate of 37%, when 5% would be expected by chance (p = .0000007, effect size = .25). In a more recent and conservative meta-analysis of 37 studies, S. Schmidt et al. (2004) found a somewhat smaller, but still significant effect (p = .001, effect size = .11).

A related group of experiments derived from the experience people often report of feeling that they are being stared at and finding, when they turn to look, that they are in fact being stared at. In these experiments the agent, instead of trying to calm or arouse the person, simply stares at him or her on a video monitor during randomly selected periods of time. Again, some autonomic measure such as electrodermal activity is measured. In 11 such studies at three labs, Schlitz and Braud (1997) found an overall success rate of 64%, when 5% would be expected by chance (p = .000054, effect size = .25). A later meta-analysis of 15 studies by S. Schmidt et al. (2004) also yielded a significant effect (p = .01, effect size = .13).

The staring studies have also revealed some interesting trends. Unlike the calm/activate studies, in which the prediction clearly is that the target person's autonomic response will be lowered during the "calm" periods and heightened during the "activate" periods, in the staring studies there is no such clear expectation of what the response will be. Some people (or people in some situations) might find the staring uncomfortable or intrusive and thus become anxious and aroused; others might be more comfortable and thus react to the connection with another person in a more positive or relaxed way; and some people might react differently depending on whether the agent is a stranger or a friend. Experiments by Braud, Shafer, and Andrews (1993a, 1993b) in fact suggested such differential responses: In early experiments the staring produced arousal or activation in the target persons; in later experiments, however, after the starer or the target person, or both, had been given "connectedness training" (i.e., instruction and exercises in how to feel comfortable with and open to relating to another person), the staring produced significant results in the opposite direction, calming instead of arousing the target person. Whether the two persons were strangers or acquaintances before the training had no effect on these results (1993b, p. 393), but scores on personality scales of introversion and social avoidance and distress were related to the staring response (pp. 400–403).

Another series of staring studies derived from the failure of one person— an avowed and vocal skeptic of psi phenomena—to replicate the original results. In this new series the skeptic, Richard Wiseman, and another experimenter who has consistently obtained highly significant results not only in staring studies but in many other DMILS and remote-viewing studies, Marilyn Schlitz, carried out experiments jointly, first in Wiseman's lab and then in Schlitz's (Wiseman & Schlitz, 1997, 1999). In these studies the experimental conditions were the same for all, except that in half of them Wiseman served as the experimenter and in half Schlitz did. In both series

Schlitz obtained significant results, whereas Wiseman obtained only chance results, suggesting that Schlitz's positive attitude and Wiseman's negative attitude influenced the results, whether directly or indirectly. These studies are, in fact, further confirmation of the "experimenter effect," long observed in psi research, which I mentioned earlier, and they raise again the questions of who the real "subject" is, or whether some kind of "rapport" or interconnection between the "subject" and "experimenter" is the crucial factor.[68]

As with all psi research, and indeed with psychological research in general, DMILS studies are not invariably replicable. Nevertheless, the history of the research shows effect sizes that are equal to, and sometimes even greater than, "some recent medical studies that have been heralded as medical breakthroughs" (Schlitz & Braud, 1997, p. 71). Clearly, these studies should be repeated and extended.

Birthmarks and Birth Defects in Cases of the Reincarnation Type

In this chapter I first examined phenomena in which a person's ideas or images seem to have generated physiological responses in his or her own body. I then expanded the scope to look at phenomena in which images or ideas or intentions in one person's mind seem to have initiated physiological reactions in another person's body. In this final section, I cross still another boundary and look at phenomena in which images or ideas that we may presume to have existed in the mind of a person who has died seem to correspond with characteristics of a living person's body.

I am referring here to a subgroup of the cases generally known as cases of the reincarnation type (CORT). These are cases in which a young child, usually about two to three years old, begins to exhibit what seem to be memories of the life of a now-deceased person. Such children often speak about other parents, or a spouse and children they believe they have, and another home; and they also often talk about how they died. In many cases they give sufficient information, such as names of people or places, so that their parents (or, more rarely, an investigator) are able to identify and locate the person about whose life the child seems to be speaking. These children also often show unusual behavior that seems appropriate for the life they are talking about. If the deceased person drowned, for example, the child may have an extreme phobia of water. If the deceased person was of the opposite sex, the child may show gender confusion or behavior appropriate for that sex. The child usually stops speaking about the other life between

68. These studies also underscore another point I made earlier: Failure of some investigators to replicate research does not automatically invalidate positive results obtained by other qualified researchers. Such failure calls, instead, for closer examination of the factors contributing to success in one study but not in another. Strong experimenter effects are hardly unknown elsewhere in psychology; biofeedback training for control of hand temperature provides another and closely related example (Taub, 1977, pp. 276–277).

the ages of five and eight, although the associated behavior may persist into adulthood. Research on these cases, which have been found all over the world, has been going on for over 40 years, and several thousand cases have been identified and studied—some in great detail—by a number of investigators, including most notably Dr. Ian Stevenson, who pioneered this line of research (for an introduction, see Stevenson, 2001; Tucker, 2005; see also the Appendix for additional literature).

Particularly relevant to this chapter are those cases, now numbering well over 200, in which the child has a birthmark or birth defect corresponding to a similar mark (usually a fatal wound) on the deceased person. Stevenson has considered these cases so important that he devoted a two-volume, 2,268-page monograph (1997) to them. A typical case is that of Hanumant Saxena (Stevenson, 1997, vol. 1, pp. 455–467), an Indian boy born with a large cluster of hypopigmented birthmarks near the center of his chest. A few weeks before he was conceived, a man in his village had been shot in the chest at close range with a shotgun, and almost immediately died. Hanumant's mother not only saw the body, but had a dream about the dead man which prepared her to think that she might have a child who would be the rebirth of this man. Between the ages of three and five, Hanumant spoke as if he were this man; but the most important feature of the case is certainly the unusual birthmark, especially since Stevenson was able to confirm by means of a post-mortem report its close correspondence with the fatal wound.

Hanumant's family believed that he was the deceased man reborn, and on this theory birthmarks such as his are somehow linked to the mental and physical effects produced in the deceased man as he was suddenly shot to death. There are, however, other possible interpretations that must be kept in mind when studying these cases. The most obvious, of course, is chance coincidence. Most people are born with some birthmarks, and certainly one of these will occasionally correspond just by chance with a mark on another person's body. Stevenson (1997, vol. 1, pp. 1131–1140) has discussed this possibility extensively. The basic argument against the chance hypothesis in most of the cases is that, unlike the common moles and nevi that many people are born with, the birthmarks and birth defects in these cases are often extremely unusual ones. Hanumant's multiple hypopigmented marks provide one example. Other cases involve extremely unusual birth defects such as unilateral brachydactyly (the lack of part or whole of the fingers on one hand), a condition otherwise practically unknown in the medical literature. Moreover, the close correspondence in shape, size, location, and other features in most cases makes the chance hypothesis exceedingly unlikely, especially since the children's families have not scoured the countryside looking for someone whose fatal wounds correspond to their child's marks. Instead, either the deceased person lived nearby—making the chance explanation even more unlikely—or the deceased person had been identified by means of statements that the child made.

Another argument against chance is that there are many cases in which there are two or more birthmarks, not in the same location as in Hanumant's case, but in two or more discrete locations. Stevenson (1997, vol. 2, pp. 1132–1134) has listed 33 examples of this type in a table. In 18 of these there were birthmarks corresponding to entry and exit gunshot wounds, often with a small birthmark corresponding to the entry wound and a larger and more irregularly shaped one corresponding to the exit wound (Stevenson, 1997, vol. 1, pp. 933–934). One such case, for example, involved a birthmark in the subject's throat. After hearing a description from the deceased man's sister of how he had shot himself in the throat, Stevenson conjectured that the subject might also have a birthmark on the top of his head. Returning to the subject, he found another, slightly larger birthmark there, covered by hair, about which he had not previously been told (Stevenson, 1997, vol. 1, pp. 728–745).

The chance interpretation is further weakened by another type of case. In discussing maternal impression cases, Myers (1892c) had urged attempts to generate them experimentally, using some benign rather than harmful image or suggestion as the stimulus (p. 335n). In some CORT cases, attempts of this sort have been made, and successfully. In some Asian countries, particularly Thailand and Burma, people sometimes mark the body of a dying or just-deceased person with, say, soot from a cooking pot, in the hope of generating a birthmark in a later-born child that will allow the family to identify the deceased person in his or her next life (Stevenson, 1997, vol. 1, pp. 803–879; Tucker, 2005, pp. 77–82; Tucker & Keil, in press). Stevenson and his colleagues have identified and studied 38 such "experimental birthmark" cases in which a child's birthmarks or birth defects correspond closely with a mark made on the deceased person's body (Tucker, 2005, p. 77). Moreover, in some African countries where infant mortality is high, particularly Nigeria, some people engage in the practice of mutilating a dead infant's body, such as by cutting off the tip of a finger, believing that this will prevent the child from dying again in infancy after its next birth. Stevenson (1997, chap. 20) has reported several cases of this type in which the correspondence between the mutilation and defects in a child born later, usually in the same family, is close and chance seems highly unlikely.

One such "experimental birthmark" case illustrates particularly well the difficulty confronting the chance hypothesis. The case involved a young Thai woman who died during surgery for a congenital heart problem; 13 months later her sister gave birth to a female child, Ma Choe Hnin Htet, who was found to have two birthmarks—a long linear hypopigmented birthmark down the middle of her chest and an irregularly shaped red birthmark on the back of her neck. Stevenson confirmed with the deceased woman's surgeon that the first birthmark corresponded closely with the surgical wound. Moreover, three of the deceased woman's friends explained that, as they were preparing the body for cremation, they had marked the back of the woman's neck with lipstick, hoping to generate an "experimental" birthmark of the kind described above. The mother of the child had of course known about the surgery on her sister. She had not, however, known about the marking of the body until after the child was born (Stevenson, 1997, vol. 1, pp. 839–852).

Here I can only refer readers to Stevenson's densely documented monograph for more information about the unusual nature of many of the birthmarks and birth defects and their close correspondence to similarly unusual marks or wounds on the deceased person; but I think it is an inescapable conclusion that chance correspondence can explain few if any of these cases.

Another possible interpretation that in some cases seems more reasonable to consider is that of maternal impressions. In most of the birthmark/birth-defect cases reported by Stevenson and others, the mother had either seen or heard about the wound on the deceased person. In Hanumant's case, for example, the hypothesis of maternal impression seems strong. This hypothesis is complicated, however, by the fact that in some cases the mother did *not* know anything whatsoever about the wound or mark on the deceased person, at least not consciously. Ma Choe Hnin Htet's case provides an example: Although her mother knew about the surgery, she knew nothing about the lipstick mark made on the back of her deceased sister's neck. Stevenson has listed 25 such cases in a table (1997, vol. 1, p. 1144). As we saw in our discussion of "sympathetic symptoms," however, a wound, pain, or other injury in one person's body was sometimes reflected in a physiological response, such as pain, in another person, even though the latter had no way of knowing normally about the injury. In such cases it was plausible to suppose that the process leading to the physiological response was guided by information obtained by the respondent in some supernormal manner. A similar process is plausible here too, and difficult to rule out decisively.

Another possible interpretation of these cases is that something in the mind of a dying or perhaps even a deceased person has somehow been translated into a mark on a developing fetus.[69] The process might thus be comparable to psychokinesis (PK) or, more precisely in this instance, to DMILS-type cases—the critical difference being that the agent may be a deceased person, still surviving in some form. Alternatively, CORT cases involving birthmarks and birth defects may be more akin to cases, such as those of stigmata, in which powerful or obsessive images in the mind of a person have produced a physiological response in that person's own body—the important difference here being that the body influenced is a *new* body,

69. The "mark" does not always involve just surface features on the skin. Stevenson (1997, chap. 21) has reported cases in which the subject has a disease corresponding to one that the previous person suffered. One such case was that of Selma Kiliç, a Turkish girl who seemed to be remembering the life of a woman who had died a year or so before Selma's birth of kidney disease; Selma herself subsequently developed kidney disease at the age of about seven (Stevenson, vol. 2, pp. 1679–1695). In a similar case, investigated by Tucker (Pasricha, Keil, Tucker, & Stevenson, 2005, pp. 379–381; Tucker, 2005, pp. 1–3), an American boy was born with defects of the pulmonary artery and heart closely similar to injuries suffered by his grandfather, a policeman, when he was fatally shot.

now being occupied by what is in some sense the same person. With this interpretation, the cases would be what most people witnessing them believe them to be—instances of rebirth or reincarnation. On any interpretation involving survival, however, it seems necessary to postulate, as has Stevenson (1997, vol. 2, pp. 2083–2092), some kind of "vehicle" or "substance" or "field" that retains memories and dispositional characteristics of a deceased person, called by Stevenson a "psychophore."

It is difficult to judge the relative plausibility of these interpretations in particular cases, and it is by no means self-evident that any one of them is always or even most frequently the best. Whatever the correct interpretation(s), however, what should be evident is that these cases are not *sui generis*, but instead constitute another large and well-documented family of extreme psychophysiological phenomena related to the various other phenomena we have examined in this chapter.

A further important question, however, remains. Many of the CORT cases involve a deceased person who was a total stranger, or perhaps only slightly acquainted with the child's family. What, therefore, is the connection or impetus, whether for the deceased person to be reborn in that family, or for the deceased person to influence that particular developing fetus, or for the mother to generate a maternal impression involving that person? The problem is not confined to these cases. As I mentioned in Chapter 2, Myers (1884–1885) pointed out that the connection between people in some telepathic or other supernormal experiences also does not seem "clearly referable either to kinship or to affection" (p. 100), since the people involved were strangers (p. 122). We are a long way from answering this question, just as we are a long way from understanding many other aspects of the phenomena described in this chapter.

Conclusion

One major goal of this chapter has been to provide an overall picture, derived from a truly enormous biomedical literature, of the remarkable range and diversity of phenomena of psychophysiological influence. Another major goal has been to show that there are well-attested phenomena demonstrating that strong emotions, beliefs, or intentions, unusually vivid imagery, and altered or dissociative states of consciousness sometimes result in striking physiological changes that, in terms of factors such as specificity of form and location, go far beyond generalized or systemic responses of the body and nervous system to stress or other emotions. Still another goal has been, following Myers, to present all these diverse phenomena in such a way as to show that they are not isolated, individual "anomalies," but instead comprise a continuum, ranging from commonplace and accepted kinds to extraordinary and dismissed ones, and moreover that they are deeply related both phenomenologically and conceptually. Recognizing this continuum also highlights the primary thesis of this chapter: Volition in general—whether of the sort that we take for granted (such as raising an arm) or rarer phenomena that more clearly challenge the currently prevailing view of mind-brain relations (such as raising a blister)—remains a challenging mystery.

Moreover, the phenomena described in this chapter illustrate that similar effects can result from quite different psychological and physiological conditions. Blisters can occur in response to a thermal stimulus, a strong emotional memory of a previous burn, or the suggestion of a hypnotist, and it seems unlikely that the physiological mechanism is the same in all three types. Symptoms of pregnancy occurring as a result of a true pregnancy seem to involve different physiological mechanisms from those occurring in association with pseudocyesis. An hallucination can be generated pathologically by physical illness, drugs, or alcohol, or by a telepathic impression. Again, we seem to be encountering volition: In contrast to purely physiological responses, many of the phenomena described in this chapter suggest the realization of an intention by whatever mechanism is available.

I have also tried to call attention to some important methodological issues inherent in the study of these refractory and puzzling phenomena. Reports of them often take the form of individual case studies involving persons who were clearly very unusual. Most of the phenomena described in this chapter occur primarily among such persons, and not among randomly selected samples of ordinary persons. For example, inducing phenomena such as psi, blisters, or vivid hallucinations with hypnotic suggestion does not occur easily or readily. As Myers stated, "they are not often evoked in answer to any rapid and, so to say, perfunctory hypnotic suggestion; they do not spring up in miscellaneous hospital practice; they need an education and a development which is hardly bestowed on one hypnotized subject in a hundred" (*HP,* vol. 1, p. 209).

Moreover, such studies of unusual persons cannot be belittled and dismissed as mere "anecdotes," in contrast with experimental studies involving larger numbers of less unusual subjects. This is particularly evident when one recognizes that most if not all of the cited observations and reports have been made by competent scientists, and that the phenomena they describe fall into a coherent overall pattern such as I have tried to display in this chapter.

Another important lesson concerns the remarkable interplay between theory and data that has generally governed the responses of scientists to the phenomena described in this chapter. On the one hand, phenomena previously regarded as suspect became more acceptable when a theory was discovered that seemed to permit their existence. Thus, for example, traditional psychosomatic medicine, long regarded with great skepticism by many physicians, has revived (albeit in modified form) with the advent of psychoneuroimmunology. On a more personal level, T. X. Barber's resistance to the evidence for extreme hypnotic phenomena collapsed once he came to believe—mistakenly—that he knew how to explain them in biological terms.

This is a two-edged sword, however. Phenomena once regarded as empirically established or "real," in part because they appeared potentially explainable in terms of an existing theory, may sometimes be unfairly demoted if that theory proves unsound. Something of this sort seems to have happened in the case of "maternal impressions," which were widely reported in the medical literature until physicians could no longer think of a pregnant woman and her fetus as a single organism—whereupon the reports sharply declined.

These tensions run throughout the spectrum of psychophysiological phenomena discussed in this chapter. Phenomena suggesting that mental activity in one person can produce physiological effects in another person clearly contradict the prevailing materialist conception of the mind-body system as a closed biological unit. They are thus unacceptable to, and dismissed by, most contemporary scientists, even though the evidence for them is in many cases as good as or better than the evidence for many other psychophysical phenomena which they *do* accept.

The latter phenomena are currently more acceptable precisely because most scientists presume that they are at least potentially explainable within the prevailing conceptual framework of biological materialism. This presumption, however, is demonstrably unsound. Certain extreme psychophysiological phenomena that occur on a within-person basis, such as Olga K.'s skin-writing, stigmata, and hypnotically induced blisters of specific geometric shapes, lie beyond the reach of current neurophysiological understanding, and seem likely to remain so. Yet these more extreme forms of psychophysiological influence, however unusual, are continuous with the many "lesser," or more commonly encountered, forms catalogued in this chapter. This continuity thus casts doubt back on the conventional "explanations" for these lesser forms themselves, raising the question of how correct, complete, or adequate they in fact are. Moreover, these conventional explanations, as we have seen throughout this chapter, are in fact typically not explanations at all, but at best redescriptions of the phenomena in vague biological terms, based on equally vague assumptions of mind-brain unity.

We have, in short, not even begun to understand how an idea generates a physiological response, whether in one's own body or in another person's body. It is clear that all the phenomena of pyschophysiological influence discussed in this chapter involve, to some degree or another, an element of volition, intention, belief, expectation, strong emotion, or some other such mental state. It is equally clear that recognizing the central role of such states tells us nothing about *how* the physiological reaction is generated. I will not belabor that point further, except to emphasize that an understanding of *suggestion* is what is required now. An early student of phenomena such as faith healing defined suggestion as "the law that any idea possessing the mind tends to materialize itself in the body" (Goddard, 1899, p. 500).[70] Hypnosis has come to be accepted in large part because its phenomena can blithely be attributed to "suggestion" conceived in this way. But as many people have recognized, explanations that invoke suggestion beg the question in that "they presuppose that the nature of suggestion has been fully clarified, which is hardly true" (Weitzenhoffer, 1953, p. 232). Myers warned that words such as suggestion are "mere names which disguise our ignorance" (*HP*, vol. 1, p. 153); and his contemporary Andrew Lang (1911), also referring to suggestion, insisted that "to 'explain the explanation' is the task for the future" (p. 546).

All the phenomena of this chapter presumably have physiological correlates of some sort that we may be able to pinpoint more precisely as research continues. But, I repeat, identifying such correlates will tell us little if anything about how the physiological processes involved are initiated and guided by an idea. The currently popular assertion that mind and brain are mind-brain—a biological, material unity—is as empty an explanation as suggestion. Recognizing this, however, does not automatically entail a return to the substance dualism that engenders such fear and loathing in the hearts and minds of most contemporary scientists. Such persons should consider more seriously Myers's insight that our expanding knowledge, about both the nature of mind and the nature of matter, suggests that "our notions of mind and matter"—as well as of the relationship between them—"must pass through many a phase as yet unimagined" (Myers, 1886c, p. 179).

More specifically, after studying phenomena such as I have covered in this chapter, Myers (1891d) was confident that "Thought and Consciousness" would emerge as a fundamental aspect of the universe, and "not, as the materialists hold them, a mere *epiphenomenon*, an accidental and transitory accompaniment of more permanent energies, a light that flashes out from the furnace-door, but does none of the work" (p. 642). The unwillingness of most scientists to confront and address the real nature and scale of the problems posed by the psychophysiological phenomena outlined in this chapter reflects the general unwillingness in psychology and neuroscience to confront the problems both of psychophysical interaction and of volition, problems at the heart of the nature of consciousness.

70. This definition anticipated—and was every bit as uninformative as—the "psychophysiological principle" that researchers on biofeedback and related effects sometimes invoke: "Every change in the physiological state is accompanied by an appropriate change in the mental-emotional state, conscious or unconscious; and conversely, every change in the mental-emotional state, conscious or unconscious, is accompanied by an appropriate change in the physiological state" (see, e.g., Norris & Fahrian, 1993, p. 234).

Chapter 4

Memory

Alan Gauld[1]

> Great is the power of memory, a fearful thing, O my God, a deep and boundless manifoldness; and this thing is the mind, and this am I myself. (St. Augustine, *Confessions*, Book X, p. 213)

> Among all the facts capable of throwing light on the psychophysiological relation, those which concern memory, whether in the normal or in the pathological state, hold a privileged position. (Bergson, 1908/1991, p.13)

Human Personality contains no chapter specifically devoted to memory, and although the book is replete with examples and discussions of oddities of memory, about the actual *nature* of memory Myers says only a little. Nevertheless, the central aim and thrust of his work—to show that certain curious phenomena are best interpreted as evidence that human personality may survive bodily death—necessarily involves memory-related issues of which Myers was certainly aware, and which since his time have been the subjects of numerous and intensive investigations. I shall discuss these under two principal headings: (1) problems to do with the doctrine of "memory traces" and the relation between memory and the brain; (2) issues to do with the role of memory phenomena in discussions of the survival problem. The latter are deeply and necessarily entangled with the philosophical problem of personal identity—the problem, that is, of the conditions under which we may properly claim that a person is the same individual person as one known to have

1. I am most grateful for the help of Ed and Emily Kelly in the preparation of this chapter.

existed at some previous time. The literature in all these areas is enormous, and all I can do is try very briefly to sketch some of the leading questions. Definitive answers are not to be had—only perhaps further questions.

Memory and the Brain

Trace Theories: General Issues

We appear to ourselves, naively, to exist in a three-dimensional universe which moves forward continuously in time. Furthermore, at any given moment we experience only some tiny part of this universe as it presents itself to our senses. Hence it is altogether natural to suppose that our ability to recall particular experiences involves some sort of physical changes which those experiences produced in our brains, changes which in some way "represent" the experiences and can travel with us in time. These changes, of course, are the putative "memory traces." This fundamental intuition, rooted in everyday experience, has dominated the history of thought about memory, finding expression in whatever technical metaphors are conveniently available, from the wax tablets of Plato to the holograms, digital computers, and connectionist networks of today (Draaisma, 2000; Sutton, 1998).

Two points should immediately be made about this fundamental presupposition. First, despite its undeniable intuitive appeal it is not logically coercive, and relies covertly on deep presumptions of a metaphysical character about the mind-brain relation and the possible forms of causal connection between events (Heil, 1978; Russell, 1921a). Although taken by most contemporary scientists and philosophers as an unquestioned and indeed unquestionable axiom, it is more properly regarded as a working principle, the merit of which must be assessed in terms of its ability to yield a theory that satisfactorily accounts for the facts of human memory. Second, to the extent that such a brain-based theory of memory is forthcoming it would appear to reduce correspondingly the prospects for post-mortem survival of any particular memories, and thus to challenge Myers's program at its core. Our first order of business must therefore be to gauge as best we can the actual level of progress, and the prospects for further progress, along contemporary mainstream lines.

I will begin with some conceptual issues in traditional "trace" theories of memory.[2] Historically, most such theories have been closely linked with the view that memories (or most of them) are fainter or less vivid revivals of

2. Many of the conceptual difficulties I will be pointing out in this chapter have been discussed previously by myself and others (e.g., Bennett & Hacker, 2003, pp. 160–164; Braude, 1979, pp. 188–202, 209–212; Bursen, 1978; Gauld, 1982, pp. 189–203, 1989; Heil, 1978; Malcolm, 1977). Most of these critiques, however, have appeared in locations frequented primarily by philosophers.

past perceptual experiences. Between revivals these "memory-images" are in some sense "stored" until summoned up by a perceptual experience similar to or associated with the one of which they are a washed-out copy. A powerful impression may create an image that remains pretty much unchanged; a series of similar images may perhaps blend like a composite photograph yielding a general idea. A conventional "trace" interpretation of what is going on would be roughly as follows: Stimulation of our sense organs brings about a complex series of brain events that culminate in our perceiving the cause of the stimulation. These brain events leave behind minute but probably widespread changes in the structure and interconnections of brain cells, the effect of which is to make us liable under certain circumstances to relive the original perceptual experience, or some blend of it with others, in a partial or diminished form, often termed a "memory image." The relevant circumstances include the occurrence of a stimulus which shares some of the properties of the original one, or of a stimulus which was concurrent with the original one and caused the formation of "associative" cross-linkages between the two sets of pathways.

This way of thinking about memory is, in one or other of its slightly updated disguises, still surprisingly common, and yet it is obviously untenable for a diversity of reasons. Take first the case of what are now termed "episodic" or "autobiographical" memories, memories of oneself witnessing things or doing or participating in events or activities. Certainly one might conceivably relive one's original experience, and indeed relive it again and again, because of the changes it had brought about in one's brain. But, as William James (1890b) put it over a century ago (and he was just one of a number who made the same point in their various terminologies):[3]

> The first element which [memory] knowledge involves would seem to be the revival in the mind of an image or copy of the original event. And it is an assumption made by many writers that the revival of an image is all that is needed to constitute the memory of the original occurrence. But such a revival is obviously not a memory, whatever else it may be; it is simply a duplicate, a second event, having absolutely no connection with the first event except that it happens to resemble it....The successive editions of a feeling are so many independent events, each snug in its own skin. (vol. 1, pp. 649–650)

James's contemporary G. T. Ladd (1893) put it even more strongly:

> There is no memory-image...that does not involve the conscious recognition of that particular image, as representative of its own past, by the same mind....All that any physiological process could possibly explain, in case we knew its nature most completely, would be why I remember one thing rather

3. See, for instance, Carpenter (1874/1882, pp. 454–455).

> than another—granted the inexplicable power of the mind to remember...at all. (pp. 429–430)[4]

Myers (1891c) had written a detailed review of James's *Principles of Psychology* and would certainly have been aware of the above problems. James, however, thought he had an answer to views such as Ladd's that the revival of a past experience in accordance with trace theory could never *per se* constitute an act of remembering. His answer, in outline, is as follows (James, 1890b, vol. 1, pp. 650–659). To think of an event as past requires that one think of it not just in its naked and timeless simplicity, but in its relations to other contemporary events, dates, names, circumstances, and so forth. In short, one thinks of it along with "a lot of contiguous associates." But, he goes on, memory involves yet more; it involves placing the event in one's own past, experiencing it with that "warmth and intimacy...characterizing all experiences 'appropriated' by the thinker as his own." When this whole bundle is "known in one integral pulse of consciousness," we have remembering. The cause of remembering is activation of the complex network of brain pathways composed of the traces of the original experience and the associated traces of its "setting" as just described.

But this is still not a solution to the problem. For all these "contiguous associates" might occur as parts or fragments or aspects or shadings of a global experience the core of which is the image of some object or event that ought thereby, according to James's theory, to become a memory-image. But it would not. The whole collection might pop into one's mind unbidden at regular intervals without conveying that it was or resembled or represented an experience one had had before. James, I fear, does not sufficiently consider the difficulties confronting his solution. I have an image—call it an apparent memory—of standing on a hillside and watching a pair of golden eagles circling each other and rising higher and higher above the adjacent valley. Do the facts that I can confidently picture and name the place, the hill, the approximate date, and the person who was with me strengthen my tendency so to regard it? In some sense almost certainly; but only because I take it for granted that my images of these further matters are also true memory-images, thereby landing us in a regress.

What of the "warmth and intimacy" which James also regards as a differentia of true memories (the cognate notion of a "feeling of familiarity" has also been quite often invoked)? He thinks that this warmth and intimacy "characteriz[es] all experiences 'appropriated' by the thinker as his own" (James, 1890b, vol. 1, p. 650). What this feeling may be is quite obscure, but insofar as one can interpret it in the light of his chapter on "The Consciousness of Self" it would appear to be a consequence of a perceived similarity between a present experience or phase of the self and a past one. However,

4. It is of course perfectly possible that one should entertain without recognition an image that replicates or resembles some object or event that one experienced in the past, and that this image should be caused by neural traces left in one's brain by the past experience. One could, if one wished, extend the term "memory" to cover such episodes (see also Ayer, 1968, pp. 252–256). But this move would not dispose of the problems confronting trace theory.

this *presupposes* and hence cannot *explain* the phenomenon of memory. Perhaps one might postulate instead that a true memory image is distinguished from an imagined fiction by some intrinsic characteristic that marks its impeccably authentic origins and gives it a metaphorical warmth and intimacy. This "mark" cannot be sheer vividness, since images of hallucinatory vividness can be quite erroneous. Let us just pretend that genuine memory experiences emerge with an ineffable stamp of genuineness that somehow influences us subliminally. It cannot be that we *learn* that such images are genuine, for that would involve memory and be regressive. The only alternative is to suppose that the stamp of genuineness somehow (perhaps innately) invests the image with an irresistible authority that makes its acceptance inevitable. Will this radical approach rescue a trace theory of memory? Of course not. Whatever the stamp of genuineness may consist in, its presence, nature, and origins lie *outside* the actual image and thus introduce into remembering some *unknown* factor over and beyond the underlying trace. But the stamp of genuineness, along with feelings of warmth, intimacy or familiarity, and so forth, are surely myths, except insofar as they are metaphorical synonyms for recognition, itself a form of memory and therefore as an explanation yet again regressive.[5]

Recognizable descendants of this "trace" theory of personal, autobiographical memory have persisted, and at times flourished, more or less down to the present. And I have talked of them as though what is meant is a kind of viewing or hearing, following the reactivation of a memory trace, of an interior picture or recording (generally attenuated and vague) of the object or event originally perceived. Such experiences are still widely called "memory-images." Now if one took these metaphors literally (as many seem to) the images would emerge as entities, almost as little objects or pictures, having a similar status to the "sense-data" or "sensa" widely written about by early to mid-20th-century philosophers, and by some thought of as known by a not too clearly defined "inner perception" or "inner sense." Such ideas lead to various problems that, whether or not insoluble, are at least decidedly tricky. For instance, the images would need interpretation before they could qualify as memory-images. Whoever "looked at" them would have in effect to say to him- or herself "that is so and so or such and such, at this, that, or the other time and place, and I know because I was there and observed or experienced it." This implies at least two further kinds of memory that have to be brought to bear on the images before they can qualify as full-blooded personal or autobiographical memory-images. The first is the matter of what makes a memory "mine," a personal memory rather than an exercise of the imagination. One can, as we saw, certainly talk of such memories possessing a certain "intimacy" ("warmth," which is a sensory property, would be misleading) and be understood; but that is simply to state the problem. The

5. Using visual pattern recognition tests, in combination with fMRI scans, Slotnick and Schacter (2004) found that correct recognition, as opposed to false recognition, was accompanied by relatively heightened activity in "early" visual processing areas (occipital areas 18 and 19). However the authors conclude that these findings most probably "reflect a non-conscious or implicit form of memory retrieval." It is not altogether clear why we should call it memory "retrieval" at all.

second is the additional requirement for a kind of memory (call it "factual" memory for the moment) bringing to bear a great deal of background information without which a putative memory-image would become impossible to interpret properly, or would at best be highly ambiguous. Thus I have a fairly vivid memory of an occasion during my military service on which the far end of the barrel of my rifle blew away on my sixth or seventh shot. But an image (such as I have) of a splayed and truncated metal tube seen from behind and slightly above, and accompanied by vaguer images, visual and tactile, of the underlying wooden stock, conveys nothing like the full force and content of the memory. The experience must include, indeed be pervaded by, an implicit understanding of such facts as what rifles are, what firearms are, what cartridges are, what explosives are, what a trigger does, how dangerous the whole thing was, and so forth. Without this understanding (which involves both a grasp of relevant concepts and further factual memories) the whole experience would be attenuated into a thin shadow of full-blooded remembering.[6] How is the requirement for that further understanding to be met without either on the one hand postulating a memory that is outside the scope of the central image or on the other hand invoking an indefinite regress of further images? Can the additional factual knowledge and the concepts required possibly be accommodated within the trace and image approach to memory? It is hardly obvious or certain that they can.

There is another way, more favored by certain philosophers than by psychologists, of talking about the images involved in personal, autobiographical memory. It is to say that you remember not by summoning up or having a memory-image but by a kind of partial reliving of the original experience of which one might say "it was rather as if I were back there again," and so forth. Such a way of talking has certain advantages, apart from avoiding overt commitment to inner objects and inner sense. It circumvents, or might be deployed so as to circumvent, some of the problems raised in the previous paragraph. If there is a kind of reliving of a whole brief episode then presumably whatever interpretations, whatever background information and deployment of concepts were involved at the time, should again be available and involved. But this still leaves substantial problems. As pointed out above, reliving an episode, whether or not the reliving is identified with neural activities shaped by that episode, does not *per se* amount to remembering it. For to describe the experience one says not "it is rather as if I am looking at" this, that, and the other, where this, that, and the other just happen to be things one personally observed, was involved in, and so forth, but "it is rather as if I were back there again," which implies that I am aware of my present experience as a kind of reliving of one of my past experiences. But what this awareness can consist in (which, as pointed out above, is of course one of the central problems of personal memory) remains unilluminated. It certainly

6. One can of course have a purely factual memory of something one personally experienced—for instance I can remember the fact that I once met a certain rather distinguished lady, though, regrettably, I cannot recollect the lady or the occasion at all—but that is not what is here in question.

cannot consist in one's grasping in the moment of recollection that there is a causal relationship between the two experiences,[7] which cannot be known independently of the present putative memory-experience.

In sum, what seems to me to be the case is that the whole experience of recollecting one's past experiences is essentially pervaded by or pregnant with the feeling that these are things from the past—one's own past. We do not as yet know how to account for the past-directedness of those personal experiences that we take as our personal ("episodic" or autobiographical) memories, nor how to account for the fact that our sense of their past-directedness (which can vary in strength) may sometimes be delusory and lead to false "recollection" (see also, Cassirer, 1957, p. 179n; Dalla Barba, 1999, pp. 168–171). These issues are closely connected with the larger problem of "intentionality," which will be touched on later.

Finally some brief comments on what may conveniently be called "factual memory." In the not very satisfactory but widely accepted modern terminology, "factual" or "propositional" memory would fall into the more general category of "semantic memory," which also covers, for instance, memory for words and their meanings, and the possession of "concepts," a particularly ambiguous term. Factual memories involve recollection not of some personally experienced object or event as such, but of some fact, general or particular, for example, the fact that Gladstone lacked the forefinger of one hand, or the fact that granite is composed of quartz, mica, and feldspar. Such memories are often mediated, accompanied, or illustrated by images, but these do not have to be "of" particular or generalized past events or objects. Indeed factual memories routinely transcend any such limited set of images or actions as the reactivation or revival of brain traces reflecting one's previous experiences might be supposed capable of generating. "Transcend" here marks the point that for any given factual memory there is typically no one image or action that fully reflects the totality of what is remembered, but generally a set (impossible to delimit sharply) of possible images and actions any one of which could, in some sense hard to define, partially reflect it. For instance I am aware of the fact that the large, reddish-brown, highly poisonous, and aggressive Brazilian wandering spider (*phoneutria fera*) is reputedly the most dangerous of all spiders. So far as I can tell, my memory-knowledge of this matter can or could result in any one of a considerable variety of mental images, none fully embodying all that I remember, and also in "imageless thoughts," in inner or outer speech, and in actions so precipitate as to preclude

7. This is a central part of modern proposals about "metarepresentation" (see, e.g., Hoerl, 2001, pp. 326–328, and Perner, 2000, pp. 300–301). B. Levine et al. (1998), discussing a patient suffering from traumatic brain injury, attributed his combination of severely impaired "episodic" (personal) memory with retained or reacquired factual ("semantic") memory relating to some of the lost events, to an impaired awareness of continuity of self over time, due to right frontal damage. But such an impairment just of the "autonoetic" aspect of memory would still have left open the possibility of the "revival" (not, however, manifested by the patient in question) of particular past experiences that he nonetheless did not recognize as from his past and that could not be regarded as "memory" in the full sense or as a justifiable basis for memory-claims.

any causation by preceding images. The images, words, and actions concerned may and often will be adapted to the varied circumstances eliciting them and may take a range of forms impossible to set limits to. It is difficult indeed to see how one might accommodate these facts within any approach that tries to reduce memory to the mere revival, in mental images or any other form, of the residua of past experiences stored in the brain as neural changes. Once again, in sum, we would have to say that the underlying "memory" knowledge (whatever it may consist in) is something over, above, and behind any delimitable set of possible expressions in thought and behavior.

Modern Approaches: Cognitive

I pass now straight to the present-day scene in which the study of memory (and practically everything else in mainstream academic psychology) is carried out largely within the traditions of "cognitive psychology" and the computational theory of the mind (CTM). As described more fully in Chapter 1, the cognitive psychological movement began in the 1950s, and represented a displacement of the traditions of stimulus-response behaviorism by ideas drawn from the interlinked sources of "information theory," linguistics, and (particularly) computer science and the general theory of computation (the ensemble, together with some aspects of neuropsychology, is often referred to as "cognitive science"). Computer science seemed to open up many possibilities for the understanding of memory, not least because the vocabulary adopted by pioneering computer engineers gave prominence to "memory" and related terms. So we still find many psychologists discussing memory (often rather unreflectingly) within a broad framework according to which the brain receives "input" "encoded" by successive stages of the sensory pathways, and this input is passed into one or more forms of short-term or working memory (a "buffer") and thence (perhaps in recoded form) to an "address" within a more permanent memory store ("external memory") from which in due course it can on the receipt of appropriate cues be "retrieved" and further processed.

Within this general coding/storage/retrieval (CSR) framework, computers are regarded from a mathematico-logical point of view as discrete-state devices which manipulate language-like symbols (that is, tokens of different symbol types) and strings of symbols, in accordance with sets of formal rules ("algorithms"), and which may store (in "memory") and later be made to resurrect (or "token") such symbols and symbol-strings. This terminology has also been found appropriate by the somewhat numerous philosophers who have fallen under the spell of cognitive science, for example Fodor (Cain, 2002) and other proponents of the CTM. According to these philosophers, the mind is "computational" because its procedures, like those of computers, involve formal rule-governed operations on "symbols," and "representational" because these symbols are or may be "representations"—of what or for whom or how remains largely obscure. Particular "mental states" consist in the system standing in one or another of various possible kinds of (generally unanalyzed) computational relations (to be identified with believing, desiring, etc.) to internal symbolic tokens or "representations" of particular propositions (e.g., the proposition that dinner is ready, or the proposition that small moas still survive in the New Zealand bush), the totality being referred to as a "propositional attitude." In such terms remembering consists in the system "tokening," and adopting a relation of belief or memory-belief towards, a representation (symbol-string) internal to the system itself. Memory "traces" *per se* are rarely mentioned, but "representations" fulfil a similar role so far as episodic and semantic memory are concerned.

Over the years we have seen assorted variations on, refinements of, or selections from the original broad framework outlined above. Rather more than a simple variation has been the emerging framework of "connectionist" and "dynamic systems" models, as summarized in Chapter 1. In models of these types the results of learning may be distributed across many cells and their connections, so that the network continues to function, though with diminishing success, even as cells and connections are being progressively eliminated (the so-called "graceful degradation"). Such networks are particularly good at recognizing patterns and spatial relationships. On the other hand they are less straightforwardly effective than traditional cognitive models at the sort of symbol manipulations supposedly required to support activities such as linguistic behavior and the solution of ordinary logical problems. Nonetheless, network thinking has become dominant among the more theoretically oriented cognitive psychologists, especially those interested in building bridges to neuroscience.[8]

There has been a certain amount of argument over the question of whether or not the internal states of connectionist networks can be said to constitute inner representations of external states of affairs (connectionists themselves commonly use the representation terminology). A given network may learn multiple tasks without mutual interference, and many units and their connections may be involved in more than one of them. But in that case not merely are the "traces" distributed across the network, but it becomes difficult to identify which subset of these interconnections, or of the patterns of activation associated with them, constitutes what representation. However, I am myself inclined to set aside such arguments and accept that connectionist networks are on the same footing as conventional digital-computer models with regard to the question of whether or not their inner states may be classified as "representations." For if (and it is a big "if"; see below) some object or state of affairs may be called a "representation" of another in virtue of some (as yet unspecified) physically determinable relationship that obtains between the two of them (and certainly both classical and connectionist modelers tend to think in terms of such relationships), the fact that connectionist representations may become in some sense blended together does not affect the issue,

8. A particularly thoroughgoing attempt to cover everything from sensory processes to conscious man in society (and embracing memory) in terms of associationism and connectionism is that by Mesulam (1998, 2000).

provided that (like holograms) they can in the end be completely and successfully disentangled by the right procedures, as they have to be to produce the correct final output. Again certain connectionists (e.g., Smolensky, Legendre, & Miyata, 1994) have adapted the mathematics of tensor calculus specifically in order to abstract from the distributed activity patterns of connectionist networks an analysis in terms of symbol structures and rules mirroring those of more conventional symbol-manipulating computational systems.

After these preliminaries we can turn to the cognitive psychology of memory insofar as it has been conducted in relative independence of brain physiology. It is characterized by a vast quantity of data, a considerable number of theories or explanatory speculations of rather limited scope, and a noticeable scarcity of broader theories (Neath & Surprenant, 2003, pp. 363–394). Much of the theorizing is conducted within the broad CTM conceptual framework outlined above, and some of the theories are actually designed and implemented as computer programs. Thus we find regular use of such terms as "information," "encoding," "computation," "representation," "store," "address," "search," "retrieval," and so forth. In general this framework is taken essentially for granted by psychologists, though with some variations, the most considerable being of course found among connectionists. The philosophers mentioned above, who find the computational approach of cognitive psychologists to "mental phenomena" congenial, have been rather more critical. They fall into two groups: first, those who, like most cognitive psychologists, are prepared to accept "mentalistic" or "folk psychological" terminology, but insist that it must be redeemed in "naturalistic" terms (i.e., roughly, terms consonant with the principles of current physical science)—no easy task; and second, those (a small group favoring connectionism) who hold such redemption impossible, and aspire to "eliminate" mentalistic terms altogether from the scientific vocabulary (e.g., Churchland, 1988).

The most obvious problem with the cognitive psychologists' framework of thought is its very unsatisfactory terminology. Several of the key terms listed above have both well-understood everyday usages and technical usages assigned to them by the pioneers of computer technology. The novel technical usages should have been enclosed in scare quotes; but somehow the scare quotes, if they were ever there, were soon forgotten. This made it easy for people to slide carelessly from one usage to another and to delude themselves that they were making progress when they were not. Let us consider in this light, because of their crucial relevance to problems of memory, the terms "store," "representation," and "information" (on the pitfalls of the first two of these, see especially Bennett & Hacker, 2003, pp. 158–171, 192–193).

Let us start with "store." The metaphors of a memory "store" and of memory "storage" have a long history (Draaisma, 2000; Sutton, 1998), and there has been a good deal of hovering between literal and metaphorical interpretations. Taken literally, a memory "store" would be something like a cupboard or a filing cabinet in the mind or brain that might contain equivalents of notes, file cards, or photographs, perhaps labeled and arranged systematically. But to retrieve, look at, and recognize these would require a person or second memory system (or "homunculus"; see Chapter 1) already possessing the relevant skills and memories. The materials stored would have only the status of *aides-mémoire,* and for the analogy to shed significant light on the nature of memory, a further and fuller and non-regressive account of this second, retrieving, system, as well as of the storage system, would be needed. Such accounts are not readily discoverable (see related critiques by Bennett & Hacker, 2003, pp. 158–171; Bursen, 1978). Latterly various semi-distinct memory "stores" have been proposed by cognitive psychologists and neuroscientists—for example, a short-term store or stores, a long-term store or stores, a stored lexicon possibly subdivided into various types of categorial stores, and so forth. However, without the backing of an adequate and non-regressive explanation of how these stores could possibly perform the functions assigned to them, these proposals amount largely to recommending ways of speaking that highlight relationships between damage to certain brain systems and various kinds of memory malfunctions, or between performance of certain memory tasks and metabolic or electrical activity in certain brain regions. As I shall argue later in the chapter, these relationships themselves are for the most part far from clear, consistent, and compelling, and their proper interpretation remains uncertain.

Next consider the term "information," which has become pervasive in cognitive psychology and neuroscience. It has a good many readily comprehensible everyday uses, as when one receives information, shares information, gleans information from the newspapers or from gossip, relays information, sells information, and so on. These uses are very different from the technical mathematical one developed by communications engineers in the late 1940s (see Shannon & Weaver, 1949/1963). In the latter, "information" presupposes a "source" of encoded messages, a finite alphabet of possible messages (which may vary in probability), and a channel connecting the source to a "receiver" that decodes the messages. The "information" conveyed by receipt of a given message is measured in terms of the number of possible alternative messages that the received message eliminates. For present purposes the point is this: "Information" thus defined is, or purports to be, a "naturalistic" concept, that is, one that can be applied objectively in a variety of different contexts and without any dependence upon scientifically suspect mentalistic concepts. This concept, however, is at best only very distantly connected with "information" in the ordinary sense, which has mainly to do with the dissemination of knowledge, of true propositions about matters of fact. Weaver (in Shannon & Weaver, 1949/1963, p. 8) makes it crystal clear that information in the technical sense is not to be confused with meaningful information in the everyday sense. "In fact," he says, "two messages, one of which is heavily loaded with meaning, and the other of which is pure nonsense, can be exactly equivalent from the present viewpoint as regards information."

The concept of information began to infiltrate psychology in the 1950s during the first stirrings of what was later to become cognitive psychology. And there it has remained. But the meaning of the term has not remained constant. Neath and Surprenant (2003) remark: "Although the original concept of information as put forth in information theory (e.g., Attneave, 1959) is no longer widely accepted, the basic idea still forms the foundation for cognitive psychology" (p. 16). Unfortunately, they nowhere pause to define how they themselves are using the term; and this is characteristic of the field as a whole. Thus there is considerable scope for easing to and fro between the more technical and the very different everyday uses of the term "information." When we find (as we often do) someone talking of encoded "information" being transmitted from short-term to long-term memory or from one part of the brain to another, or of depressive individuals processing "information" differently from non-depressives, it is commonly very hard or even impossible to work out what exactly is being proposed.[9]

Closely related to the concept of "information" is that of "representation," which is central not only to problems of memory but to cognitive psychology generally. In the ordinary sense of "representation" one thing can be a representation of another, or stand for or "stand in" for another in some context of discussion or activity, only if some *person* makes, creates, or adopts it for that purpose, or decides, decrees, accepts, or agrees with others, and so on, that it is or shall be so. Pictures, words, diagrams, equations, models, model soldiers, pebbles picked up on the beach, gestures, whatever is available or adaptable, can all be turned to account as representations of other objects or states of affairs—but only by virtue of deliberate action on the part of human beings who already possess the necessary memories, desires, intentions, skills, and conceptual capacities. Mere accidental pictorial or auditory similarity does not *per se* make one thing a representation of another, though it may facilitate something's being adopted as a representation. Occasionally a credulous person may indeed take, say, markings inside a sliced pomegranate as a picture of a religious figure, or the shimmering colors of the aurora borealis as representing warring armies; but an implicit assumption underlying such ascriptions is always that there is a purpose and an intelligence at work, albeit in such instances a superhuman one. It should be noted, too, that an effect is not *per se* a representation of its cause, however closely the latter may be reflected in, or resemble, the former. The theropod's footprint is not a representation of the theropod's foot, even though it can tell us a lot about the foot and indeed about the theropod.

If we look now at questions concerning the "inner representations" postulated by cognitive psychologists and their philosophical allies as part of their program for handling not just memory-beliefs but thought processes in general, certain obvious issues arise. One can of course in an everyday sense

---

9. The concept of information has been applied in various other areas of science, from genetics to cosmology. The source of these uses is often the close relationship between the mathematical concepts of information in information theory and of thermodynamic probability in statistical thermodynamics. In thermodynamics "entropy" is a measure of chaos or the disorderliness of a system. In information theory "information" is a measure of orderliness. Hence information has been called negentropy, or the negative of entropy. In this form it has found its way into cosmology as a measure of system order, organization, or complexity. But it is not at all clear that all or any two of these concepts can be equated with each other (see also Davies, 1995, pp. 73–77) or that any can satisfactorily be used for such a purpose.

create "inner representations" for oneself, and in certain cases seem to come upon them; one can picture to oneself some absent or imaginary state of affairs, excogitate a description of it in "inner speech," recognize hypnagogic images that pass before one's mind. But these capacities are not other than those one exercises in drawing a sketch or diagram as a sketch or diagram of some putative state of affairs, or in taking rows of model soldiers as opposing armies in a battle that is about to begin. Such capacities to create "inner representations," and "outer" ones also, are not to the cognitive scientist's way of thinking to be explained in the sort of "mentalistic" terms which we commonly use to describe them. Cognitive scientists, as noted above, are after "naturalistic" accounts, ones free of unredeemed "non-naturalistic" terms such as those of "folk psychology." This ambition has so far proved a will o'the wisp, alluring and seemingly almost within grasp, but perpetually elusive. Despite this small difficulty, many, perhaps most, psychologists seem content to drift hopefully on and accept the scientific kudos derived from using "representation" as if it were a high-flying technical term, while surreptitiously and illegitimately reverting to its everyday connotations.

We have already met rather similar situations over "store" and "information." Philosophers, even those irrevocably wedded to the idea that only computer or network models can throw light on the nature and workings of the mind, have generally been more critical. In a moment I shall briefly discuss some recent attempts by philosophers to give a naturalistic account of the relation that must obtain between two things if one of them is to be regarded as a "representation" of the other. A solution to this problem would, in the context of a representationalist theory of thought, amount to or involve a solution to the so far unresolved problem of the "intentionality" of the mental, of the fact that such "propositional attitudes" as thinking, believing, desiring, intending, and so forth, can be said to be "directed upon" or "about" states of affairs outside the immediate experience of believing, desiring, and so forth.[10]

10. Thus a desire is always a desire "for" something or "that" something should come about or be the case; a thought is a thought "of" or "about" some state of affairs; a belief is always a belief "that" something is, was, or will be the case. A full description of any such mental state must always include a specification of the state of affairs upon which it is directed. But of course we can, and often do, desire, hope for, think about, imagine, dream about, fancy that we recall, and so forth, objects or states of affairs that do not exist or obtain, and never have existed or obtained and never will. For instance Ponce de Leon (we may suppose) did many of these things in respect to the Fountain of Youth. Intentionality is therefore not a relation between the cognizing subject and some external state of affairs (it has been called "relationlike"). Furthermore, beliefs, desires, and what have you can only be about or directed upon external states of affairs as these are understood or conceived by the believer or desirer. For example, I may believe that the criminal will be caught, and the criminal may in fact be Moriarty; but if I do not know that the criminal is Moriarty, my belief will not be correctly described by the statement that I believe that Moriarty will be caught. These points have often been put more formally by saying that the sentences describing mental phenomena exhibit certain logical peculiarities. Such sentences are said, for instance, to exhibit *failure of existential generalization* ("he is riding on a horse" implies the existence of a horse, whereas "he is thinking of a centaur" does not imply the existence of a centaur), and *referential opacity* ("he recollected that Scott was the author of *Waverley*," together with "Scott was the owner

Before we turn to the kinds of solutions that have been proposed, I must say a bit about the *types* of inner representations commonly invoked by contemporary cognitive psychologists. Some have centered their discussions and practical work mainly around the role of images (and images undoubtedly do play an important part in the mental lives of many people). We have already criticized as regressive the role played in traditional trace accounts of memory by internal images conceived as faded perceptions. There is, however, one further point that is worth a brief mention. Some authors have a habit of referring to images (particularly visual ones) as "analog" representations, meaning that they can change continuously when representing changes or variations in their "intentional objects" (as, for instance, the needle on a gauge changes continuously while representing steam pressure in the boiler of a locomotive). Analog representations are conventionally contrasted with "digital" ones, for instance those constituted by the states and state transitions of a discrete state automaton such as a digital computer. But some cognitive psychologists (e.g., Kosslyn, 1980, 1981, and see also his later views, 1994, e.g., pp. 4–9) have developed "digital" models for mental images, thereby blurring this distinction.[11] Somewhere between concepts of analog and of digital representations is the notion of an "inner model" (e.g., Johnson-Laird, 1983), according to which one somehow builds up "inner" or brain "models" of one's environment or parts of it. Such models do not literally *resemble* the environment, but are said to *map on to it,* systematically, so that facts about the environment can be read off from the model by an internal scanning device (vaguely identifiable with "the mind"). As explanations of memory and related phenomena, however, "inner models" seem to me every bit as regressive as simple images (see also Gauld, 1989, pp. 112–114, 126–132).

What may be called the main line of philosophical (perhaps one should say "cognitive philosophical") theorizing about "inner representations" has lain squarely within the classic "digital" or "symbol-processing" tradition, though there have been many branch lines. It also lies squarely within the "naturalizing" tradition, the tradition that tries to avoid introducing into its speculations any concepts not demonstrably compatible with those of physical science, and accordingly looks benignly upon the CTM. How does this apply to "propositional attitudes," that is, to mental states such as belief or desire (and particularly belief, because belief includes memory-beliefs), which are held to involve a distinctive attitude towards some particular proposition? Theorists of this genre commonly suppose that in believing the believer stands in a belief relation (conceived computationally, but for our purposes we need not worry about the details) to an "inner representation" regarded on the analogy of symbols or symbol-strings in a digital computer or on its screen. It is this inner representation that purportedly carries the semantic

---

of Abbotsford," do not together imply "he recollected that the owner of Abbotsford was the author of *Waverley*").

11. Fodor (2003) attempts, with his usual panache, to assimilate David Hume's impression-idea (roughly, sensation-image) epistemology to his own preferred "Representational Theory of the Mind" (at least a first cousin to the CTM).

properties of the belief-state; in other words, it carries a semantic content that may be evaluated as true or false.[12]

In the main these content-carrying representations have been identified with words or strings of words in a putative "Language of Thought" ("LOT" or "Mentalese") encoded in the brain (Cain, 2002, pp. 51–73, 116–122; Fodor, 1975, 1981b). The referents of its symbols (at any rate its basic ones), the things the symbols pick out, are not learned but are in some way given to one. This does not mean that one innately possesses full concepts of those things; for instance one might be able to pick out horses on the basis of a few characteristics without grasping that horses are mammals, ungulates, warm-blooded, and so forth. LOT precedes the acquisition of a "natural" language, such as English, the words of which acquire their reference by becoming linked to symbols in LOT. In these terms to think of a horse is first and foremost to revive ("token") the LOT symbol HORSE, and to think of a horse jumping over a gate is to "token" the corresponding string of LOT symbols in an order and manner determined by "syntactic" rules, which Fodor regards as operating on the "formal" features of the symbols. Complex LOT representations thus consist of "tokenings" of rule-governed strings of simple symbols. The LOT hypothesis has the seeming advantage of potentially accounting for one's ability to generate an indefinitely large number of inner representations, using a finite dictionary of simple symbols and a finite set of syntactic rules. But it also encounters a good many difficulties, most of which I shall have to pass over (see Cain, 2002, pp. 51–61, 116–124, 210–211).

With this background, we can return to our central problem. What is it that makes an inner representation "of" or "about" that of which it is a representation? The problem has often been approached through the concept of information (e.g., Dretske, 1988; Jacob, 1997; Rowlands, 1999), or rather through *a* concept of "information," since the concept concerned is rather looser than the technical one discussed above. It goes along these lines: Consider two physical systems, one of which we will call *s* for "source" and the other *r* for "receiver." A lawful relation exists between them such that whenever source *s* is in state F, receiver *r* passes into state G. Then we might say that the fact that receiver *r* is in state G "carries the information" that source *s* is in state F because it is nomologically necessary (empirically always the case) that when receiver *r* is in state G, source *s* is in state F. (Of course there might actually be another state F2 of *s* such that *r* goes into G, but I will ignore this complication).

An often-used example, germane for our purposes because like memory it relates to past events, would be the width of tree rings. We might say that the growth ring *(*receiver *r)* for such and such a year is broad (is in state G), and

12. I have decided not to go into the issue of externalism versus internalism, which some would think relevant in the present context and on which there is a large literature. Roughly speaking, internalism is the view that a mental state, for example, a memory-belief, can be characterized (e.g., as the belief that so-and-so) solely in terms of factors internal to the believer, (i.e., its "narrow content"); externalism holds that reference to factors external to the believer ("broad content") may be required. For brief introductions to the issues see Segal (2000, chap. 5) and Cain (2002, chap. 6).

this carries the information that the corresponding summer *(*source *s)* was sunny (in state F) since it is nomologically necessary that if the ring is wide the summer was sunny. A next move, tempting to some, has been to say, let us call receiver *r*'s being in state G (a state which carries the "information" that source *s* is in state F) a "representation" of source *s*'s being in state F. This purportedly gives us a "naturalistic" concept of representation. It would be a very different concept from the everyday one touched on above, but that is not a problem; we have to find a different concept anyway, because the usual one is only intelligible when applied to human beings who already possess diverse intellectual capacities including memory, which is precisely what we are aiming to explain naturalistically in terms of "representations."

Nonetheless this approach will not do. As I said above, effects are not plausibly construed as "representations" of their causes. For the fact that receiver *r* is in state G is no more than a sign or clue or indication that source *s* is in state F, just as a sprinkling of cigar ash on the ground (receiver *r* is in state G) is a clue that the villain stood there smoking for five minutes (source *s* is in state F). The ash on the ground is not a symbol or a representation; it is just a sprinkling of ash. In particular we cannot evaluate the ash as true or false; but this is fatal, because however much we may change our concept of representation it must remain the case that the representational aspect of the propositional attitude of belief, memory-belief, or otherwise, is that aspect of the whole which makes it possible to evaluate the belief as true or false. In the case of the ash all that can be evaluated as true or false is the inference which Holmes draws from studying it.

To solve the problem of inner representations in conventional physicalist terms, we are thus still left with three tasks. We must devise a theory of inner representations (whether informational or not) that does not *presuppose* the intervention of an intelligent, concept-, and memory-possessing human agent. We must work out how to smuggle this proposal into our overall account of brain functioning. And we must so arrange things that a representation is not merely located in the brain but available to be "tokened" (brought up on some inner screen?) and put to use (in computations on that screen?). This last would appear to involve a shift from a third-person or observer's to a first-person "take" on representations, another interesting requirement. Alas, neither I nor anyone else, so far as I know or can judge, can find any way whatever of accomplishing these tasks, or at least any way that amounts to more than a mere neuroscientific fairy tale.

It is easy to see why the LOT approach, which has so often hidden its magic wand behind the impressive logical requirements of the inviolable CTM, has had such appeal. It solves these three problems (if "solves" is the right word) at a stroke: The symbols of LOT are basically unlearned and carry "information" conceived naturalistically. They are presumed to be in the brain. And they can be "tokened." Q. E. D. But let us probe the LOT hypothesis a little further. According to this hypothesis, to think of a horse, to activate an inner representation of a horse, requires one to "token" the LOT symbol HORSE. But what does this involve? Does one hear a little inner voice whisper HORSE (or let us say 'ιππος to give it a slight but appropriate air of strangeness) whenever one encounters a horse? Of course not; and in any case this would be of no help when it came to understanding memory, because one would still have to learn the association between 'ιππος and horses. Or, more plausibly, does the tokening of the LOT symbol simply result in a wordless intimation which might be expressed as "Ah! One of those!" Then the child, born with or very quickly developing the neural embodiments of LOT symbols, might be supposed as it encountered each new object to have the intimations "One of $those_1$, one of $those_2$, one of $those_3$," and so on.

But whatever help this form of the LOT hypothesis might give us in dealing with certain of the propositional attitudes, it will not be easy to apply to memory, that is, to memory-beliefs. For in the scheme of things we are considering, the truth or otherwise of a belief is determined by the truth evaluation of the inner representation on which the belief is directed. If (to take the simplest possible example) my belief is directed on the representation (LOT symbol) HORSE and a horse is there, the belief is true. But what if my belief is that I have seen a horse before, that is, it is a memory-belief? Then what is believed is in effect not "horse" but "horse again." But what is the force of this "again"? How might it be unpacked into symbols? The content of the belief would have to be something like: "This is a horse, I have seen one before, and what's more I can remember seeing one before." All the separate statements that are here conjoined would appear to be necessary to capture the full implications of "horse again."

However, this is more complex than would at first sight appear. For the second and third parts of this conjunction are statements about myself and my history as a continuous sentient being. It is far from obvious how or whether the elements in these statements could be supposed to be represented by special symbols of our built-in LOT. And more than that, a symbol representing remembering has to be present or implicit in the overall compound inner representation. In effect to remember something is, in part, to believe that one remembers it. But this involves one's having a propositional attitude of belief directed on a LOT sentence that includes a representation of a propositional attitude of belief directed on a LOT sentence that...and so on. But it is memory that we were hoping to analyze in terms of such inner representations and propositional attitudes directed upon them. It does not seem plausible to maintain that under these circumstances an illuminating and non-regressive account of memory can be derived from a framework of thought which regards memory as an attitude of belief directed on information-carrying inner representations consisting of symbols of a "Language of Thought."

Here, as throughout, I have had to skim very quickly over the surface of some very difficult and extensively discussed problems. The approaches to inner representations I have so far been mainly concerned with are commonly, though hardly luminously, classed under the heading of "informational semantics." They have been subjected to several additional lines of objection that I have not attempted to summarize.[13] But there are other approaches to the naturalization of meaning.[14] For example, there are approaches, not on the whole spelled out in detail, involving what has been variously called "inferential role," "causal role," or "conceptual role semantics" (Block, 1986, 1995; Cain, 2002, pp. 124–134; J. Fodor & Lepore, 1992, chap. 6). Their unifying idea is that the semantic properties of inner representations are at least in part determined by the inferential, causal, or conceptual relationships these representations bear to each other. And there is a tendency to suppose, or hope, that inferential and conceptual relationships may be reducible to causal ones, thus bringing the whole scheme into line with a "functionalist" philosophy of mind (see Chapter 1).

Certainly the question of what makes a representation a representation "of" that which it represents can hardly be considered independently of questions about the relations of one representation to other representations and of the whole complex to the things represented. To take a simple example: One might have an "inner representation" of a "hammer" as a moderate-sized T-shaped hard object, and on this basis one would do quite well at calling hammers "hammers." But this would fall seriously short of capturing the full meaning of the term. Such a T-shaped object might be a mere decoration or a religious symbol. It is essential to thinking about, wanting, having beliefs concerning or memories of, a hammer, that one knows a hammer to be a tool used in the building and related trades, and one cannot (according to the representational theory of thinking) know this except through the mediation of further representations. The question therefore arises of how these different representations interact to produce the desired result. But it would be very difficult to suppose with causal role theorists that the relations between the constitutive representations are at root *causal*. Part of the meaning of "hammer," of what would have to be embraced by an adequate inner representation, is a tool used in the building trade; and part of the meaning of "building trade" is the sort of trade in which hammers are used. And so on. Without this mutual relationship the scope of each representation would become vaguer and for most purposes less effective. What we possess here and elsewhere seems to be a whole intrinsically interrelated system of representations which cannot be picked apart without attenuating the content of each individual representation. Such relationships appear to be conceptual as opposed to causal. And yet to label them as "inferential" or "conceptual" carries its own difficulties. Consider a geological hammer. Someone who had never seen or heard of such an implement yet knew a little about hammers and about geology could nonetheless work out some of its likely features, for example, that it would be likely to have a wedge or chisel aspect for splitting rocks as well as a flat side for breaking them, and represent it accordingly. This would not be a matter of selecting aspects of a hammer-representation and aspects of a geology-representation and combining them, nor yet of each representation occasioning causal changes in the other, but of his creatively exercising what might be

13. On these standard difficulties, see, for example, Jacob (1997) and Rowlands (1999).

14. For a general account of these, see Fodor and Lepore (1992) and Loewer (1999).

called practical intelligence, in ways hardly reducible to the formal inferences of logic, about the likely purposes and requirements of geologists in relation to hammers.

There are also "teleological" theories (Millikan, 1984; Papineau, 1993) that emphasize the biological and particularly the evolutionary utility of information-carrying inner representations. Several proponents of the informational approach (e.g., Jacob, 1997; Rowlands, 1999) have attempted to mend lacunae in their positions by incorporating ideas from the teleological approaches. So has Dretske (1988), the principal pioneer of the informational approach. Dretske has further gone on to propose that to create a true inner representation, the fact of the informational relation between the (human or at least animate) receiver (call him or her *r*) being in internal state G_i and the source *s* being in state F must be learned by receiver *r*, leading to neural changes in *r* that bring about behavior appropriate to source *s*'s being in state F whenever receiver *r* is in state G_i. In effect G_i assumes charge of the behavior.

But *all* proposals of this kind encounter profound difficulties of the following sort: A certain smell reaching my nostrils in the morning air (receiver *r* moves into state G) may be a sign that sausages and bacon are being cooked in the kitchen (source *s* is in state F). Lo and behold, after a few repetitions I start turning up in the kitchen soon after the smell reaches me. But this could have come about in various ways. The rewarding effect of stumbling across food in the kitchen (source *s* is in state F) soon after the olfactory stimulation began (receiver *r* is in state G) could have strengthened the neural connections between my olfactory lobes and my leg muscles in such a way that the chemical stimulation of my nose now brings me downstairs like an automaton. But in that case I would no more have an inner representation of the connection between smell and breakfast than a slug drawn irresistibly towards spilt beer would have an inner representation of the connection between the smell of beer and beer. Suppose, on the other hand, that what I acquired was not an automatic response to the smell as a regular precursor (a "sign") of breakfast, but instead knowledge *that* the smell is a *sign* of breakfast. In that case my new memory-knowledge (my supposedly newly formed inner representation of the smell-breakfast relationship) could in principle find expression in all sorts of different ways, some entirely contrary to the automatic stimulus-response sequence described above. There is no sense in which my inner state G_i would have charge of this behavior: I would be in charge of it. For example, I might think "sausage and bacon will contravene my diet" and go for a walk instead. So now all that Dretske needs to complete his theory is to tell us (1) what the neural changes are that constitute the representation, (2) what makes them a "representation" of the smell-breakfast regularity, and (3) how the representation in question is accessed and utilized, and not only that but variably and intelligently utilized. In other words the whole problem remains to be solved.

In sum, exiguous though these accounts have necessarily been, I hope to have shown that both traditional "trace" theories of memory and their modern "inner representation" counterparts are faced with very considerable *conceptual* difficulties, difficulties which have for the most part gone unrecognized or ignored, particularly by psychologists. I am not going to claim that these difficulties are in principle insuperable—though I personally cannot see any way round them[15]—but I do claim that they cannot and should not be ignored.

Modern Approaches: Neuroscientific

The period during which Myers was writing his *Human Personality* was one of significant advance in knowledge of brain function (Hécaen & Lanteri-Laura, 1977, pp. 127–200), and he was well aware of these advances. The relevant discoveries came principally from study of the effects of brain lesions, but also, to a limited extent, from animal experimentation. The major sensory and motor regions had been located, and it was known that certain cortical areas were linked to aspects of linguistic and conceptual capacity (see, e.g., Ladd, 1893; Ladd & Woodworth, 1915; Markowitsch, 1992). But of the physical basis of "episodic" and much of "semantic" memory almost nothing was known. It was widely assumed that memory "traces," though they were never found, must be located in what before long came to be called "silent" or "association" areas, that is to say, areas of cortex ("polymodal areas"), outside the known sensory, motor, and language-related regions, on which "association fibers" from one or more sensory areas were presumed to converge and create intra- or inter-modality "associations," and perhaps also links to output pathways. This assumption could be supported by citing the loss of memory and intellect accompanying various forms of senile and other cortical degeneration,[16] while the hypothetical "memory traces" could now be conceived on the newer analogies of photographic plates, grooves in wax phonograph cylinders, or circuitry in telephone switchboards (Draaisma, 2000; Sutton, 1998).

For some decades what is now called neuropsychology continued to revolve mainly around brain lesions and brain anatomy, with a leavening of

15. My own view (Gauld & Shotter, 1977, pp. 112–116) is that there is no way of deriving the intentional (e.g., the "aboutness" of a memory-belief) from the non-intentional. See also Smythe (1992): "Cognitive theorists must come to recognize that cognitive states and processes are already meaningfully constituted prior to their theoretical interpretation" (p. 359).

16. The amnesias forming a prominent part of "Korsakoff's syndrome" were well known by 1900, but only much later was it proposed that they result from atrophy of or damage to one or more parts of the "limbic" system occasioned by thiamine deficiency consequent on chronic alcoholism. The limbic system consists of a set of interlinked structures in or surrounding the upper brain stem, and including the amygdala, the hippocampus, the mammillary bodies, certain thalamic nuclei, the fornix, and various associated regions of cortex. Most frequently involved seem to be the mammillary bodies and anterior thalamus, but the variable location of the damage and its tendency to be accompanied by general cortical degeneration, together with the somewhat muddy nature of the overall syndrome, have rather hindered speculative interpretation.

psychological speculation. But even by the early 1950s only a limited number of further discoveries had been made that bore directly on questions to do with the physiological basis of memory.[17] This was to change markedly in the late 1950s as the result of a brain operation which, undertaken to alleviate severe epilepsy, turned out to have had catastrophic side-effects. The patient, known in the literature as H. M. or Henry M., underwent bilateral removal of the hippocampus (a somewhat slug-shaped structure deep inside the medial temporal lobes) and adjacent parts of temporal cortex. He thereafter exhibited a dense and intractable "anterograde amnesia" (an inability to acquire new memories), combined with a lesser "retrograde amnesia" (a difficulty in recalling events from a certain period of time preceding the operation), despite retaining more or less normal short-term memory. Further study of H. M., and of cases analogous to his, brought vividly home the fact that here at last was a kind of brain lesion of limited scope which had a profound effect on memory. Early speculation as to the critical locus centered round the hippocampus itself, which has extensive and reciprocal linkages to other brain regions. It was suggested that the function of the hippocampus was to transfer material circulating in short-term memory to a long-term memory store in which (following some period of "consolidation") it might be indefinitely retained. No hippocampus, no further admissions to long-term memory.

In the decades between then and today, there have been many developments both in neuroscience in general and in the neuropsychology of memory.[18] Theoretical standpoints have shifted appreciably, mainly because of the infiltration or partial ousting of the older, heavily anatomical approach by the newer functional concepts, not to say jargon, of cognitive psychology, which of course has itself progressively transformed into cognitive neuroscience. In its earlier days practitioners of "cognitive neuropsychology" were less interested in the localization of psychological functions in the brain than in interpreting the psychological effects of brain damage in terms of cognitive psychological models, models often set out in the box-and-arrow manner of flow charts. They were particularly interested in finding so-called "double dissociations" of function, that is, in discovering pairs of functions, conceived as part of some cognitive psychological model, either of which can be carried on successfully even when the other is impaired by some sort of brain insult. Such dissociations were (and still commonly are) thought to shed light on the validity of functional distinctions embedded in the models—which indeed they may do when the "dissociated" functions are more exhaustively tested than is commonly the case (Shallice, 1988; Uttal, 2001). Nowadays cognitive neuropsychologists are usually well versed in brain anatomy and interested

---

17. It is interesting to note the limited progress on this front between Ladd and Woodworth (1915) and Morgan and Stellar (1950), each in its day a standard textbook of physiological psychology.

18. Useful general works here are Bear, Connors, and Paradiso (2000), Carlson (2004), Eichenbaum (2002), Eichenbaum and Cohen (2001), Heilman (2002), Heilman and Valenstein (2003), Kolb and Whishaw (2003), and Parker, Wilding, and Bussey (2002).

not only in the cognitive consequences of brain injuries but in the location and character of the injuries themselves.

More significant and ultimately more important than these shifts in theoretical standpoint have been the numerous and remarkable technological advances in our ability to observe the inner workings of the brain. As described more fully in Chapter 1, we can divide these technologies roughly into two groups: "macro" technologies which operate on scales from the whole brain down to roughly naked-eye-sized parts of it, and "micro" techniques operating down to the cellular or sub-cellular level. At present the "macro" technological advances generating the greatest interest and enthusiasm are those involving "imaging" or "scanning" of the brain by techniques which reveal the level of metabolic activity (as measured for example by blood flow, glucose consumption, or oxygen uptake) in various brain regions. These techniques—especially positron emission tomography (PET) and functional magnetic resonance imaging (fMRI)—give rise to the widely reproduced (and often seriously misleading) computerized images in which "active" areas are represented in red, less active ones in orange, and so on. Another "macro" technique, electrical stimulation of the brain (ESB), has also produced many interesting results related to memory (see, e.g., Ojemann, 1983, 1990; Penfield & Rasmussen, 1952). More recently somewhat similar results have been obtained by transcranial magnetic stimulation (TMS), which does not require opening of the skull. Each of the latter techniques has been shown capable of interfering with the maintenance or expression of certain kinds of what might be called "memory" (short-term perceptual, short-term verbal, sentence construction or production). The "micro" technological advances have been deployed mainly in studies of rudimentary learning and conditioning processes in simpler organisms, in an effort to identify and characterize at the inter- or intra-cellular levels the fundamental biochemical mechanisms likely to be at work.

So what have these technological developments, macro and micro, taught us about memory? They have certainly resulted in a vast accumulation of data, but have they brought about a revolution in our understanding of memory? It is, I think, fair to say that advances in understanding have nothing like kept pace with the accumulation of data, and that the latter has served mainly to bring out the complexity of the problems that impede the former. To justify these assertions fully would require several substantial volumes of which I have no ambition to be the author. However, to illustrate the character of recent developments it will be useful to consider various to-ings and fro-ings in the neuropsychological investigation of explicit or "declarative" memory (i.e., roughly, the sort of memories—most notably "episodic" and "semantic" memories—that can be brought to conscious awareness and reported upon).[19]

19. I have had to pass by some very curious cases of loss of memory for the qualitative properties of things. In a small number of extreme examples (see for instance Kolb & Whishaw, 2003, pp. 332–333; Zeki, 1993, pp. 265–266; and cf. Riddoch & Humphreys, 1987, pp. 1450–1451), brain damage has led not just to inability to see things in color (achromatop-

I mentioned above that in the case of H. M. and various analogous cases that came to light in succeeding years the dense anterograde amnesia that resulted from bilateral damage to or resection of the hippocampal region was generally taken to show that the hippocampus itself played a vital bridging role between short-term memory and long-term memory stores. However, during several decades of experimental work with humans and animals, this simple proposal underwent significant vagaries of fortune. It was suggested, for example, that so-called hippocampal amnesia was actually due to severance of fibers of passage (the temporal stem) that pass close by the hippocampus. This idea was apparently put out of court by the discovery of severely amnesic patients in whom the hippocampi had been bilaterally destroyed without any damage to adjacent structures (e.g., Zola-Morgan, Squire, & Amaral, 1986), but more recent studies with monkeys and humans have occasioned further rethinking. In a meta-analysis of visual recognition experiments (delayed matching to sample) with monkeys, Baxter and Murray (Baxter, 2002) concluded that lesions limited to the hippocampus have a small but reliable effect, ones limited to the neighboring perirhinal cortex have a larger but still modest one, and lesions including perirhinal cortex plus at least one other component of the hippocampal complex have a larger one still (p. 111). A further, and curious, finding (pp. 111–112) was that the greater the hippocampal damage, the less the impairment of memory, whereas with rhinal cortex lesions (the rhinal cortex includes the perirhinal cortex) the reverse held true.[20] Baxter proposes that this may be because the hippocampus operates by recall of particular events ("episodic memory") whereas the rhinal cortex operates by detecting relative familiarity. These regions accordingly make different contributions to the solution of visual recognition problems, and may compete with each other. A partially functioning but still competing hippocampus may thus produce more deleterious effects than no hippocampus at all, or a mere remnant.

In the human case too there is evidence that the hippocampus subserves episodic rather than semantic memory. Vargha-Khadem et al. (1997) report on three patients who had suffered very early bilateral damage limited to the hippocampus (their hippocampi were much reduced in volume). In addition to the problems with spatial and temporal memory commonly associated with hippocampal lesions, these patients suffered from severe antero-

---

sia) or to name the colors of things (color anomia) but to inability to recollect what it is like to experience color.

20. See also Irle and Markowitsch (1990) and criticisms by Zola-Morgan and Squire (1993). Findings in healthy humans of a negative correlation between hippocampal volume and memory performance, and also between grey matter volume and memory performance, have been surprisingly frequent (see, e.g., Van Petten et al., 2004). How far this has to do with the need for the thinning out of nerve cells and connections during early development is still a matter of discussion. The most startling examples of discrepancy between tissue volume and mental ability are certain cases of hydrocephalus described by Lorber (1983) and Lonton (1979), and see also R. Lewin (1980). Some of these individuals were able to function at a normal to high level with both cerebral hemispheres reduced to as little as five percent of the normal volume.

grade amnesia for episodic memory tasks; but semantic learning and memory were well preserved. A case of the opposite tendency is described by Kapur et al. (1994). This patient's hippocampus and surrounding structures were intact, but other medial temporal lobe structures had gone. Episodic memory was preserved, but there were moderate impairments of semantic memory. Steinvarth, Levine, and Corkin (2005) conclude from experiments with two severely amnesic but contrasting patients (H. M. and W. R.), combined with a review of other cases, that although established semantic memories may after awhile shake free of dependence on medial temporal lobe structures, episodic memories (defined, however, as bound to delimitable spatio-temporal contexts, so that genuine autobiographical episodes recollected out of context would not count) in general do not.

Various other cases seem likewise to indicate at least a partial "double dissociation" between episodic or autobiographical memory and semantic memory. For instance, Kitchener, Hodges, and McCarthy (1998) report a patient with severely impaired episodic memory, both anterograde and retrograde, but largely preserved semantic memory. A stroke had occasioned damage to the right hippocampus and severe general damage to the left medial temporal lobe. J. R. Hodges, Patterson, Oxbury, and Funnell (1992) and Murre, Graham, and Hodges (2001) describe cases of progressive "semantic dementia" with lateral temporal cortical degeneration in which the patients suffered from considerable impairment of semantic memory but had some degree of spared episodic memory. Similarly, De Renzi, Liotti, and Nichelli (1987) describe a patient with impaired semantic memory but preserved autobiographical memory in conjunction with damage to the anteromedial portion of the left temporal lobe caused by acute encephalitis. Temple and Richardson (2004) describe a case of seemingly idiopathic developmental amnesia in a 9-year-old girl with impaired semantic memory but preserved episodic. Maguire and Frith (2003) found that in a comparison of older with younger subjects, neither suffering from morphological changes in the medial temporal lobes, brain activation during episodic-autobiographical but not semantic memory tasks had switched substantially with age from the left hippocampus to the right.

With regard to the prevailing "double dissociation" interpretation of such cases, however, one can only recommend great caution. It is easy enough to suppose that semantic memory could persist in the absence of episodic memory, but vice versa is a different matter. Suppose one remembers, as I do, blowing away the end of one's army service rifle while firing rapidly. As I remarked above, one could not remember this episode in its fullness unless implicit, so to speak, in one's act of remembering were a grasp of various further remembered facts, as well as of the conceptual background against which it occurred. Without such "semantic" memory, one's recollection of the event in question would be so to speak pale and attenuated. One can perhaps imagine being able to recall *something* about an exciting episode with an elongated object of wood and metal, without having any real ("semantic") memory of what a rifle is and what it can accomplish and how it is used and of the circumstances in which it might be used or of what it was that really happened. But would that constitute a full episodic memory of the event in question? In other words, as semantic memory weakens, episodic memory inevitably must lose substance. Furthermore, such a weakening would by no means always be revealed by conventional "tests" of episodic memory such as recollection of recent events or of recently presented word lists, or discrimination of words that were versus words that were not on such lists (see also, Dalla Barba, 1999, pp. 188–189; Horner, 1990; and Ladd, 1893, p. 216, for a similar point in connection with aphasia). Conversely, it is not at all clear in cases such as that of De Renzi et al. (1987), mentioned above, that elements of semantic memory specifically relevant to the supposedly preserved autobiographical memories (e.g., of the patient's wedding) were in fact impaired; indeed, if those memories *were* fully preserved (and it would be very difficult to tell, without far more careful and direct probing than is customary), the clear implication would be that more of semantic memory was preserved than was accessible to the routine neuropsychological assessment procedures these investigators employed. The situation is not helped by the loose definitions of "semantic" and "episodic" that are in practice employed, which leave both terms liable to net an assortment of heterogeneous fish.

To summarize so far: In the first flush of excitement that followed the early studies of the case of H. M., the role of the hippocampus itself in memory (as distinct from the role of the hippocampus together with other medial temporal lobe and associated structures) was rather exaggerated and simplified, though clearly it does normally have some important role. Proposals that it might be especially involved in episodic as distinct from semantic memory suffer *inter alia* from empirical and conceptual difficulties in clearly separating the two, but are by no means to be entirely rejected. It is becoming increasingly likely, however, that there are multiple forms of amnesia in which multiple brain regions can be to a greater or lesser extent involved, and that the original hope that amnesic syndromes may be neatly classified along two or three dimensions each associated with particular brain systems is likely to be at best rather incompletely fulfilled.[21]

The emergence of the new functional neuroimaging techniques in the 1980s (PET) and early 1990s (fMRI) to an extent deflected the focus of memory studies away from the hippocampus and medial temporal lobes towards prefrontal areas. For it transpired, to everyone's surprise, that although marked prefrontal activations turned up regularly in investigations of episodic and semantic memory, hippocampal and medial temporal lobe activations, though not unknown, were less consistently observed. By 1994, Tulving

21. This was forcefully argued by Markowitsch (1984), and has been confirmed since. For example, after a lengthy and most interesting review of 20 years of work with K. C., a multiply brain-damaged and severely amnesic patient, Rosenbaum et al. (2005) conclude that implicit memory may be preserved when explicit memory has vanished, that "it is not necessarily the case that episodic and semantic memory follow the same trajectory of impairment and preservation," that there may be different types of spatial memory, and that "different types of inferences may be made on the basis of cases in which lesions are highly restricted and those like K. C. with more extensive damage" (pp. 1015, 1016).

felt able to put forward the HERA (hemispheric encoding/retrieval asymmetry) hypothesis, largely on the basis of imaging data (Tulving, Kapur, Craik, Moscovitch, & Houle, 1994). This hypothesis stated that left prefrontal regions are particularly involved in the "encoding" of episodic memories, and right ones in their retrieval (the hypothesis is just about encoding and retrieval, not about storage). It was also found that semantic retrieval activated regions overlapping with the left prefrontal episodic encoding regions, while working memory activated regions overlapping with the right prefrontal episodic retrieval regions. There were also certain recurrent links with more posterior activations, for example of episodic encoding with medial temporal activations, particularly of the parahippocampal gyrus, and of episodic retrieval with activation of the parahippocampal gyrus and of medial parietal cortex.

For some years the HERA hypothesis enjoyed considerable popularity, with a good bit of evidence apparently supporting it, but it too has largely dissolved, perhaps in part because of continuing technical and statistical developments in the field of brain imaging. For instance, a large-scale survey of brain imaging studies by Cabeza and Nyberg (2000) showed that although 23 out of 52 studies of episodic retrieval found the predicted peak activations in right frontal and prefrontal regions, additional peaks were also often found, scattered across left frontal and prefrontal cortex and also in both left and right parietal areas. M. R. Miller et al. (2002), with nine subjects carrying out an episodic retrieval task (verbal recognition), found highly significant activations of both left and right frontal and prefrontal regions, as well as the anterior cingulate gyrus and left and right lower parietal areas. There were also marked individual differences between the subjects. Six of the subjects returned for a follow-up session six months later using a similar verbal recognition task. The individual subjects exhibited fairly constant patterns of activation across the two sessions, but variations between the activation patterns of different subjects remained appreciable.[22] The authors attribute this state of affairs to there being "various conscious strategies underlying the performance of this task, rather than a common memory mechanism" (p. 1211); but this hypothesis, while not implausible, does not help a lot in the absence of an inventory of the alternative strategies that might be brought to bear even on this very simple task.

Others (e.g., Ranganath & Knight, 2002) have similarly proposed that prefrontal activity during episodic memory tasks is not due to the operations of specific encoding and retrieval mechanisms but rather to strategic, goal-directed, and evaluative processes that assist or modulate the functioning of memory mechanisms operating elsewhere. Somewhat similar explanations have occasionally been offered for the effects of brain lesions which apparently interfere with memory processes. In fact, one can draw a number of parallels between difficulties of interpretation that were widely (although slowly) acknowledged in relation to the behavioral and mental changes following brain lesions (whether experimental, accidental, or pathophysiologi-

22. Uttal (2001) and especially Harpaz (2006) make very strong claims about the pervasive lack of inter-experiment, inter-subject, or even intra-subject consistency in imaging studies.

cal) and the difficulties, increasingly recognized by professionals in the field, of interpreting the significance of brain imaging studies for the understanding of brain function (Uttal, 2001). For instance, both approaches have demonstrated that very often a given brain area may be involved in more than one function, both in the same and in different individuals. Sharply localized "dedicated" areas are rather the exception outside the motor and sensory regions of the cortex, a finding which has enhanced the popularity of connectionist ideas. Both approaches also have to cope with problems raised by the fact that the loci under investigation may have or have had inhibitory or modulatory rather than excitatory functions. And both have been accused of obliterating or minimizing the significance of individual differences by using restricted subject pools or by crudely averaging data across subjects.

Conceptual and methodological difficulties in imaging studies afflict cognitive neuroscience generally, and are discussed in greater detail in our Chapter 9, but the latter accusation in particular requires some further comment here. Individual differences in the ostensible localization of memory functions in the brain tend on balance to become more marked as one moves from the perceptual end of the scale to the verbal and conceptual. We have already noted the results of M. R. Miller et al. (2002) on verbal recognition memory. The "localization" of language functions in different left-hemisphere sites not infrequently departs grossly from standard expectations even in right-handed adults,[23] and language may be right-hemisphere based in perhaps one person in 20.

Early but persistent methods of assessing the results of PET and fMRI scans led to some breathtaking oversimplifications, particularly as the findings filtered through to the popular or popular scientific press. Especially pernicious in this regard is the so-called "subtraction" technique. In this, levels of metabolic activity observed in the brain during the performance of some task are displayed after first subtracting out the levels of brain activity during a "control" period, usually defined as "rest" or as performance of a task presumed to be identical to the experimental task except in lacking some hypothetical additional cognitive factor. The results are presented (either for individual brains or as an average across a group of brains) by coloring the most active regions in red, less active ones in orange, and so forth. This procedure was at first naively thought capable of identifying areas specifically responsible for the targeted cognitive component. However, a good part of the whole brain will have been active during the performance of *both* tasks, and the fact that some areas are zeroed out by the subtraction does not imply that these make no contribution, or the same contribution, in the situations being compared. Furthermore, the display of "significant" differences depends heavily on the filtering and thresholding employed, often trades on very small absolute differences in the actual levels of activity, and may even involve only areas of activation shared across subjects. The net result of such procedures is sometimes to leave only a tiny illuminated region, which, in extreme cases,

23. See, for example, Caplan (1987, pp. 345–402), Kertesz (1979), Ojemann (1990, pp. 303–304), Ojemann and Whitaker (1978), and Pulvermüller (1999).

may be christened by such ridiculous titles as "the God spot" or "the seat of intelligence" (see the criticisms by Sarter, Berntson, & Cacioppo, 1996).

These kinds of procedures are now widely regarded with caution, and more sophisticated ones are being adopted or are under development, but other substantial difficulties in the interpretation of PET and fMRI findings remain. For instance these findings reflect degrees of blood flow and oxygen uptake in different brain regions; but how are the latter in turn related to "information processing" in those areas? Metabolic activity within any region is more likely to be determined by the inputs to that region than by its outputs, that is, by the results of information processing (Logothetis, 2002), and in fact inputs are not infrequently inhibitory with respect to outputs. Indeed there is no obvious reason why degree of metabolic excitement in the brain should always be in synchrony with the functional importance of the task being undertaken. Again in work with brain imaging there is always a trade-off between achieving sharp definition and achieving a rapid response to changes in mental activity.

No one, I think, would deny that there are problems—conceptual, empirical, and interpretive—with imaging studies. Where differences of opinion arise is over how or whether these problems can ultimately be resolved. Some (e.g., Uttal, 2001) argue that the problems are irresolvable, that there is a certain endemic elusiveness about the relations between brain functions and psychological ones. Others, probably ranking most neuroscientists among their numbers, are more optimistic and anticipate steady progress driven by advances in imaging hardware and image-analysis techniques, perhaps combined with fractionation of brain functions and the assigning of sub-functions to different anatomical loci. One can only await developments; but I personally am unconvinced that technological developments will not multiply rather than diminish the opacities with which we are currently confronted.

Meanwhile, what are we to say of the supposed memory stores in regions of anterior and posterior "association" cortex, to which episodic memory traces are supposedly consigned, within which they are supposedly consolidated, and from which episodic and semantic memories are allegedly retrieved? There is no doubt that diffuse degeneration or metabolic impoverishment of those regions (as for example in Alzheimer's disease) may occasion or be accompanied by severe and generalized memory problems including retrograde amnesia, but interpretation of this fact is not straightforward. Many cognitive functions and personality characteristics may be drastically disrupted by the disease, which is associated with (and some say caused by) gross malfunctioning of neurotransmitter systems (especially but not exclusively cholinergic ones) centering on subcortical structures.

Things look at first sight a bit more clear-cut, perhaps, in relation to semantic memory. Specifically, there are some fairly well-established findings that have been interpreted as demonstrating the existence of semantic memory "stores" of restricted scope and limited anatomical area. Damage to certain brain areas, especially ones abutting on posterior speech areas of the left hemisphere, has long been known to produce "anomia" or "anomic aphasia." Patients have difficulty, relatively unaccompanied by other problems, in finding the right words to express what they wish to say. This disorder was initially attributed by some to interference with a "lexicon" or "word store" somewhere in the vicinity of the angular gyrus. It was also found that the difficulty could be specific to particular categories of words, for instance the names of animals or of plants or of inanimate objects or of tools, suggesting a subdivided lexicon. And it gradually became apparent that often the problems were not just in word-finding, but were more of the nature of category-specific amnesias, in which patients might suffer from difficulty in recognizing or remembering objects from certain categories, and in exhibiting a conceptual grasp of their natures. Categories particularly liable to be affected included, for example, animals, plants, artifacts, and tools or other non-living things (according to some, the biological importance of objects of these categories has led to the evolution of dedicated neural circuitry). Latterly, PET and fMRI studies with normal subjects have come up with moderately confirmatory findings as to the brain regions involved in the functions concerned (see reviews by Perani, 1999, and by the various contributors to Forde & Humphreys, 2002, and A. Martin & Caramazza, 2003). These regions overlapped a good deal but sometimes showed distinguishably different areas of peak activation, particularly in left infero-temporal, lateral temporal, occipito-temporal, and posterior parietal cortex, and (when tools are involved) ventral pre-motor cortex.

In a way these findings concerning "category-specific" areas encapsulate and bring to a head certain of the theoretical and conceptual problems about memory already raised (I pass by the purely empirical issue that there are, as always, considerable differences between the findings of different studies). For example, if we talk (as does Perani, 1999) of these findings revealing "anatomically segregated representations of semantic knowledge" (p. 69), we fall foul of the twin points: (1) that representations require interpreters who are already knowledgeable enough to comprehend them; and (2) that to understand membership of a category (say the category of animals) one must possess, or at least have a toehold in, a whole network of further concepts, with pervasive links among themselves and to other concepts, for example live versus inanimate, sensate versus insensate, reproductive versus non-reproductive, self-repairing versus inert, ingesting nutrition versus not doing so, and so on. Where are the "anatomically segregated representations" of these further areas of semantic "knowledge" to be found?

It will also prove instructive at this point to situate these issues in a larger historical context.[24] In a book now widely but undeservedly neglected, Bergson (1908/1991) had argued for a view in which consciousness "overflows the organism." Much more goes on in the mind, he thought, than can be expressed in the activity of the brain. The brain Bergson regarded as the "point of insertion of the mind in matter," an "organ of attention to life," which primarily limits and focuses mental activity in service of appropriate adjustments of the organism to its environment.

24. For the ensuing paragraphs on Bergson and Damasio, I am indebted to Ed Kelly.

Now these metaphors, while picturesque, are surely very obscure, and I do not wish to defend or endorse Bergson's general philosophical position. However, there is one specific point at which it connects directly with the issues presently before us. His book advances a variety of theoretical and empirical arguments in support of the view that "true" memory cannot be accounted for in terms of "engrams" (traces) inscribed upon the brain.[25] Among his empirical arguments the one he himself clearly thought most decisive concerned memory for words and their meanings. He was fully aware of the emerging neuropsychological story about the language system and its relationship to the clinical phenomena of aphasia. Anomia seemed to him to provide a crucial "test case," one in which he could demonstrate a fatal flaw in trace theories of memory. For most of his contemporaries the loss of specific letters, words, or groups of words following a stroke seemed to provide the first really compelling evidence for localization of specific memories at specific points in the brain. But closer study of the evidence, Bergson argued, reveals that this interpretation is incorrect. For example, a patient may recover a seemingly "lost" word if he becomes sufficiently excited, and although he cannot produce the name of some pictured object on demand, as in a typical testing context, he may produce it spontaneously in some other context, or even in the course of his circumlocutions about the pictured object itself. Thus, what appears to be damaged is not the memory *per se* but the mechanism of its retrieval. The engram theory, Bergson concluded, is false.

From our present vantage point we can see that Bergson was basically correct about the facts; specific types of knowledge or psychological function may be significantly degraded by localized lesions, but they are rarely completely abolished. His conclusion that this falsifies trace theory, however, was certainly premature and unwarranted, because the argument depends upon the incorrect premise that a materialist account of memory *must* be framed in terms of sharply localized traces, analogous to the inscription of snatches of music in the grooves of a phonographic record. As we have seen, however, virtually all contemporary neuroscientific and connectionist thinking presumes that traces are anatomically widely distributed.

But the story does not end there. Bergson's account of how "true" remembering actually works, though again basically metaphorical, comes remarkably close to the picture sketched above as emerging from the latest neuropsychological and functional neuroimaging studies. On Bergson's view the overall pattern of brain activity associated with some particular act of conscious remembering constitutes a sort of "frame," into which the memory-knowledge somehow "inserts" itself. In retrieving semantic knowledge, say of a hammer, this "frame" would tend to consist of activation of whatever brain areas would be involved in my actually perceiving and using hammers. Similar expectations flow from the general connectionist point of view, according to

---

25. Bergson sharply distinguishes "true" memory, by which in modern terminology he means declarative (semantic and episodic) memory, from "habit" memory, conceived as the totality of sensorimotor skills and adjustments acquired by the organism over the history of its interactions with the environment.

which the "cell assembly" or assemblies that supposedly contain or represent my knowledge of hammers have been shaped by the environmental regularities I have encountered in the course of my previous perceptual and motor dealings with them.

This same basic idea is also central to the influential "convergence zone framework" put forward in a long series of papers and books by the Damasios, primarily but not exclusively on the basis of neuropsychological evidence (e.g., Damasio, 1989; Damasio & Damasio, 1994, 2000). In brief, the Damasios acknowledge that the older models of language and the brain (which of course have long been heralded as a major neuropsychological success story, and are still widely reproduced in textbooks) are in fact mere "cartoons," caricatures of a much more complex reality. Although there is, especially in the left hemisphere, certainly some degree of specialization of frontal areas for speech and of posterior areas near the junction of the temporal, occipital, and parietal lobes for understanding and recognition, the territories involved are larger and more variable between persons than previously realized. This fits with the larger picture the Damasios are attempting to capture. They argue that neither conceptual/semantic knowledge nor autobiographical memories are stored "whole" at particular locations in the brain. Rather, elements of that knowledge and experience are stored in regions appropriate to them individually—for example, visual elements in the visual areas, action-related elements in the motor areas, and so on. Conscious remembering occurs in conjunction with a process of reassembly, in which the needed elements are bound together at progressively higher levels of integration (the convergence zones), these being reciprocally linked with both "upstream" and "downstream" cortical regions. This reciprocal connectivity supports elaboration of shared patterns of electrical activity, widely distributed across the relevant cortical territories, which effect and indeed constitute the reassembly. In recent publications they explicitly identify this neuroelectric reassembly mechanism with proposed solutions of the "binding" problem in perception—that is, with gamma oscillations and the like (see Chapter 1).

I will not attempt to criticize these views in any great detail, but a few general comments are certainly in order. The Damasio "framework" is of course far more detailed than Bergson's, and in that sense capitalizes appropriately on a century of further advances in our knowledge of the brain. Certainly it is expressed in more up-to-date neurophysiological jargon. Nevertheless, its driving idea is essentially the same as Bergson's, and at bottom it is hardly less metaphorical. Perhaps this is why the Damasios repeatedly characterize their proposal as a "framework" rather than as a "theory" or "model." Although none of these terms is ever really defined, their choice of "framework" seems intended to license a rather abstract and schematic "manner of speaking" that is only loosely tied to real neurophysiology. In particular, no real account is provided of what guides the reassembly process to the correct result, say my memory of a particular hammer, or of how this result would be distinguished from my perception of the same object. Nor do they attempt to deal with the generality of conceptual and factual knowledge, and its "transcendence" of specific forms of expression as discussed earlier, or with the fundamental problem of intentionality. Indeed, applied to autobiographical memory the Damasio "framework" seems to amount to little more than a traditional image theory made over in impressive-sounding neurophysiological terminology, an account that not only inherits all the problems of its image-theory predecessors but also compounds these with an additional layer of problems related to the need for a genuine specification of the hypothesized decomposition and reassembly processes.

In sum, although the Damasio "framework" seems to represent the leading edge of systems-level thinking about memory and the brain—it is cited approvingly, for example, by authorities such as Mesulam (2000, p. 61) and Schacter (1996, p. 86–87)—it appears to me not only descriptively incomplete but conceptually incoherent. Perhaps something more along the lines of Bergson's view, in which brain activity is only part of the story, needs after all to be reconsidered. Both views lead to similar expectations in terms of correlations between forms of remembering and patterns of brain activity, and so both are more or less in accord with the same facts, as we presently know them. But the theoretical gulf between them is profound, for the Damasios, unlike Bergson, presume the validity of the conventional mainstream assumption that the observed patterns of brain activity generate, or perhaps even constitute, occasions of conscious remembering.

Several kinds of observations, however, in addition to observations directly suggesting post-mortem survival of memories (which I will discuss later in this chapter), strike me as potentially telling against the Damasios. First, like the general perceptual binding model itself, the Damasio "framework" is threatened by observations involving the occurrence of normal or even enhanced mental activity under physiological conditions in which the putative mechanisms of binding are certainly disabled (see Chapters 1 and 6 for further details). Second, there are suggestions within the massive literature relating to aphasia that mental life is sometimes relatively unimpaired, perhaps surprisingly so, by strokes or other injuries that affect sizeable portions of the dominant hemisphere. Many such patients talk, for example, about knowing exactly what they wanted to say but being unable to find the correct words. Of course most such patients say or imply that their general grasp of things was diminished or clouded in some way, at least part of the time, and in many if not most patients any documented impairments are distressingly persistent. Nevertheless, there are a few scattered case reports suggesting that very significant brain injury and aphasia may sometimes co-occur with a *relative* absence of correspondingly severe effects on "the mind." Such cases can only become known, of course, by virtue of the patient recovering fully enough to tell the story of his or her experience during the illness. While such outcomes are certainly rare, and the reliability of retrospective reports must be examined critically, some of the cases already on record come from persons of recognized ability and veracity (see, e.g., the cases of Professor Lordat and Drs. Saloz and Forel in H. Gardner, 1976, pp. 397–401; and see also G. Humphrey, 1963, pp. 249–325; Moss, 1972; Wint, 1965). Additional cases of this type, especially if supported by use of modern imaging methods to provide careful characterization of the accompanying lesions, would be of great theoretical interest.

Finally, and this is really a more general comment on the theoretical import of conventional neuropsychological studies, consider the following remark by Bertrand Russell (1921a):

> The theory of the engram, or any similar theory, has to maintain that, given a body and brain in a suitable state, a man will have a certain memory, without the need of any further conditions. What is known, however, is only that he will not have memories if his body and brain are not in a suitable state. That is to say, the appropriate state of body and brain is proved to be necessary for memory, but not to be sufficient. So far, therefore, as our definite knowledge goes, memory may require for its causation a past occurrence as well as a certain present state of the brain. (p. 91)

To summarize the results of this section, what I earlier called the "macro" approach to memory and the brain, as exemplified by neuropsychological and neuroimaging investigations of "episodic" and "semantic" memory, has delivered great quantities of empirical data, but offers only rather limited help with problems of interpretation and localization, and certainly has not yet provided anything like a coherent and complete theory of memory. It is time to look briefly at the "micro" approach, and particularly at its biochemical aspects.[26]

There are many substances, the most obvious being alcohol, administration of which can produce biochemical changes that affect memory. Scopolamine and benzodiazepines, which enhance the effects of GABA (gamma-aminobutyric acid, the major inhibitory cortical neurotransmitter), have been used for pre- and post-operative medication and have the convenient effect of promoting amnesia for possibly unpleasant experiences attendant on surgery. Ingestion of glucose and the inhaling of pure oxygen have both been shown to cause transient memory improvements in the elderly. What we are after, however, are biochemical processes that are specifically linked to memory, so that the memory changes cannot be attributed to a general excitement or depression of function or to motivational or attentional changes. Much (not all) of the relevant work has been done on invertebrates (notably the sea-hare and the fruit-fly) and on rats,[27] and especially with the rat hippocampus, which permits of being removed, cut into thin but still functioning slices, and

---

26. There are useful treatments of this area in Bear et al. (2000) and Carlson (2004). A semi-popular and very readable book on biochemical and related approaches to memory is Bourtchouladze (2002); a much more technical one is Hölscher (2001).

27. Bennett and Hacker (2003, pp. 156–158) argue that research on habituation, sensitization, and classical conditioning is "not research on memory in any sense of the word," a view with which I quite agree. They remark that "an accelerated reflex or a conditioned reaction is not a form of *knowledge*. But memory is the *retention of knowledge acquired,* and remembering to…is the *use of knowledge retained*" (p. 157). And they enlarge on this theme. One might remark further that even in the human case, the subject in, say, an eyeblink conditioning experiment may well have learned *that* the CS will be followed by an unpleasant experience;

studied *in vitro*. The main aim of this work has been to explain the phenomenon of "long-term potentiation" (LTP), a process thought to be central in memory formation.

LTP is a relatively long-lasting enhancement in the excitability of a post-synaptic neuron through induced brief but high-frequency bombardments from a pre-synaptic neuron. A feature of LTP particularly attractive to mainstream memory theorists is that if a weaker stimulus arrives at the post-synaptic cell more or less concurrently with the high-frequency bombardment, the cell's response to the weaker stimulus is strengthened, thus apparently paralleling what happens in classical conditioning when, say, a warning sound comes to produce the eyeblink originally called forth by a puff of air. The attempt to provide a neurochemical account of the basis of memory has thus devolved mainly to seeking explanations of LTP and certain closely related matters (including long-term depression). No one would claim that the account is as yet anywhere near completion; but certain features stand out and seem to hold across at least some sites outside the hippocampus. One is the involvement of the excitatory neurotransmitter glutamate, which in appropriate circumstances opens receptors on the membrane of the post-synaptic cell allowing the entry of calcium ions from the extracellular fluid. This in turn activates enzymes that (after very complicated chains of events) multiply the number of receptors in the cell membrane and cause other structural changes further increasing the receptivity of the cell. It may also trigger a backward diffusion of nitric oxide into the pre-synaptic cell, which increases the production of glutamate there.

All this results, however, only in an LTP lasting for periods most appropriately counted in hours. It has become clear that what has been termed "long-lasting, long-term potentiation" requires the synthesis of new proteins in or around the receptor-bearing dendrites (branches) of the post-synaptic cell. Like the other processes we have been considering, this one also seems to be initiated during the later stages of the cascade of intra-cellular events initiated by the influx of calcium ions. The end-product of this cascade is the activation of CREB (c-amp response element binding) proteins which bind to segments of DNA and by affecting gene expression modulate protein production. How exactly this may bring about long-lasting, long-term potentiation remains a matter of speculation.

I should remark that while a fair bit of the relevant work in this area has been done directly upon *in vitro* slices of rat hippocampus, some of the proposals put forward have also been successfully tested by observing the effects which interference (chemical, psychopharmacological, genetic) with various stages of the postulated cascades of neurochemical happenings may have upon the learning capabilities of experimental animals. Certain drug companies are known to have become interested in the possible memory-enhancing effects of CREB proteins. But even so it would be pointless to pretend that

---

but his response to the CS (closing the eyes and screwing up the face) is on a much more primitive level than the application of propositional knowledge.

all, or anything like all, of the findings in this area are necessarily to be interpreted at face value.[28]

The turn of mind of many of those who have engaged in this kind of research is clearly to regard the results as evidence for good old-fashioned memory traces (henceforth, GOFMTs), often conceived in the neurological fashion introduced by the late D. O. Hebb (1949), and widely accepted in one or another form today. However, it seems to me certain that *no* theory in the GOFMT tradition will ever fully get to grips with the problems of memory, at least where by memory is meant the human capacity to acquire and deploy knowledge, rather than, say, the automatic modifications of neuromuscular reactivity acquired during procedures of classical or operant conditioning and the like. I have already touched on some of the more obvious theoretical problems. Memory is not a reliving of some past experience or of some distillate of past experiences, or the re-enactment of past behavior when like circumstances recur. Perhaps there is at times such an aspect to remembering; but that aspect would need to be supplemented by a kind of memory (one might be tempted to describe it as "memory proper") which implicitly affirms "that is how it was and I was there as witness or participant."[29] It is often assumed that such a requirement does not hold true for "semantic" as distinct from "episodic" memory, but even with that there has to be a kind of implicit affirmation of the form "I learned that somewhere or another from some reliable source or sources."

The need for such an implicit affirmation (and by "implicit" I do not mean "not conscious" but only not in general spelled out) also highlights several further difficult, interlocked, and almost universally neglected issues. I am thinking in particular of the inescapable involvement in human memory of one's "self," or of oneself conceived from a first-person point of view ("*I* was there"), and the need to offer some account of the fact that remembering (an event in the present) is often "of" or "about" a past or future event or fact (that yesterday one saw an eclipse of the moon or visited one's dentist, or that tomorrow one will see an eclipse of the moon or visit one's dentist). What is it to regard some event as in this peculiarly intimate way part of one's own history or likely future, and how can one derive the concepts of past and future from experience limited to the fleeting present? How indeed can one handle the "ofness" or "aboutness" of all propositional acts or judgments, including of course memory-judgments? This is again the perennial problem of the "intentionality" of the mental, which we ran into before as the problem of "inner representations" and their relation to that which they are held to "represent." Intentionality—"the heart of the mind" (Puccetti, 1989)—lies at the

28. Cautionary warnings concerning the alleged evidence for LTP given by the contributors to Hölscher (2001) relate to failures to repeat, changes of experimental conditions leading to failures to obtain the phenomenon, the likelihood that there is more than one kind of LTP (dependent on location and biochemistry), the likelihood that LTP may be confined or largely confined to limited areas of the hippocampus, the side-effects of the chemicals used and the genetic manipulations introduced, and the possibility that LTP may in fact be a product of widespread theta rhythms and gamma rhythms in the brain.

29. See footnote 7 on "metarepresentation."

core of all acts of occurrent remembering in which one consciously mobilizes memory knowledge, both episodic and semantic.

To make matters even more complicated, the intentionality of one's memory judgments (as of any other kind of judgment) is inescapably tied to one's possession and exercise of concepts. And here it is vital to appreciate that the acquisition of a memory can precipitate an almost instantaneous readjustment in a whole network of concepts. Suppose I quite unexpectedly witness (unobserved, let us trust) Professor Moriarty, the quiet mathematician and art collector, setting the fuse of a bomb. I shall remember this moment (if I survive) not as one in which I saw a tall, angular figure holding a peculiar round object, but as one in which I suddenly realized that the seemingly innocuous academic was in reality a much-hunted international assassin and Napoleon of crime. This requires me to possess and deploy both a Moriarty-concept and a large network of highly sophisticated social and criminological concepts, and requires also that I suddenly and radically change the former and somewhat adjust the latter in order to capture my new vision of Moriarty. And many of these concepts will be "stimulus-neutral" ones, that is, concepts of entire classes of things whose members share no special physical characteristics that they do not also share with an indefinite number of things that are not members of the class. The attempt to envisage such massive conceptual readjustments in terms of GOFMTs would require one to imagine new and appropriate dendritic spines and synapses popping out, not in minutes or hours (which has sometimes been observed), but almost instantly like a speeded-up film of mushrooms burgeoning. And even then we would have no answer to the problem of how the newly hatched synapses could be regarded as "about" or "representing" Professor Moriarty in his new context of evil. Furthermore, what would such widespread and major changes do to the remainder of the conceptual system, presumed to occupy heavily overlapping portions of the cortical network?[30]

Each one of this circle of conceptual issues has been the subject of lengthy discussion by many philosophers and by certain psychologists, and I certainly cannot probe them further here. No large measure of agreement has resulted from these discussions, and I will only remark that I do not see GOFMT theories in anything like their present form advancing them in the slightest. GOFMT theories themselves, I must also point out, are confronted with certain oddities in the empirical findings, explanatory challenges which though perhaps not insuperable are certainly significant. There are, for instance, findings that cast doubt, not on the claim that selective synaptic strengthening (occasionally perhaps synaptic pruning also) is normally involved in the establishment of memories (this seems incontrovertible, at least at a certain level), but rather on any suggestion that the self-same synaptic changes must be retained in full force for the memory to persist undiminished. For example Raichle et al. (1994, cited by Nyberg & Cabeza, 2000, p. 502) found with a verb-generation task that, as the task was mastered, the initially widespread

30. Similar issues, it should be noted, arise in regard to the phenomenon of creative insight (Chapter 7).

areas of brain activation diminished until their pattern was indistinguishable from that produced by simple word repetition. Rather similar findings have been reported by Pascual-Leone, Grafman, and Hallett (1994) with a serial button-pressing task, and by Haier et al. (1992) for the video game Tetris. Possibly related observations include the progressive shrinkage of the time-window of retrograde amnesia following closed-head injuries, and a few reports of sudden full recovery of autobiographical memory in amnesic patients with demonstrated brain lesions, where the recovery is somehow triggered by an encounter with some situation resembling a forgotten but emotionally significant event (Luchelli, Muggia, & Spinnler, 1995).

My own thinking about all this tends toward the view that while the synaptic changes investigated by the biochemical believers in GOFMTs may very well be necessary for the *formation* of memories, they may not be necessary, or necessary in anything like the same quantity or distribution, for their *maintenance*. Furthermore, to the extent that they *are* necessary we do not really know *why* they are necessary, and we have no real understanding of their contributions to whatever conditions might be sufficient for particular instances or types of remembering. These problems, moreover, become increasingly conspicuous as we ascend the scale from simple conditioning phenomena and the like to the phenomena of explicit memory in conscious human beings. The attempt to extend ideas and findings derived from the former to embrace the latter is reminiscent of, and conceptually parallel to, the hopeless attempts by early behaviorists to extend their stimulus-response theories of learning to cover the sophisticated behavior of human beings.[31] I myself think that we probably shall never be able to give a satisfactory account of the whole lot in terms of current neurochemistry. This is not to claim that no complete physical explanation of memory will ever be possible, but I do think that in order to provide one we shall *at minimum* have to move away from the accepted concepts of neurochemistry and neuroscience as they now are and into frontier areas of physics as they then may be.

Some current writers on memory are indeed already distancing themselves from the simplifications of GOFMT and adopting what they tend to refer to as a more "holistic" or "dynamic systems" approach (see Chapter 1). Among these— and such views as theirs have a distinguished lineage in neuroscience (see Hécaen & Lanteri-Laura, 1977, pp. 203–235)—are W. J. Freeman, Rose, and McIntosh. Freeman (2000), for instance, says of his work on olfactory learning in rabbits (a valuable short account of this is Freeman, 1991), as investigated by multichannel electrophysiological recordings from different cortical areas:

> First, a sensation from an odorant does not create a pattern in the brain that is fixed and stored away in a memory bank. Instead, I have observed that brain activity patterns are constantly dissolving, reforming, and changing, particularly in relation to one another. When an animal learns to respond to a new odor, there is a shift in all other patterns, even if they are not directly

31. See also footnote 27 above.

> involved with the learning. There are no fixed representations, as there are in computers; there are only meanings. Second, a sensory stimulus from an object does indeed induce the formation of a pattern in the brain, but when it is given repeatedly it does not induce precisely the same pattern in the same brain, let alone in any other brain. (p. 22)

In somewhat similar vein Rose (2003) says of his experiments with chickens:

> The seemingly paradoxical results of the first set of these experiments was that regions of the brain which were necessary for memories to be made, and which showed lasting cellular changes as a result of that learning, after an hour or so ceased to be necessary for recall. The solution to this paradox was the recognition that memories are dynamic and dispersed, located in different ways in different parts of the brain. (p. 373; see also 2005, pp. 159–163, 207–212)

Similar findings with mammals are reviewed by Shors (2004).

Again, coming to the same problems from a neuropsychological direction, McIntosh (1999) concludes an account of his own neuroimaging work on human episodic retrieval by stating:

> Right prefrontal cortical activity could be associated with the act of searching (retrieval mode) or successful retrieval depending on its relations to other [activated or deactivated] brain regions....Common to both examples is the possibility that learning and memory...may emerge from neural interactions rather than being the responsibility of particular brain areas....Memory per se is an emergent behavior of the central nervous system—it is something the brain does. (p. 542)

These ideas are less than fully worked out, but they seem to me headed in the right direction.[32] In the light of current trends in brain science one can certainly see the appeal, indeed the necessity, of regarding the brain increasingly

32. Another phenomenon that has been taken to support the view of memory "traces" as dynamic and constantly subject to revision is the recent discovery or rediscovery that established "memories" can apparently be erased if they are activated and their activation is followed shortly afterwards by the administration of a protein synthesis inhibitor (for reviews, see Alberini, 2005; Nader, 2003a). The findings have led to a renewed debate between the currently dominant "structuralist" theories of memory and supporters of a more strongly biochemical approach, with the biochemists arguing that structural "traces" could not be so quickly eradicated, and proposing instead a return to the notion (unfashionable for upwards of 30 years) that the bearers of memories must instead be complex molecules (Arshavsky, 2003; Nader, 2003b). The "memories" studied have often involved rats or chicks coming to avoid or react to an impending noxious stimulus on receipt of a warning signal, and it is less than obvious that "memory" is an appropriate term for their reactions. In some experimental situations (e.g., ones involving noxious tastes) the effect has not been found. It is as yet far from apparent whether similar findings might also be obtained with human episodic or semantic memories. What has become increasingly clear with more sharply targeted biochemical intervention is that while in general consolidation of memories and reconsolidation following reactivation share common molecular mechanisms, they are likely to involve largely different brain loci and systems, as though the memories have so to speak moved on.

as a dynamic, holistic, and self-organizing system. I hasten to add, however, that simply pointing to these changing patterns of brain activity does not of itself magically solve any of the major conceptual issues I have raised. It may in fact introduce further ones. Freeman, for example, is simply not warranted in equating his observed patterns of electrical activity with "meanings." The problems here are analogous to those of token identity theory as described in Chapter 1: Most basically, how does electrical activity in the brain translate into "meanings" at all? Furthermore, if the patterns generated by successive presentations of a given stimulus to the same or different organisms differ widely (as they do) and if the pattern of response to that stimulus is radically altered by learning a response to a different, unrelated stimulus (as it is), what is it about all these varying patterns of response that enables them to embody the *same* "meaning"?

As further illustrations of the "dynamic" and "holistic" nature of the brain activities relating to learning and memory, one might also note the sometimes extraordinary reorganizations of function that may follow, and to a fair extent compensate for, agenesis or early destruction of brain tissue. In connection with memory the most obvious examples are the quite numerous cases (especially ones involving very early damage) of apparent takeover of language functions by the right hemisphere following damage to or removal of the left (linguistic) hemisphere.[33] Very remarkable functional plasticity has also been demonstrated by motor and sensory regions of the brain. Fawcett, Rosser, and Dunnett (2001, p. 183) cite as an example patients who had suffered one-sided paralyses following strokes that damaged (as expected) the opposite motor cortex. These patients subsequently exhibited some degree of recovery and were asked to move their hands during a PET scan. Movement of the affected hands occasioned increased blood flow in sensorimotor cortex and cerebellum on both sides, which had apparently taken over the function of the damaged left motor area. As another example, the same authors also cite a PET study of blind persons who had learned to read Braille. This revealed that the tactile task of reading Braille was being sustained by visual areas of cortex, although simple touch stimuli did not activate these areas. M. H. Johnson (2005, pp. 134–135) cites evidence that congenital deafness may lead to part-allocation of auditory cortex to vision. He also notes (pp. 40–44) that rather remarkable sensory and motor plasticity has been demonstrated following experimental lesion studies in ferrets, up to and including the rerouting of visual input from visual cortex to auditory cortex deprived of its normal auditory input. Under such conditions the auditory cortex will react to visual input and may develop a systematic map of the retina. Behaviorally, animals that had learned to distinguish visual stimuli presented to the normal hemisphere from auditory ones would transfer this learning to visual

Furthermore, there may be a time effect, newly minted memories being affected by protein synthesis inhibitors, and more established ones less affected or immune.

33. See, for example, V. Anderson, Northam, Hendy, and Wrennall (2001), Basso, Gardelli, Grassi, and Mariotti (1989), and A. Smith (1983).

stimuli presented to the auditory cortex of the rewired hemisphere.[34] In some experiments a rapid (in young animals tens of minutes, in adult ones a day to several days) growth and retraction of dendritic spines (a precursor to the formation of synapses) in response to experience has been directly observed in the living animal, as for example by Trachtenberg et al. (2002) in "barrel" cortex subserving the whiskers of young adult mice.[35] In the human case it is sometimes tempting to suggest, as William James seems to hint (1890b, vol. 1, pp. 142–143), that the idea of the missing or impaired function must play some part in its restoration.

One can only wait to see what the emerging holistic-dynamic approaches to brain function may deliver, both for cognitive science generally and for the study of memory in particular. Meanwhile, let me now summarize this long and sometimes difficult survey of the accomplishments and limitations of conventional approaches to memory. With regard to good old-fashioned memory traces (GOFMTs), my conclusion was that while synaptic changes may well in many or all instances be essential to enabling conditions for the formation of memories, no full or adequate account of memory can be given in terms of the replaying of such stored traces of past events. And the proposed GOFMTs have nothing to say about such key questions as the "intentionality" of memory and the relations between concept possession and memory. Some recent writers, sensing these problems and aware of the decidedly fluctuating relations between memory processes and patterns of events in the brain, have (as I noted above) developed more dynamic and holistic views of the neural underpinnings of memory. But these views, even though no doubt an advance on GOFMTs, still offer us little enlightenment on intentionality, concept possession, and the precise role of synaptic changes, and do not as yet help us understand how it can be that the same memory can be supported by activity centering now in one brain region and now in another.

There are two very general points to bring forward with us from this part of the chapter: First, there is a good deal of evidence to indicate that normally the formation of memories is closely linked to minute structural and broader functional changes in the brain, mediated or initiated in some way by activity of the hippocampus and allied brain structures. Second, beyond this we know far less than most people imagine. We have very limited theoretical understanding of how, especially in the human case, the various changes and activities that take place in the brain during explicit remembering relate to conscious memory as we routinely experience and express it. The brain-based coding/storage/retrieval model that most contemporary workers accept without hesitation as the foundation of their efforts confronts widely ignored

34. Useful short reviews of this material will be found in Fawcett et al. (2001, chap. 13) and M. H. Johnson (2005, pp. 40–44). The re-routing studies are those of Roe, Pallas, Hahm, and Sur (1990), Sur (1993), and von Melchner, Pallas, and Sur (2000).

35. Grutzendler, Kasthuri, and Gan (2002) failed to obtain confirmatory findings; but they used mice on average rather older, examined visual rather than barrel cortex (rats and mice are not highly visual animals), and did not provide the animals with a changing environment to stimulate experience-related neural activity.

but very significant difficulties. Although the mainstream view of memory as purely a matter of brain function has for most persons hardened into a dogma that cannot be questioned, in my view it does not merit that status. It remains essentially a neurophysiological myth, appealing and widely shared and woven around an impressive collection of empirical findings, but unproven. It is still the case, as I said on an earlier occasion, that the evidence adduced in support of this view consists for the most part simply of facts that may be harmonized with it if you already happen to think it true (Gauld, 1989, p. 197).

The conceptual and empirical difficulties in modern memory work, touched upon above, suggest that a fuller understanding of human memory may ultimately require some radical change of perspective.[36] And it is conceivable that some of the odd facts collected by Myers and his colleagues may have some bearing on such a change.

The Problem of Survival

I return at last to Myers and his disciplined and long-sustained quest to find evidence that might permit, and a philosophy that might sustain, a rational belief in human survival of bodily death. It should be emphasized, perhaps, that to the extent that such a quest succeeds it will among other things undermine all theories of memory based entirely on brain processes. Myers himself was persuaded of survival by the evidence available to him, and regarded it as providing "the strongest proof which can be imagined" for the underlying unity of personality, that it can outlast not just minor disintegrations but "the crowning disintegration of bodily death" (*HP*, vol. 1, p. 11).

The principal form of evidence for the post-mortem persistence of an identifiable individual has to be the survival of his or her distinctive memories, from which questions about the post-mortem survival of his or her characteristic desires, purposes, and skills can only partially be separated. Myers himself encapsulates the evidential issues this way (*HP*, vol. 2, p. 252):

> In earth-life the actual body, in itself but a subordinate element in our thought of our friend, did yet by its physical continuity override as a symbol of identity all lapses of memory, all changes of the character within. Yet it was memory and character,—the stored impressions upon which he reacted, and his specific mode of reaction,—which made our veritable friend. How much of memory, how much of character, must he preserve for our recognition?

---

36. Attempts to find salvation by proposing cosmic memory stores in which the memories of living persons may be deposited and subsequently be accessed by those persons before their deaths and by suitably attuned other individuals ("psychics," "mediums") thereafter would be very likely to stumble over very much the same problems we have been discussing. Setting aside the "akashic records" of Hinduism, the best-known speculations of this kind are those of William James on "cosmic consciousness" (see James, 1909/1971, 1909/1986).

As will shortly become evident, it is not at all obvious how to answer this question. To some the question is not even meaningful. But before we can get any deeper into these issues, it will be well to have some preliminary sense of the character and status of the relevant evidence. This evidence consisted in Myers's time principally (but by no means entirely, because cases of apparitions of certain types, and related phenomena, also figured largely) of detailed studies of "mediums" or "sensitives" through whose organisms (as in trance speaking or automatic writing of one form or another; see Chapter 5) or by means of whose peculiar sensibilities ("seeing" clairvoyantly and "hearing" clairaudiently) the departed can allegedly communicate with the living. Since Myers's time, one further large and important category of evidence has been added, namely, the investigations by Stevenson and his collaborators of numerous cases of young children who, more or less from the time they begin to speak, ostensibly recall previous lives (see the Appendix). In a number of carefully investigated cases of both these major categories correct information with no obvious normal source has been transmitted as if from or about some deceased person.

Conventional interpretations of the proposed "evidence for survival" mostly fall into one of three broad and rough categories:

(1) Interpretations confining themselves to "normal" factors such as wishful thinking or fraud.

(2) Interpretations that postulate "supernormal" factors not including post-mortem survival of the pre-mortem personality. The most-discussed of such interpretations is the "super-ESP" hypothesis which has it that evidence, however impressive, for the post-mortem survival of someone's memories is to be attributed to supernormal or psychic abilities, sometimes necessarily of enormous scope, exercised by or between persons still living.

(3) Interpretations in terms of the post-mortem survival of the memories and character, or recognizable fragments or aspects thereof, of the formerly living individual concerned.

I do not propose to discuss these interpretations at any length. Explanations in terms of fairly obvious normal factors—in the case of mediums, fishing for information (often very rapidly and skillfully), clever reading of the sitters' appearance, expression, voice, manners, and so forth,[37] wishful thinking (not infrequently by the medium as well as by the sitter), sometimes outright fraud such as a network of informants—will carry us a long way, at least with respect to run-of-the-mill cases, but they will not, in my opinion (based on a fair amount of practical experience and a considerable acquaintance

37. It is curious how these tactics, well-known and often commented on for well over a century, have of late been christened "cold reading" and treated as though the fact of their use was some kind of new discovery. The earliest use of the term, according to Lamont and Wiseman (1999, p. 134), dates from 1977.

with the literature), cover all cases.[38] It is indeed regrettable that the interest of the substantial number of really puzzling and carefully investigated cases has tended to be obscured by the much larger quantity of inferior evidence with which the popular market has been flooded, especially in recent years.

Not least among the "puzzle cases" is Mrs. Leonora E. Piper (1859–1956) of Boston, William James's "White Crow"and one of the two "trance" mediums that most impressed Myers. Mrs. Piper was extensively investigated both in America and England (for fairly extensive accounts of her, see Gauld, 1982, and H. Holt, 1915). There is no doubt that on bad days she (or her "controls") would blatantly fish and hazard guesses; but on good days the flow of accurate, detailed, and appropriate information that sitters (including new sitters, sitters introduced under pseudonyms, etc.) might receive, as though the veritable memories of deceased persons known to them were being tapped, could be at once baffling and compelling. Although it has been convincingly argued, in this and other similar cases, that the communicating "personalities" are simply aspects or phases of the medium herself (E. M. Sidgwick, 1915)—like the various personalities of multiple personality cases they are apt to share limitations of thought and knowledge, or favorite turns of phrase and quirks of vocabulary with each other and with the medium—the problems still remain of where the apparently surviving memories come from and of how they find their way into the medium's mind.

Interpretations of categories 2 and 3 have to be taken together. Each category contains proposals other than the clear-cut super-ESP versus survival ones to which the possibilities are so often reduced. But I shall have to pass over them here and confine my remarks to the two main proposals. Initially these sound pretty straightforward, but when one comes to look for ways to decide between them testable implications prove elusive. The rival interpretations are little better than dummy emplacements behind which entrenched opposing theoreticians make a good deal of noise while waiting hopefully for decisive weaponry to arrive. Proponents of a survivalist view argue that mediums through whom deceased persons are ostensibly communicating their memories, or children who ostensibly remember previous lives, have in some instances come out with copious and correct information far exceeding anything that the medium or child could have come by normally or could have obtained supernormally from still living persons or other extant sources. Their opponents claim that we cannot with assurance set limits on what could be learned by normal or supernormal means not involving communication with the departed, and that in any case the process by which such a discar-

38. The distinguished philosopher and psychical researcher C. D. Broad (1962) offers the following summary remarks, with which I wholly agree: "Controls and ostensible communicators often display a knowledge of facts about the past lives of dead persons and about the present actions and thoughts and emotions of living ones, which is too extensive and detailed to be reasonably ascribed to chance-coincidence, and it is quite inexplicable by reference to any normal sources of information open to the medium. I do not think that this would be seriously questioned by anyone, with a reasonably open mind, who had made a careful study of the recorded facts and had had a certain amount of experience of his own in these matters; though it is often dogmatically denied by persons who lack those qualifications" (p. 259).

nate individual must be supposed to communicate information to or through a medium would itself amount to what could only be reckoned a form of "super-ESP" (or "super-PK"), albeit of a slightly less "super" variety. Resolution of the arguments does not seem imminent or in their present context even conceivable.[39]

Myers's Approach to the Problem of Survival

Myers himself has his own characteristic approach to these problems, an approach which may have been insufficiently appreciated by subsequent writers, possibly because the "super-ESP" hypothesis (though implicit in, say, the ideas of Podmore[40]) had not in their time been fully spelled out. Myers's approach may be characterized as a "broad canvas" one, in contrast to the "narrow focus" adopted by those of his successors who have concentrated mainly on the issue of whether or not the range and scope of ESP, as discovered empirically through experiment and observation, can justifiably be stretched to cover the "super-ESP" required by the "super-ESP hypothesis." In other words Myers hoped that if he placed the evidence for survival against a wide background of related and well-documented phenomena ranging from the normal, through the abnormal, to the supernormal, and all seemingly pointing to or compatible with a certain kind of explanatory framework, the power of the whole picture would overcome the doubts that some people might have felt about the interpretation of certain sections of it considered in isolation.

The background regions of Myers's "broad canvas" are set out in Chapters 2 to 5 of *Human Personality,* and what might be called the "foreground"—including direct evidence for survival—in Chapters 6 to 9. He begins in Chapter 2 by describing cases in which a second stream of consciousness with a separate chain of memories and often a different character has for extended periods displaced the ordinary or original stream. Mostly the change is disintegrative but sometimes it has been an improvement, and in some examples the second personality has shown signs of possessing enhanced or even supernormal faculties, especially telepathy. He goes on in Chapters 3–5 to consider certain phenomena to be found in rather more ordinary, or at any rate nonpathological, phases of existence, phenomena that, like secondary streams of consciousness, might likewise be called intrusive (although in a less marked way). The phenomena are:

(1) The "uprushes of imaginative power" which, often in symbolic form, "spring full-armed into our ken from the depths of our being" (*HP*, vol. 1,

39. For further discussion of these issues, see Chapter 9, as well as works listed in our Appendix.

40. See, for example, the interesting exchange on apparitions of the dead between Myers and Podmore (Myers, 1889d, 1890b; Podmore, 1890).

p. 220) without any distinctive conscious antecedents, and which have been thought characteristic of literary, musical and scientific genius (*HP*, chap. 3).

(2) The spontaneous and often unexpected material in dreams, including recollections of long-forgotten scenes and incidents or items of supernormal information, which are not ordinarily accessible to the waking consciousness (*HP*, chap. 4).

(3) In the state of hypnosis also (which Myers regarded as "an experimental development of the sleeping phase of personality"[41]), we more than ever find evidence of heightened faculty, including access to ordinarily inaccessible memories, enhanced control over physiological processes, and supernormal processes (*HP*, chap. 5).

Consideration of the phenomena of genius, dreams, and hypnosis led Myers to the view that secondary streams of consciousness are not just rare and pathological phenomena but characteristic of human beings in general. What is relatively rare is the displacement of the normal waking consciousness by a secondary or "subliminal" stream of consciousness. But the secondary streams, although hidden, are there, as it were beneath the ordinary consciousness, in all of us. Moreover, because there is evidence that dreams may develop into secondary or somnambulistic states and that memories associated with somnambulistic episodes will often be found to be part of the hypnotic memory, Myers suggested that dreams, somnambulism, and hypnosis are all rooted in the same subliminal level of consciousness.

Into this speculative background—supported, however, by a wealth of facts to which I cannot possibly do justice—Myers endeavored (in Chapters 6–9) to fit and thereby to render more convincing the evidence that he regarded as pointing towards human survival of bodily death. This evidence hinges round the notion of *automatisms,* which he defined as "subliminal emergences into ordinary life" (*HP*, vol. 1, p. 222) and which (as we describe in Chapters 2 and 5 of this volume) he divided into *sensory automatisms* and *motor automatisms*. Many such automatisms can be understood as originating in the subliminal mind of the automatist alone. The quasi-perceptual visions of crystal-gazers, many of the visual or auditory images that pop into the minds of subjects in telepathy experiments, and the vast majority of material emerging from table-tilting, ouija or planchette board operation, or automatic writing or speaking, are simply the externalization, in sensory or motor form, of material from the automatist's own mind, either conscious or subliminal. If evidence for telepathy appears in any one of these situations, as it does also in "veridical" apparitions of the living or the dying (in which information unknown to the percipient is conveyed), then this is because telepathy is a faculty specially characteristic of subliminal streams of consciousness. Even when indications of telepathy occur in the context of ostensible messages from

41. A view less widely shared today, and which had indeed begun to be questioned even in Myers's own time (see also Gauld, 1992, pp. 561–567).

purported spirit communicators, that should not weaken one's caution over accepting the communicators as genuine—imaginative romancing is another characteristic of some levels of the subliminal (see our Chapter 5).

Matters become more complex, however, when we come to apparitions of the dead in which the information conveyed was unknown normally to the percipient and seemed to have originated in the surviving memories of the deceased person. In fitting such cases into his "broad" canvas, Myers believed that it was more intelligible to suppose that the correct and sometimes copious details arose from the minds of now-deceased persons than to enter (like Podmore and other advocates of the super-ESP hypothesis) into what Myers called (*HP*, vol. 2, p. 68) the "labyrinth of complexity" involved in supposing that all the veridical details in such cases are assembled by telepathy with living sources.

One important group of cases (whose numbers have grown since Myers's time) influenced his judgment that some cases provide evidence for the active agency of a surviving deceased person. These are reciprocal or experimental apparitions, in which the apparition of a living person is seen at a certain place, and at the same time the person whose apparition it is has a vivid experience as of being at that spot (H. Hart & Hart, 1933). Such cases sometimes occur spontaneously, but sometimes they have apparently been induced by an effort of will or imagination on the part of the "sender." Myers thought that such cases provided evidence for a kind of "self-projection" or "psychical invasion" on the part of the subliminal mind, and thus for the agency or at least the participation of the person seen as the apparition. Similarly, in cases of apparitions of the dead, we may need to consider whether elements of the deceased person's surviving mind and memories may likewise be active. Myers suggested that "this self-projection is the one definite act which it seems as though a man might perform equally well before and after bodily death" (*HP*, vol. 1, p. 297). "Psychical invasion," with its implication of post-mortem survival, might therefore be a more fitting term than "telepathic impact"; and "possession" might be a more appropriate term than either.

So much for an exiguous, indeed a skeletal, précis of Myers's "broad canvas" approach, centered on the notion of the "Subliminal Self," to the interpretation of the evidence for survival. Through this approach he hoped to carry his readers over or around the difficulties that obsess those who adopt what I called above a "narrow focus" approach. I shall touch on the general notion of a "broad canvas" approach again, but first I need briefly to consider certain relevant issues that have arisen out of recent philosophical investigations of the extremely elusive notion of personal identity.

Problems of Personal Identity

It is customary to distinguish (not without some difficulty) between *qualitative* identity, the sort that holds between two or more objects if they are qualitatively indistinguishable, and *numerical* identity, the identity of the self-same object with itself through the various phases of its career. Numerical identity is not generally supposed to require qualitative identity (indeed such a requirement could rarely be met). Thus the proposition that a certain rusty length of metal found at the bottom of an old lake is numerically identical with the noted sword Excalibur, formerly the property of a 6th-century Romano-Celtic war leader, involves no misuse of terms, even though it may not be true. But if (to take a much discussed type of example) the residual good metal has been turned into a kilt-pin, and it is claimed that the kilt-pin is numerically identical with Excalibur, a certain conceptual fog would quickly set in. Different answers would be possible in different conceptual contexts. The continued personal identity of human beings (who are ongoing processes rather than stable objects) is a far more complex question than that of swords, and conceptual fog can correspondingly set in more quickly and more thickly.

Let us next distinguish between two sorts of question about personal identity, which Noonan (2003) in an extended survey of the topic[42] characterizes (p. 2) as the "constitutive" (or "metaphysical-cum-semantic") and the "evidential" questions (Paterson, 1995, pp. 21–22, calls them the "ontological" and the "epistemological" problems). The "constitutive" question is the question of what personal identity over time consists in, of what makes a person the self-same individual at different phases of his or her existence. Simple answers to this question—for example, ones in terms of a soul or "Cartesian ego," of bodily continuity, of continuity of memory, and so forth—have long ago been largely buried in the debris of protracted conflict, and modern discussions have more and more consisted of analyses of the concept of personal identity in terms of tortuous imaginary cases.[43] The "evidential" question is the question of what counts or should count as evidence that a person P2, encountered at time T2, is the self-same individual as person P1, encountered at time T1. Obviously, these questions can become deeply intertwined.

Equally obviously, they have a considerable bearing on issues related to survival. Which answers to the constitutive question do, and which do not, allow for the possibility of continued personal identity after bodily death? How far can we justifiably accept the kinds of evidence (or some of them) that are widely agreed to be appropriate for the reidentification of still embodied persons as also appropriate for the reidentification of ostensibly disembodied ones? Which has primacy—empirical evidence or constitutive theory? And so on. I want to tackle now a recurrent line of argument that attempts to resolve at a stroke important issues relating to both the constitutive and the evidential questions.

This originated from the "ordinary language" philosophers who were so prominent in Oxford philosophy and indeed world philosophy in the 1950s and 1960s. There was a tendency among these philosophers to argue that our

---

42. Useful edited works are those by Corcoran (2001), Edwards (1997), and R. Martin and Barresi (2003).

43. Some philosophers have objected to what they regard as the excessive use of such cases (see, e.g., Baillie, 1993; Donagan, 1990; and Wilkes, 1988).

ordinary concept of a human person is so tied up with concepts of a body and bodily activities that it makes no sense to talk of a person surviving in the absence of his or her body. The arguments took a variety of forms. One strand in them[44] involved the question of what, in the case of human persons, numerical identity can consist in, and suggested that the only decisive criterion of numerical identity we can have for individual items in the world (whether Excalibur or King Arthur) is continuity of spatiotemporal track. Such continuity is a necessary condition of all reidentification and can only be exhibited by a physical body. If the continuous bodily track comes to an end, identity is lost, even if a closely similar item mysteriously appears at another point in space-time. This holds true of the identity of human persons as much as of any other item, though in the human case it may for some purposes be necessary to narrow the essential part of these particular items down to part of the body, namely, the brain.

It was not long before critics began to pick holes in this kind of position,[45] but it continues to be adopted, notably by Rosenberg (1998), who states it in a particularly uncompromising way. Rosenberg (p. 107) dismisses the possibility that "the criterion of personal identity" could be continuity of a non-physical soul regarded, following Descartes, as devoid of spatial attributes (a rather unnecessary assertion, since a "Cartesian ego" could in any case only be a candidate-explanation for, and certainly not a candidate-criterion of, continued personal identity). We would be quite unable to trace the spatiotemporal path of such a soul, or to decide whether we had met up with "the same soul again." Only in respect of physical objects is such tracking and reidentification possible. Conversely (pp. 105–108, 119–121), if we were to imagine the soul as possessed of spatiotemporal properties, we would simply be turning it into some sort of highly implausible physical object (if the left barrel doesn't get you the right one will!). Thus the proper, "logically decisive" or "logically adequate" criterion (but note that Rosenberg seems here to be using the term "criterion" in an obscure and non-standard sense[46]) for continued personal identity is no different from that for the continued identity across time of any physical object (pp. 104, 105). Even if there were some non-physical element in the human person, that element could not in principle serve as the criterion for reidentifying the same person again. And even if some of my character-

44. See, for example, Flew (1987) and Penelhum (1970).

45. See, for example, Madell (1981), Noonan (2003, pp. 18–21), and Swinburne (1997).

46. The whole line of argument we are here considering has been pervaded and obfuscated by peculiar and once fashionable uses—which Mundle (1970, pp. 118–119, 234–237; see also Gauld & Shotter, 1977, pp. 154–161) has called philosophical "jargon uses"—of the term "criterion." Following such uses, continuity of spatiotemporal track, taken as "a" or "the" criterion of continued numerical identity, has been said to be "logically decisive" for or to "logically guarantee" (phrases of uncertain import having no part in formal logic and functioning largely as ways of commending one's arguments) such continued identity, including personal identity. This makes it sound as though spatiotemporal continuity is an unshakeable part, set in stone for all time, of the definition of numerical identity. But the ordinary, dictionary usage of "criterion" does not assign this degree of permanence to criteria.

istic personal memories were ostensibly to manifest again after my lamented demise, those memories could not be regarded as *my* memories.

Of course one can certainly agree that in our ordinary daily dealings with more or less stable physical objects (for instance, a can of beans on a supermarket shelf), part (and no doubt a large part) of what we mean by saying "this is the same can again," and thus assigning it a numerical identity across its various phases, is that the can now before us, given that it is constitutively similar to a can we have previously encountered, has had a continuous spatiotemporal track from our previous encounter with it to the present one. But that we can treat *all* issues of numerical identity in this cavalier and *a priori* fashion seems more than a little doubtful, even in the case of physical objects or entities.

If, for instance, the behavior of cans of beans, or of human organisms, resembled that of subatomic particles (and there is no totally clear reason why it should not), philosophers disposed to give an account of numerical identity in terms of spatiotemporal continuity would have an interesting time. In certain contexts it seems perfectly acceptable to talk of the same individual particle, say a photon or an electron, leaving a source and being detected again a split second later by an appropriate detector. At any rate many physicists do talk in this way. But all this seems to mean is that a particle has left the source and a particle has arrived at the targeted destination, and that the most appropriate way of talking (making allowance for wave-particle duality) is to say that they are one and the same. Whether the particle pursues a continuous spatiotemporal pathway from source to detector is a very different issue. For even a single particle (or atom or molecule or buckyball) may be described (as in variants of the double-slit experiment and in Feynman's "sum over histories" approach [see B. Greene, 2004, pp. 179–184]) as having pursued a doubled trajectory, or as having putatively explored or pursued every possible path to its terminus. The situation is further clouded by the Heisenberg "uncertainty principle" according to which it is impossible simultaneously to determine exactly both the position and the momentum (that is, mass times velocity in a direction) of a particle; one can determine only the one or the other. This blurs the very notion of a spatiotemporal path; and yet one might still reasonably claim that the particle which departs is the same one which arrives.

One could play with further examples, for instance the "wormholes" through space hypothesized by some cosmologists and designers of time machines. Wormholes are not, as it were, tunnels within our ordinary neighborhood space-time. When they open up they constitute "new, previously non-existent tube[s] of space" connecting one region of space-time to another, and a traveler who steps through the wormhole's mouth (its interface with his region of space) is not within the space or indeed the time of the locality he has left, nor yet in those of the locality into which he is about to emerge through the wormhole's other end. If after his precipitate arrival the wormhole through which he has passed were to collapse, the space it occupied would simply have gone.[47] In what sense (if any) and from what point of view (if any) can he be said to have pursued a continuous bodily spatiotemporal track from his departure point to his almost instantaneous arrival at a destination remote in space and time?

The upshot of these examples is that criteria for the reidentification of the same individual items again (be they objects or persons) vary according to the conceptual framework within which the question of reidentification arises; and that criteria which are appropriate in one setting may not be meaningfully applicable in another.

There has been an understandable but misguided temptation to regard the can of beans kind of case, our first example, as canonical for the reidentification of particular things in the world. If we can establish that a can of beans we observed at a given place and time pursued a continuous spatiotemporal path to a different place and time at which we perceived an apparently identical can, we may for nearly all purposes be sure that the latter was the same can again as the former. The discovery of its continuous spatiotemporal track might indeed in some rather loose sense be called "logically decisive" or "criterial" for questions of its numerical identity. Other cues to continuing identity there may be, but this one is decisive and takes precedence in the event of a clash. Note, however, that this is so only because within our everyday framework of thought for talking about everyday items the establishment of continuity of spatiotemporal track is a question-stopper. Unless the can has been incinerated and turned to powder, or emptied of its contents, or otherwise metamorphosed, there are no further relevant questions to be asked. But this framework, it should be observed, is not established by science. It is a deeply engrained feature of our societal conventions, held because for most purposes it works more effectively than any other.

This brings us to the essential point: Reidentifying a particular item (person or thing) as the same item again usually presents no problems in the context of the commonplace can of beans model within which spatiotemporal track predominates. Once we step outside the merely commonplace, however, we can find ourselves confronted with questions of reidentification which lie far outside the scope of such a model. We are entitled to talk of the identification and reidentification of particular things far beyond the scope of that model provided that the conceptual context in which we do so licenses and makes sense of such a way of talking. The everyday conceptual context which licenses and accords ultimate predominance to talk of continuous spatiotemporal tracks through three dimensions of space and one of time is not necessarily the only framework of thought within which we can sensibly talk of reidentification, whether of particles or of people—indeed L. R. Baker (1997, 2000, 2001) argues at length that even within our present everyday framework the continuity of the *person* is not to be identified with the persistence of the *organism*.

Let us now turn away from these rather abstract questions of identification and reidentification to the more immediate issue of what is in practice

47. For a lucid non-technical account of wormholes, see B. Greene (2004, pp. 461–468).

generally regarded as appropriate and potentially satisfactory *evidence* of the continued identity of ordinary human beings. Serious problems here are (discounting momentary failures of recognition and so forth) relatively rare in everyday life, though they have sometimes arisen more forcefully in the contexts of certain legal cases (for classic examples, see Rolph, 1957) or of various puzzles in historical biography. The sorts of evidence that have been advanced in such cases are fairly obvious and include a mixture of physical and psychological components: physical similarity, similarity in behavior and in psychological characteristics, production of appropriate memories, exhibition of appropriate skills, possession of relevant mementoes, recognition by friends and relatives or even (as with Odysseus) by a dog, and continuity of spatiotemporal track and matters directly related thereto (such as fingerprints, scars, birthmarks, or DNA tests). These categories of evidence are somewhat complexly interrelated. They may mutually support, or be necessary complements of, each other, and from time to time they may conflict. Assessing them is always a matter of weighing up the *tout ensemble.*

In the event of conflict between these various kinds of evidence, there is no doubt that, in Western society at least, good evidence of continuous bodily track (which can now with modern forensic methods be made almost irrefutable) will, if available, usually prevail over all other types. In fact, spatiotemporal track is so predominant that it has in effect become a "criterion," indeed the principal and generally overriding criterion, of the continued existence of any individual whose identity might be in question. In the ordinary or dictionary sense of "criterion" (and I have already pointed out that Rosenberg's use of the term appears, so far as one can tell, to differ from this ordinary usage), a criterion is simply a standard by reference to which something is or shall be deemed to be the case. Criteria are set up by convention, either a gradually evolving social convention or a deliberately established artificial one. They are adopted because they work for a given purpose, and once adopted it becomes self-contradictory, within a restricted context, to affirm the criterion and deny that something which meets it qualifies as a member of the class of which it is the criterion. But if a criterion becomes, or is found to be, unsatisfactory for its destined purpose, it can be changed or dispensed with. Criteria are absolutely not set in stone. And it is to be noted that if C is a criterion of X, it does not follow that the term "C" is part of the meaning of the term "X." Thus, for somewhat restricted legal purposes a certain breathalyser reading might be accepted as a criterion of drunkenness. But being "drunk" does not in more general usage mean or simply mean "giving breathalyser readings of more than such-and-such." It means "having imbibed too much alcohol and in consequence behaving in certain unacceptable ways." Likewise person P2's "being numerically identical with past person P1" may or may not carry as part of its meaning "having pursued a continuous spatiotemporal track from T1 to T2." We might, for instance, try (as some have done) to answer the "constitutive" problem of personal identity in terms of continuity of an individual "first-person perspective" and adopt bodily continuity as a criterion of this simply because it is a generally reliable guide.

Obviously, another kind of evidence of continued personal identity that might be reckoned to have criterial status is continuity of memory: Does the *soi-disant* John Doe remember things which he ought to remember if he is indeed John Doe? Although continuity of memory is generally outgunned, at least in Western society, if it comes into conflict with evidence for continuity of spatiotemporal track, it can come into its own when, say, we are talking on the telephone via a bad connection to someone with a slightly strange-sounding voice, and we want to decide whether he really is the old friend he claims to be; and it has taken on cardinal importance in legal cases and historical problems antedating DNA testing (and the like) or in which DNA is not available.

Just occasionally, moreover, one may find cases in which the primacy of the spatiotemporal track criterion is seriously threatened, and for some overwhelmed, by rather striking apparent manifestations of continuity of memory in the absence of accompanying continuity of bodily track. An appreciable number of the "communicators" through Mrs. Piper (see above) and certain other intensively studied mediums provide examples. So do the numerous instances of young children, laboriously investigated by Stevenson and his collaborators, who ostensibly remember previous lives (for summaries and references, see Matlock, 1990; Stevenson, 2001; Tucker, 2005), and the rare and remarkable cases in which a person's ordinary memories and characteristics have seemingly been replaced, permanently or for extended phases, and usually upon waking from a coma or serious illness, by a completely different set of memories and behavior patterns, ones corresponding to those of a deceased individual whose existence has subsequently been verified.[48]

Such cases can be peculiarly baffling or even unsettling to many Westerners, and not just because they conflict with firmly held religious or philosophical beliefs. The supremacy of the spatiotemporal track criterion is pretty well entrenched in our society and forms part of an institutionalized web of concepts, a web which, although compatible with much contemporary science, mostly reflects the world we have grown up in and social practices that work within that world. Too much shaking of such a web is apt to generate a spreading disturbance.

---

48. One such case is that of Lurancy Vennum, cited by both Myers (*HP*, vol. 1, pp. 360–368) and James (1890b, vol. 1, pp. 396–398). Similar but more recent cases are those of Shiva (Stevenson, Pasricha, & McClean-Rice, 1989) and Jasbir (Stevenson, 1974, pp. 34–52). Somewhat different is the case of Sharada (Stevenson & Pasricha, 1979; Stevenson, 1984). In this the subject was not ill at the time of the "possession," the identity of the intruding personality (from the early 19th century) was not completely established, though appropriate details were given, and the intrusions were accompanied by a sudden fluency in a language *not* (so far as could be discovered) learned normally by the subject.

Myers's "Broad Canvas" Revisited

Nonetheless, the spatiotemporal criterion of personal identity, however useful under ordinary circumstances, is, as I have argued, by no means sacrosanct. It is in fact not difficult to conceive a world that is recognizably similar to, but in some respects considerably different from, our own, in which memory would be generally accepted as a criterion of personal identity at least equal to, and sometimes capable of overriding, bodily track, and in which (for related reasons) certain sorts of supernormal phenomena (not there regarded as supernormal) might be widely accepted or indeed taken for granted. These phenomena would of course be especially the ones which Myers regarded as constituting evidence for survival of bodily death.

Imagine, for instance, a world, occupied by humans like us, in which instances of telepathy and other forms of ESP and also of PK, or telekinesis, are quite common, and in which many persons routinely undergo altered states of consciousness (ASCs) of various kinds, including vivid dreams and visions, states of dissociation, trance and secondary personality, and episodes of automatic writing and speaking. Next let it be the case that the episodes of telepathy, ESP, and PK occur with particular frequency and effectiveness when the persons undergoing or initiating them are in an ASC. And let us assume that the ESP manifesting during the ASCs takes the form not just of information or warnings about distant happenings, past, present or impending, but of messages, written or spoken, from living persons, and that on further inquiry or as the result of experiment, it turns out that these messages were intended or appropriate and that the ostensible senders were often themselves in an ASC or even undergoing an OBE in which they believed themselves to be visiting the spot at which and the person through whom the message was received. And let it further be the case that quite often messages containing correct and appropriate information be similarly received ostensibly from deceased persons.

The stage is now set for the final and most dramatic aspects of this imaginary world. Suppose, there are also many cases in which it is found that one person may be associated with more than one body, or one and the same body with more than one person. Suppose, for instance, there are cases in which a living person undergoing an OBE or NDE or in some other abnormal state manifests as a mediumistic communicator and exhibits the right kind of memories, cases in which a person has disappeared from a seriously ill or comatose body and been replaced by a totally different and lately deceased personality with a completely different but appropriate set of memories, cases in which a mediumistic communicator manifests with a continuous memory through different and independent mediums, and cases in which a mediumistic communicator of impressive authenticity announces his or her impending reincarnation and then turns up as predicted as one of Stevenson's children who ostensibly remember past lives. Into this interesting assortment of phenomena we might also throw post-mortem apparitions of various nunciative or message-bearing kinds.

In a world like this, I think it is fair to say, a socially sanctioned conceptual framework would be almost universally adopted within which survival of death would be more or less taken for granted and with it the overriding importance of memory as a criterion of personal identity. To explain the phenomena in terms of so-called "super-ESP" would involve weaving a web so tangled that "super" would be a wholly inadequate prefix to apply to the "ESP" required. But at the same time the citizens of this imaginary world, at least the more philosophically oriented ones, would be cautious about saying they had "proof" of survival. Personal survival cannot be directly demonstrated by third-person observation, as one might demonstrate (though with difficulty) that certain terrestrial bacteria can survive on Mars. Nor can it be demonstrated by theory-based logico-mathematical inference from observable phenomena to the postulated existence of something not itself directly observable, as the existence of dark matter can be mathematically inferred from its gravitational effects. In our imagined world, acceptance of survival would be almost a foundational assumption of life in society, a broad canvas picture without which the citizens could not even begin to make sense of much that they encountered on a daily basis, but within and through which many matters would be seen to fit together in ways which might in the future be refined and which would already seem to confirm the larger schema. In some ways it would be like the "foundational assumption," shared by all of us save perhaps a few psychopaths, that other people are sentient beings like ourselves. The power of the whole would derive not from its generating exact predictions but from the fact that it and it alone would render adequately comprehensible the nature of and the relations between certain classes of otherwise puzzling phenomena.

It is not hard to find partial analogies to such a situation in other and more orthodox regions of science.[49] The Darwinian theory of evolution, for instance, is (or was in its earlier days) in many respects a framework of thought with some of the characteristics of a "broad canvas" schema rather than of a precise deductive theory. Many findings, even though not precisely predictable from it, fall into place within it and combine to help us understand certain aspects of the natural world, even though (say) processes of speciation or convergent evolution in response to environmental conditions are in most circumstances impossible to observe directly, and the upshots of such processes are not derivable in detail from the broad framework.[50] Over the decades, of course, the phenomena comprehended within this framework have multiplied, and their relations with each other and with more basic data been greatly tightened.

49. There is no one template that all theories in science must fit, and probably no one continuum on which they can all be placed. Perhaps several intersecting continua would do the job! But this raises issues too complex to be gone into here.

50. A similar example might be the theory of continental drift, which brought together a diversity of findings derivable from and united by the theory largely on what might be called a commonsense basis. It encountered great hostility from geologists who regarded it as contravening established principles. Only when the global positioning system made it possible to measure the movements of tectonic plates could the theory be directly tested.

William James (1903) drew a parallel between Darwin and Myers, remarking of the latter that he showed "a genius not unlike that of Charles Darwin for discovering shadings and transitions, and grading down discontinuities in his argument" (p. 30). It will have been obvious that, in writing about my imaginary world of copious evidence for psychical phenomena and for survival, and about the overarching schema into which that evidence might be fitted, I have been trying to make clearer, as it were through magnification, the general aim and tenor of Myers's great project, both on its theoretical and on its data-collecting side. Of course our world, the "real" world, is not so generously provided with just the kinds of phenomena you might want for his purposes. Yet I never cease to be astonished at how far Myers actually got on both fronts. His *Human Personality* and his major articles contain between them one or two and often many first-hand accounts of almost all[51] the kinds of phenomena with which I chose to fill my imaginary world, and of other phenomena also. And his theory of the Subliminal Self, however one evaluates it, does indeed provide an overarching schema or "broad canvas" into which this array of phenomena can be systematically slotted with an apparent strengthening of his general position.

Myers, Memory, and the Evidence for Survival

Any attempt (not least Myers's) to systematize and interpret the ostensible evidence for human survival of bodily death has to take on board the empirical facts, so far as they are known, of the relationship between memory and the brain. Most modern neuroscientists regard memory as totally a function of the brain, a view which if justified (and it was widely enough held in Myers's own time) is fatal to the possibility that memory and related features of personality might survive death as Myers hoped, believed, and argued. It is curious how many subsequent persons who have discussed the evidence for survival and its interpretation have failed to take this crucially relevant question fully on board. I discussed the issue of memory and the brain earlier in the chapter and shall say a few concluding words on it now.

Myers himself was well abreast of the neuroscience of his time, and of the probable close relations between memory and brain function. Nonetheless, he is surprisingly relaxed about the matter and about the inseparably linked question of the general relation between mind and brain. That mental functions cannot be wholly reduced to brain functions he regards as indicated by the occurrence of telepathy, of which, he argues (e.g., *HP*, vol. 1, pp. 245–246), a physical explanation is not possible, and by the fact that in certain circumstances (for instance during what would now be called NDEs; see *HP*, vol. 2, pp. 315–323) vivid experiences, including what may have been clairvoy-

51. The major exception is examples of verified cases of ostensible reincarnation, of which in Myers's time there were very few. He had a curiously ambiguous attitude towards reincarnation. His neoplatonist leanings made him interested in the topic, but circumstances in both his personal life and his psychical research career prejudiced him against it.

ant ones, have occurred to persons who are comatose or greatly enfeebled (on this, see further our Chapter 6). With regard to memory and brain, he seems at times almost ready to accept that supraliminal memories are mediated by ordinary memory traces, though he also suggests (*HP*, vol. 2, p. 192) that, for instance in cases of temporary displacement of one set of memories by another as in some instances of alternate personalities, the same brain-cells may be involved in different and discordant memories (a suggestion to an extent compatible with modern connectionist ideas). These processes, he remarks, "are completely obscure," but may belong "to the same unknown series of operations" which ultimately lead to possession by an external spirit. The Subliminal Self he seems to think of (and this is in line with his other ideas about its nature) as enjoying a certain, and at "deeper" levels complete, freedom from the constraints of memory traces and indeed of the brain,[52] and as possibly able to select from and rearrange the restricted and trace-bound memories characteristic of the supraliminal (for hints about this see *HP*, vol. 1, pp. 105, 128, 226; vol. 2, p. 266). No doubt, also, his firm conviction that he already possessed compelling evidence for human survival of bodily death helped to persuade him in accordance with his broad canvas approach that the physical basis of memory, whatever it might turn out to consist in, could not be ultimately incompatible with this evidence.

Today memory appears a considerably tougher problem for an approach like Myers's than it was in his time (and it was tough enough then). The data demonstrating connections between memory and brain function, which were already sufficient in Myers's time to fill a library shelf or two, have now attained a detail and quantity that would fill a library or two. How within a broad canvas one might reconcile these data with the data ostensibly indicating that personal memories may survive death and disintegration is not easy to conceive, and the evidence for post-mortem survival of memory, though it has grown since Myers's time, has not grown on anything like the same scale as the evidence for some sort of linkage between memory and the brain.

At the same time, however, it must be recognized that this memory-brain linkage is nowhere near as straightforward as it is often made out to be. In the first part of this chapter I said something about modern psychological and neuroscientific approaches to memory with particular reference to "trace" theories of memory and their modern descendants. My conclusion about good old-fashioned memory traces (GOFMTs) was that while they may be

52. If this is indeed the case, and if, as Myers believed, there may be genuine cases of living persons (often ones who are asleep or comatose) manifesting as mediumistic communicators, it should be possible for the subliminal selves of persons suffering severe memory loss through brain damage to manifest likewise, relatively unimpeded by their memory problems. I can call to mind only one apparent case (Schiller, 1923) of this kind. The medium was Mrs. Piper and the "communicator" was an elderly lady in an advanced state of senile dementia. Schiller regarded this case as supporting his "transmission" theory of mind. On this theory one might suppose that if, as seems not impossible, at some time in the future it becomes possible to replace cells destroyed by Alzheimer's disease, lost memories might return; that is, transmission might be resumed; see also Chapter 6 for references to a few cases suggesting such restoration near death. My own guess is that there would be some degree of restoration, but not enough to convince those who do not antecedently believe in the theory.

all very well at the level of conditioned reflexes, avoidance learning, and so forth, they are totally inadequate to account for human declarative memory (semantic and episodic). Their modern descendants, the various forms of "inner representation" imagined by cognitive psychologists, have yet to be put in any form that coherently handles the relevant facts. In particular neither GOFMTs nor inner representations have come properly to grips with such central and inescapable issues as the "intentionality" of memory (what makes memories "of" or "about" certain events or states of affairs, and, in the case of cognitive psychology, how "inner representations" become representations "of" things external to themselves, or become, in short "representations" at all), and the relations between memory, concept possession, intentionality, and possession of a "first-person perspective."

Some writers, sensing these problems, have, as outlined earlier, developed more dynamic and holistic views of the neural underpinnings of memory. But their views, or so I suggested, do not reach anywhere near the heart of the matter.

We are left, then, with an awkward conjunction of seemingly discordant observations. First, it is a hard scientific fact that there are strong and well-established correlations between normal memory function and activities of the brain, both macroscopic and microscopic. Any adequate theory of memory must somehow accommodate and make sense of these correlations. Second, currently fashionable hard scientific accounts of memory, which attempt to build directly on these correlations and are entirely brain-based, have very marked theoretical and empirical shortcomings, as we have seen.

Finally, into this already complex situation is thrown a further complication introduced in the second part of the chapter, which here concerns us particularly; namely, that some peoples' memories—including semantic, factual, episodic, and procedural memories—have ostensibly to a greater or lesser extent survived the disintegration of their brains. The evidence for this ranges from the apparent manifestion of mere snippets of recollection to that of quite extensive and varied sequences of correct memories presented as if from an appropriate first-person perspective. Looking at these ostensible manifestations of post-mortem memory against a broad canvas, even if not quite Myers's canvas, I find it difficult not to suppose that some of them are in varying degrees somehow linked to the original person (in ways we do not understand, but not to be thought of in terms of extant records and memorabilia, the effects of pre-mortem deeds, memories lingering in the minds of the still-living, or "super-ESP" directed on all or any of these). At any rate, whatever the best explanation of the best cases may be, I can see no satisfactory means of explaining them away.

Now, if post-mortem survival of memories is a fact—and this assuredly remains at present a big "if," at least for most scientific observers—the purely brain-based mainstream approach to memory must necessarily fail. But the difficulty still remains that, so far as the deliverances of neuroscience go, a functional memory is normally strongly dependent in *some* way on a working brain. What this confluence of discordant observations suggests, in sum, is that we need to reconceptualize the nature of the linkage between memory and the brain in some fundamentally novel way.

In this dilemma, the fact that we have rejected the conventional answers to the problem of memory and brain has certain advantages. It frees us to pursue less conventional lines of attack on the problem, lines which among other things may one day conceivably help to clarify how we should best interpret the ostensible evidence for survival after death.

But what are these lines of attack to be? It seems to me, even on the basis of the very limited account of human memory and brain function that I have been able to give here, that any viable account of human declarative memory in relation to brain function (also of course any viable account of "intentional" mental phenomena in general) will eventually turn out to have features such as the following:

(1) It will be a "top down" rather than a "bottom up" theory. That is to say, it will be a theory which proposes that the elements of a system sometimes act in conformity with laws characterizing the system as a whole and not derivable from the interactions of its elements. These principles (unlike the laws of neurochemistry or the quasi-computational rules of much cognitive psychological theorizing) might be described as emerging from or supervening upon interactions of the elements, not, one should emphasize, on a moment-by-moment basis, but gradually over time and having something like the status of psychophysical laws in part tailored to each individual.

(2) It will accommodate the fact that particular declarative memories cannot be supposed tied or permanently tied to particular anatomical loci in the brain or to particular brain systems or activity patterns. There is copious evidence that such memories may be underpinned by different brain circuitry at different stages of their development or may reinstate themselves to a greater or lesser extent following extensive tissue damage and destruction.

(3) It will recognize that different memories may be intrinsically interrelated in such a way that one memory (e.g., of handling a firearm) may be as it were so pervaded by another (that firearms fire bullets propelled by explosives) that without this relationship it would become, not simply a memory of a firearm lacking some feature which it had, but not a memory of a firearm at all. This aspect of our memory-systems still awaits adequate investigation.

(4) It will regard the nerve tracts that transmit nerve impulses from one part of the brain to another not as conduits for the transmission of "information" in the loose sense commonly adopted by psychologists, but as means by which spatiotemporal patterns of activity in different regions may be fine-tuned to create overarching patterns.

From what quarter we may derive help in fleshing out the bare bones of such theoretical requirements remains to be determined. The most obvious suggestion (and I do not have a better one) is to seek new ideas about the relations of brain and memory (and also about brain and the ostensible evidence for personal survival) from the bizarre, but fascinating, frontier areas of physical science. So far only a small number of workers have even looked at this road, let alone gone far down it. Lockwood (1989), D. Hodgson (1991), and Stapp (2004a) attempt to illuminate cerebral and mental functioning and their relationships in terms of their own preferred interpretations of quantum theory. Romijn (1997) proposes, under the influence of Bohm, that a large part of mental activity, including the storage of declarative memories, takes place outside the brain at "a deeper, submanifest level." Penrose (2004), coming at the problems from the opposite direction, remarks "that a 'fundamental' physical theory that lays claim to any kind of completeness at the deepest levels of physical phenomena must also have the potential to accommodate conscious mentality" (p. 1033). He argues strongly that "computational functionalism" is not up to this task. All of these writers lay interesting possible new directions before their readers—earnests, we may hope, of developments to come. (These and related issues will be discussed further in Chapter 9.)

Perhaps, then, the best that each of us can do at the moment to subdue and render provisionally intelligible these complex and complexly interrelated areas where memory, philosophy, and psychical research meet, mix, and mystify is to work out for him- or herself some tentative sketch for a "broad canvas" picture of them that, however vague and imperfect, we may hope will provide appropriate and appropriately related spaces for features we may one day delineate more effectively. To date no one, perhaps, has had a better trial shot at this task than did Myers so long ago.

Conclusion

To recapitulate: Myers's approach to the evidence for the survival of memory and personality is rather different from the approaches taken by many of his successors. Instead of plunging *in medias res,* presenting survival evidence and arguing about the super-ESP hypothesis, he tackles the issues less directly. Before tackling the survival problem, he sets up what I called a "broad canvas" and fills it in area by area. He takes his readers though certain aspects of normal and abnormal psychology, and also through supernormal phenomena not claiming any other-worldly origin. He tries to demonstrate, from phenomena not presented as evidence for survival, that mental functioning is not so closely tied to brain functioning as is generally imagined. He is intensely interested in the frontiers of psychology and also (a less appreciated point) in the frontiers of physiology (see especially *HP*, vol. 2, pp. 505–552), from both of which he sought facts and ideas with which to buttress, enlarge, or modify his line of thought. He extends his speculations into hidden realms (the "metetherial," the "subliminal"), which he regarded as constituting a sort of "implicate order" that underlies and shapes the perceptible world. He did not expect to "prove" survival by means of one or two wonder cases, but rather sought to advance the issue by hard and patient graft (at which he was particularly good). He was, in short, trying to make survival seem a viable or more than viable option by demonstrating that the world on fuller inquiry turns out to be more like the "imaginary world" which I described above than most people would suppose. This may well be the only kind of approach to the matter that holds out any prospect of ultimate agreement. Whether or not one believes that Myers himself fully succeeded in his endeavor, one can only marvel at the dedication, the ability, the range of information, the literary skill, and the power to inspire others that he brought to it.

Chapter 5

Automatism and Secondary Centers of Consciousness

Adam Crabtree

In his classic *Varieties of Religious Experience* published in 1902, William James (1902/1958) made the following striking comment:

> I cannot but think that the most important step forward that has occurred in psychology since I have been a student of that science is the discovery, first made in 1886,[1] that, in certain subjects at least, there is not only the consciousness of the ordinary field, with its usual center and margin, but an addition thereto in the shape of a set of memories, thoughts, and feel-

---

1. There is little doubt that the 1886 date refers to a work of Myers, but there is a question as to *which* work. Powell (1979, p. 156) believes it is Myers's note on "psychical interaction" in Vol. 2 of *Phantasms of the Living* (Gurney et al., 1886) where he wrote of mental operations "below the threshold...of consciousness" (p. 285). Ignas Skrupskelis, editor of the Harvard University Press edition of *Varieties of Religious Experience,* believes that the 1886 date points to Myers's paper "Human personality in the light of hypnotic suggestion," which he says was published in 1886 in the *Proceedings of the Society for Psychical Research*; this is also the opinion of David Leary (Leary, 1990, p. 117). However, Skrupskelis and Leary are mistaken about the date of publication, which is, in fact, 1885 (Myers, 1885e). Perry (1935, vol. 2, p. 121), Fontinell (1986, p. 120), Taylor (1996, p. 87), and Barnard (1997, p. 173) state that the reference is to Myers, but do not cite a particular text. To my knowledge, the only author who believes that James is not referring to Myers in this passage is Ann Taves, who sees his words as referencing the works of Pierre Janet and indicates that it was actually Janet who made the "basic discovery" of the subconscious (Taves, 1999, p. 418). This position is weakened by the fact that, as I have pointed out elsewhere (Crabtree, 2003), Janet's understanding of the subconscious was itself largely influenced by the prior work of Myers, and that, in the passage in question, James nowhere mentions Janet or Janet's term "subconscious," but uses Myers's term "subliminal" to explicate his meaning.

> ings which are extra-marginal and outside of the primary consciousness altogether, but yet must be classed as conscious facts of some sort, able to reveal their presence by unmistakable signs. I call this the most important step forward because, unlike the other advances which psychology has made, this discovery has revealed to us an entirely unsuspected peculiarity in the constitution of human nature. No other step forward which psychology has made can proffer any such claim as this.
>
> In particular, this discovery of a consciousness existing beyond the field, or subliminally as Mr. Myers terms it, casts light on many phenomena of religious biography. (p. 188)

This remarkable tribute to Frederic Myers may be a surprise to some, but those who are familiar with James's writings know that he often pointed to Myers's work as pivotal to scientific psychology and influential in his own thinking (see, e.g., James, 1901). Indeed, much of James's later work, including *Varieties of Religious Experience* and *A Pluralistic Universe,* can be viewed as the systematic application of Myers's central theoretical ideas to problems in religion, epistemology, and metaphysics. Furthermore, those who are familiar with psychological writings in the 1880s and 1890s know that James was only one of a number of prominent figures in psychology (e.g., Theodore Flournoy[2] and Boris Sidis[3]) who were influenced by Myers's conception of the "Subliminal Self." It is now becoming clear that Myers was the first to effectively describe the psychological unconscious (see, e.g., Crabtree, 2003; Shamdasani, 1993) and that his influence on the development of what Ellenberger (1970) called "dynamic psychiatry" was considerable. What may be less known is the role played by the concept of "automatism" in the development of Myers's pivotal ideas and how the concept of "psychological automatism" provided a framework that would serve well to explain intelligent human actions not performed by the ordinary consciousness. Myers's views regarding automatism were framed in response to a contemporary debate on "unconscious cerebration," a debate with roots in the early history of mesmerism.

Historical Background

The closing decades of the 18th century witnessed a startling discovery which grew out of the practice of "animal magnetism," a healing system

2. Swiss psychologist Theodore Flournoy, author of the widely acclaimed *From India to the Planet Mars* (1900/1983), mentor to Carl Jung, and a personal friend of Myers, wrote: "Frederic Myers was one of the most remarkable personalities of our time in the realm of mental science" (Flournoy, 1911, p. 48).

3. Boris Sidis, American psychologist and pioneer in laboratory techniques at Harvard, wrote: "Psychology is especially indebted to the genius of Myers for his wide and comprehensive study of the phenomena of the subconscious, or of what he calls the manifestations of the subliminal self" (Sidis, 1898/1906, pp. 2–3).

developed by Franz Anton Mesmer. Mesmer's pupil, the Marquis de Puységur, found that certain people, when being treated for their illnesses, went into a non-ordinary state of consciousness, something he came to call "magnetic sleep" or "magnetic somnambulism." This state evinced certain characteristic qualities that were surprising and dramatic. Puységur (1784) wrote that persons in this state showed a notable alteration in personality; were highly suggestible; demonstrated a special connection with their magnetizer which Puységur called "magnetic rapport" (pp. 28–35); were able to diagnose and prescribe treatment for their own illnesses and those of others; could read the thoughts of their magnetizer; and remembered nothing of what had occurred in the magnetic state when returning to their ordinary state (Puységur, 1785, pp. 2–3). Because of the alteration of personality and post-somnambulistic amnesia, subjects when in their ordinary state did not feel that they were authors of what was done in the magnetic state. In the last quarter of the 18th century and throughout much of the 19th a great deal of healing work and experimentation was done with people in this state of magnetic sleep (Crabtree, 1993; Gauld, 1992).

Starting in the 1830s, physiologists who studied human behavior were concerned to explain the lack of connection between the ordinary waking state and the somnambulistic state. Specifically, they wanted to find out how individuals could perform intelligent actions of which they had no awareness. Some took their cue from experiments, originated by Eduard Pflüger, which were being carried out with decapitated frogs (see Maudsley, 1876, pp. 138–139). These experiments showed that even without its brain, a frog was able to respond to stimulation with seemingly purposeful movements. This stimulus/response combination was called spinal reflex activity, since the movement originated in the spinal cord. The conclusion was that, even without its brain, an animal could perform combined movements in proper sequence for an identifiable purpose. These actions came to be called "automatisms,"[4] actions that require no outside energy or direction.

Physiologists began to speculate about the application of the concept of the reflex arc to somnambulists. They developed this analogy: Like the decapitated frog, somnambulists perform purposeful actions which do not seem to arise from their ordinary consciousness; they act in ways that seem to imply thought and intention, but without the participation of their everyday awareness. These physiologists asked: Could this conundrum be explained as a kind of reflex action? The first to move in this direction was Thomas Laycock (1812–1876), professor of medicine at the University of Edinburgh, who began writing about this view in the *Edinburgh Medical and Surgical Journal* in the late 1830s. Laycock believed that there could be cerebral reflexes, comparable to spinal reflexes, by which a person's brain could convert outside stimuli into meaningful actions without the participation of the individual's consciousness. He was of the opinion that the "old metaphysics," which held that "mind considered as cause and consciousness

4. As an English word, "automatism" is of relatively recent origin, probably first occurring in 1838 (Anonymous, 1838).

were...identical" and that "reason was independent from brain function," was untenable (Laycock, 1876, p. 477). He took the position that all energies involved in human mental functioning originate in the organism and that psychological research produces no evidence showing that a separate mind or will causes changes in the brain. He termed the actual process, involving purely physiological factors, cerebral reflex action, and he declared that this principle applied even to "the highest work of intellectual faculties" (p. 1). In this way, he said, every living organism is an *automaton*, able to adapt itself to the external world without input from some extrinsic, rational, or spiritual influence (p. 486).

Similar views[5] were developed by William Carpenter (1813–1885), professor of medical jurisprudence in University College, London. Writing in his textbook *Principles of Human Physiology* (1855), he stated:

> But not only is much of our highest Mental Activity thus to be regarded as the expression of the *automatic* action of the Cerebrum:—we seem justified in proceeding further, and in affirming that the Cerebrum may act upon impressions transmitted to it, and may elaborate results such as we might have attained by the purposive direction of our minds to the subject, *without any consciousness* on our own parts; so that we only become aware of the operation which has taken place, when we compare the result, as it presents itself to our minds after it has been attained, with the materials submitted to the process. (p. 607)

Carpenter called this kind of cerebral elaboration outside awareness "unconscious cerebration," a term that immediately caught on and was incorporated into virtually all subsequent discussions of the issue. He believed unconscious cerebration accounted for everything from recall of forgotten words to the production of solutions to intellectual problems while one is sleeping and the emergence of fully formed literary or musical creations that are constructed without the conscious efforts of the author. He also believed that it explained the phenomena of somnambulism, both natural and artificial, as well as the phenomena of spiritualism.

In 1874 Thomas Huxley (1825–1895) entered the discussion of the problem of cerebral automatism through an address at Belfast to the British Association for the Advancement of Science entitled "On the Hypothesis that Animals are Automata, and its History" (Huxley, 1874). Using Descartes as his starting point, Huxley declared that it is undeniable that "reflex action" (occurring without the intervention of consciousness or will) is a part of ordinary human life. Therefore, he continued, if "actions of a certain degree of complexity are brought about by mere mechanism, why may not actions of still greater complexity be the result of a more refined mechanism?" (p. 564). Although he agreed with Descartes that animals are automata, Huxley did not accept his notion that they lacked consciousness. However, he proposed a novel way of seeing consciousness. He assumed

5. Carpenter's views were similar only up to a point, since he still held to the "old" view that Will, or Volition, was extra-physiological.

that all states of consciousness are caused by molecular changes in the brain and stated that: "The consciousness of brutes would appear to be related to the mechanism of their body simply as a collateral product of its working, and to be as completely without any power of modifying that working, as the steam-whistle which accompanies the work of a locomotive engine is without influence upon its machinery" (p. 575). Huxley went on to say that what is true of brutes is also true of human beings. Nevertheless, he insisted, this view of things does not rule out free will and does not, as some might charge, lead to fatalism, materialism, and atheism.[6]

The Views of F. W. H. Myers

Against this background of debate among physiologists and philosophers,[7] Myers was led by experimental evidence to a different picture. Experimenting with automatic writing in the early 1880s, Myers believed he had uncovered compelling evidence that a purely physiological explanation of apparently intelligent automatisms was insufficient. Myers contended that when physiologists attempted to explain mental automatisms they were operating under the mistaken assumption that consciousness is *unitary*. Philosophers had told them that consciousness and intelligence in human beings are coextensive. For the physiologist this would have to mean that if individuals perform actions of which they are not conscious, those actions have only the appearance of conscious intelligence and are really mere physiological reflexes, mere reproductions or recombinations of previous intelligent processes now repeated by rote. But, said Myers, if the consciousness of a person is not necessarily unitary, if it can be *multiple*, then new psychological vistas appear.

In an important article on automatic writing published in 1884, Myers took his initial stand against the position of the physiologists. Describing what he called the "Clelia" case of automatic writing, which included material that he considered to be evidence of telepathy, he made reference to Carpenter's formulation and stated what he believed was its inadequacy: "Throughout all these investigations we must keep *unconscious cerebration* steadily in view, and we shall, I think, find ourselves confronted with many of its results, and be induced continually to enlarge its field of action" (Myers, 1884, pp. 218–219).[8] Although here Myers was willing to keep the old terminology, by the next year he was no longer at ease with it, stating

6. One of those who did so charge was William James (see James, 1879).

7. For a more detailed discussion, see Crabtree (2003).

8. Later Myers would more explicitly spell out his objections: "I have explained that by these names [subliminal and supraliminal consciousnesses] I wish to protest against the undue extension of such phrases as 'unconscious cerebration,' and to insist that we have as good ground for attributing consciousness to some at least of these subliminal operations in ourselves as we have for attributing consciousness to the intellectual performances of our

that the facts of the Clelia case—particularly the writing of anagrams with meanings hidden to the automatist[9]—were "already overpassing very considerably the recognized limits of unconscious cerebration" (Myers, 1885b, p. 25).

Myers believed instead that the Clelia case and other cases of automatic writing indicated the presence of a second center of intelligent activity:

> It must be repeated, then, that this conclusion is already far enough from the accredited view as to the extent of the brain's unconscious operation. A *secondary self*—if I may coin the phrase—is thus gradually postulated,—a latent capacity, at any rate, in an appreciable fraction of mankind, of developing or manifesting a second focus of cerebral energy which is apparently neither fugitive nor incidental merely,—a delirium or a dream—but may possess for a time at least a kind of continuous individuality, a purposive activity of its own. (p. 27)

Myers repeatedly insisted that an adequate explanation for the phenomena in question had to be psychological, rather than physiological. In the process of developing his psychological schema, he devised a new psychological terminology—including such terms as "sub-conscious," "super-conscious," and "secondary self"—that had not existed in the literature before. Myers called for a new kind of psychology, one with a method that would ensure truly scientific results:

> The method to which I refer is that of *experimental psychology* in its strictest sense—the attempt to attack the great problems of our being not by metaphysical argument, nor by merely introspective analysis, but by a study, as detailed and exact as in any other natural science, of all such phenomena of life as have both a psychical and a physical aspect. Pre-eminently important for such a science is the study of abnormal, and I may add, of *supernormal,* mental and physical conditions of all kinds. (Myers, 1885c, p. 637)

Thus, in discussing how automatisms should be investigated, Myers made a strong plea for the establishment of a truly scientific psychology. Although he held that any purely physiological explanation of the kind of automatisms in question must fail, he insisted that if a psychological explanation of automatisms is to be believable, it must not involve elements that contradict the findings of physiology. Further, he insisted that as scientists psychological investigators must use methods that involve examining empirical data, proposing explanatory hypotheses, and devising experiments to test the validity of those hypotheses. He also stressed that to be truly scientific, psychology must investigate *all* types of human experience: the normal, the abnormal, and the supernormal—particularly not shying

---

neighbors" (Myers, 1892b, p. 327).

9. See Myers, 1885a, pp. 239–242; *HP*, vol. 1, p. 122.

away from the latter on the basis of philosophical bias (see Cook [Kelly], 1992, pp. 32–35, and Chapter 2 of this book).

Myers knew that his conception of multiple centers of consciousness operating within the psyche was novel and would not be easily accepted by conventional researchers:

> I have elsewhere endeavored to assign a wider range than orthodox science has yet admitted to the mind's unconscious operation. But the result of this further analysis has been (as I hold) not to show that ordinary physiological considerations will suffice (as Dr. Carpenter seems to suppose) to explain all the psychical problems involved, but rather to reveal the fact that these unconscious operations of the mind do not follow the familiar channels alone, but are themselves the facilitation or the starting-point of operations which to science are wholly new. (Myers, 1886a, p. lxii)

Myers stated that this new way of looking at things brought with it a whole new perspective on automatisms. His automatic writing experiments (and those of his colleague Edmund Gurney on hypnosis) were conducted with "normal" subjects, and he believed that the conclusions he arrived at were applicable to all human beings. He believed that he had adequately demonstrated that automatisms of a complex, intelligent kind, such as automatic writing, automatic speaking, automatic drawing, artistic creations that spring into consciousness fully formed, and hallucinations (such as veridical phantasms) of every kind, resulted from the action of additional centers of true conscious intelligence operating outside the normal awareness of the individual. He observed that experiences like these provide a glimpse of intelligent activity which has a brilliance that sometimes exceeds that of the ordinary self.

In an article on automatic writing published in 1889, Myers attempted to describe more completely the meaning of the word "automatism" in its psychological sense (as opposed to what he called "reflex" or "automatic" phenomena). To begin he stated that automatisms "parallel automatically whatever our conscious will, our conscious perception can discern or decree" (Myers, 1889a, p. 522). He went on to say that automatisms are, first, "independent"—that is, not related to some underlying physical pathology—and, second, "message-bearing" or "nunciative," meaning not that they bring messages from some source external to the automatist's mind, but that "they present themselves to us as messages communicated from one stratum to another stratum of the same personality. Originating in some deeper zone of a man's being, they float up into superficial consciousness as deeds, visions, words, ready-made and full-blown, without any accompanying perception of the elaborative processes that have made them what they are" (p. 524). Third, in some cases they are "veridical," that is, they correspond with objective facts not available to the automatist through normal means—an event, however, that is not to be seen as supernatural but as "supernormal" (p. 525).

Myers also made it clear that he did not conceive of the hidden secondary self as a single principle coordinate with the ordinary self, but rather pictured any number of "secondary manifestations of the self" (Myers, 1889a, p. 522). In 1888 he presented a grand formulation of his view of automatism and raised themes that became familiar in his later writings:

> I hold that hypnotism (itself a word covering a vast variety of different states) may be regarded as constituting one special case which falls under a far wider category,—the category, namely, of developments of a secondary personality. I hold that we each of us contain the potentialities of many different arrangements of the elements of our personality, each arrangement being distinguishable from the rest by differences in the chain of memories which pertains to it. The arrangement with which we habitually identify ourselves,—what we call the normal or primary self,—consists, in my view, of the elements selected for us in the struggle for existence with special reference to the maintenance of ordinary physical needs, and is not necessarily superior in any other respect to the latent personalities which lie alongside it,—the fresh combinations of our personal elements which may be evoked, by accident or design, in a variety to which we can at present assign no limit. I consider that dreams, with natural somnambulism, automatic writing, with so-called mediumistic trance, as well as certain intoxications, epilepsies, hysterias, and recurrent insanities, afford examples of the development of what I have called secondary mnemonic chains,—fresh personalities, more or less complete, alongside the normal state. And I would add that hypnotism is only the name given to a group of empirical methods of inducing these fresh personalities,—of shifting the centers of maximum energy, and starting a new mnemonic chain. (Myers, 1888a, pp. 387–388)

Myers categorized psychological automatisms under two heads: passive and active, or as he most commonly put it, sensory and motor. Motor automatisms included automatic writing, automatic speaking, automatic drawing, and use of the Chevreul pendulum. Sensory automatisms included apparitions, hallucinations, dreams, anesthesias, automatically manifested creative productions (such as literary or musical compositions), most hypnotic phenomena, and "idiot savant" phenomena. Also, the mediumistic phenomena of spiritualism, where not adjudged fraudulent, were treated as automatisms. What all psychological automatisms had in common was that they arose from some unknown inner conscious intelligence.

Automatisms include both normal and pathological manifestations. Myers believed that although the origins of these kinds of automatic phenomena are distinct, their pathways of manifestation may be held in common:

> And here I should wish to give a much wider generality to this principle, and to argue that if there be within us a secondary self aiming at manifestation by physiological means, it seems probable that its readiest *path of externalisation*—its readiest outlet of visible action,—may often lie along some track which has already been shown to be a line of low resistance

> by the disintegrating processes of disease. Or, varying the metaphor, we may anticipate that the partition of the primary and the secondary self will lie along some plane of cleavage which the *morbid* dissociations of our psychical synergies have already shown themselves disposed to follow. If epilepsy, madness, &c., tend to *split up* our faculties in certain ways, automatism is likely to split them up in ways somewhat resembling these. (Myers, 1885b, pp. 30–31)

Related Views of Some Major Contemporaries

Myers's views were noted and commented on by many of his contemporaries. Some, such as Pierre Janet, William James, T. W. Mitchell, and Morton Prince, found them stimulating and developed them in productive directions. Others, such as Sigmund Freud and William McDougall, were opposed to them in significant ways.

Pierre Janet

Pierre Janet, widely recognized for his experiments with hysterics, made use of Myers's revolutionary psychological approach to automatism to explain the existence of successive states of consciousness that were distinct from and unknown to the hysteric's ordinary awareness. In his journal articles of 1884 and 1885, Myers had already presented his novel ideas, and when Janet began to formulate his findings in 1886 he built upon Myers's work in several key areas: Myers's acknowledgment of unconscious and "sub-conscious" ideas (Myers, 1884, p. 219), his concept of secondary selves or centers of consciousness "dissociated" from the primary consciousness (Myers, 1885b, p. 31), and his recognition that these centers can act concurrently with each other (Myers, 1885a, p. 239). All of these elements show up in Janet's initial three scientific articles on his work with hysterics (Janet, 1886, 1887, 1888).

What we do *not* see in these initial publications is any significant use by Janet of the concept of automatism. That changed completely with the appearance in 1889 of Janet's doctoral thesis *L'automatisme psychologique*, where he brought together and expanded the findings of the three articles. Suddenly in this book, Myers's psychological approach to automatism becomes the central explanatory principle for the phenomena of hysteria. Janet did not explain this striking shift in perspective, but there can be little doubt that he took his lead from Myers, with whose writings he was very familiar. Janet's colleague, Alfred Binet noted the priority of Myers's work in his book on alterations of personality:

> We find here [in spiritistic phenomena], therefore, a new and curious example of mental disaggregation and division of personality. One of the authors who understands the true nature of spirit phenomena best, Mr. Myers, summed up the theory of multiple personality very exactly at a time when M. Janet's studies on somnambulism and my own on hysterical insensibility—which tend to the same result—were not yet begun. (Binet, 1896, p. 329)

William James (1901) also identified Myers as the originator of psychology's new framework:

> Myers's work on automatism led to his brilliant conception, in 1891, of hysteria. He defined it, with good reasons given, as "a disease of the hypnotic stratum." Hardly had he done so when the wonderfully ingenious observations of Binet, and especially of Janet in France, gave to this view the completest of corroborations. These observations have been extended in Germany, America, and elsewhere; and although Binet and Janet worked independently of Myers, and did work far more objective, he nevertheless will stand as the original announcer of a theory which, in my opinion, makes an epoch, not only in medical, but in psychological science, because it brings in an entirely new conception of our mental possibilities. (p. 19)

Despite these acknowledgments by Janet's own peers of Myers's priority, Janet himself was not as candid, and even today many of Myers's groundbreaking concepts are incorrectly attributed to Janet.[10] It was, however, Janet who, in *L'automatisme psychologique,* gave to the phenomenon Myers had been describing the name that has stayed with us to this day:

> We believe that one can accept simultaneously both automatism and consciousness and thereby give satisfaction to those who note in humans an elementary form of activity as completely determined as an automaton and to those who want to conserve for humans, in their simplest actions, consciousness and sensibility. In other words, it does not seem to us that in a living being the activity that manifests on the outside through movement can be separated from a certain kind of intelligence and from the consciousness that accompanies it inside, *and our goal is not only to demonstrate that there is a human activity that merits the name of automatic, but also that it is legitimate to call it a psychological automatism.* (Janet, 1889, pp. 2–3)[11]

Janet argued that the experience of hysterics indicates the existence of separate conscious centers (variously called "secondary selves," "secondary personalities," "subconscious personalities," and "new psychological existences") operating outside the field of ordinary consciousness. Furthermore, these centers were present and active in the hysteric co-temporally with ordinary consciousness; in other words, even while the individual car-

10. For a more detailed discussion of this issue, see Crabtree (2003).

11. All translations in this chapter are mine.

ried out ordinary tasks with ordinary mental involvement, these centers communicated with the researcher in a complex manner that was indistinguishable from ordinary intelligent action. Typically this communication occurred in the form of automatic writing of which the hysterical subject was unaware. Janet (1889) described the emergence of these centers in his subjects in this way:

> There can be many simultaneous subconscious personalities just as there can be many successive ones.... The conscious life of one of these subjects, of Lucie, for example, seems to be composed of three parallel streams, one under the other. When the subject is awake, the three streams exist: the first is the normal consciousness of the subject who speaks to us; the two others are groups of sensations and acts more or less associated among themselves, but absolutely unknown by the person who speaks to us. When the subject is put to sleep in the first somnambulism, the first stream is interrupted and the second surfaces. It shows itself in broad daylight and lets us see the memories it has acquired in its subterranean life. If we move on to the second somnambulism, the second stream is interrupted in its turn and only the third subsists, which then forms the whole conscious life of the individual. (pp. 333, 335)

As is well known today, Janet developed the concept of "dissociation" to describe those systems of ideas that exist in connection with a "subconscious" center of consciousness, but not connected with normal consciousness. He identified what he believed to be two laws of dissociation: first, that ideas can be conscious but not associated with that grouping of sensations and memories that make up the ordinary "I"; and second, that every phenomenon attached to a hysterical secondary personality is withdrawn from the awareness of the normal personality.

Janet conducted experiments which showed that secondary personalities can influence the ordinary consciousness of an individual without the individual having any awareness of that influence. They can, he said, operate in the background in such a way that in hypnotism, for instance, an individual may, through post-hypnotic suggestion, carry out actions that do not engage the person's ordinary consciousness. According to Janet, the dissociated and segmented life of the hysteric is the result of a pathological condition he named "psychological misery." He posited a "synthesizing force" that in normal people holds all their psychological experiences together in a unity, but in hysterics is excessively weak and fails in that task. The result is what he called a "psychological disaggregation," in which "fairly sizeable numbers of psychological phenomena are allowed to escape outside personal perception" (Janet, 1889, p. 337). Janet believed that where a person experiences traumatic events, a greater amount of synthesizing energy is needed to preserve psychic unity. In hysterics, with their congenitally low level of that force, the experiences were dissociated and led to other new subconscious personalities or were assimilated to already existing secondary personalities. Therapeutic work with hysterics, then, was aimed at uncovering the hidden secondary centers and dissolving them. In this way Janet was able to develop what might be counted as the first comprehensive and effective therapy for emotional disorders of the hysterical kind (Crabtree, 1993).

Janet considered the presence of covert centers of consciousness unknown to the individual to be invariably pathological. As a matter of fact, he claimed that if there is any subconscious activity at all, it is the result of pathology. So, said Janet, the state of perfect psychological health consists in this:

> *The power to synthesize being very great, all psychological phenomena, whatever their origin, are united in the same personal perception,* and consequently the second personality does not exist. In such a state there would be no distraction, no anesthesia (systematic or general), no suggestibility and no possibility of producing a somnambulism, since one could not develop subconscious phenomena, which would not exist. (Janet, 1889, p. 336)

Myers believed Janet's work was important but incomplete, largely because Janet worked exclusively with hysterics. Myers's experiments, on the other hand, were mostly with ordinary individuals who were able to develop automatic writing. In contrast to Janet, Myers used the unfolding data of psychological automatism to develop a wide-ranging and novel conception of the human psyche and human experience, dubbing the rich and variegated region of hidden psychological activity now emerging the "Subliminal Self." His ideas found support in many contemporary researchers, notably Binet in France (1890, 1896), Flournoy in Switzerland (1900/1983), Dessoir in Germany (1896), and, of course, James in America.

William James

Very early in his career, William James had struggled with what was called (based on the paper by Huxley quoted above) the "automaton theory." In a series of lectures titled "The Brain and the Mind" delivered in 1878 (James, 1878/1988), he argued that because we know the mind better than the nervous system, we cannot derive psychology from physiology, that is, explain psychological phenomena in purely physiological terms. Like Myers, James disagreed with Maudsley, who said that physiology is a full and sufficient basis for explaining mental experience (Perry, 1935, vol. 1, p. 28). In these lectures and in his article on Huxley's paper, James vehemently rejected the notion that automatism, as described by the physiologists, could provide an adequate basis for understanding human psychology. He insisted that the "subjective" or introspective method not only provided our most secure psychological knowledge, but it also provided a basis for interpreting the facts of brain physiology. Taking aim directly at Huxley, he wrote:

> Many persons now-a-days seem to think that any conclusion must be very scientific if the arguments in favor of it are all derived from twitching of

> frogs' legs— especially if the frogs are decapitated—& that, on the other hand, any doctrine chiefly vouched for by the feelings of human beings—with heads on their shoulders, must be benighted & superstitious. They seem to think too, that any vagary or whim, however unverified, of a scientific man must needs form an integral part of science itself; that when Huxley, for example, has ruled feeling out of the game of life, and called it a mere bystander, supernumerary, the matter is settled. I know nothing more deplorable than this indiscriminating gulping down of everything materialistic as peculiarly scientific. Nothing is scientific but what is clearly formulated, reasoned & verified. An opinion signed by the Pope if it have these merits will be a thoroughly scientific opinion. On the other hand, an opinion signed by Prof. Huxley, if it violate these requirements, will be unscientific. To talk of science as many persons do whose mental type is best represented by P. M. S. [Popular Science Monthly] is ridiculous. With these persons it is forever Science against Philosophy, Metaphysics, Religion, Poetry, Sentiment, against all that makes life worth living. (James, 1879, pp. 29–30; see also James, 1890b, chap. 5)

Although James here promoted an introspective approach as the most promising available, he had not yet arrived at a framework that comfortably embraced all available data. As indicated in the quotation of James that opens this chapter, the needed ingredient was eventually supplied by Myers and his psychologically based notion of automatism. With the advent of Myers's new perspective, James could embrace a concept of automatism that provided a psychological rather than physiological framework. In his review of Janet's *L'Automatisme psychologique* (James, 1890a), he stated his appreciation of the importance of this new perspective on automatism. Writing of the evidence produced by Janet's hysterical patients, James said: "It is therefore to no 'automatism' in the mechanical sense, that such acts are due: a self presides over them, a split-off, limited, and buried, but yet a fully conscious self" (p. 370).

Referring to the therapeutic value of Janet's work, James wrote:

> And this leads me to what, after all, is the really important part of these investigations—I mean their possible application to the relief of human misery. Let one think and say what one will about the crudity and intellectual barbarism of much of the philosophizing of our contemporary nerve-doctors; let one dislike as much as one may please the thoroughly materialistic attitude of mind which many of them show; still, their work, as a whole, is sanctified by its positive, practical fertility. Theorems about the unity of the thinking principle will always be, as they always have been, *barren*; but observations of fact lead to new issues *ad infinitum*....Who knows how many pathological states (not simply nervous and functional ones, but organic ones too) may be due to the existence of some perverse buried fragment of consciousness obstinately nourishing its narrow memory or delusion, and thereby inhibiting the normal flow of life? (pp. 371–372)

James then turned to the work of Myers on automatic writing, Edmund Gurney on hypnotism, and the findings of others, whose investigations had shown the coexistence of secondary selves with the primary one. Here, echoing Myers, he brought in his only real criticism of Janet's approach:

> My own decided impression is that M. Janet's generalizations are based on too limited a number of cases to cover the whole ground. He would have it that the secondary self is always a symptom of hysteria....The secondary and primary consciousnesses added together can, on M. Janet's theory, never exceed the normally total consciousness of the individual. This theory certainly expresses pretty well the facts which have fallen under the author's own observations, though even here, if this were a critical article, I might have something to say. But there are trances that obey another type....My *own* impression is that the trance-condition is an immensely complex and fluctuating thing, into the understanding of which we have hardly begun to penetrate, and concerning which any very sweeping generalization is sure to be premature. (p. 373)

It should not be surprising, then, that it was *Myers's* formulation of the theory of automatism to which James subscribed. In his second Lowell Lecture (E. Taylor, 1984, pp. 49–50), James defined automatism in terms drawn directly from Myers, calling them sensory and motor messages from the subliminal. He described them as physical or mental activity performed without the awareness of the conscious self, expressing a secondary but hidden dimension of personality. He gave examples of this transmission of information from the secondary to the primary self, concentrating on automatic writing, a phenomenon in which James had a particular interest (James, 1889).

On another occasion, James (1890–1896/1910) expressed his admiration for the way Myers was able to provide a framework that could bring all types of human experiences under one psychological umbrella:

> Whatever the judgment of the future may be on Mr. Myers' speculations, the credit will always remain to them of being the first attempt in any language to consider the phenomena of hallucination, hypnotism, automatism, double personality, and mediumship as connected parts of one whole subject. All constructions in this field must be provisional, and it is as something provisional that Mr. Myers offers us his formulations. But, thanks to him, we begin to see for the first time what a vast interlocked and graded system these phenomena, from the rudest motor-automatisms to the most startling sensory-apparition, form. Quite apart from Mr. Myers' conclusions, his methodical treatment of them by classes and series is the first great step toward overcoming the distaste of orthodox science to look at them at all. (p. 234)

Seeing automatisms as the key to psychopathological symptoms, James (1902/1958) noted that through the investigations of Binet, Janet, Breuer, Freud, and Prince,

> we have revealed to us whole systems of underground life, in the shape of memories of a painful sort which lead a parasitic existence, buried out-

> side of the primary fields of consciousness, and making irruptions thereinto with hallucinations, pains, convulsions, paralyses of feeling and of motion, and the whole procession of symptoms of hysteric disease of body and of mind. Alter or abolish by suggestion these subconscious memories, and the patient immediately gets well. His symptoms were automatisms, in Mr. Myers's sense of the word. (p. 193)

Before the formulations of either Myers or Janet, cases had been described in the literature of psychopathology suggesting the presence of more than one center of consciousness operating in an individual (Crabtree, 1993). The famous case of Félida X, described by Eugène Azam (1887), is one such example. At age 14 Félida began to experience bouts of profound sleep, after which she would wake up in a personality different from her ordinary one, which Azam called her "second state." Another example was Louie Vivé, who exhibited six distinct personalities, each with its own set of memories. Louie was studied by several well-known psychopathologists of the day, and his case was eventually described in detail in a book by Bourru and Burot (1888). Cases such as these were impressive evidence that one individual could house more than one source of intelligent action. But these, and most of the other examples in the literature (which begins in the late 18th century), had depicted *alternating* states and provided little evidence that the centers involved existed co-temporally. Only one case before the 1880s took that next step: the case of "Old Stump." William James (1889) himself described this case in an article on automatic writing. It concerned a woman, Anna Winsor, who had been under the care of a Dr. Ira Barrows of Providence, Rhode Island, from about 1860. The doctor's record of the case began when she was 19 and continued for several years. He described outbreaks of bizarre behavior and fits of self-destructive violence that made it impossible for the young woman to live a normal life. Shortly after he had begun treating Anna, Barrows noted a peculiar change. Her right arm suddenly became painful and then fell limp at her side. At the same time she looked at the arm in amazement, believing that it belonged to someone else and that her own right arm was drawn up behind her along her spine. Her right arm proved to be completely insensitive to pricking and other tests applied to it. Anna considered it a foreign object and a nuisance. She believed it was an arm and hand, but not hers. She also considered it intelligent and an intruder and tried to drive it away by biting it, pounding it, and pricking it. She called it "Stump" and "Old Stump."

The right arm did indeed appear to be governed by a secondary intelligence. When Anna in her delirium tried to pull her hair (with her left hand), Old Stump stopped her. Old Stump, whose intellectual development seemed more advanced than that of Anna, also wrote poetry, some of it partially in Latin (of which she "has no knowledge" [p. 553]), produced messages ostensibly from deceased individuals, made drawings, and communicated in writing with those around her—all while Anna was asleep or doing other things and not seeming to notice what Old Stump was up to. Barrows stated that when Anna was raving, Old Stump was rational, asking and answering questions in writing. Also, Old Stump seemed never to sleep, but watched over Anna during the night, seeing that she remained covered and rapping on the headboard to awaken Anna's mother when Anna experienced spasms or other problems.

This case strikingly illustrates the *concurrent* operation of two separate centers of consciousness in one individual. Each manifested as a personal system with its own ideas, intentions, and memory chains. The later work of Myers and Janet provided a great deal of additional material that indicated the co-temporal status of multiple centers. Myers's automatic writing subjects often wrote from a second center while they engaged in ordinary activities, such as reading or conversing, in their primary consciousness, and Janet's (1889) hypnotic experiments—with Léonie, for example—demonstrated the simultaneous activity of several secondary personalities. A case described by F. C. S. Schiller bears a certain resemblance to that of Anna Winsor in that a man, using two planchettes, one under each hand, simultaneously wrote two messages, dealing with entirely different subjects and purporting to come from two different personalities (*HP*, vol. 1, p. 420).

James, however, was especially interested in a further issue discussed by Myers, namely the patterns of mutual awareness holding among the concurrently active centers. Myers held that the consciousness of a subliminal personality could embrace knowledge of the thoughts and deeds of the supraliminal self. This might be thought of as a kind of inclusivity—not necessarily in the way a person's mind is inclusive of its *own* thoughts—but in some fashion which allows the thoughts of another personality to be directly perceived.[12] Myers did not speculate on whether this kind of inclusivity could also occur between two or more subliminal consciousnesses. However, he did indicate that the Subliminal Self (in the sense of the all embracing and ultimate source of unity beyond the multiplicity of an individual) encompasses all that occurs in the supraliminal and multiple subliminal centers (see Chapter 2).

James accepted and carried forward this difficult idea in his later works on problems in religion and metaphysics (see especially the conclusions of James, 1902/1958, and 1909/1971, Lecture 5). While these later efforts on the part of James to grapple with the fundamental issues raised by the scientific investigation of human experience were essentially ignored by most 20th-century psychologists as mere philosophizing, they were in fact his way of

---

12. There is no evidence that Myers believed that such a subliminal self necessarily perceives the thoughts (and actions) of the supraliminal self *as its own*—which would imply that the subliminal self would perceive itself as responsible for those thoughts (and actions). Such a position would, in fact, be hard to maintain in the face of a great many accounts in the literature of mesmerism and hypnotism in which, for example, a hypnotic personality explicitly distinguished itself from the primary personality and specifically disowned the attitudes and actions of that personality; these, and many instances of "dual personality" (e.g., Azam, 1887; Deleuze, 1813, vol. 1, p. 176; Despine, 1838, pp. 38–40; Ennemoser, 1852; Gregory, 1851, pp. 85, 486; James, 1889; Janet, 1889; Pigeaire, 1839, p. 44; Prince, 1905/1908; Richet, 1883, pp. 228–233) provide evidence that the experience of inclusivity does not necessarily, and perhaps not typically, involve a sense of common identity. Mitchell (1922, p. 223), on the other hand, said that one personality of a multiple may sometimes experience another as "part of itself."

carrying forward the thoroughly empirical spirit of Myers. And he was not alone in tackling this conceptually difficult subject. American psychologist and fellow Bostonian Morton Prince was among the foremost of Myers's contemporaries who grappled with issues relating to automatism and co-consciousness.

Morton Prince

Prince coined the word "co-consciousness" both to point to the reality of hidden centers of mental life and to convey the co-temporality of the multiple centers involved. Discussing such phenomena as automatic writing and speech, post-hypnotic suggestions, and similar phenomena, Prince (1907) wrote:

> Thus a "doubling" of consciousness results consisting of a personal self and the subconscious ideas. I prefer myself the term co-conscious to subconscious, partly to express the notion of co-activity of a second co-consciousness, partly to avoid the ambiguity of the conventional term due to its many meanings, and partly because such ideas are not necessarily *sub*-conscious at all; that is, there may be no lack of awareness of them. (pp. 67–68)

Prince also pointed out that the two centers of consciousness need not be unaware of each other. As in the case of Old Stump, there may be one-way or even mutual awareness without affecting the fact of separateness. Like Myers, Prince emphasized that secondary centers show every sign of intelligence and cannot be explained in purely physiological terms. In fact, he says, they should be treated as one might treat any separate intelligent person:

> The only grounds which I have for believing that my fellow beings have thoughts like myself are that their actions are like my own, exhibit intelligence like my own, and when I ask them they tell me they have consciousness, which as described is like my own. Now, when I observe the so-called automatic actions, I find that they are of similar character, and when I ask of whatever it is that performs these actions, Whether it is conscious or not? The written or spoken reply is, that it is and that consciously it feels, thinks and wills the actions, etc. The evidence being the same in the one case as in the other, the presumption is that the automatic intelligence is as conscious as the personal intelligence. (p. 69)

In his well-known study of the "Miss Beauchamp" case of multiple personality, Prince (1905/1908) attempted, among other things, to come to terms with the "inclusivity" aspect of co-consciousness. This case involved what Prince (1929) called three secondary personalities: BI, named "the Saint," who was characterized by piety and scrupulosity, meekness, and endless patience; BIV, named "the woman" and "the realist," who was strong, resolute, self-reliant, and easily provoked to anger; and Sally, who was mischievous, fun-loving, free from responsibility—all in all a child in character. While BI and BIV alternated with each other and became dormant when not in possession of the body, Sally was a co-conscious personality in a deeper sense. When she was not interacting in the world, she did not become dormant, but persisted and was active, often producing automatic phenomena in the other two personalities. Sally knew the thoughts, feelings, and actions of the other two personalities; also, when co-conscious, "she had perceptions of her environment which never entered the awareness of the principal consciousness. In this state she saw, heard and was generally cognizant of much that neither BI nor BIV consciously recognized" (p. 149). Prince noted that "a large mass of evidence goes to show that as a co-consciousness there were trains of thought and feelings that did not enter the conscious stream of the principal consciousness" (p. 149).

Sally maintained that she "knows everything Miss Beauchamp...does at the time she does it,—knows what she thinks, hears what she says, reads what she writes, and sees what she does; that she knows all this as a separate co-self, and that her knowledge does not come to her afterwards...in the form of a memory" (Prince, 1905/1908, p. 145). Sally would torment BI with practical jokes and called BIV an "idiot." Her whole attitude was that of a separate person with ideas and purposes of her own, who in no way felt identified with the others. Here we have another example of inclusiveness in the sense that the thoughts, feelings, and actions of one personality (or two) are known by another, without any sense of those thoughts, feelings, and actions belonging to that other.[13]

Although probably best known for his work with "Miss Beauchamp," Prince derived much of his evidence for co-consciousness from other sources, not least his work with automatic writing. Like Myers, he believed that the simultaneous functioning of two or more consciousnesses was the only possible way to explain much of the data observed. He also noted that automatic writing exhibits, as it were, grades of co-consciousness, from automatic writing produced while the writer's ordinary consciousness is completely alert and active to instances in which ordinary consciousness is nearly extinguished. He pointed out that in the latter case an argument

13. Later studies of multiple personality (e.g., Allison, 1980; Beahrs, 1982; Ludwig et al., 1972; F. W. Putnam, 1989; Ross, 1989) have also described this kind of inclusiveness, where one personality is aware of the activities of another personality "in real time," as it were, rather than, say, learning about those activities indirectly through some subsequent inner communication. Thus one personality was considered to be "co-conscious" with another when it was directly aware of what that other personality was doing while it was doing it, and "co-consciousness" referred to the internal state of a multiple in which this kind of awareness was operating. An alter personality might, for example, speak of "hearing" the thoughts of another personality or "seeing" the other personality do something. Having such awareness, however, did *not* mean experiencing the other personality as having the same identity as the alter or experiencing that other personality as part of the alter. Each of the two personalities involved would see the other as distinct in identity from him- or herself, in the same way that one human being sees another as separate and distinct.

can be made for an explanation based on alternating, rather than coexisting personalities, but that when ordinary consciousness is alert we encounter the strongest evidence for the co-temporality of the two centers, because we then see both the primary and the secondary consciousnesses operating in the same moment (Prince, 1907, pp. 72–74; for examples, see *HP*, vol. 1, pp. 169, 420, 589).

Echoing Myers, Prince insisted that the content of automatic writing rules out a purely physiological interpretation. The writings do not consist of words, phrases, and paragraphs that might be mere repetitions or memories of previous experiences, but rather are made up of original compositions. Sometimes they convey "fanciful fairy-tale-like fabrication," sometimes they provide ingenious answers to questions, and sometimes they indicate a personal character that contrasts to the normal character of the writer. He concluded: "If such a document were presented as testamentary evidence in the ordinary course of human affairs, it would seem as if the burden of proof would lie with him who would insist upon interpreting it as without psychological meaning and as only the expression of a physiological activity of the nervous system without thought" (Prince, 1907, p. 75).

Prince further pointed out that all conscious states, in our experience of them, "belong to, take part in, or help to make up a self" (p. 76). It is, in fact, difficult to conceive of a conscious state that is not associated with a self-conscious self. He stated that it would be "queer" to think of a state of consciousness or sensation or perception or idea as off by itself, not attached to anything we call a self. By emphasizing the psychological in this way, however, Prince insisted that he was not dismissing the physiological. He held that all thought is correlated with physiological activities, and he believed that the phenomena would ultimately require both a psychological and physiological explanation.

T. W. Mitchell

Thomas Walker Mitchell, physician, clinician, and editor of the *British Journal of Medical Psychology*, took a somewhat Janetian approach to explaining multiple centers of consciousness in the human psyche. Like Janet, he developed a theory of dissociation derived from his clinical experiences with hypnotism, hysteria, and multiple personality, and he had little to say about the possibility of hidden centers of consciousness that might be operating in the life of the average human being. Nevertheless, his penetrating discussion of central issues in the investigation of multiple centers renders his writings in this area important.

Mitchell accepted Myers's notion of a threshold of consciousness and said that he found the term "subliminal" most useful, because, as defined by Myers (*HP*, vol. 1, p. 14), it included every possible kind of mental phenomena occurring outside ordinary awareness. He also insisted that there was an urgent need to clear up the confusion that often showed itself in discussions of the various types of subliminal phenomena (Mitchell, 1921, p. 61). Specifically, he argued that there is a difference between what is conscious, what is unconscious, and what is dissociated (as described by Janet). He believed that Prince's terminology was best, stating that "by using Dr. Prince's term 'co-conscious,' we emphasize the important fact that in these dissociations we have an actual splitting of *consciousness*, not merely a splitting of the mind" (p. 61). By a splitting of consciousness he meant the recognition of co-conscious dissociated centers; by a splitting of the mind he meant the division between what is in some way or other conscious and what is unconscious; and by "unconscious" Mitchell meant those subliminal happenings which occur outside of consciousness and are incapable of entering into consciousness. He believed that Freud was most accurate in describing what is unconscious in this sense, but he felt that his explanation too had its faults (pp. 62–63).

Mitchell stated that dissociation can be said to occur when something that has been in consciousness becomes split off from it (p. 33). He believed that this splitting off results in an amnesia, or an inability to recall certain thoughts, feelings, or actions, and he noted that if a person who is experiencing this kind of amnesia is hypnotized, the thoughts, feelings, or actions can be reclaimed. But, he asked, when split off or dissociated, where do the thoughts and feelings go?

> Thoughts and feelings cannot be left floating about in the void, unclaimed by any thinker. We have no knowledge of any thoughts or feelings that are not the thoughts or feelings of some personal self. And we know that in becoming dissociated the split-off portions do not necessarily lose their quality of consciousness. While the patient is awake and aware of some things, dissociated sensations or perceptions may provide evidence of a concurrent discriminative awareness of other things, as effective as that which characterizes the sensory or perceptive activity of the conscious waking self. (pp. 33–34)

Mitchell was able to use his schema of dissociated ideas to successfully treat cases of multiple personality. He explained the formation of dissociated personalities in this way:

> A complex formed in relation to some event accompanied by great emotion may become dissociated from the personal consciousness, so that all recollection of the event and of the feelings and actions connected with it becomes impossible. A complex so dissociated does not cease to be capable of functioning....Many separate experiences may have taken part in the formation of a dissociated complex, but they are all bound together by some common element of feeling or emotion....[The dissociated mental complex] must somehow still form part of the structure of the mind. Did it not do so, it could never take possession of the bodily organism so as to manifest as a secondary personality....Just as we speak of a man being possessed by an idea, so we may speak of an idea developing to such an extent that it arouses a new personality. (Mitchell, 1922, pp. 105–114)

Recognizing that not all instances of multiple personality are the same, Mitchell (1912) distinguished two major types: alternating and co-conscious. In the first type,

> the split-off portions of the self seem to remain latent until the attack or alternation occurs. During their periods of latency they seem to be cut off from all experience and do not grow or develop in any way. There is a division of the self without any true doubling of consciousness. (p. 272)

This is a situation in which we simply have alternating personalities, where A is replaced by B, and then B is replaced by A. In this case neither knows the other directly—their paths never cross. In the second type, however,

> the dissociated portion of consciousness may never have formed a part of the waking self, and consequently cannot properly be described as a split-off part of the mind. When it is not in evidence as an alternating personality, it is not latent. It is co-conscious, and may have experience and grow and develop in the subconscious. There is a doubling of consciousness without any true division of the normal self. (pp. 272–273)

Here A is replaced by B, and then B by A, but B remains conscious (on a subliminal level with respect to A) and carries on with its activities while A is functioning in the world. Mitchell believed that the trance personalities (i.e., "controls") of mediums belonged in this class and attempted to clarify how they could have been formed in the first place:

> It is true that trance personalities do not, as a rule, alternate with the waking consciousness to the extent of taking possession of the whole bodily organism, and in many instances they afford no definite evidence of their existence as co-conscious activities. Yet in so far as their origin cannot be traced to any large splitting off or secession from the waking self, they seem to conform to the type of secondary personality whose growth and development take place entirely in the subconscious. I have assumed that the evolution of these personalities must be dependent on subconscious experiences in relation to the ordinary environment. But if, as some people think, man has an environment which transcends sense, it may be that this environment can affect the subconscious without having any noticeable influence on the waking self. It would then be legitimate to suppose that experience related to such an environment might sometimes take part in the formation of secondary personalities. (p. 274)

In his particular formulation of co-consciousness, Mitchell accepted the kind of inclusivity described by Myers and Prince. Like Myers, he accepted that the individual has a fundamental unity. He also believed that *alternating* manifestations of secondary selves might in principle be accounted for in terms of the activation of different neural systems. He argued, however, that this could *not* be the explanation for secondary personalities that were co-conscious with the primary. He stated the dilemma and his solution:

> A co-conscious personality's experience in so far as it is experience of the same things as that of the primary personality, must be obtained through the same sensory channels and must be subserved by the same neuronic systems. In so far as the co-conscious experience is a different experience, or an experience of different things, it must be due to the inclusion in the the functioning aggregate of a wider system of neural elements....In view of the occurrence of co-conscious personalities, we seem bound to look for some other ground of the felt unity of consciousness besides the spatial continuity of a nervous system through which a unitary soul may manifest. Such a ground may, perhaps, be found in the conception of a psychophysical threshold which delimits, though it does not constitute, personality....A permanently raised threshold will produce a curtailed personality. On the other hand, if the threshold is lowered, we get an expansion of the normal consciousness....Any considerable lowering of the threshold will produce hypnosis, and a permanently lowered threshold will lead to the formation of a hypnotic personality....Co-conscious personalities would be due to a doubling of the threshold at which consciousness can appear. The intensity of neural activity which is necessary for the appearance of *a consciousness* is not sufficient for the appearance of *the waking consciousness.* (pp. 279–281)

In a formulation which echoes that of Myers, Mitchell (1922) attempted to account for the unity in multiplicity in terms of a "soul":

> If, as the interactionists maintain, we have to postulate a soul as the ground of the unity of any consciousness, we must, of course, postulate a soul as the ground of the unity of each of the consciousnesses met with in multiple personalities of the co-conscious or hypnotic type. But there is no good reason why we should not regard one and the same soul as the effective ground in each and all of the phases of consciousness occurring in one individual. (p. 234)

Referring to the view of the philosopher Henri Bergson in regard to the relationship between body and mind, Mitchell argued that Bergson's conception of memory "helps us to understand how secondary personalities, even when exhibiting co-consciousness, may be manifestations of the activity of a single soul" (p. 235). This sounds very much like Myers's overarching Subliminal Self that contains and coordinates all that occurs in the human psyche.

William McDougall

In the process of working out his schema, Mitchell examined and rejected the solution of William McDougall, another major player in the discussion of automatism and co-consciousness. McDougall was a British psychologist who had a notable influence on psychological thinking in England and the United States in the first half of the 20th century. He was also a member of the Society for Psychical Research (SPR) and served a term as its president. McDougall was strongly critical of Myers's vision of subliminal selves, automatism, and multiple centers of consciousness. In his (1903) review of *Human Personality* (on our digital version), McDougall claimed that Myers subscribed to what William James had called "multiple monadism," the view that the individual is a system of psychic units each with its own degree of mental life, but had added to this an unacceptable additional doctrine that there is a profounder unity, the Subliminal Self, that coordinates this multiplicity (p. 515). McDougall developed a different monadic theory of the psyche, first alluded to in his book *Body and Mind* (McDougall, 1911/1961, p. 368n) and elaborated in his Presidential Address to the SPR (McDougall, 1920). Here he repudiated the views of Prince, Mitchell, and others on co-consciousness and made explicit how very different his understanding of the psyche was from that of Myers.

In this address he stated that, in *Body and Mind*, "I maintained that, however we conceive the body, we are compelled to conceive our conscious mental life as the activity of a unitary being endowed with the faculties of knowing, feeling and striving, the ego, soul, or self" (McDougall, 1920, p. 110). He went on to say that in the years intervening since the publication of that book, he had himself become involved with cases of nervous disorder that seemed at first glance to make this notion of a unitary ego untenable. These cases suggested that the self had been divided into two or more parts, each endowed with "the fundamental faculties of mind, conscious knowing, feeling and striving, a striving that expresses itself in part in the control of bodily movements" (p. 110). From such data, said McDougall, many had concluded that consciousness is a kind of stuff which can be combined, broken up, and recombined in many ways. However, he insisted that this conclusion was unjustified and that "the argument for the unity of the ego seems to me as strong and conclusive as ever" (p. 111). He did not deny the facts marshaled by those who accepted the notion of a divided self:

> I believe we are compelled to recognise that sometimes, and not infrequently, a single human organism or person is the seat of more than one stream of conscious knowing, feeling and striving, more than one train of mental activity; and that these trains may be not only distinct, but may be in acute opposition and conflict one with another, just as really as I may be in conflict with you, a conflict of purposes, of efforts towards different ends. If my former conclusion holds good, it follows that each of such distinct streams of purposive effort is the activity of a unitary self or ego. Are we then to fly to the ancient theory of possession, whenever we observe evidence of such multiplicity of distinct mental activities with a single organism? By no means. The obvious and, I believe, inevitable inference from the facts is that I who consciously address you am only one among several selves or egos which my organism, my person, comprises. I am only the dominant member of a society, an association of similar members. There are many purposive activities within my organism of which I am not aware, which are not my activities but those of my associates.... My subordinates serve me faithfully in the main, provided always that I con-

> tinue to be resolute and strong. But, when I relax my control, in states of sleep, hypnosis, relaxation and abstraction, my subordinates, or some of them, continue to work and then are apt to manifest their activities in the forms we have learnt to call sensory and motor automatisms. And if I am weak and irresolute, if I do not face the problems of life and take the necessary decisions for dealing with them, then conflict arises within our system, one or more of my subordinates gets out of hand, I lose my control, and division of the personality into conflicting systems replaces the normal and harmonious co-operation of all members in one system. And in extreme cases such a revolted subordinate, escaped from the control of the dominant member or monad, may continue his career of insubordination indefinitely, acquiring increased influence over other members of the society and becoming a serious rival to the normal ruler or dominant. (pp. 111–112)

McDougall illustrated what this conception means in concrete experience. In dreams, he stated, I, the dominant monad, become passive and inert, and my subordinates may continue to think. These thoughts are experienced as dream-images and dream-thoughts and have a quality very different from those of myself, the dominant monad. The reason is that since they emanate from a subordinate monad, they must be "more primitive, nearer to the purely organic and instinctive than my own,"—something we must assume, since they are lower in position in the hierarchy (p. 115). In hypnosis too, continued McDougall, subordinate monads are at work, independent of my control. The experience of dreams, hypnotism, and other automatisms shows that each monad retains the memory of its own activities and can obtain awareness of the actions of other monads only through hypnosis or other special techniques.

Turning to the issue of survival of death, McDougall stated that "I, if I survive the dissolution of my bodily organism, shall, by our hypothesis, retain only those functions which I have not delegated but have developed by active exercise and those memories which are most truly mine, the memories of my own activities" (p. 120). Thus, for McDougall it is the everyday "I," the dominant monad, that might survive, and I, as a monad, no longer function as the commander-in-chief of the hierarchy that characterized my earthly existence. Just what the new existence may be is not clear, but McDougall speculated that monads may form new societies after death.[14]

I have quoted at length from McDougall's talk because it represents, in clear and uncompromising terms, one very specific view of the relationship between centers of consciousness within human beings. Although McDougall agreed with Myers in accepting co-conscious centers, he conceived of their character and relationships in a way that is radically different from Myers's conception. McDougall conceived of human personality as a hier-

---

14. We cannot assume from this that McDougall was personally convinced of survival. In *Body and Mind* (1911/1961) he wrote: "A considerable mass of evidence pointing in this direction [survival] has been accumulated....Nevertheless...again and again the evidential character of the observations has fallen just short of perfection" (p. 347).

archical arrangement of conscious "monads," one which is given order from the top—the ordinary conscious self—down.[15]

This view faces a variety of empirical difficulties, however. First, we do not have any conscious awareness of planning and commanding in the sense he describes. Neither does he provide a way to understand asymmetrical consciousness between dissociated personalities, where a "subordinate" monad would know of the thoughts and activities of the dominant monad, but not vice versa; this is surprising, because McDougall (1911/1961) eventually accepted the idea that such relations exist (pp. 366–368n; 1926, pp. 255, 349–350, 490–506). Nor does he make any attempt to account for the supernormal capacities sometimes exhibited by subordinate monads, although he clearly accepted that such capacities exist (1911/1961, chap. 25). Also, in this schema the monads pre-exist, presumably from birth, but there is no way to know anything about them or how the various functions of the whole are divided among them. Speculation about what those functions might be quickly bogs down. If the dominant monad orders the movement of a hand, is there a subordinate monad, a "motor movement monad," that carries out that command? Or is there a hand monad charged with all hand activities? If the dominant monad orders the writing of an essay, what monads are involved? It is impossible to come up with anything but the most arbitrary division of monadic function in attempting to answer such questions.

In struggling with the phenomena of automatism, Myers too came to the conclusion, as we have seen, that the only possible way of explaining what occurs is to posit separate centers of consciousness with their own memory chains, centers that in some cases can be considered full-fledged personalities in the sense that in their communications they exhibit all the sorts of qualities that we normally associate with independent selves. As he investigated the phenomena further, however, Myers realized that he had opened the door to a rich and dynamic world of hidden activity in the human psyche, the world of "subliminal" or "ultra-marginal"[16] consciousness. Contrary to McDougall's notion that the unity of the individual human being is produced top-down by the everyday conscious self, a commander-in-chief overseeing lesser but autonomous selves, Myers conceived of the psyche's unity as deriving from something beyond anything ordinary consciousness can directly perceive.

Myers referred to that underlying unity as the "Self" with a capital "S" (although he was not wholly consistent with this), something distinct from other manifestations of selfhood that he described. Myers used the word "self" (small "s") as "a descriptive term for any chain of memory sufficiently continuous, and embracing sufficient particulars, to acquire what is popu-

---

15. Some years earlier, the philosopher Gerald Balfour, in his Presidential Address to the SPR, had proposed a similar view (Balfour, 1906; see also Balfour, 1935, pp. 311–314, which further develops these views in the context of an extended critique of Myers's theory of the Subliminal Self). We will return to this in Chapter 9.

16. For a discussion of James's understanding of this expression of Myers, see E. Taylor (1996).

larly called a 'character' of its own. There will thus be one distinct supraliminal self at a time; but more than one subliminal self may exist, or may be capable of being called into existence" (Myers, 1892b, pp. 305–306n).

With regard to "self" (small "s"), Myers held that all psychical action that occurs in the individual, subliminal and supraliminal, occurs with consciousness and is included in an actual or potential memory. Although he had himself sometimes done so, Myers thought that to speak of a "secondary" self could be misleading, because one might give the mistaken impression that there cannot be more selves than two and because it could cause one to believe that the supraliminal self, the empirical self of common experience, was in some way superior to the subliminal self—something that Myers explicitly denied. He insisted that "the arrangement with which we habitually identify ourselves,—what we call the normal or primary self…is not necessarily superior in any other respect to the latent personalities which lie alongside it" (Myers, 1888a, p. 387). In other words, the ordinary consciousness, the supraliminal self, had no privileged position in respect to those "arrangements" called subliminal selves or personalities. In fact, a central part of Myers's doctrine is that these normally hidden strata of the psyche have access to wider ranges of information and faculty than the everyday self. This view is in stark contrast to that of McDougall, who insisted on the superiority of the monad that is the self of everyday life. Said Myers:

> Sometimes we seem to see our subliminal perceptions and faculties acting truly in unity, truly as a Self;—co-ordinated into some harmonious "inspiration of genius," or some profound and reasonable hypnotic self-reformation, or some far-reaching supernormal achievement of clairvoyant vision or of self-projection into a spiritual world. Whatever of subliminal personality is thus acting corresponds with the highest-level centres of supraliminal life. At such moments the *subliminal* represents (as I believe) most nearly what will become the *surviving* Self. *(HP*, vol. 1, p. 73)

The views of Myers and McDougall provide strongly contrasting depictions of the organization of human personality. Elements of these two conceptions may be found in the other formulations that took shape during the course of the 20th century, but we can think of these two as the canonical forms, recurring again and again with various nonessential modifications, as we shall see below in this chapter.

It should be clear, however, that there were important issues on which McDougall agreed with Myers. Specifically, in relation to the issues of this chapter, they agreed that multiple centers of consciousness exist, that they function concurrently, that they can display awareness of each other, and that they underlie psychological automatisms. None of these views were shared by another influential contemporary, Sigmund Freud, to whom I next turn.

Sigmund Freud

The writings of Sigmund Freud present a view of mental activity outside ordinary awareness that stands in sharp contrast to those we have so far discussed. Freud paid little attention to instances of psychological automatism, so plentiful in the psychological literature, and the lack of any systematic assessment of this variegated data in his writings is striking. Nonetheless, his explanation of the concept of consciousness does have a bearing on our discussion and must be given serious attention.

Already in his *Interpretation of Dreams*, Freud took the view that what is psychical must not be considered equivalent to what is conscious. Here he wrote: "This enables us to form a quite definite view of the 'essential nature' of consciousness: we see the process of a thing becoming conscious as a specific psychical act, distinct from and independent of the process of the formation of a presentation or idea; and we regard consciousness as a sense organ which perceives data that arise elsewhere" (Freud, 1900/1964, p. 144). From this it is clear that Freud saw consciousness as unitary and ruled out any notion of multiple conscious centers. However, at this point we have little more than this simple statement on the matter, because Freud had not yet fully developed his notion of consciousness.

In a paper titled "A Note on the Unconscious in Psycho-Analysis," considered one of his most important theoretical papers, Freud went into the matter of the unicity of consciousness in greater depth. Before discussing the content of this paper, it is important to say something about factors surrounding its publication.

The paper appeared in 1912 as an article in the SPR *Proceedings*, written by Freud in response to a request from that journal to contribute to a special medical section. The significance of this publishing venue has been discussed in an intriguing article by James Keeley (2001) in which the author presents convincing arguments that Freud acquiesced to the request because he wanted to make a long delayed answer to comments made by Myers about Freud's work some 18 years earlier in the same journal. Keeley claims that there are "surprisingly close textual relations between 'A Note' and Myers's work, especially Myers's article 'The Mechanism of Hysteria'" (Myers, 1893a), in which he mentioned Freud's work. Keeley (2001) uses this and other arguments to make the case that Freud intended his article to be a strong statement—in Myers's own back yard, so to speak—not only about the central theoretical concepts of psychoanalysis, but also about how psychoanalysis had transcended its roots in late 19th-century investigations of hypnosis and concomitant phenomena—represented particularly by the work of Myers—and had thus become a fully fledged, independent, and (in his view) correct scientific psychology. Keeley states that, as Freud's first systematic theorization of the unconscious, this essay is a "crucial text in the history of psychology: the textual site of Freud's liberating himself from the influence of nineteenth-century psychology, as represented by the SPR's psychology of the subliminal self" (p. 772).

Myers, in the article mentioned above, was the first to introduce Freud and his ideas to the English-speaking world. He referred to the work of Freud and Breuer with appreciation and cited their findings as welcome confirmation from medical clinical practice of ideas he had himself developed about subliminal mental processes. At the same time, Myers implied that Freud and Breuer were latecomers to the work originally begun by himself, Edmund Gurney, and Pierre Janet. Although Myers wrote positively of Freud and Breuer, he also made the point that the investigation of psychological pathology, such as they had been engaged in, could go only so far, and that it was only through the study of subliminal phenomena in the healthy that the full story would be told (Myers, 1893a, p. 14). It is Keeley's (2001) contention that, whatever Freud may have thought about Myers's comments in 1893, by 1912 he was ready to tell the world that psychoanalysis had become a psychology of unparalleled depth that had left far behind its beginnings in the 19th-century practice of hypnotism, and embodied its own distinctive theories and methods. Keeley also believes that Myers's mention of the name of Janet (with whom Freud had in the intervening years developed a bitter rivalry) as an investigator who had priority of ideas over Freud would have provided further motivation for Freud to present his contrary views. What is important about Keeley's article for our purposes is its presentation of the ways in which Freud distinguished the "Unconscious" of psychoanalysis from Myers's "Subliminal Self" and where that put Freud in relation to the concepts of automatism, co-consciousness, and secondary personality.

Freud (1912) began "A Note" by making clear what he meant by "conscious" and "unconscious." He wrote:

> Now let us call "conscious" the conception which is present to our consciousness and of which we are aware, and let this be the only meaning of the term "conscious." As for latent conceptions, if we have any reason to suppose that they exist in the mind...let them be denoted by the term "unconscious." Thus an unconscious conception is one of which we are not aware, but the existence of which we are nevertheless ready to admit on account of other proofs or signs. (pp. 312–313)

He then tackled the belief that consciousness can be split up in such a way that some ideas or psychical acts might be said to constitute a "consciousness apart" which has become estranged from "the bulk of conscious activity" (p. 315). Freud acknowledged first that such a view might seem to be supported by cases of dual personality, such as that described by Azam (1887), which I mentioned earlier. But we are not justified, said Freud, in extending the word "conscious" so far that it includes a consciousness of which the "owner" him- or herself is not aware. He then went on to say that if philosophers find it hard to accept the existence of unconscious ideas, they should find it even more difficult to accept that there can be such a thing as an "unconscious consciousness." He suggested that, instead of talking about a "splitting of consciousness," as in the case of dual consciousness described by Azam, it would make most sense to say that we are dealing with a "shifting of consciousness," where that function simply oscillates between two different psychical complexes "which become conscious and unconscious in alternation" (p. 315).

If Myers were reading this explanation, he would object that the example Freud chose to illustrate his position, Azam's dual personality case of Félida X, is one that was widely recognized to be subject to an alternating-consciousness explanation and therefore could not serve as a test case for automatism and co-consciousness. Already in the 1870s, the case of Félida X had been understood as a shifting of consciousness from one state to another for which no further explanation was needed. What Freud would find more difficult to explain with his unitary consciousness theory would be those numerous cases in which two apparent intelligences communicate *simultaneously*. That, after all, was the kind of case that led Myers, James, Janet, and eventually many others to the notion of psychological automatism and a conception of the situation that would later be called co-consciousness. If Freud could not explain examples of psychological automatism with temporal co-consciousness, his theory was incomplete, if not erroneous.

Freud (1915/1964) returned to the issue of the unity of consciousness in *The Unconscious*, but there did little more than repeat what he had set forth in his article of 1912. In *An Autobiographical Study*, however, Freud (1925/1964) took the discussion one step further and launched an explicit, concerted attack on Pierre Janet and his idea of multiple centers of consciousness. Chafing at Janet's often repeated charge that much of psychoanalysis derived from his own work, Freud was at pains to show how little his ideas had in common with Janet's and therefore how absurd the accusation of intellectual dependence was. He stated his differences in the plainest terms possible: "Psycho-analysis regarded every thing mental as being in the first instance unconscious; the further quality of 'consciousness' might also be present, or again it might be absent" (p. 31). He took pains to chide those "philosophers" for whom "conscious" and "mental" were identical and who could not accept the notion of an "unconscious mental." Taking up Janet's view, Freud pointed out what he considered an unsolvable dilemma: "Anyone who tried to push the argument further and to conclude from it that one's own hidden processes belonged actually to a second *consciousness* would be faced with the concept of a consciousness of which one knew nothing, of an 'unconscious consciousness'—and this would scarcely be preferable to the assumption of an 'unconscious mental'" (p. 32).

To anyone who has actually read Janet (and Myers), Freud's stand is, to say the least, puzzling, and one might wonder if Freud was being deliberately obtuse in his interpretation of Janet's "unconscious mental acts." It was precisely because his hysterical subjects exhibited what he considered irrefutable evidence for a "consciousness of which one knew nothing" that Janet felt compelled to posit unconscious mental acts. It was clear even from Janet's very first writings on the matter that he used the word "unconscious" with a very specific meaning: It meant unconscious *in relation to the subject's ordinary, everyday consciousness.* He certainly never claimed that he had discovered a consciousness that was unconscious *in itself.* That absurdity, which Freud takes to be Janet's meaning, cannot be attributed to him. Whether Freud was setting up a Janetian straw man for easy destruction or simply missed the obvious meaning of Janet's statements, we cannot know. What is clear is that in this crucial theoretical matter Freud clearly separated himself from Myers, Janet, and the other authors cited above, and rejected any picture of unconscious mental activity that could be called co-conscious with ordinary, everyday awareness.

This theoretical stance made it very difficult for psychoanalysis to deal with dissociative disorders in general and multiple personality disorder in particular, something that was recognized by Freud's contemporaries. In his Presidential Address to the Medical Section of the British Psychological Society, Bernard Hart (1926) took Freud and psychoanalysis to task for failing to account for the phenomena of dissociation in their theoretical constructions (pp. 253–256).[17] In one of his few attempts to account for the possibility of multiple personalities, Freud (1923/1964) wrote:

> If [the ego's object-identifications] obtain the upper hand and become too numerous, unduly powerful, and incompatible with one another, a pathological outcome will not be far off. It may come to a disruption of the ego in consequence of the different identifications becoming cut off from one another by resistances; perhaps the secret of the cases of what is described as "multiple personality" is that the different identifications seize hold of consciousness *in turn* [italics added]. Even when things do not go so far as this, there remains the question of conflicts between the various identifications into which the ego comes apart, conflicts which cannot after all be described as entirely pathological. (pp. 30–31)

This rather strained explanation, which left the problem of co-consciousness unexplained, was, it seems, the best that could be done if the unity of consciousness was to be preserved at all costs.

Freud's idea that there can be mental acts that lack consciousness placed him in the unenviable position so ably criticized by William James when asking whether states of mind can be unconscious. James (1890b) argued persuasively that such a view was "the sovereign means for believing what one likes in psychology and of turning what might become a science into a tumbling-ground for whimsies" (vol. 1, p. 163), and James's concerns have been echoed by more recent critics of psychoanalysis.

Compelling arguments against Freud's conception of conscious and unconscious mental states have also been advanced by philosopher John Searle (e.g., Searle, 1992, pp. 165–171). He states that, since Freud sees these

---

17. Despite this criticism of psychoanalysis, Hart contended that when discussing dissociation, Janet and Freud were operating on two entirely different levels and that what appeared to be rival theories were in fact two different stages of inquiry (for a description of Hart's view, see Crabtree, 1986, pp. 97–100). Unfortunately, Hart did not tackle the crucial issue of *co-consciousness* and for that reason failed to see the incompatibility of the two positions.

states as *mental* (that is, as what Searle would call "occurrent intrinsic intentional states") even when they are unconscious, Freud is asserting that the distinction between conscious and unconscious mental states is not a distinction between two kinds of mental states—since, for him, *all* mental states are in themselves unconscious. Searle notes that Freud sees bringing such mental states to consciousness on the analogy of perceiving an object:

> What we call "consciousness" is just a mode of perception of states that are unconscious in their mode of existence. It is as if the unconscious mental states really were like furniture in the attic of the mind, and to bring them to consciousness we go up in the attic and shine the flashlight of our perception on them. Just as the furniture "in itself" is unseen, so mental states "in themselves" are unconscious. (p. 168)

Searle goes on to say that "I cannot find or invent a coherent interpretation of this theory" (p. 168). Specifically, he states that he cannot find a way to make this notion of the ontology of the unconscious consistent with current knowledge of the brain and that he cannot form a coherent analogy between perception and consciousness. In regard to the latter problem, he points out that "the model of perception works on the assumption that there is a distinction between object perceived and the act of perception" (p. 171). He argues that this distinction simply cannot apply to conscious thoughts. Further, he describes why the perception theory of consciousness cannot stand, because if bringing unconscious states into consciousness consists in having a perception of previously unconscious mental phenomena, and if this act of perceiving is itself considered a mental phenomenon (and thus "in itself" unconscious), then this act of perception requires a further, higher act of perception to bring it to consciousness, and so forth; in this way one is left with the need for ever-higher acts of perception, involving one in an "infinite regress."

It seems that the fatal flaw in Freud's view of conscious and unconscious acts is to consider that mental acts are "in themselves" unconscious. The view held by Myers might be stated as the contrary: that all mental acts are "in themselves" conscious. This view escapes the telling criticisms of James and Searle and provides a ready framework for understanding the data of automatism that remained so opaque for Freud.

Despite their major differences, Freud did have important areas of agreement with Myers. Both hoped for ultimate reconciliation between psychology and physiology but repudiated, on the basis of empirical evidence, the premature and glib reductionism of 19th-century neurology. Both also insisted that mind was not co-extensive with everyday consciousness; and both held that the "mental" which operates outside ordinary awareness is governed by laws of its own, laws whose exploration had only just begun. However, Myers's belief that the Subliminal is the source of both the pathological and the sublime, disturbance and inspired genius, the normal and the supernormal, contrasted with Freud's description of the Unconscious. Also, Freud could not agree with Myers's conviction that our everyday "terrene" consciousness cannot be considered superior to that of subliminal selves, and that there is an ultimate personal unity, referred to as the Subliminal Self (with a capital "S"), that coordinates all human experiences. Above all, Freud's rejection of the possibility of multiple subliminal centers of consciousness and his insistence that the only consciousness is the one we know in everyday life opened a great gulf between his conception of the psyche and that of Myers.

As Keeley points out, Freud's rejection of his roots in the mesmeric/hypnotic tradition[18] were stated and confirmed in "A Note." His opposition to the conception of the Subliminal Self and its offshoots had dramatic effects on the subsequent development of psychology and dynamic psychiatry, for Freud's psychoanalysis came to dominate modern clinical psychological thinking and in the process squeezed out the older tradition.[19]

Carl Jung

The psychological system of Freud's one-time protegé, Carl Jung, was more friendly to the ideas initiated by Myers. Jung studied for a time under Janet, was strongly influenced by Flournoy, with whom he had a friendship, and was acquainted with Myers's writings. Already in his doctoral thesis, Jung (1902/1983) mentions Myers, citing his "Clelia" case of automatic writing (pp. 52–53). In his "On the Nature of the Psyche," Jung (1946/1978) refers to the work of Myers when citing the passage from James's *Varieties of Religious Experience* (quoted at the start of this chapter) and points to the recognition of a mental life outside normal consciousness as the discovery by which the "old psychology was thoroughly unseated and as much revolutionized as classical physics had been by the discovery of radioactivity" (p. 167).

Jung's theory of complexes contains the notion that human beings are comprised of many fragmentary personalities. He saw complexes as a collection of images and ideas which cluster around a core that embodies one or more archetypes and are characterized by a common feeling tone (Samuels, Shorter, & Plaut, 1991, pp. 33–34). He wrote of the fact that the psyche has a tendency to split:

18. This tradition was what Ellenberger (1970) called the "first dynamic psychiatry" (p. 111).

19. Throughout the decades of the latter half of the 20th century, orthodox Freudian thinkers for the most part did not stray far from the view expressed by the master. However, some recent psychoanalytic writings have begun to move away from the strict one-consciousness view. An example of this new take on psychoanalytic theory can be found in the writings of James Grotstein, who, in his *Who is the Dreamer Who Dreams the Dream?* (2000), for example, posits an array of subselves who act from their own initiative and display all the characteristics of independently conscious centers.

> Although this peculiarity is more clearly observable in psychopathology, fundamentally it is a normal phenomenon....The tendency to split means that parts of the psyche detach themselves from consciousness to such an extent that they not only appear foreign, but lead an autonomous life of their own. It need not be a question of hysterical multiple personality, or schizophrenic alterations of personality, but merely of so-called "complexes" that come entirely within the scope of the normal. (Jung, 1937/1978, p. 121)

Jung (1934/1978) stated that "there is no difference in principle between a fragmentary personality and a complex" and that experience had showed him that complexes are really "splinter psyches" (p. 97).[20]

In "A Review of the Complex Theory" Jung explicitly associates his view of the complex with those of Janet and Morton Prince in regard to the dissociability of consciousness into "fragmentary personalities" (pp. 96–97). Although Jung says that for all practical purposes fragmentary personalities are complexes, he does not necessarily hold that all complexes are fragmentary personalities. So "splinter psyches" and "fragmentary personalities" are not clearly the same things. For that reason he can say that personality fragments "undoubtedly have their own consciousness, but whether such small psychic fragments as complexes are also capable of a consciousness of their own is a still unanswered question" (p. 97). He points out that complexes can look very much like separate consciousnesses analogous to our ego consciousness. But they seem to act differently in important ways—sometimes behaving like devils playing impish tricks, inducing embarrassing slips of the tongue or inappropriate physical actions, and sometimes taking on the role of actors in our dreams (p. 97). His hesitation to say that these complexes have their own consciousness is based on the fact that they seem to be "unteachable"—they refuse to do our bidding. He develops this idea in his "On the Nature of the Psyche," where he writes that "feeling-toned complexes" when unconscious cannot be altered the way they can be when conscious:

> Although they may be enriched by associations, they are not corrected, but are conserved in their original form, as can easily be ascertained from the continuous and uniform effect they have upon the conscious mind. Similarly, they take on the uninfluenceable and compulsive character of an automatism, of which they can be divested only if they are made conscious....These peculiarities of the unconscious state contrast very strongly with the way complexes behave in the conscious mind. Here they can be corrected. (Jung, 1946/1978, pp. 186–187)

In ruminations that remind one of the argument between Freud and Janet referred to above, Jung speculates that perhaps there is "no unconscious psychism which is not at the same time conscious" (p. 188). He says

---

20. In an early description of the formations of "unconscious personalities," Jung (1902/1983) states that they are due to the "disaggregation of psychic complexes" (p. 53).

that while it is true that as far as our ego, or ordinary consciousness, is concerned, they are for all practical purposes unconscious, yet they may, in themselves, be conscious, "for the ego may know these contents under one aspect but not know them under another aspect, when they cause disturbances of consciousness....Finally there are cases where an unconscious ego and hence a second consciousness are present, as we have already seen" (p. 188). It is clear, then, that Jung, like Janet and unlike Freud, had room for a consciousness, a fragmentary personality, that is unknown to (unconscious to) the ordinary ego, and so constitutes a secondary ego with its own separate consciousness. But whether complexes, or splinter psyches, can be considered to be conscious in the same way remains, for Jung, in doubt.

Jung's ideas were in many ways compatible with those of Myers and were not subject to the objections leveled against Freud's one-consciousness theory. His "fragmentary personalities" have qualities similar to the secondary personalities of Myers, and his concept of the Self in some ways resembles Myers's overarching, unifying Subliminal Self. Also, like Myers, Jung connected the activity of fragmentary personalities with creativity on the one hand and mediumship on the other.

Psychological Automatism: More Recent Work

The lively debates about consciousness and automatism just reviewed extended into the early 20th century but then subsided, largely due to the impact of the rise of behaviorism and the fracturing of psychology into clinical and experimental wings (see Introduction). Some interest continued on the clinical side, but for over a half century most experimental psychologists as a matter of principle would have little or nothing to do with these subjects. For many decades, William James himself was more or less drummed out of the profession by behaviorist historians of psychology such as E. G. Boring. After this extended hiatus, a new generation of psychologists began to take interest in the neglected and still unsolved problems relating to automatisms and the multiplicity of consciousness.

Ernest Hilgard

Ernest Hilgard (1977) has proposed a "neo-dissociation" schema for dealing with the problem of automatism. Echoing McDougall's "monadic" conception, Hilgard posits a hierarchical arrangement of subordinate cognitive subsystems which are controlled by an executive monitoring system. Automatisms occur when executive control is cut off from various subsystems, which then function on their own. In these cases, an amnesic barrier is formed which causes incoming information to be dissociated from consciousness.

Hilgard's (1994) theory rests on three assumptions: (1) that subordinate cognitive systems exist, each with some degree of unity, persistence, and autonomy of function, and that these systems interact, but on occasion can become somewhat isolated from each other; (2) that some kind of hierarchical control exists that normally manages the interactions among these systems, and that without such control the individual would be overwhelmed by thoughts and actions all of which would be trying to happen at once; and (3) that there must be an overarching monitoring and controlling structure which determines the hierarchical arrangement of the overall system (pp. 38–39).

In Hilgard's schema, the action of an executive ego or central control structure, apparently identified with the ordinary consciousness of everyday life, is essential to account for planning and choosing which subsystems will dominate at any particular moment. Hypnosis takes away much of the subject's normal control and changes the functions and hierarchical arrangement of the subsystems, so that motor controls may be altered, perception and memory distorted, hallucinations produced, and so on.

Like Myers, Hilgard (1977) conceives of dissociated subsystems as bearers of consciousness, analogous to ordinary consciousness, and he explicitly rejects the notion that dissociated systems of this kind are a manifestation of the archaic Unconscious of Freudian psychoanalysis:

> By contrast, in automatic writing or hypnosis, when a dissociated part of consciousness has been uncovered, the amnesic barrier is broken, and it is possible to converse *directly with the dissociated consciousness.* The same direct discourse takes place with a multiple personality, once it has emerged. This is an important difference between a psychodynamic unconscious as described previously [referring to the Unconscious of Jung and Freud] and the dissociation interpretation of divided consciousness. Morton Prince was correct in speaking of the dissociated consciousness as a coconsciousness, for it is a genuine consciousness corresponding to the familiar one. (p. 249)

Nevertheless, Hilgard considers the two approaches, the psychoanalytic/psychodynamic and the dissociation schemata, to be compatible, each with something to contribute to understanding the dynamics of the psyche (p. 250). His description of amnesia in the two explanatory systems demonstrates this view:

> In a dissociation interpretation, the barrier between the separated activities is essentially an amnesic barrier, preventing the interchange of memories, whereas, in psychoanalysis, the barrier is based primarily on repression of unacceptable impulses. I have somewhat oversimplified the relationship. I have considered the Freudian barrier a horizontal one (carrying the metaphor of the unconscious being "deeper") and the dissociative barrier a vertical one; thus the split-off parts may have equal status in their cognitive aspects....One reason for preserving the distinction between dissociation and repression is to call attention to an important

> finding noted in cases of multiple personality—that the concealed (or dissociated) personality is sometimes more normal or mentally healthy than the openly displayed one. This accords better with the idea of a split in the normal consciousness (a justification for Prince's term coconscious) rather than with the idea of a primitive unconscious regulated largely by primary process thinking. (pp. 80, 83)

One thing that Hilgard does not make clear is just how the executive ego exercises control over the subsystems. That control can hardly be conceived as consciously imposed in many of its aspects. It is one thing to say that the executive ego, aided by a central monitoring function, consciously plans and puts certain processes into action. It is quite another to say that hierarchies of subsystems are consciously arranged and rearranged. There is no evidence that such conscious interventions occur. If the executive ego is responsible for those arrangements, it must bring them about unconsciously. Hilgard says: "Central executive functions are responsible for planning in relation to goals, initiating action commensurate with those plans, and sustaining action against obstacles and distractions" (p. 220); the steps of such planning can be laid out and examined. But with many actions that are obviously intelligently devised we cannot spell out how the various subsystems were enabled to interact and successfully bring about the desired result. For instance, in the heat of an academic debate on a contentious subject, a mass of information must be sorted, the import of certain words calculated, the line of the argument charted, and so forth, and debaters will tell you that only a relatively small number of these factors are consciously analyzed and that only a limited number of the many decisions involved are consciously taken. If the executive ego is indeed setting things up so that the delivery goes well, adjusting and ordering the hierarchy of subsystems, it must be doing that largely on an unconscious level. Hilgard seems to suggest that such activity may be taking place through the executive and monitoring functions of the subsystems themselves, and therefore outside the consciousness of the central control. But if in this example we do not need the central executive and monitoring function to hierarchically arrange subsystems, when do we? To say, as Hilgard does (p. 233), that what he calls the "hidden observer"[21] is a fractionated part of the monitoring system that exists behind an amnesic barrier, is to indicate that there could also be a significant part of the central executive functioning behind that barrier.

Another problem with Hilgard's approach has to do with the notion of hierarchy and the tacit assumption that its upper levels are somehow superior to those below. This difficulty is the same as that faced by McDougall, who contended that the highest function in the human psyche is the normal consciousness of everyday life. This view is contradicted by important data of automatism, such as the fact that cognitive functions unavailable to ordi-

21. The "hidden observer" is a cognitive system that has access to information available neither to ordinary consciousness nor to hypnotic consciousness. According to Hilgard, it is discovered by using special techniques within the hypnotic state.

nary consciousness are frequently superior to those of ordinary conscious thinking and the fact that creative functions, at work on an unconscious level, consistently show themselves to be superior to processes initiated and carried out by the normal self (see our Chapter 7). As we have seen above, Hilgard himself noted that in multiple personality disorder, "the concealed (or dissociated) personality is sometimes more normal or mentally healthy than the openly displayed one" (p. 83). For that reason, if the concept of hierarchy is to have any credibility, it must be purged of any notion that because the central executive function "controls" and "arranges" subsystems, it is automatically to be considered "higher" or "superior" to those subsystems.

These difficulties arise from Hilgard's use of metaphors that are fundamentally incompatible with each other. His model of human personality posits a hierarchy of cognitive modules (or monads) specialized for particular tasks and supporting an emergent conscious self at the top. But if the normal personality is such a hierarchy of monads, how can it be broken up to form subsidiary personalities, such as those revealed by the data of automatism and dissociation? For in that case, each of the newly formed or discovered secondary conscious centers must have *all* the cognitive capabilities needed to function as a personality, and not merely those of isolated specialized modules or monads. Since, in the experimental and clinical literature, these secondary personalities show themselves as *minds* which resemble our own and are relatively complete in their own right, a model of hierarchically arranged specialized modules must fail. So although Hilgard, like Myers, accepts the existence of secondary centers of consciousness, his attempt to contemporize that notion in a form that might be acceptable to cognitive psychologists and neuroscientists does not really advance our understanding of how such centers arise or function.[22]

Stephen Braude

Stephen Braude has undertaken the investigation of automatisms and secondary personality from a philosophical point of view. In his book *First Person Plural: Multiple Personality and the Philosophy of Mind* (Braude, 1995), he examines the human experience of multiplicity and unity, concentrating on multiple personality disorder (MPD; today called dissociative identity disorder, or DID), which he believes provides a unique window into the human psyche. From his analysis of multiplicity, Braude argues that although in many ways we function as a conglomerate of distinct psychic entities, in fact we are at bottom a unity. Using language reminiscent of Myers (*HP*, vol. 1, pp. 9–11), Braude (1995) says that at issue is whether we accept that the psyche is a unity or a "colony of lower order selves" (p. 124),

22. Further critical remarks regarding Hilgard's ideas may be found in Gauld (1992, pp. 588–591).

and, like Myers, he argues that there is a unifying "Self" that exists below and beyond all multiplicity (pp. 166–180).

Braude makes the case that the alter personalities of a multiple are "distinct centers of self-awareness" (p. 68) or "apperceptive centers" (p. 78). Defining the latter term, he says that "an apperceptive center is an individual most of whose autobiographical states [states *experienced* as one's own] are indexical [states *believed to be* one's own]" (p. 78). Further, he contends that apperceptive centers are *distinct* if the autobiographical and indexical states of each are largely non-autobiographical and non-indexical for the other. The personalities of a multiple, says Braude, fulfill this requirement. He also points out that these apperceptive centers may exhibit various patterns of asymmetrical awareness "in which personality A is aware of B's thoughts or actions, but B is not aware of A's existence" (p. 43).

Having described the nature of the distinct centers of a multiple, Braude is at pains to make a further point:

> Probably the most outstanding distinguishing feature of multiplicity is this: whereas multiples seem to have more than one distinct apperceptive center at a time, this does not seem to be the case for other strong forms of dissociation. For example, a hypnotically-induced "hidden observer" is not an apperceptive center distinct from the original hypnotized individual, even though hidden observers are similar to alters in some important respects. Hidden observers report experiences of which the hypnotized subject is apparently unaware. The hidden observer's experiences are, therefore, not autobiographical for the subject. But they are indexical, at least eventually. Once the subject learns of the hidden observer's experiences he accepts those states as his own, despite their having been outside conscious awareness. More importantly, however, most (if not all) of the hypnotic subject's indexical states seem to be indexical for the hidden observer....Hence, we could say that the disparities of indexicality found in hidden observer studies are largely *asymmetrical,* whereas in cases (such as MPD) satisfying the conditions for distinct apperceptive centers, they are mostly symmetrical. (pp. 78–79)

It seems to me that Braude's contention here—that multiple personality clearly and inherently differs from other strong forms of dissociation in the way he describes—is mistaken. Specifically, I believe it is incorrect to say that what happens in hidden observer cases cannot also happen in cases of multiple personality. There is no reason to believe that one personality—say, the main functioning personality—of a multiple could not come to *believe* that the states of an alter personality are his own. After all, an intelligent multiple would be quite capable of grasping the nature of multiplicity and arriving at such a belief. In that case, according to Braude's definition, the personalities of such a multiple would not be distinct apperceptive centers. This is a problematic but, it seems to me, inevitable conclusion. For that reason, I believe that this criterion for distinctness is faulty.

The core problem with Braude's way of determining distinctness has to do with the word "believe." What would the "belief" that an alter's states are or are not one's own be for a multiple? What would it be for a hypnotic subject who develops hidden observer phenomena? Would they be the same in each case? I do not think there is any reliable way to determine how these two instances of belief might differ. For that reason, either distinctness has to be denied for both, or another criterion needs to be used.

Moreover, I disagree with Braude's statement that most, if not all, of the hypnotic subject's states seem to be indexical for the hidden observer. This certainly does not hold true, at least if we go beyond examples taken from recent "hidden observer" experiments and include in our examination the massive literature of mesmerism and hypnotism, including cases of the sort relied upon by Myers and his colleagues. As has been pointed out in the principal histories of these phenomena (Crabtree, 1993; Dingwall, 1967–1968; Ellenberger, 1970; Gauld, 1992), credible cases of this type were reported in large numbers throughout the 19th century. In this literature we encounter many examples of hypnotic personalities who see themselves as distinct from the hypnotic subject (e.g., Deleuze, 1813, vol. 1, p. 176; Gurney, 1884; Janet, 1886; Strombeck, 1814, pp. 65–70). In these "strong" instances of dissociation, the hypnotic personalities frequently deny that the states of the hypnotic subject are indexical for themselves; they explicitly reject the notion that the thoughts of the subject are their own and affirm their non-identity with the subject. An examination of the literature of automatic writing reveals the same attitude on the part of the "communicators."[23]

The difficulty with Braude's criterion for distinctness is that it falls short of establishing even the personalities of a multiple as distinct. In my opinion, the best criterion for calling something a "distinct apperceptive center" or "distinct communicating personality" remains that suggested by Prince and other early investigators of psychological automatism: If a source of automatic communication thinks and acts like a personality, for all practical purposes it *is* a personality; if the subject of the automatism experiences that source as distinct from him- or herself, for all practical purposes it *is* distinct.[24]

Despite this problem in Braude's criterion for distinctness, his overall grasp of the nature and functioning of multiple centers of consciousness is impressive, and his book represents an important step forward in establishing a sound philosophical basis for talking about psychological multiplicity. Although Braude's views were developed independently of those of Myers,

23. Braude agrees that his criterion for distinguishing DID from other strong instances of dissociation is inadequate as it stands in *First Person Plural*. His current view is that the distinction should be established partly in terms of temporal properties. A hidden observer case might manifest in a very DID–like manner, but be short-lived, whereas DID cases persist for a considerable period, long enough for at least some alters to get to be personality-like (Braude, personal communication, May 17, 2004).

24. Braude rightly points out that this criterion does not clearly distinguish DID cases from deeply-involved role playing and does not cover cases of fragmentary personalities formed for specific purposes (personal communication, May 17, 2004). Unfortunately, we do not yet have a good philosophical basis for distinguishing these two forms of automatism and so, I fear, must make do with rough determinations of this kind.

they are reminiscent of them in several important ways. He insists that experimental and clinical data have established that multiple apperceptive centers are real; he recognizes that these selves can be aware of each other in both symmetrical and asymmetrical ways; and perhaps most importantly, he presents strong empirically based arguments for an overarching unity underlying and coordinating these manifestations of multiplicity.

In his discussion of "the unity beneath multiplicity" (Braude, 1995, pp. 164–190), Braude argues against the "colonialist" view that there is no ultimate psychological unity, but only a multiplicity of independent selves or subsystems within the individual. He insists that this position cannot be maintained in the face of certain well-established facts of clinical experience, such as the commonality of language among alter personalities, their sharing of basic knowledge and capacities involved in the functions of everyday living, and the creation and maintenance of coordinated, protective psychological structures. Braude argues that the process involved in the production of dissociative centers can only make sense if there is a "pre-dissociative synthesizing self that orchestrated (and needed to orchestrate) the initial dissociations" (p. 174) and coordinated the dissociative coping strategies involved. The management of conflicting needs that occurs in the dissociative system must be accomplished by a single underlying subject. Looking at this issue from a philosophical point of view, Braude refers us to Kant, who contended that in order for us to experience things in sequence and as connected wholes, there must be an underlying subject, a transcendent ego which is a "synthesizing self [that makes] such phenomenological and conceptual connections between parts of experience" (p. 167). According to Kant, this self or subject cannot be a direct object of experience, but we are justified in positing its existence. According to Braude, this transcendental ego corresponds to the underlying self that synthesizes the psychological life of the multiple.

Braude's analysis of the reasons for accepting the notion of a unifying self beyond multiplicity provides one of the most persuasive arguments to date for the reality of Myers's ultimate Subliminal Self. Although his supporting data are drawn principally from the experiences of individuals with DID, the same conclusions could be reached from a similar examination of the production of hypnotic personalities and other secondary personalities of automatism.

Unconscious Cerebration Revisited

William Carpenter's doctrine that all automatism results from the "reflex action of the brain," expressed in the catchphrase "unconscious cerebration," has always had powerful adherents. This way of thinking, couched in more modern terminology, remains well represented among psychological thinkers today. The main representatives of this point of view are to be found among sociocognitive theorists and neurobiologically oriented psychologists. Despite the overall "unconscious cerebration" orientation of these schools of thought, there are signs of theoretical expansion as some have begun to seek an approach that will more comfortably embrace the complex data of a subliminal mental life and psychological automatism.

Sociocognitive Theorists

Perhaps the most significant contemporary challenge to a Myers-type interpretation of the phenomena of automatism is that raised by the "sociocognitive" approach to hypnosis, dissociation, and related phenomena. The spokespersons for this way of thinking are principally T. X. Barber, John Chaves, William Coe, Theodore Sarbin, Nicholas Spanos, and most recently Daniel Wegner. The most outspoken of this group is without doubt Spanos, and so it will be useful for our purposes to concentrate on his presentation of the sociocognitive position.

Spanos, a prolific author of research papers on the subjects of hypnosis, memory, imagery, suggestion, and multiple personality, summarized his key ideas in this area in his posthumously published book *Multiple Identities and False Memories: A Sociocognitive Perspective* (Spanos, 1996). It is to that book that I turn for what I presume to be his most developed thinking. This exposition will focus on sociocognitive assertions that most directly touch on the phenomenon of automatism, and pass over those that are less directly relevant. So, for example, there will be no discussion here of the diagnosis of multiple personality, possible iatrogenic factors in its production, its relationship to sexual abuse and ritual abuse, or false memories.

The sociocognitive view of automatisms can be quite simply stated. Automatisms are apparently involuntary actions produced as a result of a combination of suggestions and demands imposed on the individuals who manifest them. Those individuals may *believe* that their actions are not carried out voluntarily, that the experience "happens to them," but analysis shows that this belief is mistaken. In reality they are playing a role that is suggested to them, and they adjust their view of their experience to satisfy the unspoken demands of that role. The role is set up through subtle or not so subtle cues and is constantly being confirmed and reinforced by the social context in which the experience occurs. The result is a retrospective revision of what the experience was, a revision that goes unnoticed by the person who experiences the automatism.

The issue of multiple centers of consciousness is central to automatism. Spanos (1996) described his attitude towards psychological multiplicity in this way: "People can learn to think of themselves as possessing more than one identity or self, and can learn to behave as if they are first one identity and then a different identity" (p. 4). For Spanos, as for Freud, consciousness is always and necessarily unitary. The notion that there can be more than one center of consciousness, more than one "identity" operating in a person, is false and the result of social conditioning. Spanos believed that amnesia on the part of one identity for what might be done by another identity is simply an example of "selective recall," whereby the individual can only bring back the memories associated with the present role enactment and cannot get in touch with any other memories. Referring more specifically to MPD, Spanos wrote: "Absorption in the enactment of identity A may, to a substantial degree, function to prevent the recall of memories associated with the enactment of identity B. But what if identity B, when asked to recall identity A, claims an inability to do so? An 'inability' to recall identity A may be a requirement of the MPD role" (p. 6). The ability to remember something, said Spanos, depends on whether the role an individual is now enacting allows that recall. If it does not, then the person will experience "amnesia." This view is reflected in Spanos's conception of the nature of hypnosis:

> Hypnotic behavior, including so-called hypnotic amnesia, is shown, at its core, to be strategic behavior enacted to fulfill the subject's beliefs and expectations about hypnosis. Hypnotic subjects should not be seen as the passive automatons of the popular literature, but as voluntary actors striving to fulfill their role as they define it or as it is defined for them by the experimental or clinical situation. The notion that hypnosis can be understood as an altered state of consciousness is thus rejected....The amnesia both of the MPD patient and of the hypnotic subject may be understood as goal-directed, purposive activity. (pp. 10–11)

As these quotations indicate, Spanos used the language of voluntary action to describe how individuals go about enacting their roles. They are "voluntary actors" who carry out "goal-directed, purposive activity." When describing the "context dependent" nature of hypnotic responding, Spanos wrote that this responding "is determined by the willingness of the subjects to adopt the hypnotic role" and "their willingness and ability to use their imaginal and other cognitive skills to create the subjective experiences called for by suggestions" (pp. 19, 20). These descriptions convey unambiguously Spanos's central message—that people who experience automatisms are knowingly and willingly playing a role.

Now, Spanos knew that many people who experience automatisms do not talk about—and often in fact deny—having the conscious intention to enact a role. He noted that "the sociocognitive perspective recognizes that hypnotic subjects sometimes experience their responses as feeling involuntary" (p. 22). How can responses experienced as involuntary be examples of voluntary, goal-directed action? Here is Spanos's answer:

> Nevertheless, according to this perspective, hypnotic subjects retain control over their behavior and guide it in terms of their understanding of what is expected. Subjects report that their behavior feels involuntary, not because they have lost control over their behavior, but because they interpret their goal-directed behavior as involuntary in line with the expectations conveyed in suggestions. (p. 22)

This way of looking at things is, I submit, fatally flawed. In the experimental situation, the subject is asked for a description of his or her experience of what is happening. This must be done, since it is only the subject who can say whether something called "voluntariness" subjectively occurs. We are then told that if the subject describes the experience as involuntary, he is mistaken. On what basis? That the subject, by describing the experience as involuntary, is actually obeying ("voluntarily," by the way) some kind of interiorized social demand. If there ever was a circular proof of a position, this has to be it! If voluntariness—which can only be determined subjectively—is not to be determined by the experience of the subject, but rather by the theory of the experimenter, the term has lost all meaning. Here the explanations of the experimenter rule out results that do not fit the theory, and for no other reason than that they do not fit the theory.[25]

In examining Spanos's position, a question should also be asked about what it can mean that individuals "guide it [their behavior] in terms of their understanding of what is expected." Is this "guidance" and "understanding" conscious to them? Also, if, as previously stated, amnesia is "selective recall," is that selection a conscious action? Sociocognitive theorists certainly speak of these things as if they were conscious. But if so, why do people have no awareness of this guidance or selection? Do they have some kind of mechanism that causes them immediately to forget this conscious guidance or selection as soon as it has happened? On the other hand, if it is not conscious, are we not then talking about unconscious mental activity—something that Spanos explicitly rejects?

Voluntariness is, of course, a key issue in automatism. Automatism involves sensory or motor activity—activity that evinces intelligence—which the individual does not subjectively experience as deriving from his or her own conscious thinking or willing. The automatism seems to "happen to" the individual. How would the sociocognitive theorist explain what is really

25. This kind of rush to prove a theory is also evident in the way sociocognitive researchers typically measure "voluntariness." For example, in the protocol used by Spanos (Spanos & Gorassini, 1984; Spanos, Radtke, Hodgins, Stam, & Bertrand, 1983) in connection with testing hypnotic suggestibility, the individual was asked to rate voluntariness in this way: "During this [the arm rising] suggestion my arm felt like it rose by itself;" the subject is then given a choice of four possible answers: a) not at all; b) to a slight degree; c) to a moderate degree; d) to a great degree. Experiments of this kind rely on what the experimenters might consider a "commonsense" meaning of the words being used, but that is a naive assumption. Clinicians know that this framing of the question can be easily misunderstood by the experimental subject. When the subject is asked whether something he or she did was experienced as happening "by itself," genuine confusion may result. The subject may think: "Well, my body did it, so I cannot say that it happened 'by itself.'" In this way a *conclusion* is reached and the response is given on the basis of that conclusion, which may not reflect the subjective *experience* of the subject. If experiments of this kind are to have any validity, there will have to be greater attention devoted to making sure that the subjects questioned understand the meaning of the instructions they are being given. One further comment: In a large proportion of sociocognitive studies, the experiments are conducted with unselected undergraduate volunteers. There is no reason to think that in such samples the more impressive automatic phenomena, such as those reported in studies involving more selective groups, or in the clinical literature, will occur.

happening? If the automatist knowingly and voluntarily does what the situation demands, if the actions of the automatist and the interpretation of those actions are controlled, voluntary, goal-directed,[26] as the sociocognitive perspective insists,[27] then there seems to be only one possible way that an automatist could say that the actions are "involuntary." The automatist must consciously carry out the voluntary, goal-directed behavior, but then immediately forget that he did so. In that case, an automatism must involve repeatedly knowing and then forgetting the conscious, voluntary actions just performed, and doing so again and again in a short space of time. It must involve at one moment making conscious choices of compliance and then forgetting those choices, so that it seems to the automatist that no such choices were ever made, and then at the next moment making another deliberate goal-directed choice to comply, and then, once again, immediately forgetting it, and so on. This might be compared to the multitasking activity of a computer, which seems to perform many tasks at once, but really is carrying out discontinuous operations, constantly leaving one task to carry out a mini-step in the procedure of another task, and then returning to the first task to perform a mini-procedure there—and doing all this so quickly that there seems to be no break in the action. This kind of multitasking of knowing and forgetting might be a possible explanation, but to my knowledge the experiments that sociocognitive experimenters cite contain no evidence of such a process.[28]

Given the unproven status of such alternation of knowing and forgetting, it must be said that sociocognitive theorists have failed to demonstrate how what they posit as controlled, voluntary, goal-directed behavior (which they see as necessary to explain apparent automatisms) could derive from a unitary consciousness and yet at the same time be hidden from that consciousness. They have failed to show how an action can be both conscious and unconscious at the same time and in the same respect.

---

26. As has been pointed out, Janet (and many experimenters since him) showed that instances of psychological automatism involving negative hallucinations require the intervention of controlled, voluntary, goal-directed behavior to make the automatic movement intelligible (for instance, through suggestion an individual may be unable to see a table standing in his path, but nonetheless walk around it and avoid a collision). For Janet, the source of that behavior was a subconscious center of consciousness.

27. Robert White (1941), often cited by sociocognitive psychologists as a precursor of their thinking, made the statement: "Goal-directed striving no longer necessarily implies either awareness or intention" (p. 485). It is precisely this change in meaning of language that haunts the writing of sociocognitive thinkers and muddies the issues they deal with. How can one say that "goal-directed" striving does not involve awareness or intention? That can only happen if one moves the level of discussion from the psychological to the physiological/mechanical. In that case, a computer, for instance, might be said to carry out "goal-directed" or "purposeful" actions without the benefit of consciousness or intention if those actions are programmed to accomplish some predetermined end. But if we are going to deal with human beings, and do so on a psychological level, we do not have the luxury of so glibly excluding awareness and intention from the scene (see also Chapter 1).

28. For a further discussion of the sociocognitive position, see Gauld (1992, pp. 581–608).

Harvard psychologist Daniel Wegner (2002) has recently written a book that takes an exactly opposite and even more radical stance in regard to the issue of involuntariness. Among other matters, Wegner discusses the phenomena associated with automatism. Unfortunately, like almost all of his sociocognitive colleagues, he routinely rules out of consideration all data involving supernormal experiences, and in his discussion betrays the fact that he has only the most superficial knowledge of the relevant historical literature. Wegner rejects entirely the notion of human beings as free agents, asserting that all behavior is in fact involuntary and that the notion of conscious will is simply an illusion that facilitates social life. He points out, correctly, that there are many examples of misperception and misattribution of personal agency, but instead of dealing with the complexity that such errors reveal, he gets rid of agency altogether, at least as something that derives from conscious intention and will. By a strange twist of perspective, Wegner argues that, since in the case of automatisms we rightly recognize that we are not really the agents of what we do, automatism presents us with a truer conception of human action in general—that is, that *all* human action is automatism and lacks conscious agency. It should come as no surprise, therefore, that he repeatedly and approvingly quotes Thomas Huxley. One of those quotes very well sums up Wegner's position: "The feeling we call volition is not the cause of the voluntary act, but simply the symbol in consciousness of that state of the brain which is the immediate cause of the act" (Huxley, 1874, p. 577). The result is that not only will, but consciousness too is denied any significant contribution to mental life, and Wegner cannot escape Huxley's famous conclusion that consciousness is purely epiphenomenal, just "as the steam-whistle which accompanies the work of a locomotive engine is without influence upon its machinery" (p. 575).

What, then, happens to automatism in this schema? An automatism is simply an action produced by the individual's brain (as all our supposedly voluntary actions are), but without the illusory feeling that it is produced by conscious will. We are surprised when we experience an automatism, but, according to Wegner, we should not be, because here the true state of affairs is graphically revealed. Here we get to experience first hand that conscious agency is an illusion.[29]

The Cognitive Unconscious

Wegner's epiphenomenal stance is not philosophically new, nor it is out of step with much current theorizing in cognitive psychology, now widely thought of as cognitive neuroscience. However, in the past two decades some cognitive psychologists have begun a "reconsideration" of the unconscious (Bowers & Meichenbaum, 1984), as it became increasingly evident that large parts of our mental life and apparatus are not directly available for intro-

29. For a fuller review of Wegner's book, see E. F. Kelly (2003).

spection. No full consensus has yet emerged as to the contents, organization, and capabilities of this "cognitive unconscious," but the debate has certainly revealed the hostility that the scientific mainstream still harbors toward consciousness in *any* form. This is perhaps most completely exemplified in an article by Max Velmans (1991), "Is Human Information Processing Conscious?", which denies to consciousness and will any role in the processing of information and the determination of action. This exchange, consisting of Velmans's target presentation followed by 36 peer comments along with Velmans's response to those comments, provides a fairly good representation of current thinking. This elaborate discussion of conscious and non-conscious processes demonstrates that cognitive psychology, having embraced a one-consciousness view of mental functioning, is essentially unable to deal with the data of psychological automatism. In fact, the commentary on Velmans's article confirms that many cognitive theorists have an almost superstitious fear of the notion of ordinary consciousness itself, and if they are so spooked by *this* "ghost in the machine" (see "Damn! There goes that ghost again," Stanovich, 1991, pp. 696–697), they respond to the possibility of secondary centers of consciousness as to a veritable band of demons. A case in point is the commentary by Graham Wagstaff (1991), who writes that the idea that "full attentive processing can take place outside awareness" (p. 700), an idea discussed by Velmans in connection with Hilgard's "hidden observer," conjures up the picture of a distinct cognitive system which "*exists separately from the cognitive system represented at any particular time in awareness or 'open consciousness'*" (Wagstaff's emphasis, presumably signifying horror) and leads to questionable conceptions like "multiple personality." Wagstaff finds this possibility so distasteful that he is confident that Velmans—who must surely feel the same way—will, when he recognizes where this is going, be driven to embrace the sociocognitive explanation for such phenomena—that they are artifacts produced by compliance with task demands.

As repugnant as the idea of secondary centers of consciousness may still be to many cognitive psychologists, there are at least a few who have recognized that the data of experience *demand* some multiplicity of this kind. Some contemporary cognitive theorists, notably those associated with Hilgard and the "neo-dissociationist" school, have recently begun tentatively exploring views reminiscent of those of Myers, James, and their colleagues, relying heavily on the phenomena of psychological automatism. This trend is probably best represented in the works of John Kihlstrom.

Writing about "consciousness and me-ness," Kihlstrom (1997) reminds his colleagues that William James, in his *Principles of Psychology,* had insisted that there is an intimate relationship between consciousness and the self. Kihlstrom writes: "Consciousness comes, in James' view, when we inject ourselves into our thoughts, feelings, desires, and actions—when we take possession of them, experience and acknowledge them as our own. Consciousness is always a *personal* consciousness, and this was at least as true for memory as for any other mental faculty" (p. 451). Kihlstrom also states: "When mental representations are integrated with the self, they become part of conscious mental life; when this integration is lacking, they are not accessible to introspection, although they may influence experience, thought and action outside of phenomenal awareness" (p. 452).

Then Kihlstrom makes a bold move: "Perhaps there is not just one mental representation of the self....Considerations of the self as a concept suggest that each individual possesses a number of context-specific selves, arrayed as a set of exemplars or coexisting with a summary prototype" (p. 463). Again he cites James, who in his *Principles* wrote:

> The buried feelings and thoughts proved now to exist in hysterical anaesthetics, in recipients of post-hypnotic suggestion, etc., themselves are parts of *secondary personal selves.* These selves...are cut off at ordinary times from communication with the regular and normal self of the individual; but still they form conscious unities, have continuous memories, speak, write, invent distinct names for themselves, or adopt names that are suggested; and, in short, are entirely worthy of that title of secondary personalities which is now commonly given them. (James, 1890b, vol. 1, p. 227)

Kihlstrom (1997) does not see these selves as a part of the "psychological unconscious," properly understood. For him, dissociative phenomena cannot be understood in terms of concepts applied to preconscious and unconscious processing; they demand reference to a self (p. 464). He spells out this distinction: "In unconscious processing, procedural knowledge is executed without ever making contact with a mental representation of self. In preconscious processing, events have been so degraded that they, too, never enter working memory at the point of perception....Thus they never achieve any links with the self in the first place" (p. 464).

In an informal discussion with John Searle, Kihlstrom (1993b) further clarifies the character of mental activity associated with secondary personal selves:

> I do want to insist that these things are mental in a sense that they are representations of experiences. They are constructed through perception or reconstructed through memory or whatever, and simply have an impact on the person's ongoing experience without themselves being conscious. I don't think this is the same as playing with somebody's neurotransmitter system, which would not be mental in that sense. These are representations. I think the best evidence for the representational status is the fact that you can get conscious access to them under some conditions. The whole beauty of hypnosis and hysteria, and the reason I'm interested in hypnosis and hysteria, is that we can cancel the amnesia suggestion and the person remembers the word list perfectly well. Similarly, when a person recovers from a fugue state, the person remembers his or her past perfectly well. You have to give those things the status of mental representations; they are not merely neurotransmitters hanging around in the brain matter. (pp. 156–157)

Statements such as these on the part of some contemporary cognitive theorists bring psychology back to the core issues raised by Myers, taking them almost to the point he had already reached in 1885 when he said that a purely physiological explanation of the data in question would not do. With Kihlstrom, we can even say that these theorists have nearly come to the point of admitting that processes occurring outside primary consciousness can have a certain internal coherence, being associated with an intelligence or conscious self and attached to a specific chain of memories. In this way we might say that Kihlstrom in one fell swoop reclaims for cognitive psychology territory previously denied it, the territory opened up by Myers, Janet, James, and their colleagues as reviewed above. What is startling and distressing is that psychology has made so little progress beyond that point in over a century. We have hardly begun to look at how multiple conscious centers manifest concretely in ongoing human life, an undertaking that was already well underway at the beginning of the 20th century. We have yet to carry out the serious and thorough examination of the whole spectrum of human experience that Myers and James said was so sorely needed, paying attention to phenomena that today, as at that time, remain unpopular to establishment science. The complaint of James (1901) that the exclusion of these phenomena, such as anomalous, mediumistic, and supernormal experiences, takes place on the basis of *a priori* philosophical bias, remains as valid today as it was then.

Neurobiological Research

A small but growing body of neurobiological investigations provides additional evidence for the psychological reality of secondary centers of consciousness.[30] These have been conducted mainly in the last half of the 20th century and have focused on the phenomenon of MPD (or DID). In an early survey of psychophysiological phenomena in MPD, B. G. Braun (1983b) noted previous clinical reports indicating that striking physiological differences were sometimes observed between "alter" personalities in a multiple personality case, including alterations in handedness, rate and ability to heal, response to medication, and allergic responses. In this article, Braun also described three multiple personality cases of his own which involved the appearance and disappearance—depending on the personality in control of the body—of allergies to citrus fruit, cigarette smoke, and cats. He also described a case in which red dots (resembling cigarette burns which had been administered to the person as a child) would appear only when a certain personality was "out." Coons (1988) published a survey of

30. For additional evidence of this type and related discussions of the evidence cited here, see Chapter 3. There we address primarily the issue of changes of consciousness that induce changes in the body. Here we address the issue of the bearing of these phenomena on the psychological reality of MPD.

physiological aspects of MPD that cited other features noted by clinicians working with MPD patients. In addition to those already mentioned, he noted apparent variations in vision and sensitivity to pain, and pointed out that seizure disorders seemed abnormally common in multiple personality subjects. S. D. Miller (1989) subsequently conducted ophthalmological examinations of alter personalities to test whether MPD subjects would show greater variability in visual functioning across alter personalities than would control subjects role-playing MPD. His studies showed that the MPD subjects had 4.5 times the number of changes in optical functioning observed in simulating control subjects.

Several studies have reported large differences in autonomic function between alters. For example, Bahnson and Smith (1975) describe the results of measurements of heart rate, respiration, and skin potential taken during audio-visually recorded psychotherapy sessions with a multiple personality patient over an eight-month period. Significant differences were observed in these measurements across the four personalities involved. F. W. Putnam et al. (1990) assessed autonomic nervous system activity associated with different alter personality states of MPD subjects using measurements of skin conductance and heart rate and compared these with parallel measurements of the simulated personalities of controls. They concluded that alter personality states of MPD are physiologically distinct states of consciousness. They also noted, however, that equivalent differences could be generated by some control subjects using hypnosis.

Coons (1988) pointed out that Morton Prince was the first to measure galvanic skin responses of alter personalities. He also noted that electroencephalographic (EEG) studies of multiple personality have been carried out since the 1940s, and stated that a number of reports indicate significant variations in EEGs, particularly in alpha rhythm, across the personalities, with most investigators attributing these differences to varying degrees of arousal and tension. A more recent EEG mapping study, however, showed topographic differences among alter personalities that could not be reproduced by an actress portraying the different personalities (Hughes et al., 1990; see also F. W. Putnam, 1984). An important study of a multiple with four personalities by Ludwig et al. (1972), using EEG in combination with an autonomic measure, concluded that "all the data obtained fall into a consistent pattern and suggest that traditional skeptical explanations of pretense or role-playing are insufficient to account for the phenomena observed" (p. 298). Among other things, they demonstrated that the pattern of electrodermal response to words that had been paired with electric shocks reflected the clinically observed relations of awareness between alter personalities; thus if B claimed to be aware of A but not vice versa, B would respond not only to his own "loaded" words but also to A's, whereas A would respond only to his own. A similar study by Larmore et al. (1977) found a large variation in visually evoked responses across alter personalities that was comparable to differences between unrelated persons and far larger than those seen in identical twins. Braun (1983a) used visual evoked potential topographical maps to study the results of integration of the personalities of a multiple through psychotherapy and concluded that therapeutic procedures produced neurophysiological changes. In a survey of psychophysiological investigations of multiple personality, S. D. Miller and Triggiano (1992) stated that "psycho-physiological research using evoked potentials has provided some of the most consistent and convincing experimental evidence for the existence of MPD as a clinical entity, as well as for the distinctness of the personality states in persons with the disorder" (p. 50).

Only a few studies have so far appeared that use functional neuroimaging techniques based on hemodynamic or metabolic correlates of brain electrical activity. In one study of a multiple, measurements of blood flow in the brain showed that personality change produced significant differences in cerebral blood flow in the right temporal lobe (Mathew et al., 1985). A study some years later reported that SPECT imaging of a multiple personality with four alters showed that "visually apparent and statistically significant regional cerebral blood flow changes were observed in the left temporal lobes" (Saxe et al., 1992, p. 662). Functional magnetic resonance imaging of a multiple in 1999 indicated that personality changes were associated with changes in temporal and hippocampal activity and with nigrostriatal-system deactivation (Tsai et al., 1999). No firm conclusions can be drawn from the few studies presently available, but large between-alter effects do appear to be present that are accessible to these emerging measurement techniques.

One final topic in the neurobiological study of MPD and DID should be mentioned: Frank Putnam's investigation of the phenomenology and physiology of the "switch process" in multiple personality indicated that the state-changing that occurs as the individual switches from one personality to another has features in common with state-of-consciousness transitions observed in infants, altered states of consciousness, and psychiatric disorders. Putnam (1988) wrote: "These include the observation that states of consciousness are discrete self-organizing patterns of behavior differing along axes of affect, access to memory, attention and cognition, regulatory physiology, and a sense of self. State transitions are marked by non-linear changes in these variables" (p. 24). I might add here that there is an obvious and intriguing phenomenological similarity between the switch process in MPD and the changes of state that occur in onset and offset of mediumistic trance and possession. There seems to be good reason to anticipate that all these manifestations of secondary personalities have a great deal in common and can usefully be studied in parallel ways.

Much still remains to be done along the lines indicated here. In 1991 Putnam summarized the neurophysiological research on MPD up to that point, noting the difficulties involved in this kind of experimentation and emphasizing the need for more such work (F. W. Putnam, 1991). Miller and Triggiano (1992), while agreeing that the available studies collectively provide considerable evidence for the distinctness and genuineness of MPD alters, also stated their belief that many of the studies they reviewed lacked "appropriate experimental rigor (for example, control subjects, cohort studies, experimental blinds, valid survey instruments, etc.)" (p. 56), and suggested directions for future research.

Although the above studies successfully employed physiological markers to provide evidence for the distinctness and genuineness of alter personalities, they themselves do not provide anything like a plausible physiological theory of the formation of MPD. Indeed, some of the observed phenomena, such as changes in allergic responses and evoked potential morphologies would appear, if genuine, to threaten gravely the prospects for finding any such theory, as Myers himself might have contended. The literature on this topic is scanty, but a few points should be made.

When evidence of "duplex" personality first emerged in the 19th century, many neurologically zealous writers immediately sought to map that evidence onto the obvious anatomical duality of the brain (Harrington, 1987).[31] Myers contributed to these early debates in a particularly interesting and sophisticated way. In a series of papers on automatic writing, Myers pointed out that quite apart from issues related to its content, such writing spontaneously displays many other properties that make it extremely challenging, psychologically. For example it may be produced at extraordinary speed, or be almost invisibly minute. James (1889) described a case in which the writer, with his face the whole time buried in his elbow on the side away from his writing, first writes out an entire page without lifting the pencil from the paper, and then goes back and dots each *i* and crosses each *t* "with absolute precision and great rapidity" (p. 44). It was noted that writing can sometimes be produced by both hands simultaneously, and on different topics (*HP*, vol. 2, p. 420). It may be written with words in reverse order, or with the order of their letters reversed, or in pure mirror-image form, even starting from the bottom right and continuing to the top left of each page (James, 1889), or upside down so as to be read in the normal way by an observer facing the writer (*HP*, vol. 2, p. 448). Some of these formal peculiarities, Myers observed, also occurred in the writing of right-handed adults who had suffered damage to the left hemisphere, or in children newly learning how to write. On the basis of these and related observations Myers tentatively suggested that subliminal processes might often functionally "appropriate the energies" of the non-dominant hemisphere while the dominant hemisphere goes about its ordinary business. With characteristic prescience he further suggested that it might be possible to test this hypothesis by observing patterns of cerebral blood flow (Myers, 1885b, p. 43)—a suggestion we have only recently acquired the means to pursue. Unlike some of his contemporaries and successors, Myers did not naively imagine the secondary personality as generated by, or residing in, the non-dominant hemisphere, noting that, among other things, there is the awkward fact that the number of alter personalities is often greater than two.[32]

---

31. The same uncritical enthusiasm persists today in many pop-psychology accounts of hemispheric specialization.

32. A curious footnote to these discussions is provided by the literature on "split-brain" patients, in whom the corpus callosum is severed in order to control otherwise intractable

It is now widely recognized that any physiological correlate or substrate of MPD must be functional rather than anatomical in character. Wegner (2002) semi-seriously advances the analogy of multiple operating systems running on the same computer hardware. Passing from personality A to personality B is thus akin to shutting down Windows and booting up Linux. But this surely will not do: Apart from the fact that we have no idea what these operations consist of, physiologically, they could only account in principle for the simplest case—that of strictly alternating personalities. A much more serious proposal has recently been put forward by Edelman and Tononi (2000), in the context of a neurophysiological theory of consciousness that Edelman's group has been developing continuously for over two decades, supported by both large-scale computer simulations and neurophysiological experiments. Briefly, they conceive of a state of consciousness as the expression of a "dynamic core," a massive and distributed thalamocortical network of reciprocally interconnected neurons brought momentarily into functional relationship by, for example, the current pattern of stimulus input. It takes their whole book to explain in detail what this means, and to present the evidence supporting it, but for our purposes here the essential points are two: First, these authors have clearly recognized, like Myers, the striking analogies between psychological and neurological disconnection syndromes, and that the functional type represents the more fundamental category. In a neurological syndrome, that is, the disconnection is also functional but happens to be produced by an anatomical lesion. Second, they specifically hypothesize that MPD may reflect the operation of multiple, functionally isolated dynamic cores that form within a single nervous system. Note however that while such functionally isolated neural systems might potentially explain both alternating and co-temporal forms of MPD, it would be very difficult if not impossible to accommodate the additional property of inclusivity of awareness, as first pointed out long ago by T. W. Mitchell (1912, pp. 279–281). In sum, this is an important and potentially testable proposal, but the empirical problems here are already deeper than its authors have yet realized. Moreover, as I shall next explain, still more difficult problems remain to be faced.

---

epileptic seizures. Writers such as Gazzaniga (1970) and Sperry (1974) have argued that this procedure in effect results in the existence of two conscious persons occupying the same skull. John Sidtis (1986), on the other hand, examining split-brain patients to determine whether "neurological disconnection produces psychiatric dissociation" (p. 127), concluded: "The paradoxical absence of striking changes in general behavior after commissurotomy stands as a counter point to dissociative phenomena....The person who remains adapts to disconnection, in some ways that are behaviorally obvious, such as cross-cuing, and in other ways that we are just beginning to observe, such as by making use of semantic and spatial information that is not readily available for conscious processing....Disconnection, then, does not provide a model for dissociative phenomena" (p. 144).

I agree with this view and would point out that explanations of this type are considerably less cogent than the evidence assembled by Myers and his colleagues for multiple streams of consciousness in anatomically intact subjects. See also Nagel (1979, chap. 11, "Brain bisection and the unity of consciousness").

Automatism and Supernormal Phenomena

A cornerstone of Myers's theoretical scheme—and a major stumbling-block for many of his critics—is his contention that the subliminal is the source of supernormal phenomena, that it functions in ways beyond the competence of the everyday self and previously unknown to science. Already in his first paper on the Subliminal Self he remarked that he believed telepathic and telesthetic impressions "to be habitually received, not by aid of those adits and operations which the supraliminal self itself directly commands, but by aid of adits and operations peculiar to the subliminal self" (Myers, 1892b, p. 306). Moreover, he argued, these new faculties cannot be explained in terms of known physiological or physical principles, and this reveals that the human psyche has roots in a deeper part of reality that somehow transcends ordinary space and time.

Information acquired subliminally thus finds expression, if it does so at all, via sensory or motor automatism. The evidence that Myers marshals in support of this unifying generalization is anything but trifling or inconsequential. Between the formation of the SPR in 1882 and his death in 1901, Myers and his colleagues published in their *Proceedings* and *Journal* something over 10,000 pages of reports on supernormal phenomena, including not only extended field observations with mediums and heavily documented studies of spontaneous cases, but early attempts to study telepathy and kindred phenomena experimentally and quantitatively. The industry, thoroughness, and care manifest in these publications is unsurpassed in any scientific literature known to me.[33] Further hundreds of articles, monographs, and books written with similarly high standards were published during the same time period in continental Europe and the United States. One of the great contributions of *Human Personality* is that it distills this enormous mass of material into an orderly, coherent, and accessible scheme of presentation. The book itself is thickly documented with case reports and summaries of observations, and it repeatedly refers the reader to other reports, additional documentation, and more detailed reports on the same or related subjects. This vast literature, to which *Human Personality* itself is only an introduction, remains an unrivaled archive of information with which anyone who intends to render judgment on the phenomena must become familiar. Collectively it provides impressive—and in my view, compelling—evidence for the reality of supernormal phenomena. Any serious examination will dismiss this literature at its peril. I will next briefly discuss these connections between automatisms and supernormal phenomena under three sub-headings: creativity, motor automatisms and mediumship, and experimental psi research.

---

33. See James (1890-1896/1910): "In fact, were I asked to point to a scientific journal where hard-headedness and never-sleeping suspicion of sources of error might be seen in their full bloom, I think I should have to fall back on the Proceedings of the Society for Psychical Research" (pp. 304–305).

Automatism and Creativity

Among the various types of relevant psychological phenomena, none have been more significant in the development of the concept of automatism than the inspirations that give rise to creative works. The physiologists who originally developed the notion of automatism were struggling to explain, among other things, the subjective descriptions of the creative process given by some of the greatest literary and musical masters, who spoke of their productions as sometimes coming to them fully formed, as though they had been fashioned in some hidden workshop by artists unknown. These historical geniuses described feelings of not being part of the process that produced their greatest works, acting more like scribes than anything else.

Myers wrote at length about this phenomenon.[34] He linked genius with the classical notion of inspiration, saying that an "inspiration of Genius" is a "subliminal uprush," an emergence into supraliminal consciousness of ideas that the person has "not consciously originated, but which have shaped themselves beyond his will, in profounder regions of his being" (*HP*, vol. 1, p. 71). Another central element of creativity for Myers was the *integration* of ideas arising from subliminal regions with those of the supraliminal self, the "utilisation of a greater proportion of man's psychical being in subservience to ends desired by his supraliminal control" (*HP*, vol. 1, p. 155). The outcome of the creative process is something intended and desired by the supraliminal, and the supraliminal thus plays a key role in the completion of what begins with a subliminal uprush. The heart of the creative process is an automatism, but its culmination and completion occurs in the realm of the supraliminal. Thus, creativity is a highly desirable integration of the two aspects of the psyche and an instance of superior functioning. It is also an indication of what the human soul is capable of, because there is a hint of something "beyond," something "*incommensurable*" with "the results of conscious logical thought" (vol. 1, p. 98). Perhaps for that very reason the subliminal source does not usually present itself as a personality, as it often does in many other types of automatism. Although the result is intelligible, often brilliantly intelligible, and therefore attributable to an intelligent conscious source, that source usually remains unidentified.

Sensory and Motor Automatisms and Mediumship

Myers saw sensory automatisms as "products of inner vision or audition, externalized into quasi-percepts" (*HP*, vol. 1, p. 222), exemplified in such phenomena as dreams, crystal-visions, and apparitions. Examining these topics he proceeds in his customary fashion from cases which involve nothing obviously supernormal, through cases which begin to manifest

34. For more extensive discussion of Myers's ideas about genius, see our Chapter 2 and especially Chapter 7.

heightened perception or memory, to cases which involve definite veridical elements not accessible to ordinary perception or inference. The most significant type of sensory automatism for Myers was certainly apparitions, which form the main focus of Chapters 6 and 7 of *Human Personality* (and which we have discussed in Chapter 2). His argument here relied primarily upon well-documented spontaneous cases, many derived from the SPR's monumental publications *Phantasms of the Living* (Gurney et al., 1886) and the "Census of Hallucinations" (H. Sidgwick et al., 1894), which first documented the existence of waking hallucinations in normal persons and provided an estimate of their incidence/prevalence that agrees quite closely with current data (Bentall, 2000). The individual cases are sometimes extraordinary both in the amount and character of veridical detail and in their impact on the persons involved. Myers again leads his readers in stages, from phantasms of living persons, to those of persons in crisis, or dying, to those of the recently or remotely dead, emphasizing cases that seem to point to continuing personal agency, awareness, and memory on the part of the dead. For example, an apparition may repeatedly try to convey some useful piece of information to the percipient, or be witnessed collectively, or be witnessed by a variety of persons in the same location, but at different times. The apparition may fulfill a pre-arranged compact to appear, for example, sometimes appearing not to the intended percipient but to a companion who did not know the deceased but subsequently recognized him in a picture.

Myers himself viewed this spontaneous case material as collectively providing compelling evidence for supernormal faculty in general, and convincing evidence for post-mortem survival in particular, but he was also acutely aware of the limitations and difficulties of this approach, dependent as it is upon laborious efforts to verify and corroborate details of unpredictable and fugitive events. For him, as has been indicated in our previous discussions, *motor* automatism ultimately provided a much more abundant and quasi-experimental source of material related to his central concerns. The amount of potentially veridical information derived from automatic writing, for example, was truly staggering, and, as we shall see, some mediums used this form of expression to convey striking evidence for the operation of a supernormal faculty, and for the possibility of post-mortem survival.

Myers considered all productions of automatic writing or speaking to be psychological automatisms, whether they purported to come from spirits or were thought of as expressions of some hidden part of the writer or speaker. He insisted that even if there were cases of actual communication with spirits through these automatic means, they must first be investigated as psychological phenomena that use the same mechanisms for emergence from the subliminal into the supraliminal that all other automatisms use. If we receive messages from spirits, he insisted, they are communicated first to some subliminal level of the psyche, and only then do they rise to the supraliminal. This meant that there was no way to distinguish functionally between messages that were produced entirely by inner processes of the subliminal and those that might originate at least in part outside the individual. Myers posited a "mythopœic" faculty (*HP*, vol. 2, p. 5), existing in the subliminal consciousness of everyone, that constantly produces fantasies, stories, poetic images, and other spontaneous creations which might on occasion pass through the threshold of consciousness into supraliminal awareness. If spirits communicated, they would do so by means of this faculty. But the same might be true of manifestations of mental disorders, such as the hallucinations of "hysterics" or delusions of paranoics. Thus, the genuineness of mediumistic communications could only be determined by objective evidence deriving from the *contents* of the messages. Speaking of the work of this mythopœic faculty, Myers commented:

> One wonders to what extent this strange manufacture of inward romances can be carried. There is, I may say, a great deal more of it in the world than is commonly suspected. I have myself received so many cases of these dramatised utterances—as though a number of different spirits were writing in turn through some automatist's hand—that I have come to recognise the operation of some law of dreams, so to call it, as yet but obscurely understood. The alleged personalities are for the most part not only unidentified, but purposely unidentifiable; they give themselves romantic or ludicrous names, and they are produced and disappear as lightly as puppets on a mimic stage.[35] (*HP*, vol. 2, p. 130)

Nevertheless, Myers believed that the "ludicrousness" of the form could not of itself rule out the possibility that veridical supernormal information was sometimes being communicated. Communications could be an odd mixture of the fantastic and the telepathic, for example, as shown in his exposition of the "Clelia" case of automatic writing already mentioned (Myers, 1884). Myers recognized the difficulty in providing anything like proof that messages coming through mediums were actually from spirits. But he believed that the study of mediumship had value in its own right, apart from the question of whether or not spirits were involved, since in the process a great deal could be learned about psychological dynamics at work in us all. At the same time he clearly recognized that the complexity of subliminal processes added greatly to the difficulties to be overcome in dealing with mediumistic material. He also knew that many psychological investigators of his day, such as Janet, believed that mediumship was invariably a manifestation of mental pathology. In short, he realized that if he wanted to make the case for seriously studying mediumistic communications, he would have to do so on the basis of a well-thought-out psychological foundation.

Myers did not believe that the phenomena of mediumship were invariably indicators of pathology. Neither did Swiss psychologist Theodore

---

35. James (1890b) too commented on the stylistic peculiarities of mediumistic communications: "If he ventures on higher intellectual flights, he abounds in a curiously vague optimistic philosophy-and-water, in which phrases about spirit, harmony, beauty, law, progression, development, etc., keep recurring. It seems exactly as if one author composed more than half of the trance-messages, no matter by whom they are uttered" (vol. 1, p. 394).

Flournoy, whose study of the medium "Hélène Smith," *From India to the Planet Mars,* is considered a classic to this day.[36] Flournoy (1900/1983) had this to say about the matter:

> It is far from being demonstrated that mediumship is a pathological phenomenon. No doubt it is abnormal, in the sense of being rare, exceptional, not usual; but morbidity is another matter. It would take quite some time, several years at least, to carry out a serious and scientific investigation of the phenomena called mediumistic and be able to pronounce on its true nature. At the moment there are as many opinions on the matter as there are investigators. It is interesting to note that in the countries where these studies have been pushed the furthest—England and America—the dominant view among the *savants* who have gone deepest into the subject is not at all unfavourable to mediumship; and that, far from seeing it as a special case of hysteria, they consider it a faculty superior, advantageous, healthy—of which hysteria would be a degenerated form, a pathological parody, a morbid caricature. (p. 59)

Despite the warnings of some clinicians about the possible pathological dimensions of mediumship, many, like Myers, considered the quality of mediumistic messages to be such that they could not be simply dismissed as defective or pathological mental functioning.[37] Myers cited much high-grade evidence of an association between supernormal faculty and mediumistic automatisms. Since I can here provide only the scantiest introduction to this enormous literature (see also the Appendix), I will simply summarize the principal facts about a medium cited by Myers as providing unusually powerful evidence for the presence of supernormal capacities, and even for the continued existence of the departed.

Mrs. Leonora Piper of Boston used both trance speaking and automatic writing in her sittings. She began her mediumship in the 1880s and over a period of 40 years produced information about people, living and dead, that often astounded her observers. For 15 years she was studied, scrutinized, monitored, and even followed by detectives to rule out any possibility that she could have obtained information by normal means. For a time William James played an informal supervisory role in regard to her seances. Then Richard Hodgson of the SPR was charged with the task of investigating every aspect of her mediumship and closing any possible loophole in the precautions taken to insure the genuineness of her phenomena.[38] Despite all this, she was never discovered in deception or fraud. Details of sittings,

36. Flournoy was a proponent of Myers's "subliminal psychology" (see Flournoy, 1911, and his 1903 review of *Human Personality*, on our digital version of *HP*).

37. C. D. Broad (1962) observed: "Although instructed opinion is almost unanimous in holding that trance-mediumship supplies data which require a paranormal explanation of *some* kind, there is no consensus of experts in favour of any one suggested paranormal explanation" (p. 259).

38. See, for example, R. Hodgson (1892, 1898); Hyslop (1901); James (1909); Lang (1900); Myers, Lodge, Leaf, and James (1890); Newbold (1898); Podmore (1898); E. M. Sidgwick (1900, 1915). For biographical material on Mrs. Piper see Gauld (1968), H. Holt (1915), Hyslop

with the precautions used and information produced, were reported in various articles, mostly in the *Proceedings* of the SPR. Myers himself discussed the nature and implications of Mrs. Piper's mediumship at some length in *Human Personality* (vol. 2, pp. 237–244, 599–624).

Mrs. Piper's mediumistic productions raised many intriguing psychological questions. The experience of going in and out of the trance state was characterized by different phenomena at different periods of her mediumship. At times it was a pleasant experience, and at others it involved unpleasant happenings such as convulsive movements and grinding of teeth. While in trance Mrs. Piper could be pricked, cut, or burned and experience no pain; she could even have ammonia held under her nose without apparent effect. When she achieved the trance state, she would appear to be taken over by one or more "spirits" who would conduct the seance and/or provide the information. She would typically sit slumped over, unresponsive to outside stimuli. She might speak to one sitter while writing messages to others. When Mrs. Piper returned to her normal state, she would often spend some time in an in-between state in which she would be confused, disoriented, and exhausted. When fully awake she consistently had no memory for what had occurred in her trance state.

Mrs. Piper's mediumship went through four distinct stages, with four different principal "controls" involved—a "control" being the intelligence who is in direct communication with the medium by voice or writing (E. M. Sidgwick, 1915). In the first stage her principal control called himself "Phinuit." In this stage Phinuit spoke directly to the sitters attending the trance session. In the second stage, which began in 1892 and is evidentially the most significant, Phinuit continued to communicate by voice, but the principal control was a recently deceased man named George Pellew, referred to as "G. P.," who gradually adopted writing as his mode of communication. During the first part of this period there were frequent occasions on which Phinuit talked about one subject while at the same time G. P. wrote about another, but eventually G. P. took over as Mrs. Piper's main control.[39] George Pellew, a Washingtonian, had been killed in a riding accident only a few weeks before his communications started. Hodgson had known him slightly, but many sitters came to Mrs. Piper who were intimately acquainted with the man and his peculiarities and who were in a good position to judge the genuineness of G. P.'s information and style of communication. Of 150 sitters who were introduced to him anonymously, G. P. recognized 30 as his acquaintances in life; those 30, and only those 30, were in fact known to the living Pellew. G. P. responded to these old friends in ways that were appropriate to the actual relationships that had existed, sometimes provid-

---

(1905), Piper (1929), Sage (1903), and Salter (1950). On critics of Mrs. Piper, see Gauld (1968, Appendix B).

39. Hodgson (1898) was a witness to these instances of dual simultaneous controls operating concurrently through two different automatisms. He also reported that there were rare occasions on which right and left hands wrote separate messages while at the same time a third message was communicated by voice (p. 395).

ing large amounts of veridical information about their shared experiences and demonstrating that he knew the views and intimate concerns of each.

The third period of Mrs. Piper's mediumship started in 1897 and extended to the death of Richard Hodgson in 1905. During this phase Mrs. Piper's chief controls were a group called the "Imperator Band," ostensibly the same spirits who had previously communicated through a well-known British medium, the clergyman Stainton Moses, and whose chief communicator was called "Rector." During this period messages delivered by voice greatly decreased and writing became the main form of communication. In the fourth period, Rector remained the main control, but Hodgson himself ostensibly began to communicate (see the report by James [1909] on Mrs. Piper's "Hodgson control").

In the course of her mediumship, and particularly in the "G. P." period, Mrs. Piper routinely produced motor automatisms containing abundant veridical information that could not have been obtained by ordinary means. But it was not only the *information* that impressed observers; Mrs. Piper also reproduced with striking accuracy the mannerisms, verbal expressions, attitudes, and humor of deceased persons who were ostensibly communicating through her—especially, but by no means exclusively, in the case of her "G. P." control. All of her main contemporary investigators were convinced that *some* supernormal process gave rise to these manifestations (see Gauld, 1982, pp. 32–44). William James (1896), in his Presidential Address to the SPR, made this declaration, too little known by modern psychologists:

> If you will let me use the language of the professional logic-shop, a universal proposition can be made untrue by a particular instance. If you wish to upset the law that all crows are black, you mustn't seek to show that no crows are; it is enough if you prove one single crow to be white. My own white crow is Mrs. Piper. In the trances of this medium, I cannot resist the conviction that knowledge appears which she has never gained by the ordinary waking use of her eyes and ears and wits. What the source of this knowledge may be I know not, and have not the glimmer of an explanatory suggestion to make; but from admitting the fact of such knowledge I can see no escape. (pp. 5–6)

For many, considering the volume, complexity, and power of the best available evidence, the only reasonable explanation was that the medium got her knowledge, as claimed, from spirits of the deceased who communicated through her. There were, however, already some who thought there was a cogent alternative explanation. When writing about the medium "Hélène Smith," Flournoy had invoked Myers's notion of the "mythopœic" to express the tendency that people have to construct characters, stories, and "romances" in their subliminal minds, and, on occasion, to dramatize these romances in the form of automatisms, such as automatic writing. Flournoy believed that mediums demonstrated this tendency to an extraordinary degree, and that the "spirits" that they claimed to be in touch with were the products of this faculty. His observations of "Hélène Smith" led him to believe that almost everything that she produced could be explained in terms of the creative play of her subliminal mind, supplemented by "cryptomnesia" (unconscious recall of forgotten events) and spurred on by the need to resolve certain personal psychological problems. Although in his analysis of "Hélène Smith's" communications Flournoy allowed for the possibility that telepathy occasionally had a role, for the most part that element was played down. Flournoy's estimation of the part played by supernormal knowledge in mediumistic communications evolved, however, and his final position on the matter can be found in *Spiritism and Psychology* (Flournoy, 1911). Here he stated that he now believed that the information presented by certain mediums was so impressive that telepathy must be involved.

Flournoy's position became the seed for a conception of mediumistic psychology that slowly evolved over the 20th century and eventually came to be called the "super-psi" theory of mediumship. This theory of mediumistic communication has two components:

> (1) *Super-ESP Component.* The medium is believed to have the ability to exercise psi capacities (telepathy, clairvoyance, retrocognition, precognition, and psychokinesis) to whatever extent necessary to obtain any information needed for successful impersonation of a deceased individual. Increased powers were gradually ceded to mediums over time as experimental and anecdotal confirmation of these faculties grew, but their extension far beyond anything that had actually been proven was thus invoked as part of a speculative hypothesis that could provide an alternative explanation for the impressive veridical information gifted mediums sometimes produced.

> (2) *Superplasticity Component.* The medium is also believed to be capable of unconsciously integrating and dramatizing supernormally acquired information about an individual in such a way as to convincingly impersonate that individual. This component is based on the belief that human beings have an unconscious tendency to create stories, fables, characterizations, and even well-rounded personalities (Myers's "mythopœic faculty") and express those creative fabrications publically. This ability is characterized by playfulness, inventiveness, and an urge to dramatize that remains wholly unconscious to the medium.

Ironically, the super-ESP component of the super-psi theory, which contributed to doubting that mediumistic communications proved survival, was the result of the extraordinary success of some mediums in demonstrating telepathy and clairvoyance generally (Gauld, 1982, pp. 131–138; Stevenson, 1977, pp. 157–158). In any event, there now existed a possible interpretation of mediumistic messages that did not involve attribution of fraud, but that also was not based on survival of bodily death.

Myers himself believed that the evidence already available as he was writing *Human Personality* was sufficient to establish post-mortem survival of human personality, but he acknowledged that it might not be convincing to everyone.[40] A number of other pillars of the SPR also went from early doubt to acceptance of some concept of survival. After many years of observation of Mrs. Piper, Hodgson, who was initially skeptical, himself became convinced of continued personal existence (for a summary of his reasons, see Gauld, 1968, pp. 265–267; for the complete account, see R. Hodgson, 1898). Physicist Oliver Lodge soon (1894), and the rather skeptical Eleanor Sidgwick more slowly (1915), came to the same conclusion, although in somewhat different forms. On the other hand, James remained uncommitted to any notion of survival, and McDougall (1911/1961), although respectful of those who assented, believed that "the evidence is not of such a nature that it can be stated in a form which should produce conviction in the mind of any impartial inquirer" (p. 347).

Since Myers's time much more evidence of the types he was familiar with, plus additional types largely or totally unknown to him, has come to light (Appendix). Nevertheless, the issue of survival remains essentially deadlocked, with more or less equally able and informed parties lined up on both sides. We will revisit the extremely difficult issues related to survival in Chapter 9, but for present purposes the crucial fact is that the mediumistic literature fully documents the predicted association between automatism and supernormal phenomena, and to that extent *at minimum* supports Myers's overall theoretical outlook.

Automatism and Experimental Psi Research

Large amounts of additional work on sensory and motor automatisms were carried out following Myers's death, largely along lines originated by him, and continued to provide high-quality evidence of the postulated link between automatisms and supernormal phenomena (Appendix). Significant later landmarks in the analysis of spontaneous cases include works by Broad (1962), H. Hart (Hart et al., 1956), Stevenson (1982), and Tyrrell (1938, 1943/1953).[41] Gauld (1982) critically reviewed all contending theories of apparitions and arrived at a position very close to that of Myers himself. More recent collections of spontaneous cases, such as those assembled by Louisa Rhine (1961, 1981), have confirmed not only the general fact that spontaneous cases of the sorts studied by Myers and his colleagues continue to occur, and in substantial numbers, but also more specific expectations. For example, a majority of spontaneous psi experiences occur in connection with dreams and waking hallucinations; moreover, experiences occurring in

40. "I do not venture to suppose that the evidence set forth in these volumes, even when considered in connection with other evidence now accessible in our *Proceedings*, will at once convince the bulk of my readers that the momentous, the epoch-making discovery has been already made" (*HP*, vol. 2, p. 79). In fact, what Myers regarded as his best evidence for survival (the case of Mrs. Thompson) was never published, and his records of it disappeared after his death.

41. H. Hart, Broad, and Stevenson also provide excellent accounts of trance mediumship.

dreams tend to be superior in amount and clarity of veridical detail to those that occur in the waking state.

By the 1940s, however, work on spontaneous cases and mediumship had declined drastically in favor of the narrower experimental and statistical approaches institutionalized at Duke by J. B. Rhine and his colleagues (Mauskopf & McVaugh, 1980). In reflection and perhaps imitation of broader trends in American psychology, psychical research as conceived by the founders of the SPR thus contracted to its modern expression, "parapsychology." Without denying the importance or value of good experimental work, I wish to comment parenthetically that this narrowing of perspective seems to me to have caused considerable damage both to psychical research itself and to psychology at large. Nonetheless, the modern experimental tradition of parapsychology has itself produced much additional empirical evidence in support of Myers's model. In the first instance I should like to cite that literature in its entirety as demonstrating that supernormal phenomena, which lie at the core of Myers's conception of the Subliminal Self, do in fact occur (Appendix).

In addition, there are many studies that more specifically support Myers's concept of sensory and motor automatisms as "mediating vehicles" (Tyrrell, 1938) for the expression of psi. For example, an important series of studies at Maimonides Hospital in Brooklyn confirmed the occurrence of telepathy in dreams (for a review, see Child, 1985). Several meta-analyses, such as Schechter (1984) and Stanford and Stein (1994), have also confirmed that hypnosis can improve performance in experimental psi tasks, although it interacts in complex ways with a variety of other factors. Additional evidence came to light when laboratory workers began to adapt their experimental and statistical procedures better to the "natural history" of psi. R. A. White (1964) analyzed the self-descriptions of a number of gifted subjects and found many features in common. In particular, the importance of deep relaxation, sensory isolation, and mental quietude characteristically resulted in emergence of the requested information (in the form of involuntary visual or auditory imagery), a sensory automatism. Much laboratory work on "internal attention states" (Honorton, 1977) was catalyzed by White's paper, and repeated meta-analyses (e.g., Bem & Honorton, 1994; and Radin, 1997, 2006) have demonstrated that experiments which elicit "free" verbal or graphic responses to complex target materials under such conditions consistently produce strong and qualitatively rich psi effects, rivaling in many instances those observed in spontaneous cases.

The older style of psi experimentation involving massed forced-choice guessing of ESP cards and the like would seem to provide little scope for the operation of automatisms, but significant evidence has been found even there, and especially in connection with gifted subjects. For example E. F. Kelly, Kanthamani, Child, and Young (1975) showed in the case of their special subject BD that the target-related information was again delivered primarily in the form of spontaneous, involuntary visual imagery, confirming a central feature of that subject's self-description. Similarly, the response method of the gifted subject Van Dam in the classic experiment of Brugmans, Heymans, and Weinberg was essentially a motor automatism (Schouten & Kelly, 1978). Both of these gifted subjects, and several others as well, also showed strong tendencies to get hits in "bursts" of unusually high scoring, often accompanied by mild alterations of state suggestive of automatism. In some cases, moreover, it could be shown that virtually all of the excess hits that occurred during very long series of trials occurred during scattered episodes of this sort (E. F. Kelly, 1982).

In sum, the existing literature of experimental parapsychology provides substantial additional support for Myers's theory, by confirming both the existence of supernormal phenomena and their linkage with psychological automatism.

Conclusion

When Myers died in 1901, his masterwork *Human Personality* was very nearly complete. There we find Myers's most mature formulation regarding psychological automatism and the issues surrounding it. His formulation involves five central features:

(1) He argued that phenomena such as automatic writing, hysteria, mediumship, dreams, hypnotism, and creative inspiration force investigators to look beyond previously available physiological explanations and to posit centers of consciousness, outside the awareness of the primary consciousness, as the sources of many complex automatic actions and perceptions.

(2) He insisted that these conscious centers must be regarded, at least in well-developed cases, as personalities or selves—intelligent sources of thoughts, feelings, and actions that possess their own memory chains and exhibit a psychological cohesiveness. He indicated that these centers are not necessarily merely alternating states, but may operate concurrently with the supraliminal self and with each other.

(3) He noted that secondary or subliminal conscious centers sometimes display awareness of each other. He also wrote about a kind of "inclusiveness" in which subliminal centers may sometimes be aware of the thoughts and actions of the primary or supraliminal consciousness, as well as the environment in which the supraliminal consciousness exists. This awareness is ordinarily not reciprocal, however.

(4) He recognized that there is a strong linkage between automatisms and psi capabilities. Beginning with his study of automatic writing in the 1880s, Myers demonstrated that information produced by the communicating consciousness was sometimes veridical and could not be accounted for in terms of knowledge gained through sense experience and other "normal" means. Indications of supernormal faculty were discovered throughout the range of the sensory and motor automatisms he studied.

(5) He further hypothesized an "I" or ultimate Subliminal Self that embraces both the supraliminal and subliminal consciousness and is aware of all activity that occurs in each. This Self has roots in a transcendental environment of some sort, accounting for its supernormal capabilities. It provides the overarching unity of the psyche, reconciling its "colonial" versus "unitary" aspects, and it survives the shock of physical death.

Myers's investigation of automatisms focused on complex phenomena which demonstrated the presence of conscious intelligent activity but did not arise from the ordinary consciousness of the subject. He rejected the contemporary physiological explanation then in favor—epitomized by the term "unconscious cerebration"—as inadequate to explain the data, and he posited instead a notion of automatism which was essentially psychological. From a certain point of view, the whole history of subsequent developments concerning automatism can be looked at as a continued tension between this newly formulated psychological view of human experience and the attempt, subtle or not so subtle, to return to the "unconscious cerebration" explanation. I believe that the arguments of Myers and others against this position, based as they are on the data of experience, have, if anything, gained strength over the past century. The first four features of Myers's position, in particular, I regard as empirically established. The last feature, however, is more contentious and leads to even larger issues.

Underlying the specific debate about the interpretation of automatism is a more general controversy about the role of mind, consciousness, and volition. Myers, like James, Bergson, McDougall, and others, insisted that a psychology that gives no power to mind and consciousness is an absurdity. He was determined to hold a place for the mind and mental activity in scientific psychology, insisting that automatism was *psychological* automatism. His position was inclusive, because he believed that mind and organism stand as irreducible realities that must in the end make peace with each other.

Finally, among those who preserved a central place for consciousness and who acknowledged multiple consciousnesses as a real fact of human experience, Myers espoused a holistic rather than monadic view of the human psyche. The monadic schema, as described by McDougall, Balfour, Hilgard, or others, presents us with a hierarchical, top-down picture of mental functioning in which our ordinary consciousness stands at the top of the pyramid and, at least in healthy functioning, directly or indirectly controls all subordinate elements. In my opinion, this schema collapses in the face of the complex empirical realities of psychological automatism. Automatic veridical communication and creative inspiration tell powerfully against the structure assumed in the monadic schema. Myers, in contrast, insisted that our ordinary consciousness is not on top in any significant way, and that, as a matter of fact, what is most *sublime* in us and what is most *original*, derives from the subliminal, from what is out of sight, and from what, in the last analysis, must be our most essential Self. I believe that only this perspective can provide a framework for understanding the whole spectrum of human experience as revealed in automatism, and I believe it was the genius of Myers to so effectively give that perspective expression. We will return to these themes in a larger setting in Chapter 9.

Chapter 6

Unusual Experiences Near Death and Related Phenomena

Emily Williams Kelly, Bruce Greyson, & Edward F. Kelly

> If consciousness be a mere epiphenomenon...accompanying, but in no way guiding, certain molecular changes in the brain, we shall of course expect...that consciousness is exclusively linked with the functional disintegration of central nervous elements, and varies in its intensity with the rapidity or energy of that disintegration. And ordinary experience, at least within physiological limits, will support some view like this. Yet now and then we find a case where vivid consciousness has existed during a state of apparent coma...tranquilly and intelligently co-existing with an almost complete abeyance of ordinary vital function....Until this new field has been more fully worked—until the traces of memory which may survive from comatose, ecstatic, syncopal conditions have been revived (by hypnotic suggestion or otherwise), and carefully compared, we have no right to make any absolute assertion as to the concomitant cerebral processes on which consciousness depends. (Myers, 1891c, pp. 116–117)

The hypothesis that consciousness is the product of brain processes, or that mind is merely the subjective concomitant of neurological events, has been and remains the almost universal assumption in neuroscience and psychology. Investigations of certain extraordinary circumstances, however, reveal phenomena that call into question this assumption. An analogy can be drawn with Newtonian dynamics, which appears to explain the physics of everyday life. It was only the investigation of extraordinary circumstances, involving extremely small or large distances, speeds, or mass, that revealed the limits of the Newtonian model and the need for additional explanatory models. So too with the question of the mind-brain relationship: As Myers understood in urging his colleagues in psychology to study subliminal and other unusual psychological phenomena, exploration of extraordinary circumstances may reveal limitations of the current model of mind-brain identity and the need for a more comprehensive explanatory model.

One such extraordinary circumstance is the continued functioning of the mind when the brain appears to be inactive or impaired, such as may occur near death. Myers specifically recognized the importance of such circumstances: "It is possible that we might learn much were we to question dying persons, on their awakening from some comatose condition, as to their memory of any dream or vision during that state" (*HP*, vol. 2, p. 315), and he thus urged "much more of experiment and observation of mental conditions under anæsthetics, during recovery from fainting, and even during apparent coma" (Myers, 1891c, p. 115). He himself reported three cases of experiences occurring when a person was close to death but then revived (Myers, 1891c, 1886b, p. 305; 1892a, pp. 180–200; *HP*, vol. 2, pp. 315–323). The importance of such cases lies in the fact that "the patient, while in a comatose state, almost pulseless, and at a temperature much below normal, did, nevertheless, undergo a remarkably vivid series of mental impressions" (1892a, p. 194).

Such experiences have, in recent years, been labeled "near-death experiences," or NDEs. They are not, however, the isolated and homogeneous phenomenon that such a label suggests. Many experiences called "near-death" experiences have occurred when the person was *not* physiologically near death, and individual features associated with NDEs occur in a wide variety of conditions in which the person is also clearly not near death. We believe that the difficulties in explaining, and even in defining, the NDE stem at least in part from the failure to examine this phenomenon within the context of this larger family of related experiences. In this chapter, after outlining the general nature of the phenomena known as "NDEs" and the various explanatory models that have been proposed for them, we will then examine some of the other types of experiences that are phenomenologically related to NDEs. These include experiences in which the ordinary perceived relationship between consciousness and the body has been altered—especially "out-of-body experiences," in which a person's consciousness seems to be functioning normally, but from a spatial location outside the body. We will also discuss a variety of hallucinatory[1] experiences in which a person has

1. We wish to emphasize immediately that our use of the word "hallucination," here or elsewhere, is in no way meant to imply that the experiences we discuss in this chapter are pathological. We define "hallucination" as a perceptual experience in the absence of corresponding sensory input. Following Myers's approach, we propose that the word "hallucination" should be understood more broadly as a psychological process that can take non-pathological as well as pathological forms, depending on the circumstances in which the experiences occur. Unfortunately, the association of the word "hallucination" with pathology and delusion is so ingrained that Stevenson (1983b) has suggested that we need a new word, "idiophany," to refer

seen, heard, or otherwise sensed the presence of a dying or deceased person not physically present. Finally, we will briefly discuss religious "conversion experiences" of the sort described by James (1902/1958). These provide a bridge between NDE-type phenomena and the more extreme manifestations of noetic or life-transforming experiences associated with mysticism, to which we will devote Chapter 8.

We wish to emphasize again that all these phenomena are interrelated in some fundamental but so far poorly understood way. All involve a marked alteration in the ordinary relationship of a person's consciousness with the external world. We believe it is essential to consider the entire spectrum of experiences when proposing explanations for any one of them. We have chosen to organize this chapter specifically around the experiences known as NDEs, however, because of their extreme theoretical importance. Despite the wide variety of physiological and psychological conditions under which NDEs occur, many such experiences do clearly occur when the brain is severely impaired. At the end of this chapter we will focus specifically on this aspect of NDEs, underscoring the important theoretical implications of experiences of this type for current neurophysiological models of consciousness.

Near-Death Experiences: An Introduction

There is no universally agreed on definition of NDEs (Greyson, 1999), but they are generally understood to be the unusual, often vivid and realistic, and sometimes profoundly life-changing experiences occurring to people who have been either physiologically close to death, as in cardiac arrest or other life-threatening conditions, or psychologically close to death, as in accidents or illnesses in which they feared they would die.

The following experiences come from our collection at the University of Virginia and illustrate some of the features commonly reported. The first was reported by a woman who was in surgery after hemorrhaging severely and going into shock:

> I had floated out of my body and was looking down on all of this [the doctors and nurses working on her]. I was wearing white. I started floating down a tunnel which had rough looking sides and a blinding, bright light at the end, and I was headed for the lighted end. As I was going through the tunnel I saw my Grandfather's face, and he was smiling at me. He said something like, "It's been a long time. Welcome." He died in 1948, and I was his favorite grandchild; we were very close. I saw several faces on the wall; some of them I knew and some I did not, but they were all smiling. I

to non-pathological hallucinations. Until this is or some other word becomes widely adopted, however, we will continue to use the word "hallucination" to include the large number of experiences that go beyond sensory perception but that seem to have more in common with ordinary sensory experiences than with illusions or delusions.

> was almost to the end, and my Great-Grandmother, who helped raise me and I was very close to, appeared, and she said "Go back; you have a child who needs you. You can come here with us later." I tried to argue with her, but she told me flatly, "You go back."

Another woman, who was in surgery after suffering massive pulmonary emboli, reported:

> Some time after entering the operating room, I found myself above the scene looking down on myself, and the doctors and nurses around me. I could, of course, hear everything they were saying, and I wanted to tell them not to feel so bad, that I couldn't stand the pain any more and I liked it where I was. I was somewhere where it was so beautiful and peaceful that I wanted to stay there forever. I did not actually see anyone I knew, or anything in particular. There was a bright, but soft light, and I felt the most comforting sense of peace. Suddenly I thought "Ben [her husband] can't possibly bring up Molly alone; I had better go back," and that is the last thing I remember. I am absolutely positive that I decided to come back. Since that time I have no fear of dying.
>
> I spent ten days in intensive care, and almost a month in the hospital, but I was never able to mention this to the doctors or nurses. I have mentioned it to only a very few people in the last couple of years, and then reluctantly. I feel as though people might think I am making up a story for attention, but I assure [you] that is not so.
>
> An experience such as this does change your outlook on life and also some of your religious beliefs. I have always been an active church-goer, but only on the surface, I am afraid. Since then, I have given thought to some of the facts I was taught, and have my own way of dealing with them. I wish that people who have a loved one die suddenly, perhaps in an early stage of life, could be made to understand what this felt like, they wouldn't feel so bad.

Profound experiences near death have been reported throughout history and in many cultures.[2] Among the earliest reports is Plato's description in Book 10 of the *Republic* of the experiences of the soldier Er during the time when he had been thought dead and placed on a funeral pyre. In more recent times, numerous experiences were reported in the medical literature of the 19th and 20th centuries (for a list of some of these, see Greyson, 1998). The 19th-century physician Brierre de Boismont (1859) described two such experiences. In one of them, a woman who had been delirious and seemed to have died suddenly sighed and was revived by her attendants: "Instead, however, of thanking the persons who had taken such pains to restore her to life, she complained to them of their having recalled her soul from a condition of indescribable repose and happiness....She added that she had heard

2. See, for example, Audette (1982), C. B. Becker (1981, 1984), C. Carr (1993), Counts (1983), Feng and Liu (1992), R. Gardner (1983, p. 1932), Holck (1978), Kellehear (1993), Lundahl (1982), Osis and Haraldsson (1977/1997), Pasricha (1993), Pasricha and Stevenson (1986), Schorer (1985), and Zaleski (1987).

[while seemingly dead] the sighs and lamentations of her father, and all that had been said with regard to her funeral" (p. 263).

As we mentioned earlier, later in the 19th century Myers (1892a) reported three cases that included many of the features reported in today's experiences. In one of these, which occurred in 1889, the patient (a physician himself) seemed to have died from typhoid fever; his physician testified that "he was actually dead as fully as I ever supposed anyone dead," with no perceptible pulse, heartbeat, or respiration (p. 193). Nonetheless, the patient had a vivid and complex experience of seeming to leave his body and see it, as well as the actions of the people in the room. He then went to a place of great beauty where he felt a presence and saw the face of an unidentified person who radiated great love. He also saw a dark cloud and dark pathway (perhaps corresponding to the later descriptions by other people of a tunnel). He seemed to be given the choice of staying or returning, but when he chose to stay and tried to cross an apparent boundary, he was stopped from proceeding and then suddenly found himself back in his body. Throughout the experience, he seemed to be in a nonphysical body that had "perfect health and strength," and he reported that "memory, judgment, and imagination, the three great faculties of mind, were intact and active" (pp. 183–184).

The first systematic study was that of Heim (1892/1972), who published a report on his collection of 30 firsthand accounts (including his own) of experiences of mountain climbers who had fallen in the Alps, soldiers wounded in war, workers who had fallen from scaffolds, and individuals who had nearly died in accidents and near-drownings. This study was important for bringing together for the first time a large number of these experiences, including experiences that occur, not when the person is physiologically near death, but when he or she only thinks that death is imminent.

Similar systematic studies were conducted during the early 1970s, particularly by psychiatrist Russell Noyes (e.g., Noyes, 1972, 1976). In 1975 a popular book by the psychiatrist and philosopher Raymond Moody brought widespread attention to such phenomena, and in the past three decades there has been a surge of interest in and study of them.

As research on these experiences has increased, it has become clear that NDEs are not infrequent. Our collection at the University of Virginia now numbers 861 reports, and other researchers, including the many local and national branches of the International Association for Near-Death Studies, have also collected large numbers of cases. Early estimates of the incidence of NDEs may have been inflated by ambiguous criteria for NDEs and by biased sampling (Greyson, 1998), but studies in the past decade, using more explicit criteria and better sampling techniques suggest that NDE-like experiences may occur in about 10–20% of patients close to death (Greyson, 2003; Milne, 1995; Parnia, Waller, Yeates, & Fenwick, 2001; Schwaninger, Eisenberg, Schechtman, & Weiss, 2002; van Lommel, van Wees, Meyers, & Elfferich, 2001).

Although the widespread impression is that NDEs occur among patients who have been clinically dead and then resuscitated, they in fact occur in a wide variety of medical circumstances. An examination of medical records in cases in our collection (all of them experiences reported to us retrospectively) showed that slightly more than half of the patients, although ill enough to have been hospitalized, were at no time in danger of dying (Owens, Cook [Kelly], & Stevenson, 1990; Stevenson, Cook [Kelly], & McClean-Rice, 1989–1990); NDEs may therefore occur when patients fear they are dying even if in fact they are not. Moreover, NDEs can also occur when patients are suddenly confronted with death but escape unharmed, as in falls or near-accidents (e.g., Heim, 1892/1972).[3]

Nonetheless, there remain a substantial number of cases in which patients were clinically near death, such as during cardiac arrest or some other, usually sudden, loss of vital functions (Finkelmeier, Kenwood, & Summers, 1984; Greyson, 2003; Owens et al., 1990; Parnia et al., 2001; Sabom, 1982; Schoenbeck & Hocutt, 1991; Schwaninger et al., 2002; van Lommel et al., 2001). These include some in children who suffered cardiac arrest (Gabbard & Twemlow, 1984, pp. 154–156; M. Morse, 1983, 1994a, pp. 67–69, 1994b; Serdahely, 1990). In one recent prospective study of 344 cardiac arrest patients, 62 reported NDEs following resuscitation from cardiac arrest (van Lommel et al., 2001). In our own collection of retrospectively reported NDEs, out of 114 cases for which we have obtained and rated medical records, 35 were rated "4" on a 4-point scale of severity of condition, meaning that there was some documentation of loss of vital signs, often including cardiac arrest.

Just as NDEs can occur in a wide variety of circumstances, so do they include a wide variety of features. Frequently recurring features include feelings of peace and joy; a sense of being out of one's body and watching events going on around one's body and, occasionally, at some distant physical location; a cessation of pain; seeing a dark tunnel or void; seeing an unusually bright light, sometimes experienced as a "Being of Light" that radiates love and may speak or otherwise communicate with the person; encountering other beings, often deceased persons whom the experiencer recognizes; experiencing a revival of memories or even a full life review, sometimes accompanied by feelings of judgment; seeing some "other realm," often of great beauty; sensing a barrier or border beyond which the person cannot go; and returning to the body, often reluctantly.

Although all of these features recur frequently in large groups of cases, individual experiences are unique. The number of features reported in individual cases varies, no experience containing all features has been reported, no single feature is common to all NDEs, and features do not necessarily

3. In our studies patients are judged to be near death if the medical records indicated a loss of some vital sign such as blood pressure or pulse or if the condition was serious enough to have caused death if the patient had received no medical attention. Patients judged not to be near death were those whose medical records indicated that they had a serious, but not life-threatening condition and those who were not seriously ill. Many of these medical records were obtained years after the experience in question, and we cannot vouch for their accuracy or completeness. Nevertheless, as a group they illustrate the wide variety of physiological conditions in which these experiences can occur.

unfold in a particular fixed order. Moreover, in contrast to most NDEs, which are positive experiences, there are also NDEs that are frightening or unpleasant (Greyson & Bush, 1992).[4]

Some investigators have attempted to evaluate NDEs by quantifying their common features. The most widely used systems have been the Weighted Core Experience Index (WCEI) (Ring, 1980) and the NDE Scale (Greyson, 1983b, 1985), a 32-point rating scale that has been used primarily to determine the "richness" of, or number of features in, individual cases and has shown high internal consistency and reliability, and high correlation with Ring's WCEI ($r = .90$).

All the major features of NDEs have been reported in a wide variety of circumstances, but certain features correlate somewhat with the circumstances in which the experiences occur. For example, alterations in the sense of time, unusually rapid thinking, and a revival of memories are more common in near-death events that are sudden and unexpected than in those that may have been anticipated (Greyson, 1985). In a study in which medical records were examined to determine how close to death the person actually was, certain other features, such as an encounter with a brilliant light, enhanced cognitive function, and positive emotions, were more common among individuals who were actually close to death than in those who were not so seriously ill (Owens et al., 1990). People actually close to death were also more likely to report encounters with deceased persons than those who were not (E. W. Kelly, 2001). Although children's NDEs are generally similar to those of adults, none have been reported that include a life review, perhaps not surprisingly (Bush, 1983; M. Morse, Castillo, Venecia, Milstein, & Tyler, 1986).

One particularly noteworthy feature is that for many experiencers an NDE permanently and dramatically alters the person's attitudes, beliefs, and values, often leading to beneficial personal transformations. Aftereffects most often reported include increases in spirituality, concern for others, and appreciation of life; a heightened sense of purpose; and decreases in fear of death, in materialistic attitudes, and in competitiveness.[5] A large study of NDEs among survivors of cardiac arrest showed that, after both a two-year and an eight-year followup interval, people who had NDEs in connection with the cardiac arrest had a significant decrease in their fear of death and a significant increase in their belief in survival after death, whereas those who had not had an NDE tended not to believe in survival (van Lommel et al., 2001). More specifically (and seemingly paradoxically, given the positive nature of most experiences and the reluctance of many experiencers to return to the body), those who experience an NDE as the result of a suicide attempt rarely attempt suicide again, in contrast to most

4. Unpleasant experiences seem to be the exception, however. In our collection, for example, among cases for which we have data on this feature, only 11% described the NDE as being either "totally unpleasant" or "mostly unpleasant."

5. See, for example, Bauer (1985), Flynn (1986), Grey (1985), Greyson (1983a, 1992), Noyes (1980), Ring (1980, 1984), Sabom (1982), and van Lommel et al. (2001).

suicide attempters. This protective effect may be the result of an increased sense of purpose and appreciation for life (Greyson, 1981, 1992–1993).

Even when the NDE itself has been a positive experience, it can sometimes have negative consequences. NDEs frequently lead to significant changes in values, attitudes, and interests, and family and friends may have difficulty understanding and accepting these changes (Bush, 1991; Flynn, 1986; Greyson, 1997; Insinger, 1991). Also, some people may doubt their sanity in the aftermath of such an unexpected and powerful experience, and they may thus fail to discuss this fear or their experience with others because of a concern that they will be ridiculed or rejected (see, e.g., van Lommel et al., 2001, p. 2043).

Explanatory Models of Near-Death Experiences

Apart from the profound psychological effects that NDEs often have on individual experiencers, the importance of NDEs for psychology lies in their implications for an understanding of the relationship of mind and brain. In particular, it is the continuation and even enhancement of mental functioning at a time when the brain is physiologically impaired that presents problems for the prevailing view of mind-brain relations and thus renders NDEs of particular importance in this regard. In this section, we will review some of the explanatory models that have been proposed for NDEs, paying special attention to how well they can account for the various features of NDEs and especially for enhanced mental functioning.

Psychological and Cultural Theories

Expectation

Many observers have considered NDEs to be a defense against the threat of death. One widespread suggestion is that NDEs are products of the imagination generated to protect oneself when facing the threat of death and constructed from one's personal and cultural expectations. NDEs do seem to be a universal phenomenon—as we mentioned earlier, they have been reported throughout history and in many cultures—and they may thus be a common human reaction when confronted with death. On the other hand, there are cultural differences, suggesting that prior beliefs may have some influence on the kind of experience a person will have or report. The life review and tunnel sensation, for example, are common in some cultures but rare in others (Kellehear, 1993). Cases in India show some differences in features as compared with Western cases, primarily in the way in which the person reports being taken to an "other" realm and being sent back (Pasricha & Stevenson, 1986). Cases in north India also show differences from cases in south India (Pasricha, 1993).

Other data, however, do not support an expectation theory. Experiences often differ sharply from the individual's prior religious or personal beliefs and expectations about death (Abramovitch, 1988; Ring, 1984). People who had no prior knowledge about NDEs describe the same kinds of experiences and features as do people more familiar with the phenomenon (Greyson, 1991; Greyson & Stevenson, 1980; Ring, 1980; Sabom, 1982). Young children, who are less likely to have developed expectations about death, report NDEs with features similar to those of adults (Bush, 1983; Gabbard & Twemlow, 1984; Herzog & Herrin, 1985; M. Morse, 1983, 1994a, 1994b; M. Morse, Conner, & Tyler, 1985; M. Morse et al., 1986; Serdahely, 1990). Because many childhood experiences have been recounted only after the child has grown up, and may therefore have been influenced by the adult reporter's beliefs, Serdahely (1991) compared adult accounts of childhood NDEs with contemporary accounts by children. The features reported did not differ significantly between these two groups

If NDEs are significantly shaped by cultural expectations, we might expect that experiences occurring after 1975, when Moody's first book made NDEs such a well-known phenomenon, would conform more closely to Moody's "model" than those that occurred before that date. This does not appear to be the case (Long & Long, 2003). Similarly, a study of 24 experiences in our collection that not only *occurred* but were *reported* before 1975 found no significant differences in the features reported, when compared to a matched sample of cases occurring after 1984, except that fewer "tunnel" experiences were reported in the pre-1975 group (Athappilly, Greyson, & Stevenson, 2006).

There may therefore be a core experience underlying the varying details, and it is not the core experience that differs so much as the ways in which people in different cultures describe or interpret what they have experienced. For example, among both Indian and Western cases many people report being met by discarnate persons; but in the West these persons are usually either identified as deceased loved ones or are unrecognized, whereas in India they are often assumed to be messengers of the god of death. Similarly, in both cultures people report that they were sent back because it was "not my time"; but in the West people often feel that they were sent back because of unfinished business, whereas in India they believe that they were sent back because the messengers of death inadvertently took the wrong person (Osis & Haraldsson, 1977/1997; Pasricha & Stevenson, 1986). Other features commonly reported cross-culturally include the sense of being out of one's body, going to another realm, and seeing a light. There seems, in sum, to be an underlying core experience that is "inevitably cast in the images, concepts and symbols available to the individual" (Roberts & Owen, 1988, p. 611; see also Knoblauch, Schmied, & Schnettler, 2001).[6]

6. In this respect, NDEs are like mystical experiences. There has long been a dichotomy of opinion about mystical experiences, some emphasizing the cross-cultural differences in reports of mystical experience, others (such as James, 1902/1958, and Stace, 1960/1987) argu-

Related to the "expectation" model is the more recent suggestion that some NDEs may be the product of "false memories," that is, that "some patients, on hearing about other survivors' NDEs, would start to imagine what it would have been like if they had had the same experience" (French, 2001, p. 2010). French derives his argument from the observation that four of 37 patients in van Lommel et al.'s (2001) study did not initially report an NDE, but then did report one at a two-year followup interview. Without denying the possibility that a few reported NDEs may be the result of a false memory, we believe that for most this hypothesis is highly unlikely. Even if one discounts the claim of many people reporting NDEs that they had not previously heard about such experiences—something that we are not inclined to do—one also has to consider the fact that many people are reluctant to talk about their experiences with other persons, and may carefully choose when and to whom they do so. In our collection of cases, for example, 57% said that they had been afraid or reluctant to talk about their experience, and 27% never told anyone until more than a year afterwards. Given these observations, we are not at all surprised that four of 37 people in van Lommel et al.'s study might not have reported their experience to the investigators initially.[7]

Birth Models

In a variation on the idea that NDEs are a universal psychological reaction to the threat of dying, Sagan (1979, 1984) interpreted them—with their features of a dark tunnel, a bright light, and going to another realm—as a memory of one's birth. C. B. Becker (1982) argued, however, that newborns lack the visual, spatial, or mental capacities to register memories of being born. Even if the implicit assumption here about the dependence of episodic memory upon the brain were to prove inadequate (see Chapter 4), a more important criticism is that many NDEs do not contain the features of a tun-

---

ing that there is a core of common experience behind those differences. We discuss this issue more fully in Chapter 8.

7. We have had people tell us that they had *never* told anyone about their experience, until they contacted our research unit and told us. While interviewing a woman at her home about her NDE, one of us (EWK) learned that she had never before told her husband about her experience. Moreover, when EWK's impending visit prompted the woman to explain to her husband the reason for the visit, he told her that he too had had an NDE, which he had never told her about.

This example is not unique. K. Clark (1984) reported a similar situation: At the hospital and in the presence of his wife, a patient told Clark about his NDE, which occurred during multiple episodes of cardiac arrest. When he had finished his description, his wife told them both that she too had had an NDE, during childbirth a few years earlier, but that "she had never told anyone about this, even her husband, because he had 'always been scientific minded and I just didn't think he would accept it, and I wasn't prepared to be rejected'" (p. 249). Another patient, readmitted to Clark's unit several years after an earlier hospitalization, told her that, although she had twice asked him during the earlier hospitalization whether he had any unusual memories associated with his accident, "he had lied and denied any recollections...[because] the experience had been so personal that he needed to come to terms with it in his own mind before telling anyone about it" (p. 246).

nel or a light, and many other common features of NDEs do not seem adequately accounted for by a "birth" model. Furthermore, Blackmore (1983) found that claims of OBEs and of passing through a tunnel to another realm were equally common among persons born by caesarean section and those born by normal vaginal delivery. Grof (1975) and Grosso (1981, 1983) have generalized the birth model and suggested that NDEs reflect an archetype of birth (or rebirth), rather than an actual memory, but it is difficult to see how this theory could be tested empirically.

Depersonalization

Noyes and Kletti (1976) suggested that NDEs are a type of depersonalization, in which feelings of detachment, strangeness, and unreality protect one from the threat of death. There are significant phenomenological differences, however, between most NDEs and depersonalization (see, e.g., Gabbard & Twemlow, 1984, pp. 45–59).[8] For example, in depersonalization, "the feeling of one's own reality is temporarily lost" (p. 46), a feeling that does not occur in NDEs. Moreover, many NDEs are described instead as being vividly real. Most experiences of depersonalization are also unpleasant in nature, again in distinct contrast to most NDEs. Furthermore, in depersonalization the person may feel a certain detachment from his or her body without feeling actually out of the body.

Personality Factors

Attempts to identify personality traits or variables that predict either the occurrence of an NDE or the number and type of features occurring have generally been inconclusive, although the research has been limited so far to retrospective studies that may not reliably reflect the person's characteristics before the NDE. Experiencers have collectively been found to be as psychologically healthy as people who have not had an NDE, and they also do not differ in age,[9] gender, race, religion, religiosity, intelligence, neuroticism, extroversion, anxiety, or Rorschach measures (Gabbard & Twemlow, 1984; Greyson, 1991; Irwin, 1985; T. P. Locke & Shontz, 1983; Ring, 1980; Sabom, 1982).

Conjecturing that people who experience NDEs may be good hypnotic subjects, remember their dreams more often, and engage easily in mental imagery, some researchers have begun to examine personality variables related to hypnotic susceptibility, dream recall, or imagery. One such char-

8. Gabbard and Twemlow (1984) were actually comparing depersonalization with out-of-body experiences (OBEs), not NDEs in particular, but the features they attributed to OBEs (p. 114) apply equally to NDEs. As we will discuss later in this chapter, OBEs and NDEs are overlapping phenomena, although neither can be subsumed under the other.

9. There does seem to be a tendency for NDEs to be reported by younger persons, at least among cardiac patients (see van Lommel et al., 2001, p. 2043); but whether this is because NDEs are more likely to occur in younger people, whether it is because younger people are more likely to report NDEs, or whether older people are less likely to survive a medical condition in which an NDE might occur are questions that remain open.

acteristic is dissociation. Ring and Rosing (1990) and Greyson (2000) found that near-death experiencers scored higher than a comparison group on a dissociation scale, although their scores were much lower than those of patients with pathological dissociative disorders. Near-death experiencers may therefore be persons who respond to serious stress with dissociative behavior that is adaptive, rather than pathological (Greyson, 2001).

Related to dissociative tendencies may be *absorption*, or the ability to screen out the external world and focus one's attention either on selected sensory experiences or on internal imagery (Tellegen & Atkinson, 1974), and *fantasy proneness*, characterized by frequent and vivid fantasies and even hallucinations, intensely vivid sensory experiences, and eidetic imagery (S. C. Wilson & Barber, 1981, 1983). Empirical data regarding absorption and fantasy proneness among near-death experiencers, however, have been inconclusive. In one study people experiencing an NDE had slightly higher scores on scales of absorption or fantasy proneness, as compared with a control group (Council & Greyson, 1985); but the experiencers' scores on the measure of fantasy proneness were substantially lower than those of Wilson and Barber's fantasizers. Ring and Rosing (1990) found no such correlation, although this finding may have been partly the result of using only a brief questionnaire rather than intensive interviews (Lynn & Rhue, 1988). In any case, even a strong relationship between fantasy proneness and NDEs would not demonstrate that NDEs are nothing *but* fantasies, especially since (as we will discuss later) there are NDEs in which the person has perceived some real, verified event occurring outside the ordinary sensory range. A tendency toward fantasy proneness or absorption might instead reflect an ability to enter more readily into altered states in which the ordinary relationship of consciousness to brain activity and to the external environment has changed.

Physiological Theories

There have been numerous attempts to explain NDEs in terms of conventional biochemical or neurobiological mechanisms, acting either alone or in conjunction with other putative mechanisms. Most of these proposals are variations on the basic idea that changes in the neurochemistry of the brain, brought on by the physiological or psychological conditions accompanying a close brush with death (whether real or perceived), lead to abnormal neuroelectric activity in certain critical brain areas, usually in the limbic system or temporal lobes, that produces hallucinations. Most of these theoretical models are based on claimed similarities between the phenomenology of NDEs and that of experiences associated with the proposed neurochemical or neuroanatomical mechanisms. We will briefly review here some of these models. We should keep in mind, however, that as researchers have learned more about the variations and complexities of the conditions under which NDEs can occur, there has been a noticeable move away from attempting to find a single common mechanism underlying all NDEs, and toward recognizing that "a multi-leveled interpretation is...the most useful" (Jansen, 1997a, p. 13). Most commentators, therefore, would now acknowledge that these proposals, biological and psychological, are not mutually exclusive and that a variety of factors can lead to the occurrence of an NDE.

Blood Gases

One of the earliest and most persistent of the physiological theories proposed for NDEs is that lowered levels of oxygen (hypoxia or anoxia), perhaps accompanied by increased levels of carbon dioxide (hypercarbia), have produced hallucinations (Blackmore, 1993; Lempert, 1994; Rodin, 1980). Although such changes are potentially a factor, particularly among NDEs occurring in connection with cardiac impairment or arrest, NDEs also occur in many circumstances in which changes in oxygen or carbon dioxide levels are unlikely, such as non-life-threatening illnesses, falls, or other near-accidents. Furthermore, despite claims to the contrary, the experiential phenomena associated with such changes are only superficially similar to NDEs. One study frequently cited is that of Whinnery (1997), who compared NDEs to what he called the "dreamlets" occurring in brief periods of unconsciousness induced in fighter pilots by rapid acceleration in a centrifuge (this reduces blood flow, and therefore delivery of oxygen, to the brain). He claimed that some features common to NDEs are also found in these hypoxic episodes, including tunnel vision, bright lights, brief fragmented visual images, a sense of floating, pleasurable sensations, and, rarely, a sense of leaving the body. The primary features of acceleration-induced hypoxia, however, are myoclonic convulsions (rhythmic jerking of the limbs), impaired memory for events just prior to the onset of unconsciousness, tingling in extremities and around the mouth, confusion and disorientation upon awakening, and paralysis (Whinnery, 1997), symptoms that do not occur in association with NDEs. Moreover, contrary to NDEs, the visual images Whinnery reported frequently included living people, but never deceased people; and no life review or accurate out-of-body perceptions have been reported in acceleration-induced loss of consciousness.

Other authors have suggested that, in parallel with lowered oxygen levels, increased levels of carbon dioxide may contribute to NDEs (Blackmore, 1996, p. 74; Jansen, 1997a, p. 19). Again, this hypothesis is based on the purported similarity between NDEs and phenomena reported in connection with the proposed mechanism. For example, M. Morse, Venecia, and Milstein (1989) state that "all the reported elements of NDEs can be produced in the office setting" with inhaled carbon dioxide (p. 48). Only one study, however, is cited in support of this claim (Meduna, 1950). Meduna does mention some features that occur commonly in NDEs (such as a sense of being out of the body, a bright light, a dark void or tunnel, revival of a memory, and a sense of peace, love, or harmony with God); but these seem comparatively rare, isolated, and fragmented in this context. And other important features, such as meeting deceased persons or a life review involving many memories, are not reported. In sum, the overall phenomenology of carbon dioxide inhalation does not so far seem at all comparable to that of NDEs.[10]

Another important objection to attributing NDEs to anoxia has been noted by van Lommel et al. (2001). If anoxia and related mechanisms play an important role in the generation of NDEs, why do not most cardiac arrest patients report an NDE? Clearly, anoxia is neither a necessary nor a sufficient condition, and some other factor(s) must be involved.

Neurochemical Theories

Another early proposal of a physiological mechanism was that the release of endorphins or other endogenous opioids at a time of stress plays a major role in generating NDEs (Blackmore, 1993; D. Carr, 1981, 1982; Saavedra-Aguilar & Gómez-Jeria, 1989). This seemed a reasonable factor to examine, because endorphins are known quickly to produce cessation of pain (Oyama, Jin, & Yamaya, 1980) as well as feelings of peace and well-being, both of which are common features of NDEs. Problems with models based on the release of endorphins or similar substances soon became apparent, however. Most such neurochemicals produce long-lasting effects once they are released; the injection of endorphins in pain patients, for example, produces relief from pain lasting for hours (Oyama et al., 1980). In contrast, the onset and cessation of the NDE and its associated features are usually quite abrupt, with the pain relief lasting only as long as the NDE itself, which may be only seconds.[11] Furthermore, although the release of substances such as endorphins might account for the cessation of pain and the feelings of joy and peace, it fails to account for many other important components of NDEs, such as the out-of-body experience, seeing deceased persons, a life review, and the transformative effects.

Other, related models have thus been proposed that might overcome these limitations. Perhaps the most important of these has been the suggestion that a ketamine-like endogenous neuroprotective agent may be released in conditions of stress, acting on NMDA (N-methyl-D-aspartate) receptors located in the upper layers of the cerebral cortex and other central gray-matter structures to block the neural hyperactivation and consequent cell death that would otherwise result from the massive release of glutamate that occurs during stress. Ketamine, an anesthetic agent that selectively occupies NMDA receptors, can at subanesthetic doses produce feelings of being out of the body (Collier, 1972; Rogo, 1984). Moreover, ketamine sometimes produces other features common to NDEs, such as travel through a

---

10. Some authors have reported measurements of arterial blood gases in patients reporting an NDE that do not support the hypothesis of lowered oxygen levels or heightened carbon dioxide levels (M. Morse et al., 1989, p. 50; Parnia et al., 2001; Sabom, 1982, p. 178). Others, however, have questioned the reliability of arterial blood measurements as indicators of what may be going on in the brain (Glicksman & Kellehear, 1990).

11. This feature of sudden cessation of pain, and its return when the NDE ends, strikes us as especially difficult to explain from a conventional neurophysiological point of view.

dark tunnel into light, believing that one has died, or communing with God (Jansen, 1997a, p. 9).

This hypothesis, however, also has problems. First, it is not at all clear that ketamine experiences do in fact resemble NDEs (M. Morse, 1997, p. 61; Strassman, 1997, p. 29).[12] Unlike the vast majority of NDEs, ketamine experiences are often frightening and involve bizarre imagery, and patients usually express the wish *not* to repeat the experience (Collier, 1972; Johnstone, 1973; Strassman, 1997). Most ketamine users also recognize the illusory character of their experience (Fenwick, 1997, p. 45), in contrast to the many NDE experiencers who are firmly convinced of the reality of what they experienced and its lack of resemblance to illusions or dreams. Even if ketamine experiences do resemble NDEs in some respects, many important features of NDEs, such as seeing deceased people or a revival of memories, have not been reported with ketamine. Furthermore, ketamine typically exerts its effects in an otherwise more or less normal brain, while many NDEs occur under conditions in which brain function is severely compromised. We will return to this point later in the chapter.

Neuroanatomical Models

The need for a more comprehensive and searching comparison between the phenomenology of NDEs and that associated with various purported mechanisms for them becomes even more apparent when we examine another major component of most current physiological theories of NDEs. Behind most of these theories is an assumption that abnormal activity of the limbic system or the temporal lobes, whether produced by anoxia, endorphins, ketamine, or some other mechanism, produces NDE-like experiences. M. Morse et al. (1989), for example, proposed a model in which imbalances in serotonin or other monoamines lead to abnormal activity in the temporal lobes. Saavedra-Aguilar and Gómez-Jeria (1989) suggested that, under conditions of hypoxia and psychological stress, there is temporal lobe dysfunction and the release of endogenous neuropeptides or neurotransmitters, resulting in analgesia, euphoria, and feelings of detachment. They claim that "the list of mental phenomena seen in temporal lobe epilepsy and stereotoxic stimulation of the temporal lobe includes all the NDE phenomena" (p. 209), and they thus describe their theory as "a neurophysiological explanation for NDEs that is based on their striking similarity to temporal lobe epilepsy" (p. 217).

Many people cite electrical stimulation studies, particularly those of the neurosurgeon Wilder Penfield, as justifying this belief in the "striking similarity" between NDEs and temporal lobe epilepsy. For example, M. Morse et al. (1989) refer to the "agents that cause OBEs and NDEs," namely, "activation of areas of the temporal lobe that have been documented to cause mystical visions, out-of-body sensations, panoramic memories, and vivid hallucinations," citing Penfield (1955) and Penfield and Rasmussen (1950) in

12. Jansen (1997, p. 8) reports that he has had both types of experience and found them to be similar, but we know of no other such reports.

support of this statement (p. 47). We will discuss in more detail below the often-made claim that Penfield and others have produced OBEs by electrical stimulation of the temporal lobes, but two general points merit mention here.

First, electrical stimulation of cortex is massive and grossly unlike ordinary physiological stimulation. It does not, and cannot, result simply in a localized "activation" of the stimulated region. Indeed, as Penfield (1975) himself clearly recognized, its predominant effects are disruption of electrical activity in the immediate vicinity of the electrode, accompanied by abnormal patterns of discharge into additional cortical or subcortical areas to which the stimulated cortex itself is linked by both forward and backward projections. These remote influences, moreover, may be *either* excitatory *or* inhibitory in character. The net result, in short, is a poorly controlled, poorly characterized, and spatially widespread pattern of abnormal electrical activity. Similar comments apply to the "electrical storms" associated with epileptic attacks originating in specific cortical regions.

Second, an examination of the experiences reported by Penfield's subjects, whether during the pre-surgical electrical stimulation studies or during actual epileptic seizures, does not support sweeping claims such as those cited above about the "striking similarity" between NDEs and experiences produced by temporal lobe seizures or stimulation. Most of the experiences Penfield reported in fact bore little resemblance to actual NDEs. They consisted of hearing bits of music or singing, seeing isolated and repetitive scenes that seemed familiar and may have been fragmentary memories, hearing voices, experiencing fear or other negative emotions, or seeing bizarre imagery that was often described as dream-like (Penfield, 1955; Penfield & Perot, 1963, pp. 611–665). Subsequent studies have found similar experiential phenomena, especially fear or anxiety and fragmented, distorted experiences quite *unlike* NDE phenomenology (Gloor, 1990; Gloor, Olivier, Quesney, Andermann, & Horowitz, 1982).[13]

Persinger (1989) has also claimed that "a vast clinical and surgical literature...indicates that floating and rising sensations, OBEs, personally profound mystical and religious encounters, visual and auditory experiences, and dream-like sequences are evoked, usually as single events, by electrical stimulation of deep, mesiobasal temporal lobe structures" (p. 234). His sole reference for this strong claim is a paper by Stevens (1982). That paper, however, is confined entirely to descriptions of certain physiological observations made in studies of epileptic patients, and it contains no mention whatever of any subjective experiences or of electrical stimulation studies, much less of "a vast clinical and surgical literature" supporting Persinger's claim. Persinger goes on to claim that, using weak transcranial magnetic

---

13. Moreover, as we will discuss later in this chapter, Gloor and his colleagues called into question the assumption that it is the stimulation of the temporal lobes that produces the phenomena reported. Using both surface and depth electrodes, they showed that limbic structures associated with temporal cortex, rather than temporal cortex itself, constituted the anatomical substrate for these effects.

stimulation, he and his colleagues have produced "all of the major components of the NDE, including out-of-body experiences, floating, being pulled towards a light, hearing strange music, and profound meaningful experiences." However, we have been unable to find phenomenological descriptions of the experiences of his subjects adequate to support this claim, and the brief descriptions that he does provide in fact again bear little resemblance to NDEs (e.g., Persinger, 1994, pp. 284–285).

The discrepancy between Persinger's claim to have stimulated NDEs and the actual data from his studies is particularly obvious in Persinger (1999). In one study participants reported their experiences by completing a "debriefing questionnaire" consisting of 19 items that Persinger calls "the classic types of experiences associated with these experiments" (p. 96). Nearly all of these items, however, are completely *unlike* typical features of an NDE, and the few that might be said to resemble them ("I felt the presence of someone"; "I felt as if I left my body"; "I experienced thoughts from childhood") are too vague to be able to judge their similarity to what is experienced during an NDE. In two tables, however, Persinger gives verbatim descriptions made by two participants during the stimulation experiment (pp. 97–98). Again, neither of these descriptions resembles an NDE. Isolated elements might seem vaguely similar to those of an NDE ("I see a light"; "I see trees"; "I feel I'm not here...not in my body....I can't feel it"); but without much more detailed description, the claimed similarity between NDEs and experiences induced by transcranial magnetic stimulation is clearly premature at best.[14]

Experiences reported in other brain stimulation studies inspired by Penfield's work likewise bear little resemblance to NDEs (Horowitz & Adams, 1970, p. 19). Neurologist Ernst Rodin (1989) stated bluntly: "In spite of having seen hundreds of patients with temporal lobe seizures during three decades of professional life, I have never come across that symptomatology [of NDEs] as part of a seizure" (p. 256).

Despite the shaky foundations for assertions that NDEs are similar to experiences produced by abnormal temporal lobe activity, anoxia, ketamine, endorphins, or any other proposed physiological mechanism, most current theories of NDEs are multifactor theories in which these various hypothetical physiological and psychological mechanisms are combined *ad lib* to account for whatever constellation of features is observed in any given NDE. Blackmore (1984, 1993) and Palmer (1978), for example, have suggested that sensory isolation or increasing malfunction of the body threaten the patient's body image, leading him or her to feel detached from the body, after which the person's synesthetic or other imagery abilities produce the

14. It is also important to note that Granqvist et al. (2005; see also Larsson, Larhammar, Frederikson, & Granqvist, 2005) were unable to replicate Persinger's results. They concluded that, whereas their studies had involved a strict double-blind protocol, Persinger's participants had been inadequately blinded and therefore that "suggestibility may account for previously reported effects" (Granqvist et al., 2005, p. 1). For another skeptical evaluation of Persinger's claims—by one who has experienced Persinger's "God machine"—see Horgan (2003, pp. 91–105).

illusion of watching what is going on around the body. The release of endorphins leads to analgesia and feelings of joy and peace. With increasing cerebral anoxia, the visual system is compromised, producing the illusion of a tunnel and lights. Temporal-lobe mini-seizures stimulate a revival of memories. Visions of deceased persons and of another realm are hallucinations produced by expectations of what will happen at death.

Although physiological, psychological, and sociocultural factors may indeed interact in complicated ways in conjunction with NDEs, these and all other psychophysiological theories proposed thus far consist largely of unsupported speculations about what might be happening during an NDE. None of the proposed neurophysiological mechanisms have been adequately tested or even shown actually to occur in connection with NDEs. A naturally occurring ketamine-like substance, for example, has not been identified in humans (Strassman, 1997, p. 31). Similarly, the presence of other relevant neurochemicals or seizure activity during an NDE remains wholly conjectural, based entirely on the supposed—but questionable—similarity between experiences they are known to produce and NDEs. Moreover, some of these proposals, such as the role of expectation or the presence and effects of anoxia, have been contradicted by what little data we do have. In short, contrary to confident assertions such as "there is little doubt that the class of experiences that comprise mystical experiences in general, and NDEs in particular, is strongly correlated with temporal lobe activity" (Persinger, 1989, p. 234), there is still very much doubt.[15]

The most important objection to the adequacy of all existing psychophysiological theories, however, is that mental clarity, vivid sensory imagery, a clear memory of the experience, and a sense that the experience seemed "more real than real" are the norm for NDEs, even when they occur under conditions of drastically altered cerebral physiology. As Parnia and Fenwick (2002) point out, "any acute alteration in cerebral physiology such as occurring in hypoxia, hypercarbia, metabolic, and drug induced disturbances and seizures leads to disorganised and compromised cerebral function…[and] impaired attention," whereas "NDEs in cardiac arrest are clearly not confusional and in fact indicate heightened awareness, attention and consciousness at a time when consciousness and memory formation would not be expected to occur" (p. 6). Moreover, experiencers of NDEs in connection with cardiac arrest almost invariably retain vivid memories of their experience that change little with the passage of time (van Lommel et al., 2001), despite the fact that memory under such conditions is ordinarily seriously impaired. For most patients the involvement of the hippocampus in temporal lobe epilepsy precludes any memory afterward for what happened during a seizure; "abnormal discharges in the temporal lobe may produce confusional fragments of phenomena sometimes seen in NDEs…. This is a very long way from arguing that seizure discharges in those areas, resulting from brain catastrophe, can give rise to the clearly remembered, highly structured NDE" (Fenwick, 1997, p. 48).

15. We will revisit this claim in the context of mystical experiences in Chapter 8.

NDEs seem instead to provide direct evidence for a type of mental functioning that varies "inversely, rather than directly, with the observable activity of the nervous system" (Myers, 1891d, p. 638). Such evidence, we believe, fundamentally conflicts with the conventional doctrine that brain processes produce consciousness, and supports the alternative view that brain activity normally serves as a kind of filter, which somehow constrains the material that emerges into waking consciousness. On this latter view, the "relaxation" of the filter under certain still poorly understood circumstances may lead to drastic alterations of the normal mind-brain relation and to an associated enhancement or enlargement of consciousness. To this interpretation of NDEs, which we favor, we now turn.

"Transcendent" Aspects

Most near-death experiencers are convinced that during the NDE they temporarily separated from their physical bodies, and therefore that they may also survive the more permanent separation at death. In our collection, for example, among the people who provided information regarding these features, 81% reported feeling separated from the body during the NDE, and 82% said that the NDE had convinced them of survival after death. We have labeled this interpretation of NDEs a "transcendent" model, at the risk of alienating readers who associate such a word with unscientific beliefs, because the idea that there are aspects of the natural world inaccessible to our ordinary senses and consciousness, but perhaps reflecting some level of reality transcending the ordinary physical world, is not inherently unscientific. Although it certainly contradicts the assumptions of most contemporary psychologists and neuroscientists that the ordinary physical world *is* the only reality, the direction that physics has taken in the last century amply justifies Myers's cautionary remark that we should "sit loose" when it comes to making assumptions about the scope and the fundamental character of the natural world (*HP*, vol. 2, p. 262; see also our Chapter 9).

The popular interest in NDEs clearly derives from their suggestion that mind or consciousness may persist and continue to function even after the death of the brain. In contrast, most NDE researchers have largely ignored this question, undoubtedly because of the widespread acquiescence among psychologists and neuroscientists to the dogma that brain produces mind, or *is* the mind. Most researchers have concentrated instead on descriptive studies of the aftereffects of NDEs or on speculating about possible neurophysiological and psychological mechanisms, as described above. Several features of NDEs, however, call into question whether current psychological or physiological theories of NDEs will ever provide a full explanation of them.

Enhanced Mentation

As we mentioned earlier, perhaps the most important of these features, because it is so commonly reported in NDEs, is the occurrence of full-fledged mentation, either normal or even enhanced mental activity, at times when, according to conventional psychophysiological theory, such activity should be diminishing, or even not possible. Individuals reporting NDEs often describe the experience as being altogether unlike a dream, in that their mental processes during the NDE were remarkably clear and lucid and their sensory experiences unusually vivid, equaling or even surpassing those of their normal waking state.[16] Clearly, these are subjective impressions that we cannot verify, but the frequency and consistency of such reports is impressive. Furthermore, an analysis of cases in our collection in which we were able to examine contemporaneous medical records showed that, in fact, people reported enhanced mental functioning significantly *more* often when they were actually physiologically close to death than when they were not (Owens et al., 1990).

Another example of enhanced mental functioning during an NDE is a rapid revival of memories that sometimes extends over the person's entire life. Myers (1895d) had called attention to this phenomenon when he described "the occasional revival during drowning—or, in Charles Darwin's case, during a fall from a wall—of a series of life memories both swifter and fuller than conscious effort could have supplied" (p. 354). The philosopher Henri Bergson likewise recognized not only the occurrence but the theoretical importance of this phenomenon (e.g., Bergson, 1908/1991, p. 155). It is worth noting here also that such revivals of memory may be frequent (Myers, 1895d, p. 354). For example, an analysis of computer-coded NDE cases in our collection showed that in 24% of them there was a report of some degree of revival of memories during the NDE. We emphasize, moreover, that in contrast to the isolated and often just single brief memories evoked during cortical stimulation, those revived during an NDE are frequently described as being "many" or even as an almost instantaneous "panoramic" review of the person's entire life.[17]

Reports of NDEs from widely divergent cultures and times support the view that enhanced mental functioning can occur under conditions in which it would not be expected on current models of mind and brain. However one interprets the crosscultural differences, perhaps the most important finding

16. A recent analysis of our collection showed that 80% of near-death experiencers described their thinking during the NDE as "clearer than usual" (45%) or "as clear as usual" (35%). Additionally, 74% described their thinking as "faster than usual" (37%) or at "the usual speed" (37%); 65% described their thinking as "more logical than usual" (29%) or "as logical as usual" (36%); and 55% described their control over their thoughts as "more control than usual" (19%) or "as much control as usual" (36%).

17. In our collection, 57% of those reporting memories said that they had experienced many memories or a review of their entire life; 43% reported one or a few memories. Additionally, in an analysis of 68 published life review cases not from our collection, we found that in 71% of these the experience had involved memories of many events or of the person's whole life (Stevenson & Cook [Kelly], 1995, p. 455).

from such studies is that people have consistently reported, from different parts of the world and across different periods of history, having had complicated cognitive and perceptual experiences at times when brain functioning was severely impaired.

Veridical Out-of-Body Perceptions

Another important feature of NDEs that current theoretical models cannot adequately account for is the experience of being out of the body and perceiving events that one could not ordinarily have perceived. Near-death experiencers often report that during the NDE they viewed their bodies as if from a different point in space. A recent analysis of cases in our collection showed that 48% of the respondents reported seeing their physical bodies from a different visual perspective. Many of them also reported witnessing events going on in the vicinity of their body, such as the attempts of medical personnel to resuscitate them at the scene of an accident or in an emergency room.

Like most other features of NDEs, many of these out-of-body perceptions are entirely subjective, providing no direct evidence that the person has in fact either been separated from the body or observed contemporaneous circumstances. Some commentators (e.g., Blackmore, 1993; Saavedra-Aguilar & Gómez-Jeria, 1989; Woerlee, 2004) have argued that the belief that one has witnessed events going on around one's body is a retrospective imaginative reconstruction attributable to a persisting ability to hear, even when unconscious, or to the memory of objects or events that one might have glimpsed just before losing consciousness or while regaining consciousness, or to expectations about what was likely to have occurred.

Such explanations are inadequate, however, for several reasons. First, memory of events occurring just before or after loss of consciousness is usually confused or completely absent (Aminoff, Scheinman, Griffin, & Herre, 1988; Parnia & Fenwick, 2002; van Lommel et al., 2001). Second, claims that adequately anesthetized[18] patients retain any significant capacity to be aware of or respond to their environment in more than rudimentary ways—let alone to hear and understand—have in general not been substantiated.

18. The expression "adequately anesthetized" is intended here to exclude cases of literal awakening, or partial awakening, during surgical procedures. Such awakening is known to occur, even using present-day techniques, in something on the order of 0.1–0.3% of all general-surgery procedures (Heier & Steen, 1996; Sandin, Enlund, Samuelson, & Lennmarken, 2000). Higher rates occur, as might be expected, when muscle relaxants are used in combination with low levels of anesthetic agents. Other causes of awakening include operator errors, equipment failures, inability to use sufficient agents because of excessive loss of blood in trauma cases, and unusual tolerance of particular patients to particular agents. The phenomenology of such awakenings, however, is altogether different from that of NDEs, and often extremely unpleasant, frightening, and even painful (Osterman, Hopper, Heran, Keane, & van der Kolk, 2001; Spitellie, Holmes, & Domino, 2002). The experiences are typically brief and fragmentary, and primarily auditory or tactile, and not visual; for example, the patient may report hearing noises or snippets of speech, or briefly feeling sensations associated with intubation or with specific surgical procedures. Needless to say, anesthesiologists have strong motivation, both ethical and legal, to prevent such occurrences.

Since the earliest years of chemical anesthesia, there have been occasional reports of patients who appeared to display some degree of memory for events that occurred during surgery (Cheek, 1964, 1966). Most of these could be attributed to insufficient anesthesia, but not all (Levinson, 1965, 1990). There were also some intriguing early clinical case reports indicating that patients sometimes showed agitation following surgery in which negative comments had been made about them or their prognosis. More benignly, other patients were reported to recover more quickly when given positive suggestions during the surgery to the effect that they would do so (D. Schacter, 1996, p. 172).

Even an early review questioned the claim that people might retain some auditory perception under general anesthesia, finding numerous methodological problems with studies purporting to show this (Trustman, Dubovsky, & Titley, 1977). Moreover, more recent and better controlled studies have also not substantiated such claims (Ghoneim & Block, 1992, 1997). Studies of memory and awareness in anesthesia have been highly inconsistent, and there is no convincing evidence for adequately anesthetized patients having any explicit, or conscious, memory of events during the surgery (apart from patients who have reported such memories in connection with an NDE). What positive evidence there is for "learning and memory" during adequate general anesthesia mainly involves implicit memory phenomena such as perceptual and mnemonic "priming" and other low-level effects, which are known not to require participation of the brain systems normally involved with explicit declarative memory (Bonke, Fitch, & Millar, 1990; D. Schacter, 1996). Moreover, even these low-level effects occur inconsistently, and they depend in complex and poorly understood ways on factors such as the nature and dosage of the specific anesthetic agents used, their interactions, the specific types of memory tasks used and their conditions of administration, and the many semi-controllable stimulus events occurring during the surgery itself. Ghoneim and Block (1997) summarize the situation as follows: "We can speculate that unconscious memory occurs only in few patients, only some of the time, and during light levels of anesthesia. Learning may be more perceptual than engaging in elaborate processing of complex information and may be limited to single, relatively familiar words. Memory may be more evident if tested as soon as possible after surgery" (p. 406).

In sum, such studies as we have afford little hope for explaining NDE reports involving complex sensory experiences of events occurring during general anesthesia in terms of knowledge acquired by the impaired brain itself during the period of unconsciousness. Note also that any such explanatory claims are even less credible when, as commonly happens, the specific sensory channels involved in the reported experience have been blocked as part of the surgical routine—for example, when specifically visual experience is reported by a patient whose eyes were taped shut during the relevant period of time. We will discuss the theoretical significance of general anesthesia in relation to NDEs more fully later in this chapter.

Another reason for being cautious about attributing claims of out-of-body perceptions to retrospective reconstruction is a study by Sabom (1982), carried out specifically to examine this hypothesis. Sabom had interviewed 32 patients who reported NDEs in which they seemed to be watching what was going on around their body. Most of these were cardiac patients who were undergoing cardiopulmonary resuscitation (CPR) at the time of their NDE. Sabom then interviewed 25 "control" patients, "seasoned cardiac patients" who had *not* had an NDE during their previous cardiac-related crises, and asked them to describe a cardiac resuscitation procedure as if they were watching from a third-person perspective. Among all these patients, 80% of the "control" patients made at least one major error in their descriptions, whereas none of the NDE patients made any. Moreover, six of the 32 NDE patients related accurate details of idiosyncratic or unexpected (to them) events during their resuscitation (pp. 87–115). For example, one man, who developed ventricular fibrillation in the coronary care unit, said (among many other things) that the nurse picked up "them shocker things" and "touched them together," and then "everybody moved back away from it [the defibrillator]" (p. 96). As Sabom explained, rubbing the defibrillator paddles together to lubricate them and standing back from the defibrillator to avoid being shocked are common procedures (p. 98).

An even more difficult challenge to ordinary psychological or physiological theories of NDEs comes from cases in which experiencers report that, while out of the body, they became aware of events occurring at a distance or that in some other way would have been beyond the reach of their ordinary senses even if they had been fully and normally conscious. In our collection, 60 people have described being aware of events occurring outside the range of their physical senses. K. Clark (1984) and Owens (1995) each published a case of this type, and we have reported on 15 cases, including seven cases previously published by others and eight from our own collection (Cook [Kelly], Greyson, & Stevenson, 1998; E. W. Kelly, Greyson, & Stevenson, 1999-2000). Some of these accurate perceptions included unexpected or unlikely details, such as a woman in childbirth who reported being out of her body and seeing her mother in the waiting room smoking a cigarette; according to the daughter, the mother (a non-smoker) "admitted much later that she had 'tried' one or two because she was so nervous!" (Cook [Kelly] et al., 1998, p. 391). Additionally, Ring and Cooper (1997, 1999) reported 31 cases of blind individuals, nearly half of them blind from birth, who experienced during their NDEs quasi-visual and sometimes veridical perceptions of objects and events. Many of these people, like other NDE experiencers, also said that they saw a bright light.

A frequent—and valid—criticism of these reports of perceptions of events at a distance from the body is that they often depend on the experiencer's testimony alone. It is a frustrating fact that in many such cases people who could possibly provide verification or corroborating testimony have either moved away or died by the time of the investigation of the case. The weakness of the testimony for the majority of these claims has encouraged commentators such as Blackmore (1993, p. 262) to refuse to accept any reports of such cases as evidential, on grounds that "many of these claims are based on purely anecdotal evidence and very few have any independent corroboration" (Blackmore, 1996, p. 75) . However, some cases *have* been corroborated by others (K. Clark, 1984; H. Hart, 1954; Ring & Lawrence, 1993). Van Lommel et al. (2001, p. 2041), for example, reported a case in which a cardiac arrest victim was brought into the hospital comatose and cyanotic, and even after restoration of his circulation, he remained in a coma and on artificial respiration in the intensive care unit for more than a week. When he regained consciousness and was transferred back to the cardiac care unit, he immediately recognized one of the nurses, saying that this was the person who had removed his dentures during the resuscitation procedures. He said further that he had watched from above the attempts of hospital staff to resuscitate him in the emergency room, and he described "correctly and in detail" the room and the people working on him, including the cart in which the nurse had put his dentures. The nurse corroborated and verified his account. We ourselves (Cook [Kelly] et al., 1998, pp. 399–400) have reported a case of this type in which, in addition to numerous other details such as encountering a barrier, seeing a light and tunnel, feeling joy and peace, and meeting two deceased relatives, the patient described leaving his body and watching the cardiac surgeon "flapping his arms as if trying to fly." The surgeon verified this detail by explaining that, after scrubbing and to keep his hands from possibly becoming contaminated before beginning surgery, he had developed the idiosyncratic habit of flattening his hands against his chest, while rapidly giving instructions by pointing with his elbows.

Visions of Deceased Acquaintances

Many people who approach death and recover report that, during the time they seemed to be dying, they met deceased relatives and friends. Among the cases in our collection 42% of experiencers reported meeting one or more recognized deceased acquaintances during the NDE. Such experiences have been widely viewed as being "merely" hallucinations, caused by drugs or other physiological conditions or by the person's expectations or wishes to be reunited with deceased loved ones at the time of death. Nevertheless, a closer examination of these experiences indicates that such explanations are not adequate (E. W. Kelly, 2001).

For example, people close to death are more likely to perceive deceased persons than do healthy people, who, when they have waking hallucinations, are more likely to perceive *living* persons (Osis & Haraldsson, 1977/1997). Near-death experiencers whose medical records show that they really were close to death also were more likely to perceive deceased persons than experiencers who were ill but not close to death, even though many of the latter thought they were dying (E. W. Kelly, 2001). Moreover, numerous people, both those near death and those not near death, also perceive figures other than known deceased persons during the NDE, most of these being unrecognized. If expectation alone were driving the process, people would presumably recognize the hallucinatory figures, either as actual deceased or living people or as known religious figures, more often than was in fact the case. In our collection, however, few people reported perceiving specific religious figures such as Jesus.[19] Even fewer reported perceiving living persons, even though many of them commented that it was the thought of living people whom they were leaving that made them return to their bodies. Only two people reported perceiving deceased pets, much to the disappointment of some of those who did not. We have found that people do more often perceive deceased people with whom they were emotionally close, a finding consistent with the expectation theory—but, we add, equally consistent with that of survival after death. Nonetheless, in one-third of the cases the deceased person was either someone with whom the experiencer had a distant or even poor relationship or someone whom the experiencer had never met, such as a relative who died long before the experiencer's birth (E. W. Kelly, 2001). For example, van Lommel (2004, p. 122) reported the case of a man who had an NDE during cardiac arrest in which he saw his deceased grandmother and an unknown man. He later learned from his dying mother that he had been born out of an extramarital affair and that his father had been killed during World War II. Shown a picture of his biological father, he immediately recognized him as the man he had seen in his NDE, 10 years previously. We have a similar case in our collection, in which a man reported seeing five unknown men, one of whom he recognized several months later in a photograph as the deceased father of a girlfriend (later his wife), whom he had never met.[20]

Converging Lines of Evidence

As we mentioned earlier, the inability of any one conventional physiological or psychological hypothesis to account for all NDEs, or even all features of NDEs, has led many researchers to propose multifactorial theories, combining psychological and physiological mechanisms *ad lib.* The need, however, for increasingly complicated and composite explanations, together with the lack of an adequate empirical foundation for any of them, has led us to suggest that we should not rule out categorically that NDEs are essentially what many experiencers think they are—namely, evidence that they have temporarily separated from their body and, moreover, may survive the permanent separation that occurs at death (Cook [Kelly] et al., 1998; E. W. Kelly et al., 1999–2000). When each is examined alone and in isolation, the features described in this section, as well as other NDE features, may seem potentially explainable by some psychological or physiological hypo-

19. Many, however, did report seeing a bright or all-encompassing light which seemed to be a "Being of Light" and was often identified as God.

20. Although in neither of these cases has it been possible to obtain corroborating testimony from someone other than the person who had the experience, they illustrate a particularly important kind of experience, and we suspect that, as with many of the phenomena discussed in this chapter, we will identify more such cases if we look specifically for them.

thesis, despite the paucity of supporting evidence. When several features occur together, however, and when multiple layers of explanation must be added on *ad hoc* to account for them, these explanations become increasingly strained.

A case which conspicuously exemplifies numerous features difficult to account for in conventional psychophysiological terms is that of Pam Reynolds, reported in detail by Sabom (1998, pp. 37–51). This case is also particularly important because Sabom, a cardiologist, was able to obtain verification from participating medical personnel concerning some critical details of the operation that the patient reported observing during her experience.

This patient underwent a procedure called hypothermic cardiac arrest (Spetzler et al., 1988; Weiss et al., 1998; M. D. Williams, Rainer, Fieger, Murray, & Sanchez, 1991) for removal of an extremely large aneurysm deep in her brain that would be fatal if it ruptured and that was inaccessible by ordinary neurosurgical techniques. Her eyes were first lubricated and taped shut; then, following induction of general anesthesia (Forane, plus 50/50 nitrous oxide/oxygen), she was heavily instrumented to permit accurate monitoring of her vital functions. In addition to standard EEG and EKG monitors, special catheters provided measures of pulmonary arterial blood pressure and flow, as well as urinary temperatures in her bladder. Additional temperature recordings were taken from her esophagus, and later from the surface of her exposed brain. Molded speakers placed in her ears, and occluding the ear canals, were used to deliver loud clicks,[21] which permitted monitoring of her brainstem auditory evoked potentials. After about 90 minutes, the surgery proper began. Her skull was opened, and she was connected to a cardiopulmonary bypass machine. The circulating blood was rapidly chilled, her core temperature dropping 25° in about 10 minutes. At this point her heart, which had begun to behave erratically, was deliberately stopped with an intravenous bolus of potassium chloride. Her EEG went flat. The brainstem evoked responses further weakened as cooling progressed, and ceased entirely at 60°. She had reached "total brain shutdown." At this point, the surgical table was tilted up, and the blood was drained from her brain so that the aneurysm could be safely removed. Following repair of the aneurysm, her blood was warmed and returned to her body and her vital functions gradually restored. During the resuscitation procedures, however, her heart went into ventricular fibrillation, and she had to be shocked twice (50/100J) to restore normal rhythm.

Although the shutdown of her normal physiological functioning was carefully controlled by the medical team, by all conventional criteria this patient could be considered clinically dead during the main part of this procedure: Her electroencephalogram (EEG) was totally flat, her brainstem auditory evoked potentials had ceased, and blood was completely absent from her brain. Nevertheless, the patient reported an unusually detailed, prolonged, and continuous NDE. The experience also included some veri-

21. The clicks were 95 dB, 100 μS/ click, 11.3 clicks/sec, in successive blocks of 2,000 clicks (just under 3 minutes/block).

fiable features: First, despite having speakers in her ears that blocked all external sounds with 95 dB clicks, the experience began when she heard the sound of the special saw used to cut into her skull (a sound that she, a musician, identified as a natural "D"). She then seemed to leave her body and, from a position near the neurosurgeon's shoulders, was able to see (and subsequently describe) the saw itself. She also noted the unexpected (to her) way in which her head had been shaved, and she heard a female voice commenting that her veins and arteries were small. At some point she felt herself being pulled along a "tunnel vortex" toward a light. She also heard her deceased grandmother's voice, and then she saw numerous deceased relatives, all of them permeated by an "incredibly bright" light. Told by her relatives that she had to go back, and thinking about the young children she would be leaving, she reluctantly returned to her body. She also reported that "when I came back, they were playing 'Hotel California' and the line was 'You can check out anytime you like, but you can never leave'"—a choice of music that she later laughingly told one of her doctors had been "incredibly insensitive."

Although many of the features of her experience were subjective and unverifiable, some were not. Her description of the unusual saw was verified by the neurosurgeon and by photographs of it obtained by Sabom. Also, as the patient had heard, at the time the cardiopulmonary bypass procedure was being started, the cardiac surgeon (a female) had commented that the right femoral vessels were too small to support the bypass, so that she had to prepare the left leg. Although at the time this comment was made the patient's brainstem auditory evoked potentials had not yet disappeared, the molded speakers in her ears themselves, let alone the 95 dB clicks, would have made it impossible for her to hear the comment in the ordinary way, even had she been fully conscious at that moment.

Equally importantly, the patient reported the kind of mentation that we described earlier: She said that during her experience she was not only aware, but "the most aware that I think I have ever been in my life" (Sabom, 1998, p. 41). She further commented that her vision "was not like normal vision. It was brighter and more focused and clearer than normal vision" (p. 41) and that her hearing "was a clearer hearing than with my ears" (p. 44).

The case is not perfect. The details were not published for several years after the experience occurred. More importantly, the verifiable events that she reported observing in the operating room occurred when she was anesthetized and sensorially isolated but before and after the period of time in which she was clinically "dead." Further, it is impossible to tell exactly when during the procedure she had the experience of going into a tunnel, seeing a bright light, and conversing with her deceased relatives. Her description of the experience suggests (although of course it cannot prove) that it was continuous from the time she first heard the surgeon's saw (over an hour after she had been anesthetized) until she returned to her body and heard the song "Hotel California," near the end of the procedure, some 5½ hours later, when younger assistants had taken over from the surgeons and the background music was changed to rock music (Sabom, 1998, p. 47). Some parts of Pam's experience may therefore have occurred during the time in the procedure when she was clinically "dead" or near the end of the procedure, when she suddenly went into ventricular fibrillation. We cannot, however, say with certainty that any part of her NDE actually occurred during the period when she was clinically "dead." Even so, the extremity of her condition and her heavily anesthetized state throughout the entire procedure casts serious doubt on any view of mind or consciousness as unilaterally and totally dependent on intact physiological functioning.

The few shortcomings in this case simply highlight the need for inquiring about the experiences of other patients who have undergone hypothermic cardiac arrest or similarly drastic procedures. A major priority for future research on NDEs is to identify and study experiences that occur in conjunction with heavily monitored surgical procedures, especially cardiac procedures involving close monitoring of electrical brain activity, blood gases, neurochemical levels, or other physiological measures.

The Larger Context

Most of the proposed explanations for NDEs assume that they are the product of a "dying brain" (e.g., Blackmore, 1993; Vaitl et al., 2005, p. 102). As we have said earlier and will discuss in more detail below, one of the things that makes NDEs so important is that many of them *do* occur at a time the person is physiologically near death. Nonetheless, as we also pointed out earlier, many of them do *not* occur when the person is dying. Moreover, NDEs are by no means an isolated phenomenon. All features occurring in connection with NDEs occur in the context of other kinds of experiences in which the brain is certainly not "dying." Before we can accept any explanation of NDEs as adequate, we will need far more information than we now have concerning the actual—as opposed to conjectured—physiological and psychological conditions under which they take place. Clearly, however, they will never be understood until they are examined together with these other experiences, occurring under different conditions, that share their features. We therefore turn now to some of those other experiences.

Out-of-Body Experiences

One phenomenon obviously relevant to NDEs is the out-of-body experience (OBE). In an OBE a person's consciousness is experienced as having separated from the body, but also as continuing to function normally. The OBE is a frequent feature of NDEs, and there is some evidence that it represents an early stage that may develop into a more complex NDE with additional features if the condition is prolonged (R. Lange, Greyson,

& Houran, 2004, p. 167). As a result, many of the early collections of reports of OBEs included what we would now call NDEs because they occurred in the context of a medical or life-threatening condition (e.g., Crookall, 1964, 1972; Green, 1968b; Muldoon & Carrington, 1951/1969). On the other hand, many OBEs occur in non-medical contexts, and many NDEs do not include OBEs. Thus, it seems likely that neither OBEs nor NDEs are a subset of the other, but that both instead are manifestations of a larger class of experiences in which there has been an alteration in the ordinary experience of the self in relation to the body and the external environment.

A typical OBE is one that comes from our own collection, in which a man competing in a triathalon, after completing the swimming segment and beginning the bicycling segment, suddenly and briefly seemed to himself to be above the scene, watching the riders below, including himself, with no apparent ill effect on his ability to ride the bicycle. A more dramatic but less typical case is one from the classical literature that is frequently cited, the Wilmot case (E. M. Sidgwick, 1891, pp. 41–46; also cited in *HP*, vol. 1, pp. 682–685). In 1863 Mr. Wilmot and his sister Miss Wilmot were on a ship traveling from Liverpool, England, to New York, and for much of the journey they were in a severe storm. More than a week after the storm began, Mrs. Wilmot, in Connecticut and worried about the safety of her husband, had an experience, while she was awake during the middle of the night, in which she seemed to go to her husband's stateroom on the ship, where she saw him asleep in the lower berth and another man in the upper berth looking at her. She hesitated, kissed her husband, and left. The next morning Mr. Wilmot's roommate asked him, apparently somewhat indignantly, about the woman who had come into their room during the night. Miss Wilmot added her testimony, saying that the next morning, before she had seen her brother, the roommate asked her if she had been in to see Mr. Wilmot during the night, and when she replied no, he said that he had seen a woman come into their room in the middle of the night and go to Mr. Wilmot.[22]

22. Blackmore (1983a, pp. 143–144) thinks that she has successfully discredited the Wilmot case, and Edwards (1997, p. 20) agrees, asserting that "the case totally collapsed when it was investigated by Susan Blackmore." Blackmore claims that the entire story rests on Mr. Wilmot's testimony alone and that this testimony was unreliable because he had been seasick at the time. She further claims that "Mrs. Wilmot never reported having had an OBE at all." Although Blackmore claims to have read the original reports (citing Myers's reprinting of the case), she clearly did not read them carefully enough, and Edwards apparently relied entirely on Blackmore without reading the original report himself. In the report, both the original and Myers's reprinting of it, letters are printed not only from Mr. Wilmot but also from Mrs. Wilmot and Miss Wilmot, corroborating the essential features of his account. Although Mrs. Wilmot never explicitly said "I had an out-of-body experience," she did say "I had a very vivid sense all the [next] day of having visited my husband." She also said "I felt much disturbed at his [the man in the upper berth] presence, as he leaned over, looking at us." She further reported that "the impression was so strong that I felt unusually happy and refreshed," in contrast to the anxiety about her husband that had preceded it. We do not unfortunately have the testimony of the man in the upper berth (who had since died), but, as we mentioned above, we do have Miss Wilmot's testimony that he told her about his experience the next morning, *before* she had seen her brother and heard his account of what had happened. The case is not

The incidence of OBEs among the general population is difficult to determine, because many of the estimates have been based on questionnaire studies in which there has been no followup or investigation of the "Yes" responses to learn whether the experience truly qualified as an OBE. A tentative estimate, however, is that at least 10% of the general population has experienced one or more OBEs.[23]

As with NDEs, theories about OBEs have generally become polarized between conventional psychophysiological theories and a transcendent or "exteriorization" model in which consciousness really does function outside the body. Psychophysiological theories typically suggest that seizures or other abnormal activation of areas of the brain (usually the temporal lobes and adjacent structures) produce alterations in body perceptions or schemata, leading to depersonalization, OBEs, or "autoscopy" (experiences in which the person sees an hallucinatory double of him- or herself in external space; see below). As we mentioned earlier, research frequently cited in support of a model in which abnormal temporal lobe electrical activity produces an OBE is that of neurosurgeon Wilder Penfield (e.g., Penfield, 1955, 1958a, 1958b; Penfield & Erickson, 1941; Penfield & Perot, 1963). Penfield is widely reported as having produced OBEs and other NDE-like phenomena in the course of stimulating various points in the exposed brains of awake epileptic patients being prepared for surgery (e.g., Blackmore, 1993, pp. 212–213; M. Morse et al., 1989, p. 47; Neppe, 1989, p. 247; Tong, 2003). Only two out of his 1132 patients, however, reported anything that might be said to resemble an OBE: One patient said: "Oh God! I am leaving my body" (Penfield, 1955, p. 458). Another patient said only: "I have a queer sensation as if I am not here....As though I were half and half here" (Penfield & Rasmussen, 1950, p. 174). In later studies at the Montreal Neurological Institute (where Penfield had conducted his studies), only one of 29 patients with temporal lobe epilepsy reported "a 'floating sensation' which the patient likened at one time to the excitement felt when watching a football game and at another time to a startle" (Gloor et al., 1982, pp. 131–132). Such experiences hardly qualify as phenomenologically equivalent to OBEs.

Saavedra-Aguilar and Gómez-Jeria (1989) have similarly claimed that OBEs "appear frequently in TLE [temporal lobe epilepsy]" (p. 214), and they cite J. A. M. Frederiks (1969) as the reference for this statement. However, Frederiks made no mention at all of OBEs in connection with temporal lobe epilepsy (although he did discuss autoscopy—discussed below—which is related but not identical to OBEs). Perhaps more importantly, Frederiks specifically denied that *any* such disorders of the body schema have been localized: "No well-defined anatomical localization has yet been established nor is any likely to be established because in most cases a large, bilateral or diffuse cerebral damage is present or diffuse cerebral dysfunction can be

---

perfect, but Blackmore's and Edwards's misrepresentation of the reported facts, and offhand dismissal of testimony that conflicts with their beliefs, is indefensible at best.

23. For a review of studies estimating incidence in various populations, see Alvarado (2000, pp. 184–186).

assumed....The body schema can in my opinion not be strictly localized; it is one of the many products of the total function of the nervous system" (pp. 233, 212).

More compelling evidence for possible physiological factors associated with the occurrence of OBEs and related phenomena is summarized in a review by Devinsky, Feldmann, Burrowes, and Bromfield (1989). They reported on 10 patients of their own (identified in a prospective study of 158 seizure patients) who had experienced OBEs or autoscopic phenomena in connection with their seizures, and they also reviewed 18 earlier reports involving an additional 33 seizure patients with similar experiences. Of these 43 patients, 18 reported OBEs and 25 reported autoscopic experiences.[24] Of 30 identifiable seizure foci, only 18 involved the temporal lobes. These could occur on either or both sides, and were often accompanied by additional seizure activity, disease, or injury in frontal, parietal, or occipital cortex. These complex clinical findings also did not appear to differ in any clear or consistent way between OBE and autoscopy cases.

More recently, Olaf Blanke and colleagues (Blanke, Landis, Spinelli, & Seeck, 2004; Blanke, Ortigue, Landis, & Seeck, 2002) have provided detailed reports, including some neuroimaging results, for six neurological patients, three of whom had experiences, which Blanke et al. describe as OBEs, associated with seizure activity or with direct electrical stimulation of the exposed cortex. Three additional patients (as well as one of the three OBE patients) had autoscopic experiences in association with seizures or (in one case) with a possible ischemic attack during migraine. The imaging and stimulation results suggested involvement of a common cortical region encompassing the junction of temporal and parietal cortex (TPJ), a region which is thought normally to be involved in the integration of vestibular information with tactile, proprioceptive, and visual information regarding the body and its location in perceptual space. On this basis, the authors hypothesized that *all* such experiences involve failures of this integration, caused by "paroxysmal cerebral dysfunction of the TPJ in a state of partially and briefly impaired consciousness" (Blanke et al., 2004, p. 243).

---

24. Interestingly, four of Devinsky et al.'s own 10 patients described an OBE that sounds more like an NDE. One patient, for example, was involved in an automobile accident in which she suffered severe head trauma. Although she was unconscious for two hours and had 24 hours of retrograde amnesia, she remembered that, while unconscious, she had an OBE in which she saw the scene of the accident, including her own body, and heard a voice sending her back. Her seizures began one month later, as a result of the injuries she suffered in the accident. Another woman, who had had numerous generalized (or whole-brain) seizures (about two per month) for 21 years, reported only two OBEs, both of them occurring during seizures at times when she seemed in danger of dying (for example, by being strangled by the bedsheets in which she had become entangled). Another woman, who had frequent generalized seizures for six years, had her single OBE at a time when she thought she was dying during the seizure. The fourth patient, who had frequent absence seizures (about five a week for 17 years), had an NDE-like experience during her only generalized seizure. In this experience, she had an OBE in which she first saw her unconscious body, and then seemed to travel into space, where it was "gorgeous...[and] warm—not like heat, but security" (Devinsky et al., 1989, p. 1082). A voice then told her to go back, which she reluctantly did.

The empirical findings of Blanke and his colleagues are certainly significant, but their theoretical conclusions seem to us premature. First, the purported localization of neurologic abnormalities is less than clear and compelling. The identified region, the TPJ (encompassing the anterior part of the angular gyrus and the posterior part of the superior temporal gyrus), is only a region of "mean overlap" of individual lesions that are distributed much more widely. Furthermore, the appearance of localization derives in part from mapping results from the very different brains of all five patients onto the left hemisphere of only one of them (Blanke et al., 2004, Figures 2 and 4). In one patient no overt anatomical or functional defect could even be identified. Similarly, of Devinsky et al.'s (1989) 10 patients, three were specifically said to have fronto-temporal lesions or EEG abnormalities, two showed "generalized 3/s spike and wave discharges," and one showed no overt anatomical, neurological, or EEG abnormalities. Among the 29 additional patients for whom any information was available, the seizures of two were specifically localized to the anterior temporal lobe (which does not involve the TPJ), and only about a dozen are characterized in terms even loosely consistent with the Blanke et al. hypothesis. Furthermore, there is no clear lateralization. Among Blanke et al.'s patients and those reviewed by Devinsky et al., the location of identifiable foci was almost evenly split between the left and right hemispheres. Moreover, the studies of Gloor and his colleagues led them to "conclude that experiential phenomena, including perceptual ones, are more likely to occur in response to limbic than to temporal neocortical stimulation or seizure discharge" (Gloor et al., 1982, p. 140; see also Gloor, 1990).

Second, the generalization from these few patients with identified neurological problems to all persons experiencing an OBE, most of whom have no known neurological problem, is purely conjectural. We agree that abnormal activity in the TPJ region or some other location may sometimes contribute to the occurrence of an OBE; the fact that the experiences of some of these patients could be altered or abolished by therapeutic intervention (surgery or medication) provides evidence for this. Nevertheless, to conclude that any such activity pattern is *necessary,* in general, seems to us quite doubtful. All of the patients reported by Devinsky et al. (1989) and five of the six patients of Blanke et al. (2004) suffered moderate to severe neurological pathology; but such pathology appears generally to be absent, and certainly has not been demonstrated to be present, in the vast majority of persons who spontaneously experience OBEs. A special OBE subject studied by Tart (1968), for example, was specifically found to have a normal clinical EEG.

Furthermore, even if we assume that cortex in the vicinity of the TPJ is involved somehow in the production of at least some OBEs, that cortex itself is probably not *producing* them. This is because both seizure activity and direct electrical stimulation of a particular region of association cortex typically lead to disruption of whatever patterns of neuroelectric activity would otherwise be going on there. That is, the failure of the normal integration could be explainable by these factors, but not the production of the abnormal one (the OBE). Something else is doing that.

Moreover, there are many patients with similar neurological problems or patterns of seizure activity who do *not* experience OBEs. In Devinsky et al.'s prospective study (1989), only 10 (or 6.3%) of 158 seizure patients reported OBEs or autoscopy. Furthermore, although the 43 patients in the Devinsky et al. review had suffered numerous seizures, often over a period of many years, 10 had only one experience, and 15 others had five or fewer (p. 1082). Only two of Penfield's 1,132 patients reported even vaguely OBE-like phenomena. Moreover, as we mentioned earlier, some of Devinsky et al.'s patients had an OBE, not during an ordinary seizure, but only at a time when they were near death, or thought they were dying. These findings clearly suggest that localized abnormal activity in the brain is not only not *necessary*, but also not in general *sufficient* to produce the change in perceptual locus that is an OBE. At the very least, the sufficient neurological conditions for OBEs have not yet been fully identified.

Finally, Blanke and his colleagues, and others who have focused on the role of temporal lobe activity in the production of OBEs, have not even begun as yet to deal with certain deeper and more difficult aspects of the OBE. For example, even if we are able to associate OBEs with a certain region of the brain—something we are far from doing yet—such localization cannot account for the occurrence in many cases of veridical perceptions during loss of consciousness. More generally, it cannot account for the occurrence of *any* complex perception or mentation at a time when the abnormalities in brain functioning would normally abolish consciousness. As Devinsky et al. (1989) themselves appropriately caution, "an unresolved problem involves...the paradox of apparent consciousness during the seizure" (pp. 1087–1088). To equate OBEs with pathological "body illusions," as Blanke et al. do, seems to us to beg the question of the nature of these experiences by ignoring the complexity of their physiological, psychological, and phenomenological aspects. In short, studies such as that of Blanke et al. and Devinsky et al. have not provided anything like a complete and verified neurophysiological account of the OBE, but rather some preliminary findings and hypotheses to be pursued in further work.[25]

The polarization between those who think we must choose between an exclusively psychophysiological theory on the one hand or, on the other, a monolithic theory of OBEs as evidence for the separability of consciousness and the body seems to us too narrow a view. Before suggesting an alternative way of thinking about the problem, however, we should briefly review additional aspects of OBE cases that suggest the need for a theory that,

25. In the light of the above considerations, it strikes us as at best highly premature, and quite revealing, that the editors of *Nature* saw fit to declare triumphantly, in connection with their publication of Blanke et al. (2002), that as a result of this one study, which dealt with only one case, "the part of the brain that can induce out-of-body experiences has been located" (p. 269).

while not superseding standard psychophysiological models, goes beyond them.

The cases that present the most serious challenge to explaining OBEs in conventional terms are those that involve psi,[26] including the veridical perception of some event happening at a distance such as we saw in the Wilmot case. Blackmore (1982) correctly acknowledged that "a purely psychological theory of the OBE cannot directly account for paranormal phenomena and if they occur they demand explanation." As we pointed out earlier, however, she refuses to accept the evidentiality of any such case. She goes on to conclude that "my guess" is that psychological theories of OBEs will predominate, that these theories will simply "ignore psi altogether," and that "the question of paranormal phenomena will quietly be dropped" (p. 243). This is certainly one way of handling the problem of reports that conflict with one's beliefs. But can these reports be dismissed and "ignored" so cavalierly?

Clearly, not all OBEs—even those with impressive phenomenology—are veridical in character. A particularly striking reminder of this is an experience described by Roll (Coly & McMahon, 1995, pp. 118–119). In a vividly realistic OBE, he seemed to leave his body, travel to another part of the house, and see details of the room, including a shadow cast by the moon on the rug. Returning to his body and waking up, he went into the room, but found that there was no moonlight. He concluded that, because the details of his experience did not correspond to the actual physical environment, "this was a mental world. I was in the world that I pictured."[27] Most OBEs similarly provide no evidence that they are anything more than unusually vivid subjective experiences.

Nonetheless, not all OBEs are entirely subjective in nature; the Wilmot case is hardly unique (see, e.g, Cook [Kelly] et al., 1998; E. W. Kelly et al., 1999–2000, for reports of some NDEs that involved both OBEs and perception of events at a distance). H. Hart (1954) conducted an analysis of 288 published OBE cases in which the person reported perceiving events during the experience that he or she could not have perceived in the ordinary way. The 288 cases were all published with a description sufficient to show that, in principle, the experience fit the criteria for perception of a real event occurring at a distance. Most significantly, however, in 99 of these cases the events in question had been verified as having occurred, and the experience had been reported to someone else *before* that verification occurred. In

---

26. As we discussed in the Introduction, the authors of this book are united in the conviction that psi phenomena have been adequately demonstrated, both in spontaneous case studies and in experimental studies, even if there is as yet no adequate theoretical model to account for them. It is our hope that this volume will help catalyze the development of such a model. For readers who do not share our conviction, we refer them to reliable literature on this topic (see the Appendix).

27. One might ask whether Roll awoke from his OBE, not immediately after the experience as he thought, but later in the night, when earlier moonlight might have disappeared. The purpose here, however, is not to debate the details of this particular experience, but simply to call attention to the undeniable fact that many OBEs, however vivid, are not veridical.

many of these cases the testimony of the experiencer remains uncorroborated, and even in the corroborated cases it is often possible to poke holes in the testimony, since few of them include a written record of the experience made before the event was verified. Nevertheless, the large numbers of claims of veridical OBEs, both corroborated and uncorroborated, suggest the need for a response more robust than "quietly dropping" them.

An alternate explanation for these veridical cases might be, not that the person's consciousness in some sense literally left the body and traveled to the distant location, but that the person learned about the event in question by some psi process such as telepathy or clairvoyance, and then incorporated that knowledge into the OBE, which was simply an added hallucination. The evidence for psi from both experimental and field studies is sufficient to make this a plausible theory for many, perhaps even most, of the veridical cases. Nevertheless, another sub-group of OBEs that strains even this explanation is a group commonly called "reciprocal apparitions," again exemplified by the Wilmot case. In such cases, while one person is deliberately trying to "project," or is having a spontaneous OBE, or is having a dream in which he or she seems to go to a distant location, a person at that location, unaware of the first person's experience, sees an apparition of that person. H. Hart (1954) summarized 30 such cases that had been published up to that time (see also H. Hart & Hart, 1933). In a recent study by one of us (EWK) in which an unselected sample of people was asked about a variety of unusual experiences they may have had, five cases of this kind were reported. In one, for example, a nurse became friends with a quadraplegic man who required several hospitalizations for pneumonia and other complications. During one of these hospitalizations, the nurse, feeling guilty that she had not recently visited this patient, had a dream in which she seemed to go to him in the hospital, stood at the end of his bed, and told him to keep fighting. Shortly afterward, the patient's sister told this nurse that he had reported seeing her standing at the foot of his bed, telling him to keep fighting. None of these five cases are fully investigated or corroborated yet, but the number of them reported clearly suggests that such experiences have been, and still are being, reported in sufficient quantity to warrant taking them seriously.

In a few individuals, OBEs sometimes occur repeatedly or even under some degree of voluntary control, an important property that makes them potentially amenable to observation under controlled conditions. There have so far been only a few such studies attempting to examine veridical perceptions during OBEs. The most well known of these is Tart's (1968) study of "Miss Z," a woman who had frequent sleep-related OBEs. She was brought into Tart's lab for four nights, where she was connected to an EEG machine and asked to try, if she had an OBE, to read a five-digit number that Tart randomly selected and placed as a target on a shelf out of the range of her normal sight. She succeeded completely on one occasion, but, as Tart rightly concluded, "this evidence is not conclusive," since there was a remote possibility that she might subliminally have been able to see the target reflected in the glass surface of a clock.[28] Interestingly, Miss Z's OBE experiences occurred in conjunction with a fairly well-defined physiological pattern, developing out of Stage 1 sleep and consisting primarily of low-voltage "alphoid" EEG dominated by slow alpha frequencies. Moreover, the rapid eye movements characteristic of dreaming were absent. Miss Z unfortunately moved away shortly after this promising experiment, and Tart was unable to conduct further work with her.

In another series of experiments, a person who claimed to be able to induce OBEs at will, while awake, attempted during randomly selected experimental periods to go to a specified distant location during an OBE and influence a variety of detectors located there, including other persons, animals, and physical detectors of various sorts (R. L. Morris, Harary, Janis, Hartwell, & Roll, 1978). Although the overall psi results of the study were insignificant, there was one intriguing series of trials in which the subject's new pet kitten showed significantly less movement and less vocalizing during the OBE periods than during the control periods. Examination of physiological data showed that this subject's OBEs were also accompanied by a fairly distinctive state, consisting of deep relaxation (as evidenced by significant decline of skin potential) coupled with elements of arousal (as evidenced by significant increases of heart rate and respiration rate). There was also a large percentage decline in eye movements, although this was not statistically significant. There were no significant EEG findings.

Osis and McCormick (1980), working with another person who claimed to induce OBEs at will, conducted an experiment in which the task was to view a target in a specially constructed optical image device in which the target appears as an illusion and is visible only from a position directly in front of the viewing window. A random number generator created the target for each OBE trial by making a random composite of three features (independently drawn from four possible background colors, four quadrants, and five line drawings). In addition, unbeknownst to the subject, a strain gauge sensor was situated in a shielded chamber directly in front of the viewing window. Out of 197 such trials, there were 114 hits (a hit being defined as accurate identification of any of the three target features), which was marginally significant. Perhaps more interestingly, strain gauge activation was significantly higher during hits than during misses, both before and after target generation. Although, once again, the results can be interpreted as a combination of clairvoyance and psychokinesis, they are also in line with an hypothesis that is consistent with the subject's reported experience, namely, that he had projected his consciousness into the viewing chamber at the only point from which the target could be (optically) seen and where the strain gauge was located.

Clearly, these few existing experiments are inadequate to validate any interpretation of OBEs as involving either psi or an "exteriorization" of the mind from the body. Nevertheless, they also collectively demonstrate

---

28. It is worth noting, however, when considering this suggestion, that she called the five digits out in their correct left-right order (Tart, 1968, p. 17).

that further experimental work along these lines is feasible and potentially productive. As with NDEs, the further study of OBEs under appropriate conditions of experimental control and physiological monitoring is urgently needed. We repeat, however, our belief that advances in our understanding of NDEs, OBEs, and related phenomena are likely to come only by moving beyond the current polarization between exclusively psychophysiological models on the one hand and transcendent or "exteriorization" models on the other. OBEs, NDEs, and other such phenomena surely do not occur at random. It is reasonable to suppose that there are physiological and psychological conditions specially conducive to such experiences, and some of the psychological and physiological models proposed, sparse and conjectural as they presently are, may be converging upon some of those conditions. On the other hand, there is also a not insignificant body of evidence supporting the idea that some experiences are more than mere subjective illusions, and this body of evidence cannot simply be "quietly dropped," as Blackmore would have us do, simply because it presents problems for current models of mind and brain.

In attempting to account for reciprocal apparitions, such as those mentioned above, and for apparitions perceived simultaneously by more than one person (discussed later in this chapter), Myers (1886b) had tentatively proposed the idea that some aspect of consciousness is able in some sense to "go out" from the body and somehow produce an effect in external physical space, not in a conventional material way perceptible to ordinary senses, but nonetheless in a manner sufficient to stimulate an apparition or (as in the case of the strain gauge in Osis and McCormick's experiment or the kitten in the R. L. Morris et al. study) to affect something physical in the environment.[29] Such an idea supposes, as Myers (1886c) did, that the ordinary distinction between mind and matter may not be so straightforward as we often assume, and thus that there may be something intermediate between matter as we ordinarily perceive it and mind as we ordinarily experience it (pp. 178–179; see also our Chapter 2). We might further conjecture that under appropriate psychophysiological conditions, a wide range of experiences may emerge in which the ordinary relationship between consciousness and the body is altered, including some in which consciousness actually does separate from the body.

Autoscopy

The neurological condition known as autoscopy bears some phenomenological resemblance to OBEs. Autoscopy has sometimes been defined as "the hallucinatory projection of the body image into perceptual space" (Lukianowicz, 1958, p. 214). This definition, however, is ambiguous as to the subjective point of view from which the experience occurs, leading some authors inappropriately to equate OBEs and autoscopic experiences (e.g., Lunn, 1970). A more precise definition is "a visual experience where the

29. For an excellent brief discussion of Myers's theory, which he called "phantasmogenetic efficacy," see Gauld (1982, pp. 250–260).

subject sees an image of him/herself in external space, viewed from within his/ her own physical body" (Dening & Berrios, 1994, p. 808). That is, unlike OBEs, in which one's consciousness itself seems to be located outside the body, and one views the actual physical body from that external position, in an autoscopic experience one's consciousness seems to remain inside the body, as usual, and it is instead the hallucinatory image or "double" that seems external.[30] The autoscopic experience also differs from most spontaneously occurring OBEs, and especially from NDEs, in that it is frequently accompanied by unpleasant feelings of unreality, confusion, or depersonalization (Lukianowicz, 1958). Moreover, autoscopic experiences, as well as OBEs reported by seizure patients, usually involve "fear," "horror," "terror," or some other negative affect (Blanke et al., 2004; Dening & Berrios, 1994; Devinsky et al., 1989). Finally, people experiencing autoscopic hallucinations usually have some identified concurrent neurological or psychological pathology (e.g., Blanke et al., 2004; Damas Mora, Jenner, & Eacott, 1980; Devinsky et al., 1989; Lhermitte, 1951; Lukianowicz, 1958).[31] Nevertheless, although OBEs and autoscopic experiences are experientially different in many ways, both phenomena do involve profound alterations in the ordinary relationship between one's sense of self and sense of the body, and they may involve similar or overlapping mechanisms.

Lucid Dreams

Another phenomenon suggesting an alteration in the ordinary relationship of consciousness and the brain is that of lucid dreams. In dreams of this type the state of consciousness associated with ordinary dreaming is enhanced, in that dreamers become self-conscious, are aware that they are dreaming, and are "fully in possession of their cognitive faculties while dreaming" such that they can initiate purposive behavior (LaBerge & Gackenbach, 2000, p. 152). In a real sense, therefore, the dreamer becomes more "awake" or conscious than is ordinary in sleep and dreams. As we mentioned in Chapter 2, Myers (1887a) had recognized the importance of this particular example of enhanced awareness, saying that

> we neglect precious occasions of experiment for want of a little resolute direction of the will....[W]e ought to accustom ourselves to look on each dream, not only as a psychological *observation*, but as an observation which may be transformed into an *experiment*...to carry into our dreams enough of our waking self to tell us that they *are* dreams, and to prompt us to psychological inquiry. (p. 241)[32]

---

30. Blanke et al. (2004) and Brugger, Agosti, Regard, Wieser, and Landis (1994) also call attention to transitional experiences, called "heautoscopic," in which the subject alternates between these two perspectives, or even experiences both simultaneously.

31. This apparent association with pathology, however, may simply reflect a reporting bias, since most studies of autoscopy have been published in medical journals.

32. It was many years before anyone took up this suggestion, but one of the earliest reports about lucid dreams was published in the SPR *Proceedings* by Myers's friend and colleague, Dr. F. van Eeden (1913).

Like NDEs, lucid dreams were at first widely dismissed as impossible, and it was not until methods were found for objectively demonstrating the occurrence of such dreams that psychologists and sleep researchers accepted the phenomenon (LaBerge & Gackenbach, 2000, pp. 157–158).[33] Also, however, as with NDEs, an adequate understanding of lucid dreams will require situating them within a larger group of phenomena involving altered or enhanced mental functioning. For example, one interesting finding of recent OBE research is that people who experience OBEs are likely also to have had lucid dreams, and vice versa (Alvarado, 2000, p. 195). Lucid dreams may be a kind of precursor to simple OBEs or even to more complex, veridical ones. Several people who have frequently experienced or deliberately induced OBEs have suggested using lucid dreaming as a means of inducing OBEs (e.g., J. L. Mitchell, 1981; Muldoon & Carrington, 1929/1973, pp. 125–127; Whiteman, 1956). The two phenomena may well depend upon similar or overlapping physiological mechanisms, and research and theorizing in both areas will likely progress by joining forces.

Apparitions

We turn now to experiences in which a person has seen, heard, or otherwise sensed the presence of a dying or deceased person not physically present. Hallucinations are often defined (and often with pejorative intent) as sensory perceptions in the absence of any corresponding sensory input. By this general definition, many features of NDEs, such as seeing deceased people, a brilliant light, or "other realms," are hallucinations. The literature on hallucinations is vast, and the circumstances under which they occur are enormously varied (see, e.g., Bentall, 2000; Siegel & West, 1975). Hallucinations are reported, for example, in connection with a wide variety of psychotropic drugs or in alcohol- or disease-induced delirium; both positive and negative hallucinations[34] can be produced by hypnosis; they sometimes occur spontaneously in the drowsy states occurring just before sleep or just before awakening (hypnagogic or hypnopompic states); they are related to

33. These methods involve subjects signaling with pre-specified voluntary eye movements, verifiable by outside observers, that they are having a lucid dream (LaBerge & Gackenbach, 2000, p. 157–163).

There is another interesting parallel in the history of research on NDEs and lucid dreams: Blackmore has suggested that NDEs must occur in the moments just before losing consciousness or just before fully regaining it, when brain processes are not so seriously impaired. Similar explanations were proposed for lucid dreams by sleep researchers whose assumptions about the nature of sleep did not allow for the "paradoxical" concept of "conscious sleep"; they argued that lucid dreams must occur either in brief awakenings or in non-REM phases of sleep, until methods were developed demonstrating that lucid dreams do occur during REM sleep (LaBerge & Gackenbach, 2000, pp. 157–158).

34. A "positive" hallucination is one in which a person sees a person or object that is not physically present. A "negative" hallucination is one in which a person does *not* see a person or object that *is* present.

such phenomena as eidetic imagery, synesthesia, and imaginary playmates; they commonly occur in medical conditions such as migraine (Sacks, 1999) and Charles Bonnet syndrome (Schultz, Needham, Taylor, Shindell, & Melzack, 1996); and they can occur (especially in auditory form) in connection with psychiatric illnesses such as schizophrenia. Because the literature on such experiences is so enormous, we can here only call attention to the absolute necessity of situating NDEs, OBEs, and other such phenomena within this broader context.

One important caveat must be kept in mind here, however, and that is the converse need for the study of hallucinations in general to include, and be informed by, study of the kinds of experiences emphasized in this chapter—that is, NDEs, OBEs, and hallucinations experienced by healthy, sane people in a waking state. A recent review of research on hallucinatory experiences is unfortunately not unique in focusing almost exclusively on psychiatric patients experiencing auditory hallucinations (Bentall, 2000). We have already discussed in Chapter 2 the central place that the study of hallucinatory phenomena held in Myers's empirical and theoretical work, particularly the investigations and surveys by Myers and his colleagues of spontaneous cases of apparitions of dying or deceased persons (Gurney et al., 1886; H. Sidgwick et al., 1894). These studies, and ones reported in more recent years (e.g., Dale, White, & Murphy, 1962; Green, 1960; W. F. Prince, 1931; Rhine, 1981; Tien, 1991; D. J. West, 1948, 1990), call into serious question the long-prevailing assumption, which we mentioned at the beginning of this chapter, that hallucinations are exclusively pathological in origin, whether physiologically or psychologically generated. Even hallucinations among bereaved persons (e.g., Barbato, 1999; Grimby, 1993; Marris, 1958, p. 15; Olson, Suddeth, Peterson, & Egelhoff, 1985; Rees, 1971), although occurring in conditions of obvious psychological distress, are not considered necessarily pathological in the current edition of the *Diagnostic and Statistical Manual of Mental Disorders* (1994). Clearly, no theory of hallucinations can be adequate unless it takes into account the wide variety of conditions, physiological and psychological, under which they occur, including—importantly—apparitions reported by sane, awake, healthy individuals.

Veridical Apparitions

Additionally, just as an adequate theory of NDEs or OBEs must take into account the veridical perceptions sometimes occurring outside the person's ordinary sensory capacities, an adequate theory of hallucinatory experience must take into account reports of veridical apparitions. Particularly important examples of these are cases in which the hallucination coincided closely in time with the death or some other crisis happening to the person seen or heard in the hallucination, even though the percipient did not yet know about that death or crisis. Such cases are far from infrequent. It is no exaggeration to say that thousands of them have been investigated and reported, primarily in the pages of the *Proceedings* and *Journals* of the Society for Psychical Research and of the American Society for Psychical

Research (see, e.g., Gurney et al., 1886; E. M. Sidgwick, 1922; H. Sidgwick et al., 1894). Relatively few cases have been reported in more recent decades, but this is almost certainly the result of the sharp decline of interest among experimentally oriented parapsychologists in the investigation of spontaneous experiences, rather than of any falling off in their actual rates of occurrence. Stevenson (1995) reported three such "crisis" cases, and in a recent study by one of us (EWK), at least 18 such apparitions were reported.[35] In addition to the sheer quantity of such cases, the quality of the evidence is such that they cannot be dismissed *en masse* as unsubstantiated "anecdotes." Hart et al. (1956), for example, analyzed a collection of 165 previously published cases in which one of the criteria for inclusion was a written or oral report made of the experience, or action taken because of the experience, *before* the corresponding event was learned about normally.

Collective Apparitions

Another important group of cases suggesting that not all hallucinations are purely subjective is that of "collective" cases, in which more than one person has simultaneously seen the apparition. In one case (which provides an example both of collective perception and of the crisis apparitions mentioned above), a man and his 5-year-old son simultaneously saw at the ceiling the face of the man's father, at the time (they subsequently learned) that this person had died. The man's wife, who was sitting in the same room, corroborated having witnessed the reactions and comments of her husband and son, although she did not herself see the apparition (Gurney et al., 1886, vol. 2, pp. 248–250). Such cases are again not infrequent: Tyrrell (1943/1953) reported that he had found 130 collective cases in the literature and had "no doubt that this list is not exhaustive" (p. 69). Furthermore, although collective cases are a small fraction of *all* reported apparitions, most witnesses report being alone at the time they saw the apparition—a condition perhaps conducive to such an experience. But among cases in which more than one person *was* present, a third (H. Sidgwick et al., 1894, pp. 320–321; Tyrrell, 1943/1953, p. 23) to half (H. Hart et al., 1956, pp. 204–205) involved collective perception, although, as we saw in the case described above, not everyone present necessarily shares the experience.

Other features of collective cases likewise suggest that they are something more than subjective experiences. As Tyrrell pointed out (1943/1953), the testimony in collective cases indicates that "all the percipients see the *same* thing, each from his own point of view in space, just as though it were a material figure" (p. 70). In support of this observation, Tyrrell listed 19 features (of both solitary and collective cases) that suggest some kind of

35. Many cases identified in this study, in which the person reported simply a "sense of presence" or a "dream" coinciding with a death or other crisis, may also have involved apparitions, but even if not, they are clearly related to the apparitional cases. A "sense of presence" may in fact be an incipient apparition, as suggested by a few cases reported in which an initial sense of presence then developed into a sensory apparition (Gurney et al., 1886, vol. 1, p. 483, 527–531).

objectivity to the figure seen (pp. 77–80). For example, in one case a man reported seeing in his bedroom the figure of his brother on the night the brother was killed, and he continued to see the figure, in the same spot but from different perspectives, even when he walked around and away from it (Gurney et al., 1886, vol. 1, pp. 556–559). In another case, a woman saw an apparition of a dying friend reflected in a mirror, as well as when she turned to look directly at it (Myers, 1895e, pp. 444–446; also in *HP*, vol. 1, pp. 421–423). In still other cases, the apparition may obscure light and cast a shadow (e.g., Myers, 1889d, p. 28; this case, incidentally, was also a collective case).

It was collective cases specifically that led to the two major ways of interpreting apparitions in general. On the one hand, Gurney had argued that veridical, or "crisis," apparitions occur when the person learns telepathically[36] about, say, the death of the distant person; this information then emerges into consciousness in the form of an hallucination. Collective cases occur when one primary percipient receives the information telepathically and then "spreads" the information, also telepathically, to other persons present who are sufficiently sensitive to detect it. In contrast, Myers believed that the existence of so many cases in which multiple percipients had perceived the apparition in consistent fashion, together with certain details suggesting some kind of objectivity (such as those described in the previous paragraph), supported the idea that at least some apparitions have a more objective character than telepathic impression alone can account for. He thus proposed his idea of "phantasmogenetic efficacy," which we briefly described earlier in this chapter, in which apparitions are in some sense spatial, or affect space, without being physical in any ordinary sense.[37]

Deathbed Visions

As we also mentioned earlier, one important feature of NDEs is that of perceiving identifiable deceased persons during the experience. Closely related to this feature of NDEs are deathbed visions. Deathbed visions are experiences in which dying people seem to see or converse with people not physically present—usually deceased persons—or to perceive some environment not physically evident to bystanders. Occasionally, a bystander will also perceive what a dying person seems to be seeing (see, e.g., Howarth & Kellehear, 2001; Stevenson, 1995, pp. 359–361).

Like NDE experiencers, dying persons who see people not physically present almost invariably see deceased persons, not living ones. Deathbed visions rarely seem to involve other features prominently associated with NDEs, such as OBEs or tunnels, but these differences may be more apparent than real because an even more fundamental difference between NDEs

36. As we pointed out in Chapter 2, Myers coined the word "telepathy" in 1882 to refer to the phenomenon of one person apparently deriving information directly from another person's mind.

37. Gauld (1968, pp. 168–171; 1982, pp. 238–242, 250–260) has presented summaries of these two views. In 1968 he was clearly not persuaded by either of them, but by 1982 he took Myers's theory more seriously.

and deathbed visions is that in the latter the experiencer usually dies shortly after the experience. We therefore rarely get direct accounts from dying persons themselves; reports of what they experienced come rather from people at their bedside who heard what the dying person said about the experience or who witnessed behavior suggesting what the dying person was experiencing. As a result, we probably know little about the full extent and character of the dying person's experience. Nevertheless, the similarities between NDEs and deathbed visions suggest that, just as NDEs overlap in certain respects with OBEs, so also do they overlap, in different ways, with deathbed visions. It seems likely that all are variants of some larger class of phenomena whose nature has yet to be adequately delineated.

There has been little systematic research to date on deathbed visions. Collections of cases have been published (e.g., W. F. Barrett, 1926; Bozzano, 1906), but in modern times only Osis (1961) and Osis and Haraldsson (1977/1997) have attempted a systematic survey of such experiences. Because these surveys were based entirely on the retrospective recollections of doctors and nurses, often from many years earlier, the findings must be considered preliminary only, and they tell us little about the real incidence and character of such experiences. Nevertheless, they provide reason to believe that deathbed visions may be far more common than is presently recognized, and potentially accessible to more systematic study. Our own informal inquiries, particularly with hospice doctors and nurses, have strongly suggested that such experiences are in fact quite frequent. Moreover, in a recent study conducted by one of us (EWK), the single most common experience reported was being with a dying person who seemed to see or hear deceased loved ones; 218 out of 525 respondents reported such an experience, including 36 nurses or other hospital workers who reported witnessing such experiences, some of them on multiple occasions. Clearly, systematic research is needed to learn more about the incidence, nature, and circumstances of these theoretically important and humanly meaningful experiences.

Sufficient evidence is already available, however, to counter any facile blanket dismissal of deathbed visions as mere hallucinations of a dying brain. We need to keep in mind, first, that deathbed visions are not isolated phenomena. As we have seen, people also report seeing deceased persons in various conditions other than that of actually dying—for example in NDEs in which they were not physiologically close to death, or in apparitions experienced by awake, healthy persons. Second, Osis and Haraldsson (1977/1997) reported that patients were actually *less* likely, not more likely, to have deathbed visions if they were on medications or had illnesses affecting consciousness. Also, there are again cases that call into question even more directly this explanation of deathbed visions as subjective hallucinations. For example, in so-called "Peak in Darien" cases, the dying person apparently sees, and often expresses surprise at seeing, a person whom he or she thought was living, but who had in fact recently died. Reports of such cases are scattered and often not adequately documented; but there are enough of them to warrant giving them serious attention.[38]

An even rarer kind of deathbed experience, but one that like NDEs calls into question the absolute dependence of mental functioning on the state of the brain, are cases in which the dying person has demonstrated a sudden revival in mental functioning just before death. People sometimes appear to revive somewhat *physically* just before death. In a case in our collection, a woman, dying of congestive heart failure, was on oxygen, in a coma, and unable to communicate. At one point, however, according to her daughter, who was present, "much to my surprise she not only sat up in bed but leaped over the bottom rail of the bed, saying 'Jim [her deceased brother], wait for me, don't go....' She was looking at the wall behind where I sat and obviously saw something I did not." Her daughter and the nurses present had trouble restraining her. She did not die on this occasion, but did so a month later, after being sent home since her condition seemed to have improved.

Even more interesting than these physical revivals, however, are revivals in mental functioning. Myers (1892b) had referred to the "sudden revivals of memory or faculty in dying persons" (p. 316), and there are scattered reports of people apparently recovering from dementia shortly before death. The eminent physician Benjamin Rush, author of the first American treatise on mental illness (1812), observed that "most of mad people discover a greater or less degree of reason in the last days or hours of their lives" (p. 257). Similarly, in his classic study of hallucinations, Brierre de Boismont (1859) noted that "at the approach of death we observe that...the intellect, which may have been obscured or extinguished during many years, is again restored in all its integrity" (p. 236). Flournoy (1903, p. 48) mentioned that French psychiatrists had recently published cases of mentally ill persons who showed sudden improvement in their condition shortly before death.

In more recent years, Osis (1961) reported two cases, "one of severe schizophrenia and one of senility, [in which] the patients regained normal mentality shortly before death" (p. 24). Osis and Haraldsson (1977/1997) reported a case of a meningitis patient who had been "severely disoriented almost to the end," but who "cleared up, answered questions, smiled, was slightly elated and just a few minutes before death, came to herself" (p. 133). Turetskaia and Romanenko (1975) reported three cases involving remission of symptoms in dying schizophrenic patients. Grosso (2004, pp. 42–43) described three dementia cases that had been reported to him, one by a colleague and two by a nurse. In all three cases, the patient had not recognized family members for several years, but shortly before death they all were said to have become more coherent or alert and to have recognized family mem-

38. Reports of such "Peak in Darien" experiences may be found in W. F. Barrett (1926, pp. 10–26), Callanan & Kelley (1993, pp. 89–90, 98–99), Cobbe (1882, p. 297), Crookall (1960/1966, pp. 21–22), Gallup and Proctor (1982, pp. 13–14), Gurney and Myers (1889, pp. 459–460), Hyslop (1908, pp. 88–89), A. Johnson (1899, pp. 288–291), Kübler-Ross (1983, pp. 208–210), R. A. Moody with Perry (1988, p. 136), in *HP* (vol. 2, pp. 339–342), Osis and Haraldsson (1977/1997, p. 166), Ring (1980, pp. 207–208), E. M. Sidgwick (1885, pp. 92–93), Spraggett (1974, p. 95), and Stevenson (1959, p. 22).

bers. Such cases are few in number and not adequately documented, but the persistence of such reports suggests that they may represent a real phenomenon that could potentially be substantiated by further investigations. If so, they would seriously undermine the assumption that in such diseases as Alzheimer's the mind itself is destroyed in lockstep with the brain (e.g., Edwards, 1997, pp. 295–296). Like many of the experiences discussed in this chapter, such cases would suggest that in some conditions, consciousness may be enhanced, not destroyed, when constraints normally supplied by the brain are sufficiently loosened.

Mystical and Conversion Experiences

NDEs also have ties to still another class of phenomena that must be considered when evaluating proposed explanations. Many features of NDEs are similar to those of mystical experiences. The ineffability of the experience and the sense of being in the presence of something larger than or transcendent to oneself are features common to both NDEs and mystical experiences. Just as with NDEs, the onset of a mystical experience is often accompanied by overwhelming feelings of joy, happiness, and peace (James, 1902/1958, pp. 157, 204–205). People sometimes describe a feeling of sudden release, and although they usually seem to mean this figuratively, some reports border on an OBE: As one of Leuba's subjects said, "I cannot tell you whether I was in the body or out of the body" (Leuba, 1896, p. 372).[39]

As with NDEs, many mystical experiences involve enhanced mental functioning or heightened perception. Sometimes the "senses are much more acute," such that details of the experience and of one's physical surroundings at the time "are frequently recalled with great minuteness" (Starbuck, 1906, p. 78). One of James's (1902/1958) experiencers said that "my memory became exceedingly clear" (p. 157). A sensory phenomenon that is particularly common in mystical experiences, as well as NDEs, is the sense of seeing a bright light of unusual quality, such as "a strange light which seemed to light up the whole room (for it was dark)" (p. 202). Some people seem to be using the phrase "seeing the light" in a figurative sense, but others are clearly referring to what was to them a real and vivid sensory phenomenon.

We will discuss mystical experiences in detail in Chapter 8, but here we focus on one further and extremely significant feature common to both classes of experience—namely, the transformative aspect, especially of experiences sometimes called conversion experiences. Whatever the explanation of NDEs may be, there is no doubt that they have a profound and apparently lasting impact on many people who experience them. As we noted earlier, they often precipitate a significant change in values, attitude toward

39. This person's experience is reminiscent of the experience described by St. Paul in which he said "whether in the body, or out of the body, I cannot tell" (2 Corinthians 12:3).

death, and a new sense of purpose or meaning in life. Similarly, conversion experiences are, by definition, sudden and lasting changes in character and values such that "religious ideas, previously peripheral in...consciousness, now take central place" (James, 1902/1958, p. 162). Conversion experiences bring a "changed attitude toward life" (Starbuck, 1906, p. 360), including changes in the person's relationship with God, perception and appreciation of nature, attitude toward self, and, perhaps most significantly, attitude toward other people ("I was very selfish...now I desired the welfare of all mankind" [James, 1902/1958, p. 157]).

As we seek to evaluate various theories of NDEs, it is important to emphasize that this transformative aspect is *never*, so far as we have been able to discover, reported in connection with the various fragmentary experiences sometimes glibly equated with NDEs, such as the "dreamlets" of acceleration-induced hypoxia, experiences associated with other abnormalities of blood-gas concentrations, or experiences reported by patients receiving temporal lobe stimulation.[40] Moreover, the transformative features associated with NDEs differ from those associated with simply coming close to death but without having an NDE (Greyson, 1983a; Ring, 1984; van Lommel et al., 2001). Clearly, the profound transformative aspect of NDEs suggests that we need some explanation that goes beyond the physiological models we have so far, and even beyond the psychological experience associated with coming near death.

Many conversion experiences are said to have been preceded by a period of intense brooding, depression, and questioning, and they seem to be the result, not so much of conscious striving, but of subliminal "incubation" of these problems and thoughts, followed by a sudden intrusive experience of unexpected character that leads to a profound shift in the person's perspective and attitude (James, 1902/1958). Conversion experiences, therefore, like NDEs, mystical or religious experiences in general, and creativity and genius, may be best understood with reference to Myers's view of a larger and active subliminal consciousness from which there is occasionally an "uprush" of material into ordinary waking consciousness. Moreover, this "uprush"—and hence these experiences—may all occur more readily in people in whom the "barrier" between supraliminal and subliminal regions of the mind is, as Myers put it, more "permeable," whether constitutionally or because it has been weakened by certain psychological or physiological conditions.[41]

---

40. As we will discuss in Chapter 8, however, such transformations are commonly associated, not just with religious "conversion" experiences, but with mystical experiences in general, including the mystical-type experiences sometimes reported in connection with the use of certain drugs.

41. James interpreted conversion experiences in just this way, saying that the "discovery of a consciousness existing beyond the field of consciousness, or subliminally as Mr. Myers terms it, casts light on many phenomena of religious biography," and that "possession of a developed subliminal self, and of a leaky or pervious margin, is thus a *conditio sine qua non* of the Subject's becoming converted in the instantaneous way" (James, 1902/1958, pp. 188, 194).

Some of the literature on religious conversion experiences has followed the well-worn pathway (discussed in Chapters 7 and 8) found in the literature on mysticism and on genius by emphasizing pathological manifestations. Dewhurst and Beard (1970), for example, reviewed some of the literature on religiosity, conversion, and religious hallucinations among epileptics, including a review of evidence suggesting that many Christian mystics were in fact epileptics, and they then described six of their own epileptic patients with "mystical delusional experiences." Again, however, a more balanced picture of all these phenomena may emerge if we keep in mind Myers's argument, discussed in Chapter 2, that the psychological mechanism of a "permeable barrier" can lead to evolutive as well as dissolutive phenomena, from undeniably dysfunctional pathology to the highest levels of creative and religious experience.

A Psychological Theory?

Thus far in this chapter, we have concentrated on outlining a variety of interrelated phenomena and some of the theories that have been proposed to account for them. A major insight that emerges from such a review is the general recognition that similar experiences can occur under widely varying psychological and physiological conditions. A major problem remains, however: Why do most people, when subjected to the same or similar conditions, *not* have such experiences, whether NDEs, OBEs, apparitions, or any of the other experiences discussed in this chapter? For example, most people who suffer cardiac arrest do not report NDEs: Only 12% of the cardiac arrest patients in van Lommel et al.'s (2001) study, 10% in Greyson's (2003) study, and 6.3% in Parnia et al.'s (2001) study did so.[42]

Part of the answer undoubtedly has to do with the fact, pointed out earlier in this chapter, that many people who have unusual experiences such as NDEs are reluctant to talk about them, not only with medical personnel but even with their friends and families, including even spouses. Additionally, in some cardiac arrest patients, persisting physiological consequences of the arrest and resuscitation may have blocked memory for any experience. Van Lommel et al. (2001), for example, noted that generalized memory defects were significantly more frequent (14%) among those who did not report an NDE than among those who did (2%). But this still leaves a large reservoir of patients who apparently had no such experience. What might distinguish these patients from those who did?

Van Lommel et al. (2001) provide some intriguing clues on the physiological side. There were no significant differences in terms of the resuscitation procedures themselves—that is, factors such as the use of medications,

42. A small percentage of other cardiac arrest patients in these studies reported some memories during the arrest, but not enough to qualify for an NDE as judged by the Greyson NDE Scale (Greyson, 1983b, 1985) or the Ring WCEI (Ring, 1980).

intubation, and defibrillation. The groups also did not differ significantly in terms of other measures of proximity to death, such as the duration of arrest and unconsciousness. Both groups included patients who had cardiac arrest out of the hospital, making a precise evaluation of their actual physiological condition somewhat more difficult. Nonetheless, patients who reported an NDE were more than twice as likely to die within 30 days than those who did not. Clearly, one high priority for further research will be to characterize more precisely the relationship between actual physiological proximity to death, the likelihood of experiencing an NDE, and the phenomenological character of the experiences that do occur.

More generally, however, the occurrence of not only NDEs but also other related experiences under such a wide variety of physiological conditions, and to only some people, suggests the need to expand the search for an adequate theoretical model which includes psychological factors. General support for this idea might come from the additional finding of van Lommel et al. (2001) that reporters of NDEs were more than three times as likely as non-reporters to have had a previous NDE, even though the reporters as a group were significantly younger than the non-reporters. This suggests again that future research might profit in particular by examining all the experiences discussed in this chapter in light of Myers's model of a "permeable barrier" that controls the exchange of material between supraliminal and subliminal levels of consciousness. On this model, some people have more chronically permeable barriers than others, and in all of us the permeability can vary with changes in physiological or psychological conditions.[43] The model predicts, therefore, that people reporting NDEs, as well as other related experiences, differ from other people on measures of hypnotizability, absorption, schizotypy, dissociation, or transliminality. As we mentioned earlier, a few studies have already found some differences in dissociative tendencies, absorption, and fantasy proneness between those who have had an NDE and control groups consisting of otherwise unselected persons who have not. A more meaningful comparison, however, might be between NDE experiencers and a control group of people who have been in the same or similar physiological circumstances but did not have an NDE.

This model might also help make sense of what is currently a "loose end" in the literature on awareness during general anesthesia. We mentioned earlier that the evidence for memory of events occurring while a patient was adequately anesthetized is generally poor. Interestingly, however, the most impressive reports of explicit (or conscious) awareness of events during anesthesia have been elicited by hypnosis (Cheek, 1964, 1966; Levinson, 1965). The historically important Levinson study, for example, involved 10 highly hypnotizable subjects undergoing very similar surgical procedures carried out under a deliberately deep and uniform anesthesia regime monitored

43. Hartmann (1989, 1991) and Thalbourne (1998; Thalbourne & Delin, 1994) have proposed similar ideas about factors influencing the exchange of material between levels of the mind, and both have developed questionnaire instruments capable to some degree of measuring these factors—"boundaries" and "transliminality," respectively.

with EEG. A month later—but *only* under hypnosis—four of these patients recalled nearly verbatim, and four others recalled partially, standardized remarks made by the anesthetist in conjunction with a staged "crisis" in the procedure. These studies have never, to our knowledge, been adequately followed up, but they should be, because such results, if replicable, suggest, like NDEs, that mind is still somehow able to operate when the brain is disabled by anesthesia. Moreover, they suggest, as Myers argued, that hypnosis is a method particularly conducive to loosening the "barrier" and thus accessing subliminal levels of consciousness.

The Challenge of Near-Death Experiences

Following Myers, we have argued that explanatory models for the phenomena we have discussed in this chapter must take into account not only the full range of features and conditions associated with each individual phenomenon in isolation, but also the wide variety of related phenomena that share some of its principal features. We are not suggesting simplistically that all these phenomena will one day be brought under the rubric of one all-encompassing explanation. Nonetheless, we are arguing that if we are to understand any particular phenomenon, we must situate it in the context of related phenomena, an exercise that may then ultimately lead to a greatly expanded view of the nature of all of them. As noted several times in this chapter, the phenomena that we have discussed all suggest a marked alteration, not only in the person's state of consciousness, but more broadly in the ordinary relationship of the person's consciousness with the external world. We emphasize again that some of these alterations—sharing common characteristics despite the apparent diversity of means by which they may be brought about—suggest that there may be more to the external environment itself than our ordinary sensorimotor functioning can detect.

The challenge of NDEs in particular, however, goes beyond situating them properly within a broader framework of cognate phenomena. The challenge lies also in recognizing and accounting for one central feature that in our opinion makes this phenomenon uniquely important in any contemporary discussion of the mind-brain problem—specifically, the occurrence of vivid and complex mentation, sensation, and memory under conditions in which current neuroscientific models of the mind deem conscious experience of any significant sort impossible. The stark incompatibility of NDEs with current models of mind-brain relations is particularly evident in connection with experiences that occur under two conditions—general anesthesia and cardiac arrest. We wish now to highlight this conflict, because the theoretical significance of the many experiences occurring under these conditions has perhaps not been sufficiently appreciated. In both of these situations, we will argue, much more is at issue than some vague sense of incompatibility between the characteristics of the mentation that occurs and the physiological conditions under which it occurs.

In Chapter 1 we noted that the current mainstream doctrine of biological naturalism has coalesced neuroscientifically around the family of "global workspace" theories. Despite differences of detail and interpretation, all of these theories have in common the view that the essential substrate for conscious experience—the neuroelectric activities that make it possible and that constitute or directly reflect the necessary and sufficient conditions for its occurrence—consist of synchronous or at least coherent high-frequency (gamma-band, roughly 30–70 Hz) EEG oscillations linking widely separated, computationally specialized, regions of the brain.[44] An enormous amount of empirical evidence supports the existence of these mind-brain correlations under normal conditions of mental life, and we do not dispute this evidence. The conventional theoretical *interpretation* of this correlation, however—that the observed neuroelectric activity itself generates or constitutes the conscious experience—*must be incorrect*, because in both general anesthesia and cardiac arrest, the specific neuroelectric conditions that are held to be necessary and sufficient for conscious experience are abolished—and yet vivid, even heightened, awareness, thinking, and memory formation can still occur.[45]

General Anesthesia

Take first the case of NDEs occurring under conditions of general anesthesia: In our collection at the University of Virginia, 23% of the computer-coded cases occurred under anesthesia, and these involved the same features that characterize other NDEs, such as having an OBE and watching medical personnel working on their body, an unusually bright or vivid light, meeting deceased persons, and—significantly—thoughts, memories, and sensations that were as clear or clearer than usual. If the incidence of cases involving anesthesia in our collection is any indication of the general incidence, then conservatively many thousands of NDEs have occurred during surgical procedures involving general anesthesia.

---

44. The specific brain regions involved vary somewhat according to the tasks and theorists, but characteristically include cerebellar and limbic cortex, anterior cingulate and insular cortex, the thalamus with its dense and reciprocal connections with neocortex, and large parts of the neocortex itself, including in particular frontal and parietal cortex as well as whatever specific sensory systems may be momentarily engaged (see, e.g., Baars, 1997; Crick, 1994; Dehaene & Naccache, 2001; Edelman & Tononi, 2000; A. K. Engel et al., 2001; W. J. Freeman, 2000; John, 2001; Llinás, 2001; Mesulam, 2000; Varela et al., 2001).

45. A similar line of argument could be developed, we believe, for related conditions such as coma and persistent vegetative state, during which NDEs have also occasionally been reported. We focus here on general anesthesia and cardiac arrest only because the relevant physiological conditions are relatively well characterized and the cases already numerous.

John et al. (2001) recently carried out a massive study intended specifically to identify reliable EEG correlates of loss and recovery of consciousness during general anesthesia. They analyzed 19-channel recordings obtained from 176 surgical patients, using three common types of anesthesia regime involving diverse mechanisms of action, and they sought to characterize common properties of the EEG patterns associated with the main stages of anesthesia. Their results first confirmed and extended what has long been the main story about anesthesia and EEG, namely, that unconsciousness is associated with a pronounced shift toward lower frequencies in the delta and low theta range, with a more frontal distribution and higher power. More significantly, they showed that gamma-type EEG rhythms lost power and became decoupled across the brain when patients lost consciousness, and that these changes were reversed with return of consciousness. The whole pattern, as Baars points out in a commentary on the paper (Baars, 2001), is consistent with current neurophysiological theories of the global workspace, and appears to reflect its complete disabling under conditions of adequate anesthesia.

Additional results supportive of this conclusion derive from other recent functional imaging studies that have looked at blood flow, glucose metabolism, and other indicators of cerebral activity under conditions of general anesthesia with agents including propofol, halothane, isoflurane, and deep sedation with benzodiazapines such as midazolam (Alkire, 1998; Alkire, Haier, & Fallon, 2000; Fiset et al., 1999; Shulman, Hyder, & Rothman, 2003; Veselis et al., 1997; and N. S. White & Alkire, 2003), as well as related conditions such as persistent vegetative states and coma (see Laureys et al., 2004, and the numerous references cited there). In these studies, brain areas essential to the global workspace are consistently deactivated individually and decoupled functionally in surgically adequate anesthesia and related states of unconsciousness. Auditory and other stimuli are still able to activate their primary receiving areas in the cortex, since the sensory pathways remain relatively unimpaired, but these stimuli are no longer able to ignite the large-scale cooperative network interactions that normally accompany conscious experience.

Cardiac Arrest

The situation is even more dramatic with regard to NDEs occurring during cardiac arrest, many of which in fact occur also in conjunction with major surgical procedures involving general anesthesia. As mentioned earlier, there have been numerous reports of NDEs in connection with cardiac arrest, and, like those that occur with general anesthesia, they include the typical features associated with NDEs, most notably vivid or even enhanced sensation and mentation. A typical case is that reported by MacMillan and Brown (1971) of a cardiac arrest patient who prefaced his description of an OBE and seeing a light by saying: "I do not have words to express how vivid the experience was. The main thing that stands out is the clarity of my thoughts during the episode" (p. 889). Another typical comment was that of a 6-year-old cardiac arrest victim who insisted that "it was realer than real" (M. Morse, 1994a, p. 67).

Cardiac arrest, however, is a physiologically brutal event. Cerebral functioning shuts down within a few seconds. Whether the heart actually stops beating entirely or goes into ventricular fibrillation, the result is essentially instantaneous circulatory arrest, with blood flow and oxygen uptake in the brain plunging swiftly to near-zero levels. EEG signs of cerebral ischemia, typically with global slowing and loss of fast activity, are visually detectable within 6–10 seconds, and progress to isoelectricity (flat-line EEGs) within 10–20 seconds of the onset of arrest. In sum, full arrest leads rapidly to establishment of three major clinical signs of death—absence of cardiac output, absence of respiration, and absence of brainstem reflexes—and provides the best model we have of the dying process (DeVries, Bakker, Visser, Diephuis, & van Huffelen, 1998; Parnia & Fenwick, 2002; van Lommel et al., 2001; Vriens, Bakker, DeVries, Wieneke, & van Huffelen, 1996). Nevertheless, in five published studies alone, over 100 cases of NDEs occurring under conditions of cardiac arrest have been reported (Greyson, 2003; Parnia et al., 2001; Sabom, 1982; Schwaninger et al., 2002; van Lommel et al., 2001), and there are many more in other collections, including our own.

The case of Pam Reynolds, described earlier in this chapter, is a notable example of an NDE that occurred under conditions involving both deep general anesthesia and cardiac arrest of a particularly extreme form. As pointed out in our earlier discussion, we do not know precisely when in the surgical procedure Pam had her experience, other than to say that the early parts of the experience, including the OBE, occurred when she was not yet "brain dead" but already deeply anesthetized. Nonetheless, even if we assume for the sake of discussion that her entire experience occurred during these earlier stages of the procedure, brain activity even at that time was inadequate to support organized mentation, according to current neurophysiological doctrine.

How might scientists intent upon defending the conventional view respond to the challenge presented by cases occurring under conditions like these? First, it will undoubtedly be objected that even in the presence of a flat-lined EEG there still could be undetected brain activity going on. Current scalp-EEG technology detects only activity common to large populations of suitably oriented neurons, mainly in the cerebral cortex; and so perhaps future improvements in technology will allow us to detect additional brain activity not visible to us at present. This objection may seem to have some force, because both experimental and modeling studies show that certain kinds of electrical events in the brain, such as highly localized epileptic spikes, do not appear in scalp recordings (Pacia & Ebersole, 1997). Moreover, recordings carried out under conditions of general anesthesia comparable to those used with Pam Reynolds provide direct evidence that some residual electrical activity can appear subcortically or in the neighborhood of the ventricles, even in combination with an essentially flat scalp EEG (Karasawa et al., 2001).

This first objection, however, completely misses the mark. *The issue is not whether there is brain activity of any kind whatsoever, but whether there is brain activity of the specific form regarded by contemporary neuroscience as the necessary condition of conscious experience.*[46] Activity of this form is eminently detectable by current EEG technology, and as we have already shown, it is abolished both by adequate general anesthesia and by cardiac arrest. In cardiac arrest, even neuronal action-potentials, the ultimate physical basis for any possible coordination of neural activity between widely separated brain regions, are rapidly abolished (van Lommel, 2006). Moreover, cells in the hippocampus, the region thought to be essential for memory formation (see Chapter 4), are known to be especially vulnerable to the effects of anoxia (Vriens et al., 1996). In short, it is not credible to suppose that NDEs occurring under conditions of adequate general anesthesia, let alone cardiac arrest, can be accounted for in terms of some hypothetical residual capacity of the brain to process and store complex information under those conditions.

A somewhat more credible line of defense, perhaps, is to suggest that the experiences do not occur when they appear to occur, during the actual episodes of brain insult, but at a different time, perhaps just before or just after the insult, when the brain is more or less normally functional. After all, we do know that large amounts of vivid experience can occur in just a few seconds, for example in conjunction with the fall of an alpine climber (Heim, 1892/1972). This suggestion too encounters serious problems, however. First, episodes of ordinary unconsciousness produced by physiological events such as ventricular fibrillation or cardiac arrest characteristically leave their subjects amnesic and confusional for events immediately preceding and following these episodes, the more so in proportion to their duration and severity (Aminoff et al., 1988; Parnia & Fenwick, 2002; van Lommel et al., 2001). In addition, the confusional experiences occurring as a person is losing or regaining consciousness *never*, to our knowledge, have the life-transforming impact so characteristic of NDEs. Second, a substantial number of NDEs, like Pam Reynolds's, contain apparent time "anchors," in the form of verifiable reports of events occurring during the period of insult itself. For example, the cardiac-arrest victim described by van Lommel et al. (2001) had been discovered lying in a meadow 30 minutes or more prior to his arrival at the emergency room, comatose and cyanotic, and yet days later, having recovered, he was able to describe accurately various circumstances occurring in conjunction with the ensuing resuscitation procedures in the hospital.

We have observed two kinds of critical responses, totally divergent, to verifiable time-anchor events of this sort. The first, favored by mainstream critics, is essentially to deny that the reported events have occurred or that they have any force. They are mere "anecdotes," without value as scien-

46. Representative of people who have completely missed the mark here is Woerlee (2004).

tific evidence. We will make only two comments regarding this attitude, in relation to the entire body of evidence presently available. First, it is scientifically inappropriate to approach each such "anecdote" in complete isolation, as though it stands on its own as the only evidence in existence for phenomena in which people have obtained information about situations from which they were sensorially isolated. As stated in our Introduction and documented in the Appendix, phenomena of this type are independently known to exist; what is unusual here is only the specific circumstances of their occurrence. Second, as emphasized especially by Bergson (1913) in his Presidential Address to the SPR, many reports of veridical spontaneous experiences (including those associated with NDEs) are not simply vague or general statements but contain very specific details, and the correspondence of these details with remote events must be recognized as highly unlikely to have occurred by chance, even if we cannot compute their improbability with any great exactitude.

The other critical response comes from persons who take the available veridical reports seriously, like ourselves, but interpret them differently. Their suggestion, essentially, is that the NDE is simply an imaginative reconstruction, and one which can sometimes incorporate paranormally derived information, obtained when the brain is fully functional, about events occurring during the period of unconsciousness. We will again make just two brief comments in response: First, this form of counter-explanation will presumably provide little solace to mainstream critics, since it incorporates as an essential ingredient psi processes which are themselves equally inconsistent with current mainstream views. Second, although this time-displaced psi interpretation, like other "super-psi" hypotheses, cannot be decisively refuted, it simply ignores, in our opinion, the essential core of NDE phenomenology—that these intense and vivid experiences are subjectively timed to the moment of the reported and verifiable events and are remembered that way for years or decades afterwards. It would also need to explain why the reports always follow, never precede, the events in question, and why their subjects characteristically show little or no evidence of psi capacities in any other context before the NDE.

Two further critical responses merit only still briefer mention. One is to suggest that these supposedly verifiable NDEs are being inadvertently misreported, whether by the subjects of the experiences themselves or by their investigators. That is certainly always a possibility to be guarded against in individual cases; but when this suggestion is used repeatedly and without supporting evidence as a blanket defense against the entire body of evidence, it should be recognized for what it is, which is simply an unwillingness to examine that evidence in a truly scientific spirit. The same response applies, but even more so, to any suggestion that the investigators of NDEs are just making it all up. As the philosopher Henry Sidgwick (1882) pointed out in his initial Presidential Address to the SPR in 1882: "We have done all that we can when the critic has nothing left to allege except that the investigator is in the trick. But when he has nothing else left to allege he will allege that" (p. 12).

Conclusion

In sum, the central challenge of NDEs lies in asking how these complex states of consciousness, including vivid mentation, sensory perception, and memory, can occur under conditions in which current neurophysiological models of the production of mind by brain deem such states impossible. This conflict between current neuroscientific orthodoxy and the occurrence of NDEs under conditions of general anesthesia and/or cardiac arrest is head-on, profound, and inescapable. In our opinion, no future scientific or philosophic discussion of the mind-brain problem can be fully responsible, intellectually, without taking these challenging data into account. We refer readers back to the quotation from Myers with which we began this chapter, and to the challenge that he issued over a century ago. Only when researchers approach the study of NDEs and their associated physiological conditions with this question firmly in mind will we progress in our understanding of NDEs beyond the sorts of ill-founded neuroscientific and psychological speculations that abound in the contemporary literature. Similarly, however, only when neuroscientists and psychologists examine current models of mind in light of NDEs and related phenomena such as those discussed in this chapter will we progress in our understanding of consciousness and its relation to brain.

Chapter 7

Genius

Edward F. Kelly and Michael Grosso

> In conformity with a rule which seems applicable to every science of observation...it is the exceptional phenomenon which is likely to explain the usual one; and, consequently, whatever we can observe that has to do with invention, is capable of throwing light on psychology in general. (Hadamard, 1949, p. 136)

> I think that a materialist definition of genius is impossible, which is why the idea of genius is so discredited in an age like our own, where materialist ideologies predominate. (Bloom, 2002, p. 12)

In his beautiful memorial tribute to F. W. H. Myers, William James (1901) endorsed Myers's broad vision of a scientific psychology, contrasting it with the much narrower vision produced by a different type of scientific imagination, the "classic-academic" type, which he describes in terms almost equally applicable to present-day mainstream cognitive psychology:

> The human mind, as it is figured in this literature, was largely an abstraction. Its normal adult traits were recognized. A sort of sunlit terrace was exhibited on which it took its exercise. But where that terrace stopped, the mind stopped; and there was nothing farther left to tell of in this kind of philosophy but the brain and the other physical facts of nature. (p. 14)

Thanks to Myers and other "romantic improvers," however, "a mass of mental phenomena are now seen in the shrubbery beyond the parapet," and "the world of mind is shown as something infinitely more complex than was suspected" (p. 14). James explicitly characterizes Myers as the leader of this expansionist movement: "Through him for the first time, psychologists are in possession of their full material, and mental phenomena are set down in an adequate inventory" (p.16). Moreover, Myers was more than just a prodigious collector; he had shown a Darwin-like genius for organizing and coordinating this mass of material in service of what James regarded as the first serious scientific attempt to delineate the constitution of this transmarginal or subliminal background of the mind. This problem—henceforward to be known as "*the problem of Myers*"—"still awaits us as the problem of far the deepest moment for our actual psychology, whether his own tentative solutions of certain parts of it be correct or not" (p. 18).

Chapter 2 presented a general account of Myers's theory, but here we will concentrate in much greater detail on just one of the empirical topics that Myers himself dealt with explicitly—genius. This topic, we will argue, provides another important arena within which Myers's views, when revisited in light of the much larger body of relevant evidence available today, can be recognized as preferable in a variety of ways to the alternatives that mainstream psychological theory and research have so far provided.

Genius is obviously a topic of great human interest and significance, to all of us as individuals and to civilization as a whole. It also seems self-evident, as Wind's principle and our first epigraph suggest, that a cognitive science capable of accommodating the fully-developed phenomena of genius would be capable *a fortiori* of accommodating cognitive phenomena in general. However, despite this seemingly crucial importance of genius as a kind of benchmark and navigational aid for progress in scientific psychology, its treatment to date for the most part reflects the general history of 20th-century psychology, as summarized in our Introduction, and has been anything but satisfactory or illuminating.

In the first four decades following the rise of Watson's radical behaviorism, for example, the mainstream American psychological literature was practically devoid of relevant studies. In his landmark Presidential Address to the American Psychological Association J. P. Guilford (1950) reported that only 186 of the roughly 121,000 entries in *Psychological Abstracts* up to that date had addressed this vital topic. Guilford bemoaned this "appalling" neglect, and his challenge provoked a modest increase in research output which has continued and even slowly intensified up to the present. Nevertheless, even now such research represents a relatively tiny and specialized sub-field of psychology. Moreover, by far the greatest proportion of research to date has been carried out in the framework of Guilford's own psychometric tradition, dating back to Galton and Binet, which revolves mainly around measurement of "divergent thinking," "fluency," "flexibility," puzzle-solving behaviors, and the like, typically in student volunteers.

We do not wish to disparage unduly the modern research tradition, and we hasten to add that it includes many other threads, such as the early work of Gestalt psychologists on "insight," psychoanalytic investigations of "primary process" thinking, and detailed studies of life history and personality characteristics in demonstrably productive individuals, some of which we will touch upon later.

For purposes of this introduction, however, the important bottom-line fact is that even to many of its practitioners, not to mention outside observers such as ourselves, modern "creativity" research appears mired, overall, in a rather dismal state. A number of the contributors to the recent *Handbook of Creativity* (R. J. Sternberg, 1999)—the explicit goal of which was "to provide the most comprehensive, definitive, and authoritative single volume review available in the field"—candidly acknowledge this sorry state of affairs, which also is fully apparent in the most current state-of-the-art review consulted by us (Runco, 2004). In effect, we suggest, the study of the real thing—"genius"—has largely degenerated in modern times into the study of diluted cognates such as "creativity" or even "talent," which happen to be relatively accessible to the more "objective" means of investigation currently favored by most investigators.

Myers consciously and deliberately took an approach targeted throughout to genius in its fullest expressions—what "the highest minds have bequeathed to us as the heritage of their highest hours" (*HP*, vol. 1, p. 120). We will show that by means of this approach, honoring Wind's principle, Myers produced an account of genius which anticipates to a remarkable degree most of what has been best in more recent work, while also accommodating various unusual phenomena, such as psychological automatisms and secondary streams of consciousness, altered states of consciousness, unusual forms of symbolic thinking, and psi, that are inescapably bound up with this topic but scarcely touched upon in contemporary mainstream accounts. His views also have been confirmed at various important points by more recent empirical and theoretical investigations, and they have important implications for the further evolution of scientific psychology more generally.

To substantiate these claims we will present Myers's account of genius in considerable detail, situating it as we proceed with respect to the main relevant trends in more recent psychological research. Our presentation is necessarily telegraphic and selective, for the existing literature on "creativity," though but a tiny proportion of the psychology literature as a whole, harbors something upwards of 10,000 papers and books; our purpose is not to survey this enormous literature comprehensively, but to advance and defend a particular point of view.

Myers's Theory of Genius: General Features and Scope

Myers's chapter on genius in *Human Personality* is almost identical to his earlier paper on this subject (Myers, 1892d). The chapter itself is conspicuously atypical in form, in that it is very short and less densely empirical than its siblings, and lacks an appendix. Yet there can be no doubt that it both illustrates and provides support for some of Myers's most central and deeply-felt convictions regarding the subliminal realm and its role in human mental life. His chapter on genius is itself a work of genius, so full of bold and challenging observations and speculations that it will require the balance of our present chapter and all of the next to do it reasonably full justice.

Myers begins by setting forth the general character of his conception of genius. In his previous chapter he had characterized hysteria as a disintegrative or "dissolutive" process involving loss of control of normally supraliminal elements of the personality. Genius for Myers presents the opposite situation. Specifically, in genius an increased "strength and concentration of the inward unifying control" (*HP*, vol. 1, p. 70) results in enhanced coordination and integration of the supraliminal and subliminal phases of personality. In effect genius stands in relation to ordinary personality roughly as ordinary personality itself stands in relation to hysteria. Genius represents the evolution of personality toward a more ideal form of psychic functioning, and therefore toward a truer standard of "normality."

In taking this position Myers directly opposed a sizeable cadre of writers including Max Nordau, John Nisbet, and Cesare Lombroso, who at that time were busily engaged in deflating "genius" by characterizing it as nothing more than a form or manifestation of "degeneracy" or "madness" of one or another supposedly well-understood type.[1]

Myers's basic response to this deflationary movement, then in full flood, incisively encapsulates the main features of his own very different view (*HP*, vol. 1, p. 71):

> On this point I shall join issue; and I shall suggest, on the other hand, that Genius—if that vaguely used word is to receive anything like a psychological definition—should rather be regarded as a power of utilising a wider range than other men can utilise of faculties in some degree innate in all;—a power of appropriating the results of subliminal mentation to subserve the supraliminal stream of thought;—so that an "inspiration of Genius" will be in truth a *subliminal uprush*, an emergence into the current of ideas which the man is consciously manipulating of other ideas which he has not consciously originated, but which have shaped themselves beyond his will, in profounder regions of his being. I shall urge that there is here no real departure from normality; no abnormality, at least in the sense of degeneration; but rather a fulfilment of the true norm of man, with suggestions, it may be, of something *supernormal*;—of something which tran-

1. A striking exception to this widely circulated degeneracy interpretation of genius is the book by German psychiatrist William Hirsch (1896), translated anonymously into English by James's philosophical colleague C. S. Peirce. That James himself held views similar to and strongly influenced by those of Myers is apparent from his 1896 Lowell Lectures, as reconstructed by E. Taylor (1984).

> scends existing normality as an advanced stage of evolutionary progress transcends an earlier stage.[2]

Note first Myers's insistence on a *psychological* definition of genius. Some later investigators have focused instead primarily on its objective manifestations, so that "genius" becomes an inference backwards from the appearance of *products* that are regarded as useful or valuable or satisfying by some audience at some point in time. In the work of Lange-Eichbaum (1932), representing this tendency of thought at its extreme, the personality of the genius essentially vanishes, the term "genius" implying only a relation of approval between products of creative activity and the relevant community of evaluators. The recently articulated "systems perspective" of Csikszentmihalyi (1988, 1996) and others similarly downplays the psychological dimensions of the subject in favor of cultural, social, and situational factors.

Myers, however, deliberately takes the opposite tack. He first clearly acknowledges that a work of genius conventionally satisfies two distinct sorts of requirements: "It must involve something original, spontaneous, unteachable, unexpected, and it must also win for itself in some way the admiration of mankind" (*HP*, vol. 1, p. 75). But he immediately makes clear that *his* concern is with the first sort of criterion, which corresponds to a real psychological class. As he puts it:

> What the poet feels while he writes his poem is a psychological fact in *his* history; what his friends feel while they read it may be a psychological fact in *their* history, but does not alter the poet's creative effort, which was what it was, whether any one but himself ever reads his poem or no.

Thus for example Hartley Coleridge seemed to Myers to have manifested the characteristic psychological marks of genius even though he never produced anything tangible that commanded wide attention.

Myers's central concern and goal, in sum, is to elucidate the psychological processes involved in undeniable manifestations of genius, and to discern their broader implications for the theory of human personality. We will present and discuss his more detailed arguments under these headings.

The Creative Process: A Descriptive Model

A traditional descriptive model of the creative process, based on the self-observation and testimony of large numbers of variously eminent persons, provides a useful organizing framework for this discussion. Credit for

2. E. Taylor (1984, pp. 162–163) uses this very passage—almost verbatim and without identifying it as Myers's—by way of characterizing Myers's theory of genius as the chief background for James's final Lowell Lecture.

explicitly formulating this model is usually given to Graham Wallas (1926), a political scientist and administrator primarily concerned with pedagogical matters, but it was also formulated in nearly identical terms and in greater detail by psychologist Eliot Dole Hutchinson (1931, 1939). The model posits four phases or stages that can often be discerned in high-level creative effort: (1) *preparation*; (2) *incubation*; (3) *illumination*; and (4) *verification*. Briefly, *preparation* refers primarily to the initial stages of intense voluntary effort on a particular work or problem (although it is sometimes generalized to include the typically lengthy period of time in which high-level technical skills relevant to the task are laboriously acquired). If this initial effort fails, the work or problem may temporarily be put aside in frustration, this being the stage of *incubation* or renunciation, in which conscious effort seems to be largely or wholly absent. Something more than simple rest or dissipation of inhibitions seems to be involved during the incubation period, for then comes *illumination*, inspiration, or insight, in which radically new ideas intrude into consciousness, often suddenly, copiously, and with strong accompanying affect. This leads to a further stage of voluntary effort, *verification*, in which the new material may be evaluated, elaborated, and worked into the structure of the evolving product.[3]

Only in rare cases can these "stages" accurately be pictured as unrolling in a rigid sequence, or at a single level. Normally they go forward concurrently at multiple, overlapping, and recursively interacting levels in regard to different elements of the total problem situation. The incubation and inspiration stages, which form the psychological heart of the model, are not invariably or necessarily discernible in individual episodes of creative activity, and even when recognizably present they can vary widely in duration, character, and importance (Ghiselin, 1952; Hutchinson, 1931, 1939; Koestler, 1964; Wallas, 1926).

A descriptive model of this general sort is accepted by nearly everyone who has studied the subject of genius seriously. There is, however, a modern "deflationary" tradition, exemplified by Weisberg (1986, 1999) and Perkins (1981, 2000), that we must comment upon at least briefly before proceeding. This school wishes to deny that there is anything special or unusual about the character of the mental processes occurring in genius-level creativity, and in particular to deny that genius ever depends upon or utilizes any special sort of "unconscious" work. Nothing more is involved, on this view, than unusually tenacious, disciplined, and incremental application of cognitive processes of the ordinary sort. Not surprisingly, this contrarian view arises mainly in the context of laboratory studies of puzzle-solving behaviors and other sorts of on-demand "creativity," mostly in student volunteers. The fact that the alleged phenomena of incubation and illumination cannot

3. Wallas identified the first three stages in an 1891 lecture by Helmholtz, on the occasion of his 70th birthday, in which he described how his best scientific ideas had come to him, and the fourth in the famous account by Poincaré of some of his mathematical discoveries (see Hadamard, 1949, or Ghiselin, 1952). Hutchinson arrived at his formulation through study of hundreds of accounts involving not only scientists and mathematicians but artists, musicians, and literateurs, mostly persons of lesser magnitude than Helmholtz and Poincaré.

readily and reliably be evoked under their preferred laboratory conditions disposes such workers to conclude that the phenomena do not exist, or are of only minor importance. Their existence and importance in any event cannot be established by first-person testimony from any number of witnesses, no matter how eminent, because such testimony is merely "anecdotal" and always subject to corruption by well-known hazards such as limitations of observation, failures of memory, motivated distortions in service of public personae, and so on.

With all due respect, this "nothing-special" view of genius seems to us a particularly egregious example of "methodolatry" (see Introduction), coupled with willful disregard of an enormous and fundamentally coherent mass of evidence deriving from persons especially well positioned and qualified, generally speaking, to observe and report the phenomena of greatest psychological interest. As Ghiselin (1952) remarks, "the fundamentals...are all but inescapable" (p. 11). The unwillingness of many modern literary scholars to confront genius in its full-blown phenomenological reality has recently provoked Harold Bloom (2002) to castigate them as "cultural levelers, quite immune from awe" (p. 7), and in our view that judgment applies equally here. We also find it especially ironic, and revealing, that in the end both Weisberg and Perkins are forced to acknowledge that even the "ordinary" cognitive operations to which they aspire to reduce all manifestations of genius—operations such as remembering, recognizing, realizing, seeing-as, noticing, and reasoning—remain *themselves* at bottom (and again in accordance with Wind's principle) unexplained. It is also ironic, of course, that their repudiation of the possibility of unconscious mental work in genius comes just as many other mainstream psychologists are re-admitting such things in the form of the "cognitive unconscious." As in Chapter 5, the real issue before us therefore becomes that of the *scope* and *character*, rather than the existence *per se*, of the mental activity that goes on behind the scenes, outside the purview of ordinary waking consciousness.

Myers's Psychology of Creative Inspiration

Let us presume, then, that the Wallas/Hutchinson model is broadly correct, descriptively. Myers directs *his* analysis straight to the psychological core of this model, to its most critical, mysterious, and controversial component—specifically, to the phase of "illumination," or in his own more theory-laden terminology, "subliminal uprush." Three main features of his analysis—*continuity*, *automatism*, and *incommensurability*—will command the bulk of our attention.

Continuity

Myers emphasizes the fundamental continuity between the mental processes at work in genius and those of more everyday character. He is a thoroughgoing naturalist, and for him genius is first and foremost an intensification of phenomena already observable in germ in the central, supraliminal part of the mental "spectrum" (Chapter 2), rather than some sort of supernatural gift of faculty altogether new. *Some* degree of cooperation between supraliminal and subliminal elements of personality, he points out,

> is constantly occurring on a smaller scale in the inner life of most of us. We identify ourselves for the most part with a stream of voluntary, fully conscious ideas,—cerebral movements connected and purposive as the movements of the hand which records them. Meantime we are aware also of a substratum of fragmentary, automatic, *liminal* ideas, of which we take small account. These are bubbles that break on the surface; but every now and then there is a stir among them. There is a rush upwards as of a subaqueous spring; an inspiration flashes into the mind for which our conscious effort has not prepared us. This so-called inspiration may in itself be trivial or worthless; but it is the initial stage of a phenomenon to which, when certain rare attributes are also present, the name of genius will naturally be given. (*HP*, vol. 1, p. 77)

As described in Chapter 2, Myers conceives of the subliminal as being in all of us restrained or released in accord with dynamic adjustments in the level of some sort of "threshold"—or in the permeability of a membrane or "diaphragm"—which regulates its supraliminal expression. In most of us this dynamic process is evidenced by occurrences such as nocturnal dreams and the mild dissociative fluctuations, such as daydreams and hypnagogic states, that mark daily life. In genius, however, these dynamic adjustments are somehow amplified, providing correspondingly greater supraliminal access to products or elements of subliminal mentation.

Not all such products are of equal value, however, for "hidden in the deep of our being is a rubbish-heap as well as a treasure-house" (*HP*, vol. 1, p. 72). Myers takes pains to guard against any naive or unchecked romanticism:

> I shall be obliged in this chapter to dwell on valuable aid rendered by subliminal mentation; but I do not mean to imply that such mentation is *ipso facto superior* to supraliminal, or even that it covers a large proportion of practically useful human achievement. When I say "The differentia of genius lies in an increased control over subliminal mentation," I express, I think, a well-evidenced thesis, and I suggest an important inference, namely, that the man of genius is for us the best type of the normal man, in so far as he effects a successful co-operation of an unusually large number of elements of his personality—reaching a stage of integration slightly in advance of our own. This much I wish to say: but my thesis is not to be pushed further:—as though I claimed that all our best thought was sub-

> liminal, or that all that was subliminal was potentially "inspiration." (*HP*, vol. 1, p. 72)

For Myers the subliminal realm has a complex hierarchical organization marked by successively higher levels of integration, each with its own characteristic functional properties or "adits and operations." In deliberate analogy with Hughlings Jackson's evolutionary model of hierarchical organization in the human nervous system (see our Chapter 2), Myers pictures the subliminal tentatively and broadly as comprising three such levels: The lowest involves the "minimal psychic concomitant, whatever that may be" (*HP*, vol. 1, p. 74), of bare vegetative functions of the sort governed by Jackson's lowest-level physiological centers, as well as mechanical effects due to habit, adaptation, stimulus inputs that escape conscious detection, and the like. A middle region, the "hypnotic stratum," is associated with automatisms such as the dissociative phenomena of hysteria and deep hypnosis, but it also supplies the content of ordinary dreaming, daydreaming, and imagining and is the source of the "mythopœic" function, an incessant "strange manufacture of inward romances" (*HP*, vol. 2, p. 130).[4] The deepest region is the least known and hardest to describe, but is above all the locus of various forms of supernormal contact with the outside world, including both psi phenomena and the intuitions and inspirations of genius.

These "strata" are not to be conceived in quasi-geological fashion as if they are static, immobile, or rigidly separated by impassable barriers: "They are strata (so to say) not of immovable rock, but of imperfectly miscible fluids of various densities, and subject to currents and ebullitions which often bring to the surface a stream or bubble from a stratum far below" (Myers, 1892b, p. 307). Thus, although the metaphor of "depth" used by Myers and other theoreticians of the subliminal almost inevitably suggests an essentially "geographical" interpretation, for Myers its principal connotations are meant to be *functional* rather than *spatial*. Within this basic functional scheme, engagement of the "deepest" strata of subliminal activity is specifically associated for Myers with those profoundest inspirations of genius in which the Self or Individuality comes closest to full and harmonious manifestation of its capabilities, including its supernormal capabilities (*HP*, vol. 1, p. 73).

Inspirations of genius in general involve successful appeal to the deeper subliminal levels, with success being due to some combination of intensity in the appeal itself (via the preparatory labor) and a favorable psychological constitution (traits) or conditions (states) that provide an unusual "permeability" or openness to the subliminal. Myers's views here are very similar to those of later observers such as Wallas (1926), Hutchinson (1931, 1939), Ghiselin (1952), and Kubie (1958), among many others. Hutchinson (1939),

4. Ellenberger (1970, pp. 150, 314–318) specifically credits this term and concept to Myers (although he uses the alternate spelling "mythopœtic") and laments its general neglect by subsequent workers in dynamic psychiatry. A major exception is Myers's colleague and admirer the Swiss psychologist Flournoy, whose studies of the medium Hélène Smith we will come to shortly.

for example, comments that the characteristic phenomenology of illumination is most pronounced in connection with cases of especially brilliant insight, "where the degree of difficulty and frustration is great and the drive toward accomplishment persistently strong" (p. 232). Myers also emphasizes that the phenomenology intensifies in proportion to "depth." He focuses in particular on two further psychological characteristics of creative inspiration, both of which flow from, and support, his broader theoretical picture.

Automatism

Myers holds that the subliminal uprushes of genius belong to the more general category of psychological automatisms (see our Chapter 5) and therefore are inevitably associated not only with automatism itself but with related phenomena such as mediumistic trance and kindred altered states of consciousness. He develops this picture, characteristically, in stages.

Calculating Prodigies

Myers turns first to a discussion of "calculating boys," who for him illustrate the essential psychological workings of higher forms of genius in a usefully "diagrammatic," verifiable, and semi-quantitative form.[5] The scant information then available in regard to some 15 such cases either previously published or known to him personally was sufficient to reveal the affinity of this "computative gift" to other phenomena of subliminal origin, such as hallucinations, rather than to products of ordinary voluntary effort. For example, despite its seemingly necessary connections with more general mathematical knowledge and insight, it is distributed almost at random, appearing among persons of ordinary or even extremely low intelligence as well as in mathematical geniuses such as Gauss and Ampère. It also has a "critical-period" aspect, tending to appear and disappear suddenly in childhood, and if it disappears without being integrated into the general pattern of voluntary skills, it usually leaves behind no memory whatsoever of the processes involved. Most significantly, perhaps, among the dull prodigies it usually operates in the apparent absence of steady conscious effort, or even while the calculator is consciously occupied with other matters. The answer simply appears, usually though not always visually, all at once and with no trace of the steps or processes that led to it. Indeed, the calculator may not even be able to grasp the elementary arithmetical operations that an ordi-

---

5. See also our Chapter 1. Myers states clearly that he would rather have used illustrations drawn from higher mathematics, were sufficient data available, and he appeals to mathematicians for accounts of the mental processes accompanying attainment of their highest results (*HP*, vol. 1, pp. 78–79). This may have precipitated a subsequent survey of mathematicians carried out by Claparède and Flournoy, which in turn stimulated the famous account by Poincaré in 1904 of his inventive processes (see Hadamard, 1949, pp. 10–11). Hadamard's own book answers Myers's appeal more definitively, combining Poincaré's account with a substantial number of others, and strikingly confirms Myers's general outlook.

nary person would use to solve, much more laboriously, the same problem. Myers also noted that there was a possible hint of special involvement of the right hemisphere in these phenomena, inasmuch as the two cases for which relevant information was available showed a pronounced tendency toward ambidexterity.

Myers's observations on prodigious but retarded calculators such as Dase and Fuller have been sustained and generalized in the subsequent century, primarily through further study of what is now called the "savant syndrome," in which islands of considerable or sometimes spectacular ability appear in the midst of otherwise generalized and profound disability. A particularly valuable survey is that of Treffert (1989), who estimates that something like 100 such "prodigious" cases of the sort that interested Myers have so far been reported, of whom roughly one or two dozen, including "the twins" of Sacks (1987), are currently living. In addition to prodigious calculators, there have been prodigious mechanical, artistic, and especially musical savants, all of whom characteristically display narrow but deep attention coupled with extraordinary memory.[6] Treffert speculatively links the savant syndrome to hypothetical abnormalities in development and functional organization of memory and attentional systems in the savant brain, and sensibly calls for anatomical and functional imaging studies (which to our knowledge are just getting underway in earnest) to investigate these. But in the end, echoing Penfield (1975), he acknowledges misgivings as to whether the brain alone can provide the full answer. Both Treffert and Sacks are skilled and caring clinicians with long and first-hand experience of the savant syndrome, and both remain—appropriately, in our opinion—openly awed by it. They also share with Myers a recognition of its deep connections with the mystery of genius.

"Organic" Senses

Myers next presses on to consider more briefly some further instances of apparent subliminal cooperation, instances which share with arithmetic calculation the properties of definiteness and verifiability of result, but which involve *sensory* phenomena of various sorts. His first examples concern "perceptions of a less specialized kind which underlie our more elaborate modes of cognizing the world around us"—specifically the sense of the passage of time, and the sense of weight or muscular resistance, which rank

6. Various other kinds of supernormal abilities have also been reported in such individuals. For example, when Sacks accidentally dropped a large box of matches on the floor, both twins instantly perceived that there were 111 matches in all, and that this number is the product of the prime numbers 37 and 3. According to Scripture (1891, pp. 20, 39–40), this unusual capacity for immediate perceptual grasping of numerosity ("subitizing") is universal among calculating prodigies. Dase, for example, could instantly determine the number of sheep in a herd, or of books in a book-case, or of window-panes on the side of a large house. Yet for most of us such judgments remain accurate only to something at best on the order of the usual 7 ± 2 items (Mandler & Shebo, 1982; G. A. Miller, 1956). Rimland (1978, and personal communication, November, 1978) has also reported finding in his survey of savant-type skills in early infantile autism a few cases in which recurrent spontaneous psi phenomena were conspicuously present.

"among the profoundest elements in our organic being" (*HP*, vol. 1, p. 85). He cites several cases, drawn mainly from "a sane and waking person" whose acquaintance he had made, in which correct knowledge of some objective state of affairs such as the time of day, or the weight of an animal hide, had appeared spontaneously and in quasi-hallucinatory form, in advance of verification and accompanied by a strong sense of conviction. Myers suggests that such occurrences are best explained as the result of some sort of subliminal calculation, analogous to those of arithmetical prodigies, rather than to any sort of direct or supernormal knowledge.

Hypnotism provides many further analogies to the process of subliminal uprush in genius, as Myers (1898b) had himself argued earlier in an address to the British Medical Association. When a deeply hypnotized girl produces the suggested hallucination of a black cat, for example, she reveals a degree of creativity comparable to that of her dreams but normally unavailable to her waking consciousness. Thus, comments Myers, "as the Sistine Madonna was to Raphael, so to the hypnotized girl is the delusive cat." Additional examples are provided by successful posthypnotic suggestions, in which the suggested thoughts or actions emerge into consciousness or behavior, suddenly and involuntarily, upon the appearance of a prespecified but consciously forgotten cue. Of special interest among these in the present connection are cases in which the "cue" consists in the passage of a specified amount of time. Careful work by Myers's colleagues Gurney, Delboeuf, and especially Bramwell had shown that in deeply hypnotizable subjects this sense of the passage of time can sometimes reach astonishing levels of precision, with errors on the order of one part in 2000 or better over intervals of many thousands of minutes.[7] McDougall (1911/1961, pp. 353–354) comments favorably on this work, and mentions in a footnote that he had himself encountered the same phenomenon—interestingly enough, in a highly hypnotizable subject who had also proven capable of producing blisters and extravasation of blood from the skin. McDougall further points out that this phenomenon poses a severe challenge to any attempted explanation based on unconscious monitoring of physiological rhythms, because "we know of no bodily rhythm sufficiently constant to serve as the basis of so accurate an appreciation of duration as would have enabled the subject to carry out the suggestion with the high degree of accuracy shown" (p. 353). To our limited knowledge of research on biorhythms, this argument remains valid today, but little further work, unfortunately, appears to have been carried out along these lines.[8]

---

7. Myers gives a condensed account of this work in his chapter on hypnotism (*HP*, vol. 1, pp. 194–195, plus supporting appendices), but a much fuller account, including descriptions of the precautions against various potential sources of error, appears in Bramwell (1903, pp. 114–139).

8. There may also be an "absolute" time-sense, analogous to the well-known sense of absolute or perfect pitch which is common in the musically gifted (though neither necessary nor sufficient for high achievement) and apparently universal among musical savants (Treffert, 1989). One of us (EFK), as a teenager, was briefly acquainted with a younger boy, in other respects ordinary, who always somehow "knew," with startlingly small error, what time it

Hallucinatory Syndromes

Myers turns next to Sir John Herschel, the former royal astronomer, for an example of subliminal products of *visual* type. Herschel, it turns out, was subject to vivid and kaleidoscopic visual imagery of a highly regular and geometric sort. This imagery occurred involuntarily, usually when he was lying awake in darkness (though twice in broad daylight and twice also in conjunction with chloroform anesthesia for minor surgeries), and was not accompanied by illness or discomfort. Herschel himself had interpreted these hallucinatory phenomena as providing "evidence of a thought, an intelligence, working within our own organization distinct from that of our own personality" (*HP*, vol. 1, p. 88). Myers agreed, viewing them as expressions of an "indwelling general perceptive power" which we all have, and credited Herschel with having thus originated at least in germ his own more comprehensive theory of subliminal consciousness.

Contemporary research on hallucinatory syndromes lends support to Myers's conception, although the situation now looks more complex and interesting. To begin, Herschel himself can now be recognized as a migraineur, one of the roughly 1% of the total population who experience migraine aura without accompanying headache (Sacks, 1999, chap. 17; Wilkinson, 2004). Second, "geometrical spectres" like those of his migraine aura are now known to occur under a wide variety of additional circumstances including in particular "hypnagogic" or "twilight" states at sleep onset and offset, the intoxications produced by various hallucinogenic substances such as mescaline and LSD, psychotic breakdowns, fever-induced delirium, stroboscopic visual stimulation at critical frequencies, and sensory deprivation (Klüver, 1966; Sacks, 1999; Siegel, 1977).

The most primitive or elementary forms of such activity typically involve single or multiple points or spots of light, possibly colored, that may organize progressively into a variety of characteristic and simple geometries. Drawing mainly upon his own studies with mescaline, Klüver (1966, p. 66) identified the principal building blocks, or "hallucinatory form constants," from which more complicated imagery might subsequently evolve. In his original analysis these were just four in number: (1) gratings, lattices, fretworks, filigrees, honeycombs, or chessboards; (2) cobwebs; (3) tunnels, funnels, alleys, cones, or vessels; and (4) spirals.[9]

The central impulse of mainstream reductionist science, exemplified with particular clarity in the cases of migraine aura (Sacks, 1999; Wilkinson, 2004) and hypnagogic imagery (Mavromatis, 1987; D. Schacter, 1976), has always been to "explain" these recurrent formal characteristics of visual hallucinatory experience as direct expressions in consciousness of events,

---

was. Treffert (1989, pp. 97–98) describes two similar cases, one involving "Ellen," a blind musical savant who also displayed spontaneous ESP abilities.

9. Klüver himself was not entirely clear or consistent about this classification, which seems to us somewhat arbitrary, and Siegel (1977) and colleagues, working mainly with psychoactive drugs, subsequently identified additional *form* constants as well as a variety of *color* and *movement* constants. These details need not concern us here, however.

structures, or processes within the visual pathway. Early accounts of hypnagogia, for example, were relentlessly "peripheralist," and sought to trace most if not all of the reported phenomenology to "entoptic" sources—that is, to events or structures within the eye itself. Although such sources certainly do play *some* role in the formation of hypnagogic imagery, presumably by triggering or supplying raw materials for some more central constructive process, few if any now take seriously the notion that hypnagogic imagery, even in its most elementary forms, is in effect generated within the eye.

This general discussion has recently reached a more interesting stage in the context of the migraine aura. The core phenomenology of the aura consists of parallel groups of extremely bright, jagged, scintillating lines, sometimes bounding closed regions described as "fortifications" that expand and move with increasing speed toward the edge of the visual field in a highly stereotypical manner, usually with a region of "scotoma" or temporary blindness trailing behind.[10] Early thinking emphasized "static" properties of the aura, viewing it essentially as a kind of phenomenological photograph of the microanatomy of visual cortex, but Lashley (1941), himself a migraineur, introduced the currently dominant "dynamic" view: Specifically, careful comparisons between the evolution of his own aura phenomenology and the known geometry and organization of primary visual cortex led him to hypothesize that the aura results from a traveling wave of neural excitation/depression moving through the cortex at a constant rate of about 3 mm/minute. More generally, the modern idea is that the dynamics of migraine aura phenomenology are to be explained entirely in terms of time-dependent interactions between a spreading-depression process and the functional architecture of visual cortex. Thus for example the phenomenology of jagged boundaries, with short line segments joining at sharp angles, is thought to reflect the classic Hubel/Wiesel architecture of feature detectors, orientation columns, and the like in primary visual cortex (Sacks, 1999; Wilkinson, 2004).

In recent years Lashley's converging-operations approach has been enriched by the advent of functional neuroimaging and computer modeling methods, both of which have provided additional support for a spreading-wave model (Bressloff, Cowan, Golubitsky, Thomas, & Wiener, 2001; Dahlem, Engelmann, Löwel, & Müller, 2000; Hadjikhani et al., 2001). That some sort of abnormal pattern of physiological activation is present in visual cortex during migraine aura is now widely accepted, although details of the abnormality and its pathophysiological origins remain to be elucidated.

Much less certain, however, is the precise role of this abnormal activity pattern in production of the conscious experience of aura. There are undoubtedly some who, like the early "entoptic" theorists of hypnagogia, imagine visual experience in general to be directly generated by or isomorphic with activity in the visual pathway itself, but we now know that the reality is more complicated. Under normal circumstances, activity in visual cortical areas is in general necessary but not sufficient for the correspond-

10. For further details see Sacks (1999) and Wilkinson (2004).

ing elements of conscious visual experience (e.g., Dehaene & Naccache, 2001; Haynes & Rees, 2005; Kamitani & Tong, 2005). Something further upstream must interpret or take account of the input-driven activity pattern, which thus initiates, constrains, and guides, but does not fully determine, the conscious experience.

Several further considerations point in the same direction. It may be doubted, for example—and indeed Sacks (1999, p. 289) himself does doubt— whether the standard traveling-wave model really can account in detail for the full-blown phenomenology of the aura. The strain becomes particularly evident as soon as one goes beyond the abstract notion of form constants or other carefully selected aura properties such as the size and speed of motion of "fortifications." Klüver had noted that his form constants are not restricted to the visual modality, and must therefore have a more central origin. Thus for example one can experience a cobweb on one's tongue, or feel one's legs turning into a spiral. Klüver pointed out a number of further properties of hallucinatory experience, moreover, and he himself acknowledged that these more complex phenomena are invariably of far greater salience and impressiveness to the *subjects* of such experience.

The elementary structures identified as visual form constants, for example, are typically elaborated into ever more complex patterns by an endless and dynamic *geometrization*, with the elementary forms repeating themselves indefinitely at multiple spatial scales. The boundaries of forms are often other forms. There may be microscopic clarity of detail, with lines almost vanishingly thin, and a kaleidoscopic play of color, brightness, and movement in the evolving structures. Colors themselves may be unnaturally bright, rich, and textured. These visions sometimes can be viewed with the eyes open, in which case they may superimpose upon, alter, or even replace the visual scene itself, in part or in whole, and they often change dramatically in response to tactile or auditory stimuli. Particularly in cases other than migraine aura, the hallucinatory process may generate full-blown dreamlike scenes or stories, sometimes involving additional sensory modalities and incorporating locations, events, or persons long forgotten (Siegel, 1977). As in dreams themselves, this imaginative activity is truly creative and goes far beyond simple literal reproduction of past experience. For example one may observe oneself carrying out novel activities of various sorts, or observe familiar scenes from unfamiliar perspectives.[11]

In short, in migraine aura as well as the other circumstances in which hallucinatory activity appears, some process is triggered or released which

---

11. Sacks's own worries remain at the level of Klüver's form-constants, and he seeks to ameliorate them by appealing to the modern vogue of non-linear dynamic systems, conceived as operating within the visual system itself to produce more global forms of self-organized activity that are not so closely tied to the hard-wired cortical architecture and thus might capture the required properties. This approach barely begins to address the real complexities of the problem, as indicated in the text, and even on its own narrower terms the simulation results provided by Sacks are hardly very encouraging. The results of Bressloff et al. (2001) are far more impressive, and yet these authors explicitly acknowledge various limitations of their model.

under varying degrees of voluntary control and in service of its ongoing construction of phenomenological reality can utilize, reinterpret, or even ignore (as in negative hallucinations) patterns of neural activity appearing in visual cortex.

Further support for such a view derives from recent investigations of another hallucinatory syndrome, the Charles Bonnet syndrome (Schultz & Melzack, 1991). This syndrome (CBS) occurs primarily in otherwise normal elderly persons, in conjunction with loss of vision due to conditions such as cataracts, glaucoma, or macular degeneration. Under such conditions, up to 30% of patients report experiencing complex and involuntary visual hallucinations while otherwise fully and normally conscious. The real incidence may be substantially higher, since patients are understandably chary of reporting bizarre experiences to medical personnel. These hallucinations typically appear to their subjects as occupying external space, with visual quality higher than that of their residual vision. The precipitating circumstance, in this as in other sensory-deprivation syndromes including dreaming, is not so much the *presence* of an abnormal activity pattern (as in migraine aura) as the *absence* of normal input-driven ones.

The especially interesting finding from recent EEG and fMRI imaging studies is that the self-reported phenomenology of hallucinations in CBS patients correlates with increased activation in the corresponding, functionally specialized subregions of (ventral) visual cortex (ffytche, Howard, Brammer, David, & Williams 1998; Santhouse, Howard, & ffytche, 2000). Thus for example if patients hallucinated in color, increased activation was found in the color area (V4). This finding is early and tentative, but if correct it poses problems for a conventional causal account. Clearly, *some* sort of subliminal process must be organizing and driving these complex, widespread, and coordinated activation patterns, because they cannot plausibly be expected to arise by chance from the spontaneous background activity of the input-deprived visual cortex itself. Analogous though less clear-cut activation patterns are found in the case of *voluntary* imagery, when subjects deliberately attempt to visualize some pre-specified state of affairs (Kosslyn, 1994), but in CBS, as in dreams and waking apparitions, the imagery is completely unexpected, surprising, and involuntary. Might this not reflect the operation of something very like Myers's subliminal consciousness, establishing appropriate patterns of brain activity in the process of delivering its products to the supraliminal consciousness? Such a model might also explain the further result of ffytche et al. (1998), unexpected by them, that their fMRI signals arose *before* emergence of the corresponding qualitative features into subjects' hallucinatory experiences.

A conventional global-workspace theorist might respond by agreeing that a subliminally formed template or plan of some sort drives the hallucinatory process, while insisting that it be unconscious and inhabit some other part of the brain. This move, however, would not accommodate at least two additional lines of evidence that support a more Myers-like view. First, as already pointed out in Chapter 5, psychological automatisms in the form of involuntary visual imagery and hallucinatory states such as dreaming are known in general to be especially fruitful sources of strong psi effects, showing that the hallucinatory process has access to information beyond the reach of the brain itself. A direct connection to CBS can be made by way of Gurney et al. (1886, vol. 1, pp. 389–456), who discussed the hypnagogic state at length, noting that the number of veridical apparitions occurring under these conditions in their sample of 701 spontaneous cases was far higher than would be expected from the sheer proportion of time we humans pass in such states. The fertility of their analysis has been abundantly confirmed in subsequent work, including later studies of spontaneous cases (Sherwood, 2002) and contemporary experimental studies using the "Ganzfeld" sensory-deprivation technique and other means of inducing hypnagogic-like states.[12] Given this background, in fact, we will venture two further predictions in relation to CBS itself: First, inasmuch as CBS amounts to a long-term though partial Ganzfeld condition, we expect that sympathetic and open-minded investigation will reveal it to be a fertile source of spontaneous psi effects as well, potentially adaptable for experimental purposes. Second, just as "shell-hearing," like crystal-gazing or "scrying," can elicit psi-conducive forms of hallucinatory activity in normal persons (E. F. Kelly & Locke, 1981a), there ought to be an auditory analog of CBS with similarly psi-conducive properties.

The second line of evidence is of course that developed in detail in our previous chapter. To recapitulate, we showed there that full-blown or even abnormally heightened conscious awareness can occur under conditions of general anesthesia and/or cardiac arrest, conditions in which the specific neurophysiological mechanisms believed by current mainstream neuroscience to be necessary for consciousness have been rendered inoperative. This argument, if correct, shows even more clearly than the argument from psi phenomena that the roots of the hallucinatory process—Myers's "indwelling general perceptive power"—lie *outside* the material brain as conventionally understood.

In summary of this section on hallucinatory syndromes, Herschel and Myers now appear to have been rather too hasty in thinking that Herschel's "geometrical spectres" provided a direct, unmediated window into the operations of the subliminal mind, but in the end they may have been more right than wrong. This topic occupies just over a page in Myers's own chapter, and it is not particularly essential to his main argument since he could certainly have employed other relevant examples such as post-hypnotic visual hallucinations. We have dwelt upon it at length, however, because these recent empirical developments have more clearly exposed and sub-

12. The success rate of the Ganzfeld might actually prove much higher, we surmise, if attention were confined more narrowly to those subjects and conditions that produce altered states of consciousness with hypnagogic-like, vivid, and autonomous visual imagery, as contrasted with more ordinary forms of free-associative thought. Much of what goes on under conventional short-term Ganzfeld conditions is almost certainly of the latter type, as indicated both by the character of typical mentation reports and by the EEG studies of Wackermann, Pütz, Büchi, Strauch, and Lehmann (2002). See also Alvarado (1998).

stantiated the deep connections among the various forms of hallucinatory activity, and their compatibility with Myers's conception of a fundamental subliminal power or faculty of *imagination* that enters into the highest expressions of genius.[13]

Automatisms in Genius

Myers turns next to his main topic, the natural history of inspiration itself—"the records, namely, left by eminent men as to the element of subconscious mentation, which was involved in their best work" (*HP*, vol. 1, p. 89). We will recapitulate the main threads of his exposition, departing for reasons of expository convenience from strictly textual order and emphasizing points of special theoretical significance to Myers. As we proceed, we will also attempt to show how his overall picture of genius has been corroborated and extended through various lines of subsequent research and scholarship.

Myers begins by briefly quoting 10 typical illustrations of the automatic character of inspiration, selecting these from a much larger number of records obtained by Paul Chabaneix, a French physician, through direct inquiry with eminent contemporary artists, philosophers, and writers. Two points are immediately noteworthy here: First, Myers explicitly declined to make use of similar material that had been collected on a much larger scale, but in a far less disciplined manner, by von Hartmann in his then-popular book, *Philosophy of the Unconscious*, a work which Myers bluntly characterizes as "to me especially distasteful, as containing what seems to me the loose and extravagant parody of important truth" (*HP*, vol. 1, p. 89). Second, and more importantly, the basic phenomenological picture that Myers seeks to convey here has been confirmed and amplified in many subsequent collections.[14]

Ghiselin's introductory essay provides a particularly thoughtful, insightful, and concise descriptive account of the creative process, based on first-person reports of creative activity in a wide variety of fields. His account is also highly consistent with Myers's as far as it goes, though lacking Myers's more richly elaborated conception of subliminal operations, and was arrived at independently, making the confirmation of Myers's general outlook even more striking. In regard to automatism, Ghiselin (1952) could hardly be more definite:

> [There is] a sense of self-surrender to an inward necessity inherent in something larger than the ego and taking precedence over the established order....Production by a process of purely conscious calculation seems

---

13. Our conception of this cosmogonic, world-generating, or virtual-reality system has much in common with that of Brann (1991), who provides a systematic exposition and defense of the thesis that an imaginative capacity of this sort constitutes a fundamental and neglected dispositional property of the mind.

14. See, in addition to those of Wallas (1926) and Hutchinson (1931, 1939), valuable works by Abrams (1958), Bowra (1949, 1955), Ghiselin (1952), Hadamard (1949), Harding (1948), Koestler (1964), Kubie (1958), and Prescott (1922).

> never to occur....More or less of such automatism is reported by nearly every worker who has much to say about his processes, and no creative process has been demonstrated to be wholly free from it. (pp. 15–16)

Inspiration is essentially the intrusion into supraliminal consciousness of some novel form of order that has gestated somewhere beyond its customary margins. The content of such inspirations can vary widely in character, scope, and completeness, but psychologically the process is fundamentally the same throughout its range. The novelty appears

> sometimes in the form of a mere glimpse serving as a clue, or like a germ to be developed; sometimes a fragment of the whole, whether rudimentary and requiring to be worked into shape or already in its final form; sometimes essentially complete, though needing expansion, verification, or the like. Spontaneous appearance of inventions very fully formed is not extremely rare, but it is by no means ordinary. Spontaneity is common, but what is given is usually far from complete. (p. 15)

Thus for Ghiselin as for Myers the essence of genius is unusually effective cooperation between supraliminal and subliminal elements of the personality. Neither is sufficient by itself to support the highest forms of creative achievement. Skilled and persistent voluntary effort is almost invariably necessary, both to initiate and shape the subliminal work and to evaluate its products, the materials delivered to waking consciousness in moments of inspiration. But persons of genius throughout history have testified consistently that such moments were the characteristic and essential accompaniment of their best work.

These moments often reach extreme levels of phenomenological impressiveness. Material may suddenly appear that is surprising, unfamiliar, even strange, flowing with extraordinary ease and copiousness, accompanied by intense affect and excitement, and in the absence of any feeling of personal responsibility for what comes. Many examples of such events can be found in the sources cited above, and we need not repeat them in profusion here, but it is precisely in light of such extreme and unusual manifestations that Myers seeks to establish the fundamental kinship between subliminal uprushes of genius and other forms of psychological automatism.

Sleep and dreams provide a first sort of example, relatively close to ordinary experience. Myers pictures the genius as successfully coordinating the waking and sleeping phases of his existence: "He is carrying into sleep the knowledge and the purpose of waking hours;—and he is carrying back into waking hours again the benefit of those profound assimilations which are the privilege of sleep" (*HP*, vol. 1, p. 90). Robert Louis Stevenson provides the chief example here: In his well-known chapter on dreams in *Across the Plains,* Stevenson describes how he progressively harnessed his abundant dream-life in service of his writing. His "Brownies," the "little people" who manage his internal theater,

> are near connections of the dreamer's, beyond doubt; they share in his financial worries and have an eye to the bank-book; they share plainly in his training;...they have plainly learned like him to build the scheme of a considerate story and to arrange emotion in progressive order; only I think they have more talent; and one thing is beyond doubt;—they can tell him a story piece by piece, like a serial, and keep him all the while in ignorance of where they aim. (*HP*, vol. 1, p. 91)

The Brownies are thus capable of "really guileful craftsmanship," and though occasionally guilty of absurdities they generally fashion "better tales than he could fashion for himself." Stevenson concludes that his unseen collaborators do the bulk of his creative work: "That part which is done while I am sleeping is the Brownies' part beyond contention; but that which is done when I am up and about is by no means necessarily mine, since all goes to show the Brownies have a hand in it even then" (*HP*, vol. 1, p. 91).

In his following chapter on sleep (section 417 and its appendix), Myers notes several additional instances of nocturnal problem-solving, which in that chapter provide him with stepping-stones toward dreams more clearly involving acquisition of supernormal knowledge. In three of these instances the solution emerged during a dream, while in the fourth (Professor Lamberton) it appeared upon awakening. The last is in some ways the most interesting: Lamberton had tried in vain for over a week to solve algebraically a certain problem in analytic geometry, but upon awakening that morning he found the solution standing before his eyes in the form of a complex hallucinatory diagram drawn upon the opposite wall, formerly a blackboard. This impressed him greatly, as he had made no previous efforts to solve the problem geometrically, was in general a poor visualizer, and had no other waking hallucinatory experiences either before or after this one.

Mazzarello (2000) summarizes the well-known cases of scientific discovery involving Kekulè, Loewi, and Mendeleyev, and many other cases of creative solutions obtained during sleep, dreams, and hypnagogic states have been collected by D. Barrett (2001), Mavromatis (1987), and Van de Castle (1994), among others. We will cite one more, which would have been especially welcomed by Myers as a demonstration of subliminal contributions to higher mathematics. The distinguished mathematician Hadamard (1949) states that:

> One phenomenon is certain and I can vouch for its absolute certainty: the sudden and immediate appearance of a solution at the very moment of sudden awakening. On being very abruptly awakened by an external noise, a solution long searched for appeared to me at once without the slightest instant of reflection on my part—the fact was remarkable enough to have struck me unforgettably—and in a quite different direction from any of those which I had previously tried to follow. (p. 8)[15]

15. It is of interest, and will be relevant to subsequent discussion, that Hadamard had read Myers and acknowledges (p. 22) that he himself was capable of automatic writing.

More generally, drawing not only upon his own experiences of mathematical discovery but also upon extensive and direct interactions with many other leading mathematicians and scientists, Hadamard declares that any doubt as to the existence of unconscious work "can hardly arise" (p. 21). Indeed, "strictly speaking, there is hardly any completely logical discovery. Some intervention of intuition issuing from the unconscious is necessary at least to initiate the logical work" (p. 112).

We jump now to section 327 of *HP*, in which Myers begins to develop more fully the deep and overlapping interconnections among genius, automatism, and trance. All, of course, involve subliminal influences upon the supraliminal consciousness, but these can vary greatly in terms of their intensity, the degree to which they alter the normal functioning of that consciousness. Just as trance, when habitual, tends to engender automatic writing or speech, and prolonged automatism tends to induce trance, the subliminal uprushes of genius can be arranged in a hierarchy of increasing involvement of these more extreme manifestations.

At the near or shallow end of this progression in depth is the momentary flash of inspiration, a brief automatism. Myers illustrates this with lines from Wordsworth describing how "Some lovely image in the song rose up / Full-formed, like Venus rising from the sea," adding that "such a sudden poetic creation, like the calculating boy's announcement of the product of two numbers, resembles the sudden rush of planchette or pencil, in haste to scrawl some long-wished-for word" (*HP*, vol. 1, p. 104).

A transition from ordinary facility to something involving more significant contributions from the subliminal can sometimes be recognized in connection with *improvisation*. Myers first acknowledges the important contributions of memory and conventional rules or habits to ordinary musical or oratorical improvisation, following lines quite similar to those subsequently taken by Boden (1991) in regard to computer simulations of jazz improvisation and the like. But in George Sand ordinary facility evolved into

> an unusual vigour and fertility of literary outflow going on in an almost dreamlike condition; a condition midway between the actual inventive dreams of R. L. Stevenson and the conscious labour of another man's composition...a continuous and effortless flow of ideas, sometimes with and sometimes without an apparent *externalisation* of the characters who spoke in her romances. (*HP*, vol. 1, p. 106)

Similarly, Charles Dickens was highly prone to hypnagogic-like reveries (Mavromatis, 1987) and alluded often to the tendency of his imaginary characters toward "independence"; for example, "Mrs. Gamp, his greatest creation, spoke to him, he tells us (generally in church), as with an inward monitory voice" (*HP*, vol. 1, p. 106).

Myers next describes the even more extreme case of M. de Curel, a distinguished French dramatist, of which a long account had been published by the psychologist Alfred Binet in 1894. In de Curel, Myers observes, the waking experience of creation approaches that of Stevenson in dreams:

> He begins in an ordinary way, or with even more than the usual degree of difficulty and distress in getting into his subject. Then gradually he begins to feel the creation of a number of quasi-personalities within him;—the characters of his play, who speak to him;—exactly as Dickens used to describe Mrs. Gamp as speaking to him in church. These personages are not clearly visible, but they seem to move round him in a scene—say a house and garden—which he also dimly perceives, somewhat as we perceive the scene of a dream. He now no longer has the feeling of composition, of creation, but merely of literary revision; the personages speak and act for themselves, and even if he is interrupted while writing, or when he is asleep at night, the play continues to compose itself in his head. Sometimes while out shooting, &c., and not thinking of the play, he hears sentences rising within him which belong to a part of this play which he has not yet reached. He believes that subliminally the piece has been worked out to that further point already. M. de Curel calls these minor duplications of personality a *bourgeonnement* or budding of his primary personality;—into which they gradually, though not without some painful struggle, re-enter after the play is finished. (*HP*, vol. 1, p. 107)

Myers goes on at this point to other topics to which we will return shortly, but we will first point out just a few of the many additional examples that can be found in collections like those cited earlier, in which works of genius are mediated at least in part by automatism, sometimes accompanied by trance-like altered states of consciousness.

Parallels to the literary improvisation of George Sand, for example, can be found in dance, in the work of choreographer George Balanchine:

> He started doing this movement and that, showing the dancers what they had to do. Then at a certain moment it became something much more than just himself and his ideas. He started to work as a somnambulist, without knowing what he was doing. And all this was quickly done, with the greatest assurance. When he finished, he would sit and ask the dancers to show him what he had done, and he would seem to be very astonished. That is what I call inspiration. (Teachout, 2004, pp. 18–19)

A. E. Housman (1952) described how the inspiration for much of his best poetry occurred during afternoon walks, following a pint of beer at lunch. As he strolled along, absent-mindedly looking about,

> there would flow into my mind, with sudden and unaccountable emotion, sometimes a line or two of verse, sometimes a whole stanza at once, accompanied, not preceded, by a vague notion of the poem which they were destined to form part of. Then there would usually be a lull of an hour or so, then perhaps the spring would bubble up again....I happen to remember distinctly the genesis of the piece which stands last in my first volume. Two of the stanzas, I do not say which, came into my head, just as they are printed, while I was crossing the corner of Hampstead Heath between Spaniard's Inn and the footpath to Temple Fortune. A third stanza came with a little coaxing after tea. One more was needed, but it did not come: I had to turn to and compose it myself, and that was a laborious business.

> I wrote it thirteen times, and it was more than a twelvemonth before I got it right. (p. 91)

William Blake, who with Wallace Stevens was "an extremist of the imagination" (Brann, 1991, p. 509), wrote his friend Butts that his prophetic poem *Milton* was written "from immediate dictation, twelve or sometimes twenty or thirty lines at a time, without premeditation and even against my will. The time it has taken in writing was thus rendered non-existent, and an immense poem exists which seems to be the labour of a long life, all produced without labour or study....I may praise it, since I dare not pretend to be other than the secretary" (Damon, 1958, p. 202).[16]

The hypermnesic, possibly eidetic, and mammothly prolific writer Thomas Wolfe (1952) describes the onset of the process that generated three enormous novels in 4½ years:

> An extraordinary image remains to me from that year, the year I spent abroad when the material of these books first began to take on articulate form. It seemed that I had inside me, swelling and gathering all the time, a huge black cloud, and that this cloud was loaded with electricity, pregnant, crested, with a kind of hurricane violence that could not be held in check much longer; that the moment was approaching fast when it must break. Well, all I can say is that the storm did break. It broke that summer while I was in Switzerland. It came in torrents, and it is not over yet.
>
> I cannot really say the book was written. It was something that took hold of me and possessed me, and before I was done with it—that is, before I finally emerged with the first completed part—it seemed to me that it had done for me. It was exactly as if this great black storm cloud I have spoken of had opened up and, mid flashes of lightning, was pouring from its depth a torrential and ungovernable flood. Upon that flood everything was swept and borne along as by a great river. And I was borne along with it. (p. 187)

Nietzsche (1952) recounts in similarly extreme terms in *Ecce Homo* how he was "invaded" by *Thus Spake Zarathustra*:

> Can any one at the end of this nineteenth century possibly have any distinct notion of what poets of a more vigourous period meant by inspiration? If not, I should like to describe it. Provided one has the slightest remnant of superstition left, one can hardly reject completely the idea that one is the mere incarnation, or mouthpiece, or medium of some almighty power. The notion of revelation describes the condition quite simply; by which I mean that something profoundly convulsive and disturbing suddenly becomes visible and audible with indescribable definiteness and exactness. One hears—one does not seek; one takes—one does not ask who gives: a thought flashes out like lightning, inevitably without hesita-

16. Myers, like Brann (1991), regards Blake as an example of strong imagination insufficiently controlled by supraliminal discipline: "Throughout all the work of William Blake (I should say) we see the subliminal self flashing for moments into unity, then smouldering again in a lurid and scattered glow" (*HP*, vol. 1, p. 73).

> tion—I have never had any choice about it. There is an ecstasy whose terrific tension is sometimes released by a flood of tears, during which one's progress varies from involuntary impetuosity to involuntary slowness. There is the feeling that one is utterly out of hand, with the most distinct consciousness of an infinitude of shuddering thrills that pass through one from head to foot;—there is a profound happiness in which the most painful and gloomy feelings are not discordant in effect, but are required as necessary colors in this overflow of light. There is an instinct for rhythmic relations which embraces an entire world of forms (length, the need for a widely extended rhythm, is almost a measure of the force of inspiration, a sort of counterpart to its pressure and tension). Everything occurs quite without volition, as if in an eruption of freedom, independence, power and divinity. The spontaneity of the images and similes is most remarkable; one loses all perception of what is imagery and simile; everything offers itself as the most immediate, exact, and simple means of expression. (pp. 202–203)

Harding (1948, chap. 2) cites a large number of additional cases in which the sense of being possessed by some external force and compelled to create is especially pronounced. One involves Goethe, who described how his poems sometimes

> have come suddenly upon me, and have insisted on being composed immediately, so that I have felt an instinctive and dreamy impulse to write them down on the spot. In such a somnambulistic condition, it has often happened that I have had a sheet of paper lying before me all aslant, and I have not discovered it till all has been written, or I have found no room to write any more. I have possessed many such sheets written diagonally. (p. 12)

Automatism also figures prominently in an especially curious case involving the great 20th-century poet James Merrill, and in particular his masterpiece, *The Changing Light of Sandover* (1980/1993). On the cover of this book Harold Bloom expresses particular admiration for one of its chapters: "I don't know that *The Book of Ephraim*, at least after some dozen readings, can be over-praised, as nothing since [by] the greatest writers of our century equals it in demonic force." Yet the book was produced in its entirety by means of a ouija board operated jointly by Merrill and his longtime friend "R." In its opening pages Merrill describes the instant the ouija board came to life: "YES a new and urgent power YES / Seized the cup. It swerved, clung, hesitated, / Darted off, a devil's darning needle / Gyroscope our fingers rode bareback / (But stopping dead the instant one lost touch)." Thus if either Merrill or his partner took his finger off the cup, it stopped dead. But when it worked, it was astonishing: "Yet even the most fragmentary message—/ Twice as entertaining, twice as wise / As either of its mediums—enthralled them." It is of course difficult if not impossible to determine exactly who is contributing what to the creative process in a case of this sort, but the suggestion that the results outstrip what either could accomplish alone is especially intriguing and worthy of further investigation.[17]

Bowra (1955) summarizes in more general terms the involuntary character of inspiration as experienced and reported by many poets:

> [It] manifests itself in a manner which no one can mistake. The poet unaccountably finds himself dominated by something which absorbs his being and excludes other interests from his mind. It is not easy to define exactly what this is, but we may mark certain elements in it. Central to it is something which may be called an idea, though in some ways it is too vague to deserve the name. It has a powerful character and atmosphere of its own, and though at first it is too indefinite for intellectual analysis, it imposes itself on the poet with the majesty and authority of vision. Even if he does not fully understand it, he feels it and almost sees it. (p. 4)

In sum, Myers seems to us certainly correct in pointing out connections of genius with trance and automatism. Indeed, these same connections can also be recognized from the opposite direction—that is, from cases in which the aspects of trance and automatism predominate, but which also give rise to high-level creative production. We turn next to these.

Genius in Automatists

In the first instance it should be noted that considerable amounts of "creativity" are necessarily involved in the production of characteristic dissociative phenomena such as glove anesthesias, negative hallucinations in hypnosis, and "alter" or "multiple" personalities formed in response to overwhelming trauma. Philosopher Stephen Braude (2002) has shown with particular clarity that such phenomena cannot be conceived in terms of atomic mental states or contents that are statically segregated by fixed and passive boundaries of some sort. Rather, successful maintenance of the dissociation requires continuous, active, adaptive—in short, creative—subliminal improvisation in response to the subject's ongoing and constantly-changing interactions with his environment. Mediumistic dramatizations of deceased personalities also sometimes display (at minimum) remarkable histrionic capacities, reproducing voice, tone, mannerisms, characteristic turns of phrase, and other traits of the deceased with verisimilitude sufficient to convince even knowledgeable and critical sitters of their continuing post-mortem existence.

Cases involving emergence of secondary personalities with characteristics superior to those of the primary personality are also relevant here. One such case is that of Old Stump, described in Chapter 5. Another is de Puységur's patient Victor Race, suffering from an inflamed lung, who manifested when mesmerized a secondary personality remarkably more gifted than Victor in his normal state: "Though ordinarily a simple and tongue-tied peasant, he would, in the somnambulic state, converse in a fluent and

17. Similar group dynamics have sometimes been observed, incidentally, in the production of unusually strong psychokinetic effects (Batcheldor, 1984).

elevated manner....Victor assumed management of his own case, diagnosing and prescribing for his illness, and predicting its course. More than this: on being brought into contact with other patients, he seemed able to do the same for them" (Gauld, 1992, p. 41).

Still more important is the well-studied case of the Swiss medium "Hélène Smith" (Catherine Elise Müller). Myers (*HP*, vol. 2, pp. 130–144) provides a précis based on the initial investigation by Flournoy (1900/1963), using this as his primary example of the action of the mid-level "mythopœic" subliminal centers that engage perpetually in a "strange manufacture of inward romances" (an interpretation approved by Ellenberger, 1970, pp. 150, 317–318). The initial stages of Hélène Smith's trance mediumship were replete with automatisms of various kinds but consisted mainly of lengthy descriptions of her supposed adventures in a series of increasingly exotic settings, including India and the planet Mars. Some of these reports seemed to contain considerable amounts of plausible historical and geographical detail, encouraging her admirers to agree with her that she was recounting her own actual experiences of previous lives. Flournoy and Myers, however, saw these tales rather as moderately creative productions of her subliminal, drawing upon a faculty of "cryptomnesia" (Stevenson, 1983a), or subliminal access to materials long ago encountered but inaccessible to ordinary conscious recall. Flournoy's book recounts in detail how he was able by laborious investigation to track down probable sources for much of the content of her romances, although he did in the end conclude that they also contained at least a few elements of probable supernormal origin (Flournoy, 1911).

The story does not end there, however. Hélène Smith's mediumship continued to evolve, eventually supplanting her previous waking life as a department manager in a large shop in Geneva. Flournoy was unfortunately not privy to these later developments, as she and her followers had become irritated with his deflationary zeal and punished him by refusing further cooperation. Of particular interest is a large volume of automatic drawings and paintings, many of which are reproduced in a massive study by Deonna (1932). Even in reproductions without color her paintings are well composed, smoothly executed with defined images, exuding a surreal religiosity comparing favorably with the paintings of Frida Khalo. Yet Hélène Smith apparently painted without a brush, using her fingers in a trance-like condition. N. Fodor (1966) quotes her own description of the process:

> On the days when I am to paint I am always roused very early—generally between five and six in the morning—by three loud knocks at my bed. I open my eyes and see my bedroom brightly illuminated, and immediately understand that I have to stand up and work. I dress myself in the beautiful iridescent light, and wait a few moments, sitting in my armchair, until the feeling comes that I have to work. It never delays. All at once I stand up and walk to the picture. When about two steps before it I feel a strange sensation, and probably fall asleep at the same moment. I know, later on,

> that I must have slept because I notice that my fingers are covered with different colours, and I do not remember at all to have used them. (p. 350)[18]

A related case of perhaps even greater theoretical significance is that of "Patience Worth," first studied and reported in depth by Walter Franklin Prince (1927/1964). The medium in this case was Pearl Curran, a midwestern American housewife of modest education who possessed, so far as Prince could determine through extensive and careful investigation, no special interests or aptitude in language, literature, or poetry. In Pearl's 31st year, in the course of some half-hearted experimentation with a ouija board, the personality identifying itself as Patience Worth, ostensibly a 17th-century Englishwoman, made its first appearance. Her ensuing collaboration with Pearl lasted almost 25 years, and ultimately produced some 29 volumes or 4,375 single-spaced pages of novels, poems, proverbs, aphorisms, witticisms, and conversational repartee (Braude, 2003).

Far more important than the sheer *volume* of this material, however, are several aspects of its *character*. First, it was generated automatically, initially by means of the ouija board, later by automatic vocalization of single letters, then words, apparently accompanied by panoramas of vivid visual imagery illustrating or dramatizing the spoken content. Pearl occasionally carried out directly competing tasks such as writing a letter to a friend while this was going on. Second is the extreme fluency and virtuosity of the performance. Patience typically produced her material without delay and faster than a stenographer could write it down, pausing only to let the stenographer catch up. This was the case even in response to difficult challenges posed on the spot by Prince—for example, to improvise a poem on a given theme, or to write alternating lines or passages on different subjects or in different literary styles. Interrupted by Prince in the middle of a sentence or passage, Patience could resume on demand and without break or pause, sometimes weeks or months later. Her material was consistently of high quality even as initially produced, and she almost never revised anything. She also displayed extensive and accurate knowledge of the various times and places figuring in her novels, and portrayed them with impressive verisimilitude. Perhaps most remarkable of all, she possessed an extensive repertoire of archaic Anglo-Saxon words deriving from multiple periods and localities, many of which were known at the time, if at all, only to a few professional philologists.

In short, Patience Worth, who had emerged essentially fully-formed in those first sessions with the ouija board, differed radically from the relatively staid and ordinary Pearl Curran, and not only in matters of personality, style, and attitude but also in knowledge, intelligence, and creative capacities. Her performances, as Prince (1927/1964) points out, required "phenomenal memory, phenomenal speed, and phenomenal complexity of mental operations" (p. 487). Summing up the results of his "arduous and

---

18. Two additional cases of this type were reported by Osty (1928a, 1928b), both involving pronounced aspects of automatism and trance.

unremitting labor," Prince (1927/1964) advances the following proposition: "*Either our concept of what we call the subconscious must be radically altered, so as to include potencies of which we hitherto have had no knowledge, or else some cause operating through but not originating in the subconsciousness of Mrs. Curran must be acknowledged*" (p. 509). We can only second this theoretical challenge, as does Schiller (1928), as well as Braude (2003) in his valuable summary and analysis of the case.

Additional examples of the connection between mediumship and genius are presented and discussed in Grosso (in press). One we cannot resist mentioning here, to conclude this section, concerns the role of Myers and automatism in Surrealism, which was perhaps the most important artistic movement of the 20th century. Cubism, Dada, Futurism, Abstract Expressionism, and Minimalism were all important but limited innovations, primarily technical and thematic. Surrealism alone challenged fundamental premises about art and creativity, shifting the focus from conscious to unconscious processes, introducing the role of chance in the creative process, and treating that process as not merely aesthetic but political, social, and metaphysical. Although it is widely supposed that Surrealism was inspired wholly by Freud, that is certainly not correct: Its chief theoretician, André Breton, published in 1933 an article specifically acknowledging its indebtedness to "the gothic psychiatry of F. W. H. Myers" (Breton, 1933/1997). Myers's work on automatism in fact provided the key psychological mechanism that Surrealism would attempt to exploit in novel ways: "Surrealism has above all worked to bring inspiration back into favor, and we have for that purpose promoted the use of automatic forms of expression" (p. 15). The goal of Surrealism is essentially to unify the personality, which means for Breton what Myers meant by genius, the successful coordination and interpenetration of dream and waking life. As Breton (1924/1972) puts it in his *Manifestoes of Surrealism*: "I believe in the future resolution of these two states, dream and reality, which are seemingly so contradictory, into a kind of absolute reality, a *surreality*, if one may so speak" (p. 14). It would be an interesting study, but one which would take us too far afield for present purposes, to explore in greater detail the role actually played by psychological automatisms in the production of particular works of Surrealist art.

To summarize the discussion so far: Myers argues, and we think he is correct, that whereas momentary "flashes of inspiration" are essentially brief automatisms, more or less continuous with much of what goes on in ordinary mental life, in more extreme cases of real genius the subliminal uprush becomes more intense and protracted, and arises from deeper subliminal strata that utilize different modes of operation and may have access to additional sources of information. This leads to the third major feature of his analysis of inspiration, and—surprisingly—to a cluster of issues lying at the heart of contemporary cognitive theory.

Incommensurability

Myers introduces this theme in section 322 (*HP*, vol. 1, p. 98).

> And thus there may really be something at times *incommensurable* between the inspirations of genius and the results of conscious logical thought. Just as the calculating boy solves his problems by methods which differ from the methods of the trained mathematician, so in artistic matters also that "something of strangeness" which is in "all excellent beauty", may be the expression of a real difference between subliminal and supraliminal modes of perception.

Non-Linguistic Symbolisms

In the next six pages, one of the most condensed and difficult but important parts of the chapter, Myers develops his central ideas: Subliminal mentation is less closely bound than supraliminal mentation to *language*, either ordinary spoken and written language or the specialized languages of science and mathematics; but it is not for that reason to be presumed *inferior*, that it "in some way falls short of the standard implied in articulate speech" (*HP*, vol. 1, p. 98).

Myers clearly acknowledges the primacy of language as the privileged means of ordinary communication. It is an absolute necessity of intellectual life and the foundation of all civilization. But it is not the whole story: "There is, however, no *a priori* ground for supposing that language will have the power to express all the thoughts and emotions of man" (*HP*, vol. 1, p. 99). Indeed, the study of automatisms in general and the inspirations of genius in particular reveal that other forms of symbolism become increasingly important as we access deeper strata of the subliminal. There is a "hidden habit of wider symbolism, of self-communion beyond the limits of speech" that is better adapted to expression of "that pre-existent but hidden concordance between visible and invisible things, between matter and thought, between thought and emotion, which the plastic arts, and music, and poetry do each in their own special field discover and manifest for human wisdom and joy" (*HP*, vol. 1, p. 101).

Myers goes on in section 326 to make some extremely condensed and penetrating remarks elaborating this basic conception with respect to poetry, music, and the plastic arts in turn. We encourage interested readers to savor thoughtfully these remarks, which anticipate in a remarkable way attempts by later philosophers such as Brann (1991), Cassirer (1955–1996), Langer (1956), and Whitehead (1938/1968) to temper the linguistic obsessions of modern analytic philosophy with an appreciation of non-discursive or "presentational" modes of symbolism. Langer (1956) says of music, for example, that "there are certain aspects of the so-called 'inner life'—physical or mental—which have formal properties similar to those of music—patterns of motion and rest, of tension and release, or agreement and disagreement, proportion, fulfillment, excitation, sudden change, etc." (p. 185). By virtue of such isomorphisms a musical configuration can become expressive of an emotional state, so that "music sounds the way emotions feel."

But let us return now to mainstream cognitive psychology, where a similar imbalance in favor of discursive and propositional forms of thought has long dominated the scene, and especially since the rise of the computational theory of the mind (CTM; Chapter 1). We wish first simply to reiterate Myers's central *empirical* claim, that subliminal contributions to creative activity generally, and to the more extreme "inspirations of genius" in particular, tend strongly to take the form of unusually intense and often involuntary imagery, predominantly though not exclusively visual, accompanied by strong affect and a profound sense of surprise and wonder at its beauty, harmony, elegance, and proportion or fitness to the consciously intended purpose. That this claim is broadly correct, descriptively, seems to us beyond reasonable doubt, as we have already indicated. What we want next to discuss in greater depth concerns rather the manner in which scientific psychology subsequent to Myers has dealt with such matters.

The CTM itself in its classical symbol-processing form scarcely touches these subjects at all, with one important exception—*analogy*—that we will discuss in more detail below. Most of the remaining work, surveyed by Boden (1991; updated in Boden, 1999), involves attempted computer simulations of processes of scientific discovery, musical improvisation, or the creation of simple stories, poems, and the like. The authors of these various scientific-discovery programs have been widely faulted for setting things up in advance in such a way as to make their "discoveries" inevitable, a criticism with which we generally agree, and in that light the overall assessment of this work by Boden herself, generally an uncritical enthusiast of the CTM, is telling: "The success of programs for scientific discovery, limited though it is, is not matched by programs for producing poems or (especially) stories" (Boden, 1999, p. 359).

We will leave this part of the subject there, adding only that the reasons for these failures, in our view, are essentially the central defects of the CTM as identified by critics such as Searle and Dreyfus and summarized in Chapter 1. It is also worth noting, however, that Hofstadter and FARG (1995) arrive at an equally negative overall assessment from the opposite, CTM-friendly, point of view. It should also be pointed out, we think, that all such attempts to explain genius as a completely rule-bound process conflict with a deep intuition, shared by many, that genius by definition breaks old rules and makes new ones: As Kant (1790/1951) put the point so clearly, "genius is a talent for producing that for which no definite rule can be given; it is not a mere aptitude for what can be learned by a rule" (p. 150). Indeed, he says, "Genius is the talent (or natural gift) which gives the rule to art."

Associationism and Its Limits

By far the largest proportion of attempts to explain the creative process have invoked the core doctrines of "associationism," in forms ranging from the 17th-century mechanical theory of association of ideas to its modern descendant, connectionism, which speaks in terms of waves of excitation reverberating through neural networks (Chapter 1). (As J. Fodor [2001] remarks, perhaps a bit too caustically: "That's what's so nice about empiricist cognitive science: You can drop out for a couple of centuries and not miss a thing" [p. 49].) Wallas (1926), for example, thought of unconscious or preconscious ideas as existing ready-made in a Jamesian-style "fringe" of consciousness, in effect a remote part of the "upper cortex," which he and others of that period naively conceived as a kind of vast telephone switchboard. The creative person is one in whom trains of association set in motion by the preparatory labor somehow penetrate that remote region during the incubation phase and deliver useful ideas back to consciousness in the form of inspiration. Ghiselin (1952) expresses very similar views in a slightly updated neurophysiological terminology.

Later accounts by psychologists followed similar lines but sought to impose a more mechanistic flavor consistent with the observations of Guilford (1950) and others regarding the importance of "divergent thinking" and the like. So, for example, Mednick (1962) advanced an associationist theory according to which creativity is found in persons and conditions in which the associative hierarchies linking concepts are relatively equipotential or "flat," permitting large numbers of remote and surprising associations, in contrast with "steep" hierarchies that permit only relatively small numbers of obvious or stereotypical ones. Mendelsohn (1976) related these characteristics to attentional processes, emphasizing that "defocusing" of attention increases the range of possible associations and combinations of ideas and hence, it is presumed, creativity.

Martindale (1995, 1999) has recently updated these ideas within the framework of contemporary neural-network and connectionist theorizing, seeking in effect a neurobiology of the creative process. He reviews, for example, a variety of evidence suggesting that the flat associative hierarchies and defocused attention that supposedly account for creativity correlate to some degree with brain conditions such as reduced cortical arousal and reduced frontal-lobe control, (possibly) accompanied by relatively greater right-hemisphere involvement.[19] The relentless psychometrician Hans Eysenck (1995) welcomes these "state" formulations, treating them as complementary to his own "trait" concept of "psychoticism" as a biologically grounded propensity toward remote but relevant associations (p. 267). For both Martindale and Eysenck, however, as for many other leading creativity theorists, the central notion that "remote associations" comprise the essence of the creative process goes essentially unchallenged.

The fundamental idea of associationist theories of creativity is that the incubation/inspiration cycle can satisfactorily be conceptualized in terms of

19. We comment parenthetically that the conditions identified by Martindale are also associated with the hypnagogic state and its vivid, involuntary imagery, which commonly plays a role in creative activity as noted above. More generally, his neurobiological observations are also consistent with a Myers-like view in which global impairment of the normal supraliminal mode of mind-brain operation can lead to proportional disinhibition or release of normally inaccessible subliminal modes.

retrieval and combination of ideas already in the network, by means of some process of spreading activation. This conception seems plausible enough, we would agree, in connection with certain rudimentary forms of the phenomena to be explained. It might well account, for example, for what goes on when we finally retrieve a temporarily forgotten word following unsuccessful attempts to do so in the tip-of-the-tongue (TOT) state (A. S. Brown, 1991; R. Brown & McNeill, 1966; James, 1890b, vol. 1, p. 251). As many observers have noted, such occasions seem to involve—at least in germ—all four stages of the Wallas model, so why not regard TOT as a suitable prototype for the whole domain?

Coleridge and the Theory of Imagination

Forceful answers can be found, we submit, in a source rarely consulted by contemporary psychologists, namely the investigations by 19th-century English romantic poets, Coleridge in particular, into the nature of human imagination.[20] The gist of the story goes as follows: Coleridge had felt a strange power in certain early poems by his friend Wordsworth, poems that he recognized as markedly superior to his own. Seeking to understand this puzzling but important effect, and thus to harness it in service of his own poetry, he turned first to the mainstream psychological theory of his day, the theory of association of ideas as developed by figures such as Hobbes, Locke, Hume, and Hartley. This theory represented a deliberate and self-conscious attempt to extend the triumphs of classical mechanistic physics into the domain of the mind. The "atoms" of the new science were "ideas," typically conceived as fainter replicas of former perceptions, or as the simpler qualities or parts into which such perceptions could be analyzed. Their commerce was to be governed by "laws of association" analogous to Newton's laws of motion, based in particular on factors such as contiguity in time or place, resemblances of one or another sort, and connections of cause and effect. Imagination, in this framework, was to be conceived in terms of novel combinations or recombinations of these independent, self-existent atomic parts. Thus the prototypical example of the imagination at work became the Chimera of Greek mythology, a fire-breathing monster which conjoined the head of a lion with a goat's body and serpent tail. Correspondingly, imagination was regarded as fundamentally delusive, and figu-

---

20. See especially Coleridge (1817/1967); good secondary sources here are Abrams (1958), Brann (1991), Hill (1978), and I. A. Richards (1960). It seems certain that Myers would have been intimately familiar with the original literature of this movement, and fully aware of its deep affinities with the theory of genius he articulates in *HP*. Most fundamentally, perhaps, for Coleridge as for Myers, the role of imagination in genius is secondary to its role as "the living Power and prime Agent of all human Perception" (Coleridge, 1817/1967, p. 167). For both, that is, perception becomes imagination constrained by sensory input. It is also somewhat ironic, even sad, that Coleridge is mainly cited by contemporary psychologists in connection with his much-maligned stories regarding the composition of *Kubla Khan* in an opium dream. He is of far greater importance to psychology, we think, as a theorist and exemplar of the imagination (see also Lowes, 1927).

rative and metaphorical language were viewed as serving purely ornamental functions.

Coleridge struggled to reconcile this mechanistic theory with what he could directly observe in the workings of real human imagination as manifested in creative geniuses such as Wordsworth, Shakespeare, Milton, and himself, among sundry others. Imagination, he concluded, *cannot* be fully understood in these terms; moreover, the unexplained residue lies at the very heart of creative imagination, and encompasses its most significant properties. Coleridge sought to explicate these properties in terms of his famous distinction between mere *fancy* and *imagination* proper: Fancy seems within reach of associationist theories; mechanical and passive, it associates, aggregates, collates, collocates, juxtaposes, transposes, rearranges, and mirrors, giving rise in such ways to low-grade products like the infamous Chimera. Imagination, by contrast, "that synthetic and magical power," is for Coleridge something radically different and altogether superior: Imagination is organic and active; it assimilates, dissolves and recreates, fuses, synthesizes, and unifies. It transmutes the chaos of raw materials provided by everyday experience, forging and shaping them by means of its inherent "coadunating," "alembic," and "esemplastic" powers into truly novel creations that balance or reconcile seemingly opposite or discordant qualities in harmonious unity. It is above all a unique form of thought, and one of the principal powers of the human mind.

A fuller appreciation of Coleridge's concept of imagination can best be obtained by studying the numerous examples adduced in the sources cited above. We ourselves have no doubt that it poses severe challenges, not only to classical association theories but to cognitive science more generally, and we think that cognitive science can only be enriched by paying greater attention to these long-neglected but very high-level discussions. Two further observations may serve to reinforce this contention.

The first has to do with the subsequent history of Coleridge's attempted distinction between fancy and imagination, which has so far been pursued mainly in the context of literary theory and criticism. Most such observers have found Coleridge's distinction ultimately untenable, but in an interesting and important way: Specifically, what they deny is *not* that imagination has the sorts of properties that Coleridge ascribes to it, but rather that these difficult properties can be prevented from invading the supposedly lesser realm of fancy. That is (and again in accord with Wind's principle), even relatively *ordinary* forms of cognition, when more closely examined, are inescapably saturated with properties of the sort that Coleridge viewed as beyond the reach of any mechanistic association theory (Abrams, 1958; I. A. Richards, 1960).

Second, we wish to comment briefly on the few other recent psychological publications known to us to have made contact with this older literature. The first (Sutton, 1998) attempts to deny that there is any problem. Specifically, Sutton claims that certain secondary strains within classical associationism, epitomized in particular by Hartley, are the true ancestors of contemporary connectionism, and that these are immune to critiques such as Coleridge's which supposedly apply only to its less sophisticated forms. In fact, however, Coleridge knew Hartley's work intimately and used *his* version of associationism as the principal vehicle for his critical analyses. In our view, Sutton simply avoids coming to grips with the real cognitive issues, appealing to abstract connectionist principles such as "distributed representations" and "superimposition" that in fact do little even to help solve problems of ordinary memory function (Chapter 4), let alone those of creative imagination.

Similar comments apply to Boden's (1991) chapter on "creative connections," the setting for which is the remarkable investigation by Lowes (1927) of the workings of Coleridge's own poetic imagination in the production of *Kubla Khan* and *The Ancient Mariner*. Having dutifully acknowledged the properties of strong imagination that both Coleridge and Lowes themselves regarded as truly fundamental, Boden proceeds to treat the subject as if it really were mostly a matter of associative connections, and explainable at least in general terms by the elementary properties (which she describes) of connectionist networks. She forthrightly acknowledges the limitations of current models, and that "the intuitive understanding offered by Livingston Lowes is incalculably richer, and more subtle, than any connectionist explanation" (p. 130), but glibly reassures her readers that these gaps will be closed in due course by the "more powerful" computer systems of the future.

No warrants have as yet been provided for these computationalist promissory notes, and as explained in Chapter 1 we strongly doubt that they can ever be fulfilled. The situation is to us strongly reminiscent of the one that provoked the destructive review by Chomsky (1959) of Skinner's book on verbal behavior, in that connectionist notions which so far explain rather little when deployed in a careful and technically rigorous manner are being brandished about metaphorically by less scrupulous enthusiasts as the answer to everything. A telling commentary on the real state of things in regard to connectionist modeling of creative imagination is that neither "creativity" nor "imagination," let alone cognate terms such as "inspiration" or "genius," even appear in the indexes of connectionist handbooks such as Bechtel and Abrahamson (2002) and Harnish (2002).

Our third example is an important paper by N. J. T. Thomas (1999), who approaches the subject of imagination in the context of a review of the "imagery debates" mentioned in Chapter 1. Thomas recognizes that current imagery theories fall far short of providing an adequate theory of imagination, and that the Romantic-era theorists of the imagination had important things to say—sentiments with which we wholly agree. He goes on, however, to a summary dismissal of Coleridge and his allies on grounds that, although descriptively on target, they left us only "a mixture of warmed-over associationist notions, clearly inadequate to the demands being placed upon them, and fragments of grandiose idealist metaphysics, ripe for mystificatory appropriation" (p. 232). Thomas himself turns instead to "perceptual activity" theory, which takes "seeing-as" as the fundamental capacity of imagination, and seeks to derive imagination from an account of perception inspired mainly by recent work in robotics. To this we would respond first that his investment of such high hopes in robotics seems forlorn; but more importantly, (1) that the Coleridge/Myers view is much more like his own than he appreciates (the entire first half in particular of the statement quoted above is simply inaccurate), and (2) that its empirical and philosophical foundations are far stronger than he realizes, as demonstrated both by *HP* itself and by the present volume.

Despite these caveats, we welcome Thomas's paper as one of several recent developments within mainstream psychology itself that indicate growing recognition of the need to deal with creative imagination as it actually is, rather than as most contemporary workers have pictured it to be. Even the hard-core experimentalist George Mandler (1994) was moved to remark that "there may well be conditions in which such spreading or fanning out [of network activation] reaches recesses of the unconscious that dynamic psychology has considered, but experimental psychology has not" (p. 25). Another recent example is the "creative cognition" approach (S. M. Smith, Ward, & Finke, 1995; Ward, Finke, & Smith, 1995; Ward, Smith, & Finke, 1999; Ward, Smith, & Vaid, 1997), which in its emphasis on continuity and the role in creative thinking of "pre-inventive structures" such as imagery, analogy, and symbolism, has also begun moving beyond the current frontiers of mainline cognitive theory in a Myers-like direction, albeit in what seems to us so far an excessively timid and limited way.

In sum, what seems to be in the offing is a revival of psychological interest in creative imagination as a distinctive and powerful mode of thought. Just as "genius" has degenerated in recent times into "creativity," the original Greek *phantasia* with its connotations of world-fashioning or cosmogonic power has degenerated over the centuries into mere "fantasy," escapist day-dreaming of little or no cognitive import. Like Brann (1991), we believe psychology must now reverse this pernicious trend; the "sober romanticism" which she champions in her monumental interdisciplinary compilation of thinking about the imagination is in fact highly consistent with Myers's views, and would have been greatly enriched by those views had only she known them.

Psychoanalytic Theory: Primary and Secondary Process

We said "revival" in the previous paragraph because imagination has not always been so neglected by psychology as in recent decades. In particular, and as hinted in the statement above by George Mandler, psychodynamic theories associated with the clinical wing of the field have always paid far more attention to this subject. In their terms, the "incommensurability" that Myers pointed out between subliminal and supraliminal modes of functioning maps rather nicely onto a famous distinction between "primary" and "secondary" process, first introduced by Freud in his *Interpretation of Dreams* (1900/1964, chap. 6). In Freud's original formulation, secondary process is more or less clearly understood as ordinary wakeful thinking, which is voluntary, discursive, more or less logical, and reality-oriented—a product, in short, of the conscious ego. Primary process, by contrast, Freud regarded as instinct-dominated, oriented only toward gratification of infantile wishes, and rooted in the unconscious id. In Freud's theory of dream formation, as expounded by Fliess (1959), primary process expresses itself in the various properties of dreams which allow them to serve as acceptable forms of manifest expression for clearly formulated but unacceptable wishes latent in the unconscious. The properties in question include, for example, picturization, symbolization, condensation, concretization, allusion, displacement, and representation through opposites.

The psychoanalytic conception of primary process is approximately convergent, *descriptively*, with creative imagination as conceived by Myers, Coleridge, Brann, and others. Where it originally differed, of course, was in its profound devaluation of imagination, its relentlessly "archeological" approach to non-verbal symbolism, and more generally its close ties to the sometimes bizarre formulations of orthodox Freudian metapsychology. These differences have been substantially eroded, however, by subsequent revisionary trends within psychoanalysis itself, driven at least in part by trenchant empirical critiques of Freud's dream theory by Hall (1953) and others. Primary process is no longer conceived as rigidly distinct from and opposed to secondary process, or as a mere slave of the Freudian unconscious—that boiling cesspool of primitive sexual and aggressive urges. Rather, it represents a distinctive mode of cognition existing alongside secondary process, complementary to and interactive with it, and potentially available in service of creative activity. Kubie (1958) in particular has emphasized the versatility, brilliance, and speed of this "preconscious" system, and its role as the wellspring of creativity:

> In the adult who is not hamstrung by conscious or unconscious fear and guilt, preconscious processes make free use of analogy and allegory, superimposing dissimilar ingredients into new perceptual and conceptual patterns, thus reshuffling experience to achieve that fantastic degree of condensation without which creativity in any field of activity would be impossible. In the preconscious use of imagery and allegory many experiences are condensed into a single hieroglyph, which expresses in one symbol far more than one can say slowly and precisely, word by word, on the fully conscious level. This is why preconscious mentation is the Seven–League Boot of intuitive creative functions. This is how and why preconscious condensations are used in poetry, humor, the dream, and the symptom. (pp. 34–35)

Even a few mainstream psychologists from Hilgard (1962), Neisser (1963), and Shepard (1978) to Eysenck (1995) and Sloman (1996) have recognized that this psychoanalytic concept of primary process, liberated from its Freudian origins, corresponds to something which is vital in human cognitive makeup generally, and especially significant in relation to creative thinking.[21] The same recognition lies at the core of the account by Koestler (1964) of creative inspiration as "bisociation," or association of ideas across normally separate domains. Indeed, Koestler states flatly that "we find all the bisociative patterns that I have discussed prominently displayed in the dream" (p. 179).

These trends within neo-Freudian psychoanalytic thinking in regard to primary process and creativity have been documented in many places, including Erdelyi (1985), Fromm (1978–1979), Kris (1952), Kubie (1958), Rapaport (1951), and Suler (1980). They coalesce around the concept of "regression in service of the ego," introduced by Ernst Kris (1952). Stripped of its heavy encrustation in the technical vocabulary of psychoanalysis, this amounts essentially to voluntary, controlled exposure to the free play of imagination (primary process) in service of adaptive purposes such as creativity, wit, and humor (Schafer, 1958). Clearly, this notion is substantially congruent with Myers's general conception of genius as effecting greater than normal cooperation between supraliminal and subliminal forms of mentation. Kris's (1952) conception of *inspiration* likewise is closely similar to Myers's, except that his clinical perspective and experience compel him to point out the associated psychological hazards as well: "Inspiration—the 'divine release from the ordinary ways of man,' a state of 'creative madness' (Plato), in which the ego controls the primary process and puts it into its service—need be contrasted with the opposite, the psychotic condition, in which the ego is overwhelmed by the primary process" (p. 60). Koestler (1964, p. 659) speaks in very similar terms of genius as reaching deep underground sources of inspiration through a *reculer pour mieux sauter*, as contrasted with pathological conditions representing a *reculer sans sauter*.

The Crucial Role of Analogy and Metaphor

The psychoanalytic concepts of primary process and regression in service of the ego provide useful ways of talking about subliminal contributions to creative activity, but they remain primarily descriptive and rely upon a psychological theory which derives mainly from clinical practice and observation. E. F. Kelly (1962) attempted to account for the same descriptive properties in more mechanistic fashion, utilizing Heinz Werner's (1957) broader-based comparative psychology of mental development. Creative inspiration was again portrayed in much the same terms, emphasizing the emergence into consciousness of pregnant figurative constructs—images, symbols, metaphors, analogies, and the like—organized at an unconscious level; the main novelty, only partly successful, consisted in an attempt to show how such constructs might form spontaneously in accordance with

21. Not all mainstream psychologists agree, however. R. J. Sternberg and Lubart (1999), for example, provide just a two-paragraph summary of psychoanalytic contributions, and then dismiss the entire subject from further consideration, saying only that "although the psychodynamic approach may have offered some insights into creativity, psychodynamic theory was not at the center of the emerging scientific psychology" (p. 6).

Werner's account of the mechanisms involved in "primitive" perceptual and conceptual processes.

Common to all these pre-CTM 20th-century accounts was a recognition of the fundamental role of *analogizing* in creative activity, and more generally of *metaphor*, broadly construed, as the language of the imagination. Such recognition was hardly original with them, of course: According to Aristotle, for example, the "greatest thing by far is to have a command of metaphor. This alone cannot be imparted by another; it is the mark of genius, for to make good metaphors implies an eye for resemblances" (Butcher, 1951, p. 87). For Emerson as for Myers, analogy represented the fundamental movement of thought, its capacity to penetrate to hidden affinities linking things behind the diversity of their surface appearances. Emerson's godson William James (1890b) accorded analogy a similarly prominent position within his psychology, declaring the *grasping of sameness* to be "the very keel and backbone of our thinking" (vol. 1, p. 459). Indeed, for him it lies at the very heart of genius: "*Some people are far more sensitive to resemblances, and far more ready to point out wherein they consist, than others are.* They are the wits, the poets, the inventors, the scientific men, the practical geniuses. *A native talent for perceiving analogies* is reckoned by Prof. Bain, and by others before and after him, as *the leading fact in genius of every order*" (vol. 1, pp. 529–530). Large-scale analogies have unquestionably played an important historical role in shaping scientific thought, two prominent examples being Laplace's clockwork universe and contemporary efforts to construe the mind as some sort of computational system. At a lower level Draaisma (2000) has documented the role of technological metaphors in the evolution of memory theory, and ironically enough even Perkins (2000), who has explicitly argued *against* the importance of analogy in creative thinking, develops his "nothing-special" theory in the context of an elaborate and sustained analogy between creative effort and prospecting for gold in Alaska (his "Klondike space" metaphor). The capacity for metaphor, in sum, plays an important role even in scientific thinking, and it represents an important element of our overall cognitive organization.

The Failure of Computational Theories of Analogy

As noted in Chapter 1, mainstream cognitive science of the last few decades has rediscovered these truths. In addition to the important descriptive studies of metaphor by linguist George Lakoff and his colleagues (Lakoff, 1993, 1995; Lakoff & Turner, 1989), a large amount of computer modeling of analogy processes has been carried out under the auspices of the CTM, work collectively characterized by practitioners Holyoak and Thagard (1995) as having produced "great progress" and constituting what is "undoubtedly one of the success stories of cognitive science" (p. 251).

We respectfully demur, and must now attempt at least briefly to explain why. Our goal here will be to cut through a large and complex literature to what we perceive as its core problem, which is essentially the inability of all existing computational models to address the fundamental issues of semantics or meaning and the intentional activity of knowing human subjects—the heart of the mind (Chapter 1). Non-specialist readers are forewarned that this section may prove hard going on a first reading.

A comprehensive state-of-the-art survey of recent analogy work is provided by Gentner, Holyoak, and Kokinov (2001), but we will begin with two leading exemplars, the structure-mapping theory of Gentner (1983), implemented primarily in the form of their "structure-mapping engine" (SME; Falkenhainer, Forbus, & Gentner, 1989; Forbus, Gentner, & Law, 1994), and the "multiconstraint" theory of Holyoak and Thagard (1995), implemented primarily in the form of their "analogical constraint mapping engine"(ACME; Holyoak & Thagard, 1989) and programs for "analogical retrieval by constraint satisfaction" (ARCS; Hummel & Holyoak, 1997; Thagard, Holyoak, Nelson, & Gochfeld, 1990). There are many significant differences among these models, but for our purposes what matters more is their similarities. We will now sketch these common properties, acknowledging that our description is necessarily terse and that interested readers may need to consult the original sources to gain a fuller appreciation of what we are talking about.

Like all cognitive models inspired by the CTM, these models of analogy processing incorporate two principal components: (1) representations of the model's knowledge in some cognitive domain or domains, and (2) computational processes that operate on these representations to produce the desired behavior. In almost all of the analogy work, as in classical cognitive science generally, "knowledge" is represented in some sort of predicate-calculus-like logical format which identifies the objects talked about, their properties (the predicates that apply to them), and the relations (possibly multiplace) in which they can participate. Expressions incorporating these elements can serve as arguments in higher-order expressions, permitting very complex propositional structures to be built up. Two important things to note here are: first, that *English words* are routinely used to identify the various properties, functions, and relations that make up the knowledge representation language; and second, that the representations used by the analogy-mapping programs are typically *hand-crafted* by their human designers.

SME and ACME are concerned only with *interpretation* of analogies, and not with their *production*, which is a far harder problem. "Interpretation" amounts here to identifying the best-possible mapping between knowledge in a *source* domain and knowledge in a *target* domain, each characterized by a representation of the above-indicated sort. ACME does this (in what seems to us a somewhat more realistic manner, psychologically speaking) by using a connectionist network to settle on the most coherent way of picking out the cross-domain correspondences between elements of the same type—that is, correspondences of objects with objects, predicates with predicates, and relations with relations—given the available knowledge representations. In this way, for example, Socrates' description of himself as "a midwife of ideas" is said to be correctly interpreted when this constraint-satisfaction mechanism discovers that the expression:

(1) cause ((helps (obj-midwife obj-mother)) (give_birth_to (obj-mother obj-child)))

which expresses the system's knowledge in the midwifery (source) domain, maps onto:

(2) cause ((helps (Socrates obj-student)) (knows_truth_or_falsity (obj-student obj-idea)))

in the Socrates (target) domain in such a way that Socrates bears the same relationship to ideas as midwives do to babies (Holyoak & Thagard, 1989, pp. 344–347). Boden (1991, p. 174) gushes over this result, characterizing it as a step toward understanding what takes place in the mind of a human reader of Shakespeare's famous passage in Macbeth about "sleep that knits up the ravelled sleave of care," and Holyoak and Thagard (1995, p. 258) thank her for her "fine overview" of their work on analogy.

We feel obliged to register our astonishment that anyone could take this example, representative of many similar examples in the broader analogy literature, so seriously. To us it seems utter caricature of real human understanding, "explaining" nothing. We feel certain, too, that John Searle would agree with this judgment, finding clear parallels to the hyperbole about computer "story understanding" that originally provoked his critique of the CTM, all of which applies here (Chapter 1).

In this case, however, we can also call upon one further witness who is even more important, because he differs from both Searle and ourselves in sharing the basic philosophical commitments of the CTM, and has himself worked extensively on the subject of analogy. We refer to computer scientist Douglas Hofstadter, who with his "Fluid Analogies Research Group" (FARG) has tenaciously pursued a radically different and highly innovative approach to analogy that is rooted in the study of "microdomains" such as letter-string problems rather than "macrodomain" or high-level analogies of the Socrates/midwife sort. Hofstadter and FARG (1995) provide not only an illuminating history of their own efforts, packed with important psychological and computational insights, but trenchant critiques of their "real-world" competitors, including in particular SME and ACME, as well as many other leading projects in cognitive psychology and artificial intelligence including scientific-discovery and story-writing programs.

We will mention here just a few of Hofstadter's most telling criticisms of SME and ACME, which are also the ones most important for our own purposes. First, these "real-world" approaches essentially bypass the crucial issue as to how concepts or representations are acquired or constructed in the first place, leaving it to the designers to provide all the necessary "knowledge" in precisely the right form. Both systems lack the dynamic flexibility of human cognition and depend too strongly on the detailed structure of the representations provided them in advance. Hofstadter wonders, appropriately, what would happen if these "source" and "target" knowledge representations were coded *independently* by different persons. Most importantly, and like many other AI projects, SME and ACME engender a strong "Eliza" effect (Weizenbaum, 1976)—that is, an atmosphere of meaningfulness which depends strongly upon the use of English-like words and expressions in their representational notations. Such notations, even if intended simply as mnemonic aids, covertly engage the semantic capabilities of designers or observers of the system and encourage them to project these capabilities into the system itself (the homunculus problem; Chapter 1). But, Hofstadter argues, SME and ACME are in reality "hollow," semantically empty; they *know* nothing about Socrates, midwifery, or anything else, and *operate* entirely syntactically, in terms of the *forms* employed in the notation. To underscore this last point Hofstadter suggests replacing the English-like words and expressions of the original notation with letters or numbers. In that case everything would work exactly as before, except that the specious atmosphere of meaningfulness would be dispelled.[22]

Hofstadter's critique of these high-level analogy programs, in our opinion, is fair, thorough, and devastating. We wish only to add one further point related specifically to ARCS, the program for retrieving suitable analogs of a given word from long-term memory. Both Boden (1991, p. 174) and Holyoak and Thagard (1995, p. 252) make much of the fact that ARCS utilizes information from WordNet, an electronic thesaurus of English developed independently at Princeton by George Miller and colleagues (Miller, Beckwith, Fellbaum, Gross, & Miller, 1990). Boden in particular suggests that ARCS thereby gains access to a significant part of the conceptual system underlying English, but this suggestion needs to be carefully qualified. As Miller and Fellbaum (1991, pp. 200–201) made clear, WordNet is not "*constructive*" but merely "*differential*": It explicitly labels a variety of semantic properties of entries and semantic relations that hold between entries, but it does not attempt to represent the *meanings* of entries directly; rather, it simply provides brief definitions ("glosses") sufficient to allow fluent speakers of English to *identify* meanings which they are presumed already to possess. Although WordNet helps ARCS retrieve words semantically related to a target word, it does so *syntactically*, by virtue of the labels provided, and has no understanding of word meanings themselves.

If meaning cannot successfully be captured by standard forms of high-level symbolic cognitive architecture, how then are we to deal with it? Hofstadter believes that he has the answer, and that *his* approach, radically different, ratifies the fundamental connectionist faith that "human cognitive phenomena are emergent statistical effects of a large number of small, local, and distributed subcognitive effects with no global executive" (Hofstadter & FARG, 1995, p. 291). Abandoning the forlorn hopes of those who attempt to get at high-level semantics *directly*, Hofstadter turns instead to a variety of microdomains in which, he believes, all the essential features of human cognition are present, but in more tractable form. His goal, as the book's

22. This same exercise, incidentally, was suggested by E. F. Kelly (1975, p. 72) as a way to strip the "semantic markers" of J. J. Katz and Fodor (1964) of their atmosphere of telegraphic speech.

subtitle indicates, is to develop "computer models of the fundamental mechanisms of thought."

The centerpiece of this work is *Copycat*, a computer program which generates solutions to analogy problems of the following sort: Suppose the letter-string *aabc* were changed to *aabd*; how would you change the letter-string *ijkk* in the "*same way*"? No brief description can possibly do justice to the marvelous ingenuity of this program, but we must attempt to convey enough of its flavor to get to our central point (full details can be found in Hofstadter & FARG, 1995; and M. Mitchell, 1993). The program's architecture includes three main components: First is the "slipnet," which represents *Copycat*'s pre-supplied or "Platonic" knowledge and plays a crucial role in its dynamic behavior. This knowledge includes the letters of the alphabet and the numbers 1-5, with each successive pair of each group linked by labeled connections indicating their successor/predecessor relationships, and a variety of other things including pairs such as *first* and *last*, *leftmost* and *rightmost*, and *predecessor* and *successor*, all of which are again explicitly labeled as "opposites" (M. Mitchell, 1993, p. 47). Second is the "workspace," essentially a short-term or working memory in which candidate solution structures are dynamically assembled in parallel fashion. Finally, the "coderack" contains a large repertoire of "codelets," essentially micro-level programs or "agents" that launch themselves opportunistically, when their conditions of execution are satisfied by structures appearing in the workspace, or occasionally if they are selected by a random process.[23]

Each of *Copycat*'s problem runs is dominated at first by bottom-up or "open-minded" influences consisting of competitive interactions among a host of codelets operating in parallel, but as processing continues and larger candidate solution structures begin to form, top-down or "closed-minded" influences come increasingly into play, reflecting "pressures" created both by the emerging structures themselves and by the changing configuration of the slipnet, which is "rubbery" and dynamically adjusts the "distances" among its concepts in response to the situation at hand. These dynamic properties represent Hofstadter's way of modeling the context-dependent conceptual halos and "slippages" that he regards as crucial properties of human thinking. A measure of "temperature" falls as the level of "goodness" or order in the workspace increases, but that order itself emerges spontaneously from the collective activity of these low-level processes. There is no central executive.

That will have to do by way of description of *Copycat*. No one who studies this program can fail to admire its ingenuity, but what is its real sig-

23. On pp. 291–295 Hofstadter makes some especially interesting remarks concerning the position of *Copycat's* computational architecture with respect to that of conventional symbolic and connectionist models. It is not a hybrid or mixture of these, but intermediate between the two. Most importantly, it embodies a fundamental operational distinction between *types* (the Platonic constituents of the slipnet) and *tokens* (their instances in the workspace), a distinction which Hofstadter believes is essential to all cognitive activity but cannot be captured by conventional connectionist models. His arguments here are in fact strikingly parallel to those of J. Fodor (2001), who has abandoned the CTM altogether.

nificance? Commentators from the "real-world" faction have been inclined to dismiss Hofstadter's microdomain approach simply on grounds that it seems too tiny, too remote from the high-level problems of interest to them, but Hofstadter defends himself repeatedly and ably against such facile responses. The real core issue, he argues, has nothing to do with the size or subject matter *per se* of problem domains, but rather with their ability to engender real progress on fundamental issues of cognitive theory, and especially progress on the core problem of *meaning*.

We agree with this view, and here we come to the crux of the matter: Hofstadter believes there is a fundamental difference between *Copycat* and the semantically empty "real-world" analogy programs, in that symbols in *Copycat*, such as "successor," "acquire at least some degree of genuine meaning, thanks to their correlation with actual phenomena, even if those phenomena take place in a tiny and artificial world" (Hofstadter & FARG, 1995, p. 290). Unlike SME and ACME, he argues, *Copycat* can survive the label-substitution test—for example, replacing "successor" with "SIGMA"—for the following reason: "An astute human watching the performance of *Copycat* and seeing the term 'SIGMA' evoked over and over again by the presence of successor relationships and successorship groups in many diverse problems would be likely to make the connection after a while, and then might say, 'Oh, I get it—it appears that the Lisp atom 'SIGMA' stands for the idea of successorship'" (p. 290).

But this core argument, we submit, is specious: In his zeal to sustain the CTM, Hofstadter has simply confused what a conscious, intelligent human observer can learn about *Copycat* by observing its behavior with what *Copycat* itself "knows." He has failed to recognize that the really essential feature of this microdomain consists in the fact that he is able to limit all relevant "meanings" to those which can be transformed into *formal* or syntactic properties of letters and letter-strings, as defined by the slipnet. Like SME and ACME, *Copycat* itself "knows" nothing about successorship or anything else. The claimed contrast with real-world analogy programs is therefore not fundamental, and the problems of meaning and intentionality in knowing subjects remain unsolved.[24]

In sum, *neither* the "real-world" analogy programs nor Hofstadter's microdomain approach have as yet done much to illuminate even analogical thinking of quite pedestrian forms, let alone the more dramatic forms of metaphor and symbolism accompanying inspirations of genius.

---

24. It is a bit ironic, in this light, that despite his own earlier warnings about the Eliza effect in high-level analogy programs, Hofstadter himself begins talking ever more loosely about *Copycat* as "seeing," "knowing," "judging," "understanding," "focusing its attention," "believing," and so on. On the other hand, it is no surprise that he loathes the "biochauvinism" of philosophers such as John Searle (p. 290) and that he applauds the linguistic achievements of Terry Winograd's SHRDLU without mentioning Winograd's subsequent defection from AI (p. 311; see also our Chapter 1).

Implications for Cognitive Theory

But the problems go even deeper, in fact, than we have so far indicated: Analogical thinking cannot properly be thought of as some sort of special case, to be handled by mechanisms isolated from the main parts of our cognitive system. Rather, it is simply a relatively conspicuous expression of a cognitive capacity which pervades even the most mundane uses of everyday language, but which has not yet received the attention it deserves. We refer here to the ubiquitous phenomenon of generality in word meaning, discussed in detail in E. F. Kelly (1975). This is something very different from "slippage," the primary implementation in *Copycat* of Hofstadter's important and general ideas about the role of "fluidity" in human thinking. "Slippage" for him means a discrete shift from one sharply-defined concept to a different but related concept—for example, from "successor" to "predecessor"—whether triggered by "pressures" or by a random decision. *Generality*, by contrast, involves the deployment of a single concept in semantically appropriate ways to a diversity of novel circumstances. This is distinct on the one hand from *polysemy*, the possession by a general term of multiple distinct senses, and on the other from *vagueness*, under which we include not only human-type uncertainty about the applicability of a general term to particular cases, but also failures of discrimination, as in a connectionist network.

The main thrust of the lengthy discussion in E. F. Kelly (1975), which we will not repeat here, is to show that generality of word meaning is far more pervasive than most psychologists and linguists realize. Its pervasiveness and importance only become apparent when one is forced to confront large numbers of everyday usages of common words side-by-side, an experience that few contemporary cognitive scientists have had. Note also that this fundamental property of word meaning is closely related to the manner in which memory-knowledge "transcends" or "overflows" its expressions in specific episodes of remembering, as discussed in Chapter 4. Neither phenomenon is adequately accounted for by current cognitive theories of "representation," and both have been largely ignored in the vast psychological literature on "concepts" (Komatsu, 1992; Medin & Heit, 1999; E. E. Smith & Medin, 1981). We can only concur with Hofstadter and FARG (1995) that "the question 'what is a concept?' could be said to lie at the crux of cognitive science, and yet concepts still lack a firm scientific basis" (p. 294).

Meanwhile, what must be fully appreciated is that the domain of *metaphor*, which scholars have tended to identify with lofty flights of poetic and artistic imagination and to think of as something special, extends in reality downward to the most pedestrian figures of speech of everyday parlance, where it shades over into ordinary generality. As Emerson (1837/1983) remarked, "language is fossil poetry" (p. 457). But there is an evident inner unity linking highest to lowest, and all are expressions in varying degrees of a fundamental and still-unexplained activity of our cognitive organization.[25]

This already has serious implications for cognitive science, but there is still more to be said. Let us continue for a moment with metaphor and related modes of symbolism. Above all else, these represent attempts to understand, construe, or express something in terms of something else. Philosopher Max Black (1962, 1990) has done a particularly good job, we think, of characterizing this process in a psychologically realistic way. Metaphor breaks rules, but in service of a deeper fidelity. It is inherently creative, for "there can be no rules for 'creatively' violating rules" (Black, 1990, p. 55). Good metaphors illuminate; they express and promote insight, through a sort of tension or "*interanimation*" between individual concepts or large conceptual domains which are kept simultaneously in view. As emphasized particularly by Black, this interanimation often goes far beyond the sort of abstract or literal point-by-point comparison between prespecified and static attributes and relations contemplated by structure-matching theorists such as Gentner (1983). Indeed, and as Myers also suggested, in the most important cases the subject being construed or expressed may itself only become *known*, or at least better known, *as a result* of this symbolic process. Bowra (1955) nicely captures this in his continuing description of creative inspiration: "What begins by being almost unconscious becomes conscious; what is at the start an outburst of energy infused with a vague idea or an undifferentiated vision becomes concrete and definite; what is outside the poet's control is gradually made to submit to his will and judgment" (pp. 5–6).

The critical point here is once again that these more extreme forms of "interanimation" have pedestrian analogs at the core of everyday cognition. This is in fact implied by the phenomenon of generality of word meaning discussed above: Examination of the entries given by desk dictionaries for common words such as "make," "take," "turn," "hand," or "go" reveals that the number of psychologically real meanings is far lower than the number of usages listed, and indeed those numbers vary enormously among commercial dictionaries for every such word. But if this is the case, comprehension of words in context becomes not a matter of *selecting* among large numbers of pre-existing, highly specific, and static meanings, but of mutual adjustment or interanimation involving smaller numbers of more general and elastic ones. E. F. Kelly (1975) argued that an appropriate model or pro-

25. To *describe* this activity, of course, is not to *explain* it. Common to all recent attempts by cognitive psychologists to explain it, from Tversky (1977) to the real-world analogy theorists, is the idea that we can structure the *representations* of the relevant concepts and things in such a way that their "similarity" is intrinsic and can be directly computed from properties of those representations themselves. Formidable difficulties stand in the way of any such project, however, as shown in particular by philosophers such as McClendon (1955) and Goodman (1972). As Goodman summarizes his results, "similarity tends under analysis either to vanish entirely or to require for its explanation just what it purports to explain" (p. 446). For a notable recent attempt to find a way through these difficulties, see Goldstone (1994); but see also our Chapter 1 and below.

totype for contextual understanding is therefore not enforcement of "selection restrictions" (J. J. Katz & Fodor, 1964), but the philosophical notion of "syncategorematicity," originally developed in relation to evaluative concepts such as "good." The basic idea is that the meaning of "good" changes systematically when predicated of violinists, horses, ideas, and so on, but in a manner that is intelligible in terms of the varying natures of the things so labeled. Similarly, the phrases "eat bread" and "eat soup" do not involve different meanings of "eat" (Weinreich, 1966, p. 411) but an adjustment of one more general sense to the different things eaten; a "tiny" elephant is far larger than a "gigantic" mouse, and so on, without end.

Here again we connect with frontline issues in cognitive theory. Whereas most of the work to date on concepts deals only with *categorization*, the principles by which diverse things are grouped together or recognized as instances of a single concept, we wish instead to emphasize the closely related and even more fundamental problem of conceptual *combination*. A similar basic impulse clearly underlies other recent developments such as the work of Lakoff and his colleagues on metaphor, the "generative lexicon" of Pustejovsky (1995), the "cognitive grammar" of Langacker (1990, 1999), the "construction-integration" model of discourse comprehension by Kintsch (1998), and the mutual-constraint "coherence" model of Holyoak and Thagard (1995), subsequently generalized by Thagard (1997, 2000) and applied not only to creativity but to a host of related topics in psychology and philosophy. We welcome all these developments as headed in the right direction, but find all of them fatally flawed by their dependence on the grossly inadequate notational devices presently available for representation and combination of "knowledge." One good example here is that of the real-world analogy programs, discussed above. More generally, most of the work carried out so far on "conceptual combination" hardly gets beyond hackneyed specimens of the "colorful ball" or "pet fish" type. Sooner or later we are going to have to come to grips with the full-blown phenomenology of creative imagination—its coadunative, alembic, and esemplastic powers as conceived by persons such as Coleridge and Myers.

There is one last and even more basic point we wish to highlight here, without much argument, before concluding this section. Cognitive science is also going to have to give up its reliance on the fundamentally flawed idea that semantics can be treated as intrinsic to the sorts of representational structures it employs. In the first instance it is seldom if ever the case that a concept can plausibly be regarded as having a single, fixed structure independent of the circumstances in which it is used. Even more importantly, no such structure, however complex, can fully determine the conditions of its own application. That gap can only be bridged by the intentional activity of a conscious mind with the capacity to use representational forms of *all* sorts—be they words, phrases, sentences, analogies, metaphors, parables, allegories, images, symbols, charts, maps, equations, diagrams, blueprints, models, sketches in sand, or whatever—to achieve and express *insight* about states of affairs in the world. These problems are immensely difficult, and despite the efforts of the early Gestalt psychologists (Mayer, 1995, 1999) present-day cognitive science remains very far from solving them. We can again only concur with Hofstadter when he says candidly that "though few seem to recognize or admit it, ours is a field still searching for its foundations" (Hofstadter & FARG, 1995, p. 376). For related discussion see Chapters 1, 4, and 9.

Summary

Let us now try to summarize this long discussion of "incommensurability," all of it precipitated by Myers's trenchant comments on differences between supraliminal and subliminal forms of mentation. Recent decades have witnessed a welcome renewal of interest among mainstream psychologists in topics such as imagery, analogy, and metaphor that are deeply intertwined with the psychology of genius. In regard to analogy in particular, serious attempts have been made to account for routine "real-world" forms of the phenomenon using conventional cognitive formalisms, but despite claims to the contrary these attempts have produced little if any real progress. The unconventional "microdomain" approach of Hofstadter and FARG (1995) has fared little better, although it is in many ways more interesting. Meanwhile, it has also become evident that the aspects or properties of cognition that make these mid-level problems so intractable in computationalist terms reach not only *upward*, to the even more difficult phenomena associated with genius, but *downward*, to the most mundane forms of everyday cognition. In consonance with Wind's principle, an adequate cognitive psychology of genius will surely accommodate the psychology of everyday cognition, but a truly adequate psychology of everyday cognition is probably not attainable without it.

In this light, more intensive investigation of the cognitive character of subliminal contributions to genius-level creativity is certainly needed. Older psychological theories of creative inspiration, such as those of the various psychoanalysts, as well as E. F. Kelly (1962) and Koestler (1964), have grappled more directly with these core phenomena, descriptively, but fall short of explaining them in a satisfying way. All, significantly, share one central theoretical commitment, which is to seek explanations of creative inspiration entirely in terms of regression to developmentally prior or more "primitive" forms of symbolic activity that persist alongside the more advanced, adult, reality-oriented forms associated with ordinary language. Myers has a different and more radical idea: For him, that "something of strangeness" and the sheer *complexity* as well as the prodigious memory and speed of mental operations displayed by calculating boys, by automatists such as Hélène Smith and Patience Worth, and by major inspirations of genius, all point to something which *transcends* ordinary forms of cognition rather than simply preceding them developmentally. We will return to this theme shortly.

The Creative Personality

Any theory of the creative process entails consequences for a theory of creative personality, and Myers's unusually rich conception of inspiration as subliminal uprush entails a correspondingly rich variety of implications regarding personality structure, both in geniuses themselves and in humanity at large. His views in this area again not only correctly anticipate the main trends in subsequent research, but in some cases point significantly beyond them.

Genius and Mental Illness

We can conveniently begin to delineate these implications by reverting briefly to Myers's discussion of the 19th-century "degeneracy" theorists such as Lombroso, Nisbet, and Nordau. A tradition associating genius with "madness" had of course existed since classical or even pre-classical times, receiving its most influential early expression in Plato's *Phaedrus*. The 17th-century poet John Dryden articulated a widely held view with his famous epigram that "Great wits are sure to madness near allied / And thin partitions do their bounds divide." The degeneracy theorists, however, took this much further. Self-consciously wrapping themselves in the mantle of science, authors of this stripe issued numerous and widely circulated polemics which in effect *identified* genius with "madness," "insanity," or "degeneracy," claiming that such an identification was fully justified by advances in 19th-century biological psychology.

Myers was one of the few who disputed this facile reductionism, and his reasons were cogent. Beginning in section 315 of *HP*, he comments directly on Lombroso as representative of the degeneracy movement. There is first a sampling problem, in that Lombroso included along with real geniuses many persons whose eminence derived from sheer hard work or historical accidents rather than the characteristic psychological qualities of genius itself. Second, his piling up of "anecdotes of the follies and frailties" (*HP*, vol. 1, p. 91) of the eminent is certainly insufficient to establish his central thesis: For one thing, the availability of such stories may reflect little more than the relatively intense scrutiny such persons receive. Subjected to similar scrutiny, Myers points out, "hardly a good easy man among us but might be analysed into half neuropath and half Philistine if it would serve a theory" (*HP*, vol. 1, p. 91).[26]

26. This is particularly true, we should point out, given the excessive latitude of Lombroso's criteria for "eccentricity." These are sometimes bizarre by modern diagnostic standards, including things such as short stature, odd physiognomy or skull shape, left-handedness, leanness, rickets, and excessive yawning. His procedures also share with those of modern investigators such as Jamison (1993) a problem of circularity due to direct overlap between features of creativity itself and features supposedly diagnostic of the form of psychopathol-

Despite these defects in Lombroso's procedures, however, Myers recognizes that "there are underlying facts of great importance which give to his view such plausibility as it possesses" (*HP*, vol. 1, p. 92). What Myers denies is not the *existence* of a relationship between genius and madness, but its *interpretation* by the degeneracy theorists. Abnormality in a statistical sense is not necessarily pathological, Myers contends. What matters is the causal structure underlying the observed correlation. For him that correlation reflects the fact that genius and madness share, as an essential common feature, an unusual openness to the subliminal. The degeneracy theorists, however, had missed a crucial difference—namely, that genius masters its subliminal uprushes, whereas the insane are overwhelmed by theirs.[27] Genius is not degenerate but "progenerate," reflecting increased strength and concentration of inward unifying control (*HP*, vol. 1, p. 70) and increased utilization of subliminal forms of mentation in service of supraliminal purpose. Indeed, in its highest developments genius represents the truest standard of excellence, and a more appropriate criterion of "normality" than conformity to a statistical average.

William James was largely in agreement with these views and expanded on them in the culminating lecture of his Lowell series on "exceptional mental states" (E. Taylor, 1984). Subject to depressive episodes himself, James took special pains to examine in a more detailed way the arguments of the degeneracy theorists, and he identified at least two additional problems of a general sort. First was the issue of overdiagnosis, based on inadequate diagnostic criteria: Against any presumption that hallucinations are invariably diagnostic for psychopathology, for example, James pointed to the demonstrations by Myers and his colleagues that waking hallucinations are not uncommon in the lives of otherwise normal persons (Bentall, 2000; Gurney et al., 1886). Secondly, there are many examples of geniuses, even poetic geniuses, who were paragons of balance and stability. Here James cites Schiller, Browning, and George Sand, along with various members of his own community such as Emerson, Longfellow, Lowell, Whittier, and Oliver Wendell Holmes. Madness therefore is certainly not *necessary* for genius, although it may sometimes combine with intellect and will to produce it. What madness provides in such cases—what *really* is necessary, and can also occur in its absence—is uprushes from the "seething cauldron" of the subliminal, as described by Myers.

This basic Myers/James interpretation of relations between genius and mental illness has been confirmed and refined by subsequent research, including not only clinical and biographical investigations but also experi-

---

ogy with which it is being compared. For Lombroso, for example, "eccentricity" is also indicated by characteristics such as word-coining, originality, and flights of imagination.

27. Compare this statement by Charles Lamb from his remarkable three-page essay "Sanity of True Genius": "The ground of the mistake is, that men, finding in the raptures of the higher poetry a condition of exaltation, to which they have no parallel in their own experience, besides the spurious resemblance of it in dreams and fevers, impute a state of dreaminess and fever to the poet. But the true poet dreams being awake. He is not possessed by his subject but has dominion over it" (E. V. Lucas, 1903, pp. 187–189).

mental and quantitative studies of various types. We will next briefly survey some highlights of this large literature.

The clinical side of things was of course at first mainly in the custody of the Freudian school of psychodynamic theorists, which to a considerable extent followed the degeneracy theorists in emphasizing regressive, unconsciously determined, and seemingly pathological aspects of genius to the exclusion of those aspects of rational, conscious control that Myers and James recognized as equally fundamental to success of the creative enterprise. Freud himself was profoundly ambivalent toward genius and the imagination, greatly admiring them but deeply suspicious of their origins (Storr, 1972). Creative imagination, like the dream, was viewed by Freud as substitute gratification, the disguised expression of unacceptable wishes and impulses. Behind it all there is nothing but a deep inability to confront "reality." Leonardo da Vinci, for example, was characterized by Freud as a repressed homosexual who sublimated his unacceptable urges into scientific curiosity and the production of great works of art. Of course there is little if any historical evidence that Leonardo himself was a closet homosexual, and there have certainly been a great many repressed homosexuals, but few Leonardos. Freud was apparently undeterred by such considerations, however, and legions of his disciples followed his example, producing speculative accounts of wildly varying plausibility of the neurotic origins of various great works of art and literature (see, e.g., W. Phillips, 1957). These psychoanalytic accounts mainly addressed supposed neurotic conflicts of creative geniuses in relation to the thematic content of their works, for as Freud himself had acknowledged in his study of Leonardo, the creative act itself remained unexplained.

We have already described in relation to the creative process how orthodox Freudian theory gradually gave way to reformists such as Kris (1952) and Kubie (1958), who adopted views much closer to those of Myers and James. Kubie's conception of the "preconscious" in particular has a great deal in common with Myers's conception of the subliminal; it is the home of imagination, and the vital source of creativity and dreams, rich in affectively loaded symbolism, analogy, and imagery. While retaining Freud's conception of a truly inaccessible dynamic unconscious which harbors actively repressed and unacceptable wishes and urges, Kubie (1958) treats this as the source not of creativity itself, as in Freud's view, but of limitations and distortions in an otherwise healthy psychological process: In a nutshell, "neurosis corrupts, mars, distorts, and blocks creativeness in every field" (p. 142). Correspondingly, the creative person is one who enjoys an unusual degree of conflict-free intimacy with preconscious processes, and who thus for Kubie as for Myers is a model of psychological health. Closely similar views in regard to art and neurosis were expressed from the point of view of literary theory in an excellent essay by Lionel Trilling (1953).

The psychoanalytic concept of "neurosis" of course corresponds to relatively mild forms of "insanity" or "madness" as understood by the 19th-century degeneracy theorists. As psychiatry advanced and its diagnostic categories and procedures evolved, attention also focused on relations between genius and more severe forms of mental illness, including in particular schizophrenia and the affective spectrum disorders (manic-depressive or bipolar disorder, major depression, etc.). A sizeable literature developed in which increasingly refined diagnostic procedures were applied either retrospectively, to the biographies or autobiographies of outstandingly creative historical personages, or in clinical-type research with living persons of varying degrees of eminence.

We can quickly summarize the main results of this research, which are clear and consistent (Eysenck, 1995; Jamison, 1993; Juda, 1949; Ludwig, 1995; Nettle, 2001; Post, 1994; R. L. Richards, 1981): There is definitely an elevated incidence of significant mental illness among highly creative persons, and in particular an elevated incidence of affective spectrum disorders among poets, writers, and artists. However, this statistical linkage provides no warrant for any direct or thoroughgoing identification between such illnesses and the psychological conditions of creative activity. Even among poets and writers, for example, where the incidence of affective disorders is highest, it falls far short of universality. Conversely, the vast majority of victims of bipolar disorder and severe depression are certainly not creative geniuses. There may also be some overestimation of incidences, since even modern diagnostic manuals have included aspects of creativity as criteria for the relevant diagnostic entities. The DSM-III used by Jamison (1993), for example, included among its criteria for hypomania "sharpened and unusually creative thinking" and "increased productivity, often with unusual and self-imposed working hours" (p. 265). Furthermore, even when overt psychopathology is incontrovertibly present—as it clearly sometimes is—its causal relation to the creativity is not always clear. The higher incidence of depression among artists and writers, for example, may partly be a consequence rather than a cause of the creative life, owing to the relatively greater risks and uncertainties of such life for them as compared, say, with scientists. Conversely, the suffering occasioned by mental illness may translate more directly for them than for scientists into experiences potentially useful for their creative purposes. There is also the important issue of temporal relations between creative production and outbursts of disorder. Severe and chronic disorders such as schizophrenia, for example, typically put an end to whatever of creativity was present beforehand, and severe depression commonly does so as well, at least temporarily.

Most importantly, a central recurring theme amidst all the reported psychopathology is its coexistence with unusual levels of ego strength, manifested in characteristics such as industry, drive, perseverance, organization, discipline, independence of judgment, tolerance of ambiguity and frustration, and determination to master the subject at hand using any available means of expression (Barron, 1958, 1963, 1968, 1969; Dellas & Gaier, 1970, p. 63; Eysenck, 1995, p. 114). Even Jamison (1993, pp. 97–99), despite her somewhat Lombroso-like tendency to emphasize the pathological, clearly acknowledges this characteristic: "There is a great deal of evidence to suggest that, compared to 'normal' individuals, artists, writers, and creative people in general, are both psychologically 'sicker'—that is, they score higher on a wide variety of measures of psychopathology—and psychologically healthier (for example, they show quite elevated scores on measures of self-confidence and ego strength" (p. 97).[28]

This paradoxical combination of characteristics is evident even in the extreme case of manic-depressive illness, which has been especially common in poets and is Jamison's special interest. She cites as emblematic Seamus Heaney's extraordinary description, which Myers would certainly have relished, of the poet Robert Lowell:

> [Lowell] had in awesome abundance the poet's first gift for surrender to those energies of language that heave to the fore matter that will not be otherwise summoned, or that might be otherwise suppressed. Under the ray of his concentration, the molten stuff of the psyche ran hot and unstanched. But its final form was as much beaten as poured, the cooling ingot was assiduously hammered. A fully human and relentless intelligence was at work upon the pleasuring quick of the creative act. He was and will remain a pattern for poets in this amphibiousness, this ability to plunge into the downward reptilian welter of the individual self and yet raise himself with whatever knowledge he gained there out on the hard ledges of the historical present. (Jamison, 1993, p. 99)

Genius occurring in conjunction with manic-depressive illness, in sum, is not a model of genius in general but a special case of the more general model set forth by Myers. It has one key characteristic, however, that makes it especially inviting as a subject for further research. Specifically, the stages of the creative process are in this case temporally segregated to a considerable degree, with the "uprush" of imaginative material—the "touch of fire"—strongly linked to the hypomanic phase of the illness cycle.[29] This circumstance cries out for within-subject neurophysiological and imaging studies of brain conditions accompanying the cyclic emergence of imaginative activity, as Jamison herself observes (pp. 112–113). Not much has yet been accomplished, unfortunately, along these lines.

Together with the other affective-spectrum disorders, manic-depressive illness also forms part of an even larger picture of biological conditions

---

28. Compare Barron (1958, p. 164). Much of the extensive research that Jamison cites in this connection derives from Frank Barron and the Institute for Personality Assessment and Research (IPAR). Interestingly enough, Barron (1969, preface) has revealed that his transition from philosophy to psychology was spurred by reading Myers's *Human Personality* in combination with James's *Principles*, and that this experience profoundly influenced all of his subsequent work.

29. Jamison (1993, pp. 105–113) identifies two principal characteristics which connect the thinking that occurs during this period with imagination as conceived by Myers, James, and Coleridge, among others: First, its extreme fluency, speed, and flexibility; second, its *formal* properties, including unusual forms of categorization and combination, merging of percepts, ideas, and images, highly original associations and analogies, and elevated mood. For her prime illustration of these characteristics, interestingly, she turns to Coleridge.

conducive to creativity. Specifically, Eysenck (1995), Jamison (1993), Nettle (2001), and R. L. Richards, Kinney, Lunde, Benet, and Merzel (1988) have assembled data showing that a capacity for "strong imagination," which may express itself either in psychosis or in creativity, is at least partly heritable. Thus for example healthy relatives of mental patients show much higher levels of creative accomplishment than members of the general population (J. L. Karlsson, 1984), first-degree relatives of creative persons show higher incidence of mental illness (Andreasen, 1987), and genius, like manic-depressive illness, tends to distribute along family lines even when the descendants are adopted by other families (Jamison, 1993; McNeill, 1971). Exactly what the relevant genetic conditions are, and how they translate into brain conditions conducive to strong imaginative activity, again remains to be elucidated, although Eysenck in particular thinks of imagination primarily in terms of "remote associations" and gravitates toward Martindale's account of biological conditions conducive to these. Nettle in effect turns degeneracy theory on its head: Not only does psychosis *not* explain genius, he suggests, but the social value of strong imagination in the form of genius may itself explain the persistence of psychosis, which partially shares its genetic underpinnings.

To summarize the discussion so far, extensive modern research on relations between genius and mental illness has strongly confirmed Myers's central conception of genius as successful cooperation between supraliminal and subliminal modes of cognition. Further confirmation derives from the neglected subject of "art in the insane," which we can discuss only briefly here (see also Grosso, in press). Whereas most of us rely excessively on supraliminal modes of cognition, and fail to reach our full creative potential due to insufficient access to the subliminal, these individuals represent the opposite problem—superabundance of subliminal uprush unchecked by the necessary supraliminal control. As Kris reported (1952), "every mental institution in western civilization has its inmates who cover every scrap of paper, every free place on wall or window sill, with words or shapes; there are some who carve with any instrument at hand in any material to which they can gain access or who model in bread if there is no clay" (p. 153).

These phenomena, which have largely been suppressed by the advent of antipsychotic medications, formerly occurred in something like 1–2% of hospitalized patients, usually schizophrenics (Kris, 1952). The creative activity typically began spontaneously, often in persons with no relevant prior training or experience, and went on at great intensity for periods ranging from weeks to decades. The sheer volume of the material, as well as its symbolic richness and complexity, is sometimes staggering: Adolf Wölfli, for example, a paranoid schizophrenic, worked from 1908 to 1930 on a massive narrative that amounts to a personal mythology, a mixture of authentic personal history and cosmic fantasy, interwoven with prose, poetry, pictorial illustrations, and musical compositions. His corpus ultimately comprised some 25,000 packed pages, along with hundreds of drawings, many of which now hang next to the work of Paul Klee in Switzerland (Spoerri,

1997). Morganthaler (1921/1992) was fascinated by Wölfli's relentless creative output and observed the inmate at his worktable as he wrote and drew. Wölfli would talk about the content of the work but had no idea how he did what he did. Morganthaler observed that he worked from no previous sketch and without conscious plan, yet the entire ongoing oeuvre seemed guided by a single, compulsive, unifying intelligence (MacGregor, 1989).

These phenomena clearly have more to do with automatism than with conscious craft, and belong with the family of mediumistic creativity discussed above. Wölfli shares with Hélène Smith in particular a profile of extraordinary multi-modal creativity powerfully shaped by persistent automatisms. All this of course is consistent with Myers's notion of subliminal intelligence. Prinzhorn (1972/1995) viewed the phenomena in very Myers-like terms as outpourings of a distinct and fundamental image-making or world-generating capacity of the human mind, whereas Kris (1952) interpreted them from his orthodox Freudian perspective as unusually clear expressions of the primary-process mechanisms at work in ordinary dream-formation. From either point of view, the art of the insane provides a potentially important window on the workings of creative imagination and deserves greater attention in that light.

Genius as Personality in Transformation

The brunt of our effort so far has been devoted to showing that Myers's central conception of genius as successful cooperation between supraliminal and subliminal forms of mentation has been strongly confirmed by subsequent research, and that this has significant ramifications even for contemporary mainstream cognitive science. This is by no means the whole story, however, for his theory of genius as described so far is embedded within a more comprehensive theoretical framework that pushes the envelope of current mainstream thinking about both genius itself and human personality in general even further (Chapter 2). We will conclude by sketching these even more challenging features of his theory of genius.

For Myers, as we have said, genius is "evolutive," in contrast to the "dissolutive" phenomena associated with hysteria and other mental disorders. He was profoundly influenced by Darwin, and strove to remain broadly consistent with Darwin's evolutionary outlook while accommodating the special facts being brought to light by psychical research. Myers portrays genius as the norm of the future, representing a condition of improved psychic integration. The genius thus stands for him among the vanguard on an evolutionary track which humanity as a whole is pursuing, a track that leads "in the direction of greater complexity in the perceptions which he forms of things without, and of greater concentration in his own will and thought,—in that response to perceptions which he makes from within" (*HP*, vol. 1, pp. 77–78). This evolution, moreover, consists "not only of gradual *self-adaptation* to a known environment, but of *discovery* of an environment, always there, but unknown" (*HP*, vol. 1, p. 95). In Myers's "cosmical" theory of evolution, this process of progressive discovery itself reflects progressive mobilization of faculties initially latent in the subliminal, including faculties (such as telepathy) which he believed cannot be regarded as products of ordinary Darwinian ("planetary" or "terrene") evolution.

Although the main lines of Myers's argument for this more comprehensive and obviously controversial view of evolution are initially deployed in his chapter on genius, we need not attempt to evaluate them here. Myers himself recognized that the phenomena of genius, while *consistent* with his enlarged conception of the subliminal, cannot in themselves suffice to *establish* it: "The 'inspirations of genius' which seem to spring full-armed into our ken from the depths of our being must count as a form of subliminal faculty, although no theory of such faculty could be based solely upon mental products so closely interwoven with supraliminal or voluntary thinking" (*HP*, vol. 1, p. 220). Following Myers's own lead, therefore, we will defer discussion of his larger evolutionary theory to Chapter 9, when we will have a larger supply of relevant facts at hand, and focus instead more narrowly here on its expressions in the realm of genius.

The Creative *Nisus*: A Drive Toward Wholeness

For Myers, the essential link between genius and madness is that they both reflect, in their differing ways, a "perturbation which masks evolution," an instability caused by the evolving dynamic interplay between supraliminal and subliminal modes of mentation. Genius, however, effects fuller "co-operation of the submerged with the emergent self" (*HP*, vol. 1, p. 96), and in this way it expresses a *nisus* (striving or drive) toward greater psychic integration or wholeness that Myers sees as a fundamental property of human nature. Thus, he says, the waking personality "will endeavor to attain an ever completer control over the resources of the personality, and it will culminate in what we term *genius* when it has unified the subliminal as far as possible with the supraliminal in its pursuit of deliberate waking ends" (*HP*, vol. 1, p. 152). Genius, in short, draws upon hidden resources of the Self or Individuality in service of a more flourishing conscious life.

Expressions of such a *nisus* can be discerned in all the various forms and levels of creative activity described above. It can be mobilized, for example, in the treatment of cases of secondary personality (MPD/DID; see our Chapter 5). Thus, Victor Race eventually began to take on the superior qualities of his secondary personality, and early investigators such as Janet and Binet came to understand more generally that their patients' multiple selves represented opportunities for re-integration, healing, and enlargement of the waking personality. Similar positions have been reached by two thoughtful contemporary students of MPD, Stephen Braude (1995) and Adam Crabtree (1985), from their distinctive vantage points in philosophy of mind and clinical practice, respectively. Crabtree (1985) specifically recommends that the goal of therapy in such cases should be "to assist the creation of a full-blown personality that embodies mixed elements already existing within the individual in a disorganized way" (p. 225).

Similar integrative tendencies can often be seen at work in the related but more benign domain of mediumistic creativity. The highly functional Hélène Smith, for example, said of herself that "I have never been so clear-sighted, so lucid, so capable of judging rapidly on all points, as since I have been developed as a medium" (*HP*, vol. 2, p. 131). No one disputed these observations, according to Myers, and his colleague Flournoy, who studied her extensively, went even further, declaring that those who have looked into mediumship most deeply "see in it a faculty superior, advantageous, healthy, of which hysteria is a form of degenerescence, a pathological parody, a morbid caricature" (*HP*, vol. 2, p. 132). Prince (1927/1964) responded in similar fashion to Professor Cory's characterization of Pearl Curran as "disintegrated," noting that "to all appearances, and judging by her ability to meet the crises and tests of life, she is splendidly integrated" (p. 462). Indeed, Prince continues, "since somehow remarkable literature has resulted, and according to all testimony her own mentality has been improved and her life made happier and more effective since the arrival of 'Patience Worth', it seems a pity that we cannot start an epidemic of disintegration." We generally agree with these sentiments, and we deplore the fact that the scientific study of trance mediumship, so ably begun by persons of the stature of Myers, James, Flournoy, Prince, and others has been so neglected in more recent times. The psychology and neurophysiology of trance mediumship, and its impact on the development of personality, cries out for further investigation using modern research tools.[30]

A drive toward integration is also observable among creative persons suffering from various forms of overt psychopathology. Even Wölfli, for example, appeared through his writing and art to gain some degree of mastery over the sexual and aggressive impulses that had led to his hospitalization. Writers such as Kubie (1958) and Trilling (1953) discuss in depth how highly creative persons in effect utilize creative work to overcome the fragmentation of their own personalities by neurotic conflicts, and in so doing may help us to overcome ours. Jamison (1993) and especially Storr (1972) articulate similar views regarding the healing power of art, extending them to more extreme forms of mental illness including in particular manic-depressive illness.

Relatively healthy geniuses display a similar *nisus*, however. Ghiselin (1952) states that in general "the inventor, whether artist or thinker, creates the structure of his psychic life by means of his words" (p. 13). This theme also pervades the discussion by critic Harold Bloom (2002) of 100 geniuses of literature. Genius in Bloom's view reflects an "aboriginal" compulsion

---

30. We do not mean to deny, however, that careless or superficial engagement with mediumship and associated practices such as the use of ouija boards and the like can sometimes result from or lead to psychological problems. We also wish to dissociate ourselves from most current commercial, stage, or TV "mediumship."

toward the expansion of human consciousness, and thus at the top of his list stands Shakespeare—"a consciousness shaped by all the consciousnesses that he imagined. He remains, presumably forever, our largest instance of the uses of literature for life, which is the work of augmenting consciousness" (p. 12). Storr (1972) takes as paradigmatic a statement by composer Aaron Copland, who, having first explained that the compulsion to create is at bottom a need for self-expression, continues as follows:

> But why is the job never done? Why must one always begin again? The reason for the compulsion to renewed creativity, it seems to me, is that each added work brings with it an element of self-discovery. I must create in order to know myself, and since self-knowledge is a never-ending search, each new work is only a part-answer to the question "Who am I?" and brings with it the need to go on to other and different part-answers. (p. 223)

The polymath Johann Wolfgang von Goethe beautifully exemplifies Myers's view: "What he wanted was *totality*; he fought the mutual extraneousness of reason, senses, feeling, and will...he disciplined himself to wholeness, he *created* himself," says Nietzsche of Goethe in the *Twilight of the Gods*. This "resplendent instance of jovial genius" himself confirmed, in a letter to von Humboldt, that he strove incessantly toward a synthesis of the practical and imaginative elements of his nature, a condition in which "consciousness and unconsciousness will interact like warp and weft, an image I am so fond of, uniting the human faculties" (Beddow, 1989, p. 111).

It is significant here that Goethe also epitomized for the Swiss analytical depth-psychologist Carl Jung the process of *individuation*, "the central concept of my psychology" (Jung, 1961/1965, p. 209). We mentioned in Chapter 5 the influence which Myers apparently exerted on Jung, and this concept of a drive to individuation, essentially equivalent to Myers's *nisus*, provides one striking expression of that influence. More generally, it would not be too much of a caricature to say that whereas Freud and his school became preoccupied with the "rubbish heap" side of Myers's broad conception of the subliminal, Jung tended like Myers himself in the opposite direction, toward a preoccupation with the subliminal as "treasure house." Jung was much more in the grip of von Hartmann and the extremist wing of the German romantic tradition, however, and his writing has a tendency to dissolve into depths of obscurity which we like many others sometimes find impenetrable. Nevertheless, we feel there is much of value in his work, especially in regard to creativity. Jungians in general adopt a far more positive stance than Freud toward imagination, symbolism, and creativity, emphasizing their role in self-discovery and self-integration (Storr, 1972, chap. 16 & chap. 18). In contrast to Freud, for example, Neumann (1959) treats Leonardo's genius, and genius in general, as a fundamentally transformative and integrative process of personal growth. The Jungian practice of "active imagination" combines creativity with psychotherapy in a manner also consistent with Myers's view of genius. Described by Barbara Hannah (1981) as the "most powerful tool in Jungian psychology for achieving wholeness" (p. 2), this is essentially a technique for actively engaging the subliminal; one waits, for example, for emotionally charged imagery to well up from below, and then actively attempts to express its meanings concretely in paint, words, gesture, or vocalization.

Similar views regarding the contributions of imagination to psychotherapy, and more generally of creativity to personal growth or "self-actualization," have been advanced by persons such as Achterberg (1985), Assagioli (1965/1971), Maslow (1968), Sheikh (1984), and Storr (1972), among many others. This leads inexorably to the potentially important but currently vexed practical topic of creativity "training," around which a large and lucrative commercial industry has in recent decades sprung up. We agree for the most part with critics such as Beyerstein (1999), R. J. Sternberg and Lubart (1999), and Weisberg (1986) that existing training procedures are not grounded in an adequate psychological theory of creativity, and that empirical evidence of their validity and effectiveness is in extremely short supply. Nevertheless, we also feel with Nickerson (1999) cautious optimism that real progress in this direction may be possible—particularly, we suggest, in the context of Myers's theoretical and practical investigations of subliminal processes.

Myers himself distinctly foresaw this possibility: "Man is in course of evolution," he says, and "it may be in his power to hasten his own evolution in ways previously unknown" (*HP*, vol. 1, p. 23). "What advance can we make in inward mastery?" he wonders; "how far extend our grasp over the whole range of faculty with which we are obscurely endowed?" (*HP*, vol. 1, p. 70). Although Myers himself does not explicitly address these questions, it follows from his general theory that any procedures which encourage increased but controlled interaction with the subliminal can potentially move us in the desired direction. In addition to "active imagination" and creative work themselves, one thinks naturally in terms of cultivating phenomena such as ordinary dreams, lucid dreaming, and hypnagogia, which most persons can probably do, and perhaps—in those with the requisite susceptibilities—activities such as automatic writing or drawing, crystal-gazing or scrying, trance mediumship, and deep hypnosis.

We should also mention in this connection that there is a very large cross-cultural literature dealing with procedures for controlled production of altered states of consciousness and associated phenomena. The shaman, as a specialist in these "archaic techniques of ecstasy," represents in effect the creative genius of preliterate society (Eliade, 1964; Nettle, 2001). M. Murphy (1992) has situated this form of genius within an even larger context, drawing upon a vast array of anthropological, psychological, and biomedical data to provide a comprehensive natural history of psychophysical transformative practices. From this larger point of view the shamanistic vocation can be seen as one species of a broader genus of personality-development technologies (Grosso, in press). In addition to utilizing particular techniques of the sorts identified above, such personality-development processes might wisely begin by identifying and building upon whatever creative inclinations each person antecedently displays. The range of such inclinations, Myers suggests, could be wide, for "genius may be recognized in every region of thought and emotion. In each direction a man's everyday self may be more or less permeable to subliminal impulses" (*HP*, vol. 1, p. 116). Comic genius or wit, for example, has been recognized by authorities as divergent in outlook as Freud, Kris, Bergson, and Koestler as being closely related to the higher forms of genius in its manner of drawing upon subliminal operations.

Art as Transformative

Creativity in a given domain might also be enhanced more directly, through exposure to outstanding examples of genius in that domain. We have in mind here the obscure but important topic of the response of receptive human observers to great works of art. That something more is involved than purely intellectual appreciation seems certain. Freud in his characteristic way pathologizes this "something extra." Art provides substitute gratification, a means of escape from reality, and the artist enables us to derive aesthetic pleasure from his fantasies by formally disguising their forbidden origins in the unconscious (Freud, 1920/1968, pp. 384–385). For Jung, in typical contrast, art provides more than aesthetic pleasure; indeed, to the extent that we can imaginatively involve ourselves in a great work of art we vicariously participate in the transformative, integrative process effected by its creator, and are in some measure transformed and integrated ourselves. Some such "resonance" effect may account, for example, for John Stuart Mill's famous declaration that he was healed by reading Wordsworth's poetry, and for the fact that Shakespeare "augments" not just his own consciousness, but ours as well. Thus a major goal of creative education in general, as for Harold Bloom (2002), should be "to activate the genius of appreciation" in students, potentiating the transfer of this transformative power (p. 3). It is surely also relevant here that persons who rate high on objective scales of aesthetic judgment also tend to rate high on measures of creativity (Child, 1973, pp. 65–67).

But there is more to be said, for not *all* works of art have such transformative effects, or have them to the same degree. As theoreticians of aesthetics from Longinas forward have almost unanimously contended, there seems to be a deep inner connection between the psychological phenomenon of inspiration and the transformative power of art. At the level of *persons*, for example, it is simply an empirical fact that virtually every major contributor to the western cultural canon who has commented on the creative process has spoken appreciatively of the role of inspiration (Ghiselin, 1952). And the relationship goes even deeper, apparently, for it is typically not their creative work in general but their *best* work that is described as so benefitting.

That this is not simply the opinion of the creator but also involves qualities inherent in the creative product itself is argued explicitly in the case of poetry by Bowra (1955, pp. 19–25). "Poems which are known to have been conceived by their authors in inspired moments are often those which move us most powerfully," he says, stating a potentially testable hypothesis. Furthermore, "if we look into the question, we see that inspired poetry has certain qualities which are responsible for its hold on us and for our continued delight in it." The qualities that Bowra goes on to identify need not occupy us in detail, for they overlap strongly, and unsurprisingly, with the qualities of creative imagination as delineated by persons such as Coleridge and Myers.

Transpersonal Roots of Genius

And here we return at last to the main thread of Myers's own explicit argument—the thread we temporarily put aside at the end of our discussion of "incommensurability" between supraliminal and subliminal modes of expression. As we indicated there, Myers does not believe that creative imagination can be fully explained in terms of facts of personal biography, developmentally earlier or more "primitive" forms of symbolic activity, and the like. In the last 14 pages of the genius chapter he develops his alternative view, according to which the roots of imagination, of expression, and indeed of genius itself, lie much deeper.

The essence of Myers's conception is that both human personality and nature as a whole have complex, multilevel organizations, that these organizations are in some meaningful sense "parallel," and that "inner" and "outer" somehow mingle at the deepest level. Like Coleridge, who warred incessantly against "the despotism of the eye," Myers believes that ordinary supraliminal perceptual and cognitive processes reveal only relatively superficial aspects of the far wider and deeper environment, mostly unknown, in which we are continuously immersed. The subliminal reaches further into this complex reality, however, and can report what it finds using its own characteristic modes of symbolic expression. Thus genius, the distinctive characteristic of which is "the large infusion of the subliminal in its mental output" (*HP*, vol. 1, p. 97), provides means for *discovery* of this hidden environment.

Views of this sort were of course especially characteristic of the 19th-century English romantic poets (Abrams, 1953; Bowra, 1955; Prescott, 1922), although contemporary American writers of the "transcendentalist" school held similar views. Emerson (1837/1983), for example, says of the genius that "in going down into the secrets of his own mind, he has descended into the secrets of all minds" (p. 64); and not just of minds, but of nature as well, for "nature is the opposite of the soul, answering to it part for part. One is seal, and one is print. Its beauty is the beauty of his own mind. Its laws are the laws of his own mind" (p. 56).

Among later psychologists, the figure who comes closest to Myers is again Carl Jung (1952), who speaks like Myers of true symbolic expression as "the expression of something existent in its own right, but imperfectly known" (p. 215). Jung specifically argues that in the highest or "visionary" mode of poetic creation, epitomized for him by Part 2 of Goethe's *Faust*, what is expressed derives from the deepest stratum of the psyche, a transpersonal region which he calls the "collective unconscious," where inner and outer come together (see also Neumann, 1959). We ourselves think that the sorts of comparative and cross-cultural investigations of "archetypal" symbolism carried out both by Jung himself and by others such as Joseph Campbell are broadly consistent with, and potentially enrich, Myers's conception of the subliminal and its operation, but it cannot be denied that Jung's own writings about archetypes and the collective unconscious are especially obscure, and certainly they have had little if any impact on mainstream psychology.

Creativity and Psi

Why then should the mainstream pay more attention to Myers than to Jung in regard to transpersonal aspects of genius? In a nutshell, because here as elsewhere Myers's system is far better grounded empirically, as demonstrated both by the present book and by *HP* itself. In his characteristic way, Myers begins in section 331 of *HP* to marshal arguments for his enlarged conception of the roots of genius. Other parts of *HP* serve to demonstrate that subliminal products are prone in general to be carriers of supernormal knowledge, and the question therefore naturally arises whether this is also true of the subliminal uprushes associated with genius.

Myers asks first whether such uprushes, like those of a medium or sensitive, tend to display supernormal knowledge of "definite facts." There is of course a tradition going back to classical times that links these two domains: The Muses, for example, were the daughters of Memory and possessed the gift of prophecy. Although Myers recognizes that these gifts may be somewhat separable in the subliminal region, he clearly expects them to overlap to some degree, and he declares unequivocally that remarkable instances of supernormal knowledge in persons of genius "undoubtedly do exist" (*HP*, vol. 1, p. 108). He declines to discuss "the most conspicuous and most important" of such instances, by which he means events in the lives of the great personages of various religions, and he refers briefly instead to two other historical geniuses—Socrates and Joan of Arc—whom he himself had investigated extensively. Both cases, details of which are provided elsewhere (Myers, 1889a; *HP*, vol. 2, pp. 95–103), involved conspicuous episodes of trance and automatism, accompanied (more clearly in the case of Joan) by infusions of definite supernormal knowledge.

Myers drops the subject at this point and moves on, but in light of subsequent developments more can now be said. First, many additional instances have come to light of spontaneous psi experiences in the lives of eminent persons, a particularly good collection being that of Prince (1928/1963). These demonstrate clearly that psi occurs in highly creative persons, but not necessarily that it occurs more frequently or dramatically in them than in the less creative. Two lines of modern experimental evidence, however, more clearly confirm Myers's expectation of linkages between creativity and psi.

Both trace back to a seminal paper by R. A. White (1964), who sought to identify psychological conditions associated with the unusual levels of success in some older "free-response" ESP experiments (these had used materials such as objects and drawings, rather than ESP cards or the like, as the targets). Her resulting "recipe" for psi success strikingly parallels the Wallas/Hutchinson model of the creative process: Specifically, following an initial period of sensory isolation and relaxation, it prescribes a deliberate demand for the needed information (preparation) followed by waiting and release of effort (incubation), spontaneous emergence of information into consciousness (inspiration, usually in the form of involuntary visual or auditory imagery), and evaluation or elaboration of the information so retrieved (verification). White's analysis was one of the main influences leading to Honorton's (1977) model of psi and internal attention states, and to the large body of successful psi research using "Ganzfeld" procedures (Alvarado, 1998; Braud, 1978; see also the Appendix).

A number of additional experimental studies have sought more directly to measure relationships between creativity and psi performance. Both creativity and psi have generally been in short supply in these studies, unfortunately, and most have relied excessively, in our opinion, on psychometrically suspect "creativity" measures of the conventional sorts ("divergent thinking" and the like; see, e.g., Barron & Harrington, 1981; Dellas & Gaier, 1970; Hocevar, 1981). Nevertheless, some order has begun to emerge, particularly since the advent of the Ganzfeld procedures. Free-response Ganzfeld studies carried out by a variety of investigators and laboratories have now also clearly indicated that "creative" groups such as musicians, artists, and writers perform conspicuously better than unselected subjects, averaging something over 40% direct hits where only 25% would be expected by chance (Dalton, 1997; N. J. Holt, Delanoy, & Roe, 2004; Schlitz & Honorton, 1992).

In sum, although much remains to be done to sort out details of the relationship between creativity and psi, that such a relationship exists now seems beyond reasonable doubt. We emphasize again that this confirms a specific expectation flowing directly from Myers's theory of genius.[31]

Genius and Mysticism

Beyond occasionally providing supernormal access to definite facts of the ordinary kind, the subliminal uprushes of genius reveal, Myers thinks, that we are "capable of a deeper than sensorial perception, of a direct knowledge of facts of the universe outside the range of any specialised organ" (*HP*, vol. 1, p. 111). In support of this thesis he appeals first to the

31. Another aspect of this relationship, which we will not attempt to develop further here, concerns possible psi contributions to the creative process itself, and perhaps to some cases of "simultaneous discovery." Mark Twain (1900), who was a firm believer in "mental telegraphy," took special interest in this subject.

poet Wordsworth, and especially to his unique autobiographical poem *The Prelude*, published posthumously and dedicated to his friend Coleridge (see Wordsworth, Abrams, & Gill, 1979). "Most poets have been Platonists," Myers observes, and "their influence tends to swell that ancient stream of idealistic thought which lies at the root of all civilised religions" (*HP*, vol. 1, p. 109). Wordsworth, a member of Bloom's top 100, is typical in experiencing his moments of inspiration as moments of entrance or insight into a normally hidden spiritual environment that somehow undergirds or interpenetrates the everyday, observable world. By means of the "auxiliar light" of his poetic imagination, Myers suggests, Wordsworth obtained "a vague but genuine consciousness" of this invisible world. His poetry, which had earlier provoked Coleridge's extensive investigations of the creative imagination, epitomizes for Myers the symbolic process essential to all great art, "which abandons logical definiteness of statement for the sake of a nearer approach to truth hidden in the ideal world" (*HP*, vol. 1, p. xxx). Wordsworth's testimony on these matters was especially convincing to Myers, not merely because of its unmatched volume and evident candor, but because "he, if any man, has kept his mind, as Bacon advised, concentric to the universe" (*HP*, vol. 1, p. 111).[32]

The outreach of the subliminal, moreover, is not purely intellectual or "telaesthetic" in character, for it is motivated and guided by affective factors, and in particular by a sense of *beauty*. Here Myers appeals to Plato himself, drawing upon his conception of love as expressed by the prophetess Diotima in the *Symposium* (192–212). Love for Myers is the foundation of both genius and religion, religion being conceived in its essence as genius of the spiritual realm. Love draws the genius ever forward, ascending stage by stage in Plato's characteristic fashion from beautiful *objects* to beautiful *ideas* and ultimately to the archetype of absolute beauty itself, whereupon "beholding beauty with the eye of the mind, he will be enabled to bring forth, not images of beauty, but realities (for he has hold not of an image but of a reality)" (Jowett, 1892/1937, p. 335). For Myers as for Plato, love, beauty, and truth ultimately merge in a state of exalted consciousness.

Having expressed in such soaring terms his deepest personal intuitions, Myers concludes by contrasting his view of genius with the conventional one, reverting for this purpose to his "diagrammatic" example of genius, the calculating boy. What is the ultimate source of this strange ability, he wonders. He acknowledges that some sort of spontaneous genetic variation may be involved; indeed, this hypothesis, "being hardly more than a mere restatement of the facts,...cannot help being true, so far as it goes" (*HP*, vol. 1, p. 117). But Myers doubts that the biological variation itself can explain those facts. His own answer is that the ultimate source of Dase's computational faculty lies in some sort of ideal world in which "the multiplication

---

32. It is also of some importance here that Myers was socially connected to Wordsworth's family, had met him as a child, and had previously written a monograph about him informed by intimate acquaintance with the poet's family history and private correspondence (Myers, 1880/1929).

table is, so to speak, in the air" (*HP*, vol. 1, p. 119). Thus, as in the case of other supernormal phenomena of subliminal origin, biological variation did not *create* but only *revealed* Dase's ability: "By some chance of evolution—some sport—a vent-hole was opened at this one point between the different strata of his being, and a subliminal uprush carried his computative faculty into the open day" (*HP*, vol. 1, p. 119).[33] The progress of evolution, epitomized in genius, consists largely in the progressive revelation and integration of such latent subliminal faculty and, in this way, fuller discovery of this ideal world.

Myers ends here, acknowledging that his grand theoretical vision of genius as personality in evolution goes beyond what the science of his day can guarantee, and returns to the sober exposition of matter-of-fact issues that characterizes the great bulk of his book. How does all this relate, we must now ask, to a contemporary psychology of genius?

It probably could go without saying that few if any mainstream psychologists of the past century would have taken these more challenging elements of Myers's theory of genius at all seriously, had they ever been exposed to them. Nor have the various humanistic and transpersonal psychologists who have advocated Myers-like views from the margins of the field shown much awareness of the additional strength their positions could derive from Myers's relentlessly empirical approach to an enlarged scientific psychology. Both groups, we suggest, would do well to revisit Myers's theoretical challenge in light of more recent developments.

To begin, the Neoplatonic elements in Myers's account of genius no longer appear as radical as they might have even a few decades ago. The sense of beauty, for example, has increasingly been recognized as playing a vital role in creative activity in all fields from mathematics and science to the arts. Koestler (1964) in particular had urged this view upon the early cognitive psychologists, without much success, declaring for example that "beauty is a function of truth, truth a function of beauty. They can be separated by analysis, but in the lived experience of the creative act—and of its re-creative echo in the beholder—they are as inseparable as thought is inseparable from emotion" (p. 331). A. I. Miller (2001) documents in detail the role played by a sense of beauty in both Picasso and Einstein. Even Poincaré, in what surely is one of the most mechanistic accounts ever provided of the creative process, invoked the notion of a subliminal aesthetic "sieve" that would only pass through to waking consciousness, among the innumerable "combinations of mental atoms" mechanically formed by unconscious processes, those whose "elegance" would make them of real mathematical interest. The contemporary computationalist Hofstadter makes the point even more directly, saying "I feel that responsiveness to *beauty*, and its close

33. Treffert (1989) comes fairly close to Myers here, concluding that we must conceive the skills of prodigious savants as emerging out of some sort of "collective unconscious." In such persons, Treffert says, "access to the rules of music or rules of mathematics, for example, is so extensive that some ancestral (inherited) memory must exist to account for that access" (p. 220). Unlike Myers, of course, Treffert hopes to locate this "ancestral memory" in the biology.

cousin, *simplicity*, plays a central role in high-level cognition, and I expect that this will gradually come to be more clearly recognized as cognitive science progresses" (Hofstadter & FARG, 1995, p. 318). That it is in fact being so recognized is evident, for example, from R. J. Sternberg and Davidson's (1995) book on the nature of insight, in the foreword to which Janet Metcalfe welcomes this as something novel; many of the contributors, she says, "remark on the joy that is felt with creative insights and also on the appreciation for beauty that characterizes creative people. This aspect of the phenomenology of insight, until very recently, has been neglected as being too warm and soft for cool, hard Cognitive Science" (p. xi).

Most mainstream psychologists will of course hold out hope that the sense of beauty itself will ultimately prove within reach of conventional biologically-based thinking. We doubt it, but will not argue that point here. Much more serious problems, however, are posed by the "telaesthetic" aspect of creative intuition, its capacity to penetrate beyond the current horizon of knowledge to real "facts of the universe."

Myers in fact considerably *underestimated* the strength of his case in this area, for poets are not the only Platonists, and the products of creative intuition are often anything but vague. We refer here especially to pure mathematicians and mathematical physicists, nearly all of whom are Platonists of some description. For Einstein, for example, music and physics were closely linked:

> He imagined Mozart plucking melodies out of the air as if they were ever present in the universe, and he thought of himself as working like Mozart, not merely spinning theories but responding to Nature, in tune with the cosmos....He thought of both musical and physical truths as Platonic forms that the mind must intuit. Great music cannot be "created" any more than great physics can be deduced strictly from experimental data. Some aesthetic sense of the universe is necessary for both. (A. I. Miller, 2001, p. 186)[34]

Another Nobel laureate in physics, Eugene Wigner (1960), has spoken of "the unreasonable effectiveness of mathematics," its ability to describe fundamental processes in the physical world to astonishing levels of accuracy. This Platonic theme has been developed most vigorously and explicitly in recent years by mathematician Roger Penrose (1989, 1994, 1997), chiefly in relation to mathematical concepts although he clearly presupposes that such a Platonic world may contain "other absolutes, such as the Good and the Beautiful" as well (Penrose, 1997, p. 1).

---

34. Myers held similar views in regard to music, which for him was a quintessential expression of subliminal faculty. "We know the difficulty of explaining its rise on any current theory of the evolution of human faculty. We know that it is like something discovered, not like something manufactured;—like wine found in a walled-up cellar, rather than like furniture made in the workshop above" (*HP*, vol. 1, p. 103). Mozart, for Myers as for Einstein, is the prime example. Although we will not pursue this subject further here, music remains even now resistant to conventional forms of explanation.

Further examples can readily be found in the realm of pure mathematics. Hadamard (1949, chap. 8) briefly discusses some cases of "paradoxical" intuition, including in particular discoveries by Fermat, Riemann, and Galois of correct mathematical results that were not obvious and that went far beyond any possibility of proof by means of the mathematics available at the time. Indeed, some of the proofs were only accomplished following development of whole new areas of mathematics over periods ranging from decades to centuries. Hadamard himself specifically suggests, like Myers, that such intuitions arise from unusually deep strata of the psyche, and that they sometimes emerge in the form of automatisms.

These properties are also found in the extraordinary and well-documented life of the modern mathematical genius Srinivas Ramanujan (Eysenck, 1995, pp. 195–201; Kanigel, 1991; Newman, 1948). There were no recognizable mathematicians in Ramanujan's family, and he received only a patchy formal training in the course of a generally unhappy educational experience in the schools of his native south India. Nevertheless, between the ages of 16 and 26, ignited by what amounted to little more than a dry compendium of some 5000 known mathematical equations, this largely self-taught prodigy managed not only to recapitulate single-handedly a sizeable fraction of the history of Western mathematics but to generate an astonishing volume and variety of novel results in number theory as well. Discovered in 1913 by the distinguished British mathematician G. H. Hardy, Ramanujan continued this prodigious outpouring until his untimely death in 1920 at the age of 33. Some of his most important theorems have already taken decades to prove, and his crammed notebooks will continue to occupy mathematicians for generations to come. His work has found application in areas as diverse as blast-furnace design, manufacture of plastics and telephone cables, cancer research, statistical mechanics, and computer science. On Hardy's informal scale of natural mathematical ability, on which most of us would rate close to 0 and Hardy placed himself only at 25, the magnificent David Hilbert ranks an 80, and Ramanujan stands all by himself at 100.

All the main ingredients of Myers's conception of genius are conspicuously present in this case. First there is extraordinary memory; Hardy recounts, for example, that upon his informing Ramanujan of the number of a taxi in which he had just arrived for a visit, Ramanujan exclaimed at once that this number, 1729, is the smallest integer expressible as the sum of two cubes in two different ways.

Second and more important, his biography is replete with signs of automatism. Some examples: "It was the goddess Namagiri, he would tell his friends, to whom he owed his mathematical gifts. Namagiri would write the equations on his tongue. Namagiri would bestow mathematical insight in his dreams" (Kanigel, 1991, p. 36). "Another time, in a dream, he saw a hand write across a screen made red by flowing blood, tracing out elliptic integrals" (p. 66). This appearance of drops of blood in his dreams signified the presence of the god Narahimsa; then "scrolls containing the most complicated mathematics used to unfold before his eyes" (p. 281). Unfortunately, neither Hardy nor apparently Ramanujan himself took much interest in observing or reporting these psychological phenomena.

Ramanujan's theorems were "elegant, unexpected, and deep" (p. 206). Mathematicians of great ability, including Hardy among many others, were "enraptured" by his work, and specifically by "its richness, beauty, and mystery—its sheer mathematical loveliness" (pp. 349–350). He was not often wrong, and even when he *was* wrong (as in some early work on the distribution of prime numbers), the incorrect results still exuded this peculiar atmosphere of mathematical beauty. Yet, as Hardy himself observed, "all his results, new or old, right or wrong, had been arrived at by a process of mingled argument, intuition, and induction, of which he was entirely unable to give any coherent account" (p. 216).

Ramanujan was also an overt Platonist, Indian style. "He pictured equations as products of the mind of God" (p. 282). Mathematical reality exists independently of us, and is discovered, not made; "for him, numbers and their mathematical relationships fairly threw off clues to how the universe fit together. Each new theorem was one more piece of the Infinite unfathomed" (p. 66). In this matter at least, Ramanujan, the apotheosis of intuition, was in complete accord with his colleague and mentor Hardy, the master of proof.

Creative imagination on this scale, we submit, fairly beggars the theoretical apparatus available to contemporary cognitive science, its "associations," predicate-calculus "representations," and all the rest. We make no exception here of the recent attempt by Lakoff and Núñez (2000) to account for the origins of mathematics in terms of Lakoff's more general theory of "embodied cognition." In brief, these authors argue that a fundamental cognitive process of "conceptual metaphor" can fully explain the progressive elaboration of systems of increasingly abstract mathematical ideas, both historically and ontogenetically. From this point of view, moreover, they summarily dismiss the Platonic "romance of mathematics" as mere pre-scientific mythology, a folk-theory, immune to empirical evidence and acceptable only as a matter of *a priori* faith.

Apart from its pedagogical implications, which appear substantial, we find this theoretical position deeply flawed, and if writing a full review we would develop the following as our main points of rebuttal: (1) Lakoff and Núñez insufficiently appreciate the fact that inventions of pure mathematics have often been discovered only long after the fact to have profound physical parallels. (2) The realization of a concept such as "number" in alternative and seemingly inconsistent mathematical forms does not invalidate a Platonist view, since even on their own terms this is compatible with the possible existence of the "idea" of number at some deeper psychological or ontological level. (3) More generally, they persistently confound issues related to the *ontological status* of mathematical ideas with issues as to the *means by which we acquire them.* (4) They also persistently caricature the Platonist position, claiming for example that it implies that mathematical ideas are literally *in* or *part of* the observable world, and that classical symbolic computationalism is the correct theory of the mind; yet the Platonist mathematician Roger Penrose, who explicitly rejects both of these views, is nowhere discussed. (5) On their own side, meanwhile, they consistently overstate the progress of cognitive science generally, and of George Lakoff in particular; simply to *label* the phenomenon of "conceptual metaphor," for example, does nothing whatever to explain it. (6) Finally, a plethora of *ex cathedra* pronouncements scattered through their book demonstrates that Lakoff and Núñez themselves are guilty of precisely the same sort of faith-based *a priori* theoretical commitment they attribute to their Platonist adversaries: Specifically, they themselves accept, without question, the current mainstream dogma that everything in the mind must be generated by brain processes, period. But this quasi-religious doctrine, which they incorrectly claim "has been scientifically established by means of convergent evidence within cognitive science" (p. 363), is itself falsified by a wider range of empirical evidence of the sorts originally marshaled by Myers and updated in the present volume. Within that larger framework, we conclude, *some* sort of "Platonic" construal of mathematics remains an empirically viable possibility.[35]

With this as background, then, let us return briefly to Ramanujan. Even the normally ebullient Hans Eysenck (1995) sheepishly acknowledges that this case "shows just how much distance there is between that which we have to explain, and our puny achievements in explaining it" (p. 201). Kanigel himself, struggling to come to terms with the extreme character of Ramanujan's genius, begins to wonder whether it is entangled somehow with his pronounced mystical streak, and his general immersion in south Indian mystical culture. He notes the consistency of such a view with longstanding majority tradition in both East and West, and cites approvingly a passage from Hadamard which explicitly links that tradition to both Myers and James:

35. See also A. Baker (2005), for a philosophic defense based on the prime-numbered lifecycle lengths of cicadas. We specifically decline here to embrace any specific philosophical conception of the "ideal" realm, whether that of Plato himself or any of its historical variants. Like Myers and James, we tend to think that issues as to its ultimate character and composition will only be resolved, if ever, by expanded forms of empirical inquiry involving systematic exploration of altered states of consciousness. There is one point of Platonic doctrine, however, that is especially relevant to the subject of genius and deserves at least brief mention here. Myers was in general very ambivalent about the possibility of pre-existence, and he specifically rejected Plato's conception of learning as "reminiscence"—the idea that Dase, for example, might have acquired his knowledge of the multiplication tables through "individual training" in some previous state of existence (*HP*, vol. 1, p. 119). We tend to agree with Myers in regard to Dase himself, but in light of the large body of evidence that has subsequently accumulated in support of reincarnation (see the Appendix), we would not rule out its possible contributions to some otherwise puzzling cases of extreme precocity. There are many such cases, possible examples including Mozart with his pronounced tendencies toward automatism, and Picasso, who drew skillfully before he could talk and whose first words were "piz, piz," Spanish baby-talk for "pencil" (A. I. Miller, 2001, p. 10). Stevenson (2000, p. 654) has identified several instances of unusual precocity that occurred without familial counterparts, but we currently lack any such case that is accompanied by verifiable memories of an appropriate previous life.

> That unconsciousness may be something not exclusively originating in ourselves and even participating in Divinity seems already to have been admitted by Aristotle. In Leibniz's opinion, it sets the man in communication with the whole universe, in which nothing could occur without its repercussion in each of us; and something analogous is to be found in Schelling; again, Divinity is invoked by Fichte; etc.
>
> Even more recently, a whole philosophical doctrine has been built on that principle in the first place by Myers, then by William James himself.... According to that doctrine, the unconscious would set man in connection with a world other than the one which is accessible to our senses and with some kinds of spiritual beings. (Hadamard, 1949, pp. 40–41)

What Myers and James *really* said, of course, is not that the subliminal connects us to another world, but that it connects us to the one existing world in novel ways. The more extreme phenomena of genius, and especially phenomena of the sorts adduced by Myers and amplified here, show that the roots of genius reach into or through a part of our being which somehow transcends ordinary biological functioning in space and time. The deepest affinity of genius lies with this transcendent or transpersonal aspect of our psychological constitution, and hence with the world-wide phenomenon of mysticism.

It is no accident, therefore, that Myers selects as his culminant example of genius, the completest type of humanity, "the eagle soaring over the tomb of Plato"—the Alexandrian mystical philosopher Plotinus (*HP*, vol. 1, p. 120). But before proceeding further with this theme we must take special pains to correct a misapprehension which is already rampant in the psychological literature. Notwithstanding assertions to the contrary by R. J. Sternberg and Lubart (1999), Boden (1991), Weisberg (1986), and many others, *mysticism does not imply supernatural intervention*. It is true that in pointing out these psychological connections with mysticism Myers hews close to the classical origins of the terms *genius* and *creation*, with their well-known supernatural connotations. But the essence of what he is doing is to respect the impressive *phenomenology* of genius—reflected in the concept of "inspiration" as being literally "breathed into" by the Muses, a god or daemon, or whatever—while reinterpreting it in entirely naturalistic, functional terms. As we will show in the following chapter, the term "mystical" properly refers to a very large and important class of real human experience which is not necessarily or even primarily "religious." It does not deserve to be used pejoratively, and it is not synonymous with "unscientific." To attempt, as many do, to dichotomize accounts of genius into those that are mystical, as opposed to those that are supposedly scientific, is altogether specious.

Conclusion

From a purely historical point of view, Myers correctly anticipated most of what we think has been best in the first century of psychological work on "creativity." His basic conception of the creative process as successful cooperation between supraliminal and subliminal modes of cognition, for example, anticipated the most mature developments in 20th-century psychodynamic theorizing, and led him to an interpretation of relationships between creativity and mental illness that has been strongly confirmed in subsequent research. In a qualified sense his emphasis on "continuity" also anticipates the nascent efforts by present-day cognitive theorists to characterize creativity in terms of extraordinary use of ordinary cognitive abilities.

Still to be taken up, however, are a variety of further challenges which Myers's theory of genius poses both for the psychology of genius itself and for psychology more generally. All derive from the fact that Myers, unlike most contemporary mainstream psychologists, deliberately focused on genius in its most extreme manifestations rather than on "creativity" of the more readily available forms. The account of genius which he developed in this way has implications in at least four key areas:

The first concerns the need for cognitive psychology to expand its scope to deal more effectively with non-verbal forms of expression in general and with full-fledged creative imagination in particular. Interest in these matters appears to be increasing, but the "imagery debates" and so on of recent decades constitute in our view only the barest beginnings of such an enlargement. Important but neglected resources here include studies of the creative imagination by Coleridge and the romantic poets, investigations of "primary process" thinking by psychodynamic theorists, and investigations of the hallucinatory syndromes induced by psychedelics and various other means.

The second concerns the homunculus problem, and our persisting inability even to recognize, let alone explain, the ubiquitous phenomena of intentionality, seeing-as, and insightful grasping of meanings as central aspects of human mental life. These phenomena occur in conjunction with all forms of symbolic activity, both discursive and non-discursive, from the highest flights of poetic metaphor and symbolism to the altogether mundane phenomenon of generality of word meaning in ordinary discourse. Cognitive science has a serious "inattentional blindness" problem, we believe, and *meaning* is the unseen gorilla in the room (Simons & Chabris, 1999).

A third challenge involves Myers's conception of *nisus* and the transformative power of creation both for genius itself and for those who interact with its products. Although this theme too is already present in the literature to some extent, we think much more research could be carried out along these lines. Myers's work leads both directly and indirectly, for example, to a variety of novel possibilities for creativity enhancement that merit further investigation. We see this as one aspect of the larger subject of "transformative practices," which we will address more fully in the following chapter.

Finally, Myers led the way in exposing an inescapable connection between genius and mysticism at the foundations of human personality. Mysticism, even more than genius itself, has been a topic actively avoided and even despised by most mainstream psychologists, but like Myers and James we believe that it will ultimately prove not only significant but *central* to an empirically adequate scientific psychology. We turn next to this.

Chapter 8

Mystical Experience

Edward F. Kelly and Michael Grosso

> No philosophy of human personality is worth very much unless it takes full account of the data of mystical experience. (Price, 1954, pp. 52–53)

> I think it more likely than not that in religious and mystical experience men come into contact with some Reality or some aspect of Reality which they do not come into contact with in any other way. (Broad, 1953, p. 173)

> That which lies at the root of each of us lies at the root of the Cosmos too. (Myers, *HP*, vol. 2, p. 277)

Modern mainstream psychology has so far had comparatively little to say about what is arguably the most extraordinary of all human experiences. The present chapter attempts to address this deficiency. Like H. H. Price, we believe that psychology *must* take account of the full range of human experience or be reduced to a caricature, a defacing, of what it means to be human. Unfortunately, there was a long interlude in the development of modern psychology in which mystical experiences, together with all other phenomena of consciousness, virtually disappeared from the scientific literature. In large part because of its undeniable connections with the scientifically unpopular subject of religion, mysticism in particular, even more than its near-relative genius, has yet to recover from this systematic and undeserved neglect.

The central aim of this chapter is to abet further the return of the repressed, by helping to restore the long-avoided and often-despised topic of mystical experience to what we believe is its proper place in the foreground of a worthy scientific psychology. We approach this task with considerable trepidation, however. The literature of mysticism is vast, ramified, and deeply intertwined with longstanding and emotionally charged controversies in disciplines such as theology and comparative religion. We certainly claim no special expertise in these areas, and like most scientists would generally prefer to avoid becoming entangled with them to the extent possible. Our intention therefore is to focus primarily on the psychological character and biological accompaniments of these powerful experiences.

Nevertheless, questions related to the objective significance of mystical experience (or lack thereof) are intellectually inescapable. Indeed, at the heart of the many controversies surrounding mysticism, particularly in the West, lies a profound and implacable historical opposition between traditional religious supernaturalism and the reductive-materialist attitudes that have dominated modern mainstream scientific literature on the subject. We will not shrink from addressing these difficult issues. Our plan is to pursue a middle course, close in empirical spirit to the approaches of F. W. H. Myers and William James, which takes the phenomena of mysticism seriously but soberly and attempts to draw out their significant implications for contemporary theories of personality and cognition. Traversing the enormous worldwide literature pertaining to mysticism in a selective and focused manner, we will marshal evidence and argument demonstrating the deep consistency of mystical experience and its concomitants with the expanded scientific naturalism pioneered by Myers and James and advocated throughout this book. Interpretation of mystical experience from this larger point of view, we believe, potentially overcomes the great traditional oppositions and can heal the analogous divisions that have appeared within scientific psychology itself through the rise of its humanistic and transpersonal subcurrents. The position we are advocating, to put the matter as succinctly if crudely as we can, strongly endorses the fundamental "expansionist" impulse of these recent splinter movements, but also insists, equally strongly, on unreserved commitment to the empirical and theoretical discipline characteristic of mainstream science (see also Child, 1973).

It could perhaps go without saying that any attempt to steer such a middle course through these turbulent regions is certain to encounter significant opposition from both flanks. As James himself evidently feared in regard to his classic *Varieties of Religious Experience* (henceforth, *VRE*), we fear that our treatment of mysticism may prove "too biological for the religious, too religious for the biologists" (Perry, 1935, vol. 2, p. 326). Nevertheless, we hope to convince many if not all readers that the position we develop in regard to mysticism is scientifically the most comprehensive and responsible position available and that it lends itself to further empirical elaboration in a large number of interesting and feasible directions.

Phenomenology of Mystical Experience: An Introduction

The psychological literature on mysticism is conveniently bracketed by two "bookend" publications—the *VRE* of James (1902/1958) and a recent survey by Wulff (2000). The former, almost everyone would agree, shows how well begun the subject already was, over a century ago. The latter provides a useful overview, somewhat weighted toward clinical considerations, of the modest scientific progress achieved since that time.

James's treatment of mysticism in *VRE* remains the *locus classicus* and natural starting point for serious psychological discussions, even after a hundred years, and we will rely heavily upon it here. He begins by underscoring the central importance of mystical states of consciousness to the subject matter of his entire book—"the vital chapter from which the other chapters get their light" (p. 292).[1] How shall such states be identified and characterized? Rejecting out of hand all pejorative uses of the terms "mysticism" and "mystical," James provisionally selects four principal marks, two major and two minor, which suffice to delimit the family of states most relevant to his expository purposes.[2]

The first major characteristic, *ineffability*, is negative. The subject of such an experience typically declares

> that it defies expression, that no adequate report of its contents can be given in words. It follows from this that its quality must be directly experienced; it cannot be imparted or transferred to others. In this peculiarity mystical states are more like states of feeling than like states of intellect. No one can make clear to another who has never had a certain feeling, in what the quality or worth of it consists. (pp. 292–293)

The beauty of a spectacular sunset or the passions of love would be difficult if not impossible to communicate to anyone unacquainted with such experiences, and mystical experience is for some inherent reason still more difficult to convey adequately in words, even for geniuses of language such as Dante or Rumi.

Ineffability, though a useful mark, tells us little that is positive about the mystical experience itself. But the second major characteristic of mystical states, emphasized throughout by James, is their *noetic quality*:

> Although so similar to states of feeling, mystical states seem to those who experience them to be also states of knowledge. They are states of insight into depths of truth unplumbed by the discursive intellect. They are illu-

1. James goes on immediately to acknowledge as a possible limitation of his treatment that "my own constitution shuts me out from their enjoyment almost entirely, and I can speak of them only at second hand" (p. 292). We must acknowledge suffering for the most part from similar limitations, but we have also followed James in striving throughout to overcome these by being as "objective and receptive" as we can.

2. All four, we note immediately, are also relevant to full-blown NDEs, which (as we mentioned in Chapter 6) commonly include a mystical or transcendent aspect (Greyson, 1985).

> minations, revelations, full of significance and importance, all inarticulate though they remain; and as a rule they carry with them a curious sense of authority for after-time. (p. 293)

Subjects of profound mystical experience thus typically feel sure that they have gained fundamental insight into the nature of "reality," and yet find themselves unable to express their discoveries adequately in a form intelligible to the rest of us. It is chiefly this strange combination of cognitive properties, so characteristic of mystical experience, that has given rise to the heated controversies regarding its objective significance.

Two further characteristics—*transiency* and *passivity*—James regards as less sharply marked and not to the same degree definitive, but still commonly present, particularly in association with experiences that occur spontaneously. Mystical experiences are typically very intense and usually though not always can be sustained only for short periods ranging from a few seconds to perhaps a few hours, although sometimes also recurring over time with an appearance of progressive development. Even when cultivated by voluntary practices such as meditation, moreover, they tend to break in upon and engulf the subject as though originating from a region outside normal consciousness.

Having described in the abstract these characteristics of strong mystical experiences, James turns to providing concrete examples. It is important to note here that in doing so he deliberately employs Myers's taxonomic method (p. 294; see also Chapter 2), situating his examples of true mystical experience as extreme cases on a continuum stretching upward through various phenomena of more rudimentary but related type. He begins with the sense of heightened significance that can suddenly attach itself to a word, a phrase, a passage of poetry or music, or the play of light and sound, when the mind is suitably attuned, remarking that "we are alive or dead to the eternal inner message of the arts according as we have kept or lost this mystical susceptibility" (p. 295). Next in line come *déjà vu* and related experiences; "dreamy" states of various kinds; states induced by intoxicants and anesthetics such as alcohol, nitrous oxide, and chloroform; borderline mystical states awakened in various persons by scenes of great natural beauty; and finally, as his culminant example of a spontaneous mystical experience, the case of Canadian psychiatrist R. M. Bucke, whose single and brief but impressive experience at age 36 of what he later termed "cosmic consciousness" led him to devote the remainder of his life to investigating and reporting its occurrence in others (Bucke, 1901/1969). We reproduce in full Bucke's own description of this experience, as quoted by James from a privately printed pamphlet that preceded the main work.[3] All four of James's marks are clearly present:

---

3. The corresponding passage in the latter (Bucke, 1901/1969, pp. 9–10), although very similar in content to the version quoted by James, shows signs of theoretical elaboration in light of Bucke's subsequent research.

> I had spent the evening in a great city, with two friends, reading and discussing poetry and philosophy. We parted at midnight. I had a long drive in a hansom to my lodging. My mind, deeply under the influence of the ideas, images, and emotions called up by the reading and talk, was calm and peaceful. I was in a state of quiet, almost passive enjoyment, not actually thinking, but letting ideas, images, and emotions flow of themselves, as it were, through my mind. All at once, without warning of any kind, I found myself wrapped in a flame-colored cloud. For an instant I thought of fire, an immense conflagration somewhere close by in that great city; the next, I knew that the fire was within myself. Directly afterward there came upon me a sense of exultation, of immense joyousness accompanied or immediately followed by an intellectual illumination impossible to describe. Among other things, I did not merely come to believe, but I saw that the universe is not composed of dead matter, but is, on the contrary, a living Presence; I became conscious in myself of eternal life. It was not a conviction that I would have eternal life, but a consciousness that I possessed eternal life then; I saw that all men are immortal; that the cosmic order is such that without any peradventure all things work together for the good of each and all; that the foundation principle of the world, of all the worlds, is what we call love, and that happiness of each and all is in the long run absolutely certain. The vision lasted a few seconds and was gone; but the memory of it and the sense of the reality of what it taught has remained during the quarter of a century which has since elapsed. I knew that what the vision showed was true. I had attained to a point of view from which I saw that it must be true. That view, that conviction, I may say that consciousness, has never, even during periods of the deepest depression, been lost. (pp. 306–307)

James next goes on, using the relatively scanty comparative materials available at that time, to provide a sampling of reports concerning states of consciousness methodically cultivated in accord with the Hindu, Buddhist, Islamic (Sufi), and Christian mystical traditions. By far the largest amount of space is devoted to the Christian mystics, with whom James undoubtedly felt himself more thoroughly and reliably familiar. His emphasis throughout is on the key properties of *ineffability* and *noetic quality*, which emerge together in conjunction with states of consciousness that somehow pass beyond all ordinary forms of sensation and cognition and yet seemingly into contact or even unity with some sort of higher reality. An elegant illustration is provided by St. John of the Cross in his *Dark Night of the Soul* (Book 2, chap. 17[3]), in a passage in which he attempts to explain why the infusion of spiritual knowledge or wisdom in mystical states is ineffable or "secret":[4]

> [The soul] can find no suitable way or manner or similitude by which it may be able to describe such lofty understanding and such delicate spiri-

4. We quote from an authoritative English translation of the original Spanish by Allison Peers (1959, pp. 159–160), whereas James apparently provided his own English translation of an earlier translation into French. The central message of both English versions is the same, despite some differences in detail.

> tual feeling. And thus, even though the soul might have a great desire to express it and might find many ways in which to describe it, it would still be secret and remain undescribed. For, as that inward wisdom is so simple, so general and so spiritual that it has not entered into the understanding enwrapped or cloaked in any form or image subject to sense, it follows that sense and imagination (as it has not entered through them nor has taken their form and color) cannot account for it or imagine it, so as to say anything concerning it, although the soul be clearly aware that it is experiencing and partaking of that rare and delectable wisdom.

We hope that the material presented so far will suffice to convey, even to readers having no prior acquaintance with the subject, some initial feeling for the impressive phenomenology of mystical experience. Additional examples will be provided below, and many more can be found in important collections such as those of Bucke (1901/1969), Happold (1963/1970), Stace (1960/1987), Underhill (1911/1974), and Woods (1980).

But now what is the real significance of these powerful experiences? Are they revelations of hidden realities, as the mystics themselves believe, or are they instead purely subjective phenomena, mere delusions fabricated by disordered brains? As pointed out above, contemporary Western culture remains deeply divided on these issues, with the positive and negative attitudes tending to parcel out along religious versus scientific lines, respectively.

Even more poignantly, both attitudes can sometimes be found coexisting uneasily in the same person, as in the case of the rationalist philosopher Bertrand Russell. Russell was deeply appreciative of mystical philosophers such as Plato and Spinoza, and even said of Heraclitus that "in such a nature we see the true union of the mystic and the man of science—the highest eminence, as I think, that it is possible to achieve in the world of thought" (Russell, 1921b, p. 4). Yet Russell also remained deeply and generally distrustful of mystical experience, declaring with characteristic sarcasm, for example, that "from a scientific point of view, we can make no distinction between the man who eats little and sees heaven and the man who drinks much and sees snakes. Each is in an abnormal physical condition, and therefore has abnormal perceptions" (Russell, 1935/1974, p. 188).

On the other hand, many eminent scientists have been more or less openly religious, and receptive to mysticism in particular. Einstein (1949), for example, remarked that "the religious geniuses of all ages have been distinguished by this kind of [cosmic] religious feeling....In my view it is the most important function of art and science to awaken this feeling and keep it alive in those who are capable of it....I maintain that cosmic religious feeling is the strongest and noblest incitement to scientific research" (pp. 26–28).

Such remarkable diversity of attitudes underscores once again our need, both culturally and individually, to resolve the fundamental question as to the "truth" (James) or objective significance of mystical experience. In order to begin framing the relevant issues more narrowly, we will conclude this introduction by briefly contrasting the contemporary opinions of Bucke and James.

Bucke displays in abundance the characteristic certitude of persons who have themselves experienced "cosmic consciousness." Nevertheless, and to his credit, he recognizes that *certitude* does not entail *certainty*, and he therefore also provides several arguments for its objective significance (Bucke, 1901/1969, pp. 70–71). First, mystical consciousness, in contrast with all forms of "insanity," tends to produce moral elevation, enhanced self-control, and the like, as demonstrated by the roughly 50 cases catalogued in his book. In addition, civilization as a whole clearly rests upon foundational religious careers profoundly shaped by it. Most importantly, the question of mystical "truth" seems to Bucke entirely on a par, epistemologically, with that of the truth of ordinary perceptual judgments. Everyone can agree that the tree is really there across the field because all adequately sighted observers see and report it in essentially the same way. Similarly, Bucke thinks, the objective reality of what mystics experience is straightforwardly established by an argument from unanimity:

> Just in the same way do the reports of those who have had cosmic consciousness correspond in all essentials, though in detail they doubtless more or less diverge (but these divergences are fully as much in our misunderstanding of the reports as in the reports themselves). So there is no instance of a person who has been illumined denying or disputing the teaching of another who has passed through the same experience. (p. 71)

It seems evident that Bucke's critical faculties were overwhelmed here by the impressiveness of his own first-person experience. The unanimity he perceives seems at least partly an artifact of his procedures, for most of the 11 features he uses to characterize the supposedly common experience are directly transcribed from his own, and clearly influenced his identification of it in others. Thus, for example, he thinks the experience occurs primarily in well-developed males between the ages of 30 and 40, and acknowledges his immediate suspicion of cases purportedly occurring under different circumstances (p. 75). Most importantly, he overlooks the obvious and problematic fact that unanimous judgments are sometimes uniformly *wrong*, as in the case of mirages or incorrigible visual illusions of various kinds.

James, the third-person observer, adopts a more nuanced, subtle, and cautious stance, despite the fact that he clearly has great personal sympathy for the driving impulse behind Bucke's argument. In regard to near-unanimity at the core of religious mysticism, for example, he says :

> This overcoming of all the usual barriers between the individual and the Absolute is the great mystic achievement. In mystic states we both become one with the Absolute and we become aware of our oneness. This is the everlasting and triumphant mystical tradition, hardly altered by differences of clime or creed. In Hinduism, in Neoplatonism, in Sufism, in Christian mysticism, in Whitmanism, we find the same recurring note, so

> that there is about mystical utterances an eternal unanimity which ought to make a critic stop and think. (*VRE*, p. 321)[5]

Nonetheless, where Bucke sees only unanimity James recognizes and respects diversity as well, and in his provisional assessment of the "truth" of mysticism he carefully hedges (*VRE*, pp. 323–328). It is true and appropriate, as a matter of psychological fact, that mystical experiences are typically authoritative for those who have them. Nevertheless, "no authority emanates from them which should make it a duty for those who stand outside of them to accept their revelations uncritically" (p. 324).

In particular, they do not by anything intrinsic to their character warrant any of the specific theological or ecclesiastical doctrines with which they have commonly been associated. Any naive argument from unanimity is unsound, in part because that is at bottom only an appeal to numbers, which has no logical force, but more importantly because the supposed unanimity itself appears to James to break down to some degree upon closer inspection: Not only do mystical states ally themselves freely with a great diversity of mutually incompatible theological and metaphysical doctrines, but they have pathological counterparts, such as acute psychotic states, which seem to emanate from the same or similar subliminal regions of the psyche. This leads James to his crucial practical conclusion:

> That region contains every kind of matter: "seraph and snake" abide there side by side. To come from thence is no infallible credential. What comes must be sifted and tested, and run the gauntlet of confrontation with the total context of experience, just like what comes from the outer world of sense. Its value must be ascertained by empirical methods, so long as we are not mystics ourselves. (p. 326)[6]

For James, therefore, it remains an open question, to be resolved by empirical means, whether higher mystical states do or do not in fact provide more enveloping points of view, windows through which we glimpse normally hidden aspects of a larger, more comprehensive reality. James himself clearly is sympathetic to this possibility, and he insists—repeatedly—that

---

5. James's personal attitudes are brought out even more clearly in a letter he wrote in 1904 (Perry, 1935, vol. 2, pp. 350–351) to his colleague James Leuba, an arch-reductionist: "I find it preposterous to suppose that if there be a feeling of unseen reality shared by large numbers of best men in their best moments, responded to by other men in their 'deep' moments, good to live by, strength-giving,—I find it preposterous, I say, to suppose that the goodness of that feeling for living purposes should be held to carry no objective significance.…Now, although I am so devoid of *Gottesbewusstsein* in the directer and stronger sense, yet there is *something in me* which *makes response* when I hear utterances from that quarter made by others. I recognize the deeper voice. Something tells me:— '*thither lies truth*'— and I am sure it is not old theistic prejudices of infancy.…Call this, if you like, my mystical *germ*."

6. As discussed in Chapter 2, the diversity of the content of the subliminal, ranging from "dissolutive" to "evolutive" manifestations, was an important aspect of Myers's theory: "Hidden in the deep of our being is a rubbish-heap as well as a treasure-house;—degenerations and insanities as well as beginnings of higher development" (*HP*, vol. 1, p. 72).

at minimum "the existence of mystical states absolutely overthrows the pretension of non-mystical states to be the sole and ultimate dictators of what we may believe" (p. 327).

In sum, the problem of evaluating the objective significance of mystical experience resolves itself into two closely related sub-problems: First, to what degree are mystical experiences in their full world-wide distribution truly similar in their most important characteristics? Is there in fact a highest type, or universal core? Second, if such a core experience exists, what if anything about that experience or its concomitants might be brought to bear on the question of objective significance?

One of the most searching, thoughtful, and provocative examinations of these questions carried out to date, in our opinion, remains that of analytic philosopher W. T. Stace (1960/1987). We will anchor our presentation to his.

The Problem of the Universal Core

Stace shares with many earlier writers including Bucke and James the general sense that deep mystical experiences have something important in common that sets them off sharply from ordinary states of consciousness. He is dissatisfied, however, with previous attempts to say what that something is, and he takes as his first and logically primary task to establish and characterize this universal core in a more rigorous and empirically well-grounded way.

This requires in the first place sampling from a wider than normal cultural and temporal variety of reported experiences. In addition to numerous examples drawn from the Judeo-Christian, Islamic, Hindu, Buddhist, and Taoist religious traditions, therefore, Stace also examines reports provided by historically prominent but "unattached" mystics such as Plotinus, and less well-known reports from recent times such as that of Arthur Koestler (1954).

Of course we have direct access only to mystics' reports (or perhaps even translations or descriptions of their reports) and not to their experiences themselves. These records, moreover, are sometimes saturated with highly figurative language, or with language that clearly goes beyond simple *description* of an experience to its *interpretation*, where by "interpretation" Stace means "anything which the conceptual intellect adds to the experience for the purpose of understanding it, whether what is added is only classificatory concepts, or a logical inference, or an explanatory hypothesis" (p. 37). In most cases the relevant conceptual apparatus is of course that provided by the theological or institutional context in which the experience occurs.

Although this distinction seems clear enough in principle, it is often hard to apply in practice, and to varying degrees in different cases. Stace is not at all naive about these difficulties, however, and requires only that he be able to separate the descriptive or phenomenological aspects of reports from their interpretive or theological parts in sufficient degree, and in a sufficient number of cases, to delineate with reasonable confidence the main features of the underlying states of consciousness.

Proceeding in this fashion, Stace identifies two principal classes of deep mystical states, strongly overlapping, which he calls the "extrovertive" and "introvertive" types. Each of these types is characterized by a family-resemblance relation involving seven specific features that empirically co-occur with high regularity, although not all seven need be present in any given case. Each type is also accompanied by borderline or transitional cases showing lesser degrees of conformity to the central, defining pattern.

Five of the features that Stace identifies are common to both of these main classes and echo properties of mystical experience previously identified or emphasized by writers such as Bucke, James, Underhill, and others. The first of these five is a sense of the "objectivity" or "reality" of the experience, which corresponds to James's "noetic quality" and Bucke's "intellectual illumination." Second is strong positive affect, with feelings of calm, peace, blessedness, joy, bliss, and the like. Third is a feeling, closely related to the previous, that what is apprehended or contacted in the experience is somehow holy, or sacred, or divine. That is, there is an aspect of emotionally charged or numinous contact with something powerful or awesome, a *mysterium tremendum* (Otto, 1923/1970). Fourth is *paradoxicality*, a sense that the experience somehow inherently defies or overpasses ordinary rules of logic, permitting or demanding simultaneous application of normally incompatible predicates such as active/inactive, full/empty, light/dark, and so on. We will give a few examples below, and Stace himself devotes an entire chapter to this puzzling aspect. Closely connected with this paradoxicality, of course, is the last of the five features shared by all mystical experience, its alleged *ineffability*, as discussed previously.[7]

Although all strong mystical experiences thus have much in common, the extrovertive and introvertive types are distinguished by two remaining characteristics which also reveal them to be two species of a common genus. The extrovertive form is perhaps more common in spontaneous cases and at earlier stages of the mystic way, although it can also occur following "enlightenment" experiences of the introvertive type. Its primary

7. Stace adds the qualification "alleged" to underscore the peculiarity that virtually all mystics, having declared that their experience cannot be described in words, immediately go on to describe it, often at prodigious length. In a separate chapter devoted to this subject he argues that mystics are in fact providing literal descriptions of remembered experiences which were themselves inherently paradoxical. Price (1962) resists this interpretation, however, suggesting that the difficulty is more akin to that of one who, not having acquired the concept of "Scotch mist," must describe the meteorologic condition to which that concept applies as both "raining" and "not raining." Although we cannot pursue these interesting issues in greater detail here, we suspect that Price may be correct in suggesting that more widespread first-person familiarity with mystical experience could lead to reduction of the apparent paradoxicality through a similar process of "ostensive definition," and more generally that we need to extend and refine our currently impoverished methods of phenomenological description and analysis.

distinguishing feature is that the ordinary perceptual world remains, but in transfigured form. A multiplicity of objects and events may continue to be perceived through the physical senses, but now they are apprehended as both distinct and yet at the same time mysteriously identical, pervaded by some sort of shared inner subjectivity or consciousness, or light, or life which binds all elements of the perceptual field both to each other and to the perceiving subject. It is as if the multiplicity itself somehow discloses a normally hidden unity. As Meister Eckhart concisely remarks, "here all blades of grass, wood, and stone, all things are One" (Stace, 1960/1987, p. 63). One example is the experience of Bucke, quoted above. Another is a well-known experience of Jacob Boehme, a German shoemaker and family man of modest education: "Sitting one day in his room his eyes fell upon a burnished pewter disk, which reflected the sunshine with such marvelous splendor that he fell into an inward ecstasy, and it seemed to him as if he could now look into the principles and deepest foundations of things" (Bucke, 1901/1969, p. 180). Fearing that this might be just a trick of his imagination, Boehme went outside to test it: "Here he remarked that he gazed into the very heart of things, the very herbs and grass, and that actual Nature harmonized with what he had inwardly seen," says one biographer; and "viewing the herbs and grass of the field in his inward light, he saw into their essences, use and properties," says another (Underhill, 1911/1974, p. 256).

Both Stace and Underhill remark that a number of mystical poets such as Blake, Tennyson, Whitman, and Wordsworth often seem to verge upon this sort of experience. Blake, for example, much influenced by Boehme, sees "a world in a grain of sand, and heaven in a wildflower," and Myers (1880/1929) in his biography of Wordsworth characterizes the poet explicitly as operating in a realm "midway between mystic intuition and delicate observation" (p. 137). The same sort of apprehension of hidden unity and expansion of self in and through nature is approached but not quite realized in the case of Richard Jefferies, which Bucke (1901/1969, pp. 319–322) treats as a borderline case of cosmic consciousness. Bucke quotes from Jefferies's autobiography his description of an experience at age 18 in which a sense of hidden inward unity underlying the perceptible world first began to flood into him as he lay alone in the grass:

> Having drunk deeply of the heaven above and felt the most glorious beauty of the day, and remembering the old, old sea,...I now became lost, and absorbed into the being or existence of the universe. I felt down deep into the earth, under, and high above into the sky, and farther still to the sun and stars. Still farther beyond the stars into the hollow of space, and losing thus my separateness of being came to seem like part of the whole.

We turn now to mystical experiences of the *introvertive* type, which seem to us both psychologically and philosophically to form the real heart of the subject. As Stace points out, these are far more prominent in the worldwide literature of mysticism in that they occur predominantly in advanced stages of the mystic vocation and are clearly regarded as the higher type by persons such as Meister Eckhart who have experienced both. They are also easily recognized, even by third-person observers such as ourselves, as a more radical and complete expression of the central impulse of the extrovertive mystical states described above. The core experience is again one of *unity*, but in this case the unity is even more profound, and it is achieved in a startlingly different manner. In these experiences one's perceptual world is not merely transfigured but abolished, along with all other contents of ordinary consciousness such as specific thoughts, images, memories, and the like. But what results—confuting the expectations of empiricists such as David Hume—is not some sort of blank or dim or unconscious condition, but an extraordinary inward experience of pure, contentless, undifferentiated, unitary consciousness. "*This undifferentiated unity is the essence of the introvertive mystical experience*" (Stace, 1960/1987, p. 87).

A few examples here may help to flesh out this description. We cite first a passage from the Mandukya Upanishad which distills the essence of India's psychological teachings. Beyond ordinary consciousness, dreaming consciousness, and dreamless sleep, say their ancient sages, lies a higher form of consciousness—*Turiya*, the Fourth:

> The Fourth, say the wise, is not subjective experience, nor objective experience, nor experience intermediate between these two, nor is it a negative condition which is neither consciousness nor unconsciousness. It is not the knowledge of the senses, nor is it relative knowledge, nor yet inferential knowledge. Beyond the senses, beyond the understanding, beyond all expression, is The Fourth. It is pure unitary consciousness, wherein awareness of the world and multiplicity is completely obliterated. It is ineffable peace. It is the supreme good. It is One without a second. It is the Self. Know it alone! (Prabhavananda & Manchester, 1957, p. 51)

Many passages from the Christian mystical tradition further attest to the existence of such non-ordinary conscious states devoid of multiplicity. Stace characteristically emphasizes examples from highly cerebral Christian mystics such as Ruysbroeck and especially Meister Eckhart, but he also goes to some pains (pp. 100–104) to argue that St. Teresa's highest unitive experiences, although described in relatively unsophisticated and theology-laden language superficially dissimilar from Meister Eckhart's, must have been in essence the same.[8]

---

8. Stace's argument here turns on the fact that St. John of the Cross, whose descriptions of unitive experience are often extremely similar to Meister Eckhart's, was also St. Teresa's principal spiritual advisor and confessor and apparently largely agreed with her as to the principal psychological characteristics of unitive states. An important translator, student, and admirer of the great Spanish mystics, Peers (1951) confirms this latter point, adding that "the complementary nature of the works of the two saints is very noticeable: they seldom disagree, though each relies largely on personal experience, and a synthesis of their writings would form an account of the mystical life, we may safely say, approached by very few other syntheses, and surpassed by none" (p. 232). St. John, for example, is known to have deliberately avoided writing on "lower" mystical phenomena such as voices and visions, which he felt St. Teresa had already described in adequate detail. A joint and in-depth psychological study of these two individuals clearly would be of great interest and value.

This "*vacuum*" or negative aspect of introvertive mystical experience is highlighted by descriptors such as "emptiness," "void," "obscurity," "darkness," "nothingness," "silence," which recur throughout the mystical literature. Inasmuch as our ordinary sense of space and time is strongly bound up with (and perhaps even a condition of) the normal multiplicity of perceptual and cognitive experience, the obliteration of this multiplicity may also account for the further property that the experience typically seems to its subjects as somehow outside or beyond space and time. Yet this vacuum, paradoxically, is at the same time a "*plenum*," with the obscurity "dazzling," the desert "teeming," and so on. It is especially these further, positive, but "ineffable" aspects of unitive mystical experience that seem to us to constitute its central mystery and challenge.

Based on her comprehensive survey of Christian mysticism, Underhill (1911/1974) captures both the vacuum and plenum aspects of unitive experience and draws our attention to still another crucial characteristic:

> In this experience the departmental activities of thought and feeling, the consciousness of I-hood, of space and time—all that belongs to the World of Becoming and our own place therein—are suspended. The vitality which we are accustomed to split amongst these various things, is gathered up to form a state of "pure apprehension": a vivid intuition of—or if you like conjunction with—the Transcendent...[the mystic's] consciousness escapes the limitations of the senses, rises to freedom, and is united for an instant with the "great life of the All." (p. 367)

The feature we wish to emphasize here is the alteration of "I-hood"—the sense of self. What happens seems again in part explainable as a consequence of the obliteration of multiplicity. Everyday consciousness is typically felt, with varying degrees of clarity, as structured in terms of a polarity between ourselves as conscious egos or subjects and whatever it is that we are currently doing or experiencing. To the degree that this distinction along with all others is obliterated during unitive experience, it seems inevitable that the mystic's habitual sense of self must undergo some sort of radical transformation.

There can be no doubt that this is in fact the case. Stace devotes an entire section to this subject, which he titles "the dissolution of individuality" (pp. 111–123). This label is accurate insofar as reports of introvertive mystical experience do often describe the fading, dimming, melting, dissolving, loss, or death of the ordinary finite self. The Sufis even have a special term for this, *fana*, which literally mean "passing away." But this is only one aspect of the transformation, its negative side. If this were the entirety of what occurs, genuine mystical experience might be difficult to distinguish from pathological forms of "depersonalization." The ordinary self is not literally *obliterated*, of course, since after all it normally returns, although often uplifted and transformed in ways we will discuss subsequently. The Sufis, for example, also speak of *baqa*, revival, the return to an enhanced self. During the experience, however, the ordinary, everyday self is *transcended*, in a dramatic and remarkably consistent way. Specifically, in its place there characteristically emerges a vastly amplified sense of self—a Self—that almost inevitably experiences itself as being in a state of direct contact, or union, or identity with some reality variably conceived as a Universal Self, the One, the Absolute, the Ground of Being, or God (Stace, 1960/1987, p. 93).

This fundamental characteristic of introvertive mystical experience appears with particular clarity and force in another of its classic descriptions, this one by the Neoplatonist philosopher Plotinus, who appears in history at or near the original confluence of the Greek and Oriental mystical traditions and is arguably a principal fountainhead of modern Western mystical traditions as well. The passages we quote from are widely known, and in varying translations have been cited as representative and authoritative by both Stace and Underhill, among many others.[9] The testimony of Plotinus (1969) seems to us especially significant, as it constitutes a serious effort by a philosopher of the first rank to characterize as clearly as he can an extraordinary experience of union which he is known to have entered into himself, on at least four occasions (p. 17). Based largely on this description, moreover, Underhill (1911/1974, p. 372) specifically endorses the fundamental identity between the unitive experiences of Plotinus and those of the great Christian mystics. Its affinities with the description from the Mandukya Upanishad, quoted above, will be equally apparent.

The key passage appears in the 6th *Ennead*, tractate 9, section 10, of which we quote only a small part.[10] Plotinus is attempting to describe the supreme good, the "flight of the one to the One," which can only be realized in full through a mode of direct apprehension which he finds greatly superior to ordinary reason:

> In our self-seeing There, the self is seen as belonging to that order, or rather we are merged into that self in us which has the quality of that order. It is a knowing of the self restored to its purity. No doubt we should not speak of seeing; but we cannot help talking in dualities, seen and seer, instead of boldly, the achievement of unity. In this seeing, we neither hold an object nor trace distinction; there is no two. The man is changed, no longer himself nor self-belonging; he is merged with the Supreme, sunken into it, one with it: centre coincides with centre, for centres of circles, even here below, are one when they unite, and two when they separate; and it is in this sense that we now (after the vision) speak of the Supreme as separate. This is why the vision baffles telling; we cannot detach the Supreme to state it; if we have seen something thus detached we have failed of the Supreme which is to be known only as one with ourselves.

---

9. Myers, who was intimately familiar with the *Enneads*, uses the same passages (in his own slightly different translation, naturally) in an interesting essay on "Tennyson as Prophet" (Myers, 1889h).

10. Like Stace we have relied on the famous translation by Stephen McKenna, but ours is a later (4th) edition, revised by B. S. Page, and differs slightly from the version quoted by Stace (p. 104).

The same sort of radical transformation in the sense of self is evident in two modern "borderline" introvertive cases involving distinguished persons not attached to any specific mystical tradition. The first, originally publicized by James, involves Tennyson, who describes an experience he frequently had in solitude:

> This has come upon me through repeating my own name to myself silently, till all at once, as it were out of the intensity of the consciousness of individuality, individuality itself seemed to dissolve away into boundless being, and this not a confused state but the clearest, the surest of the surest, utterly beyond words—here death was an almost laughable impossibility—the loss of personality (if so it were) seeming no extinction, but the only true life. I am ashamed of my feeble description. Have I not said the state is utterly beyond words? (*VRE*, p. 295)[11]

The second and perhaps even more interesting case involves Arthur Koestler (1954, pp. 345–363), who reports a series of mystical experiences precipitated under the harrowing conditions of his imprisonment during the Spanish Civil War in 1937. Koestler, a scientifically well-educated person, was at that time strongly committed to Socialist/Communist politics and decidedly materialist and anti-religious. Placed in solitary confinement by his Fascist captors, he had undergone a prolonged hunger strike and found himself in a state of chronic exhaustion, expecting constantly to be taken from his cell and beaten or executed like many other prisoners. The first experience supervened upon his profoundly gratifying success in reconstructing Euclid's proof that there is an infinity of prime numbers. Suddenly, he reports,

> I was floating on my back in a river of peace, under bridges of silence. It came from nowhere and flowed nowhere. Then there was no river and no I. The I had ceased to exist.
>
> It is extremely embarrassing to write down a phrase like that when one has read *The Meaning of Meaning* and nibbled at logical positivism and aims at verbal precision and dislikes nebulous gushings. Yet, "mystical" experiences, as we dubiously call them, are not nebulous, vague or maudlin—they only become so when we debase them by verbalisation. However, to communicate what is incommunicable by its nature, one must somehow put it into words, and so one moves in a vicious circle. When I say "the I had ceased to exist," I refer to a concrete experience that is verbally as incommunicable as the feeling aroused by a piano concerto, yet just as real—only much more real. In fact, its primary mark is the sensation that this state is more real than any other one has experienced before—that for the first time the veil has fallen and one is in touch with "real reality," the hidden order of things, the X-ray texture of the world, normally obscured by layers of irrelevancy.

---

11. James adds this further statement by Tennyson, as reported by Tyndall: "By God Almighty! there is no delusion in the matter! It is no nebulous ecstasy, but a state of transcendent wonder, associated with absolute clearness of mind."

> What distinguishes this type of experience from the emotional entrancements of music, landscapes or love is that the former has a definitely intellectual, or rather noumenal, content. It is meaningful, though not in verbal terms. Verbal transcriptions that come nearest to it are: the unity and interlocking of everything that exists, an inter-dependence like that of gravitational fields or communicating vessels. The "I" ceases to exist because it has, by a kind of mental osmosis, established communication with, and been dissolved in, the universal pool. It is this process of dissolution and limitless expansion which is sensed as the "oceanic feeling", as the draining of all tension, the absolute catharsis, the peace that passeth all understanding. (p. 352)

This experience could not be voluntarily induced, but it recurred spontaneously, initially as often as two or three times a week and at slowly lengthening intervals thereafter. Koestler credits it with catalyzing a fundamental transformation in his attitudes and personality, and with directly inspiring the four books he produced in the following five years in an effort to digest its meaning. Later, in response to direct questioning by Stace, Koestler himself also interpreted his experience as an incipient or incomplete form of the full-fledged introvertive experience described in the Mandukya Upanishad.

We have now done about as much as we can by way of describing the principal psychological characteristics of introvertive mystical experience. Its extreme developments are perhaps most concisely encapsulated by the famous Vedic formula "Sat-Chit-Ananda"—pure being or existence, pure awareness or consciousness, and pure bliss, amplified without limit. Many further descriptions and examples can be found in the sources cited above, and readers may find it useful to consult these, but mystics themselves declare unanimously that full appreciation of such extraordinary states of consciousness comes only to those fortunate enough or determined enough to experience them directly.

Stace (1960/1987) concludes his descriptive survey of mystical experiences by explicitly identifying the central, crucial property, common to both the introvertive and extrovertive forms, which constitutes its true universal core: "In this general experience of a unity which the mystic believes to be in some sense ultimate and basic to the world, we have the very inner essence of all mystical experience...the nucleus round which the other and more peripheral characteristics revolve" (pp. 132–133).

Stace himself next turns immediately to the task of evaluating this central claim of mystics to have made contact with something in nature that is real, though normally inaccessible—the problem of "objective reference," as he calls it. We will shortly follow him there, but we must first deal with a controversy that his characterization of the universal core has provoked.

Steven Katz and the Contructivist Backlash

Stace was a philosophically sophisticated member of what has come to be known as the "perennialist" school (A. Huxley, 1944/1970), which seeks out and emphasizes *commonalities* in religion generally and in the mystical or primordial wisdom tradition in particular (H. Smith, 1976). There have always been opposing voices, however, who for one or another reason have preferred to emphasize the existence of significant and possibly irreducible *differences*. William James characteristically found merit in both points of view, although clearly tending philosophically toward the perennialist camp, but these contrasting tendencies have recently come into sharp conflict over Stace's taxonomy of mystical experience.

The success of Stace's enterprise depends crucially, of course, on the feasibility of applying successfully in practice his theoretical distinction between experience and interpretation—in effect, to peer through the diversity of concrete surface forms in which mystical experience has found written expression in different times, places, and religious traditions, and to discern the essential psychological characteristics of the underlying experiences. Is it really possible to perform this psychological extraction? With certain qualifications to be introduced below, we think so; we count ourselves among those persuaded that Stace demonstrated, by actually doing it, that this *is* possible, at least to a degree sufficient to sustain his characterization of the universal core.[12]

Not everyone agrees, however. An opposing position, "constructivism," was formulated with particular force and clarity in an influential essay by Steven Katz (1978) and rapidly became dominant among contemporary scholars in comparative religion. Its essence is contained in a characteristically vehement passage from that essay:

> *There are NO pure (i.e. unmediated) experiences.* Neither mystical experience nor more ordinary forms of experience give any indication, or any grounds for believing, that they are unmediated. That is to say, *all* experience is processed through, organized by, and makes itself available to us in extremely complex epistemological ways. The notion of unmediated experience seems, if not self-contradictory, at best empty....the experience itself as well as the form in which it is reported is shaped by concepts which the mystic brings to, and which shape, his experience. (p. 26)

Thus, on the view of Katz and his constructivist allies, if one is a Christian one necessarily has a distinctively Christian experience, a Taoist's experience will be structured by Taoist assumptions, a Jew can never escape from the shaping power of his Jewish upbringing, and so on. There can therefore be no ultimate type or universal core of mystical experience, independent

12. We especially recommend here a thoughtful and appreciative contemporary review by the eminent philosopher of perception H. H. Price (1962).

of factors such as time, context, gender, race, and culture. There is only a multiplicity of distinctive, culturally conditioned states of consciousness.

We believe this doctrine is seriously flawed, both psychologically and philosophically. Although we cannot go deeply into details of the controversy, we must attempt at least briefly to indicate our principal reasons for thinking so.

Katz evidently believes that his primary epistemological axiom—his italicized statement in the passage above—represents the fundamental novelty in his position and the source of his differences with Stace and other perennialists. If so, however, he is certainly mistaken. In the first place the axiom itself is not a novelty, because Stace himself accepts it; he states clearly, for example, that "there is no such thing as an absolutely pure experience without any interpretation at all" (p. 203).

Second and more importantly, the axiom by itself does not suffice to undermine Stace's project, because it leaves uncertain the degree to which *particular* experiences are in fact shaped by cultural conditioning. This is the real source of their differences. Stace nowhere claims that *all* reported mystical experiences are completely *un*mediated, but only that enough of them are sufficiently so to permit us to grasp their common psychological characteristics. Katz, by contrast, clearly presumes that experiences in general, and mystical experiences in particular, are *completely* determined by cultural conditionings. In this crucial respect Katz and other radical constructivists seem to us driven, at bottom, by an unexamined *a priori* commitment to the sort of relentless "postmodernism"—characteristic of so much contemporary scholarship in the humanities and social sciences—that abhors absolutes and universal narratives of any kind.

This sort of radical constructivism, however, is known to require heavy qualification even in the case of *ordinary* perceptual and cognitive experience, as shown for example by the old controversies over the "linguistic relativity" hypothesis of Sapir and Whorf. The fact that Eskimos have many more words than we do for specific types of snow, for example, does not entail that we are incapable of having the corresponding perceptual experiences, or of making the same distinctions (recall here too the "Scotch mist" example). Conversely, many perceptual illusions are "cognitively impenetrable" in the sense of J. Fodor (1983), and not alterable by any sort of voluntary efforts, or by knowledge of their underlying mechanisms.

It cannot be denied, of course, that most of us operate most of the time in the grip of linguistic habits, beliefs, and expectations that powerfully shape and color what we experience and report. It is equally certain that many kinds of phenomena reported by mystics, particularly in the early stages of their vocation, are shaped in similar ways. Thus, for example, whereas a Catholic mystic might report a visionary experience of Jesus or the Virgin Mary, his Hindu counterpart would naturally report a vision of Krishna, Kali, or some other personality drawn from his own religious tradition.

The radical constructivist position, however, becomes increasingly strained as we progress toward the deeper regions of mystical experience, which are precisely the ones of greatest interest both to Stace and to us. In the first place it ignores the fundamental relationship between the *character* of such experience and the practical teachings of mystics as to *how it can be achieved.* The central objective of mystical teachings and practices everywhere is essentially the same—specifically, to overcome conditionings and attachments of everyday life that get in the way of a mystical receptivity which is presumed to exist in all of us. To what degree we can in fact palliate or transcend these cultural and psychological conditionings is exactly the question at hand, and this is an empirical question. We all know from experience that it is to some degree possible to reflect upon one's beliefs, attitudes, and habits of perception and thought; to take a position for or against them; to choose to intensify and prolong or reject and eradicate them; and so on. Mysticism is a domain of human experience in which this capacity, not highly developed in most of us, is seized upon and exploited in the highest degree.

The great systematizer of Yogic practices Patanjali, for example, defines the technique of Yoga succinctly as "inhibition of the modifications of the mind" (Taimni, 1972, p. 6). Eliade (1958) characterizes these practices collectively as a process of systematic deconditioning which results in "*rebirth to a nonconditioned mode of being*" (p. 4). This "rebirth," moreover, constitutes "one of India's greatest discoveries: that of consciousness as witness, of consciousness freed from its psychophysiological structures and their temporal conditioning" (p. xx). To achieve this state, "the yogin undertakes to 'reverse' normal behavior completely. He subjects himself to a petrified immobility of body (asana), rhythmical breathing and arrest of breath (pranayama), fixation of the psychomental flux (ekagrata), [and] immobility of thought" (p. 362). The ultimate goal of Yogic training, in short, is specifically to overcome the conditionings that keep us culturally and psychologically bound, and that prevent us from experiencing what we can become in a deconditioned state.

The same principle is also evident in the various forms of Buddhism. For example, the Madyamaka school of Mahayana Buddhism, founded by Nagarjuna in the 1st century B. C. E., is explicit about the practice of progressively and systematically deconditioning the beliefs and assumptions of one's working epistemology, leading to a state of pure consciousness called the Middle Way or Emptiness. Goleman (1977) and D. P. Brown (1977) have shown respectively, and in detail, that Buddhaghosa's *Visuddhimagga* (the "path to purification") and a collection of Tibetan Buddhist meditation texts, the *Mahamudra*, can also be interpreted in these terms. Similarly, a contemporary Tibetan monk and associate of the Dalai Lama describes as the fundamental method for achieving states of emptiness or nirvana a relentless analysis of the contingent conceptualizations that permeate ordinary experience. The fundamental insight sought is that all such experience is "conceptually designated." Thus he writes: "As you look around at different objects and events, mentally comment, 'This is simply a conceptual designation.' As you do so, try to identify the basis of designation of these various objects that you identify, and see how you label things that have no label in themselves" (Lamrimpa, 1999, p. 37). One trains oneself to observe how from moment to moment one "conceptually designates" one's experience, and constructs one's contingent notions of the real, one's values, interpretations, and beliefs, or in sum the entire busy apparatus of one's everyday mental life. The central Buddhist practice is again to identify, deconstruct, and root out of consciousness these mental fabrications, and thus to realize nirvana, release, transcendence—in short, deconditioned consciousness.

The same sort of disciplined effort to overcome ordinary conditionings is also central to the practices of Plotinus and many Christian mystics. For example, Dionysius the Areopagite, one of the founders of Christian mysticism, emphasized the idea of the *via negativa* (Happold, 1963/1970, pp. 211–217). It is a way of not doing, forgetting, letting go. For Dionysius the mystical project is to "leave behind the senses and the operations of the intellect" and enter the "dazzling obscurity." In the way of negation, we deliberately go beyond all conditioned attributes "in order that, without veil, we may know that Unknowing" (p. 215).

St. John of the Cross, whose description of "secret" or ineffable wisdom we quoted earlier, also explains in complementary fashion how that infusion of wisdom is to be attained :

> A soul is greatly impeded from reaching this high estate of union with God when it clings to any understanding or feeling or imagination or appearance or will or manner of its own, and cannot detach and strip itself of all these. For, as we say, the goal which it seeks lies beyond all this, yea, beyond even the highest thing that can be known or experienced; and thus a soul must pass beyond everything to unknowing. (Peers, 1958, pp. 88–89)

Meister Eckhart's short treatise *On Detachment* (1981, pp. 285–294) is also exemplary: "I find no other virtue better than a pure detachment from all things; because all other virtues have some regard for created things, but detachment is free from all created things." Perfect detachment leads to the "annihilation of self." This language of "annihilation" and "nothingness" is of course parallel to the Sufi *fana* or fading and the early Buddhist *sunyata* or void, emptiness. By emptying the ordinary self of all sensations, images, thoughts, and volitions one arrives at the experience of pure consciousness, the Self, and as Eckhart observes, "the less there is of self, the more there is of Self" (H. Smith, 2000, p. 73).

A non-theistic Chinese text from the 8th-century T'ang Dynasty sets forth a psychological dynamic of mystical experience closely similar to that described by Meister Eckhart. The text, by Hui Hai, *On Sudden Illumination*, is a manual consisting of questions and answers regarding the attempt to achieve nirvana, the experience that offers "deliverance while still in this life" (Blofeld, 1962, p. 77). Hui Hai uses plain language, without theological metaphors and assumptions, to describe the necessary discipline: "Just let things happen without making any response," he says, "and keep your minds from dwelling on anything whatsoever; for he who can do this thereby enters Nirvana." The expression "anything whatsoever" is equivalent to Meister Eckhart's "all created things," except that the latter has an obvious theological connotation that "anything whatsoever" does not. To *not dwell* on anything whatsoever is an expression that Hui Hai keeps using, and its meaning is clear. To not dwell on something is to detach oneself from it. The quotation continues: "Attained, then, is the condition of no rebirth, otherwise called the gate of non-duality, the end of strife (peace and calm)....Why so? Because it is ultimate purity" (Blofeld, 1962, p. 77). Thus, comparing the Christian Meister Eckhart with the Chinese Buddhist, whose accounts are relatively uncluttered by mythic and theological baggage, we find that both the experience itself and the procedures for inducing it are described in practically identical terms.

Many further examples of this sort could readily be provided, but this would serve little purpose here. Our essential point is that crucial features of the introvertive mystical experience as characterized by Stace—in particular its aspects of undifferentiated unity, devoid of all multiplicity—are precisely what would be expected to follow from successful practice of these central mystical disciplines. These "vacuum" properties, moreover, are the ones most critical to Stace's subsequent philosophical arguments, and they are also the ones most amenable to direct confirmation by first-person testimony of the sort that he marshals. It seems clear to us, in sum, that when mystics talk about inhibiting the modifications of the mind and going beyond or becoming detached from all "created" (read, *constructed*) things, they understand their challenge precisely as that of systematically overcoming the sorts of conditioning that Katz and his allies assume without question cannot be overcome. Deikman's (1966) well-known characterization of meditation as "de-automatization" embodies the same basic idea. Perovich (1990) takes it to the philosophical limit by characterizing constructivism as a misapplication of Kant's epistemology to experiences which inherently transcend the shaping or filtering effects even of our most fundamental perceptual categories such as space, time, causality, and selfhood. Important commonalities in the resulting experiences, moreover, can be seen as direct expressions of corresponding commonalities in the means that mystics have discovered for accomplishing this deconditioning and thus reducing or even escaping altogether, at least temporarily, the normal influence of this Kantian "filter."

Several related observations further undermine the alleged causal potency of cultural conditionings in shaping all details of mystical experience. There is first an abundant historical record, particularly in the Western theistic traditions, of tensions resulting from the tendency of mystical experiences as actually lived to break through the crust of local ecclesiastical culture. Happold (1963/1970, p. 249), for example, points to Sufism as a prime example of this tendency; indeed, several Sufi mystics are known to have been put to death for heresy after reporting their unitive experiences with unguarded candor and enthusiasm. Meister Eckhart got into trouble with the Catholic Church for similar reasons, and in his emphasis on the potential for each individual to discover a Godhead hidden within, he can perhaps even be viewed as a precursor to the Reformation. At a lower level one can find many instances of the phenomenon of "redogmatization" (Neumann, 1968/1970) in which a mystic's initial report is subsequently altered, whether by himself or by someone else such as a secretary or ecclesiastical authority, in order to bring it into better alignment with local doctrinal requirements. Stace (1960/1987, pp. 154–161) treats the changing interpretations by Martin Buber of his own introvertive mystical experience as an example of this phenomenon. Among other things, this points up the hazards of relying exclusively on mystical *texts*, particularly when original authorship or the adequacy of translations is uncertain. As Stace points out, direct investigation of contemporary cases affords the enormous methodological advantage that ambiguities and uncertainties about the details of experiences as initially reported can potentially be resolved through interaction with their subjects.

One further argument against the position of Katz and other radical constructivists seems to us even more decisive. Powerful mystical experiences of the types identified by Stace have often occurred spontaneously in "naive" persons who previously had no commitment to, or involvement in, *any* particular religious or mystical tradition. The first or foundational experiences within such traditions presumably must have been of this type, and in cases such as that of Arthur Koestler they have occurred in persons antecedently hostile to the entire subject. We emphasize that in cases of these sorts the constructivist picture of causal dependence is not simply unsupported but *inverted*, in that it is often the experiences themselves that impel such persons to develop or seek out an interpretive conceptual framework capable of rendering them intelligible. Grinspoon and Bakalar (1979/1997) have argued that it is in fact precisely in this way that the psychedelic movement of the 1960s quickly affiliated itself with the Oriental wisdom traditions.

Folklorist David Hufford (1985, 2005) has also pointed out that in these respects mystical experiences (and NDEs) appear strikingly analogous to the "supernatural assault" or sleep-paralysis experiences that have been the primary focus of his own research (Hufford, 1982). By being more careful than previous investigators about the phenomenological details, Hufford was able to show that these sleep-paralysis experiences have their own "universal core," a consistent underlying phenomenology that gets interpreted in varying terms in different historical and cross-cultural contexts: "The actual details of the experience do not vary according to the victim's background, prior beliefs, or knowledge of a cultural model for the experience" (Hufford, 1982, p. 120). In this case the experiential uniformity clearly reflects a corresponding uniformity in the biological conditions under which sleep-paralysis experiences occur, and Hufford surmises that this will prove the case in regard to mystical experiences as well.[13]

---

13. Similar comments apply, of course, to NDEs, which overlap phenomenologically with both mystical and psychedelic experiences (see Chapter 6, and Ring, 1988).

We conclude, then, that the constructivist critique falls short, and that Stace's characterization of a most-extreme form or universal core in mystical experiences remains valid. This is *not* to claim, however, that all mystical experiences are the same. The domain is large and heterogeneous, and the constructivists are certainly correct in maintaining that cultural conditioning plays an important role in shaping large parts of it. But the domain also appears to be stratified more or less in the way Stace describes, with its psychologically and philosophically most significant region lying beyond the reach of purely constructivist principles. One can certainly honor and investigate the real differences among mystical traditions, as constructivists advocate, without denying the reality of these vital commonalities. Considerable further support for this position, especially in regard to the existence and importance of states of pure, undifferentiated consciousness, can be found in an important series of books by philosopher Robert Forman (1990, 1998, 1999), himself apparently a subject of such states.

Although we are indebted to Stace for his taxonomic labors, some critical points also need to be made. We agree first with Price (1962) that he puts rather too much emphasis on cool intellectual mystics such as Meister Eckhart at the expense of more devotional or emotional ones such as St. Teresa of Avila. Stace constantly reminds his readers that Teresa is naive, uncritical, not quite up to par philosophically, and—no doubt worst of all—drunk with love. Yet the available evidence clearly suggests that both reason and emotion, each in their own way, can serve—when rightly deployed—as tools of mystical self-development. The Hindu tradition, for example, recognizes the Bhakti or devotional path as equally valid, and Plato, the Sufis, and other great Christian mystics such as St. John of the Cross would certainly agree. James clearly admires St. Teresa's psychological self-descriptions, and Peers (1951, p. xvii) even characterizes her as the central unifying personality among the great Spanish mystics. In short, Stace's personal predilections as an analytic philosopher seem to have led him to underrate the potential contributions of religious emotion to the genesis of mystical states.[14]

Second, we must insist that Stace was misguided in excluding voices, visions, and allied subjects from the class of "genuine" mystical phenomena (pp. 47–55). These are indeed very different from the more extreme phenomena that are especially germane to his own philosophical agenda, and they are widely recognized by mystics and scholars alike as belonging primarily to earlier, lower, or less advanced stages of mystical development. Nevertheless, they comprise a variety of unusual and interesting psychological phenomena which form an important part of the total worldwide literature of mysticism. Moreover, as we will soon show, they occupy a natural place within the sort of psychological model advanced by Myers and James.

---

14. Ironically, philosopher John E. Smith (1983) takes William James to task in exactly the opposite direction—that is, for not adequately appreciating the potential contribution of abstract metaphysical reasoning to the genesis of mystical states, as illustrated by the case of St. Bonaventure.

To banish them summarily as Stace does is to overlook and obscure these important psychological continuities.

The Problem of Objective Significance

The consistency with which mystics describe their deepest experiences demonstrates that they are testifying more or less correctly about unusual states of consciousness that really do occur, and that are profoundly impressive to their subjects. As we have already seen, however, this unanimity of the great mystics about their experience, although *necessary*, is not by itself *sufficient* to establish any thesis regarding its objective significance. It could still be entirely subjective, a shared illusion, a mirage, as the great majority of contemporary scientists undoubtedly suppose.

On the other hand, it should be equally clear that identification of some biological condition or conditions under which mystical experience occurs would not by itself *disprove* its objective significance. Reductionist scientists have always been inclined to overlook this rather elementary logical point, and the recent spate of facile and triumphant neurologizing about "God Spots" and the like is only the latest installment in a long and dismal history. William James went to considerable pains to disarm this unthinkingly skeptical attitude in the very first chapter of *VRE*: Medical materialism "has no physiological theory of the production of these its favorite states [i.e., ordinary states], by which it may accredit them; and its attempt to discredit the states which it dislikes, by vaguely associating them with nerves and liver, and connecting them with names connoting bodily affliction, is altogether illogical and inconsistent" (p. 30). All ordinary perceptual and cognitive experience goes forward in conjunction with biological processes in our bodies and brains, but nobody denies for that reason that such experience can teach us important things about the reality in which we find ourselves situated. It could also be the case, as the mystics themselves believe, that *their* experience contains lessons of at least equal importance in regard to that reality. As James himself concluded, mystical experience like all other experience "must be sifted and tested, and run the gauntlet of confrontation with the total context of experience" (*VRE*, p. 326).

James, as we saw earlier, was led by his own survey to a carefully guarded epistemological position: Mystics do gravitate in certain definite philosophical directions, but they are less than fully unanimous about this, and however impressive their experiences may be individually, collectively they warrant no specific propositions about the nature of reality to which those of us who are non-mystics need assent. This remained more or less the received opinion among philosophers for many decades, as illustrated by the quotations above from Bertrand Russell and by old standard texts in epistemology such as Montague (1925). Stace, however, builds upon his characterization of the universal core in a serious effort to carry the subject further. Specifically, he offers a novel—indeed, startling—philosophical argument in support of the view that mystical experience literally is, as the mystics themselves claim, in an important way *transsubjective.*

Stace's Philosophical Argument for Objective Significance

A sense of self-transcendence is inherent in the introvertive mystical experience, and closely tied to its noetic quality. In this state of pure, unitary consciousness,

> the boundary walls of the separate self fade away, and the individual finds himself passing beyond himself and becoming merged in a boundless and universal consciousness....The conclusion which the mystic draws—not however by way of a reasoned conclusion, but as something immediately experienced—is that what he has reached is not merely his individual pure ego but the pure ego of the universe; or, otherwise put, that his individual self and the universal self are somehow one and the same. (Stace, 1960/1987, pp. 147–148)

Now comes the startling part: Speculative philosophical reasoning, Stace argues, leads necessarily to the same conclusion. For if any two persons A and B have each attained a state of pure, unitary, undifferentiated consciousness, there is no longer any property that could individuate or distinguish these states. They are therefore identical, both to each other and to any other such states. For the same reason, moreover, there can be only one pure ego in the universe. "Hence," Stace concludes, "the mystic who has reached what seems at first to be his own private pure ego has in fact reached the pure ego of the universe, the pure cosmic ego" (p. 151). The same sort of argument, he adds, shows that the extrovertive "One" and the introvertive "One" are one and the same.

This argument is assuredly breathtaking, but is it sound? Like Price (1962), we think not, although for slightly different reasons. At its base lies a logical principle sometimes attributed to Leibniz called "the identity of indiscernibles." The crucial point about this principle is that any identity claim based upon it is falsified by discovery of any property whatsoever that differentiates the things identified.[15] Price points out that two *minds* are always differentiated by more than their *occurrent* contents, their conscious states alone. *Dispositional* properties such as memories, skills, habits, and the like also count, and these clearly survive the mystic's conscious experience of undifferentiated unity.

Price's argument here is undoubtedly correct, and Stace certainly left himself open to it by speaking explicitly and repeatedly in terms of identity of *minds*. Stace might have responded, we surmise, by restricting his identity

15. Discovery of such properties, for example, is what forced abandonment of early mind-brain identity theories; see Kim (1998, chap. 3) and our Chapter 1.

claim more carefully to the conscious states themselves; but even this cannot save the argument, for it relies too heavily upon his own very abstract characterization of the *vacuum* aspect of introvertive mystical experiences. In reality, things are more complicated. Even Meister Eckhart, for example, who provides Stace with many classic descriptions of unitary consciousness, points out repeatedly that some tiny spark or thread of individuality always remains, even in his "deepest" states, which enables his return to the ordinary state.

More generally, our reading of the mystical literature suggests that there is ample room for differentiation of introvertive mystical states on the *plenum* side, in terms of their positive characteristics. Affectively, for example, they seem to range from relatively bland or neutral (or perhaps even somewhat negative, as in the very atypical case of J. A. Symonds; see *VRE*, pp. 296–297) to blissful beyond comparison; as James remarks, "the deliciousness of some of these states seems to be beyond anything known to ordinary consciousness" (p. 316).

What this points to again, in our opinion, is the need for a more detailed, precise, and empirically well-grounded phenomenological cartography of mystical states. Many such cartographies have already been advanced within the world's mystical traditions, of course, often in mind-numbing detail. The difficulties of this profoundly interesting subject are unfortunately greatly magnified by the increasing inability of ordinary language to convey adequately the properties of the relevant states and experiences as one ascends the mystical scale. Although these schemes certainly bear generic resemblances to one another (as indeed they must, if Stace and other perennialists are right about a common core), we cannot agree with those such as H. Smith (1976) who apparently think this mapping of mystical states has already been successfully completed, and that the wisdom traditions themselves provide alternative but equivalent descriptions of the same, well-established empirical realities. We will not attempt to argue this point here, but the actual level of resemblance among the traditional taxonomies seems to us rather more like that of a group of garden shrubs, similar in global shape but differing markedly in internal detail. Nor do we find any compelling reason to suppose that any one of these traditions is empirically complete and has correctly worked out the whole story, or even is significantly ahead of all the others in attempting to do so. We do not doubt that much can be learned through comparative study of the wisdom traditions, but we also think a complementary approach to the problem using modern scientific methods is urgently needed, and long overdue.

In sum, Stace's abstract philosophical argument for the objective significance of mystical experience does not quite succeed. Stace himself acknowledges that it cannot be regarded as conclusive, although he personally finds it strong (p. 202). But at the very least it deserves admiration as a unique attempt to theorize about mystical experiences in a manner commensurate in boldness with the extraordinary character of the experiences themselves. It may yet prove true, that is, that the mystic arrives at what

Plotinus calls the center of the sphere, the single point at which all of its great circles intersect—"the still point of the turning world," in T. S. Eliot's memorable phrase.

Empirical Arguments for Objective Significance

Stace himself turns next to various ontological matters outside the scope of this chapter. There is much more still to be said, however, in regard to the objective significance of mystical experience. Specifically, we will now present some additional, *empirical*, arguments supporting the view that mystics do in fact make contact with reality in novel ways.

Mysticism and Genius

As already suggested near the end of the previous chapter, there are profound and inescapable interconnections, both historical and psychological, between mysticism and genius. Historically, for example, it is brute fact that the two co-occur to a conspicuous degree. Bucke's roster of 50 actual and borderline subjects of cosmic consciousness includes not only outstanding religious personalities such as Jesus, Paul, Mohammed, Ramakrishna, and the Buddha, but literary and philosophic luminaries including Socrates, Plotinus, Dante, Pascal, Spinoza, Blake, Balzac, Emerson, Whitman, Wordsworth, Tennyson, Pushkin, and Thoreau. Most of the latter also appear on Bloom's (2002) roster of the 100 all-time greatest writers, along with several others such as Plato, Virgil, and St. Augustine who could have appeared on Bucke's list as well. Other writers on Bucke's list such as Edward Carpenter and Richard Jefferies were highly regarded in their own time, and a number of significant contemporary writers including not only Koestler but Gerard Manley Hopkins, John Masefield, Romain Rolland, Rabindranath Tagore, and Simone Weil are also known to have had mystical or near-mystical experiences. There are undoubtedly many additional literary cases not known to us, and similar patterns are known to exist among artists, musicians, and possibly even scientists. The tradition linking music with mysticism goes back at least as far as Pythagoras, and a list of Western composers subject to mystical-type experience would almost certainly include not only Bach, Mozart, and Beethoven, but numerous others such as Cage, Elgar, Holst, Liszt, Messiaen, Satie, Scriabin, and the jazz artist John Coltrane.[16]

In sum, whether one looks from the genius side or from the mysticism side, one observes what appears to be a highly significant historical linkage between these rare and highly valued human attributes.[17] Indeed, it is no

16. We are indebted to concert pianist Lorin Hollander for this information (personal communication, April 9, 2006).

17. Many difficulties stand in the way of evaluating this association in a rigorous way using only historical documents, but for us it satisfies what statisticians jokingly refer to as the "IOT" ("InterOcular Trauma") test—it socks you right between the eyes.

exaggeration to say with Bucke that mystical consciousness pervades the foundations of all civilization. The correlation is less than perfect, to be sure, for there have been geniuses who are not recognizably mystics and vice versa. Nevertheless, we predict with confidence (as would Myers) that if one administered standardized instruments for measurement of creativity and mysticism to a sufficiently large sample of subjects, one would find a significant overrepresentation of persons scoring extremely high on both dimensions simultaneously. Some preliminary evidence of such a relationship has in fact already been found by Thalbourne and Delin (1994, 1999). These authors go on, moreover, to suggest that this association results from a shared personality factor that they call "transliminality," tentatively defined as "a largely involuntary susceptibility to, and awareness of, large volumes of inwardly generated psychological phenomena of an ideational and affective kind" (Thalbourne & Delin, 1994, p. 25). Although they apparently developed this concept on their own, its affinity with Myers's spectrum psychology is evident. Indeed, they even epitomize their conception using the remark by Underhill (1911/1974), essentially paraphrasing Myers, that "a 'mobile threshold' may make a man a genius, a lunatic, or a saint" (p. 62).[18]

Mystical experiences also drive *within*-person creative production in various ways. It is hardly surprising, for example, that persons who have been the subjects of such powerful experiences will often seek to publicize them using whatever powers of expression they antecedently possess. Thus, Dante produces the *Paradiso*, Tennyson's recurrent experience of self-transcendence finds it way into *The Ancient Sage*, Koestler grinds out his four books in five years, and—for good or ill—Jacob Boehme generates thick tomes crammed with impenetrable Hermetic symbolism.

There is one further connection, however, which to our knowledge remains poorly documented but which if real is of potentially considerable significance to cognitive science. Specifically, mystical experience may sometimes transform an individual's perceptual, cognitive, and expressive capacities themselves. Bucke (1901/1969), for example, regards such sudden increases in mental powers as one aspect of an objective "transfiguration" produced by genuine experiences of cosmic consciousness. His primary example is Walt Whitman, whose published works he studied diligently and whom he knew personally as well. Bucke asserts that "in the case of Whitman (as in that of Balzac) writings of absolutely no value were *immediately* followed (and, at least in Whitman's case without practice or study) by pages...covered not only by a masterpiece but by such vital sentences as have not been written ten times in the history of the race" (p. 226). We our-

18. There is some irony here, for Underhill herself certainly *was* familiar with Myers's depth psychology. She cites him explicitly only once, but shows considerable general acquaintance with the subject matter of *HP*, and liberally invokes key Myers concepts such as those of automatisms, uprushes, and subliminal mentation. She in fact uses Myers in much the same way as does James in *VRE*, while apparently distancing herself rather deliberately, for reasons we can only surmise, from both. One wonders how subsequent mysticism scholarship might have been altered had she been less reticent about these scientific connections, and less of an apologist for Christianity.

selves have encountered several individuals who informally reported noting sudden and dramatic increases in their perceptual acuity, reading speed, problem-solving ability, memory capacities, and the like following moderately intense mystical experiences. These changes were further described as either permanent or slowly fading over periods of weeks to months. Effects of these types, although relatively mundane, could much more readily be measured and documented using conventional cognitive instruments.

In sum, the within-subject impact of mystical experience on cognitive capacities in general and on creative activity in particular seems to us a topic ripe for more careful investigation. But let us now attempt to draw out more fully the deep psychological parallels between mysticism and genius. In the previous chapter, it will be recalled, we showed how Myers characterized inspirations of genius in terms of three primary features—*continuity*, *automatism*, and *incommensurability*. The same three features are also conspicuously present in relation to mystical experience and the mystic vocation.

Continuity, for example, was already apparent on a global scale in the sequence of proto-mystical phenomena assembled by James in *VRE*. Myers (*HP*, chap. 9) examines the upper portion of this range in greater psychological detail, tracing out a continuum that leads from trance mediumship and its parallels in the lower forms of shamanism "straight into the inmost sanctuary of mysticism" (*HP*, vol. 2, p. 259)—the ecstatic flights of Plotinus and the other great mystics. Thus:

> From the medicine-man of the lowest savages up to St. John, St. Peter, St. Paul, with Buddha and Mahomet on the way, we find records which, though morally and intellectually much differing, are in psychological essence the same....We thus show continuity and reality among phenomena which have seldom been either correlated with each other or even intelligibly conceived in separation. With our new insight we may correlate the highest and the lowest ecstatic phenomena with no injury whatever to the highest. (p. 260)[19]

In deliberate pursuit of the mystic vocation, moreover, each individual describes a unique trajectory along this dimension of depth, determined in part by his own characteristics and in part by the tradition in which he operates. This is brought out most clearly in relation to the role of *automatism*, the second feature shared with genius.

19. Although we agree in general terms with their conception of an underlying continuity between the highest mystical phenomena and phenomena of lower types, we must comment here that both Myers and James seem to us to share the characteristic cultural chauvinism of their time in being rather too ready to exalt Christianity at the expense of other religions, and to presume that pre-literate peoples are incapable of the higher forms of religious experience. We dare not elaborate on the former, but in regard to the latter see for example the Plains Indian specialist Joseph Epes Brown (1991), who defends core elements of Native American traditions as legitimate and independent expressions of the perennial philosophy, and Eliade (1964), who finds examples of genuine mystical states among Siberian shamans.

William James was fully aware of the connections between automatism and *passivity*, his fourth marker of mystical states. When a genuine mystical state breaks in, he observes, "the mystic feels as if his own will were in abeyance, and indeed sometimes as if he were grasped and held by a superior power. This latter peculiarity connects mystical states with certain definite phenomena of secondary or alternative personality, such as prophetic speech, automatic writing, or the mediumistic trance" (*VRE*, p. 293). Unlike phenomena of the latter types, however, which tend to be merely interruptive and produce no lasting effects, advanced mystical states of consciousness always leave behind some degree of memory for their content, accompanied by conviction of their importance, and they often exert profound transformative effects on the inner lives of their subjects. Thus they fall into place in a natural way as higher or more developed forms of the sorts of psychological automatisms discussed in Chapter 5.

There can be little doubt, moreover, that the trajectory of individual mystics often consists in considerable part of progression from the lower to the higher forms. This is particularly evident in the relatively well-documented lives of the Christian mystics as presented for example by Underhill (1911/1974) and Maréchal (1927/2004). Lower stages of the mystic path are replete with voices, visions, automatic writing and speaking, and kindred phenomena. Underhill points to Madam Guyon, for example, as being almost as much medium as mystic:

> When she was composing her works she would experience a sudden and irresistable inclination to take up her pen; though feeling wholly incapable of literary composition, and not even knowing the subject on which she would be impelled to write. If she resisted this impulse it was at the cost of the most intense discomfort. She would then begin to write with extraordinary swiftness; words, elaborate arguments, and appropriate quotations coming to her without reflection, and so quickly that one of her longest books was written in one and a half days. (p. 66)

The psychological resemblance here between Mme. Guyon and creative mediums such as Hélène Smith (Chapter 7) is unmistakable. Underhill cites a number of additional cases including those of Jacob Boehme and St. Teresa in which automatisms were pronounced, and she also points out their general psychological kinship with the phenomenon of creative inspiration.

In both domains, moreover, the value of what is produced can be seen to increase as the process reaches progressively deeper into the psyche. Low-grade forms of mystical vision mainly reflect ordinary forms of personal experience and conventional religious symbolisms, but the contribution of automatisms to deliberate mystical development is systematic and progressive, ultimately breaking through the shell of the ordinary individuality. Underhill quotes an elegant synopsis by Delacroix, based on intensive case studies, which Myers would certainly have applauded:

> [These automatisms] are governed by an interior aim; they have, above all, a teleological character. They indicate the continuous intervention of a being at once wiser and more powerful than the ordinary character and reason; they are the realization, in visual and auditory images, of a secret and permanent personality of a superior type to the conscious personality. They are its voice, the exterior projection of its life. They translate to the conscious personality the suggestions of the subconscious: and they permit the continuous penetration of the conscious personality by these deeper activities. They establish a communication between these two planes of existence, and, by their imperative nature, they tend to make the inferior subordinate to the superior. (p. 273)

At the higher stages of the mystic path, moreover, automatisms progressively shed their quasi-sensory character, while becoming ever more illuminating and transformative to their subjects. Thus, for example, as St. Teresa advances from her *Life* to *The Interior Castle*, her "visions" become increasingly abstract, or "intellectual," and decoupled from conventional symbolisms.[20] And this is as it must be, for as her own mentor St. John of the Cross also advises, an aspirant to the highest unitive states "must be careful not to lean upon imaginary visions, forms, figures, and particular intelligible objects, for these things can never serve as proportionate or proximate means to so great an end; yea, rather they are an obstacle in the way, and therefore to be guarded against and rejected" (Peers, 1958, p. 156).

In the limit, as Stace demonstrates, the great mystics succeed in emptying themselves altogether of cognitive particulars, whereupon they experience that extraordinary inflowing of boundless, pure, undifferentiated consciousness—an introvertive mystical experience. At this point the third shared characteristic, *incommensurability*, becomes even more pronounced than in the case of genius, for all observers from Bucke and James forward agree that such states are startlingly different from everyday consciousness—discrete altered states of consciousness as described by Tart (1975a). Indeed, it is precisely from this appearance of uncovering something normally hidden but radically distinct from and superior to ordinary consciousness that mystical states derive their psychological impact and interest, for subjects and observers alike.

Mysticism and Supernormal Phenomena

One further property shared by mysticism with genius, and potentially decisive in regard to the question of its objective significance, is its association with supernormal phenomena of various sorts. Indeed, explicit claims

20. The modern mystical experience of Jungian psychologist Genevieve Foster (1985) was closely similar to some of Teresa's "intellectual visions," as Foster herself eventually discovered upon reading Underhill. Its core feature was an overwhelming sense of numinous contact with a loving but invisible being whose presence was keenly felt and sharply localized in space. This "vision" lasted for some five days, and it transformed her life. See also Hufford's (1985) interesting commentary on this case, and Maréchal (1927/2004), who makes the "feeling of presence," in a hierarchy of progressively intense forms, central to his account of mystical development.

regarding such an association are far more widespread and conspicuous in regard to mysticism, suggesting once again that mysticism at its core involves an even more extreme development of the psychological processes and results so skillfully delineated by Myers in relation to genius.[21]

Biographies of the founding personalities of the great religions are of course replete with reports of "miraculous" doings of various sorts. These reports are of little or no scientific value, however, and like Myers we shall decline to discuss or invoke them. We will begin instead by returning to the subject of Yoga, which for our purposes provides a more promising starting point.[22]

Within the Hindu tradition, an enormous body of theoretical and practical information pertaining to Yoga was collected, systematized, and crystallized in the form of 196 aphorisms or "Sutras" by Patanjali somewhere near the beginning of the Christian era. This remarkable work, still widely regarded as an authoritative source of practical information on Yoga, outlines within its four brief chapters a sophisticated doctrine regarding human psychophysical organization, which supplies in turn the theoretical basis for a comprehensive program of self-development. The claimed results of this program, catalogued at considerable length, explicitly include the systematic appearance of both higher states of consciousness and a variety of supernormal capacities.

There have been many translations and expositions of the Yoga Sutras and associated commentaries, but the most helpful ones known to us are those of Dasgupta (1924/1970), Eliade (1958, 1969), and Taimni (1972). These systematically expand the extremely compressed and often difficult language of the Sutras, presenting thorough expositions of Patanjali's doctrines and locating them in the larger matrix of orthodox Hindu philosophy.[23]

Central to Patanjali's practical psychology is a process of progressive intensification of attention, culminating in unwavering absorption in its objects. Three progressively deeper stages are distinguished—concentration (*dharana*), meditation (*dhyana*), and the highest state or states of absorption (*samadhi*). This threefold process, *Samyama*, represents much

---

21. William James himself verges upon this argument at various points in *VRE* (see, e.g., pp. 313, 314, 378), but always holds back, confining the relevant remarks to brief asides, allusions, and footnotes. His conservatism may have been "politically" wise in the academic environment of the Gifford lectures, and indeed his very first words were: "It is with no small amount of trepidation that I take my place behind this desk, and face this learned audience." Nevertheless, that James did not more systematically and openly bring the findings of psychical research to bear on the problem of mystical "truth" seems to us an unfortunate instance, rare for him, of missed opportunity. It certainly does not reflect any ambivalence or uncertainty on his part regarding the value of these findings (see, e.g., James, 1890–1896/1910).

22. In this section we have adapted some material previously published in E. F. Kelly and Locke (1981b). We thank the Parapsychology Foundation for permission to use this material.

23. Readers should be forewarned, however, that Taimni occasionally injects superfluous elements of Theosophical doctrine into his interpretations of Patanjali's meaning. See also Jain and Jain (1973) for a useful summary of Patanjali's system by contemporary biomedical scientists.

more than a movement within the range of ordinary states of consciousness. Indeed the central thrust of Patanjali's exposition is to describe how the practice of *Samyama*, systematically intensified, will lead through a hierarchy of increasingly exalted discrete states to the ultimate mystical objective of pure, undifferentiated, limitless consciousness. The emergence of supernormal capacities or *siddhis* is reported in matter-of-fact fashion as a by-product of this central movement, their value consisting mainly in providing markers on the developmental path.[24]

The Yoga Sutras thus contain an explicit and elaborate theoretical statement of relationships between mystical states and supernormal phenomena, one which in principle lends itself to empirical verification. In spirit, Patanjali's treatise is really a scientific work more than a religious or philosophical one, although it predates this kind of academic dismemberment of its subject matter. Its central doctrines are presented not as authoritarian dogma simply to be believed, but as empirical realities that can be experientially verified through assiduous practice of specified disciplines.

From a modern experimentally oriented point of view, unfortunately, the state of evidence directly pertinent to these claims is still unsatisfactory. Although there are innumerable supportive anecdotes and field observations of varying impressiveness, there is still little hard evidence documenting the occurrence of high-grade psi in meditative adepts. This may be due at least in part to systematic reluctance on the part of such persons to demonstrate psi abilities; Patanjali himself remarks, and the traditions for the most part agree, that preoccupation with the *siddhis* is to be avoided, for it draws the mind outward and thus creates obstacles to achievement of unitive consciousness, the mystic's proper goal. Skeptics will naturally suspect that this is merely an excuse, and we ourselves do not doubt that this may sometimes be the case. In our experience with serious meditators, however, it seems far more commonly a genuinely held attitude. One can readily appreciate the dangers of paying too much and the wrong kind of attention to these phenomena, as emphasized especially by Underhill, but to ignore and denigrate them in a wholesale manner seems equally a mistake in view of their important bearing on the issue of mystical "truth."[25] Good psi experiments with truly accomplished meditators would represent landmark scientific events in both fields. We ourselves would welcome such opportunities, and perhaps other groups such as the Dalai Lama's Mind and Life Institute will ultimately venture in this direction as well.

Meanwhile, a modest amount of progress has already been made in linking lower-grade forms of meditation experimentally with psi. Honor-

---

24. An interesting detail arises here: Although the Yogic discipline of meditation is emphasized as providing the main pathway to the *siddhis,* Patanjali also acknowledges that they may arise "abnormally" in certain other contexts. The relevant sutra (vol. 1, sutra 19) is particularly obscure, but Taimni argues plausibly that it can be construed as referring specifically to capacities for trance mediumship.

25. For similar reasons we deplore the curious tendency of transpersonal psychology to distance itself from parapsychology, at least in part out of what looks to us like unthinking compliance with the prevailing negative attitude of the wisdom traditions.

ton (1977) pointed out that the eight limbs of Yogic practice as outlined by Patanjali can be understood at minimum as a system of progressive psychophysical noise reduction leading to a state characterized by physical relaxation, isolation from the normal sensory environment, and intensely focused inwardly directed attention. This is strikingly consistent with the self-descriptions of gifted ESP subjects (R. A. White, 1964), and it would therefore not be surprising if even modest practice of Yoga and its central techniques of meditation should produce conditions favorable for the occurrence of psi. And indeed this appears to be the case, as indicated by an increasing variety and number of experimental studies of psi performance in relation to meditation and similar low-noise conditions (Braud, 1978; Honorton, 1977, 1997; Rao & Palmer, 1987).

Although the linkage identified by Patanjali between the achievement of deep meditative and mystical states and the emergence of strong psi phenomena has barely begun to be verified and explored experimentally, significant further support for such a linkage derives indirectly from comparative study of the wisdom traditions themselves. It is noteworthy first that Patanjali's catalog of *siddhis* is anything but unique. Other mystical traditions, including relatively remote ones such as Sufism, Catholicism, and the many expressions of Shamanism in preliterate societies, have discovered and catalogued many of the same phenomena in strikingly parallel ways. These parallels are drawn out in considerable detail by M. Murphy (1992), who provides what is by far the most systematic attempt to date to construct a "natural history" of the entire domain.

More importantly, this domain is not populated solely by unverifiable oral reports of ancient anecdotal lore, as many skeptical observers might casually suppose. Significant empirical anchorage can be found, for example, in an important but neglected work by Herbert Thurston (1952). Thurston, a Jesuit scholar, performed the heroic service of digesting innumerable volumes of Catholic hagiography in search of serious evidence of supernormal phenomena in the lives of the saints. Most of what he found falls within the ambiguous domain of extreme psychophysiological influence—what Myers referred to generically as "hyperboulia," or "increased power over the organism" (*HP*, vol. 1, p. xiii). Relevant phenomena here include stigmata (appearance of the wounds of Christ), tokens of espousal (deformation of the skin to produce structures with the appearance of wedding rings or other symbols of the mystical marriage), "incendium amoris" (production of intense bodily heat), inedia (not eating for weeks, months, or years), capacity to sustain prolonged contact with fire, boiling water, and so forth, without pain or injury, several peculiarities manifested by saintly corpses (prolonged incorruption, continued bleeding, or absence of rigidity), and luminous phenomena.[26] Other phenomena investigated by Thurston, how-

26. Luminous phenomena form a complex and fascinating subject deserving of detailed treatment on its own. The introvertive mystical state of consciousness is often described as "self-effulgent," and Bucke takes this sense of unusual subjective light as one of the defining marks of cosmic consciousness. Something of this sort is in fact commonly reported in con-

ever, fall well within the traditional domain of psi research, including both ESP phenomena of various kinds and macroscopic PK phenomena including in the most extreme cases outright bodily levitation.

Thurston's method is to adduce evidence systematically for each of the targeted phenomena in turn, based on the lives of saints (mainly post-16th-century) who reportedly manifested them. The evidence cited comes primarily from the written records of formal proceedings instituted by the Church for the purposes of determining whether these particular individuals merited beatification or canonization. However, Thurston also goes to considerable pains to point out instances of analogous phenomena documented outside the Church. In particular, he seems to have been quite familiar with the early work of the SPR and with its standards of evidence.

How seriously should scientifically minded persons take this rather mind-boggling assortment of material? Although this must always remain to some degree a matter of personal judgment, conditioned by individual knowledge and sensibilities, we ourselves believe, for reasons we will next briefly explain, that it deserves to be taken very seriously indeed.

Four main features of Thurston's evidence seem to us significant. First is its sheer *volume*. Many individual events of very unsubtle type were observed and reported consistently by large numbers of people and/or on repeated occasions, with some of this testimony coming from initially hostile or skeptical witnesses. Some of the reports also appear to be independent in the sense that persons manifesting or reporting a particular phenomenon appear unlikely to have known of other contemporaneous or previous manifestations of that same phenomenon. Furthermore, most of the categories of phenomena, in particular those that do not depend on specifically Christian doctrine, have been reported to recur independently in a variety of settings, and some, such as the phenomena of extreme psychophysical influence, have been independently confirmed and amplified by a variety of modern scientific evidence (Chapter 3).

Second is the general *quality* of the evidence. Beatification and canonization proceedings are serious business, not unlike secular trials. Although *bona fide* "miracles" might make good advertisements for the faith, the Church is a conservative institution with considerable investment in avoiding potentially embarrassing and damaging error. Evidence presented in favor of a candidate is systematically attacked by a "devil's advocate" or *promotor fidei* whose specific task is to find weaknesses sufficient to throw out the case. The records distinguish among types and grades of evidence—for example, first-hand versus second-hand testimony, skeptical versus docile witnesses, and so forth—and important witnesses are whenever possible

---

junction not only with religious mystical states but also with OBEs, NDEs, shamanic journeys, and apparitional experiences of many sorts (see Chapter 6). The unusual luminosities, moreover, are sometimes "objective" in the sense that they may be visible to some though not necessarily all potential observers, or on rare occasions even photographed or detected by optical instruments such as photomultiplier tubes (Alvarado, 1987; Joines, Baumann, Kim, Zile, & Simmonds, 2004). Intellectual or spiritual "illumination" and "enlightenment," in short, may sometimes involve more than mere metaphors.

formally deposed. On the whole, the quality of evidence seems to be fairly comparable to that appearing in the spontaneous case material assembled by Gurney et al. (1886) and their SPR colleagues.

Third is the *attitude* of these individuals toward their phenomena. There is usually scarcely a trace of any sense of pride or ownership. Indeed, many of the cases reveal not only humility but acute embarrassment often coupled with active efforts to *conceal* the supernormal events, lest they should draw too much attention and disrupt the individual's central spiritual practices. Any superficial attempt to simulate these attitudes in hopes of promoting chances of eventual sainthood would likely have been detected by the *promotor fidei.*

Finally and most germane to the central concerns of this chapter, a strong association is evident in this material between the occurrence of the various supernormal phenomena and the achievement of exalted states of consciousness through intense spiritual practice. In many cases, in fact, the supernormal events are specifically stated to have occurred during episodes of spiritual ecstasy.

We will briefly describe here just a single case which exemplifies in extreme form the challenges posed by this material. Levitation, a phenomenon reported by mystics of many traditions, was a principal feature in the case of Fr. Joseph of Copertino, a 17th-century Franciscan monk, for whom "ecstatic flight" appeared to become a literal reality. Joseph was observed in flight on over a hundred occasions, and by a large number and variety of witnesses, including hostile ones, whose sworn testimony was obtained within a few years of the events. His flights occurred both indoors and outdoors, covered distances ranging from a few feet to 30 yards or more, and sometimes caused him to remain for substantial periods of time in the branches of nearby trees. Of special interest is the fact that during his canonization proceedings, the *promotor fidei* was none other than the great humanist Prosper Lambertini, later Pope Benedict XIV, also principal codifier of the Church's standardized rules of procedure and evidence for canonization. Lambertini was initially hostile to Joseph's cause, but upon thorough and searching review of all details of the case, including the sworn depositions, he concluded that the ecstatic flights had indeed occurred essentially as reported. Subsequently, as Pope, he himself published the decree of Joseph's Beatification.

We hasten to acknowledge here that so brief a description of this extraordinary case is sure—and rightly so—to leave many readers incredulous at best. Anyone tempted to dismiss the case offhand, however, should first study the more detailed accounts of it by Braude (1986/1991), Eisenbud (1979), and M. Murphy (1992), as well as Thurston (1952) himself. Nor is this case unique: Thurston cites several other well-attested Catholic cases including that of St. Teresa, and M. Murphy (1992, p. 633) lists 21 more. Braude also reviews at length the cases of well-investigated mediums including Eusapia Palladino and D. D. Home who produced not only levitations of large objects including themselves but other phenomena from Thurston's catalog such as immunity to fire, luminosities, and bodily distortions.

In summary, through its deep connections both with genius and with supernormal phenomena of various kinds, mysticism poses essentially the same sorts of problems posed for contemporary mainstream psychological science by genius itself, but in still more extreme form. In both, the individual reaches deep within his own personality, yet somehow, paradoxically, makes novel forms of contact with some reality or aspect of reality without, if indeed these spatial metaphors continue to have any meaning.[27] But whereas genius *per se* presses only to the deepest levels of recognizable symbolic activity, already uncomfortably beyond the horizon of current cognitive theory, mysticism in its most extreme developments transcends those limits altogether, moving beyond tangible products of all sorts to radically different forms of consciousness. What could any "computational theory of the mind," for example, possibly have to say about the introvertive mystical experience of pure undifferentiated consciousness?

Taking it as established, then, that mystical experiences are both real and important, our next task is to survey what has so far been learned—very little, regrettably—about their conditions of occurrence.

Neurobiological Approaches to Mysticism

In this section we will first briefly canvas the principal attempts known to us to say something meaningful about aspects or patterns of brain-body activity associated with mystical experience. None of these is very successful, in our opinion, and all exemplify in varying degrees several characteristic faults of the existing literature, in particular: (1) failure to come to grips with the full-blown phenomenology of mystical experiences; (2) paucity of directly supporting empirical data; and (3) excessive willingness to spin out elaborate neurophysiological just-so stories that purport to "explain" mystical experience in terms of currently understood neuroscience.

Mysticism and Temporal Lobe Epilepsy

We begin with the widely circulated hypothesis of a special linkage between mystical experiences and epileptic seizures, especially seizures associated with temporal-lobe or temporo-limbic epilepsy (TLE). Claims of this sort have long been invoked by reductive materialists in efforts to

27. Stace (1960/1987, pp. 196–197) explicitly likens the ontological status of the "cosmic ego" encountered by mystics to that of other "universals" as conceived by Plato, Aristotle, and many philosophers of mathematics. See Chapter 7 regarding the modified Platonism underlying Myers's account of genius.

"debunk" religious personalities such as St. Paul and Joan of Arc, and are foundational to the work of contemporary God-in-the-Brain theorists such as Mandell (1980) and Persinger (1987). They seem even to have become widely accepted as an element of medical folklore; according to Ramachandran and Blakeslee (1998), for example, "every medical student is taught that patients with epileptic seizures originating in this part of the brain can have intense, spiritual experiences during the seizures" (p. 175; see also Mesulam, 2000, chap. 8).

The actual evidence for such a linkage, however, is in fact very sparse, as is apparent even in a recent attempt by Saver and Rabin (1997) to summarize the observations supporting it. We focus here on their discussion of ictal (during-seizure) experiences in TLE, in particular the intellectual "auras" or altered states of consciousness that sometimes accompany the abnormal neuroelectric activity. Most such experiences are in the first place only "religious" in a very broad sense having little to do with mystical states *per se.* They include, for example, dreamy states, feelings of depersonalization or unreality, and feelings of being detached, far away, or "not in this world." The one point of seemingly genuine contact concerns so-called "ecstatic seizures," for which the historical prototype is Dostoevsky's famous description of Prince Myshkin in *The Idiot.* This indeed sounds like a real mystical experience, and Saver and Rabin therefore include Dostoevsky, along with St. Paul, St. Teresa, and Joan of Arc, in a long table summarizing 15 cases of "historical-religious" personalities known or surmised to have been epileptic. These diagnoses are in most cases transparently circumstantial, however, and they often depend on behaviors that are associated primarily with early stages of the mystic vocation and are equally well or better interpreted as psychological automatisms (Chapter 5). In only two of their 15 cases, in fact, is a medical diagnosis of epilepsy certain: In the first, that of Dostoevsky, it is not certain either that he was a temporal-lobe case or even that he himself had the experiences he describes (see below); the other, oddly enough, involves Myers's own brother, the physician Arthur Myers, who was a patient of Hughlings Jackson (1888, 1898; see also D. C. Taylor & Marsh, 1980) and who was found on autopsy to have a small left temporal lesion, but who was by no stretch of the imagination subject to mystical states of any kind.

Saver and Rabin (1997) next go on to identify 10 "well-studied modern clinical cases of ecstatic seizure all [of which] appear to have had a temporolimbic substrate" (p. 503). In seven of these, however, all appearing in a single article (D. Williams, 1956), the "ecstasy" is more aptly described as "pleasure," and the main point of the article is that even this is extremely rare. Two of the other three arguably enter the genuinely mystical range, but fall considerably short even of Dostoevsky's description, let alone the full-blown introvertive mystical experience.[28]

---

28. In the best of these (Cirignotta, Todesco, & Lugaresi, 1980), a brief ecstatic episode fortuitously occurred during a polygraphic recording including eight channels of EEG, in a patient in whom the diagnosis of TLE had been confirmed by the presence of spike-and-wave

And what about Dostoevsky himself? Saver and Rabin conspicuously neglect to cite an important paper by Gastaut (1978) which deals in depth with this subject. Temporal-lobe or "psychomotor" epilepsy, it turns out, came into focus as a well-defined clinical entity only in the late 1940s, and Gastaut, a distinguished French epileptologist, had himself been the person chiefly responsible for entry into that literature—with Dostoevsky as the canonical example—of the concept of ecstatic auras. In the 1978 paper, however, Gastaut totally repudiated his own earlier position. First, close study of much newly discovered biographical material had led him to conclude that Dostoevsky mainly suffered not from TLE with organic pathology of the temporal region but from primary or common generalized functional epilepsy. Second, it now seemed probable that his vivid descriptions of ecstatic auras were not autobiographical reports but imaginative creations, largely reflecting his more general religious preoccupations and knowledge. Most importantly for our purposes here, Gastaut's detailed review of the relevant medical literature revealed that even garden-variety levels of euphoria or joy, let alone true mystical ecstasy, had extremely rarely if ever been a component of epileptic auras. In virtually every case in which any affective tone whatever had been reported, it was typically negative—fear, terror, anxiety, apprehension, or anger. Among literally thousands of cases studied directly by himself and several other prominent clinical epileptologists, Gastaut could not find even one unambiguous example of an ecstatic aura. Dostoevsky's real contribution to epileptology, he concludes, lies not in the unsupported concept of mystical auras in TLE, but rather in a recognition that his genius flourished *despite* his epilepsy, not because of it, and could not be diminished or impaired by decades of severe and frequent *grand mal* seizures. He was a living disproof, in short, of the "degeneracy" theories of genius advanced by 19th-century writers such as Lombroso and Lelut (p. 198; see also Chapter 7).[29]

Several studies involving direct electrical stimulation of temporal and limbic cortex in TLE patients have similarly failed to disclose any clear-cut connection with genuine mystical experience. Only about 10% of the 520 TLE patients studied by Penfield and Perot (1963), for example, reported any experiential phenomena at all, either in response to electrical stimulation or as part of their normal seizure pattern, and none of the reported experiences bears any significant resemblance to mystical states of consciousness. Subsequent reports by Halgren, Walter, Cherlow, and Crandall (1978), Halgren (1982), Gloor et al. (1982), and Gloor (1990) confirm these patterns,

---

activity in right temporal cortex during slow-wave sleep. Although abnormal electrical activity localized to the right temporal region may therefore have *preceded* the ecstatic experience, its *causal* role is unclear because the experience itself occupied just "a few instants," of uncertain temporal location, in a record that lasts for over a minute and displays rapidly changing large-scale patterns of unusual brain activity. Future studies of this type, using more EEG channels, common-reference (versus bipolar) recordings, and markers for onset/offset of the targeted conscious states, could help to pinpoint their actual electrophysiological correlates.

29. In a subsequent paper Gastaut (1984) slightly qualifies his diagnosis of Dostoevsky's epilepsy but not his attack on the concept of ecstatic auras in TLE.

and all of them emphasize like Gastaut both that affective responses of any kind are relatively rare and that they consist almost exclusively of fear and anxiety. Gloor et al. (1982), using implanted multichannel electrodes which permitted stimulation and recording at both temporal neocortical and limbic sites in the same subject, showed in addition that experiential phenomena occur only when *limbic* structures are activated, whether or not an afterdischarge propagates to temporal cortex, whereas stimulation of temporal neocortex produces experiential responses only if it is strong enough to propagate afterdischarges into limbic structures. Experiential responses, moreover, can change dramatically with repeated stimulation of the same limbic site, have no fixed relationship to the precise locus of that site, and can reoccur after the tissue surrounding the site has been surgically removed, all suggesting that the conscious experiences actually originate somewhere else altogether (Halgren, 1982).[30]

In sum, we find no credible evidence of any generalized association between epileptic seizure activity and genuine mystical experience. Extremely few if any well-documented epileptics have reported true mystical experiences, and there is little or no cogent evidence of epilepsy in the great majority of historically prominent mystics about whose lives we have sufficient information to judge. It may still be true that epilepsy sometimes produces neurobiological conditions conducive to mystical experience, but as yet we have no clear picture as to what, precisely, those conditions are. Meanwhile, TLE *per se*, as a gross clinical entity, is certainly neither necessary nor sufficient.

Gellhorn and Ergotropic/Trophotropic Systems

A second group of neurobiological approaches, now a little outdated, revolves around the work of neurophysiologist Ernst Gellhorn on autonomic/somatic integration. In a long series of publications, Gellhorn had identified and characterized two large-scale anatomically distinct physiological systems—broadly, "ergotropic" or activating and "trophotropic" or quieting—whose interactions support a wide range of ordinary behavioral and psychological states. Each system is elaborately organized, with visceral

30. Note the structural analogy here with migraine auras and related hallucinatory phenomena discussed in Chapter 7. Among other things, these stimulation results render it exceedingly unlikely, in our opinion, that "God experiences" can be induced by weak impressed magnetic fields of the sort applied by Persinger (1999, 2001). The experiences Persinger reports are at best distantly related to the genuinely mystical, and they appear highly vulnerable to distortion by subject expectancies and demand characteristics created by his experimental conditions. Our long-standing suspicions in this regard have recently been confirmed by the failure of an attempt to replicate his findings using his own apparatus under strictly double-blind conditions (Granqvist et al., 2005). More generally, the numerous papers and books in which Persinger has claimed to explain all sorts of supernormal phenomena in terms of largely hypothetical patterns of abnormal temporal lobe activity seem to us of little scientific value (see also Chapter 6; and Horgan, 2003, pp. 91–105).

or autonomic, skeletal-muscular, and cerebral components integrated in hierarchical fashion. These hierarchies, moreover, are parallel in structure in such a way that at each level they generally interact in a competitive or reciprocally inhibitory manner. Thus, for example, the sympathetic branch of the autonomic nervous system, a major component of the ergotropic system, interacts with the (trophotropic) parasympathetic branch in regulating functions such as total cardiac output and the distribution of blood to its target organs. Over a wide range of normal conditions, these systems function in internally consistent ways and work together smoothly to achieve a "tuning" of their reciprocal interactions appropriate to the behavioral situation at hand.[31] Gellhorn also explored, however, various circumstances such as anoxia and sensory deprivation in which the normal congruence and reciprocity break down, leading to pathological or paradoxical outcomes of various kinds.

With this large body of prior research providing the scientific background, Gellhorn and Kiely (1972) ventured some quite modest and tentative suggestions about possible neurophysiological underpinnings of mystical states. Most of their article is actually about meditation, and more specifically about sitting, concentrative forms of meditation, which they interpreted as producing a generalized shift toward trophotropic dominance. The mere act of sitting in a fixed and relaxed position, for example, drastically reduces one major source of ergotropic activation, proprioceptive feedback from the skeletal musculature. Most of the scanty experimental findings then available regarding meditation—such as slowing of dominant EEG frequencies and increases in skin resistance—were consistent with this view. Gellhorn and Kiely also pointed out that meditation is similar in these respects to other psychosomatic quieting disciplines such as autogenic training and progressive relaxation, and thus can be expected to have a variety of potentially significant psychological and medical benefits.

As described so far, Gellhorn and Kiely correctly anticipated the confluence with behavioral medicine that has been overwhelmingly the central preoccupation of subsequent meditation research (Andresen, 2000; M. Murphy & Donovan, 1997). More relevant to our purposes here, however, are their relatively sparse remarks in regard to states of actual mystical ecstasy. Their primary example is the EEG study of Das and Gastaut (1957), in which reported Yogic ecstasy occurred in conjunction with a physiological state that paradoxically combined extreme cortical arousal with profound inhibition of skeletal musculature.[32] The general picture they seem to have in mind is that as Yogic meditation deepens, progressively shifting the

31. Although this classical conception remains substantially correct, it has recently been expanded and refined in ways summarized by Hugdahl (1996).

32. Gellhorn and Kiely also make a somewhat overdrawn comparison here between Yogic ecstasy and REM (dreaming) sleep, which displays partly similar physiological properties, and they make the prescient suggestion that the transitions to these states, and to somewhat similar psychedelic and psychotic states, might be mediated by overlapping or similar mechanisms (see below).

"tuning" toward trophotropic dominance, it will at some point pass beyond the region within which the total physiological system is dynamically stable, and thus will lead to paradoxical "rebound" or state-transition effects which decouple cerebral/experiential states from their normal lower-level physiological moorings. They make no attempt to provide further details as to either the locations of these switching points, the specific mechanisms that drive and guide the switching, or the character of the resulting states. They clearly regard this "model" as merely provisional and descriptive, an abstract conceptual framework that might prove heuristically useful in guiding collection and interpretation of further empirical data.

Julian Davidson (1976) provides an excellent and appreciative assessment of Gellhorn's contribution and suggests several extensions that help bring it in line with an expanded range of empirical observations. First and foremost among these is the recognition that mystical states can also be approached from the *ergotropic* side. Here Davidson draws upon earlier and somewhat eccentric publications by Sargant (1975) and Fischer (1971). Sargant, in particular, catalogs a variety of circumstances, drawn from many cultures, in which intense and prolonged "excitement" induced by dancing, drumming, singing, hyperventilation, self-mutilation, ritual sex, psychoactive drugs, and the like result in "collapse" and the sudden emergence of extreme changes in physiological and mental state. Sargant's physiology is antiquated, and his psychology of altered states empirically inadequate and impoverished, but the induction of profound altered states of consciousness by ergotropic maneuvers is unquestionably a real phenomenon (see also E. F. Kelly & Locke, 1981b; R. G. Locke & Kelly, 1985).[33]

How does it come to pass that driving the system beyond its customary limits in these seemingly divergent (trophotropic versus ergotropic) directions can eventuate in mystical states of consciousness having so much in common? Davidson recognizes this as a problem (p. 365), but has little to offer by way of solution. Instead, he trails off into a highly speculative discussion as to how the conscious experience of an altered state might be determined jointly by physiological conditions and cognitive variables such as beliefs and attitudes; in this way, he suggests, states which are actually physiologically diverse might be experienced as similar by virtue of common beliefs or expectations. His model here, however, is the classic experiment of S. Schacter and Singer (1962), in which the experience of physiologically *similar* states was made to *diverge* through manipulations of expectancies and social settings. The other new element he brings in—inevitably, in that period—is the possibility that shifts in ergotropic/trophotropic tuning might also alter the balance of contributions from the differentially specialized cerebral hemispheres. Ineffability, for example, might result from a shift of dominance from the more linguistically sophisticated and analytical left hemisphere toward the more non-verbal, "intuitive," and "holistic"

33. Sargant himself has no use for any of these states and seeks merely to discredit them as variant forms of "brain-washing," explainable in full in terms of mechanisms of generalized inhibition identified by Pavlov in his studies of experimental neurosis in dogs.

right. Much like the physiologically oriented creativity theorists discussed in our previous chapter, Davidson also suggests that the psychoanalytic distinction between primary and secondary process maps at least roughly onto right versus left hemisphere dominance, with mystical experience, like inspirations of genius, representing a kind of regression in service of the ego.

We do not wish to argue that these speculations are entirely without merit, and indeed they may in particular have some bearing on the lower stages of mystical development. Two crucial limitations, however, require special emphasis here: First, it is certain that proposals of these sorts cannot possibly accommodate the full-blown phenomenology of introvertive mystical experience, because that phenomenology passes beyond the reach of ordinary cognitive "mechanisms" of all types. Second, they are virtually devoid of any serious factual basis. The simple truth of the matter is that we know next to nothing about the relevant physiological conditions. It seems more likely to us, as to Hufford (2005) and many other observers, that neurobiological conditions associated with mystical experiences of the universal-core type will prove to be correspondingly homogeneous in some crucial way, whether they arise in the contemplative Meister Eckhart or in a whirling Sufi dervish. But what are those conditions, and how do we arrive at them from such disparate directions?

The only way to get adequate answers, we believe, is through direct investigation of genuine mystical states. Very little further progress has been made in this regard, unfortunately, in the last several decades. The current state of things is well exemplified, at least for purposes of this chapter, by two recent and widely circulated attempts to explain mystical experience in neurobiological terms.

The Model of d'Aquili and Newberg

The first comes from (now-deceased) anthropologist/physician Eugene d'Aquili, a long-time student of neurobiological aspects of religion, and Andrew Newberg, a specialist in SPECT/PET neuroimaging. In a series of semi-scientific and popular papers and books, these authors have attempted to formulate and test an expanded model of mystical states grounded in contemporary cognitive neuroscience (d'Aquili & Newberg, 1993, 1999; Newberg & d'Aquili, 2000, 2002). Their model, originally presented in the 1993 *Zygon* paper, has persisted more or less unchanged in subsequent books and papers, but we will focus on d'Aquili and Newberg (1999), which contains its most elaborate presentation and illustrates the main defects of their approach. In this book, we first get an introduction to brain science, clearly intended for non-scientists, which can only be described as largely outdated, superficial, and simplistic. It also greatly overstates what we actually know about many mysterious aspects of ordinary mental activity, as for example when they assert (p. 34) that the distinction between self and world arises within left superior posterior parietal cortex. This is followed by an even more idiosyncratic and controversial analysis of what they call "cognitive operators" and their associations with specific brain regions. For example, whereas most contemporary cognitive neuroscientists think of perceptual integration or "binding" as a large-scale process involving numerous and widely distributed areas of the brain, d'Aquili and Newberg (p. 52) speak glibly of a "holistic operator" which itself grasps the entire present situation as a unified Gestalt, and which resides in the right superior posterior parietal lobe and adjacent cortical areas.

Finally, drawing mainly upon their own inadequate characterizations of both brain and mind, they present their model of what might be happening during unitive mystical experience. The model builds upon Gellhorn's conception of ergotropic/trophotropic systems, but extends it by postulating a considerable number of specific dynamic interactions among various neocortical and limbic areas. An elaborate narrative is provided, complete with box-and-arrow diagrams, that amounts to little more than a re-description of mystical phenomenology in quasi-neurophysiological language. The unitive mystical state occurs, they declare, when simultaneous maximal activation of both ergotropic and trophotropic systems coincides with complete functional deafferentation, initiated by conscious intentions issuing from prefrontal cortex, of both left and right superior posterior parietal orientation association areas (p. 116). Deafferentation on the left supposedly obliterates the self-world dichotomy, while deafferentation on the right results in an experience of pure space devoid of specific contents, and so on.

There is little point in belaboring these descriptions further here. The d'Aquili/Newberg "model" of mystical states, in our view, is little more than a neurophysiological fairy tale, concocted by means of radical extrapolation beyond the primitive basis afforded by contemporary cognitive neuroscience, and spelled out in far greater detail than is warranted by anything we really know about mystical states themselves. Certainly there is little or no independent empirical justification for key elements of their model, and some, such as their identification of spatial awareness with right posterior parietal cortex, have been seriously undermined by more recent work (Karnath, Ferber, & Himmelbach, 2001). D'Aquili and Newberg themselves have presented only a few shreds of crude neuroimaging data suggesting the expected decreases of parietal activation correlative with increases in frontal areas, but others such as Kjaer et al. (2002), Lou et al. (1999), and Vollenweider (1998) have identified very different patterns. Furthermore, in no case is there much reason to feel confident that any true mystical experiences occurred. In short, although we applaud their long-term goals, and their relatively positive attitude toward mysticism, we cannot say the same in regard to their science, at least so far. More effort directed to publication of improved experimental studies in refereed neuroscience journals would be very much in order.

James Austin's *Zen and the Brain* (1999)

This book is far more substantial scientifically, but also ultimately unsatisfying, and for partly similar reasons. Austin is a very experienced clinical neurologist and research neuropharmacologist. What is especially unusual, however, is that he has also been a practitioner of Zen for over 30 years, in the course of which he has himself experienced a number of unusual states, including in particular what sounds like a brief but genuine extrovertive mystical experience—"Kensho," in the terminology of Zen (p. 536)—in 1982. These experiences clearly impressed him enormously, and his book appears to be the product of decades of serious effort to understand them in terms of available brain science—a kind of avocation or labor of love evolving in parallel with his conventional scientific preoccupations.

The result is a quite extraordinary and massive volume that interweaves large amounts of serious brain science with liberal interludes of personal narrative and Zen lore. It is perhaps somewhat ironic that anyone could produce an 844-page book devoted to the importance of getting beyond words, but for anyone willing to make the necessary effort it is worth the trip. Austin's basic strategy is to provide grounding in both Zen practice and brain science, and then to explore their unfolding relationships as practice deepens. Disproportionate space is devoted to the more dramatic experiences, and especially to his Kensho experience, again testifying to their impact on him.

A great deal of good results from this approach. Although we cannot possibly do justice here to the details, Austin provides a comprehensive and informative survey of existing meditation research, packed with interesting insights and suggestions for further research. Not surprisingly, given his scientific background, he is especially strong in regard to neglected basic-neuroscience aspects such as the role of neurochemistry and dynamically interacting slow biological rhythms, subjects conspicuously absent from the model of d'Aquili and Newberg (1999) among others. He also constantly underscores the need for more research, and especially for neuroimaging studies with advanced meditators, with which we heartily agree.[34] Finally, he is uncommonly alert to the fundamental role that neuroplasticity might play in reshaping the brains even of adult meditators. Indeed, for him the ultimate goal of Zen practice is to strip away the neural underpinnings of

34. With one significant technical caveat, however: Austin is not as aware as he should be of the emerging neurophysiological story in regard to global workspace theory and the putative role of large-scale shared cortical neuroelectric activity in solving the "binding" problem (although this seems to be changing—see Austin, 2000). Perhaps for this reason, he also shares with many other neuroimaging enthusiasts a failure to appreciate the potential contributions of high-density EEG (and MEG) imaging. These electrophysiological methods are complementary, not alternative, to currently more popular PET and fMRI methods, and have enjoyed major technical advances in recent years. Briefly, under conditions substantially more comfortable for subjects, they provide relatively direct measures of shared neural activity, on a frequency-specific basis and on a time scale more relevant to experience and behavior. See also Nunez and Silberstein (2000) and E. F. Kelly, Lenz, Franaszczuk, & Truong (1997).

the egocentric space-time framework in which ordinary conditioned experience takes place. He even proposes at one point that his hypothesized cytotoxic "pruning" of the ordinary self might be detectable in post-mortem microscopic autopsies of what he thinks is its essential neural substrate, a subcortical triad comprised of the amygdala, hypothalamus, and central grey matter.[35]

Despite these considerable strengths, what matters more for purposes of this chapter are the systematic limitations of Austin's approach. It is unfortunate first that he takes so much the role of an apologist for Zen. This was hardly necessary, and it undoubtedly makes his book less attractive than it might otherwise have been—and deservedly so—to a scientific audience. More importantly perhaps, this deliberate narrowness of perspective deprived him of access to a much larger inventory of phenomenological observations potentially germane to his neurologizing perspective.

One significant example here is his "absorption" experience (p. 469), in which a luminous and exquisitely detailed image of a small red maple leaf suddenly appears in the far upper left corner of an otherwise empty, vast, and jet-black visual field. As a clinical neurologist, Austin immediately recognizes that something like this could not happen under normal circumstances. This is one of a number of examples, including in particular his far more potent Kensho experience, in which cognitive phenomena emerging in meditation dramatically surpass ordinary cognitive operations in speed, precision, complexity, and integrative power. It is certainly to Austin's credit that he recognizes these, and this in fact illustrates the value and importance of collecting detailed introspective reports from advanced meditators, and studying them from an informed neurological perspective. In his protracted ruminations about the neurophysiological underpinnings of this surprising event, however, Austin places unwarranted emphasis on the fact that the image appeared on his *left*, implying for him an origin in right temporoparietal cortex. Yet even a casual acquaintance with the broader literature of mysticism would have made him aware that such events, as for example the various visions of St. Teresa, can crop up anywhere around the subject in spherical space.[36] Even when relevant and potentially helpful, in short, his neurologizing is too dependent both on idiosyncracies of the Zen tradition and on his own quite limited personal experience of unusual states.

35. Note that Austin differs here both from d'Aquili and Newberg, who think the self is specially associated with left posterior parietal cortex, and from most other cognitive neuroscientists, who presume that it is part of a neural "executive" system which resides within the frontal lobes.

36. The precise spatial distribution of such events within and between subjects remains to be determined in detail, however. We leave aside here the related matter of Austin's premature endorsement of a "copy" or "image" theory of memory, encouraged in part by his subsequent discovery of a photograph that he himself had earlier made of the same maple leaf (see also our Chapter 4).

The final limitation, however, is far more fundamental.[37] The neurologizing itself becomes increasingly unsatisfactory and speculative as we approach the most interesting and important phenomena, and increasingly saturated with terms such as "might," "maybe," "perhaps," "suppose," and so on. What this reflects is Austin's clearly acknowledged determination to construct "explanations" of mystical experience, no matter how far-fetched and hypothetical, that are wholly based on standard contemporary neuroscience.

At its core this book represents an extraordinary collision of relentlessly conventional and rigid mainstream scientific sensibilities with conscious experiences so powerful that they threaten the very foundations of Austin's orthodox outlook. Like psychology as a whole, Austin defends himself—perhaps unconsciously—by carefully circumscribing his encounter with mysticism in such a way as to avoid contact with dimensions of the subject that would still more seriously threaten his preconceived views. Austin accepts without hesitation that Zen masters have developed ways of cultivating extraordinary states of consciousness that are characterized by many unusual and interesting properties, but anything further they might say is mere Oriental nonsense unworthy of attention; thus we must "strip off the heavy baggage of centuries of mystical, philosophical, and doctrinal speculations" (p. 53). Austin's own brief taste of Kensho had such impact upon him that even he, setting aside these scruples, cannot refrain from characterizing it with metaphysically loaded terms such as "absolute reality," "ultimate perfection," "eternity," and so on. Nevertheless, he goes to some pains to assert at numerous points in his book, and apparently with complete self-assurance, that there is nothing whatever of scientific significance in talk of ESP, NDEs, or supernormal phenomena of any kind—this despite the fact that the wisdom traditions in general, including the Zen masters he quotes in profusion, take such things seriously. Unfortunately for him, it is also quite obvious from what he *does* say about these subjects that he knows practically nothing about the real scientific literature concerning them. This, we submit, is bad scientific practice—not only for Austin personally, but for psychology as a whole.

37. Here our views largely coincide with those expressed in a thoughtful review by cognitive scientist Eleanor Rosch (1999), although we are not comfortable with some of the examples she invokes in support of her challenge to neuroscientists.

Mysticism and Psychedelics

There is one further topic that is inescapably linked to the neurobiology of mystical experience, but that so far falls mainly under the heading of opportunities sadly lost, or at least postponed. We refer, of course, to the psychedelic dimension.[38]

That there are potentially important connections between psychoactive substances and mysticism was already apparent to William James, and in his taxonomy of protomystical phenomena in *VRE* he comments in this regard upon alcohol, nitrous oxide, and other anesthetics such as ether and chloroform. The sway of alcohol over mankind, for example, seems to James to reside in its capacity to stir, however transiently, the mystic sense: "Sobriety diminishes, discriminates, and says no; drunkenness expands, unites, and says yes. It is in fact the great exciter of the *Yes* function in man. It brings its votary from the chill periphery of things to the radiant core. It makes him for the moment one with truth" (*VRE*, p. 297). These "whiffs and gleams" of the mystical, however, belong chiefly to the fleeting early stages of drunkenness, which "in its totality is so degrading a poisoning."

Nitrous oxide is an even more powerful stimulant of mystical states. James was familiar with the contemporary writings of Benjamin Blood, and had been deeply impressed by the effects on himself of this anesthetic gas. It was in fact in this specific context that James wrote what is surely one of the most widely quoted passages in all of psychology:

> One conclusion was forced upon my mind at that time, and my impression of its truth has ever since remained unshaken. It is that our normal waking consciousness, rational consciousness as we call it, is but one special type of consciousness, whilst all about it, parted from it by the filmiest of screens, there lie potential forms of consciousness entirely different. We may go through life without suspecting their existence; but apply the requisite stimulus, and at a touch they are there in all their completeness, definite types of mentality which probably somewhere have their field of application and adaptation. No account of the universe in its totality can be final which leaves these other forms of consciousness quite disregarded....They forbid a premature closing of our accounts with reality. (p. 298)[39]

---

38. We prefer the term *psychedelic*, which means "mind-manifesting," to more theoretically loaded cognate terms whether negative (such as *psychotomimetic*, *hallucinogenic*, and so on) or positive (such as *entheogenic*). For an interesting account by Humphry Osmond of his invention of this term in friendly competition with Aldous Huxley, see Cavanna and Ullman (1968, pp. 124–125).

39. Myers also self-experimented with nitrous oxide. In his review of the *Principles* (Myers, 1891c) he strongly endorses James's call for further experiments with anesthetics, and adds this personal note: "Having myself, by mere good fortune, once attained under nitrous oxide to the state of 'impersonal consciousness'...I have endeavoured in vain to repeat the experience. Yet the psychological instructiveness of this unique sensation is so great that it should, I think, be a matter of course for the experimental psychologist to test fully his own capacity of getting down into that diffusive sense of scarce-conditioned existence from whence the notion

James (p. 301) cites two further instances in which quasi-mystical experience occurred in conjunction with surgical anesthesia, under chloroform in one case and ether in the other.[40] Indeed, the emergence of both of these agents as drugs of abuse in the late 19th century may well have resulted in part from their capacity to engender such experiences (L. Lewin, 1927/1998). We are not aware of any modern attempt to collect and systematize observations of this sort, but the effort to do so would undoubtedly be worthwhile, since similar experiences are almost certainly occurring in connection with modern anesthetic regimes, and they bear strongly on the central themes of this chapter (see also H. Smith, 2000, pp. 70–71). It will also be recalled from Chapter 6 that NDEs, which often have a mystical dimension, sometimes occur in conjunction with general surgical anesthesia.

We now reach the heart of the subject, the major psychedelics, including both plant-derived substances such as mescaline and psilocybin and the later synthetic agents, above all LSD-25. Their turbulent cultural and legal history has been told in detail many times, perhaps most notably in the sober and balanced treatment by Grinspoon and Bakalar (1979/1997). Had Myers and James lived long enough, they would certainly have participated actively in these developments, and indeed James himself is known to have consumed peyote, though only once because it made him violently ill without any compensatory psychedelic effects (Grinspoon & Bakalar, 1979/1997, p. 59).

Although the extraordinary psychedelic properties of LSD had already been discovered by Albert Hofman in 1943, an overt linkage in Western popular culture between psychedelics and mysticism was initially forged by the perennialist Aldous Huxley (1954/1990), based mainly on his own early encounters with mescaline.[41] This was of course followed by the mostly infamous doings at Harvard under the inauspicious leadership of Timothy Leary, the hysterical culture wars of the 1960s, and the near-total government shutdown by 1970 of psychedelic research with humans (Grob, 1998). Because of this decades-long ban on new research, much of the following discussion is based on very old work, some of it certainly falling short in various ways of today's research standards. Nevertheless, the main points we want to make appear to us fully justified by the evidence already available.

First and foremost among these points is that the major psychedelics can and sometimes do produce genuine mystical experiences. In fact, they appear capable of producing or at least helping to produce the entire range

---

of personality itself, and the specialized senses severally, seem slowly to define themselves, not only as an advance and a development, but as a loss and a limitation" (pp. 115–116).

40. The latter, interestingly, also included an aspect of "panoramic life review" (see Chapter 6).

41. An interesting historical footnote is provided here by neuroscientist J. R. Smythies (1983), who reveals that he provided mescaline not only to Huxley but also to other intellectuals interested in its philosophical implications, including C. D. Broad, H. H. Price, and R. C. Zaehner.

of mystical phenomena, from the lowest forms of trance and automatism to unitive experiences which seem virtually indistinguishable, phenomenologically, from those reported by religious mystics. This conclusion is supported in the first place by a large volume of cross-cultural and historical evidence, much of which has come to light only in the last few decades, documenting the contributions of psychoactive agents to religious traditions worldwide. Psychedelics figure heavily in shamanistic practices, for example, particularly among pre-literate societies of Siberia, Central America, and the Amazon Basin (de Rios, 1984; de Rios & Janiger, 2003; Furst, 1972; Grinspoon & Bakalar, 1979/1997; Schultes & Hofmann, 1979/1992). They have also been implicated in the formation of some major religious traditions. The sacred Soma plant glorified in the ancient Hindu *Rig Veda* was tentatively identified by Wasson (1968) as the red bulbous mushroom *amanita muscaria* or fly-agaric, rich in the psychedelic agent psilocybin, and thus some of the foundational mystical scriptures of India may at least in part reflect experiences engendered by this psychedelic mushroom (see also H. Smith, 2000). Similarly, the principal rite of popular Greek mystery religion, celebrated annually for two thousand years, culminated in drinking a potion which appears to have consisted in part of a derivative of ergot having properties like those of LSD (Wasson, Ruck, & Hofman, 1978). Many other examples can be found in and through the sources cited (see also Lukoff, Zanger, & Lu, 1990).

Similar conclusions follow from the initial modern attempts to study psychedelic effects directly in human volunteers. One major landmark here is the dissertation research of Walter Pahnke (1966; see also Pahnke & Richards, 1966), who in an attempted double-blind study randomly assigned either 30 mg of psilocybin or nicotinic acid (an active control which produces mild skin tingling and flushing) to 10 matched pairs of divinity students and 10 (mostly faculty) "guides," all of whom then spent the next several hours together, listening in a dedicated room to a live Good Friday service piped in from a nearby chapel.

Subjects' experiences were assessed through a combination of self-report, interview, and questionnaire methods within one week and again after six months, and scaled on both occasions by "blind" judges for the degree to which they satisfied Stace's criteria for mystical experience. Briefly, the experimental subjects scored high on average on measures of all seven of Stace's criteria, and far higher than their matched controls. These large differences, moreover, had become even more pronounced by the time of a 25-year followup carried out by Doblin (1991), who somehow managed to identify 19 of the original 20 participants and was able to readminister the original six-month measurement procedures to 16 of these including seven from the psilocybin group. Despite some issues having to do especially with the rapid and total collapse of the attempted double-blind, the results of these studies collectively show that psilocybin is definitely capable under favorable conditions of producing intense mystical-type experiences that have profound and persistent life-shaping effects. Additional support for this conclusion derives from the testimony of Huston Smith (2000, pp. 100-101), who as it turns out was one of Pahnke's "guides," received the psilocybin, and acknowledges that the Good Friday experiment provided him with "the most powerful cosmic homecoming I have ever experienced."

Further evidence comes from Masters and Houston (1966), who administered psychedelics (mainly LSD or peyote) in varying dosages to 206 subjects of their own and interviewed some 214 others who under a variety of circumstances had taken the same or similar drugs. Although the great preponderance of the effects they report are perceptual and imaginative, particularly at low dosages or early in the sessions, they also devote an entire chapter to experiences of more religious or mystical character, and state specifically that six of their own 206 subjects appeared to have reached a "deepest phenomenological stratum" corresponding to the full-fledged introvertive mystical experience as described by Stace (1960/1987, p. 307). All six, interestingly, were over 40 years of age, of superior intelligence, well adjusted, and creative.

More recently, Strassman (2001) has reported experiences induced by DMT (dimethyltryptamine), a fast-acting and powerful psychedelic that may be produced endogenously by the pineal gland.[42] Among these, once again, are experiences that clearly reach well into the mystical range. One subject, for example, says:

> I immediately saw a bright yellow-white light directly in front of me. I chose to open to it. I was consumed by it and became part of it. There were no distinctions—no figures or lines, shadows or outlines. There was no body or anything inside or outside. I was devoid of self, of thought, of time, of space, of a sense of separateness or ego, or of *anything* but the white light. There are no symbols in my language that can begin to describe that sense of pure being, oneness, and ecstasy. (p. 244)

Many further examples of this sort can be found in the reports of other researchers who have worked extensively with LSD and related psychedelics, such as Grof (1975, 1985) and de Rios and Janiger (2003), and in the popular psychedelic literature. Although deep mystical experiences certainly do not occur automatically or routinely, especially among unprepared recreational users exposed to drugs of unknown composition and quality, that such experiences can and do occur fairly often among well-prepared, mature, and stable persons in suitably structured and comfortable settings seems to us a certainty. Indeed, like Pahnke and Richards (1966, p. 193), we think that the reproducibility of mystical-type experiences under such conditions is in principle sufficient to support their investigation using modern experimental methods, if only the current legal barriers can be relaxed.[43]

---

42. Strassman also paints a grim picture of the regulatory hurdles he had to overcome in conducting this research.

43. Groups working in support of such changes include the Heffter Research Institute, the Albert Hofmann Foundation, the Council on Spiritual Practices (CSP), and the Multidisci-

Some religious scholars such as Zaehner (1957/1978) and Katz (see Horgan, 2003, pp. 44–45) have strongly resisted such conclusions, but their resistance seems to us transparently motivated by factors such as pre-existing commitment to one or another theological position and perhaps a certain horror at the thought that genuine religious experience might sometimes be obtained by popping a pill, without the protracted austerities characteristic of traditional mystic self-disciplines.[44] Any such horror ought to be mitigated at least somewhat, however, by the realization that psychedelics can be regarded, much like other widely recognized and accepted "triggers" of genuine mystical experience, as somehow establishing or permitting conditions in the brain that are conducive to its occurrence. The key question, of course, is precisely what those conditions are.

Although psychedelics clearly afford unique opportunities to produce and study the relevant conditions experimentally, little has so far been accomplished along these lines, mainly because of the legal restrictions currently in place. Nevertheless, some sense of the possibilities in this direction can already be gleaned from recent PET imaging studies carried out with humans by psychiatrist F. X. Vollenweider and colleagues in Switzerland, where these restrictions are less severe (Gamma et al., 2004; Vollenweider, 1994, 1998; Vollenweider & Geyer, 2001; Vollenweider, Leenders, Øye, Hell, & Angst, 1997; Vollenweider, Leenders, Scharfetter, Antonini, et al., 1997; Vollenweider, Leenders, Scharfetter, Maguire, et al., 1997). The most relevant of these studies examined patterns of brain activity (glucose utilization) and associated states of consciousness produced in healthy normal volunteers by moderate doses of psilocybin and ketamine. Briefly, these agents were found to produce strikingly similar global effects, despite altogether divergent primary actions on cortical neurotransmission. Metabolic activity increased over much of the brain, and especially in areas generally associated with the "global workspace," including in particular frontal, temporal, and parietal cortex, the insula, and the thalamus. Vollenweider intreprets these results, which conflict both with the model of d'Aquili and Newberg (1999) and with the "transient hypofrontality" hypothesis of Dietrich (2003), as revealing previously hidden interactions among the major neurotransmitter systems. The common final outcome, he suggests, results from the fact that *both* psilocybin (a partial agonist of [5-HT_2] serotonin receptors) and ketamine (an antagonist of glutamate at NMDA receptors) lead, by different pathways, to top-down inhibition of a gating or filtering of incoming information normally exerted at the level of the thalamus. The

---

plinary Association for Psychedelic Studies (MAPS), all easily accessible on the worldwide web.

44. Austin (1999) acknowledges the overlap between mystical and psychedelic experience, but discourages the use of drugs on the grounds that they effect rapidly and violently the same kinds of changes in brain function that he thinks are produced more gradually, voluntarily, and controllably by practice of meditation. We have considerable sympathy for this point of view, but genuinely adverse effects even of the major psychedelics are not common (Strassman, 1984), and we wonder also whether "gentler" psychedelics yet to be discovered might not some day prove more trustworthy adjuncts to meditative practice.

opening of this thalamic gate, he argues, leads in turn to cortical "overload" or "flooding," cognitive "fragmentation," and acutely psychotic states of consciousness.

This work is interesting and important, in particular because it leads on its own strictly neurobiological premises to the central idea that psychedelic and mystical states result from breakdowns of a filtering action normally exerted somewhere in or by the brain. It is just a beginning, however, and has a number of serious limitations as well. Many details of the postulated neurophysiological mechanisms, for example, are sketchy and hypothetical. The PET imaging results have inherently low spatial and temporal resolution, are obtained by averaging across subjects, cannot distinguish between excitation and inhibition (in particular at the level of the thalamus), and cannot be correlated in a fine-grained manner with dynamic variations and individual differences in the associated states of consciousness. It is not clear, moreover, how the theory could be extended to cover mystical-type states induced by sensory *deprivation* and other known triggering conditions. Nor, finally, does it do adequate justice, within its fundamentally pathologizing intellectual framework, to the positive, integrative, and transformative potentials of psychedelic experience.[45]

We must next say something in regard to contemporary *psychological* accounts or models of psychedelic experience. The main such efforts known to us that are based on large amounts of direct experience with the effects of LSD and related agents on human subjects are those of de Rios and Janiger (2003), Grof (1975, 1980, 1985), and Masters and Houston (1966), all deriving from the mid-20th-century. These authors are broadly in agreement on a number of important points: First, psychedelic experiences are strongly dependent on set and setting, and enormously variable both within and between subjects and sessions. Second, what happens at any given point seems less the product of some highly specific neuropharmacological action than an amplification or release of more general psychological functions and materials that would normally be latent but inaccessible. Third, the resulting experiences are conspicuously stratified in depth: The "aesthetic" forms (altered perceptions, hallucinatory sensory phenomena, and the like) are by far the most common but also the least significant. With higher or repeated doses these tend to give way to more highly imaginative, creative, symbolic, or even mythic forms of cognitive activity, and finally, in relatively few instances, we may pass altogether beyond the realm of ordinary cognition and personal biography, with dissolution of the everyday ego and emergence of unitive mystical experience.

---

45. We also mention in passing that even on its own purely neurobiological terms Vollenweider's current model neglects at least one other important source of "filtering" action in the brain, namely, the NMDA (N-methyl-D-aspartate) receptor system of the upper cortical layers. As summarized for example by Kohn and Whitsel (2002) and Flohr (2000), this activity-dependent system plays a critical role in habituation to repeated stimuli and other short-term dynamic adjustments of cortical function, and also is specifically and selectively disabled by agents such as ketamine and PCP.

The deepest parts of this continuum are of course our primary concern here.[46] Arguably the most systematic attempt to date to map this "transpersonal" region of psychedelic experience is that of psychiatrist Stanislav Grof, based on literally thousands of sessions spanning 17 years of clinical research and personal experimentation with LSD. The conclusions Grof wishes to draw from this mass of material were already largely in place by the time of his first book (Grof, 1975), in which he describes how the experiences he encountered in himself and his patients forced him beyond the orthodox Freudianism of his psychoanalytic training in Czechoslovakia to a greatly expanded conception of the human unconscious. Briefly, he identifies four large classes or stages of LSD experience which he terms "abstract and aesthetic," "psychodynamic," "perinatal," and "transpersonal." The last two of these represent the principal novelties of his expanded conceptual scheme: Perinatal experiences revolve around ostensible memories of psychologically formative events occurring near the time of birth, and transpersonal experiences include, in addition to mystical experiences proper, the emergence of "archetypes" and other products of the Jungian collective unconscious, encounters with superhuman spiritual entities, ostensible memories of past lives, and a score of other experiences that to say the least are extremely odd.

Grof himself quickly recognized strong affinities between his expanded conception of the psychodynamic unconscious and the transpersonal psychologies associated with the primordial tradition (Tart, 1975b), and he has spent much of his subsequent career working out these parallels in greater detail. Huston Smith (1976, 2000) also recognized these similarities, and has even gone so far as to characterize Grof's work as in effect scientifically corroborating that tradition. It is hardly surprising in this light that Grof is widely regarded as one of the pillars of contemporary transpersonal psychology (Walsh & Vaughan, 1980, 1993).

Grof surely deserves credit for helping to open up this potentially important area of research, but in our opinion his actual scientific accomplishments, as represented in his published works, cannot carry this much theoretical weight. Perhaps reflecting his clinical background and training, his reports seem to us to consist mainly of Grof himself presenting, at one remove from the actual experiences of his subjects, what amount to summary narratives sketching his overall impressions and interpretations of their character and meaning. This procedure is certainly insufficient to justify strong and radical empirical claims of the sorts that he makes throughout his books. Readers are apparently expected simply to trust his judgment, primarily on the strength of oft-repeated general reassurances as to the supposedly thorough, cautious, and conservative nature of his procedures for

46. Note, however, that the existence of a "middle" region in which strikingly different and in some ways superior modes of symbolism and cognition emerge is in line with the account of genius developed in Chapter 7. Psychedelics could thus in principle facilitate further experimental investigation of these processes, and indeed of creativity itself (de Rios & Janiger, 2003).

collecting and analyzing data, when what we really need are details of the actual evidence supporting specific factual claims. In regard to ostensible memories of past lives, to take one especially significant example, detailed presentation of verified supporting evidence after the manner of Stevenson (1997, 2001) is surely crucial; yet Grof presents practically no such evidence, and most of what little he does present was apparently discovered by the subjects themselves. Unlike Masters and Houston (1966), who suggest that many aspects of LSD experience "may constitute subliminal triumphs of *Time*, *Life*, *Newsweek*" (p. 306), Grof also shows little or no awareness of the potential for cryptomnesia to explain much of his data (Stevenson, 1983a). More generally, he seems to us altogether too prone to regard the intense phenomenology of LSD experiences as itself somehow warranting their empirical truth. In sum, although we find Grof's work in many ways interesting and suggestive, in its current form it falls far short of empirically establishing his central transpersonal claims.[47]

One point all psychological students of psychedelics agree upon is that these agents somehow activate or provide access to important psychological materials and processes normally latent somewhere beyond the margins of waking consciousness. In this, psychedelic states are again closely akin to mystical states. In both, as James puts it, "we pass from out of ordinary consciousness as from a less into a more, as from a smallness into a vastness" (*VRE*, p. 319). What could be more natural, under these circumstances, than to conceive of *ordinary* consciousness as a contracted or reduced form of some sort of larger and more potent consciousness latent within—to think, that is, in terms of a "filter" or "transmission" theory of the sort advocated by Myers, James, and Bergson, and discussed throughout this book, in which the normal functions of the brain with its sensory and motor systems are in substantial part *eliminative* rather than *productive*?

Even the physiologist Vollenweider, as we saw, moves partway in this direction, and many psychologically oriented students of psychedelics in addition to Grof have explicitly adopted a full-fledged transpersonal filter model of some sort. A. Huxley (1954/1990, pp. 22–27) does so, for example, relying upon the following passage from C. D. Broad (1953), which was originally written in relation to the problems posed for conventional mind-brain theory by psi phenomena:

> Each person is at each moment potentially capable of remembering all that has ever happened to him and of perceiving everything that is happening anywhere in the universe. The function of the brain and nervous system is to protect us from being overwhelmed and confused by this mass of largely useless and irrelevant knowledge, by shutting out most of what

47. Despite these scientific limitations of his published work, Grof certainly does not deserve the sneering Voltaire-style abuse heaped upon him by Edwards (1996). It remains possible in our view that more information may yet be mined from Grof's original records, and that future research by others will substantiate at least some of his transpersonal claims. Similarly non-dismissive attitudes are expressed by scientific commentators as diverse as Austin (1999), Wulff (2000), and especially Grinspoon and Bakalar (1979/1997).

> we should otherwise perceive or remember at any moment, and leaving only that very small and special selection which is likely to be practically useful. An extension or modification of this type of theory seems to offer better hopes of a coherent synthesis of normal and paranormal cognition than is offered by attempts to tinker with the orthodox notion of events in the brain and nervous system *generating sense-data*. (pp. 22–23)

On such a view, Huxley suggests, we are all potentially "Mind at Large." However, "to make biological survival possible, Mind at Large has to be funneled through the reducing valve of the brain and nervous system. What comes out at the other end is a measly trickle of the kind of consciousness which will help us to stay alive" (p. 23). Huxley sees psychedelic agents as impairing or suspending this filtering action and thus permitting the inflowing or uprush of Mind at Large with its intrinsically greater capacities:

> As Mind at Large seeps past the no longer watertight valve, all kinds of biologically useless things start to happen. In some cases there may be extra-sensory perception. Other persons discover a world of visionary beauty. To others again is revealed the glory, the infinite value and meaningfulness of naked existence, of the given, unconceptualized event. In the final stage of egolessness there is an "obscure knowledge" that All is in all—that All is actually each. (p. 26)

A full-fledged transpersonal filter model of this sort has also commended itself to various scientists approaching psychedelics from a diversity of perspectives. One of the first was Stevenson (1957), who explicitly invoked a filter model and remarked that "these drugs may bring us, at least partially, into contact with a world of which we know little and should know a great deal more" (p. 439). Similarly, Pahnke, in his 1968 Ingersoll lecture, specifically endorsed James's (1898/1900) formulation of the transmission theory on the same formal occasion 70 years earlier: "Our LSD patients who have had the psychedelic mystical experience and who previously knew nothing of this transmission theory are supplying data which precisely fit this hypothesis. Their threshold seems to be lowered so that they directly experience this Vaster Consciousness in an Eternal Now, beyond time and space" (Pahnke, 1969, p. 16).

Strassman (2001) playfully analogizes the brain to a television receiver, with DMT as an agent which at high enough doses enables us to "switch channels" and thus connect with novel dimensions of reality that are always present, but normally remain hidden. Similarly, in a postscript to the presentation and defense of his ketamine model of NDEs, Jansen (1997b) reports that he has moved away from his former reductive materialism and toward a transpersonal perspective, aligning himself with those "who see drugs as just another door to a space, and not as actually producing that space.…Ketamine is a door to a place we cannot normally get to; it is definitely not evidence that such a place does not exist" (pp. 94–95). We should point out here that in one particular respect ketamine is an especially interesting psychedelic agent. Its psychedelic and anesthetic effects are known to derive from its capacity to bind non-competitively and selectively to the NMDA receptor complex found in the upper layers of all central gray-matter structures (alcohol and nitrous oxide, interestingly, have somewhat similar although weaker selectivities), and Flohr (2000) in particular has argued that this receptor system provides the essential neurophysiological substrate for ordinary consciousness by supporting rapid formation of large-scale cell assemblies ("binding"; see Chapter 1). At sufficiently high doses this binding process is completely blocked, in his view, leading to unconsciousness, whereas at lower doses it is merely impaired, giving rise to what he regards as purely pathological "disturbances" of consciousness. This model, in our opinion, again fails to do justice to the phenomenological richness and complexity of ketamine-induced experiences, which are more in line with the transpersonal filter model advocated here by Jansen, and also by ourselves. As indicated in Chapter 6 we do not accept Jansen's thoroughgoing identification of NDEs with ketamine experiences, but rather see all these experiences—psychedelic experiences in general, NDEs, and mystical experiences proper—as being related and overlapping but not individually homogeneous or identifiable with each other. Nevertheless, Jansen's revised, transpersonal interpretation of ketamine experience seems to us basically correct as far as it goes.[48]

Other thoughtful students, however, such as Vollenweider (1998) and especially Grinspoon and Bakalar (1979/1997), have declined to embrace such transpersonal interpretations of psychedelic effects even though they do explicitly embrace filter models of more conventional sort. Vollenweider's exclusive focus on a thalamic gate is certainly too narrow, even in purely biological terms, but how far do the data actually drive us in the transpersonal direction? Grinspoon and Bakalar appear intellectually open to the transpersonal perspective (see especially their Chapter 7), but they consistently fail to appreciate the degree to which it is in principle empirically testable and has in fact already to some degree been successfully tested. This amounts once again to Stace's problem of objective reference, in a slightly different guise. What we wish to suggest here is that what psychedelics have in common with all other means of producing mystical states may consist not in the engagement of any highly specific final common neurophysiological pathways, mechanisms, or modules, but rather in some sort of more global disruption or "loosening" of the normal mind-brain connection, which in turn enables fuller expression of an objectively real transpersonal component of human personality.

Several further considerations lend support to such a view, in regard both to psychedelic experience and to mystical experience generally. First is the sheer diversity of the circumstances known to trigger mystical experiences (Grinspoon & Bakalar, 1979/1997, p. 36; Wulff, 2000, p. 410). These include not only chemical agents both simple and complex, inorganic and

---

48. We also suspect that it could be particularly fruitful to explore possible ways of recovering conscious experiences that may occur at a deeper stratum of personality during ketamine anesthesia (see also Grace, 2003; H. Smith, 2000, pp. 70–71).

organic, but all the various induction procedures both trophotropic and ergotropic devised by literally thousands of human societies, over thousands of years, in service of their production (R. G. Locke & Kelly, 1985). It seems to us unlikely that *all* of these heterogeneous means of engendering mystical experience can have anything more in common than a capacity to disrupt or destabilize the normal mode of operation of the mind-brain system. Why some kinds of "disruption" produce this "loosening" while others do not remains to be elucidated.[49]

Second is the curious phenomenon of synesthesia, or fusion of the senses, which is a common accompaniment of both psychedelic and mystical experiences. Although we do not wish to press the point too hard, this seems just the sort of thing one might expect if the normal sharp differentiation of the special senses is effected by coupling of a more general imaginative power with the specific environment of the brain and its sensory organs, and is partially undone by a decoupling effect of psychedelic agents.[50] Suggestions by Cytowic (1995) and others that synesthesia is more common in writers, artists, and musicians and also associated with increased incidence of psi phenomena could, if upheld in further research, support such an interpretation.

Third, the full-fledged transpersonal filter model receives direct support from the body of evidence reviewed in Chapter 6 showing that NDEs—which, as we have said before, often have a mystical or transcendent aspect—sometimes occur under conditions in which the specific physiological mechanisms thought by mainstream neuroscientists to be necessary for the production of conscious states have been largely or totally disabled.

Finally, states of consciousness produced by psychedelic agents, like mystical states in general, appear likely to be strongly psi-conducive, although the evidence for this too is currently less than satisfactory. The existence of such connections is presumed by the worldwide shamanic tradition and also deeply ingrained in contemporary psychedelic folklore, including the publically expressed expectations of neuroscientist John Smythies and various eminent persons to whom he provided mescaline (see footnote 41). However, there has so far been little meaningful experimental work on this important topic. During the brief period when psychedelics were widely available for use with humans, formal ESP testing of all sorts was unfortunately carried out almost without exception using forced-choice card-guessing methods that are singularly ill-suited for use with persons undergoing intense psychedelic experiences. Nevertheless, even the scanty data currently available suggest that the association is real and accessible to more imaginative forms of experimentation. Grof (1975) in typical fashion makes many strong claims but provides little if any credible evidence.

---

49. Similar issues arise in relation to NDEs, as discussed in Chapter 6.

50. See Myers (1892f), where he suggested that synesthesia was "a kind of vestige of that undifferentiated continuous sensitivity from which we suppose our existing senses to have been specialised in the struggle for life" (p. 529). See also his comments on nitrous oxide in footnote 39.

Masters and Houston (1966, pp. 113–122), in contrast, report some quite striking albeit informal results using both forced-choice and free-response procedures, with the latter clearly emerging as the preferred testing strategy for any future work. Tart (1977) summarizes most of the existing studies and suggests additional methodological refinements for future work. There seems ample reason to expect that such work will be successful, provided that it heeds the lessons of the past (Grob, 1998).

In summary of this section, it seems to us beyond reasonable doubt that in principle psychedelics afford vital opportunities for wide-ranging and illuminating experimental studies of mystical-type experiences, their neurobiological accompaniments, and associated cognitive phenomena of many kinds including psi phenomena. Whether our culture can muster the courage and wisdom to permit such explorations remains to be seen, however. At present the major psychedelics are treated simply as drugs of abuse, under a legal system which in fact does little to prevent abuse but has been highly successful in suppressing research that could contribute significantly to reshaping scientific understanding of human personality and mind-body relations. We refer readers here especially to Grinspoon and Bakalar (1979/1997, chap. 8), who sharply highlight the manner in which the existing medical-legal control system has itself in effect become a means of defending the entrenched mainstream reductionist-materialist conception of human mind and personality. As they trenchantly observe, "we have a mysticism problem as well as a drug problem" (p. 302).

Psychodynamic Approaches to Mysticism: Toward a Working Model

Much of the scanty theoretical effort so far directed to mysticism by scientific psychology has arisen within its clinical wing and relies chiefly upon the psychodynamic models of human personality advanced by Freud, Jung, and their followers. These developments have followed a trajectory generally parallel to that of psychodynamic theorizing about *genius*, as reviewed in Chapter 7, which is to be expected in view of the evident psychological overlap, discussed above, between these domains. Nevertheless, the resulting positions in regard to mysticism are more sharply differentiated in terms of their overall attitude toward its meaning and significance. We next briefly canvas these developments (for more detail see Wulff, 2000, and especially Parsons, 1999).

Freud and Jung

The "classical" phase, dominated by orthodox Freudian psychoanalysis, was almost unremittingly hostile to all expressions of religiosity, mysticism included. Freud regarded religion in general as merely a defense, much like the protection afforded by a strong father, against infantile feelings of helplessness. To be religious is for him merely to regress to a more primitive developmental level, to abandon the reality principle in response to unmanageable stress. His attitudes toward mystical experience *per se*, however, developed mainly through his interactions with the French scholar and novelist Romain Rolland, and are slightly more nuanced. Rolland was apparently subject to mystical experiences and regarded them as the real foundation of religious life, something altogether different from religions themselves as social institutions. This positive attitude on the part of a highly valued friend evidently discomfited Freud, and in Chapter 1 of *Civilization and Its Discontents* he formulated his initial and best-known response. He acknowledges the occurrence in Rolland and many others of a "peculiar feeling," which he characterizes as "a sensation of 'eternity', a feeling as of something limitless, unbounded—as it were 'oceanic'...a feeling of an indissoluble bond, of being one with the external world as whole" (Freud, 1961, pp. 11–12). Freud can discover no trace of such feelings in himself, however, and despite the disturbing testimony of Rolland he cannot accept that they might play a role in religion comparable in importance to the feelings of infantile helplessness and longing for the father (p. 19). He tentatively concludes that mystical states represent the restoration of a "boundless narcissism," much like that of an infant at the breast in a primitive phase of ego-development antedating the discrimination between self and world.

Freud ends this brief discussion of mysticism on a curious note of ambivalence which persisted through his continuing interactions with Rolland (Parsons, 1999). His orthodox followers, however, generally devalued and pathologized the subject without any such reservations (Wulff, 2000, p. 419),[51] and theirs was undoubtedly the majority psychodynamic viewpoint even as recently as the so-called "GAP report" (Group for the Advancement of Psychiatry, 1976). This stunningly arrogant yet ill-informed position paper is in our opinion a low point in the modern psychiatric literature. Echoing the crudest early psychoanalytic characterizations of genius as merely an expression of mental illness, it defends a thoroughgoing pathological-regression interpretation of mysticism by focusing almost exclusively on marginal or secondary phenomena that lend themselves to such interpretations, while utterly failing to come to grips with the central empirical realities of the subject.

---

51. We include in this group the work of Leuba (1925), who sought to analyze the highest experiences of Christian mystics in terms of a reductive psychodynamics of sexual repression and sublimation having much in common with Freudian psychoanalysis while not embracing it overtly. For a destructive critique of Leuba's efforts along these lines, informed by a much deeper acquaintance with Christian mysticism, see Maréchal (1927/2004).

To be sure, unusual and distinctly odd forms of thought and behavior can often be identified in the literature of mysticism, sometimes reaching the level of true psychopathology. Pushkin, for example, appears on the rosters not only of Bucke (1901/1969) and Bloom (2002), but also that of Jamison (1993) as an instance of bipolar disorder. Nevertheless, and again as in the case of genius, any presumption of a universally pathological origin for mystical phenomena is belied by a broader acquaintance with the subject. Anyone who widely samples the lives of the great mystics, for example, with their intense and difficult psychological disciplines and their extraordinary practical, creative, and ethical achievements, must surely find it difficult to take seriously the claim that their psychology is fundamentally and universally rooted in some sort of infantile narcissism.[52] We are reminded here of the cautionary remark by Myers (1886a), just as apt today as it was then, that modern "thinkers know well that man can fall *below* himself; but that he can rise *above* himself they can believe no more" (vol. 1, p. lvi).

The GAP committee's clinically based pathologizing also directly conflicts with a wide variety of empirical evidence (much of which was already available, starting with James's *VRE*, had they chosen to look at it) showing that religious, supernormal, and mystical-type experiences tend to occur, in modern Western industrial societies at least, in persons who on average are at least as well-adjusted, physically healthy, affluent, educated, and creative as their peers (Greeley, 1974, 1975, 1987; Hay, 1994; Hay & Morisy, 1978; Koenig et al., 2001; Laski, 1961; Maslow, 1964, 1973; Privette, 1983; Spilka, Hood, & Gorsuch, 1985; Wulff, 2000).

As in the case of genius, therefore, the radical pathologizing associated with classical Freudian psychoanalysis has gradually given way to adaptive ("regression in service of the ego") and transformative/transpersonal schools of thought (Parsons, 1999; Wulff, 2000) which regard religious and mystical experience far more positively. One significant and desirable result of these trends is that the occurrence of mystical experiences, NDEs, and the like is no longer automatically taken by clinicians, as it once was, to be diagnostic of mental disorder (Lukoff, Lu, & Turner, 1992). It seems now to be more widely appreciated, in sum, that such experiences often exert profoundly positive and even transformative effects on human personality, including (as exemplified by the reports of Bucke and Tennyson) reduction or even elimination of the fear of death.

Among the major psychoanalytic theorists, the one most attuned to these positive, transformative, and transpersonal aspects of religious and mystical experience was undoubtedly Carl Jung. Indeed, Jung's more accepting attitude toward these matters was one of the main causes of his break with Freud. In brief, whereas for Freud the unconscious was entirely a function of personal biography and biology, Jung conceived it as containing in addition a deeper functional stratum, the collective unconscious, which is a repository of universal templates, themes, or "archetypes" of experience and the principal source of supernormal and transpersonal phenomena.

52. See especially Underhill (1911/1974).

Jung saw the central process of *individuation*, the growth and integration of personality, as driven and shaped by numinous encounters between the conscious ego and this deeper unconscious or "dark" region of the psyche. For him and his followers, as for Myers, genius and mysticism are profoundly related, with both reflecting an inherent drive or *nisus* toward more comprehensive consciousness and more complete psychic integration. According to Neumann (1968/1970), we are in fact at bottom *homo mysticus*: The mystical is "a fundamental category of human experience" (p. 383) and "the profoundest source of creative life" (p. 385). Indeed, "man's very center is an unknown creative force which lives within him and molds him in ever-new forms and transformations" (p. 415). Mystical experiences involve mutually transformative contacts between the ordinary ego and this hidden center, which Jungians term the self, and thus they can energize and guide that overall shift in the center of gravity of the personality from ego toward self which constitutes the essence of individuation. Jung's views here approach those of Underhill (1911/1974), for whom "the essence of the mystic life consists in the remaking of personality," leading when successful to the "Mystical Marriage" or "Unitive Life," a more or less permanent or recurrent state of "conscious relation with the absolute" (p. 375).

For further detail we must refer readers to the elaborate and sometimes difficult expositions provided by the Jungians themselves.[53] Although it is true in a general way that Jung's theory is more comprehensive than Freud's and more consistent with the full range of available data, it can hardly be claimed that it provides an empirically satisfactory or complete psychodynamic account of mystical experience. Jung's arguments for archetypes and the collective unconscious, for example, rest primarily on his own clinically based investigations of art and literature, comparative mythology, dreams, and psychosis, and like most other developments in transpersonal psychology have so far generally been viewed by more mainstream psychologists as undisciplined, uncritical, and largely irrelevant to scientific psychology. Nevertheless, some additional support for his ideas can be found in further studies of comparative mythology by J. Campbell (1949/2004) and perhaps also in observations from psychedelic investigations. Grof (1985), for example, asserts that the latter "have repeatedly confirmed most of Jung's brilliant insights" and that Jung's system, although not yet encompassing the full spectrum of psychedelic phenomena, "requires the least revisions or modifications of all the systems of depth psychology" in order to do so (p. 190).

Such "confirmations" are of course hardly independent of Jung's original formulations, and it remains to be seen whether or to what degree they will be supported in further investigations along similar lines. Moreover,

---

53. A. Huxley (1961) explicitly contrasts the rich documentation with concrete facts that is so characteristic of Myers with "those psycho-anthropologico-pseudo-genetic speculations which becloud the writings of the sage of Zurich." Nevertheless, there are also important similarities and hidden links between the views of Myers and Jung that certainly merit further exploration.

quite apart from serious and still unresolved issues as to the character, number, and thematic content of "archetypes," there are at least two significant ways in which Jungian accounts of mystical experience seem to us inadequate, empirically. In the first place, such experiences certainly cannot all be regarded as "archetypal," for archetypes only reach overt expression in the form of *images*, broadly construed, and as shown by Stace and others the innermost core of mystical experience unfolds in a region beyond images and all other distinctive mental particulars. This is closely connected with the second and more serious limitation. What Jung clearly found most congenial in his encounters with religious mysticism generally and Eastern mysticism in particular was the wealth of myth, symbolism, and imagery that he could readily assimilate to his core doctrine of individuation and the collective unconscious, as described above. A central feature of that doctrine, however, is Jung's conviction that the *ego* is the primary bearer of consciousness. Thus for example, he says:

> Consciousness is inconceivable without an ego; it is equated with the relation of contents to an ego. If there is no ego there is nobody to be conscious of anything. The ego is therefore indispensable to the conscious process.... I cannot imagine a conscious mental state that does not relate to a subject, that is, to an ego. (Jung, 1969b, p. 484)[54]

This theoretical commitment seems to have rendered Jung systematically unable to come fully to grips with introvertive mystical experiences of the sort described by Stace and others. For him, disappearance of the ordinary conscious ego during a numinous encounter with the collective unconscious can only mean that the conscious ego has been flooded, or contaminated, or engulfed by the inherently dark contents of that unknown part of psyche. As a result, consciousness itself supposedly dims or contracts, ultimately to some sort of void, nothingness, or state of egoless unconsciousness (e.g., Jung, 1969a, pp. 287–288; Jung, 1969b, pp. 484–485, 491, 496, 498, 504–505, 560; see also Neumann, 1968/1970, pp. 379, 381, 383, 392, 397, 399, 403).[55]

This kind of description of mystical states, however, which follows from Jung's strong identification of consciousness with the ordinary ego, is flatly contradicted by the unanimous testimony of great mystics of all times and places that their highest states are not dim or *un*conscious, but if anything "*super*conscious." The ingredient crucially absent from the Jungian model, in short, is precisely Myers's central theoretical move, his repudiation of that identification in favor of his own core conception of the Subliminal Self—"a more comprehensive consciousness, a profounder faculty, which for the most part remains potential only," but which expresses itself in

54 Jung (1969a, p. 283) also makes explicit that the same characterization applies to whatever consciousness accompanies any "complexes" or secondary personalities that may form under pathological conditions (see Chapter 5).

55. A similar picture of the limitations of Jung's understanding of mystical experience is presented in scholarly detail by Coward (1985).

greater or lesser degree as a function of fluctuating conditions in the organism (*HP*, vol. 1, p. 12).

Myers and James

And here we arrive at a central message of this chapter, directed not only to students of comparative religion but also to humanistic and transpersonal psychologists generally and to any mainstream scientists who might develop an increased interest in mysticism as a result of our labors here. It is this: The best way forward, we believe, is not through any sort of minor adjustment of traditional clinically based psychodynamic models of the sorts advanced by Freud and Jung, as advocated for example by Parsons (1999), nor by uncritically embracing the "perennialist" psychologies of persons such as H. Smith (1976) and Grof (1975, 1985), but by building upon the conceptually more adequate and empirically more secure foundation already created by Myers and carried forward by James.[56]

The importance of James's connections with Myers, we believe, has not yet been adequately appreciated by most students of mysticism and religion. James's biographers, including his "official" biographer Perry (1936), have generally downplayed or ignored altogether his deep involvement with psychical research, and even E. Taylor (1996, p. 96), who knows better, cites as a summary of James's "own position" a passage from *VRE* (p. 366) in which James in essence is paraphrasing Myers (and anticipating Maslow). It can be argued that a large proportion of James's late work revolves specifically around his attempts to draw out in detail consequences for the psychology of religion, and for epistemology and metaphysics, of Myers's theory of the Subliminal Self.

These connections are perhaps especially apparent in regard to *VRE*. There, James not only uses Myers's "taxonomic" expository methods throughout, organizing his case material serially and placing special emphasis on the most extreme and challenging phenomena, but clearly acknowledges in various ways and places that the theoretical apparatus he brings to bear on their explanation is that provided by Myers (e.g., see *VRE*, pp. 366, 386). His treatments in *VRE* of the psychology of religion generally, and of mysticism in particular, can be regarded, not unfairly we believe, as consisting in the main of an attempt to make more fully explicit views that in Myers are already clearly present but remain for the most part implicit.

---

56. Recall here that Huxley, who as we saw had himself advanced a filter theory of psychedelic and mystical experience, apparently came to the same conclusion when he discovered *Human Personality*. In an introduction written for a one-volume edition (1961), he explains why he finds Myers's conceptual framework far more congenial than those of Freud and Jung, and declares: "How strange and how unfortunate it is that this amazingly rich, profound, and stimulating book should have been neglected in favor of descriptions of human nature less complete and of explanations less adequate to the given facts!" We could hardly agree more.

But James also went further and extended Myers's thinking in novel and important ways. In particular, as shown with particular clarity by Leary (1990), he continued throughout his final decade to pursue tenaciously the problem that was always closest to his heart, the problem of the self. Most psychologists are aware of James's elaborate discussions in the *Principles* of the self and the stream of consciousness, and of his famous doctrine of the thought itself as the only thinker. Relatively few, however, are aware of his own dissatisfaction with these views, of his continuing struggles after 1890 to get beyond them, and of the more radical position at which he eventually arrived.

The linchpin of these late developments is *VRE*, because in religious and especially mystical experiences James found himself able to begin tracing that "something more" that he had always obscurely sensed to be hidden behind the subjective pole of everyday states of consciousness (James, 1890b, vol. 1, p. 305). In mystical experiences we come into contact with something in ourselves that is wiser than the ordinary self yet somehow of the same type or quality. James states as one of his principal conclusions in *VRE* that "we have in *the fact that the conscious person is continuous with a wider self through which saving experiences come*, a positive content of religious experience which, it seems to me, *is literally and objectively true as far as it goes*" (p. 388). This "wider self" James explicitly identifies (p. 386) with the Subliminal Consciousness as characterized by Myers (1892b): "Each of us is in reality an abiding psychical entity far more extensive than he knows—an individuality which can never express itself completely through any corporeal manifestation" (p. 305). On its "near side" this wider self abuts everyday consciousness and provides "exactly the mediating term" required to describe accurately, and at least partly explain, not only dissolutive phenomena of various sorts but automatisms, inspirations of genius, and all the central phenomena of religious life—the divided self, the struggle, prayer, conversion, the sense of influx of helping power, joy and security, saintliness, and mystical experience itself.

But what about the "far side," the remoter margin of this vast subliminal region? Here James begins to diverge from Myers in an important way. Myers was deeply acquainted with mystical philosophers and poets such as Plato, Plotinus, Wordsworth, and Tennyson, and he himself was evidently at least somewhat susceptible to mystical experiences, both natural and drug-induced. Although a strong undercurrent of sympathy for the mystical therefore pervades his thinking, it rarely finds overt expression in his scientific writings, including *HP*, and in fact he himself never discusses the subject of mysticism explicitly in a continuous and connected fashion. From various scattered evidence it appears certain that he imagined the subliminal region revealed by mystical experience as reaching all the way to a sort of "World Soul" or "God" (see, e.g., Gauld, 1968, chap. 13; Myers, 1895e, pp. 585–593; *HP*, chap. 10), but he refrains from any systematic attempt to spell out his cosmological views in greater detail. Indeed, he explicitly declines to address such larger issues, saying that his aim is not "to shape the clauses of the great Act of Faith, but merely...*to prove the preamble of all religions*... that a spiritual world exists—a world [that is] not a mere 'epiphenomenon' or transitory effect of the material world" (1900b, pp. 116–117).

James, however, was less preoccupied with personal survival and less convinced of its existence, and it is he who picks up and develops further this largely implicit cosmological thread in Myers's thinking. Mystical experience shows that there is something in us or connected with us which is both *other* and *larger* than our ordinary conscious selves, something which produces real effects, and which in its highest expressions is "godlike" though not necessarily corresponding precisely to any extant conception of God. How shall we conceive the nature and organization of this something within?

In *A Pluralistic Universe* (1909/1971) James delivers on the promise first made in his postscript to *VRE*, setting forth in general terms his sense of the right sort of answer—specifically, a "pluralistic panpsychism" along lines originally suggested by Gustav Fechner.[57] The facts of ordinary psychology, together with those of psychopathology, psychical research, and religious experience, establish for James a "decidedly *formidable* probability" in favor of such a view: "The drift of all the evidence we have seems to me to sweep us very strongly toward the belief in some form of superhuman life with which we may, unknown to ourselves, be coconscious" (p. 268). James pictures this coconscious life as having a complex structure of its own, taking the form of a hierarchy of progressively comprehensive integrations of the consciousnesses appearing at lower levels. "Integration" here involves more than mere summation; following Fechner, James likens it to what we find in our own experience. Just as the meaning of a sentence is something above and beyond a summation of the meanings of its constituent words,

> our mind is not the bare sum of our sights plus our sounds plus our pains, but in adding these terms together also finds relations among them and weaves them into schemes and forms and objects of which no one sense in its separate estate knows anything....It is as if the total universe of inner life had a sort of grain or direction, a sort of valvular structure [normally] permitting knowledge to flow in one way only, so that the wider might always have the narrower under observation, but never the narrow the wider. (p. 202)[58]

57. This is the same Gustav Fechner, the physicist, known to most psychologists only as the founder of psychophysics.

58. This Fechner/James concept of integration or compounding is explicitly rejected by Balfour (1935) and McDougall (1911/1961), both of whom also reject Myers's closely related conception of the Subliminal Self. Both, however, seriously misrepresent it. Balfour, for example, states that "the unity resulting from the compounding of consciousness is nothing but the components themselves, although nevertheless each component retains its separate individuality inside the unity" (p. 270). With typical sarcasm, McDougall characterizes compounding instead as a kind of blending or averaging process: "Suppose my consciousness is filled with the glory of colour of a sunset sky, while yours, as you lie near by under your motor-car, is filled with a problem in mechanics. What sort of consciousness would these two make

James conceives of this integration as an ongoing, evolving process, the current highest stage of which is a conscious reality of some sort corresponding to the common person's notion of God. But his is a finite and imperfect God which falls short of *total* integration; the one thing James is sure about is that the monistic Absolute Idealism of philosophic colleagues such as Royce and Bradley is false. Its abstract God is to him a foreign and monstrous fiction, the pernicious result of intellectualizing unconstrained by empirical data. For James the issues raised by religious experience are *empirical* issues, and the proper way forward is clear: "Let empiricism once become associated with religion, as hitherto, through some strange misunderstanding, it has been associated with irreligion, and I believe that a new era of religion as well as of philosophy will be ready to begin" (1909/1971, p. 270).[59]

James's own final appraisal of the topography of the subliminal or transmarginal region is sketched in one of his last published essays, "Confidences of a Psychical Researcher" (1909/1986). There he first goes on record for the commonness of psychological phenomena originating from that region, including automatisms such as trance mediumship and automatic writing, and for the occurrence among them—in the midst of much humbug—of "really supernormal knowledge" (p. 372). Then comes the following extraordinary passage:

> Out of my experience, such as it is (and it is limited enough) one fixed conclusion dogmatically emerges, and that is this, that we with our lives are like islands in the sea, or like trees in the forest. The maple and the pine may whisper to each other with their leaves, and Conanicut and Newport hear each other's fog-horns. But the trees also commingle their roots in the darkness underground, and the islands also hang together through the ocean's bottom. Just so there is a continuum of cosmic consciousness, against which our individuality builds but accidental fences, and into which our several minds plunge as into a mother-sea or reservoir. Our "normal" consciousness is circumscribed for adaptation to our external earthly environment, but the fence is weak in spots, and fitful influences from beyond leak in, showing the otherwise unverifiable common connexion. Not only psychical research, but metaphysical philosophy and speculative biology are led in their own ways to look with favor on some such "panpsychic" view of the universe as this. Assuming this common reservoir of consciousness to exist, this bank upon which we all draw, and in which so many of earth's memories must in some way be stored, or mediums would not get at them as they do, the question is, What is its own structure? What is its inner topography? This question, first squarely formulated by Myers, deserves to be called "Myers's problem" by scientific

---

if compounded? Presumably a gorgeously coloured problem in mechanics" (p. 169). We will return to this subject in Chapter 9.

59. Myers expresses the same view: "Bacon foresaw the gradual victory of observation and experiment—the triumph of actual analyzed fact—in every department of human study;—in every department save one. The realm of 'Divine things' he left to authority and faith. I here urge that that great exemption need be no longer made" (*HP*, vol. 2, p. 279).

> men hereafter.[60] What are the conditions of individuation or insulation in this mother-sea? To what tracts, to what active systems functioning separately in it, do personalities correspond? Are individual "spirits" constituted there? How numerous, and of how many hierarchic orders may these then be? How permanent? How transient? And how confluent with one another may they become?
>
> What again, are the relations between the cosmic consciousness and matter? Are there subtler forms of matter which upon occasion may enter into functional connexion with the individuations in the psychic sea, and then, and then only, show themselves?—So that our ordinary human experience, on its material as well as on its mental side, would appear to be only an extract from the larger psycho-physical world? (pp. 374–375)

In *VRE* James portrays the "axis of reality" as running through the subjective poles of all conscious experiences, which themselves are "strung upon it like so many beads" (p. 377). Introvertive mystical experience can be viewed as essentially revealing the origin of that axis and thus, as our Myers epigraph to this chapter suggests, the innermost subjective core of James's hierarchical scheme. For these deep mystical states of pure, undifferentiated, unitary consciousness, in which consciousness takes itself as its own intentional object and self gives way to Self, appear to expose the normally hidden roots of everyday forms of intentionality and selfhood.

Here the profound theoretical gulf between conventional mainstream conceptions of human personality and the radically different conception advanced by Myers and James expands to its fullest extent. On the conventional view we are essentially *closed*, encapsulated within our skulls, in the sense that everything in mind and consciousness is *generated* by the electrochemical activity of our brains. For Myers and James, however, we are *open*, in some way profoundly interconnected with each other and with the entire universe, and what we consciously experience is somehow *selected* by our brains from a much larger field of conscious activities originating at least in part beyond the margins of everyday consciousness, and perhaps even beyond the brain itself.

We will return to these theoretical matters in Chapter 9. Meanwhile, we end this section by noting that among the various kinds of evidence marshaled in this book which load the scales in favor of "open," "transmission," or "filter" models, that provided by mystical experience and its associated phenomena was for Myers and James both especially pivotal, personally. We resonate strongly with their sense of its importance. Furthermore, and contrary to anti-scientific critics such as H. Smith (1976), we believe both that a great deal remains to be learned about mysticism and that much *can* be learned through further development and application of conventional

60. James (1901, pp. 17–18) first delineated this as "Myers's problem" in his obituary of Myers, which is included on our digital version of *HP*.

scientific methods and practices.[61] We will conclude this chapter, therefore, by briefly outlining some particularly attractive possibilities of this sort.

Opportunities for Further Research

Most of the useful work to date on mysticism, from James onward, has been based upon close study of biographical documents and other writings produced by identified historical mystics and their interpreters. In addition to illuminating individual cases, these studies have provided raw materials for the valuable "natural histories" of James, Stace, Thurston, and M. Murphy, among others. Although such work has therefore been valuable and should surely continue, our purpose here is to emphasize possibilities for additional, complementary forms of empirical research that can potentially shed new light on all of the issues discussed above.

General Considerations

To speak first in the most general terms, a foundational principle of all such research, and a condition for its success, will be to utilize what is best in *both* of the relevant intellectual traditions—specifically, the third-person observational tradition currently dominant in Western science and the first-person introspective disciplines associated primarily with the Oriental wisdom traditions. This is entirely in the spirit of Myers's "tertium quid" or "breadth" approach, as described in Chapter 2.

Imaging studies with persons undergoing mystical-type experiences, for example, would clearly be of enormous value, the more so to the extent that they combine state-of-the-art neuroimaging methods having appropriate technical properties (targeting of relevant physiological parameters, high spatial/temporal resolution, subject-friendliness, and so on) with improved means of tracking and reporting the characteristics of unusual states of consciousness. Neuroimaging technology has made spectacular progress in recent decades and will undoubtedly continue to do so, given its fundamental role in most if not all areas of cognitive neuroscience. The more challenging problems lie rather on the first-person side of our science, which is in far less satisfactory shape. We have yet to recover fully from the decades-long hegemony of behaviorism, with its strictures against introspection and the study of conscious states, but significant progress is now being made on this

61. We find especially repugnant the often-expressed view that only persons who themselves have had full-blown mystical experiences can contribute anything of value to the study of mysticism. Anyone tempted by this doctrine should consider the examples of Myers, James, and Stace, among many others, which belie it. This is not to deny, however, that personal experience of mystical (and psychedelic) states could be helpful in many ways in shaping their scientific investigation (see also Tart, 1972).

front as well. It seems now widely appreciated, for example, that "objective" and "subjective" methods differ more in degree than in kind, and that the collapse of classical introspectionism had less to do with any inherent problems than with the ascendency of the behaviorist juggernaut itself (K. Danziger, 1980; Varela, 1996).

There *are* problems to be sure, as with any other method of scientific observation, but also an increasing variety and sophistication of means for coping with these. For excellent general introductions to methodological issues in altered-states research, see Tart (1975a) and Pekala and Cardeña (2000). What is especially needed, we think, is further refinement and adaptation of these methodologies to the specific environment of research on meditative, psychedelic, and mystical states. We already have some questionnaire-type instruments with respectable psychometric properties (reliability and validity) that sample these overlapping domains. These include Hood's mysticism scale (Hood, 1975; Hood, Morris, & Watson, 1993), which is based directly on Stace's analysis; Dittrich's (1994, 1998) APZ, which has become standard for psychedelic studies in Europe; and Pekala's PCI and DAQ (Phenomenology of Consciousness Inventory, Dimensions of Attention Questionnaire; see Pekala & Cardeña, 2000, p. 65), which are more general-purpose tools for quantitative characterization of altered states of consciousness. In addition, MacDonald, LeClair, Holland, Alter, and Friedman (1995) present a comprehensive survey of existing measures of transpersonal constructs and a good general discussion of the strengths and limitations of the psychometric approach. Further effort to identify the major dimensions of variation in altered states of consciousness and to standardize their measurement should be a high priority, for by mapping a diversity of experiences into common coordinates the use of such instruments can undoubtedly help bring some order into studies of mysticism, as has the use of Greyson's (1985) scale in studies of NDEs.

These psychometric efforts must be closely coordinated, however, with attempts to refine and enrich our currently impoverished resources for phenomenological description of the relevant states (Gifford-May & Thompson, 1994; Lukoff & Lu, 1988; Varela, 1996; Walsh, 1995). Further comparative study of the traditional "cartographies" of meditative and mystical states, as noted earlier, can surely be of help here, but these cartographies can and must also be cross-checked wherever possible through independent investigations using contemporary subjects and methods. In-depth interviews will be crucial to such efforts, and pose problems for the most part analogous to those successfully confronted on a daily basis by skilled workers in areas such as cultural anthropology, neuropsychology, psychotherapy, and developmental psychology—namely, the task of fathoming "foreign" states of mind and consciousness by means of searching yet sensitive questioning and observation.

Good subjects will also be uncommonly vital to future research on altered states of consciousness—co-investigators, really, or sometimes even the investigators themselves in an alternate role—and will often be selected or trained to help ensure its success. Above all, they must strive to describe their conscious experiences as accurately and in as much detail as possible, and with a minimum of interpretation as emphasized especially by Stace. In order to optimize the possibility of correlating physiological and psychological events, moreover, subjects should be enabled to report unusual experiences (or at least to register them for subsequent reporting). Similarly, experimenters should be enabled to collect reports of experiences occurring in conjunction with any unusual physiological events or states they detect in their subjects, preferably at or near the time of detection. It can be anticipated with confidence that our understandings of what we most need to measure on both the physiological and experiential sides, and how to do so, are likely to undergo considerable evolution as research of this sort proceeds.

All of these general considerations would clearly apply, for example, to further research with psychedelic agents, which would provide means for producing strong mystical-type states under reasonably well-controlled experimental conditions. On this front, unfortunately, we can do little at present except to encourage our European colleagues to expand their intellectual horizons beyond the current preoccupation with "psychotomimetic" properties of psychedelic experience, while reiterating our hope that suitable relaxation of existing regulations will soon facilitate the resumption of such research here in the U.S. as well.

Sources of Relevant Phenomena

Where else, meanwhile, might we find sources of the sorts of experiences we wish to study? In the first place it seems certain that spontaneous mystical experiences of various kinds are continuing to occur, at least sporadically, and that persons who have such experiences, if not the experiences themselves, are in principle available for more detailed study. Bucke (1901/1969) readily discovered a number of contemporaneous cases, as did both Laski (1961) and Maslow (1964, 1973) more recently. Similarly, Happold's (1963/1970) interest in mysticism was prompted by experiences of his own, Stace had direct and productive interactions with both Arthur Koestler and the philosophically astute mescaline subject "N. M.," and Hufford (1985) was able to interview Genevieve Foster repeatedly regarding aspects of her visionary experience.

From a different direction Greeley (1975) has reported similarly encouraging results based upon a large national multistage probability sample acquired using the resources of the National Opinion Research Center. Of some 1,460 respondents, Greeley reports that 35% answered affirmatively his main question, "Have you ever felt as though you were very close to a powerful, spiritual force that seemed to lift you out of yourself," with almost half of these describing themselves as having had such experiences "several times" (12%) or "often" (5%). Closely similar results were reported shortly afterward by Hay and Morisy (1978) for a large sample of adults in Great Britain.

Greeley's question is rather vague, however, and it seems certain that a sizeable proportion of the affirmative answers reflect experiences falling well short of the full-blown mystical type. This is already evident from Greeley's own data, for among those who answered the main question affirmatively, the proportions who also accepted key items on an accompanying checklist of "descriptors" of mystical experience were often quite low, on the order of 25% or less (p. 65). Moreover, followup studies by Hufford (1985) and by L. Thomas and Cooper (1980) demonstrated directly, by investigating in greater detail the experiences that gave rise to "Yes" answers, that relatively few could be regarded as genuinely mystical. In the latter study, in fact, only about 1% of the total sample appeared to have had such experiences.

Although the prevalence of deep mystical experiences is therefore undoubtedly much lower than Greeley's numbers suggest, the more important fact is that they do occur. Even if their incidence were far lower still, say even on the order of one per million adults per year, there would potentially be hundreds or even thousands of new cases annually, world-wide, if we could just find them. We could then not only systematically collect detailed reports of contemporary mystical experiences but also investigate their conditions of occurrence (triggers), their short-term and long-term effects, and the cognitive and personality characteristics of those predisposed to have them. Some sort of larger-scale, better-funded, and better-publicized international registry, structured along lines pioneered in the U.K. by Alister Hardy's Religious Experience Research Unit (Hardy, 1979; http://www.religiousexperience.co.uk) and in the U. S. by Rhea White's Exceptional Human Experience network (S. Brown, 2000; http://www.ehe.org), would ideally serve these purposes and could perhaps even facilitate collaborative connections between especially promising subjects and appropriate research groups. Leading educational and membership organizations involved in the promotion and study of meditation and other transformative practices, such as Esalen, the Institute for Noetic Sciences, the Institute for Transpersonal Psychology, and the California Institute for Integral Studies, might also participate.

Much more also remains to be learned through cross-cultural investigation of procedures for controlled production of altered states of consciousness. The very large anthropological literature dealing with this subject shows that over 90% of the world's roughly 4,000 recognized societies harbor one or more institutionalized procedures for induction of altered states of consciousness, typically combining elements such as fasting, sleep deprivation, and other ascetic practices with the use of psychoactive substances and "driving" procedures such as drumming, dancing, clapping, and chanting, often carried on at great intensity and for protracted periods of time. Indeed, the great social value attached to the resulting altered states of consciousness—which are universally believed to confer supernormal abilities such as divination, healing, and control of pain—is directly reflected in the extremity of the measures that participants willingly endure in service of their production. As argued in detail elsewhere, more systematic analysis of this large but uneven literature, supplemented in the future by better-informed and better-equipped field studies and by parallel studies in the laboratory, can be expected with high confidence to elucidate the psychophysiological basis of these powerful effects, and thus potentially lead to more efficient means of inducing them (E. F. Kelly & Locke, 1981b; R. G. Locke & Kelly, 1985).

At present, however, the most promising and available pathway toward experimental study of mystical states clearly lies in their methodical cultivation using the central meditative disciplines developed by the wisdom traditions. As indicated earlier, these traditions are fundamentally coherent in their overall psychological contours, though differing in many details, and their deep convergence on matters of both method and results gives to the whole, in our minds, the appearance of nascent psychological fact.

There has been a steady growth of interest in meditation since the 1960s, but the amount of research progress has so far remained rather disappointing, especially from the perspective of this chapter. To be sure, it has been shown repeatedly that even elementary practice of meditation techniques can lead to a variety of clinically significant psychophysiological consequences, and the resulting marriage of meditation research with behavioral medicine and psychotherapy undoubtedly represents a public-health development of considerable practical importance (Andresen, 2000; Lehrer & Woolfolk, 1993; M. Murphy & Donovan, 1997; Shapiro & Walsh, 1984). We have barely scratched the surface, however, in terms of using meditation to gain experimental access to the higher forms of transformative ecstatic and mystical experience that comprise its principal long-term objective. Although this subject is much too large to review in detail here, we wish to record a few basic observations on the status and prospects of such research.

As in the case of contemporary experimental work on hypnotism, a large proportion of existing research on meditation fails even to make significant contact with the intended subject matter. Many published studies reflect an appalling ignorance of the traditional literatures, assuming that the word "meditation" refers both to some single universal technique and to a correspondingly unitary state of consciousness, and that practice of the technique, however elementary, is operationally equivalent to induction of that state. A large proportion of existing studies are superficial and perfunctory, relying for their subjects upon convenience samples of undergraduates and other meditation beginners whose attainments surely fall far short of the point at which most traditional meditation manuals even begin their instruction. It should hardly be surprising that such studies have generally produced correspondingly banal results (Davidson, 1976; M. Murphy & Donovan, 1997; Schuman, 1980; Shapiro & Walsh, 1984; M. A. West, 1987).

The relatively small amount of work so far carried out with advanced practitioners, however, has already produced a variety of more intriguing findings suggestive of what potentially lies ahead. As Michael Murphy, himself a very experienced meditator, puts it in his overview of meditation research (M. Murphy & Donovan, 1997): "Contemporary research does not illumine the full range of experience described in the contemplative scriptures and the oral traditions from which they come. Modern studies give us only a first picture of the foothills, with a few glimpses of the peaks. Still, what they give us corresponds in several ways with the traditional accounts" (p. 44). We will next briefly review just a few of these more promising "glimpses." The crucial feature these examples have in common is that they involve an apparent conjunction between unusual conscious states or events and physiological conditions or events that also lie well outside the normal range.

First is the conjunction of mystical experience with "deathlike" states in the body. As James observes in *VRE*, "in the condition called *raptus* or ravishment by theologians, breathing and circulation are so depressed that it is a question among the doctors whether the soul be or be not temporarily dissevered from the body" (p. 316). Underhill (1911/1974) similarly states that in prolonged instances of rapture "the body is cold and rigid, remaining in the exact position which it occupied at the oncoming of the ecstasy, however difficult and unnatural this pose may be. Sometimes entrancement is so deep that there is complete anesthesia" (p. 359). Myers reports Socrates as having remained standing in one place under such conditions, immobile, for periods ranging from several hours to more than a day (*HP*, vol. 2, p. 99). Several modern cases of this sort, involving meditating Yogis buried in airtight chambers, were reviewed in Chapter 3, and see Arbman (1968) for more.

Several more recent experimental studies have also indicated the existence of a lower-level version of the same or similar phenomena in advanced practitioners of Transcendental Meditation (TM)—specifically, the occurrence of spontaneous respiratory suspensions, more frequent and of longer duration than those occurring in control subjects, which tend strongly to be associated with episodes of pure or "transcendental" consciousness and a fairly consistent pattern of correlated changes in measures of autonomic and cortical activity (Baddawi, Wallace, Orme-Johnson, & Royzere, 1984; Farrow & Hebert, 1982; Travis & Wallace, 1997). Whether these physiological occurrences are causes or consequences of the transient alterations in conscious state is not clear, but they provide at minimum simple and effective markers for use in further studies. The association with breathing patterns is also especially interesting inasmuch as the respiratory system is a transitional system having both involuntary and voluntary levels of control, and deliberate manipulation of breathing patterns *(pranayama,* in Patanjali's system) has always been a major component of meditative disciplines. It is certain that such practices can strongly influence the concentrations of blood gases, among other things, and hence directly or indirectly affect many autonomic and central nervous system functions. For example, recent studies indicate that meditation techniques involving deliberately slow breathing produce pronounced oscillations and high variability of heart rate, a sensitive indicator of autonomic tuning (Peng et al., 1999), and that forced unilateral breathing through individual nostrils, a common component of *pranayama* and related techniques, produces both systematic shifts in cerebral dominance and correlated changes in performance on hemispherically specialized cognitive tasks (Jella & Shannahoff-Khalsa, 1993; K. Morris, 1998). Clearly, this area will provide a rich field for further investigation (see also Austin, 1999, chap. 22).[62]

We next give two further examples involving apparent correlations between unusual conscious states and unusual states of the central nervous system, as reflected in the behavior of EEG measures. Our primary historical source for both sorts of effects is the remarkable paper by Das and Gastaut (1957), which we regard—despite its imperfections—as a landmark in the field and a model of how to proceed. Crucial to their success was the circumstance that Das, a native Indian, had been closely associated since infancy with a Yogic community, and consequently was able to recruit from among its members seven very advanced practitioners of a local form of concentrative meditation. The experiments themselves, some 20 in all, were carried out in Calcutta, in a plain but air-conditioned room, using portable physiological instrumentation supplied by Gastaut.[63] Following preparations for recording (four channels of EEG recorded in a variety of derivations from 10 scalp electrodes, two channels EKG or heart activity, and two channels EMG or muscle activity recorded from the quadriceps via concentric needles), subjects assumed the cross-legged lotus position on a large couch, performed some preliminary breathing exercises, and began their meditations. Physiological data were recorded continuously on paper strip-charts, and subsequently transported to Marseille for analysis by Gastaut.

The results, in a word, are stunning. First, these highly trained subjects were able to remain for *hours* in a state of perfect physical immobility and relaxation, with no visible trace of muscle activity in quadriceps EMG or frontal EEG leads. During this time, moreover, progressive and systematic changes of a dramatic sort occurred in their EEGs. Most significantly, the deepest stages of meditation, including at least one reported episode of Yogic ecstasy, were accompanied by the emergence of fast rhythmic activity all over the scalp at progressively increasing frequencies of 20, 30, and ultimately even 40 Hz. During the ecstasy itself, this fast (gamma-range) EEG activity also reached extraordinary amplitudes, on the order of 150 microvolts peak-to-peak (Figure 3, F). Das and Gastaut interpret these EEG results as revealing a state of extreme cortical excitation accompanying the

62. Following the imposition of governmental restrictions on use of LSD in research with humans, Grof developed a technique he calls "holotropic breathwork," a kind of music-assisted hyperventilation which he claims produces similar, if less dramatic effects. Although we have not specifically investigated it, this claim seems to us rather dubious and reinforces our more general concerns about the possible role of expectancies and demand characteristics throughout Grof's research, including his psychedelic research (see also Wulff, 2000).

63. This is the same Henri Gastaut, distinguished French epileptologist, who figured in our earlier discussion of Dostoevsky's "ecstatic seizures."

unusual concentration of inwardly focused attention that these subjects were evidently able to achieve. In support of the latter they also remark in passing that the high-frequency, high-amplitude EEG rhythms, once established, were completely unaffected by any form of auditory, visual, tactile, or nociceptive (painful) stimulation.

This paper is brief, lacks important information regarding details of the stimulation and recording procedures, contains no statistical analyses, and in various other ways falls short of what we might now routinely expect from state-of-the-art psychophysiology research reports. Nevertheless, we believe it deserves to be taken very seriously.[64] The physiological findings are startling, to be sure, but in a way that makes considerable sense. Furthermore, and more importantly, they have been corroborated at least in part in a number of subsequent studies, and in particular by those relatively few studies which exhibit a similar degree of selectivity in regard to the qualifications of subjects and the choice of data epochs subjected to analysis.

The reported absence of responsiveness to external stimulation, for example, would naturally be expected in anyone who has achieved what Patanjali terms *pratyahara*, withdrawal of the senses, or isolation from the sensory environment. Additional and very striking examples of this phenomenon were soon provided by Anand et al. (1961a), again working in India with Yogis purportedly capable of entering states of *samadhi*. In two of these, strong auditory, visual, tactile, and thermal stimuli which invariably produced blocking of ongoing EEG in the normal state failed to do so during meditation. Two other Yogis showed no changes in parietal EEG during protracted (45–55 minute) immersion of their hands in near-freezing water (4°C). A later EEG study of advanced TM practitioners by Banquet (1973) similarly showed that the EEG patterns accompanying brief episodes of "deep meditation" or "transcendence" were not altered by flash and click stimuli.

Unresponsiveness to external stimuli during deep states of concentrative meditation seems to us surely a real phenomenon. Indeed, it seems an exaggerated and voluntary form of a phenomenon of selective attention that all of us encounter spontaneously from time to time in the course of everyday life, a stock example here being the football player so intent upon the game that he fails to realize until afterward that he has suffered a painful injury.[65] A natural extension of the existing studies would be to compare the psychophysiological responses of advanced meditators to identical stimuli delivered *inside* versus *outside* episodes of increased absorption, as indexed for example by momentary breath suspension. On the psychophysical side

64. Recall here too that this study provided Gellhorn and Kiely (1972) with the principal stimulus for their theoretical ruminations about neurophysiological correlates of mystical states.

65. We mention in passing that a widely cited debunking study by D. E. Becker and Shapiro (1981) has no impact here, because it deals only with *habituation* of the EEG blocking normally produced by sensory stimulation, and not with the abnormal *absence* of blocking, even by very strong stimuli, observed by others under conditions of deep meditative absorption. Indeed, we see little sign in their data that any such states occurred.

we would expect stimuli delivered during such episodes to be both less detectable and of lower subjective magnitude when successfully detected. Furthermore, analysis of the associated evoked potentials could reveal precisely where this blockage occurs, whether at the level of the thalamus, as hypothesized by Austin (1999), or somewhere else in the CNS .

The gamma-frequency EEG activity reported by Das and Gastaut is of even greater interest, and we believe this too is a real phenomenon. It certainly cannot be casually dismissed, as it was for example by Fenwick (1987, p. 106), as EMG artifact arising from the scalp musculature. Das and Gastaut themselves were fully aware of this possibility and provide no less than seven arguments against it. Most fundamentally, the activity is not "diffuse" or wideband but "fusiform" or spindle-shaped, nearly monochromatic at a dominant frequency, and equally visible in regions such as the top of the head (vertex) that are relatively remote from scalp muscles. Moreover, this dominant rhythm itself shifts progressively toward the higher frequencies characteristic of deep meditative states and then remains there, stable, for hours. The original paper gives only a few small-scale illustrations of the relevant phenomena, but in subsequent correspondence with one of us (EFK), Gastaut himself, who had of course examined all of the original recordings in detail, stood firmly behind these published descriptions.

Supportive findings have again also appeared in relevant parts of the subsequent EEG literature.[66] In the Banquet (1973) study, for example, the EEG patterns that accompanied the deepest meditative states, and only these, specifically included spatially generalized moderate-amplitude fast activity in the vicinity of 40 Hz. Even stronger confirmatory evidence has recently been found in a study of eight highly experienced Tibetan Buddhist meditators by Lutz, Grieschar, Rawlings, Ricard, and Davidson (2004), who also point out the theoretical connection between coherent large-scale gamma oscillations of this sort and perceptual "binding" as conceived by contemporary global-workspace theorists. Also potentially relevant here is the curious fact that nitrous oxide, a known psychedelic agent, has been shown to produce high-amplitude gamma-band EEG activity, mainly in frontal areas (Yamamura, Fukuda, Takeya, Goto, & Furukawa, 1981).

The central point of this highly selective review is not to claim that anything has yet been definitively established in regard to physiological correlates of deep meditative and mystical states, but only that we already have substantial, empirically grounded indications that such correlates exist and are accessible to well-conceived imaging studies of the sorts outlined above. We will conclude with three further observations concerning the future of such research.

66. One possible exception here is the study of Anand et al. (1961a), who specifically state that they did *not* observe the high-frequency, high-amplitude EEG activity reported by Das and Gastaut. It is not clear, however, whether their experimental conditions, physiological instrumentation, and EEG recording procedures were fully comparable.

Further Guidelines for Future Research and Theory

First and foremost, we emphasize again, and again as in the case of genius, the vital importance of focusing more future research on the real thing—here, genuinely deep meditative and mystical states and persons who experience these—rather than on conveniently available but inadequate surrogates. Furthermore, although it would now be technically possible and certainly worthwhile to carry out more comprehensive and penetrating field studies of the Das and Gastaut sort, it should not really be necessary to travel to places such as India or Japan to find suitable subjects. One long-term consequence of the culture wars of the 1960s is the creation throughout the Western world of sizeable cadres of individuals seriously engaged with meditation and other transformative practices, at least some of whom would surely be willing to participate in meaningful scientific research conducted by sympathetic investigators.

Second, collection of new data should be far the highest priority until we really know something about what is going on in these unusual individuals and states. Most of the theorizing that we have seen so far is very premature, and implicitly presupposes that information derived from neurophysiological and neuropsychological investigations of "ordinary" cognitive functions can be extrapolated freely and without limit to "extraordinary" ones. This approach fails to take into consideration recent neuroscientific research revealing a previously unrecognized degree of plasticity even in the adult nervous system. The human brain is heavily weighted toward top-down anatomical connectivity and shows remarkable functional adaptability at all time scales, from milliseconds upward, with numerous mechanisms available to make some of these functional changes—for good or ill—persistent or even permanent (Gilbert, 1998; Kohn & Whitsel, 2002; Merzenich, Recanzone, Jenkins, Allard, & Rudo, 1988; Taub, Uswatte, & Elbert, 2002; see also Chapter 1). Such effects seem *a priori* likely to be reflected in the anatomical structure and functional organization of the brains of long-term practitioners of meditation and other transformative disciplines (as well as in persons who have undergone powerful mystical-type experiences), and indeed some evidence of topographically specific anatomical changes in meditators has recently appeared (Lazar et al., 2005). We should study these anatomical and functional arrangements directly, and with minimal presuppositions regarding their possible form.

This need for better empirical grounding also bears strongly upon our final suggestion, which is this: The more we can learn about the nature of *essential* physiological changes associated with deep meditative and mystical states, the better will be our chances of learning how to encourage or reproduce these states under controlled experimental conditions, which in turn will permit us to study both the states themselves and associated supernormal phenomena in greater detail. What is to be avoided here is the premature closing of scientific accounts that gave rise in the 1970s to the first generation of EEG biofeedback devices. During that period, some promising early demonstrations of a possible association between EEG alpha abundance and pleasurable mental states spawned a cottage industry of electronics entrepreneurs manufacturing low-cost alpha trainers, which were then purchased by other experimenters, who used them to conduct further studies of the same sort, and so on. We need to break out of this kind of vicious circularity by first gaining a much fuller and clearer picture of what the relevant physiological conditions are, and only then trying to find improved ways of creating or supporting them. We think the long-term prospects for providing improved access to mystical experiences in this way are actually rather good, and that society as a whole could only benefit in consequence. Myers and James would surely agree.

Conclusion

Mysticism has largely been ignored by mainstream psychology and philosophy for most of the past century. The encyclopedic *Oxford Companion to the Mind*, for example, barely mentions the subject, and in a recent and massive scholarly anthology on philosophy and consciousness (Block, Flanagan, & Güzeldere, 1997) the word "mysticism" and its cognates appear *nowhere* in the index. The central aim of the present chapter has been to help restore this neglected topic to what earlier thinkers such as Myers and James believed to be its proper place in the foreground of a worthy scientific psychology.

At first it seemed as if 20th-century psychology was well on the way to reducing consciousness to a scientific nullity. This perverse trend has been reversed, however, and consciousness has reappeared on the map of science, although it is still viewed by many as if it were some sort of alien intruder, or "nomological dangler," something best excised, whenever possible, like a hanging nail. But a serious study of mysticism forces us to go beyond merely acknowledging that consciousness is "real" and needs to be explained, to a recognition that it plays a uniquely significant role in cognition generally, and that its reality is of a different order than anything else encountered in the empirical world.

In the first place it is an incontrovertible and empirically grounded fact that the mystical domain comprises large numbers of real human experiences—experiences, moreover, which are often uniquely powerful and transformative—and that experiences of this sort lie at or near the foundations of religions generally and thus even of civilization itself.

Furthermore, careful survey and analysis of the reported experiences reveals that at the core of this domain lies a robust, deeply significant, and still mysterious psychological phenomenon—the introvertive mystical experience of pure, unitary, undifferentiated, self-reflexive consciousness—the singular properties of which pose profound challenges to all mechanist, physicalist, and computationalist theories of human mind and personality.

Mysticism assigns to consciousness a central and even supreme reality. Its fundamental lesson is that there are experiences, forms of consciousness, and modes of being with characteristics *not* mechanical, physical, or computable. The introvertive mystical experience appears to transcend time and space, the sensory, the imaginal, and the rational; yet it also involves more than mere subjective illusion, for the associations of mysticism with genius and with supernormal phenomena show that it makes contact with some reality or aspect of reality beyond the normal limits of the mind-body system as conventionally understood. Indeed, it appears to reveal the underlying source of our ordinary, everyday experience of intentionality and selfhood. Mysticism, in short, is a topic of vital importance to psychology.

This has consequences, however. In concluding his own review, Wulff (2000) states that "the valorizing of mystical experience is risky for the field of psychology, for to take mysticism seriously—to view it as in some sense a healthy and veridical response to the world—is to open onself to a world view that fundamentally challenges the assumptions, theories and procedures of modern psychology" (p. 430). This is for the most part a fair assessment. The facts of mysticism do pose fundamental challenges to mainstream reductionistic physicalism. Wulff nevertheless thinks, and so do we, that scientific psychology must open itself more fully to these genuinely transpersonal aspects of the human psyche.

Transpersonal psychology thus has a real subject matter. But to put the matter bluntly, it must put its scientific house in better order, and notwithstanding the unfortunate proclivity of some of its adherents toward inflammatory rhetoric about supposedly insurmountable "clashes" or "collisions" between the primordial tradition and mainstream science, we can discover no essential obstacle to doing so. As we have shown, mystical experiences and associated phenomena are available for study from a variety of perspectives, and there exist numerous important opportunities for further scientific research.

But mainstream psychology itself will also benefit from such efforts, for what we are advocating here is not its rejection or overthrow but an *expansion*, to dimensions at last fully commensurate with those inherent in its subject matter. Mystical and transpersonal experience is a real and vitally important facet of human psychology, and we must somehow come to terms with it. Restoring the mystical to its proper place will go far toward restoring the humanity of our science. The mystical roots of conscious experience also reveal a deep human identity, transcending all national, rational, personal, and theological differences. What better reason to investigate these remarkable, transformative experiences?

Finally, we have suggested that the development of an expanded psychology of mysticism can best be guided by a working model grounded in leading ideas and data provided by Myers, James, and Bergson. The main elements of this model include: Myers's empirically rich hypothesis of the Subliminal Self; the James-Bergson conception of the mind-brain relation—their "transmission" hypothesis, the idea of the brain as an organ which somehow limits, shapes, or "filters," not creates, consciousness; and James's late thinking in regard to pluralistic panpsychism. Such a model, we believe, makes use of the most important insights provided by previous work in dynamic psychiatry and philosophy, is potentially consistent with all relevant facts of present-day neuroscience and neuropsychology, and can accommodate additional facts—including psi phenomena and mystically tinged NDEs occurring in conjunction with general anesthesia and cardiac arrest—that are beyond the reach of conventional mainstream views. Its further development can also capitalize on important resources not available to Myers and James themselves, including a more highly developed and comparative scholarship of mysticism, the world-wide growth and consolidation of transformative practices, and the development of more powerful research technologies including the new functional neuroimaging methods. We will now attempt, in our final chapter, to develop and justify this model in a more systematic and comprehensive way.

Chapter 9

Toward a Psychology for the 21st Century

Edward F. Kelly

> The problem of Myers still awaits us as the problem of far the deepest moment for our actual psychology, whether his own tentative solutions of certain parts of it be correct or not. (James, 1901, p. 18)
>
> The rejection of any source of evidence is always treason to that ultimate rationalism which urges forward science and philosophy alike. (Whitehead, 1929/1958, p. 61)
>
> The truest success of this book will lie in its rapid supersession by a better. (Myers, *HP*, vol. 1, p. 9)

We come now to the hardest task of all, that of weaving together the various threads of this book into an overall reassessment of Myers's work and its implications for the future of scientific psychology. I will begin with what some major contemporaries had to say.

Contemporary Reviews of *Human Personality*

There were many early reviews of *HP*, ranging in tone from scornful derision to unalloyed praise (see Gauld, 1968, chap. 12), but the most useful for our purposes are those of Stout (1903), McDougall (1903), and James (1903), each of which offers serious criticism in combination with actual knowledge of the contents of the book. All are included on our digital version of *HP*.

The assessment by Stout, a distinguished British psychologist of that period, is wholly negative and proceeds along lines that many present-day mainstream reviewers would undoubtedly be inclined to follow. Precisely for these reasons, it is worth examining here in some detail. It will become evident that the fundamental issue at stake is that of unconscious cerebration (Stout) versus subliminal or transmarginal consciousness (Myers), as discussed in Chapters 2 and 5. Unconscious cerebration, in today's terminology, comprises all the sorts of things a "cognitive unconscious" might accomplish by means of automatic brain activity.

Stout (1903) begins by describing what he regards as the principal novelty of *HP*:

> The theory represented by Mr. Myers diverges in a startling way from all the various forms of the doctrine of subconscious or unconscious mental states and processes which have ever been current among psychologists. The theory has at least as much affinity with such conceptions as that of a tutelary genius or a guardian angel. The Subliminal Self is not to be identified with any organized system of mental traces or dispositions formed in the course of the conscious experience of the ordinary self....The Subliminal Self is rather to be conceived as a primary and independent stream of personal consciousness having its own separate system of mental traces and dispositions formed in the course of its own separate experience. (pp. 45–46)

Despite Stout's attempts to justify this description using quotes from *HP*, it is a caricature of Myers's actual views. Myers does hold that *some* contents of the subliminal region do not derive from the conscious experience of the ordinary self, but he certainly does not hold that *all* of its contents are of this sort. Indeed, as shown in Chapters 2 and 5, Myers admits all the conventionally recognized forms of transmarginal content, including everything from momentarily forgotten or incompletely processed material to Janet's well-characterized clinical cases of dissociated consciousness, and seeks only to extend these existing conceptions in order to embrace a still wider range of documented empirical phenomena. One of the strengths of his theory, in fact, is that it identifies previously unrecognized relationships and continuities underlying an enormous range and variety of phenomena, both normal and supernormal.

Stout next deploys his own caricature of Myers's conception in an attempt to turn the generality itself into an argument against him. Specifically, the central strategy of Stout's critique is to argue that the Subliminal Self as he has described it *must* provide at least part of the explanation of all "normal" phenomena, as well as any supernormal ones, and hence that if any normal phenomenon can be explained without recourse to it, Myers's general theory is false. He then proceeds to describe how unconscious cerebration alone might explain recollection of momentarily forgotten names, problem-solving, alternate personalities, sleep and dreams, hypnosis, and other generally accepted phenomena discussed by Myers.

Two principal features of Stout's "explanations," however, merit special emphasis—first, his heavy reliance on promissory materialism in regard to accepted or "normal" phenomena, and second, his systematic unwillingness to take seriously Myers's heavy documentation of supernormal phenomena. Both tendencies are fully evident in regard to hypnosis, for example:

> Setting aside alleged cases of telepathy, clairvoyance, etc., hypnosis presents no phenomena so extraordinary as to justify our regarding them as beyond the reach of explanation in accordance with the ordinary methods and principles of physiology and psychology. The way is dark, but it is not blocked by unsurmountable barriers. We need not have recourse to a flying-machine. (p. 57)

I cannot resist noting here the irony that Stout's dismissive final sentence was penned in the same year in which the Wright brothers made their first successful flight at Kitty Hawk. More to the point scientifically, however, are the many parts of our Chapter 3 that undermine his unquestioning faith in the reach of conventional forms of explanation, even in regard to the psychophysiological aspects of hypnotism. Similar comments apply to the other "normal" phenomena he discusses.

Finally, having resorted repeatedly to his "setting aside" approach to Myers's documentation of psi-type phenomena occurring in conjunction with hypnosis, dreams, and so on, and mistakenly believing himself already to have successfully disproven Myers's general theory of the Subliminal Self, Stout turns to a brief statement (pp. 62–64) of his own "personal attitude" toward psi phenomena generally. He acknowledges "that after all criticisms are allowed for, the evidence is still decidedly impressive, and that it is sufficient to constitute a good case for further investigation," but he is not persuaded by it. Most of the "reasons" he offers in defense of this attitude, however, amount to generic suspicions, devoid of reference to specific experiments or cases, about possible failures of memory, conscious or unconscious cheating, and the like, issues that had long since been identified and controlled in ongoing investigations by Myers and his SPR colleagues. The one specific opinion he advances is that a proposed skeptical explanation of ostensible evidence for telepathy in terms of "unconscious whispering" is "peculiarly probable." What Stout neglects to mention here, however, is that this hypothesis—also eagerly embraced by the even more skeptical American psychologist Titchener in the pages of *Science*—had been thoroughly discredited in papers already published by William James and Henry Sidgwick (see Burkhardt, 1986, chap. 22; E. Taylor, 1996, pp. 108–111). In short, like many present-day scientists Stout is simply unable to come fully to grips with the relevant evidence and chooses instead to ignore it.

McDougall and James, unlike Stout, accept the reality of psi phenomena and find much to admire in the character and content of Myers's book, but they too have problems with his general theory. McDougall's complaints run partly parallel to Stout's and rest on the same primary misapprehensions, in particular that Myers fails to recognize routine contributions of unconscious cerebration to everyday mental life, and that he holds a rigidly duplex theory in regard to the supraliminal and subliminal streams of consciousness.[1] Two additional factors also seem to drive his somewhat convoluted and turgid critique: First, he is already beginning to develop his own very different "monadic" theory (discussed in Chapter 5), according to which the everyday consciousness or self is the real self, and the apex of personality. This leads him to be hostile to Myers's conception of psychological automatisms as expressions of a larger and in some ways superior transmarginal consciousness. Secondly, he thinks that Myers has failed to appreciate his true "main difficulty" (p. 526), the fact that post-mortem survival seems to be precluded by the normal dependence of mind and consciousness on an intact brain. Although McDougall's language here is carefully guarded, he appears at this time to hold something close to a standard production model of mind-brain relations.

Two crucial points should be noted, however. First, McDougall himself soon moved beyond the production model, driven in part by the findings of psychical research and also by his own ruminations on other topics, such as memory, meaning, and the unity of consciousness, discussed in the present volume. His book *Body and Mind* (1911/1974) is in fact subtitled "A History and a Defense of Animism," where by animism he means the following:

> The essential notion, which forms the common foundation of all varieties of Animism, is that all, or some, of those manifestations of life and mind which distinguish the living man from the corpse and from inorganic bodies are due to the operation within him of something which is of a nature different from that of the body, an animating principle generally, but not necessarily or always, conceived as an immaterial and individual being or soul. (p. xx)

McDougall ultimately arrived at a variety of animism, his "psychophysical dualism," which embraces the notion of a psyche or soul without presuming it to be ontologically distinct from the body or capable of surviving bodily death. Indeed, McDougall himself was not convinced of survival. The principal obstacle remained for him the same "main difficulty" he had identified in his review of *HP*, a difficulty which he found the survival evidence then available insufficient—though just barely—to overcome: "Again and again the evidential character of the observations has fallen just short of perfection; the objections that stand between us and the acceptance of the conclusion seem to tremble and sway, but still they are not cast down" (McDougall, 1911/1974, p. 347).

---

1. See Chapter 2. McDougall continued throughout his career to misrepresent Myers in these ways, as can be seen for example in his *Outline of Abnormal Psychology* (McDougall, 1926, p. 523).

Here, however, the second point comes into play. McDougall seems never to have taken fully on board the significance of James's (1898/1900) discussion of transmission theory (see our Chapter 1). It is not even mentioned in his review of *HP* as a possible way around the difficulty, and one, moreover, that is compatible with Myers's theory. In addition, when McDougall later does come to discuss it, in the last chapter of *Body and Mind*, he grossly misrepresents James's actual views, as I will demonstrate later.

Meanwhile, let us turn even more briefly to the appraisal of Myers's work by William James. The two main sources for this are his 1901 memorial address and his 1903 review of *HP* (both on our digital version of *HP*). Both pieces are vintage James, marvels of incisiveness, clarity, warmth, and felicity of expression, and I beg all readers—especially my fellow psychologists—to study them with care in conjunction with this chapter. James was more intimately acquainted with Myers and his work than either Stout or McDougall, understood the theory better, and appreciated it far more:

> It is a vast synthesis, but a coherent one, notwithstanding the vagueness of some of the terms that figure in it. No one of the dots by which his map is plotted out, no one of the "corners" required by his triangulation, is purely hypothetical. He offers empirical evidence for the concrete existence of every element which his scheme postulates and works with. In logical form the theory is thus a scientific construction of a very high order. (James, 1903, p. 30)

As to the *truth* of Myers's theory, however, as distinct from its formal merits, James withholds final judgment, for three primary reasons: First, he thinks some of the "corners" or "stepping-stones" may themselves be too frail, or insufficiently well documented. Second, he wonders whether Myers perhaps generalized too hastily from conditions that in fact have been adequately documented only in a few special situations, such as deep hypnosis and multiple personality disorder, involving small numbers of highly unusual persons. Third, and for James the most troubling, is Myers's inability to explain to his satisfaction how the subliminal region can serve equally as "rubbish-heap" and "treasure-house" (*HP*, vol. 1, p. 72), "so impartially the home of both evolutive and of dissolutive phenomena" (James, 1903, p. 32). All of these concerns are legitimate and remain relevant today, and I shall attempt to deal with them in the course of what now follows.

A Re-assessment of Myers's Theory of Personality

Principles which I have tried to follow in constructing this assessment, and which I must ask readers to follow as well, include in particular the following four: First, many contemporary readers, and especially scientific readers, are likely to find certain aspects of Myers's writing at times jarring or even distasteful. His sentences are often long and complex, his prose sometimes startlingly ornate and lyrical, and the text loaded with quotations from multiple foreign languages including in particular Greek and Latin.[2] All of this can make for hard going, but it involves only superficial stylistic matters characteristic of Myers and his time. The effort necessary to penetrate his meanings is almost always worthwhile, in my opinion, and it must be made in order to appreciate in full the richness and beauty of his theory. Related to this, what we must attempt now to appraise is the theory that Myers actually held, and not the sorts of caricatures of it served up by critics such as Stout and McDougall, and by Freud's biographer and disciple Ernest Jones (1918, p. 122) in service of their own very different theoretical outlooks. Third, we must respond to the *whole* theory and take *all* the associated data into account, not artificially restricting our attention, as did Stout, to those elements of Myers's vision with which we happen to be comfortable at the moment. Finally, and most importantly, we must try to take into account all of the additional relevant evidence that has come forward in the intervening century, most of which has been summarized, or at least pointed to, in the present volume.

Our assessment will proceed at three general levels: (1) Myers's methodological principles and commitments; (2) his natural history of the mind; and (3) the theoretical structure which he elaborated in order to account for his data. The first two of these sections can be relatively short and should, I think, be uncontroversial.

Myers's Methodological Principles

Myers was reared chiefly on literature and history, with primary interests in poetry and religion, but that he successfully transformed himself into a serious scientist can scarcely be doubted by anyone who takes the trouble to study his contributions to psychology. As described in Chapter 2, he was deeply committed to the ultimate lawfulness of nature, and to the use of empirical methods in ferreting out its secrets. Where he differs from most contemporary scientists is in refusing to rest content with scientific theories, facts, or methods in their existing state of development. No topic is to be banned *a priori* as beyond the reach of science. Indeed, Myers's central impulse and long-term goal is to overcome the historical opposition between science and religion by means of an expanded and enlightened science capable of penetrating into the psychological territory previously occupied by the historical religions alone, with their mutually inconsistent teachings and decidedly mixed impacts on human welfare. He aspires ultimately to re-ground this entire domain of vital human experience in real scientific knowledge rather than faith and dogma; see, for example, his "Provisional Sketch of a Religious Synthesis" in *HP* (vol. 2, pp. 284–292).

2. To assist modern readers, we have provided on our digital version of *HP* translations of all non-English passages.

In pursuit of this and all the related goals of psychical research, what seems to him most needed is not unthinking mechanical application of any existing method to every new problem, but constant effort to adapt our research methods creatively to all new situations as they arise, and as we find them.

Myers would therefore certainly have lamented—correctly, I believe—the subsequent withering of psychical research, and of psychology more generally, into disciplines preoccupied to the extent they presently are with laboratory-based experimental investigations as the only road to knowledge.[3] This is not because he doubted the value of experimentation, when appropriate, but because he also appreciated the value of other kinds of empirical research such as detailed individual case studies and field investigations. Both *HP* itself and the present volume illustrate, I believe, the power of the broader concept of empiricism advocated by Myers and James for psychology as a whole.

It also merits emphasis here that there are many scientific options in the region between one-shot case studies and full-fledged factorial experimental designs. Methodologists D. T. Campbell and Stanley (1966), for example, identified numerous useful though less rigorous experimental designs that are still capable of producing reliable and valid scientific knowledge, and they explicitly stated that the goal of their efforts was to "encourage an open-minded and exploratory orientation to novel data-collection arrangements and a new scrutiny of some of the weaknesses that accompany routine utilizations of the traditional ones" (p. 61). From the opposite direction, cases initially studied and reported in detail individually, such as apparition cases, NDEs, and cases of the reincarnation type, can also be encoded according to appropriate descriptive schemes and entered into cumulative databases which, when they become sufficiently large, afford important new opportunities for quantitative study of internal patterns, predictive relationships, and so on, governing the relevant domains.[4]

A broadened empiricism has similarly been advocated for psychology as a whole by Toulmin and Leary (1985):

> It is not only *thinking* that suffered because of American psychology's cult of empiricism....Empiricism itself suffered because of the rigid, experimental fetters that were placed upon it. Surely there should be room too for a retreat, at least by some, from *experimental* empiricism. All science, and probably all speculation, originates at a more basic level of empiricism: the level of experience. In a discipline that is often confused about its subject matter, it is not a bad idea to return to basic experience from time to time. The natural taxonomy that arises therefrom is much more likely

3. In fact, in reviews of two annual volumes of *L'année psychologique* published shortly before his death Myers had already begun to lament the direction that scientific psychology was taking toward limited and ultimately trivial experimental studies (see our Chapter 2).

4. At the University of Virginia, for example, 836 cases of NDEs and 1,200 cases of young children who claim to remember a previous life have been entered into such computerized databases.

to provide a useful framework for experimental work than the artificial taxonomies that structure so much of the field today. (p. 612) [5]

Myers's Natural History of the Mind

This leads immediately, of course, to Myers's own "taxonomy," and on this subject all serious students agree. His natural history of the mind, quite apart from the theoretical constructions he based upon it, has been hailed by many as a scientific achievement of great value in itself. Let James again speak here for all: In his 1901 memorial address he describes Myers as "the pioneer who staked out a vast tract of mental wilderness and planted the flag of genuine science upon it" (p. 23), largely through exercise of the kind of taxonomic genius described in our Chapter 2. In his later review of *HP*, James (1903) was if anything even more explicit:

> Reading him afresh in these two volumes, I find myself filled with an admiration which almost surprises me. The work, whatever weaknesses it may have, strikes me as at least a masterpiece of co-ordination and unification. The voluminous arsenal of "cases" of which the author's memory disposes might make the most erudite naturalist or historian envy him, and his delicate power of serially assorting his facts, so as to find always just the case he needs to fit into a gap in the scheme, is wholly admirable. He shows indeed a genius not unlike that of Charles Darwin for discovering shadings and transitions, and grading down discontinuities in his argument. (p. 30)

One of the "weaknesses" James had in mind, as indicated above, was the possible frailty of some individual elements of Myers's taxonomy. James unfortunately does not identify which particular elements he had in mind, but in any event it seems to me undeniable that this "natural history" aspect of Myers's work has only been further strengthened by the large amounts of additional evidence generated during the subsequent century and summarized in the present volume. We now have far more detailed evidence, for example, regarding the existence of psi phenomena in general and their association with altered states of consciousness such as dreams and hypnosis (see Appendix), supernormal control of bodily processes (Chapter 3),

---

5. Parenthetically, the 20th-century contraction of "psychical research" to its desiccated modern descendant, "parapsychology," was if anything even more extreme than that experienced by psychology generally. At the hands of J. B. Rhine, the field suffered a kind of "identification with the aggressor"—that is, with the experimental behaviorism of the early-to-mid 20th century—and confined itself in large part not merely to experimental and statistical methods but to methods of an unnecessarily primitive and limited sort (Burdick & Kelly, 1977). Although this has begun to change in recent decades, parapsychology still falls far short of what the founders of psychical research envisioned, as reflected in particular by the tendency of many modern parapsychologists to treat psi phenomena as free-floating "anomalies" rather than trying, like Myers, to incorporate them within a larger framework of interrelated psychological phenomena.

problems in regard to conventional trace theories of memory (Chapter 4), psychological automatisms including the full-blown dissociative phenomena of automatic writing, hypnosis, and MPD/DID (Chapter 5), NDEs and OBEs occurring under extreme physiological conditions (Chapter 6), genius (Chapter 7), and mystical and psychedelic experiences (Chapter 8), all of which maps smoothly onto—and hence reinforces—Myers's basic descriptive framework. I should also reiterate here that Myers not only provided a useful taxonomy of subliminal contents and processes but also strove to develop or improve various means of putting these "on tap" for more efficient experimental investigation (Chapter 2). It seems to me a virtual certainty that we have barely scratched the surface in terms of exploiting these techniques—such as hypnosis, automatic writing, and crystal-gazing or "scrying"—in the manner Myers envisaged (E. F. Kelly & Locke, 1981a).

I turn now to the third level of our reassessment, a far more difficult subject.

Myers's General Theory of the Psyche: The Subliminal Self

Chapter 2 has set forth what we believe to be the correct understanding of what Myers (1885c) really meant by his "Subliminal Self" (uppercase)—briefly, the totality of the psyche, soul, or Individuality, comprising both supraliminal and subliminal elements, regions, or functional systems. The supraliminal or everyday self constitutes only a small portion of the psyche, formed out of some few of its "elements" (p. 387) in response to the demands of the environment. One or more "subliminal selves" (lower-case) may also occasionally emerge in a similar way under certain unusual conditions. But the Subliminal Self—the underlying, comprehensive Self—is the centerpiece of Myers's theoretical construct, for it is at this level that he seeks to reconcile the "colonial" (Ribot) versus "unitary" (Reid) accounts of human personality in favor of a more profound unity.[6]

As noted in Chapter 2, there has been much confusion about this conception in the literature, and it cannot be denied that Myers himself was to

---

6. It has been overlooked that Myers's colleague Edmund Gurney had apparently arrived at closely similar views, and for reasons at least partly independent of Myers, prior to his untimely death in 1888. In Gurney et al. (1886) he first points out that phenomena of hypnosis and secondary personality render it difficult "to measure human existence by the limits of the phenomenal self." Moreover, he goes on, "the very nature of this difficulty cannot but suggest a deeper solution than the mere connection of various streams of psychic life in a single organism. It suggests that a single individuality may have its psychical being, so to speak, on different planes; that the strong fragments of 'unconscious intelligence,' and the alternating selves of 'double consciousness,' belong really to a more fundamental unity, which finds in what we call life very imperfect conditions of manifestation; and that the self which ordinary men habitually regard as their proper individuality may after all be only a partial emergence" (vol. 1, p. 231).

For philosophic elaboration and justification of such a conception Gurney also appeals to Du Prel (1889/1976). Recall here too that Braude (1995) independently reached a similar position based on his philosophical analysis of multiple personality disorder (see our Chapter 5).

a considerable extent responsible for it. His terminology is unfortunate and confusing, and even Myers himself did not use it altogether consistently. It seems likely, though we cannot be sure, that he was still ironing out details of the exposition at the time of his death. This might have helped clarify things, but it is certain in any event that the conception is not only inherently difficult, but also highly counter-intuitive for many commentators—myself included. Nevertheless, I have come to think that it is more or less correct, for reasons I will next try to explain.

The starting point for Myers's scheme, his "measured base," consists of various forms of evidence for the existence of dissociated streams of consciousness existing outside the awareness of the ordinary self, rising in complexity and coherence in some cases to the level of true secondary personalities or "subliminal selves." As shown in Chapters 2 and 5, James and many others found the evidence Myers marshaled for this purpose already cogent, and much additional evidence of related types has subsequently come to light that is further supportive of his interpretations. Chapter 5, for example, provides what to me is a convincing demonstration that there have been cases of multiple personality which cannot be satisfactorily interpreted in terms of "periodic sharp alterations in a *single* stream of consciousness" (Gauld, 1968, p. 279). In this light it is rather sad to find unconscious cerebration once again being trumpeted as the proper explanation of all psychological automatisms, as though these old and vigorous debates had never occurred (see, e.g., Wegner, 2002, and its review by E. F. Kelly, 2003), and despite the fact that other modern workers such as Hilgard (1977), Kihlstrom (1993b), and Oakley (1999) have moved toward positions much closer to that adopted by Myers and James over a century ago.

Chapter 5 in effect provides what might be called an "existence proof" for the possibility that multiple, concurrent, and overlapping streams of consciousness can sometimes coexist in conjunction with a single human organism. Much of that evidence, however, derives from very unusual persons and circumstances. Myers argued that subliminal consciousness of this sort is at work in all of us, all the time, but this raises James's second issue: Is such far-reaching generalization justifiable? This is a fair and realistic concern, but Myers himself addresses it fairly effectively, I think, and we can certainly do substantially better today. To document this adequately would take much more space than can be devoted to it here, but let me at least briefly indicate the main lines along which the argument would run.

For one thing the database of individuals displaying major automatisms of the sort relied upon by Myers has greatly expanded in the subsequent century. Many additional and sometimes even better cases of multiple personality, automatic writing and drawing, and trance mediumship, for example, have come to light more recently here in the West. Furthermore, the enormous 20th-century expansion of cultural anthropology has made evident that the core phenomena of psychological automatism have a truly world-wide distribution and reflect in all likelihood fundamental capacities which we all to some degree share. Like the trance medium Mrs. Piper, for example, shamans sometimes report ecstatic journeys undertaken during periods when to external observers they appeared to be ritually possessed by identifiable spirits, displaying behaviors appropriate to that state. Also relevant here is the fact that ritualized procedures for induction of trance and possession trance in preliterate societies often exert powerful effects on Western bystanders or observers, sometimes including quite skeptical ones intent upon defeating any such effects (Deren, 1972; Sargant, 1975). Myers certainly knew about this in general terms, but he could scarcely have imagined the wealth of relevant evidence that has since become available (Bourguignon, 1973; E. F. Kelly & Locke, 1981b; R. G. Locke & Kelly, 1985).

Myers also underestimated, if anything, the relevance of *dreaming* and allied phenomena to his central argument. Subsequent research has amply confirmed his original contention that dreams have a strong propensity to serve as carriers of supernormal information, both spontaneously (e.g., Stevenson, 1970, p. 2) and in experimental studies (Child, 1985). But what modern research has also shown, and Myers did not know, is that this intensified power of involuntary inward visualization, a sensory automatism, is essentially universal among humans, as revealed in particular by the subsequent discovery of physiological correlates of dreaming itself (REM sleep) as well as by investigations of psychedelic agents, sensory deprivation, and other "hallucinogenic" conditions (Siegel & West, 1975). Although we humans differ widely in terms of access to this "cosmogonic" capacity, we all apparently have it, and as argued especially by Schiller (1905, 1915) the maker of these phantasms must be recognized as some sort of highly creative agency that resides within the personality but is distinct from everyday consciousness in the way postulated by Myers (see also Globus, 1987). That this agency is constantly at work behind the scenes is further suggested by the phenomenology of hypnagogia, in which involuntary dream-like mentation unstably commingles with drowsy ordinary consciousness (Mavromatis, 1987), by intrusive apparitional experiences occurring under conditions of full waking consciousness (Chapter 6), and by the "subliminal uprushes" of genius, which can occur at any time of day or night (Chapter 7).

I will return to the generality issue shortly in a different context, but let me first say a word about James's third concern, the mingling of rubbish-heap and treasure-house in the subliminal region, the fact that "the parasitic ideas of psycho-neurosis, and the fictitious personations of planchette-writing and mediumship reside there side by side with the inspirations of genius, with the faculties of telepathy and telæsthesia, and with the susceptibility of genuine spirit control" (James, 1903, p. 32). The key words here are "side by side," which are more James's than Myers's. James immediately goes on to acknowledge the manner in which Myers himself actually sought to deal with this problem—that is, through his conception of the subliminal region as *stratified*—but finds this conception "deficient in clearness."

I will make just three comments in response to this complaint. First, Myers himself would certainly have agreed that his conception is "deficient in clearness" in the sense that much still needs to be done to identify more fully the number and character of these strata, or more generally to map out in greater detail the structural and functional organization of the subliminal region. Nevertheless, James seems to me to overstate somewhat the difficulties here. He may have been thinking of strata as essentially geological in character, rigid and static, whereas Myers was more inclined to think of them in terms of his image of imperfectly miscible fluids of varying density, "subject to currents and ebullitions which often bring to the surface a stream or a bubble from a stratum far below" (Myers, 1892b, p. 307). On this latter view the psyche is a dynamic system constantly in flux, with currents initiated in the deeper layers boiling toward the surface and, depending on their inherent energies, emerging there in forms varyingly intermingled with material derived from intermediate layers. Such a picture, metaphoric though it is, seems naturally to accommodate the frequent but by no means invariable "smothering" of supernormal phenomena in degenerative accompaniments that so troubled James. Myers also emphasized repeatedly that the character of final outcomes—evolutive or dissolutive—is determined in large part by what the supraliminal consciousness itself is able to do with the subliminal products it receives (see our Chapter 7). Finally, another issue lurking here for James, and barely touched upon by Myers, concerns the "depth" to which operations of the subliminal parts of the mind might map directly onto operations of the brain. This general issue—how Myers's psychological theory can be reconciled with contemporary brain science—will be discussed in detail in a later section.

We move on now to the conceptual heart of Myers's theory of the Subliminal Self, its postulation in all of us of a more comprehensive consciousness, indeed an all-inclusive consciousness embracing the entirety of our conscious mental activity both supraliminal and subliminal, evolutive and dissolutive. The primary alternative to such a view (at least among those prepared to recognize the reality of subliminal streams of awareness) is the family of "monadic" views exemplified in particular by McDougall (1911/1961, 1920) and Balfour (1935).[7]

McDougall's monadic theory of personality has already been discussed in Chapter 5. The essence of such theories is that they picture everyday consciousness as emerging at the apex of a hierarchy of lesser integrations of lower-level individuals. Under normal conditions, on this view, the ordinary self or "dominant monad" thus represents the true and only self. Balfour (1935, p. 175) candidly states, speaking for many, that "my own instinctive conviction is that my own true self is 'the me as I know myself'." This intuition certainly corresponds both with everyday experience and with all conventional mainstream theories of personality, but it cannot be presumed to

7. The analysis of Myers's theory by Balfour, a philosopher, is the most serious and sustained attempt known to me to grapple directly with its central conceptual difficulties. Balfour undertook this effort in conjunction with his intensive study of communications delivered by the trance medium "Mrs. Willett" from the ostensibly surviving personalities of Myers and Gurney. If nothing else this material illustrates, on Balfour's view, the automatic production of intellectual activity outstripping the known capacities of the medium in her ordinary state, as in the case of Patience Worth (Balfour, 1935, p. 300).

be self-evidently reliable or self-validating. As Myers puts it (*HP*, vol. 1, p. 13):

> This is, no doubt, the apparent dictum of consciousness, but it is nothing more. And the apparent dicta of consciousness have already been shown to need correction in so many ways which the ordinary observer could never have anticipated that we surely have no right to trust consciousness, so to say, a step further than we can feel it,—to hold that anything whatever—even a separate consciousness in our own organisms—can be proved *not* to exist by the mere fact that we—as we know ourselves—are not aware of it.

In Chapter 5 we described how James (1902/1958, p. 188) celebrated the discovery in 1886 of "an entirely unsuspected peculiarity in the constitution of human nature," the transmarginal consciousness identified and explored by Myers. Balfour, by contrast, wishes to reject Myers's conception for precisely that reason, complaining that "we are asked to believe that our true self is a self the very existence of which the vast majority of mankind have never even suspected" (p. 273). But this argument too is clearly unsound. For one thing, many peculiarities of the *physical* world had remained undiscovered for thousands of years, including rather momentous ones such as radioactivity (Schiller, 1905). Certainly no one now believes that we routinely have full access to the structure and content of our minds. Moreover, Myers-like conceptions of a larger consciousness latent within us *have* in fact emerged, and repeatedly, within the world's mystical traditions (Chapter 8).

Human personalities, like biological organisms and even society itself, have a homeostatic aspect and must constantly strive for balance between growth and preservation. But the discomfort that many of us undoubtedly experience in seriously entertaining Myers's conception is undermined by the widespread occurrence of experiences of psychological "expansion" or "opening" that appear to support it—whether these be spontaneous or produced by psychedelic agents, meditation, or other transformative practices. It is relevant and worth repeating here that Myers and James themselves displayed a strong affinity for the mystical that was in part intellectual but also derived in part from their own mystical-type experiences, including powerful experiences induced by nitrous oxide (Chapter 8).

Myers of course also adduced a great deal of empirical evidence directly contradicting commonsense intuitions as to the supremacy of the supraliminal in our mental life, including for example extreme manifestations of bodily control, secondary personalities whose capabilities exceed those of the everyday self, genius-level creativity, hypermnesia and calculating prodigies, OBEs/NDEs and mystical experiences, psi capacities linked to dreams and other automatisms, and all the rest. Both his taxonomy of relevant phenomena and his unifying generalizations—in particular that these "supernormal" phenomena take the form of psychological automatisms arising from deeper levels of the psyche, and manifest themselves in proportion to the abeyance of the supraliminal consciousness—have been strengthened at many points by subsequent research, as demonstrated in this book.

But now we come to what I think is the logical crux of the matter. Myers conceives the supraliminal consciousness as somehow functioning simultaneously both as itself and (possibly together with one or more subliminal streams of consciousness) as part of a larger, more comprehensive consciousness, the Subliminal Self, which provides for the overarching unity of the psyche or Individuality. Both McDougall and Balfour explicitly reject this core conception. In his review of *HP*, McDougall (1903, p. 518) simply jibes in passing that he finds it comparable in obscurity to that of the Christian Trinity. Balfour (pp. 270–271) explicitly recognizes its formal resemblance to Fechner's conception of the integration or "compounding" of consciousness across individuals, and he acknowledges the appeal of that conception to James (1909/1971). Yet he too summarily dismisses it, on grounds that the theory of compounding itself "presents formidable logical difficulties" and that Fechner's solution seems to him "frankly mystical."

Although this difficult topic really deserves a much more thorough scholarly treatment in itself, I wish to argue at least briefly here against Balfour and McDougall and on behalf of Myers and James. Both Balfour and McDougall seem to me excessively committed, *a priori*, to everyday consciousness as the supreme psychological achievement. Neither has much use for anything "mystical," and certainly McDougall devotes no chapter to that subject in his otherwise comprehensive *Body and Mind*. Neither seems fully to have grasped Myers's conception, for neither distinguishes systematically between subliminal selves and the Subliminal Self. As we saw, both also seriously misrepresent, in different ways, the character of higher-order compounds or integrations of conscious experience as conceived by Fechner and James (Chapter 8, footnote 58).

The issues come to a head in a particularly relevant way in a brief discussion by McDougall (1911/1961, pp. 358–363), in which he attempts to repudiate the transmission theory as formulated by James (1898/1900) in favor of his own preferred form of animism, his psychophysical dualism or soul theory. Although this disagreement appears at first sight to involve a head-on collision between intellectual freight-trains, what actually happens proves more akin to a passing of great ships in the night. McDougall begins by asserting that the formulations of transmission theory by James and Bergson agree on the following "essential points":

> Both reject the claims of mechanism to rule in the organic world; both regard all psychical existence as of the form of consciousness only; both assume that consciousness exists independently of the physical world in some vast ocean or oceans of consciousness; both maintain that the consciousness or psychical life of each organism is a ray from this source; that the bodily organisation of each creature is that which determines individuality; that the brain is a mechanism which lets through, or brings into operation in the physical world, a stream of consciousness which is copious in proportion to the complexity of organisation of the brain. (p. 358n)

Two features of McDougall's portrayal of transmission theory are especially relevant here: First, he treats it as depending essentially upon the doctrine of "mind-stuff," the notion that consciousness exists ultimately in the form of "atoms" that can be combined into larger aggregates while retaining their individual identities. Second, he portrays the brain as the organ which assembles and disassembles such compounds, and hence takes it as a necessary corollary that "the brain is the ground of our psychic individuality" (p. 358).

This latter feature, however, had already been explicitly denied by James in a crucial clarification of his own original statement of the transmission theory. This clarification, added to the second edition in the form of a preface, is so important that I will quote from it at length.[8] James begins by stating that he intends to remove an objection raised by many critics of his original formulation:

> If our finite personality here below, the objectors say, be due to the transmission through the brain of portions of a preëxisting larger consciousness, all that can remain after the brain expires is the larger consciousness itself as such, with which we should thenceforth be perforce reconfounded, the only means of our existence in finite personal form having ceased.
>
> But this, the critics continue, is the pantheistic idea of immortality, survival, namely, in the soul of the world; not the Christian idea of immortality, which means survival in strictly personal form.
>
> In showing the possibility of a mental life after the brain's death, they conclude, the lecture has thus at the same time shown the impossibility of its identity with the personal life, which is the brain's function....
>
> The plain truth is that *one may conceive the mental world behind the veil in as individual form as one pleases, without any detriment to the general scheme by which the brain is represented as a transmissive organ*.
>
> If the extreme individualistic view were taken, one's finite mundane consciousness would be an extract from one's larger, truer personality, the latter having even now some sort of reality behind the scenes. And in transmitting it—to keep to our extremely mechanical metaphor, which confessedly throws no light on the actual *modus operandi*—one's brain would also leave effects on the part remaining behind the veil; for when a thing is torn, both fragments feel the operation.
>
> And just as (to use a very coarse figure) the stubs remain in a checkbook whenever a check is used, to register the transaction, so these impressions on the transcendent self might constitute so many vouchers of the finite experiences of which the brain had been the mediator; and ultimately they might form that collection within the larger self of memories of our earthly passage, which is all that, since Locke's day, the continu-

8. Parenthetically, it seems very unlikely that McDougall would not have been aware of this clarification. It had long been in the literature when McDougall was writing *Body and Mind*, and in his memorial address McDougall (1911) describes James as having been "for many years the largest influence affecting my intellectual life" (p. 12). We can be sure in any case that this clarification would have been one of the first points James brought to McDougall's attention, had they ever discussed the subject.

> ance of our personal identity beyond the grave has by psychology been recognized to mean.
>
> It is true that all this would seem to have affinities rather with preëxistence and with possible re-incarnations than with the Christian notion of immortality. But my concern in the lecture was not to discuss immortality in general. It was confined to showing it to be *not incompatible* with the brain-function theory of our present mundane consciousness. I hold that it is so compatible, and compatible moreover in fully individualized form. (James, 1898/1900, pp. v–viii)

The overall resemblance between the picture sketched here by James and Myers's model of human personality is unmistakable.

The bulk of McDougall's attack upon transmission theory is directed at the "mind-stuff" doctrine, and more specifically at James's attempt in *A Pluralistic Universe* to defend the very sort of self-compounding of mental states that he himself had destructively criticized in the *Principles*. McDougall clearly thinks that in doing this he is attacking the transmission theory itself, but in this he is again off the mark, for what is primarily at stake in their disagreement is not the *existence* of complex mental states but alternative accounts of how they come into being. We can therefore bypass the tortuous details of these arguments (although I must comment in passing that like McDougall I find James's revised treatment of "compounding" ultimately unconvincing) and proceed instead to what for our purposes is a more critical question. Does everyday consciousness represent the highest level of consciousness within us, as McDougall and Balfour and virtually all contemporary mainstream psychologists presume, or could there really be within many or all of us a more comprehensive consciousness of the sort postulated by Myers and James? McDougall correctly identifies the two main sources of evidence relied upon by James and Myers—psychological automatisms and related dissociative phenomena, and mystical experience—but he does not discuss this evidence at all, apparently thinking (mistakenly) that his theoretical arguments against the transmission theory have already discredited their view. I must now say a little more about this evidence.

James (1909/1971) clearly thought that phenomena of divided personality, hypnosis, automatic writing and speech, and trance mediumship collectively demonstrate the existence of inclusive or higher-order consciousness as a real psychological phenomenon:

> For my own part I find in some of these abnormal or supernormal facts the strongest suggestions in favor of a superior coconsciousness being possible. I doubt whether we shall ever understand some of them without using the very letter of Fechner's conception of a great reservoir in which the memories of earth's inhabitants are pooled and preserved, and from which, when the threshold lowers or the valve opens, information ordinarily shut out leaks into the mind of exceptional individuals among us. (p. 264)

The main evidence from these sources for inclusive forms of co-consciousness has been summarized in Chapters 2 and 5 and need not be repeated here; I will only say again that I too find it convincing in that regard (but see Balfour, 1935, pp. 272–276, and Gauld, 1968, pp. 296–299 for different views).[9]

In the Conclusions chapter of *A Pluralistic Universe*, James turns to religious and mystical experience for additional evidence:

> The sort of belief that religious experience of this type naturally engenders in those who have it is fully in accord with Fechner's theories. To quote words which I have used elsewhere [i.e., in the Conclusions chapter of *VRE*], the believer finds that the tenderer parts of his personal life are continuous with a *more* of the same quality which is operative in the universe outside of him and which he can keep in working touch with, and in a fashion get on board of and save himself, when all his lower being has gone to pieces in the wreck. In a word, the believer is continuous, to his own consciousness, at any rate, with a wider self from which saving experiences flow in. Those who have such experiences distinctly enough and often enough to live in the light of them remain quite unmoved by criticism, from whatever quarter it may come, be it academic or scientific, or be it merely the voice of logical common sense. They have had their vision and they *know*—that is enough—that we inhabit an invisible spiritual environment from which help comes, our soul being mysteriously one with a larger soul whose instruments we are. (p. 267)

Mystical experience in its higher forms seems to me to strengthen Myers's position in several important ways. First, it cannot be denied that the most relevant cases of multiple personality are not only rare but distinctly pathological in character, in that a more inclusive secondary personality often, though not always, experiences itself as distinct from, and even alien and hostile to, the primary personality. Balfour (1935) correctly points out that this is not what we should expect on Myers's theory of the normal personality, for (ignoring Balfour's incorrect terminology) "if the subliminal 'phase' of a man's consciousness represented his true self, we might actually expect that, on ceasing to be subliminal, it would absorb into itself the supraliminal phase, and the two phases would be as one self" (pp. 273–274). But as James above suggests, and as we showed in greater detail in Chapter 8, something of just this expected sort *does* regularly happen in conjunction with profound mystical experiences, in which the everyday self opens up, widens or expands, and becomes at least temporarily identified with some sort of larger, wiser, and benign self hidden within. The supra-

9. Even McDougall (1911/1961) himself seems at times to verge on acceptance of the Myers/James view. For example, he accepts the existence of inclusive *memory* in multiple personality cases such as that of Miss Beauchamp (p. 369), and at one point he even suggests that "by conceiving the animating principle of each organism as but relatively individual, as a bud from the tree of life, it seems possible dimly to foreshadow a synthesis of the Animism of James and Bergson with the hypothesis [his soul-theory] discussed in these concluding paragraphs" (p. 377).

liminal self is not condemned, obstructed, or obliterated but transcended, in a highly positive direction and with powerful transformative aftereffects that appear in many instances to be objectively measurable.

Evidence from the mystical domain also bears strongly on the generality issues discussed earlier. In the first place, there have certainly been thousands if not millions of deep mystical experiences in the course of human history, many involving quite ordinary and unprepared persons, and the mystical traditions are unanimous in believing that all of us are capable of achieving such experiences through appropriate sorts of transformative practice. Furthermore, although the occurrence of such an experience does not itself necessarily imply that the larger consciousness had been there all along, as Myers and James suppose, that is certainly the way most mystics have experienced and reported it—that is, as something already present within, which they had uncovered or found. Indeed, the course of the mystic vocation often involves a kind of oscillation between these concentric surface and depth poles of the psyche, as its center of gravity shifts toward the latter, and in more permanent states of deep mystical realization these dual foci may sometimes even be maintained simultaneously (Forman, 1999, chap. 9).

It also seems highly relevant, and psychologically plausible, that the deeper focus is typically characterized as a passive knower or witness, rather than as an actor in its own right; thus for example the Upanishads repeatedly invoke the metaphor of "two birds on the self-same tree, always companions, one of which looks on while the other eats the sweet fruit." The same picture underlies Patanjali's practical system of yoga and its theoretical companion, the Samkhya system of orthodox Hindu philosophy. In the normal situation, that is, the surface and depth foci are more or less concentric or in alignment, and only when the deeper consciousness with its more potent faculties and more comprehensive point of view finds the supraliminal getting out of alignment, so to speak, would it exert its influence through psychological automatisms of the sorts described by Myers and James—saving religious experiences, uprushes of genius, veridical apparitions, phenomena of extreme psychophysical influence, and so on.

The net status of Myers's conception of the Subliminal Self seems to me presently as follows. The conception itself is admittedly counterintuitive and logically difficult. I find especially challenging, for example, its aspect of *inclusiveness*, and wonder whether the Subliminal Self might better be conceived as "more comprehensive" in some weaker sense.[10] The evidence presently supporting Myers's conception is also less than compelling, and

10. The central and very obscure difficulty here, also recognized by McDougall, is that the activity of a mind involves more than its occurrent aspect, the stream of consciousness, with specific isolable contents such as particular images, thoughts, and the like. Knowing, for example, that someone has in mind the image of an elderly bearded man would tell you very little of what is actually going on in that person's mind. For the Subliminal Self to be fully inclusive of the supraliminal self, it would have to be somehow inclusive of its hidden dispositional properties and point of view as well. Much more is involved in "inclusiveness," that is, than merely treating the Subliminal Self or Individuality as a large set of discrete "elements

certainly it falls far short of the form proposed by Gauld (1968) as necessary for a "conclusive" demonstration—specifically, "the bringing to light in a large number of people of a hidden stream of consciousness which could give a coherent and testable account of its own past history and actions" (p. 299). Nevertheless, it seems to me definitely possible and perhaps even probable, especially in light of the evidence flowing from mystical experiences, that Myers and James really have identified a more or less correct account of the overall structure and dynamics of the human psyche—one, furthermore, that is capable of accommodating in a natural way a far wider array of empirical observations than any of its rivals. In sum, although Myers's theory of the Subliminal Self is by no means proven, it constitutes at minimum, in my estimation, a viable and useful working model capable of guiding further research.

Post-Mortem Survival

And now what about Myers's most central concern—whether there is or is not personal survival of bodily death? Survival is not ruled out *a priori* and in general by filter or transmission models of mind and personality, as it is by all conventional production models. On the other hand, animistic or filter models themselves do not as a class necessarily *entail* survival, although they do render it in varying degrees less improbable.

Myers clearly regarded survival as an almost inevitable corollary of the specific type of personality theory that he elaborates in *HP*, and indeed to demonstrate this forms the central strategy and goal of his exposition (his "broad-canvas" approach; see our Chapters 2 and 4). At the same time, it should be recognized that the empirical case for survival does not depend on the correctness of this particular theory. I wish next to summarize the collective sense of our group as to the empirical status of this problem.

The basic issues have already been framed in Chapters 4 and 5. Briefly, detailed and specific information has sometimes come forward—under conditions which rule out "normal" explanations involving conscious or unconscious cheating, cryptomnesia, defects of memory or reporting, cold reading, and the like—which suggests the possible continued existence in some form of previously living persons. In the best such cases the potentially viable explanations appear reduced to two principal candidates, either survival itself or some sort of extreme supernormal (psi) process involving only living persons.

Myers was convinced by the evidence available to him—while acknowledging that it might not be as convincing to others (*HP*, vol. 2, p. 79)—that survival is a fact of nature: "It seems to me now that the evidence for communication with the spirits of identified deceased persons through the trance-

of personality," some subset of which can be told off into the supraliminal self or personality and shared by both (see also Braude, 1979).

utterances and writings of sensitives apparently controlled by those spirits is established beyond serious attack" (*HP*, vol. 1, p. 29). Myers's acceptance of personal survival seemed to many of his colleagues at the time, and still seems to us, premature. This impression, however, may in part reflect the fact that much of what Myers himself regarded as his best evidence was either never published at all or could not be published in a manner that adequately conveys the impact of evidential details and their verisimilitude available privately to him. His well-known emotional interest in survival, in any event, seems unlikely to have biased his judgment, as he himself pointed out (*HP*, vol. 2, p. 294; see also our Chapter 2).

A considerable amount of additional evidence suggestive of survival has accumulated in the subsequent century, some of it of very high quality. Most of this evidence is of types already known to Myers, although acquired in larger amounts and with various methodological refinements, while some—such as cases of the reincarnation type, including those involving birthmarks and birth defects (Chapter 3)—is almost entirely new. The net result of this accumulation of evidence has been to bring the conflict between survival and "super-psi" interpretations into ever-sharper relief, as pro-survival researchers have sought to identify phenomena and testing procedures that increasingly strain the relative credibility of super-psi interpretations.

For example, it might initially seem plausible that a medium could acquire information sufficient to impersonate some deceased individual through telepathic interactions with sitters, especially if a single sitter is present who has exactly the relevant information. That plausibility may seem to diminish, however, when no such person is present, as in a "proxy" sitting; or in sittings when a "drop-in" communicator appears, unknown to anyone present but subsequently identified as a formerly living person; or when the necessary information is distributed across multiple individuals, some of whom are not present; or when some of that information is also contained in obscure documents not even known at that moment to exist. Conversely, survival seems to become more plausible to the degree that many sources of relevant information are potentially available, with some conflicting, yet the ostensible communicator delivers information circumscribed precisely to that which the deceased person himself would have known, in a manner demonstrably in accord with his intentions, and with his characteristic mannerisms, diction, humor, and the like.[11]

11. See the Appendix. Another interesting kind of survival evidence involves the display not only of appropriate information but of high-level *skills* such as the linguistic skills involved in "responsive xenoglossy," the capacity to speak fluently a foreign language not learned by normal means. Stevenson, for example, has documented extensively the case of Sharada, in which a secondary personality in a young Hindu woman spoke and wrote an archaic form of Bengali appropriate to the life she claimed to have led some 150 years earlier. She also provided factual details about that life that Stevenson was able to verify, but only by means of an extremely laborious investigation of obscure historical records (Stevenson, 1984; Stevenson & Pasricha, 1979; see also Braude, 2003, chap. 4).

This brief and abstract description will serve, I hope, to illustrate the general flavor of these debates, which seem to many well-informed observers to have arrived at a logical impasse. The core problem hinges on the fact that information provided by an ostensibly surviving communicator can only be verified by reference to information which is known to some living person or persons, or objectively documented in some other fashion, and hence which is also in principle potentially accessible to some sort of psi process. It is therefore always possible to invent scenarios according to which apparent evidence of survival can be "explained" alternatively in terms of psi processes involving only living persons. Such scenarios may need to be fantastically complex, but psi has been shown in various experimental contexts to operate in a "goal-oriented" manner unaffected by the apparent "complexity" of its tasks (H. Schmidt, 1987), and consequently they cannot be decisively refuted. But note the real logical peculiarity here: It is not that we have positive knowledge that psi processes *can* accomplish the extraordinary things required by such explanations, but rather that we are presently unable to prove they *cannot.*[12]

Let me conclude this section with a few general observations on the net status of this debate. First, it involves a large body of relevant empirical evidence which at present is virtually unknown to the great majority of laypersons and scientists alike. Our Appendix provides many pointers into this literature, emphasizing sources which illustrate in cogent form properties of the sorts characterized above as particularly suggestive of survival. We insist that anyone who wishes to participate meaningfully in discussions of the survival question must study this literature, thoughtfully and with an open mind.

Second, the core issue of super-psi versus survival cannot be decisively resolved at the present time. Persons sufficiently determined to deny survival while accepting the reality of psi can continue to do so rationally, but provisional acceptance of the survival hypothesis is also rationally warranted by the evidence available. One might also choose, of course, to defer commitment either way, pending further information.

As a matter of historical fact, able and informed students such as Braude (2003), Broad (1962), Dodds (1934), Ducasse (1961, 1969), Gauld (1982), G. Murphy (1945), Price (1966), and Stevenson (e.g., 1977; 1997, chap. 26), among numerous others, have divided more or less equally, and for the most part narrowly, along the two sides of this divide. Some have remained undecided, and Stephen Braude, for many years a particularly determined defender of super-psi interpretations, has recently moved tentatively to a mildly pro-survival position much like our own.

Our general attitude toward super-psi explanations, in the first place, is essentially that of Ducasse (1969):

12. The survival hypothesis itself, of course, must also invoke psi processes of some sort to account for information flows between mediums and communicators.

> When Occam's razor is alleged to shave off survival as a superfluous hypothesis, and to leave ESP as sufficient to account for all the facts in evidence, it turns out that ESP cannot do it without being arbitrarily endowed with an *ad hoc* "beard" consisting not of capacity for more far-reaching *perception*, but of capacity for reasoning, inventing, constructing, understanding, judging; i.e. for *active thinking*; and more specifically for the particular modes of such thinking which *only* the particular mind whose survival is in question is *known* to have been equipped with. (p. 41)

Secondly, the totality of the evidence now available seems to us to have tilted the balance somewhat further in favor of the survival hypothesis. Of particular significance in this regard, in our opinion, are mediumistic cases involving proxy sitters (E. W. Kelly, in press) and drop-in communicators (for references to this research, see Braude, 2003, chap. 2; and Gauld, 1982, chap. 5), cases of the reincarnation type (e.g., Stevenson, 1997, 2001), and NDEs occurring under extreme physiological conditions (our Chapter 6). The last may in the long run prove especially critical, for they arise from the very heart of mainstream biomedical science, and seem likely to become more numerous and compelling as our capacity to rescue physiologically monitored human beings from the borderland of death increases.

Finally, and perhaps most importantly, the broader theoretical setting that frames this debate is itself shifting, and in a manner that makes survival appear to us more likely. In Chapter 3 we highlighted the dynamic interplay between fact and theory in the specific context of phenomena of extreme psychophysical influence, showing how previously suspect empirical phenomena suddenly become acceptable once scientists find a theory that appears to permit them. We think a process of this sort is already underway in regard to the entire range of interrelated empirical phenomena discussed in this book and that this will ultimately vindicate Myers's "broad-canvas" approach to the survival question itself.

More specifically, we think that if other things were anywhere near equal, most rational persons would conclude, on the basis of the available evidence, that survival in some form is at least possible, and perhaps even a demonstrated empirical reality. The problem, of course, is that "other things" seem to most scientists nowhere near equal, because of the seemingly overwhelming antecedent improbability of survival in the context of present-day mainstream science and philosophy. As G. Murphy and Dale (1961) had already remarked, "it is the biological and the philosophical difficulty with survival that holds us back, not really the unacceptability of the evidence as such" (p. 213). We believe, however, that these theoretical difficulties can be greatly attenuated or even removed, and in a way that potentially accommodates most or all of the rogue phenomena we have discussed, survival included.

We will attempt shortly to demonstrate this in some detail. Meanwhile, although we ourselves are collectively disposed to regard survival in some form as at minimum an empirical possibility, and perhaps even a probability, I hasten to add that we expressly disavow any more specific claims, at present, as to its incidence and nature. A wide range of possible forms can be discriminated (Broad, 1962, Epilogue), and there exists at least some evidence consistent with each of them. These range from mere transient persistence of at least a few memories, to persistence of something much like the earthly personality with evidence of thought, planning, conscious will, and so on (Ducasse, 1961, 1969), to merging into some sort of transpersonal field (G. Murphy, 1945). It may seem plausible to suppose like Myers that if anyone survives in personal form we all do, but in making this particular leap Myers was certainly too hasty, for survival could perfectly well occur in widely differing forms and durations for different persons, or not at all, depending on a host of factors we currently know nothing about.[13]

I will leave the matter there for present purposes. Whether or not readers are swayed by our assessment of the survival issue, we will be satisfied if we have convinced them of the difficulty and importance of the problem, and of the fact that it is amenable to empirical investigation. We also wish to emphasize in concluding this section that a choice must ultimately be made between super-psi and survival interpretations of the survival evidence. *Both* horns of this dilemma are in our view fatal to the current mainstream materialist synthesis, but the occurrence of survival in particular—of any form—would decisively resolve the conflict between production and transmission models of mind-brain relations in favor of some sort of transmission model.

Myers's Generalized Concept of Evolution

As Chapters 2 and 7 have already indicated, the concept of evolution is central to Myers's theory of personality (*HP*, vol. 1, p. 19). He accepted Darwin's doctrine of natural selection as the basis of organic evolution, but sought to integrate it with his own conception of human personality as rooted in a hidden, wider environment that underlies and interpenetrates the world of ordinary experience, at bottom a spiritual or "metetherial" realm lying beyond the material as classically conceived.

The main novelty of this broadened conception of evolution is set forth in his chapter on genius (*HP,* vol. 1, pp. 93–98, 111–120). Like conventional evolutionary theorists, Myers recognizes that new capacities emerge in conjunction with the sorts of "protoplasmic" changes played upon by natural selection. Unlike such theorists, however, he thinks of these capacities as being not so much *generated* by the organic changes as *released* by them from the subliminal or metetherial realm, in which in some sense they already existed, latent but unrealized. Thus,

> I hold, of course, that sports or variations occur, which are at present unpredictable, and which reveal in occasional offspring faculties which

13. The same comment applies, of course, in relation to the evidence for reincarnation.

> their parents showed no signs of possessing. But I differ from those who hold that the faculty itself thus manifested is now for the first time initiated in that stock by some chance combination of hereditary elements. I hold that it is not initiated, but only revealed; that the "sport" has not called a new faculty into being, but has merely raised an existing faculty above the threshold of supraliminal consciousness. (*HP*, vol. 1, p. 118)

Myers acknowledges that at most points his view is essentially indistinguishable from the conventional view:

> No fresh mystery is in fact introduced. All human powers, to put the thing broadly, have somehow or other to be got into protoplasm and then got out again. You have to explain first how they became implicit in the earliest and lowest living thing, and then how they have become thus far explicit in the latest and highest. All the faculties of that highest being, I repeat, existed *virtually* in the lowest, and in so far as the admitted faculties are concerned the difference between my view and the ordinary view may be said to be little more than a difference as to the sense which that word *virtually* is here to assume. (*HP*, vol. 1, p. 118)

The real difference between the two conceptions becomes apparent, however, in regard to certain additional capacities—such as telepathy and telæsthesia—which Myers regards as inherently and necessarily beyond the reach of any explanation based on material factors alone. Inasmuch as capacities of this sort definitely do exist, less unusual ones can perhaps also be re-conceptualized in analogous fashion. On such a view, for example, one might even suppose with Myers that "the specialised forms of terrene perception were not real novelties in the universe, but imperfect adaptations of protoplasm to the manifestation of the indwelling general perceptive power" (*HP*, vol. 1, p. 118). To illustrate the hypothesized "release" of subliminal capacities by novelties of biological constitution, Myers appeals to the example of the calculating prodigy Dase, as described in our Chapter 7. But the central thrust of his argument is that our highest human attributes—including our capacities for music, art, poetry, beauty, pure mathematics, truth, and love—are of this sort, and not merely "sports" or "spandrels," by-products of organic evolution itself. Myers thus conceives of evolution as having a "cosmical" as well as a "planetary" aspect, tending globally toward progressive release of these higher attributes and hence toward "constantly widening and deepening perception of an environment infinite in infinite ways" *(HP*, vol. 1, p. 96). On his view this does not happen according to any preset or inevitable plan, however; our evolutionary fate remains uncertain, and it is very much in our own hands.

Myers freely acknowledges that this generalized conception of evolution is a speculative hypothesis founded upon his more fundamental and empirically grounded conception of the subliminal realm. Yet this view, he insists,

> is not one whit remoter or more speculative than the view which, *faute de mieux*, is often tacitly assumed by scientific writers. My supposed opponent and I are like two children who have looked through a keyhole at the first few moves in a game of chess,—of whose rules we are entirely ignorant. My companion urges that since we have only seen the *pawns* moved, it is probable that the game is played with the pawns alone; and that the major pieces seen confusedly behind the pawns are only a kind of fringe or ornament of the board. I reply that those pieces stand on the board like pawns; and that since they are larger and more varied than the pawns, it is probable that they are meant to play some even more important rôle in the game as it develops. We agree that we must wait and see whether the pieces are moved; and I now maintain that I have seen a piece moved [i.e., telepathy], although my companion has not noticed it.
>
> The chessboard in this parable is the Cosmos; the pawns are those human faculties which make for the preservation and development on this planet of the individual and the race; the pieces are faculties which may either be the mere by-products of terrene evolution, or on the other hand may form an essential part of the faculty with which the human germ or the human spirit is originally equipped, for the purpose of self-development in a cosmical, as opposed to a merely planetary, environment. (*HP*, vol. 1, pp. 93–94)

Having briefly described Myers's general conception of evolution, I must now attempt to evaluate it. To this end I shall begin with James (1901), who clearly acknowledges the significance of that conception, while not attempting to adjudicate as to its truth:

> I feel sure that [it] is a hypothesis of first-rate philosophic importance. It is based, of course, on his conviction of the extent of the Subliminal, and will stand or fall as that is verified or not; but whether it stand or fall, it looks to me like one of those sweeping ideas by which the scientific researches of an entire generation are often molded. (p. 21)

I think we can go slightly further now, but I must preface the following brief remarks by saying that I intend to tread very lightly here, in part because of my own very limited acquaintance with evolutionary biology, and in part because of the super-heated cultural conflicts currently swirling around this topic.

I do think there has been a small net movement in the direction of Myers's view. First, as the present book seeks to demonstrate, his general picture of mind and personality has in fact continued to accumulate various kinds of empirical support, even as theoretical and empirical difficulties and limitations have come to light in competing accounts of conventional materialist/reductionist sort, such as the CTM (Chapter 1). As James pointed out, this in itself tends to work in favor of Myers's larger view.

Second, there has recently been some motion in this direction from within evolutionary biology itself. Let me speak very carefully here. Myers was certainly no creationist, nor even an "intelligent design" theorist unless in the most attenuated sense. All he requires is that there be some global creative tendency in the universe, however slight, that results over time in increasing richness and complexity of biological forms.[14] But even some mainstream evolutionary biologists seem prepared to accept pictures of this sort. Commentator Robert Wright (1999), for example, while explicitly denying that evolution is directed specifically toward us—Homo sapiens—points out that the average complexity of species has in fact risen in general, driven by competitive pressures ("arms races") within and between species, and that mammalian lineages in particular have tended toward increased "braininess." Certain useful properties such as vision and flight have also been reinvented repeatedly during the course of evolution, and Wright explicitly proposes that similar built-in tendencies may exist with respect to higher-order properties, such as intelligence, altruism, and love, that are of course central to Myers's vision. Similarly, both Wright himself and the evolutionary biologist Lumsden (1999) point to an increasing recognition among neo-Darwinian theorists that in humans the evolution of the genome has become strongly intertwined with the evolution of civilization itself, so that they cannot be thought of as proceeding independently on separate tracks. Lumsden even goes so far as to state flatly that "human creativity is the fire that drives gene-culture coevolution" (p. 160).[15]

Views of these latter sorts seem within range of rapprochement with Myers's generalized concept of evolution. Modern neo-Darwinists certainly have achieved a greatly expanded mechanistic understanding of the material side of evolution, but I think Myers would unhesitatingly endorse that aspect of their science. The main residual difference lies rather in the presumption, shared by most evolutionary biologists with virtually all other contemporary mainstream scientists, that genius along with all other human mental functions can be fully and satisfactorily explained in terms of classical physicalist principles. This presumption was firmly rejected by both Myers and James, and the central theme of the present volume has been to substantiate that they were correct in doing so. Myers's generalized picture of evolution, in sum, may yet prove closer to the truth.

---

14. Parenthetically, major 20th-century philosophers such as Alexander, Bergson, and Whitehead, in addition to James, maintained generically similar views.

15. I find it especially ironic that sophisticated evolutionary biologists like Lumsden find fault with "Darwinian" creativity models of the sorts proposed by psychologists such as D. T. Campbell (1960), Perkins (1995), and Simonton (1995) on grounds that biological evolution itself is not as simplistically mechanistic as they appear to think. I agree, together with diverse critics from Hadamard (1949) to Koestler (1964), Boden (1991), and Eysenck (1995), that any conception which takes random variation as the basis of real human creativity is fundamentally flawed—a bad metaphor and little else.

Myers/James Filter Theory and Contemporary Science: Toward Reconciliation

Up to this point I have been arguing on behalf of the Myers/James picture as a purely psychological theory, urging its provisional acceptance as a useful working model of the overall structure and organization of the human psyche. I have also tentatively endorsed the reality of post-mortem survival as an empirical phenomenon, while reserving judgment on Myers's generalized evolutionary doctrine pending further information.[16]

The appeal of Myers's theory derives for me from two principal factors: First, it encompasses an enormous range of empirical phenomena, including a variety of phenomena which lie beyond the reach of mainstream materialist views. One aim of this book has been to show that many such "rogue" phenomena exist, as Myers and James both firmly believed, and that the evidence for them has in general become far stronger during the subsequent century. Furthermore, these empirical phenomena—both "normal" and "supernormal"—are interconnected in such a way that one cannot provide an empirically satisfactory treatment of any one of them without necessarily becoming entangled with others as well. One cannot deal adequately with psi phenomena, for example, without recognizing and somehow accommodating their deep associations with topics such as dreaming, genius, and mysticism. The power of Myers's theory derives not so much from an incontrovertible superiority in explaining any of these phenomena individually as in providing a coherent and plausible scheme of interpretation for all of them at once. And this is a great virtue of Myers's theory, as pointed out by Schiller (1905): "A synthesis which embraces such a multitude of facts does not rest solely on any one set of them, and in a sense grows independent of them all. That is, the mere coherence of the interpretation becomes a great point in its favour as against a variety of unconnected alternatives" (p. 70).

Myers's theory also has predictive value, at least in the sense of directing our attention toward additional types of phenomena that might be expected both to exist and to be accessible to empirical investigation. Myers himself, for example, seems to have anticipated both NDEs in general (see our Chapter 6) and the "mindsight" phenomenon reported tentatively by Ring and Cooper (1997, 1999), in which congenitally blind persons undergoing NDEs report a kind of quasi-visual awareness of their physical surroundings (Myers, 1891c, pp. 126–127). The demonstrated association of psi with altered states such as dreaming, hypnagogia, and twilight states emerging under Ganzfeld conditions also is broadly consistent with his general principle that subliminal functions emerge in proportion to the abeyance of normal supraliminal functioning. Similarly, his concept of a "permeable" boundary between the supraliminal and subliminal regions implies that

16. This applies especially to a part of his doctrine I did not discuss—namely, his conviction that individual human personalities may continue to develop or "evolve" in the post-mortem state. To my knowledge, there is presently little or no credible evidence for such a view.

persons whose boundaries are demonstrably more permeable, as measured for example by the scales of Thalbourne (1998; Thalbourne & Delin, 1994) and Hartmann (1991), should show more evidence of subliminal functioning, such as creativity, psi, involuntary imagery and other automatisms, and recall of dreams and early childhood events, all of which have been at least tentatively confirmed. Another such implication, which is rumored to be true but to my knowledge has not yet been seriously investigated, is that psi phenomena should be prominently associated with dissociative disorders such as MPD/DID, and perhaps especially with those "alters" that are deepest or most comprehensive. Many other examples have been provided in earlier chapters, and more will be supplied below.

But are these considerations sufficient to *justify* Myers's theory? The "correct" answer here ultimately depends on one's answer to the prior philosophical question as to precisely what criteria are appropriate for justification of a psychological theory of this sort. This general and very difficult problem is the subject of ongoing discussion within our Esalen theory group, and I will certainly not attempt to resolve it here. However, the basic issues come into sharper focus in the context of a less favorable appraisal of Myers's theory by Gauld (1992):

> The broad framework is not one that can be used to derive the details of the phenomena that are used to support it. It may "make sense" of the phenomena, but it does not enable us unequivocally to predict any particular phenomenon. This situation obtains commonly enough in psychology, but it would generally be thought undesirable in the "hard" sciences and by philosophers. A partial parallel, however, is provided by the Darwinian theory of evolution. Here too we have a broad and abstract hypothesis which "makes sense" of a great mass of observations; yet it would be hard to maintain that the details of the data can be directly derived from the theory. Of course since Darwin's time certain paths have been established which fill some of the space between the theory and particular features of the phenomena. Nothing similar has been accomplished in respect of Myers's theory of the subliminal self [*sic*]. If it had been, Myers would perhaps now be as famous as Darwin. (pp. 399–400)

I will make just two main comments on this relatively negative assessment. First, I think the demand for derivation of phenomena in all details is too strong a requirement for justification of large-scale psychological theories, although I will not attempt to argue this point here. I also think, as indicated above, that Myers's theory does in fact have significant predictive value, albeit of a weaker sort than that characteristic of the "hard" sciences. Second, although Gauld certainly is correct in pointing to the subsequent "filling in" of Darwin's theory as having contributed in major ways to its justification, I think he overstates the contrast between Darwin and Myers in this respect. In the first place, as indicated above, a good deal of descriptive filling-in has already occurred, in the sense of more and better documentation for phenomena already utilized by Myers himself in developing his scheme, and the discovery of additional phenomena consistent with it.

One major gap remains, however. It was specifically the rise of new scientific disciplines such as population genetics and molecular biology that did more than anything else to fill in and buttress the original Darwinian theory. Similarly, a psychological theory of the sort advanced by Myers and James cannot be sustained unless it can somehow be reconciled with the enormous advances of the ensuing century in what we know about the brain. The central task of this section, therefore, is to demonstrate that such reconciliation may in fact be possible.

We believe that the empirical evidence marshaled in this book is sufficient to falsify all forms of biological naturalism, the current physicalist consensus on mind-brain relations.[17] The mind is "irreducible" in a stronger sense than that intended by epiphenomenalists, including Chalmers,[18] or even by those like Searle who are at least committed to salvaging mind and consciousness as causal factors in behavior, but cannot explain how to do so in conventional physicalist terms. There is apparently at least one fundamental bifurcation in nature that cannot be accounted for in these terms, and we therefore seem driven toward *some* sort of animist or pluralist alternative.

Although the primary purpose and merit of our book consist in the marshaling of the evidence itself, we also think it is now possible to see at least dimly how a psychological "filter" theory of the Myers/James sort can be adapted to the framework of contemporary science, and we wish to provide at least in outline some more positive characterization of these possibilities. We emphasize at the outset that this account is necessarily provisional and very incomplete; our goal is simply to suggest a variety of potentially fruitful directions for further investigation. We also urge readers to bear in mind as they work through this section, as we have in developing it, the wise counsel of H. H. Price (1939): "We may safely predict that it will be the timidity of our hypotheses, and not their extravagance, which will provoke the derision of posterity" (p. 341).

We must begin by making clearer what we mean by "a psychological filter theory of the Myers/James sort." In the first place, in lumping Myers and James together in this way we do not mean to imply that they hold

17. From here on I will speak more consistently in the first person plural, reflecting the fact that what follows is to a much greater extent the product of very extensive discussions involving all authors of the present book and many additional parties as well. The opinions stated are in all cases strong majority positions, but I am primarily responsible for details of their formulation, and not all of us are in full accord on all points. We *are*, however, unanimous in regard to certain more general attitudes, including in particular an admiration for Myers and his synoptic naturalism, skepticism about the current received wisdom in psychology and neuroscience, openness to unorthodox findings where properly evidenced, and a conviction that the world is at bottom a much more puzzling place than contemporary mainstream science admits. Individual authors are of course responsible for opinions expressed in their own chapters.

18. That Chalmers is an epiphenomenalist follows from his arguments for the conceivability of "zombies," creatures that lack consciousness but nonetheless are equivalent to us cognitively. We reject both the epiphenomenalism and his endorsement of strong artificial intelligence.

identical views on all subjects, but only that their overall conceptions of the psyche are far more similar to each other than to any materialist/reductionist theory past or present.

We also need to specify more carefully our interpretation of James's "transmission" or "filter" theory, originally introduced in Chapter 1 and recurring intermittently thereafter throughout this book.[19] As invoked informally and loosely so far, this amounts only to a family of related but somewhat cloudy metaphors bearing a variety of unexamined connotations and implications regarding the role of the brain in our mental life. "Transmission," for example, suggests faithful conveyance from one place to another, but this is certainly *not* what Myers had in mind with his theory of the Subliminal Self and its relations with the supraliminal self. The related term "filter," which like Aldous Huxley's "reducing valve" suggests selection, narrowing, and loss, is much more appropriate to that relationship, and for that reason we greatly prefer it as a shorthand description of Myers's theory.

But how does this relate to the brain? Myers's theory as he himself developed it is entirely psychological, not philosophical, and he also says extremely little about the brain. It is rather James, the psychologist and philosopher, who explicitly links these notions of transmission and filtering with the brain. James in fact suggests a variety of metaphors, but the one that has most commonly been seized upon by others is that of optical devices such as colored glass, lenses, and prisms. The common feature is that a beam of integral white light presented to such devices comes out the other side filtered, reduced, focused, redirected, or otherwise altered in some systematic fashion.

Subsequent advocates of transmission or filter models have tended naturally to update this basic picture with reference to emerging technologies such as radio and television. Thus for example we find Strassman (2001) comparing the brain to a TV receiver, and likening entry into the altered states produced by psychedelics to changing the channel. There are two generic problems with accounts of this sort, however, that we must attempt to avoid. First, all metaphors of the radio and TV variety clearly engender homunculus problems of the sorts described in Chapter 1; after all, who is it that is watching Strassman's TV and changing the channels? More gener-

19. There is a strangely incomplete or asymmetric pattern of connections among James, Myers, Schiller, and Bergson—all early advocates of filter-type theories—which invites further historical investigation. James (1898/1900) is usually given primary credit for formulating the transmission theory, yet he himself acknowledged that Schiller (1891/1894) had already worked it out in greater detail. James's formulation relies heavily on Fechner's concept of the psychophysical threshold or limen, but he does not point out the close parallel with Myers's ideas, invoking Myers only as an investigator of supernormal phenomena. Myers, meanwhile, makes no explicit reference to transmission theory as formulated by either James, Schiller, or Bergson, and references Schiller and Bergson only in regard to a single case study each. Nonetheless Schiller (1905, p. 66) explicitly identifies Myers's general theory as a splendid example of transmission theory and laments that Myers himself did not describe it in those terms. Yet James corresponded extensively with both Myers and Schiller around the time of the Ingersoll lecture, and with Bergson later on (Perry, 1935), and all four were members of the SPR.

ally, we must not endow the "filter" with all the properties we are trying to account for in the mind itself—properties such as high-level thinking, memory, imagination, conceptual grasp, and so on.

The common feature of these metaphors, and the root of their conceptual problems, is the idea of passage *through* the filter. There is a way around this, however. Recall that the central goal of James's original analysis was to show that even perfect correlation between brain events and mental events entails neither the impossibility of post-mortem survival nor the truth of the conventional materialist production theory of brain-mind relations. Those views derive from interpreting the admitted facts of functional dependence—mind-brain correlations—in one particular way. Other possibilities exist, however: "When we think of the law that thought is a function of the brain, we are not required to think of productive function only; *we are entitled also to consider permissive or transmissive function*. And this the ordinary psychophysiologist leaves out of his account" (James, 1898/1900, p. 15).

Most subsequent advocates of James's analysis, as we have seen, have invoked its "transmission" thread, so much so that the whole picture is now widely known by that name alone. We think this unfortunate, because it is actually the other thread—permission—that is theoretically the more promising. More generally, we wish now to argue that by thinking of the brain as an organ which somehow constrains, regulates, restricts, limits, and enables or permits expression of the mind in its full generality, we can obtain an account of mind-brain relations which potentially reconciles Myers's theory of the Subliminal Self with the observed correlations between mind and brain, while circumventing the conceptual difficulties identified above in transmission models. We in fact see a spectrum of potentially viable theoretical possibilities of this sort. We will next canvas these under two broad headings—non-Cartesian dualist-interactionist models and neutral-monist models—that seem to us to bracket the range.

Non-Cartesian Dualist-Interactionist Models

When theories need to be changed in order to accommodate discordant observations, it usually makes sense, as a matter of scientific policy, to change them in ways that seem to do the least possible violence to the existing theories, while enabling us to explain those additional observations. This attitude leads in the present case to the family of what we are calling "non-Cartesian dualist-interactionist models," and more specifically to a subset of such models corresponding to the psychological filter theory elaborated by Myers (Chapter 2) and carried forward by James (Chapter 8), which can be viewed as the most highly developed example so far among models of this sort.[20] The driving idea is that associated with each human organism, a physical thing in the ordinary sense, is a second thing, a mind or psyche, which interacts in some way with that organism. Based upon the evidence summarized in this book, we will also presume for the sake of discussion that the psyche has the kind of internal organization and dynamics assigned to it by Myers and James, and that it may under various circumstances, including circumstances involving serious bodily injury or death, be able to function in some manner on its own. What we want to focus on here is how we can conceive of its *normal* interactions with the associated organism.

We will begin by briefly noting that there have been previous efforts along dualist lines by modern scientists, including some very distinguished 20th-century neuroscientists.[21] One group includes Charles Sherrington and two of his students, John Eccles and Wilder Penfield. All three expressed the conviction that the properties of minds cannot be reduced to or identified with those of brains, and all attempted to support that conviction by reference to empirical data of various kinds. In all cases, however, the evidence marshaled, although readily *interpretable* within a dualist-interactionist framework, was insufficient to *establish* it, since alternative explanations based on the conventional viewpoint were nowhere decisively excluded. Popper and Eccles (1977) suffered the additional liability that their attacks were directed mainly at associationist-type theories that had already largely disappeared from cognitive psychology.[22] In Eccles's case it was also clear, as shown for example by his last (1994) book, that he had embraced dualism early in life and for largely non-scientific reasons (his Catholicism, possibly supplemented by an OBE), and had sought throughout his career simply to tell this unchanging dualist story in the most up-to-date neurophysiological language. The net result, in any case, was that the dualistic views of all three have largely been ignored by mainstream psychologists and neuroscientists.

Next comes another major neuroscientist, Roger Sperry (e.g., 1980, 1993), who also sought to salvage the mind but in a slightly different way, essentially by splitting the difference between mainstream physicalist views

20. In an unpublished essay on Myers that he was still developing at the time of his death, C. D. Broad concluded that this was Myers's own philosophic position. This unfinished essay, "The Life and Work of F. W. H. Myers," can be found among Broad's papers in the archives of Trinity College, Cambridge.

21. There has recently been a modest revival of interest in dualism among philosophers as well; see for example J. Foster (1991), E. J. Lowe (1996), Madell (1988), and Smythies and Beloff (1989). Unfortunately, these philosophic discussions often fail to make contact with relevant empirical literature; in Corcoran (2001), for example, the possibility of post-mortem survival is assessed almost exclusively in light of the apparent *a priori* viability of philosophical theories that seem to permit it, and without reference to the available empirical evidence.

22. See Mandler (1978). Of course associationist theories have subsequently revived in the form of "connectionism," as described in Chapter 1. Note the irony here that the anti-associationist arguments of Popper and Eccles, as well as those of William James and numerous other early critics including in particular the Gestalt psychologists, have once again become relevant. See also J. Fodor (2001).

and an outright dualism. He undoubtedly took note of the hostile reception accorded his fellow Nobel prize winner Eccles, and hoped to avoid a similar fate. His compromise position, "monistic dualism," holds that mind and consciousness "emerge" from brain processes when these processes reach a certain threshold of complexity. The emergent properties are said then to seize control of lower-level aspects of brain function, much as, for example, an eddy generated by the turbulent flow of a stream "enslaves" the leaves that circulate within it. The problem is that Sperry essentially *stipulates* the emergence without really accounting for it in physicalist terms; both the emergent and the enslaved phenomena are unambiguously physical in all his analogies.[23] His emergent consciousness appears miraculously and then takes on a life of its own, so to speak; but this radical kind of emergence has been specifically rejected as incoherent by more consistent physicalists such as Searle (1992) and Kim (1998). McDougall (1911/1961) had also rejected such views, which already existed at the end of the 19th century, as "animism of the lowest or most meagre degree" (p. 357); they seemed to him to sacrifice the advantages of the mainstream materialist doctrine, and to introduce all the problems of dualism without any of its potentially compensating advantages. In sum, Sperry's attempted compromise also failed to take hold.

Preceding chapters of this book have already shown that a much stronger *empirical* case for some sort of interactive dualism can now be made. But before attempting to move any further in this theoretical direction we must next deal with several conceptual issues that have seemed to many observers to constitute serious or even fatal *a priori* obstacles to doing so. To begin, we reject categorically the apparent presumption of most contemporary scientists and philosophers that any departure from the currently fashionable materialist monism is necessarily antiscientific, and that to move toward pluralism in any form is in and of itself inescapably tantamount to abandoning several centuries of scientific achievement, releasing the black flood of occultism, and reverting to primitive supernaturalist beliefs characteristic of bygone times. As John Searle (1992) correctly observes, only this prevailing terror of dualism can explain the mainstream's willingness to put forward, and to tolerate, the various kinds of patently unsatisfactory materialist accounts of mind-brain relations that we have seen over the past hundred years. We agree with Searle's diagnosis, of course, but not with his solution. We think, and will attempt to show, that Myers-like theories can be framed in ways that not only can potentially accommodate most or all of the relevant psychological and neurophysiological data, but also are fully compatible with front-line physical science itself.

We certainly do *not* advocate return to an unmodified Cartesianism. We can immediately abandon the most controversial parts of the Cartesian conceptual apparatus, including in particular the notion of mind and body as ontologically distinct "substances" with essential or criterial attributes of

23. Note that similar analogies are regularly invoked by dynamic systems theorists such as W. J. Freeman (1999, 2000).

thinking and extension, respectively. A conceptual distinction can be made between mind and brain without presupposing this kind of ontological division, as recognized clearly by McDougall (1911/1961). The absolute dichotomy set up by Descartes between mind and body has been substantially undermined, historically. For one thing, the phenomenological solidity of matter has proved evanescent in the face of advances on the physical side. Furthermore, at least some forms of mental activity such as perception and visual imagery inherently have quasi-spatial phenomenological properties, as emphasized particularly by writers such as Brann (1991), Price (1953), Smythies (1994), and Velmans (1996). As Myers himself clearly recognized (Chapter 2), the Cartesian gulf has already narrowed and may be bridged, or bridgeable, by further advances from either or both sides; thus, "It is no longer safe to assume any sharply-defined distinction of mind and matter....Our notions of mind and matter must pass through many a phase as yet unimagined" (Myers, 1886c, pp. 178–179). Myers himself anticipated the possible eventual discovery of a single common something, a Tertium Quid, that would bring the two poles together, while others have imagined a whole series of intermediate levels, still in some sense "physical," that could serve as "vehicles of consciousness" (Poortman, 1954/1978).

These developments have immediate impact on the argument that has most commonly been made against interactive dualism, the causal argument. Once Descartes had made mind and body so utterly different, it is alleged, there is no longer any way for them to interact causally, and therefore dualism must be false. Searle (1992) takes this line. However, whatever force this argument ever had certainly has been diminished by the subsequent blurring of the supposed ontological divide between mind and body. Moreover, it is not apparent to us that the argument had any real force to begin with. Descartes himself took psychophysical interaction as a given, an explanatory primitive, and resisted attempts to construe it on the contact-interaction model of classical physical causation (Richardson, 1982). Causal relations are not necessarily transparent, and ever since Hume we have tended to interpret them in terms of consistent covariation. Hume's argument has in fact recently been embraced by arch-skeptic Paul Edwards (1996, chap. 17) in support of his "brain-dependence" thesis—the claim that brain processes unilaterally generate conscious mental experience. But surely if causality can work in *that* direction, it might in principle work in the other as well (Broad, 1925/1960).

The other common argument against dualism appeals to energy conservation laws and their supposed violation by mental causation. As noted in Chapter 2 this was especially popular in the 19th century, the heyday of classical physics, but it is also implicit in many modern discussions and resurfaces explicitly in Dennett (1991). However, Broad (1925/1960, pp. 103–109) had already shown that even in the context of classical physics, which Dennett mistakenly describes as "standard" physics, such arguments are inconclusive.

Even when the issues are framed in conventional physicalist terms, therefore, the main traditional arguments against interactive dualism appear to us less than compelling. Furthermore, and more fundamentally, it is no longer scientifically appropriate even to frame the issues in this way. Although a principle of causal closure of the physical world *as classically conceived* is assumed as the starting point of practically all contemporary scientific and philosophic discussions of mind-brain issues, it is hardly self-evident that this principle applies without restriction to a world that also contains minds. It assumes precisely what we are challenging, that classical physicalism is correct and complete, and can fully explain both brains and minds. But that classical conception of the physical world has long since been shattered by developments within physics itself, particularly by the advent of quantum theory in the early years of the 20th century.[24]

Among the small but growing number of systematic attempts to understand the implications of these developments for mind-brain theory, we regard as especially promising, and will summarize here, the work of quantum physicist Henry Stapp. There are several reasons for this choice. First, unlike many more popular writers Stapp knows the physics inside out. Second, he is consistently conservative and orthodox in his use of quantum theory, staying as close as possible to its empirically proven foundations and postulating no exotic quantum states or processes. Third, he is serious about establishing connections with mainline psychology and neuroscience. Finally, he has provided useful comments on a variety of related quantum-theoretic proposals (including those of Bohm, Eccles, and Penrose and Hameroff), which tend in broadly similar directions but are less satisfactory on various technical grounds (Stapp, 2005a, 2005b, in press a, in press b).

Few working psychologists and neuroscientists, let alone the public at large, have any conception of the fundamental significance of quantum theory. Classical concepts and approximations are often sufficient to support the concerns of the special physical sciences, and quantum mechanics is scarcely mentioned in the context of general education even at the college level. Yet it cannot be emphasized too strongly that the classical physics consensus that underwrites practically everything now going on in psychology, neuroscience, and philosophy of mind has in fact been completely undermined by this tectonic shift in the foundations of physics.

This is one of Stapp's main points. He describes vividly how the founders of quantum mechanics discovered, to their extreme discomfiture, that the fundamental ideas of classical physics were not just limited but *wrong*, leading repeatedly to clear predictions that were falsified by experiment. The theory they were driven to in response, quantum theory, is a more fundamental and better physical theory that explains everything explainable in classical terms, and a vast number of additional things as well, often to extraordinary levels of accuracy. No experimental outcome predicted by it has ever been falsified.

---

24. For authoritative but readable surveys see for example Capek (1961), Whitehead (1925/1953, 1938/1968), and Stapp (2004a, 2005a).

Furthermore, it is crucial to appreciate that human consciousness, which had deliberately been excluded from the classical physics of the three preceding centuries, plays an essential role in this improved physical theory. Orthodox quantum theory is intrinsically a *psychophysical* theory, "a weaving of psychologically described realities into the framework of mathematical physics" (Stapp, 2005a). "The founders of quantum mechanics made the revolutionary move of bringing conscious human experiences into the basic physical theory in a fundamental way. In the words of Niels Bohr the key innovation was to recognize that 'in the great drama of existence we ourselves are both actors and spectators'" (Stapp, 2005a).[25]

Quantum theory also is necessarily relevant to brain science, for according to the principles of contemporary physics it *must* be used to explain the behaviors of all macroscopic systems that depend sensitively on the behavior of their atomic constituents, and brains are certainly systems of this kind.[26] Stapp himself has identified and carefully analyzed one particular element of brain dynamics to which quantum theory certainly applies. This is the process of *exocytosis*, in which neurotransmitter molecules are released into the synaptic cleft. The release is triggered by arrival of calcium ions at critical sites in the transmitter storage areas, the vesicles. But as these small ions pass through their membrane channels (diameter circa 1 nanometer) their positions become nearly fixed; hence, by Heisenberg's uncertainty relation, what happens next must be represented as a cloud of possible trajectories in the vicinity of the vesicle. This injection of a true quantum uncertainty—that is, an uncertainty involving more than incomplete knowledge of classically conceived details—goes on constantly at every one of the trillions of active synapses in the waking human brain, and this by itself is sufficient to establish that the brain is subject to quantum principles. This necessary entry of quantum uncertainties is also consistent with the findings of dynamic system theorists, who emphasize that in the waking state the brain operates continually on the edge of instability, with small changes in input potentially leading to large changes in overall behavior.[27]

25. Eugene Wigner (1962, p. 285) similarly remarked that the laws of quantum mechanics cannot be formulated consistently without recourse to the concept of consciousness. Although Wigner himself subsequently retreated from this position, Stapp (2004a) shows that his reasons for doing so are not compelling.

26. Physicist and brain theorist Paul Nunez (1995) remarks that "an appreciation of the grand conceptual leap required in the transition from classical to quantum systems may give us some vague feeling for how far from current views neuroscience may eventually lead. Such humbling recognition will perhaps make us especially skeptical of attempts to 'explain away' (that is with tautology) data that do not merge with common notions about consciousness, such as multiple conscious entities in a single brain, hypnosis, and so on" (p. 158).

27. Eccles had originally proposed that this dynamic instability might be exploited by "triggering" certain "critically poised" neurons, using the quantum indeterminacy associated with neurotransmitter molecules in the synaptic cleft itself to effect the triggering without violation of conservation laws. It soon became evident, however, that these molecules are too large, and the distances too long. Eccles himself subsequently settled on the exocytosis mechanism as a critical site (Beck & Eccles, 1992; Eccles, 1994).

Unfortunately, most brain researchers have not yet recognized the relevance of quantum-theoretic considerations to their science. A few others have considered the possibility but dismissed it out of hand for wholly inadequate reasons. For example, E. Roy John (2001) asserts that: "There is no evidence that quantum mechanical processes can apply to the slow processes which transpire in the brain in times on the order of milliseconds and involve many cubic centimeters of cells at body temperature" (p. 200). These statements are simply incorrect, as Stapp (2005a) explains. Body temperature has a negative bearing only on proposals which, unlike his own, postulate creation and maintenance of large-scale quantum coherence or other exotic physical states under the normal conditions of brain operation. Stapp's proposal, moreover, is entirely consistent with the observed spatial and temporal scales of brain activity in relation to experience and behavior. Most fundamentally, in light of the demonstration that the behavior of low-level brain constituents is necessarily saturated with quantum effects, combined with the revolution that has occurred at the foundations of physics, the burden of proof here falls upon those who deny, not those who affirm, the relevance of quantum theory to brain science.

Stapp further argues that of the various formulations of quantum theory the one that most naturally applies to neuroscience, and indeed *must* be applied in that setting, is that of mathematician John von Neumann (1932/1955). The basic reason for this is straightforward: In the course of developing his rigorous formalization of quantum mechanics, von Neumann (1932/1955, chap. 6) proved that the separation originally introduced by the founders of quantum theory between a very small observed physical system described in mathematical language and an observing system described in empirical/phenomenal terms can be progressively shifted in such a way that the physical, mathematically described part ultimately includes the entire body and brain of an observing human agent, while the empirical/phenomenal part becomes that agent's stream of conscious experience. In this restructured framework, identified by Wigner as the "orthodox" interpretation of quantum mechanics, the operations of the complete mind-brain system necessarily involve more than the deterministic, locally-acting, bottom-up mechanical processes described by classical physics. There continue to be bottom-up and locally-acting mechanical processes (which von Neumann calls Process 2), but these now take the form prescribed by quantum-mechanical generalizations of the laws of classical mechanics and incorporate all of the uncertainties entailed by the quantum principles. Operating alone, Process 2 would rapidly generate a vast proliferation of possible brain states, simultaneously existing in a state of "potentiality." What actually happens, according to the quantum principles, is determined at least in part by a second process (Process 1) of fundamentally different character, which von Neumann (1932/1955) himself specifically characterized as arising from, or leading into, the human mind, "the intellectual inner life of the individual" (p. 418). These influences are entirely free, in the sense of not being determined by anything in the physics itself. Consciousness itself, in short, is needed to complete the quantum dynamics.

In Stapp's minimal and physically justified elaboration of this basic scheme, the conscious mental activity of the observer is portrayed as operating top-down, and in an inherently non-local manner, to select or enforce large-scale, quasi-stable patterns of oscillatory brain activity from the multitude of possible patterns generated by Process 2. Note that these sorts of global activity patterns, expected in light of Stapp's physics-based theory, correspond in a natural way to neural correlates of mental activity, as conventionally conceived.

For fuller explanations of all aspects of the theory, interested readers should consult the original sources. The net effect of these quantum-theoretic developments, we emphasize, is to bring consciousness back into *both* physical science *and* brain theory at the foundational level. As Stapp (2004a) remarks, his model "makes consciousness causally effective, yet it is compatible with all known laws of physics, including the law of conservation of energy" (p. 23). This totally deflates the main arguments, summarized above, that have routinely been advanced against interactive dualism. Indeed, far from *ruling out* dualism, as alleged by Dennett (1991) and numerous others, "*Contemporary physical theory allows, and in its orthodox von Neumann form entails, an interactive dualism*" (Stapp, 2005a, italics added).

Stapp's theory as described so far remains abstract and mathematical, grounded most securely at the physics end. Certainly a great deal remains to be done to flesh it out in psychological and neuroscientific detail, particularly on the perceptual/cognitive (versus motor) side. Nevertheless, Stapp himself has already identified a variety of important psychological phenomena that he thinks his model can successfully explain, and in a manner uniquely consistent with these basic-physics considerations. The key factor here is the ability of Process 1 to hold a conscious mental intention in place despite the strong disruptive tendencies inherent in the mechanical Process 2. This is accomplished, in accordance with a well-studied physical phenomenon known as the quantum Zeno effect, by allowing the relevant Process 1 "intentions" or "permissions" to be issued repeatedly, as needed, but only up to some maximum possible rate. Stapp correctly points out the striking consistency between this picture and William James's vivid phenomenological descriptions of attention as the essential phenomenon of will. The model also potentially explains in a natural way certain other characteristic features of conscious experience, such as the attentional "bottleneck" of Pashler (1998) and the properties of the "global workspace" as conceived by many contemporary brain theorists—broadly, the fact that a serial, integrated, and very limited stream of consciousness somehow emerges in association with a nervous system that is distributed, massively parallel, and of huge capacity (Baars, 1993). Top-down effects of the sort emphasized in Chapter 1 also fall directly and naturally out of such a model: "Quantum theory, unlike classical physics, can yield mathematically specified top-down effects of mind on brain that are *not determined* by the bottom-up local-deterministic process" (Stapp, 2005a).[28] For examples of such top-down effects Stapp mainly relies upon recent clinical research on "self-directed neuroplasticity," in which psychiatric patients are taught to modify, voluntarily, their maladaptive psychological (and neurophysiological) responses to emotionally challenging stimuli (J. Schwartz, Stapp, & Beauregard, 2003, 2005). Additional relevant studies would presumably include those showing that by voluntarily altering their perceptual interpretation of an ambiguous visual stimulus, subjects can systematically alter patterns of brain activity even as "early" as primary visual cortex (e.g., Kamitani & Tong, 2005).

We are sympathetic to these empirical arguments, but we doubt whether many psychologists and neuroscientists will find them compelling in themselves. Up to this point Stapp's *empirical* case for his interactive-dualist model appears to us to suffer essentially the same liabilities as the evidence marshaled by Popper and Eccles (1977) in support of theirs. That is, his interpretations may well be correct, but none of the empirical phenomena he has adduced so far are clearly or decisively beyond the reach of more conventional types of explanation. In particular, the neurophysiological global workspace models of people such as Damasio, Dehaene, Edelman, Llinás, and others are as relentlessly conventional and classical as anything else in mainstream cognitive neuroscience; adherents of such models would certainly take the view that at least in principle they can explain *all* top-down effects, including the results on self-directed neuroplasticity, in terms of the dense reciprocal connections that are known to link cortical elements of the global workspace directly or indirectly to all other parts of the brain.

The situation changes, however, when Stapp's theoretical model is combined with the kinds of "rogue" phenomena catalogued in the present book. We must first acknowledge that in making this move we are going beyond anything Stapp himself has yet suggested or embraced in his published work. He does not explicitly characterize the relationship he conceives as holding between the source of Process 1 events, the conscious mind of the individual, and the bodily processes with which it interacts, and it is not clear to what degree he himself regards them as actually or potentially separable. Nevertheless, we see no objection in principle to extending his basic model in this way, provided that the extension is empirically justified.

A natural starting point is provided by the phenomena of extreme psychophysical influence, such as geometric blisters and skin-writing, that we have shown cannot be produced *directly* by mechanisms under the control of the brain and nervous system (Chapter 3). Process 1 is inherently non-local, and therefore it can plausibly be imagined as enabling control of events in the skin that lie beyond the reach of mechanisms known to conventional

28. We note in passing that the received causal doctrine of conventional neuroscience, that system-level properties of the brain are produced by bottom-up local interactions of its constituent microentities, is the one-dimensional historical residue of a much richer causal doctrine dating back to the Greeks, one that specifically incorporates downward mental or "ontic" causation. For a sustained philosophic argument in support of ontic causation, informed by modern developments in cognitive neuroscience, see Pols (1998).

present-day neuroscience. In this case the relevant events would also be quantum-level events of the same type as those Stapp has already shown are subject to quantum effects and fundamental to CNS dynamics—namely, that is, passage of calcium and other small ions through their membrane channels, resulting in a spatially patterned local release of inflammatory or vasoactive substances from structures in the skin and its vasculature. Learning to do this could be viewed as analogous, perhaps, to the situation in early development, which Stapp portrays as consisting in substantial part of the child's gradually learning how to bring mental events or intentions into proper correspondence with environmental events by selecting the appropriate large-scale patterns of brain activity. Analogous special situations can perhaps also be identified in adult life, as for example in the conscious use of feedback signals to develop exquisitely detailed voluntary control of single motor units (Basmajian, 1977). It is interesting in this regard, and consistent with Stapp's general outlook, that rare phenomena such as the formation of hypnotic blisters of specific geometric shape seem to occur mainly under conditions of extreme attention to, or preoccupation with, the relevant psychological material. The same sort of explanation might extend naturally to other phenomena of extreme psychophysical influence discussed in Chapters 3 and 8, including stigmata and allied phenomena, transitional phenomena such as the "maternal impression" cases, and perhaps even PK-type events occurring further outside one's own body.[29] We will give additional examples as we proceed.

To summarize the argument so far: Although many important issues clearly remain to be resolved, Stapp and his quantum-theoretic allies have already successfully undermined the basic-science foundations of present-day materialist-monist psychology and neuroscience. In so doing they also have opened a path toward alternative mind-brain theories of dualist-interactionist character that are more consistent both with fundamental science and with everyday experience, and that have the potential to explain at least some of the critical empirical phenomena catalogued in this book. Surely these are enormous theoretical virtues. There seems to be no insuperable obstacle to moving further in this direction, and we will now attempt to do so.

The basic pathway for reconciling the Myers/James filter theory with neuroscience seems clear enough in principle: Brain processes somehow shape the manner in which the associated psychic entity variably manifests its intrinsic properties and capabilities in the form of our ordinary or "supra-

29. Clearly on this view the occurrence of such phenomena depends partly on conditions within the mind or consciousness of the agent, partly on conditions having to do with the character of the targeted physical system itself, and partly, perhaps, on the availability of appropriate feedback. This invites further work, both theoretical and experimental, to delineate more precisely what the relevant conditions are, and how they can be instantiated or exploited experimentally. We also note in passing that this sort of view seems to us preferable to the view apparently held by Myers (*HP*, vol. 2, pp. 505–554), according to which the Subliminal Self *consciously* manipulates all necessary low-level details of the neural and biochemical machinery in order to produce the targeted effects.

liminal" conscious mental life. The "permeability" of the "membrane" that Myers conceptualized in psychological terms as modulating supraliminal expression of the Subliminal Self would thus have its neurophysiological counterpart in some aspect or aspects of brain activity. Effects of evolution, development, fatigue, fasting, psychedelics, meditation, thumps on the head, electrical brain stimulation, and the like all seem potentially interpretable in such terms.[30] But the broad and abstract justification deriving from James's (1898/1900) original argument (that such correlations can be interpreted in terms of *permission* or *transmission* rather than *production* theories) is not sufficient for our present purposes. We want now to get at least in outline a more detailed positive characterization of how such a mind-brain system might normally operate, and try to reconcile that with a broad range of existing neuroscientific data. The ultimate goal would be to explain in a quite specific way, for example, why it is that conscious experience of such-and-such types should be correlated with the patterns of brain activation revealed by functional neuroimaging studies, and why specific types of brain injury produce the kinds of alterations of mental functioning that they do. The following pages suggest possible elements of such a reconciliation.

We will start by rejecting the extreme localizationism characteristic of much recent research and theory in cognitive neuroscience. Functional neuroimaging and neuropsychological studies are commonly regarded, especially by cognitive psychologists, as providing conclusive and unqualified support for the view that the mind is entirely "modular" in its constitution and generated by corresponding structures and processes in the nervous system. The brain itself is typically conceived by such persons as a functionally complete system of "organs of computation" developed over the course of biological evolution for performance of particular, highly specialized, computational tasks. The postulated organs or modules thus represent the neurophysiological implementation of some cognitive model or models of the box-and-arrow variety, where the boxes represent supposed cognitive components and the arrows represent relations among them, directions of "information flow," and the like (J. Fodor, 1983; Pinker, 1997; see Chapter 1). It is further presumed that brain activities portrayed in the model give rise to, or in some sense are, the associated mental activities and experiences.

The confidence that many scientists apparently have in such a picture, however, is quite unwarranted: In the first place, James's (1898/1900) original argument does show that even if the correlations between brain activity and mental activity were as detailed, clear, and compelling as many people imagine them to be, that would not of itself be sufficient to *establish* the production model as against a permission or transmission model. Furthermore, things are in fact anything but that clear, and they become less so as we move toward the more central attributes of the mind.

30. Following Myers, we presume that the intelligence which determines precisely what products of subliminal activity achieve supraliminal expression under particular brain conditions is itself subliminal.

The widely cited views of J. Fodor (1983) concerning "modularity" are much more subtle than most of those who casually cite him realize. Fodor himself attributed modularity (as defined by most or all of nine specific criteria) only to the hierarchically organized and relatively hardwired perceptual (and presumably motor) systems, and he in fact specifically *denied* that the central domains of the mental have these characteristics. For these more crucial general-purpose or "horizontal" capacities, such as memory, thinking, and imagination, the association with brain activity seemed to Fodor himself relatively global and nonspecific. Furthermore, in his judgment the failure of cognitive science to deal adequately with these capacities over decades of work had been "pretty nearly absolute" (p. 126)—indeed, so much so that he gloomily concluded: "The ghost has been pushed further back into the machine, but it has not been exorcised" (p. 127). Hard-core adherents of the CTM have of course berated Fodor for not attributing modularity to the mind itself (see, e.g., Cain, 2002, pp. 194–208), but his own more recent statements have become if anything even stronger. For example, in Fodor (2001) he explicitly repudiates the CTM in both its classical/symbolic and connectionist forms, and declares in conclusion: "So far, what our cognitive science has found out about the mind is mostly that we don't know how it works" (p. 100).

Fodor's original characterization remains largely applicable today, despite two further decades of work supported by the advent of the new functional neuroimaging technologies. In cognitive neuroscience generally and in functional neuroimaging studies in particular, the modularity doctrine has held up best with regard to early-stage sensory functions and the like, and relatively poorly with regard to the mind proper. This pessimistic view of the situation is argued forcefully in an important critical book by psychologist William Uttal (2001), which should be required reading for anyone interested in these issues.[31] Most of the mind-imaging industry, Uttal argues, consists of attempts to correlate poorly defined psychological constructs with poorly defined and indirect measures of neural activity. On the psychological side, for example, there is theoretical chaos. Many workers have sought to identify "components" of the mind, supposedly distinct cognitive functions potentially identifiable with particular brain regions or structures. However, there is little or no evidence of progress toward agreement as to how many such components exist or what they do. The numbers of components proposed by different investigators mainly reflect their personal interests, industriousness, methodological commitments, and so on, and have ranged from a few to literally hundreds. Both Uttal (2001) and Pols (1998) argue for the contrasting view, which we share, that mind proper has a fundamentally unitary character underlying the diversity of its appearances as mind-in-action. That is, existing taxonomies of supposed mental "com-

31. We refer here especially to Uttal's discussion of experimental and logical issues in neuroimaging research; better introductions to the imaging techniques themselves can be found elsewhere. Related diatribes regarding problems in neuroimaging research can be found at http://www.human-brain.org.

ponents" mainly reify aspects or properties of the mind that are brought into action under particular task conditions or circumstances.[32]

Things are hardly better on the neurophysiological side, despite the sophistication and elegance of the new functional neuroimaging technologies. The dramatic and modular-looking "brain activation" pictures now routinely displayed in fMRI/PET imaging articles in our journals and news media are often seriously misleading. The brain does not neatly decompose either anatomically or functionally, especially at the cortical level, into well-delineated structures or regions that are identifiable with specific components of mind and whose contributions to cognitive performances can be inserted or removed without influence on the rest of the system. The *appearances* of modularity in these images in fact result to a considerable and insufficiently appreciated degree from the complex processes involved in image acquisition and analysis itself.

Measuring brain "activation" is not a simple or standardized process like reading a meter on a physical instrument or performing routine assays of blood chemistry. The intrinsic resolution of the imaging hardware is compromised by preliminary data-conditioning operations such as spatial and temporal smoothing or filtering, and there are deep statistical issues, with no fully satisfactory solutions, related to control of Type 1 and Type 2 errors (false positives and false negatives) in final images that may still contain hundreds or even thousands of correlated elements. Small variations in a long sequence of analytical decisions can result in strikingly different-looking final maps, each portraying well-demarcated regions that ostensibly contain all the physiologically "significant" activation, from the same raw image data. Attempts to overcome the high variability of anatomical and functional organization across subjects by mapping their individual data onto standardized brains or coordinate systems can result in spurious "localizations" existing in none of them. The mechanisms of neurovascular coupling that underlie the measured responses are extremely complex and only partly understood, involve multiple layers of interdependent mechanism operating on different spatial and temporal scales, and may differ in detail from region to region and even across layers of the cortex. The measured responses themselves are spatially and temporally imprecise, relate only indirectly to the neural activity of primary interest, and correlate well only in limiting cases with more direct measures of neuroelectrical activity such as EEG and MEG (Huettell et al., 2004; Nunez & Silberstein, 2000; Wikswo et al., 1993). PET and fMRI also have little capacity at present to distinguish between excitatory and inhibitory neural activity within a given brain area

32. Analogous comments certainly apply to our presently impoverished means for describing and differentiating states of consciousness in general. Similar positions as to the unitary character of mind were staked out much earlier by commentators such as James (1890b), McDougall (1911/1961), and Broad (1925/1960). Uttal himself concludes that we should fall back to a more sophisticated form of behaviorism (p. 206); however, his working list of the great questions of scientific psychology (his Appendix A) suggests that he may also be open to more radical theoretical options of the sort we are advocating here, at least if they are forced upon us by data (as we believe they are).

or to track the rapidly changing patterns of functional interaction between areas. As pointed out in Chapter 4, the widely-used "subtraction" methodology (Kosslyn, 1994; Posner & Raichle, 1994) is both logically unsound and neurophysiologically implausible, and "double-dissociation" imaging studies suffer from logical problems similar to those previously identified in the context of neuropsychological investigations of the effects of brain injury (Shallice, 1988). Replicability of imaging results is also far lower than commonly assumed, and not only *between* but also *within* subjects. Many of these concerns, we must add, apply even in the realm of early-stage sensory processes, where the localizationist picture is most nearly correct.

Despite the great promise of the new functional neuroimaging techniques, we are still on a steep learning curve and a long way from having them under full control. Meanwhile, the overall state of evidence supporting localizationist views of the mind is far less clear and compelling than typical journal articles and textbook accounts suggest. Chapter 4, for example, demonstrated in some detail that this generalization holds even in relation to the representation of *linguistic* functions, historically the primary inspiration for such views. Furthermore, what evidence remains for modularity often can be accounted for equally well by distributed network models that are potentially consistent with our more "global" view of mind-brain interaction (Farah, 1994; Plaut & Farah, 1990; Van Orden, Jansen op de Haar, & Bosman, 1997). Some additional imaging findings also seem conspicuously more consistent with such a view—for example, recent findings on binocular rivalry, switching of response patterns to ambiguous figures such as the Necker cube, and the work on self-directed neuroplasticity. The key feature common to these is that massive changes occur in the *overall* patterns of brain response to an unchanging stimulus, changes that reflect the subject's altered perception or judgment.

Neurophysiological studies of the consequences of brain injury point, we think, in similar directions. It is certainly true that deficits resulting from similar injuries tend to be more alike, and in characteristic ways, than deficits resulting from very dissimilar ones, but this generalization again holds best for injuries to relatively peripheral parts of the sensory and motor systems. Although the whole subject is clouded by difficulties related to precise specification of the brain injuries that have actually occurred, together with their local and distant sequelae in space and time, the higher mental functions seem rarely if ever to be totally destroyed (short, that is, of death or permanent vegetative states), and there is enormous and largely unexplained variability both between and within individuals who have suffered serious injuries of any particular type. Indeed, as indicated in Chapter 4, in the relatively few cases in which the overall condition of such persons has been investigated or reported in adequate depth, it is hard not to be impressed by the degree to which the core of self and mind can sometimes be preserved, even in combination with catastrophic brain injuries including separation of the hemispheres (H. Gardner, 1976).[33]

In sum, far from supporting the idea that cognition is entirely and extremely modular in its organization, with patterns of brain activity directly reflecting that modularity, modern neuroimaging and neuropsychological studies have instead provided evidence that the association between conscious, effortful mental activity and brain activity is more global in character. The broad consensus that has recently emerged around the family of neurophysiological "global workspace" theories in part reflects an increasing recognition that this is the case.

The anatomical makeup of the global workspace varies to some extent dynamically, in accord with the demands imposed by ongoing activity, but it is noteworthy that by all accounts it invariably includes areas such as frontal cortex and posterior parietal cortex whose total volume has greatly increased in the course of mammalian evolution—that is, areas of "uncommitted," "association," or "intrinsic" cortex above and beyond those specifically dedicated to the more modular and hard-wired pathways and mechanisms associated with more peripheral parts of the sensory and motor systems. The functional architecture of this tissue is substantially uniform, with the same cell types, patterns of microconnectivity, neurotransmitter/receptor mechanisms, and columnar organization repeated everywhere (Edelman & Mountcastle, 1982). It seems clear that the normal supraliminal expression of mind proper depends strongly, in a manner like that suggested by global workspace theories, on the total amount and functional status of this more general-purpose tissue. General intelligence, for example, has long been known to correlate modestly (around .4) with overall brain size, and recent work has shown this relationship to be driven primarily by the volume of areas belonging to the global workspace, especially frontal cortex (Haier et al., 2004). In this respect, global workspace theories in fact match up rather well with the views of Myers and Bergson, who viewed the brain as predominantly a sensorimotor device, the "organ of attention to life," an instrument adapted by evolution to enable the mind to gain information about, and to act upon, the everyday physical environment. Mainstream global-workspace theorists themselves of course invariably accept the more fundamental orthodox conception that the underlying brain activity itself, *whatever* its form, *produces* or in some sense *is* the corresponding mental activity. Rejection of that deeper view, however, we regard as necessitated by the other lines of evidence marshaled earlier in this book.

33. James (1890b, vol. 1, pp. 141–142) went so far as to suggest that the preserved concept of a lost or diminished mental function may somehow participate directly in the recovery of that function through appropriate repairs or modifications of the associated brain activity. We think this idea has merit, as did Myers (1891c, p. 116), but Myers was also certainly correct in cautioning as to the practical difficulties in evaluating it (see also Finger, LeVere, Almli, & Stein, 1988).

We think this modified-holist view of mind-brain relations is substantially correct.[34] Before taking it further in a dualist-interactionist direction, however, we must first deal with another possible conceptual obstacle. At the time of the *Principles* William James (1890b) was very sympathetic to pictures of this general sort. In describing the generic dualist-interactionist or "soul" theory, the sort of view unhesitatingly endorsed both by virtually all ordinary persons and by the scholastic philosophers, he said:

> If there be such entities...they may possibly be affected by the manifold occurrences that go on in the nervous centers. To the state of the entire brain at a given moment they may respond by inward modifications of their own. These changes of state may be pulses of consciousness, cognitive of objects few or many, simple or complex....I confess, therefore, that to posit a soul influenced in some mysterious way by the brain-states and responding to them by conscious affections of its own, seems to me the line of least logical resistance, so far as we have yet attained. (vol. 1, p. 181)

Despite the appeal that such a theory clearly held for him, James declined to accept it, offering instead his famous doctrine of the stream of consciousness, according to which the only thinker that psychology needed to recognize became the thought itself. Only much later did James give full expression to the logical scruple that had prevented him from endorsing dualism, a difficulty whose seriousness is underscored by the fact that George Mandler (1978) made it the centerpiece of his hostile commentary on the dualism of Popper and Eccles (1977). Here is James's (1909/1971) statement:

> It is not for idle or fantastical reasons that the notion of the substantial soul, so freely used by common men and the more popular philosophies, has fallen upon such evil days, and has no prestige in the eyes of critical thinkers. It only shares the fate of other unrepresentable substances and principles. They are without exception all so barren that to sincere inquirers they appear as little more than names masquerading—*Wo die Begriffe fehlen da stellt ein Wort zur rechten Zeit sich ein.* You see no deeper into the fact that a hundred sensations get compounded or known together by thinking that a "soul" does the compounding than you see into a man's living eighty years by thinking of him as an octogenarian, or into our having five fingers by calling us pentadactyls. Souls have worn out both themselves and their welcome, that is the plain truth. Philosophy ought to get the manifolds of experience unified on principles less empty. Like the word

---

34. "Holism," according to which the brain acts as an undifferentiated whole, goes back to antiquity and has waned and waxed and waned again in popularity across the history of modern neuroscience. The 19th century witnessed an upsurge of localization driven by the early discoveries of people like Fritsch and Hitzig, Broca, and Wernicke, but this produced an extreme holistic backlash in the 20th at the hands of Pierre Marie, Kurt Goldstein, Henry Head, and Karl Lashley. Lashley's famously unsuccessful effort to locate "engrams" (memory traces) in animal brains was particularly influential in American psychology during the behaviorist period, but localizationists regained the ascendancy during the cognitive revolution. Current global workspace theories thus represent a compromise position, with partial reversion toward holism.

"cause," the word "soul" is but a theoretic stopgap—it marks a place and claims it for a future explanation to occupy. (p. 221)

The problem is essentially that in taking a dualistic-interactionist position on the mind we may seem simply to be giving up, in effect moving things that we might have hoped to explain in terms of brain processes and the like into an inaccessible inner realm. We do not accept this objection, however: In the first place, it seems to us clear that the conventional physicalist approaches themselves are not adequate to the task, and that the richness of the conscious human mind simply cannot be explained by homunculus-free computational models or by classical mechanical brain-processes operating alone. Like McDougall (1911/1961, p. 362), who specifically rebuked James for giving up the idea of a psychic being or soul, we think that psychology must postulate *minds* or *psyches* to explain some of its most significant mental and behavioral phenomena (including "rogue" phenomena of the sorts catalogued in this book), just as physics postulates unobservable entities and processes to help explain *its* observable phenomena. The work of Henry Stapp and allied quantum theorists provides strong additional warrant for this attitude (and see also Braude, 2003, chap. 9).

The picture we are moving to is thus that the main dispositional properties or capabilities of the mind (J. Fodor, 1983) reside in the associated psychic entity, which is at least in part outside the brain as conventionally conceived. We normally experience these capabilities as they express themselves in conjunction with our organism, in a manner determined at least in part by its ongoing states and processes, as suggested above and discussed in greater detail below. The capabilities in question specifically include memory, thinking, and the cosmogonic imagination or "virtual-reality" system. More elaborate inventories of the attributes of mind have been presented by McDougall (1911/1961), Broad (1925/1960,1962), Stevenson (1981), and Pols (1998), along with a half-dozen or so of the psychologists and neuroscientists canvassed by Uttal (2001). Pols (1998), for example, building upon the inventory given by Descartes in book II of the *Meditations*, says:

> Here, then, is a list of the mind's functions, not perhaps as comprehensive as it could be, but more comprehensive than most such lists; mind knows, makes (that is, forms, produces, creates), understands, thinks, conceives, perceives, remembers, anticipates, believes, doubts, attends, intends, affirms, denies, wills, refuses, imagines, values, judges, and feels. (p. 98)

Pols emphasizes that these attributes, though *distinguishable*, are overlapping and interconnected rather than discrete or separable, and can be viewed for the most part as modes of operation of a more pervasive conscious unity. He is close to McDougall (1911/1961) in this, though much more detailed.

The normal mind-brain relationship is certainly one of peculiar mutual dependence and intimacy. That was very clear to Descartes himself: "Nature...teaches me by these sensations of pain, hunger, thirst, etc., that I am not only lodged in my body as a pilot in a vessel, but that I am very closely united to it, and so to speak so intermingled with it that I seem to compose with it one whole" (Haldane & Ross, 1931, vol. 1, p. 192). This intimacy unfortunately disappeared from many later dualistic accounts including in particular that of Eccles, who often speaks in terms of a completely disembodied "self-conscious mind" that stands apart from and inspects or influences the activity of cortical columns, rather like an immaterial piano-player playing the keys of the bodily piano. That sort of picture is clearly no good, because except by way of very indirect technical arrangements we normally have no *conscious* contact whatsoever with low-level physiological events occurring in our brains. Eccles's picture also seems inconsistent with many neuropsychological phenomena such as the confusion that typically accompanies hemineglect due to parietal-lobe injuries (Stapp, 2004a, p. 167).

Problems of this sort can probably be circumvented, however. Gauld (1968) points out that a person can be conceived as relating to his brain in more intimate fashion, perhaps in a manner somewhat analogous to that of a parasite to its host, and that such a picture could potentially accommodate many relevant facts of neuropsychology: "Malfunctioning of a host may cause malfunctioning of a parasite, and vice-versa; none the less, malfunctioning host and malfunctioning parasite might regain their health if they were separated. Similarly, could a person disengage himself from his damaged brain, he might once more function properly" (at least temporarily, we might add) (p. 348). Something very much like the latter in fact appears to happen in the case of NDEs occurring under conditions of cardiac arrest or general anesthesia (Chapter 6). Philosopher C. D. Broad (1925/1960, 1962) repeatedly invoked the somewhat similar metaphor of a chemical compound, which in some respects seems slightly better: In the formation of table salt from sodium and chlorine, for example, a unique entity, something distinctly new, emerges. The components may also give up something in forming the compound, but they retain their separate identities and the potential to revert to their previous dissociated state. That is, there is also a dynamic aspect, with the components able to exist either conjoined or apart, and a sort of "energy hump" in between so that they tend to do one or the other depending on whatever conditions are relevant.

The very biological-looking critical-period aspect of cases of the reincarnation type (Stevenson, 1997, 2001), in which pre-existing memories of a previous life seem to get progressively overlaid by the subsequent learning of the new personality, appears consistent with such a metaphor. Here it looks as though what otherwise might normally be a fast and automatic forgetting process is somehow getting interrupted or delayed. The high incidence in such cases of violent death in the previous personality is especially intriguing in this regard.[35] More generally, the notion that we begin neonatal life

---

35. See especially Stevenson (1997). There may also be a parallel here with trance mediumship, in that a number of the really successful communicators such as "G.P." (see Gauld, 1968, 1982) have also suffered violent or sudden death. Perhaps "unfinished business" is somehow conducive to remembering, as in the well-known "Zeigarnik" effect.

with a great deal of our personality already in place is broadly consistent with recent trends in developmental psychology, and Stevenson (2000) has pointed out a variety of ways in which the reincarnation hypothesis could potentially explain residual variability not otherwise explainable in terms of "normal" genetic or environmental factors.

Taking the "entry" metaphor seriously requires us to predict that corresponding phenomena of "withdrawal" may sometimes occur. For example, in persons suffering from progressive senile dementias it may sometimes happen that the mind of the dying person becomes disengaged sufficiently from the diseased brain, near the point of death, that relatively normal functioning briefly reappears (provided that suitable expressive capacities are still available). Phenomena of this type were already being reported by early observers such as de Boismont (1859), Flournoy (1903), and Rush (1812), as mentioned in Chapter 6, and recent interactions between several of the authors of the present book and medical personnel at several hospices and clinics strongly suggest that such phenomena are still occurring and potentially accessible to systematic study. Severe Alzheimer-type neuropathology has also sometimes been found in autopsies of persons exhibiting normal or even above-normal pre-mortem mental function (Davis, Schmitt, Wekstein, & Markesberg, 1999). Mental revivals in the context of severe neurodegenerative disease clearly merit further research, not least because materialist critics such as Edwards (1996, chap. 17) have emphatically denied that they can occur.

The everyday or supraliminal self as we normally experience it comes into conscious action in conjunction with the associated brain, whenever that brain achieves some threshold level of overall activation or "arousal" characterized by the predominance of intrinsic electrical rhythms of roughly 8–12 Hz and higher. All the major proposals regarding neurophysiological correlates of normal conscious experience point to the importance of synchronous (or at least coherent) neural oscillations in the gamma frequency range, oscillations that link and perhaps somehow "bind" the electrical activity of widely distributed regions of the brain. In the context of the non-Cartesian dualist-interactionist model this suggests that there is normally some sort of mutually constraining or resonant linkage between this large-scale brain activity and the associated psyche which limits, focuses, funnels, unifies, and stabilizes the supraliminal mental life, while whatever additional strata of mental or psychic organization may be present, per Myers and James, remain active behind the scenes. The stabilization or mutual-constraint aspect is revealed, perhaps, by the fact that in NDE cases involving life-threatening injury, the subject often initially remains at least briefly in a more or less normal state of consciousness before beginning to experience the more drastic alterations associated with a full-blown NDE (Chapter 6). One can also readily imagine, as explicitly suggested by James (1898/1900), that the normal ongoing interactions between mind and brain might result in modifications on *both* sides, although the details of how this could work again remain obscure.

The patterns of brain activity accompanying normal conscious experience also seem to have an overall functional architecture that in a meaningful sense is parallel to, or isomorphic with, the characteristic perceiver/perceived or knower/known phenomenological structure of that experience. At least two proposals from recent mainstream literature in neurophysiology are consistent with this basic idea. Crick and Koch (2003) explicitly acknowledge this universal phenomenological property, which they call the "homuncular" structure of experience, and suggest that it probably reflects some large-scale feature of brain organization. They themselves think it may reflect the fact that the front of the brain, more involved in executive functions and the like, is "looking at" activity in the back of the brain, which contains the main sensory systems. This rough and metaphorical way of formulating the basic idea seems broadly consistent with most current consciousness theories of the global workspace type. A more elaborate and neurophysiologically justified model, however, flows from the specific variant of workspace theory deriving from Penfield (1975), Newman and Baars (1993), and especially Llinás et al. (1998), which emphasizes the role of the extended reticular activating system and the massive reciprocal connections linking the thalamus with the cerebral cortex. Llinás's group has discovered a thalamocortical "scanning" rhythm, in the neighborhood of 40 Hz, which sweeps repeatedly across the cortex in a front-to-back direction (Joliot, Ribary, & Llinás, 1994). They interpret this as a process by which a thalamus-driven readout mechanism periodically interrogates the cortex and synthesizes or binds the various processes going on there into the momentary global state. Apart from the physiological evidence directly supporting it, this proposal, unlike that of Crick and Koch (2003), is also consistent with a large body of clinical evidence showing that small lesions in the upper brainstem and thalamus completely abolish ordinary consciousness itself, whereas cortical lesions, even large ones, typically abolish or alter only relatively specific elements of its phenomenological content.

The Llinás model also maps fairly well onto a sizeable body of data regarding "the psychological moment" (Stroud, 1955). In simple reaction-time experiments, for example, the within-subject distribution across trials of the time it takes to press a button in response to a flash or tone turns out not to be continuous, as initially expected, but to consist instead of multiple discrete peaks separated by intervals of a few tens of milliseconds (Dehaene, 1993). Another example is provided by the "wagon-wheel" illusion often seen in movies, in which the wheels of the stagecoach seem to turn erratically, or even in the wrong direction. This previously had been thought due entirely to "aliasing" effects associated with the varying relations between the rate of rotation of the wheel and the fixed presentation rate of the movie frames, but it turns out to occur even with wheel-like visual objects that rotate continuously under continuous illumination (Purves, Paydartar, & Andrews, 1996). The conclusion appears inescapable that there is an inherent *discreteness* in sensorimotor activity, corresponding in a striking way to James's notion of "pulses of consciousness." Note also that effects of this sort, variable between individuals and tasks, are inherent in Stapp's model, inasmuch as Process 1 in itself imposes a task-dependent framing on the otherwise continuous evolution of Process 2.[36]

Even when the normal, ongoing adult engagement of mind and brain is in force (whatever that relationship amounts to in detail), the mind appears to retain at least a limited ability to operate more independently, and potentially in very different ways, when that engagement is altered or ruptured in various ways by changes in the functional status of the brain. The dramatic and rapid within-subject fluctuations in mental status often observed in brain-damaged patients (H. Gardner, 1976), for example, might reflect corresponding fluctuations in patients' capacities to interact normally with their malfunctioning brains. Sleep and dreams also can clearly be thought about in this way—a kind of regulated quasi-periodic "stretching" or other modification of the normal linkage—and certainly the lack of satisfactory progress on these subjects despite a century or so of serious scientific effort provides motivation to try thinking about them in a new and different way. Slow-wave sleep, for example, involves significant modifications in the overall level and pattern of brain activity, modifications that partially mimic those produced by general anesthesia, and these non-REM sleep states are already known to be accompanied by fragmentary mental activity very different in character from that of ordinary dreams (Foulkes, 1962). Vivid REM-sleep dreaming itself, interestingly, has recently been shown in both imaging (A. R. Braun et al., 1998) and neuropsychological (Solms, 1997) studies to be associated with *reduced* activity in prefrontal and occipital cortex, consistent with Myers's principle that the subliminal is liberated by the abeyance of the supraliminal and its associated forms of outwardly directed activity. Recently identified phenomena of "paradoxical function facilitation," in which previously unrecognized skills or abilities emerge following brain injury (Kapur, 1996; B. L. Miller et al., 1998), may in some cases merit a similar interpretation.

The "dreams" that are sometimes reported as occurring in connection with general anesthesia itself also deserve more careful study than they have received to date, to characterize more precisely their phenomenological properties and physiological conditions of occurrence. For these to occur at all under conditions of deep general anesthesia would conflict—like the occurrence of NDEs (Chapter 6)—with current neuroscientific opinion regarding conditions necessary for conscious experience. They would be expected, however, from the Myers/James point of view, and especially in persons open to subliminal influence, such as persons of high "transliminality," with thin or permeable "boundaries." An observation consistent

---

36. Another possible manifestation of this "framing" process is the EEG "microstates" discovered by Dietrich Lehmann and colleagues (Lehmann, Ozaki, & Pal, 1987; Pascual-Marqui, Michel, & Lehmann, 1995). These are brief episodes of relatively stable topography in the scalp-recorded potential field, lasting on the order of 50–150 milliseconds and separated by sharp transitions. The manner and degree to which such segmentation of scalp potential fields corresponds to the rapidly changing structure of conscious experience remains to be determined, however.

with this expectation is provided by Hejja and Galloon (1975), who showed that "dreaming" in conjunction with ketamine anesthesia occurred overwhelmingly among patients who also recalled dreaming at home. A full 50 of their reported ketamine dreams occurred among the 68 patients who also reported dreaming at home, while only two others were reported by an additional 82 patients who did not.

The NDE literature (Chapter 6) further indicates that the normal linkage can sometimes be so severely stretched or otherwise modified that the mental system spontaneously begins to operate in radically different ways. It seems especially significant in this regard that NDEs involving subjectively enhanced cognitive functioning tend to occur more commonly in persons who in fact are closer to death physiologically (Owens et al., 1990). But NDEs can also occur in persons who are continuously and fully conscious, as for example in mountain climbers during serious falls, and similar experiences also can arise following ingestion of various psychedelic agents, and in connection with transformative practices such as meditation, where their physiological accompaniments are surely very different and can more readily be studied in detail and across time (Chapter 8). The sheer diversity of circumstances under which similar kinds of experience can occur itself suggests that their common cause may involve some overall alteration of the normal mind-brain relationship, rather than engagement of specific neurophysiological final common pathways or mechanisms.

The strength of mind-brain coupling may also vary systematically between *persons* in ways that could be measured, and that might again shed light on the nature of the coupling itself. Successful trance mediums like Mrs. Piper, for example, might be viewed (and were viewed by Myers) as persons in whom the coupling is unusually "loose," permitting the psyche to disengage partially or wholly from its customary entanglements and thus to provide temporary access for potential "communicators."[37] Unfortunately, practically nothing of significance is presently known about the great trance mediums (or for that matter about exceptional psi subjects of any other kind) in terms of relevant characteristics of physiological function, personality, or cognitive style.

Our basic functional picture of the normal waking situation, like that of most neuroscientists including Crick and Koch (2003) in their discussion of "zombie modes," is that mind and consciousness get involved in ongoing activity only to the extent they need to, while things that are simple, or fully learned or overlearned, can run on more or less automatically via brain processes. Such a division of labor can readily be accommodated within the basic framework of Stapp's model, because to the degree that the proliferation of possible brain states by Process 2 is directly constrained by interactions between the organism and its environment, the need for Pro-

37. Conversely, aphasia-like phenomena which often accompany the emergence of a new communicator (such as difficulties in speaking or writing the right words) might be viewed as expressions of the difficulties that psyche encounters in "operating" a partly unfamiliar organism. See Myers (*HP*, vol. 2, p. 254) for some interesting remarks on this subject.

cess 1 contributions would be correspondingly reduced. Such a picture is consistent not only with everyday experiences such as driving a car while carrying on a conversation, but also with neuroimaging results showing that the numerous and widely distributed brain territories initially engaged by a complex task massively deactivate and contract as the task is progressively mastered (e.g., Haier et al., 1992; John, 1976). Consistent with our modified-holist view, this looks more like changing degrees of engagement of one large, common structure than all-or-none selective engagement/disengagement of highly localized and specific computational "modules." Similarly, human cortical neurons involved in working-memory tasks have recently been shown to produce gamma-band EEG activity under *all* the task conditions, but in amounts proportional to the overall memory "load" associated with each task (Howard et al., 2003). Another relevant observation involves electrical stimulation of the small thalamic regions that produce petit mal epileptic "absences"; Penfield (1975, pp. 37–43) interpreted this as reversibly disrupting the connection of mind to brain and releasing the brain as a kind of sensorimotor automaton to operate temporarily on its own, for example in playing the piano or driving a car (both poorly, in the absence of the normal conscious fine-tuning).

We have now said about as much as we need to, or at this point usefully can, in terms of justifying the non-Cartesian dualist-interactionist model and fleshing it out in neurophysiological terms. Although we have perhaps made some progress in this regard, it is only candid to acknowledge that we ourselves remain less than fully satisfied with this approach. The traditional dualist problems regarding mental causation and energy conservation seem to be overcome, but there remain further deep problems with no good solutions in sight. We still have no real understanding of the ultimate nature of the relationship between brain processes and mental activity, and certainly no solution of Chalmers's "hard problem"—why conscious experiences with their specific qualitative characteristics should arise at all in connection with the associated patterns of brain activity. It is not clear which aspects of the "cognitive unconscious" go with the brain, which with the associated psyche, and how their respective contributions get coordinated. We have talked about mind-brain relations primarily in relation to the functioning of an adult human, presuming the existence of an associated psyche, but where do these psyches come from in the course of individual human development, or in the evolution of species? Where and how, exactly, does consciousness enter the picture? These are difficult problems, to say the least (and see Griffin, 1997, chap. 3, for related discussion). Finally, we have said practically nothing about further difficult problems having to do with the properties of that adult psyche itself. We conceive that the psyche or at least some part of it may be capable of operating in some fashion on its own, independent of the brain, but what could be the character or mode of subsistence of such an entity? Broad (1962, Epilogue), who discusses this problem in considerable depth, ultimately adopts the conventional scientific view (disputed by Braude, 2003, pp. 294–301) that any dispositional properties of a mind must be grounded in or explained by minute structure and processes in *some* sort of material substrate. From this viewpoint, post-mortem survival of human personality or consciousness would necessarily occur in conjunction with some sort of "subtle" physical body or bodies, perhaps of the types conceived by the wisdom traditions and summarized by Poortman (1954/1978). Although such a picture does not seem to be ruled out by our present knowledge of physics, and deserves further investigation, we suspect that a more fundamentally novel way of approaching the problems *may* in the end yield a better solution. We turn next to this.

Neutral-Monist Models

The key to moving in this more radical direction is to recognize that our entire discussion of non-Cartesian dualist-interactionist models has implicitly, and perhaps mistakenly, taken the classical "matter" side of the Cartesian bifurcation for granted. To recapitulate: The body conceived conventionally as a physiological machine has proven unable to account for all the properties of minds, and so we must try to find a different theory that can better account for the empirical data. In a first attempt to do so we proceeded in what probably seems the most natural and conservative direction, at least to most persons reared like ourselves in the intellectual tradition of Western reductionist science. Specifically, following the main lead suggested by James (1898/1900), we left the Cartesian body in place but re-introduced the psyche, conceived as a second and distinct type of existent (itself possibly at least in part physical in some extended sense) with which that body is somehow associated. This approach, however, gave rise to difficulties analogous to those of the traditional Cartesian causal dilemma. In particular, we have struggled with only limited success to understand how and why these two species of existents normally interact in the production of conscious mental life. We want now to take a different approach, by examining more closely the *body* side of the mind-body relation.

We have all grown accustomed to the idea that the phenomenological table that we see and touch is not the "real" table, as described by physics. In this case we have no difficulty accepting that ordinary perceptual experience is not a reliable guide to the ultimate nature of things. Yet it is extremely difficult if not impossible for most of us to adopt that same attitude with respect to the phenomenological solidity, the felt presence, of our own bodies. They seem just inescapably there, brute facts, existing on their own as classical Cartesian objects. It is this intuition, however, that we will now challenge.[38]

To begin, consider the character of what we experience in dreams. Those of us who dream vividly encounter a phenomenological world similar in

38. For additional help in this regard, see the all-out assault on this everyday intuition by Harrison (1989).

many salient respects to the world we all experience in the waking state. We experience ourselves as embodied, and we move purposefully among other solid, three-dimensional objects, including at times other persons, that seem to exist independently of ourselves and that also behave for the most part in more or less customary ways. Both we and the persons we encounter seem to have both an "outside" and an "inside." If we smash violently into something, we may appear to bleed, and it usually hurts. Those other persons act as though they have their own thoughts and motivations, and they sometimes tell us things that we ourselves do not consciously know. Yet all this vivid dream-world experience, so like what we experience in ordinary waking life, occurs in the near-total absence of corresponding sensory input (Globus, 1987).

The seeming reality of the dream of course evaporates, for most of us anyway, when we awaken in the ordinary way to the phenomenologically similar world presented in everyday experience. *This* world seems to most of us unquestionably real, existing "out there" and independently of ourselves. Yet as we saw in Chapter 8, great mystics of all traditions have reported entering states of consciousness relative to which that everyday reality itself proves evanescent in the same way as a dream. The material world given in everyday experience, they declare, is not what it seems. Matter as we customarily experience it does not exist, at least not in the way we naively believe it to exist.

In our attempt to develop the non-Cartesian dualist-interactionist model we relied heavily on a first major consequence of quantum theory, that it brings consciousness back into physics at the foundational level and in a causally effective manner. There is a second major consequence, however, no less profound but even less widely appreciated. It is this: There is no such thing as matter as classically conceived. Physics is not ultimately about an independently existing objective world of classically conceived material entities, but rather about our knowledge, and about relationships among experiences. Thus our *ontology*, our conception of the basic "stuff" of which the universe is composed, also must undergo fundamental revision. Stapp (2004a) summarizes the situation this way:

> The physical world thus becomes an evolving structure of information, and of propensities for experiences to occur, rather than a mechanically evolving mindless material structure. The new conception essentially fulfills the age-old philosophical idea that nature should be made out of a kind of stuff that combines in an integrated and natural way certain mind-like and matter-like qualities, without being reduced to either classically conceived mind or classically conceived matter. (p. 268)

Before proceeding further in this direction we will briefly digress, for reasons that are both historically and conceptually significant. We are acutely aware that many scientifically minded readers, even among those who have stayed with us to this point, may have gagged at our emphasis on the word "ontology." Ontology is a branch of metaphysics, and scientists tend to pride themselves on having nothing to do with such arcane matters. William James himself clearly shared that attitude at the time he was writing the *Principles;* in his preface and elsewhere he declares that the proper business of psychology as a natural science consists simply in ascertaining the correlations that ordinarily hold between states of mind and brain-states, and that to attempt to explain these correlations in terms of anything more fundamental would be to trespass into metaphysics. But Myers (1891c), in his remarkable review of the *Principles*, chided James for taking this narrow view, and for failing to recognize the degree to which more penetrating empirical investigations of the mind-brain connection might be able to shed light on its ultimate character. Undoubtedly influenced in considerable part by Myers, James (1892) by the time of his *Briefer Course* had already abandoned the position adopted in the *Principles* and concluded that there can in fact be no such thing as a metaphysics-free science of psychology:

> When, then, we talk of "psychology as a natural science" we must not assume that we mean a sort of psychology that stands at last on solid ground. It means just the reverse: it means a psychology particularly fragile, and into which the waters of metaphysical criticism leak at every joint, a psychology all of whose elementary assumptions and data must be reconsidered in wider connections and translated into other terms. (pp. 467–468)

So far we have "only the hope of a science," and its actual state of development requires us "to understand how great is the darkness in which we grope, and never to forget that the natural-science assumptions with which we started are provisional and revisable things" (James, 1892, p. 468). In his Presidential Address to the American Psychological Association in December 1894 James again stated flatly: "I have become convinced...that no conventional restrictions *can* keep metaphysical and so-called epistemological inquiries out of the psychology-books" (James, 1895/1978, p. 88; see also E. Taylor, 1996, chap. 7). The real issue, in short, is not whether we will have metaphysics, but whether we will have good metaphysics or bad.

This of course marks the point at which behavioristically oriented historians of psychology characteristically portray James as ceasing to be a psychologist and becoming instead a "mere" philosopher. But there can be no doubt that James himself did *not* see things this way. We have already shown (Chapter 8) that much of James's later work, especially *The Varieties of Religious Experience* (1902/1958) and *A Pluralistic Universe* (1909/1971), can be understood in considerable part as direct applications of Myers's model of the psyche to problems in religion and philosophy. What we have not yet emphasized, however, is that there is a further dimension of James's later work that connects directly with the matters now before us.

Our account of the non-Cartesian dualist-interactionist model rested directly upon the formulation of "transmission" theory by James (1898/1900). Yet even at that early date James was already searching for a way to get beyond dualism. In a crucial footnote he remarks:

> The philosophically instructed reader will notice that I have all along been placing myself at the ordinary dualistic point of view of natural science and of common sense. From this point of view mental facts like feelings are made of one kind of stuff or substance, physical facts of another. An absolute phenomenalism, not believing such a dualism to be ultimate, may possibly end by solving some of the problems that are insoluble when propounded in dualist terms. (pp. 50–51)

This brief statement encapsulates and foreshadows the doctrine of "radical empiricism" that James was systematically developing during the last years of his life. This involved far more than the methodological principle (which he also endorsed) that we must be willing to look at all relevant data in approaching any scientific problem. Rather, James was driving toward a comprehensive metaphysical system grounded wholly and directly in actual human experience, experience of all forms up to and including mystical experience (see Perry, 1935, vol. 2, Part 6).

James's ambitious program remained unfinished at his death in 1910, but it was subsequently taken up and integrated with emerging developments in physics by the Anglo-American mathematician, philosopher of science, and metaphysician Alfred North Whitehead. It is no accident, in this light, that in his last book Whitehead (1938/1968, p. 2) identified James as one of the four greatest thinkers of the Western tradition, along with Plato, Aristotle, and Leibniz. But Whitehead also had a profound understanding of emerging developments in physics and clearly recognized their ontological implications. His work in fact represents the most systematic effort to date to elaborate a comprehensive metaphysical system specifically intended to be compatible *both* with the new basic science *and* with all available facts of human experience.[39]

Whitehead's system is provisional, unfinished, open-ended, and vast in scope, but altogether naturalistic in spirit and character. It is far too complex and difficult to present here in any detail, but we can quickly summarize its central, driving ideas. The root cause of our present mind-brain difficulties, Whitehead argues, is the ontological bifurcation originally imposed on nature by Descartes and his 17th-century supernaturalist allies. Classical physics, as it evolved over subsequent centuries in the work of Galileo, Newton, Laplace, and their successors, dealt only with the "matter" side of this Cartesian ontology. But its core concept of lifeless mechanical matter has now proven to be a vicious abstraction, vitiated by what was left out at the very beginning. Modern physical theory invites us instead to conceive of nature as in some sense alive throughout, with even its lowest-level con-

39. Just as we have not taken Henry Stapp to be any sort of final or ultimate authority but rather as the primary representative of a group of quantum theorists whom we see as moving in broadly similar directions in regard to mind-brain relations, we are here taking Whitehead as representative of a larger group of "process" theorists working in what we are calling the neutral-monist tradition. Among these we include (in addition to Leibniz, the later James, and Whitehead himself in his Harvard period) major figures such as Charles Sanders Peirce, Henri Bergson, Bertrand Russell, Charles Hartshorne, and David Ray Griffin. We thank Eric Weiss for particularly helpful comments on this section.

stituents having both exterior/objective and interior/subjective aspects. The fundamental stuff of the universe, on this view, is not lifeless bits of classically conceived matter moving in fields of force, but "occasions of experience." These occasions, from the point of view of other such occasions, appear as "events." But Whitehead's analysis of events suggests that every event to *some* degree "feels" causes from the past, "imagines" possibilities for the future, and "makes decisions" as to what it will become.[40] Thus the definiteness and particularity that distinguish each event from all others are precisely a result of its "mental pole," however rudimentary.

Whitehead's fundamental move is thus to re-situate mind in matter as the fundamental factor by which determinate events emerge out of a background of possibilities. The behavior of the lowest or most matter-like occasions is determined almost completely by efficient causes from the past; such an event is influenced by or "feels" its past but engages in an absolute minimum of "imagination" or "decision." There is, however, a creative evolutionary drive inherent in nature which leads to the progressive elaboration, across time, of more complex events associated with correspondingly more complex, sophisticated, and self-determining experiential interiors. Events are interdependent, moreover, in ways more subtle and complex than those contemplated by Descartes and his modern successors. The classical conception of matter arose predominantly in association with the most recently evolved forms of perceptual experience, especially vision and hearing, but these are secondary or derivative acquisitions that do not fully disclose the nature of the ways in which events can potentially affect each other. They in fact conceal a profound continuity between ourselves and lower forms of organization in terms of more primitive forms of interrelatedness and experience which reflect a global interconnectedness that is fundamental to nature: "Any local agitation shakes the whole universe. The distant effects are minute, but they are there" (Whitehead, 1938/1968, p. 138).[41] The fundamental concepts in this "organismic" view of nature are process, activity, transition, and change, all orchestrated in service of "creative advance."[42]

40. The scare quotes in this sentence are meant to emphasize that the mentalistic terms employed here are being used broadly and metaphorically, and not as they would normally apply to the mental activity of a conscious human being. How far down nature can plausibly be viewed as manifesting such "mentalistic" properties remains an open question, but the threshold, if one exists, is undoubtedly much further down than most of us commonly assume. McDougall (1911/1969, pp. 258–260) found signs of unified and purposive behavior even in one-celled organisms such as the Amoeba and the Paramecium, and Seager (1998) has advanced somewhat similar arguments in regard to elemental units of inanimate nature itself.

41. Recall that very similar ideas in regard to "panaesthesia" as a more fundamental or primitive capacity for experience were expressed by Myers (Chapter 2).

42. Whitehead's magnum opus, *Process and Reality* (1929/1978), is an extremely difficult book, but an excellent and readable introduction to his main ideas can be found in his last book (Whitehead, 1938/1968), especially Chapters 7 and 8. Griffin (1997, 1998, 2000) and Hosinski (1993) provide accurate and readable secondary sources, and G. R. Lucas (1989) and Griffin, Cobb, Ford, Gunter, and Ochs (1993) situate his work within the larger philosophic tradition.

It would carry us far beyond the purposes and scope of the present book to present or discuss Whitehead's views here in greater depth. We certainly do not mean to endorse his views wholesale, but we do wish to record here our collective sense that he was moving in a direction that is both theoretically promising and fundamentally consistent with the ontological implications of quantum theory. The latter is perhaps especially surprising and impressive in that Whitehead apparently arrived at his ontological ideas mainly by generalizing from his own earlier work on relativity theory and foundational concepts of physics such as space, time, motion, and causality, rather than by way of quantum theory itself. He was certainly familiar with emerging developments in quantum theory, but he apparently saw these primarily as illustrating or confirming ideas that he had arrived at on his own and from a different direction (V. Lowe, 1951, p. 90). Many quantum physicists including Henry Stapp (2004b) apparently agree with this judgment, finding Whitehead's general outlook intuitively appealing and at least potentially compatible with their understanding of the physics. There also appears to be growing interest among such physicists in exploring and deepening these connections, through a process of cross-fertilization and mutual adjustment in which Whitehead's original philosophical system is being progressively "modernized" in light of continuing developments in physics, while serving as a fruitful source of suggestions toward rounding out the ontological side of quantum theory itself (Shimony, 1993; Eastman & Keeton, 2004).[43]

In addition to being deeply compatible with basic science, a Whitehead-like neutral-monist outlook seems to afford new possibilities for progress on substantive issues relevant to mind-brain relations. First, as argued in particular by Griffin (1997, chap. 3; 1998) one can readily appreciate at least in principle how a neutral-monist solution *might* overcome the unresolved problems—common to both materialism and dualism as traditionally conceived, and probably unresolvable in those terms—of accounting for the emergence of mind and consciousness in the course of biological evolution and individual human development. Griffin (1993, 1994, 1997, 1998, 2000) has also made serious and generally well-received efforts to accommodate the data of psychical research, including survival data, within his basically Whiteheadian framework.[44] We ourselves can also glimpse at least in general

43. See Eastman and Keeton's on-line resource guide to physics and Whitehead, which is available at http://www.ctr4process.org/publications/PSS. It is also worth noting here that a similar neutral-monist position has tentatively been reached, from still another direction, by Chalmers (1996); see also his and other contributions to Shear (1998). Chalmers hardly mentions Whitehead at all, anchoring his neutral-monist sympathies instead in the work of Russell (1927). For critical comparative analysis of the neutral monisms of Russell and Whitehead, see Lovejoy (1930/1960) and G. R. Lucas (1989, chap. 7).

44. Parenthetically, physicist Oliver Lodge (1929) was probably the first to recognize the relevance of Whitehead's metaphysics to the survival problem. Affinities between psi phenomena and the picture of "entangled" reality revealed by quantum theory have been carefully drawn out by Radin (2006), and Stapp (in press a), in his discussion of the Libet experiments, provides a potential solution for Griffin's problems concerning precognition.

terms how such a framework *might* ultimately provide viable explanations of allied phenomena such as NDEs occurring under conditions of general anesthesia and cardiac arrest (Chapter 6) and the various still-unexplained properties of human memory (Chapter 4).[45]

Whitehead's original theory has problems of its own, however. Some of his most central technical notions and terms, such as "prehension" and "concrescence," remain for us extremely difficult and obscure. The precise manner in which lower-grade "actual entities" combine to form higher-grade entities with new, emergent properties seems particularly in need of further explication, and the importance of this can readily be appreciated from a testy exchange between Searle and Chalmers recorded in Searle (1997). Chalmers (1996) had unwisely mused at length regarding the possible mental life of thermostats, but Searle ridiculed these "panpsychist" speculations on grounds that thermostats lack the kind of biological organization that he thinks we know to be necessary for any form of conscious experience. This kind of attempted *reductio ad absurdum* has been a common response to the views of Whitehead and the other neutral monists, but as emphasized especially by Griffin (1998, chap. 9) it ignores a long tradition, extending from Leibniz to Whitehead, Hartshorne, and Griffin himself, that attempts to distinguish systematically between mere "aggregates" (such as rocks and thermostats) and "compounds" (such as earthworms and ourselves) in terms of their respective levels and types of organization. Clearly, to the degree that these distinctions can be grounded in an adequate understanding of the process of composition, the Searle-type *reductio* can be circumvented. Previous philosophic attempts to accomplish this, however, including Griffin's, seem to us mainly *descriptive* rather than *explanatory*.[46]

Even if the composition problem can be successfully resolved, further difficulties are already in sight. For example, it is not clear to us at present whether neutral monism is truly distinguishable from an interactive dualism

45. Related suggestions regarding NDEs and memory have recently been offered by Romijn (1997), who draws upon the generically similar quantum-mechanical theory of consciousness developed by David Bohm in his later years. Bohm himself attempted to use that same theory to explain psi phenomena, which he evidently took seriously (Bohm, 1986), and his neutral-monist conception of the "implicate order" has also been enlisted by Karl Pribram (1979, 1986, 1991) in support of "holonomic" explanations of brain function, perception, and (receptive) psi, though with only limited success (Braude, 1979; Draaisma, 2000; see also Stapp, in press a, in press b, regarding technical problems in Bohm's quantum mechanics).

46. A possible way forward is suggested by physicist and philosopher of science Abner Shimony in his critical response to Roger Penrose (1997) from the point of view of a "modernized Whiteheadianism" which "applies the framework of quantum theory to an ontology that is *ab initio* mentalistic" (Shimony, 1997, p. 154). Shimony portrays the emergence of conscious states from an ensemble of neurons, for example, as due to large-scale quantum entanglement, analogous to the demonstrated emergence in relatively small quantum systems of novel properties transcending those of their constituents. Quantum theory, that is, already encompasses a mode of composition that has no analogue in classical physics. Penrose himself subsequently endorsed these suggestions, stating that "although I had not explicitly asserted, in either *Emperor* or *Shadows*, the need for mentality to be 'ontologically fundamental in the universe', I think that something of this nature is indeed necessary" (1997, pp. 175–176). See also Seager (1998).

of the sort sketched earlier. This is the central theme of Lovejoy's (1930/1960) examination of the doctrines advanced by Russell and Whitehead, and Griffin's descriptive term for his own position, "nondualist interactionism," seems perilously close to an oxymoron. In addition, Whitehead's theory as described so far is a purely bottom-up theory in which our normal, supraliminal consciousness emerges at the apex of a hierarchy of lesser integrations. This picture is similar to the monadic theories of McDougall and Balfour, and we have already argued that such theories deal poorly with the fully-developed phenomena of psychological automatism and secondary personality, as well as genius and mysticism (Chapters 5, 7, 8). More generally, they cannot easily accommodate any of the evidence assembled by Myers, James, and their colleagues for the existence in all or at least some of us of normally hidden levels of psychic organization characterized by increasing scope, precision, speed, and complexity of mental function. It appears possible in principle, however, to accommodate such phenomena, while remaining within the basic neutral-monist framework, by incorporating elements of a complementary top-down tradition (represented in the West by historical figures such as Plato, Plotinus, and the German idealists, and in the East by the higher schools of Hindu philosophy and the wisdom traditions) that sees consciousness itself as the fundamental reality in nature, flowing outward or downward to its most matter-like aspects, and then back up again in the course of cosmic evolution (Poortman, 1954/1978). Whitehead's own system in its full development incorporates such ideas in a form having much in common with James's vision of an unfinished pluralistic universe (see our Chapter 8). It is also worth mentioning, perhaps, that considerable sympathy for views of this general type has been expressed by theoretical physicists such as Schrödinger (1959, Epilogue), d'Espagnat (1976), and Haag (1996).

Within such a top-down neutral-monist framework, human personality would be pictured as a complex system made up of the same kind of "stuff" throughout. The system consists of a hierarchy of levels or strata of the types recognized in particular by Myers, James, and the wisdom traditions. Each level is characterized by its own form of psychophysical organization and has both interior and exterior aspects that allow it to participate in some form of experienced world appropriate to itself. The activities of these different strata are somehow interconnected, and coordinated in greater or lesser degree, by something like Myers's Subliminal Self, or by a consciousness that somehow underlies or pervades the whole structure. The fundamental cleavage in nature suggested in particular by the survival evidence would on such a view be interpreted not *ontologically*, as the separation of an entire "psyche" from its associated "body," but *functionally*, as a shift within that complex system, following dissolution of its outermost psychophysical shell, to a different mode of operation based on whatever levels remain. Such a picture would be theoretically attractive in that it incorporates *both* of the fundamental insights of quantum theory and overcomes the residual dualism of the non-Cartesian dualist-interactionist model, while also potentially accommodating all of the relevant empirical data. To what degree it is actually correct, and can be fleshed out in both empirical and theoretical detail, remains to be seen.

To recapitulate: Both Myers and James believed that the only way we can get consciousness out of a theory is to build it into the theory *somewhere* at the beginning.[47] The neutral-monist options identified here—strictly bottom-up, strictly top-down, or possibly some higher-level integration of the two—seem to bracket the possible ways of doing so. Our own collective sympathies tend currently, but less than unanimously, toward the last of these somewhat dizzying abstractions, which clearly has a great deal in common with the views held by Myers and James. We will not attempt to develop them further or adjudicate among them at the present time, however, for to do so is the central goal of our ongoing Esalen discussions and the expected subject of our next book.

Meanwhile, what we think will ultimately prove most helpful in catalyzing further theoretical progress will be thoroughgoing application—determined and disciplined, but also sympathetic and flexible—of Western-style scientific imagination to the phenomenological realities revealed by the great contemplative traditions, both East and West. We need to chart more fully and accurately the natural history of these "higher" or "deeper" subliminal realms. How many meaningfully distinguishable states or levels of consciousness actually or potentially exist within us, with what properties and what relationships to each other? Under what sorts of conditions do they occur, and what sorts of consequences do they have? Can we harness the benefits of potentially useful states by developing improved means of facilitating their occurrence? Partial or preliminary answers to some of these questions may be obtainable through careful and scientifically informed comparative study of the existing literature of the wisdom traditions themselves, but what will contribute most in the long run, in our opinion, is intensified experimental and phenomenological investigation of altered states of consciousness of *all* types, whether spontaneously occurring or induced by meditation, psychedelics, hypnosis, or other means. Only in this way, if ever, will we finally get to the bottom of what James called "Myers's problem." There are many lifetimes' worth of exciting and important science to be done here, work unlikely to be undertaken by persons immured in the current mainstream consensus.

47. James (1890b) remarks that "*if evolution is to work smoothly, consciousness in some shape must have been present at the very origin of things*" (vol. 1, p. 149). See also the critique by Griffin (1998) of conventional accounts by Dennett, Humphrey, and others of the supposed incremental "emergence" of consciousness in the course of evolution.

Summary and Prospectus

For an enlarged scientific picture of human mind and personality to emerge, two things need to happen: First, it must be demonstrated that the currently dominant physicalist theories of mind-brain relations are inadequate in principle; and second, an alternative theory must be found that remedies these defects.

The present volume has sought mainly to address the first of these tasks, by assembling in one place large amounts of credible evidence for a wide variety of empirical phenomena that appear difficult or impossible to explain in conventional physicalist terms. We find this evidence cumulatively overwhelming, and expect to have persuaded many open-minded readers that this is the case. At the same time, we are also acutely aware that the continuing scientific resistance to many of these phenomena derives in large part from their apparent conflict with current physicalist orthodoxy. Nothing would do more to hasten their wider recognition and acceptance, we believe, than identification of an alternative theoretical outlook that is scientifically defensible and that would permit and perhaps ultimately even explain them. In this concluding chapter, therefore, we have attempted to show at least in a provisional way that such theoretical expansion appears possible.

Our theoretical reconnaissance proceeded at two primary levels. In the first half of the chapter we argued that the psychological theory advanced by Myers and developed further by James in his late period has been considerably strengthened by many related scientific findings of the subsequent century. We ourselves strongly suspect that they were already approaching a more or less correct overall picture of the structure of the human psyche, but at the very least they provided a useful working model which brings the entire range of relevant empirical phenomena into intelligible relationship within a coherent descriptive framework, and which suggests a variety of potentially fruitful directions for further research.

This theory was not disproven but simply displaced, forgotten—a casualty of the changes wrought in scientific psychology by the advent of behaviorism. Its near-total absence from contemporary discussions of consciousness seems to us the worst yet among many unfortunate examples of scientific amnesia (Draaisma, 2000; Harrington, 1987; Koch & Leary, 1985), and to help overcome this amnesia has been one of the central objectives of our book.

In the second half of the chapter we attempted to go further by showing in a provisional way that more comprehensive psychological theories of the Myers/James type are also potentially reconcilable with the relevant aspects of present-day science. In this first stage of an ongoing theoretical effort we have attempted only to sketch out the main directions in which further progress seems possible, and is urgently needed. Theories of the types indicated share several major advantages relative to those that currently dominate mainstream science and philosophy: In particular, they are more deeply compatible with leading-edge physical science itself; they appear potentially capable of explaining most and perhaps all of the "rogue" empirical phenomena catalogued in this book; and they ratify, rather than reject, our everyday experience of ourselves as purposeful, causally effective, conscious agents. We wish here to underscore this last point, because it brings out in perhaps the most dramatic and humanly relevant way the stark contrast between the sorts of theory we are advocating and those that dominate the current scene.

The self was absolutely central to the psychology of William James (Leary, 1990). In the *Principles* (1890b) he says: "The universal conscious fact is not 'feelings and thoughts exist' but 'I think' and 'I feel'. No psychology...can question the *existence* of personal selves. The worst a psychology can do is so to interpret the nature of these selves as to rob them of their worth" (vol. 1, p. 226). The self is something the presence of which we can feel almost constantly at the innermost subjective pole of our experience. Its ultimate origins remain mysterious, and as we saw in Chapter 8 James himself traced them into the recesses of the subliminal consciousness, and even to the hypothesis of a World-Soul as the ultimate foundation and root of our individualized conscious selves. But however it arises, the self is the active element in the stream of consciousness, expressing the dispositional basis of our conscious mental life:

> It is what welcomes or rejects. It presides over the perception of sensations, and by giving or withholding its assent it influences the movements they tend to arouse. It is the home of interest,—not the pleasant or the painful, nor even pleasure or pain as such, but that within us to which pleasure and pain, the pleasant and the painful, speak. It is the source of effort and attention, and the place from which appear to emanate the fiats of the will. (vol. 1, pp. 297–298)

This is essentially James's answer to Hume, who had famously declared that upon looking within he could only find particular sensations, images, feelings, and thoughts, and never his "self." But the dominant position in contemporary psychology, neuroscience, and philosophy derives from Hume, not from James. Particularly with the recent rise of connectionism and dynamic systems theory (Chapter 1), our experience of ourselves as causally effective agents has come increasingly to be portrayed as mere illusion, with consciousness itself at best a causally ineffectual by-product of the grinding of our neural machinery. There is in reality nobody in charge, no executive. We are nothing but self-organizing packs of neurons. "Subjectless processes" do all the work. Pronouncements of this general type abound, for example, in recent books and papers by prominent figures such as the Churchlands, Francis Crick, Daniel Dennett, Jean-Pierre Dupuy, Gerald Edelman, Walter Freeman, Douglas Hofstadter, Steven Pinker, and numerous others.

Possibly the most extreme specimen to date of this genre is the book by Harvard psychologist Daniel Wegner (2002). Having identified Dennett in his preface as a primary intellectual influence, and having then quoted on page 1 Laplace's 1814 description of the mechanical clockwork universe as an epitome of the scientifically proper view of things, Wegner proceeds with no apparent sense of irony or paradox to generate some 400 pages of argument in support of Thomas Huxley's original claim that our experience of conscious will as causally efficacious is entirely illusory. Nothing could more aptly summarize our own estimation of such views than the caustic remark by Whitehead (1929/1958) that "scientists animated by the purpose of proving themselves purposeless constitute an interesting subject for study" (p. 16). Could anything possibly be more remote from the views of William James, for whom conscious will was a living and undeniable reality, and the active regulation of our conscious mental life its essential manifestation?[48]

We believe that these extraordinary mainstream conclusions, so deeply at odds with the most fundamental deliverances of everyday experience, result from correctly perceiving what are in fact necessary consequences of the classical materialist-monist premises from which practically all of contemporary psychology, neuroscience, and philosophy derive. We further contend that disastrous consequences of this magnitude ought to be recognized by everybody for what they really are, a *reductio ad absurdum* of those materialist-monist premises themselves. The only possible justification for clinging to results so monstrous must be the belief that there is no alternative, no scientifically legitimate way of avoiding them. But we have clearly shown, we submit, that this belief is mistaken.

In sum, then, to move in the theoretical directions outlined here seems to us both necessitated by a wide range of empirical data and scientifically justified at the foundational level of physics itself. Which of the main types of theory we have distinguished will ultimately prove most satisfactory, and indeed whether they *are* in the end meaningfully different types of theory, remains to be seen. But *something* along these lines seems to us sure to emerge, however long this may take, and we predict with high confidence that psychology will not end up, as many have feared, being cannibalized either by neurophysiology or by sociology.

Our theoretical suggestions are responsive to Chomsky's repeated pleas for "unification" between an empirically adequate psychology and a deepened conception of its physical basis (Introduction), and they restore the most mature concerns of our most luminous predecessor, William James—which have been systematically ignored by mainstream psychology for over a century—to the place which he himself believed they should rightfully occupy at the center of our science. In effect we seem to have come full circle, to a view of human nature much like that advanced by Myers, James, and their

---

48. This is not to say, of course, that *all* of our actions are *fully* under conscious supraliminal control. Both Myers and James recognized that aspects of experience and behavior are sometimes controlled in part or in whole by transmarginal influences of various kinds, whether automatic or "infrared" processes originating in the organism or "ultraviolet" influences exerted by a wider subliminal consciousness.

colleagues. But we emphatically do not see this as a matter of going backward to something already fully formed, already completed and perfected at their hands and ready to be adopted *as is*. It would be more accurate to say that we have reached the corresponding point on the next higher turn of a spiral. For their basic picture of the human psyche can now be anchored to physical science at a much deeper level, and the further development of that picture can surely capitalize on the tremendous methodological and technical advances that have been achieved in the intervening century.

The expanded scientific psychology that would result from such efforts can potentially overcome the great historical divisions within psychology, while also strengthening its principal domains individually. In general terms we can readily foresee, for example, a deepened cognitive mainstream in which the present elevation of the physical or physiological at the expense of consciousness and the mental has been essentially inverted. Computational modeling in all its forms would be downgraded from a general theory of the mind to a useful but limited applications technology (Searle, 1992). Consciousness would be more widely recognized as *the* constitutive problem of the field (G. A. Miller, 1985), and far greater resources and effort would be allocated than at present to research focused upon relationships between unusual states of consciousness and brain processes, as for example in psychophysiological and neuroimaging studies of OBEs and NDEs, psychedelics, meditation and related transformative practices, mystical experience, and other altered states. More penetrating investigations of psychophysical influence and psychological automatisms along lines suggested in Chapters 3 and 5 are surely in order, and there would also be greatly increased emphasis on currently unsolved problems in cognitive and personality theory—in particular, unsolved problems in regard to intentionality, meaning, symbolism, memory, personal identity, selfhood, and volition—that are deeply intertwined and central to our concerns as human beings.

We can also imagine a revitalization of dynamic psychiatry, complementary to the current vogue in biological psychiatry, that would result in development of new and potentially more effective forms of dynamic therapy, fuller exploration of the "mythopœtic" dimensions of human personality (Ellenberger, 1970), and more satisfactory approaches to socially and personally vital issues such as end-of-life care. Transpersonal psychology, similarly, can certainly be brought into better relationship with the mainstream, with its central impulses and concerns grounded primarily in real empirical knowledge rather than faith in the wisdom traditions. We also anticipate the development of a new generation of improved transformative practices, tools for refashioning ourselves in accordance with the enlarged psychology, that will enable many more of us to draw more efficiently and systematically upon normally inaccessible interior resources of imagination, creativity, and spirituality.

The key to this fundamentally optimistic vision, we repeat, is to build upon the foundation prepared by Myers and James. No other system of psychology has seriously rivaled its unique combination of unremitting commitment to empirical rigor with courage to embrace the supernormal and transpersonal phenomena that are essential to a fuller understanding of human mind and personality. Not that it should be regarded as a finished product, of course—surely the last thing either of them would have imagined or wished. It is rather a working guide, a provisional map of the territory, to be fleshed out and further improved by the labors of coming generations. Indeed, we can do no better here, in concluding both this chapter and our book as a whole, than to appropriate one last statement from Myers himself, as relevant today as when he first wrote it:

> The research on which my friends and I are engaged is not the mere hobby of a few enthusiasts. Our opinions, of course, are individual and disputable; but the *facts* presented here and in the S.P.R. *Proceedings* are a very different matter. Neither the religious nor the scientific reader can longer afford to ignore them, to pass them by. They must be met, they must be understood, unless Science and Religion alike are to sink into mere obscurantism. And the one and only way to understand them is to learn more of them; to collect more evidence, to try more experiments, to bring to bear on this study a far more potent effort of the human mind than the small group who have thus far been at work can possibly furnish. Judged by this standard, the needed help has still to come. Never was there a harvest so plenteous with labourers so few. (*HP*, vol. 2, p. 80)

Appendix

Introductory Bibliography of Psychical Research

This annotated list is intended only to provide an entry into the vast literature of serious psychical research. It is by no means complete or even comprehensive, and it reflects to some degree our personal preferences, although many if not most of our selections would probably also appear on similar lists compiled by other knowledgeable professionals. Many of the entries cited contain extensive bibliographies of their own. For additional references to some of the basic literature of the field, see http://www.pflyceum.org/106.html.

Introductory and General Scientific Literature

Broughton, Richard S. (1992). *Parapsychology: The Controversial Science.* New York: Ballantine. A good general introduction to the problems, findings, and implications of the science of parapsychology.

Edge, Hoyt L., Morris, Robert L., Rush, Joseph H., & Palmer, John (1986). *Foundations of Parapsychology: Exploring the Boundaries of Human Capability.* London: Routledge & Kegan Paul. An advanced, textbook-style survey of methods and findings in modern parapsychology, emphasizing experimental studies.

Krippner, Stanley (Ed.) (1977–1997). *Advances in Parapsychological Research* (8 vols.). An ongoing series reviewing recent research on a wide variety of topics of current interest to parapsychologists, including occasional bibliographic updates of the literature.

Murphy, Michael (1992). *The Future of the Body: Explorations into the Further Evolution of Human Nature.* New York: Tarcher/Putnam. An extensive survey and classification of phenomena bearing on the question of the evolution of human nature, as suggested in particular by latent, or as yet not fully realized, attributes and capacities for transcendence and transformation. In this context the author describes a variety of effects of mental states on the body, as well as numerous transformative practices. Several appendices and a large bibliography guide the reader to an enormous wealth of literature on the topics surveyed.

Pratt, J. G., Rhine, J. B., Smith, B. M., Stuart, C. E., & Greenwood, J. A. (1940). *Extra-Sensory Perception After Sixty Years: A Critical Appraisal of the Research in Extra-Sensory Perception*. New York: Henry Holt. One of the classics of experimental parapsychology which, despite its age, is still a valuable overview of the early research at Duke. Includes responses to all meaningful experimental and statistical criticisms advanced up to that date.

Radin, Dean R. (1997). *The Conscious Universe: The Scientific Truth of Psychic Phenomena*. New York: Harper Edge. An excellent recent survey, particularly good in terms of its overall assessments of several large areas of contemporary experimental psi research.

Radin, Dean R. (2006). *Entangled Minds: Extrasensory Experiences in a Quantum Reality*. New York: Simon & Schuster. The author presents updated meta-analyses for several large areas of psi research (including Ganzfeld research) and argues that the "entangled" reality revealed by quantum mechanics is more congenial to psi than that postulated by classical physics.

Rao, K. Ramakrishna (Ed.) (2001). *Basic Research in Parapsychology* (2nd ed.). Jefferson, NC: McFarland. A collection of previously published journal reports of important experimental studies.

Tyrrell, G. N. M. (1961). *Science and Psychical Phenomena* and *Apparitions*. New Hyde Park, NY: University Books. The first title in this volume contains an overview of spontaneous cases of psi, experimental evidence, and trance mediumship. The second title is a classic discussion of studies of apparitions and the several interpretations of them, including Tyrrell's own.

Ullman, Montague, & Krippner, Stanley (with Alan Vaughan) (1989). *Dream Telepathy* (2nd ed.). Jefferson, NC: McFarland. A report of the experiments on telepathic dreams conducted at Maimonides Medical Center in New York, plus a limited survey of spontaneous dream telepathy cases.

Wolman, B. B. (Ed.) (1985). *Handbook of Parapsychology*. Jefferson, NC: McFarland (first published in 1977 by Van Nostrand Reinhold). A large book with technical papers on a wide variety of topics, written by specialists mainly for scientists, but containing abundant details and references to other publications for readers wishing to study the subject more deeply.

Spontaneous Case Studies

Gurney, Edmund, Myers, Frederic, & Podmore, Frank (1886). *Phantasms of the Living* (2 vols.). London: Trübner. A classic and the first major publication of the Society for Psychical Research, primarily reporting hundreds of spontaneous cases investigated and documented by the authors, with emphasis on apparitions coinciding with the death of a distantly located person. Indispensable reading for anyone seriously interested in psychical research. Contains sophisticated discussions of problems of evidence and methods for investigating spontaneous cases.

Prince, Walter Franklin (1963). *Noted Witnesses for Psychic Occurrences.* New Hyde Park, NY: University Books. Prince collected in this volume numerous first-hand accounts from well-known scientists, artists, statesmen, and professionals from a wide variety of fields, describing apparently paranormal experiences that they themselves had. Prince believed that such reports from people who were otherwise known to be responsible, intelligent observers and who had reputations that could be damaged by a fraudulent or fictional account would help raise the credibility of all reports of spontaneous paranormal experiences.

Rhine, Louisa E. (1981). *The Invisible Picture: A Study of Psychic Experiences.* Jefferson, NC: McFarland. Summary of the author's research, spanning several decades, on reports of spontaneous psychic experiences.

Sidgwick, Eleanor Mildred (1962). *Phantasms of the Living.* New Hyde Park, NY: University Books. A volume consisting of two classic studies of spontaneous cases: A survey, first published by Mrs. Sidgwick in 1922, of spontaneous cases of telepathy and apparitions reported to the Society for Psychical Research between 1886 and 1920; and an abridged version of the 1886 volume *Phantasms of the Living* by Gurney, Myers, and Podmore (see above).

Sidgwick, H., Johnson, A., Myers, A. T., Myers, F. W. H., Podmore, F., & Sidgwick, E. (1894). Report of the Census of Hallucinations. *Proceedings of the Society for Psychical Research, 10,* 25–422. Report of a survey of 17,000 persons which demonstrated the frequent occurrence of hallucinatory experiences in normal, healthy persons in a waking state. Many of the experiences reported coincided closely in time with a crisis, such as the death of a distant person, and the authors made quantitative evaluations suggesting that such experiences occur more often than can be expected by chance.

Stevenson, Ian (1970). *Telepathic Impressions: A Review and Report of 35 New Cases.* Charlottesville: University Press of Virginia. A review and analysis of 160 previously published cases in which a person has a strong impression about something happening to another person who is physically distant, followed by reports of Stevenson's investigations of 35 new cases.

Philosophical Literature

Braude, Stephen E. (1979). *ESP and Psychokinesis: A Philosophical Examination.* Philadelphia: Temple University Press. A discussion of some of the experimental evidence for psi phenomena, as well as conceptual and philosophical issues associated with them.

Braude, Stephen E. (1986). *The Limits of Influence: Psychokinesis and the Philosophy of Science.* New York, London: Routledge & Kegan Paul. Braude examines evidence for large-scale phenomena of psychokinesis, arguing that much of the evidence is of high quality and that it can and must be incorporated into the framework of science.

Broad, C. D. (1962). *Lectures on Psychical Research.* New York: Humanities Press. Primarily a series of lectures given in 1959–1960 at Cambridge University by Broad, a philosopher at Cambridge, presenting and discussing some of the experimental evidence, trance mediumship, and studies of what Broad called "hallucinatory quasi-perceptions" (including apparitions, dreams, and out-of-body experiences).

Griffin, David Ray (1997). *Parapsychology, Philosophy, and Spirituality: A Postmodern Exploration.* Albany: SUNY Press. A review of the evidence from psi research, with an emphasis on the empirical evidence for post-mortem survival, in the context of Griffin's contention that psi research has been largely rejected or ignored because it challenges both the supernaturalism of religion and the materialism of modern science. He argues that it provides the framework for a much-needed postmodern world view that can go beyond this dichotomy and reconcile the two within a larger perspective.

Price, H. H. (1995). *Philosophical Interactions with Parapsychology: The Major Writings of H. H. Price on Parapsychology and Survival* (Frank B. Dilley, Ed.). New York: St. Martin's Press. In this volume Dilley brings together many of the extensive and important writings of H. H. Price (1899–1984), an Oxford philosopher, about the theoretical implications of psi research in general and about theoretical issues underlying the notion of post-mortem survival.

Wheatley, J. M. O., & Edge, H. (1976). *Philosophical Dimensions of Parapsychology.* Springfield, IL: Charles C Thomas. A collection of articles by 21 philosophers and scientists, published between 1937 and 1973, on the implications of various kinds of psi phenomena for philosophy and science.

Survival and Mediumship

Braude, Stephen E. (2003). *Immortal Remains: The Evidence for Life after Death.* Lanham, MD: Rowman & Littlefield. Braude examines various kinds of evidence for survival, including mental mediumship, reincarnation and possession cases, hauntings, and out-of-body experiences, especially in the context of the survival/super-psi interpretations of them. He concludes that the cumulative weight of the evidence may be tipping the scales slightly toward survival.

Dodds, E. R. (1934). Why I do not believe in survival. *Proceedings of the Society for Psychical Research, 42*, 147–172. A classic statement advocating the super-psi interpretation of survival evidence, written by a keen student of the literature.

Ducasse, C. J. (1961). *A Critical Examination of the Belief in Life After Death.* Springfield, IL: Charles C Thomas. A philosophical examination of the idea of life after death, encompassing religious, scientific, philosophical, and empirical views. Contains an extensive discussion of the concept of reincarnation.

Gauld, Alan (1982). *Mediumship and Survival: A Century of Investigations.* London: Heinemann. A review of different types of evidence for survival, especially mental mediumship, but also reincarnation, possession, out-of-body experiences, and apparitions. Gauld also discusses theoretical positions, as well as methodological and philosophical problems. See also his earlier and briefer discussion of the same material: Gauld, A. (1977). Discarnate survival. In B. B. Wolman (Ed.), *Handbook of Parapsychology* (pp. 577–630). New York: Van Nostrand Reinhold.

Hart, Hornell (1959). *The Enigma of Survival.* Springfield, IL: Charles C Thomas. A review of some of the evidence for post-mortem survival from mediumship and from apparitions, followed by a comprehensive review of the arguments both for and against the competing interpretations of this evidence.

Murphy, Gardner (1945). (a) An outline of survival evidence; (b) Difficulties confronting the survival hypothesis; (c) Field theory and survival. *Journal of the American Society for Psychical Research, 39*, 2–34, 67–94, 181–209. These papers by a distinguished American psychologist bring the difficulties of the survival debate into sharp focus.

Myers, Frederic W. H. (1903). *Human Personality and Its Survival of Bodily Death* (2 vols.). London: Longmans, Green. A major classic of early psychical research, and indeed of psychology, in which Myers describes a wide range of subliminal psychological phenomena, including dissociation, sleep, genius, hypnotism, automatisms, and trance, within the context of his theory of human personality as extending beyond the confines of normal psychophysiological functioning.

Salter, W. H. (1950). *Trance Mediumship: An Introductory Study of Mrs. Piper and Mrs. Leonard.* London: Society for Psychical Research. Contains introductory discussions of two of the most important trance mediums, as well as a valuable bibliography of the research literature on mediumship.

Saltmarsh, H. F. (1930). *Evidence of Survival from Cross-Correspondences.* London: G. Bell. A readable introduction to one of the most interesting but difficult bodies of evidence suggestive of post-mortem survival.

Stevenson, Ian (1984). *Unlearned Language: New Studies in Xenoglossy.* Charlottesville: University Press of Virginia. Certainly the best account to date of this rare but important phenomenon, in which a person demonstrates the ability to speak responsively a language not learned normally. Includes detailed reports of two cases that Stevenson investigated.

Stevenson, Ian (1977). Research into the evidence of man's survival after death: A historical and critical survey with a summary of recent developments. *Journal of Nervous and Mental Disease, 165,* 152–170. A brief but scholarly and well-documented summary of the main lines of research on post-mortem survival.

Reincarnation

Shroder, Tom (1999). *Old Souls: The Scientific Evidence for Past Lives.* New York: Simon & Schuster. In 1997 Tom Shroder, an editor at the *Washington Post,* accompanied Dr. Ian Stevenson through India, Lebanon, and the United States as Dr. Stevenson investigated cases of children who seem to remember previous lives. This is Shroder's book about those experiences. Now also out in paperback as *Old Souls: Compelling Evidence from Children Who Remember Past Lives* from Fireside Books.

Stevenson, Ian (1974). *Twenty Cases Suggestive of Reincarnation* (2nd ed., revised and enlarged). Charlottesville: University Press of Virginia. Dr. Stevenson's first book on what has become an extensive body of research. Includes detailed reports of 20 cases of children (from five different countries) who claimed to remember previous lives.

Stevenson, Ian (1975–1983). *Cases of the Reincarnation Type* (vols. 1–4). Charlottesville: University Press of Virginia. Reports of 44 cases of the reincarnation type in India, Sri Lanka, Lebanon, Turkey, Burma, and Thailand, investigated extensively by the author.

Stevenson, Ian (1997). *Reincarnation and Biology: A Contribution to the Etiology of Birthmarks and Birth Defects* (2 vols.). Westport, CT: Praeger. These volumes deal with an important subset of cases of the reincarnation type, cases in which living subjects manifest birthmarks or birth defects, often of extremely unusual character, usually corresponding to injuries that killed the ostensible previous person. Contains reports of over 200 cases, as well as important discussions of the relationship between this phenomenon and other kinds of phenomena demonstrating the effects of mental states on the body. (A 200-page synopsis of this work is available in *Where Reincarnation and Biology Intersect.* Westport, CT: Praeger, 1997.)

Stevenson, Ian (2003). *European Cases of the Reincarnation Type.* Jefferson, NC: McFarland. With this volume Dr. Stevenson shows that cases of the reincarnation type occur in modern Western cultures, many of them similar to those from Asian countries in which a belief in reincarnation is widespread. He describes some cases from early in the 20th century, and then reports 32 cases that he himself investigated.

Stevenson, Ian (2001). *Children Who Remember Previous Lives: A Question of Reincarnation* (Rev. ed.). Jefferson, NC: McFarland. Dr. Stevenson describes, for the general reader, research conducted over the past 40 years on the phenomenon of young children who seem to remember a previous life. He also addresses some of the questions frequently asked about these cases.

Tucker, Jim B. (2005). *Life Before Life: A Scientific Investigation of Children's Memories of Previous Lives.* New York: St. Martin's. An excellent introduction for the general reader to investigations, conducted by Dr. Tucker, Dr. Ian Stevenson, and other colleagues, of cases suggestive of reincarnation among young children. Included are discussions of the memories reported by the children, unusual behavior in the children, and birthmarks and birth defects apparently related to the previous life.

History of Psychical Research

Beloff, John (1997). *Parapsychology: A Concise History.* New York: St. Martin's. A brief historical survey of the field from its origins in renaissance magic, mesmerism, and spiritualism, through 19th-century psychical research, early 20th-century psychical research and experimental parapsychology, to more recent developments.

Gauld, Alan (1968). *Founders of Psychical Research.* New York: Schocken Books. The best available treatment of the persons and events involved in the formation and early work of the Society for Psychical Research.

James, William (1986). *The Works of William James: Essays in Psychical Research.* Cambridge: Harvard University Press. A comprehensive collection of all of James's known writings on the subject of psychical research, from 1869–1909, including papers, reviews, and correspondence. Includes all the works published in an earlier volume (Murphy, Gardner, & Ballou, Robert O. [1961]. *William James on Psychical Research.* London: Chatto & Windus).

Mauskopf, Seymour H., & McVaugh, Michael R. (1980). *The Elusive Science: Origins of Experimental Psychical Research.* Baltimore, London: Johns Hopkins University Press. A comprehensive, well-documented, and scholarly history of the development of experimental psi research, concentrating primarily on the period from 1920–1940.

Meta-Analyses, Reviews, and Selected Journal Articles on Experimental Studies

DMILS (Distant Mental Influence on Living Systems)

Braud, W. (2003). *Distant Mental Influence.* Charlottesville, VA: Hampton Roads. A collection of papers previously published by Braud and colleagues of experimental studies showing that the intentions of one person can influence physiological processes of other organisms, including other persons. See also Chapter 3 in the present volume for additional references.

Ganzfeld

Bem, D. J., & Honorton, C. (1994). Does psi exist? Replicable evidence for an anomalous process of information transfer. *Psychological Bulletin, 115*, 4–18. Report and meta-analysis of a series of psi Ganzfeld experiments, in which subjects in a condition of sensory deprivation attempt to identify a randomly chosen target image. A critical response to this paper was Milton, J. & Wiseman, R. (1999). Does psi exist? Lack of replication of an anomalous process of information transfer. *Psychological Bulletin, 125*, 378–391. A reply to these criticisms appeared in Bem, D. J., Palmer, J., & Broughton, R. S. (2001). Updating the Ganzfeld database: A victim of its own success? *Journal of Parapsychology, 65*, 207–218.

Honorton, C. (1985). Meta-analysis of the psi ganzfeld research: A response to Hyman. *Journal of Parapsychology, 49*, 51–91.

Honorton, C., Berger, R., Varvoglis, M., Quant, M., Derr, P., Schechter, E., & Ferrari, D. (1990). Psi communication in the ganzfeld: Experiments with an automated testing system and a comparison with a meta-analysis of earlier studies. *Journal of Parapsychology, 54*, 99–139.

Hyman, R. & Honorton, C. (1986). A joint communiqué: The psi Ganzfeld controversy. *Journal of Parapsychology, 50*, 351–364. In response to their continuing debate about the status of the Ganzfeld research, Honorton, a parapsychologist, and Hyman, a skeptic, issued here a set of guidelines for conducting and reporting future research that they both agreed would constitute adequately stringent standards. The papers by Honorton et al. (1990) and Bem and Honorton (1994) (see above) report research conducted using these guidelines.

Rosenthal, R. (1986). Meta-analytic procedures and the nature of replication: The ganzfeld debate. *Journal of Parapsychology, 50*, 315–336.

Hypnosis and Psi

Honorton, C., & Krippner, S. (1969). Hypnosis and ESP performance: A review of the experimental literature. *Journal of the American Society for Psychical Research*, *63*, 214–252.

Schechter, E. (1984). Hypnotic induction vs. control conditions: Illustrating an approach to the evaluation of replicability in parapsychological data. *Journal of the American Society for Psychical Research*, *78*, 1–27.

Stanford, R. G., & Stein, A. G. (1994). A meta-analysis of ESP studies contrasting hypnosis and a comparison condition. *Journal of Parapsychology*, *58*, 235–269.

Van De Castle, R. L. (1969). The facilitation of ESP through hypnosis. *American Journal of Clinical Hypnosis*, *12*, 37–56.

Statistics and Meta-Analyses

Honorton, C., & Ferrari, D. (1990). "Future telling": A meta-analysis of forced-choice precognition experiments, 1935–1987. *Journal of Parapsychology*, *53*, 281–308.

Honorton, C., Ferrari, D., & Bem, D. (1998). Extraversion and ESP performance: A meta-analysis and a new confirmation. *Journal of Parapsychology*, *62*, 255–276.

Radin, D., & Ferrari, D. (1991). Effects of consciousness on the fall of dice: A meta-analysis. *Journal of Scientific Exploration*, *5*, 61–83.

Radin, D., & Nelson, R. D. (1989). Consciousness-related effects in random physical systems. *Foundations of Physics*, *19*, 1499–1514.

Utts, J. (1991). Replication and meta-analysis in parapsychology. *Statistical Science*, *6*, 363–403.

The Psi Controversy

This is a small but representative selection from a very large literature, intended to illustrate the character of the debates. Some of the books and articles listed above also include substantial discussions of the critical literature, including Broad (1962), Broughton (1991), Griffin (1997), and Radin (1997).

Alcock, J. (1990). *Science and Supernature: A Critical Appraisal of Parapsychology.* Buffalo, NY: Prometheus. Alcock, a social psychologist and committed skeptic, argues that there is no persuasive evidence for any paranormal phenomena and that it is a belief system rather than science.

Child, I. L. (1985). Psychology and anomalous observations: The question of ESP in dreams. *American Psychologist, 40*, 1219–1230. Reviews the Maimonides dream telepathy studies (see Ullman & Krippner volume, above) and criticisms of them by skeptical psychologists.

Druckman, D., & Swets, J. A. (Eds.). (1988). *Enhancing Human Performance: Issues, Theories, and Techniques*, pp. 169–231. Washington, DC: National Academy Press; Palmer, J. A., Honorton, C., & Utts, J. (1988). *Reply to the National Research Council Study on Parapsychology.* Research Triangle Park, NC: Parapsychological Association. A report from the National Research Council which concluded that research in parapsychology has provided "no scientific justification...for the existence of parapsychological phenomena." In the reply, the authors show that the scope of this review was severely restricted to conform to the authors' pre-existing beliefs, even to the extent of asking a prominent psychologist to withdraw his favorable conclusions.

Hansel, C. E. M. (1966). *ESP: A Scientific Evaluation*. New York: Charles Scribner's Sons; and (1980). *ESP and Parapsychology: A Critical Re-evaluation.* Buffalo, NY: Prometheus. One of the best-known of the critical books, but one which demonstrates the lengths to which critics must go to uphold their conclusions. The second volume took no account of the serious criticisms of the first volume, such as Honorton, C. (1967). *ESP: A Scientific Evaluation*. C. E. M. Hansel, Review. *Journal of Parapsychology, 31*, 76–82; Pratt, J. G., & Woodruff, J. L. (1961). Refutation of Hansel's allegation concerning the Pratt-Woodruff series. *Journal of Parapsychology, 25*, 114–129; Rhine, J. B., & Pratt, J. G. (1961). A reply to the Hansel critique of the Pearce-Pratt series. *Journal of Parapsychology, 25*, 92–98; or Stevenson, I. (1967). An antagonist's view of parapsychology. A review of Professor Hansel's *ESP: A Scientific Evaluation. Journal of the American Society for Psychical Research, 61*, 254–267.

Kurtz, Paul (Ed.) (1985). *A Skeptic's Handbook of Parapsychology.* Buffalo, NY: Prometheus. A large volume of papers primarily by critics of the field, published under the auspices of the Committee for the Scientific Investigation of Claims of the Paranormal.

Price, George R. (1955). Science and the supernatural. *Science, 122*, 359–367. A paper often cited by skeptics, who nonetheless rarely if ever mention Price's later apology to Rhine for the accusations of fraud that he made against him in this paper (Price, George R. [1972]. Letter to the editor. *Science, 175*, 359).

Rao, K. R. & Palmer, J. (1987). The anomaly called psi: Recent research and criticism. *Behavioral and Brain Sciences, 10*, 539–643. A lead positive review article on the then current status of experimental psi research, followed by a second, negative target article by James Alcock, with numerous commentaries on both articles and responses from their authors.

Utts, J. (1996). An assessment of the evidence for psychic functioning; Hyman, R. (1996). Evaluation of a program on anomalous mental phenomena; Utts, J. (1996). Response to Hyman. *Journal of Scientific Exploration, 10,* 3–61. The evaluations by a statistician and a skeptical psychologist primarily of remote-viewing experiments carried out in some government-sponsored research programs.

Zusne, L., & Jones, W. H. (1989). *Anomalistic Psychology: A Study of Magical Thinking* (2nd ed.). Hillside, NJ: Lawrence Erlbaum. A textbook intended to show students that there are normal psychological explanations for a variety of apparently anomalous phenomena involving psychophysiology, perception, and memory. The authors also discuss the psychology of belief in the context of the occult and of magic, and conclude that parapsychology is "bad science" on grounds that most of it, they claim, involves either inappropriate or fraudulent research.

References

Abbot, N. C. (2000). Healing as a therapy for human disease: A systematic review. Journal of Alternative and Complementary Medicine, 6, 159–169.

Abramovitch, H. (1988). An Israeli account of a near-death experience: A case study of cultural dissonance. *Journal of Near-Death Studies, 6*, 175–184.

Abrams, M. H. (1958). *The Mirror and the Lamp: Romantic Theory and the Critical Tradition*. New York: Norton.

Achterberg, J. (1985). *Imagery in Healing*. Boston: New Science Library.

Ader, R. (1997). The role of conditioning in pharmacotherapy. In A. Harrington (Ed.), *The Placebo Effect: An Interdisciplinary Exploration* (pp. 138–165). Cambridge: Harvard University Press.

Ader, R. (2000). The placebo: If it's all in your head, does that mean you only think you feel better? *Advances in Mind-Body Medicine, 16*, 7–11.

Ader, R., & Cohen, N. (1975). Behaviorally conditioned immunosuppression. *Psychosomatic Medicine, 37*, 333–340.

Agnati, L. F., Bjelke, B., & Fuxe, K. (1992). Volume transmission in the brain. *American Scientist, 80*, 362–373.

Alberini, C. M. (2005). Mechanisms of memory stabilization: Are consolidation and reconsolidation similar or different processes? *Trends in Neurosciences, 28*, 51–56.

Albin, R. L. (2002). Sham surgery controls: Intracerebral grafting of fetal tissue for Parkinson's disease and proposed criteria for use of sham surgery controls. *Journal of Medical Ethics, 28*, 322–325.

Alcock, J. E. (1981). *Parapsychology: Science or Magic? A Psychological Perspective*. Oxford: Pergamon.

Aldrich, C. K. (1972). A case of recurrent pseudocyesis. *Perspectives in Biology and Medicine, 16*, 11–21.

Alkire, M. T. (1998). Quantitative EEG correlations with brain glucose metabolic rate during anesthesia in volunteers. *Anesthesiology, 89*, 323–333.

Alkire, M. T., Haier, R. J., & Fallon, J. H. (2000). Toward a unified theory of narcosis: Brain imaging evidence for a thalamocortical switch as the neurophysiologic basis of anesthetic-induced unconsciousness. *Consciousness and Cognition, 9*, 370–386.

Allison, R. (1980). *Mind in Many Pieces*. New York: Rawson, Wade.

Alvarado, C. S. (1987). Observations of luminous phenomena around the human body: A review. *Journal of the Society for Psychical Research*, *54*, 38–60.

Alvarado, C. S. (1989). Dissociation and state-specific psychophysiology during the nineteenth century. *Dissociation*, *2*, 160–168.

Alvarado, C. S. (1998). ESP and altered states of consciousness: An overview of conceptual and research trends. *Journal of Parapsychology*, *62*, 27–63.

Alvarado, C. S. (2000). Out-of-body experiences. In E. Cardeña, S. J. Lynn, & S. Krippner (Eds.), *Varieties of Anomalous Experience: Examining the Scientific Evidence* (pp. 183–218). Washington, DC: American Psychological Association.

Amanzio, M., & Benedetti, F. (1999). Neuropharmacological dissection of placebo analgesia: Expectation-activated opioid systems versus conditioning-activated specific subsystems. *Journal of Neuroscience*, *19*, 484–494.

Aminoff, M. J., Scheinman, M. M., Griffin, J. C., & Herre, J. M. (1988). Electrocerebral accompaniments of syncope associated with malignant ventricular arrhythmias. *Annals of Internal Medicine*, *108*, 791–796.

Anand, B. K., Chhina, G. S., & Singh, B. (1961a). Some aspects of electroencephalographic studies in yogis. *Electroencephalography and Clinical Neurophysiology*, *13*, 452–456.

Anand, B. K., Chhina, G. S., & Singh, B. (1961b). Studies on Shri Ramanand Yogi during his stay in an air-tight box. *Indian Journal of Medical Research*, *49*, 82–89.

Anderson, J. A., & Rosenfeld, E. (Eds.). (1988). *Neurocomputing: Foundations of Research*. Cambridge, MA: MIT Press.

Anderson, J. R. (1978). Arguments concerning representations for mental imagery. *Psychological Review*, *85*, 249–277.

Anderson, V., Northam, E., Hendy, J., & Wrennall, J. (2001). *Developmental Neuropsychology: A Clinical Approach*. Hove: Psychology Press.

Andreasen, N. C. (1987). Creativity and mental illness: Prevalence rates in writers and their first-degree relatives. *American Journal of Psychiatry*, *144*, 1288–1292.

Andreasen, N. (1997). Linking mind and brain in the study of mental illnesses: A project for a scientific psychopathology. *Science*, *275*, 1586–1593.

Andresen, J. (2000). Meditation meets behavioural medicine: The story of experimental research on meditation. *Journal of Consciousness Studies*, *7*, 17–73.

Angell, M. (1985). Editorial: Disease as a reflection of the psyche. *New England Journal of Medicine*, *312*, 1570–1572.

Anonymous. (1838). On the supposed sensibility and intelligence of insects. *Blackwood's Magazine*, *43*, 589–606.

Arbman, E. (1968). *Ecstasy and Religious Trance* (Vol. 2). Uppsala, Sweden: Humanistic Foundation.

Arshavsky, Y. I. (2003). Long-term memory: Does it have a structural or chemical basis? *Trends in Neurosciences, 26,* 465–466.

Asher, R. (1956). Respectable hypnosis. *British Medical Journal, 1,* 309–313.

Assagioli, R. (1971). *Psychosynthesis.* New York: Viking. (Original work published 1965)

Astin, J. A., Harkness, E., & Ernst, E. (2000). The efficacy of "distant healing": A systematic review of randomized trials. *Annals of Internal Medicine, 132,* 903–910.

Astin, J. A., Shapiro, S. L., Eisenberg, D. M., & Forys, K. L. (2003). Mind-body medicine: State of the science, implications for practice. *Journal of the American Board of Family Practitioners, 16,* 131–147.

Athappilly, G. K., Greyson, B., & Stevenson, I. (2006). Do prevailing societal models influence reports of near-death experiences? A comparison of accounts reported before and after 1975. *Journal of Nervous and Mental Disease, 194,* 218–222.

Athwal, B. S., Halligan, P. W., Fink, G. R., Marshall, J. C., & Frackowiak, R. S. J. (2001). Imaging hysterical paralysis. In P. W. Halligan, C. Bass, & J. C. Marshall (Eds.), *Contemporary Approaches to the Study of Hysteria* (pp. 216–234). Oxford: Oxford University Press.

Attneave, F. (1959). *Applications of Information Theory to Psychology.* New York: Holt, Rinehart & Winston.

Audette, J. (1982). Historical perspectives on near death episodes and experiences. In C. R. Lundahl (Ed.), *A Collection of Near Death Readings* (pp. 21–43). Chicago: Nelson Hall.

Austin, J. H. (1999). *Zen and the Brain.* Cambridge, MA: MIT Press.

Austin, J. H. (2000). Consciousness evolves when self dissolves. In J. Andresen & R. K. C. Forman (Eds.), *Cognitive Models and Spiritual Maps: Interdisciplinary Explorations of Religious Experience* (pp. 209–230). Thorverton, UK: Imprint Academic.

Aviles, J. M., Whelan, E., Hernke, D. A., Williams, B. A., Kenny, K. E., O'Fallon, W. M., & Kopecky, S. L. (2001). Intercessory prayer and cardiovascular disease progression in a coronary care unit population: A randomized controlled trial. *Mayo Clinic Proceedings, 76,* 1192–1198.

Ayer, A. J. (1952). *Language, Truth, and Logic.* New York: Dover.

Ayer, A. J. (1968). *The Origins of Pragmatism: Studies in the Philosophy of Charles Sanders Peirce and William James.* London: Macmillan.

Azam, E. (1887). *Hypnotisme, double conscience, et altérations de la personnalité.* Paris: J. B. Baillière.

Baars, B. J. (1988). *A Cognitive Theory of Consciousness.* Cambridge: Cambridge University Press.

Baars, B. J. (1993). How does a serial, integrated and very limited stream of consciousness emerge from a nervous system that is mostly unconscious, distributed, parallel and of enormous capacity? In G. R. Bock & J. Marsh (Eds.), *Experimental and Theoretical Studies of Consciousness* (pp. 282–290). Chichester, UK: Wiley-Interscience.

Baars, B. J. (1997). *In the Theater of Consciousness: The Workspace of the Mind.* New York: Oxford University Press.

Baars, B. J. (2001). The brain basis of a "consciousness monitor": Scientific and medical significance. *Consciousness and Cognition, 10,* 159–164.

Bacon, F. (1960). *The New Organon and Related Writings.* New York: Liberal Arts Press. (Original work published 1620)

Badash, L. (1972). The completeness of nineteenth-century science. *Isis, 63,* 48–58.

Baddawi, K., Wallace, R. K., Orme-Johnson, D., & Royzere, A. M. (1984). Electrophysiologic characteristics of respiratory suspension periods occurring during the practice of the Transcendental Meditation program. *Psychosomatic Medicine, 46,* 267–276.

Bahnson, C. B., & Smith, K. (1975). Autonomic changes in a multiple personality. *Psychosomatic Medicine, 37,* 85–86.

Bailar, J. C. (2001). The powerful placebo and the Wizard of Oz. *New England Journal of Medicine, 344,* 1630–1632.

Baillie, J. (1993). *Problems in Personal Identity.* New York: Paragon House.

Bain, A. (1874). *Mind and Body: The Theories of Their Relation.* New York: D. Appleton. (Original work published 1872)

Bakan, D. (1967). *On Method: Toward a Reconstruction of Psychological Investigation.* San Francisco: Jossey-Bass.

Baker, A. (2005). Are there genuine mathematical explanations of physical phenomena? *Mind, 114,* 223–238.

Baker, L. R. (1997). Persons in metaphysical perspective. In L. E. Hahn (Ed.), *The Philosophy of Roderick M. Chisholm* (pp. 433–453). La Salle, IL: Open Court.

Baker, L. R. (2000). *Persons and Bodies: A Constitution View.* Cambridge: Cambridge University Press.

Baker, L. R. (2001). Materialism with a human face. In K. Corcoran (Ed.), *Soul, Body and Survival* (pp. 159–180). Ithaca, NY: Cornell University Press.

Balfour, G. (1906). Presidential address. *Proceedings of the Society for Psychical Research, 19,* 373–396.

Balfour, G. (1935). A study of the psychological aspects of Mrs. Willett's mediumship, and of the statements of the communicators concerning process. *Proceedings of the Society for Psychical Research, 43,* 41–318.

Banquet, J. P. (1973). Spectral analysis of the EEG in meditation. *Electroencephalography and Clinical Neurophysiology, 35,* 143–151.

Barahal, H. S. (1940). The psychology of sudden and premature graying of hair. *Psychiatric Quarterly, 14,* 786–799.

Barahal, H. S., & Freeman, N. (1946). Sudden graying of hair, alopecia, and diabetes mellitus of psychogenic origin. *Psychiatric Quarterly, 20*, 31–38.

Barbato, M. (1999). Parapsychological phenomena near the time of death. *Journal of Palliative Care, 15*, 30–37.

Barber, B. (1961). Resistance by scientists to scientific discovery. *Science, 134*, 596–602.

Barber, T. X. (1961). Physiological effects of "hypnosis." *Psychological Bulletin, 58*, 390–419.

Barber, T. X. (1963). The effects of "hypnosis" on pain. *Psychosomatic Medicine, 25*, 303–333.

Barber, T. X. (1965). Physiological effects of "hypnotic suggestions": A critical review of recent research (1960-1964). *Psychological Bulletin, 63*, 201–222.

Barber, T. X. (1978). Hypnosis, suggestions, and psychosomatic phenomena: A new look from the standpoint of recent experimental studies. *American Journal of Clinical Hypnosis, 21*, 13–27.

Barber, T. X. (1984). Changing "unchangeable" bodily processes by (hypnotic) suggestions: A new look at hypnosis, cognitions, imagining, and the mind-body problem. In A. A. Sheikh (Ed.), *Imagination and Healing* (pp. 69–127). New York: Baywood Publishing. (Also published in 1984 in *Advances: Journal of the Institute for the Advancement of Health* [now *Advances in Mind-Body Medicine*], *1*, 7–40)

Barker, J. C. (1965). Scared to death? [letter]. *British Medical Journal, 2*, 591.

Barker, J. C. (1966). Scared to death [letter]. *Journal of the American Medical Association, 198*, 176.

Barker, J. C. (1968). *Scared to Death: An Examination of Fear, Its Causes and Effects*. London: Frederick Muller.

Barnard, G. W. (1997). *Exploring Unseen Worlds: William James and the Philosophy of Mysticism*. Albany: State University of New York Press.

Barrett, D. (1988). Trance-related pseudocyesis in a male. *International Journal of Clinical and Experimental Hypnosis, 36*, 256–261.

Barrett, D. (2001). *The Committee of Sleep*. New York: Crown.

Barrett, W. F. (1926). *Death-Bed Visions*. London: Methuen.

Barrett, W. F., Gurney, E., Hodgson, R., Myers, A. T., Myers, F. W. H., Ridley, H. N., Stone, W. H., Wyld, G., Robertson, C. L., & Podmore, F. (1883). Third report of the committee on mesmerism. *Proceedings of the Society for Psychical Research, 2*, 12–23. (Report written by Barrett & Gurney)

Barrett, W. F., Gurney, E., Myers, F. W. H., Ridley, H. N., Stone, W. H., Wyld, G., & Podmore, F. (1883). First report of the committee on mesmerism. *Proceedings of the Society for Psychical Research, l*, 217–229. (Report written by Barrett, Gurney, Myers, & Podmore)

Barrett, W. F., Massey, C. C., Moses, W. S., Podmore, F., Gurney, E., & Myers, F. W. H. (1883). Report of the literary committee. *Proceedings of the Society for Psychical Research, 1,* 116–155. (Report written by Gurney & Myers)

Barron, F. (1958). The psychology of imagination. *Scientific American, 199,* 150–166.

Barron, F. (1963). *Creativity and Psychological Health.* Princeton, NJ: Van Nostrand.

Barron, F. (1968). *Creativity and Personal Freedom* (Rev. ed.). New York: Van Nostrand.

Barron, F. (1969). *Creative Person and Creative Process.* New York: Holt, Reinhart, & Winston.

Barron F., & Harrington, D. (1981). Creativity, intelligence, and personality. *Annual Review of Psychology, 32,* 439–476.

Bartrop, R. W., Lazarus, L., Luckhurst, E., Kiloh, L. G., & Penny, R. (1977). Depressed lymphocyte function after bereavement. *Lancet, 1,* 834–836.

Barzun, J. (1983). *A Stroll with William James.* Chicago: University of Chicago Press.

Basmajian, J. V. (1977). Learned control of single motor units. In G. E. Schwartz & J. Beatty (Eds.), *Biofeedback: Theory and Research* (pp. 415–431). New York: Academic Press.

Basso, A., Gardelli, M., Grassi, M. P., & Mariotti, M. (1989). The role of the right hemisphere in recovery from aphasia: Two case studies. *Cortex, 25,* 555–566.

Batcheldor, K. J. (1984). Contributions to the theory of PK induction from sitter-group work. *Journal of the American Society for Psychical Research, 78,* 105–122.

Bauer, W. (1985). Near-death experiences and attitude change. *Anabiosis: The Journal for Near-Death Studies, 5,* 39–47.

Baxter, M. G. (2002). Memory and the medial temporal lobes: Differentiating the contribution of the primate rhinal cortex. In A. Parker, E. L. Wilding, & T. J. Bussey (Eds.), *The Cognitive Neuroscience of Memory: Encoding and Retrieval* (pp. 103–120). Hove: Psychology Press.

Beahrs, J. (1982). *Unity and Multiplicity: Multilevel Consciousness of Self in Hypnosis, Psychiatric Disorder and Mental Health.* New York: Brunner/Mazel.

Bear, M. F., Connors, B. W., & Paradiso, M. A. (2000). *Neuroscience: Exploring the Brain* (2nd ed.). Philadelphia: Lippincott Williams & Wilkins.

Bechtel, W., & Abrahamsen, A. (2002). *Connectionism and the Mind: Parallel Processing, Dynamics, and Evolution in Networks* (2nd ed.). Oxford: Blackwell.

Beck, F. C., & Eccles, J. C. (1992). Quantum aspects of brain activity and the role of consciousness. *Proceedings of the National Academy of Sciences USA, 89,* 11357–11361.

Becker, C. B. (1981). The centrality of near-death experiences in Chinese pure land Buddhism. *Anabiosis: The Journal for Near-Death Studies, 1,* 154–171.

Becker, C. B. (1982). The failure of Saganomics: Why birth models cannot explain near-death phenomena. *Anabiosis: The Journal for Near-Death Studies, 2*, 102–109.

Becker, C. B. (1984). The pure land revisited: Sino-Japanese meditations and near-death experiences of the next world. *Anabiosis: The Journal for Near-Death Studies*, *4*, 51–68.

Becker, D. E., & Shapiro, D. (1981). Physiological responses to clicks during Zen, Yoga, and TM meditation. *Psychophysiology*, *18*, 694–699.

Beddow, M. (1989). Goethe on genius. In P. Murray (Ed.), *Genius: The History of an Idea* (pp. 166–180). Oxford: Basil Blackwell.

Beecher, H. K. (1955). The powerful placebo. *Journal of the American Medical Association*, *159*, 1602–1606.

Beecher, H. K. (1961). Surgery as placebo: A quantitative study of bias. *Journal of the American Medical Association*, *176*, 1102–1107.

Beer, R. D. (2000). Dynamical approaches to cognitive science. *Trends in Cognitive Science*, *4*(3), 91–99.

Bellis, J. M. (1966). Hypnotic pseudo-sunburn. *American Journal of Clinical Hypnosis*, *8*, 310–312.

Bem, D. J., & Honorton, C. (1994). Does psi exist? Replicable evidence for an anomalous process of information transfer. *Psychological Bulletin, 115*, 4–18.

Benedetti, F., Collaco, L., Torre, E., Lanotte, M., Melcarne, A., Pesare, M., Bergamasco, B., & Lopiano, L. (2004). Placebo-responsive Parkinson patients show decreased activity in single neurons of subthalamic nucleus. *Nature Neuroscience*, *7*, 587–588.

Benedetti, F., Pollo, A., Lopiano, L., Lanotte, M., Vighetti, S., & Rainero, I. (2003). Conscious expectation and unconscious conditioning in analgesic, motor, and hormonal placebo/nocebo responses. *Journal of Neuroscience*, *23*, 4315–4323.

Bennett, M. R., & Hacker, P. M. S. (2003). *Philosophical Foundations of Neuroscience*. Oxford: Blackwell.

Benor, D. J. (1990). Survey of spiritual healing research. *Complementary Medical Research*, *4*, 9–33.

Benson, H., Dusek, J. A., Sherwood, J. B., Lam, P., Bethea, C. F., Carpenter, W., Levitsky, S., Hill, P. C., Clem, D. W., Jr., Jain, M. K., Drumel, D., Kopecky, S. L., Mueller, P. S., Marke, K., Rollins, S., & Hibberd, P. L. (2006). Study of the therapeutic effects of intercessory prayer (STEP) in cardiac bypass patients: A multicenter randomized trial of uncertainty and certainty of receiving intercessory prayer. *American Heart Journal*, *151*, 934–942.

Benson, H., & Epstein, M. D. (1975). The placebo effect: A neglected asset in the care of patients. *Journal of the American Medical Association*, *232*, 1225–1227.

Benson, H., Lehmann, J. W., Malhotra, M. S., Goldman, R. F., Hopkins, J., & Epstein, M. D. (1982). Body temperature changes during the practice of g Tum-mo yoga. *Nature*, *295*, 234–236.

Benson, H., & McCallie, D. P. (1979). Angina pectoris and the placebo effect. *New England Journal of Medicine*, *300*, 1424–1429.

Bentall, R. P. (2000). Hallucinatory experiences. In E. Cardeña, S. J. Lynn, & S. Krippner (Eds.), *Varieties of Anomalous Experience: Examining the Scientific Evidence* (pp. 85–120). Washington, DC: American Psychological Association.

Bergson, H. (1913). Presidential address (H. W. Carr, Trans.). *Proceedings of the Society for Psychical Research*, *27*, 157–175.

Bergson, H. (1991). *Matter and Memory* (N. M. Paul & W. S. Palmer, Trans.). New York: Zone Books. (Original 5th edition published 1908)

Berk, L. S., Tan, S. A., Fry, W. F., Napier, B. J., Lee, J. W., Hubbard, R. W., Lewis, J. E., & Eby, W. C. (1989). Neuroendocrine and stress hormone changes during mirthful laughter. *American Journal of the Medical Sciences*, *298*, 390–396.

Berne, R. M., & Levy, M. N. (1993). *Physiology* (3rd ed.). St. Louis: Mosby.

Besterman, T. (1929). Report of a four months' tour of psychical investigation. *Proceedings of the Society for Psychical Research*, *38*, 409–480.

Bethune, H. C., & Kidd, C. B. (1961). Psychophysiological mechanisms in skin diseases. *Lancet*, *2*, 1419–1422.

Bettley, F. R. (1952). Ichthyosis and hypnosis [letter]. *British Medical Journal*, *2*, 996.

Beyerstein, B. L. (1999). Pseudoscience and the brain: Tuners and tonics for aspiring superhumans. In S. Della Salla (Ed.), *Mind Myths: Exploring Popular Assumptions About the Mind and Brain* (pp. 59–82). Chichester, UK: John Wiley & Sons.

Biggs, M. H. (1887). Cases received by the literary committee. *Journal of the Society for Psychical Research*, *3*, 100–103.

Binet, A. (1890). *On Double Consciousness*. Chicago: Open Court.

Binet, A. (1896). *Alterations of Personality* (H. G. Green, Trans.). New York: D. Appleton. (Original work published 1891)

Binet, A., & Féré, C. (1888). *Animal Magnetism*. New York: Appleton.

Birnbaum, M. H., & Thomann, K. (1996). Visual function in multiple personality disorder. *Journal of the American Optometric Association*, *67*, 327–334.

Bishay, E. G., Stevens, G., & Lee, C. (1984). Hypnotic control of upper gastrointestinal hemorrhage: A case report. *American Journal of Clinical Hypnosis*, *27*, 22–25.

Bivin, G. D., & Klinger, M. P. (1937). *Pseudocyesis*. Bloomington, IN: Principia Press.

Black, M. (1962). *Models and Metaphors*. Ithaca, NY: Cornell University Press.

Black, M. (1990). *Perplexities: Rational Choice, the Prisoner's Dilemma, Metaphor, Poetic Ambiguity, and Other Puzzles*. Ithaca, NY: Cornell University Press.

Black, S., Humphrey, J. H., & Niven, J. S. F. (1963). Inhibition of Mantoux reaction by direct suggestion under hypnosis. *British Medical Journal*, *1*, 1649–1652.

Blackmore, S. (1982). *Beyond the Body: An Investigation of Out-of-the-Body Experiences*. London: Heinemann.

Blackmore, S. (1983a). Are out-of-body experiences evidence for survival? *Anabiosis: The Journal for Near-Death Studies, 3,* 137–155.

Blackmore, S. (1983b). Birth and the OBE: An unhelpful analogy. *Journal of the American Society for Psychical Research, 77,* 229–238.

Blackmore, S. (1984). A psychological theory of the out-of-body experience. *Journal of Parapsychology, 48,* 201–218.

Blackmore, S. (1993). *Dying to Live: Near-Death Experiences*. Buffalo, NY: Prometheus.

Blackmore, S. (1996). Near-death experiences. *Journal of the Royal Society of Medicine, 89,* 73–76.

Blanke, O., Landis, T., Spinelli, L., & Seeck, M. (2004). Out-of-body experience and autoscopy of neurological origin. *Brain, 127,* 243–258.

Blanke, O., Ortigue, S., Landis, T., & Seeck, M. (2002). Stimulating illusory own-body perceptions. *Nature, 419,* 269–270.

Block, N. (1986). Advertisement for a semantics for psychology. In P. A. French, T. E. Uehling, Jr., & H. K. Wettstein (Eds.), *Midwest Studies in Philosophy, Vol. 10: Studies in the Philosophy of Mind* (pp. 159–181). Minneapolis: University of Minneapolis Press.

Block, N. (1995). An argument for holism. *Proceedings of the Aristotelian Society, 95,* 151–169.

Block, N., Flanagan, O., & Güzeldere, G. (Eds.) (1997). *The Nature of Consciousness*. Cambridge, MA: MIT Press.

Blofeld, J. (1962). *The Zen Teaching of Hui Hai*. London: Rider.

Bloom, H. (2002). *Genius: A Mosaic of One Hundred Exemplary Creative Minds*. New York: Warner.

Bock, G. R., & Marsh, J. (Eds.) (1993). *Experimental and Theoretical Studies of Consciousness* (Ciba Foundation Symposium 174). Chichester, UK: John Wiley & Sons.

Boden, M. A. (1990). Escaping from the Chinese room. In M. A. Boden (Ed.), *The Philosophy of Artificial Intelligence* (pp. 89–104). New York: Oxford University Press.

Boden, M. A. (1991). *The Creative Mind: Myths and Mechanisms*. New York: Basic Books.

Boden, M. A. (1999). Computer models of creativity. In R. J. Sternberg (Ed.), *Handbook of Creativity* (pp. 351–372). New York: Cambridge University Press.

Bohm, D. J. (1986). A new theory of the relationship of mind to matter. *Journal of the American Society for Psychical Research, 80,* 113–135.

Boismont, A. B. de (1859). *On Hallucinations* (R. T. Hulme, Trans.). London: Henry Renshaw.

Boitnott, J. K., Friesinger, G. C., & Slavin, R. E. (1967). Clinicopathologic conference: Case presentation. *Johns Hopkins Medical Journal, 121*, 186–199.

Bonke, B., Fitch, W., & Millar, K. (Eds.) (1990). *Memory and Awareness in Anaesthesia.* Amsterdam: Swets & Zeitlinger.

Boring, E. G. (1933). *The Physical Dimensions of Consciousness.* London: Century.

Bourgignon, E. (1973). *Religion, Altered States of Consciousness and Social Change.* Columbus: Ohio State University Press.

Bourru, H., & Burot, P. (1888). *Variations de la personnalité.* Paris: J. B. Baillière.

Bourtchouladze, R. (2002). *Memories Are Made of This.* London: Weidenfeld & Nicolson.

Bowers, K. S. (1979). Hypnosis and healing. *Australian Journal of Clinical and Experimental Hypnosis, 7*, 261–277.

Bowers, K., & Meichenbaum, D. (1984). *The Unconscious Reconsidered.* New York: John Wiley & Sons.

Bowra, C. M. (1949). *The Romantic Imagination.* Cambridge: Harvard University Press.

Bowra, C. M. (1955). *Inspiration and Poetry.* London: Macmillan; New York: St. Martin's.

Bozzano, E. (1906). Apparitions of deceased persons at death-beds. *Annals of Psychic Science, 3*, 67–100.

Brading, A. (1999). *The Autonomic Nervous System and Its Effectors.* Oxford: Blackwell Science.

Bramwell, J. M. (1896). Personally observed hypnotic phenomena. *Proceedings of the Society for Psychical Research, 12*, 176–203.

Bramwell, J. M. (1903). *Hypnotism: Its History, Practice and Theory.* New York: Julian Press.

Brann, E. T. H. (1991). *The World of the Imagination.* Lanham, MD: Rowman & Littlefield.

Braud, W. G. (1978). Psi-conducive conditions: Explorations and interpretations. In B. Shapin & L. Coly (Eds.), *Psi and States of Awareness* (pp. 1–34). New York: Parapsychology Foundation.

Braud, W. (1993). On the use of living target systems in distant mental influence research. In L. Coly & J. D. S. McMahon (Eds.), *Psi Research Methodology: A Re-examination* (pp. 149–181). New York: Parapsychology Foundation. (Reprinted as chap. 6 in Braud [2003])

Braud, W. (2003). *Distant Mental Influence.* Charlottesville, VA: Hampton Roads.

Braud, W., & Schlitz, M. (1989). A methodology for the objective study of transpersonal imagery. *Journal of Scientific Exploration, 3*, 43–63. (Reprinted as chap. 1 in Braud [2003])

Braud, W., & Schlitz, M. (1991). Consciousness interactions with remote biological systems: Anomalous intentionality effects. *Subtle Energies, 2*, 1–46. (Reprinted as chap. 4 in Braud [2003])

Braud, W., Shafer, D., & Andrews, S. (1993a). Reactions to an unseen gaze (remote attention): A review, with new data on autonomic staring detection. *Journal of Parapsychology, 57*, 373–390. (Reprinted as chap. 7 in Braud [2003])

Braud, W., Shafer, D., & Andrews, S. (1993b). Further studies of autonomic detection of remote staring: Replication, new control procedures, and personality correlates. *Journal of Parapsychology, 57*, 391–409. (Reprinted as chap. 8 in Braud [2003])

Braude, S. (1979). *ESP and Psychokinesis: A Philosophical Examination*. Philadelphia: Temple University Press.

Braude, S. (1991). *The Limits of Influence*. London: Routledge. (Original work published 1986)

Braude, S. (1995). *First Person Plural: Multiple Personality and the Philosophy of Mind* (Rev. ed.). Lanham, MD: Rowman & Littlefield.

Braude, S. (2002). The creativity of dissociation. *Journal of Trauma and Dissociation, 3*, 5–26.

Braude, S. (2003). *Immortal Remains: The Evidence for Life after Death*. Lanham, MD: Rowman & Littlefield.

Braun, A. R., Balkin, T. J., Wesenstein, N. J., Gwadry, F., Carson, R. E., Varga, M., Baldwin, P., Belenky, G., & Herscovitch, P. (1998). Dissociated pattern of activity in visual cortices and their projections during human rapid eye movement sleep. *Science, 279*, 91–95.

Braun, B. G. (1983a). Neurophysiologic changes in multiple personality due to integration: A preliminary report. *American Journal of Clinical Hypnosis, 26*, 84–92.

Braun, B. G. (1983b). Psychophysiologic phenomena in multiple personality and hypnosis. *American Journal of Clinical Hypnosis, 26*, 124–137.

Brende, J. O. (1984). The psychophysiologic manifestations of dissociation. *Psychiatric Clinics of North America, 7*, 41–50.

Brentano, F. (1995). *Psychology from an Empirical Standpoint* (A. C. Rancurello, D. B. Terrell, & L. L. McAlister, Trans.). London: Routledge. (Original work published 1874)

Bressler, B., Nyhus, P., & Magnussen, F. (1958). Pregnancy fantasies in psychosomatic illness and symptom formation. *Psychosomatic Medicine, 20*, 187–202.

Bressloff, P. C., Cowan, J. D., Golubitsky, M., Thomas, P. J., & Wiener, M. C. (2001). Geometric visual hallucinations, Euclidean symmetry and the functional architecture of striate cortex. *Philosophical Transactions of the Royal Society of London–B, 356*, 299–330.

Breton, A. (1972). *Manifestoes of Surrealism* (R. Seaver & H. R. Lane, Trans.). Ann Arbor: University of Michigan Press. (Original work published 1924)

Breton, A. (1997). *The Automatic Message.* London: Atlas Press. (Original work published 1933)

Brett, G. S. (1921). *A History of Psychology. Vol. III: Modern Psychology.* London: George Allen & Unwin.

Breuer, J., & Freud, S. (1957). On the psychical mechanism of hysterical phenomena: Preliminary communication. In J. Breuer & S. Freud, *Studies on Hysteria* (J. R. Strachey, Trans.) (pp. 3–17). New York: Basic Books. (Original work published 1893)

British Medical Journal. (1910). *1,* 1453–1497.

Broad, C. D. (1953). *Religion, Philosophy and Psychical Research.* New York: Harcourt, Brace.

Broad, C. D. (1960). *The Mind and Its Place in Nature.* Patterson, NJ: Littlefield, Adams. (Original work published 1925)

Broad, C. D. (1962). *Lectures on Psychical Research.* London: Routledge & Kegan Paul.

Brockman, J. (Ed.) (2003). *The New Humanists: Science at the Edge.* New York: Basic Books.

Brody, E. B. (1979). [Review of] *Cases of the Reincarnation Type. Volume II. Ten Cases in Sri Lanka. Journal of the American Society for Psychical Research, 73,* 71–81.

Brody, H. (1980). *Placebo and the Philosophy of Medicine.* Chicago: University of Chicago Press.

Brown, A. S. (1991). A review of the tip-of-the-tongue phenomenon. *Psychological Bulletin, 109,* 204–223.

Brown, D. P. (1977). A model for the levels of concentrative meditation. *International Journal of Clinical and Experimental Hypnosis, 25,* 236–273.

Brown, E., & Barglow, P. (1971). Pseudocyesis: A paradigm for psychophysiological interactions. *Archives of General Psychiatry, 24,* 221–229.

Brown, J. E. (1991). *The Spiritual Legacy of the American Indian.* New York: Crossroad.

Brown, R., & McNeill, D. (1966). The "tip of the tongue" phenomenon. *Journal of Verbal Learning and Verbal Behavior, 5,* 325–337.

Brown, S. (2000). The exceptional human experience process: A preliminary model with exploratory map. *International Journal of Parapsychology, 11,* 69–111.

Brugger, P., Agosti, R., Regard, M., Wieser, H.-G., & Landis, T. (1994). Heautoscopy, epilepsy, and suicide. *Journal of Neurology, Neurosurgery, and Psychiatry, 57,* 838–839.

Bucke, R. M. (1969). *Cosmic Consciousness.* New York: Dutton. (Original work published 1901)

Buckley, W. (1968). *Modern Systems Research for the Behavioral Scientist.* Chicago: Aldine.

Burdick, D. S., & Kelly, E. F. (1977). Statistical methods in parapsychological research. In B. B. Wolman (Ed.), *Handbook of Parapsychology* (pp. 81–130). New York: Van Nostrand Reinhold.

Burkhardt, F. (Ed.) (1986). *The Works of William James: Essays in Psychical Research*. Cambridge, MA: Harvard University Press.

Bursen, H. A. (1978). *Dismantling the Memory Machine*. Dordrecht, Holland: Reidel.

Burt, C. (1968). *Psychology and Psychical Research*. London: Society for Psychical Research.

Bush, N. E. (1983). The near-death experience in children: Shades of the prison-house reopening. *Anabiosis: The Journal for Near-Death Studies, 3*, 177–193.

Bush, N. E. (1991). Is ten years a life review? *Journal of Near-Death Studies, 10*, 5–9.

Butcher, S. H. (1951). *Aristotle's Theory of Poetry and Fine Art*. New York: Dover.

Butler, C., & Steptoe, A. (1986). Placebo responses: An experimental study of psychophysiological processes in asthmatic volunteers. *British Journal of Clinical Psychology, 25*, 173–183.

Byerly, H. (1976). Explaining and exploiting placebo effects. *Perspectives in Biology and Medicine, 19*, 423–436.

Byrd, R. C. (1988). Positive therapeutic effects of intercessory prayer in a coronary care unit population. *Southern Medical Journal, 81*, 826–829.

Cabeza, R., & Nyberg, L. (2000). Imaging cognition II: An empirical study of 275 PET and fMRI studies. *Journal of Cognitive Neuroscience, 12*, 1–47.

Cain, M. J. (2002). *Fodor: Language, Mind and Philosophy*. Cambridge: Polity.

Callanan, M., & Kelley, P. (1993). *Final Gifts: Understanding the Special Needs, Awareness, and Communications of the Dying*. New York: Bantam.

Campbell, D. T. (1960). Blind variation and selective retention in creative thought as in other knowledge processes. *Psychological Review, 67*, 380–400.

Campbell, D. T., & Stanley, J. C. (1966). *Experimental and Quasi-Experimental Designs for Research*. Chicago, IL: Rand McNally.

Campbell, J. (2004). *The Hero with a Thousand Faces*. Princeton, NJ: Princeton University Press. (Original work published 1949)

Cannon, W. (1942). "Voodoo" death. *American Anthropologist, 44*, 169–181. (Reprinted in *Psychosomatic Medicine, 19*, 182–190, 1957.)

Capek, M. (1961). *The Philosophical Impact of Contemporary Physics*. Princeton, NJ: Van Nostrand.

Caplan, D. (1987). *Neurolinguistics and Linguistic Aphasiology: An Introduction*. Cambridge: Cambridge University Press.

Cardeña, E., & Kirsch, I. (2000). What is so special about the placebo effect? *Advances in Mind-Body Medicine, 16*, 16–18.

Carlson, N. R. (2004). *Physiology of Behavior* (8th ed.). Boston: Pearson Educational.

Carpenter, W. (1855). *Principles of Human Physiology* (5th ed.). London: John Churchill.

Carpenter, W. (1882). *Principles of Mental Physiology.* London: Kegan Paul. (Original work published 1874)

Carr, C. (1993). Death and near-death: A comparison of Tibetan and Euro-American experiences. *Journal of Transpersonal Psychology, 25,* 59–110.

Carr, D. (1981). Endorphins at the approach of death. *Lancet, 1,* 390.

Carr, D. (1982). Pathophysiology of stress-induced limbic lobe dysfunction: A hypothesis for NDEs. *Anabiosis: The Journal for Near-Death Studies, 2,* 75–89.

Carrel, A. (1950). *The Voyage to Lourdes.* New York: Harper.

Casdorph, H. R. (1976). *The Miracles.* Plainfield, NJ: Logos International.

Cassirer, E. (1955–1996). *The Philosophy of Symbolic Forms* (4 vols.) (R. Manheim, Trans.). New Haven, CT: Yale University Press.

Cassirer, E. (1957). *The Philosophy of Symbolic Forms. Vol. 3: The Phenomenology of Knowledge* (R. Manheim, Trans.). New Haven, CT: Yale University Press.

Cavanna, R., & Ullman, M. (1968). *Psi and Altered States of Consciousness.* New York: Parapsychology Foundation.

Chadwick, O. (1975). *The Secularization of the European Mind in the Nineteenth Century.* Cambridge: Cambridge University Press.

Challis, G. B., & Stam, H. J. (1990). The spontaneous regression of cancer: A review of cases from 1900 to 1987. *Acta Oncologica, 29,* 545–550.

Chalmers, D. (1996). *The Conscious Mind: In Search of a Fundamental Theory.* New York: Oxford University Press.

Chapman, L. F., Goodell, H., & Wolff, H. G. (1959). Changes in tissue vulnerability induced during hypnotic suggestion. *Journal of Psychosomatic Research, 4,* 99–105.

Cheek, D. B. (1964). Surgical memory and reaction to careless conversation. *American Journal of Clinical Hypnosis, 6,* 237.

Cheek, D. B. (1966). The meaning of continued hearing sense under general chemoanesthesia: A progress report and report of a case. *American Journal of Clinical Hypnosis, 8,* 275–280.

Chibnall, J. T., Jeral, J. M., & Cerullo, M. A. (2001). Experiments on distant intercessory prayer: God, science, and the lesson of Massah. *Archives of Internal Medicine, 161,* 2529–2536.

Child, I. L. (1973). *Humanistic Psychology and the Research Tradition.* New York: John Wiley.

Child, I. L. (1985). Psychology and anomalous observations: The question of ESP in dreams. *American Psychologist, 40,* 1219–1230.

Chomsky, N. (1957). *Syntactic Structures*. The Hague: Mouton.

Chomsky, N. (1959). [Review of] *Verbal Behavior*, by B. F. Skinner. *Language, 35*, 26–58.

Chomsky, N. (1963). Formal properties of grammars. In R. D. Luce, R. R. Bush, & E. Galanter (Eds.), *Handbook of Mathematical Psychology* (Vol. 2, pp. 323–418). New York: John Wiley.

Chomsky, N. (1993). *Language and Thought*. Wakefield, RI: Moyer Bell.

Churchland, P. M. (1988). *Matter and Consciousness* (Rev. ed.). Cambridge, MA: MIT Press.

Cirignotta, F., Todesco, C. V., & Lugaresi, E. (1980). Temporal lobe epilepsy with ecstatic seizures (so-called Dostoevsky epilepsy). *Epilepsia, 21*, 705–710.

Clark, A. (2001). *Mindware: An Introduction to the Philosophy of Cognitive Science*. New York: Oxford University Press.

Clark, K. (1984). Clinical interventions with near-death experiencers. In B. Greyson & C. P. Flynn (Eds.), *The Near-Death Experience: Problems, Prospects, Perspectives* (pp. 242–255). Springfield, IL: Charles C Thomas.

Clawson, T. A., & Swade, R. H. (1975). The hypnotic control of blood flow and pain: The cure of warts and the potential for the use of hypnosis in the treatment of cancer. *American Journal of Clinical Hypnosis, 17*, 160–169.

Clifford, W. K. (1874). Body and mind. *Fortnightly Review, 16* (n.s.), 714–736.

Cobb, L. A., Thomas, G. I., Dillard, D. H., Merendino, K. A., & Bruce, R. A. (1959). An evaluation of internal-mammary-artery ligation by a double-blind technic. *New England Journal of Medicine, 260*, 1115–1118.

Cobbe, F. P. (1882). *The Peak in Darien*. Boston: George H. Ellis.

Cohen, L. M. (1982). A current perspective of pseudocyesis. *American Journal of Psychiatry, 139*, 1140–1144.

Cohen, S. I., Bondurant, S., & Silverman, A. J. (1960). Psychophysiological influences on peripheral venous tone. *Psychosomatic Medicine, 22*, 106–117.

Coleridge, S. T. (1967). *Biographia Literaria*. London: J. M. Dent & Sons. (Original work published 1817)

Collier, B. B. (1972). Ketamine and the conscious mind. *Anaesthesia, 27*, 120–134.

Coly, L., & McMahon, J. D. S. (Eds.) (1995). *Parapsychology and Thanatology*. New York: Parapsychology Foundation.

Condon, W. S., Ogston, W. D., & Pacoe, L. V. (1969). Three faces of Eve revisited: A study of transient microstrabismus. *Journal of Abnormal Psychology, 74*, 618–620.

Conn, L., & Mott, T. (1984). Plethysmographic demonstration of rapid vasodilation by direct suggestion: A case of Raynaud's Disease treated by hypnosis. *American Journal of Clinical Hypnosis, 26*, 166–170.

Cook [Kelly], E. W. (1992). *Frederic W. H. Myers: Parapsychology and Its Potential Contribution to Psychology.* Unpublished doctoral dissertation, University of Edinburgh, Scotland.

Cook [Kelly], E. W., Greyson, B., & Stevenson, I. (1998). Do any near-death experiences provide evidence for the survival of human personality after death? Relevant features and illustrative case reports. *Journal of Scientific Exploration, 12,* 377–406.

Coons, P. M. (1988). Psychophysiologic aspects of multiple personality disorder: A review. *Dissociation, 1,* 47–53.

Coons, P. M., Milstein, V., & Marley, C. (1982). EEG studies of two multiple personalities and a control. *Archives of General Psychiatry, 39,* 823–825.

Corcoran, K. (Ed.) (2001). *Soul, Body and Survival: Essays on the Metaphysics of Human Persons.* Ithaca, NY: Cornell University Press.

Council, J. R., & Greyson, B. (1985, August). *Near-death experiences and the "fantasy-prone" personality: Preliminary findings.* Paper presented at the 93rd Annual Convention of the American Psychological Association, Los Angeles.

Counts, D. A. (1983). Near-death and out-of-body experiences in a Melanesian society. *Anabiosis: The Journal for Near-Death Studies, 3,* 115–135.

Cousins, N. (1976). Anatomy of an illness (as perceived by the patient). *New England Journal of Medicine, 295,* 1458–1463.

Coward, H. (1985). *Jung and Eastern Thought.* Albany: State University of New York Press.

Crabtree, A. (1985). *Multiple Man: Explorations in Possession and Multiple Personality.* London: Holt, Rinehart, & Winston.

Crabtree, A. (1986). Explanations of dissociation in the first half of the twentieth century. In J. Quen (Ed.), *Split Minds/Split Brains: Historical and Current Perspectives* (pp. 85–107). New York: New York University Press.

Crabtree, A. (1993). *From Mesmer to Freud: Magnetic Sleep and the Roots of Psychological Healing.* New Haven: Yale University Press.

Crabtree, A. (2003). "Automatism" and the emergence of dynamic psychiatry. *Journal of the History of the Behavioral Sciences, 39,* 51–70.

Craik, K. J. W. (1943). *The Nature of Explanation.* Cambridge: Cambridge University Press.

Crasilneck, H. B., & Hall, J. A. (1959). Physiological changes associated with hypnosis: A review of the literature since 1948. *International Journal of Clinical and Experimental Hypnosis, 7,* 9–50.

Crasilneck, H. B., & Hall, J. A. (1975). *Clinical Hypnosis: Principles and Applications.* New York: Grune & Stratton.

Crawford, H. J., Knebel, T., Kaplan, L., Vendemia, J. M. C., Xie, M., Jamison, S., & Pribram, K. H. (1998). Hypnotic analgesia: 1. Somatosensory event-related potential changes to noxious stimuli and 2. Transfer learning to reduce chronic low back pain. *International Journal of Clinical and Experimental Hypnosis, 46,* 92–132.

Crawford, H. J., Knebel, T., & Vendemia, J. M. C. (1998). The nature of hypnotic analgesia: Neurophysiological foundation and evidence. *Contemporary Hypnosis, 15*, 22–33.

Crawford, H. J., Wallace, B., Nomura, K., & Slater, H. (1986). Eidetic-like imagery in hypnosis: Rare but there. *American Journal of Psychology, 99*, 527–546.

Crick, F. (1994). *The Astonishing Hypothesis: The Scientific Search for the Soul.* New York: Simon & Schuster.

Crick, F., & Koch, C. (2003). A framework for consciousness. *Nature Neuroscience, 6*, 119–126.

Crookall, R. (1964). *More Astral Projections: Analyses of Case Histories.* London: Aquarian Press.

Crookall, R. (1966). *The Study and Practice of Astral Projection.* New Hyde Park, NY: University Books. (Original work published 1960)

Crookall, R. (1972). *Case-Book of Astral Projection 545–746.* Secaucus, NJ: University Books.

Csikszentmihalyi, M. (1988). Society, culture, and person: A systems view of creativity. In R. J. Sternberg (Ed.), *The Nature of Creativity* (pp. 325–339). Cambridge: Cambridge University Press.

Csikszentmihalyi, M. (1996). *Creativity: Flow and the Psychology of Discovery and Invention.* New York: Harper Collins.

Curran, A. P. (1976). Cure and canonisation. *The Month, 237* (n.s. 9), 333–335.

Cytowic, R. E. (1995). Synesthesia: Phenomenology and neuropsychology—A review of current knowledge. Psyche, 2. Retrieved February 7, 2004, from http://psyche.cs.monash.edu.au/v2/psyche-2-10-cytowic.html

Dahinterova, J. (1967). Some experiences with the use of hypnosis in the treatment of burns. *International Journal of Clinical and Experimental Hypnosis, 15*, 49–53.

Dahlem, M. A., Engelmann, R., Löwel, S., & Müller, S. C. (2000). Does the migraine aura reflect cortical organization? *European Journal of Neuroscience, 12*, 767–770.

Dale, L. A., White, R., & Murphy, G. (1962). A selection of cases from a recent survey of spontaneous ESP phenomena. *Journal of the American Society for Psychical Research, 61*, 3–47.

Dalla Barba, G. (1999). Confabulation and temporality. In L.-G. Nilsson & H. J. Markowitsch (Eds.), *Cognitive Neuroscience of Memory* (pp. 163–192). Seattle: Hogrefe & Huber.

Dallas, H. A. (1900). Correspondence. *Journal of the Society for Psychical Research, 9*, 288–289.

Dalton, K. (1997). Exploring the links: Creativity and psi in the ganzfeld. *Proceedings of the 40th Parapsychological Association Convention* (pp. 119–134). Brighton, England.

Damas Mora, J. M. R., Jenner, F. A., & Eacott, S. E. (1980). On heautoscopy or the phenomenon of the double: Case presentation and review of the literature. *British Journal of Medical Psychology, 53*, 75–83.

Damasio, A. R. (1989). Time-locked multiregional retroactivation: A systems-level proposal for the neural substrates of recall and recognition. *Cognition, 33*, 25–62.

Damasio, A. R. (1999). The brain behind the mind. In Neuroscience: A New Era of Discovery. Retrieved November 16, 2001, from http://www.sfn.org/nas/summaries/Damasio.html

Damasio, A. R., & Damasio, H. (1994). Cortical systems for retrieval of concrete knowledge: The convergence zone framework. In C. Koch & J. L. Davis (Eds.), *Large-Scale Neuronal Theories of the Brain* (pp. 61–74). Cambridge, MA: MIT Press.

Damasio, A. R., & Damasio, H. (2000). Aphasia and the neural basis of language. In M.-M. Mesulam (Ed.), *Principles of Behavioral and Cognitive Neurology* (2nd ed.) (pp. 294–315). Oxford: Oxford University Press.

Damon, S. F. (1958). *William Blake: His Philosophy and Symbols*. Gloucester, MA: Peter Smith.

Danziger, K. (1980). The history of introspection reconsidered. *Journal of the History of the Behavioral Sciences, 16*, 241–262.

Danziger, N., Fournier, E., Bouhassira, D., Michaud, D., De Broucker, T., Santarcangelo, E., Carli, G., Chertock, L. & Willer, J. C. (1998). Different strategies of modulation can be operative during hypnotic analgesia: A neurophysiological study. *Pain, 75*, 85–92.

d'Aquili, E. G., & Newberg, A. B. (1993). Religious and mystical states: A neuropsychological model. *Zygon, 28*, 177–197.

d'Aquili, E. G., & Newberg, A. B. (1999). *The Mystical Mind: Probing the Biology of Religious Experience*. Minneapolis, MN: Fortress.

Darwin, F. (Ed.) (1958). *The Autobiography of Charles Darwin and Selected Letters*. New York: Dover. (Original work published 1892)

Das, H. H., & Gastaut, H. (1957). Variations de l'activité électrique du cerveau, du coeur, et des muscles squelletiques au cours de la méditation et de l'extase yogique. *Electroencephalography and Clinical Neurophysiology*, supplement 6, 211–219.

Dasgupta, S. (1970). *Yoga as Philosophy and Religion*. Port Washington, NY: Kennikat. (Original work published 1924)

Daston, L. J. (1978). British responses to psycho-physiology, 1860–1900. *Isis, 69*, 192–208.

Daston, L. J. (1982). The theory of will versus the science of mind. In W. R. Woodward & M. G. Ash (Eds.), *The Problematic Science: Psychology in Nineteenth-Century Thought* (pp. 88–115). New York: Praeger.

Davidson, J. (1976). The physiology of meditation and mystical states of consciousness. *Perspectives in Biology and Medicine, 19*, 345–379.

Davies, P. (1995). *The Cosmic Blueprint: Order and Complexity at the Edge of Chaos.* London: Penguin.

Davis, D. G., Schmitt, F. A., Wekstein, D. R., & Markesberg, W. R. (1999). Alzheimer neuropathologic alterations in aged cognitively normal subjects. *Journal of Neuropathology and Experimental Neurology, 58*, 376–388.

Davison, G. C., & Singleton, L. (1967). A preliminary report of improved vision under hypnosis. *International Journal of Clinical and Experimental Hypnosis, 15*, 57–62.

Decker, H. S. (1986). The lure of nonmaterialist Europe: Investigations of dissociative phenomena, 1880–1915. In J. M. Quen (Ed.), *Split Minds/Split Brains: Historical and Current Perspectives* (pp. 31–62). New York & London: New York University Press.

Deese, J. (1972). *Psychology as Science and Art.* New York: Harcourt Brace Jovanovich.

Dehaene, S. (1993). Temporal oscillations in human perception. *Psychological Science, 4*, 264–270.

Dehaene, S., & Naccache, L. (2001). Towards a cognitive neuroscience of consciousness: Basic evidence and a workspace framework. *Cognition, 79*, 1–37.

Deikman, A. J. (1966). De-automatization and the mystic experience. *Psychiatry, 29*, 329–343.

Delanoy, D. (2001). Anomalous psychophysiological responses to remote cognition: The DMILS studies. *European Journal of Parapsychology, 16*, 30–41.

Delbœuf, J. (1892). De l'appréciation du temps par les somnambules. *Proceedings of the Society for Psychical Research, 8*, 414–421.

Deleuze, J. (1813). *Histoire critique de magnétisme animal* (2 vols.). Paris: Mame.

Dellas, M., & Gaier, E. L. (1970). Identification of creativity: The individual. *Psychological Bulletin, 73*, 55–73.

Dening, T. R., & Berrios, G. E. (1994). Autoscopic phenomena. *British Journal of Psychiatry, 165*, 808–817.

Dennett, D. C. (1978). *Brainstorms: Philosophical Essays on Mind and Psychology.* Cambridge, MA: MIT Press.

Dennett, D. C. (1991). *Consciousness Explained.* Boston: Little, Brown.

Dennett, D. C., & Kinsbourne, M. (1992). Time and the observer: The where and when of consciousness in the brain. *Brain and Behavioral Sciences, 15*, 183–247.

Deonna, W. (1932). *De la Planéte Mars en Terre Sainte: Art et Subconscient.* Paris: E. De Boccard.

Deren, M. (1972). *Divine Horsemen: The Voodoo Gods of Haiti.* New York: Dell.

De Renzi, E., Liotti, M., & Nichelli, P. (1987). Semantic amnesia with preserved autobiographical memory. *Cortex, 23*, 575–597.

De Rios, M. D. (1984). *Hallucinogens: Cross-Cultural Perspectives.* Albuquerque: University of New Mexico Press.

De Rios, M. D., & Janiger, O. (2003). *LSD, Spirituality, and the Creative Process.* Rochester, VT: Park Street.

Despine, C. (1838). *Observations de médecine pratique. Faites aux Bains d'Aix-en-Savoie.* Anneci: Burdet.

Dessoir, M. (1896). *Das Doppel-Ich* (2nd ed.). Leipzig: E. Günther.

Devane, G. W., Vera, M. I., Buhi, W. C., & Kalra, P. S. (1985). Opioid peptides in pseudocyesis. *Obstetrics and Gynecology, 65,* 183–187.

Devinsky, O., Feldmann, E., Burrowes, K., & Bromfield, E. (1989). Autoscopic phenomena with seizures. *Archives of Neurology, 46,* 1080–1088.

DeVries, J. W., Bakker, P. F. A., Visser, G. H., Diephuis, J. C., & van Huffelen, A. C. (1998). Changes in cerebral oxygen uptake and cerebral electrical activity during defibrillation threshold testing. *Anesthesiology and Analgesia, 87,* 16–20.

Dewhurst, K., & Beard, A. W. (1970). Sudden religious conversions in temporal lobe epilepsy. *British Journal of Psychiatry, 117,* 497–507.

Diagnostic and Statistical Manual of Mental Disorders (4th ed.) (1994). Washington DC: American Psychiatric Association.

Diamond, M., Scheibel, A., Murphy, G., & Harvey, T. (1985). On the brain of a scientist: Albert Einstein. *Experimental Neurology, 88,* 198–204.

Dientsfrey, H. (1999). Mind and mindlessness in mind-body research. *Advances in Mind-Body Medicine, 15,* 229–233.

Dietrich, A. (2003). Functional neuroanatomy of altered states of consciousness: The transient hypofrontality hypothesis. *Consciousness and Cognition, 12,* 231–256.

Dimond, E. G., Kittle, C. F., & Crockett, J. E. (1958). Evaluation of internal mammary artery ligation and sham procedure in angina pectoris. *Circulation, 18,* 712–713.

Dingwall, E. (1967-1968). *Abnormal Hypnotic Phenomena: A Survey of Nineteenth-Century Cases* (4 vols.). New York: Barnes & Noble.

Dittrich, A. (1994). Psychological aspects of altered states of consciousness of the LSD type: Measurement of their basic dimensions and prediction of individual differences. In A. Pletscher & K. Ladewig (Eds.), *50 Years of LSD: Current Status and Perspectives of Hallucinogens* (pp. 101–118). New York: Parthenon.

Dittrich, A. (1998). The standardized psychometric assessment of altered states of consciousness (ASCs) in humans. *Pharmacopsychiatry, 31* (supplement), 80–84.

Doblin, R. (1991). The Good Friday experiment: A long-term followup and methodological critique. *Journal of Transpersonal Psychology, 23,* 1–28.

Dodds, E. R. (1934). Why I do not believe in survival. *Proceedings of the Society for Psychical Research, 42,* 147–172.

Donagan, A. (1990). Real persons. *Logos, 11,* 1–16.

Dowling, J. (1984). Lourdes cures and their medical assessment. *Journal of the Royal Society of Medicine, 77,* 634–638.

Draaisma, D. (2000). *Metaphors of Memory: A History of Ideas about the Mind.* Cambridge: Cambridge University Press.

Dreaper, R. (1978). Recalcitrant warts on the hand cured by hypnosis. *Practitioner, 220,* 305–310.

Dretske, F. (1988). *Explaining Behavior: Reasons in a World of Causes.* Cambridge, MA: MIT Press.

Dreyfus, H. L. (1972). *What Computers Can't Do: A Critique of Artificial Reason.* New York: Harper & Row.

Ducasse, C. J. (1951). *Nature, Mind, and Death.* LaSalle, IL: Open Court.

Ducasse, C. J. (1961). *A Critical Examination of the Belief in a Life After Death.* Springfield, IL: Charles C Thomas.

Ducasse, C. J. (1969). *Paranormal Phenomena, Science, and Life After Death* (Parapsychological Monographs No. 8). New York: Parapsychology Foundation.

Dunbar, H. F. (1954). *Emotions and Bodily Changes* (4th ed.). New York: Columbia University Press.

Du Prel, C. (1976). *The Philosophy of Mysticism.* New York: Arno Press. (Original work published 1889)

Dupuy, J. -P. (2000). *The Mechanization of the Mind: On the Origins of Cognitive Science* (M. B. DeBevoise, Trans.). Princeton, NJ: Princeton University Press.

Early, L. F., & Lifschutz, J. E. (1974). A case of stigmata. *Archives of General Psychiatry, 30,* 197–200.

Eastman, T. E., & Keeton, H. (2004). *Physics and Whitehead: Quantum, Process, and Experience.* Albany: State University of New York Press.

Eccles, J. C. (1994). *How the Self Controls Its Brain.* Berlin: Springer.

Eckhart, Meister (1981). *The Essential Sermons, Commentaries, Treatises, and Defense* (E. Colledge & B. McGinn, Trans.). Mahwah, NJ: Paulist Press.

Edelman, G. M., & Mountcastle, V. B. (1982). *The Mindful Brain: Cortical Organization and the Group-Selective Theory of Higher Brain Function.* Cambridge, MA: MIT Press.

Edelman, G. M., & Tononi, G. (2000). *A Universe of Consciousness: How Matter Becomes Imagination.* New York: Basic Books.

Edwards, P. (1996). *Reincarnation: A Critical Examination.* Amherst, NY: Prometheus.

Edwards, P. (Ed.) (1997). *Immortality.* Amherst, NY: Prometheus.

Eichenbaum, H. (2002). *The Cognitive Neuroscience of Memory.* New York: Oxford University Press.

Eichenbaum, H., & Cohen, N. J. (2001). *From Conditioning to Conscious Recollection: Memory Systems of the Brain.* Oxford: Oxford University Press.

Einstein, A. (1949). *The World As I See It* (A. Harris, Trans.). New York: Philosophical Library.

Eisenbud, J. (1979). How to make things null and void: An essay-review of Brian Inglis' *Natural and Supernatural. Journal of Parapsychology, 43*, 140–152.

Eliade, M. (1958). *Yoga: Immortality and Freedom* (W. R. Trask, Trans.). New York: Bollingen Foundation.

Eliade, M. (1964). *Shamanism: Archaic Techniques of Ecstasy* (W. R. Trask, Trans.). Bollingen Series LXXVI. Princeton, NJ: Princeton University Press.

Eliade, M. (1969). *Patanjali and Yoga* (C. L. Markmann, Trans.) New York: Funk & Wagnalls.

Elkington, A. R., Steele, P. R., & Yun, D. D. (1965). Scared to death? [letter]. *British Medical Journal, 2*, 363–364.

Ellenberger, H. F. (1970). *The Discovery of the Unconscious: The History and Evolution of Dynamic Psychiatry.* New York: Basic Books.

Elliotson, J. (1843). *Numerous Cases of Surgical Operations Without Pain in the Mesmeric State.* Philadelphia: Lea & Blanchard.

Ellis, F. R. (1965). Scared to death? [letter]. *British Medical Journal, 2*, 821.

Emerson, R. W. (1983). *Essays and Lectures.* New York: Viking Press. (Original work published 1837)

Engel, A. K., Fries, P., & Singer, W. (2001). Dynamic predictions: Oscillations and synchrony in top-down processing. *Nature Reviews: Neuroscience, 2*, 704–716.

Engel, G. L. (1966). A psychological setting of somatic disease: The "giving up-given up" complex. *Proceedings of the Royal Society of Medicine, 60*, 553–555.

Engel, G. L. (1968). A life setting conducive to illness: The giving-up–given-up complex. *Bulletin of the Menninger Clinic, 32*, 355–365.

Engel, G. L. (1971). Sudden and rapid death during psychological stress. Folklore or folk wisdom? *Annals of Internal Medicine, 74*, 771–782.

Engel, G. L. (1977). The need for a new medical model: A challenge for biomedicine. *Science*, *196*, 129–136.

Engel, G. L. (1978). Psychological stress, vasodepressor (vasovagal) syncope, and sudden death. *Annals of Internal Medicine, 89*, 403–412.

Engelhardt, H. T., Jr. (1975). John Hughlings Jackson and the mind-body relation. *Bulletin of the History of Medicine, 49*, 137–151.

Ennemoser, J. (1852). *Anleitung zur Mesmerischen Praxis.* Stuttgart and Tübingen: J. G. Cotta.

Ephraim, A. J. (1959). On sudden or rapid whitening of the hair. *Archives of Dermatology, 79*, 228–236.

Erdelyi, M. H. (1985). *Psychoanalysis: Freud's Cognitive Psychology.* New York: W. H. Freeman.

Erickson, M. H. (1943). Hypnotic investigation of psychosomatic phenomena: Psychosomatic interrelationships studied by experimental hypnosis. *Psychosomatic Medicine, 5*, 51–58.

Erickson, M. H. (1965). Acquired control of pupillary responses. *American Journal of Clinical Hypnosis, 7*, 207–208.

Erickson, M. H. (1977). Control of physiological functions by hypnosis. *American Journal of Clinical Hypnosis, 20*, 8–19.

Ernst, E. (2003). Distant healing — An "update" of a systematic review. *Wiener Klinische Wochenschrift, 115*, 241–245.

Ernst, E., & Resch, K. L. (1995). Concept of true and perceived placebo effects. *British Medical Journal, 311*, 551–553.

Esdaile, J. (1846). *Mesmerism in India and Its Practical Application in Surgery and Medicine.* London: Longman, Brown, Green, & Longmans.

Espagnat, B. d' (1976). *Conceptual Foundations of Quantum Mechanics* (2nd ed. rev.). Reading, MA: W. A. Benjamin.

Everson, S. A., Goldberg, D. E., Kaplan, G. A., Cohen, R. D., Pukkala, E., Tuomilehto, J., & Salonen, J. T. (1996). Hopelessness and risk of mortality and incidence of myocardial infarction and cancer. *Psychosomatic Medicine, 58*, 113–121.

Ewin, D. M. (1974). Condyloma acuminatum: Successful treatment of four cases by hypnosis. *American Journal of Clinical Hypnosis, 17*, 73–78.

Ewin, D. M. (1979). Hypnosis in burn therapy. In G. D. Burrows, D. R. Collison, & L. Dennerstein (Eds.), *Hypnosis 1979* (pp. 269–275). Amsterdam: Elsevier.

Ey, H. (1982). History and analysis of the concept. In A. Roy (Ed.), *Hysteria* (pp. 3–19). Chichester, UK: John Wiley & Sons.

Eysenck, H. J. (1995). *Genius: The Natural History of Creativity.* New York: Cambridge University Press.

Falkenhainer, B., Forbus, K. D., & Gentner, D. (1989). The structure-mapping engine: An algorithm and examples. *Artificial Intelligence, 4*, 1–63.

Farah, M. J. (1994). Neuropsychological inference with an interactive brain: A critique of the "locality" assumption. *Behavioral and Brain Sciences, 17*, 43–104.

Farrow, J. T., & Hebert, J. R. (1982). Breath suspension during the transcendental meditation technique. *Psychosomatic Medicine, 44*, 133–153.

Fava, G. A., & Sonino, N. (2000). Psychosomatic medicine: Emerging trends and perspectives. *Psychotherapy and Psychosomatics, 69*, 184–197.

Favill, J., & White, P. D. (1917). Voluntary acceleration of the rate of the heart beat. *Heart, 6*, 175–188.

Fawcett, J. W., Rosser, A. E., & Dunnett, S. B. (Eds.) (2001). *Brain Damage, Brain Repair.* Oxford: Oxford University Press.

Faymonville, M. E., Laureys, S., Degueldre, C., DelFiore, G., Luxen, A., Franck, G., Lamy, M., & Maquet, P. (2000). Neural mechanisms of antinociceptive effects of hypnosis. *Anesthesiology, 92*, 1257–1267.

Feigenbaum, E. A., & Feldman, J. (1963). *Computers and Thought*. New York: McGraw-Hill.

Feigl, H. (1958). The "mental" and the "physical." In H. Feigl, M. Scriven, & G. Maxwell (Eds.), *Minnesota Studies in the Philosophy of Science* (Vol. 2, pp. 370–497). Minneapolis: University of Minnesota Press.

Feng, Z. & Liu, J. (1992). Near-death experiences among survivors of the 1976 Tangshan earthquake. *Journal of Near-Death Studies, 11*, 39–48.

Fenwick, P. (1987). Meditation and the EEG. In M. A. West (Ed.), *The Psychology of Meditation* (pp. 104–117). Oxford: Clarendon.

Fenwick, P. (1997). Is the near-death experience only *N*-methyl-*D*-aspartate blocking? *Journal of Near-Death Studies, 16*, 43–53.

ffytche, D. H., Howard, R. J., Brammer, M. J., David, A., & Williams, S. (1998). The anatomy of conscious vision: An fMRI study of visual hallucinations. *Nature Neuroscience, 1*, 738–742.

Fields, H. L., & Price, D. D. (1997). Toward a neurobiology of placebo analgesia. In A. Harrington (Ed.), *The Placebo Effect: An Interdisciplinary Exploration* (pp. 93–116). Cambridge: Harvard University Press.

Finger, S., LeVere, T. E., Almli, R., & Stein, D. G. (1988). Recovery of function: Sources of controversy. In S. Finger, T. E. LeVere, R. Almli, & D. G. Stein (Eds.), *Brain Injury and Recovery: Theoretical and Controversial Issues* (pp. 351–361). New York: Plenum.

Finkelmeier, B. A., Kenwood, N. J., & Summers, C. (1984). Psychologic ramifications of survival from sudden cardiac death. *Critical Care Quarterly, 7*, 71–79.

Fischer, R. (1971). A cartography of the ecstatic and meditation states. *Science, 174*, 897–904.

Fiset, P., Paus, T., Daloze, G., Plourde, G., Meuret, P., Bonhomme, V., Hajj-Ali, N., Backman, S. B., & Evans, A. C. (1999). Brain mechanisms of propofol-induced loss of consciousness in humans: A positron emission tomographic study. *Journal of Neuroscience, 19*, 5506–5513.

Fisher, J. G., & Kollar, E. J. (1980). Investigation of a stigmatic. *Southern Medical Journal, 73*, 1461–1463.

Fisher, S. (2000). "Is there really a placebo effect, professor?" *Advances in Mind-Body Medicine, 16*, 19–21.

Flanagan, O. (1991). *The Science of the Mind* (2nd ed.). Cambridge, MA: MIT Press.

Flew, A. G. N. (1987). *The Logic of Mortality*. Oxford: Blackwell.

Fliess, R. (1959). On the nature of human thought: The primary and secondary processes as exemplified by the dream and other psychic productions. In M. Levitt (Ed.), *Readings in Psychoanalytic Psychology* (pp. 213–220). New York: Appleton-Century-Crofts.

Flohr, H. (2000). NMDA receptor-mediated computational processes and phenomenal consciousness. In T. Metzinger (Ed.), *Neural Correlates of Consciousness: Empirical and Conceptual Questions* (pp. 245–258). Cambridge, MA: MIT Press.

Flournoy, T. (1903). [Review of *Human Personality and its Survival of Bodily Death*, by F. W. H. Myers.] *Proceedings of the Society for Psychical Research, 18*, 42–52. (On our digital version of *HP*)

Flournoy, T. (1911). *Spiritism and Psychology* (H. Carrington, Trans.). New York: Harper & Brothers.

Flournoy, T. (1963). *From India to the Planet Mars*. New Hyde Park, NY: University Books. (Original work published 1900)

Flournoy, T. (1983). *Des Indes à la planète Mars*. Paris: Éditions du Seuil. (Original work published 1900)

Flynn, C. P. (1986). *After the Beyond: Transformation and The Near-Death Experience*. NY: Prentice-Hall.

Fodor, J. A. (1975). *The Language of Thought*. Cambridge, MA: Harvard University Press.

Fodor, J. A. (1981a). The mind-body problem. *Scientific American, 244*, 114–123.

Fodor, J. A. (1981b). *Representations: Philosophical Essays on the Foundations of Cognitive Science*. Hassocks: Harvester.

Fodor, J. (1983). *The Modularity of Mind: An Essay on Faculty Psychology*. Cambridge, MA: MIT Press.

Fodor, J. (2001). *The Mind Doesn't Work That Way: The Scope and Limits of Computational Psychology*. Cambridge, MA: MIT Press.

Fodor, J. (2003). *Hume Variations*. Oxford: Oxford University Press.

Fodor, J. A., & Lepore, E. (1992). *Holism: A Shopper's Guide*. Oxford: Blackwell.

Fodor, N. (1966). *Encyclopedia of Psychic Science*. New Hyde Park, NY: University Books.

Fontinell, E. (1986). *Self, God, and Immortality: A Jamesian Investigation*. Philadelphia: Temple University Press.

Forbus, K. D., Gentner, D., & Law, K. (1994). MAC/FAC: A model of similarity-based retrieval. *Cognitive Science, 19*, 141–205.

Forde, E. M. E., & Humphreys, G. W. (Eds.) (2002). *Category Specificity in Brain and Mind*. New York: Psychology Press.

Forman, R. K. C. (1990). *The Problem of Pure Consciousness*. New York: Oxford University Press.

Forman, R. K. C. (1998). *The Innate Capacity: Mysticism, Psychology and Philosophy*. New York: Oxford University Press.

Forman, R. K. C. (1999). *Mysticism, Mind, Consciousness*. Albany: State University of New York Press.

Forrest, K. A. (2001). Toward an etiology of dissociative identity disorder: A neurodevelopmental approach. *Consciousness and Cognition, 10,* 259–293.

Foster, G. (1985). *The World Was Flooded With Light.* Pittsburgh: University of Pittsburgh Press.

Foster, J. (1991). *The Immaterial Self: A Defence of the Cartesian Dualist Conception of the Mind.* London: Routledge.

Foulkes, D. (1962). Dream reports from different stages of sleep. *Journal of Abnormal and Social Psychology, 65,* 14–25.

Frank, J. D. (1975). The faith that heals. *Johns Hopkins Medical Journal, 137,* 127–131.

Frankel, F. H., & Misch, R. C. (1973). Hypnosis in a case of long-standing psoriasis in a person with character problems. *International Journal of Clinical and Experimental Hypnosis, 21,* 121–130.

Frederick, A. N., & Barber, T. X. (1972). Yoga, hypnosis, and self-control of cardiovascular functions. *Proceedings of the Annual Convention of the American Psychological Association, 7,* 859–860.

Fredericks, L. E. (1967). The use of hypnosis in hemophilia. *American Journal of Clinical Hypnosis, 10,* 52–55.

Frederiks, J. A. M. (1969). Disorders of the body schema. In P. J. Vinken & G. W. Bruyn (Eds.), *Handbook of Clinical Neurology. Vol. 4: Disorders of Speech, Perception, and Symbolic Behavior* (pp. 207–240). New York: American Elsevier.

Freed, C. R., Greene, P. E., Breeze, R. E., Tsai, W.-Y., DuMouchel, W., Kao, R., Dillon, S., Winfield, H., Culver, S., Trojanowski, J. Q., Eidelberg, D., & Fahn, S. (2001). Transplantation of embryonic dopamine neurons for severe Parkinson's disease. *New England Journal of Medicine, 344,* 710–719.

Freeman, T. B., Vawter, D. E., Leaverton, P. E., Godbold, J. H., Hauser, R. A., Goetz, C. G., & Olanow, C. W. (1999). Use of placebo surgery in controlled trials of a cellular-based therapy for Parkinson's disease. *New England Journal of Medicine, 341,* 988–992.

Freeman, W. J. (1991). The physiology of perception. *Scientific American, 264,* 34–41.

Freeman, W. J. (1998). Foreword. In E. Basar (Ed.), *Brain Function and Oscillations* (pp. ix–xiii). Berlin: Springer-Verlag.

Freeman, W. J. (1999). Consciousness, intentionality and causality. *Journal of Consciousness Studies, 6,* 143–172.

Freeman, W. J. (2000). *How Brains Make Up Their Minds.* New York: Columbia University Press.

Freinkel, A. (1998). An even closer look at therapeutic touch [letter]. *Journal of the American Medical Association, 280,* 1905.

French, C. C. (2001). Dying to know the truth: Visions of a dying brain, or false memories? *Lancet, 358,* 2010–2011.

Freud, S. (1912). A note on the unconscious in psycho-analysis. *Proceedings of the Society for Psychical Research, 26*, 312–318.

Freud, S. (1961). *Civilization and Its Discontents*. New York: W. W. Norton.

Freud, S. (1964). The interpretation of dreams. In J. Strachey (Ed.), *Standard Edition of the Complete Psychological Works of Sigmund Freud* (Vol. 4). London: Hogarth Press. (Original work published 1900)

Freud, S. (1964). The unconscious. In J. Strachey (Ed.), *Standard Edition of the Complete Psychological Works of Sigmund Freud* (Vol. 14, pp. 166–171). London: Hogarth Press (Original work published 1915)

Freud, S. (1964). The ego and the id. In J. Strachey (Ed.), *Standard Edition of the Complete Psychological Works of Sigmund Freud* (Vol. 19, pp. 12–66). London: Hogarth Press. (Original work published 1923)

Freud, S. (1964). An autobiographical study. In J. Strachey (Ed.), *Standard Edition of the Complete Psychological Works of Sigmund Freud* (Vol. 20, pp. 7–74). (Original work published 1925)

Freud, S. (1968). *A General Introduction to Psychoanalysis*. New York: Washington Square. (Original work published 1920)

Fried, P. H., Rakoff, A. E., Schopbach, R. R., & Kaplan, A. J. (1951). Pseudocyesis: A psychosomatic study in gynecology. *Journal of the American Medical Association, 145*, 1329–1335.

Fromm, E. (1978–1979). Primary and secondary process in waking and in altered states of consciousness. *Journal of Altered States of Consciousness, 4*, 115–128.

Fry, A. (1965). Scared to death? [letter]. *British Medical Journal, 2*, 591.

Fuente-Fernández, R. de la (2004). Uncovering the hidden placebo effect in deep-brain stimulation for Parkinson's disease. *Parkinsonism and Related Disorders, 10*, 125–127.

Fuente-Fernández, R. de la, Phillips, A. G., Zamburlini, M., Sossi, V., Calne, D. B., Ruth, T. J., & Stoessl, A. J. (2002). Dopamine release in human ventral striatum and expectation of reward. *Behavioural Brain Research, 136*, 359–363.

Fuente-Fernández, R. de la, Ruth, T. J., Sossi, V., Schulzer, M., Calne, D. B., & Stoessl, A. J. (2001). Expectation and dopamine release: Mechanism of the placebo effect in Parkinson's disease. *Science, 293*, 1164–1166.

Fuente-Fernández, R. de la, Schulzer, M., & Stoessl, A. J. (2002). The placebo effect in neurological disorders. *Lancet Neurology, 1*, 85–91.

Fuller, A. K., & Fuller, A. E. (1986). Who introduced the English-speaking world to Sigmund Freud? *American Journal of Psychiatry, 143*, 1056–1057.

Furst, P. T. (1972). *Flesh of the Gods: The Ritual Use of Hallucinogens*. Washington, DC: Praeger.

Gabbard, G. O. (2000). A neurobiologically informed perspective on psychotherapy. *British Journal of Psychiatry, 177*, 117–122.

Gabbard, G. O., & Twemlow, S. W. (1984). *With the Eyes of the Mind: An Empirical Analysis of Out-of-Body States*. New York: Praeger.

Galishoff, M. L. (2000). God, prayer, and coronary care unit outcomes: Faith vs works? [letter]. *Archives of Internal Medicine, 160*, 1877.

Gallup, G., & Proctor, W. (1982). *Adventures in Immortality: A Look Beyond the Threshold of Death*. New York: McGraw-Hill.

Galton, F. (1872). Statistical inquiries into the efficacy of prayer. *Fortnightly Review, 12*, 125–135. (Also published in F. Galton, *Inquiries into Human Faculty and Development*, London: Macmillan, 1883, pp. 277–294)

Gamma, A., Lehmann, D., Frei, E., Iwata, K., Pascual-Marqui, R. D., & Vollenweider, F. X. (2004). Comparison of simultaneously recorded [$H_2{}^{15}O$]-PET and LORETA during cognitive and pharmacologic activation. *Human Brain Mapping, 22*, 83–96.

Gardner, H. (1976). *The Shattered Mind: The Person after Brain Damage*. New York: Vintage.

Gardner, H. (1985). *The Mind's New Science: A History of the Cognitive Revolution*. New York: Basic Books.

Gardner, R. (1983). Miracles of healing in Anglo-Celtic Northumbria as recorded by the Venerable Bede and his contemporaries: A reappraisal in the light of twentieth century experience. *British Medical Journal, 287*, 1927–1933.

Garner, J. (1974). Spontaneous regressions: Scientific documentation as a basis for the declaration of miracles. *Canadian Medical Association Journal, 111*, 1254–1264.

Gastaut, H. (1978). Fyodor Mikhailovitch Dostoevsky's involuntary contribution to the symptomatology and prognosis of epilepsy. *Epilepsia, 19*, 186–201.

Gastaut, H. (1984). New comments on the epilepsy of Fyodor Dostoevsky. *Epilepsia, 25*, 408–411.

Gauld, A. (1968). *The Founders of Psychical Research*. London: Routledge & Kegan Paul.

Gauld, A. (1982). *Mediumship and Survival*. London: Heinemann.

Gauld, A. (1988). Reflections on mesmeric analgesia. *British Journal of Experimental and Clinical Hypnosis, 5*, 17–24.

Gauld, A. (1989). Cognitive psychology, entrapment and the philosophy of mind. In J. R. Smythies & J. Beloff (Eds.), *The Case for Dualism* (pp. 187–253). Charlottesville: University Press of Virginia.

Gauld, A. (1990). The early history of hypnotic skin marking and blistering. *British Journal of Experimental and Clinical Hypnosis, 7*, 139–152.

Gauld, A. (1992). *A History of Hypnotism*. Cambridge: Cambridge University Press.

Gauld, A., & Shotter, J. D. (1977). *Human Action and Its Psychological Investigation*. London: Routledge & Kegan Paul.

Gazzaniga, M. (1970). *The Bisected Brain*. New York: Appleton-Century-Crofts.

Gellhorn, E., & Kiely, W. F. (1972). Mystical states of consciousness: Neurophysiological and clinical aspects. *Journal of Nervous and Mental Disease*, *154*, 399–405.

Gentner, D. (1983). Structure-mapping: A theoretical framework for analogy. *Cognitive Science*, *7*, 155–170.

Gentner, D., Holyoak, K. J., & Kokinov, B. K. (2001). *The Analogical Mind: Perspectives from Cognitive Science*. Cambridge, MA: MIT Press.

Ghiselin, B. (1952). *The Creative Process*. New York: New American Library.

Ghoneim, M. M., & Block, R. I. (1992). Learning and consciousness during general anesthesia. *Anesthesiology, 76*, 279–305.

Ghoneim, M. M., & Block, R. I. (1997). Learning and memory during general anesthesia: An update. *Anesthesiology*, *87*, 387–410.

Gidro-Frank, L., & Bowersbuch, M. K. (1948). A study of the plantar response in hypnotic age regression. *Journal of Nervous and Mental Disease*, *107*, 443–458.

Gifford-May, D., & Thompson, N. L. (1994). "Deep states" of meditation: Phenomenological reports of experience. *Journal of Transpersonal Psychology*, *26*, 117–138.

Gilbert, C. D. (1998). Adult cortical dynamics. *Physiological Review*, *78*, 467–485.

Ginandes, C., Brooks, P., Sando, W., Jones, C., & Aker, J. (2003). Can medical hypnosis accelerate post-surgical wound healing? Results of a clinical trial. *American Journal of Clinical Hypnosis*, *45*, 333–351.

Glicksman, M. D., & Kellehear, A. (1990). Near-death experiences and the measurement of blood gases. *Journal of Near-Death Studies*, *9*, 41–43.

Globus, G. (1987). *Dream Life, Wake Life: The Human Condition Through Dreams*. Albany: State University of New York Press.

Gloor, P. (1990). Experiential phenomena of temporal lobe epilepsy: Facts and hypotheses. *Brain*, *113*, 1673–1694.

Gloor, P., Olivier, A., Quesney, L. F., Andermann, F., & Horowitz, S. (1982). The role of the limbic system in experiential phenomena of temporal lobe epilepsy. *Annals of Neurology*, *12*, 129–144.

Goddard, H. (1899). The effects of mind on body, as evidenced by faith cures. *American Journal of Psychology*, *10*, 431–502.

Goetz, C. G., Leurgans, S., Raman, R., & Stebbins, G. T. (2000). Objective changes in motor function during placebo treatment in PD. *Neurology*, *54*, 710–714.

Golden, K. M. (1977). Voodoo in Africa and the United States. *American Journal of Psychiatry*, *134*, 1425–1427.

Golden, K. M. (1982). Voodoo in the hospital: A diagnostic and treatment dilemma. *American Journal of Social Psychiatry*, *11* (3), 39–43.

Goldstein, A., & Hilgard, E. R. (1975). Failure of the opiate antagonist naloxone to modify hypnotic analgesia. *Proceedings of the National Academy of Sciences USA*, *72*, 2041–2043.

Goldstone, R. L. (1994). The role of similarity in categorization: Providing a groundwork. *Cognition, 52*, 125–157.

Goleman, D. (1977). *The Varieties of the Meditative Experience.* New York: E. P. Dutton.

Goodman, N. (1972). Seven strictures on similarity. In N. Goodman (Ed.), *Problems and Projects* (pp. 437–446). New York: Bobbs-Merrill.

Gorton, B. E. (1949). The physiology of hypnosis: A review of the literature. *Psychiatric Quarterly, 23*, 317–343, 457–485.

Grabowska, M. J. (1971). The effect of hypnosis and hypnotic suggestion on the blood flow in the extremities. *Polish Medical Journal, 10*, 1044–1051.

Grace, R. F. (2003). The effect of variable dose-diazepam on dreaming and emergence phenomena in 400 cases of ketamine-fentanyl anaesthesia. *Anaesthesia, 58*, 904–910.

Gracely, R. H. (1995). Hypnosis and hierarchical pain control systems. *Pain, 60*, 1–2.

Graff, N. I., & Wallerstein, R. S. (1954). Unusual wheal reaction in a tattoo. *Psychosomatic Medicine, 16*, 505–515.

Granqvist, P., Fredrikson, M., Unge, P., Hagenfeldt, A., Valind, S., Larhammar, D., & Larsson, M. (2005). Sensed presence and mystical experiences are predicted by suggestibility, not by the application of transcranial weak complex magnetic fields. *Neuroscience Letters, 379*, 1–6.

Gravitz, M. A. (1981). The production of warts by suggestion as a cultural phenomenon. *American Journal of Clinical Hypnosis, 23*, 281–283.

Greeley, A. M. (1974). *Ecstasy: A Way of Knowing.* Englewood-Cliffs, NJ: Prentice-Hall.

Greeley, A. M. (1975). *The Sociology of the Paranormal: A Reconnaisance.* Beverly Hills, CA: Sage.

Greeley, A. M. (1987). Mysticism goes mainstream. *American Health, 6*, 47–49.

Green, C. (1960). Analysis of spontaneous cases. *Proceedings of the Society for Psychical Research, 53*, 97–161.

Green, C. (1968a). *Lucid Dreaming.* London: Hamish Hamilton.

Green, C. (1968b). *Out-of-the-Body Experiences.* New York: Ballantine Books.

Greene, B. (2004). *The Fabric of the Cosmos: Space, Time and the Texture of Reality.* London: Allen Lane.

Greene, W. A., Goldstein, S., & Moss, A. J. (1972). Psychosocial aspects of sudden death. *Archives of Internal Medicine, 129*, 725–731.

Gregory, W. (1851). *Letters to a Candid Enquirer, on Animal Magnetism.* London: Taylor, Walton, & Maberly.

Grey, M. (1985). *Return from Death.* London: Arkana.

Greyson, B. (1981). Near-death experiences and attempted suicide. *Suicide and Life-Threatening Behavior, 11*, 10–16.

Greyson, B. (1983a). Near-death experiences and personal values. *American Journal of Psychiatry, 140*, 618–620.

Greyson, B. (1983b). The near-death experience scale: Construction, reliability and validity. *Journal of Nervous and Mental Disease, 171*, 369–375.

Greyson, B. (1985). A typology of near-death experiences. *American Journal of Psychiatry, 142*, 967–969.

Greyson, B. (1991). Near-death experiences precipitated by suicide attempt: Lack of influence of psychopathology, religion, and expectations. *Journal of Near-Death Studies, 9*, 183–188.

Greyson, B. (1992). Reduced death threat in near-death experiences. *Death Studies, 16*, 533–546.

Greyson, B. (1992–1993). Near-death experiencers and antisuicidal attitudes. *Omega, 26*, 81–89.

Greyson, B. (1997). The near-death experience as a focus of clinical attention. *Journal of Nervous and Mental Disease, 185*, 327–334.

Greyson, B. (1998). The incidence of near-death experiences. *Medicine & Psychiatry, 1*, 92–99.

Greyson, B. (1999). Defining near-death experiences. *Mortality, 4*, 7–19.

Greyson, B. (2000). Dissociation in people who have near-death experiences: Out of their bodies or out of their minds? *Lancet, 355*, 460–463.

Greyson, B. (2001). Posttraumatic stress symptoms following near-death experiences. *American Journal of Orthopsychiatry, 71*, 358–373.

Greyson, B. (2003). Incidence and correlates of near-death experiences in a cardiac care unit. *General Hospital Psychiatry, 25*, 269–276.

Greyson, B., & Bush, N. E. (1992). Distressing near-death experiences. *Psychiatry, 55*, 95–110.

Greyson, B., & Stevenson, I. (1980). The phenomenology of near-death experiences. *American Journal of Psychiatry, 137,* 1193–1196.

Griffin, D. R. (1993). Parapsychology and philosophy: A Whiteheadian postmodern perspective. *Journal of the American Society for Psychical Research, 87,* 217–288.

Griffin, D. R. (1994). Dualism, materialism, idealism, and psi: A reply to John Palmer. *Journal of the American Society for Psychical Research, 88*, 23–39.

Griffin, D. R. (1997). *Parapsychology, Philosophy, and Spirituality: A Postmodern Examination.* Albany: State University of New York Press.

Griffin, D. R. (1998). *Unsnarling the World Knot: Consciousness, Freedom and the Mind-Body Problem.* Berkeley: University of California Press.

Griffin, D. R. (2000). *Religion and Scientific Naturalism: Overcoming the Conflicts.* Albany: State University of New York Press.

Griffin, D. R., Cobb, J. B., Ford, M. P., Gunter, P. A. Y., & Ochs, P. (1993). *Founders of Constructive Postmodern Philosophy: Peirce, James, Bergson, Whitehead, and Hartshorne*. Albany: State University of New York Press.

Grimby, A. (1993). Bereavement among elderly people: Grief reactions, post-bereavement hallucinations and quality of life. *Acta Psychiatrica Scandinavia, 87,* 72–80.

Grinspoon, L., & Bakalar, J. B. (1997). *Psychedelic Drugs Reconsidered.* New York: Lindesmith Center. (Original work published 1979)

Grob, C. S. (1998). Psychiatric research with hallucinogens: What have we learned? *Heffler Review of Psychedelic Research, 1,* 8–20.

Grof, S. (1975). *Realms of the Human Unconscious: Observations from LSD Research.* New York: Viking.

Grof, S. (1980). Realms of the human unconscious: Observations from LSD research. In R. N. Walsh & F. Vaughan (Eds.), *Beyond Ego: Transpersonal Dimensions in Psychology* (pp. 87–99). Los Angeles: J. P. Tarcher.

Grof, S. (1985). *Beyond the Brain: Birth, Death, and Transcendence in Psychotherapy.* Albany: State University of New York Press.

Grosso, M. (1981). Toward an explanation of near-death phenomena. *Journal of the American Society for Psychical Research, 75,* 37–60.

Grosso, M. (1983). Jung, parapsychology, and the near-death experience: Toward a transpersonal paradigm. *Anabiosis: The Journal for Near-Death Studies, 3,* 3–38.

Grosso, M. (2004). *Experiencing the Next World Now.* New York: Paraview.

Grosso, M. (in press). Mediumship and creativity. In L. Coly, C. S. Alvarado, & N. L. Zingrone (Eds.), *The Study of Mediumship: Interdisciplinary Perspectives.* New York: Parapsychology Foundation.

Grotstein, J. (2000). *Who is the Dreamer Who Dreams the Dream?* Hillsdale, NJ: Analytic Press.

Group for the Advancement of Psychiatry (1976). *Mysticism: Spiritual Quest or Psychic Disorder?* New York.

Grutzendler, J., Kasthuri, N., & Gan, W.-B. (2002). Long-term dendritic spine stability in the adult cortex. *Nature, 420,* 812–816.

Guilford, J. P. (1950). Creativity. *American Psychologist, 5,* 444–454.

Guin, J. D., Kumar, V., & Petersen, B. H. (1981). Immunofluorescence findings in rapid whitening of scalp hair. *Archives of Dermatology, 117,* 576–578.

Gurney, E. (1884). The stages of hypnotism. *Proceedings of the Society for Psychical Research, 2,* 61–72. (Also published in *Mind, 9,* 110–121, 1884)

Gurney, E. (1885). Hallucinations. *Proceedings of the Society for Psychical Research, 3,* 151–189.

Gurney, E. (1887a). [Comment on case reported by Dr. Biggs.] *Journal of the Society for Psychical Research, 3,* 103–105.

Gurney, E. (1887b). Peculiarities of certain post-hypnotic states. *Proceedings of the Society for Psychical Research*, *4*, 268–323.

Gurney, E. (1887c). Stages of hypnotic memory. *Proceedings of the Society for Psychical Research*, *4*, 515–531.

Gurney, E. (1887d). *Tertium Quid: Chapters on Various Disputed Questions* (2 vols). London: Kegan Paul, Trench.

Gurney, E. (1888). Recent experiments in hypnotism. *Proceedings of the Society for Psychical Research*, *5*, 3–17.

Gurney, E., & Myers, F. W. H. (1883). Mesmerism. *Nineteenth Century*, *9*, 695–719.

Gurney, E., & Myers, F. W. H. (1884a). Apparitions. *Nineteenth Century*, *15*, 791–815.

Gurney, E., & Myers, F. W. H. (1884b). Visible apparitions. *Nineteenth Century*, *16*, 68–95.

Gurney, E., & Myers, F. W. H. (1885). Some higher aspects of mesmerism. *Proceedings of the Society for Psychical Research*, *3*, 401–423.

Gurney, E., & Myers, F. W. H. (1889). On apparitions occurring soon after death. *Proceedings of the Society for Psychical Research*, *5*, 403–485.

Gurney, E., Myers, F. W. H., & Podmore, F. (1886). *Phantasms of the Living* (2 vols.). London: Trübner.

Haag, R. (1996). *Local Quantum Physics*. Berlin: Springer.

Haas, D. C., Davidson, K. W., Schwartz, D. J., Rieckmann, N., Roman, M. J., Pickering, T. G., Gerin, W., & Schwartz, J. E. (2005). Depressive symptoms are independently predictive of carotid atherosclerosis. *American Journal of Cardiology*, *95*, 547–550.

Hadamard, J. (1949). *The Psychology of Invention in the Mathematical Field* (enlarged ed.). Mineola, NY: Dover.

Hadfield, J. A. (1917). The influence of hypnotic suggestion on inflammatory conditions. *Lancet*, *2*, 678–679.

Hadjikhani, N., Sanchez del Rio, M., Wu, O., Schwartz, D., Bakker, D., Fischl, B., Kwong, K. K., Cutrer, F. M., Rosen, B. R., Tootell, R. B. H., Sorensen, A. G., & Moskowitz, M. A. (2001). Mechanisms of migraine aura revealed by functional MRI in human visual cortex. *Proceedings of the National Academy of Sciences USA*, *98*, 4687–4692.

Hadley, E. E. (1929–1930). Axillary "menstruation" in a male. *American Journal of Psychiatry*, *9*, 1101–1111.

Hahn, R. A. (1997). The nocebo phenomenon: Scope and foundations. In A. Harrington (Ed.), *The Placebo Effect: An Interdisciplinary Exploration* (pp. 56–76). Cambridge, MA: Harvard University Press.

Hahn, R. A., & Kleinman, A. (1983). Belief as pathogen, belief as medicine: "Voodoo death" and the "placebo phenomenon" in anthropological perspective. *Medical Anthropology Quarterly*, *4*(3), 16–19.

Haier, R. J., Jung, R. E., Yeo, R. A., Head, K., & Alkire, M. T. (2004). Structural brain variation and general intelligence. *NeuroImage, 23*, 425–433.

Haier, R. J., Siegel, B. V., Jr., MacLachlan, A., Soderberg, E., Lotternberg, S., & Buchsbaum, M. S. (1992). Regional glucose metabolic changes after learning complex visuospatial/motor task. *Brain Research, 570*, 134–143.

Haldane, E., & Ross, G. R. T. (1931). *The Philosophical Works of Descartes*. Cambridge: Cambridge University Press.

Halgren, E. (1982). Mental phenomena induced by stimulation in the limbic system. *Human Neurobiology, 1*, 251–260.

Halgren, E., Walter, R. D., Cherlow, D. G., & Crandall, P. H. (1978). Mental phenomena evoked by electrical stimulation of the human hippocampal formation and amygdala. *Brain, 101*, 83–117.

Hall, C. (1953). A cognitive theory of dream symbols. *Journal of General Psychology, 48*, 169–186.

Halligan, P. W., & David, A. S. (1999). Conversion hysteria: Towards a cognitive neuropsychological account. *Cognitive Neuropsychiatry, 4*, 161–163.

Hamill, R. W. (1996). Peripheral autonomic nervous system. In D. Robertson, P. A. Low, & R. J. Polinsky (Eds.), *Primer on the Autonomic Nervous System* (pp. 12–25). San Diego, CA: Academic Press.

Hammond, D. C., Keye, W. R., & Grant, C. W., Jr. (1983). Hypnotic analgesia with burns: An initial study. *American Journal of Clinical Hypnosis, 26*, 56–59.

Hannah, B. (1981). *Encounters with the Soul: Active Imagination as Developed by C. G. Jung*. Ft. Collins, CO: Sigo Press.

Hansel, C. E. M. (1966). *ESP: A Scientific Evaluation*. New York: Charles Scribner's Sons.

Happold, F. C. (1970). *Mysticism*. Baltimore: Penguin. (Original work published 1963)

Harding, R. E. M. (1948). *An Anatomy of Inspiration and an Essay on the Creative Mind* (3rd ed.). Cambridge: W. Heffer & Sons.

Hardy, A. (1979). *The Spiritual Nature of Man: A Study of Contemporary Religious Experience*. Oxford: Oxford University Press.

Harnish, R. M. (2002). *Minds, Brains, Computers: An Historical Introduction to the Foundations of Cognitive Science*. Oxford: Blackwell.

Harpaz, Y. (2006). Misunderstanding in cognitive brain imaging [on-line]. Available: http://human-brain.org/imaging.html.

Harrington, A. (1987). *Medicine, Mind, and the Double Brain*. Princeton, NJ: Princeton University Press.

Harrington, A. (1997). Introduction. In A. Harrington (Ed.), *The Placebo Effect: An Interdisciplinary Exploration* (pp. 1–11). Cambridge: Harvard University Press.

Harris, W. S., Gowda, M., Kolb, J. W., Strychacz, C. P., Vacek, J. L., Jones, P. G., Forker, A., O'Keefe, J. H., & McAllister, B. D. (1999). A randomized, controlled trial of the effects of remote, intercessory prayer on outcomes in patients admitted to the coronary care unit. *Archives of Internal Medicine, 159*, 2273–2278.

Harrison, S. (1989). A new visualization of the mind-brain relationship: Naive realism transcended. In J. R. Smythies & J. Beloff (Eds.), *The Case for Dualism* (pp. 113–165). Charlottesville: University Press of Virginia.

Hart, B. (1926). The conception of dissociation. *British Journal of Medical Psychology, 6*, 241–263.

Hart, H. (1954). ESP projection: Spontaneous cases and the experimental method. *Journal of the American Society for Psychical Research, 48*, 121–146.

Hart, H., & collaborators (1956). Six theories about apparitions. *Proceedings of the Society for Psychical Research, 50*, 153–239.

Hart, H., & Hart, E. B. (1933). Visions and apparitions collectively and reciprocally perceived. *Proceedings of the Society for Psychical Research, 41*, 205–249.

Hartmann, E. (1975). Dreams and other hallucinations: An approach to the underlying mechanism. In R. K. Siegel & L. J. West (Eds.), *Hallucinations: Behavior, Experience, and Theory* (pp. 71–79). New York : John Wiley & Sons.

Hartmann, E. (1989). Boundaries of dreams, boundaries of dreamers: Thin and thick boundaries as a new personality measure. *Psychiatric Journal of the University of Ottawa, 14*, 557–560.

Hartmann, E. (1991). *Boundaries in the Mind: A New Psychology of Personality*. New York: Basic Books.

Hashish, I., Harvey, W., & Harris, M. (1986). Anti-inflammatory effects of ultrasound therapy: Evidence for a major placebo effect. *British Journal of Rheumatology, 25*, 77–81.

Haxthausen, H. (1936). The pathogenesis of hysterical skin-affections. *British Journal of Dermatology and Syphilis, 48*, 563–567.

Hay, D. (1994). "The biology of god": What is the current status of Hardy's hypothesis? *International Journal for the Psychology of Religion, 4*, 1–23.

Hay, D., & Morisy, A. (1978). Reports of ecstatic, paranormal, or religious experience in Great Britain and the United States—A comparison of trends. *Journal for the Scientific Study of Religion, 17*, 255–268.

Haynes, J.-D., & Rees, G. (2005). Predicting the orientation of invisible stimuli from activity in human primary visual cortex. *Nature Neuroscience, 8*, 686–691.

Hebb, D. O. (1949). *The Organization of Behavior*. New York: Wiley.

Hécaen, H., & Lanteri-Laura, G. (1977). *Evolution des connaissances et des doctrines sur les localisations cérébrales*. Paris: Desclée de Brouwer.

Heier, T., & Steen, P. A. (1996). Awareness in anaesthesia: Incidence, consequences and prevention. *Acta Anaesthesiologica Scandinavica, 40*, 1073–1086.

Heil, J. (1978). Traces of things past. *Philosophy of Science, 45*, 60–72.

Heil, J. (1981). Does cognitive psychology rest on a mistake? *Mind, 90*, 321–341.

Heil, J. (1998). *Philosophy of Mind: A Contemporary Introduction*. London: Routledge.

Heilman, K. M. (2002). *Matters of Mind: A Neurologist's View of Brain-Behavior Relationships*. New York: Oxford University Press.

Heilman, K. M., & Valenstein, E. (2003). *Clinical Neuropsychology* (4th ed.). Oxford: Oxford University Press.

Heim, A. v. St. G. (1972). The experience of dying from falls (R. Noyes & R. Kletti, Trans.) *Omega*, *3*, 45–52. (Original work published 1892)

Hejja, P., & Galloon, S. (1975). A consideration of ketamine dreams. *Canadian Anesthesia Society Journal*, *22*, 100–105.

Helm, F., & Milgrom, H. (1970). Can scalp hair suddenly turn white? *Archives of Dermatology*, *102*, 102–103.

Herzog, D. B., & Herrin, J. T. (1985). Near-death experiences in the very young. *Critical Care Medicine, 13*, 1074–1075.

Hilgard, E. (1962). Impulsive versus realistic thinking: An examination of the distinction between primary and secondary processes in thought. *Psychological Bulletin*, *59*, 477–488.

Hilgard, E. (1977). *Divided Consciousness*. New York: John Wiley & Sons.

Hilgard, E. (1994). Neodissociation theory. In S. Lynn & J. Rhue (Eds.), *Dissociation: Clinical and Theoretical Perspectives* (pp. 32–51). New York: Guilford Press.

Hilgard, E. R., & Hilgard, J. R. (1983). *Hypnosis in the Relief of Pain* (Rev. ed.). Los Altos, CA: William Kaufmann. (Original work published 1975)

Hill, J. S. (1978). *Imagination in Coleridge*. Totowa, NJ: Rowman & Littlefield.

Hirsch, W. (1896). *Genius and Degeneration: A Psychological Study* (2nd ed.). New York: D. Appleton.

Ho, K. H., Hashish, I., Salmon, P., Freeman, R., & Harvey, W. (1988). Reduction of post-operative swelling by a placebo effect. *Journal of Psychosomatic Research*, *32*, 197–205.

Hocevar, D. (1981). Measurement of creativity: Review and critique. *Journal of Personality Assessment*, *45*, 450–464.

Hodges, J. R., Patterson, K., Oxbury, S., & Funnell, E. (1992). Semantic dementia: Progressive fluent aphasia with temporal lobe atrophy. *Brain, 121*, 1313–1327.

Hodges, R. D., & Scofield, A. M. (1995). Is spiritual healing a valid and effective therapy? *Journal of the Royal Society of Medicine*, *88*, 203–207.

Hodgson, D. (1991). *The Mind Matters: Consciousness and Choice in a Quantum World*. Oxford: Oxford University Press.

Hodgson, R. (1891). A case of double consciousness. *Proceedings of the Society for Psychical Research*, *7*, 221–257.

Hodgson, R. (1892). A record of observations of certain phenomena of trance. *Proceedings of the Society for Psychical Research*, *8*, 1–167.

Hodgson, R. (1898). A further record of observations of certain phenomena of trance. *Proceedings of the Society for Psychical Research, 13*, 284–582.

Hoenig, J. (1968). Medical research on yoga. *Confinia Psychiatrica, 11*, 69–89.

Hoerl, C. (2001). The phenomenology of episodic recall. In C. Hoerl & T. McCormack (Eds.), *Time and Memory* (pp. 315–335). Oxford: Oxford University Press.

Hofstadter, D., & FARG (1995). *Fluid Concepts and Creative Analogies: Computer Models of the Fundamental Mechanisms of Thought*. New York: Basic Books.

Holck, F. H. (1978). Life revisited: Parallels in death experiences. *Omega, 9*, 1–11.

Holden, C. (1978). Cancer and the mind: How are they connected? *Science, 200*, 1363–1369.

Hölscher, C. (Ed.) (2001). *Neuronal Mechanisms of Memory Formation: Concepts of Long-Term Potentiation and Beyond*. Cambridge: Cambridge University Press.

Holt, H. (1915). *On the Cosmic Relations* (2 vols.). London: Williams & Norgate.

Holt, N. J., Delanoy, D. L., & Roe, C. H. (2004, August). *Creativity, subjective paranormal experiences and altered states of consciousness*. Paper presented at the 47th Parapsychological Association Convention, Vienna, Austria.

Holt, R. R. (1964). Imagery: The return of the ostracized. *American Psychologist, 12*, 254–264.

Holyoak, K. J., & Thagard, P. (1989). Analogical mapping by constraint satisfaction. *Cognitive Science, 13*, 295–335.

Holyoak, K. J., & Thagard, P. (1995). *Mental Leaps: Analogy in Creative Thought*. Cambridge, MA: MIT Press.

Honorton, C. (1977). Psi and internal attention states. In B. B. Wolman (Ed.), *Handbook of Parapsychology* (pp. 435–472). New York: Van Nostrand Reinhold.

Honorton, C. (1997). The ganzfeld novice: Four predictors of initial ESP performance. *Journal of Parapsychology, 61*, 143–158.

Honorton, C., & Krippner, S. (1969). Hypnosis and ESP: A review of the experimental literature. *Journal of the American Society for Psychical Research, 63*, 214–252.

Hood, R. W., Jr. (1975). The construction and preliminary validation of a measure of reported mystical experience. *Journal for the Scientific Study of Religion, 14*, 29–41.

Hood, R. W., Jr., Morris, R. J., & Watson, P. J. (1993). Further factor analysis of Hood's mysticism scale. *Psychological Reports, 3*, 1176–1178.

Horgan, J. (2003). *Rational Mysticism: Dispatches from the Border between Science and Spirituality*. Boston: Houghton Mifflin.

Horner, M. D. (1990). Psychobiological evidence of the distinction between episodic and semantic memory. *Neuropsychology Review, 1*, 281–321.

Hornig, S., & Miller, F. G. (2002). Is placebo surgery unethical? *New England Journal of Medicine, 347*, 137–139.

Horowitz, M. J., & Adams, J. E. (1970). Hallucinations on brain stimulation: Evidence for revision of the Penfield hypothesis. In W. Keup (Ed.), *Origin and Mechanisms of Hallucinations* (pp. 13–22). New York: Plenum.

Hosinski, T. E. (1993). *Stubborn Fact and Creative Advance: An Introduction to the Metaphysics of Alfred North Whitehead*. Lanham, MD: Rowman & Littlefield.

Housman, A. E. (1952). The name and nature of poetry. In B. Ghiselin (Ed.), *The Creative Process* (pp. 86–91). New York: New American Library.

Howard, M. W., Rizzuto, D. S., Caplan, J. B., Madsen, J. R., Lisman, J., Aschenbrenner-Scheibe, R., Schulze-Bonhage, A., & Kahana, M. J. (2003). Gamma oscillations correlate with working memory load in humans. *Cerebral Cortex, 13*, 1369–1374.

Howarth, G., & Kellehear, A. (2001). Shared near-death and related illness experiences. *Journal of Near-Death Studies, 20*, 71–85.

Hróbjartsson, A., & Gøtzsche, P. C. (2001). Is the placebo powerless? An analysis of clinical trials comparing placebo with no treatment. *New England Journal of Medicine, 344*, 1594–1602.

Hubel, D. H., & Wiesel, T. N. (1962). Receptive fields, binocular interaction and functional architecture in the cat's visual cortex. *Journal of Physiology, 160*, 106–154.

Huettell, S. A., McKeown, M. J., Song, A. W., Hart, S., Spencer, D. D., Truett, A., & McCarthy, G. (2004). Linking hemodynamic and electrophysiological measures of brain activity: Evidence from functional MRI and intracranial field potentials. *Cerebral Cortex, 14*, 165–173.

Hufford, D. (1982). *The Terror That Comes in the Night: An Experience-Centered Study of Supernatural Assault Traditions*. Philadelphia: University of Pennsylvania Press.

Hufford, D. (1985). Commentary: Mystical experience in the modern world. In G. Foster, *The World Was Flooded With Light* (pp. 87–183). Pittsburgh: University of Pittsburgh Press.

Hufford, D. (2005). Sleep paralysis as spiritual experience. *Transcultural Psychiatry, 42*, 11–45.

Hugdahl, K. V. (1996). Cognitive influences on human autonomic system function. *Current Opinion in Neurobiology, 6*, 252–258.

Hughes, J. R., Kuhlman, D. T., Fichtner, C. G., & Gruenfeld, M. J. (1990). Brain mapping in a case of multiple personality. *Clinical Electroencephalography, 21*, 200–209.

Hummel, J. E., & Holyoak, K. J. (1997). Distributed representations of structure: A theory of analogical access and mapping. *Psychological Review, 104*, 427–466.

Humphrey, G. (1963). *Thinking*. New York: Wiley.

Humphrey, N. (1996). *Leaps of Faith: Science, Miracles, and the Search for Supernatural Consolation*. New York: Basic Books.

Hunter, J. D. W. (1965). Scared to death? [letter]. *British Medical Journal, 2*, 701.

Hutchinson, E. D. (1931). Materials for the study of creative thinking. *Psychological Bulletin, 28*, 392–410.

Hutchinson, E. D. (1939). Varieties of insight in humans. *Psychiatry, 2*, 323–332.

Huxley, A. (1961). Foreword. In S. Smith (Ed.), abridged volume of *Human Personality and Its Survival of Bodily Death*, by F. W. H. Myers (pp. 7–8). New Hyde Park, NY: University Books.

Huxley, A. (1970). *The Perennial Philosophy*. New York: Harper & Row. (Original work published 1944)

Huxley, A. (1990). *The Doors of Perception*. In A. Huxley, *The Doors of Perception and Heaven and Hell* (pp. 7–79). New York: Perennial Library. (Original work published 1954)

Huxley, T. H. (1874). On the hypothesis that animals are automata, and its history. *Fortnightly Review*, n.s. *16*, 555–580.

Huxley, T. H. (1892). Science and pseudo-science. In *Essays Upon Some Controverted Questions* (pp. 265–297). London: Macmillan. (Original work published 1887)

Huxley, T. H. (1892). Prologue. In *Essays Upon Some Controverted Questions* (pp. 1–53). London: Macmillan.

Huxley, T. H. (1898). The struggle for existence in human society. In *Evolution and Ethics and Other Essays* (pp. 195–236). London: Macmillan. (Original work published 1888)

Huxley, T. H. (1913). *Life and Letters of Thomas Henry Huxley* (2nd ed.) (L. Huxley, Ed.). London: Macmillan.

Hyslop, J. H. (1901). A further record of observations of certain trance phenomena. *Proceedings of the Society for Psychical Research, 16*, 1–649.

Hyslop, J. H. (1905). *Science and a Future Life*. Boston: Turner.

Hyslop, J. H. (1908). *Psychical Research and the Resurrection*. Boston: Small, Maynard.

Ikemi, Y., & Nakagawa, S. (1962). A psychosomatic study of contagious dermatitis. *Kyushu Journal of Medical Science, 13*, 335–350.

Ikemi, Y., Nakagawa, S., Nakagawa, T., & Sugita, M. (1975). Psychosomatic consideration on cancer patients who have made a narrow escape from death. *Dynamic Psychiatry, 31*, 77–92.

Inglis, B. (1983). Retrocognitive dissonance. In W. G. Roll, J. Beloff, & R. A. White (Eds.), *Research in Parapsychology 1982* (pp. 69–72). Metuchen, NJ: Scarecrow. [Abstract]

Insinger, M. (1991). The impact of a near-death experience on family relationships. *Journal of Near-Death Studies, 9*, 141–181.

Irle, E., & Markowitsch, H. J. (1990). Functional recovery after limbic lesions in monkeys. *Brain Research Bulletin, 25*, 79–92.

Irwin, H. J. (1985). *Flight of Mind: A Psychological Study of the Out-of-Body Experience*. Metuchen, NJ: Scarecrow Press.

Jackson, J. H. (1884). The Croonian lectures on evolution and dissolution of the nervous system. *British Medical Journal, 2*, 591–593.

Jackson, J. H. (1888). On a particular variety of epilepsy ("intellectual aura"), one case with symptoms of organic brain disease. *Brain, 11,* 179–207.

Jackson, J. H. (1898). Case of epilepsy with tasting movements and "dreamy state"—Very small patch of softening in the left uncinate gyrus. *Brain, 21,* 580–590.

Jackson, J. H. (1931–1932). *Selected Writings of John Hughlings Jackson* (2 vols). London: Hodder & Stoughton.

Jacob, P. (1997). *What Minds Can Do: Intentionality in a Non-Intentional World.* Cambridge: Cambridge University Press.

Jacobs, S., & Ostfeld, A. (1977). An epidemiological review of the mortality of bereavement. *Psychosomatic Medicine, 39*, 344–357.

Jain, M., & Jain, K. M. (1973). The science of yoga: A study in perspective. *Perspectives in Biology and Medicine, 16*, 93–102.

James, W. (1879). Are we automata? *Mind, 4*, 1–22.

James, W. (1887). [Review of] *Phantasms of the Living. Science, 9*, 18–20.

James, W. (1889). Notes on automatic writing. *Proceedings of the American Society for Psychical Research, 1*, 548–564.

James, W. (1890a). The hidden self. *Scribner's Magazine, 7*, 361–373.

James, W. (1890b). *The Principles of Psychology* (2 vols.). New York: Henry Holt.

James, W. (1892). *Psychology: Briefer Course*. New York: Henry Holt.

James, W. (1896). Address by the President. *Proceedings of the Society for Psychical Research, 12*, 2–10. (Reprinted in *The Works of William James: Essays in Psychical Research,* pp. 127–137, F. H. Burkhardt, ed., 1986, Cambridge, MA: Harvard University Press)

James, W. (1900). *Human Immortality: Two Supposed Objections to the Doctrine* (2nd ed.). Boston & New York: Houghton, Mifflin. (Original work published 1898)

James, W. (1901). Frederic Myers's service to psychology. *Proceedings of the Society for Psychical Research, 17*, 1–23. (On our digital version of *HP*)

James, W. (1903). [Review of] *Human Personality and Its Survival of Bodily Death. Proceedings of the Society for Psychical Research, 18*, 22–33. (On our digital version of *HP*)

James, W. (1909). Report on Mrs. Piper's Hodgson-control. *Proceedings of the Society for Psychical Research, 23,* 2–121.

James, W. (1910). What psychical research has accomplished. In *The Will to Believe and Other Essays in Popular Philosophy* (pp. 299–327). London: Longmans, Green. (Composed of segments originally published 1890, 1892, and 1896)

James, W. (1920). *The Letters of William James* (H. James, ed.). Boston: Little, Brown.

James, W. (1958). *The Varieties of Religious Experience.* New York: Mentor. (Original work published 1902)

James, W. (1971). *A Pluralistic Universe*. In *Essays in Radical Empiricism and A Pluralistic Universe* (pp. 121–284). New York: E. P. Dutton. (Original work published 1909)

James, W. (1978). The knowing of things together [1894 Presidential Address to the American Psychological Association]. In F. H. Burkhardt (Ed.), *The Works of William James. Vol. 5: Essays in Philosophy* (pp. 71–89). Cambridge, MA: Harvard University Press. (Original work published 1895)

James, W. (1986). The confidences of a psychical researcher. In F. H. Burkhardt (Ed.), *Essays in Psychical Research* (pp. 361–375). Cambridge, MA: Harvard University Press. (Original work published 1909)

James, W. (1986). *Essays in Psychical Research* (F. H. Burkhardt, Ed.). Cambridge, MA: Harvard University Press.

James, W. (1988). The brain and the mind. In I. K. Skrupskelis (Ed.), *Manuscript Lectures* (pp. 16–43). Cambridge, MA: Harvard University Press. (Lecture delivered in 1878)

Jamison, K. R. (1993). *Touched With Fire: Manic-Depressive Illness and the Artistic Temperament*. New York: Simon & Schuster.

Janet, P. (1886). Les actes inconscients et le dédoublement de la personnalité pendant le somnambulisme provoqué. *Revue philosophique, 22*, 577–592.

Janet, P. (1887). L'anesthésie systématisée et la dissociation des phénomènes psychologiques. *Revue philosophique, 23*, 449–472.

Janet, P. (1888). Les actes inconscients et la mémoire pendant le somnambulisme. *Revue philosophique, 25*, 238–279.

Janet, P. (1889). *L'automatisme psychologique: Essai de psychologie expérimental sur les formes inférieures de l'activité humaine*. Paris: Félix Alcan.

Janet, P. (1968a). Report on some phenomena of somnambulism (B. S. Koppell, Trans.). *Journal of the History of the Behavioral Sciences, 4*, 124–131. (Original work published 1886)

Janet, P. (1968b). Second observation of sleep provoked from a distance and the mental suggestion during the somnambulistic state (B. S. Koppell, Trans.). *Journal of the History of the Behavioral Sciences, 4*, 258–267. (Original work published 1886)

Janet, P. (1901). *The Mental State of Hystericals: A Study of Mental Stigmata and Mental Accidents* (C. R. Corson, Trans.). New York: G. P. Putnam's Sons. (Original work published 1893)

Janet, P. (1920). *The Major Symptoms of Hysteria* (2nd ed.). New York: Macmillan. (Original work published 1907)

Janet, P. (1961). [Autobiographical chapter.] In C. Murchison (Ed.), *A History of Psychology in Autobiography* (pp. 123–133). New York: Russell & Russell. (Original work published 1930)

Jänig, W. (1990). Functions of the sympathetic innervation of the skin. In A. D. Loewy & K. M. Spyer (Eds.), *Central Regulation of Autonomic Functions* (pp. 334–348). New York: Oxford University Press.

Jansen, K. L. R. (1997a). The ketamine model of the near-death experience: A central role for the *N*-methyl-*D*-aspartate receptor. *Journal of Near-Death Studies, 16*, 5–26.

Jansen, K. L. R. (1997b). Response to commentaries on "The ketamine model of the near-death experience." *Journal of Near-Death Studies, 16*, 79–95.

Jastrow, J. (1900). *Fact and Fable in Psychology.* Boston & New York: Houghton, Mifflin.

Jastrow, J. (1903). The status of the subconscious. *American Journal of Psychology, 14*, 343–353.

Jastrow, J. (1906). *The Subconscious.* Boston & New York: Houghton, Mifflin.

Jelinek, J. E. (1973). Sudden whitening of the hair. *Cutis, 11*, 513–530.

Jella, S. A., & Shannahoff-Khalsa, D. S. (1993). The effects of unilateral forced nostril breathing on cognitive performance. *International Journal of Neuroscience, 73*, 61–68.

John, E. R. (1976). A model of consciousness. In G. Schwartz & D. Shapiro (Eds.), *Consciousness and Self-Regulation* (pp. 6–50). New York: Plenum.

John, E. R. (2001). A field theory of consciousness. *Consciousness and Cognition, 10*, 184–213.

John, E. R., Prichep, L. S., Kox, W., Valdés-Sosa, P., Bosch-Bayard, J., Aubert, E., Tom, M., diMichele, F., & Gugino, L. D. (2001). Invariant reversible QEEG effects of anesthetics. *Consciousness and Cognition, 10*, 165–183.

Johnson, A. (1899). Coincidences. *Proceedings of the Society for Psychical Research, 14*, 158–330.

Johnson, A. G. (1994). Surgery as a placebo. *Lancet, 344*, 1140–1142.

Johnson, M. H. (2005). *Developmental Cognitive Neuroscience: An Introduction* (2nd ed.). Oxford: Blackwell.

Johnson, R. F. Q., & Barber, T. X. (1976). Hypnotic suggestions for blister formation: Subjective and physiological effects. *American Journal of Clinical Hypnosis, 18*, 172–181.

Johnson, R. F. Q., & Barber, T. X. (1978). Hypnosis, suggestions, and warts: An experimental investigation implicating the importance of "believed-in efficacy." *American Journal of Clinical Hypnosis, 20*, 165–174.

Johnson-Laird, P. N. (1983). *Mental Models: Towards a Cognitive Science of Language, Inference, and Consciousness.* Cambridge: Cambridge University Press.

Johnstone, R. E. (1973). A ketamine trip. *Anesthesiology, 39*, 460–461.

Joines, W. T., Baumann, S. B., Kim, J., Zile, J. M., & Simmonds, C. (2004, August). *The measurement and characterization of charge accumulation and electromagnetic emission from bioenergy healers.* Paper presented at the 47th Parapsychological Association Convention, Vienna, Austria.

Joliot, M., Ribary, U., & Llinás, R. (1994). Human oscillatory brain activity near 40 Hz coexists with cognitive temporal binding. *Proceedings of the National Academy of Sciences USA, 91*, 11748–11751.

Jones, E. (1918). *Papers on Psycho-Analysis* (Rev. and enlarged). Toronto: Macmillan.

Jones, E. (1961). *The Life and Work of Sigmund Freud* (L. Trilling & S. Marcus, Eds.). New York: Basic Books.

Jones, R. (1902). Grey hair and emotional states: An anthropological note. *Lancet, 1*, 583–585.

Jowett, B. (Trans.) (1937). *The Dialogues of Plato*. New York: Random House. (Original work published 1892)

Juda, A. (1949). The relationship between highest mental capacity and psychic abnormalities. *American Journal of Psychiatry, 106*, 296–309.

Julesz, B. (1971). *Foundations of Cyclopean Perception*. Chicago: University of Chicago Press.

Jung, C. G. (1952). Psychology and literature. In B. Ghiselin (Ed.), *The Creative Process* (pp. 208–223). New York: New American Library.

Jung, C. G. (1965). *Memories, Dreams, Reflections*. New York: Vintage. (Original work published 1961)

Jung, C. G. (1969a). *The Archetypes and the Collective Unconscious* (R. F. C. Hull, Trans.) (2nd ed.). In *The Collected Works of C. J. Jung* (Bollingen Series 20, vol. 9, part 1). Princeton, NJ: Princeton University Press.

Jung, C. G. (1969b). *Psychology and Religion: West and East* (R. F. C. Hull, Trans.) (2nd ed.). In *The Collected Works of C. J. Jung* (Bollingen Series 20, vol. 11). Princeton, NJ: Princeton University Press.

Jung, C. (1978). A review of the complex theory. In *The Structure and Dynamics of the Psyche* (*The Collected Works of C. G. Jung*, vol. 8, pp. 92–104). Princeton, NJ: Princeton University Press. (Original work published 1934)

Jung, C. (1978). Psychological factors determining human behavior. In *The Structure and Dynamics of the Psyche* (*The Collected Works of C. G. Jung*, vol. 8, pp. 114–125). Princeton, NJ: Princeton University Press. (Original work published 1937)

Jung, C. (1978). On the nature of the psyche. In *The Structure and Dynamics of the Psyche* (*The Collected Works of C. G. Jung*, vol. 8, pp. 150–234). Princeton, NJ: Princeton University Press. (Original work published 1946)

Jung, C. (1983). On the psychology and pathology of so-called occult phenomena. In *Psychiatric Studies* (*The Collected Works of C. G. Jung*, vol. 1, pp. 3–88). Princeton, NJ: Princeton University Press. (Original work published 1902)

Kamitani, Y., & Tong, F. (2005). Decoding the visual and subjective contents of the human brain. *Nature Neuroscience, 8*, 679–685.

Kamiya, J., Barber, T. X., DiCara, L. V., Miller, N. E., Shapiro, D., & Stoyva, J. (1971). *Biofeedback and Self-Control*. Chicago: Aldine Atherton.

Kandel, E. R., Schwartz, J. H., & Jessell, T. M. (1991). *Principles of Neural Science* (3rd ed.). New York: Elsevier.

Kanigel, R. (1991). *The Man Who Knew Infinity: A Life of the Genius, Ramanujan.* New York: C. Scribner's.

Kant, I. (1951). *Critique of Judgment* (J. H. Bernard, Trans.). New York: Hafner's. (Original work published 1790)

Kaprio, J., Koskenvuo, M., & Rita, H. (1987). Mortality after bereavement: A prospective study of 95,647 widowed persons. *American Journal of Public Health, 77,* 283–287.

Kaptchuk, T. J. (1998). Powerful placebo: The dark side of the randomised controlled trial. *Lancet, 351,* 1722–1725.

Kaptchuk, T. J. (2002). The placebo effect in alternative medicine: Can the performance of a healing ritual have clinical significance? *Annals of Internal Medicine, 136,* 817–825.

Kaptchuk, T. J., Goldman, P., Stone, D. A., & Stason, W. B. (2000). Do medical devices have enhanced placebo effects? *Journal of Clinical Epidemiology, 53,* 786–792.

Kapur, N. (1996). Paradoxical functional facilitation in brain-behaviour research: A critical review. *Brain, 119,* 1775–1790.

Kapur, N., Ellison, D., Parkin, A. J., Hunkin, N. M., Burrows, E., Sampson, S. A., & Morrison, E. A. (1994). Bilateral temporal lobe pathology with sparing of medial temporal lobe structures: Lesion profile and pattern of memory disorders. *Neuropsychologia, 32,* 23–38.

Karambelkar, P. V., Vinekar, S. L., & Bhole, M. V. (1968). Studies on human subjects staying in an air-tight pit. *Indian Journal of Medical Research, 56,* 1282–1288.

Karasawa, H., Sakaida, K., Noguchi, S., Hatayama, K., Naito, H., Hirota, N., Sugiyama, K., Ueno, J., Nakajima, H., Fukada, Y., & Kin, H. (2001). Intracranial electroencephalographic changes in deep anesthesia. *Clinical Neurophysiology, 112,* 25–30.

Karlsson, H. E. (2000). Concepts and methodology of psychosomatic research: Facing the complexity. *Annals of Medicine, 32,* 336–340.

Karlsson, J. L. (1984). Creative intelligence in relatives of mental patients. *Hereditas, 100,* 177–181.

Karnath, H. O., Ferber, S., & Himmelbach, M. (2001). Spatial awareness is a function of the temporal not the posterior parietal lobe. *Nature, 411,* 950–953.

Katz, J. J., & Fodor, J. (1964). The structure of a semantic theory. In J. Fodor & J. J. Katz (Eds.), *The Structure of Language* (pp. 479–518). New York: Prentice-Hall.

Katz, S. T. (Ed.) (1978). *Mysticism and Philosophical Analysis.* New York: Oxford University Press.

Keeley, J. P. (2001). Subliminal promptings: Psychoanalytic theory and the Society for Psychical Research. *American Imago, 58,* 767–791.

Kellehear, A. (1993). Culture, biology, and the near-death experience: A reappraisal. *Journal of Nervous and Mental Disease, 181,* 148–156.

Kelly, E. F. (1962). *Creative Thinking and Creative Personality Structure.* Unpublished honor's thesis, Yale University, New Haven, CT.

Kelly, E. F. (1975). Some theoretical problems of word meaning. In E. F. Kelly & P. J. Stone, *Computer Recognition of English Word Senses* (pp. 50–119). Amsterdam: North-Holland.

Kelly, E. F. (1979). Converging lines of evidence on mind/brain relations. In B. Shapin & L. Coly (Eds.), *Brain/Mind and Parapsychology* (pp. 1–31). New York: Parapsychology Foundation.

Kelly, E. F. (1982). On grouping of hits in some exceptional psi performers. *Journal of the American Society for Psychical Research, 76,* 101–142.

Kelly, E. F. (2003). [Review of] *The Illusion of Conscious Will,* by D. Wegner. *Journal of Scientific Exploration, 17,* 166–171.

Kelly, E. F., Kanthamani, H., Child, I., & Young, F. (1975). On the relation between visual and ESP confusion structure in an exceptional ESP subject. *Journal of the American Society for Psychical Research, 69,* 1–31.

Kelly, E. F., Lenz, J. E., Jr., Franaszczuk, P., & Truong, Y. K. (1997). A general statistical framework for frequency-domain analysis of EEG topographic structure. *Computers and Biomedical Research, 30,* 129–164.

Kelly, E. F., & Locke, R. G. (1981a). A note on scrying. *Journal of the American Society for Psychical Research, 75,* 221–227.

Kelly, E. F., & Locke, R. G. (1981b). *Altered States of Consciousness and Psi: An Historical Survey and Research Prospectus* (Parapsychological Monographs No. 18). New York: Parapsychology Foundation.

Kelly, E. F., & Stone, P. J. (1975). *Computer Recognition of English Word Senses.* Amsterdam: North-Holland.

Kelly, E. W. (2001). Near-death experiences with reports of meeting deceased people. *Death Studies, 25,* 229–249.

Kelly, E. W. (in press). Mediumship and the survival question. In L. Coly, C. S. Alvarado, & N. L. Zingrone (Eds.), *The Study of Mediumship: Interdisciplinary Perspectives.* New York: Parapsychology Foundation.

Kelly, E. W., Greyson, B., & Stevenson, I. (1999–2000). Can experiences near death furnish evidence of life after death? *Omega, 40,* 513–519.

Kelso, J. A. S. (1995). *Dynamic Patterns: The Self-Organization of the Brain and Behavior.* Cambridge, MA: MIT Press.

Kendler, K. S. (2001). A psychiatric dialogue on the mind-body problem. *American Journal of Psychiatry, 158,* 989–1000.

Kennedy, J. E., & Taddonio, J. L. (1976). Experimenter effects in parapsychological research. *Journal of Parapsychology, 40,* 1–33.

Kertesz, A. (1979). *Aphasia and Associated Disorders: Taxonomy, Localization, and Recovery.* New York: Grune & Stratton.

Kidd, C. B. (1966). Congenital ichthyosiform erythroderma treated by hypnosis. *British Journal of Dermatology, 78,* 101–105.

Kienle, G. S., & Kiene, H. (1997). The powerful placebo: Fact or fiction? *Journal of Clinical Epidemiology, 50*, 1311–1318.

Kiernan, B. D., Dane, J. R., Phillips, L. H., & Price, D. D. (1995). Hypnotic analgesia reduces R-III nociceptive reflex: Further evidence concerning the multifactorial nature of hypnotic analgesia. *Pain, 60*, 39–47.

Kihlstrom, J. F. (1993a). Discussion. In G. R. Bock & J. Marsh (Eds.), *Experimental and Theoretical Studies of Consciousness* (p. 215). Chichester, UK: John Wiley.

Kihlstrom, J. F. (1993b). The psychological unconscious and the self. In G. R. Bock & J. Marsh (Eds.), *Experimental and Theoretical Studies of Consciousness* (pp. 147–156). Chichester, UK: John Wiley & Sons.

Kihlstrom, J. F. (1997). Consciousness and me-ness. In J. Cohen & J. Schooler (Eds.), *Scientific Approaches to Consciousness* (pp. 451–468). Mahwah, NJ: Lawrence Erlbaum Associates.

Kim, J. (1998). *Philosophy of Mind.* Boulder, CO: Westview.

Kimble, G. A. (1990). A search for principles in *Principles of Psychology. Psychological Science, 1*, 151–155.

Kintsch, W. (1998). *Comprehension: A Paradigm for Cognition.* Cambridge: Cambridge University Press.

Kirkpatrick, R. A. (1981). Witchcraft and lupus erythematosus. *Journal of the American Medical Association, 245*, 1937.

Kirsch, I. (2004). Conditioning, expectancy, and the placebo effect: Comment on Stewart-Williams and Podd (2004). *Psychological Bulletin, 130*, 341–343.

Kirsch, I., & Sapirstein, G. (1999). Listening to prozac but hearing placebo: A meta-analysis of antidepressant medication. Prevention and Treatment, 1 (APA electronic journal available at http://journals.apa.org/prevention).

Kitchener, E. G., Hodges, J. R., & McCarthy, R. (1998). Acquisition of post-morbid vocabulary and semantic facts in the absence of episodic memory. *Brain, 121*, 1313–1327.

Kjaer, T. W., Bertelsen, C., Pircini, P., Brooks, D., Alving, J., & Lou, H. C. (2002). Increased dopamine tone during meditation-induced change of consciousness. *Cognitive Brain Research, 13*, 255–259.

Klauder, J. V. (1938). Stigmatization. *Archives of Dermatology and Syphilology, 37*, 650–659.

Kleijnen, J. (2000). Placebo and randomized controlled trials. *Advances in Mind-Body Medicine, 16*, 42.

Klein, H. (1991). Couvade syndrome: Male counterpart to pregnancy. *International Journal of Psychiatry in Medicine, 21*, 57–69.

Kline, M. V. (1952-1953). The transcendence of waking visual discrimination capacity with hypnosis: A preliminary case report. *British Journal of Medical Hypnotism, 4*, 32–33.

Klopfer, B. (1957). Psychological variables in human cancer. *Journal of Projective Techniques, 21*, 331–340.

Klüver, H. (1966). *Mescal and Mechanisms of Hallucinations.* Chicago: University of Chicago Press.

Knoblauch, H., Schmied, I., & Schnettler, B. (2001). Different kinds of near-death experiences: A report on a survey of near-death experiences in Germany. *Journal of Near-Death Studies, 20,* 15–29.

Koch, S. (Ed.) (1959–1963). *Psychology: A Study of a Science* (6 vols.). New York: McGraw-Hill.

Koch, S. (1961). Psychological science versus the science-humanism antinomy: Intimations of a significant science of man. *American Psychologist, 16,* 629–634.

Koch, S., & Leary, D. E. (1985). *A Century of Psychology as Science.* New York: McGraw-Hill.

Koenig, H. G., McCullough, M. E., & Larson, D. B. (2001). *Handbook of Religion and Health.* Oxford: Oxford University Press.

Koestler, A. (1954). *The Invisible Writing.* Boston: Beacon.

Koestler, A. (1964). *The Act of Creation: A Study of the Conscious and Unconscious in Science and Art.* New York: Dell.

Kohn, A., Metz, C., Quibrera, M., Tommerdahl, M., & Whitsel, B. (2000). Functional neocortical microcircuitry demonstrated with intrinsic signal optical imaging in vitro. *Neuroscience, 95,* 51–62.

Kohn, A., Metz, C., Tommerdahl, M., & Whitsel, B. (2002). Stimulus-evoked modulation of sensorimotor pyramidal neuron EPSPs. *Journal of Neurophysiology, 88,* 3331–3347.

Kohn, A., & Whitsel, B. L. (2002). Sensory cortical dynamics. *Behavioural Brain Research, 135,* 119–126.

Kolb, B., & Whishaw, I. Q. (2003). *Fundamentals of Neuropsychology.* New York: Worth.

Komatsu, L. K. (1992). Recent views of conceptual structure. *Psychological Bulletin, 112,* 500–526.

Kosslyn, S. M. (1973). Scanning visual images: Some structural implications. *Perception and Psychophysics, 14,* 90–94.

Kosslyn, S. M. (1980). *Image and Mind.* Cambridge, MA: Harvard University Press.

Kosslyn, S. M. (1981). The medium and the message in mental imagery. In N. Block (Ed.), *Imagery* (pp. 207–244). Cambridge, MA: MIT Press.

Kosslyn, S. M. (1994). *Image and Brain: The Resolution of the Imagery Debate.* Cambridge, MA: MIT Press.

Kosslyn, S. M., Thompson, W. L., Costantini-Ferrando, M. F., Alpert, N. M., & Spiegel, D. (2000). Hypnotic visual illusion alters color processing in the brain. *American Journal of Psychiatry, 157,* 1279–1284.

Kothari, L. K., Bordia, A., & Gupta, O. P. (1973a). The yogi claim of voluntary control over the heart beat: An unusual demonstration. *American Heart Journal, 86,* 282–284.

Kothari, L. K., Bordia, A., & Gupta, O. P. (1973b). Studies on a yogi during an eight-day confinement in a sealed underground pit. *Indian Journal of Medical Research*, *61*, 1645–1650.

Koutstaal, W. (1992). Skirting the abyss: A history of experimental explorations of automatic writing in psychology. *Journal of the History of the Behavioral Sciences*, *28*, 5–27.

Kris, E. (1952). *Psychoanalytic Explorations in Art*. New York: International Universities Press.

Kropotov, J. D., Crawford, H. J., & Polyakov, Y. I. (1997). Somatosensory event-related potential changes to painful stimuli during hypnotic analgesia: Anterior cingulate cortex and anterior temporal cortex intracranial recordings. *International Journal of Psychophysiology*, *27*, 1–8.

Krucoff, M. W., Crater, S. W., Green, C. L., Maas, A. C., Seskevich, J. E., Lane, J. D., Loeffler, K. A., Morris, K., Bashore, T. M., & Koenig, H. G. (2005). Music, imagery, touch, and prayer as adjuncts to interventional cardiac care: The Monitoring and Actualisation of Noetic Trainings (MANTRA) II randomised study. *Lancet*, *366*, 211–217.

Kubie, L. (1958). *Neurotic Distortion of the Creative Process*. Lawrence: University of Kansas Press.

Kübler-Ross, E. (1983). *On Children and Death*. New York: Macmillan.

Kuhn, T. (1962). *The Structure of Scientific Revolutions*. Chicago: University of Chicago Press.

Kurtz, P. (1985). Is parapsychology a science? In P. Kurtz (Ed.), *A Skeptic's Handbook of Parapsychology* (pp. 503–518). Buffalo, NY: Prometheus.

LaBerge, S. (1985). *Lucid Dreaming*. Los Angeles: Jeremy P. Tarcher.

LaBerge, S., & Gackenbach, J. (2000). Lucid dreaming. In E. Cardeña, S. J. Lynn, & S. Krippner (Eds.), *Varieties of Anomalous Experience: Examining the Scientific Evidence* (pp. 151–182). Washington, DC: American Psychological Association.

Lachman, S. J. (1982-1983). A psychophysiological interpretation of voodoo illness and voodoo death. *Omega*, *13*, 345–360.

Lader, M. (1973). The psychophysiologicy of hysterics. *Journal of Psychosomatic Research*, *17*, 265–269.

Ladd, G. T. (1893). *Outlines of Physiological Psychology*. London: Longmans, Green.

Ladd, G. T., & Woodworth, R. S. (1915). *Elements of Physiological Psychology*. New York: Charles Scribner's Sons.

Laidlaw, T. M., Booth, R. J., & Large, R. G. (1996). Reduction in skin reactions to histamine after a hypnotic procedure. *Psychosomatic Medicine*, *58*, 242–248.

Lakoff, G. (1987). *Women, Fire, and Dangerous Things: What Categories Reveal about the Mind*. Chicago: University of Chicago Press.

Lakoff, G. (1993). Contemporary theory of metaphor. In A. Ortony (Ed.), *Metaphor and Thought* (2nd ed.) (pp. 202–251). Cambridge: Cambridge University Press.

Lakoff, G. (1995). The neurocognitive self: Conceptual system research in the twenty-first century and the rethinking of what a person is. In R. Solso & D. Massaro (Eds.), *The Science of the Mind: 2001 and Beyond* (pp. 221–243). New York: Oxford University Press.

Lakoff, G., & Núñez, E. (2000). *Where Mathematics Comes From: How the Embodied Mind Brings Mathematics into Being*. New York: Basic Books.

Lakoff, G., & Turner, M. (1989). *More Than Cool Reason: A Field Guide to Poetic Metaphor*. Chicago: University of Chicago Press.

Lamont, P., & Wiseman, R. (1999). *Magic in Theory*. Hatfield: University of Hertfordshire Press.

Lamrimpa, G. (2002). *Realizing Emptiness: Madhyamaka Insight Meditation* (A. Wallace, Trans.). Ithaca, NY: Snow Lion.

Lang, A. (1900). Reflections on Mrs. Piper and telepathy. *Proceedings of the Society for Psychical Research, 15*, 39–52.

Lang, A. (1911). Psychical research. In *Encyclopedia Britannica* (11th ed., Vol. 22, pp. 544–547). New York: Encyclopedia Britannica.

Langacker, R. W. (1990). *Concept, Image, and Symbol: The Cognitive Basis of Grammar*. New York: Mouton de Gruyter.

Langacker, R. W. (1999). *Grammar and Conceptualization*. New York: Mouton de Gruyter.

Lange, R., Greyson, B., & Houran, J. (2004). A Rasch scaling validation of a "core" near-death experience. *British Journal of Psychology, 95*, 161–177.

Lange, R. A., & Hillis, L. D. (1999). Transmyocardial laser revascularization. *New England Journal of Medicine, 341*, 1074–1076.

Lange-Eichbaum, W. (1932). *The Problem of Genius*. New York: Macmillan.

Langer, S. K. (1956). *Philosophy in a New Key: A Study in the Symbolism of Reason, Rite, and Art*. New York: Mentor.

Laplace, P.-S. (1995). *Philosophical Essay on Probabilities* (A. I. Dale, Trans.). New York: Springer-Verlag. (Original 5th ed. published 1825)

Larmore, K., Ludwig, A. M., & Cain, R. L. (1977). Multiple personality—An objective case study. *British Journal of Psychiatry, 131*, 35–40.

Larsson, M., Larhammar, D., Fredrikson, M., & Granqvist, P. (2005). Reply to M. A. Persinger and S. A. Koren's response to Granqvist et al. "Sensed presence and mystical experiences are predicted by suggestibility, not by the application of transcranial weak magnetic fields." *Neuroscience Letters, 380*, 348–350.

Lashley, K. S. (1941). Patterns of cerebral integration indicated by scotomas of migraine. *Archives of Neurology and Psychiatry, 46*, 331–339.

Lashley, K. S. (1950). In search of the engram. *Symposia of the Society for Experimental Biology, 4*, 454–482.

Lashley, K. S. (1951). The problem of serial order in behavior. In L. A. Jeffress (Ed.), *Cerebral Mechanisms in Behavior* (pp. 506–528). New York: Wiley.

Laski, M. (1961). *Ecstasy in Secular and Religious Experiences*. London: Cresset.

Laureys, S., Faymonville, M.-E., de Tiège, X., Peigneux, P., Berré, J., Moonen, G., Goldman, S., Maquet, P. (2004). Brain function in the vegetative state. In C. Machado & D. A. Shewmon (Eds.), *Advances in Experimental Medicine and Biology. Vol. 550: Brain Death and Disorders of Consciousness* (pp. 229–238). New York: Kluwer/Plenum.

Laycock, T. (1876). Reflex, automatism, and unconscious cerebration. *Journal of Mental Science, 21*, 477–498; *22*, 1–17.

Lazar, S. W., Kerr, C. E., Wasserman, R. H., Gray, J. R., Greve, D. N., Treadway, M. T., McGarvey, M., Quinn, B. T., Dusek, J. A., Benson, H., Rauch, S. L., Moore, C. I., & Fischl, B. (2005). Meditation experience is associated with increased cortical thickening. *NeuroReport*, *16*, 1893–1897.

Leary, D. (1990). William James on the self and personality: Clearing the ground for subsequent theorists, researchers, and practitioners. In M. G. Johnson & T. B. Henley (Eds.), *Reflections on The Principles of Psychology: William James After a Century* (pp. 101–137). Hillsdale, NJ: Lawrence Erlbaum.

Lee, J. (1998). An even closer look at therapeutic touch [letter]. *Journal of the American Medical Association*, *280*, 1905–1906.

Lehmann, D., Ozaki, H., & Pal, I. (1987). EEG alpha map series: Brain micro-states by space-oriented adaptive segmentation. *Electroencephalography and Clinical Neurophysiology*, *67*, 271–288.

Lehrer, P. M., & Woolfolk, R. L. (Eds.). (1993). *Principles and Practice of Stress Management* (2nd ed.). New York: Guilford.

Lempert, T. (1994). Syncope and near-death experience. *Lancet*, *344*, 829–830.

Leuba, J. H. (1896). The psychology of religious phenomena. *American Journal of Psychology*, *7*, 309–385.

Leuba, J. H. (1925). *The Psychology of Religious Mysticism*. London: Routledge & Kegan Paul.

Leuchter, A. F., Cook, I. A., Witte, E. A., Morgan, M., & Abrams, M. (2002). Changes in brain function of depressed subjects during treatment with placebo. *American Journal of Psychiatry*, *159*, 122–129.

Levin, J. S. (1994). Religion and health: Is there an association, is it valid, and is it causal? *Social Science and Medicine*, *38*, 1475–1482.

Levine, B., Black, S. E., Cabeza, R., Sinden, M., McIntosh, A. R., Toth, J. P., Tulving, E., & Stuss, D.T. (1998). Episodic memory and the self in a case of isolated retrograde amnesia. *Brain*, *121*, 1951–1973.

Levine, J. D., Gordon, N. C., & Fields, H. L. (1978). The mechanism of placebo analgesia. *Lancet*, *2*, 654–657.

Levinson, B. W. (1965). States of awareness during general anaesthesia: Preliminary communication. *British Journal of Anaesthesia*, *37*, 544–546.

Levinson, B. W. (1990). The states of awareness in anaesthesia in 1965. In B. Bonke, W. Fitch, & K. Millar (Eds.), *Memory and Awareness in Anaesthesia* (pp. 11–18). Amsterdam: Swets & Zeitlinger.

Levy, R., & Mushin, J. (1973). The somatosensory evoked response in patients with hysterical anaesthesia. *Journal of Psychosomatic Research, 17*, 81–84.

Lewin, L. (1998). *Phantastica*. Rochester, VT: Park Street. (Original work published 1927)

Lewin, R. (1980). Is your brain really necessary? *Science, 210*, 1232–1234.

Lewis, A. (1951). Henry Maudsley: His work and influence. *Journal of Mental Science, 97*, 259–277.

Lewis, A. (1975). The survival of hysteria. *Psychological Medicine, 5*, 9–12.

Lex, B. W. (1974). Voodoo death: New thoughts on an old explanation. *American Anthropologist, 76*, 818–823.

Lhermitte, J. (1951). Visual hallucination of the self. *British Medical Journal, 1*, 431–434.

Lifschutz, J. E. (1957). Hysterical stigmatization. *American Journal of Psychiatry, 114*, 527–531.

Lindsay, P. H., & Norman, D. A. (1972). *Human Information Processing: An Introduction to Psychology*. New York: Academic Press.

Lipowski, Z. J. (1977). Psychosomatic medicine in the seventies: An overview. *American Journal of Psychiatry, 134*, 233–244.

Lipowski, Z. J. (1984). What does the word "psychosomatic" really mean? A historical and semantic inquiry. *Psychosomatic Medicine, 46*, 153–171.

Lipowski, Z. J. (1986). Psychosomatic medicine: Past and present. Part 1. Historical background. *Canadian Journal of Psychiatry, 31*, 2–7.

Llinás, R. (2001). *I of the Vortex: From Neurons to Self*. Cambridge, MA: MIT Press.

Llinás, R., & Paré, D. (1996). The brain as a closed system modulated by the senses. In R. Llinás & P. S. Churchland (Eds.), *The Mind-Brain Continuum* (pp. 1–18). Cambridge, MA: MIT Press.

Llinás, R., & Ribary, U. (1994). Perception as an oneiric-like state modulated by the senses. In C. Koch & J. L. Davis (Eds.), *Large-Scale Neuronal Theories of the Brain* (pp. 111–124). Cambridge, MA: MIT Press.

Llinás, R., Ribary, U., Contreras, D., & Pedroarena, C. (1998). The neuronal basis for consciousness. *Philosophical Transactions of the Royal Society of London-B, 353*, 1841–1849.

Locke, R. G., & Kelly, E. F. (1985). A preliminary model for the cross-cultural analysis of altered states of consciousness. *Ethos, 13*, 3–55.

Locke, T. P., & Shontz, F. C. (1983). Personality correlates of the near-death experience: A preliminary study. *Journal of the American Society for Psychical Research, 77*, 311–318.

Lockwood, M. (1989). *Mind, Brain and the Quantum: The Compound "I."* Oxford: Blackwell.

Lodge, O. (1894). On the difficulty of making crucial experiments as to the source of the extra or unusual intelligence manifested in trance-speech, automatic writing, and other states of apparent mental inactivity. *Proceedings of the Society for Psychical Research, 10*, 14–24.

Lodge, O. (1929). On the asserted difficulty of the spiritualistic hypothesis from a scientific point of view. *Proceedings of the Society for Psychical Research, 38*, 481–516.

Loewer, B. (1999). A guide to naturalizing semantics. In B. Hale & C. Wright (Eds.), *A Companion to the Philosophy of Language* (pp. 108–126). Oxford: Blackwell.

Loftus, E. (1979). *Eyewitness Testimony.* Cambridge, MA: Harvard University Press.

Logothetis, N. K. (2002). The neural basis of the blood-oxygen-level-dependent functional magnetic resonance signal. *Philosophical Transactions of the Royal Society of London-B, 357*, 1003–1037.

Long, J. P., & Long, J. A. (2003). A comparison of near-death experiences occurring before and after 1975: Results from an internet study. *Journal of Near-Death Studies, 22*, 21–32.

Lonton, A. P. (1979). The relationship between intellectual skills and the computerised axial tomograms of children with spina bifida and hydrocephalus. *Zeitschrift für Kinderchirurgerie und Grenzgebiete, 28*, 368-374.

Lorber, J. (1983). Is your brain really necessary? In D. Voth (Ed.), *Hydrocephalus im frühen Kindesalter: Fortschritte der Grundlagenforschung, Diagnostik und Therapie* (pp. 2–14). Stuttgart: Enke Verlag.

Lorenz, J., Kunze, K., & Bromm, B. (1998). Differentiation of conversive sensory loss and malingering by P300 in a modified oddball task. *NeuroReport, 9*, 187–191.

Lou, H. C., Kjaer, T. W., Friberg, L., Wildochiotz, G., Holm, S., & Nowak, A. (1999). A ^{15}O-H_2O PET study of meditation and the resting state of normal consciousness. *Human Brain Mapping, 7*, 98–105.

Lovejoy, A. O. (1960). *The Revolt Against Dualism* (2nd ed.). LaSalle, IL: Open Court. (Original work published 1930)

Lowe, E. J. (1996). *Subjects of Experience.* Cambridge: Cambridge University Press.

Lowe, E. J. (1998). There are no easy problems of consciousness. In J. Shear (Ed.), *Explaining Consciousness—The Hard Problem* (pp. 117–123). Cambridge, MA: MIT Press.

Lowe, V. (1951). The development of Whitehead's philosophy. In P. A. Schilpp (Ed.), *The Philosophy of Alfred North Whitehead* (2nd ed., pp. 15–124). New York: Tudor.

Lowes, J. L. (1927). *The Road to Xanadu: A Study in the Ways of the Imagination.* Boston, MA: Houghton Mifflin.

Lucas, E. V. (Ed.) (1903). *The Works of Charles and Mary Lamb. Vol. II: Elia and the Last Essays of Elia*. London: Methuen.

Lucas, G. R. (1989). *The Rehabilitation of Whitehead: An Analytic and Historical Assessment of Process Philosophy*. Albany: State University of New York Press.

Luchelli, F., Muggia, S., & Spinnler, H. (1995). The "Petites Madeleines" phenomenon in two amnesic patients: Sudden recovery of forgotten memories. *Brain, 118*, 167–183.

Ludwig, A. M. (1972). Hysteria: A neurobiological theory. *Archives of General Psychiatry, 27*, 771–777.

Ludwig, A. M. (1983). The psychobiological functions of dissociation. *American Journal of Clinical Hypnosis, 26*, 93–99.

Ludwig, A. M. (1995). *The Price of Greatness: Resolving the Creativity and Madness Controversy*. New York: Guilford Press.

Ludwig, A. M., Brandsma, J. M., Wilbur, C. B., Bendfeldt, F., & Jameson, D. H. (1972). The objective study of a multiple personality. *Archives of General Psychiatry, 26*, 298–310.

Lukianowicz, N. (1958). Autoscopic phenomena. *AMA Archives of Neurology and Psychiatry, 80*, 199–220.

Lukoff, D., & Lu, F. (1988). Transpersonal psychology research review topic: Mystical experience. *Journal of Transpersonal Psychology, 20*, 161–184.

Lukoff, D., Lu, F., & Turner, R. (1992). Toward a more culturally sensitive DSM-IV: Psychospiritual and religious problems. *Journal of Nervous and Mental Disease, 180*, 673–682.

Lukoff, D., Zanger, R., & Lu, F. (1990). Transpersonal psychology research review: Psychoactive substances and transpersonal states. *Journal of Transpersonal Psychology, 22*, 107–148.

Lumsden, C. J. (1999). Evolving creative minds: Stories and mechanisms. In R. J. Sternberg (Ed.), *Handbook of Creativity* (pp. 153–168). New York: Cambridge University Press.

Lundahl, C. R. (1982). Near-death experiences of Mormons. In C. R. Lundahl (Ed.), *A Collection of Near-Death Research Readings* (pp. 165–179). Chicago: Nelson-Hall.

Lunn, V. (1970). Autoscopic phenomena. *Acta Psychiatrica Scandinavica*, suppl. *219*, 118–125.

Luparello, T., Lyons, H. A., Bleecker, E. R., & McFadden, E. R. (1968). Influences of suggestion on airway reactivity in asthmatic subjects. *Psychosomatic Medicine, 30*, 819–825.

Luria, A. R. (1966). *Higher Cortical Functions in Man*. New York: Basic Books.

Luria, A. R. (1968). *The Mind of a Mnemonist* (L. Solotaroff, Trans.). New York: Avon Books.

Luskin, F. (2000). Review of the effect of spiritual and religious factors on mortality and morbidity with a focus on cardiovascular and pulmonary disease. *Journal of Cardiopulmonary Rehabilitation*, *20*, 8–15.

Lutz, A., Greischar, L. L., Rawlings, N. B., Ricard, M., & Davidson, R. J. (2004). Long-term meditators self-induce high-amplitude gamma synchrony during mental practice. *Proceedings of the National Academy of Sciences USA*, *101*, 16369–16373.

Lynn, S. J., & Rhue, J. W. (1988). Fantasy proneness: Hypnosis, developmental antecedents, and psychopathology. *American Psychologist, 43*, 35–44.

MacDonald, D. H., LeClair, L., Holland, C. J., Alter, A., & Friedman, H. L. (1995). A survey of measures of transpersonal constructs. *Journal of Transpersonal Psychology*, *27*, 171–235.

MacGregor, J. M. (1989). *The Discovery of the Art of the Insane*. Princeton, NJ: Princeton University Press.

MacMillan, R. L., & Brown, K. W. G. (1971). Cardiac arrest remembered. *Canadian Medical Association Journal*, *104*, 889–890.

Madell, G. (1981). *The Identity of the Self.* Edinburgh: University Press.

Madell, G. (1988). *Mind and Materialism*. Edinburgh: University Press.

Madden, J. (1903). Wounds produced by suggestion. *American Medicine*, *5*, 288–290.

Maguire, E. A., & Frith, C. D. (2003). Aging affects the engagement of the hippocampus during autobiographical memory retrieval. *Brain*, *126*, 1511–1523.

Malcolm, N. (1977). *Memory and Mind*. Ithaca, NY: Cornell University Press.

Malitz, S., & Kanzler, M. (1971). Are antidepressants better than placebo? *American Journal of Psychiatry*, *127*, 41–47.

Mallock, W. H. (1903). The gospel of Mr. F. W. H. Myers. *Nineteenth Century*, *53*, 628–644.

Mandell, A. (1980). Toward a psychobiology of transcendence: God in the brain. In J. M. Davidson & R. J. Davidson (Eds.), *The Psychobiology of Consciousness* (pp. 379–464). New York: Plenum.

Mandler, G. (1978). An ancient conundrum [review of *The Self and Its Brain*, by K. R. Popper and J. C. Eccles]. *Science*, *200*, 1040–1041.

Mandler, G. (1994). Hypermnesia, incubation, and mind-popping: On remembering without really trying. In C. Umiltà & M. Moscovitch (Eds.), *Conscious and Nonconscious Information Processing* (electronic resource) (pp. 3–33). Cambridge, MA: MIT Press.

Mandler, G., & Shebo, B. J. (1982). Subitizing: An analysis of its component processes. *Journal of Experimental Psychology: General*, *111*, 1–22.

Maréchal, J. (2004). *The Psychology of Mystics* (A. Thorold, Trans.). Mineola, NY: Dover. (Original work published 1927)

Margnelli, M. (1999). An unusual case of stigmatization. *Journal of Scientific Exploration*, *13*, 461–482.

Margolis, C. G., Domangue, B. B., Ehleben, C., & Shrier, L. (1983). Hypnosis in the early treatment of burns: A pilot study. *American Journal of Clinical Hypnosis, 26*, 9–15.

Markowitsch, H. J. (1984). Can amnesia be caused by damage to a single brain structure? *Cortex, 20*, 27–45.

Markowitsch, H. J. (1992). *Intellectual Functions and the Brain: An Historical Perspective*. Seattle, WA: Hogrefe & Huber.

Marr, D. (1982). *Vision: A Computational Investigation into the Human Representation and Processing of Visual Information*. San Francisco: W. H. Freeman.

Marris, P. (1958). *Widows and Their Families*. London: Routledge & Kegan Paul.

Marsden, C. D. (1986). Hysteria—A neurologist's view. *Psychological Medicine, 16*, 277–288.

Marshall, J. C., Halligan, P. W., Fink, G. R., Wade, D. T., & Frackowiak, R. S. J. (1997). The functional anatomy of a hysterical paralysis. *Cognition, 64*, B1–B8.

Martin, A., & Caramazza, A. (Eds.) (2003). *The Organisation of Conceptual Knowledge in the Brain: Neuropsychological and Neuroimaging Perspectives*. Hove: Psychology Press.

Martin, R., & Barresi, J. (Eds.) (2003). *Personal Identity*. Oxford: Blackwell.

Martindale, C. (1995). Creativity and connectionism. In S. M. Smith, T. B. Ward, & R. A. Finke (Eds.), *The Creative Cognition Approach* (pp. 250–268). Cambridge, MA: MIT Press.

Martindale, C. (1999). Biological bases of creativity. In R. J. Sternberg (Ed.), *Handbook of Creativity* (pp. 137–152). New York: Cambridge University Press.

Maslow, A. (1964). *Religions, Values, and Peak Experiences*. Columbus: Ohio State University Press.

Maslow, A. (1968). *Toward a Psychology of Being*. New York: Van Nostrand.

Maslow, A. (1973). *The Farther Reaches of Human Nature*. New York: Viking.

Mason, A. A. (1952). A case of congenital ichthyosiform erythroderma of Brocq treated by hypnosis. *British Medical Journal, 2*, 422–423.

Mason, A. A. (1955a). Ichthyosis and hypnosis [letter]. *British Medical Journal, 2*, 57–58.

Mason, A. A. (1955b). Surgery under hypnosis. *Anæsthesia, 10*, 295–299.

Mason, A. A. (1960). Hypnosis and suggestion in the treatment of allergic phenomena. *Acta Allergologica*, supplement 7, 332–338.

Mason, A. A. (1961). Hypnotic suggestion [letter]. *British Medical Journal, 2*, 956–957.

Mason, A. A., & Black, S. (1958). Allergic skin responses abolished under treatment of asthma and hayfever by hypnosis. *Lancet, 274*, 877–880.

Masters, R. E. L., & Houston, J. (1966). *The Varieties of Psychedelic Experience*. New York: Dell.

Mathew, R. J., Jack, R. A., & West, W. S. (1985). Regional cerebral blood flow in a patient with multiple personality. *American Journal of Psychiatry, 142*, 504–505.

Mathis, J. L. (1964). A sophisticated version of voodoo death. *Psychosomatic Medicine, 26*, 104–107.

Matlock, J. G. (1990). Past life memory case studies. In S. Krippner (Ed.), *Advances in Parapsychological Research 6* (pp. 184–267). Jefferson, NC: McFarland.

Matthews, D. A., McCullough, M. E., Larson, D. P., Koenig, H. G., Swyers, J. P., & Milano, M. G. (1998). Religious commitment and health status. *Archives of Family Medicine, 7*, 118–124.

Maudsley, H. (1868). *Physiology and Pathology of Mind* (2nd rev. ed.). London: Macmillan.

Maudsley, H. (1876). *The Physiology of Mind.* London: Macmillan.

Maudsley, H. (1879). Materialism and its lessons. *Popular Science Monthly, 15*, 667–683.

Mauskopf, S., & McVaugh, M. (1980). *The Elusive Science: Origins of Experimental Psychical Research.* Baltimore: Johns Hopkins University Press.

Mavromatis, A. (1987). *Hypnagogia: The Unique State of Consciousness Between Wakefulness and Sleep.* London: Routledge & Kegan Paul.

Mayberg, H. S., Silva, J. A., Brannan, S. K., Tekell, J. L., Mahurin, R. K., McGinnis, S., & Jerabek, P. A. (2002). The functional neuroanatomy of the placebo effect. *American Journal of Psychiatry, 159*, 728–737.

Mayer, R. (1995). The search for insight: Grappling with Gestalt psychology's unanswered questions. In R. J. Sternberg & J. E. Davidson (Eds.), *The Nature of Insight* (pp. 3–32). Cambridge, MA: MIT Press.

Mayer, R. (1999). Fifty years of creativity research. In R. J. Sternberg (Ed.), *Handbook of Creativity* (pp. 449–460). New York: Cambridge University Press.

Mazzarello, P. (2000) What dreams may come? *Nature, 408*, 523.

McAvoy, B. R. (1986). Death after bereavement. *British Medical Journal, 293*, 835–836.

McClendon, H. J. (1955). Uses of similarity of structure in contemporary philosophy. *Mind, 64*, 79–95.

McClure, C. M. (1959). Cardiac arrest through volition. *California Medicine, 90*, 440–441.

McCord, H. (1968). Hypnotic control of nosebleed. *American Journal of Clinical Hypnosis, 10*, 219.

McCullough, M. E., Larson, D. B., Hoyt, W. T., Koenig, H. G., & Thoresen, C. (2000). Religious involvement and mortality: A meta-analytic review. *Health Psychology, 19*, 211–222.

McCulloch, W. S., & Pitts, W. (1943). A logical calculus of the ideas immanent in nervous activity. *Bulletin of Mathematical Biophysics, 5*, 115–133.

McDermott, R. A. (1986). Introduction. In W. James, *Essays in Psychical Research* (F. H. Burkhardt, Ed.) (pp. xiii–xxxvi). Cambridge, MA: Harvard University Press.

McDougall, W. (1903). [Review of] *Human Personality and Its Survival of Bodily Death*, by F. W. H. Myers. *Mind, 12*, 513–526. (On our digital version of *HP*)

McDougall, W. (1908). The state of the brain during hypnosis. *Brain, 31*, 242–258.

McDougall, W. (1911). In memory of William James. *Proceedings of the Society for Psychical Research, 25*, 11–29.

McDougall, W. (1920). Presidential address. *Proceedings of the Society for Psychical Research, 31*, 105–123.

McDougall, W. (1926). *Outline of Abnormal Psychology.* New York: Charles Scribner's Sons.

McDougall, W. (1961). *Body and Mind: A History and A Defense of Animism.* Boston: Beacon. (Original work published 1911)

McFadden, E. R., Luparello, T., Lyons, H. A., & Bleecker, E. (1969). The mechanism of action of suggestion in the induction of acute asthma attacks. *Psychosomatic Medicine, 31*, 134–143.

McGinn, C. (1999). *The Mysterious Flame: Conscious Minds in a Material World.* New York: Basic Books.

McGuirck, J., Fitzgerald, D., Friedmann, P. S., Oakley, D., & Salmon, P. (1998). The effect of guided imagery in a hypnotic context on forearm blood flow. *Contemporary Hypnosis, 15*, 101–108.

McIntosh, A. R. (1999). Mapping cognition in the brain through neural interactions. In J. K. Foster (Ed.), *Neuroimaging and Memory* (pp. 515–548). Hove: Psychology Press.

McNeill, T. F. (1971). Prebirth and postbirth influence on the relationship between creative ability and recorded mental illness. *Journal of Personality, 39*, 391–406.

McPeake, J. D. (1968). Hypnosis, suggestions, and psychosomatics. *Diseases of the Nervous System, 29*, 536–544.

McRae, C., Cherin, E., Yamazaki, T. G., Diem, G., Vo, A. H., Russell, D., Ellgring, J. H., Fahn, S., Greene, P., Dillon, S., Winfield, H., Bjugstad, K. B., & Freed, C. R. (2004). Effects of perceived treatment on quality of life and medical outcomes in a double-blind placebo surgery trial. *Archives of General Psychiatry, 61*, 412–420.

Meador, C. K. (1992). Hex death: Voodoo magic or persuasion? *Southern Medical Journal, 85*, 244–247.

Meares, A. (1977). Atavistic regression as a factor in the remission of cancer. *Medical Journal of Australia, No. 2,* 132–133.

Meares, A. (1979). Meditation: A psychological approach to cancer treatment. *The Practitioner, 222*, 119–122.

Meares, A. (1980). What can the cancer patient expect from intensive meditation? *Australian Family Physician*, *9*, 322–325.

Meares, A. (1981). Cancer, psychosomatic illness, and hysteria. *Lancet*, *2*, 1037–1038.

Meares, A. (1983). Psychological mechanisms in the regression of cancer. *Medical Journal of Australia*, No. 1, 583–584.

Medin, D. L., & Heit, E. (1999). Categorization. In B. M. Bly & D. E. Rumelhart (Eds.), *Cognitive Science* (pp. 99–143). San Diego: Academic Press.

Mednick, S. A. (1962). The associative basis for the creative process. *Psychological Review*, *69*, 220–232.

Meduna, L. J. (1950). *Carbon Dioxide Therapy: A Neurophysiological Treatment of Nervous Disorders*. Springfield, IL: Charles C Thomas.

Melchner, L. von, Pallas, S. L., & Sur, M. (2000). Visual behaviour mediated by retinal projections directed to the auditory pathway. *Nature*, *404*, 871–876.

Mendelsohn, G. A. (1976). Associative and attentional processes in creative performance. *Journal of Personality*, *44*, 341–369.

Merrill, J. (1993). *The Changing Light of Sandover: A Poem*. New York: Alfred A. Knopf. (Original work published 1980)

Merzenich, M. M., Recanzone, G., Jenkins, W., Allard, T. T., & Nudo, R. J. (1988). Cortical representational plasticity. In P. Rakic & W. Singer (Eds.), *Neurobiology of Neocortex* (pp. 41–67). New York: Wiley.

Mesulam, M.-M. (1998). From sensation to cognition. *Brain*, *121*, 1013–1052.

Mesulam, M.-M. (2000). *Principles of Behavioral and Cognitive Neurology* (2nd ed.). New York: Oxford University Press.

Mill, J. S. (1874). *A System of Logic, Ratiocinative and Inductive*. New York: Harper & Row. (Original work published 1843)

Mill, J. S. (1910). *The Letters of John Stuart Mill* (2 vols.; H. S. R. Elliott, Ed.). London: Longmans, Green.

Miller, A. I. (2001). *Einstein, Picasso: Space, Time, and the Beauty That Causes Havoc*. New York: Basic Books.

Miller, B. L., Cummings, J., Mishkin, F., Boone, K., Prince, F., Ponton, M., & Cotman, C. (1998). Emergence of artistic talent in frontotemporal dementia. *Neurology*, *51*, 978–982.

Miller, E. (1987). Hysteria: Its nature and explanation. *British Journal of Clinical Psychology*, *26*, 163–173.

Miller, E. (1999). Conversion hysteria: Is it a viable concept? *Cognitive Neuropsychiatry*, *4*, 181–191.

Miller, G. A. (1956). The magic number seven, plus or minus two: Some limits on our capacity for processing information. *Psychological Review*, *63*, 81–97.

Miller, G. A. (1985). The constitutive problem of psychology. In S. Koch & D. E. Leary (Eds.), *A Century of Psychology as Science* (pp. 40–45). New York: McGraw-Hill.

Miller, G. A., Beckwith, R., Fellbaum, C., Gross, G., & Miller, K. (1990). Introduction to Word Net: An on-line lexical database. *International Journal of Lexicography, 3*, 235–244.

Miller, G. A., & Fellbaum, C. (1991). Semantic networks of English. *Cognition, 41*, 197–229.

Miller, G. A., Galanter, E., & Pribram, K. H. (1960). *Plans and the Structure of Behavior.* New York: Henry Holt.

Miller, M. R., Van Horn, J. D., Wolford, G. L., Handy, T. C., Valsangkar-Smyth, M., Inati, S., Grafton, S., & Gazzaniga, M. S. (2002). Extensive individual differences in brain activations associated with episodic retrieval are reliable over time. *Journal of Cognitive Neuroscience, 14*, 1200–1214.

Miller, S. D. (1989). Optical differences in cases of multiple personality disorder. *Journal of Nervous and Mental Disease, 177*, 480–486.

Miller, S. D., Blackburn, T., Scholes, G., White, G. L., & Mamalis, N. (1991). Optical differences in multiple personality disorder: A second look. *Journal of Nervous and Mental Disease, 179*, 132–135.

Miller, S. D., & Triggiano, P. J. (1992). The psychophysiological investigation of multiple personality disorder: Review and update. *American Journal of Clinical Hypnosis, 35*, 47–61.

Miller, W. R., & Thoresen, C. E. (2003). Spirituality, religion, and health: An emerging research field. *American Psychologist, 58*, 24–35.

Millikan, R. (1984). *Language, Thought and Other Biological Categories.* Cambridge, MA: MIT Press.

Milne, C. T. (1995). Cardiac electrophysiology studies and the near-death experience. *CACCN: Journal of the Canadian Association of Critical Care Nurses, 6*(1), 16–19.

Milton, G. W. (1973). Self-willed death or the bone-pointing syndrome. *Lancet, 1*, 1435–1436.

Minsky, M. (Ed.) (1968). *Semantic Information Processing.* Cambridge, MA: MIT Press.

Minsky, M. (1975). A framework for representing knowledge. In P. H. Winston (Ed.), *The Psychology of Computer Vision* (pp. 211–277). New York: McGraw-Hill.

Minsky, M. (1985). *The Society of Mind.* New York: Simon & Schuster.

Minsky, M., & Papert, S. (1968). *Perceptrons.* Cambridge, MA: MIT Press.

Mitchell, J. L. (1981). *Out-of-Body Experiences.* Jefferson, NC: McFarland.

Mitchell, M. (1993). *Analogy-Making as Perception.* Cambridge, MA: MIT Press.

Mitchell, T. W. (1912). Some types of multiple personality. *Proceedings of the Society for Psychical Research, 26*, 257–285.

Mitchell, T. W. (1921). *The Psychology of Medicine*. London: Methuen.

Mitchell, T. W. (1922). *Medical Psychology and Psychical Research*. London: Methuen.

Moerman, D. E. (1983). General medical effectiveness and human biology: Placebo effects in the treatment of ulcer disease. *Medical Anthropology Quarterly, 4*, 3, 13–16.

Moerman, D. E. (2000). Cultural variations in the placebo effect: Ulcers, anxiety, and blood pressure. *Medical Anthropology Quarterly, 14*, 51–72.

Moll, A. (1901). *Hypnotism* (5th ed.). London: Walter Scott.

Montague, W. P. (1925). *The Ways of Knowing*. London: Allen & Unwin.

Montgomery, G. H., & Kirsch, I. (1997). Classical conditioning and the placebo effect. *Pain, 72*, 197–213.

Montgomery, P. R. (1967). White overnight? [letter]. *British Medical Journal, 1*, 300.

Moody, R. A. (1975). *Life after Life*. Covington, GA: Mockingbird Books.

Moody, R. A., with Perry, P. (1988). *The Light Beyond*. New York: Bantam.

Moody, R. L. (1946). Bodily changes during abreaction. *Lancet, 2*, 934–935.

Moody, R. L. (1948). Bodily changes during abreaction. *Lancet, 1*, 964.

Moore, L. E., & Kaplan, J. Z. (1983). Hypnotically accelerated burn wound healing. *American Journal of Clinical Hypnosis, 26*, 16–19.

Morgan, C. T., & Stellar, E. (1950). *Physiological Psychology* (2nd ed). New York: McGraw-Hill.

Morganthaler, W. (1992). *Madness and Art: The Life and Works of Adolf Woelfli* (A. H. Esman, Trans.). Lincoln: University of Nebraska Press. (Original work published 1921)

Morris, K. (1998). Meditating on yogic science. *Lancet, 351*, 1038.

Morris, R. L., Harary, S. B., Janis, J., Hartwell, J., & Roll, W. G. (1978). Studies of communication during out-of-body experiences. *Journal of the American Society for Psychical Research, 72*, 1–21.

Morse, J. M., & Mitcham, C. (1997). Compathy: The contagion of physical distress. *Journal of Advanced Nursing, 26*, 649–657.

Morse, M. (1983). A near-death experience in a 7-year-old child. *American Journal of Diseases of Children, 137*, 959–961.

Morse, M. (1994a). Near death experiences and death-related visions in children: Implications for the clinician. *Current Problems in Pediatrics, 24*, 55–83.

Morse, M. (1994b). Near-death experiences of children. *Journal of Pediatric Oncology Nursing, 11*, 139–144.

Morse, M. (1997). Commentary on Jansen's paper. *Journal of Near-Death Studies, 16*, 59–62.

Morse, M., Castillo, P., Venecia, D., Milstein, J., & Tyler, D. C. (1986). Childhood near-death experiences. *American Journal of Diseases of Children, 140*, 1110–1114.

Morse, M., Conner, D., & Tyler, D. (1985). Near-death experiences in a pediatric population. *American Journal of Diseases of Children, 139*, 595–600.

Morse, M., Venecia, D., & Milstein, J. (1989). Near-death experiences: A neurophysiological explanatory model. *Journal of Near-Death Studies, 8*, 45–53.

Moseley, J. B., O'Malley, K., Peterson, N. J., Menke, T. J., Brody, B. A., Kuykendall, D. H., Hollingsworth, J. C., Ashton, C. M., & Wray, N. P. (2002). A controlled trial of arthroscopic surgery for osteoarthritis of the knee. *New England Journal of Medicine, 347*, 81–88.

Moss, C. S. (1972). *Recovery with Aphasia*. Urbana: University of Illinois Press.

Mueller, P. S., Plevak, D. J., & Rummans, T. A. (2001). Religious involvement, spirituality, and medicine: Implications for clinical practice. *Mayo Clinic Proceedings, 76*, 1225–1235.

Muldoon, S., & Carrington, H. (1969). *The Phenomena of Astral Projection*. London: Rider. (Original work published 1951)

Muldoon, S., & Carrington, H. (1973). *The Projection of the Astral Body*. New York: Samuel Weiser. (Original work published 1929)

Mullins, J. F., Murray, N., & Shapiro, E. M. (1955). Pachyonychia congenita. *Archives of Dermatology, 71*, 265–268.

Mundle, C. W. K. (1970). *A Critique of Linguistic Philosophy*. Oxford: Oxford University Press.

Murphy, G. (1929). *An Historical Introduction to Modern Psychology*. London: Kegan Paul, Trench, Trübner, and New York: Harcourt & Brace.

Murphy, G. (1945). *Three Papers on the Survival Problem*. New York: American Society for Psychical Research. (Also published in *Journal of the American Society for Psychical Research*, 1945)

Murphy, G. (1954). Introduction. In F. W. H. Myers, *Human Personality and Its Survival of Bodily Death* (Vol. 1, pp. i-vi). New York: Longmans, Green.

Murphy, G., & Ballou, R. O. (Eds.) (1960). *William James on Psychical Research*. London: Chatto & Windus.

Murphy, G., with L. A. Dale (1961). *Challenge of Psychical Research*. New York: Harper.

Murphy, M. (1992). *The Future of the Body: Explorations into the Future Evolution of Human Nature*. New York: Jeremy P. Tarcher.

Murphy, M., & Donovan, S. (1997). *The Physical and Psychological Effects of Meditation* (2nd ed.). Sausalito, CA: Institute for Noetic Sciences.

Murray, J. L., & Abraham, G. E. (1978). Pseudocyesis: A review. *Obstetrics and Gynecology, 51*, 627–631.

Murre, J. M. J., Graham, K. S., & Hodges, J. R. (2001). Semantic dementia: Relevance to connectionist models of long-term memory. *Brain, 124*, 647–675.

Myers, A., & Dewar, H. A. (1975). Circumstances attending 100 sudden deaths from coronary artery disease with coroner's necropsies. *British Medical Journal, 37,* 1133–1143.

Myers, A. T. (1888). Recent experiments by M. Charles Richet on telepathic hypnotism. *Journal of the Society for Psychical Research, 3,* 222–226.

Myers, A. T., & Myers, F. W. H. (1893). Mind-cure, faith-cure, and the miracles at Lourdes. *Proceedings of the Society for Psychical Research, 9,* 160–209.

Myers, F. W. H. (1881). M. Renan and miracles. *Nineteenth Century, 10,* 90–106.

Myers, F. W. H. (1884). On a telepathic explanation of some so-called spiritualistic phenomena. *Proceedings of the Society for Psychical Research, 2,* 217–237.

Myers, F. W. H. (1884–1885). Specimens of the classification of cases for "Phantasms of the Living." *Journal of the Society for Psychical Research, l,* 54–56, 77–83, 94–103, 114–130, 142–152, 157–165, 182–193, 213–220, 238–245.

Myers, F. W. H. (1885a). Automatic writing, or the rationale of planchette. *Contemporary Review, 47,* 233–249.

Myers, F. W. H. (1885b). Automatic writing—II. *Proceedings of the Society for Psychical Research, 3,* 1–63.

Myers, F. W. H. (1885c). Human personality. *Fortnightly Review, 38,* 637–655.

Myers, F. W. H. (1885d). Further notes on the unconscious self. *Journal of the Society for Psychical Research, 2,* 122–131.

Myers, F. W. H. (1885e). Human personality in the light of hypnotic suggestion. *Proceedings of the Society for Psychical Research, 4,* 1–24.

Myers, F. W. H. (1886a). Introduction. In E. Gurney, F. W. H. Myers, & F. Podmore, *Phantasms of the Living* (Vol. 1, pp. xxxv–lxxi). London: Trübner.

Myers, F. W. H. (1886b). Note on a suggested mode of psychical interaction. In E. Gurney, F. W. H. Myers, & F. Podmore, *Phantasms of the Living* (Vol. 2, pp. 277–316). London: Trübner.

Myers, F. W. H. (1886c). On telepathic hypnotism, and its relation to other forms of hypnotic suggestion. *Proceedings of the Society for Psychical Research, 4,* 127–188.

Myers, F. W. H. (1886d). [Remarks.] *Journal of the Society for Psychical Research, 2,* 155–157.

Myers, F. W. H. (1886e). [Report of some experiments in Paris.] *Journal of the Society for Psychical Research, 2,* 443–453.

Myers, F. W. H. (1887a). Automatic writing—III. *Proceedings of the Society for Psychical Research, 4,* 209–261.

Myers, F. W. H. (1887b). Note on certain reported cases of hypnotic hyperæsthesia. *Proceedings of the Society for Psychical Research, 4,* 532–539.

Myers, F, W. H. (1888). Greek oracles. In F. W. H. Myers, *Essays Classical* (pp. 1-105). London: Macmillan. (Original work published 1880)

Myers, F. W. H. (1888a). French experiments in strata of personality. *Proceedings of the Society for Psychical Research*, *5*, 374–397.

Myers, F. W. H. (1888b). The work of Edmund Gurney in experimental psychology. *Proceedings of the Society for Psychical Research*, *5*, 359–373.

Myers, F. W. H. (1889a). Automatic writing—IV. The dæmon of Socrates. *Proceedings of the Society for Psychical Research*, *5*, 522–547.

Myers, F. W. H. (1889b). Binet on the consciousness of hysterical subjects. *Proceedings of the Society for Psychical Research*, *6*, 200–206.

Myers, F. W. H. (1889c). Dr. Jules Janet on hysteria and double personality. *Proceedings of the Society for Psychical Research*, *6*, 216–221.

Myers, F. W. H. (1889d). On recognised apparitions occurring more than a year after death. *Proceedings of the Society for Psychical Research*, *6*, 13–65.

Myers, F. W. H. (1889e). [Review of] Professor Janet's "Automatisme Psychologique." *Proceedings of the Society for Psychical Research*, *6*, 186–198.

Myers, F. W. H. (1889f). [Review of] *Das Doppel-Ich*, by M. Dessoir. *Proceedings of the Society for Psychical Research*, *6*, 207–215.

Myers, F. W. H. (1889g). [Review of] Janet's *Psychological Automatism. Nineteenth Century*, *26*, 341–343.

Myers, F. W. H. (1889h). Tennyson as prophet. *Nineteenth Century*, *25*, 381–396.

Myers, F. W. H. (1890a). Correspondence. *Journal of the Society for Psychical Research*, *4*, 244–248.

Myers, F. W. H. (1890b). A defence of phantasms of the dead. *Proceedings of the Society for Psychical Research*, *6*, 314–357.

Myers, F. W. H. (1890c). [Review of] A. Aksakof's *Animismus and Spiritismus. Proceedings of the Society for Psychical Research*, *6*, 665–674.

Myers, F. W. H. (1891a). Abstract of "The mechanism of suggestion." *Journal of the Society for Psychical Research*, *5*, 170–172.

Myers, F. W. H. (1891b). Abstract of "Problems of personality." *Journal of the Society for Psychical Research*, *5*, 83, 98–105.

Myers, F. W. H. (1891c). [Review of William James's] *The Principles of Psychology. Proceedings of the Society for Psychical Research*, *7*, 111–133.

Myers, F. W. H. (1891d). Science and a future life. *Nineteenth Century*, *29*, 628–647.

Myers, F. W. H. (1892a). On indications of continued terrene knowledge on the part of phantasms of the dead. *Proceedings of the Society for Psychical Research*, *8*, 170–252.

Myers, F. W. H. (1892b). The subliminal consciousness. Chapter 1: General characteristics and subliminal messages. *Proceedings of the Society for Psychical Research*, *7*, 298–327.

Myers, F. W. H. (1892c). The subliminal consciousness. Chapter 2: The mechanism of suggestion. *Proceedings of the Society for Psychical Research*, *7*, 327–355.

Myers, F. W. H. (1892d). The subliminal consciousness. Chapter 3: The mechanism of genius. *Proceedings of the Society for Psychical Research, 8*, 333–361.

Myers, F. W. H. (1892e). The subliminal consciousness. Chapter 4: Hypermnesic dreams. *Proceedings of the Society for Psychical Research, 8*, 362–404.

Myers, F. W. H. (1892f). The subliminal consciousness. Chapter 5: Sensory automatisms and induced hallucinations. *Proceedings of the Society for Psychical Research, 8*, 436–535.

Myers, F. W. H. (1893a). The subliminal consciousness. Chapter 6: The mechanism of hysteria. *Proceedings of the Society for Psychical Research, 9*, 3–25.

Myers, F. W. H. (1893b). The subliminal consciousness. Chapter 7: Motor automatism. *Proceedings of the Society for Psychical Research, 9*, 26–128.

Myers, F. W. H. (1894). A proposed scheme of apparitions. *Proceedings of the Society for Psychical Research, 10*, 415–422.

Myers, F. W. H. (1894–1895). The drift of psychical research. *National Review, 24*, 190–209.

Myers, F. W. H. (1895a). Abstract of "The progression from subliminal phenomena to phenomena claiming to be obtained under spirit control." *Journal of the Society for Psychical Research, 7*, 21–25.

Myers, F. W. H. (1895b). Obituary: Robert Louis Stevenson. *Journal of the Society for Psychical Research, 7*, 6–7.

Myers, F. W. H. (1895c). Resolute credulity. *Proceedings of the Society for Psychical Research, 11*, 213–234.

Myers, F. W. H. (1895d). The subliminal self. Chapter 8: The relation of supernormal phenomena to time;—Retrocognition. *Proceedings of the Society for Psychical Research, 11*, 334–407.

Myers, F. W. H. (1895e). The subliminal self. Chapter 9: The relation of supernormal phenomena to time;—Precognition. *Proceedings of the Society for Psychical Research, 11*, 408–593.

Myers, F. W. H. (1896a). Glossary of terms used in psychical research. *Proceedings of the Society for Psychical Research, 12*, 166–174.

Myers, F. W. H. (1896b). Recent experiments in normal motor automatism. *Proceedings of the Society for Psychical Research, 12*, 316–318.

Myers, F. W. H. (1897). Summary of "Hysteria and genius." *Journal of the Society for Psychical Research, 8*, 50–59, 69–71.

Myers, F. W. H. (1898a). Abstract of "Discussion of some reciprocal and other cases received." *Journal of the Society for Psychical Research, 8*, 318–325.

Myers, F. W. H. (1898b). The psychology of hypnotism. *Proceedings of the Society for Psychical Research, 14*, 100–108.

Myers, F. W. H. (1898c). [Review of] *L'année psychologique. Proceedings of the Society for Psychical Research, 14*, 146–147.

Myers, F. W. H. (1899). Dr. Morton Prince's "Experimental study of visions." *Proceedings of the Society for Psychical Research, 14*, 366–372.

Myers, F. W. H. (1900a). In memory of Henry Sidgwick. *Proceedings of the Society for Psychical Research, 15*, 452–464.

Myers, F. W. H. (1900b). Presidential address. *Proceedings of the Society for Psychical Research, 15*, 110–127.

Myers, F. W. H. (1900c). Pseudo-possession. *Proceedings of the Society for Psychical Research, 15*, 384–415.

Myers, F. W. H. (1900d). The range of the subliminal. *Journal of the Society for Psychical Research, 9*, 288–292.

Myers, F. W. H. (1900e). [Review of] *L'année psychologique. Proceedings of the Society for Psychical Research, 15*, 105–107.

Myers, F. W. H. (1902). On the trance-phenomena of Mrs. Thompson. *Proceedings of the Society for Psychical Research, 17*, 67–74.

Myers, F. W. H. (1903). *Human Personality and Its Survival of Bodily Death* (2 vols.). London: Longmans, Green.

Myers, F. W. H. (1929). *Wordsworth*. London: Macmillan. (Original work published 1880)

Myers, F. W. H. (1961). *Fragments of Inner Life*. London: Society for Psychical Research. (Original work published 1893)

Myers, F., Lodge, O., Leaf, W., & James, W. (1890). A record of observations of certain phenomena of trance. *Proceedings of the Society for Psychical Research, 6*, 436–660.

Nader, K. (2003a). Memory traces unbound. *Trends in Neurosciences, 26*, 65–72.

Nader, K. (2003b). Response to Arshavsky: Challenging the old views. *Trends in Neurosciences, 26*, 466–468.

Nagel, T. (1979). *Mortal Questions*. Cambridge: Cambridge University Press.

Nagel, T. (1993a, March 4). The mind wins [Review of *The Rediscovery of the Mind*, by J. Searle]. *New York Review of Books*, 37.

Nagel, T. (1993b). What is the mind-body problem? In G. R. Bock & J. Marsh (Eds.), *Experimental and Theoretical Studies of Consciousness* (p. 107). Chicester, England: John Wiley.

Neath, I., & Surprenant, A. M. (2003). *Human Memory: An Introduction to Research, Data, and Theory* (2nd ed.). Belmont, CA: Wadsworth.

Needles, W. (1943). Stigmata occurring in the course of psychoanalysis. *Psychoanalytic Quarterly, 12*, 23–39.

Neher, A. (1980). *The Psychology of Transcendence*. Englewood Cliffs, NJ: Prentice-Hall.

Neisser, U. (1963). The multiplicity of thought. *British Journal of Psychology, 54*, 1–14.

Neisser, U. (1967). *Cognitive Psychology*. New York: Appleton-Century-Crofts.

Neisser, U. (1976). *Cognition and Reality: Principles and Implications of Cognitive Psychology*. San Francisco: W. H. Freeman.

Nelson, S. R. C. (1965). Scared to death? [letter]. *British Medical Journal, 2*, 821.

Nemiah, J. C. (2000). A psychodynamic view of psychosomatic medicine. *Psychosomatic Medicine, 62*, 299–303.

Neppe, V. M. (1989). Near-death experiences: A new challenge in temporal lobe phenomenology? Comments on "A neurobiological model for near-death experiences." *Journal of Near-Death Studies, 7*, 243–248.

Nettle, D. (2001). *Strong Imagination: Madness, Creativity and Human Nature.* Oxford: Oxford University Press.

Neumann, E. (1959). *Art and the Creative Unconscious.* Princeton, NJ: Princeton University Press.

Neumann, E. (1970). Mystical man. In J. Campbell (Ed.), *The Mystic Vision: Papers from the Eranos Yearbooks* (Bollingen Series XXX, pp. 375–415; R. Manheim, Trans.). (Original work published 1968)

Newberg, A. B., & d'Aquili, E. G. (2000). The neuropsychology of religious and spiritual experience. In J. Andresen & R. K. C. Forman (Eds.), *Cognitive Models and Spiritual Maps: Interdisciplinary Explorations of Religious Experience* (pp. 251–266). Thorverton, UK: Imprint Academic.

Newberg, A. B., & d'Aquili, E. (2002). *Why God Won't Go Away: Brain Science and the Biology of Belief.* New York: Ballantine.

Newbold, W. R. (1898). A further record of observations of certain phenomena of trance. *Proceedings of the Society for Psychical Research, 14*, 6–49.

Newell, A. (1990). *Unified Theories of Cognition.* Cambridge, MA: Harvard University Press.

Newell, A., & Simon, H. A. (1972). *Human Problem Solving.* Englewood Cliffs, NJ: Prentice-Hall.

Newman, J. (1948). Srinivas Ramanujan. *Scientific American, 178*, 54–57.

Newman, J., & Baars, B. J. (1993). A neural attentional model for access to consciousness: A global workspace perspective. *Concepts in Neuroscience, 4*, 255–290.

Newton, I. (1964). *Principia Mathematica* (F. Cajori, Ed.). Berkeley: University of California Press. (Original work published 1687)

Nickerson, R. S. (1999). Enhancing creativity. In R. J. Sternberg (Ed.), *Handbook of Creativity* (pp. 392–430). New York: Cambridge University Press.

Nietzsche, F. (1952). Composition of *Thus Spake Zarathustra.* In B. Ghiselin (Ed.), *The Creative Process* (pp. 201–203). New York: New American Library.

Nixon, W. C. W. (1965). Scared to death? [letter]. *British Medical Journal, 2*, 700–701.

Noonan, H. W. (2003). *Personal Identity* (2nd ed.). London: Routledge.

Norris, P. A., & Fahrian, S. L. (1993). Autogenic feedback. In P. M. Lehrer & R. L. Woolfolk (Eds.), *Principles and Practice of Stress Management* (2nd ed.) (pp. 231–262). New York: Guilford.

Noyes, R. (1972). The experience of dying. *Psychiatry, 35*, 174–184.

Noyes, R. (1976). Depersonalization in the face of life-threatening danger: A description. *Psychiatry*, *39*, 19–27.

Noyes, R. (1980). Attitude change following near-death experience. *Psychiatry*, *43*, 234–242.

Noyes, R., & Kletti, R. (1976). Depersonalization in the face of life-threatening danger: An interpretation. *Omega, 7*, 103–114.

Nunez, P. L. (1995). *Neocortical Dynamics and Human EEG Rhythms*. New York: Oxford University Press.

Nunez, P. L., & Silberstein, R. B. (2000). On the relationship of synaptic activity to macroscopic measurements: Does co-registration of EEG with fMRI make sense? *Brain Topography*, *13*, 79–96.

Nyberg, L., & Cabeza, R. (2000). Brain imaging of memory. In E. Tulving & F. I. M. Craik (Eds.), *Oxford Handbook of Memory* (pp. 501–520). Oxford: Oxford University Press.

Oakley, D. A. (1999). Hypnosis and conversion hysteria: A unifying model. *Cognitive Neuropsychiatry*, *4*, 243–265.

Obler, L. K., & Fein, F. (Eds.) (1988). *The Exceptional Brain: Neuropsychology of Talent and Special Abilities*. New York: Guilford.

Ogden, E., & Shock, N. W. (1939). Voluntary hypercirculation. *American Journal of the Medical Sciences*, *198*, 329–342.

O'Grady, J. P., & Rosenthal, M. (1989). Pseudocyesis: A modern perspective on an old disorder. *Obstetrical and Gynecological Survey*, *44*, 500–511.

Ojemann, G. A. (1983). Brain organization for language from the perspective of electrical stimulation mapping. *Behavioral and Brain Sciences, 6*, 189–239.

Ojemann, G. A. (1990). Organization of language cortex derived from investigations during neurosurgery. *Seminars in the Neurosciences, 2*, 297–305.

Ojemann, G. A., & Whitaker H. A. (1978). Language localization and variability. *Brain and Language, 6*, 239–260.

Olson, P. R., Suddeth, J. A., Peterson, P. J., & Egelhoff, C. (1985). Hallucinations of widowhood. *Journal of the American Geriatric Society*, *33*, 543–547.

O'Regan, B., & Hirshberg, C. (1993). *Spontaneous Remission: An Annotated Bibliography*. Sausalito, CA: Institute of Noetic Sciences.

Ornsteen, A. M. (1930). Discussion. *Archives of Neurology and Psychiatry*, *24*, 416.

Osis, K. (1961). *Deathbed Observations by Physicians and Nurses*. New York: Parapsychology Foundation.

Osis, K., & Haraldsson, E. (1997). *At the Hour of Death* (3rd ed.). Norwalk, CT: Hastings House. (Original work published 1977)

Osis, K., & McCormick, D. (1980). Kinetic effects at the ostensible location of an out-of-body projection during perceptual testing. *Journal of the American Society for Psychical Research*, *74*, 319–329.

Osler, W. (1910). The faith that heals. *British Medical Journal, 1*, 1470–1472.

Osterman, J. E., Hopper, J., Heran, W. J., Keane, T. M., & van der Kolk, B. A. (2001). Awareness under anesthesia and the development of posttraumatic stress disorder. *General Hospital Psychiatry, 23*, 198–204.

Osty, E. (1928a). Aux confins de la psychologie classique et de la psychologie métapsychique. II. M. Augustin Lesage, peintre sans avoir appris. *Revue Métapsychique, No. 1,* 1–36.

Osty, E. (1928b). Aux confins de la psychologie classique et de la psychologie métapsychique. III. Marjan Gruzewski, peintre sans avoir apris. *Revue Métapsychique, No. 2,* 85–126.

Osty, E. (1929). Ce que la médicine doit attendre de l'étude expérimentale des propriétés psychiques paranormales de l'homme. *Revue Métapsychique, No. 2,* 79–148.

Otto, R. (1970). *The Idea of the Holy* (J. W. Harvey, Trans.). London: Oxford University Press. (Original work published 1923)

Owens, J. E. (1995). Paranormal reports from a study of near-death experience and a case of an unusual near-death vision. In L. Coly & J. D. S. McMahon (Eds.), *Parapsychology and Thanatology* (pp. 149–167). New York: Parapsychology Foundation.

Owens, J. E., Cook [Kelly], E. W., & Stevenson, I. (1990). Features of "near-death experience" in relation to whether or not patients were near death. *Lancet, 336*, 1175–1177.

Oyama, T., Jin, T., & Yamaya, R. (1980). Profound analgesic effects of ß-endorphins in man. *Lancet, 1*, 122–124.

Pacia, S. V., & Ebersole, J. S. (1997). Intracranial EEG substrates of scalp ictal patterns from temporal lobe foci. *Epilepsia, 38*, 642–654.

Pahnke, W. (1966). Drugs and mysticism. *International Journal of Parapsychology, 8*, 295–313.

Pahnke, W. (1969). The psychedelic mystical experience in the human encounter with death. *Harvard Theological Review, 62*, 1–32.

Pahnke, W., & Richards, W. (1966). Implications of LSD and experimental mysticism. *Journal of Religion and Health, 5*, 175–208.

Palmer, J. (1978). The out-of-the-body experience: A psychological theory. *Parapsychology Review, 9*(5), 19–22.

Papert, S. (1988). One AI or many? In S. Graubard (Ed.), *The Artificial Intelligence Debate: False Starts, Real Foundations* (pp. 1–14). Cambridge, MA: MIT Press.

Papineau, D. (1993). *Philosophical Naturalism*. Oxford: Blackwell.

Parker, A., Wilding, E. L., & Bussey, T. J. (Eds.) (2002). *The Cognitive Neuroscience of Memory: Encoding and Retrieval*. Hove: Psychology Press.

Parnia, S., & Fenwick, P. (2002). Near death experiences in cardiac arrest: Visions of a dying brain or visions of a new science of consciousness. *Resuscitation, 52*, 5–11.

Parnia, S., Waller, D. G., Yeates, R., & Fenwick, P. (2001). A qualitative and quantitative study of the incidence, features and aetiology of near death experiences in cardiac arrest survivors. *Resuscitation, 48*, 149–156.

Parry, D. P. (1861). Sudden whitening of the hair. *Dublin Medical Press, 45–46*, 332.

Parsons, W. B. (1999). *The Enigma of the Oceanic Feeling: Revisioning the Psychoanalytic Theory of Mysticism.* New York: Oxford University Press.

Pascual-Leone, A., Grafman, J., & Hallett, M. (1994). Modulation of cortical motor output maps during development of explicit into implicit knowledge. *Science, 265*, 1600–1601.

Pascual-Marqui, R. D., Michel, C. M., & Lehmann, D. (1995). Segmentation of brain activity into microstates: Model estimation and validation. *IEEE Transactions on Biomedical Engineering, 42*, 658–665.

Pashler, H. (1998). *The Psychology of Attention.* Cambridge, MA: MIT Press.

Pasricha, S. (1993). A systematic survey of near-death experiences in south India. *Journal of Scientific Exploration, 7*, 161–171.

Pasricha, S. K., Keil, J., Tucker, J. B., & Stevenson, I. (2005). Some bodily malformations attributed to previous lives. *Journal of Scientific Exploration, 19*, 359–383.

Pasricha, S., & Stevenson, I. (1986). Near-death experiences in India. *Journal of Nervous and Mental Disease, 174*, 165–170.

Paterson, R. W. K. (1995). *Philosophy and the Belief in Life after Death.* London: Macmillan.

Pattie, F. A. (1941). The production of blisters by hypnotic suggestion: A review. *Journal of Abnormal and Social Psychology, 36*, 62–72.

Paul, G. L. (1963). The production of blisters by hypnotic suggestion: Another look. *Psychosomatic Medicine, 25*, 233–244.

Pawlowski, E. J., & Pawlowski, M. M. F. (1958). Unconscious and abortive aspects of pseudocyesis. *Wisconsin Medical Journal, 57*, 437–440.

Peers, E. A. (1951). *Studies of the Spanish Mystics, Vol. 1* (2nd ed. rev.). New York: Macmillan.

Peers, E. A. (Ed. and Trans.) (1958). *Ascent of Mount Carmel*, by St. John of the Cross (3rd ed. rev.). Garden City, NY: Image Books.

Peers, E. A. (Ed. and Trans.) (1959). *Dark Night of the Soul*, by St. John of the Cross (3rd ed. rev.). Garden City, NY: Image Books.

Pekala, R. J., & Cardeña, E. (2000). Methodological issues in the study of altered states of consciousness and anomalous experiences. In E. Cardeña, S. J. Lynn, & S. Krippner (Eds.), *Varieties of Anomalous Experience: Examining the Scientific Evidence* (pp. 47–82). Washington, DC: American Psychological Association.

Penelhum, T. (1970). *Survival and Disembodied Existence.* London: Routledge & Kegan Paul.

Penfield, W. (1955). The role of the temporal cortex in certain psychical phenomena. *Journal of Mental Science, 101,* 451–465.

Penfield, W. (1958a). *The Excitable Cortex in Conscious Man.* Liverpool: Liverpool University Press.

Penfield, W. (1958b). Functional localization in temporal and deep Sylvian areas. *Research Publications of the Association for Research in Nervous and Mental Disorders, 36,* 210–226.

Penfield, W. (1975). *The Mystery of the Mind: A Critical Study of Consciousness and the Human Brain.* Princeton, NJ: Princeton University Press.

Penfield, W., & Erickson, T. C. (1941). *Epilepsy and Cerebral Localization.* Springfield, IL: Charles C Thomas.

Penfield, W., & Perot, P. (1963). The brain's record of auditory and visual experience: A final discussion and summary. *Brain, 86,* 595–696.

Penfield, W., & Rasmussen, T. (1950). *The Cerebral Cortex of Man: A Clinical Study of Localization of Function.* New York: Macmillan.

Peng, C.-K., Mietus, J. E., Liu, Y., Khalsa, G., Douglas, P. S., Benson, H., & Goldberger, A. L. (1999). Exaggerated heart rate oscillations during two meditation techniques. *International Journal of Cardiology, 70,* 101–107.

Penrose, R. (1989). *The Emperor's New Mind: Concerning Computers, Minds, and the Laws of Physics.* New York: Oxford University Press.

Penrose, R. (1994). *Shadows of the Mind: A Search for the Missing Science of Consciousness.* Oxford: Oxford University Press.

Penrose, R. (1997). *The Large, the Small, and the Human Mind.* Cambridge: Cambridge University Press.

Penrose, R. (2004). *The Road to Reality: A Complete Guide to the Physical Universe.* London: Jonathan Cape.

Perani, D. (1999). The functional basis of memory: PET mapping of the memory system in humans. In L.-G. Nilsson & H. J. Markowitsch (Eds.), *Cognitive Neuroscience of Memory* (pp. 55–78). Seattle: Hogrefe & Huber.

Perkins, D. N. (1981). *The Mind's Best Work.* Cambridge, MA: Harvard University Press.

Perkins, D. N. (1995). Insight in minds and genes. In R. J. Sternberg & J. E. Davidson (Eds.), *The Nature of Insight* (pp. 495–533). Cambridge, MA: MIT Press.

Perkins, D. N. (2000). *The Eureka Effect: The Art and Logic of Breakthrough Thinking.* New York: W. W. Norton.

Perner, J. (2000). Memory and theory of mind. In E. Tulving & F. I. M. Craik (Eds.), *Oxford Handbook of Memory* (pp. 297–312). Oxford: Oxford University Press.

Perovich, A. N., Jr. (1990). Does the philosophy of mysticism rest on a mistake? In R. K. C. Forman (Ed.), *The Problem of Consciousness: Mysticism and Philosophy* (pp. 237–253). New York: Oxford University Press.

Perry, R. B. (Ed.) (1935). *The Thought and Character of William James* (2 vols.). Boston: Little, Brown.

Persinger, M. A. (1987). *Neuropsychological Basis of God Beliefs.* New York: Praeger.

Persinger, M. A. (1989). Modern neuroscience and near-death experiences: Expectancies and implications. Comments on "A neurobiological model for near-death experiences." *Journal of Near-Death Studies, 7,* 233–239.

Persinger, M. A. (1994). Near-death experiences: Determining the neuroanatomical pathways by experiential patterns and simulation in experimental settings. In L. Bessette (Ed.), *Healing: Beyond Suffering or Death* (pp. 277–286). Chabanel, Québec: Publications MNH.

Persinger, M. A. (1999). Near-death experiences and ecstasy: A product of the organization of the human brain? In S. Della Sala (Ed.), *Mind Myths: Exploring Popular Assumptions About the Mind and Brain* (pp. 85–99). Chichester, UK: John Wiley.

Persinger, M. A. (2001). The neuropsychiatry of paranormal experiences. *Neuropsychology and Clinical Neuroscience, 13,* 515–524.

"Pertinax" (1965). Without prejudice. *British Medical Journal, 2,* 876.

Peters, R. M. (1999). The effectiveness of therapeutic touch: A meta-analytic review. *Nursing Science Quarterly, 12,* 52–61.

Peterson, M. D. (1970). *Thomas Jefferson and the New Nation.* New York: Oxford University Press.

Petrovic, P., Kalso, E., Petersson, K. M., & Ingvar, M. (2002). Placebo and opioid analgesia—Imaging a shared neuronal network. *Science, 295,* 1737–1740.

Phillips, D. P., & King, E. W. (1988). Death takes a holiday: Mortality surrounding major social occasions. *Lancet, 332,* 728–732.

Phillips, D. P., Liu, G. C., Kwok, K., Jarvinen, J. R., Zhang, W., & Abramson, I. S. (2001). The *Hound of the Baskervilles* effect: Natural experiment on the influence of psychological stress on timing of death. *British Medical Journal, 323,* 1443–1446.

Phillips, D. P., Ruth, T. E., & Wagner, L. M. (1993). Psychology and survival. *Lancet, 342,* 1142–1145.

Phillips, D. P., & Smith, D. G. (1990). Postponement of death until symbolically meaningful occasions. *Journal of the American Medical Association, 263,* 1947–1951.

Phillips, W. (1957). *Art and Psychoanalysis.* New York: Criterion.

Piddington, J. G. (1903). The trance phenomena of Mrs. Thompson. *Journal of the Society for Psychical Research, 11,* 74–76.

Pigeaire, J. (1839). *Puissance de l'électricité animal, ou Du magnétisme vital et de ses rapports avec la physique, la physiologie et la médecine.* Paris: Dentu & G. Baillière.

Pinker, S. (1997). *How the Mind Works.* New York: W. W. Norton.

Pinker, S., & Mehler, J. (Eds.) (1988). *Connections and Symbols*. Cambridge, MA: MIT Press.

Piper, A. (1929). *The Life and Work of Mrs. Piper*. London: Kegan Paul.

Pitblado, C., & Cohen, J. (1984). State-related changes in amplitude, latency, and cerebral asymmetry of average evoked potentials in a case of multiple personality. *International Journal of Clinical Neuropsychology, 6*, 70.

Place, U. T. (1956). Is consciousness a brain process? *British Journal of Psychology, 42*, 44–50.

Planck, M. (1950). *Scientific Autobiography* (F. Gaynor, Trans.). London: Williams & Norgate.

Plaut, D. C., & Farah, M. J. (1990). Visual object representation: Interpreting neurophysiological data within a computational framework. *Journal of Cognitive Neuroscience, 2*, 320–343.

Plotinus (1969). *The Enneads* (S. McKenna, Trans., 4th ed.). New York: Pantheon.

Podiapolsky, P. P. (1909). On vasomotor disturbances caused by hypnotic suggestion. *Zhurnal Neuropatologii I Psikhiatrie, 9*, 101–109.

Podmore, F. (1890). Phantasms of the dead from another point of view. *Proceedings of the Society for Psychical Research, 6*, 229–313.

Podmore, F. (1894). *Apparitions and Thought-Transference*. London: Walter Scott.

Podmore, F. (1898). Discussion of the trance-phenomena of Mrs. Piper. *Proceedings of the Society for Psychical Research, 14*, 50–78.

Polanyi, M. (1966). *The Tacit Dimension*. New York: Doubleday.

Pols, E. (1998). *Mind Regained*. Ithaca, NY: Cornell University Press.

Poortman, J. J. (1978). *Vehicles of Consciousness: The Concept of Hylic Pluralism*. Utrecht: Theosophical Publishing House. (Original work published 1954)

Popper, K. R., & Eccles, J. C. (1977). *The Self and Its Brain: An Argument for Interactionism*. Berlin: Springer-Verlag.

Port, R. F., & van Gelder, T. (Eds.) (1998). *Mind as Motion*. Cambridge, MA: MIT Press.

Posner, M. I., & Raichle, M. E. (1994). *Images of Mind*. New York: Scientific American Library.

Post, F. (1994). Creativity and psychopathology: A study of 291 world-famous men. *British Journal of Psychiatry, 165*, 22–34.

Powell, L. H., Shahabi, L., & Thoresen, C. E. (2003). Religion and spirituality: Linkages to physical health. *American Psychologist, 58*, 36–52.

Powell, R. (1979). The "subliminal" versus the "subconscious"in the American acceptance of psychoanalysis, 1906–1910. *Journal of the History of the Behavioral Sciences, 15*, 155–165.

Prabhavananda, Swami, & Manchester, F. (1957). *The Upanishads: Breath of the Eternal*. New York: New American Library.

Prescott, F. C. (1922). *The Poetic Mind.* Ithaca, NY: Great Seal.

Pribram, K. H. (1979). A progress report on the scientific understanding of paranormal phenomena. In B. Shapin & L. Coly (Eds.), *Brain/Mind and Parapsychology* (pp. 143–172). New York: Parapsychology Foundation.

Pribram, K. H. (1986). The cognitive revolution and mind/brain issues. *American Psychologist, 41,* 507–520.

Pribram, K. H. (1991). *Brain and Perception.* Hillsdale, NJ: Lawrence Erlbaum.

Price, H. H. (1939). Presidential address: Haunting and the "psychic ether" hypothesis. *Proceedings of the Society for Psychical Research, 45,* 324–343.

Price, H. H. (1953). Survival and the idea of "another world." *Proceedings of the Society for Psychical Research, 50,* 1–25.

Price, H. H. (1954). [Review of] *The Imprisoned Splendour,* by R. C. Johnson. *Journal of Parapsychology, 18,* 51–64.

Price, H. H. (1962). [Review of] *Mysticism and Philosophy,* by W. T. Stace. *Proceedings of the Society for Psychical Research, 41,* 299–312.

Price, H. H. (1966). Mediumship and human survival. *Journal of Parapsychology, 24,* 199–219.

Prince, M. (1900). The development and genealogy of the Misses Beauchamp: A preliminary report of a case of multiple personality. *Proceedings of the Society for Psychical Research, 15,* 466–483.

Prince, M. (1907). A symposium on the subconscious. *Journal of Abnormal Psychology, 5,* 67–80.

Prince, M. (1908). *The Dissociation of a Personality* (2nd ed.). London: Longmans, Green. (Original work published 1905)

Prince, M. (1929). Miss Beauchamp: The theory of the psychogenesis of multiple personality. In *Clinical and Experimental Studies in Personality* (pp. 130–208). Cambridge, MA: Sci-Art Publishers.

Prince, M., & Peterson, F. (1908). Experiments in psycho-galvanic reactions from co-conscious (subconscious) ideas in a case of multiple personality. *Journal of Abnormal Psychology, 3,* 114–131.

Prince, W. F. (1931). Human experiences. *Boston Society for Psychic Research, Bulletin 14.* Boston: Boston Society for Psychic Research.

Prince, W. F. (1963). *Noted Witnesses for Psychic Occurrences.* New Hyde Park, NY: University Books. (Original work published 1928)

Prince, W. F. (1964). *The Case of Patience Worth.* New Hyde Park, NY: University Books. (Original work published 1927)

Prinzhorn, H. (1995). *Artistry of the Mentally Ill* (E. von Brockdorff, Trans.). New York: Springer-Verlag. (Original work published 1972)

Privette, G. (1983). Peak experience, peak performance, and flow: A comparative analysis of positive human experiences. *Journal of Personality and Social Psychology, 45,* 136–138.

Puccetti, R. (1989). The heart of the mind: Intentionality vs. intelligence. In J. R. Smythies & J. Beloff (Eds.), *The Case for Dualism* (pp. 255–264). Charlottesville: University Press of Virginia.

Pulvermüller, F. (1999). Words in the brain's language. *Behavioral and Brain Sciences, 22*, 253–279.

Purves, D., Paydartar, J. A., & Andrews, T. J. (1996). The wagon wheel illusion in movies and reality. *Proceedings of the National Academy of Sciences USA, 93*, 3693–3697.

Pustejovsky, J. (1995). *The Generative Lexicon*. Cambridge, MA: MIT Press.

Putnam, F. W. (1984). The psychophysiologic investigation of multiple personality disorder: A review. *Psychiatric Clinics of North America, 7*, 31–39.

Putnam, F. W. (1986). The scientific investigation of multiple personality disorder. In J. M. Quen (Ed.), *Split Minds/Split Brains: Historical and Current Perspectives* (pp. 109–125). New York and London: New York University Press.

Putnam, F. (1988). The switch process in multiple personality disorder. *Dissociation, 1*, 24–32.

Putnam, F. (1989). *Diagnosis and Treatment of Multiple Personality Disorder*. New York: Guilford Press.

Putnam, F. W. (1991). Recent research on multiple personality disorder. *Psychiatric Clinics of North America, 14*, 489–502.

Putnam, F. W., Guroff, J. J., Silberman, E. K., Barban, L., & Post, R. M. (1986). The clinical phenomenology of multiple personality disorder: Review of 100 recent cases. *Journal of Clinical Psychiatry, 47*, 285–293.

Putnam, F. W., Zahn, T. P., & Post, R. M. (1990). Differential autonomic nervous system activity in multiple personality disorder. *Psychiatry Research, 31*, 251–260.

Putnam, H. (1967). Psychological predicates. In W. H. Capitan & D. D. Merrill (Eds.), *Art, Mind and Religion* (pp. 37–48). Pittsburgh, PA: University of Pittsburgh Press.

Putnam, H. (1998). *Representation and Reality* (6th ed.). Cambridge, MA: MIT Press. (Original work published 1988)

Puységur, A. M. J. de C., Marquis de (1784). *Mémoires pour servir à l'histoire et à l'établissement du magnétisme animal*. Paris: Dentu.

Puységur, A. M. J. de C., Marquis de (1785). *Suite de mémoires pour servir à l'histoire et à l'établissement du magnétisme animal*. Paris and London: n.p.

Pylyshyn, Z. (1973). What the mind's eye tells the mind's brain: A critique of mental imagery. *Psychological Bulletin, 8*, 1–14.

Pylyshyn, Z. (1984). *Computation and Cognition: Toward a Foundation for Cognitive Science*. Cambridge, MA: MIT Press.

Radin, D. I. (1997). *The Conscious Universe: The Scientific Truth of Psychic Phenomena*. New York: HarperEdge.

Radin, D. I. (2006). *Entangled Minds: Extrasensory Experiences in a Quantum Reality.* New York: Simon & Schuster.

Raginsky, B. B. (1959). Temporary cardiac arrest induced under hypnosis. *International Journal of Clinical and Experimental Hypnosis, 7,* 53–68.

Rainville, P., Carrier, B., Hofbauer, R. K., Bushnell, M. C., & Duncan, G. H. (1999). Dissociation of sensory and affective dimensions of pain using hypnotic modulation. *Pain, 82,* 159–171.

Rainville, P., Duncan, G. H., Price, D. D., Carrier, B., & Bushnell, M. C. (1997). Pain affect encoded in human anterior cingulate but not somatosensory cortex. *Science, 277,* 968–971.

Ramachandran, V. S., & Blakeslee, S. (1998). *Phantoms in the Brain: Probing the Mysteries of the Human Mind.* New York: William Morrow.

Ranganath, C., & Knight, R. T. (2002). Prefrontal cortex and episodic memory: Integrating findings from neuropsychology and functional brain imaging. In A. Parker, E. L. Wilding, & T. J. Bussey (Eds.), *The Cognitive Neuroscience of Memory: Encoding and Retrieval* (pp. 83–99). Hove: Psychology Press.

Rantasalo, I., & Penttinen, K. (1959). Stigmatisation: A case with herpes simplex virus in the lesion. *Annales Paediatriae Fenniae, 5,* 145–148.

Rao, K. R., & Palmer, J. (1987). The anomaly called psi: Recent research and criticism. *Behavioral and Brain Sciences, 10,* 539–555.

Rapaport, D. (1951). *Organization and Pathology of Thought: Selected Sources.* New York: Columbia University Press.

Ratnoff, O. (1969). Stigmata: Where mind and body meet. *Medical Times, 97,* 150–163.

Rees, W. D. (1971). The hallucinations of widowhood. *British Medical Journal, 4,* 37–41.

Reinders, A. A. T. S., Nijenhuis, E. R. S., Paans, A. M. J., Korf, J., Willemsen, A. T. M., & den Boer, J. A. (2003). One brain, two selves. *NeuroImage, 20,* 2119–2125.

Reiter, P. J. (1965). The influence of hypnosis on somatic fields of function. In L. M. LeCron (Ed.), *Experimental Hypnosis* (pp. 241–263). New York: Citadel Press.

Rhine, L. E. (1961). *Hidden Channels of the Mind.* New York: Morrow.

Rhine, L. E. (1962). Psychological processes in ESP experiences: Part 1. Waking experiences. *Journal of Parapsychology, 26,* 88–111.

Rhine, L. E. (1967). Hallucinatory experiences and psychosomatic psi. *Journal of Parapsychology, 31,* 111–134.

Rhine, L. E. (1981). *The Invisible Picture: A Study of Psychic Experiences.* Jefferson, NC: McFarland.

Ribot, T. (1882). *Diseases of Memory: An Essay in the Positive Psychology.* London: Kegan Paul, Trench.

Ribot, T. (1898). *The Diseases of Personality* (3rd rev. ed.). Chicago: Open Court.

Richards, I. A. (1960). *Coleridge on Imagination* (3rd ed.). Bloomington: Indiana University Press.

Richards, R. L. (1981). Relationship between creativity and psychopathology: An evaluation and interpretation of the evidence. *Genetic Psychological Monographs, 103*, 261–324.

Richards, R. L., Kinney, D. K., Lunde, I., Benet, M., & Merzel, A. P. C. (1988). Creativity in manic-depressives, cyclothymes, their normal relatives, and control subjects. *Journal of Abnormal Psychology, 97*, 281–288.

Richardson, R. C. (1982). The "scandal" of Cartesian interactionism. *Mind, 91*, 20–37.

Richet, C. (1883). La personnalité et la mémoire dans le somnambulisme. *Revue philosophique, 15*, 225–242.

Richet, C. (1888). Relation de diverses expériences sur la transmission mentale, la lucidité, et autres phénomènes non explicables par les données scientifiques actuelles. *Proceedings of the Society for Psychical Research, 5*, 18–168.

Richter, C. P. (1957). On the phenomenon of sudden death in animals and man. *Psychosomatic Medicine, 19*, 191–198.

Riddoch, M. J., & Humphreys, G. W. (1987). A case of integrative visual agnosia. *Brain, 110*, 1431–1462.

Rimland, B. (1978). Inside the mind of the autistic savant. *Psychology Today, 12* (August), 69–78.

Ring, K. (1980). *Life at Death: A Scientific Investigation of the Near-Death Experience.* New York: Coward, McCann & Geoghegan.

Ring, K. (1984). *Heading Toward Omega: In Search of the Meaning of the Near-Death Experience.* New York: Morrow.

Ring, K. (1988). Paradise is paradise: Reflections on psychedelic drugs, mystical experience, and the near-death experience [guest editorial]. *Journal of Near-Death Studies, 6*, 138–148.

Ring, K., & Cooper, S. (1997). Near-death and out-of-body experiences in the blind: A study of apparent eyeless vision. *Journal of Near-Death Studies, 16*, 101–147.

Ring, K., & Cooper, S. (1999). *Mindsight: Near-Death and Out-of-Body Experiences in the Blind.* Palo Alto, CA: William James Center/Institute of Transpersonal Psychology.

Ring, K., & Lawrence, M. (1993). Further evidence for veridical perception during near-death experiences. *Journal of Near-Death Studies, 11*, 223–229.

Ring, K., & Rosing, C. J. (1990). The Omega Project: An empirical study of the NDE-prone personality. *Journal of Near-Death Studies, 8*, 211–239.

Roberts, G., & Owen, J. (1988). The near-death experience. *British Journal of Psychiatry, 153*, 607–617.

Robinson, D. N. (1977). Preface. In D. N. Robinson (Ed.), *Significant Contributions to the History of Psychology 1750–1920* (Vol. 10, pp. xxi–xxxvi). Washington, DC: University Publications of America.

Robinson, D. N. (1978). *The Mind Unfolded: Essays on Psychology's Historic Texts.* Washington, DC: University Publications of America.

Roddie, I. C. (1983). Circulation to skin and adipose tissue. In J. T. Shepherd & F. M. Abboud (Eds.), *The Cardiovascular System* (Vol. 3, *Handbook of Physiology,* section 2, pp. 285–317). Bethesda, MD: American Physiological Society.

Rodin, E. (1980). The reality of death experience: A personal perspective. *Journal of Nervous and Mental Disease, 168,* 259–263.

Rodin, E. (1989). Comments on "A neurobiological model for near-death experiences." *Journal of Near-Death Studies, 7,* 255–259.

Roe, A. W., Pallas, S. L., Hahm, J.-O., & Sur, M. (1990). A map of visual space induced in primary auditory cortex. *Science, 250,* 818–820.

Rogo, D. S. (1984). Ketamine and the near-death experience. *Anabiosis: The Journal for Near-Death Studies, 4,* 87–96.

Rolph, C. H. (1957). *Personal Identity.* London: Michael Joseph.

Romijn, H. (1997). About the origin of consciousness: A new, multidisciplinary perspective on the relationship between brain and mind. *Proceedings of the Koninklijke Nederlandse Akademie van Wetenschappen, 100,* 181–267.

Rosa, L., Rosa, E., Sarner, L., & Barrett, S. (1998). A close look at therapeutic touch. *Journal of the American Medical Association, 279,* 1005–1010.

Rosch, E. (1999). Is wisdom in the brain? *Psychological Science, 10,* 222–224.

Rosch, E., & Lloyd, B. B. (Eds.) (1978). *Cognition and Categorization.* Hillsdale, NJ: Lawrence Erlbaum.

Rose, S. (2003). *The Making of Memory* (Rev. ed.). London: Vintage.

Rose, S. (2005). *The 21st-Century Brain: Explaining, Mending and Manipulating the Mind.* London: Jonathan Cape.

Rosenbaum, R. S., Köhler, S., Schacter, D. L., Moscovitch, M., Westmacott, R., Black, S. E., Gao, F., & Tulving, E. (2005). The case of K. C.: Contributions of a memory-impaired person to memory theory. *Neuropsychologia, 43,* 989–1021.

Rosenberg, J. F. (1998). *Thinking Clearly About Death.* Indianapolis: Hackett.

Rosenblatt, F. (1962). *Principles of Neurodynamics: Perceptrons and the Theory of Brain Mechanisms.* Washington, DC: Spartan Books.

Rosenblueth, A., Wiener, N., & Bigelow, J. (1943). Behavior, purpose and teleology. *Philosophy of Science, 10,* 18–24.

Rosenthal, R., & Rubin, D. R. (1978). Interpersonal expectancy effects: The first 345 studies. *Behavioral and Brain Sciences, 3,* 377–415.

Ross, C. (1989). *Multiple Personality Disorder: Diagnosis, Clinical Features, and Treatment.* New York: Wiley.

Rowbotham, D. J. (2001). Endogenous opioids, placebo response, and pain. *Lancet, 357,* 1901–1902.

Rowlands, M. (1999). *The Body in Mind: Understanding Cognitive Processes.* Cambridge: Cambridge University Press.

Rozanski, A., Blumenthal, J. A., & Kaplan, J. (1999). Impact of psychological factors on the pathogenesis of cardiovascular disease and implications for therapy. *Circulation, 99*, 2192–2217.

Ruesch, J. (1947). What are the known facts about psychosomatic medicine at the present time? *Journal of Social Casework, 28*, 291–296.

Rumelhart, D. E., & McClelland, J. (Eds.) (1986). *Parallel Distributed Processing: Explorations in the Microstructure of Cognition* (2 vols.). Cambridge, MA: MIT Press.

Runco, M. A. (2004). Creativity. *Annual Review of Psychology, 55*, 657–687.

Rush, B. (1812). *Mental Inquiries and Observations upon Diseases of the Mind.* Philadelphia: Kimber & Richardson.

Russell, B. (1921a). *The Analysis of Mind.* London: Allen & Unwin.

Russell, B. (1921b). *Mysticism and Logic, and Other Essays.* London: Longmans, Green.

Russell, B. (1927). *The Analysis of Matter.* London: Kegan Paul.

Russell, B. (1974). *Religion and Science.* London: Oxford University Press. (Original work published 1935)

Ryan, T. J. (1991). Cutaneous circulation. In L. A. Goldsmith (Ed.), *Physiology, Biochemistry, and Molecular Biology of the Skin* (2nd ed.) (Vol. 2, pp. 1019–1075). New York: Oxford University Press.

Ryle, G. (1949). *The Concept of Mind.* New York: Barnes & Noble.

Saavedra-Aguilar, J. C., & Gómez-Jeria, J. S. (1989). A neurobiological model for neardeath experiences. *Journal of Near-Death Studies, 7*, 205–222.

Sabom, M. (1982). *Recollections of Death: A Medical Investigation.* New York: Harper & Row.

Sabom, M. (1998). *Light and Death: One Doctor's Fascinating Account of Near-Death Experiences.* Grand Rapids, MI: Zondervan.

Sacks, O. (1987). *The Man Who Mistook His Wife For A Hat.* New York: Simon & Schuster.

Sacks, O. (1999). *Migraine* (Rev. ed.). New York: Vintage Books.

Sagan, C. (1979). *Broca's Brain: Reflections on the Romance of Science.* New York: Random House.

Sagan, C. (1984). The amniotic universe. In B. Greyson & C. P. Flynn (Eds.), *The Near-Death Experience: Problems, Prospects, Perspectives* (pp. 140–153). Springfield, IL: Charles C Thomas.

Sage, M. (1903). *Mrs. Piper and the Society for Psychical Research* (N. Robertson, Trans.). London: Brimley Johnson.

Salter, W. (1950). *Trance Mediumship: An Introductory Study of Mrs. Piper and Mrs. Leonard.* London: Society for Psychical Research.

Samuels, A., Shorter, B., & Plaut, F. (1991). *A Critical Dictionary of Jungian Analysis.* London: Routledge.

Sandin, R. H., Enlund, G., Samuelsson, P., & Lennmarken, C. (2000). Awareness during anaesthesia: A prospective case study. *Lancet, 355*, 707–711.

Sandweiss, D. A. (2000). P value out of control [letter]. *Archives of Internal Medicine, 160*, 1872.

Santhouse, A. M., Howard, R. J., & ffytche, D. H. (2000). Visual hallucinatory syndromes and the anatomy of the visual brain. *Brain, 123*, 2055–2064.

Sargant, W. (1975). *The Mind Possessed.* New York: Penguin.

Sarter, M., Berntson, G. G., & Cacioppo, J. T. (1996). Brain imaging and cognitive neuroscience: Toward strong inference in attributing function to structure. *American Psychologist, 51*, 13–21.

Saver, J. L., & Rabin, J. (1997). The neural substrates of religious experience. *Journal of Neuropsychiatry and Clinical Neuroscience, 9*, 498–510.

Saxe, G. N., Vasile, R. G., Hill, T. C., Bloomingdale, K., & van der Kolk, B. A. (1992). SPECT imaging and multiple personality disorder. *Journal of Nervous and Mental Disease, 180*, 662–663.

Schacter, D. (1976). The hypnagogic state: A critical review of the literature. *Psychological Bulletin, 83*, 452–481.

Schacter, D. (1996). *Searching for Memory: The Brain, the Mind, and the Past.* New York: Basic Books.

Schacter, S., & Singer, J. E. (1962). Cognitive, social, and psychological determinants of emotional state. *Psychological Review, 69*, 379–399.

Schafer, R. (1958). Regression in the service of the ego: The relevance of a psychoanalytic concept for personality assessment. In G. Lindzey (Ed.), *Assessment of Human Motives* (pp. 119–147). New York: Rinehart.

Schank, R. C., & Colby, K. M. (Eds.) (1973). *Computer Models of Thought and Language.* San Francisco: W. H. Freeman.

Schechter, E. I. (1984). Hypnotic induction vs. control conditions: Illustrating an approach to the evaluation of replicability in parapsychological data. *Journal of the American Society for Psychical Research, 78*, 1–27.

Schiller, F. C. S. (1894). *Riddles of the Sphinx: A Study in the Philosophy of Evolution* (2nd ed.). London: Swan Sonnenschein and New York: Macmillan. (Original work published 1891)

Schiller, F. C. S. (1905). The progress of psychical research. *Fortnightly Review, 77*, 60–73.

Schiller, F. C. S. (1915). Review: *The Unconscious, The Fundamentals of Human Personality, Normal and Abnormal*, by M. Prince. *Proceedings of the Society for Psychical Research, 27*, 492–506.

Schiller, F. C. S. (1923). A case of apparent communication through a medium by a person living, but suffering from senile dementia. *Journal of the Society for Psychical Research, 21*, 87–92.

Schiller, F. C. S. (1928). Review: *The Case of Patience Worth*, by W. F. Prince. *Proceedings of the Society for Psychical Research, 36*, 573–576.

Schleifer, S. J., Keller, S. E., Camerino, M., Thornton, J. C., & Stein, M. (1983). Suppression of lymphocyte stimulation following bereavement. *Journal of the American Medical Association*, *250*, 374–377.

Schlitz, M., & Braud, W. (1997). Distant intentionality and healing: Assessing the evidence. *Alternative Therapies*, *3*, 62–73. (Reprinted as chap. 11 in Braud [2003])

Schlitz, M., & Honorton, C. (1992). Ganzfeld ESP performance within an artistically gifted population. *Journal of the American Society for Psychical Research*, *86*, 83–98.

Schmidt, H. (1987). The strange properties of psychokinesis. *Journal of Scientific Exploration*, *1*, 103–118.

Schmidt, S., Schneider, R., Utts, J., & Walach, H. (2004). Distant intentionality and the feeling of being stared at: Two meta-analyses. *British Journal of Psychology*, *95*, 235–247.

Schneck, J. M. (1954). Ichthyosis treated with hypnosis. *Diseases of the Nervous System*, *15*, 211–214.

Schneck, J. M. (1966). Hypnotherapy for ichthyosis. *Psychosomatics*, *7*, 233–235.

Schoenbeck, S. B., & Hocutt, G. D. (1991). Near-death experiences in patients undergoing cardiopulmonary resuscitation. *Journal of Near-Death Studies*, *9*, 211–218.

Schopbach, R. R., Fried, P. H., & Rakoff, A. E. (1952). Pseudocyesis: A psychosomatic disorder. *Psychosomatic Medicine*, *14*, 129–134.

Schorer, C. E. (1985). Two native American near-death experiences. *Omega*, *16*, 111–113.

Schouten, S. A. (1993a). Psychic healing and complementary medicine. *European Journal of Parapsychology*, *9*, 35–91.

Schouten, S. A. (1993b). Applied parapsychology: Studies of psychics and healers. *Journal of Scientific Exploration*, *7*, 375–401.

Schouten, S. A., & Kelly, E. F. (1978). On the experiment of Brugmans, Heymans, and Weinberg. *European Journal of Parapsychology*, *2*, 247–290.

Schrödinger, E. (1959). *Mind and Matter.* Cambridge: Cambridge University Press.

Schultes, R. E., & Hofmann, A. (1992). *Plants of the Gods: Their Sacred, Healing, and Hallucinogenic Powers.* Rochester, VT: Healing Arts Press. (Original work published 1979)

Schultz, G., & Melzack, R. (1991). The Charles Bonnet syndrome: "Phantom mental images." *Perception*, *20*, 809–825.

Schultz, G., Needham, W., Taylor, R., Shindell, S., & Melzack, R. (1996). Properties of complex hallucinations associated with deficits in vision. *Perception*, *25*, 715–726.

Schulz, R., Beach, S. R., Ives, D. G., Martire, L. M., Ariyo, A. A., & Kop, W. J. (2000). Association between depression and mortality in older adults: The cardiovascular study. *Archives of Internal Medicine*, *160*, 1761–1768.

Schuman, M. (1980). The pyschophysiological model of meditation and altered states of consciousness: A critical review. In J. M. Davidson & R. J. Davidson (Eds.), *The Psychobiology of Consciousness* (pp. 333–378). New York: Plenum.

Schwaninger, J., Eisenberg, P. R., Schechtman, K. B., & Weiss, A. N. (2002). A prospective analysis of near-death experiences in cardiac arrest patients. *Journal of Near-Death Studies, 20*, 215–232.

Schwartz, E. L. (1999). Computational neuroanatomy. In R. A. Wilson & F. C. Keil (Eds.), *MIT Encyclopedia of the Cognitive Sciences* (pp. 164–166). Cambridge, MA: MIT Press.

Schwartz, G. E., & Beatty, J. (Eds.) (1977). *Biofeedback: Theory and Research*. New York: Academic Press.

Schwartz, J., Stapp, H., & Beauregard, M. (2003). The volitional influence of the mind on the brain, with special reference to emotional self-regulation. In M. Beauregard (Ed.), *Consciousness, Emotional Self-Regulation and the Brain* (pp. 195–238). Amsterdam and New York: John Benjamin.

Schwartz, J., Stapp, H., & Beauregard, M. (2005). Quantum physics in neuroscience and psychology: A neurophysical model of mind-brain interaction. Philosophical Transactions of the Royal Society of London–B, 360, 1309–1327. (Also available at www.physics.lbl.gov/~stapp/stappfiles.html)

Schwarz, B. E., Bickford, R. G., & Rasmussen, W. C. (1955). Hypnotic phenomena, including hypnotically activated seizures, studied with the electroencephalogram. *Journal of Nervous and Mental Disease, 122*, 564–574.

Scripture, E. W. (1891). Arithmetical prodigies. *American Journal of Psychology, 4*, 1–59.

Seager, W. (1998). Consciousness, information, and panpsychism. In J. Shear (Ed.), *Explaining Consciousness—The "Hard" Problem* (pp. 269–286). Cambridge, MA: MIT Press.

Searle, J. R. (1980). Minds, brains, and programs. *Behavioral and Brain Sciences, 3*, 417–424.

Searle, J. R. (1984). *Minds, Brains and Science*. Cambridge, MA: Harvard University Press.

Searle, J. R. (1990). Is the brain's mind a computer program? *Scientific American, 262*, 26–31.

Searle, J. R. (1992). *The Rediscovery of the Mind*. Cambridge, MA: MIT Press.

Searle, J. R. (1997). *The Mystery of Consciousness*. New York: New York Review of Books.

Searle, J. R. (2000). Consciousness. *Annual Review of Neuroscience, 23*, 557–578.

Seeman, T. E., Dubin, L. F., & Seeman, M. (2003). Religiosity/spirituality and health. *American Psychologist, 58*, 53–63.

Segal, G. M. A. (2000). *A Slim Book about Narrow Content*. Cambridge, MA: MIT Press.

Selye, H. (1956). *The Stress of Life*. New York: McGraw-Hill.

Serdahely, W. J. (1990). Pediatric near-death experiences. *Journal of Near-Death Studies, 9*, 33–39.

Serdahely, W. J. (1991). A comparison of retrospective accounts of childhood near-death experiences with contemporary pediatric near-death experience accounts. *Journal of Near-Death Studies, 9*, 219–224.

Shadlen, M. N., & Movshon, J. A. (1999). Synchrony unbound: A critical evaluation of the temporal binding hypothesis. *Neuron, 24*, 67–77.

Shallice, T. (1988). *From Neuropsychology to Mental Structure*. Cambridge: Cambridge University Press.

Shamdasani, S. (1993). Automatic writing and the discovery of the unconscious. *Spring, 54*, 100–131.

Shannon, C. E., & Weaver, W. (1963). *The Mathematical Theory of Communication*. Urbana: University of Illinois Press. (Original work published 1949)

Shapiro, D. H., & Walsh, R. N. (Eds.) (1984). *Meditation: Classic and Contemporary Perspectives*. New York: Aldine.

Sharpe, M., Gill, D., Strain, J., & Mayou, R. (1996). Psychosomatic medicine and evidence-based treatment. *Journal of Psychosomatic Research, 41*, 101–107.

Shear, J. (Ed.) (1998). *Explaining Consciousness—The "Hard Problem."* Cambridge, MA: MIT Press.

Sheehan, E. P., Smith, H. V., & Forest, D. W. (1982). A signal detection study of the effects of suggested improvement on the monocular visual acuity of myopes. *International Journal of Clinical and Experimental Hypnosis, 30*, 138–146.

Sheikh, A. A. (Ed.) (1984). *Imagination and Healing*. Farmingdale, NY: Baywood.

Sheikh, A. A., Kunzendorf, R. G., & Sheikh, K. S. (1996). Somatic consequences of consciousness. In M. Velmans (Ed.), *The Science of Consciousness: Psychological, Neuropsychological and Clinical Reviews* (pp. 140–161). London: Routledge.

Shepard, R. N. (1978). The mental image. *American Psychologist, 33*, 125–137.

Sherwood, S. J. (2002). Relationship between the hypnagogic/hypnopompic states and reports of anomalous experiences. *Journal of Parapsychology, 66*, 127–150.

Shetty, N., Friedman, J. H., Kieburtz, K., Marshall, F. J., Oakes, D., & the Parkinson Study Group. (1999). The placebo response in Parkinson's disease. *Clinical Neuropharmacology, 22*, 207–212.

Shimojo, S., & Shams, L. (2001). Sensory modalities are not separate modalities: Plasticity and interactions. *Current Opinion in Neurobiology, 11*, 505–509.

Shimony, A. (1993). *Search for a Naturalistic World View* (2 vols.). Cambridge: Cambridge University Press.

Shimony, A. (1997). On mentality, quantum mechanics and the actualization of potentialities. In R. Penrose, *The Large, the Small, and the Human Mind* (pp. 144–160). Cambridge: Cambridge University Press.

Shors, T. J. (2004). Memory traces of trace memories: Neurogenesis, synaptogenesis and awareness. *Trends in Neurosciences, 27*, 250–256.

Shulman, R. G., Hyder, F., & Rothman, D. L. (2003). Cerebral metabolism and consciousness. *Comptes Rendus Biologies, 326*, 253–273.

Sicher, F., Targ, E., Moore, D., & Smith, H. S. (1998). A randomized double-blind study of the effect of distant healing in a population with advanced AIDS: Report of a small scale study. *Western Journal of Medicine, 169*, 356–363.

Sidgwick, E. M. (1885). Notes on the evidence, collected by the Society, for phantasms of the dead. *Proceedings of the Society for Psychical Research, 3*, 69–150.

Sidgwick, E. M. (1891). On the evidence for clairvoyance. *Proceedings of the Society for Psychical Research, 7*, 30–99.

Sidgwick, E. M. (1900). Discussion of the trance phenomena of Mrs. Piper. *Proceedings of the Society for Psychical Research, 15*, 16–38.

Sidgwick, E. M. (1915). A contribution to the study of the psychology of Mrs. Piper's trance phenomena. *Proceedings of the Society for Psychical Research, 28*, 1–657.

Sidgwick, E. M. (1922). Phantasms of the living. *Proceedings of the Society for Psychical Research, 33*, 23–429.

Sidgwick, H. (1882). Address by the President at the first general meeting. *Proceedings of the Society for Psychical Research, 1*, 7–12.

Sidgwick, H., Johnson, A., Myers, A. T., Myers, F. W. H., Podmore, F., & Sidgwick, E. M. (1894). Report on the census of hallucinations. *Proceedings of the Society for Psychical Research, 10*, 25–422.

Sidgwick, H., & Myers, F. W. H. (1892). [Report on] The Second International Congress of Experimental Psychology. *Proceedings of the Society for Psychical Research, 8*, 601–611.

Sidis, B. (1906). *The Psychology of Suggestion: A Research into the Subconscious Nature of Man and Society*. New York: D. Appleton. (Original work published 1898)

Sidis, B. (1912). The theory of the subconscious. *Proceedings of the Society for Psychical Research, 26*, 319–343.

Sidis, B., & Goodhart, S. P. (1905). *Multiple Personality: An Experimental Investigation into the Nature of Human Individuality*. New York: D. Appleton.

Sidtis, J. (1986). Can neurological disconnection account for psychiatric dissociation? In J. Quen (Ed.), *Split Minds/Split Brains: Historical and Current Perspectives* (pp. 127–147). New York: New York University Press.

Siegel, R. K. (1977). Hallucinations. *Scientific American, 237*(4), 132–140.

Siegel, R. K., & West, L. J. (Eds.) (1975). *Hallucinations: Behavior, Experience, and Theory*. New York: John Wiley.

Sierra, M., & Berrios, G. E. (1999). Towards a neuropsychiatry of conversive hysteria. *Cognitive Neuropsychiatry, 4*, 267–287.

Signer, S. F., Weinstein, R. P., Munoz, R. A., Bayardo, J. F., Katz, M. R., & Saben, L. R. (1992). Pseudocyesis in organic mood disorder: Six cases. *Psychosomatics, 33*, 316–323.

Silva, J. A., Leong, G. B., & Weinstock, R. (1991). Misidentification syndrome and male pseudocyesis. *Psychosomatics, 32*, 228–230.

Simons, D. J., & Chabris, C. F. (1999). Gorillas in our midst: Sustained inattentional blindness for dynamic events. *Perception, 28*, 1059–1074.

Simonton, D. K. (1995). Foresight or insight? A Darwinian answer. In R. J. Sternberg & J. E. Davidson (Eds.), *The Nature of Insight* (pp. 465–494). Cambridge, MA: MIT Press.

Simpson, C. J. (1984). The stigmata: Pathology or miracle? *British Medical Journal, 289*, 1746–1748.

Sinclair-Gieben, A. H. C., & Chalmers, D. (1959). Evaluation of treatment of warts by hypnosis. *Lancet, 2*, 480–482.

Singer, W. (1998). Consciousness and the structure of neuronal representations. *Philosophical Transactions of the Royal Society of London-B, 353*, 1829–1840.

Slavney, P. R. (1990). *Perspectives on "Hysteria."* Baltimore: Johns Hopkins University Press.

Sloan, R. P., Bagiella, E., & Powell, T. (1999). Religion, spirituality, and medicine. *Lancet, 353*, 664–667.

Sloman, S. A. (1996). The empirical case for two systems of reasoning. *Psychological Bulletin, 119*, 3–22.

Slotnick, S. J., & Schacter, D. L. (2004). A sensory signature that distinguishes true from false memories. *Nature Neuroscience, 7*, 664–650.

Small, G. W. (1986). Pseudocyesis: An overview. *Canadian Journal of Psychiatry, 31*, 452–457.

Smart, J. J. C. (1959). Sensations and brain processes. *Philosophical Review, 68*, 141–156.

Smith, A. (1983). Overview or underview? Comment on Satz and Fletcher's "Emergent trends in neuropsychology: An overview." *Journal of Consulting and Clinical Psychology, 31*, 768–775.

Smith, A., & Sugar, O. (1975). Development of above normal language and intelligence 21 years after left hemispherectomy. *Neurology, 25*, 813–818.

Smith, E. E., & Medin, D. L. (1981). *Categories and Concepts*. Cambridge, MA: Harvard University Press.

Smith, G. R., McKenzie, J. M., Marmer, D. J., & Steele, R. W. (1985). Psychologic modulation of the human immune response to varicella zoster. *Archives of Internal Medicine, 145*, 2110–2112.

Smith, H. (1976). *Forgotten Truth: The Primordial Tradition*. New York: Harper & Row.

Smith, H. (2000). *Cleansing the Doors of Perception: The Religious Significance of Entheogenic Plants and Chemicals*. New York: Jeremy Tarcher/Putnam.

Smith, J. E. (1983). William James's account of mysticism: A critical appraisal. In S. T. Katz (Ed.), *Mysticism and Religious Tradition* (pp. 247–279). New York: Oxford University Press.

Smith, S. M., Ward, T. B., & Finke, R. A. (Eds.) (1995). *The Creative Cognition Approach*. Cambridge, MA: MIT Press.

Smolensky, P. (1988). On the proper treatment of connectionism. *Behavioral and Brain Sciences, 11*, 1–23.

Smolensky, P., Legendre, G., & Miyata, Y. (1994). *Principles for an Integrated Connectionist/Symbolic Theory of Higher Cognition*. Cambridge, MA: MIT Press.

Smythe, W. E. (1992). Conceptions of interpretation in cognitive theories of representation. *Theory in Psychology, 2*, 339–362.

Smythies, J. R. (1983). The impact of psychedelic drugs on philosophy and psychical research. *Journal of the Society for Psychical Research, 52*, 194–200.

Smythies, J. R. (1994). *The Walls of Plato's Cave*. Avebury: Aldershot.

Smythies, J. R., & Beloff, J. (Eds.) (1989). *The Case for Dualism*. Charlottesville: University Press of Virginia.

Snyder, A. W., & Mitchell, D. J. (1999). Is integer arithmetic fundamental to mental processing? The mind's secret arithmetic. *Proceedings of the Royal Society of London-B, 266*, 587–592.

Society for Psychical Research. (1882). Objects of the Society. *Proceedings of the Society for Psychical Research, 1*, 3–6.

Solfvin, J. (1984). Mental healing. In S. Krippner (Ed.), *Advances in Parapsychological Research* (Vol. 4, pp. 31–63). Jefferson, NC: McFarland.

Solms, M. (1997). *The Neuropsychology of Dreams: A Clinico-Anatomical Study*. Mahwah, NJ: Lawrence Erlbaum.

Solomon, G. F. (1993). Whither psychoneuroimmunology? A new era of immunology, of psychosomatic medicine, and of neuroscience. *Brain, Behavior, and Immunity, 7*, 352–366.

Solomon, G. F., & Moos, R. H. (1964). Emotions, immunity, and disease. *Archives of General Psychiatry, 11*, 657–673.

Solso, R. D. (Ed.) (1997). *Mind and Brain Sciences in the 21st Century*. Cambridge, MA: MIT Press.

Solso, R. D., & Massaro, D. W. (Eds.) (1995). *The Science of the Mind: 2001 and Beyond*. New York: Oxford University Press.

Spanos, N. P. (1996). *Multiple Identities and False Memories: A Sociocognitive Perspective*. Washington, DC: American Psychological Association.

Spanos, N. P., & Chaves, J. F. (1989). Hypnotic analgesia and surgery: In defence of the social-psychological position. *British Journal of Experimental and Clinical Hypnosis, 6*, 131–139.

Spanos, N. P., & Gorassini, D. (1984). Structure of hypnotic test suggestions and attributions of responding involuntarily. *Journal of Personality and Social Psychology, 46*, 688–696.

Spanos, N. P., Radtke, L., Hodgins, D., Stam, H., & Bertrand, L. (1983). The Carleton University Responsiveness to Suggestion Scale: Normative data and psychometric properties. *Psychological Reports, 53*, 523–535.

Spanos, N. P., Stenstrom, R. J., & Johnston, J. C. (1988). Hypnosis, placebo, and suggestion in the treatment of warts. *Psychosomatic Medicine, 50*, 245–260.

Spanos, N. P., Williams, V., & Gwynn, M. I. (1990). Effects of hypnotic, placebo, and salicylic acid treatments on wart regression. *Psychosomatic Medicine, 52*, 109–114.

Spence, S. A., Crimlisk, H. L., Cope, H., Ron, M. A., & Grasby, P. M. (2000). Discrete neurophysiological correlates in prefrontal cortex during hysterical and feigned disorder of movement. *Lancet, 355*, 1243–1244.

Sperry, R. W. (1974). Lateral specialization in the surgically separated hemispheres. In F. O. Schmitt & F. G. Worden (Eds.), *The Neurosciences: Third Study Program* (pp. 5–10). Cambridge, MA: MIT Press.

Sperry, R. W. (1980). Mind-brain interaction: Mentalism, yes; dualism, no. *Neuroscience, 5*, 195–206.

Sperry, R. W. (1993). The impact and promise of the cognitive revolution. *American Psychologist, 48*, 878–885.

Spetzler, R. F., Hadley, M. N., Rigamonti, D., Carter, L. P., Raudzens, P. A., Shedd, S. A., & Wilkinson, E. (1988). Aneurysms of the basilar artery treated with circulatory arrest, hypothermia, and barbiturate cerebral protection. *Journal of Neurosurgery, 68*, 868–879.

Spiegel, D., Bierre, P., & Rootenberg, J. (1989). Hypnotic alteration of somatosensory perception. *American Journal of Psychiatry, 146*, 749–754.

Spiegel, D., Kraemer, H., & Carlson, R. W. (2001). Is the placebo powerless? [letter]. *New England Journal of Medicine, 345*, 1276.

Spiegel, H. (1997). Nocebo: The power of suggestibility. *Preventive Medicine, 26*, 616–621.

Spieker, L. E., Hürlimann, D., Ruschitzka, F., Corti, R., Enseleit, F., Shaw, S., Hayoz, D., Deanfield, J. E., Lüscher, T. F., & Noll, G. (2002). Mental stress induces prolonged endothelial dysfunction via endothelin-A receptors. *Circulation, 105*, 2817–2820.

Spilka, B., Hood, R., & Gorsuch, R. (1985). *The Psychology of Religion: An Empirical Approach*. Englewood, NJ: Prentice-Hall.

Spiro, H. M. (2000). A contribution to the debate. *Advances in Mind-Body Medicine, 16*, 26–27.

Spitellie, P. H., Holmes, M. A., & Domino, K. B. (2002). Awareness during anesthesia. *Anesthesiology Clinics of North America, 20*, 555–570.

Spoerri, E. (1997). *Adolf Wölfli: Draftsman, Writer, Poet, Composer*. Ithaca, NY: Cornell University Press.

Spraggett, A. (1974). *The Case for Immortality*. New York: Signet.

Springer, S. P., & Deutsch, G. (1985). *Left Brain, Right Brain* (Rev. ed.). San Francisco: W. H. Freeman. (Original work published 1981)

Stace, W. T. (1987). *Mysticism and Philosophy*. New York: Oxford University Press. (Original work published 1960)

Stanford, R. G., & Stein, A. G. (1994). A meta-analysis of ESP studies contrasting hypnosis and a comparison condition. *Journal of Parapsychology, 58*, 235–269.

Stanovich, K. (1991). Damn! There goes that ghost again! [Peer commentary on M. Velmans, "Is Human Information Processing Conscious?"]. *Behavioral and Brain Sciences, 14*, 696–698.

Stapp, H. P. (2004a). *Mind, Matter, and Quantum Mechanics* (2nd ed.). Berlin: Springer-Verlag.

Stapp, H. P. (2004b). Whiteheadian process and quantum theory. In T. E. Eastman & H. Keeton (Eds.), *Physics and Whitehead: Quantum, Process, and Experience* (pp. 92–102). Albany: State University of New York Press.

Stapp, H. P. (2005a). The Mindful Universe. Retrieved April 2005 from http://www-physics.lbl.gov/~stapp/stappfiles.html.

Stapp, H. (2005b). Quantum interactive dualism: An alternative to materialism. *Journal of Consciousness Studies, 12*, 43–58.

Stapp, H. (in press a). Quantum approaches to consciousness. In P. D. Zelazo, M. Moscovitch, & E. Thompson (Eds.), *The Cambridge Handbook of Consciousness*. Cambridge: Cambridge University Press.

Stapp, H. (in press b). Quantum mechanical theories of consciousness. In M. Velmans & S. Schneider (Eds.), *A Companion to Consciousness*. Oxford: Blackwell.

Starbuck, E. D. (1906). *The Psychology of Religion*. New York: Walter Scott Publishing.

Starkman, M. N., Marshall, J. C., la Ferla, J., & Kelch, R. P. (1985). Pseudocyesis: Psychologic and neuroendocrine interrelationships. *Psychosomatic Medicine, 47*, 46–57.

Stein, D. J., & Mayberg, H. (2005). Placebo: The best pill of all. *CNS Spectrums, 10*, 440–442.

Stein, M., Miller, A. H., & Trustman, R. L. (1991). Depression, the immune system, and health and illness: Findings in search of a meaning. *Archives of General Psychiatry, 48*, 171–177.

Steinvorth, S., Levine, B., & Corkin, S. (2005). Medial temporal lobe structures are needed to re-experience remote autobiographical memories: Evidence from H. M. and W. R. *Neuropsychologia, 43*, 479–496.

Sternbach, R. A. (1964). The effects of instructional sets on autonomic responsivity. *Psychophysiology, 1*, 67–72.

Sternberg, E. M. (2001). *The Balance Within: The Science Connecting Health and Emotions*. New York: W. H. Freeman.

Sternberg, E. M. (2002). Walter B. Cannon and "voodoo death": A perspective from 60 years on. *American Journal of Public Health, 92*, 1564–1566.

Sternberg, E. M., & Gold, P. W. (2002). The mind-body interaction in disease. *Scientific American, 12*, 82–89.

Sternberg, R. J. (Ed.) (1999). *Handbook of Creativity.* New York: Cambridge University Press.

Sternberg, R. J., & Davidson, J. E. (Eds.) (1995). *The Nature of Insight.* Cambridge, MA: MIT Press.

Sternberg, R. J., & Lubart, T. I. (1999). The concept of creativity: Prospects and paradigms. In R. J. Sternberg (Ed.), *Handbook of Creativity* (pp. 3–15). New York: Cambridge University Press.

Stevens, J. R. (1982). Sleep is for seizures: A new interpretation of the role of phasic events in sleep and wakefulness. In M. B. Sternman, M. N. Shouse, & P. Passount (Eds.), *Sleep and Epilepsy* (pp. 249–264). New York: Academic Press.

Stevenson, I. (1957). Comments on the psychological effects of mescaline and allied drugs. *Journal of Nervous and Mental Disease, 125*, 438–442.

Stevenson, I. (1959). The uncomfortable facts about extrasensory perception. *Harper's Magazine, 219*, 19–25.

Stevenson, I. (1965). Single physical symptoms as residues of an earlier response to stress. *Annals of Internal Medicine, 70*, 1231–1237.

Stevenson, I. (1970). *Telepathic Impressions: A Review and Report of 35 New Cases.* Charlottesville: University Press of Virginia.

Stevenson, I. (1974). *Twenty Cases Suggestive of Reincarnation* (2nd ed. rev.). Charlottesville: University Press of Virginia.

Stevenson, I. (1977). Research into the evidence of man's survival after death. *Journal of Nervous and Mental Disease, 165*, 152–170.

Stevenson, I. (1978). Some comments on automatic writing. *Journal of the American Society for Psychical Research, 72*, 315–332.

Stevenson, I. (1981). Can we describe the mind? In W. G. Roll & J. Beloff (Eds.), *Research in Parapsychology 1980* (pp. 130–142). Metuchen, NJ: Scarecrow. [Abstract]

Stevenson, I. (1982). The contribution of apparitions to the evidence for survival. *Journal of the American Society for Psychical Research, 76*, 341–358.

Stevenson, I. (1983a). Cryptomnesia and parapsychology. *Journal of the Society for Psychical Research, 52*, 1–30.

Stevenson, I. (1983b). Do we need a new word to supplement "hallucination"? *American Journal of Psychiatry, 140*, 1609–1611.

Stevenson, I. (1984). *Unlearned Language: New Studies in Xenoglossy.* Charlottesville: University Press of Virginia.

Stevenson, I. (1985). Birth defects from cursing? A case report. *British Medical Journal, 290*, 1813.

Stevenson, I. (1987). Why *investigate* spontaneous cases? *Journal of the American Society for Psychical Research, 81*, 101–109.

Stevenson, I. (1989). A case of severe birth defects possibly due to cursing. *Journal of Scientific Exploration, 3*, 201–212.

Stevenson, I. (1992a). A new look at maternal impressions: An analysis of 50 published cases and reports of two recent examples. *Journal of Scientific Exploration, 6*, 353–373.

Stevenson, I. (1992b). Birthmarks and birth defects corresponding to wounds on deceased persons. *Journal of Scientific Exploration, 7*, 403–416.

Stevenson, I. (1995). Six modern apparitional experiences. *Journal of Scientific Exploration, 9*, 351–366.

Stevenson, I. (1997). *Reincarnation and Biology: A Contribution to the Etiology of Birthmarks and Birth Defects* (2 vols.). New York: Praeger.

Stevenson, I. (2000). The phenomenon of claimed memories of previous lives: Possible interpretations and importance. *Medical Hypotheses, 54*, 652–659.

Stevenson, I. (2001). *Children Who Remember Previous Lives: A Question of Reincarnation* (Rev. ed.). Jefferson, NC: McFarland.

Stevenson, I., & Cook [Kelly], E. W. (1995). Involuntary memories during severe physical illness or injury. *Journal of Nervous and Mental Disease, 183*, 452–458.

Stevenson, I., Cook [Kelly], E. W., & McClean-Rice, N. (1989-1990). Are persons reporting "near-death experiences" really near death? A study of medical records. *Omega, 20*, 45–54.

Stevenson, I., & Pasricha, S. K. (1979). A case of secondary personality with xenoglossy. *American Journal of Psychiatry, 136*, 1591–1592.

Stevenson, I., Pasricha, S. K., & McClean-Rice, N. (1989). A case of the possession type in India with evidence of paranormal knowledge. *Journal of Scientific Exploration, 3*, 81–101.

Stewart-Williams, S., & Podd, J. (2004). The placebo effect: Dissolving the expectancy versus conditioning debate. *Psychological Bulletin, 130*, 324–340.

Stoessl, A. J., & de la Fuente-Fernández, R. (2004). Willing oneself better on placebo—Effective in its own right. *Lancet, 364*, 227–228.

Storr, A. (1972). *The Dynamics of Creation*. London: Secker & Warburg.

Stout, G. F. (1903). Mr. F. W. H. Myers on "Human Personality and Its Survival of Bodily Death." *Hibbert Journal, 2*, 44–64. (On our digital version of *HP*)

Strassman, R. (1984). Adverse reactions to psychedelic drugs: A review of the literature. *Journal of Nervous and Mental Disease, 172*, 577–595.

Strassman, R. (1997). Endogenous ketamine-like compounds and the NDE: If so, so what? *Journal of Near-Death Studies, 16*, 27–41.

Strassman, R. (2001). *DMT: The Spirit Molecule*. Rochester, VT: Park Street.

Stratton, G. M. (1917). The mnemonic feat of the "Shass Pollak." *Psychological Review, 34*, 244–247.

Strombeck, F. K. von (1814). *Histoire de la guérison d'une jeune personne, par le magnétisme animal, produit par la nature elle-mème. Par un témoin oculaire de ce phénomène extraordinaire. Traduit de l'Allemand.* Paris: Librairie Grecque, Latine, Allemande.

Stromeyer, C. F. III (1970). Eidetikers. *Psychology Today, 4*, 76–80.

Stromeyer, C. F. III, & Psotka, J. (1970). The detailed texture of eidetic images. *Nature, 225*, 346–349.

Stroud, J. M. (1955). The fine structure of psychological time. In H. Quasten (Ed.), *Information Theory in Psychology* (pp. 174–207). Glencoe, IL: Free Press.

Suler, J. (1980). Primary process thinking and creativity. *Psychological Bulletin, 88*, 144–165.

Sulzberger, M. B., & Wolf, J. (1934). The treatment of warts by suggestion. *Medical Record, 140*, 552–557.

Sur, M. (1993). Cortical specification: Microcircuits, perceptual identity, and overall perspective. *Perspectives on Developmental Neurobiology, 1*, 109–113.

Surman, O. W., Gottlieb, S. K., & Hackett, T. P. (1972). Hypnotic treatment of a child with warts. *American Journal of Clinical Hypnosis, 15*, 12–14.

Surman, O. W., Gottlieb, S. K., Hackett, T. P., & Silverberg, E. L. (1973). Hypnosis in the treatment of warts. *Archives of General Psychiatry, 28*, 439–441.

Sutton, J. (1998). *Philosophy and Memory Traces: Descartes to Connectionism*. Cambridge: Cambridge University Press.

Swinburne, R. (1997). *The Evolution of the Soul* (Rev. ed.). Oxford: Oxford University Press.

Szechtman, H., Woody, E., Bowers, K. S., & Nahmias, C. (1998). Where the imaginal appears real: A positron emission tomography study of auditory hallucinations. *Proceedings of the National Academy of Sciences USA, 95*, 1956–1960.

Taimni, I. K. (1972). *The Science of Yoga*. Wheaton, IL: Theosophical Publishing House.

Targ, E. (1997). Evaluating distant healing: A research review. *Alternative Therapies, 3*, 74–78.

Tart, C. T. (1968). A psychophysiological study of out-of-the-body experiences in a selected subject. *Journal of the American Society for Psychical Research, 62*, 3–27.

Tart, C. T. (1972). States of consciousness and state-specific sciences. *Science, 176*, 1203–1210.

Tart, C. T. (1975a). *States of Consciousness*. New York: Dutton.

Tart, C. T. (1975b). *Transpersonal Psychologies*. New York: Harper & Row.

Tart, C. T. (1977). Drug-induced states of consciousness. In B. B. Wolman (Ed.), *Handbook of Parapsychology* (pp. 500–525). New York: Van Nostrand Reinhold.

Tart, C. T. (1993). Mind embodied: Computer-generated virtual reality as a new, dualistic-interactive model for transpersonal psychology. In K. R. Rao (Ed.), *Cultivating Consciousness: Enhancing Human Potential, Wellness and Healing* (pp. 123–137). Westport, CT: Praeger.

Taub, E. (1977). Self-regulation of human tissue temperature. In G. E. Schwartz & J. Beatty (Eds.), *Biofeedback: Theory and Research* (pp. 265–300). New York: Academic Press.

Taub, E., Uswatte, G., & Elbert, J. (2002). New treatments in neurorehabilitation founded on basic research. *Nature Reviews: Neuroscience, 3*, 228–236.

Taves, A. (1999). *Fits, Trances, and Visions: Experiencing Religion and Explaining Experience from Wesley to James*. Princeton, NJ: Princeton University Press.

Taylor, D. C., & Marsh, S. M. (1980). Hughlings Jackson's Dr. Z: The paradigm of temporal lobe epilepsy revealed. *Journal of Neurology, Neurosurgery, and Psychiatry, 43*, 758–767.

Taylor, E. (1984). *William James on Exceptional Mental States: The 1896 Lowell Lectures*. Amherst: University of Massachusetts Press.

Taylor, E. (1996). *William James on Consciousness Beyond the Margin*. Princeton, NJ: Princeton University Press.

Teachout, T. (2004). *All in the Dances: A Brief Life of George Balanchine*. Orlando, FL: Harcourt.

Tellegen, A., & Atkinson, G. (1974). Openness to absorbing and self-altering experiences ("absorption"), a trait related to hypnotic susceptibility. *Journal of Abnormal Psychology, 83*, 268–277.

Temple, C. M., & Richardson, P. (2004). Developmental amnesia: A new pattern of dissociation with intact episodic memory. *Neuropsychologia, 42*, 764–781.

Ter Riet, G., de Craen, A. J. M., de Boer, A., & Kessels, A. G. H. (1998). Is placebo analgesia mediated by endogenous opioids? A systematic review. *Pain, 76*, 273–275.

Thagard, P. (1997). Coherent and creative conceptual combinations. In T. B. Ward, S. M. Smith, & J. Vaid (Eds.), *Creative Thought: An Investigation of Conceptual Structures and Processes* (pp. 129–141). Washington, DC: American Psychological Association.

Thagard, P. (1998). *Mind: Introduction to Cognitive Science*. Cambridge, MA: MIT Press.

Thagard, P. (2000). *Coherence in Thought and Action*. Cambridge, MA: MIT Press.

Thagard, P., Holyoak, K. J., Nelson, G., & Gochfeld, D. (1990). Analog retrieval by constraint satisfaction. *Artificial Intelligence, 46*, 259–310.

Thalbourne, M. A. (1998). Transliminality: Further correlates and a short measure. *Journal of the American Society for Psychical Research, 92*, 402–419.

Thalbourne, M A., & Delin, P. S. (1994). A common thread underlying belief in the paranormal, creative personality, mystical experience and psychopathology. *Journal of Parapsychology, 58*, 2–38.

Thalbourne, M A., & Delin, P. S. (1999). Transliminality: Its relation to dream life, religiosity, and mystical experience. *International Journal for the Psychology of Religion, 9*, 35–43.

Thigpen, C. H., & Cleckley, H. (1954). A case of multiple personality. *Journal of Abnormal and Social Psychology, 49*, 135–151.

Thigpen, C. H., & Cleckley, H. M. (1957). *The Three Faces of Eve.* New York: McGraw-Hill.

Thomas, L. (1979). Warts. *Human Nature, 2*, 58–59.

Thomas, L., & Cooper, P. (1980). Incidence and psychological correlates of intense spiritual experiences. *Journal of Transpersonal Psychology, 12*, 75–85.

Thomas, N. J. T. (1999). Are theories of imagery theories of imagination? An *active perception* approach to conscious mental content. *Cognitive Science, 23*, 207–245.

Thompson, W. G. (2005). *The Placebo Effect and Health: Combining Science and Compassionate Care.* Amherst, NY: Prometheus.

Thomson, K. S. (1996). The revival of experiments on prayer. *American Scientist, 84*, 532–534.

Thouless, R., H., & Wiesner, B. P. (1947). The psi-process in normal and "paranormal" psychology. *Proceedings of the Society for Psychical Research, 48*, 177–196.

Thurston, H. (1922). The phenomena of stigmatization. *Proceedings of the Society for Psychical Research, 32*, 179–208.

Thurston, H. (1952). *The Physical Phenomena of Mysticism.* Chicago: Henry Regnery.

Tien, A. Y. (1991). Distributions of hallucinations in the population. *Social Psychiatry and Psychiatric Epidemiology, 26*, 287–292.

Tiihonen, J., Kuikka, J., Viinamäki, H., Lehtonen, J., & Partanen, J. (1995). Altered cerebral blood flow during hysterical paresthesia. *Biological Psychiatry, 37*, 134–135.

Tinling, D. C. (1967). Voodoo, root work, and medicine. *Psychosomatic Medicine, 29*, 483–490.

Toga, A. W., & Mazziotta, J. C. (1996). *Brain Mapping: The Methods.* San Diego, CA: Academic Press.

Tong, F. (2003). Out-of-body experiences: From Penfield to present. *Trends in Cognitive Science, 7*, 104–106.

Toulmin, S., & Leary, D. E. (1985). The cult of empiricism in psychology, and beyond. In S. Koch & D. E. Leary (Eds.), *A Century of Psychology as Science* (pp. 594–617). New York: McGraw-Hill.

Trachtenberg, J. T., Chen, B. E., Knott, G. W., Feng, G., Sanes, J. R., Welker, E., & Svoboda, K. (2002). Long-term *in vivo* imaging of experience-dependent synaptic plasticity in adult cortex. *Nature, 420*, 788–794.

Travis, F., & Wallace, R. K. (1997). Autonomic patterns during respiratory suspensions: Possible markers of transcendental consciousness. *Psychophysiology, 34*, 39–46.

Treffert, D. A. (1989). *Extraordinary People: Understanding "Idiot Savants."* New York: Harper & Row.

Trilling, L. (1953). *The Liberal Imagination: Essays on Literature and Society*. Garden City, NY: Anchor-Doubleday.

Trustman, R., Dubovsky, S., & Titley, R. (1977). Auditory perception during general anesthesia—Myth or fact? *International Journal of Clinical and Experimental Hypnosis, 25*, 88–105.

Tsai, G., Condie, D., Wu, M., & Chang, I. (1999). Functional magnetic resonance imaging of personality switches in a woman with dissociative identity disorder. *Harvard Review of Psychiatry, 7*, 119–122.

Tucker, J. B. (2005). *Life Before Life: A Scientific Investigation of Children's Memories of Previous Lives*. New York: St. Martin's.

Tucker, J. B., & Keil, J. (in press). Experimental birthmarks: New cases of an Asian practice. *International Journal of Parapsychology, 13*.

Tuke, D. H. (1884). *Illustrations of the Influence of the Mind upon the Body in Health and Disease* (2nd ed.). Philadelphia: Henry C. Lea's Son.

Tulving, E., Kapur, S., Craik, F. I. M., Moscovitch, M., & Houle, S. (1994). Hemispheric encoding/retrieval asymmetry in episodic memory: Positron emission tomography findings. *Proceedings of the National Academy of Sciences USA, 91*, 2016–2020.

Turetskaia, B. E., & Romanenko, A. A. (1975). Agonal remission in the terminal stages of schizophrenia (M. H. Pertzoff, Trans.). *Journal of Neuropathology and Psychiatry, 75*, 559–62.

Turing, A. M. (1950). Computing machinery and intelligence. *Mind, 59*, 433–460.

Turner, E. K. (1960). Teratogenic effects on the human fœtus through maternal emotional stress: Report of a case. *Medical Journal of Australia, 47*, 502–503.

Turner, M. (1999). Malingering, hysteria, and the factitious disorders. *Cognitive Neuropsychiatry, 4*, 193–201.

Tversky, A. (1977). Features of similarity. *Psychological Review, 84*, 327–352.

Twain, M. (1900). Mental telegraphy. In *The American Claimant* (pp. 375–396). New York: Harper & Brothers.

Tyndall, J. (1879). Apology for the Belfast address. In *Fragments of Science: A Series of Detached Essays, Addresses, and Reviews* (Vol. 2, pp. 204–225). London: Longmans, Green. (Original work published 1874)

Tyndall, J. (1879). Professor Virchow and evolution. In *Fragments of Science: A Series of Detached Essays, Addresses, and Reviews* (Vol. 2, pp. 375–420). London: Longmans, Green.

Tyrrell, G. N. M. (1938). *Science and Psychical Phenomena.* New York: University Books.

Tyrrell, G. N. M. (1953). *Apparitions.* London: Duckworth. (Original work published 1943)

Ullman, M. (1947). Herpes simplex and second degree burn induced under hypnosis. *American Journal of Psychiatry, 103,* 828–830.

Ullman, M. (1959). On the psyche and warts. I. Suggestion and warts: A review and comment. *Psychosomatic Medicine, 21,* 473–488.

Ullman, M., & Dudek, S. (1960). On the psyche and warts. II. Hypnotic suggestion and warts. *Psychosomatic Medicine, 22,* 68–76.

Ullman, M., & Krippner, S., with A. Vaughan (1973). *Dream Telepathy.* New York: Macmillan.

Underhill, E. (1974). *Mysticism* (12th ed.). New York: Meridian. (Original work published 1911)

Uttal, W. R. (2001). *The New Phrenology: The Limits of Localizing Cognitive Processes in the Brain.* Cambridge, MA: MIT Press.

Vaitl, D., Birbaumer, N., Gruzelier, J., Jamieson, G. A., Kotchoubey, B., Kübler, A., Lehmann, D., Miltner, W. H. R., Ott, U., Pütz, P., Sammer, G., Strauch, I., Strehl, U., Wackermann, J., & Weiss, T. (2005). Psychobiology of altered states of consciousness. *Psychological Bulletin, 131,* 98–127.

Vakil, R. J. (1950). Remarkable feat of endurance by a yogi priest. *Lancet, 2,* 871.

Van de Castle, R. L. (1969). The facilitation of ESP through hypnosis. *American Journal of Clinical Hypnosis, 12,* 37–56.

Van de Castle, R. L. (1994). *Our Dreaming Mind.* New York: Ballantine.

Van Eeden, F. (1913). A study of dreams. *Proceedings of the Society for Psychical Research, 26,* 431–461.

Van Gelder, T. (1998). The dynamical hypothesis in cognitive science. *Behavioral and Brain Sciences, 21,* 615–628.

Van Lommel, P. (2004). About the continuity of our consciousness. In C. Machado & D. A. Shewmon (Eds.), *Brain Death and Disorders of Consciousness: Advances in Experimental Medicine and Biology* (Vol. 550, pp. 115–132). New York: Kluwer Academic/Plenum.

Van Lommel, P. (2006). Near-death experience, consciousness, and the brain: A new concept about the continuity of our consciousness based on recent scientific research on near-death experience in survivors of cardiac arrest. *World Futures, 62,* 134–151.

Van Lommel, P., van Wees, R., Meyers, V., & Elfferich, I. (2001). Near-death experiences in survivors of cardiac arrest: A prospective study in the Netherlands. *Lancet, 358,* 2039–2045.

Van Orden, G. C., Jansen op de Haar, M. A., & Bosman, A. M. T. (1997). Complex dynamic systems also predict dissociations, but they do not reduce to autonomous components. *Cognitive Neuropsychology, 14*, 131–165.

Van Pelt, S. J. (1965). The control of the heart rate by hypnotic suggestion. In L. M. LeCron (Ed.), *Experimental Hypnosis* (pp. 268–275). New York: Citadel.

Van Petten, C., Plante, E., Davidson, P. S. R., Kuo, T. Y., Bajuscak, L., & Glisky, E. L. (2004). Memory and executive function in older adults: Relationships with temporal and prefrontal gray matter volumes and white matter hyperintensities. *Neuropsychologia, 42*, 1313–1335.

Varela, F. J. (1996). Neurophenomenology: A methodological remedy for the hard problem. *Journal of Consciousness Studies, 3*, 330–349.

Varela, F. J., Lachaux, J.-P., Rodriguez, E., & Martinerie, J. (2001). The brainweb: Phase synchronization and large-scale integration. *Nature Reviews: Neuroscience, 2*, 229–239.

Vargha-Khadem, F., Gadian, D. G., Watkins, K. E., Connelly, A., Van Paesschen, W., & Mishkin, M. (1997). Differential effects of early hippocampal pathology on episodic and semantic memory. *Science, 277*, 376–380.

Vasiliev, L. L. (1976). *Experiments in Distant Influence*. New York: E. P. Dutton.

Velmans, M. (1991). Is human information processing conscious? *Behavioral and Brain Sciences, 14*, 651–726.

Velmans, M. (Ed.) (1996). *The Science of Consciousness: Psychological, Neuropsychological and Clinical Reviews*. London: Routledge.

Veselis, R. A., Reinsel, R. A., Beattie, B. J., Mawlawi, O. R., Feshchenko, V. A., DiResta, G. R., Larson, S. M., & Blasberg, R. G. (1997). Midazolam changes cerebral blood flow in discrete brain regions: An $H_2{}^{15}O$ positron emission topography study. *Anesthesiology, 87*, 1106–1117.

Vollenweider, F. X. (1994). Evidence for a cortical-subcortical imbalance of sensory information processing during altered states of consciousness using positron emission tomography and [^{18}F] fluorodeoxyglucose. In A. Pletscher & D. Ladewig (Eds.), *50 Years of LSD: Current Status and Perspectives of Hallucinogens* (pp. 67–86). New York: Parthenon.

Vollenweider, F. X. (1998). Recent advances and concepts in the search for biological correlates of hallucinogen-induced altered states of consciousness. *Heffler Review of Psychedelic Research, 1*, 21–32.

Vollenweider, F. X., & Geyer, M. A. (2001). A systems model of altered consciousness: Integrating natural and drug-induced psychoses. *Brain Research Bulletin, 56*, 495–507.

Vollenweider, F. X., Leenders, K. L., Øye, I., Hell, D., & Angst, J. (1997). Differential psychopathology and patterns of cerebral glucose utilisation produced by (*S*)- and (*R*)-ketamine in healthy volunteers using positron emission tomography (PET). *European Neuropsychopharmacology, 7*, 25–38.

Vollenweider, F. X., Leenders, K. L., Scharfetter, C., Antonini, A., Maguire, P., Missimer, J., & Angst, J. (1997). Metabolic hyperfrontality and psychopathology in the ketamine model of psychosis using positron emission tomography (PET) and [^{18}F] fluorodeoxyglucose (FDG). *European Neuropsychopharmacology, 7*, 9–24.

Vollenweider, F. X., Leenders, K. L., Scharfetter, C., Maguire, P., Stadelmann, O., & Angst, J. (1997). Positron emission tomography and fluorodeoxyglucose studies of metabolic hyperfrontality and psychopathology in the psilocybin model of psychosis. *Neuropsychopharmacology, 16*, 357–372.

Von der Malsburg, C. (1995). Binding in models of perception and brain function. *Current Opinion in Neurobiology, 5*, 520–526.

Von Neumann, J. (1955). *Mathematical Foundations of Quantum Mechanics* (R. T. Beyer, Trans.). Princeton, NJ: Princeton University Press. (Original work published 1932)

Von Neumann, J. (1956). Probabilistic logics and the synthesis of reliable organisms from unreliable components. In C. E. Shannon & J. McCarthy (Eds.), *Automata Studies* (pp. 43–98). Princeton, NJ: Princeton University Press.

Von Neumann, J. (1958). *The Computer and the Brain*. New Haven: Yale University Press.

Vriens, E. M., Bakker, P. F. A., DeVries, J. W., Wieneke, G. H., & van Huffelen, A. C. (1996). The impact of repeated short episodes of circulatory arrest on cerebral function. Reassuring electroencephalographic (EEG) findings during defibrillation threshold testing at defibrillator implantation. *Electroencephalography and Clinical Neurophysiology, 98*, 236–242.

Vuilleumier, P., Chicherio, C., Assal, F., Schwartz, S., Slosman, D., & Landis, T. (2001). Functional neuroanatomical correlates of hysterical sensorimotor loss. *Brain, 124*, 1077–1090.

Vygotsky, L. (2000). *Thought and Language* (A. Kozulin, Trans.). Cambridge, MA: MIT Press. (Original work in English published 1986)

Wackermann, J., Pütz, P., Büchi, S., Strauch, I., & Lehmann, D. (2002). Brain electrical activity and subjective experience during altered states of consciousness: Ganzfeld and hypnagogic states. *International Journal of Psychophysiology, 46*, 123–146.

Wager, T. D., Rilling, J. K., Smith, E. E., Sokolik, A., Casey, K. L., Davidson, R. J., Kosslyn, S. M., Rose, R. M., & Cohen, J. D. (2004). Placebo-induced changes in fMRI in the anticipation and experience of pain. *Science, 303*, 1162–1167.

Wagstaff, G. (1991). No conscious or co-conscious? [Peer commentary on M. Velmans, "Is Human Information Processing Conscious?" *Behavioral and Brain Sciences, 14*, 700.

Wall, P. D. (1977). Why do we not understand pain? In R. Duncan & M. Weston-Smith (Eds.), *Encyclopedia of Ignorance* (pp. 361–368). Oxford: Pergamon.

Wall, P. D. (1993). Pain and the placebo response. In G. R. Bock & J. Marsh (Eds.), *Experimental and Theoretical Studies of Consciousness* (pp. 187–216). Chichester, UK: John Wiley.

Wall, P. D. (1996). The placebo effect. In M. Velmans (Ed.), *The Science of Consciousness: Psychological, Neuropsychological, and Clinical Reviews* (pp. 162–180). London and New York: Routledge.

Wallace, R. K. (1970). Physiological effects of transcendental meditation. *Science, 167,* 1751–1754.

Wallace, R. K., & Benson, H. (1972). The physiology of meditation. *Scientific American, 226,* 85–90.

Wallas, G. (1926). *The Art of Thought.* London: J. Cape.

Walsh, R. N. (1995). Phenomenological mapping: A method for describing and comparing states of consciousness. *Journal of Transpersonal Psychology, 27,* 25–56.

Walsh, R. N., & Vaughan, F. (Eds.) (1980). *Beyond Ego: Transpersonal Dimensions in Psychology.* Los Angeles: J. P. Tarcher.

Walsh, R. N., & Vaughan, F. (1993). *Paths Beyond Ego: The Transpersonal Vision.* New York: Tarcher/Putnam.

Walters, M. J. (1944). Psychic death: Report of a possible case. *Archives of Neurology and Psychiatry, 52,* 84–85.

Ward, T. B., Finke, R. A., & Smith, S. M. (1995). *Creativity and the Mind: Discovering the Genius Within.* New York: Plenum.

Ward, T. B., Smith, S. M., & Finke, R. A. (1999). Creative cognition. In R. J. Sternberg (Ed.), *Handbook of Creativity* (pp. 189–212). New York: Cambridge University Press.

Ward, T. B., Smith, S. M., & Vaid, J. (Eds.) (1997). *Creative Thought: An Investigation of Conceptual Structures and Processes.* Washington, DC: American Psychological Association.

Wardell, D. W., & Weymouth, K. E. (2004). Review of studies of healing touch. *Journal of Nursing Scholarship, 34,* 147–154.

Wasson, G. (1968). *Soma: Divine Mushroom of Immortality.* New York: Harcourt Brace & World.

Wasson, G., Ruck, C., & Hofman, A. (1978). *The Road to Eleusis.* New York: Harcourt Brace Jovanovich.

Watson, A. A. (1973). Death by cursing—A problem for forensic psychiatry. *Medicine, Science, and the Law, 13,* 192–194.

Watson, J. B. (1913). Psychology as a behaviorist views it. *Psychological Review, 20,* 158–177.

Watson, M., Haviland, J. S., Greer, S., Davidson, J., & Bliss, J. M. (1999). Influence of psychological response on survival in breast cancer: A population-based cohort study. *Lancet, 354,* 1331–1336.

Wegner, D. M. (2002). *The Illusion of Conscious Will.* Cambridge, MA: MIT Press.

Weinreich, U. (1966). Explorations in semantic theory. In J. Sebeok (Ed.), *Current Trends in Linguistics* (Vol. 3, pp. 395–477). The Hague: Mouton.

Weisberg, R. W. (1986). *Creativity: Genius and Other Myths.* New York: W. H. Freeman.

Weisberg, R.W. (1999). Creativity and knowledge: A challenge to theories. In R. J. Sternberg (Ed.), *Handbook of Creativity* (pp. 251–272). New York: Cambridge University Press.

Weiss, L., Grocott, H. P., Rosanaia, R. A., Friedman, A., Newman, M. F., & Warner, D. S. (1998). Case 4–1998. Cardiopulmonary bypass and hypothermic circulatory arrest for basilar artery aneurysm clipping. *Journal of Cardiothoracic and Vascular Anesthesia, 12*, 473–479.

Weitzenhoffer, A. M. (1951). The discriminatory recognition of visual patterns under hypnosis. *Journal of Abnormal Social Psychology, 46*, 388–397.

Weitzenhoffer, A. M. (1953). *Hypnotism: An Objective Study in Suggestibility.* New York: John Wiley & Sons.

Weizenbaum, J. (1976). *Computer Power and Human Reason: From Calculation to Judgment.* San Francisco: W. H. Freeman.

Wenger, M. A., & Bagchi, B. K. (1961). Studies of autonomic functions in practitioners of yoga in India. *Behavioral Science, 6*, 312–323.

Werner, H. (1957). *Comparative Psychology of Mental Development* (Rev. ed.). New York: International Universities Press.

West, D. J. (1948). A mass-observation questionnaire on hallucinations. *Journal of the Society for Psychical Research, 34*, 187–196.

West, D. J. (1957). *Eleven Lourdes Miracles.* London: Gerald Duckworth.

West, D. J. (1990). A pilot census of hallucinations. *Proceedings of the Society for Psychical Research, 57*, 163–207.

West, M. A. (Ed.) (1987). *The Psychology of Meditation.* New York: Oxford University Press.

Whelan, C. I., & Stewart, D. E. (1990). Pseudocyesis—A review and report of six cases. *International Journal of Psychiatry in Medicine, 20*, 97–108.

Whinnery, J. E. (1997). Psychophysiologic correlates of unconsciousness and near-death experiences. *Journal of Near-Death Studies, 15*, 231–258.

White, N. S., & Alkire, M. T. (2003). Impaired thalamocortical connectivity in humans during general-anesthetic-induced unconsciousness. *NeuroImage, 19*, 402–411.

White, R. (1941). A preface to the theory of hypnotism. *Journal of Abnormal and Social Psychology, 36*, 477–505.

White, R. A. (1964). A comparison of old and new methods of response to targets in ESP experiments. *Journal of the American Society for Psychical Research, 58*, 21–56.

White, R. A. (1976). The limits of experimenter influence on psi test results: Can any be set? *Journal of the American Society for Psychical Research, 70*, 333–369.

Whitehead, A. N. (1953). *Science and the Modern World.* New York: Free Press. (Original work published 1925)

Whitehead, A. N. (1958). *The Function of Reason*. Princeton, NJ: Princeton University Press. (Original work published 1929)

Whitehead, A. N. (1968). *Modes of Thought*. New York: Free Press. (Original work published 1938)

Whitehead, A. N. (1978). *Process and Reality* (D. R. Griffin & D. W. Sherburne, Eds.). New York: Free Press. (Original work published 1929)

Whiteman, J. H. M. (1956). The process of separation and return in experiences fully "out of the body." *Proceedings of the Society for Psychical Research, 50*, 240–274.

Whitlock, F. A. (1967). The aetiology of hysteria. *Acta Psychiatrica Scandinavica, 43*, 144–162.

Whitlock, F. A., & Hynes, J. V. (1978). Religious stigmatization: An historical and psychophysiological enquiry. *Psychological Medicine, 8*, 185–202.

Wiener, N. (1961). *Cybernetics: Control and Communication in the Animal and the Machine* (2nd ed.). New York: John Wiley.

Wigner, E. P. (1960). The unreasonable effectiveness of mathematics in the natural sciences. *Communications on Pure and Applied Mathematics, 13*, 1–14.

Wigner, E. P. (1962). Remarks on the mind-body question. In I. J. Good (Ed.), *The Scientist Speculates: An Anthology of Partly-Baked Ideas* (pp. 284–302). New York: Basic Books.

Wikswo, J. P., Jr., Gevins, A., & Williamson, S. J. (1993). The future of the EEG and MEG. *Electroencephalography and Clinical Neurophysiology, 87*, 1–9.

Wilkes, K. (1988). *Real People*. Oxford: Oxford University Press.

Wilkinson, F. (2004). Auras and other hallucinations: Windows on the visual brain. *Progress in Brain Research, 144*, 305–320.

Willard, R. D. (1977). Breast enlargement through visual imagery and hypnosis. *American Journal of Clinical Hypnosis, 19*, 195–200.

Williams, D. (1956). The structure of emotions reflected in epileptic experience. *Brain, 79*, 29–67.

Williams, H. C., & Pembroke, A. C. (1988). Naevus of Jamaica. *Lancet, 2*, 915.

Williams, J. R. (2005). Depression as a mediator between spousal bereavement and mortality from cardiovascular disease: Appreciating and managing the adverse health consequences of depression in an elderly surviving spouse. *Southern Medical Association, 98*, 90–95.

Williams, M. D., Rainer, W. G., Fieger, H. G., Murray, I. P., & Sanchez, M. L. (1991). Cardiopulmonary bypass, profound hypothermia, and circulatory arrest for neurosurgery. *Annals of Thoracic Surgery, 52*, 1069–1075.

Willis, W. D., Jr. (1999). Dorsal root potentials and dorsal root reflex: A double-edged sword. *Experimental Brain Research, 124*, 395–421.

Wilson, R. A., & Keil, F. C. (Eds.) (1999). *MIT Encyclopedia of the Cognitive Sciences*. Cambridge, MA: MIT Press. (Also available on-line at http://cognet.mit.edu/MITECS)

Wilson, S. C., & Barber, T. X. (1981). Vivid fantasy and hallucinatory abilities in the life histories of excellent hypnotic subjects ("somnambules"): Preliminary report with female subjects. In E. Klinger (Ed.), *Imagery: Vol. 2. Concepts, Results, and Applications* (pp. 133–149). New York: Plenum.

Wilson, S. C., & Barber, T. X. (1983). The fantasy-prone personality: Implications for understanding imagery, hypnosis, and parapsychological phenomena. In A. A. Sheikh (Ed.), *Imagery: Current Theory, Research, and Application* (pp. 340–390). New York: Wiley.

Wind, E. (1967). *Pagan Mysteries in the Renaissance.* Harmondsworth, England: Penguin.

Wink, C. A. S. (1961). Congenital ichthyosiform erythroderma treated by hypnosis. *British Medical Journal, 2,* 741–743.

Winograd, T. (1972). Understanding natural language. *Cognitive Psychology, 3,* 1-191.

Winograd, T., & Flores, F. (1986). *Understanding Computers and Cognition: A New Foundation for Design.* Norwood, NJ: Ablex.

Winston, P. H. (Ed.) (1975). *The Psychology of Computer Vision.* New York: McGraw-Hill.

Wint, G. (1965). *The Third Killer.* London: Chatto & Windus.

Wiseman, R., & Schlitz, M. (1997). Experimenter effects and the remote detection of staring. *Journal of Parapsychology, 61,* 197–207.

Wiseman, R., & Schlitz, M. (1999). Experimenter effects and the remote detection of staring: A replication [abstract]. *Journal of Parapsychology, 63,* 232–233.

Wittstein, I. S., Thiemann, D. R., Lima, J. A. C., Baughman, K. L., Schulman, S. P., Gerstenblith, G., Wu, K. C., Rade, J. J., Bivalacqua, T. J., & Chamption, H. C. (2005). Neurohumoral features of myocardial stunning due to sudden emotional stress. *New England Journal of Medicine, 352,* 539–548.

Woerlee, G. M. (2004). Cardiac arrest and near-death experiences. *Journal of Near-Death Studies, 22,* 235–249.

Wolfe, T. (1952). The story of a novel. In B. Ghiselin (Ed.), *The Creative Process* (pp. 186–199). New York: New American Library.

Woods, R. (Ed.) (1980). *Understanding Mysticism.* Garden City, NY: Doubleday.

Wordsworth, J., Abrams, M. H., & Gill, S. (1979). *William Wordsworth: The Prelude, 1799, 1805, 1850.* New York: W. W. Norton.

Wright, R. (1999, December 13). The accidental creationist: Why Steven Jay Gould is bad for evolution. *New Yorker,* 56–65.

Wright, S. H. (1999). Paranormal contact with the dying: 14 contemporary death coincidences. *Journal of the Society for Psychical Research, 63,* 258–267.

Wulff, D. M. (2000). Mystical experience. In E. Cardeña, S. J. Lynn, & S. Krippner (Eds.), *Varieties of Anomalous Experience* (pp. 397–440). Washington, DC: American Psychological Association.

Wulsin, L. R. (2000). Editorial: Does depression kill? *Archives of Internal Medicine, 160*, 1731–1732.

Wulsin, L. R., Vaillant, G. E., & Wells, V. W. (1999). A systematic review of the mortality of depression. *Psychosomatic Medicine, 61*, 6–17.

Yamamura, T., Fukuda, M., Takeya, H., Goto, Y., & Furukawa, K. (1981). Fast oscillatory EEG activity induced by analgesic concentrations of nitrous oxide in man. *Anesthesia and Analgesia, 60*, 283–288.

Yazíci, K. M., & Kostakoglu, L. (1998). Cerebral blood flow changes in patients with conversion disorder. *Psychiatry Research: Neuroimaging Section, 83*, 163–168.

Young, P. J. W. (1965). Scared to death? [letter]. *British Medical Journal, 2*, 701.

Young, R. M. (1968). The functions of the brain: Gall to Ferrier (1808-1886). *Isis, 59*, 251–268.

Young, R. M. (1970). *Mind, Brain, and Adaptation in the Nineteenth Century: Cerebral Localization and Its Biological Context from Gall to Ferrier*. Oxford: Clarendon.

Zaehner, R. C. (1978). *Mysticism: Sacred and Profane*. New York: Oxford University Press. (Original work published 1957)

Zaleski, C. (1987). *Otherworld Journeys: Accounts of Near-Death Experience in Medieval and Modern Times*. Oxford: Oxford University Press.

Zeki, S. (1993). *A Vision of the Brain*. Oxford: Blackwell.

Zola-Morgan, S., & Squire, L. R. (1993). Neuroanatomy of memory. *Annual Review of Neuroscience, 16*, 547–563.

Zola-Morgan, S., Squire, L. R., & Amaral, D. G. (1986). Human amnesia and the medial temporal region: Enduring memory impairment following a bilateral lesion limited to field CA1 of the hippocampus. *Journal of Neuroscience, 9*, 1922–1936.

Zubieta, J.-K., Bueller, J. A., Jackson, L. R., Scott, D. J., Xu Y., Koeppe, R. A., Nichols, T. E., & Stohler, C. S. (2005). Placebo effects mediated by endogenous opioid activity on μ-opioid receptors. *Journal of Neuroscience, 25*, 7754–7762.

Zusne, L. (1985). Magical thinking and parapsychology. In P. Kurtz (Ed.), *A Skeptic's Handbook of Parapsychology* (pp. 685–700). Buffalo, NY: Prometheus.

Index

About the Authors

Edward F. Kelly is currently Research Professor in the Department of Psychiatric Medicine at the University of Virginia. He received his undergraduate degree in psychology from Yale and a Ph.D. from Harvard with primary interests in psycholinguistics and cognitive science. His most recent research, carried out at the University of North Carolina–Chapel Hill as part of a large neuroscience research program, involved non-invasive study of normal and abnormal plasticity in human somatosensory cortex using high-resolution EEG and fMRI techniques. He had previously spent over 10 years working full time in experimental parapsychology, initially at J. B. Rhine's Institute for Parapsychology in Durham, NC, and subsequently through the Department of Electrical Engineering at Duke University. He is author of *Computer Recognition of English Word Senses* (with Philip J. Stone); and *Altered States of Consciousness and Psi: An Historical Survey and Research Prospectus* (with Ralph G. Locke). His central long-term interests revolve around mind-brain relations and functional neuroimaging studies of unusual states of consciousness and associated cognitive phenomena.

Emily Williams Kelly is currently Research Assistant Professor in the Department of Psychiatric Medicine at the University of Virginia. She received her undergraduate degree in English literature from Duke University, an M.A. in religious studies from the University of Virginia, and a Ph.D. in psychology from the University of Edinburgh. Her dissertation focused on the development of scientific psychology in the late 19th century, with an emphasis on F. W. H. Myers and his contributions to psychology. She has been associated with the Department of Psychiatric Medicine since 1978, working primarily with Dr. Ian Stevenson in research on cases of the reincarnation type and near-death experiences. In recent years her research has focused on other kinds of phenomena suggestive of survival after death, including apparitions, deathbed visions, and mediumship.

Adam Crabtree is currently on the faculty of the Centre for Training in Psychotherapy, Toronto. He received an M.A. in philosophy from the University of Toronto and a Ph.D. in therapeutic counseling from the Open International University for Complementary Medicines. He is particularly interested in the history of hypnotism, psychotherapy, and dissociative disorders. His books include *Multiple Man: Explorations in Possession and Multiple Personality; Animal Magnetism, Early*

Hypnotism, and Psychical Research: An Annotated Bibliography; and *From Mesmer to Freud: Magnetic Sleep and the Roots of Psychological Healing.*

Alan Gauld, M.A., Ph.D., and D.Litt, is a retired Reader in Psychology, School of Psychology, University of Nottingham. As an undergraduate he read History and Natural Sciences (Psychology) at Emmanuel College, Cambridge. He spent a post-graduate year at Harvard, returned to Emmanuel as a Research Fellow, and then moved to Nottingham, where he principally taught biological psychology and neuropsychology. He has written or co-authored five books: *The Founders of Psychical Research*; *Human Action and its Psychological Investigation* (with John Shotter); *Poltergeists* (with Tony Cornell); *Mediumship and Survival*; and *A History of Hypnotism.* He is a past president of the Society for Psychical Research, received from the Parapsychological Association the Award for Outstanding Contributions to Parapsychological Research, and was awarded the Myers Memorial Medal of the Society for Psychical Research.

Bruce Greyson is the Chester F. Carlson Professor of Psychiatry and Director of the Division of Perceptual Studies at the University of Virginia. He was one of the founders of the International Association for Near-Death Studies, and for the past 25 years has edited the *Journal of Near-Death Studies.* Dr. Greyson majored in psychology at Cornell University, received his medical degree from the SUNY Upstate Medical College, and completed his psychiatric residency at the University of Virginia. He practiced and taught psychiatry at the University of Michigan and the University of Connecticut, where he was Clinical Chief of Psychiatry, before returning to the University of Virginia 11 years ago. Dr. Greyson's research for the past three decades has focused on the aftereffects and implications of the near-death experience. He is co-editor (with Charles P. Flynn) of *The Near-Death Experience: Problems, Prospects, Perspectives.*

Michael Grosso, though nominally retired, is currently teaching at the University of Virginia's School of Continuing Education. He received his Ph.D. from Columbia University in philosophy with an M.A. in classical Greek, and has taught philosophy at Marymount College, John F. Kennedy University, City University of New York, and New Jersey City University. His main current interests focus on developing a theory of mind adequate to the available empirical data and developing methods of 21st-century philosophical practice. These interests come together in his ongoing attempt to develop a new philosophical therapy that is based on a radically expanded understanding of human mental capacities. He is currently a director of the American Philosophical Practitioner's Association and Review Editor of the *Journal of Philosophical Practice.* His recent books include *The Millennium Myth; Experiencing the Next World Now*; and *The Misunderstood Savior: Epicurus and Philosophical Practice* (forthcoming).